AutoCAD LT 98
Fundamentals and Applications

by

Ted Saufley
CAD Manager
A-dec, Inc.
Newberg, Oregon

Autodesk.
Certified Instructor

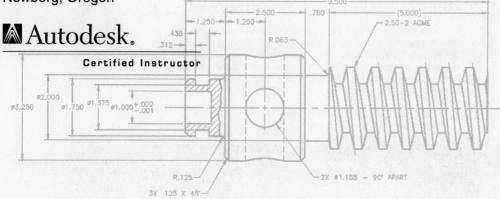

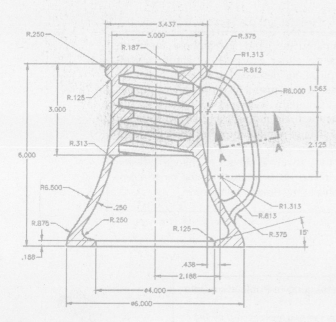

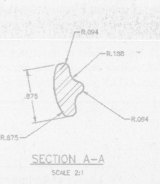

SECTION A-A
SCALE 2:1

Autodesk.
Registered Author/Publisher

Publisher
The Goodheart-Willcox Company, Inc.
Tinley Park, Illinois

AutoCAD LT—Fundamentals and Applications is not an Autodesk product. Autodesk takes no responsibility with regard to the selection, performance, or use on Non-Autodesk products. All understandings, agreements, or warranties must take place directly between Goodheart-Willcox and the prospective users. AUTODESK SPECIFICALLY DISCLAIMS ALL WARRANTIES, EXPRESSED OR IMPLIED, INCLUDING, BUT NOT LIMITED TO, THE IMPLIED WARRANTIES OF MERCHANTABILITY AND FITNESS FOR A PARTICULAR PURPOSE.

The Autodesk logo is registered in the U.S. Patent and Trademark Office by Autodesk, Inc.

Copyright 1999

by

THE GOODHEART-WILLCOX COMPANY, INC.

All rights reserved. No part of this book may be reproduced, stored in a retrieval system, or transmitted in any form or by any means, electronic, mechanical, photocopying, recording, or otherwise, without the prior written permission of The Goodheart-Willcox Company, Inc. Manufactured in the United States of America.

Library of Congress Catalog Card Number 98-48493
International Standard Book Number 1-56637-525-8

1 2 3 4 5 6 7 8 9 10   99   03 02 01 00 99

"The Goodheart-Willcox Company, Inc., and the authors make no warranty or representation whatsoever, either expressed or implied, with respect to any of the software or applications described or referred to herein, their quality, performance, merchantability, or fitness, for a particular purpose.

Further, The Goodheart-Willcox Company, Inc., and the authors specifically disclaim any liability whatsoever for direct, indirect, special, incidental, or consequential damages arising out of the use or inability to use the software or applications described or referred to herein.

The contents of the AutoCAD LT software is subject to change between maintenance releases. The material in this book is based on the most recent AutoCAD LT software release available at the time of publication."

Library of Congress Cataloging-in-Publication Data

Saufley, Ted.
    AutoCAD LT 98 : fundamentals and applications / by Ted Saufley.
        p. cm.
    Includes index
    ISBN 1-56637-525-8
    1. Computer graphics. 2. AutoCAD LT for Windows.
I. Title.
T385.S265 1999
604.2'0285'5369--dc21   98-48493
                                                            CIP

AutoCAD LT

Introduction

AutoCAD LT—Fundamentals and Applications is a text and workbook combination that provides complete instruction in mastering AutoCAD LT™ commands and drawing techniques. Typical applications of AutoCAD LT are presented with basic and advanced concepts. The topics are covered in an easy-to-understand sequence, and progress in a way that allows you to become comfortable with the commands as your knowledge builds from one chapter to the next. In addition, *AutoCAD LT—Fundamentals and Applications* offers the following features:

- Step-by-step use of AutoCAD LT commands.
- Easily understandable explanations of how and why the commands function as they do.
- Numerous illustrations to reinforce concepts.
- Professional tips explaining how to use AutoCAD LT effectively and efficiently.
- Exercises and tutorials involving tasks to reinforce chapter section topics.
- Chapter tests for reviewing commands and key AutoCAD LT concepts.
- Chapter problems to supplement each chapter.
- Material specific to AutoCAD LT 97 highlighted in blue for easy identification.

Objectives

It is the goal of *AutoCAD LT—Fundamentals and Applications* to provide a step-by-step approach in mastering AutoCAD LT 98 and 97 commands. Each topic is presented in a logical sequence that permits the user to progress from the most basic drawing commands to the more advanced editing and dimensioning functions. Additionally, the reader also becomes acquainted with:

- Quick and efficient drawing construction techniques.
- Dimensioning applications and practices, as interpreted through accepted standards.
- Drawing sectional views and creating custom hatch patterns.
- Creating special shapes and symbols for multiple use.
- Isometric drawing and dimensioning practices.
- Plotting and printing drawings.
- Using the Windows 98/95/NT Explorer for drawing file management.
- Customizing the AutoCAD LT graphical user environment and menu system.
- Using clipboard graphics and Object Linking and Embedding (OLE).

Fonts Used in this Text

Different type faces are used throughout the chapters to define terms and identify AutoCAD LT commands. Important terms always appear in ***bold-italic face, serif*** type. AutoCAD LT menus, commands, variables, dialog box names, and button names are printed in **bold-face, sans serif** type. Filenames, directory names, paths, and keyboard-entry items appear in the text in Roman, sans serif type. Keyboard keys are shown inside brackets [ ] and appear in Roman, sans serif type. For example, [Enter] means to press the Enter (Return) key.

Prompt sequences are set apart from the body text with space above and below, and appear in Roman, sans serif type. Keyboard entry items in prompts appear in **bold-face, sans serif** type. In prompts, the [Enter] key is represented by the enter symbol (⏎).

AutoCAD LT 97 Compatibility

AutoCAD LT 98 is the newest version of Autodesk's AutoCAD LT package. This version was released one year after it predecessor, AutoCAD LT 97, was released. Despite the brief time between releases, there are many significant additions in AutoCAD LT 98. Although the focus of this text is primarily on AutoCAD LT 98, it is also completely compatible with AutoCAD LT 97. In those instances where AutoCAD LT 97 commands and/or procedures differ from AutoCAD LT 98, the text outlining those differences appears in blue.

Checking the AutoCAD LT 98 Getting Started Guide

No other AutoCAD LT reference should be needed when using this worktext. However, the author has referenced the major topic areas to the corresponding *AutoCAD LT 98 Getting Started Guide* chapters for your convenience. You will find the icon (shown here) in the margin next to most major headings in this text.

The number indicates the chapter in the *AutoCAD LT Getting Started Guide*. For example, a reference such as this one refers to Chapter 8 of the *AutoCAD LT 98 Getting Started Guide*.

Introducing the AutoCAD LT Commands

There are several ways to select AutoCAD LT drawing and editing commands. The format is slightly different when typing commands from the keyboard when compared to selecting commands from the toolbar, digitizing tablet, or pull-down menus. All commands and related options in this text are introduced by providing all of the command entry methods

Unless otherwise specified, all AutoCAD LT command entries are shown as if they were typed at the keyboard. This allows you to see the full command name and the prompts that appear on screen. Since you are encouraged to enter commands in the most convenient manner, shortened command aliases are also presented. Commands, options, and values you must enter are given in **bold** text as shown in the following example. Pressing the [Enter] key is indicated with the enter symbol (⏎). (Also, refer to the earlier section *Fonts Used in this Text*.)

```
Command: LINE or L⏎
From point: 2,2⏎
To point: 4,2⏎
To point: ⏎
```

General input tasks such as picking a point or selecting an object are presented in *italics*.

> Command: **LINE** *or* **L**↵
> From point: *(pick a point)*
> To point: *(pick another point)*
> To point: ↵

The command line, pull-down menu, and toolbar button entry methods are presented throughout the text. When a command is introduced, these methods are illustrated in the margin next to the text reference. The toolbar in which the button is located is also identified. The example in the margin next to this paragraph illustrates the various methods of initiating the **LINE** command.

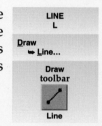

LINE
L

<u>Draw</u>
↪ Line...

Draw
toolbar

Line

Prerequisites

AutoCAD LT—Fundamentals and Applications has been developed for the user or student with prior exposure to Microsoft Windows, but it is by no means required. The text takes you through the entire AutoCAD LT command structure and applies AutoCAD LT functions to basic drafting concepts. Thus, readers should already possess a good working knowledge of drafting principles, such as orthographic projection, line and lettering standards, and industrial dimensioning practices.

Flexibility in Design

Flexibility is the key word when using *AutoCAD LT—Fundamentals and Applications*. This worktext is an excellent training aid for individual, as well as classroom instruction. *AutoCAD LT—Fundamentals and Applications* teaches you AutoCAD LT and its applications to common drafting tasks. It is also a useful resource for professionals using AutoCAD LT in the work environment.

There are a variety of notices you will see throughout the text. These notices consist of technical information, hints, and cautions that will help you develop your AutoCAD LT skills. The notices that appear in the text are identified by icons and rules around the text. The notices are as follows:

PROFESSIONAL TIP  These are ideas and suggestions aimed at increasing your productivity and enhancing your use of AutoCAD LT commands and techniques.

NOTES A note alerts you to important aspects of the command or activity that is being discussed.

CAUTIONS A caution alerts you to potential problems if instructions or commands are used incorrectly, or if an action could corrupt or alter files, folders, or disks. If you are in doubt after reading a caution, always consult your instructor or supervisor.

The chapter exercises, tests, and drawing problems are set up to allow an instructor to select individual or group learning goals. Thus, the structure of *AutoCAD LT—Fundamentals and Applications* lends itself to the development of a course devoted entirely to AutoCAD LT training. To that end, several optional course syllabi are provided in the *Solution Manual* for you to use or revise to suit individual classroom needs.

AutoCAD LT—Fundamentals and Applications offers several ways for you to evaluate your performance. Included are:

- **Tutorials.** Several of the chapters include mini-tutorials that offer step-by-step instructions for producing AutoCAD LT drawings. The tutorials also serve to help reinforce key chapter concepts.

- **Exercises.** Each chapter is divided into short sections covering various aspects of AutoCAD LT. An exercise composed of several instructions is found at the end of most sections. These exercises help you become acquainted with the commands just introduced.

- **Chapter Tests.** Each chapter also includes a written test. Questions may require you to provide the proper command, option, or response to perform a certain task.

- **Drawing Problems.** A variety of drawing problems follow each chapter. These problems are presented as "real-world" CAD drawings and, like some real-world applications, may contain mistakes, inaccuracies, or omissions. Always be sure to modify the drawings as needed and apply accurate dimensions to the completed drawings where required. The problems are designed to make you think, solve problems, research proper drafting standards, and correct possible errors in the drawings. Each drawing problem deals with one of five technical disciplines. Although doing all of the problems will enhance AutoCAD LT skills, you may have a particular discipline upon which you wish to focus. The discipline that a problem addresses is indicated by a text graphic in the margin next to the problem number. Each graphic and its description is as follows:

Mechanical Drafting	• These problems address mechanical drafting and design applications, such as a manufactured part.
Architectural Drafting	• These problems address architectural drafting and design applications, such as floor plans and presentation drawings.
Electronics Drafting	• These problems address electronics drafting and design applications, such as electronic schematics, logic diagrams, and electrical part design.
Graphics	• These problems address graphic design applications, such as text creation, title blocks, and page layout.
General	• These problems address a variety of general drafting and design applications, and should be attempted by everyone learning AutoCAD LT for the first time.

About the Author

Ted Saufley is the CAD Manager at A-dec, Inc., the world's leading manufacturer of dental equipment and dental furniture, located in Newberg, Oregon. As an Autodesk Certified Instructor (ACI), Ted spent 12 years developing and conducting classes in Computer-Aided Drafting, AutoCAD, AutoCAD LT, Animator, 3D Studio, and Mechanical Desktop for the Premier Authorized Autodesk Training Center at Clackamas Community College, Oregon City, Oregon. In addition to community college experience, Ted was also an AutoCAD instructor at the University of Oregon Continuation Center in Portland, Oregon. In both 1992 and 1995, he was recognized by Autodesk as one of the top rated AutoCAD instructors in the Autodesk Training Center network. Ted has extensive industrial experience in both mechanical and software engineering, and has been involved with CAD/CAM for nearly two decades as a user, software developer, and consultant. He is the author of Goodheart-Willcox's *AutoCAD LT Fundamentals and Applications—Windows 3.1* and *AutoCAD AME—Solid Modeling for Mechanical Design*, and the coauthor of *AutoCAD and its Applications—Release 12 for Windows.*

Notice to the User

This worktext is designed as a complete entry-level AutoCAD LT teaching tool. The author presents a typical point of view. Users are encouraged to explore alternative techniques for using and mastering AutoCAD LT. The author and publisher accept no responsibility for any loss or damage resulting from the contents of information presented in this text. This text contains the most complete and accurate information that could be obtained from various authoritative sources at the time of production. The publisher cannot assume responsibility for any changes, errors, or omissions.

Acknowledgments

Denis Cadu, Autodesk, Inc.

Contribution of Materials

Melissa Martin, Geo Engineers, Portland, OR
Doug Millican, Pesznecker Bros., Clackamas, OR

Special thanks to...

Joanne Reid for her contributions to Chapters 24 and 25 of this text.

Contents at a Glance

Table of Contents

AutoCAD LT

Chapter *1*

Getting Started with AutoCAD LT

Learning Objectives

After you have completed this chapter, you will be able to:
- ○ Load AutoCAD LT from the Windows 98, Windows 95, or Windows NT Programs folder.
- ○ Describe the AutoCAD LT graphics window and user interface.
- ○ Understand the function and components of dialog boxes.
- ○ Select and use the various keyboard and function keys and identify their command equivalents.
- ○ Use the **HELP** command and other on-line services for assistance.

Introduction to AutoCAD LT

AutoCAD LT is a low cost, but full-featured CAD (Computer-Aided Drafting) software package. With it, you can prepare engineering drawings for mechanical objects, architectural floor plans for residential and commercial structures, or site plans for subdivided parcels of land. Sharing the same easy-to-use interface and command syntax as its "big brother" AutoCAD, AutoCAD LT has quickly emerged as a powerful, but inexpensive desktop solution for performing 2D drawing and dimensioning functions.

Because AutoCAD LT does not have the solid modeling and rendering features, external database links, or AutoLISP language programming capabilities of AutoCAD, many people mistakenly believe that the "LT" in AutoCAD LT means "Lite." In actuality, LT really does not mean anything. Because AutoCAD LT requires less *random access memory (RAM)* and hard disk space than full AutoCAD, it can be installed and run on relatively modest laptop and notebook computers. As you experiment with the exercises, tutorials, and drawing problems found in this text, you will probably come to agree with thousands of other users that there is nothing light about AutoCAD LT.

The latest version of the program upon which this text is based, AutoCAD LT 98 operates under the Windows 98, Windows 95, and Windows NT operating systems only. The program is contained on a CD-ROM that contains an installation program called SETUP.EXE. Instructions are given on-screen during the installation process to assist you in proper installation. The setup program automatically transfers files from the CD-ROM to subfolders it creates on your computer's hard disk, and then creates a new *folder* in the Programs section of the Start menu. The program may then be started by first clicking the Start button and then clicking Programs. Next, click

AutoCAD LT 98 from the AutoCAD LT 98 program folder to start the program. The Program and AutoCAD LT 98 folders for Windows 98, Windows 95, and Windows NT are shown in **Figure 1-1.** Regardless of the operating system you are using, the installation procedure also creates a desktop shortcut which may be used to quickly launch AutoCAD LT.

Figure 1-1.
AutoCAD LT 98 is started by clicking the Start button, then selecting the Programs folder, and finally selecting AutoCAD LT 98 from the AutoCAD LT 98 folder. The Windows 98 desktop is shown in A, the Windows 95 desktop is shown in B, while the Windows NT desktop appears in C.

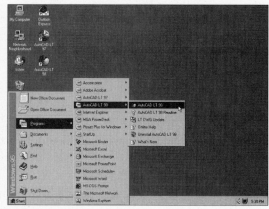

A   B

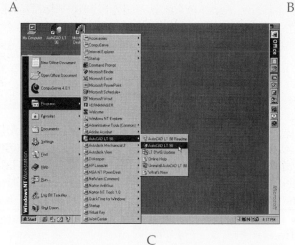

C

 NOTE

Observe that a README file appears in the AutoCAD LT 98 program folder in all three operating systems. This file includes useful information about AutoCAD LT and special functions and limitations which may not be covered in the printed *AutoCAD LT 98 Getting Started Guide.* Be sure to read this additional documentation after installing AutoCAD LT on your hard disk.

Also note that on-line help is available. Using On-line Help and other on-line services is covered at the end of this chapter. If you wish to remove AutoCAD LT from your computer, select Uninstall AutoCAD LT 98 from the program folder. The program can also be uninstalled by clicking the Add/Remove Programs icon in the Microsoft Windows Control Panel. Be sure to check with your supervisor or instructor before doing so.

Once you select AutoCAD LT 98 from the program folder, AutoCAD LT begins loading into memory and a small hourglass icon appears along with the AutoCAD LT 98 logo in the center of your screen. You are then presented with the **Start Up** dialog box shown in **Figure 1-2**. *Dialog boxes* are widely used in Windows-based applications to request information about a task you are performing, provide information or options you may require, or to display important warning messages. Dialog boxes and their components are described in detail in a later section of this chapter.

The **Start Up** dialog box allows you to quickly and easily set up drawing parameters, such as drawing size and units. For now, just click the **Cancel** button at the upper-right of the dialog box. The dialog box then disappears, AutoCAD LT finishes loading, and the Command: prompt appears at the bottom of the graphics window. It is within the AutoCAD LT graphics window that all drawing and editing operations are performed. With the graphics window now fully displayed, you are ready to begin exploring the AutoCAD LT user interface.

Figure 1-2.
The **Start Up** dialog box is displayed as AutoCAD LT is loaded and provides a handy means of setting up new drawing parameters.

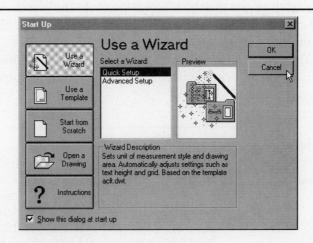

NOTE   The drawing setup parameters offered in the **Start Up** dialog box are covered in detail in *Chapter 2* of this text. Other functions available in this dialog box are more fully described in *Chapter 17*.

The AutoCAD LT User Interface

The AutoCAD LT user interface consists of all the items you will need to interact with the program. These items consist of the graphics and text windows, drawing window, command window, status bar, pull-down menus, tablet menu, toolbars, keyboard buttons, and dialog boxes.

The AutoCAD LT Graphics Window

The AutoCAD LT graphics window is composed of various elements and buttons. See **Figure 1-3A**. Located at the very top of the screen display is the *title bar*, which tells you the name of the current drawing file. The drawing name appears as [Drawing.dwg] until the file is first saved. Just below the title bar, the ten AutoCAD LT pull-down menus may be found on the *menu bar*. Directly beneath the menu bar, you will find the *Standard toolbar* which contains tools that are used as shortcuts to some of the more frequently used file management and display control commands. The

Object Properties toolbar is located directly beneath the **Standard Toolbar**. Both the *Command window* and *Status bar* are located at the bottom of the graphics window. Each of these graphics window components is discussed in detail in the following sections.

Several items in the graphics window may be freely moved about and located in new positions as desired. These types of items are referred to as *floating windows*. When in the floating state, these windows are identified with their own standard borders and title bars and are moved and sized similar to any other window in the Windows 98/95/NT operating systems. A floating window can be anchored, or *docked*, at one of the edges of the graphics window. You may freely move and dock objects at any time during a drawing session.

In AutoCAD LT, the **Draw** and **Modify** toolbars are docked at the left side of the graphics window by default. This configuration is illustrated in **Figure 1-3A.** To convert a docked window to a floating state, simply select the docked window at its border, press and hold the pick button of your pointing device and drag it to any location you wish in the graphics window. Once the window is located to your satisfaction, release the pick button. In **Figure 1-3B**, the **Draw** and **Modify** toolbars, as well as the command window, are shown as floating windows. Note that the title bar and border are automatically restored when a docked window is returned to a floating state. However, a docked window becomes part of the graphics window and loses its title bar and standard border.

NOTE

The **Content Explorer** window is automatically displayed at the right side of the graphics window the first time AutoCAD LT is launched after installation. See **Figure 1-3C.** **Content Explorer** provides an easy, convenient method for inserting frequently used symbols, hatch patterns, locating drawing files, and viewing symbol images and descriptions. All of these powerful features are fully explored in *Chapter 15* of this text.

However, you may find that **Content Explorer** obscures too much of the available drawing area to your liking. If so, click the **Minimize** button (represented by a dash) in the upper-right corner of the **Content Explorer** window to minimize the application. If you wish to close the application, click the **Close** button (represented by an "X") in the upper-right corner of the **Content Explorer** window. The majority of the screen examples illustrated in this text show the graphics window with **Content Explorer** disabled.

Standard Screen Layout

The standard screen layout provides a large drawing area or *drawing window*. The drawing window is bordered by the **Object Properties** toolbar at the top, and the command window at the bottom. In its uncustomized format, the drawing window is white and the text appearing in the command window is black on a white background. Look at your screen now while referring to **Figure 1-3A.**

Figure 1-3.
A—The standard AutoCAD LT 98 graphics window. Note the default locations of the docked **Draw** and **Modify** toolbars, as well as the **Command** window. B—The **Draw** and **Modify** toolbars, as well as the **Command** window, are shown in their floating states. C—The **Content Explorer** window is displayed at the right side of the graphics window the first time AutoCAD LT is started after initial installation. If desired, minimize or close **Content Explorer** as described in the text.

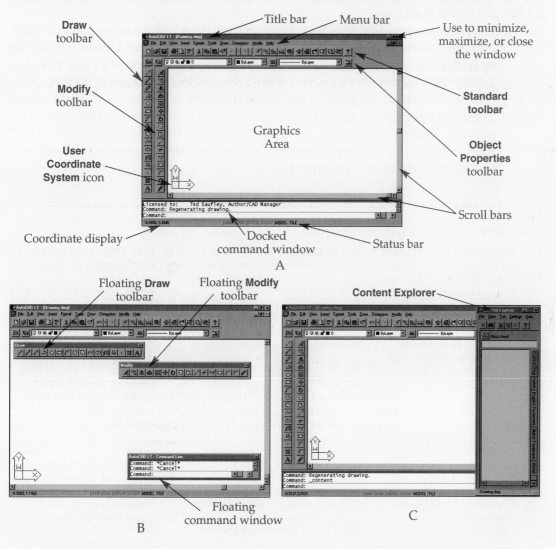

NOTE

Do not be alarmed if your display screen may appear differently than that shown in **Figure 1-3.** Various factors, chiefly screen resolution, affect the appearance of the AutoCAD LT graphics window. At high screen resolutions, for example, it is possible to display more toolbars along the edges of the graphics window than can be displayed at low resolutions. The screen examples illustrated in this text are at 800 × 600 resolution.

Take a few moments to become familiar with the various areas and functions of the AutoCAD LT graphics window. Doing so will quickly increase your comfort level with the program and shorten the learning curve. The following list describes each area of the graphics window:

- **Command window.** The *command window* consists of three text lines docked along the bottom of the graphics window and displays the Command: prompt. This area is also referred to as the *command line* or *command prompt* area. The commands that you enter, and the messages and prompts issued by AutoCAD LT, are displayed here. Since this area of the graphics window is your primary communication with AutoCAD LT, make a habit of glancing at the command line from time to time as you are working. As shown in **Figure 1-3,** the command window may be in a docked (the default) or floating state.

- **Scroll bars.** Two *scroll bars,* one horizontal and the other vertical, allow you to pan the display in the graphics area. Pan operations are described in *Chapter 4* of this text.

- **Graphics cursor.** The *graphics cursor* is used to select drawing objects, tools, and buttons as well as to make pull-down menu selections. Depending on the operation, the cursor can appear as a small crosshair cursor or as an arrow. See *Chapter 20* to learn how you may adjust the size of the graphics cursor.

- **Standard Toolbar.** By default, the **Standard Toolbar** is located directly below the menu bar and just above the graphics area. This toolbar contains an assortment of buttons which provide handy shortcuts for accessing AutoCAD LT file management and display control commands. These buttons are illustrated and briefly described in **Figure 1-4.**

Figure 1-4.
The **Standard Toolbar** and its components.

A— **New.** Starts a new drawing session.

B— **Open.** Allows you to work with an existing drawing.

C— **Save.** Saves the drawing to disk.

D— **Print.** Prints or plots to a selected output device.

E— **Print Preview.** Shows how the drawing will look when printed or plotted.

F— **Spelling.** Activates a spell checker for the drawing text.

G— **Cut.** Cuts a specified area of the drawing and stores it in the Windows Clipboard.

H— **Copy.** Copies a specified area of the drawing and stores it in the Windows Clipboard.

I— **Paste.** Pastes the contents of the Windows Clipboard into the AutoCAD LT drawing window.

J— **Property Painter.** Copies properties, such as color or linetype, from one object to other objects.

K— **Undo.** Reverses, or undoes, the most recent operation or command.

L— **Redo.** Reverses the effects of the last **Undo** operation.

M— **PolarSnap Settings.** Constrains cursor movement to specified angles and radial distances.

N— **Snap Points Flyout.** Presents a series of buttons used to select drawing objects at precise pick points.

O— **UCS Flyout.** Displays a series of buttons to create and manage user-definable coordinate systems.

P— **Inquiry Commands Flyout.** Presents a series of buttons used to verify drawing data and accuracy.

Q— **Draw Order.** Changes the display order of images and other objects.

R— **Aerial View.** Opens the **Aerial View** window.

S— **Views Flyout.** This flyout provides a series of buttons to obtain different views of drawing objects.

T— **Pan RealTime.** Moves the drawing display in the current viewport in realtime.

U— **Zoom RealTime.** Zooms the drawing display in realtime.

V— **Zoom Window Flyout.** Presents a series of buttons to perform conventional zooming operations.

W—**Zoom Previous.** Restores the previous view.

X— **Help.** Activates AutoCAD LT's **Online Help** service.

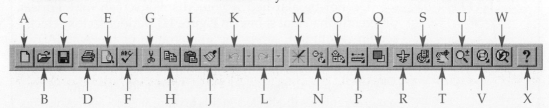

When you move your pointing device over the toolbar, the crosshair cursor reverts to the Windows arrow pointer. If you momentarily pause over one of the tool buttons, the corresponding AutoCAD LT command name appears in a small text box near your cursor. These handy command identifiers are called *tooltips*. The **Save** command tooltip is shown in **Figure 1-5A.** Observe that several buttons display a small black triangle in the lower-right corner. These types of buttons are called *flyouts*. As shown in **Figure 1-5B,** if you click and hold the pick button on your pointing device while pointing at a flyout, a related series of tool buttons is displayed.

- **Object Properties toolbar.** This toolbar appears just below the **Standard Toolbar** and directly above the graphics area. It contains tool buttons that control and modify properties of drawing objects as shown in **Figure 1-6.** These properties include color, layer, linetype, etc., and are explained fully in later chapters.

Figure 1-5.
A—A corresponding tooltip identifier appears when you pause your pointing device over a tool button. B—A related series of tool buttons is displayed if you click and hold the pick button on your pointing device while pointing at a flyout.

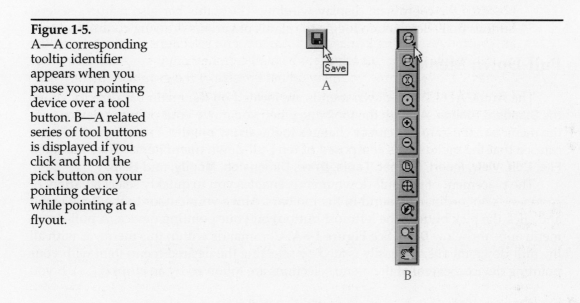

Figure 1-6.
The **Object Properties** toolbar and its components.

A— **Make Object's Layer Current.** Makes the layer of a selected object the current layer.

B— **Layers.** Activates the **Layer & Linetype Properties** dialog box where you create and manage drawing layers.

C— **Layer Control.** Displays the current layer name. Clicking on the down arrow at the right displays a drop-down list of the layers defined in the drawing. Selecting a layer from the drop-down list quickly sets the selected layer current. The **Layer Control** list is also used to control the status of drawing layers.

D— **Color Control.** Displays the current system color. Clicking on the down arrow at the right displays a drop-down list from which a different color may be chosen.

E— **Linetype.** Activates the **Layer & Linetype Properties** dialog box from which various linetypes may be loaded and set current.

F— **Linetype Control.** Displays the current linetype name. Clicking on the down arrow at the right displays a drop-down list of the linetypes loaded in the drawing. Selecting a linetype from the drop-down list quickly sets the selected linetype current.

G— **Properties.** This button activates the **DDMODIFY** command when only one drawing object is selected. When more than one object is selected, the **DDCHPROP** command is activated. Both commands may be used to modify the properties of existing drawing objects.

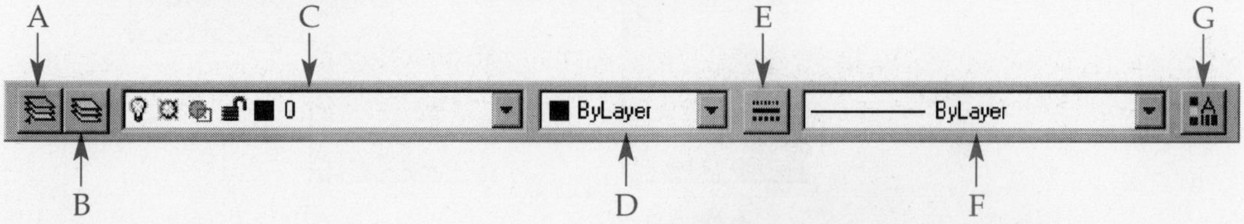

- **Docked toolbars.** *Docked toolbars*, like floating toolbars, contain tool buttons to quickly activate AutoCAD LT commands. As previously mentioned, the **Draw** and **Modify** toolbars are docked at the left side of the graphics window by default. Both floating and docked toolbars may be moved, modified, or hidden from view as desired.
- **UCS icon.** The **UCS** (*User Coordinate System*) **icon** at the lower-left of the drawing window represents the orientation of the UCS axes and the location of the current UCS origin. It also represents the viewing direction relative to the XY plane.
- **Status bar.** The *status bar* appears at the very bottom of the graphics window. It contains a small window at the far left that display, the current screen coordinates. The displayed coordinates reflect the units of measurement currently in use by AutoCAD LT. By default, the units are four-place decimals. Whenever you point at a tool button or a pull-down menu item, a brief description of the corresponding command is displayed at the far left of the status bar and obscures the coordinate display window. The status bar also features several buttons that allow you to toggle the status of various drawing control features.

Pull-Down Menus

The AutoCAD LT pull-down menus are located on the menu bar directly above the **Standard Toolbar**. As with the toolbars, when you move your pointing device over the menu bar, the graphics cursor changes to the arrow pointer. From **Figure 1-7,** you can see that the menu bar is composed of ten pull-down menu items. They are titled **File, Edit, View, Insert, Format, Tools, Draw, Dimension, Modify,** and **Help.**

The placement of the pull-down menus enables you to quickly select a variety of commands not ordinarily found in the toolbars. Move your cursor to the **Draw** menu and click the pick button (the leftmost button) on your pointing device. A pull-down menu appears below **Draw.** See **Figure 1-8A.** Commands within this menu, as with all the pull-down menus, are easily issued by selecting the desired menu item with your pointing device. Several of the menu selections are followed by an *ellipsis* (...). If you

---

Figure 1-7.
Shown are the ten pull-down menu titles on the menu bar.

| File | Edit | View | Insert | Format | Tools | Draw | Dimension | Modify | Help |

Figure 1-8.
A—The **Draw** pull-down menu.
B—When a pull-down menu item followed by an arrow is selected with your pointing device, a cascading submenu of command suboptions appears.

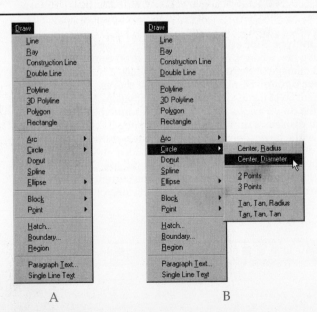

A   B

pick one of these items, a dialog box is displayed. Dialog boxes are discussed in a later section of this chapter.

You will observe that several of the commands in the **Draw** pull-down menu have a small arrow to the right. When one of these items is selected with the pointing device, a *cascading submenu* appears. This submenu offers you additional options for the selected command. See **Figure 1-8B.** Each of these commands and suboptions are discussed in the appropriate chapters of this text.

If you pick the wrong pull-down menu, simply move the cursor to the menu you want and click on it. The first menu is removed and the one you clicked is displayed. The pull-down menu disappears after you pick an item from the menu, pick a point in the drawing window, or type on the keyboard.

Accessing Pull-Down Menus from the Keyboard

Even the most casual perusal of the pull-down menu titles on the menu bar will reveal one underlined character in each of the menu names. This is consistent with the Microsoft Windows 98/95/NT user interfaces that permit access to any pull-down menu from the keyboard using an [Alt] key combination shortcut. For instance, the **File** menu may be accessed by pressing [Alt]+[F]. Pressing [Alt]+[E] accesses the **Edit** menu, and so on. These types of key combinations are called *accelerator keys*.

NOTE AutoCAD LT 98 has been designed to be a *Microsoft Office Compatible* product. That means that the pull-down menus, toolbars, and accelerator keys are similar to those found in Microsoft Office suite applications, such as Access, Excel, PowerPoint, and Word. If you use any or all of these programs, you are probably already familiar with accelerator keys.

Once a pull-down menu is displayed, a menu item within it may be selected using a single character key. As an example, suppose you wanted to construct a circle defined by its center point and its radius. Referring once again to **Figure 1-8B**, you first press [Alt]+[D] to access the **Draw** menu, then press [C] to select the **Circle** command, and then press [R] to select **Center, Radius**. These single key shortcuts for pull-down menu items are called *mnemonic keys*.

Admittedly, it is far more efficient to make your menu selections with your pointing device than from the keyboard. However, if your pointing device should suddenly become inoperative and stop responding, the accelerator and mnemonic keys provide a handy means of exiting the program without rebooting your computer.

NOTE There are many individual character key and key combination shortcuts available for Windows and Windows-based applications. Refer to the documentation supplied with your version of Microsoft Windows for a complete list of keyboard shortcuts.

Dialog Boxes

As previously mentioned, any time you select a pull-down menu item followed by an ellipsis, a dialog box is displayed. In their simplest form, dialog boxes are used to display informational or warning messages to you. These types of dialog boxes are often called *alert* boxes and remain on the screen until you acknowledge the displayed message by clicking the **OK** button. See **Figure 1-9.**

Since many of the features of dialog boxes are common throughout Microsoft Windows and Windows-based applications like AutoCAD LT, spend a few moments getting acquainted with the various components found within them. Remember that a wide variety of the items you need to select and set to complete your drawings are found in dialog boxes.

Common dialog boxes all contain the same basic areas, and work the same way regardless of the application you are using. One type of common dialog box you will encounter is illustrated in **Figure 1-10.** This is the **Save Drawing As** dialog box. Observe that its name is clearly shown at the top of the dialog box in the *title bar*. This type of dialog box contains a listing of folders on your computer and is commonly used when saving a drawing or other type of file. The other areas of common dialog boxes are described as follows:

- **Text box.** A *text box* is used to insert a single line of textual information such as a filename or a numeric value. When a text box is empty, a flashing vertical bar called the *insertion point* appears at the far left of the box. See **Figure 1-11.** The text you type starts at this point. In the example shown in **Figure 1-10,** a user has typed in the name bracket in the **File name:** text box. If the text box you want to use already contains text, the existing text is highlighted. You can type over the text if you choose, or press the [Delete], [Backspace], or [Spacebar]

Figure 1-9.
The simplest dialog boxes display informational messages as shown in A, or warnings as shown in B. For each type, you must click the **OK** button to acknowledge the message.

Figure 1-10.
The basic areas of a common dialog box.

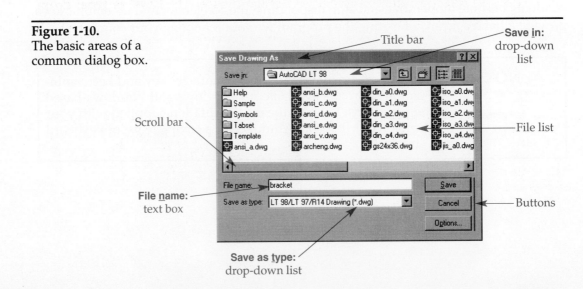

AutoCAD LT—Fundamentals and Applications

Figure 1-11.
You can enter a
filename, numeric
value, or any single
line of information
in a text box.

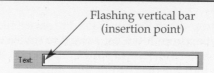

Flashing vertical bar
(insertion point)

Text:

keys on your keyboard to remove the existing text from the text box. You can edit the existing text using the keyboard cursor keys, [Home], [End], [→], and [←]. The [Home] key moves the cursor to the beginning of the line of text and the [End] key moves to the end of the line. The [→] and [←] keys move the cursor one character to the right or to the left, respectively. By using the [Ctrl] key in conjunction with the right arrow or left arrow key, you can move the cursor to the next word or the previous word, respectively.

- **List box.** Every type of common dialog box used for file operations, such as opening or saving a drawing, displays a *list box*. This is the bordered area in the middle of the dialog box that contains a listing of existing files or folders. See **Figure 1-10.** You can *open* one of the folders by *double-clicking* its name in the list. Once opened, the contents of the folder are then listed. You can use your pointing device to select a file from the list or type in the desired file-name in the text box as previously described. When the list of filenames is long, you can use a *horizontal scroll bar* to view the files that exist beyond the rightmost border of the box. If filenames in a list box appear *grayed-out*, they are not available for selection.

- **Scroll bars.** *Scroll bars* can appear in either vertical or horizontal orientations depending on the particular application. As shown in **Figure 1-12,** a scroll bar contains a scroll arrow and a scroll box. Use the scroll arrow to scroll up or down one line at a time. You can scroll continuously if you hold down the pick button on your pointing device. If you click just above or below the scroll box in a vertical scroll bar, you can scroll a whole page at a time. For a horizontal scroll bar like that shown in the **Save Drawing As** dialog box, click to the left or right of the scroll box.

- **Drop-down lists.** A *drop-down list* is a rectangular box that displays a list of choices. The list of available items does not appear, however, until you click the down arrow in the small box at the right. Two types of drop-down lists occur in the sample dialog box shown in **Figure 1-10.** The **Save in:** drop-down list at the top of the dialog box displays the currently open folder and can be used to select a different folder or storage device. The **Save as type:** drop-down list allows you to save your AutoCAD LT drawing in a variety of file formats. See **Figure 1-13.** This capability is provided to ensure compatibility with earlier versions of both AutoCAD LT and AutoCAD. In both drop-down list examples, the current selection is shown highlighted in the list.

Figure 1-12.
Both vertical and
horizontal scroll
bars contain scroll
arrows and a
scroll box.

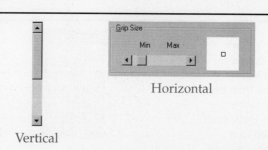

Grip Size

Min   Max

Horizontal

Vertical

Figure 1-13.
A—The **Save in:** drop-down list box is used to save a file to a different folder or storage device.
B—The **Save as type:** drop-down list is used to save a drawing or template file in a format compatible with earlier versions of AutoCAD LT and AutoCAD. In both examples, the highlighted items indicate the current selections.

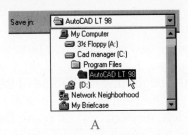

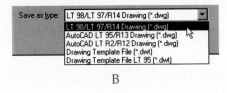

A

B

- **Command buttons.** These buttons usually appear at the far right or the bottom of dialog boxes and are used to initiate an immediate action. The **OK** and **Cancel** buttons are the most common type of command buttons. Click **OK** to accept the changes or information shown in a dialog box. To discard any changes made, click the **Cancel** button. Clicking a button that contains an ellipsis opens another dialog box, or what is often called a *subdialog box.* Several examples of these types of buttons are shown in **Figure 1-14.** Note the appearance of the **OK** button in this illustration. Observe that this button is displayed with a heavier border and is also highlighted with a dashed rectangle. This means that it is the default selection and may be quickly selected by simply pressing the [Enter] key on your keyboard.
- **Check boxes.** Clicking inside a *check box* makes a setting active. An active check box is indicated with a check mark (✓). See **Figure 1-15A.** To deactivate the setting, click the check box and the check mark is removed. As shown in the illustration, more than one check box setting can be active at a time.
- **Option buttons.** *Option buttons* are used the same way as check boxes. As shown in **Figure 1-15B,** an option button is active when the circle is filled. Simply click the desired option button to activate a setting. Unlike check boxes, however, only one option button may be active at a time. As soon as you click a different option button in a group, the previous selection is deactivated.

Figure 1-14.
A button label with a ellipsis (…) opens another dialog box. The heavier border around the **OK** button indicates that this is the default selection.

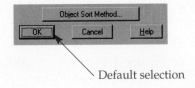

Default selection

Figure 1-15.
A—An check mark (✓) in a check box indicates an active setting. More than one check box may be selected. B—Only one option button in a group can be active at any one given time.

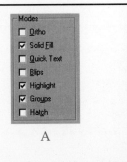

A

B

- **Image tiles.** Several of the dialog boxes in AutoCAD LT use pictorial images to display the available options. See **Figure 1-16.** These pictorial images are called *image tiles*. They are also sometimes referred to as *icon menus*. Simply click the graphical representation to change the option. Once the desired option is in the image tile, click the **OK** button. The dialog box is closed and the option you selected is made current.

Figure 1-16.
Some dialog boxes contain image tiles that graphically display options or selections.

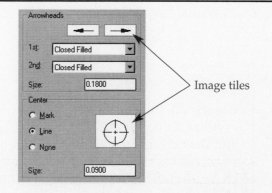

Image tiles

PROFESSIONAL TIP

As a new user, you may occasionally find yourself inside a dialog box without realizing how you got there. If you find yourself in just such a situation, be sure to click the **Cancel** button to exit the dialog box. You can also press the [Esc] key on your keyboard to quickly exit the dialog box. Doing so will discard any unnecessary (and undesirable) changes you may have made inadvertently.

The AutoCAD LT Tablet Menu

If you have a digitizing tablet, it may be used to draw objects, select items in the drawing window, and issue frequently used commands. The pointing device supplied with your tablet may be a multibutton puck, or pen-like stylus. By attaching a *tablet menu overlay*, most, but not all, AutoCAD LT commands may be selected directly from the tablet. The AutoCAD LT 98 tablet menu overlay is shown in **Figure 1-17.** Refer to the Appendix of this text for the AutoCAD LT 97 tablet menu.

The tablet menu may be customized to suit organizational or individual needs. However, remember that your digitizing tablet must first be configured before it can be used. See *Chapter 23* for more information about configuring the tablet and customizing the tablet menu. Also refer to *Appendix B* of the *AutoCAD LT 98 Getting Started Guide* for complete tablet information.

NOTE

Be aware that a digitizing tablet can only be used with AutoCAD LT if it is Wintab-compatible. *Wintab* is a Windows specification that permits you to use your tablet both as a system pointer and a pointing device. Therefore, the tablet and tablet puck (or stylus) is used in place of a conventional mouse for *all* your Windows programs, not just AutoCAD LT.

Figure 1-17.
The AutoCAD LT 98 tablet menu. (*Autodesk, Inc.*)

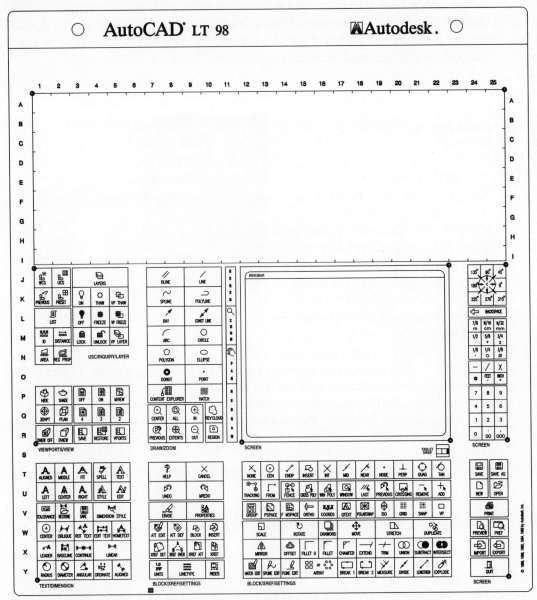

Selecting AutoCAD LT Commands

You will soon learn that there are usually several different ways to accomplish exactly the same task in AutoCAD LT. Apart from the toolbars, pull-down menus, tablet menu, and dialog boxes, commands may also be entered from the keyboard.

The advantage in using the toolbar buttons, as well as the pull-down menus, is that you do not have to remove your eyes from the screen. The disadvantage of a digitizing tablet is that you must take your eyes away from the screen as you search for the desired command on the tablet menu overlay. Additionally, unless you are an excellent typist, typed commands also require that you look away from the screen. However, the commands and their options can be learned more quickly by typing them. Therefore, the examples shown in this text illustrate each of the AutoCAD LT commands as they appear when typed at the Command: prompt. Many commands may be entered from the keyboard as one-, two-, or three-character abbreviations. These shortened command forms are called *command aliases*. Command aliases and other command entry forms are presented throughout this text where appropriate.

Control Keys and Function Keys

Earlier in this chapter, you learned how accelerator and mnemonic keys can be used to activate and make selections from the ten AutoCAD LT pull-down menus. Other functions may be performed with keyboard shortcuts as well. Many of these tasks are activated using *control key* combinations. To perform a control key function, simply press and hold the key labeled [Ctrl] while pressing another key. The available control key combinations and their functions are as follows:

- **[Ctrl]+[A].** Selects all drawing objects on the screen.
- **[Ctrl]+[B].** Toggles **SNAP** mode on and off.
- **[Ctrl]+[C].** Issues the **COPYCLIP** command where selected objects are copied from AutoCAD LT and placed in the Windows Clipboard.
- **[Ctrl]+[D].** Toggles the coordinate display on the Status bar on and off.
- **[Ctrl]+[E].** Toggles through the right, left, and top **ISOPLANE** modes for isometric constructions.
- **[Ctrl]+[F].** Activates the **Osnap Settings** dialog box.
- **[Ctrl]+[G].** Toggles the **GRID** on and off.
- **[Ctrl]+[H].** Works the same as the [Backspace] key.
- **[Ctrl]+[L].** Toggles **ORTHO** mode on and off.
- **[Ctrl]+[N].** Issues the **NEW** command.
- **[Ctrl]+[O].** Issues the **OPEN** command.
- **[Ctrl]+[P].** Issues the **PLOT** command.
- **[Ctrl]+[S].** Issues the **SAVE** command.
- **[Ctrl]+[T].** Toggles **TABLET** mode on and off.
- **[Ctrl]+[V].** Issues the **PASTECLIP** command where Clipboard objects are pasted into the AutoCAD LT graphics window.
- **[Ctrl]+[X].** Issues the **CUTCLIP** command where selected objects are cut from AutoCAD LT and placed in the Windows Clipboard.
- **[Ctrl]+[Y].** Issues the **REDO** command.
- **[Ctrl]+[Z].** Issues the **UNDO** command.

An even easier method for instant access to commands exists through the use of *function keys*. The function keys are usually located at the very top of your keyboard and are labeled F1 through F12. Eight of the function keys are preprogrammed by AutoCAD LT to perform the following tasks:

- **[F1].** Invokes the **On-Line Help** system.
- **[F2].** Toggles between the graphics window and the text window. The text window is a window that displays prompts, messages, and the command history for the current drawing session. You can use it to view the lengthy output of certain commands, as well as to review previously entered commands. You can also display the text window by first selecting **Display** from the **View** pull-down menu, and then selecting **Text Window** from the cascading submenu. From the keyboard, enter the **TEXTSCR** command. Return to the graphics window by pressing [F2] or entering the **GRAPHSCR** command. A typical text window display appears in **Figure 1-18.**
- **[F3].** Activates the **Osnap Settings** dialog box (same as [Ctrl]+[F]).
- **[F4].** Toggles **TABLET** mode on and off (same as [Ctrl]+[T]).
- **[F5].** Toggles the **ISOPLANE** mode (same as [Ctrl]+[E]).
- **[F6].** Toggles the coordinate display on and off (same as [Ctrl]+[D]).
- **[F7].** Toggles the **GRID** on and off (same as [Ctrl]+[G]).
- **[F8].** Toggles **ORTHO** mode on and off (same as [Ctrl]+[L]).
- **[F9].** Toggles **SNAP** mode on and off (same as [Ctrl]+[B]).
- **[F10].** Toggles the Status bar display on and off.

Figure 1-18.
The **AutoCAD LT Text Window** displays all prompts, messages, and commands for the current drawing session.

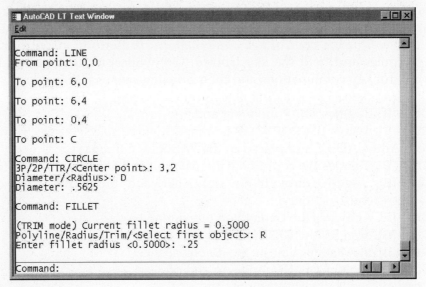

```
Command: LINE
From point: 0,0

To point: 6,0

To point: 6,4

To point: 0,4

To point: C

Command: CIRCLE
3P/2P/TTR/<Center point>: 3,2
Diameter/<Radius>: D
Diameter: .5625

Command: FILLET

(TRIM mode) Current fillet radius = 0.5000
Polyline/Radius/Trim/<Select first object>: R
Enter fillet radius <0.5000>: .25

Command:
```

PROFESSIONAL TIP   Try not to be overwhelmed with the many different command options offered by AutoCAD LT. Remember there is no *right* or *wrong* way of issuing a command. Everyone has their own particular preferences when working with the program. Experiment with the different interface options and then use the method that works best for you.

Getting Help

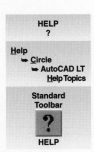

HELP
?

Help
↳ Circle
↳ AutoCAD LT
   Help Topics

Standard
Toolbar

?
HELP

If you need some help with a specific command, option, or program feature, AutoCAD LT provides a powerful and convenient online Help system. There are several ways to access online Help. The two fastest methods are to simply click the **Help** button on the **Standard Toolbar** or press the [F1] function key on your keyboard. Either action displays the **AutoCAD LT 98 Help System** window. See **Figure 1-19.** You can also display this window by selecting **AutoCAD LT Help Topics** from the **Help** pull-down menu, or by entering HELP or a ? at the Command: prompt.

Complete information for using AutoCAD LT is contained in the **AutoCAD LT 98 Help System.** As shown in **Figure 1-19,** the left frame of the window displays the table of contents and tabs providing quick access to the index and search functions. Clicking on the **Index** tab displays a list of **Help** topics in the left frame. See **Figure 1-20.** Once a topic is selected, it is displayed in the right frame of the window. The **Search** tab lists topics based on a word or words you enter in a keyword field at the top of the tab. As with the **Index** tab, a topic is displayed in the right frame of the window once it is selected from the list. When you wish to exit the **Help** system and return to the AutoCAD LT graphics window, click the close button (represented by an X) at the upper-right corner of the window.

Figure 1-19.
The **AutoCAD LT 98 Help System** window.

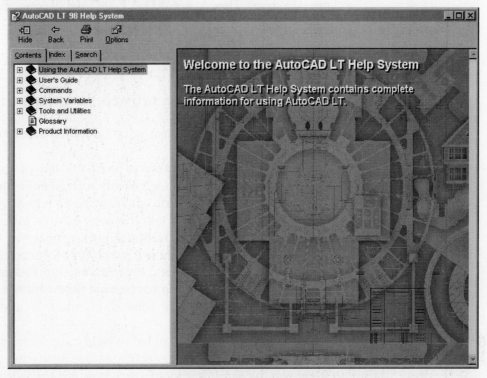

Figure 1-20.
The **Index** tab includes a list of index entries. When an entry is accessed the topic information is displayed in the right frame.

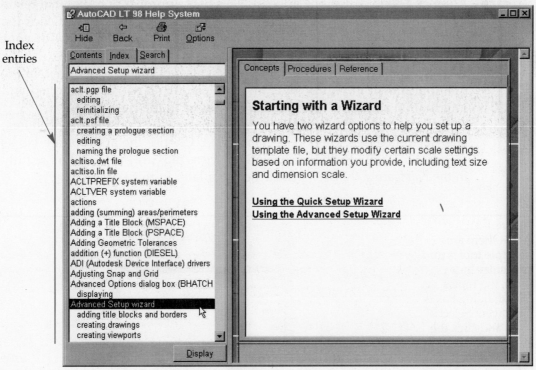

> **NOTE**   Online help requires Microsoft Internet Explorer 4.0 (or later) to run. The AutoCAD LT 98 installation program installs it for you automatically if not detected on your workstation.

Using the Contents, Index, and Search tabs to Find Information

Information can be located in three ways by using the **Contents, Index**, or **Search** tabs. These tabs are described as follows:

- **Contents.** The **Contents** tab displays a table of contents list of topics and subtopics. Use this tab when you want to narrow your search quickly by selecting and expanding topics. Because you can always see where you are in the **Help** system when using the **Contents** tab, it is very easy to quickly jump to other topics. A window with three additional tabs appears in the right frame of the **Contents** tab to provide a choice of the type of information to display. The three tabs are labeled **Concepts, Procedures**, and **Reference**. See **Figure 1-20.** These tabs let you select from a conceptual description, a step-by-step procedure, or a reference to other related commands and system variables.

- **Index.** The **Index** tab displays an alphabetical list of **Help** index entries. Use the index when you want information about a specific feature, keyword, or procedure. To find an item, use the scroll bar to advance through the list or type in a key word and the list will advance to that item. After finding an item in index list, double-click on the item or click on the item and click the **Display** button at the bottom of the **Help** window. At this point, one of the following three things may happen:

  - A **Topics Found** dialog box appears. This lists a number of topics that relate to the item selected. See **Figure 1-21.** Select one of the topics and click the **Display** button. You can also double-click the topic of interest with your pointing device. Now, information is displayed in the right frame.

  - Information about the selected item is displayed in the right frame. In the example shown in **Figure 1-22,** the **ARC** command has been selected and information about the command is displayed in the right frame.

  - A window appears in the right frame displaying the **Concepts, Procedures**, and **Reference** tabs previously mentioned. Choose the appropriate tab as required to obtain further information. These tabs are explained more fully in the *Navigating the User's Guide* heading later in this section.

Figure 1-21.
When there are multiple topics for a particular index entry, the **Topics Found** dialog box is displayed. Select a topic and click the **Display** button to view that topic information.

Figure 1-22.
Index topics with a
simple definition
and usage
information are
described
immediately in the
right frame.

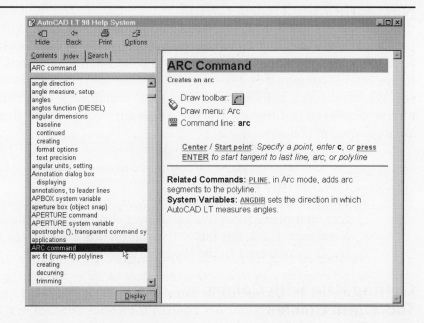

- **Search.** The **Search** tab displays an alphabetical list of **Help** index entries that contain the word or words you enter in the keyword field at the top. The list is not generated until you press the **List Topics** button. Once the list is displayed, select a topic and click the **Display** button at the bottom of the tab. You can also double-click the topic of interest with your pointing device. The topic is then displayed in the right frame of the **Search** tab. In the example shown in **Figure 1-23**, the words "dimension arrowheads" have been entered in the keyword field. The **List Topics** button is then clicked and the **Choosing Dimension Arrowheads** topic is selected from the generated list. The topic is then fully explained, and sometimes graphically illustrated, in the right frame of the **Search** tab. The **Search** tab is a new online Help feature in AutoCAD LT 98 only. If you are using AutoCAD LT 97, use the **Index** tab instead.

Figure 1-23.
The **Search** tab
displays a list of
topics based on the
word or words
entered in the
keyword field. Once
a topic is selected
and the **Display**
button clicked, the
topic is then
displayed in the
right frame of the
Search tab. The
Search tab is not
available in
AutoCAD LT 97.

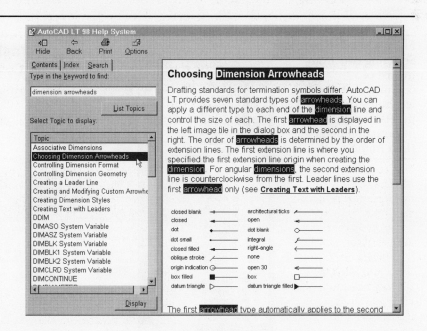

Navigating the User's Guide

As stated in the **Help System** window, the **User's Guide** provides quick access to conceptual descriptions, procedures, and associated commands. The **User's Guide** topics offer three tabs that allow you to choose the type of information you wish to see. When you click a different tab, the topic remains the same but the type of information displayed is different. The three tabs are located above the topic window and are explained as follows:

- **Concepts.** The **Concepts** tab describes an AutoCAD LT feature or function. As the default tab, it is automatically activated when a topic is selected from the **User's Guide**.
- **Procedures.** The **Procedures** tab displays step-by-step instructions for common procedures related to the selected **User's Guide** topic.
- **Reference.** Click this tab to list commands and system variables related to the current **User's Guide** topic.

Getting **Help** with **Commands, System Variables, Tools, and Utilities**

While in the **Contents** tab, the **Commands** feature is used when you need help with a specific command and its options. A list starting with the label **A commands** running through **Z commands** is displayed in the left frame of the **Help** window. In the example shown in **Figure 1-24**, the **R** commands are first selected for listing. Next, the **RAY** command is selected from the list. Information about the **RAY** command is immediately displayed in the right frame of the **Help** window.

The **System Variables** feature works identically to the **Commands** feature. System variables control the drawing, editing, and dimensioning environment by changing the way certain commands work. You will be introduced to many of the system variables used in AutoCAD LT as you progress through the chapters of this textbook.

The **Tools and Utilities** feature provides help with various tools that can be used while a command is in progress, as well as several utilities that convert data and AutoCAD LT files.

Figure 1-24.
Selecting **RAY** from the list of commands in the left frame displays the **RAY** command information in the right frame.

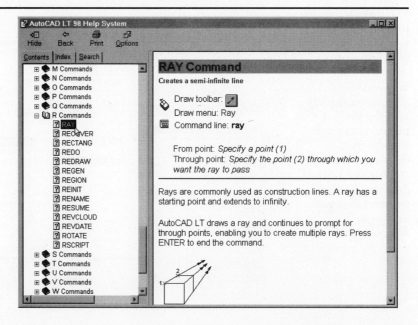

Using the Online Glossary

Just as you might look up a topic in a textbook by using the book's index to locate a particular word, you can also research AutoCAD LT topics using a single word or phrase. To do so, select the **Glossary** feature from the online **Help** system. In the example shown in **Figure 1-25,** all words and topics starting with the letter *L* are first selected by clicking the **L** button in the top row of buttons at the top of the dialog box. Use your pointing device to scroll through the glossary listing until the topic you are seeking is displayed.

Figure 1-25.
The **Glossary** is used to get help with a specific word or phrase. The highlighted text indicates the blue underlined text, which accesses additional information when clicked.

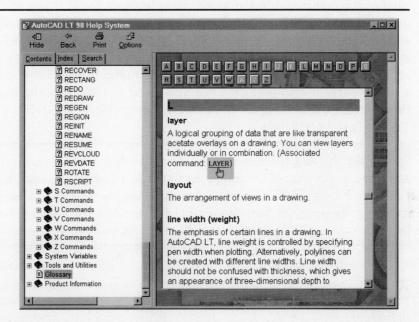

PROFESSIONAL TIP

Many **Help** topics contain blue underlined text. Move your pointing device to the blue text and the pointer assumes the appearance of a hand. See **Figure 1-25.** Now, simply click the blue text to see a definition of the underlined word or phrase.

Interpreting the Help System Buttons

The four buttons located in the upper-left of the **Help System** window can assist in your use of **Online Help**. The buttons are described below:

- **Hide.** The **Hide** button reduces the size of the **Help** window by hiding the table of contents, index, and search frames. The reduced window size is helpful when displaying procedures while you work on a drawing. Once reduced, the **Hide** button becomes the **Show** button.
- **Show.** Click the **Show** button when you wish to restore the full size of the **Help System** window. Once restored, the **Show** button once again reverts to the **Hide** button.
- **Back.** Use this button when you wish to return to the previous **Help System** topic.
- **Refresh.** The **Refresh** button appears in AutoCAD LT 97 only and is used to reload the current topic in the **Help System** window. This button is rarely used.

- **Print.** Click the **Print** button to send the current **Help** topic to your printer for off-line reading and reference.
- **Options.** The **Options** button displays a pull-down menu that offers several additional display features. The **Options** button is not available in AutoCAD LT 97.

Using Context-Oriented Help

It is also possible to ask for help while you are working inside another command. For example, suppose you are using the **PLINE** command and forget the meaning of each of the command line options. Simply press the [F1] key and the help you need for that command and its options are then displayed in the **Help** window. You can accomplish the same thing by entering either an apostrophe and a question mark, or an apostrophe and the word HELP at the Command: prompt for any command. The ability to get help while inside another command is called *context-oriented help.* It is a particularly useful feature since you need not spend valuable time scanning the **Help** topics or searching for key words.

PROFESSIONAL TIP AutoCAD LT need not be running for you to get help with AutoCAD LT commands and functions. Remember that you can get help at any time by clicking Online Help from the AutoCAD LT 98 program folder.

Other Online Services

AutoCAD LT offers several other online services with which you should become familiar. These services differ between AutoCAD LT 98 and AutoCAD LT 97, but may be accessed from either the AutoCAD LT program folder in the Start menu or the **Help** pull-down menu. The services are described in the following sections.

Finding Out What's New in AutoCAD LT 98

Users already familiar with earlier versions of AutoCAD LT can quickly learn what is new and/or improved in the new release by clicking **What's New** from the AutoCAD LT 98 program folder. This application displays the screen shown in **Figure 1-26.** The available selections textually and graphically describe all of the new features of AutoCAD LT 98. The **What's New** feature is also available in AutoCAD LT 97 and is shown in **Figure 1-27.**

Figure 1-26.
Using **What's New** allows users of previous releases of AutoCAD LT to learn all about the new features offered with AutoCAD LT 98.

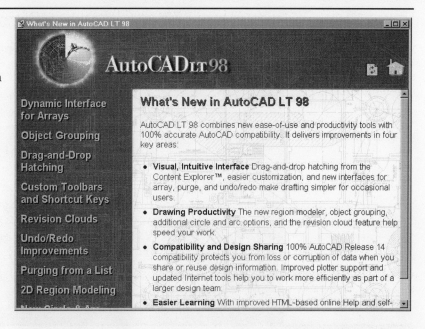

Figure 1-27.
What's New is also available for users of AutoCAD LT 97.

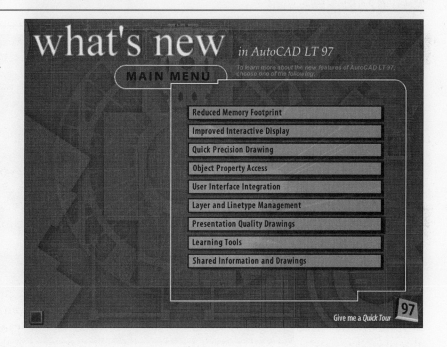

Take a Quick Tour

Users of AutoCAD LT 97 can receive a quick introduction to the program by selecting **Quick Tour** from the **Help** pull-down menu. This application displays the screen shown in **Figure 1-28.** The screen is part of a multimedia application that graphically explains how to navigate through the **Quick Tour.** Once the instructions are concluded, the **Main Menu** is presented. There are two selections available. **See Figure 1-29.** Choose **Introducing AutoCAD LT 97** if you wish to tour the user interface and review the use of online help. If you would like a broad overview of AutoCAD LT 97's capabilities, select **Drawing with AutoCAD LT 97** instead. **Quick Tour** features buttons in the upper-right corner of the display screen enables you to pause the tour, return to the **Main Menu**, or move forward and backward through the tour as you like.

When you are through visiting **Quick Tour**, press the [Esc] key on your keyboard or click the red button at the lower-left to exit and return to AutoCAD LT.

Figure 1-28.
The **Quick Tour**
program in
AutoCAD LT 97
starts with an
animation that
graphically explains
how to navigate the
program.

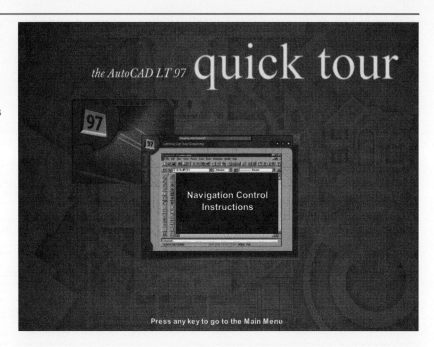

Figure 1-29.
Quick Tour
introduces the
novice user to
computer-aided
drafting using
AutoCAD LT 97.

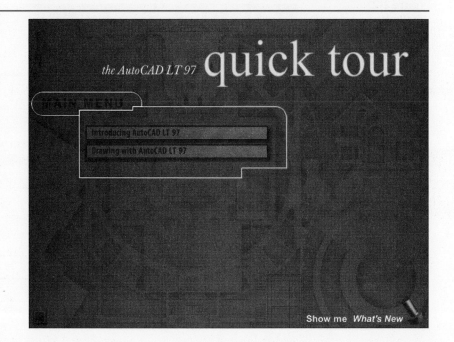

Learning Assistance

Included with both AutoCAD LT 98 and AutoCAD LT 97, and located in the **Help** pull-down menu, is a powerful learning tool called **Learning Assistance**. It is comprised of **Tutorials**, **Fast Answers**, and **Concepts**. **Learning Assistance** is an interactive, multimedia application that makes use of text, graphics, sound, and animations. As such, it is both entertaining and highly informative.

As with AutoCAD LT, **Learning Assistance** is supplied on a separate CD-ROM and must first be installed on your computer's hard disk before it can be used. The installation procedure creates a desktop shortcut which may be used to quickly launch the program outside of AutoCAD LT. It may also be started by first selecting **Programs** from the **Start** menu and then selecting **AutoCAD LT Learning Assistance**.

PROFESSIONAL TIP   Although AutoCAD LT 98 or AutoCAD LT 97 need not be running for you to use the **Learning Assistance** program, the *Learning Assistance CD* must be in the CD-ROM drive of your computer to use **Learning Assistance**.

Chapter Test

Write your answer in the space provided.

1. *True or False?* The "LT" in AutoCAD LT stands for "Lite". _____
_____
_____

2. What are the names of the four default toolbars in AutoCAD LT? _____
_____
_____

3. What is a flyout and how is it accessed? _____
_____
_____

4. Which area displays the primary communication between AutoCAD LT and the user? _____
_____

5. What is the difference between floating and docked windows? _____
_____
_____
_____

6. What is a tooltip? _____
_____
_____

7. What is an accelerator key? What is a mnemonic key? How are they used? Give an example of each. _____
_____
_____
_____
_____

8. List the ten AutoCAD LT pull-down menus. _____
_____
_____

9. What are the functions of the following control keys?

   A. [Ctrl]+[B]— _____

   B. [Ctrl]+[D]— _____

   C. [Ctrl]+[E]— _____

   D. [Ctrl]+[G]— _____

   E. [Ctrl]+[L]— _____

   F. [Ctrl]+[N]— _____

10. Name the function keys that execute the same task as the following control keys.

Control key	**Function key**
A. [Ctrl]+[B]—	_____
B. [Ctrl]+[D]—	_____
C. [Ctrl]+[E]—	_____
D. [Ctrl]+[G]—	_____
E. [Ctrl]+[L]—	_____

11. What is the text window and which function key displays it? _____

_____

_____

_____

_____

12. What type of pull-down menu has an arrow to the right of the item? _____

_____

13. What does an ellipsis (…) after a menu item represent? _____

_____

_____

_____

14. What is an image tile? Where might you find one? _____

_____

_____

_____

15. Describe the purpose of a scroll bar and how it is used. _____

_____

_____

_____

_____

16. What is the difference between a check box setting and an option button setting?

_____

_____

_____

_____

17. If you find yourself inadvertently in a dialog box, what should you do? Why?

_____

_____

18. What is the purpose of a digitizing tablet and tablet menu overlay? _____

_____

_____

_____

_____

19. *True or False?* AutoCAD LT must be running to access **Online Help**. _____
20. How do you exit **Online Help**? _____

_____

_____

Chapter Problems

1. If you are using AutoCAD LT 97, start the program as described earlier in this chapter and spend a few moments exploring the **Quick Tour** program. In preparation for the topics to be discussed in *Chapter 2*, select the Drawing with AutoCAD LT 97 menu item and carefully read the *Setting Up Your Drawing* topic.

   General

2. Draw a freehand sketch of the **Standard** and **Object Properties** toolbars. Using your very best upper-case block lettering, label each button with its corresponding tooltip.

   General

3. Launch **Learning Assistance** and activate the **Orientation** program and read the section titled **Using Drawing Tools**. Based on what you learn from this section, draw a freehand sketch of the **Draw** toolbar and label the appropriate buttons with the name of the traditional drafting instrument that would perform the same function on a drafting board.

   General

AutoCAD LT

Drawing Setup and File Operations

Learning Objectives

After you have completed this chapter, you will be able to:
- ○ Set up drawing parameters as you begin a new drawing session.
- ○ Select appropriate measurement styles.
- ○ Size the drawing area.
- ○ Understand and use grid and snap settings.
- ○ Describe the purpose and advantage of template files.
- ○ Save your work and access existing drawing files.
- ○ Maintain file compatibility with earlier versions of AutoCAD LT and AutoCAD.
- ○ Use the **Browse** and **Search** functions to locate drawing files.
- ○ End a drawing session.

If you have ever created engineering or architectural drawings on a drafting board, you know that there are several factors to be considered before you start any new drawing. First, you must carefully study the object you intend to draw so that you can decide how many views are required to adequately describe the object. Second, you need to determine if any additional detail, section, or auxiliary views are required. It is only then that you know what size sheet of drafting media (vellum or mylar) to tape down to your drafting board.

Planning ahead is just as important when using AutoCAD LT. In this chapter, you will learn to set up new drawings to your exact specifications using the various AutoCAD LT measurement styles and drawing aids. You will also learn to save your work, access existing drawings, and end a drawing session.

Starting a Drawing Session

Getting Started Guide 5

A new drawing session is launched automatically by simply starting up AutoCAD LT. After the program is finished loading, you are presented with the **Start Up** dialog box. See **Figure 2-1.** The **Start Up** dialog box contains several buttons on the left that determine how you set up a new drawing.

NOTE Although not recommended, you can disable the **Start Up** dialog box by deactivating the **Show this dialog at start up** check box in the lower-left corner of the dialog box.

Figure 2-1.
The **Start Up** dialog box provides a handy means of setting up new drawing parameters.

Select to use
a wizard to start
a drawing

List of available
wizards

Description of
highlighted wizard

Check box turns
the **Start Up** dialog
box on and off

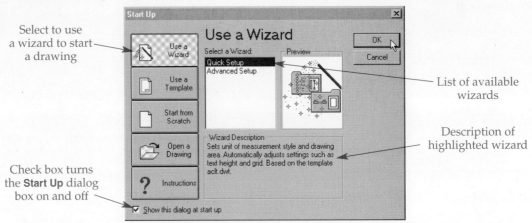

When you create a new drawing, you have the option to use a *template*, or proto-type, that contains standard, or default, drawing settings. You may choose from several templates supplied with AutoCAD LT, or you can select your own customized template. The **Use a Template** button in the **Start Up** dialog box is designed expressly for this purpose. Using and customizing templates is discussed later in this chapter.

You also have the option to select one of two drawing setup wizards. A *wizard* is an automated procedure used by Microsoft Windows to help add and remove software programs. Wizards are also used to set up operating system and program parameters and help facilitate *plug and play* hardware installations.

> **NOTE**
> If AutoCAD LT is already running and you begin a new drawing using the **NEW** command, then the **Start Up** dialog box is titled **Create New Drawing**. The **NEW** command is covered later in this chapter.

The **Start from Scratch** Button

By default, AutoCAD LT uses the English system of feet and inches for all new drawings. If your application requires metric measurements, click the **Start from Scratch** button at the left of the **Start Up** dialog box. You are then provided the option of selecting **Metric** default settings, rather than **English**. The measurement system you select is then used with the other startup options.

Using the **Quick Setup** Wizard

To use the **Quick Setup** wizard, click the **Use a Wizard** button at the upper left of the **Start Up** dialog box. (Since this is the default method for new drawing setup, this button should already be active.) Next, be sure that the **Quick Setup** selection is high-lighted in the **Select a Wizard** option list and then click the **OK** button. This accesses the **Quick Setup** dialog box. See **Figure 2-2**. **Quick Setup** is a two-step procedure. Step 1 permits you to select the appropriate measurement style for your drawing. Step 2 lets you specify the size, or limits, of the drawing area.

Figure 2-2.
The **Units** tab in the **Quick Setup** subdialog box allows you to select from five styles of linear measurement.

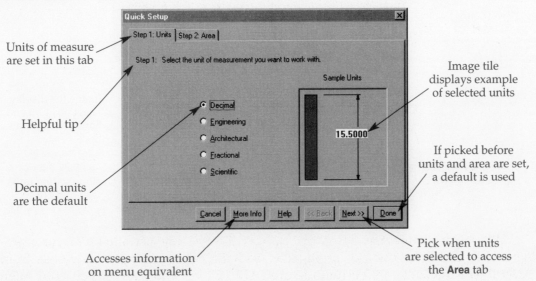

Units of measure are set in this tab

Helpful tip

Decimal units are the default

Image tile displays example of selected units

If picked before units and area are set, a default is used

Accesses information on menu equivalent

Pick when units are selected to access the **Area** tab

Step 1: Units tab

The **Quick Setup** subdialog box appears with this tab activated. This tab provides you with five measurement styles from which to choose. The five systems are **Decimal** (the default measurement style), **Engineering**, **Architectural**, **Fractional**, and **Scientific**. You can select the desired system of units by clicking the appropriate option button in the subdialog box. For each measurement style, AutoCAD LT displays an example in the image tile to the right of the option buttons. To better understand the format of each style, the dialog box examples are repeated below:

System	Sample
Decimal	15.5000
Engineering	1'-3.5000"
Architectural	1'-3 1/2"
Fractional	15 1/2
Scientific	1.5500E+01

The measurement style that you select is used for all displayed numeric values in the current drawing. That applies to the values shown in the **Command** window, in dialog boxes, and the coordinate display on the **Status** bar.

Step 2: Area tab

Perhaps the greatest difference between computer-aided drafting and traditional, paper-based drafting is the ability to draw nearly anything imaginable at full scale using CAD. Whether you are drawing a jumbo jetliner or a threaded fastener, a residential deck or a commercial shopping mall, everything is drawn at full scale. The finished size of a drawing is determined at plotting time. Plotting parameters and plot scales are discussed in *Chapter 14* of this text.

Although AutoCAD LT can draw virtually anything at full scale, it is usually a good idea to size the drawing area on the screen before beginning a new drawing. This makes it much easier to use title blocks with your drawings as well as helping to determine the final plot scale. Sizing the drawing area is also known as setting the *drawing limits*. After you have selected the desired measurement style, click the **Step 2: Area** tab, or the button labeled **Next** 》, to display the next step or "page" of the **Quick Setup** subdialog box. See **Figure 2-3**. AutoCAD LT places the origin of the drawing at the lower-left corner (0,0) of the drawing window, while the upper-right

Figure 2-3.
The **Area** tab in the **Quick Setup** subdialog box allows you to size the drawing area using "real-world" units.

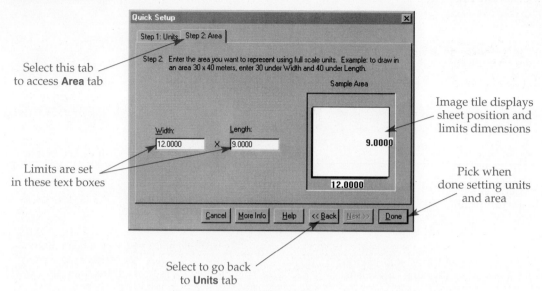

Select this tab to access **Area** tab

Limits are set in these text boxes

Select to go back to **Units** tab

Image tile displays sheet position and limits dimensions

Pick when done setting units and area

corner is set to 12 units on the X axis and 9 units on the Y axis (12,9). This is the default drawing area which represents an architectural A-size sheet of paper.

You can increase or decrease the drawing area using the **Width:** and **Length:** text boxes. For example, to construct a drawing that is to be fitted onto a mechanical A-size (8-1/2 × 11) sheet, set the drawing width to 11 inches and the drawing length to 8.5 inches. For a mechanical C-size sheet, set the drawing width to 22 inches and the drawing length to 17 inches, etc. Remember to always use "real-world" units when you size the drawing area, such as feet, inches, or millimeters. The units you enter should be consistent with the measurement style that was selected in the **Step 1: Units** tab.

Once you have sized the drawing area as required, click the button labeled **Done**. The subdialog box closes and the graphics window should appear. See **Figure 2-4**. Note the display of dots centered in the drawing window. These dots are called the *grid*, which is one of several drawing aids in AutoCAD LT. It is very similar to grid

Figure 2-4.
The drawing screen as it appears after using the **Quick Setup** wizard.

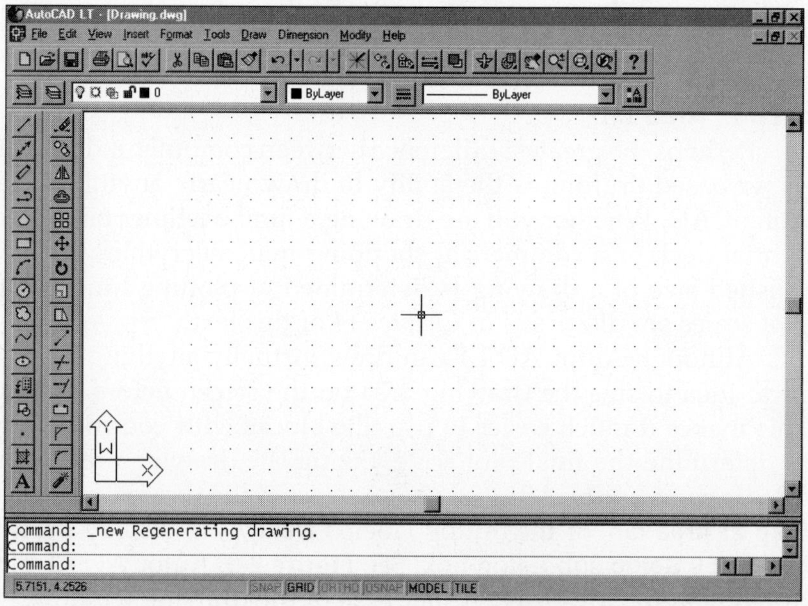

paper with which you are probably already familiar. However, unlike grid paper which uses lines, the AutoCAD LT grid is a series of dots on the screen. You can specify the spacing between the dots on both the horizontal (X) and vertical (Y) axes. The grid is covered in more detail later in this chapter.

EXERCISE 2-1

❑ Start AutoCAD LT as described in Chapter 1 of this text.
❑ When the **Start Up** dialog box appears, click the **Use a Wizard** button and select **Quick Setup** from the **Select a Wizard:** list. Click the **OK** button when you are finished.
❑ Set Architectural units.
❑ Access the **Step 2: Area** tab.
❑ Set the drawing width to 80′ and the drawing length to 60′.
❑ The **Quick Setup** subdialog box should appear as shown below. Click the **Done** button when you are finished.

❑ Using your pointing device, move the cursor around the drawing window. The coordinate display at the lower left of the Status bar should be displaying feet and inch units.
❑ Enter the **QUIT** command at the Command: prompt to exit AutoCAD LT. When the dialog box appears prompting you to save the changes, click the **No** button.

Using the Advanced Setup Wizard

When you use the **Quick Setup** wizard for a new drawing, your setup options are somewhat limited. For example, you cannot select a measurement style for angular values. Additionally, the **Quick Setup** wizard affects only model space. *Model space* is where you construct your drawing, or model. Normally, this is precisely the space you want to be working in. There may be instances, however, when you want to enter paper space. *Paper space* may be used to arrange the final layout of your drawing prior to plotting. AutoCAD LT can use paper space or model space to insert a border or title block, as well as a time and date stamp, on your drawing.

When you wish to perform a more detailed drawing setup, select the **Advanced Setup** option from the **Select a Wizard** dialog box. This option allows you to set the angular measurement style and angle direction, add a border or title block to your drawing, and lets you choose whether to work in the model space or paper space environments. The **Advanced Setup** wizard displays the subdialog box with options shown in **Figure 2-5.** Although seven option tabs are available, you may find several

Figure 2-5.
Linear units of measurement as well as the degree of precision may be selected using the **Advanced Setup** wizard.

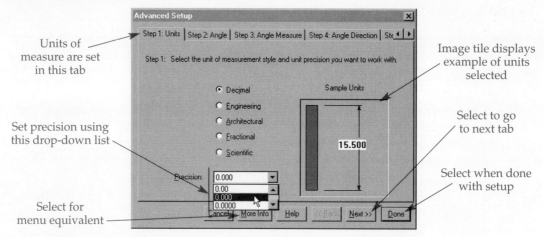

Units of measure are set in this tab

Image tile displays example of units selected

Set precision using this drop-down list

Select to go to next tab

Select when done with setup

Select for menu equivalent

of the tabs obscured depending on your current screen resolution. If this is the case, simply click the right arrow at the upper right of the dialog box to display the obscured option tabs. Use the left arrow when you wish to display the option tabs at the left of the dialog box.

Step 1: Units tab

Note the addition of the **Precision:** drop-down list to the **Units** tab. Keep in mind that AutoCAD LT defaults to four digits of precision for **Decimal**, **Engineering**, and **Scientific** linear measurement styles. If you want to change the number of displayed digits to the right of the decimal point, use the **Precision:** drop-down list to select the number of places of precision. In the example shown, the **Decimal** option button is activated, and three decimal places of precision are selected from the drop-down list. Observe that the **Sample Units** image tile at the right is automatically updated to reflect the change.

Step 2: Angle tab

AutoCAD LT uses decimal degrees as the default angular measurement style. If you wish to change the angular units, click the **Angle** tab. See **Figure 2-6.** You may choose from one of five different styles of angular measurement. The styles are **Decimal Degrees**, **Degrees/Minutes/Seconds**, **Gradians**, **Radians**, and **Surveyor's** units. As with linear measurements, you can also change the degree of accuracy for displayed angular values. The format for each of the angle styles are as follows:

Angular Measurement	Sample Angle
Decimal Degrees	90
Deg/Min/Sec	90d
Grads	100g
Radians	2r
Surveyor	N

In the example shown in **Figure 2-6,** the **Surveyor** option button is activated, and the **Precision:** drop-down list is used to increase the accuracy of the displayed surveyor angular values.

Figure 2-6.
Angular units of measurement as well as the degree of precision may be selected using the **Advanced Setup** wizard.

Select angle measurement

Precision of angle measurement selected in this drop-down list

Image tile displays angle measurement selected

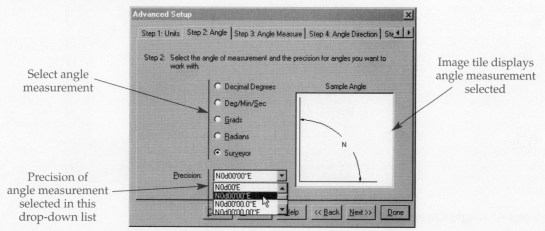

NOTE

Keep in mind the number of decimal places you select for linear or angular measurement is for display purposes only. These displayed values are used by **AutoCAD LT** on the command line, the coordinate display on the **Status** bar, and in dialog boxes. They are also used when you query the system for the length of a line, the radius of a circle, or the area of a closed shape, for example. But regardless of the number of decimal places you specify, AutoCAD LT's database is accurate to 14 decimal places. See *Chapter 8* for detailed information on inquiry commands.

Step 3: Angle Measure tab

AutoCAD LT uses the polar coordinate system to measure angles. With this system, all angles are measured in a *positive*, or counterclockwise, direction. Thus, 0° is to the right (east), 90° is straight up (north), 180° is to the left (west), and 270° is straight down (south). This convention is illustrated in **Figure 2-7.** If you want to measure angles in a clockwise fashion, simply enter the angles as negative (–) values.

You can change the direction from which angles are measured by clicking the **Angle Measure** tab in the **Advanced Setup** subdialog box. Doing so displays the option buttons and image tile shown in **Figure 2-8.** If you want to set some arbitrary direction for angle 0, click the option button labeled **Other**. You can then enter the desired angle in the text box to the right of the option button.

Figure 2-7.
AutoCAD LT measures angles in a positive, or counterclockwise, direction.

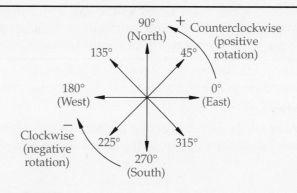

Figure 2-8.
You can change the
location of angle 0
using the **Angle
Measure** tab.

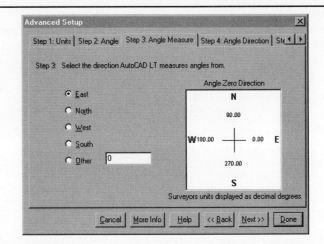

Step 4: Angle Direction tab

If you wish to measure angles in a clockwise direction (negative), rather than counterclockwise, click the **Angle Direction** tab and activate the appropriate option button as required. See **Figure 2-9**.

Figure 2-9.
The direction of
angular
measurement can be
changed using the
Angle Direction tab.

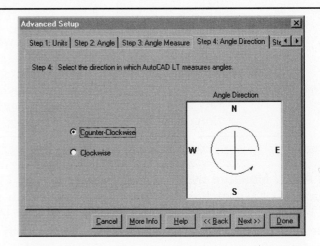

PROFESSIONAL TIP

Unless there is a compelling reason to do otherwise, it is suggested that you leave the angle measure and direction control settings at their default values. This is because you will very likely be sharing drawing files with other AutoCAD LT users—clients, coworkers, classmates, etc. These users will be expecting angular measurement to follow the default convention. Changing the system without good reason will cause undue confusion.

Step 5: Area tab

The **Area** tab is used to change the size of the drawing area. Use this tab in the same manner described earlier in the **Quick Setup** wizard section.

Step 6: Title Block tab

Click the **Title Block** tab if you wish to insert a border (the default) or title block around the limits of your drawing. A drawing with a plain border appears in **Figure 2-10**.

If you want to use a title block sheet instead of a plain border, use the **Title Block Description:** drop-down list to obtain a list of available title block formats. From the example shown in **Figure 2-11**, a C-size title block is selected from the list. This particular title block is drawn in accordance with the American National Standards Institute (ANSI) specification, ANSI Y14.1 *Drawing Sheet Sizes and Format*. Hence the appropriate title block name ANSI C. Use the vertical scroll bar in the list box to display a complete listing of title blocks provided by AutoCAD LT. In addition to ANSI title blocks, there are also title blocks conforming to ISO (*International Organization for Standardization*), DIN (*Deutsches Institut Fuer Normung*), and JIS (*Japanese Industry Standard*) drafting standards.

Figure 2-10.
The **Title Block** tab is used when you wish to insert a border (shown) or predefined title block format around the limits of your new drawing.

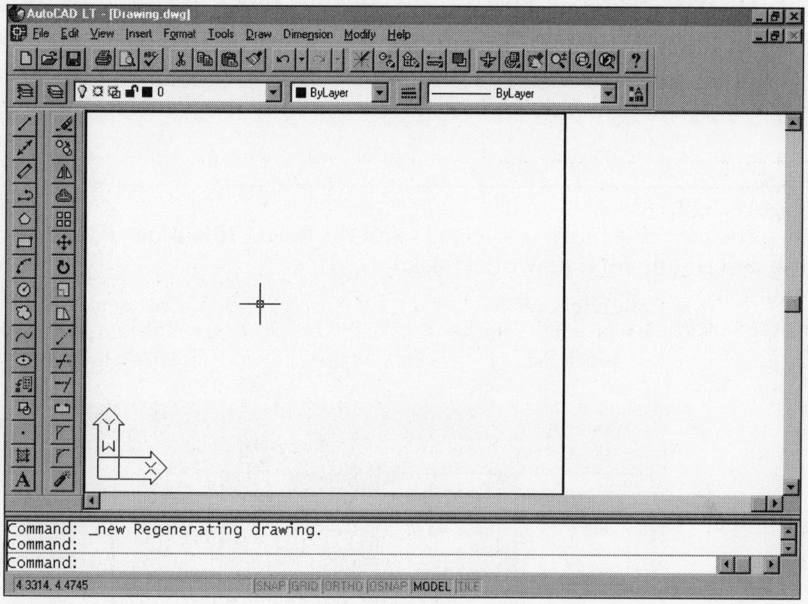

Figure 2-11.
A list of available title blocks is shown in the **Title Block Description:** drop-down list.

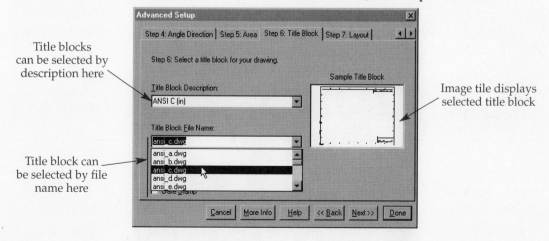

Title blocks can be selected by description here

Title block can be selected by file name here

Image tile displays selected title block

NOTE   The ANSI V option in the list is also an A size title block, but it is in vertical format. The ANSI A option is a title block in horizontal format.

Additional title block options.   Each of the available title blocks are separate drawing files that reside in the AutoCAD LT 98 folder. This folder, and the title blocks themselves, are created by the SETUP.EXE installation program. Take care *not* to delete these files or you will lose your automatic access to title block formats. Additionally, you can easily customize these title block drawings to make them more closely conform to your school or company standards, if you like.

Note the **Add...** and **Remove** buttons located just below the **Title Block File Name:** list box. These buttons and their respective functions are as follows:

- **Add....**Use this button if you have additional title blocks that you would like to add to the list. Consider the example shown in **Figure 2-12A.** Here a user has created a custom E-size title block for architectural applications. After clicking the **Add...** button, the **Select Title Block File** subdialog box is displayed. So that AutoCAD LT can find the new title block, the user first opens the AutoCAD LT 98 folder and then enters the name of the title block,

Figure 2-12.
A—The new title block is selected from the **Select Title Block File** subdialog box. B—Entering the description for a new title block.

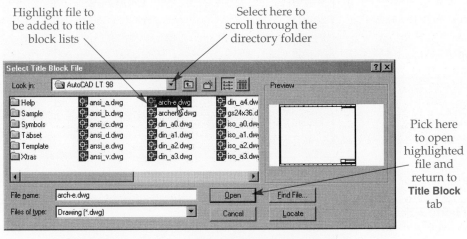

A

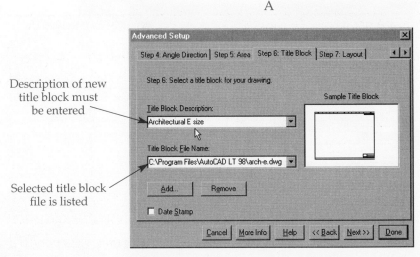

B

arch-e, in the **File name:** text box (or selects the arch-e file from the file list) and then clicks the **Open** button. The previous subdialog box is redisplayed so that an appropriate description can be added in the **Title Block Description:** drop-down list text box. See **Figure 2-12B.** After clicking the **Done** button, the new architectural E-size title block is then automatically added to the title block list for future use.

- **Remove.** To permanently remove one or more title blocks from the list, first select the title block name so that it is highlighted, and then click the **Remove** button. The title block is removed from the list only, and not from the hard disk. Should you accidentally remove a title block from the list, use the **Add...** button to add it back.

CAUTION   Be sure to first check with your supervisor or instructor before changing or removing any of the AutoCAD LT-supplied title blocks.

Adding a time and date stamp to the title block. If you like, the **Advanced Setup** wizard will conveniently add the user name, date, time of day, and drawing name to the title block format you select. This option is activated by clicking the **Date Stamp** check box at the lower left of the **Advanced Setup** subdialog box. If you select one of the horizontal title block formats for your drawing, the date stamp is placed outside the left vertical margin of the title block. See **Figure 2-13A.** If a vertical title block format is selected, such as ANSI V, the date stamp is placed outside the top horizontal margin. See **Figure 2-13A.** The date stamp option is not available if you choose to have just a border for your drawing, (the **No title block** option). However, the time and date stamp can later be added to the border.

It may be necessary to adjust the screen display somewhat so that the date stamp can be seen. To do so, you must enter paper space, issue the **ZOOM** command with the **All** option, and then return to model space to begin drawing. These operations are performed as follows:

      Command: **PSPACE** *or* **PS**↵
      Command: **ZOOM** *or* **Z**↵
      All/Center/Extents/Previous/Scale(X/XP)/Window/⟨Realtime⟩: **A**↵
      Command: **MSPACE** *or* **MS**↵

Figure 2-13. A—The ANSI A title block. B—The ANSI V title block. Note the location of the date stamp on each drawing.

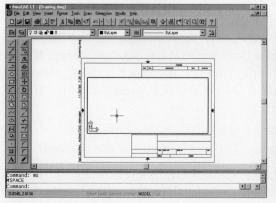
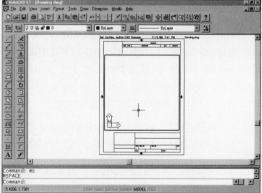

        A   B

PROFESSIONAL TIP

Be aware that by double-clicking the **MODEL/PAPER** button on the **Status** bar, you can quickly toggle between model space and paper space and save yourself some typing. Paper space is covered in detail in *Chapter 17* of this text. Refer to *Chapter 4* for more information about the **ZOOM** command.

Revising the date stamp information. Every new drawing started in AutoCAD LT is automatically given the name drawing.dwg until it is first saved with a specific name. Saving your drawing files is covered in a later section of this chapter. Because a new drawing is unnamed, the date stamp cannot yet show the proper name that the drawing will have when it is complete. This also applies to the date shown on the drawing. You may begin a new drawing on Monday, yet not finish it until Thursday. How can you update the drawing name, date, and time information on a drawing when it is finished?

Fortunately, this capability is provided by selecting **Time and Date Stamp** from the **Tools** pull-down menu. See **Figure 2-14.** This menu item enables the **REVDATE** command and automatically updates the date stamp information on your drawing. This command can be used at anytime. To enter it from the keyboard, enter REVDATE, or RD, at the Command: prompt.

Figure 2-14.
Selecting **Time and Date Stamp** from the **Tools** pull-down menu updates the date stamp information on a drawing.

Adding a time and date stamp to a border only. You can also use the **REVDATE** command to add date stamp information to a drawing that has no date stamp. If you choose to have just a border for your drawing, (the **No title block** option), then the date stamp location can be specified when AutoCAD LT prompts you on the command line with the following:

REVDATE block insertion point ⟨0,0⟩: *(enter coordinates or press* [Enter]*)*
REVDATE block rotation (0 or 90 degrees) ⟨0⟩: *(enter* 0 *or* 90 *and press* [Enter]*)*

Whenever you see alpha or numeric data enclosed within angle brackets like the examples shown above, that means those values are the default settings. Unless you enter a different X and Y location, the date stamp is inserted at the 0,0 drawing origin.

To accept the default insertion point values shown in the angle brackets, simply press the [Enter] key. If you want the date stamp information to read left to right in a horizontal orientation (0°), simply press [Enter] again. On the other hand, if you would prefer to have the date stamp read from the bottom to the top in a vertical orientation, type in 90 before you press [Enter].

Step 7: Layout tab

If you choose to insert a border or title block, it is important to keep in mind that the borders and title blocks are inserted in paper space by default. The ANSI A title block is shown in **Figure 2-13A** and the ANSI V title block appears in **Figure 2-13B**. Observe that a rectangular border appears inside both title blocks. This border is a *floating viewport*. A viewport is a bounded area that displays some portion of a drawing in model space. It is in model space that all of our drawing and editing tasks are typically performed. This is why the grid and graphics cursor are only displayed inside the viewport and not outside.

To fill out the title block information, you will need to work outside the boundary of the floating viewport. To do this, you must exit model space and enter paper space. As mentioned previously, this is easily accomplished by double-clicking the **MODEL/PAPER** button on the **Status** bar. When you are in paper space, the button is labeled **PAPER**. The button is labeled **MODEL** when you are in model space. To return to model space and your drawing, simply double-click the **MODEL/PAPER** button again, or enter MSPACE, or MS, at the Command: prompt.

The **Layout** tab allows you to determine whether paper space or model space will be used for the new drawing session. As shown in **Figure 2-15**, the tab offers several options. The question at the top of the tab asks:

Do you want to use advanced paper space layout capabilities?

Remember that paper space is the default as evidenced by the activated option button labeled **Yes**. If you choose to ignore paper space and work entirely in model space, click the option button labeled **No**. Next, click the **Done** button to exit the **Advanced Setup** wizard and begin working on your new drawing. The tab also asks:

How do you want to start?

If you choose to use paper space layout capabilities, there are three options available to you. These three options are described as follows:

- **Work on my drawing while viewing the layout.** This is the default option. As shown by the image tile in **Figure 2-15A**, the graphics cursor is confined within the model space boundary of the floating viewport. It is then necessary to enter paper space to complete the title block information as previously described. Compare the image tile in the subdialog box with the illustrations shown in **Figure 2-13**.
- **Work on my drawing without the layout visible.** This option disables the paper space layout environment. It is therefore equivalent to answering **No** to the question: Do you want to use advanced paper space layout capabilities? As shown by the image tile in **Figure 2-15B**, no floating viewports are created.
- **Work on the layout of my drawing.** This option creates a floating viewport and activates paper space. As shown by the image tile in **Figure 2-15C**, the graphics cursor is not confined to the floating viewport and may be freely moved about the drawing window. With this option, you must enter model space to construct and edit your drawing.

Once you have selected the desired layout option, click the **Done** button at the lower right of the subdialog box to exit the **Advanced Setup** wizard and begin working on your new drawing.

Figure 2-15.
The options offered in the **Layout** tab determine whether your new drawing is begun in model space or paper space.

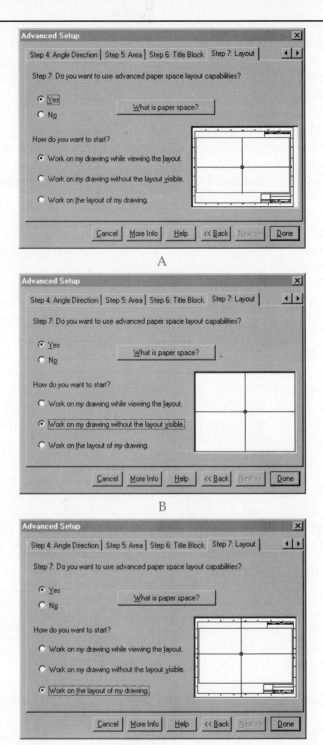

A

B

C

PROFESSIONAL TIP

If you make a typing error when entering characters from the keyboard, you can use the [Backspace] key to fix the error. Remember that the [Ctrl]+[H] key combination works the same as the [Backspace] key. If you are in the middle of a command and would like to cancel, press the [Esc] key instead. The [Esc] key is located at the very upper-left corner of most computer keyboards. Remember that you can use the [Esc] key to cancel out of a dialog box, also.

EXERCISE 2-2

❏ Start AutoCAD LT.
❏ When the **Start Up** dialog box appears, click the **Use a Wizard** button and select **Advanced Setup** from the **Select a Wizard:** list. Click the **OK** button when you are finished.
❏ Do not change the linear measurement style, but access the **Step 2: Angle** tab, and set the angle of measurement to **Degrees/Minutes/Seconds**.
❏ Set the angular display precision to 0d00'00".
❏ Access the **Step 5: Area** tab and set the drawing width to 17.0000 and length to 11.0000. These values represent a B-size drawing.
❏ Access the **Step 6: Title Block** tab.
❏ Select ANSI B (in) title block and activate the date stamp. Click the **Done** button when you are finished.
❏ So you can see the date and time stamp on the drawing, perform the **PSPACE** and **ZOOM** command operations previously described.
❏ Now, return to model space.
❏ Leave this exercise displayed on your screen and do not exit AutoCAD LT.

Template Files

Getting Started Guide 5

As previously mentioned, a template file is a prototype, or framework, that is used to create new drawings. A typical template file can contain the default settings for linear and angular measurement styles, as well as the size of the drawing area or limits. Other settings might include grid and snap spacings, layers, colors, and linetypes, as well as text and dimension styles. (These types of settings are covered in later sections of this text.) Thus, you can create template files to reflect settings consistent with your specific discipline, design application, or company standards.

AutoCAD LT provides several template files that you can use "right-out-of-the-box", or you can create your own. The template files are stored in the C:\Program Files\AutoCAD LT 98\Template folder on your hard disk. This folder is created automatically by the SETUP.EXE installation program. To use a template, first click the **Use a Template** button in the **Start Up** dialog box. See **Figure 2-16**. You will observe the filename aclt.dwt appears highlighted in the file list just to the right of the dialog box buttons. The default template file used by AutoCAD LT is called aclt.dwt (all of the supplied

Figure 2-16.
Click the **Use a Template** button in the **Start Up** dialog box to begin a new drawing based on a predefined template file.

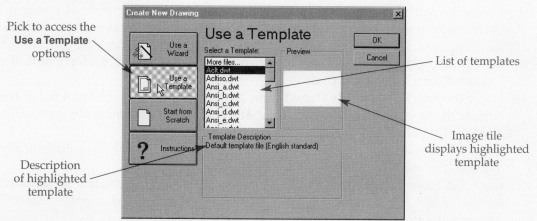

AutoCAD LT template files have the file extension .DWT). The reason that AutoCAD LT defaults to decimal units of measurement with four digits to the right of the decimal point is because the aclt.dwt template is set up this way. Similarly, the reason that every new drawing defaults to 12,9 for the upper-right corner drawing area is because the aclt template has these limits set. For that matter, *all* of the settings in the aclt template carry over into every new AutoCAD LT drawing, unless you specify a different template file.

Selecting a Template File

If you would like to use a template file other than aclt.dwt, use the vertical scroll bar to scroll through the **Select a Template:** list. Keep in mind that *any* drawing may be used as a template. From the file list, note the template file named acltiso.dwt. This template contains metric settings in accordance with the International Organization for Standardization (ISO). It is automatically used when you change from English to metric units by clicking the **Start from Scratch** button as previously described in this chapter. Also observe that each of the title blocks available with AutoCAD LT appear in the template file list, as well.

NOTE   Clicking the **Cancel** button in the **Start Up** dialog box is the equivalent to starting a new drawing using the aclt.dwt template file.

Advantages of Template Files

The key to using AutoCAD LT productively is to *never perform the same operation twice*. If you are an architect, it is far more efficient to have a template file set up for architectural drafting than it is to set architectural units and limits every time you begin a new drawing. Once you have a drawing with architectural parameters set, save it as a template for future use. The same can be said for mechanical or civil engineering applications. When you create your templates, give them logical names like mech.dwt, arch.dwt, or civil.dwt so they can easily be identified. Once you have completed the remainder of this text, you will have learned all of the other types of settings and variables that control the AutoCAD LT drawing and dimensioning environment. You will then be better prepared to make your template files as complete as possible.

Because the entire concept of template files is to construct one drawing based on another, you can easily create similar types of drawings very quickly. As an example, consider the three simple objects illustrated in **Figure 2-17.** Except for the hole patterns, observe that all three drawings are identical. To quickly produce the three drawings, you would do the following:

1. Create the part1 drawing. Be sure to make the drawing as complete as possible.
2. Once the drawing is complete, use the **SAVEAS** command to save it as a template file. When the **Save Drawing As** dialog box appears, use the **Save in:** drop-down list at the top of the dialog box to open the AutoCAD LT 98 folder inside the Program Files folder on the C: drive.
3. Select **Drawing Template File (*.dwt)** from the **Save as type:** drop-down list at the bottom of the dialog box. See **Figure 2-18.** This action automatically opens the AutoCAD LT 98\Template folder.
4. Enter the name part1 in the **File name:** text box. AutoCAD LT automatically appends the .dwt file extension to the name you enter.
5. Click the **Save** button. You are then presented with the **Template Description** subdialog box. This subdialog box allows you to enter a description for the template file that you are saving.

Figure 2-17.
The template drawing method can be used to quickly produce similar drawings.

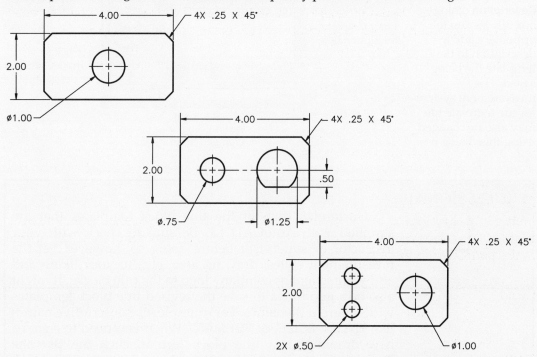

Figure 2-18.
The **Save Drawing As** dialog box is used to save a drawing as a template file to the AutoCAD LT 98\Template folder.

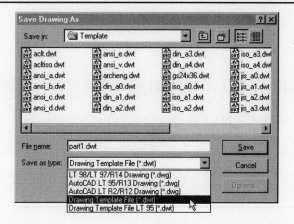

6. As shown in **Figure 2-19**, an appropriate description may be entered before clicking the **OK** button. Click the **Cancel** button if you do not wish to enter a description. Observe from the illustration that you can also change the measurement system from English to Metric for the template file using the **Measurement** drop-down list. Whether you choose to enter a description or not, once the **OK** or **Cancel** button is clicked the drawing is then saved with the name part1.dwt in the AutoCAD LT 98\Template folder.

7. Now begin a new drawing session. When the **Create New Drawing** dialog box appears, click the **Use a Template** button and select part1.dwt from the template list. Click **OK** when you are finished.

8. A copy of the part1 template is displayed in the graphics window. Make the required changes to the hole pattern

9. Use the **SAVEAS** command as previously described to save the new template as part2.dwt.

10. Repeat the procedure for the part3 drawing.

Figure 2-19.
The **Template Description** dialog box allows you to optionally add a description to the template file being saved. The measurement system for the template file may also be changed using this dialog box.

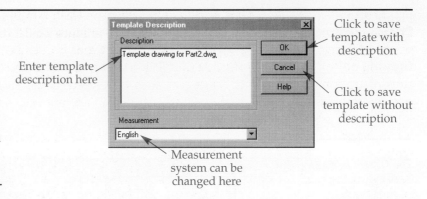

Enter template description here

Click to save template with description

Click to save template without description

Measurement system can be changed here

PROFESSIONAL TIP

Customize each of the title block templates that are supplied with AutoCAD LT. Be sure to check with your instructor or supervisor before doing so, however. Set the measurement styles, drawing area, etc., to your liking and add your school or company logo to the title blocks. It might also be a good idea to save the revised title block templates with different filenames. For example, use descriptive names like TITLEA, BSIZE, or FORMATC. When you need to create a new drawing in a title block format, click the **Use the Template** button and select the appropriate size title block from the template file list. See *Chapter 15* for additional ideas on title block customization.

Getting Started Guide 5

NEW
N
[Ctrl]+[N]

File
↳ New...

Standard Toolbar

New

Beginning a New Drawing with the NEW Command

Once AutoCAD LT is running and you are working on a drawing, you can begin an entirely new drawing by issuing the **NEW** command. The **NEW** command is accessed by entering NEW, or N, at the Command: prompt, selecting **New...** from the **File** pull-down menu, pressing [Ctrl]+[N], or clicking the **NEW** button on the **Standard Toolbar**.

CAUTION

If the current drawing in the graphics window has not yet been saved, AutoCAD LT displays an alert box prompting you to save or discard the changes before starting a new drawing. See **Figure 2-20.** This alert box gives you the option to save your drawing changes, discard them, or cancel the command entirely. Always slow down and think a moment before clicking the appropriate button.

Figure 2-20.
AutoCAD LT displays an alert box if you attempt to begin a new, or open an existing, drawing without saving any changes to the current drawing.

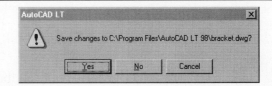

Regardless of the method you use to issue the **NEW** command, the **Create New Drawing** dialog box is automatically displayed. See **Figure 2-21.** Note that this dialog box is identical to the **Start Up** dialog box, except that it does not feature the **Open a Drawing** button. Keep in mind that the **NEW** command defaults to the previously used startup option. If a different startup option is desired, be sure to select the desired option from this dialog box. This was described in the previous sections.

Figure 2-21.
The **Create New Drawing** dialog box is displayed whenever the **NEW** command is issued. Apart from the missing **Open a Drawing** button, this dialog box and its options are identical to the **Start Up** dialog box.

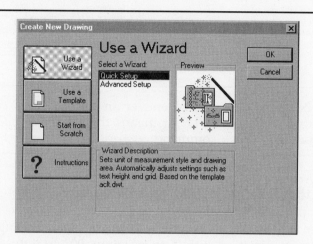

Alternative Drawing Setup Options

From the previous sections you have learned it is quick and easy to specify various drawing setup parameters using wizards whenever you start up AutoCAD LT. However, what if you wanted to change your measurement style, or perhaps increase or decrease the drawing area for an existing drawing? Fortunately, it is not necessary to start all over again. You can easily change the units of measurement or drawing limits for any drawing at any time. Both of these options are located in the **Format** pull-down menu. See **Figure 2-22.**

Figure 2-22.
The **Format** pull-down menu contains the commands needed for changing measurement styles and drawing limits without beginning a new drawing.

Selecting Units of Measurement Using DDUNITS

You can change the linear and angular measurement styles for an existing drawing using the **DDUNITS** command. Entering DDUNITS, or UN, at the Command: prompt, or selecting **Units...** from the **Format** pull-down menu displays the **Units Control** dialog box. See **Figure 2-23.** Simply click the appropriate option button for the linear and/or angular measurement style you desire, and select the number of places of display precision using the corresponding drop-down lists.

DDUNITS
UN

Format
➡ Units...

Chapter 2   Drawing Setup and File Operations

Figure 2-23.
The **DDUNITS**
command displays
the **Units Control**
dialog box.

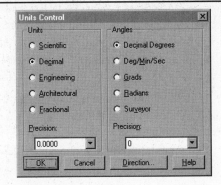

NOTE   Whenever an AutoCAD LT command is prefaced with
"DD", it means that a *dynamic dialog* box is used with the
command.

Using the Direction Control subdialog box

As previously mentioned, AutoCAD LT uses the polar coordinate system to measure angles. With this system, you may recall, all angles are measured in a counterclockwise direction with 0° to the right, 90° straight up, 180° to the left, and 270° straight down.

You can change this default method of angular measurement by clicking the **Direction...** button in the **Units Control** dialog box. This displays the **Direction Control** subdialog box. See **Figure 2-24.** If you want to set some arbitrary direction for angle 0, click the option button labeled **Other**. You can then enter the desired angle in the **Angle:** text box. Alternatively, you can click the **Pick ⟨** button and then pick a point in the drawing window to represent angle 0.

Figure 2-24.
You can change the
location of angle 0
and direction of
angular
measurement using
the **Direction Control**
subdialog box.

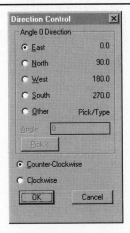

Changing Drawing Limits with the LIMITS Command

Remember that although AutoCAD LT can draw virtually any object at virtually any scale, it is still helpful to size the drawing area before beginning construction. Normally, the drawing limits are determined using the setup wizards when AutoCAD LT is started, but can be changed at anytime using the **LIMITS** command. Before setting the drawing limits, be sure to set the measurement style accordingly. In other words, if you want to size the drawing area large enough to accommodate a residential or commercial structure, first set architectural units before changing the limits. The same provision applies for mechanical or civil engineering drawings. To specify new limits using the **LIMITS** command, enter LIMITS, or LM, at the Command: prompt or select **Dra̲wing Limits** from the **Fo̲rmat** pull-down menu. Once the command is initiated, its syntax and options are as follows:

LIMITS
LM

Format
➥ Dra̲wing Limits

> Reset Model space limits:
> ON/OFF/⟨Lower left corner⟩⟨0.0000,0.0000⟩: *(specify a point, enter on or off, or accept the default)*
> Upper right corner ⟨12.0000,9.0000⟩: *(specify a point or accept the default)*

From the prompt above, you can see that AutoCAD LT is asking for the lower-left corner of the drawing area. It is usually a good idea to leave the corner at the default 0,0 values, so just press [Enter] at this prompt. If you do decide to change the values though, always set the limits by first entering the horizontal distance, followed by a comma, and then entering the vertical distance. Also notice that the **LIMITS** command allows you to turn the limits **ON** and **OFF**. The limits are off by default. That means that even though you set the lower-left and upper-right boundaries of the drawing area, you may still freely draw outside those specified points. However, if you attempt to draw outside the defined boundaries when the limits are turned on, then you are prevented from doing so and receive the following error message:

> **Outside limits.

Turning the limits on is also called *limits checking*. Should you find yourself constrained by limits checking in any of your drawings, simply return to the **LIMITS** command and turn the limits off.

After specifying the lower-left corner, you are then prompted to set the upper-right corner of the drawing area. The default values are 12 units on the X (horizontal) axis, and 9 units on the Y (vertical) axis. It is often useful to set the upper-right values to match the size of the media on which you intend to plot the finished drawing. As an example, if you intend to plot on a B-size piece of vellum or mylar, set the upper-right corner to 17,11. For a D-size drawing, set the upper-right corner to 34,22. Once you have manually set your new limits, do not forget to zoom your screen to display them. This is accomplished using the **ZOOM All** option. This option zooms the screen to the drawing limits or to the drawing extents—whichever is greater. The command sequence is as follows:

> Command: **ZOOM** or **Z**↵
> All/Center/Extents/Previous/Scale(X/XP)/Window/⟨Realtime⟩: **A**↵
> Command:

One of the benefits of setting the limits with the **Quick Setup** or **Advanced Setup** wizards is that the screen is zoomed for you automatically. The **ZOOM** command and each of its options is covered in *Chapter 4* of this text.

Setting the Grid

AutoCAD LT provides several handy drawing aids to help you draw accurately in the drawing window. As previously mentioned, one of these drawing aids is called the *grid*. Remember that unlike grid paper which uses lines, the grid created by AutoCAD LT is a series of dots on the screen. The grid is automatically displayed when you use the **Quick Setup** wizard. Unfortunately, however, using the wizard does not allow you to specify the spacing between the dots on both the horizontal (X) and vertical (Y) axes.

To set the grid X and Y spacing independently using the **GRID** command, enter GRID, or G, at the Command: prompt. Once the **GRID** command is initiated, its syntax and options are as follows:

GRID
G

> Grid spacing(X) or ON/OFF/Snap/Aspect ⟨current⟩: *(specify a value, enter an option, or accept the default)*

Chapter 2   Drawing Setup and File Operations   **65**

This **GRID** options are described as follows:

- ⟨*current*⟩. The current grid spacing for both X and Y axes is displayed here. By default, this value is set to .5 units.
- **ON/OFF.** Turns the grid on and off. This is the same as pressing function key [F7], double-clicking the **GRID** button on the **Status** bar, or using the [Ctrl]+[G] key combination.
- **Snap.** This handy option sets the grid spacing equal to the current snap spacing. The **SNAP** command is discussed in the next section.
- **Aspect.** The **Aspect** option lets you set the grid X spacing differently than the Y spacing.

In the example shown in **Figure 2-25**, both the X and Y grid spacing have been set to .5 units. The drawing window covered by the grid corresponds to the current drawing limits. If you want to increase or decrease the size of the grid, increase or decrease the drawing limits accordingly. After setting your new limits, remember to zoom your screen as previously described to display them.

The **GRID Aspect** option lets you set the grid X and Y spacing independently. In the example shown in **Figure 2-26**, the X spacing is set to .5 units, but the Y spacing has been set to 1 unit. If you set the grid spacing too close, AutoCAD LT cannot display it and you will receive the following message:

Grid too dense to display

Keep in mind that the grid dots are for construction purposes only. They will not plot, neither can they be erased. Remember that when you no longer want to see the grid, it can quickly be turned off by pressing function key [F7], double-clicking the **GRID** button on the **Status** bar, or by using the [Ctrl]+[G] key combination.

Figure 2-25.
In this example, the drawing limits are set to 0,0 and 17,11 (B-size) and both the grid X and Y values are set to .5 units. A **ZOOM All** operation has been performed to zoom the display to the screen limits.

Grid pattern

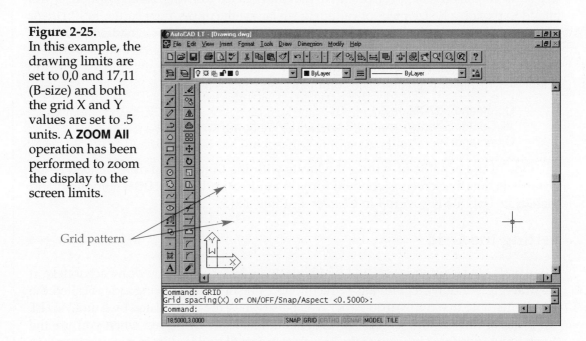

Figure 2-26.
Once again the drawing limits are set to 0,0 and 17,11 (B-size), but the grid Y spacing is set to 1 unit while the X spacing remains at .5. As in the previous example, a **ZOOM All** operation has been performed to zoom the display to the screen limits.

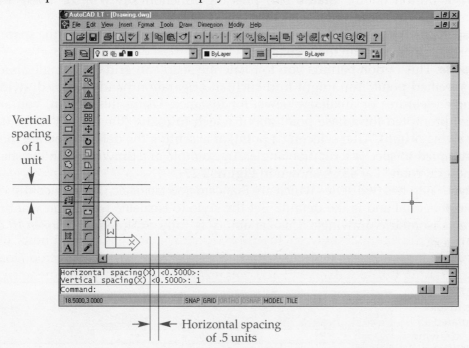

NOTE Remember that the grid display matches the current drawing limits. To increase or decrease the grid coverage, increase or decrease the drawing limits, and perform a **ZOOM All**. Also, do not be concerned that the drawing limits and grid do not extend all the way to the right side of the screen. This is because drawing limits are calculated in "real-world" units and the aspect ratio (ratio of horizontal width to vertical height) of a computer display monitor usually differs from the aspect ratio of standard drawing sheet sizes. Remember too, that you may freely draw both inside and outside the drawing limits unless limits checking has been enabled.

Setting the Snap

While the grid is a handy visual aid, its real value becomes apparent when used in conjunction with another drawing aid called *snap*. Normally, the screen graphics cursor can be freely moved about the drawing window. When the snap function is enabled, the cursor movement is restricted to user-specified increments. The cursor then jumps from snap point to snap point. The grid does not have to be on to use snap. However, by setting grid and snap spacing to be equal, you can draw lines and other objects by snapping onto the displayed grid dots. If you set the snap spacing smaller than the grid spacing, you can draw between the grid dots.

To access the **SNAP** command, enter SNAP, or SN, at the Command: prompt. Observe that the **SNAP** command offers features nearly identical to that of the **GRID** command. Once the **SNAP** command is initiated, its syntax and options are as follows:

SNAP
SN

Snap spacing or ON/OFF/Aspect/Rotate/Style ⟨*current*⟩: (*specify a value, enter an option, or accept the default*)

- ⟨*current*⟩. The current snap spacing for both X and Y axes is displayed here. As with the grid spacing, the snap spacing defaults to .5 units.
- **ON/OFF.** Turns snap mode on and off. This is the same as double-clicking the **SNAP** button on the **Status** bar, pressing function key [F9], or using the [Ctrl]+[B] key combination.
- **Aspect.** As with the **GRID** command, the Aspect option lets you set the snap X spacing different than the Y spacing.
- **Rotate.** This option permits you to rotate the snap and grid at an angle about a specified point. You might find such an orientation handy when drawing angled features or auxiliary views, for instance. Using this option, you are first prompted for a base point about which to rotate (the default is the 0,0 drawing origin). After selecting a point, or accepting the default, you are then prompted to specify a rotation angle. An example of a drawing with the snap and grid rotated at 45° is shown in **Figure 2-27.**
- **Style.** Snap has two styles which are Standard and Isometric. The Standard style is orthogonal and is the default. Set the style to Isometric when you want to create isometric drawings. This capability is fully explored in *Chapter 16* of this text.

Figure 2-27.
Both the grid and snap are rotated 45° around the drawing origin. Note the appearance of the graphics cursor at the far right.

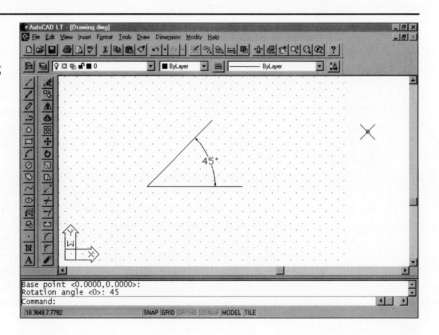

NOTE Entering the **SNAP** and **GRID** commands from the keyboard automatically turns on the snap and grid.

Setting the Snap and Grid Using a Dialog Box

Perhaps the easiest way to specify or change snap and grid settings is with the **Drawing Aids** dialog box. See **Figure 2-28.** You can access this dialog box at anytime during a drawing session by issuing the **DDRMODES** (Dynamic DRawing Modes) command. To do so, enter DDRMODES at the Command: prompt or select **Drawing Aids...** from the **Tools** pull-down menu.

In the example shown in **Figure 2-28,** the snap spacing is set to .2500 and the grid spacing to .5000. After setting the spacing, click the **Snap** and **Grid** check boxes to activate the snap and grid. When you are done, click the **OK** button to exit the dialog box.

You may recall from the previous discussion of the **SNAP** command and its options that it is possible to rotate the entire snap and grid around a base point at a specified angle. To obtain a rotated orientation, enter the desired rotation angle in the **Snap Angle** text box. Normally, the drawing is rotated about the 0,0 origin, but if you want to rotate about some other coordinate, enter the appropriate X and Y values in the **X Base** and **Y Base** text boxes.

Other drawing aids appear at the far left of the dialog box in the area labeled **Modes.** Each of these items will be discussed later in this text as they are encountered. You will also note that the lower right of the dialog box contains a section labeled **Isometric Snap/Grid.** These options are covered in *Chapter 16* of this text.

DDRMODES

Tools
↳ Drawing
   Aids...

Figure 2-28.
The **Drawing Aids** dialog box.

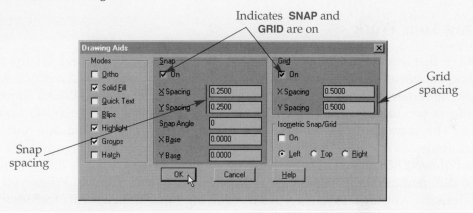

PROFESSIONAL TIP

Here are two quick ways to set the X and Y snap and grid spacing equal using the **Drawing Aids** dialog box. First turn both snap and grid on by activating the **Snap** and **Grid** check boxes. Next, double-click inside the snap **X Spacing** text box and enter the value you desire. Now, simply click inside the snap **Y Spacing** text box and its value changes to match that of the X spacing. Repeat the procedure with the grid X and Y spacing text boxes.

The second method is even faster. After setting the X spacing for either the snap or grid, simply press the [Enter] key. The Y spacing is set to match that of the X spacing automatically.

❏ Exercise 2-2 should still be displayed on your screen.

❏ Issue the **NEW** command. Do not save the current drawing when prompted to do so.

❏ When the **Create New Drawing** dialog box appears, click the **Use a Template** button and use the Aclt.dwt file from the template file list. Click **OK** when you are finished.

❏ Open the **Drawing Aids** dialog box and set the snap X and Y spacing to .5 units and the grid X and Y spacing to 1 unit. Be sure to activate the **Snap** and **Grid** check boxes before exiting the dialog box.

❏ Use the **LIMITS** command to set the limits for a C-size title block drawing (lower left 0,0 and upper right 22,17).

❏ Zoom the display to the new drawing limits.

❏ Using your pointing device, move the cursor around the drawing area. Observe the motion of the cursor as it snaps from one grid dot to the next.

❏ Now, turn the snap off using the button on the **Status** bar, function key, or control key combination. Do you notice the difference in the cursor movement?

❏ Also, try turning the grid on and off using the button on the **Status** bar, function key, or control key combination.

❏ When you are done, continue reading the following sections. Do not exit AutoCAD LT .

Saving Your Work

Now that you know how to begin a new drawing session and set up a few drawing parameters, it is time you learned how to save your work. An AutoCAD LT drawing assumes the name drawing.dwg until it is saved. It is the **SAVEAS** command that allows you to provide a name for your drawing while simultaneously saving it to disk. This command also allows you to redirect the drawing to a different drive and/or folder. Once a drawing has been given a name, the **SAVE** command is used instead of **SAVEAS**. Of course, if you want to save a drawing with a different name, or to a different folder, then the **SAVEAS** command should be used. When you save your drawing, you also save the current drawing environment. This includes your limits, snap, and grid settings.

SAVE
SA
[Ctrl]+[S]

File
↳ **S**ave

Standard
Toolbar

Save

To save a drawing, enter SAVE, or SA, at the Command: prompt, click the **Save** button on the **Standard Toolbar**, press [Ctrl] +[S], or select **S**ave from the **F**ile pull-down menu.

If the drawing has not yet been saved, AutoCAD LT automatically invokes the **SAVEAS** command instead of **SAVE** so that a name can be provided for the drawing. The **SAVEAS** command displays the **Save Drawing As** dialog box. See **Figure 2-29**. In this example, a user has entered the name bracket in the **File name:** text box. It is not necessary to append the file extension .dwg to the drawing name—AutoCAD LT does this for you automatically. In the example shown, bracket.dwg is being saved to the AutoCAD LT 98 folder by default. Use the same drop-down list if you wish to save the drawing to a different storage device, such as your floppy disk. After providing a name for the drawing, click the **S**ave button to save the drawing and exit the dialog box.

Figure 2-29.
The **Save Drawing As** dialog box is used to save a drawing with a different name or to a different folder or storage device.

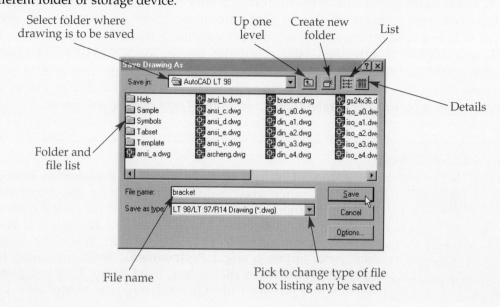

Select folder where drawing is to be saved

Up one level

Create new folder

List

Details

Folder and file list

File name

Pick to change type of file box listing any be saved

Naming Drawings

Because the Windows 98/95/NT operating systems allow a maximum of 256 characters for a filename, it is possible to give descriptive names to your drawing files. You can use spaces as well as most punctuation symbols. However, the following characters cannot be used: quotation mark ("), asterisk (*), forward slash (/), backward slash (\), and question mark (?). Thus, it is possible to provide a name such as the following:

Drive Linkage Baseplate.Machined.Sheet 2

PROFESSIONAL TIP

It is good practice to save your drawings in a folder other than the default AutoCAD LT 98 folder. As an example, you might create a folder called *mechanical* in which you store all mechanical drawings you are working on. Other folders might be called *architectural, sheet metal, projects,* etc.

Also, if you are working in an environment that includes Windows 3.1 users with Windows 98/95/NT users, and drawing files are regularly exchanged between the two groups, it might be a good idea to restrict file names to the old MS-DOS convention of eight characters or less with no spaces. This practice will ensure consistent file names between users of AutoCAD LT 98, AutoCAD LT 97, AutoCAD LT for Windows 95, and AutoCAD LT for Windows 3.1.

Saving Work Automatically

It is critically important to save your drawing on a frequent basis. Doing so protects you from losing work due to hardware or electrical power failures. A good rule of thumb is to save every 10-15 minutes. If something should go wrong, the most work you will lose is only about fifteen minutes worth. AutoCAD LT has a system variable called **SAVETIME** that can be set to save your work automatically at regular intervals. To set this variable using a dialog box, enter PREFERENCES, or PR, at the Command: prompt, or select **Preferences**... from the **Tools** pull-down menu.

PREFERENCES
PR

Tools
➥ Preferences...

PROFESSIONAL TIP

A quick and easy way to open the **Preferences** dialog box, is to move your pointing device over the Command window at the bottom of the screen. Next, click the button that corresponds to the [Enter] key on your keyboard. If you are using a mouse, this is the right button. When the *right-click menu* appears, select **Preferences**... from the menu to open the **Preferences** dialog box. See *Chapter 3* for complete information about right-clicking and the AutoCAD LT shortcut menu.

Once the **Preferences** dialog box is displayed on your screen, click the **System** tab at the top and locate the **Automatic save every** section in the middle of the dialog box. See **Figure 2-30.** Enter the desired time interval in minutes (or use the up and down arrows) in the text box. When you are through setting the time interval, click the **OK** button to exit the dialog box. Once this feature is enabled, AutoCAD LT automatically saves your drawing with the name auto1.sv$ after the specified time interval has elapsed.

Assume that you have set the automatic save feature to save your drawing every 15 minutes. If you are in the middle of a drawing or editing command when 15 minutes has elapsed, AutoCAD LT will wait until you are finished before saving the drawing. You will not be interrupted. As the drawing is saved, the following message appears in the command line area at the bottom of the graphics window:

Automatic save to C:\WINDOWS\TEMP\auto1.sv$...

The Command: prompt reappears when the automatic save is complete. If you should ever need to work on this file inside AutoCAD LT, you will need to rename it.

Figure 2-30.
The **Preferences** dialog box can be used to automatically save your drawing at specified time intervals.

Turns automatic backup off and on

Check to save work automatically

Enter time of desired interval of automatic saves

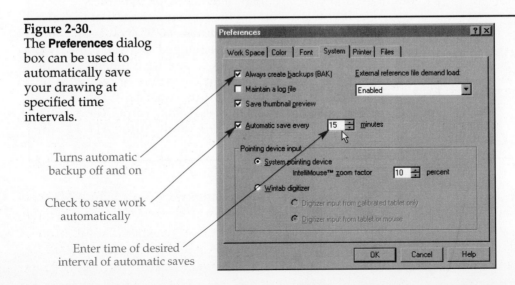

This is because AutoCAD LT will not read a file with the extension .SV$. It must be renamed with a .DWG file extension. To accomplish this, use the Windows Explorer file management program that is supplied with Windows 98, Windows 95, and Windows NT. If you are not familiar with Windows Explorer, be sure to read *Chapter 25* of this text.

> **NOTE**
> Many of the options available in the **Preferences** dialog box are covered in *Chapter 20*. Other **Preferences** dialog box options are covered in later chapters of this text where pertinent.

Saving a Drawing at Automatic Intervals Using the Command Line

The **SAVETIME** system variable lets you set automatic save intervals at the Command: prompt rather than using the **Preferences** dialog box. In the example that follows, the time interval is set to 15 minutes.

    Command: SAVETIME↵
    New value for SAVETIME ⟨120⟩: 15↵
    Command:

Backup (.BAK) Files

The first time a new drawing is saved to disk, AutoCAD LT automatically appends the file extension .DWG to the drawing. After 10-15 minutes of additional work, the drawing is saved again. What happens to the original drawing on disk?

The second time that the drawing is saved, the original .DWG file is renamed with a .BAK (backup) file extension. The newly saved drawing is now the .DWG file. Thus, AutoCAD LT always maintains the previous version of a drawing as a .BAK file. This can be very handy should you make several changes to a drawing, save it, and then realize that you do not need the revisions after all. To retrieve the earlier version, you must first delete the unwanted drawing from the disk. Then, since AutoCAD LT will not read a .BAK file, rename the backup version .BAK file extension to a .DWG extension. The older version may now be used by AutoCAD LT.

When you are sure that you no longer need earlier backup versions of your drawings, delete the .BAK files from your hard drive to conserve disk space.

> **NOTE**
> Although *strongly* not recommended, you can disable the automatic creation of backup files by deactivating the **Always create backups (BAK)** check box under the **System** tab in the **Preferences** dialog box. See **Figure 2-30.**

Saving AutoCAD LT 98 Drawings in Previous Version Formats

This text is based upon AutoCAD LT 98—the latest version of AutoCAD LT. This version of the program runs under Windows 98, Windows 95, and Windows NT only and is compatible with AutoCAD Release 14. The previous version of AutoCAD LT, called AutoCAD LT 97 is also compatible with AutoCAD Release 14, but may not be fully compatible with Windows 98. Its predecessor, AutoCAD LT for Windows 95, is compatible with AutoCAD Release 13. The earliest versions of AutoCAD LT, Releases 1 and AutoCAD LT for Windows 3.1, are compatible with AutoCAD Release 12.

The file formats between AutoCAD LT 98 and AutoCAD LT 97 and previous LT versions are markedly different. Therefore, if a drawing created with AutoCAD LT 98/97 is to be read by an earlier version of AutoCAD LT or AutoCAD, the drawing must be saved in a compatible file format. This can be accomplished using the **SAVEAS** command. As shown in **Figure 2-31**, the drawing file named plotplan is being saved in the **AutoCAD LT R2/R12 Drawing (*.dwg)** format, by selecting that file format from the **Save as type:** drop-down list. You may recall from the previous discussion in this chapter regarding template files that this drop-down list is also used to save a drawing as a template. If you wish to save the drawing file with a different name, enter the name in the **File name:** text box. When you are finished, click the **Save** button at the right to save the drawing in the selected format.

Figure 2-31.
The **Save as type:** drop-down list in the **Save Drawing As** dialog box can be used to save AutoCAD LT 98/97 drawings in formats that are compatible with earlier versions of AutoCAD LT or AutoCAD.

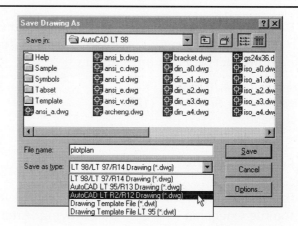

CAUTION

Saving a drawing in an earlier version format may result in some data loss. If the drawing has already been saved in the AutoCAD LT 98/97 format, be sure to provide a different name for the drawing you intend to save in an earlier AutoCAD LT format. This will preserve the current format version on disk.

EXERCISE 2-4

❏ Exercise 2-3 should still be displayed on your screen.
❏ Use the **Preferences** dialog box or the **SAVETIME** system variable to save the drawing every 10 minutes.
❏ Use the **SAVEAS** command to save the drawing with the name MYFIRST.
❏ Once saved, use the **REVDATE** command to revise the date stamp on your drawing. Observe that the stamp now reflects the current drawing name.
❏ Issue the **SAVE** command. Since the drawing now has a name, it is quickly saved without displaying a dialog box.
❏ Exit AutoCAD LT by issuing the **QUIT** command.
❏ Next, click the Start button on the taskbar and open the _Programs folder. Select Windows Explorer from this folder.
❏ Open the AutoCAD LT 98 folder. You should have two versions of the MYFIRST drawing; .BAK and .DWG.

Accessing an Existing Drawing

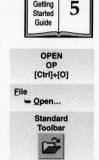

Before you can work with a previously created drawing file, it must first be opened using the **OPEN** command. To initiate this command, enter OPEN, or OP, at the Command: prompt, click the **Open** button on the **Standard Toolbar**, press [Ctrl]+[O], or select **Open...** from the **File** pull-down menu.

As previously mentioned, if the drawing you are currently working with has not yet been saved, AutoCAD LT displays the alert box shown in **Figure 2-20**. You then have the option to save your drawing changes, discard them, or cancel the command entirely. Whether you choose to save your changes or not, you are next presented with the **Select File** dialog box. See **Figure 2-32**.

Figure 2-32.
The **Select File** dialog box. Notice the drawing frame.dwg has been selected from the file list and appears in the **File name:** text box. A bitmap preview image appears at the right of the dialog box.

Highlighted file to be opened

Preview of highlighted file

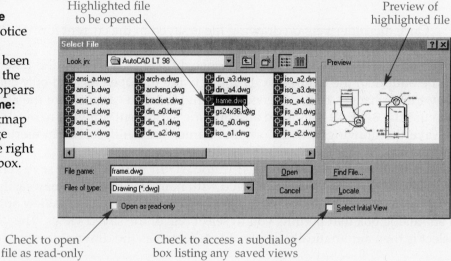

Check to open file as read-only

Check to access a subdialog box listing any saved views

PROFESSIONAL TIP

Remember you can also open an existing drawing as AutoCAD LT is initially starting up by clicking the **Open a Drawing** button in the **Start Up** dialog box. See **Figure 2-33**. Observe that the four most recently opened drawing files are listed. You may select one of these files to open, or select **More files...** from the top of the list to access the **Select File** dialog box.

If the file you want to open is in a different folder or on a different storage device, use the **Look in:** drop-down list as appropriate. As with other common file dialog boxes of this type, enter the desired file name in the **File name:** text box or use your pointing device to select a file from the file list in the middle of the dialog box.

Once you have selected a file from the file list or entered the file name in the text box, a bitmap preview image of the drawing is then displayed in the **Preview** image tile. The preview image only appears if the drawing you selected has been saved in AutoCAD LT 98/97/AutoCAD R14 or AutoCAD LT for Windows 95/AutoCAD R13 format. If the drawing you select is from a previous version of AutoCAD LT or AutoCAD, no bitmap image appears in the **Preview** image tile in the dialog box. As the earlier version drawing is opened, the following message is displayed on the command line:

Converting old drawing.

Figure 2-33.
A drawing may also be opened at startup using the **Open a Drawing** dialog box.

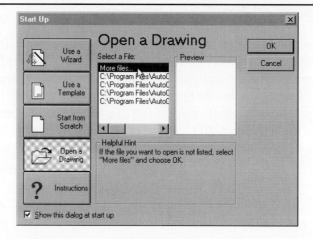

Once this older version drawing file is saved in the current format, it will display a bitmap preview image when next opened.

Notice also the two check boxes labeled **Open as read-only** and **Select Initial View** at the bottom of the dialog box. If you activate the **Open as read-only** check box, you may make changes to the opened drawing, but you cannot save the changes unless you use the **SAVEAS** command and provide a different drawing name. If you attempt to save the drawing with its original name, you will receive an alert box message informing you that the drawing is write-protected.

As you will learn in *Chapter 4*, AutoCAD LT allows you to save specified views of your drawing. The views are saved with names so that they may easily be restored for viewing, or deleted when no longer needed. The **Select Initial View** option displays a subdialog box that permits you to select one of the saved views. The view that you select is then automatically displayed on screen as the drawing is opened.

Opening a Drawing Using the Locate Button

There may be occasions when a drawing exists in a different folder than that which is currently open. If the folder can be found in the AutoCAD LT search path, the drawing can be quickly opened by entering the drawing name in the **File name:** text box and then clicking the **Locate** button in the lower-right corner of the **Select File** dialog box. An alert box is displayed if AutoCAD LT cannot find the drawing in the current search path.

Using the Find File... Button to Locate Drawing Files

There may be instances when you wish to open an existing drawing file, but you cannot remember the drawing name or where the drawing resides on disk. Additionally, there may be occasions when you have even forgotten what the drawing looks like! You can locate a drawing file by its appearance, as well as by its name, type, date or time created, by clicking the **Find File...** button in the **Select File** dialog box. This displays the **Browse/Search** subdialog box. See **Figure 2-34.**

Using the Browse function

The **Browse** tab is active by default. This allows you to graphically search through bitmap images of the AutoCAD LT 98/97 (and AutoCAD R13/R14) drawings stored on your computer. You may choose to display small (the default), medium, or large bitmap images of your drawings by selecting the desired size from the **Size:** drop-down list at the lower right of the subdialog box. Use the **Directories:** file list box and **Drives:** drop-down list if the drawing you are searching for resides in

Figure 2-34.
The **Browse/Search** subdialog box. The **Browse** tab lets you graphically search through bitmap images to locate drawing files.

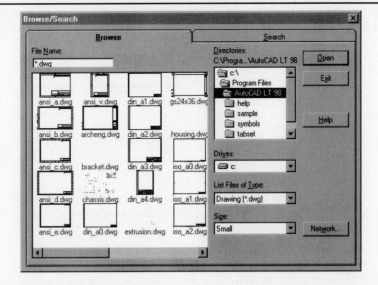

a different folder or on a different drive. Once you have found the desired file, it may be opened by clicking its bitmap image and then clicking the **Open** button. An even faster way to open the file is by simply double-clicking the bitmap image.

Using the Search function

Click the **Search** tab when you wish to locate a drawing file by its name, type, date or time created. See **Figure 2-35.** To locate a file with this function, do the following:

1. Select the type of file you want to find from the **File Types:** drop-down list. You may search for .dwg, .dxf, and .dwt file types only. Drawing Interchange Files (.dxf) are discussed in *Chapter 25.*

2. If desired, use the **Time:** and **Date:** text boxes to limit the search to files created after a time or date (or both) that you specify. When you use these features, you must follow these formats:

   Date *mm-dd-yy*
   Time *hh:mm:ss*

3. Use the **Drive:** drop-down list to specify the drive you want searched.

Figure 2-35.
Clicking the **Search** tab lets you search for files on different drives and in other folders. The search can be limited by the date and/or time when the files were created.

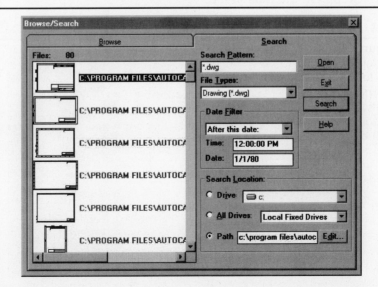

Figure 2-36.
The **Edit Path** subdialog box. The Program Files\Mechanical folder on the C: drive has been added to the search path.

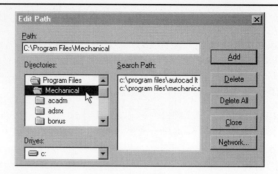

4. Activate the **All Drives:** option button and choose from the drop-down list if you wish to search local drives (the drives installed on your computer), or all drives, including the network.
5. Activate the **Path** option button and enter the desired path in the corresponding text box if you wish to restrict the search to a designated path. In the example illustrated, the search path is restricted to the C:\Program Files\AutoCAD LT 98 folder.
6. Click the **Search** button to start the search.

When the search is completed, the list box on the left side of the **Search** tab displays the names of the files that matched the search criteria. In the example shown, a total of 80 .dwg files were found in the C:\Program Files\AutoCAD LT 98 folder. To open a drawing from the list, double-click the file name in the list or click once on the file name and then click the **Open** button at the upper right of the dialog box.

Building a search path. Normally AutoCAD LT searches the AutoCAD LT folder only when the **Search** button is clicked. However, you can have AutoCAD LT search a number of folders on the same drive or on different drives by building a search path. To build a search path, do the following:

1. Click the **Edit...** button at the lower right of the **Search** tab. The **Edit Path** subdialog box appears. See **Figure 2-36.**
2. In the **Drives:** and **Directories:** list boxes, locate the folders you want searched, highlight each folder, and click the **Add** button to add them to the search path. Any folders you select will appear in the **Search Path:** list box. If you later decide to delete a folder from the **Search Path:** list box, highlight it and click the **Delete** button. In the example shown in **Figure 2-36**, the Program Files\Mechanical folder on the C: drive has been selected and added to the search path.
3. Click the **Close** button to close the **Edit Path** subdialog box and update the **Path** text box in the **Search** tab.

Figure 2-37.
AutoCAD LT lists the four most recently opened drawings at the bottom of the **File** pull-down menu.

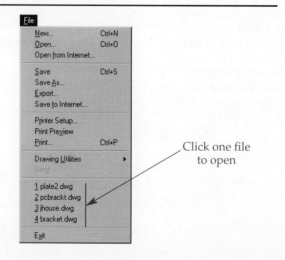

Click one file to open

Opening a Drawing from the File Pull-Down Menu List

AutoCAD LT remembers up to a maximum of four drawing files most recently opened. These file names are listed at the bottom of the **File** pull-down menu. See **Figure 2-37.** Any one of these files may be quickly opened by clicking the file name with your pointing device. The drive and folder for each drawing is included with the file name if the drawing is not located in the default folder (C:\Program Files\AutoCAD LT 98). If you should try to open one of these drawing files using this method after it has been deleted or moved to a different drive or folder, AutoCAD LT will be unable to locate it and display an error message in an alert box.

Ending a Drawing Session

When you wish to end a drawing session, enter EXIT or QUIT at the Command: prompt or select **Exit** from the **File** pull-down menu. If your drawing has not yet been saved, AutoCAD LT displays the dialog box shown in **Figure 2-20.** Click the **No** button to discard your changes and exit AutoCAD LT when you have just been experimenting with the program and have no intent on saving the drawing. Should you decide that you want to save the drawing after all, click the **Yes** button. If the drawing does not yet have a name, the **Save Drawing As** dialog box is then displayed. Click the **Cancel** button to continue drawing if you decide not to exit AutoCAD LT.

```
EXIT
QUIT

File
 ➥ Exit
```

Chapter Test

Write your answer in the space provided.

1. What is the difference between the **Start Up** and **Create New Drawing** dialog boxes? _____

    _____

    _____

2. *True or False?* The setup wizards may be used to specify grid and snap settings.

3. What is the default number of digits to the right of the decimal point in AutoCAD LT? _____

4. How many types of linear measurement styles are available in AutoCAD LT? How many types of angular styles? _____

    _____

5. What are the default drawing limits in AutoCAD LT? _____

    _____

6. *Yes or No?* Is it possible to turn off the grid, but still use snap? _____

7. Which setup wizard is used to place a title block around the drawing limits?

    _____

8. *Yes or No?* Can a title block be created in both paper space and model space?

9. The AutoCAD LT database is accurate to how many decimal places of precision?

    _____

    _____

    _____

10. Which command lets you set the grid and snap using a dialog box?_____

11. Identify two ways to begin a new drawing using metric measurements. _____
    _____
    _____
    _____

12. List two different ways to exit paper space. _____
    _____
    _____
    _____

13. How do you update the date stamp information on a drawing? _____
    _____
    _____

14. How do you cancel a command in progress? _____

15. What must you do after sizing the drawing area with the **LIMITS** command?
    _____

16. AutoCAD LT keeps displaying the error message **Outside limits. What is wrong
    and how can it be corrected? _____
    _____

17. Name the command that lets you set measurement styles using a dialog box.
    _____

18. Identify two different ways to have AutoCAD LT automatically save your
    drawing at specified time intervals. _____
    _____

19. What are the advantages of using a template drawing? _____
    _____
    _____
    _____
    _____

20. What are some of the differences between the **SAVE** and **SAVEAS** commands?
    _____
    _____
    _____
    _____

21. Every time you attempt to save your drawing, you receive a message stating that
    the drawing is write-protected. What is the cause of this message? _____
    _____

22. What must be done before a .BAK backup file can be read by AutoCAD LT?____
    _____

23. How do you access the **Browse** and **Search** functions of AutoCAD LT? _____
    _____
    _____

24. Identify the keyboard shortcuts for the **NEW**, **SAVE**, and **OPEN** commands._____

_____

25. Which two commands can be used to end an AutoCAD LT drawing session?

_____

_____

Chapter Problems

1. Begin a new drawing from scratch and set the following parameters:

   a. Linear decimal units with 3 digits to the right of the decimal point.

   b. Angular decimal degrees with 0 digits to the right of the decimal point.

   c. Snap spacing = .25

   d. Grid spacing = .5

   e. Limits set to 0,0 (lower-left) and 11, 8.5 (upper-right). Perform a **ZOOM All** after setting the limits.

   f. Save the drawing as a template file with the name TEMPLATEA.DWT (for A-size template).

   g. Add the description A-size template drawing to the **Template Description** dialog box.

      This template file will be used for many of the subsequent drawing problems in this text.

   General

2. Begin a new drawing using the TEMPLATEA template. Change the drawing limits to 17,11 for the upper-right corner. Remember to zoom the drawing after changing the limits. Save the new drawing as a template file with the name TEMPLATEB.DWT. As with the previous problem, add an appropriate description for the template file. This B-size template drawing will also be used for future drawing problems.

   General

3. Begin a new drawing using the TEMPLATEB template. Change the drawing limits to 22,17 for the upper-right corner. Once again, zoom the drawing after changing the limits. Save the new drawing as a template file with the name TEMPLATEC.DWT and add an appropriate description in the **Template Description** dialog box. As with TEMPLATEA and TEMPLATEB, this C-size template file will be used for subsequent drawing problems.

   General

4. Begin a new drawing using the AutoCAD LT-supplied template file ansi_a.dwt. Set the grid, snap, etc., as described in Problem 2-1. Save the revised title block drawing as a template file with the name TITLEA.DWT. Add the description A-size title block drawing to the **Template Description** dialog box. Your new title block template will be used for future drawing problems in this text.

   General

5. Perform identical operations with the supplied ansi_b and ansi_c title block template files. Set the limits accordingly for each and do not forget to zoom afterwards. Save the revised title block templates with the names TITLEB.DWT and TITLEC.DWT, respectively. Add template file descriptions similar to Problem 2-4.

   General

AutoCAD LT

Chapter 3

Drawing and Erasing Lines

Learning Objectives

After you have completed this chapter, you will be able to:
- Understand and use **Direct Distance Entry** for drawing lines.
- Use **ORTHO** mode, **PolarSnap**, and the coordinate display box as drawing aids.
- Undo, redo, and continue line segments.
- Enter absolute, relative, and polar coordinates for line constructions.
- Erase unwanted lines and restore them again.
- Understand and use selection set options.
- Describe the difference between verb/noun and noun/verb object selection.
- Undo and redo AutoCAD LT commands.

Perhaps the most frequently used function of any CAD system is drawing lines. In AutoCAD LT, lines are the most commonly drawn *objects*, or entities. In this chapter, you will learn to construct lines using a variety of techniques. Since some of the lines you draw will invariably have to be erased, you will also learn the various methods used to select objects for erasing and other editing functions.

Accuracy and Scaling

Precision is, or should be, the standard for every drafter, designer, and engineer. In a truly integrated CAD working environment, precise geometry creation is of great importance. This is because the electronic geometry contained in the CAD file is used to drive most, if not all, downstream operations. In mechanical engineering, such operations include prototype and production manufacturing, testing and analysis, as well as technical documentation such as product manuals and illustrations. In such cases, the original CAD geometry is used to satisfy those functions. Indeed, it is quite common for a *numerical control (N/C)* programmer or machinist to completely ignore the dimensions on a CAD drawing and generate the machining tool paths on the displayed geometry alone. Inaccurate geometry results in inaccurate tool paths—inaccurate tool paths result in inaccurate parts.

Accurate and precise geometry construction is important in the *AEC (Architecture, Engineering, Construction)* trades also. It is now quite common for subcontractors and vendors to share a set of CAD working drawings electronically. Since the same drawings are used for a variety of applications, including wiring, piping, landscaping, *HVAC (heating, ventilating, air-conditioning)*, it is critically important that the drawings are as precise as possible. A single geometric error in a simple residential floor plan can cause serious downstream repercussions for everyone involved in the building project.

Sloppy, imprecise geometry is often called *dirty geometry*. This usually occurs because of incorrect coordinate entry, as well as through the improper use of the AutoCAD LT editing commands. Other instances of dirty geometry occur when objects are inadvertently duplicated one upon another or corners do not meet. Such mistakes can be a major source of grief for other users who must work with these drawing files.

One of the most common ways of creating inaccurate geometry is through the practice of rounding off, or truncating, decimal values when entering decimal coordinates. When using decimal units to construct your geometry, always enter decimal values in full. For examples use .0625 for 1/16, .09375 for 3/32, .21875 for 7/32, etc. A fraction-to-decimal conversion chart appears in the appendices of this text. Remember that AutoCAD LT's database is accurate to 14 decimal places. Use this high degree of accuracy to your advantage when entering decimal coordinates. Proper coordinate entry will eliminate rounding errors and/or tolerance build-up.

If you prefer to enter your coordinates using fractional units, the numerator and denominator must be whole numbers greater than zero. When entering values greater than one that contain fractions, there must be a hyphen between the whole number and the fraction—for example, 3-1/2. You must use a hyphen (-) as a separator because a space (pressing the spacebar) acts just like pressing the [Enter] key. This will end the command line input.

Another common mistake made by users new to CAD is failing to create drawings at full scale. From the previous chapter you learned that AutoCAD LT can draw virtually anything at virtually any size. The drawings are scaled up or down as necessary using a predetermined scale factor at plot time. Think of the scale factor as the size of what is being drawn relative to the size of the plotted drawing. It is important to consider the appropriate scale factor to ensure that drawing annotation, such as notes and dimensions, have the proper lettering height when plotted. Creating text and dimensions with the correct height is covered in later chapters of this text. For complete information on plotting and plot scales, refer to *Chapter 14* of this text.

Drawing Lines

A line is drawn in AutoCAD LT by using the **LINE** command and specifying a starting point and an ending point for the line. The endpoints of the line can be selected interactively by simply picking points on the screen with your cursor, or by entering precise coordinates. To access the **LINE** Command, enter LINE, or L, at the Command: prompt, select **Line** from the **Draw** pull-down menu, or click the **Line** button in the **Draw** toolbar. See **Figure 3-1**. After the line command is initiated, you are presented with the following prompts:

> From point: *(pick a start point for the line)*
> To point: *(pick an endpoint for the line)*
> To point: *(pick another point or press [Enter] to end the command)*

AutoCAD LT draws a single-line segment between the From point: and To point: prompts. The **LINE** command continues to prompt for points, so you can continue drawing additional lines. No matter how many line segments you draw, however, each segment is a separate object. When you are done drawing lines, click the right button on your mouse or press [Enter] to end the command.

In the example illustrated in **Figure 3-2**, a line is drawn between two points selected with the graphics cursor. When you draw lines interactively using the cursor,

Figure 3-1.
The **LINE** command can be issued by selecting **Line** from the **Draw** pull-down menu.

Figure 3-2.
Line segments are drawn between selected points in the drawing window.

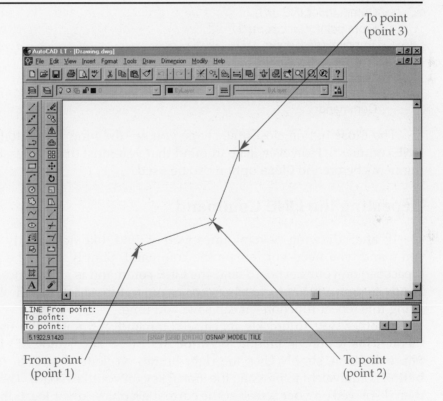

To point
(point 3)

From point
(point 1)

To point
(point 2)

a *rubberband* line connects to the end of the last point selected. As you move your pointing device around the drawing window, the rubberband line follows the motion of your cursor.

The **Close** Option

When you want to draw a closed shape using lines, it is a simple matter to have the **LINE** command draw a line automatically back to its starting point. This capability is provided with the **Close** option. To obtain a clearer understanding, refer to the object illustrated in **Figure 3-3.** In this example, the user picks point 1 on the screen at the From point: prompt. Points 2, 3, and 4 are then picked at the next three **To point:**

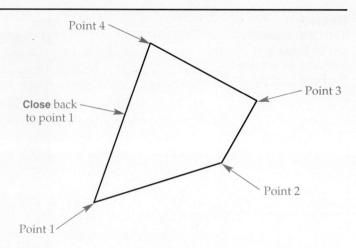

Figure 3-3.
The **Close** option creates a closed shape by automatically drawing a line segment back to the starting point.

Point 4

Point 3

Close back to point 1

Point 2

Point 1

prompts. After picking point 4, the shape is closed back to point 1 by entering CLOSE, or C, at the To point: prompt. The sequence of steps to draw the object shown in **Figure 3-3** looks like this:

> Command: **LINE** *or* **L**↵
> From point: *(pick point 1)*
> To point: *(pick point 2)*
> To point: *(pick point 3)*
> To point: *(pick point 4)*
> To point: **CLOSE** *or* **C**↵
> Command:

The **Close** option closes the shape you are drawing and automatically ends the **LINE** command. However, keep in mind that you must draw at least two or more line segments before the **Close** option can be used.

Repeating the LINE Command

If after drawing several lines you would like to quickly repeat the **LINE** command, you need not reissue the command. Simply press the [Enter] key or the [Spacebar] on your keyboard, and the **LINE** command is automatically repeated. This handy feature applies to nearly every command in AutoCAD LT. Get in the habit of using this repeat function—it can save you time.

Another way to quickly repeat a command is through the use of the **Shortcut** menu. This feature is unique to AutoCAD LT 98 and AutoCAD LT 97. To use the **Shortcut** menu, simply click the right button on your mouse. In AutoCAD LT, this button is equivalent to pressing the [Enter] key on your keyboard. The **Shortcut** menu is then displayed on your screen at the current graphics cursor location. See **Figure 3-4A.** Select **Repeat LINE** from the top of the menu (or press [R] on your keyboard) to continue drawing lines. Observe that the **Shortcut** menu always displays the last command used as well as several other functions pertinent to that command. These functions may vary depending on the type of command just used. The commands in the shortcut menu will also vary depending on whether you right-click in the drawing window, text window, or command window.

Using Your Mouse to Enter Commands

The right button of your mouse can be used in place of the [Enter] key for all command entry in AutoCAD LT. As an example, enter in LINE or L on the command line. Now, instead of pressing [Enter] on your keyboard, click the right mouse button.

As expected, the **Shortcut** menu appears on screen at the current graphics cursor location but appears somewhat different. See **Figure 3-4B.** To enter the **LINE** command, select <u>**Enter**</u> **L** from the top of the menu (or press [L] on your keyboard).

NOTE   The **Shortcut** menu is also called the *right-click menu*. This is because pressing the right mouse button is often referred to as *right-clicking.* You can still make use of the **Shortcut** menu if you are using a digitizing tablet instead of a mouse. Tablets are equipped with a puck (or some other type of pointing device) that includes a button is equivalent to the [Enter] key on your keyboard. Since the button mapping varies between manufacturers, be sure to read the product documentation supplied with your digitizer.

Figure 3-4. A—The **Shortcut** menu is used to quickly repeat the previous command. B—It can also be used as an alternative to the keyboard [Enter] key for command re-entry.

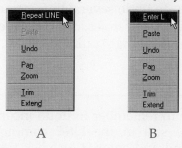

A   B

Using the MULTIPLE Command

Commands may be continually repeated using the **MULTIPLE** command. To use this method, enter MULTIPLE at the Command: prompt and press [Enter] or the [Spacebar]. You are then prompted for the command to continually repeat:

> Command: **MULTIPLE**↵
> Multiple command: **LINE** *or* **L**↵

AutoCAD LT then continually repeats the command until you cancel by pressing the [Esc] key on your keyboard. You can use the **MULTIPLE** command with most of the drawing and editing commands in AutoCAD LT. However, it cannot be used with dialog box commands.

The Continuation Option

There will be occasions when you inadvertently end the **LINE** command without drawing all of the lines you had intended. You can easily repeat the **LINE** command and have AutoCAD LT automatically pick up where it left off. First, use one of the methods previously described to repeat the **LINE** command. At the From point: prompt, simply press [Enter] or the [Spacebar]. The new line is automatically connected to the endpoint of the last line drawn. This method of reattachment is called the *continuation* option. Once attached, you may continue to draw more line segments.

Undoing Line Segments

No matter how careful or attentive, you will occasionally draw a line segment incorrectly. AutoCAD LT provides an **Undo** option that permits you to remain in the **LINE** command, remove the incorrect segment, and continue on with line construction. To use this option, simply enter UNDO, or U, or while you are still in the **LINE** command as shown below:

> Command: **LINE** or **L.**⏎
> From point: *(pick point 1)*
> To point: *(pick point 2)*
> To point: *(pick point 3)*

UNDO
U

Standard
Toolbar

Undo
LT 97 only

You suddenly realize that the line just drawn between points 2 and 3 is incorrect. Use the **Undo** option to remove the segment as follows:

> To point: **UNDO** or **U.**⏎
> To point: *(pick a new location for point 3)*

If you are using AutoCAD LT 97, you can also click the **Undo** button on the toolbar to undo a line segment. To undo several line segments as far back as needed, enter U followed by [Enter] a number of times, or successive clicks of the toolbar **Undo** button. Remember that if you are using AutoCAD LT 98, you cannot use the **Undo** button in the middle of a command.

Standard
Toolbar

Redo

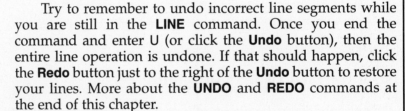

CAUTION   Try to remember to undo incorrect line segments while you are still in the **LINE** command. Once you end the command and enter U (or click the **Undo** button), then the entire line operation is undone. If that should happen, click the **Redo** button just to the right of the **Undo** button to restore your lines. More about the **UNDO** and **REDO** commands at the end of this chapter.

Using Ortho Mode

Ortho is an AutoCAD LT drawing aid that constrains cursor movement to horizontal or vertical directions only. That means that no matter how hard you try, you cannot draw a diagonal line with your cursor when **Ortho** is on. Therefore it becomes much easier to draw perfectly horizontal or vertical lines using **Ortho**. **Ortho** is particularly handy when you have found that you have drawn two views too closely together and there is not enough room for dimensions. You simply move one of the views left or right (or up and down) to increase the spacing between the views. With **Ortho** on, motion is constrained about the horizontal and vertical axes so that the views maintain perfect alignment. There are several ways to enable **ORTHO** mode. One way is to use the **ORTHO** command as follows:

> Command: **ORTHO** or **OR.**⏎
> ON/OFF ⟨*current*⟩: *(type ON or OFF as desired)*

However, it is faster to use the [Ctrl]+[L] keyboard combination, press function key [F8], or simply double-click the **Ortho** button on the **Status** bar. Like **GRID** and **SNAP** modes, **ORTHO** can be toggled on and off right in the middle of a drawing command.

EXERCISE 3-1

❏ Load Windows and start AutoCAD LT.

❏ Begin a new drawing using the TEMPLATEA template drawing you created in *Problem 1* of *Chapter 2*. If you did not complete this drawing problem, set the snap spacing to .25 and the grid spacing to .5.

❏ Use the **LINE** command with grid and snap turned on to draw the objects shown below. Do not be concerned with dimensions. Size the objects so that they are proportional to those shown.

❏ As you draw, experiment with the **Undo, Close,** and **Continuation** options described in the preceding text.

❏ Now, turn off the grid and snap and try drawing several of the objects.

❏ Turn on **Ortho** mode, or double-click the **Ortho** button on the **Status** bar, and try drawing the two triangles. What happens?

❏ Finally, use the **MULTIPLE** command to automatically repeat the **LINE** command. Remember to cancel to exit the **LINE** command.

❏ When you are done, save the drawing with the name EX3-1.

Drawing a Line Using Direct Distance Entry

Getting Started Guide 8

Direct Distance Entry is a construction method that allows you to specify a point by moving your cursor to indicate a direction and then typing a distance from the first point selected. The *Direct Distance Entry* method can be used for nearly every command in AutoCAD LT that requests points. With the **LINE** command, it allows you to quickly specify a line of a specific length. For example, when you are in the **LINE** command and the **To point:** prompt is displayed, you enter a real value instead of using your pointing device to indicate a distance. However, before you enter the line length value you must move your cursor in the direction you want the line to be drawn. Do not pick a point, though—just move your cursor. AutoCAD LT starts drawing from the last point you selected and draws (in the direction of the cursor) a line segment with the length you specified. The line will be perfectly straight if **Ortho** is on. If **Ortho** is off, the line will be drawn at the angle formed by the last specified point and the current cursor location.

You can quickly draw the rectangle shown in **Figure 3-5** by turning **Ortho** mode on and then using the following procedure:

> Command: **LINE** *or* **L**↵
> From point: *(pick a location for point 1)*

Figure 3-5.
A rectangle drawn
using **Direct
Distance Entry.**
Notice that the
Ortho button on the
Status bar is active.

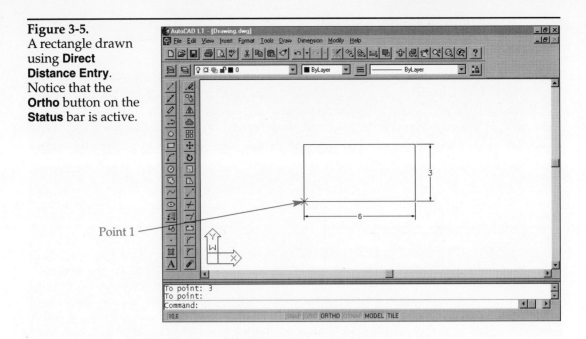

Point 1

Now, move your cursor to the right but do *not* pick a point.

> To point: **6**↵

Move your cursor up. Again, do *not* pick a point.

> To point: **3**↵

Now move your cursor to the left.

> To point: **6**↵

Finally, move your cursor down.

> To point: **3**↵
> To point: ↵
> Command:

Remember that the **Close** option is a better alternative than entering 3 for the last line segment.

EXERCISE 3-2

❑ Begin a new drawing session. It is not necessary to use one of your template drawings for this exercise. Use the **Start from Scratch** button instead.
❑ Turn **Ortho** on and use the **LINE** command with **Direct Distance Entry** to draw the rectangle shown in **Figure 3-5.**
❑ Try drawing the rectangle with **Ortho** off. What happens?
❑ Turn **Ortho** back on and draw several other rectangular and square-shaped objects with **Direct Distance Entry** using any length values you like.
❑ When you are done, save the drawing as EX3-2.

AutoCAD LT—Fundamentals and Applications

Drawing Lines Using Coordinates

While *Direct Distance Entry* is certainly quick and easy, there will be occasions when other means of point entry are required. Most of the point entry methods in AutoCAD LT use the *Cartesian*, or rectangular, coordinate system with which you are probably already familiar. With this system, all X and Y values are related to the drawing origin (usually at the very lower left of the drawing window) where X=0 and Y=0. Point distances are measured along the horizontal X axis and the vertical Y axis. Positive X values are to the right, or east, and positive Y values are to the top, or north as shown in **Figure 3-6.** It follows, therefore, that negative X values are to the left, or west, and negative Y values are to the bottom, or south.

NOTE

Since AutoCAD LT is a true 3D software program, it also has a Z axis that is perpendicular, or normal to the screen. Positive Z values are out of the screen toward you, the viewer, while negative Z values go into the screen, or away from you. The three XYZ axes, therefore, form 90° mutually perpendicular planes which allow six degrees of freedom for 3D geometry construction. Basic 3D viewing and drawing commands are introduced in *Chapter 19* of this text.

Figure 3-6.
In the Cartesian coordinate system, the positive X direction is to the right and the positive Y direction is up. The negative X direction is to the left and the negative Y direction is down.

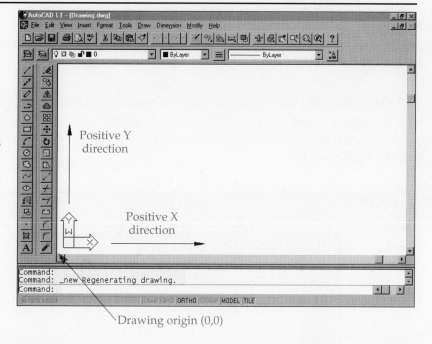

The World Coordinate System (WCS)

The Cartesian coordinate system described above is fixed in 3D space and may not be moved or altered. Because it is universal, AutoCAD LT refers to it as the *World Coordinate System*, or *WCS*. Whenever a new drawing file is created in AutoCAD LT, the drawing window defaults to a single viewport which corresponds to the WCS. In this view, the user is looking down along the positive Z axis onto the XY plane. This viewing angle is referred to as the *plan view*, or *plan to the WCS* as it is commonly called. All of the coordinates are measured along the X and Y axes relative to the 0, 0 origin at the lower left. Most of the 2D drawings that you will create using this text-

---

book will be in the plan view with the World Coordinate System. An alternative to the WCS is the *UCS*, or *User Coordinate System*. With the UCS, a user may redefine the location of 0,0 and the direction of the XYZ axes. This capability is absolutely essential for 3D geometry construction, but can also be used for certain 2D applications. Those applications and the UCS will be discussed more fully in later chapters.

Using Absolute Coordinates

Absolute coordinates are the most basic of the point entry methods used in AutoCAD LT. With absolute coordinates, all points are measured relative to the drawing origin (0,0). As an example, refer to the object shown in **Figure 3-7.** This is the same 6 × 3 rectangle that you created using **Direct Distance Entry** in the previous exercise. In this example, the object is created using absolute coordinate entry. Observe that the lower-left corner of the rectangle has the absolute coordinate 3,3. This means that AutoCAD LT measures 3 units horizontally (the positive X direction), and 3 units vertically (the positive Y direction) from the drawing origin (0,0) to locate the starting point of the first line. If you are seated at your computer, use the command sequence below to construct the rectangle. Remember to separate the Y coordinate from the X coordinate with a comma (,). If you make a typing mistake, use the [Backspace] key to correct the error. If you draw a line segment incorrectly, use the **U** option to undo it while you are still in the **LINE** command.

> Command: **LINE** *or* **L**↵
> From point: **3,3**↵
> To point: **9,3**↵
> To point: **9,6**↵
> To point: **3,6**↵
> To point: **C**↵
> Command:

Of course, you can enter the final coordinate of 3,3 and then press [Enter] to close the rectangle. However, typing C and then [Enter] as shown in the syntax above is a much quicker method to close the shape and end the **LINE** command all in one simple operation.

Figure 3-7.
The 6 × 3 rectangle drawn using absolute coordinates.

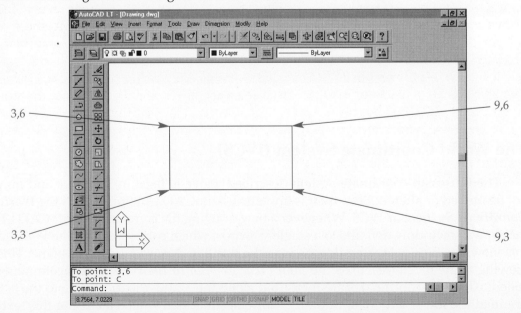

❑ Begin a new drawing session. It is not necessary to use one of your template drawings for this exercise. Use the **Start from Scratch** button instead.

❑ Use the **LINE** command with the following absolute coordinates to draw the object shown below.

Point	Coordinate	Point	Coordinate	Point	Coordinate
1	4,2	5	7.75,3.5	9	8,5.875
2	8,2	6	7.75,4.375	10	4,5.875
3	9,3	7	9,4.375	11	4,2 *or*
4	9,3.5	8	9,4.875		CLOSE

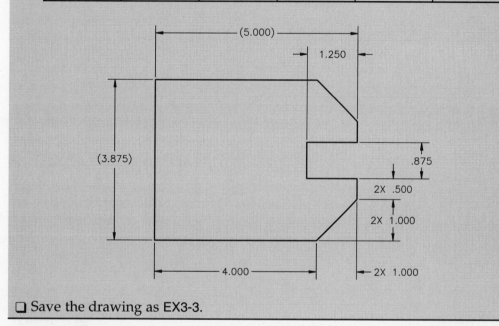

❑ Save the drawing as EX3-3.

Using Relative Coordinates

While absolute coordinates are useful, they are not very efficient. To explain further, think about the traditional, paper-based drafting process. If you were to work on a drafting board using the equivalent of absolute coordinates, then every line drawn would have to be measured from the very lower-left corner of the sheet of vellum taped to your board. Drafting would become very laborious and time-consuming, indeed!

It is far better to draw lines and other drawing objects *relative to each other*, rather than relative to the drawing origin. This is the method commonly used on a drafting board. AutoCAD LT allows for this type of point entry using *relative coordinates*. With this method, the coordinates you enter are in relation to previously entered coordinates. To tell AutoCAD LT that you want to use relative coordinates, you must precede your coordinate entry with the *at symbol (@)*. It is located on the number 2 key on the top row of your keyboard so you must use the [Shift] key to access it.

What does the @ symbol really represent? Every time you locate a point in the drawing area, the X, Y (and Z) coordinates of the cursor position are stored in an AutoCAD LT system variable called **LASTPOINT**. As you move your cursor around the screen and pick points, the **LASTPOINT** values constantly change. When you use the @ symbol, AutoCAD LT reads and uses the XYZ coordinates stored in **LASTPOINT**. This is why AutoCAD LT always knows where you left off in your drawing!

From **Figure 3-8**, you can see how relative coordinates define the 6 × 3 rectangle that was previously drawn using **Direct Distance Entry** and absolute coordinates. If you are seated at your computer, try the following command sequence to draw the rectangle using relative coordinates. Do not forget to use the @ symbol, or your line segments will be drawn relative to 0,0.

> Command: **LINE** *or* **L**↵
> From point: **3,3**↵
> To point: **@6,0**↵
> To point: **@0,3**↵
> To point: **@-6,0**↵
> To point: **C**↵
> Command:

Figure 3-8.
The 6 × 3 rectangle drawn using relative coordinates.

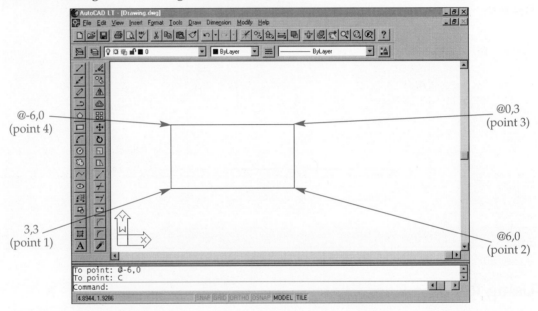

EXERCISE 3-4

❑ Begin a new drawing session. It is not necessary to use one of your template drawings for this exercise. Use the **Start from Scratch** button instead.
❑ Draw the same object as in Exercise 3-3, but using the following relative coordinates:

Point	Coordinate	Point	Coordinate	Point	Coordinate
1	4,2	5	@–1,0	9	@–1,1
2	@4,0	6	@0,.875	10	@-4,0
3	@1,1	7	@1,0	11	@0,–3.875 *or*
4	@0,.5	8	@0,.5		CLOSE

❑ Save the drawing as EX3-4.

AutoCAD LT—Fundamentals and Applications

Using Polar Coordinates

From *Chapter 2* you learned that AutoCAD LT uses a *polar coordinate system* to measure angles. Remember that in this system, angles are measured in a positive, or counterclockwise, direction where 0° is to the right (east), 90° is straight up (north), 180° is to the left (west), and 270° is straight down (south). This convention is graphically illustrated in **Figure 3-9.**

Polar coordinates can be used to locate a point by specifying its distance and angle from an existing point. To use relative polar coordinates, enter the @ symbol, the distance, a less-than sign (⟨), and then the angle (@*distance⟨angle*). Refer to **Figure 3-10** to see how several lines are drawn using polar coordinates. If you think of the angle as direction, you can see that polar coordinates use distance and direction values, and not X and Y values at all.

From **Figure 3-11**, observe how polar coordinates are used to draw the 6 × 3 rectangle that was previously drawn using the *Direct Distance Entry*, absolute, and relative coordinate methods. Once more, try the following command sequence to draw the rectangle using polar coordinates if you are seated at your computer.

```
Command: LINE or L↵
From point: 3,3↵
To point: @6⟨0↵
To point: @3⟨90↵
To point: @6⟨180↵
To point: C↵
Command:
```

Figure 3-9.
In the polar coordinate system, angles are measured in a positive, or counterclockwise, direction.

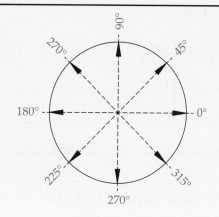

Figure 3-10.
Lines drawn using polar coordinates.

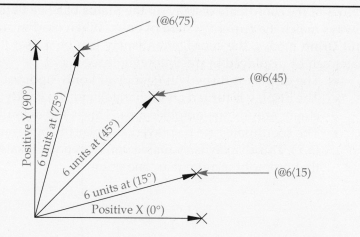

Figure 3-11.
The 6 × 3 rectangle drawn using polar coordinates.

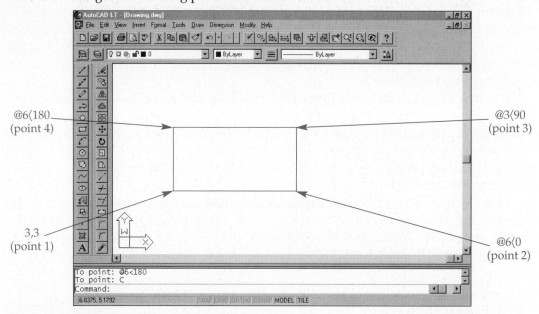

EXERCISE 3-5

❑ Begin a new drawing session. It is not necessary to use one of your template drawings for this exercise. Use the **Start from Scratch** button instead.
❑ Draw the same object as in the previous three exercises, but using the following polar coordinates:

Point	Coordinate	Point	Coordinate	Point	Coordinate
1	4,2	5	@1⟨180	9	@1.414⟨135
2	@4⟨0	6	@.875⟨90	10	@4⟨180
3	@1.414⟨45	7	@1⟨0	11	@3.875⟨270 *or*
4	@.5⟨90	8	@.5⟨90		CLOSE

❑ Save the drawing as EX3-5 and QUIT.

Using the Coordinate Display Box

AutoCAD LT displays the current cursor location with a pair of XY coordinate values in the coordinate display on the **Status** bar. See **Figure 3-12.** These coordinates always match the current system of units. When used in conjunction with **Grid**, **Snap**, and **Ortho** modes, the coordinate display can be a useful drawing aid. The coordinates can be displayed in the following three ways:

- The display is turned off (static) and only updates when you specify a point.
- The display is turned on (dynamic) and constantly updates as you move your cursor around the graphics area. This is the default setting.
- The coordinates are displayed as polar (distance⟨angle) rather than Cartesian (XY). This display is available only when you draw lines or other object types that prompt for more than one point.

Figure 3-12.
When activated, the coordinate display indicates the cursor location using the current units of measurement.

Command:

6.5000,3.5000 ◄———————————— Coordinates displayed here

In *Chapter 1* you learned that the coordinate display can be toggled on and off using function key [F6], or the control key combination [Ctrl]+[D]. You can also turn the coordinate display on and off by simply double-clicking anywhere inside the coordinate display with your pointing device. While in the middle of a drawing command, you can use any one of these methods to cycle through the three coordinate display states or you can use the **COORDS** system variable as follows:

Command: **COORDS.**↵
New value for COORDS ⟨*current*⟩: (*enter* 0, 1, *or* 2 *and press* [Enter])

By default, **COORDS** is set to 1 (on). To turn off the display, set **COORDS** to 0 (zero). Set **COORDS** to 2 if you want to use a polar display.

EXERCISE 3-6

❑ In this exercise, you will once again draw the 6 × 3 rectangle. However, this time you will rely solely on drawing aids to create the object.
❑ Begin a new drawing using your **TEMPLATEA** template drawing.
❑ Be sure that snap and grid are turned on and set **COORDS** to 2.
❑ Issue the **LINE** command. At the **From point:** prompt, pick a starting point somewhere near the lower-left corner of the screen. Observe the coordinate display on the **Status** bar as you move your cursor to the right.
❑ Pick a second point when the display reads: 6⟨0. It may be helpful to turn on **Ortho** mode.
❑ Move your cursor up and pick a point when the display reads: 3⟨90.
❑ Now move your cursor to the left and pick a third point when the display reads: 6⟨180.
❑ Finally, use the **Close** option to close the shape. It is not necessary to save this exercise.

Drawing Lines Using PolarSnap Settings

PolarSnap is a feature introduced in AutoCAD LT 97. Used in conjunction with **Ortho** mode, **PolarSnap** restricts rubber-band cursor movement to precise angles and distances. You can specify the snap angle, snap distance or both using the **Ortho/Polar Settings** dialog box shown in **Figure 3-13**. This dialog box is opened by entering POLAR at the Command: prompt or clicking the **PolarSnap Settings** button on the **Standard Toolbar**. The available options offered in the **Ortho/Polar Settings** dialog box are described below:

- **On.** Activate this check box when you wish to use **Ortho** or **PolarSnap** settings. Until activated, each of the other options in the dialog box appear "grayed-out" and are unavailable. If you have already enabled **Ortho** mode by pressing [F8], [Ctrl]+[L], or double-clicking the **ORTHO** button on the status bar, this check box will be active.
- **Polar: Angle Snap.** Activate this option button when you wish to draw a line with a variable length but at a precise angle. Use the **Angle** text box to enter the desired angle. See **Figure 3-13B**. Since the angle defaults to 15°, the cursor snaps at 0°, 15°, 30°, 45°, and so on.

- **Polar: Distance Snap.** This option permits you to draw lines at incremental lengths at any angle. By default, this option draws lines at 1 unit increments. See **Figure 3-13C.** If you set the distance to 3, then the cursor snaps from the first point specified to lengths of 3, 6, 9, 12, and so on. Use the Distance text box to enter the desired distance.
- **Polar: Distance & Angle Snap.** This last option is particularly handy since it allows you to draw a line at any incremental length and at any angle. See **Figure 3-13D.** Use the **Angle** and **Distance** text boxes to set the desired values.
- **Polar ToolTip.** Active by default, this option displays a floating tooltip that displays the distance and/or angle from the last specified point. See **Figure 3-14.** It is similar to that displayed when you pause your pointing device over a tool button. Although an extremely useful drawing aid, it can be disabled by deactivating the **Polar ToolTip** check box.

Figure 3-13.
A—**Ortho** mode must be activated to use the **Ortho/PolarSnap Settings** dialog box options.
B—Activate the **Polar: Angle Snap** option button when you wish to draw a line at any length, but with a specified angle. C—The **Polar: Distance Snap** option is used when you wish to draw a line with an incremental length. D—Activate the **Polar Angle & Distance Snap** option when you wish to draw a line of an incremental length and at a specified angle.

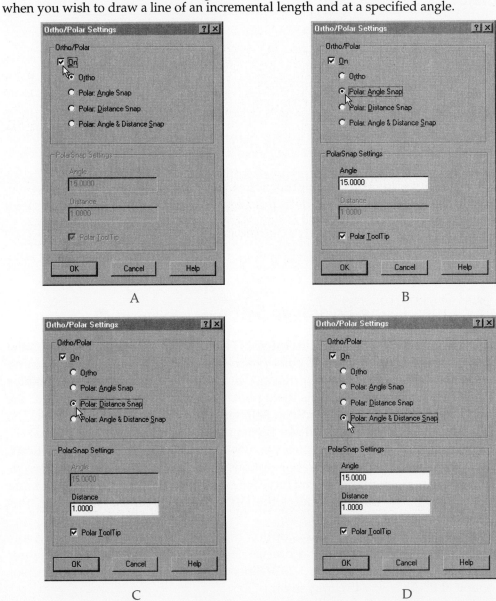

A

B

C

D

AutoCAD LT—Fundamentals and Applications

Figure 3-14.
A floating tooltip displays the distance and/or angle from the last specified point when using **PolarSnap**.

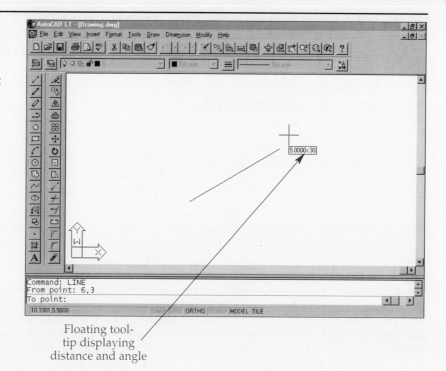

Floating tool-tip displaying distance and angle

The **POLAR** command is one of a small subset of AutoCAD LT commands that may be invoked *transparently*, which means the command may be used while inside another command. Once a transparent command is complete, the previous command is resumed. To use a transparent command, preface the command with an apostrophe ('). In the sequence that follows, you can see how **POLAR** can be invoked to make changes to PolarSnap settings while still in the middle of the **LINE** command.

> Command: **LINE** *or* **L**↵
> From point: *(pick point 1)*
> To point: *(pick point 2)*
> To point: *(pick point 3)*
> To point: **'POLAR**↵

The **Ortho/Polar Settings** dialog box is then displayed. Make any required setting changes and click the **OK** button.

> Resuming LINE command.
> To point: *(pick another point or press* [Enter] *to end the command)*

In the example above, **POLAR** could also be transparently invoked by clicking the **PolarSnap Settings** button on the **Standard Toolbar** rather than entering '**POLAR** on the command line.

NOTE   As with Direct Distance Entry, **SNAP** mode, and **ORTHO** mode, AutoCAD LT overrides **PolarSnap** when you enter coordinates on the command line as described earlier in this chapter. For Direct Distance Entry, only the **PolarSnap** distance setting is overridden—not the angle setting.

❏ Begin a new drawing. Use the **Start from Scratch** button rather than one of your template drawings.

❏ Using the correct **PolarSnap** angle settings, draw the objects shown below. Each of the short line segments on Object 2 is 1.0000 long.

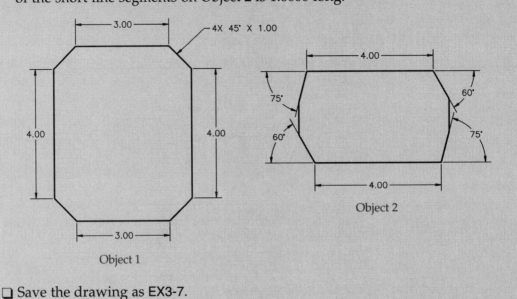

Object 1

Object 2

❏ Save the drawing as EX3-7.

Editing and the ERASE Command

When you modify a drawing to correct mistakes or to revise a design, you are editing the drawing. Whether you select only one object to edit, or many hundreds of objects, you create a *selection set*. There are a variety of ways to create selection sets for editing. Each of the selection set options described in the following sections apply to erasing objects. However, the selection options are used the same way with most of the editing commands in AutoCAD LT whenever you receive the Select objects: prompt.

Erasing unwanted drawing objects is one of the most basic editing functions. To do so, enter ERASE, or E, at the Command: prompt or click the **Erase** button in the **Modify** toolbar. You may also issue the **ERASE** command by selecting **Erase** from the **Modify** pull-down menu or by selecting **Clear** from the **Edit** pull-down menu. See **Figure 3-15.** The **ERASE** command prompts you to select objects to be erased:

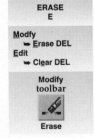

> Command: **ERASE** *or* **E**↵
> Select objects: *(select an object)*
> Select objects: *(select another object or press* [Enter] *to end the command)*

When the Select objects: prompt appears, the graphics cursor is replaced with a small box called the *pickbox*. Move your pointing device to place the pickbox over the object you want to select and pick. As shown in **Figure 3-16A**, a picked object assumes a dotted or dashed appearance. AutoCAD LT calls this *highlighting*. The **Select objects:** prompt remains active in case you want to select another object. When you are done picking, press [Enter] to end the **ERASE** command. The object(s) you select is then erased from the screen and the Command: prompt reappears. See **Figure 3-16B.**

Figure 3-15.
The **ERASE** command may be issued by selecting **Erase** from the **Modify** pull-down menu or by selecting **Clear** from the **Edit** pull-down menu.

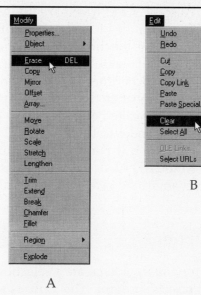

A

B

Figure 3-16.
A—Locate the pickbox over the object to be erased, pick it and press [Enter]. B—Select another object or press [Enter] to end the command. The object is erased.

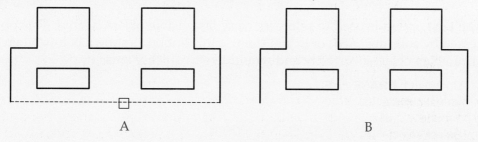

A

B

> **NOTE**
>
> You can turn off highlighting using the **HIGHLIGHT** system variable (0=OFF, 1=ON). However, since highlighting lets you know that an object has been selected, it is suggested that it be left on. Highlighting can also be turned on and off in the **Drawing Aids** dialog box. This dialog box is accessed by entering DDRMODES at the Command: prompt or selecting **Drawing Aids...** from the **Tools** pull-down menu.

The OOPS Command

If you find that you have erased objects mistakenly, those objects may be restored using the **OOPS** command. This appropriately named command is accessed by entering OO at the Command: prompt. However, keep in mind that the **OOPS** command can only restore objects erased with the very last **ERASE** operation.

Sizing the Pickbox

The size of the pickbox can be increased to allow for a larger picking area, or decreased to provide more accurate picking when objects are spaced closely together. Use the **PICKBOX** system variable if you want to change the size of the pickbox.

> Command: **PICKBOX**↵
> New value for PICKBOX⟨3⟩: *(enter an integer value)*

The pickbox can also be sized transparently while inside another command by entering 'PICKBOX. The size of the pickbox is measured in *pixels*. Pixels, or *pels*, stands for picture elements and are the tiny dots that make up what is displayed on a computer monitor. The default value is 3 pixels, but most users prefer a slightly larger pickbox of 5 or 6 pixels. Try experimenting with various sizes to find the one that suits your preferences. Once you change the size of the pickbox, the new value is stored in an external configuration file called aclt5.cfg. If you are using AutoCAD LT 97, the file is called aclt4.cfg. This file resides in the root AutoCAD LT folder and is created when you first install AutoCAD LT. It contains hardware configuration settings that are used for all of your AutoCAD LT drawings. Therefore, changing the pickbox size in the current drawing changes the pickbox size for all of your drawings.

Selection Set Options

As mentioned previously, you create a selection set when you select one or more objects at the Select objects: prompt. The various selection set options include **Last, Previous, All, Window, Crossing, WPolygon, CPolygon, Undo, Remove,** and **Add**. Each of these options are described in the following sections.

Last and Previous Options

The **Last** option is used to select the very last visible object created. This option is accessed by entering LAST, or L. You can use this option as shown below when you have drawn an object incorrectly and would like to quickly erase it.

```
Command: ERASE or E↵
Select objects: L↵
1 found
Select objects: ↵
Command:
```

AutoCAD LT remembers the most recent object selection. For example, suppose you erase a group of objects and decide to restore them with the **OOPS** command. You then realize that you want to erase the objects after all. You can quickly reselect the restored objects to erase using the **Previous** option by entering PREVIOUS, or P, as follows:

```
Command: ERASE or E↵
Select objects: PREVIOUS or P↵
n found
Select objects: ↵
Command:
```

All, Window, and Crossing Options

When you want to select every object on your drawing for an editing operation, use the **All** option. Be careful, because even objects not displayed in the current viewport, such as objects off the screen or on layers that have been turned off, are selected with this option. However, any objects on frozen layers are ignored. See *Chapter 5* of this text for more information about layers and their various states.

The **All** option can quickly be invoked by choosing **Select <u>A</u>ll** from the **<u>E</u>dit** pull-down menu or by pressing [Ctrl]+[A] from the keyboard. You may also enter ALL (not just A) as follows:

> Command: **ERASE** *or* **E**⏎
> Select objects: **ALL.**⏎ *(or press* [Ctrl]+[A]*)*
> *n* found
> Select objects: ⏎
> Command:

You can also select a large number of objects by enclosing them within a selection window. As shown in **Figure 3-17A**, the window is defined by picking two diagonally opposite corners. Thus, the window box can be square or rectangular in shape and is displayed on screen in a solid line representation. It is important to note that only objects that lie *completely within* the window are selected. The results of the window selection are shown in **Figure 3-17B**. To use the **Window** option, enter WINDOW, or W, as follows:

> Command: **ERASE** *or* **E**⏎
> Select objects: **WINDOW** *or* **W**⏎
> First corner: *(pick a point)* Other corner: *(pick a second diagonal point)*
> *n* found
> Select objects: ⏎
> Command:

A second type of window selection method available in AutoCAD LT is called a *crossing*. Like a window box, a crossing box is also defined with two diagonal corners and is square or rectangular in shape. Also like a window box, any objects enclosed within the crossing box are selected. The major difference is that, in addition to all the objects within the box that are selected, any objects that cross over the box are also selected. From the example illustrated in **Figure 3-18A**, you can see that the same two diagonal corners are selected as in the previous example. Also note that unlike a

---

Figure 3-17.
A—The **Window** option requires two diagonal corners. Note that a window box is represented with a solid line. B—After pressing [Enter], all of the objects completely enclosed within the **Window** box are erased.

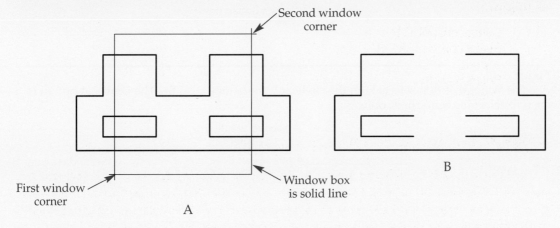

window box, the crossing box is represented with a dotted, or dashed, line instead of a solid line. Compare the results using a **Crossing, Figure 3-18B**, with those using a **Window, Figure 3-17B**. To use the **Crossing** option, type CROSSING, or C, as follows:

Command: **ERASE** *or* **E**↵
Select objects: **CROSSING** *or* **C**↵
First corner: *(pick a point)* Other corner: *(pick a second diagonal point)*
n found
Select objects: ↵
Command:

To further illustrate the difference between the **Window** and a **Crossing** option, consider the circle with centerlines shown in **Figure 3-19A**. As you will learn in *Chapter 12* of this text, AutoCAD LT sometimes creates centerlines with individual line segments depending on the method used. When this occurs, a centerline is comprised of six separate lines. Such a centerline is shown in **Figure 3-19A**. To erase all the centerlines, you might be inclined to use the **Window** option. Unfortunately, the circle gets included in the selection set as well. Although the **Remove** option can be used to remove the circle from the selection set, it requires an additional step, which will be covered later in this chapter.

Figure 3-18.
A—The **Crossing** option also requires two diagonal corners. Observe that a crossing box is represented with a dotted, or dashed, line. B—After pressing [Enter], all of the objects enclosed within or crossing over the **Crossing** box are erased.

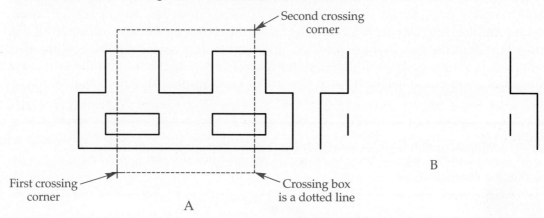

Figure 3-19.
A—The **Window** option selects both the circle and the centerlines. B—The **Crossing** option is used to select the centerlines only.

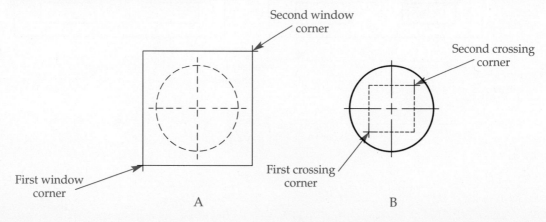

A far more efficient way to select only the centerlines is shown in **Figure 3-19B**. Use the **Crossing** option and pick the two diagonal corners indicated. The portion of the centerlines that are completely enclosed within the box are selected, as well as the portions that cross over the box. The circle is ignored entirely.

Using Implied Windowing

Because window and crossing boxes are so frequently used for editing operations, AutoCAD LT allows you to automatically create a window or crossing without first typing W or C. This method is called *implied windowing*. When the Select objects: prompt appears, pick the first corner point in an empty area of the drawing window; AutoCAD LT then prompts you for the other corner point. If you drag your cursor from left to right, a window box is automatically created. Dragging your cursor from right to left automatically creates a crossing box. Implied windowing is on by default in AutoCAD LT, but may be turned off using the **PICKAUTO** system variable.

Verb/Noun vs. Noun/Verb Selection

From the examples given so far, you can see that to perform an editing operation, such as **ERASE**, you first enter the command and then select the objects to be edited. AutoCAD LT calls this method *Verb/Noun selection*. An alternative method for object selection is called *Noun/Verb*. This second method allows you to select the objects first, and then enter the command you want to use on the selection set. As shown in **Figure 3-20A**, you can use implied windowing to preselect objects with a **Window** box without even being in a command. Simply pick a corner point on an empty area of the screen and drag to the right to completely enclose the objects. Once the objects are selected, you then enter the editing command that you wish to use with them. The small squares that appear on the preselected objects are called *grips* and are discussed in detail in *Chapter 10*. If you inadvertently preselect screen objects and want to remove the grips from the display, press the [Esc] key twice. To automatically preselect objects with a crossing selection, pick a corner point on an empty area of the screen and drag to the left. See **Figure 3-20B**. The noun/verb selection method is on by default in AutoCAD LT, but may be turned off using the **PICKFIRST** system variable.

Figure 3-20.
A—Picking a corner and dragging to the right automatically creates a **Window** box.
B—Picking a corner and dragging to the left creates a **Crossing** box.

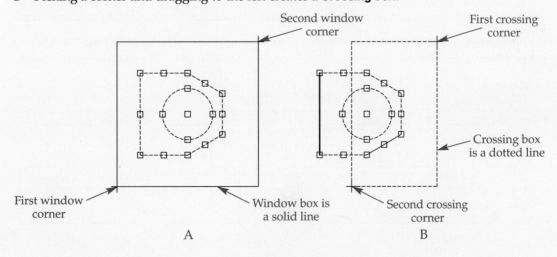

CAUTION Setting the **PICKFIRST** variable to 0 disables the **Shortcut** menu described earlier in this chapter.

PROFESSIONAL TIP You can quickly erase drawing objects by first selecting them without issuing the **ERASE** command. Once highlighted, simply press [Delete] on your keyboard to erase the selected objects.

WPolygon, CPolygon, and Fence Options

Because the **Window** selection set option places a square or rectangle around objects, it is sometimes difficult to select the objects you want without others being selected as well. The **WPolygon** selection set option is similar to **Window**, but it lets you designate an irregular polygon (a closed figure with three or more sides) around the objects you want to select. You can draw a polygon of any shape, but it cannot touch or cross itself. Like a **Window** box, the **WPolygon** outline is drawn with a solid line. To better understand the **WPolygon** option, refer to **Figure 3-21A**. To use the **WPolygon** option, enter WPOLYGON, or WP, as follows:

Command: **ERASE** *or* **E**↵
Select objects: **WPOLYGON** *or* **WP**↵
First polygon point: *(pick point 1)*
Undo/⟨Endpoint of line⟩: *(pick point 2 or enter* U *to undo)*
Undo/⟨Endpoint of line⟩: *(pick point 3 or enter* U *to undo)*
Undo/⟨Endpoint of line⟩: *(pick point 4 or enter* U *to undo)*
Undo/⟨Endpoint of line⟩: ↵
n found
Select objects: ↵
Command:

As with the **Window** option, any objects completely enclosed by the **WPolygon** are selected. See **Figure 3-21B**.

Figure 3-21.
A—Objects are selected by using an irregular polygon with the **WPolygon** option. B—After pressing [Enter], all of the objects completely enclosed within the polygon outline are erased.

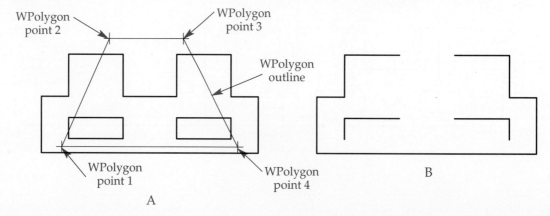

There is also a **CPolygon** option that is similar to **WPolygon** but has the same characteristics as **Crossing**. In other words, objects completely enclosed or crossed over with a **CPolygon** outline are selected. Also, the **CPolygon** outline is drawn with a dotted, or dashed, line like a **Crossing** box. See **Figure 3-22A.** To use the **CPolygon** option, enter CPOLYGON, or CP, as follows:

Command: **ERASE** *or* **E**⏎
Select objects: **CPOLYGON** *or* **CP**⏎
First polygon point: *(pick point 1)*
Undo/⟨Endpoint of line⟩: *(pick point 2 or U to undo)*
Undo/⟨Endpoint of line⟩: *(pick point 3 or U to undo)*
Undo/⟨Endpoint of line⟩: *(pick point 4 or U to undo)*
Undo/⟨Endpoint of line⟩: ⏎
n found
Select objects: ⏎
Command:

The results of the **CPolygon** operation are shown in **Figure 3-22B.**

An additional method used to select more than one object at a time exists with the **Fence** selection set option. A **Fence** is a multisegmented line that is drawn to select objects it passes through. It is somewhat similar to **CPolygon**, but it does not close the last segment drawn. The **Fence** can be drawn straight or staggered and is represented with a dashed line. Refer to the lower object shown in **Figure 3-23A.** To use the **Fence** option, enter FENCE, or F, as follows:

Command: **ERASE** *or* **E**⏎
Select objects: **FENCE** *or* **F**⏎
First Fence point: *(pick point 1)*
Undo/⟨Endpoint of line⟩: *(pick point 2 or U to undo)*
Undo/⟨Endpoint of line⟩: *(pick point 3 or U to undo)*
Undo/⟨Endpoint of line⟩: *(pick point 4 or U to undo)*
Undo/⟨Endpoint of line⟩: ⏎
n found
Select objects: ⏎
Command:

The results of the **Fence** selection are shown in **Figure 3-23B.**

Figure 3-22.
A—Objects are selected by using an irregular polygon with the **CPolygon** option. Note the dotted or dashed **CPolygon** outline. B—After pressing [Enter], all of the objects completely enclosed within or crossing over the polygon outline are erased.

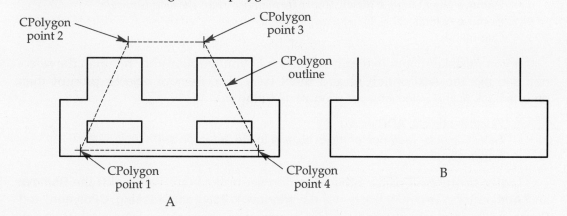

Figure 3-23.
A—A fence line may be straight or staggered. B—After pressing [Enter], all of the objects passed through with the fence line are erased.

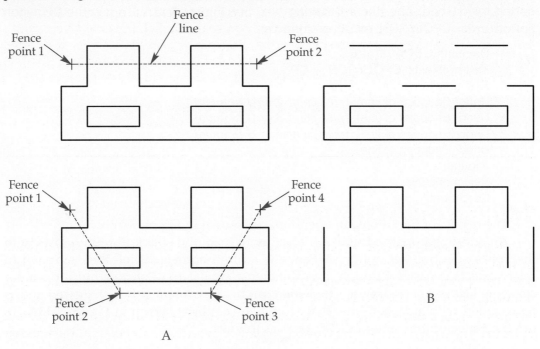

Undo, Remove, and Add Options

There will be instances when you mistakenly select an object for editing. You can undo your selection using the **Undo** selection set option. This option works identically to the **LINE** command **Undo** option described earlier in this chapter. Simply type U to remove the highlighting from the selected object while the Select objects: prompt is still displayed. If you are using AutoCAD LT 97, you can also click the **Undo** button on the **Standard Toolbar** to remove an object from the selection set.

On other occasions, it is likely that you will include one or more objects inadvertently in a selection set. This can often happen when you use the **Window** and **Crossing** options. Objects can be removed from a selection set using the **Remove** option as follows:

    Command: **ERASE** *or* **E.**⏎
    Select objects: *(pick one or more objects)*
    Select objects: **REMOVE** *or* **R.**⏎
    Remove objects: *(pick the objects to be removed from the selection set)*
    Remove objects: ⏎
    Command:

If you mistakenly remove some objects that you would rather retain in the selection set, use the **Add** option to add them back. The Remove objects: prompt then reverts back to the Select objects: prompt as follows:

    Remove objects: **ADD** *or* **A.**⏎
    Select objects: *(add one or more objects to the selection set)*
    Select objects: ⏎

Lastly, because all of the other selection set options are valid with the **Remove** and **Add** options, you may freely use the **Window, WPolygon, Crossing, CPolygon,** and **Fence** methods to add or remove a large number of objects to or from a selection set.

PROFESSIONAL TIP

Here is a fast and easy way to remove an object from a selection set without using the **Remove** option. When the Select objects: prompt is displayed, pick the object you want to remove while simultaneously pressing and holding the [Shift] key. You can also use this method to remove objects from a selection set using the **Window** and **Crossing** options. Press and hold the [Shift] key while picking an empty spot in the drawing window. Now, move your pointing device to the right to obtain a **Window** box—move to the left to get a **Crossing** box.

Selecting Objects Close Together

Regardless of how you have sized the object selection pickbox, it is often difficult to select objects that are spaced closely together or that overlap each other. To illustrate this point, consider the objects shown in **Figure 3-24.** Observe that the circle, centerline, and line objects all fall within the boundary of the pickbox. Therefore, it is anybody's guess as to which of the three objects gets selected during a pick operation. Fortunately, AutoCAD LT offers a handy feature called *object cycling* which allows you to cycle through each object until you reach the one you want.

To use object cycling, press the [Ctrl] key and pick a location as close as possible to the object you want. Continue to hold down the [Ctrl] key as you successively click the pick button on your pointing device. When the object you want is highlighted, release the [Ctrl] key and press [Enter] to select the desired object.

Customizing Object Selection

Apart from the selection set options previously described, there are several other selection modes available to you. These modes are set in the **Object Selection Settings** dialog box. This dialog box is accessed by entering DDSELECT, or SE, at the Command: prompt, or by selecting **Selection...** from the **Tools** pull-down menu. See **Figure 3-25A.**

Figure 3-24.
To use object cycling, press and hold the [Ctrl] key as you successively click the pick button on your pointing device. When the desired object is highlighted, release the [Ctrl] key and press [Enter] to select the object.

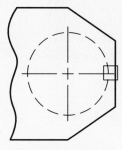
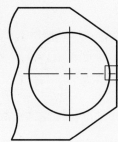
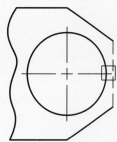

| Starts Cycling from Circle | Cycles to Part of Center Line | Cycles to Object Line |

The **Object Selection Settings** dialog box is shown in **Figure 3-25B.** Each of the options available in this dialog box are described in the following section. The **Selection Modes** area contains four check boxes that perform the following functions:

- **Noun/Verb Selection.** Activating the **Noun/Verb Selection** check box allows you to select objects first, and then enter the command you want to use on the selection set as described previously in this chapter. This option is on by default. Remember that another way to activate or deactivate this option is with the **PICKFIRST** system variable.

- **Use Shift to Add.** This check box controls how you add objects to an existing selection set. When checked, it activates an additive selection mode, in which you must press and hold down the [Shift] key while adding more objects to the selection set. While this mode is not very efficient, it is consistent with several other graphics software programs commercially available. The **Use Shift to Add** mode is off by default. You can also use the **PICKADD** system variable to turn this mode on and off.

- **Press and Drag.** This option controls how selection windows are drawn. When active, you must press and hold down the pick button on your pointing device as you diagonally drag your cursor to create a **Window** or **Crossing** box selection. Release the button to complete the window or crossing at its second diagonal corner. As with the **Use Shift to Add** option, this method is not very efficient but it is consistent with several other commercially available software products. By default, the **Press and Drag** mode is off, but you can also use the **PICKDRAG** system variable to toggle this option on and off.

- **Implied Windowing.** As discussed previously, implied windowing allows you to automatically create a selection window when the Select objects: prompt appears by picking first and second diagonal corner points in empty areas of the screen. Drawing the selection window from left to right creates a **Window** box, while drawing the selection window from right to left creates a **Crossing** box. Enabled by default, **Implied Windowing** may be disabled using this check box or the **PICKAUTO** system variable.

Figure 3-25.
A—The **DDSELECT** command can be issued by picking **Selection...** from the **Tools** pull-down menu. B—The **Object Selection Settings** dialog box.

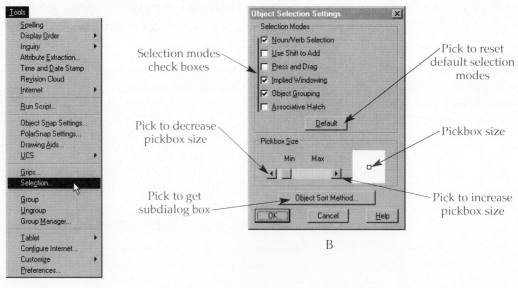

A

B

- **Object Grouping.** Active by default, this setting selects an entire group when you pick a member of the group. This setting is also controlled using the **PICKSTYLE** system variable. See *Chapter 15* for more information about groups and the **GROUP** command. This check box does not appear in AutoCAD LT 97.
- **Associative Hatch.** If this check box is activated, boundary objects are also selected when an associative hatch pattern is picked. Associative hatching and boundaries are described in *Chapter 13* of this text. This check box does not appear in AutoCAD LT 97.
- **Default.** Click the **Default** button to reset the six selection mode check boxes to their original default settings. That is, **Noun/Verb Selection, Implied Windowing**, and **Object Grouping** are activated, and **Use Shift to Add, Press and Drag**, and **Associative Hatch** are deactivated.

Earlier in this chapter you learned that the **PICKBOX** command may be used to adjust the size of the pickbox. You can also use the horizontal slider bar in the **Pickbox Size** area to accomplish the same task. As you move the slider button left or right, the pickbox size dynamically changes as illustrated in the pickbox image tile to the right of the slider bar.

Clicking the **Object Sort Method...** button displays the **Object Sort Method** subdialog box shown in **Figure 3-26.** The six check boxes that appear in this subdialog box allow you to process objects in the order in which they occur in the database. That is, in the order in which the objects were created. As an example, check the **Redraws** and **Regens** check boxes to assure that redraws and regenerations always draw objects in the order in which they were created. Regenerations are covered in *Chapter 4* of this text. Redraws are discussed in *Chapter 7* of this text. To ensure that objects selected by the **Window** and **Crossing** options go into the selection set in a predictable order, check the **Object Selection** check box.

PROFESSIONAL TIP

By default, only **Plotting** and **PostScript Output** are object sorted as shown in **Figure 3-26.** Unless the drawing you are working on or the application you are using depends on object order, it is recommended that you do not change the default settings in the other check boxes. This is because selecting additional sorting methods usually increases processing time and slows down system performance. This is particularly true for large drawings.

Figure 3-26.
The **Object Sort Method** subdialog box.

Object sort method check boxes

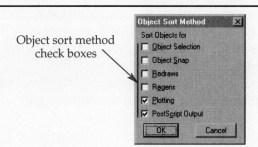

Undoing the Effects of a Command

Earlier in this chapter you learned how an incorrectly drawn line segment can be removed using the **Undo** option in the **LINE** command. You also learned that the **OOPS** command can restore erased objects by essentially undoing the **ERASE** command. AutoCAD LT provides two other commands that reverse the most recent operation. These two commands are the **U** and **UNDO** commands. AutoCAD LT also provides the **REDO** command, which reverses an **UNDO** operation.

The U Command

U

Edit
↳ Undo

Standard
toolbar

Undo

The **U** command reverses, or undos, the most recent AutoCAD LT operation. Operations external to the current drawing, such as plotting or saving a drawing to disk, cannot be undone however. To use the **U** command, simple enter U at the Command: prompt. You can also access the **U** command by clicking the **Undo** button on the **Standard Toolbar**, or selecting **Undo** from the **Edit** pull-down menu. You can enter U as many times as you like, backing up one step at a time. Be careful, because too many U's can take you all the way back to the beginning of the current drawing session.

The UNDO Command

The **UNDO** command is similar to the **U** command but with a variety of available options. Some of the options let you undo several commands at once and perform special operations, such as marking a point to return to in case things go wrong. The **UNDO** command must be entered at the Command: prompt because choosing **Undo** from the **Edit** pull-down menu or clicking the **Undo** button on the **Standard Toolbar** invokes the **U** command—not the **UNDO** command. The **UNDO** command sequence is as follows:

Command: **UNDO**↵
Auto/Control/BEgin/End/Mark/Back/⟨*number*⟩:

Each of the options offered by the **UNDO** command are described below:
- ⟨*number*⟩. The default option lets you specify the number of preceding operations to be undone. Entering 3 reverses the previous three operations. Entering 1 is the equivalent of using the **U** command.
- **Auto.** Selecting **Auto** prompts you with the following:

  ON/OFF ⟨*current*⟩: (*enter* ON *or* OFF *and press* [Enter])

  When **Auto** is on, (its default setting), AutoCAD LT commands are automatically grouped together to perform certain operations, no matter how complicated. This grouping occurs *behind the scenes* with no action necessary on your part. Each of the commands in the group are then removed as a single command when a **U** or **UNDO** operation is performed. If **Auto** is turned off, then each command in a group of commands is treated separately and several repetitions of **U** or **UNDO** are required.
- **Control.** The **Control** option limits the **UNDO** operation or disables it completely. Selecting **Control** prompts you with the following suboptions:

  All/None/One ⟨All⟩:

  - **All.** The **All** suboption enables all of the **UNDO** options. This is the default setting.
  - **None.** Selecting **None** disables the **U** and **UNDO** commands.
  - **One.** The **One** suboption limits the **UNDO** command to a single operation, so that it operates similar to the **U** command. The **Auto** and **Mark** options are not available when **One** is in effect.

- **BEgin and End.** These options are used together. When you use the **BEgin** option, a group of commands is treated as a single command for the purposes of **U** and **UNDO**. Select the **End** option to terminate the command grouping. To explain further, suppose you enable the **BEgin** option and then perform three separate drawing commands. Because **BEgin** is enabled, all three commands are grouped together as if one. Then you return to the **UNDO** command, and enable the **End** option. If you now issue the **U** or **UNDO** commands, all three commands are undone at the same time. Any commands performed after using the **End** option are treated separately by the **U** and **UNDO** commands.
- **Mark.** The **Mark** option makes a special mark in the undo information. Use the **Back** option to undo back to the mark. AutoCAD LT informs you when you reach the mark if you undo one operation at a time. If the **BEgin** option is enabled, **Mark** and **Back** cannot be used.
- **Back.** The **Back** option reverses every operation back to the beginning of the current drawing session. You are prompted with:

  This will undo everthing. OK? ⟨Y⟩ *(answer* Y *or* N *and press* [Enter]*)*

If a mark has been inserted using the **Mark** option, then **Back** takes the drawing back to the state it was in when the mark is encountered.

The REDO Command

It is inevitable that you will eventually undo an operation accidentally. Since pressing [Enter] or the spacebar automatically repeats the previous command in AutoCAD LT, you can see that performing a **U** command, and then inadvertently pressing [Enter] a second time would perform two undos! To reverse an unwanted undo, enter REDO at the Command: prompt, click the **Redo** button on the **Standard Toolbar**, or select **Redo** from the **Edit** pull-down menu. However, keep in mind that the **REDO** command must be issued *immediately* after performing the **U** command. If you attempt to perform a **REDO** after executing several other commands since the unwanted undo, the following message is displayed:

REDO

Edit
↳ Redo

Standard
Toolbar

Redo

Previous command did not undo things.

PROFESSIONAL
TIP

Observe from the **Edit** pull-down menu in **Figure 3-27A** that there are keyboard shortcuts for the **U** and **REDO** commands. Press [Ctrl]+[Z] when you wish to issue the **U** command. Pressing [Ctrl]+[Y] is the equivalent of invoking the **REDO** command. The **Undo** and **Redo** buttons on the **Standard Toolbar** are shown in **Figure 3-27B.** For AutoCAD LT 98 users, these buttons are *grayed-out* and unavailable at the beginning of a new drawing session. Only until one or more commands are issued, does the **Undo** button become active. The **Redo** button remains *grayed-out* until at least one **Undo** operation is performed.

Also, remember that the **OOPS** command can only be used to reverse the very last erase operation. The **U** and **UNDO** commands can reverse *all* drawing and editing operations. It is also important to keep in mind that the **REDO** command can only reverse one **U** or **UNDO** operation. Therefore, take care when undoing commands. Save your drawing often as a precaution against one-too-many undos!

Undoing and redoing a specific number of actions

The ability to undo or redo several actions at once has been added to AutoCAD LT 98. The ability to undo or redo several actions at once is not available in AutoCAD LT 97. To explain further, consider the example shown in **Figure 3-28A.** Clicking the down arrow to the right of the **Undo** button on the **Standard Toolbar** displays a drop-down list of the most recently used commands. You can use your pointing device to select one or more commands from the list to undo. The commands appear in the list in the reverse order in which they were executed. Make your selection(s) by starting at the top of the list and pressing and holding the pick button on your pointing device as you move down to select additional commands to undo. The number of commands you select is reported at the bottom of the drop-down list. When you are done selecting, release the pick button on your pointing device to initiate the undo operation. In the example shown, the **ERASE, ARC,** and **CIRCLE** command operations are selected for undoing.

Once one or more commands has been undone, the **Redo** button on the **Standard Toolbar** is no longer *grayed-out* and is available for selection. Click the down-arrow to the right of the **Redo** button to display a list of the most recently reversed commands. To redo one or more of the commands, press and hold the pick button on your pointing device and move down through the list making your selection. Release the pick button to initiate the redo operation.

You can also perform multiple redos on the command line using the **MREDO** command. The procedure looks like this:

> Command: **MREDO** or **MR** ↵
> All/Last/⟨Number⟩: *(select an option or press* [Enter]*)*

Figure 3-27.
A—Both the **U** and **REDO** commands may be accessed from the **Edit** pull-down menu.
B—The **Undo** and **Redo** buttons on the **Standard Toolbar**.

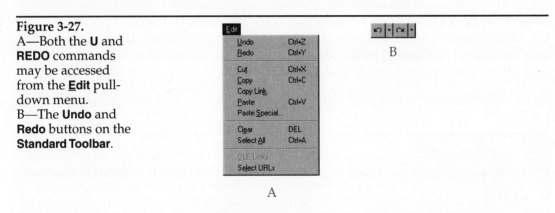

A

B

Figure 3-28.
A—Simultaneously undoing three commands in AutoCAD LT 98.
B—Using the **Redo** button in AutoCAD LT 98 to redo one (or more) commands.

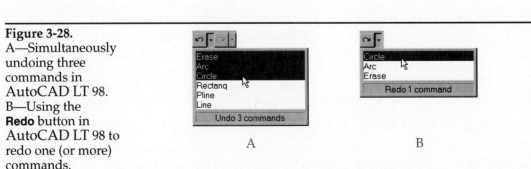

A   B

Selecting **All** redos all of the previous undo operations. The **Last** option redos the last undo operation only. Entering a positive number at the default ⟨Number⟩ option redos precisely that number of undo operations. Pressing [Enter] at the ⟨Number⟩ prompt is the equivalent of entering 1. Therefore, only the last undo operation is redone. This is also the same as using the **MREDO Last** option.

NOTE

Selecting one or more operations to undo using the button on the AutoCAD LT 98 **Standard Toolbar** is equivalent to issuing the **UNDO** command at the Command: prompt and entering a specific number of commands to undo.

EXERCISE 3-8

❑ Open drawing EX3-1.DWG that you completed earlier in this chapter.
❑ Experiment with the **Last, Previous, All, Window, Crossing, Wpolygon, CPolygon, Undo, Fence, Remove,** and **Add** selection set options as you erase portions of the drawing. Use the **OOPS** command to restore the erased objects.
❑ Draw several lines and use the **U** or **UNDO** commands to remove them. Use the **REDO** command to get them back.
❑ If you are using AutoCAD LT 98, try undoing and redoing several actions simultaneously using the buttons on the **Standard Toolbar**.
❑ When you are done experimenting, quit the session.

Chapter Test

Write your answers in the spaces provided.

1. Why is precise coordinate entry important? _____
   _____
   _____
   _____

2. What is a transparent command? What must you type to use one? Give an example. _____
   _____
   _____
   _____
   _____

3. List two methods to quickly repeat the previous command. _____
   _____
   _____

4. How can you tell AutoCAD LT to close a shape back to its starting point? _____
   _____
   _____
   _____

5. Why should you undo an incorrect line segment while still in the **LINE** command? _____

_____

_____

6. What is the continuation option? How is it used? _____

_____

_____

7. What is **Ortho** mode? List two ways to toggle **Ortho** mode on and off. _____

_____

_____

_____

8. Define *Direct Distance Entry.*_____

_____

_____

_____

9. How do absolute coordinates differ from relative coordinates? What symbol must you type to tell AutoCAD LT that you want to use relative coordinates?

_____

_____

_____

_____

10. What is the **LASTPOINT** system variable? _____

_____

11. What are polar coordinates? How are they used? _____

_____

12. List four ways to change the status of the coordinate display._____

_____

_____

_____

13. When an object is picked, it assumes a dotted or dashed appearance. What is this appearance called?_____

_____

14. What is the difference between the **Last** and **Previous** selection set options? ____

_____

15. Describe the similarities between a *window box* and a *crossing box*. How are they different? _____

_____

_____

_____

16. List two methods to remove an object from a selection set. _____

_____

_____

17. What is the purpose of the **PICKFIRST** variable? _____

_____

_____

18. Which option of the **UNDO** command reverses every operation back to the beginning of the current drawing session? _____

_____

19. List three ways to access the **REDO** command. _____

_____

_____

_____

20. What are the three **PolarSnap** options? Describe them. _____

_____

_____

_____

21. *True or False?* **Ortho** mode must be active to use **PolarSnap**._____
22. What is the purpose of object cycling? Describe its use. _____

_____

_____

_____

Chapter Problems

1. Using TEMPLATEA as your template drawing, draw the two views of the object shown below. Note that the dimensions for this object are in fractional format. You need not set fractional units to enter fractional coordinates on the AutoCAD LT command line. When entering these fractions, do not forget to separate the whole number from the fractional value with a hyphen (-). Save the completed drawing as P3-1.

Mechanical Drafting

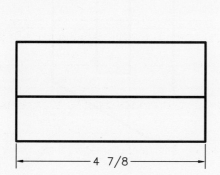
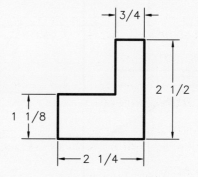

2. Once again using TEMPLATEA as your template, draw the object shown. Note that the decimal dimensions are expressed with 3 digits to the right of the decimal point. Two of the dimensions (1.188 and 1.063) are really 4-place decimals. Since accuracy is of paramount importance, be sure to refer to the decimal/fractional equivalency chart in the appendices at the end of this text so that these two coordinates may be entered without rounding error. Save the completed drawing as P3-2.

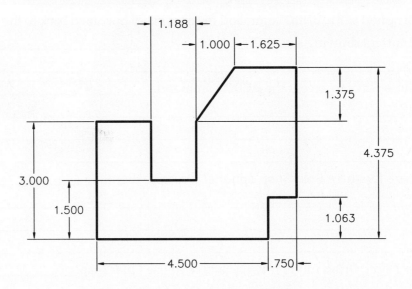

3. Using TEMPLATEA as your template, draw the object shown. Start this object at a known coordinate such as 0,0 or 1,1 so that it is easier to locate the internal features. Save the completed drawing as P3-3.

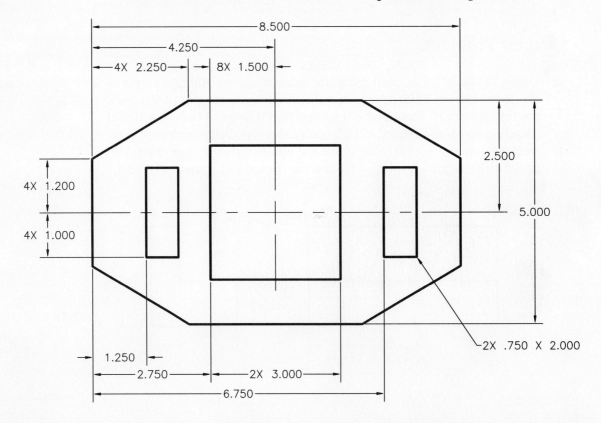

4. Draw this object using **TEMPLATEB** as your template drawing. To facilitate the construction of this object's internal cutout, set your grid to 1/8 and your snap to 1/16. Note that each of the dimensions are expressed as two-place decimals. As with **P3-2**, be sure to refer to the decimal/fractional equivalency chart in the appendices at the end of this text so that all coordinates are entered without rounding error. Save the completed drawing as **P3-4**.

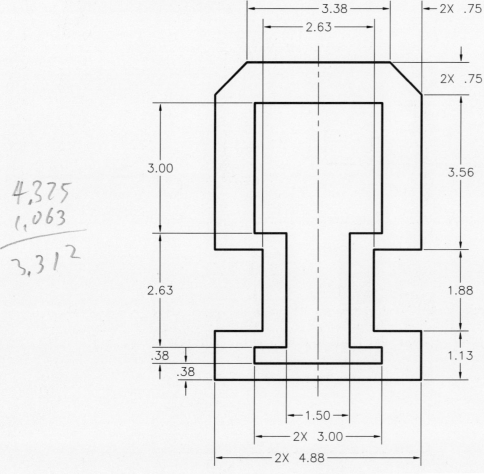

AutoCAD LT

Chapter *4*

Display Commands

Learning Objectives

After you have completed this chapter, you will be able to:
- ○ Zoom selected drawing areas to magnify details.
- ○ Pan the drawing window to change the viewing area.
- ○ Invoke and navigate the **Aerial View** window.
- ○ Save, recall, and delete named views.
- ○ Divide the drawing window into multiple viewports.
- ○ Describe the difference between a screen redraw and a screen regeneration.

There are several ways to view the various parts of your drawing using the AutoCAD LT display commands. The **ZOOM** command lets you change the magnification of selected drawing areas, or the entire drawing itself. Using the **PAN** command, you can reposition the drawing display in the current viewport. The **DSVIEWER** command enables the **Aerial View** window. This allows you to see the entire drawing in a separate display window, locate the particular area you want to view, and move to it using both zoom and pan functions. Once a view is displayed to your satisfaction, you can then use the **VIEW** command to save the view with a name. Named views may be listed, restored, or deleted at any time. Finally, you can also divide the screen into multiple viewing areas using the **VPORTS** command.

Magnifying Drawing Details with the **ZOOM** Command

It is the **ZOOM** command that allows you to magnify (*zoom in*) or shrink (*zoom out*) the image in the drawing window. Think of the zoom function as you would a telephoto lens on a camera. Just as a telephoto lens does not actually change the absolute size of objects, neither does zooming. So when you zoom, the apparent size of the view in the drawing window changes—not the actual size of the objects. However, unlike a telephoto lens, the potential zoom ratio in AutoCAD LT is 10 trillion to one! This is another reason why AutoCAD LT can draw virtually anything at full scale.

ZOOM
Z

View
➥ Zoom ⟩

Each of the **ZOOM** command options may be directly accessed from a cascading submenu by selecting **Zoom** from the **View** pull-down menu. See **Figure 4-1A.** Additionally, many of the zoom functions may be selected from the **Zoom** button flyout on the **Standard Toolbar**. See **Figure 4-1B.** When you enter the **ZOOM** command at the Command: prompt, you are presented with the following options:

> Command: **ZOOM** or **Z↵**
> All/Center/Extents/Previous/Scale(X/XP)/Window/⟨Realtime⟩: *(select an option)*

Each of the **ZOOM** options are described in the following sections.

Zooming to the Drawing Limits—ZOOM All Option

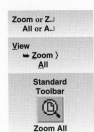

Zoom or Z↵
All or A↵

View
➥ Zoom ⟩
All

Standard
Toolbar

Zoom All

Use **ZOOM All** after changing your limits or when you want to display your entire drawing. This is because the **All** option zooms the display to the current drawing limits or to the drawing extents, whichever is greater.

> Command: **ZOOM** or **Z↵**
> All/Center/Extents/Previous/Scale(X/XP)/Window/⟨Realtime⟩: **ALL** or **A↵**

A zoomed-up portion of a wrench handle is shown in **Figure 4-2A.** After performing a **ZOOM All**, the entire wrench drawing is displayed. See **Figure 4-2B.**

Zooming About a Center Point—ZOOM Center Option

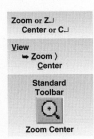

Zoom or Z↵
Center or C↵

View
➥ Zoom ⟩
Center

Standard
Toolbar

Zoom Center

You can zoom about the center of a selected point using the **ZOOM Center** option. After selecting a point about which to zoom, you are prompted to enter a magnification or height scale factor.

> Command: **ZOOM** or **Z↵**
> All/Center/Extents/Previous/Scale(X/XP)/Window/⟨Realtime⟩: **CENTER** or **C↵**
> Center point: *(select a point)*
> Magnification or Height ⟨*current height*⟩: *(enter a value and press* [Enter]*)*

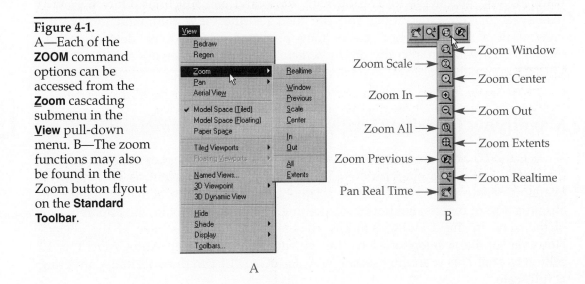

Figure 4-1.
A—Each of the **ZOOM** command options can be accessed from the **Zoom** cascading submenu in the **View** pull-down menu. B—The zoom functions may also be found in the Zoom button flyout on the **Standard Toolbar**.

The height represents the current screen height in the current units. Enter a smaller height value to zoom up the view; enter a larger height value to zoom out. You can also zoom the image with a magnification scale factor. Refer to the wrench shown in **Figure 4-3A.** In this example, a center point is first located and the view is zoomed up with a magnification scale factor of 4X. Remember to always enter X when you use the magnification option, otherwise AutoCAD LT will interpret the number you enter as a height value. The results of the **ZOOM Center** option are shown in **Figure 4-3B.**

Zooming All the Objects in the Drawing—ZOOM Extents Option

The **ZOOM Extents** option displays the largest possible view of all the objects in the drawing. It also automatically centers the drawing within the drawing window. If nothing has been drawn yet, then **ZOOM Extents** zooms to the screen limits.

Command: **ZOOM** *or* **Z.**↵
All/Center/Extents/Previous/Scale(X/XP)/Window/⟨Realtime⟩: **EXTENTS** *or* **E.**↵

Refer to **Figure 4-4** to see the effect of a **ZOOM Extents** operation on the wrench drawing.

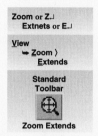

Zoom or Z.↵
Extnets or E.↵

<u>V</u>iew
➥ **Zoom** ⟩
   Extends

Standard
Toolbar

Zoom Extends

Figure 4-2.
A—Current view of the wrench. B—The view after performing a **ZOOM All.**

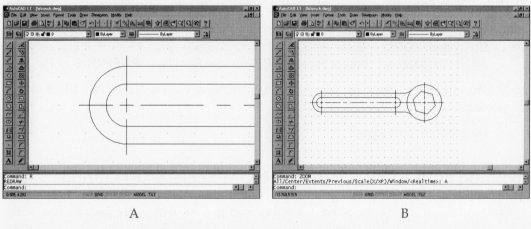

A   B

Figure 4-3.
A—**ZOOM Center** requests a center point around which the zoom is performed. Note the location of the graphics cursor. B—The result of **ZOOM Center** at 4X scale.

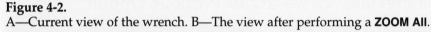
Center
point

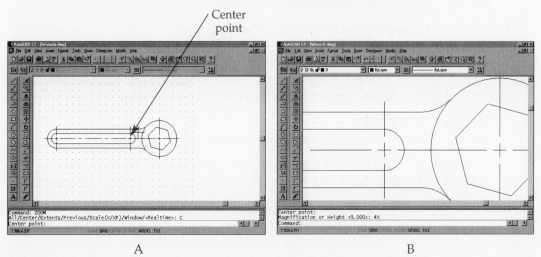

A   B

Chapter 4   Display Commands

123

Figure 4-4.
The wrench
drawing after
performing a **ZOOM
Extents**.

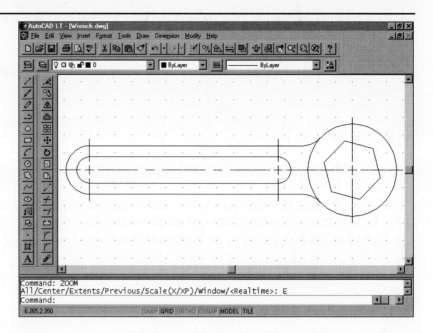

Returning to a Previous View—ZOOM Previous Option

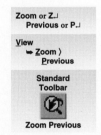

Zoom or Z↵
   Previous or P↵

View
  ➥ Zoom ⟩
     Previous

Standard
Toolbar

Zoom Previous

The **ZOOM Previous** option lets you quickly return to a previous view. You can restore up to 10 previous views.

> Command: **ZOOM** or **Z**↵
> All/Center/Extents/Previous/Scale(X/XP)/Window/⟨Realtime⟩: **PREVIOUS** or **P**↵

If you attempt to back up more than 10 previous views, AutoCAD LT displays the message:

> No previous view saved.

Zooming with a Scale Factor—ZOOM Scale(X/XP) Options

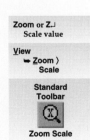

Zoom or Z↵
   Scale value

View
  ➥ Zoom ⟩
     Scale

Standard
Toolbar

Zoom Scale

You can also zoom the screen display using a known scale factor. The scale factor can be relative to the current drawing limits (**ZOOM Scale**), the current display (**ZOOM Scale X**), or a paper space view (**ZOOM Scale XP**). To zoom with a scale *relative to the drawing limits*, enter the desired scale factor as follows:

> Command: **ZOOM** or **Z**↵
> All/Center/Extents/Previous/Scale(X/XP)/Window/⟨Realtime⟩: **.5** ↵

The result of this operation is shown in **Figure 4-5A.**

It is often better to zoom an image *relative to the current display* rather than relative to the drawing limits. The result of the zoom operation is more predictable. To scale the image relative to the current display, you must enter a scale factor appended with an "X" as shown below. Do not put a space between the value and the letter X.

> Command: **ZOOM** or **Z**↵
> All/Center/Extents/Previous/Scale(X/XP)/Window/⟨Realtime⟩: **.5X**↵

This method is illustrated in **Figure 4-5B.** Observe that the wrench drawing has been zoomed by another factor of one-half relative to the display shown in **Figure 4-5A.**

To zoom the model space display relative to paper space, type XP after the scale factor as follows:

Command: **ZOOM** *or* **Z**↲
All/Center/Extents/Previous/Scale(X/XP)/Window/⟨Realtime⟩: **.5XP** ↲

Refer to **Figure 4-6** to obtain a clearer understanding of the **XP** option. In this example, a D-size title block is drawn in paper space. Now imagine cutting three rectangular cutouts through the title block sheet with a pair of scissors. The three cutouts represent paper space viewports through which a model space drawing (such as the wrench) can be viewed. The **Scale XP** option scales the contents of each viewport (model space) relative to the D-size sheet (paper space). At the upper left, the wrench is scaled 1:1 (1XP) relative to paper space. In the middle, the wrench is scaled 1:2 (.5XP) relative to paper space. The viewport at the bottom right displays the wrench scaled 1:4 (.25XP) relative to paper space. See *Chapter 17* in this text for more information on paper space and floating viewports.

Figure 4-5.
A—Zooming with a scale factor zooms the display relative to the drawing limits. B—Using **Scale X** to scale the image relative to the current display.

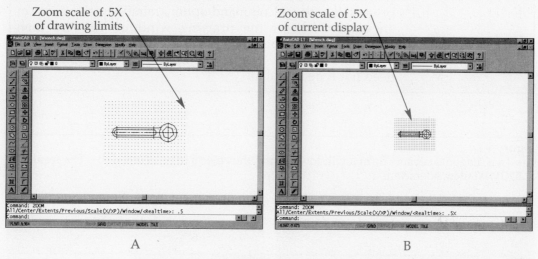

A

B

Figure 4-6.
The **Scale XP** option zooms the view in each viewport relative to paper space.

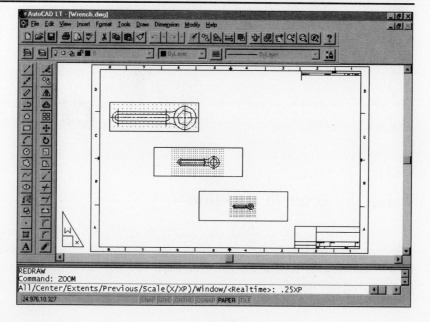

Zooming with a Window—ZOOM Window Option

Zoom or Z↵
Window or W↵

View
→ Zoom ⟩
Window

Standard
Toolbar

Zoom Window

The **ZOOM Window** option is probably the most often used of the **ZOOM** options. It is used the same way as the **Window** selection set option described in *Chapter 3* of this text. Simply pick a corner point, and then select a diagonal corner point to form a square or rectangular window around the area to be zoomed. See **Figure 4-7A.**

Command: **ZOOM** *or* **Z.**↵
All/Center/Extents/Previous/Scale(X/XP)/Window/⟨Realtime⟩: **WINDOW** *or* **W.**↵
First corner: *(pick a corner)* Other corner: *(pick a second corner)*

The result of the **ZOOM Window** operation is shown in **Figure 4-7B.**

PROFESSIONAL TIP

As previously mentioned, zooming with a window is probably the most frequently used zoom function. Here are two quick ways to perform this operation.

Perhaps the fastest method is to click the **ZOOM Window** button on the **Standard Toolbar**. If you prefer to use the command line, first issue the **ZOOM** command and, when presented with the command options, simply pick a point in an empty area of the drawing window. You are then prompted: Other corner. Now pick a diagonal corner point forming a window around the objects to be zoomed. You need not type a W at all.

Figure 4-7.
A—Two diagonal corners form a window around the objects to be zoomed. B—The result of a **ZOOM Window** operation.

Zoom corner 1

Zoom corner 2

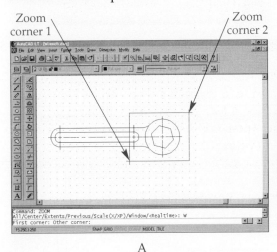

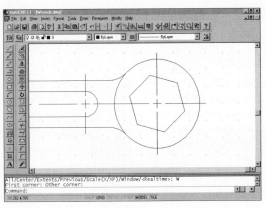

A

B

Using the **Zoom In** Function

View
→ Zoom ⟩
In

Standard
Toolbar

Zoom In

You can quickly double the zoom magnification factor of your drawing by selecting **In** from the **Zoom** cascading submenu or clicking the **Zoom In** button located in the **Zoom** tool flyout on the **Standard Toolbar**. Zooming in is the equivalent of performing a **Zoom Scale** 2X.

Using the Zoom Out Function

If you wish to quickly reduce the screen display by a factor of one-half, select **Out** from the **Zoom** cascading submenu or click the **Zoom Out** button also located in the **Zoom** tool flyout on the **Standard Toolbar**. Zooming out is the same as performing a **Zoom Scale** .5X.

Zooming with the Realtime Function

Zooming in realtime lets you use your pointing device to change the apparent size of objects in the current viewport with continuous visual feedback. To use this powerful feature, enter RTZOOM at the Command: prompt, pick **Realtime** from the **Zoom**⟩ cascading submenu in the **View** pull-down menu, click the **Zoom Realtime** button on the **Standard Toolbar**, or simply press [Enter] when the **ZOOM** command options are displayed on the command line. The command sequence is as follows:

Command: **RTZOOM**↵
Press Esc or Enter to exit, or right-click to activate pop-up menu.

Or,

Command: **ZOOM** *or* **Z**↵
All/Center/Extents/Previous/Scale(X/XP)/Window/⟨Realtime⟩: ↵
Press Esc or Enter to exit, or right-click to activate pop-up menu.

When you use this function, an icon representing a magnifying glass appears in the drawing window. See **Figure 4-8A.** The following message is displayed on the status bar:

Press pick button and drag vertically to zoom.

Press and hold the pick button of your pointing device and drag up or down (not left or right) to change the magnification of your drawing. When the drawing is zoomed to your satisfaction, press [Esc] or [Enter] to terminate the command.

Using the ZOOM Pop-Up Menu

When you use the **Zoom Realtime** option, AutoCAD LT displays a message on the command line informing you that performing a right-click operation activates a pop-up menu. This menu is shown in **Figure 4-8B.** Observe that it allows you to perform **Zoom Extents, Zoom Previous,** and **Zoom Window** functions as described in the previous sections. If you select **Zoom Window,** the icon shown in **Figure 4-8C** appears in the drawing window. Move your pointing device to pick a second corner forming a rectangle around the area you wish to zoom.

Notice that the pop-up menu also features a **Pan** function. Panning is covered in the next section.

Shifting the Display with the PAN Command

The **PAN** command moves or shifts the drawing display in the current viewport without changing the magnification. Panning may be accomplished in realtime or by selecting points in the drawing window. These pan functions may be accessed from a cascading submenu by selecting **Pan** from the **View** pull-down menu. See **Figure 4-9.**

Figure 4-8.
A—The **Zoom Realtime** option displays a magnifying glass icon in the drawing window. Press and hold the pick button on your pointing device as you drag up and down to zoom the display. B—Several zoom functions are available in the pop-up menu. C—This icon appears when **Zoom Window** is selected from the pop-up menu. Use it to form a window around the area you wish to magnify.

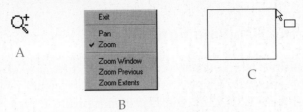

Figure 4-9.
Each of the **PAN** command functions can be accessed from the **Pan** cascading submenu in the **View** pull-down menu.

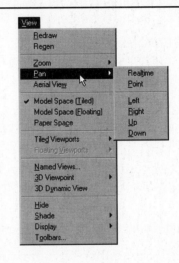

Performing a Realtime Pan

PAN or P↵
RTPAN

View
  ➡ Pan ⟩
      Realtime

Standard
Toolbar

Pan Realtime

Panning in realtime lets you use your pointing device to shift the display in the current viewport with continuous visual feedback. To use this function, select **Pan ⟩** from the **View** pull-down menu and then select **Realtime**, click the **Pan Realtime** button on the **Standard Toolbar**, or enter PAN, or P or RTPAN, at the Command: prompt as follows:

Command: **PAN, P,** *or* **RTPAN**↵
Press Esc or Enter to exit, or right-click to activate pop-up menu.

When you use this function, an icon representing a hand appears in the drawing window. See **Figure 4-10.** The following message is displayed on the status bar:

Press pick button and drag to pan.

Press and hold the pick button on your pointing device and drag in any direction to shift the display of your drawing in the current viewport. When the view is panned to your satisfaction, press [Esc] or [Enter] to terminate the command.

As with the **Zoom Realtime** function, the pop-up menu may be activated by performing a right-click operation with your pointing device.

Figure 4-10.
The **Pan Realtime** option displays an icon that resembles a hand in the drawing window. Press

AutoCAD LT—Fundamentals and Applications

Panning the Display Using Two Points

View
→ Pan 〉
Point

To pan the display using two points select **Pan**〉 from the **View** pull-down menu and then select **Point**. If you choose to pan the display using the **Point** function, it may be accomplished in one of two different ways.

Specifying one point

With the first method, you specify a single point that indicates the relative displacement of the drawing with respect to the drawing window. When prompted for the second point, press [Enter]. The command sequence is as follows:

> Command: '_-pan Displacement: *(pick a point on the screen)* Second point:⏎

This method, unfortunately, shifts the view so that the lower-left origin of the drawing is moved to the point you specify. The results are often unpredictable and undesirable.

Specifying two points

With the second panning method, you specify two points instead of just one. AutoCAD LT then computes the screen displacement from the first point to the second point and displays the drawing accordingly. This method is far more predictable than the first method described and is illustrated in **Figure 4-11A**. The command sequence is as follows:

> Command: '_-pan Displacement: *(pick a point on the screen)* Second point: *(pick a second point)*

The result of the pan operation on the wrench drawing is shown in **Figure 4-11B.**

Figure 4-11.
A—The **Pan Point** function shifts the display with a displacement equal to the distance and angle between two specified points. B—The result of the pan operation.

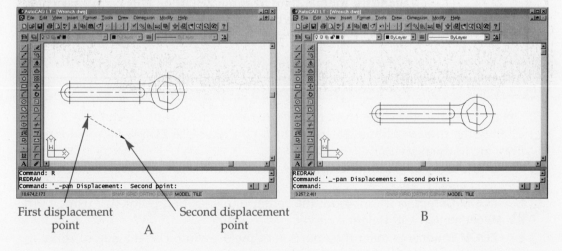

First displacement point   Second displacement point   A   B

Using Scrollbars to Pan the Display

In addition to the pan methods described above, you may also pan the display using the horizontal and vertical scrollbars in the graphics window. The horizontal scrollbar located just above the command prompt area may be used to scroll the display left or right. If you wish to pan the display up or down, use the vertical scrollbar at the far right of the graphics window.

The scrollbars are enabled by default, but may be turned off if you would like to increase the active drawing area. To do so, enter the **PREFERENCES** command or select **Preferences...** from the **Tools** pull-down menu to display the **Preferences** dialog box. If necessary, first click the **Work Space** tab and then locate the **Display scrollbars** check box at the upper left of the dialog box. See **Figure 4-12.** Remove the check mark to deactivate the scrollbars.

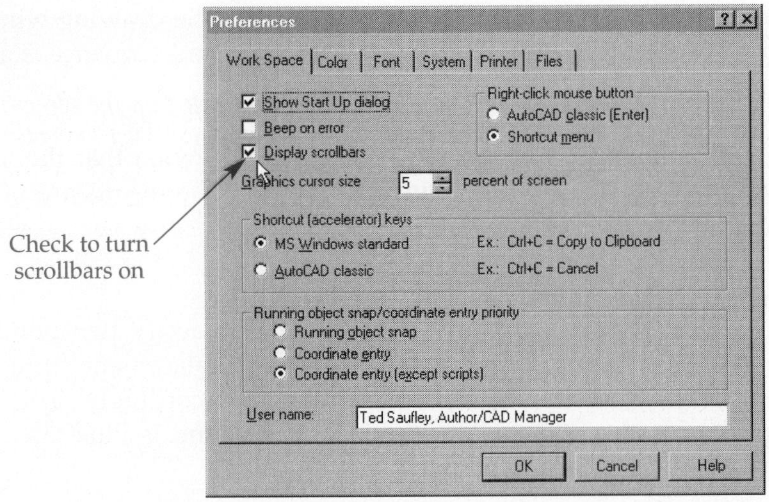

Figure 4-12.
Deactivate the **Display scrollbars** check box in the **Preferences** dialog box to turn off the horizontal and vertical pan scrollbars in the drawing window.

Check to turn scrollbars on

NOTE

The **ZOOM** and **PAN** commands, like the **PICKBOX** and **POLAR** commands discussed in previous chapters, are several other AutoCAD LT commands that may be used transparently. However, it is much quicker to access the **Pan Realtime** button and each of the **Zoom** buttons on the **Standard Toolbar** than to enter 'ZOOM or 'PAN because each of the buttons may be used transparently.

EXERCISE 4-1

❑ Open one of the drawings from the *Chapter 3* exercises or problems.
❑ Change the drawing limits to any values you like. Use **ZOOM All** to zoom the drawing to the new limits.
❑ Use **ZOOM Extents** to fill the drawing window with your drawing. Return to the previous view.
❑ Use **ZOOM Center** to zoom about the center of a specified point. Try using both the **Magnification** and **Height** options.
❑ Use **ZOOM Window** to magnify a portion of the drawing. Use it again to zoom in a little closer.
❑ Zoom the display using the zoom realtime function.
❑ Experiment with the **ZOOM Scale** and **Scale X** options. In your opinion, which of the options seems more predictable?
❑ Try performing a few transparent zoom operations while drawing some lines.
❑ Shift the display up and down, or left and right with the various pan functions, including the scrollbars. Be sure to try realtime panning, also.
❑ Do not save the drawing when you are finished experimenting.

Using the Microsoft IntelliMouse

If you are using a Microsoft IntelliMouse as your pointing device, it may also be used to zoom and pan the drawing window—without using any AutoCAD LT commands! The *Microsoft IntelliMouse* is a two-button mouse with a small wheel between the buttons. The wheel is used to zoom and pan the display. To zoom in or out, rotate the mouse wheel forward to zoom in, backward to zoom out. To pan, hold down the wheel button and drag the mouse.

PROFESSIONAL TIP   You can also zoom using the mouse by pressing and holding the [Ctrl] key on your keyboard as you rotate the mouse wheel forward and backward.

Setting the IntelliMouse zoom factor

As you rotate the IntelliMouse wheel, the amount by which the zoom increases or decreases is controlled by the *zoom factor*. By default, the zoom factor is set to 10%. This means the zoom level changes by 10% with each increment in the wheel rotation. You can adjust the zoom factor using the **PREFERENCES** command. When the **Preferences** dialog box appears, click the **System** tab and make your adjustments in the **Pointing device input** area of the dialog box.

Using the Aerial View Window

When you work on a large drawing, you can spend a lot of time zooming and panning the drawing window trying to locate a particular detail or feature. One of the most powerful features in AutoCAD LT is the **Aerial View** window. **Aerial View** is a navigation tool that lets you see the entire drawing in a separate window, locate the detail or feature you want, and move to it quickly. You can zoom in on an area, change the magnification, and pan the display using **Aerial View**. Best of all, you can use the **Aerial View** **Zoom**, **Pan**, and **Locate** functions while a drawing or editing command is in progress.

DSVIEWER
DS

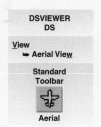

View
➥ Aerial View

Standard
Toolbar

Aerial

To open the **Aerial View** window, enter DSVIEWER, or DS, at the Command: prompt, click the **Aerial View** button on the **Standard Toolbar**, or select **Aerial View** from the **View** pull-down menu.

Whatever view is currently displayed in the drawing window then appears in the **Aerial View** window at the lower right of the display. See **Figure 4-13**. Like floating toolbars, the **Aerial View** window can be moved to any convenient location on the screen. To do so, simply click in the title bar of the **Aerial View** window, press and hold the pick button on your pointing device, and drag the **Aerial View** window to a new location. You may also resize the **Aerial View** window by dragging its border left or right, or up and down as desired. If you drag the border by one of its corners, the window is resized both horizontally and vertically so that the correct aspect ratio is maintained.

When you wish to exit **Aerial View**, click the **Close** button at the upper right of the **Aerial View** window, click the **Aerial View** button on the **Standard Toolbar**, or enter DSVIEWER or DS on the command line.

Figure 4-13.
Whatever is currently displayed in the drawing window appears in the **Aerial View** window at the lower right of the screen.

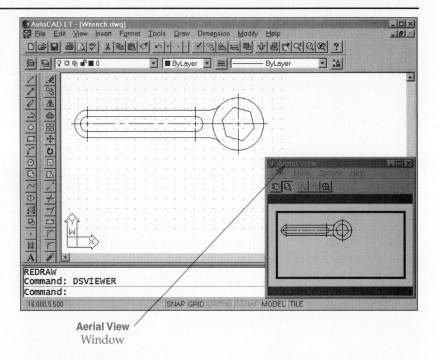

Aerial View Window

<table>
<tr><td>NOTE</td><td>The **Aerial View** window can be moved, resized, minimized, maximized, restored, and closed using the **Aerial View** control pull-down menu. To access this menu, click the aircraft icon in the upper-left corner of the **Aerial View** window.</td></tr>
</table>

Aerial View Window Description

The **Aerial View** window contains three pull-down menus and six toolbar buttons. See **Figure 4-14.** Each of these is described as follows:

- **View pull-down menu.** This pull-down menu features options that let you zoom the image in the **Aerial View** window in and out. **Zoom In** doubles the magnification of the image in the **Aerial View** window, while **Zoom Out** reduces the magnification by one-half. Select **Global** when you wish to restore the entire drawing in the **Aerial View** window. The **View** menu options are also accessible by clicking the **Zoom In**, **Zoom Out**, or **Global** buttons on the **Aerial View** toolbar.

- **Mode pull-down menu.** This pull-down menu is used to switch between **Pan** and **Zoom** modes. Keep in mind that the **Aerial View** zoom and pan functions may be used at anytime while a drawing or editing command is in progress.

  - **Pan**—When **Pan** mode is selected, the view box appears as shown in **Figure 4-15.** The *view box* is displayed with a heavy solid border. If zooming with **Aerial View** has just been performed, the view box is the same size as the current zoom window. If no zooming has been performed, the view box is the same size as the **Aerial View** window. Press and hold the pick button on your pointing device as you move the view box around the **Aerial View** window. As you move your pointing device, the area displayed within the view box is simultaneously panned in realtime in the drawing window.

- **Zoom**—If you select **Zoom** mode, crosshairs appear in the **Aerial View** window. Using the crosshairs, click to set one corner of the view box. As you move the cursor to select an opposite corner, the area displayed within the view box is simultaneously zoomed in realtime in the drawing window. The view box is shown in **Figure 4-16.** Once the object is zoomed to your satisfaction, release the pick button on your pointing device. Note that the **Mode** menu functions may also be used by clicking the **Pan** or **Zoom** buttons on the **Aerial View** toolbar.
- **Options pull-down menu.** This menu features the options described as follows:
  - **Auto Viewport**—When multiple model space viewports of a drawing exist, the default ON status of this toggle displays the active, or current, viewport in the **Aerial View** window. When toggled off, you must click the **Aerial View** title bar to update the window so it matches the current viewport. Creating multiple viewports in model space is described later in this chapter.

Figure 4-14.
The **Aerial View** window toolbar buttons.

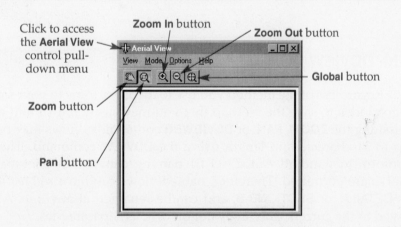

Figure 4-15.
When panning, the view box is represented with a heavy solid border.

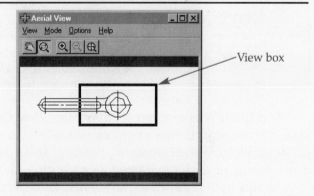

Figure 4-16.
When zooming, the view box is represented with a lighter solid border.

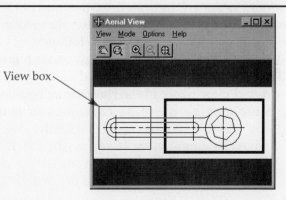

- **Dynamic Update**—As you edit a drawing, the **Aerial View** window is automatically updated to reflect the drawing changes. You can conserve system resources by toggling **Dynamic Update** off when performing extensive editing operations.
- **RealTime Zoom**—On by default, this option controls whether or not the drawing window updates in realtime as you zoom in the **Aerial View** window.

EXERCISE 4-2

❏ Open the JHOUSE drawing in the Program Files\AutoCAD LT 98\Sample folder. Notify your instructor or supervisor if this drawing cannot be found on your workstation.
❏ Activate the **Aerial View** window and use **Zoom** mode to window in SECTION A-A.
❏ Next, use **Pan** mode to pan down to the drawing title block. Zoom up the area until the drawing title can be clearly read.
❏ Do not save the JHOUSE drawing when you are finished experimenting.

The **DDVIEW** Command

Regardless of the method you use to display a view to your satisfaction, it is often a good idea to save the view so that you may easily return to it at any time without reissuing the **ZOOM**, **PAN**, or **DSVIEWER** commands. Views may be saved with names up to 31 characters in length using the **DDVIEW** command. The view names must conform to standard AutoCAD LT naming convention—no spaces or punctuation marks are permitted. Therefore, named views can have *real-world* descriptions such as DETAILA, or SECTIONB-B, and can be renamed at anytime. All named views are saved in the current drawing—not on disk as separate files.

NOTE   A named object, like a view, may contain a dollar sign ($), hyphen (-), and underscore (_) in its name. Refer to the *AutoCAD LT 98 Getting Started Guide* for a complete description of valid names and wild-card characters.

DDVIEW
V

View
↳ Named Views...

Standard
Toolbar

Named Views

The **DDVIEW** command displays the **View Control** dialog box which is used to save, restore, and delete views as necessary. To issue the **DDVIEW** command, enter DDVIEW, or V, at the Command: prompt, select **Named Views...** from the **View** pull-down menu, or click the **Named Views** button on the **Standard Toolbar**.

As shown in **Figure 4-17**, all named views saved in the current drawing are listed in the **View Control** dialog box. The current view name is also listed as *CURRENT*. Views saved in model space are indicated by the word MSPACE at the right, while views saved in paper space are indicated by the word PSPACE. The buttons appearing in the **View Control** dialog box are as follows:

- **New....** Click this button when you wish to save a new view. You are then presented with the **Define New View** subdialog box. As shown in **Figure 4-18**, enter the desired view name in the **New Name:** text box at the top. Remember the view name may be up to 31 characters in length, but no spaces are permitted. By default, whatever is currently displayed in the drawing window is saved as a new view. If you wish to define a different view, activate the **Define Window** option button and then click the button labeled **Window⟨**. The dialog box closes and you are prompted on the command line

Figure 4-17.
The **View Control**
dialog box.

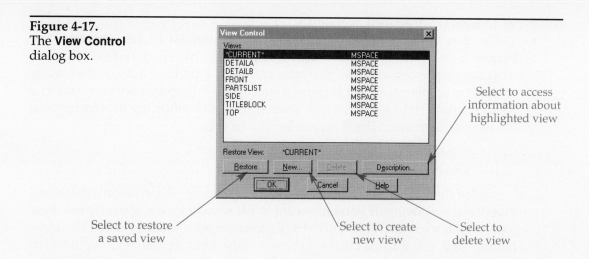

Select to restore
a saved view

Select to access
information about
highlighted view

Select to create
new view

Select to
delete view

Figure 4-18.
Saving a view using
the **Define New View**
subdialog box.

Activate to define a
different view using
the **Window**〈 button

Enter name of
new view

Pick to save new view
and to return to **View
Control** dialog box

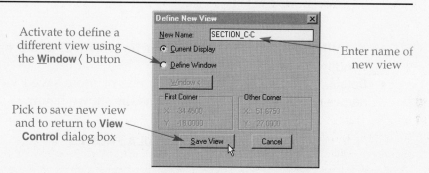

to select two diagonal corners that define a new view window. After the two
corners are selected, the subdialog box reappears. Now, click the **Save View**
button to save the new view and exit the **Define New View** subdialog box. The
View Control dialog box reappears and the new view name appears in the
Views list. Click the **OK** button to exit the dialog box.

- **Restore.** To restore a saved view in the current viewport, first select the view
  you want from the **Views** list in the **View Control** dialog box using your
  pointing device. Then, click the **Restore** and **OK** buttons to display the saved
  view. Keep in mind that to restore model or paper space views, you must be
  in the space in which the view was created.
- **Delete.** To delete a saved view, first select the view you want from the **Views**
  list in the **View Control** dialog box and then click the **Delete** button. The view
  is immediately deleted from the drawing file and removed from the **Views** list.
- **Description....** This button opens a subdialog box that lists information about
  the selected view. See **Figure 4-19.** Information about a three-dimensional
  view obtained with the **DVIEW** command is also listed in this subdialog box.
  Refer to *Chapter 19* for more information about the **DVIEW** command.

Using the VIEW Command

Views may also be saved, restored, deleted, and listed using the **VIEW** command.
To use the **VIEW** command, enter VIEW, or –V, at the Command: prompt. The command
sequence is as follows:

> Command: **VIEW** *or* **–V**↵
> ?/Delete/Restore/Save/Window: *(select an option)*

VIEW
–V

The **VIEW** options are described as follows:

- **?.** The **?** option lists all saved views in the **AutoCAD LT Text Window**. See **Figure 4-20.** This option is particularly handy when you find yourself working with a drawing file that was created a long time ago, or with a file created by another user. An M (model space) or a P (paper space) appears in a column to the right of each view name in the list to indicate in which space the view was created. The **?** option looks like this:

    ?/Delete/Restore/Save/Window: **?**↵
    View(s) to list ⟨*⟩: ↵

    Since the asterisk is a *wildcard* character, pressing [Enter] lists all the views saved in the drawing. If you only want to list several views, separate the view names with a comma; FRONT,TOP,SIDE. Do not put a space between the view names. The graphics window automatically flips to the text window to display the view names. If no views exist in the drawing, the following message is displayed:

    No matching views found.

    When you are done, press function key [F2] to flip back to the graphics window.

- **Delete.** The **Delete** option removes one or more saved views. Multiple view names must be separated by commas as shown below.

    ?/Delete/Restore/Save/Window: **D**↵
    View name(s) to delete: **DETAILA,FRONT**↵

Figure 4-19.
The **View Description** subdialog box lists information about a saved view.

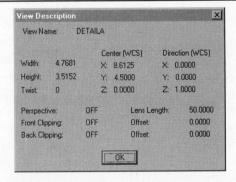

Figure 4-20.
The **?** option of the **VIEW** command lists all saved views in the **AutoCAD LT Text Window**.

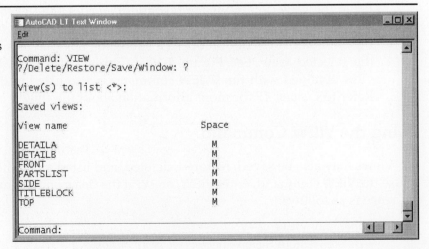

AutoCAD LT—Fundamentals and Applications

- **Restore.** Use the **Restore** option to display a saved view in the current viewport.

> ?/Delete/Restore/Save/Window: **R**↵
> View name to restore: **SECTIONB-B**↵

- **Save.** Once you have a view that you want to save displayed in the current viewport, use this option and provide a name for the view. Be advised that no warning is issued if a view is saved with the same name of an existing view, however.

> ?/Delete/Restore/Save/Window: **S**↵
> View name to save: **LEFTSIDE**↵

- **Window.** This option lets you define a new view with two diagonal points. The view is named and saved, but not displayed until the **Restore** option is invoked.

> ?/Delete/Restore/Save/Window: **W**↵
> View name to save: **PARTSLIST**↵
> First corner: *(pick a point)* Other corner: *(pick a point)*

The **Select Initial View** Option

AutoCAD LT permits a saved view name to be specified for display *before* entering the drawing editor. This procedure is performed using the **Select File** dialog box illustrated in **Figure 4-21A.** With this method, you issue the **OPEN** command and select the drawing file you wish to load into AutoCAD LT as you normally would. Next, activate the **Select Initial View** check box in the lower-right corner of the dialog box and then click the **OK** button to exit the **Open Drawing** dialog box. This displays the **Select Initial View** subdialog box. See **Figure 4-21B.** Use this subdialog box to select the named view you wish to preload. After clicking the **OK** button, the view you selected from the list is then displayed in the drawing window.

Figure 4-21.
A—The **Select Initial View** check box is activated at the lower right of the **Select File** dialog box. B—The **Select Initial View** subdialog box lists all saved views in the drawing.

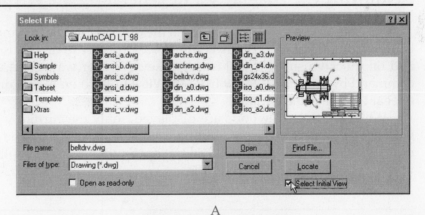

A

B

Renaming a Saved View

DDRENAME
REN

Format
➡ Rename...

Views may be renamed at anytime with the **DDRENAME** command. This command permits you to rename your saved views, and other AutoCAD LT named objects, using a dialog box. Enter DDRENAME, or REN, at the Command: prompt or select **Rename...** from the **Format** pull-down menu to display the **Rename** dialog box. See **Figure 4-22.**

The **Named Objects** list appears in the upper-left corner of the dialog box and contains the types of objects that may be named or renamed in AutoCAD LT. Each of these objects will be explored fully as they are encountered in this text. From the example, observe that View has been selected from the list at the left. A listing of all the views saved in the current drawing appears at the right of the dialog box. To rename view DETAILB, first select the view name from the list. The name of the view you select is then displayed in the **Old Name:** text box. With your pointing device, click anywhere inside the **Rename To:** text box and enter the new view name. In the example, view DETAILB is renamed to SECTIONB-B. When you are done typing, click the **Rename To:** button and the new view name appears in the list at the right of the dialog box. When you are finished renaming objects, click the **OK** button to exit the **Rename** dialog box.

It is also possible to rename objects from the command line instead of using a dialog box. In the following example, the **RENAME**, or **–REN**, command is used to perform the identical renaming operation described above.

```
Command: RENAME or –REN↵
Block/Dimstyle/LAyer/LType/Style/Ucs/VIew/VPort: VI↵
Old view name: DETAILB↵
New view name: SECTIONB-B↵
Command:
```

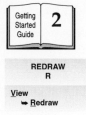

Getting Started Guide 2

Redrawing the Display vs. Regenerating the Display

REDRAW
R

View
➡ Redraw

It is sometimes necessary to refresh the drawing screen to remove stray pixels left behind by drawing and editing commands. One way to do this is to turn the grid on and off quickly using the [F7] function key. A better way exists using the **REDRAW** command by selecting **Redraw** from the **View** pull-down menu, or entering REDRAW or R at the Command: prompt.

When multiple viewports are displayed, only the current viewport is redrawn with the **REDRAW** command. Multiple viewports are described at the end of this chapter. **REDRAW** may also be used transparently by preceding the command name with an apostrophe; **'REDRAW,** or **'R**.

Figure 4-22.
Using the **Rename** dialog box to rename a saved view.

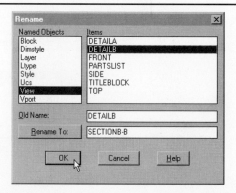

The other command that may be used to refresh the drawing display is the **REGEN** command. **REGEN** *regenerates*, or *rebuilds*, the entire drawing as it reindexes the drawing database for optimum display and object selection performance. The **REGEN** command also recomputes the screen coordinates for all objects. In AutoCAD LT the information for each drawing object is stored as a real, or double-precision floating point, number. When a regeneration occurs, the floating point values in the database are converted to the appropriate screen coordinates. Because this process can be somewhat slow, expect some delay when regenerating a large drawing. When multiple viewports are displayed, only the contents of the current viewport are regenerated. Some commands regenerate the drawing for you automatically; other commands require that you force the regeneration manually. To do so, select **Regen** from the **View** pull-down menu or enter REGEN, or RE, at the Command: prompt. Unlike **REDRAW**, **REGEN** may not be used transparently.

Blips and the BLIPMODE Variable

When the **BLIPMODE** variable is turned on, points you select in the drawing window are marked with small crosses called *blips*. These are temporary markers that appear when a location is indicated with an entered coordinate or a pointing device, like your mouse. Blips are also left on the screen after an erase operation.

Consider the example shown in **Figure 4-23A**. Because **BLIPMODE** is on, blips appear on the screen as objects are constructed. In **Figure 4-23B**, the objects have been selected for erasure using a window box. After erasing the objects, the blips remain on the screen as reference points. See **Figure 4-23C**. Even though they do not plot, blips are a minor annoyance and may be quickly removed using the **REDRAW** command.

Figure 4-23.
A—Blips appear in the drawing window during drawing and editing operations. B—Erasing all objects using a window box. C—Blips remain after erasing, but can be removed with the **REDRAW** command.

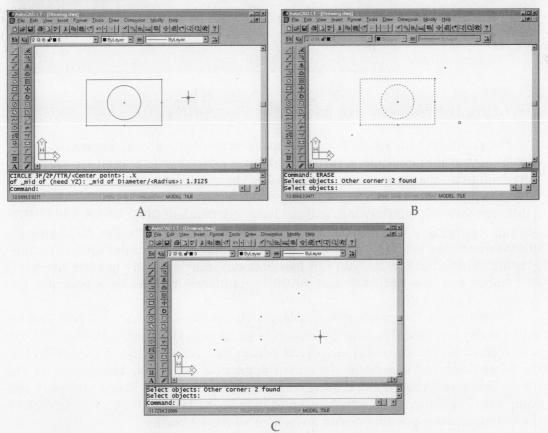

In AutoCAD LT 98 and AutoCAD LT 97, the **BLIPMODE** variable is off by default. This is different from earlier versions of the program. With blips turned off, fewer redraws need to be performed. However, there are certain instances when blips can be of value. Such an example is described in *Chapter 8* of this text.

You can use a dialog box to turn blips on and off. To do so, select **Drawing Aids...** from the **Tools** pull-down menu. The **Drawing Aids** dialog box then appears. See **Figure 4-24**. You may recall from *Chapter 2* that this dialog box can also be used to set grid and snap spacing. Use the **Blips** check box at the left of the dialog box to turn blips on or off as desired.

Blips may also be turned on and off on the command line. To do so, enter **BLIPMODE** at the Command: prompt as follows:

Command: **BLIPMODE.**⏎
ON/OFF ⟨OFF⟩: *(enter* ON *or* OFF *as desired and press* [Enter]*)*

> **NOTE**
>
> The status of the **BLIPMODE** variable is stored in the current drawing only. Therefore, if you wish blips to be on (or off) in all of your drawings, set **BLIPMODE** as required in your template files.

Figure 4-24.
Blips can be turned on and off using the **Drawing Aids** dialog box.

Use to turn blips on and off

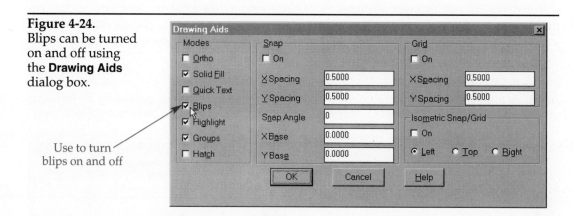

Dividing the Screen into Multiple Viewports

The AutoCAD LT **VPORTS** command allows you to divide the model space display screen into multiple viewing windows, or *viewports*. Several typical viewport configurations are shown in **Figure 4-25**. The viewports are *tiled*; which means they are adjacent to one another with no gaps in between. Each viewport can display a different view of your drawing, and can have independent **GRID**, **SNAP**, and **LIMITS** settings. However, if **ORTHO** mode is on, it is on in all viewports. For 3D drawings, one viewport may take an isometric, or pictorial, style, while the others remain orthographic. Whether 2D or 3D, you can pan or zoom independently in each viewport. Remember that the **REDRAW** and **REGEN** commands redraw or regenerate the current viewport only.

Regardless of the number of displayed viewports, only one viewport can be active at any one time. The active viewport is surrounded by a wider border, and the screen crosshair cursor is only displayed within that viewport. See **Figure 4-26.** For the other displayed viewports, the cursor appears as an arrow. The viewports are interactive; thus a drawing or editing command may be started in one viewport, but completed in another. An inactive viewport may be made current by a simple click of the button on your pointing device anywhere within its border.

Figure 4-25.
The display screen may be divided into 2, 3, or 4 multiple viewports in a variety of configurations.

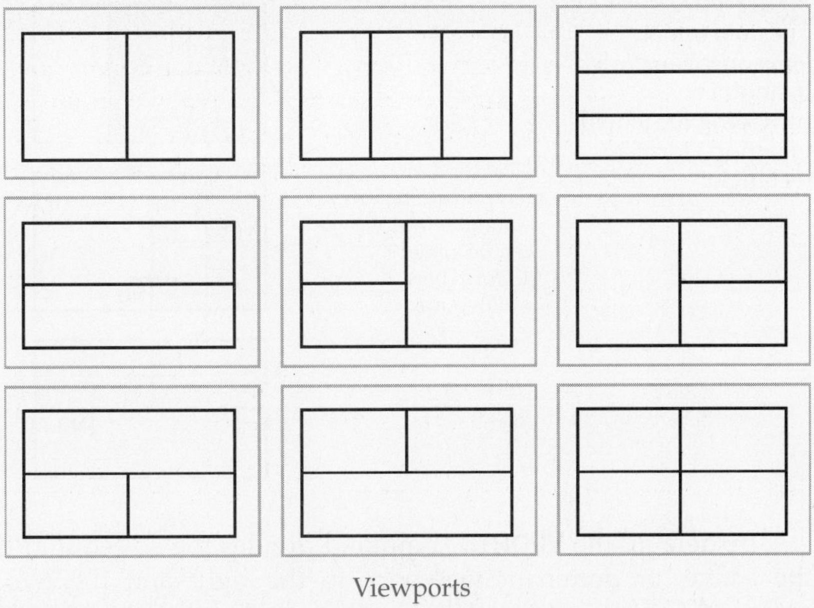

Viewports

Figure 4-26.
The active viewport is represented with a wide border and displays the graphics cursor.

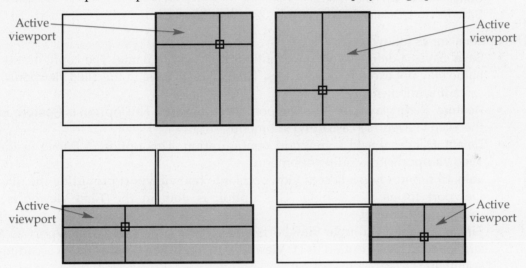

Active viewport

Active viewport

Active viewport

Active viewport

The **VPORTS** command has similar functionality to the **DDVIEW** and **VIEW** commands in that it allows a multiple viewport configuration to be saved with a name, restored, listed, or deleted. Single viewports can be returned to at anytime, and more than one configuration can be saved. Like view names, viewport configuration names can be up to 31 characters in length and the same naming restrictions apply. Furthermore, an inactive viewport can be joined to an active viewport providing that the resulting viewport forms a rectangle. See **Figure 4-27.** You may find that joining viewports together can be quicker than defining an entirely new viewport configuration. However, keep in mind that the newly joined viewport inherits all aspects of the dominant viewport to which it was joined—**LIMITS, GRID, SNAP**, etc.

Figure 4-27.
The **Join** option joins one viewport to another providing the joined viewports form a rectangle.

The shaded viewports form rectangles and can be joined to form new viewports

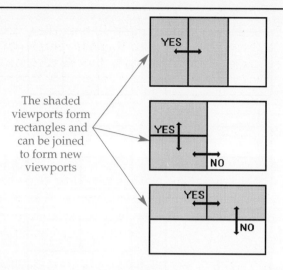

VPORTS
VW

View
➥ Tiled
    Viewports ⟩

By default, the **VPORTS** command divides the screen into three viewports with the active, or dominant viewport, to the right and the two inactive viewports arranged in a vertical orientation to the left. To access the **VPORTS** command options, select **Tiled Viewports⟩** in the **View** pull-down menu or enter VPORTS, or VW, at the Command: prompt as follows:

Command: **VPORTS** *or* **VW.**↵
Save/Restore/Delete/Join/SIngle/?/2/⟨3⟩/4: *(select an option)*

The options are as follows:

- **Save.** Saves a defined viewport configuration with a name. The configuration name may not exceed 31 characters. This option is **S̲ave** in the **Tile̲d Viewports⟩** cascading submenu.
- **Restore.** Redisplays a saved viewport configuration. This option is **R̲estore** in the **Tile̲d Viewports⟩** cascading submenu.
- **Delete.** Deletes a saved viewport configuration. This option is **D̲elete** in the **Tile̲d Viewports⟩** cascading submenu.
- **Join.** Combines two adjacent viewports into one viewport providing the new viewport forms a rectangle. This option is **J̲oin** in the **Tile̲d Viewports⟩** cascading submenu.
- **Single.** Disables multiple viewports and displays the current viewport as a single view. This option is **1̲ Viewport** in the **Tile̲d Viewports⟩** cascading submenu.
- **?.** Lists any or all saved viewport configurations in the **AutoCAD LT Text Window**. The listing includes a unique identification number and coordinate location for each viewport. The coordinate location is based on the lower left of the display screen as 0.0000, 0.0000 and the upper right of the display as 1.0000, 1.0000. This option is not found in the **Tile̲d Viewports⟩** cascading submenu.
- **2.** Divides the current viewport into two viewports. You can choose between a horizontal or vertical division. This option is **2̲ Viewports** in the **Tile̲d Viewports⟩** cascading submenu.
- **3.** Divides the current viewport into three viewports. The dominant viewport may be placed to the right (the default), to the left, above, or below the other two viewports. This option is **3̲ Viewports** in the **Tile̲d Viewports** cascading submenu.
- **4.** Divides the current viewport into four equally sized viewports. This option is **4̲ Viewports** in the **Tile̲d Viewports⟩** cascading submenu.

NOTE	The **Layout...** option in the **Tiled Viewports〉** cascading submenu accesses the **Tiled Viewport Layout** dialog box. This dialog box is discussed in the next section.

Creating Multiple Viewports Using a Dialog Box

You can quickly and easily divide your screen into multiple viewports using the **Tiled Viewport Layout** dialog box shown in **Figure 4-28.** To open this dialog box, select **Layout...** in the **Tiled Viewports〉** cascading submenu. You can select the viewport configuration you wish by clicking the appropriate image tile, or selecting from the list of configurations at the left of the dialog box as shown. After making your selection, click the **OK** button to exit the dialog box.

View
➥ Tiled
  Viewports 〉
  ➥ Layout...

Observe that two viewport configurations appear in this dialog box that are not otherwise available. Can you identify them?

While multiple viewports have their greatest benefit for 3D modeling, they can also be useful for 2D applications. Consider the assembly drawing illustrated in **Figure 4-29.** In this example, the screen is divided into two vertical viewports. The drawing parts list is created in the right viewport, while the left viewport displays the relevant portion of the assembly drawing for reference purposes.

Finally, keep in mind that when plotting multiple viewports, only the current viewport is plotted.

PROFESSIONAL TIP 	Named viewport configurations, like named views, take up space in a drawing file. Create and save only those views and multiple viewports necessary to detail your drawing. Should you no longer require certain views or viewport configurations, remove them using the **Delete** option of the **DDVIEW**, **VIEW**, or **VPORTS** commands.

Figure 4-28.
The **Tiled Viewport Layout** dialog box.

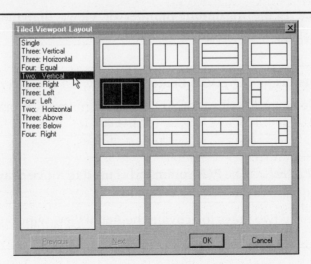

Figure 4-29.
A practical application of 2D viewports. The drawing parts list is created in the right viewport, while the assembly drawing is referenced in the left viewport.

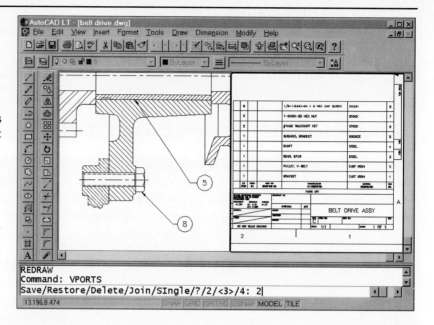

Chapter Test

Write your answers in the spaces provided.

1. Which **ZOOM** option automatically centers your drawing on the screen? _____

2. Which **ZOOM** option should be used after changing the drawing limits? _____

3. Which **ZOOM** option should be used to display every object in the drawing? ___

4. Describe the difference between **ZOOM Scale** and **ZOOM Scale X**. _____

5. What is the maximum number of views that may be recalled using **ZOOM Previous**? _____

6. When using the **ZOOM Center** option, what character should be entered with the scale factor to tell AutoCAD LT to use magnification instead of height? _____

7. *True or False?* The **PAN** command is used to move drawing objects to a new screen location. _____

8. Identify two ways to activate the **Aerial View** window. _____

9. *Yes or No?* Can **Aerial View** zooming and panning functions be used transparently?

10. What is the purpose of the **VIEW** command? _____

    _____

11. Which option of the **VIEW** command allows you to save a view without having
    the view displayed? _____

    _____

12. Which option of the **VIEW** command allows you to display a previously saved view?

    _____

13. What is the maximum number of characters permitted for a view name? Are
    spaces allowed? _____

    _____

14. *True or False?* When using the **VIEW** command, AutoCAD LT alerts you if you
    attempt to save a new view with the name of an existing view. _____

15. *Yes or No?* Can each viewport in a multiple viewport configuration have separate
    grid and snap settings? _____

16. Which **VPORTS** option is used to display one viewport? _____

17. *True or False?* All the viewports in a multiple viewport configuration can be
    plotted simultaneously. _____

18. *True or False?* Redraws and regenerations occur in the current viewport only.

    _____

19. How do you turn off the drawing window scroll bars? _____

    _____

    _____

    _____

20. What are blips and how can they be removed from the screen? _____

    _____

    _____

    _____

    _____

21. How do you activate the **ZOOM** pop-up menu? _____

    _____

22. Describe how the *Microsoft IntelliMouse* can be used as a display control device.

    _____

    _____

    _____

Chapter Problems

General

1. Begin a new drawing using your TEMPLATEA template drawing that was created in *Chapter 2.* If you have not done this already, refer to *Chapter 2* and do so now.

    A. Using the **LINE** command, draw a square, triangle, and rectangle as shown. Make the objects proportional to the drawing limits.

    B. Save a view of all displayed objects. Name the view ALL.

    C. Create one saved view of each shape. The view names should be SQUARE, TRIANGLE, and RECTANGLE.

    D. Set up a four viewport configuration and save it with the name 4VIEWS.

    E. Activate the upper-left viewport and restore view SQUARE.

    F. Activate the lower-left viewport and restore view TRIANGLE.

    G. Activate the upper-right viewport and restore view RECTANGLE.

    H. Activate the lower-right viewport and restore view ALL.

    I. Use **PAN** or **Aerial View** to center each view in its respective viewport.

    J. Save the drawing as P4-1.

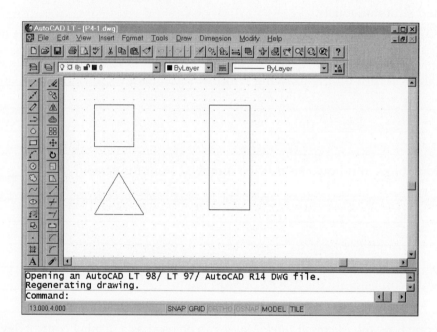

2. Open the sample drawing plate2.dwg from the Program Files\AutoCAD LT 98 \Sample folder. Notify your instructor or supervisor if this drawing cannot be found on your workstation.

A. Zoom in on the notes at the lower left of the drawing. Save the view with the name **NOTES**.

B. Zoom in on the title block information at the lower right of the drawing. Save the view with the name TITLE_BLOCK.

C. Zoom in on the right (front) view of the friction plate. Save the view with the name FRONT.

D. Create a three viewport configuration with the dominant viewport to the left. Save the viewport configuration with the name 3VIEWS.

E. Activate the upper-right viewport and restore view NOTES.

F. Activate the lower-right viewport and restore view TITLE_BLOCK.

G. Activate the left viewport and restore view FRONT.

H. Save the drawing as P4-2.

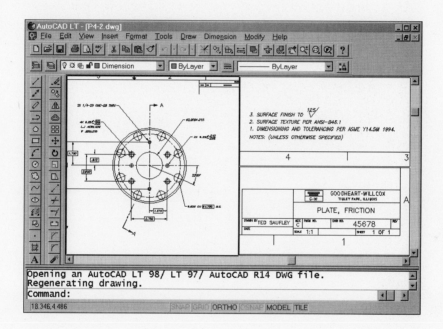

Chapter 5

AutoCAD LT

Colors, Linetypes, and Layers

Learning Objectives

After you have completed this chapter, you will be able to:
- ○ Select and use the colors available in AutoCAD LT.
- ○ Load and use various linetypes.
- ○ Create your own custom linetypes using both AutoCAD LT and the Microsoft Windows Notepad editor.
- ○ Create and manage drawing layers.
- ○ Change the properties of existing objects.
- ○ Purge unused linetypes and layers from your drawing.

Controlling the objects in your drawings plays a very important role in the efficient use of AutoCAD LT. Using various colors adds clarity and visual appeal to CAD drawings. It is also necessary to use various linetypes to describe objects without ambiguity and to comply with industry standards. In the traditional, paper-based drafting environment, transparent overlays are often used to separate various drawing elements. For an architectural application, one overlay may feature doors and windows, while another might include piping symbols. The overlays are perfectly aligned with one another. Other drawing elements, like receptacles, floor plans, and foundations may also be created on separate overlays. AutoCAD LT provides a similar capability using *layers*. With layers, you can separate your drawing objects into logically named groupings. Colors and linetypes may be assigned to individual layers, and the layers can be made visible or invisible as required. Objects can be moved from one layer to another, and linetypes and layers can be purged from a drawing if not required.

Using Colors

There are 255 colors available for your use in AutoCAD LT. Every color has a number assigned by the **AutoCAD Color Index**, or **ACI**. The first seven colors can also be addressed by their names. AutoCAD LT refers to these first seven colors as the *standard colors*. Their names and numbers are given on the next page:

Color Number	Color Name
1	R *or* Red
2	Y *or* Yellow
3	G *or* Green
4	C *or* Cyan
5	B *or* Blue
6	M *or* Magenta
7	W *or* White

Color 7 is the default color in AutoCAD LT. It is white on a dark background and black on a light background.

When printing or plotting your drawing, individual colors can be set to print/plot at different line widths. See *Chapter 14* of this text for complete information about plotter pens and colors.

Setting a Color from a Dialog Box

DDCOLOR
COL

Format
➥ Color...

You can use the **Select Color** dialog box to set a color for new drawing objects as shown in **Figure 5-1.** To access this dialog box, enter DDCOLOR, or COL, at the **Command:** prompt, select **Color...** from the **Format** pull-down menu, or select **Other...** from the **Color Control** drop-down list on the **Object Properties** toolbar. See **Figure 5-2.**

In the example illustrated in **Figure 5-1,** the color red is selected from the **Standard Colors** section at the top of the **Select Color** dialog box. Observe that the color name appears in the **Color:** text box at the bottom and a color swatch is displayed in the image tile just to the right of the text box. Colors 8 through 255 do not have names. If one of these is selected, the color swatch and color number only appears in the text box. After selecting the desired color, click **OK** to exit the **Select Color** dialog box. The new color is then displayed in the **Color Control** drop-down list on the **Object Properties** toolbar.

The **DDCOLOR** command may also be used transparently by entering 'DDCOLOR, or 'COL, while in the middle of another command. If you are using AutoCAD LT 97, you must enter 'CO instead of 'COL to use **DDCOLOR** transparently. However, be aware that for some AutoCAD LT commands, the new color does not take effect until the current command is terminated.

Figure 5-1.
The **Select Color**
dialog box.

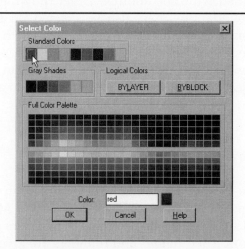

Figure 5-2.
Select **Color...** from
the **Format** pull-
down menu or
select **Other...** from
the **Color Control**
drop-down list on
the **Object
Properties** toolbar to
open the **Select
Color** dialog box.

Components of the **Select Color** dialog box

The other sections of the **Select Color** dialog box are described below.

- **Gray Shades.** This area displays color numbers 250-255. Use this section to specify a shade of gray for new objects.

- **Logical Colors.** The two buttons in this section specify how color assignments are made. In the default **BYLAYER** mode, new objects assume the color of the layer upon which they are drawn (layers are described in a later section of this chapter). If you select **BYBLOCK** mode, AutoCAD LT draws new objects in the default color. That color is white or black, depending on your screen background color, and is maintained until the objects are made into a block. A *block* is one or more objects grouped together into a single object. When the block is inserted into a drawing, the objects in the block inherit the current setting of the **DDCOLOR** command. See *Chapter 15* for a complete description of blocks and block attributes.

- **Full Color Palette.** This section contains color numbers 10-249. Your display device determines the number of colors that are available from the **Full Color Palette**. Most, if not all, color monitors and graphics cards available today display at least 256 colors. Some graphics cards feature *true color* capabilities, which means that these graphics cards can display up to 16.7 million colors. AutoCAD LT does not use more than 256 colors, however.

NOTE

Although there are 256 colors in AutoCAD LT, only 255 are available to you because, as previously mentioned, color number 7 can be either black or white depending on your screen background color.

Setting a Color at the **Command:** Prompt

It is also possible to set a different color for new drawing objects at the Command: prompt. To do so, use the **COLOR** command and enter the first letter of the color name, the full color name, or the color number. In the following example, the color green is selected.

> Command: **COLOR**↵
> New object color ⟨*current*⟩: (*type* 3 *or* G *or* GREEN *and press* [Enter])

The **COLOR** command may also be used transparently by entering 'COLOR. As with setting a color using the dialog box, the new color does not take effect for some commands until the current command is terminated. The new color is then displayed in the **Color Control** drop-down list on the **Object Properties** toolbar.

EXERCISE 5-1

- ❏ Begin a new drawing from scratch. It is not necessary to use one of your templates for this exercise.
- ❏ Using the **Color Control** drop-down list on the **Object Properties** toolbar, draw a line with each of the seven standard colors.
- ❏ Now, use **DDCOLOR** to draw lines using each of the available gray shades.
- ❏ Use **DDCOLOR** again to draw lines using any of the colors in the **Full Color Palette.**
- ❏ It is not necessary to save the drawing when you are finished.

Getting Started Guide 5

Standard Linetypes

All of the lines you have drawn in the exercises and problems from the previous chapters have been in a solid, unbroken linetype. In drafting terminology, you might refer to this linetype as an object line. AutoCAD LT calls it the *continuous linetype*. The continuous linetype is the default linetype in AutoCAD LT and is always loaded and ready for use in every new drawing. There are many other linetypes available to you as well. From **Figure 5-3**, you can see that each linetype is a repeating pattern of dashes or dots separated with blank spaces. The linetypes are defined in an external linetype file called aclt.lin in the AutoCAD LT 98 folder. Metric versions of the linetypes are defined in a second linetype file called acltiso.lin. This linetype file is used automatically if you click the **Start from Scratch** button and select metric settings when beginning a new drawing. Regardless of the linetype file you select, a linetype must first be loaded into the program and set current before it can be used.

Figure 5-3.
The standard linetypes defined in the aclt.lin linetype file.

Continuous	————————	Acad_iso02w100	— — — — — —
Border	— — — — — —	Acad_iso03w100	— — — — —
Border2	— — — — — — — —	Acad_iso04w100	—·—·—·—·—·
Borderx2	—— —— ——	Acad_iso05w100	——·——·——·
Center	—— — —— — ——	Acad_iso06w100	——··——··——
Center2	—— - —— - ——	Acad_iso07w100	··················
Centerx2	——— — ——— —	Acad_iso08w100	— — ·— — ·—
Dashdot	— · — · — · — ·	Acad_iso09w100	— — ··— — ··
Dashdot2	-·-·-·-·-·-·-	Acad_iso10w100	—·—·—·—·—·
Dashdotx2	—— · —— · ——	Acad_iso11w100	——·——·——·
Dashed	— — — — — —	Acad_iso12w100	——··——··——
Dashed2	- - - - - - - - - -	Acad_iso13w100	——·——·——·
Dashedx2	—— —— ——	Acad_iso14w100	——·—·——·—·
Divide	— · · — · · — ·	Acad_iso15w100	——·——·——·
Divide2	-··-··-··-··-··	Fenceline1	—o—o—o—
Dividex2	——··——··——	Fenceline2	—□—□—□—
Dot	···················	Gas_line	— GAS — GAS —
Dot2	··················	Hot_water_supply	— HW — HW —
Dotx2	· · · · · · · · ·		
Hidden	- - - - - - - - - -	Tracks	+++++++++++++
Hidden2	- - - - - - - - - - - -		
Hiddenx2	— — — — — —	Zigzag	/\/\/\/\/\/\
Phantom	— — — — — —		
Phantom2	- - — - - — - - —	Batting	∞∞∞∞∞∞∞∞∞
Phantomx2	—— — —— — ——		

Loading Linetypes Using a Dialog Box

One or more linetypes can easily be loaded using the **Layer & Linetype Properties** dialog box shown in **Figure 5-4.** Once a linetype is loaded, this dialog box may also be used to set it current. To access the **Layer & Linetype Properties** dialog box, enter LINETYPE, or DDLTYPE or LT, at the Command: prompt, select **Linetype...** from the **Format** pull-down menu, or click the **Linetype** button on the **Object Properties** toolbar.

The dialog box displays only linetypes that have been loaded. When you begin a new drawing without using a customized template, the three listed options are **ByLayer**, **ByBlock**, and **Continuous**. Each section of the **Layer & Linetype Properties** dialog box is described as follows:

- **Show:**. This drop-down list can be used to restrict the display of linetypes in the dialog box in several ways. You can show all of the loaded linetypes (the default), only those that are used in the drawing, or just those that are unused. You may also choose to display any linetypes that belong to dependent objects. See *Chapter 15* for more information about dependent objects.

LINETYPE
DDLTYPE or LT

F**o**rmat
↪ Li**n**etype...

Object Properties
toolbar

Linetype

Figure 5-4. The **Layer & Linetype Properties** dialog box.

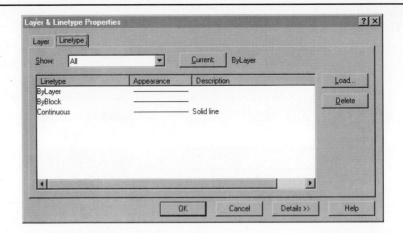

- **Current:.** To draw with a different loaded linetype, first select the linetype from the list using your pointing device. The selected linetype name then appears highlighted. Next, click the **Current:** button at the top center of the dialog box to make your selection active.
- **Load....** To load additional linetypes, click this button at the upper right of the dialog box. Doing so displays the **Load or Reload Linetypes** subdialog box shown in **Figure 5-5A.** The components of this subdialog box are described as follows:
    - **Available Linetypes**—This list displays all of the linetypes in the default aclt.lin linetype file. Use your pointing device to select the linetypes you wish to load from this list. To select more than one linetype from the list, press and hold the [Ctrl] key as you make your selections. This method allows you to select linetypes in a random order. In the example shown, the **Hidden** and **Phantom** linetypes are selected using this method. If you wish to select linetypes in a consecutive order, pick the first linetype in the list you want. Then press and hold the [Shift] key as you select the last linetype you want from the list. Every linetype between the first pick and the second pick is selected in consecutive order. If you wish to remove a highlighted linetype from the list, press and hold the [Ctrl] key as you make your selection. If you right-click with your pointing device, a small cursor menu appears as shown in **Figure 5-5B.** Click **Select All** if you want to load *all* of the available linetypes. (You can also press

Figure 5-5.
A—The **Load or Reload Linetypes** subdialog box is used to load linetypes from a selected linetype file. B—Right-clicking displays a pop-up menu to facilitate linetype selection.

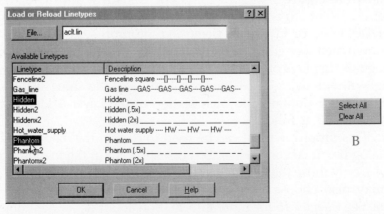

A

[Ctrl]+[A] on your keyboard to select all the linetypes.) However, be aware that loading unneeded linetypes increases the drawing file size and takes up valuable disk space unnecessarily. If you are dissatisfied with the linetype(s) you select, click the **Clear All** button to clear your selection.

- **File...**—When you wish to load a linetype that resides in a linetype file other than aclt.lin, click this button at the upper-left to open the **Select Linetype File** subdialog box. See **Figure 5-6.** Observe that linetype files have a *.lin* file extension. In the example shown, the acltiso.lin file is selected from the file list at the top of the subdialog box. After selecting the desired linetype file, click the **Open** button to return to the **Load or Reload Linetypes** subdialog box. The linetypes contained in the selected linetype file are then displayed in the **Available Linetypes** list.

After loading the desired linetype(s), click the **OK** button in the **Load or Reload Linetypes** subdialog box. The **Layer & Linetype Properties** dialog box appears once again and displays the linetypes you selected for loading. See **Figure 5-7.** Several other buttons available in this dialog box are described below:

- **Delete.** When you no longer need a linetype in the current drawing, select it from the list using any of the methods previously described and click this button. The linetype(s) you select are removed from the current drawing only—not the linetype file. Deleting unneeded linetypes helps to reduce file size and conserve disk space. If you select a linetype that cannot be deleted, AutoCAD LT displays the alert box shown in **Figure 5-8.** It is also possible to remove unneeded linetypes using the **PURGE** command. This command is described at the end of this chapter.

Figure 5-6.
Selecting a linetype file from the **Select Linetype File** subdialog box. The acltiso.lin file is used for metric drawings.

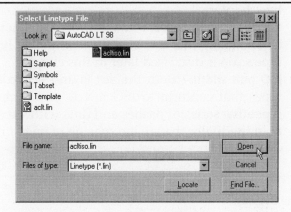

Figure 5-7.
The newly loaded linetypes appear in the **Layer & Linetype Properties** dialog box.

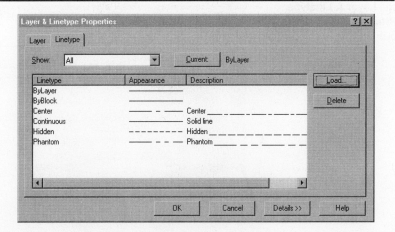

Figure 5-8.
Certain linetypes
cannot be deleted as
evidenced by the
message in this alert
box.

- **Details》**. After selecting a linetype from the list, click this button to display an expanded version of the **Layer & Linetype Properties** dialog box. See **Figure 5-9.** When you are done working with the expanded version of the **Layer & Linetype Properties** dialog box, click the **Details《** button to return to the default, unexpanded version. Finally, click the **OK** button to exit the **Layer & Linetype Properties** dialog box. The options available in this expanded version are explained as follows:
  - **Name:**—This text box displays the currently selected linetype and may be used to edit the linetype name. As with other named objects, a linetype name may contain up to 31 characters. It may also contain a dollar sign ($), a hyphen (-), and an underscore (_). No spaces are permitted in the linetype name, however. Be advised that the **ByLayer**, **ByBlock**, and **Continuous** linetypes may not be renamed.
  - **Description:**—A brief, and editable, description of the selected linetype appears in this text box.
  - **Global scale factor:**—This text box displays the global scale factor for all linetypes. Global linetype scale factors are discussed in a later section of this chapter.
  - **Current object scale:**—You can set the linetype scale for newly created objects using this text box. As with global linetype scale, individual linetype scale is discussed later in this chapter.
  - **ISO pen width:**—Both the aclt.lin and acltiso.lin linetype files contain linetypes that conform to ISO metric standards. These linetypes also use a repetitive series of dashes and dots with varying spacing. When you wish to individually change the spacing of one of these linetypes, first select the

Figure 5-9.
Clicking the **Details》**
button displays an
expanded version of
the **Layer & Linetype
Properties** dialog
box.

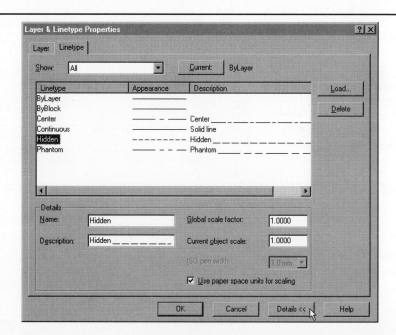

AutoCAD LT—Fundamentals and Applications

linetype from the list in the **Layer & Linetype Properties** dialog box. Next, select the desired size from the **ISO pen width:** drop-down list. The available sizes range from .13mm to 2mm. Any new objects created with the modified linetype reflect the change in gap spacing.

- **Use paper space units for scaling**—This check box is active by default. It ensures that linetypes are scaled identically in both model space and paper space. This setting can also be controlled at the Command: prompt using the **PSLTSCALE** system variable. See *Chapter 17* for more information about the model space and paper space drawing environments.

Setting a Linetype Current

Once a linetype is loaded, it must be set current before you can draw with it. Only one linetype can be current at a time. There are several ways to make a linetype current. The first way is to select the linetype from the **Layer & Linetype Properties** dialog box and then click the **Current:** button as previously mentioned. Remember that only linetypes that have been loaded appear in this dialog box. When you are finished, click the **OK** button to exit the **Layer & Linetype Properties** dialog box.

Setting a Linetype Current using the Linetype Control Drop-Down List

Loaded linetypes also appear in the **Linetype Control** drop-down list. This list appears just to the right of the **Linetype** button on the **Object Properties** toolbar. In the example shown in **Figure 5-10**, the Hidden linetype is selected from the list. The current linetype name is then displayed on the **Object Properties** toolbar. Keep in mind that using this method is the fastest and easiest way to set a different linetype current.

Figure 5-10.
Setting a linetype current using the **Linetype Control** drop-down list.

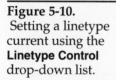
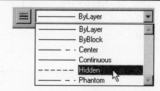

Setting a Linetype Current at the Command: Prompt

You may also set a linetype current using the **CELTYPE** system variable on the command line. In the following example, the Phantom linetype is set current:

```
Command: CELTYPE↵
New value for CELTYPE ⟨current⟩: PHANTOM↵
Command:
```

Using the -LINETYPE command

To use the **-LINETYPE** command to load and set linetypes, enter -LINETYPE, or -LT, at the Command: prompt. This command also allows you to list available linetypes and create your own custom linetype. Creating custom linetypes is discussed later in this chapter. The command sequence is as follows:

```
Command: -LINETYPE or -LT↵
?/Create/Load/Set: (select an option)
```

The **-LINETYPE** options are described as follows:

- **?.** The **?** option is used to list the available linetypes. When you select the list option, you are presented with the **Select Linetype File** subdialog box shown in **Figure 5-6.** Select the linetype file that you wish to list and click the **Open...** button. The graphics window automatically flips to the text window to display the linetypes available in the file you selected. See **Figure 5-11.** After listing each of the linetypes, the **-LINETYPE** command options are redisplayed. Select an option or press [Enter] to end the command. Press [F2], or select **Display** and then **Text Window** from the **View** pull-down menu to flip back to the graphics window.

- **Create.** As previously mentioned, you may define your own custom linetypes. This capability is discussed in a later section of this chapter.

- **Load.** Use the **Load** option to load one or more linetypes into the drawing editor. You must enter the linetype name(s) in full—abbreviations are not accepted. When loading multiple linetypes, separate each linetype name with a comma as shown below:

> Command: **-LINETYPE** *or* **-LT**↵
> ?/Create/Load/Set: **L**↵
> Linetype(s) to load: **CENTER,HIDDEN,PHANTOM**↵

After you enter the linetype name(s) and press [Enter], you are presented with the **Select Linetype File** subdialog box. Select the linetype file that you wish to load from and click the **Open...** button. AutoCAD LT then loads the linetypes you requested and redisplays the **-LINETYPE** command options. Select another option or press [Enter] to end the command. If you would like to quickly load all the linetypes defined in a linetype file, enter the * wildcard character at the **Linetype(s) to load:** prompt. However, remember that loading unneeded linetypes increases the drawing file size unnecessarily.

- **Set.** Use this option to set current a loaded linetype. In the following example, the Hidden linetype is set current:

> Command: **-LINETYPE** *or* **-LT**↵
> ?/Create/Load/Set: **S**↵
> New object linetype (or ?) ⟨*current*⟩: **HIDDEN**↵

Figure 5-11.
The **-LINETYPE** command **?** option displays the available linetypes in the **AutoCAD LT Text Window**.

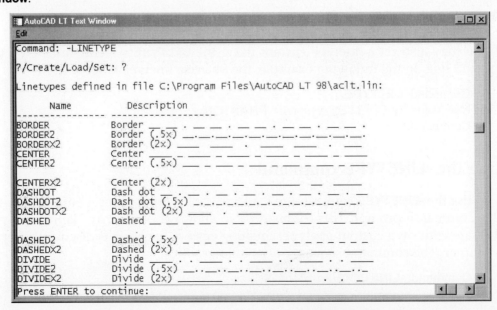

If you forget the name of the linetype you wish to set current, use the **?** option to list the loaded linetypes as follows:

New object linetype (or ?) ⟨*current*⟩: **?**↵
Linetype(s) to list ⟨*⟩: ↵

Since the * symbol is a wildcard character, simply press [Enter] to list all loaded linetypes. After setting a linetype current, the **-LINETYPE** command options are redisplayed. Select another option or press [Enter] to end the command.

PROFESSIONAL TIP

If you wish to change a linetype transparently, enter '-LT, not 'LINETYPE or 'LT at the Command: prompt.

Linetype Scale Factors

Occasionally, you will draw a line that is too short to hold even one dash sequence. This often occurs when you are drawing very short hidden or centerlines in a confined area, such as a narrow side view. In these instances, AutoCAD LT uses the Continuous linetype instead. The problem can be corrected by changing the linetype scale factor. There are two ways to accomplish this task. One method allows you to set the scale factor individually for a linetype as it is being loaded. The other method is global in nature and therefore affects all the linetypes displayed on the screen. Both methods are described in the following sections.

Setting Individual Linetype Scale Using a Dialog Box

You can individually set the linetype scale for a loaded linetype using the expanded version of the **Layer & Linetype Properties** dialog box. In the example shown in **Figure 5-12**, the Hidden linetype is first selected from the list and then the **Details ⟩⟩** button is clicked to display the expanded version of this dialog box. Next,

---

Figure 5-12.
Setting individual linetype scale for a single loaded linetype using the expanded version of the **Layer & Linetype Properties** dialog box.

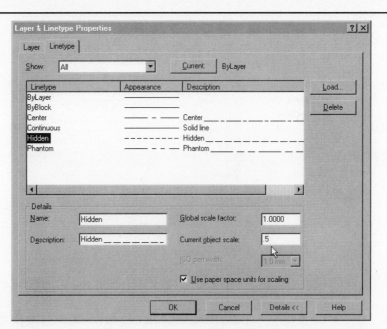

the linetype scale is set to .5 in the **Current object scale:** text box. A value greater than one increases the length of dashed and dotted linetypes; a value less than one decreases the length. Negative values are not permitted. After setting the linetype scale, click **OK** to exit the dialog box. All new objects drawn with this linetype reflect the revised scale factor. Previously drawn objects are not affected by the change and neither are objects drawn with a different linetype.

Setting Individual Linetype Scale at the **Command:** Prompt

The linetype scale for the currently loaded linetype may also be set using the **CELTSCALE** system variable on the command line. The procedure looks like this:

> Command: **CELTSCALE.**⌐
> New value for CELTSCALE ⟨*current*⟩: **2.**⌐
> Command:

Whether you set individual linetype scale using the dialog box or on the command line, remember that the change affects only newly created objects that use the modified linetype. Objects already created or drawn with a different linetype are not affected.

Globally Setting Linetype Scale with the **LTSCALE** System Variable

Use the **LTSCALE** variable when you wish to change the linetype scale for *every* linetype, other than Continuous, in your drawing. As with individual linetype scaling, **LTSCALE** changes the relative length of dashed and dotted linetypes per drawing unit. A value greater than one increases the length; a value less than one decreases the length and negative values are not permitted. You can also change **LTSCALE** by using the expanded version of the **Layer & Linetype Properties** dialog box. Enter the value you desire in the **Global scale factor:** text box as shown in **Figure 5-13.** On the command line the sequence is as follows:

> Command: **LTSCALE** *or* **LTS.**⌐
> New scale factor ⟨*current*⟩: *(enter a positive value and press* [Enter]*)*
> Command:

Figure 5-13.
Setting global linetype scale for all loaded linetypes using the expanded version of the **Layer & Linetype Properties** dialog box.

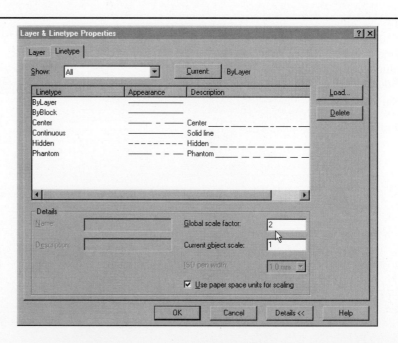

Several examples of lines with varying linetype scales appear in **Figure 5-14.** However, keep in mind that changing the global linetype scale factor automatically forces a drawing regeneration. Remember also that the **LTSCALE** variable affects both previously drawn and newly created objects in your drawing.

Figure 5-14.
Several examples of linetype scale factors using **LTSCALE**.

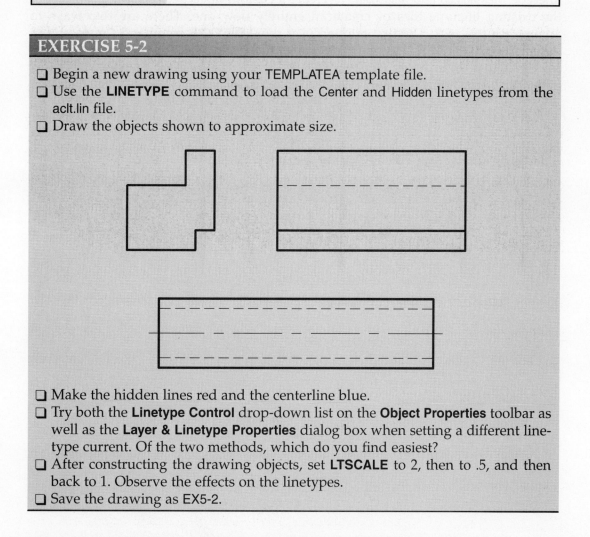

LTSCALE = 1

LTSCALE = 2

LTSCALE = .5

PROFESSIONAL TIP

As an alternative to individual linetype scaling, you can change the linetype scale for specific objects by selecting one of the variations from the aclt.lin or acltiso.lin linetype files. As an example, if you are satisfied with the scale of the hidden lines on your drawing but would like to increase the spacing of the centerlines only, use the Centerx2 linetype instead of Center or Center2.

EXERCISE 5-2

- ❏ Begin a new drawing using your TEMPLATEA template file.
- ❏ Use the **LINETYPE** command to load the Center and Hidden linetypes from the aclt.lin file.
- ❏ Draw the objects shown to approximate size.

- ❏ Make the hidden lines red and the centerline blue.
- ❏ Try both the **Linetype Control** drop-down list on the **Object Properties** toolbar as well as the **Layer & Linetype Properties** dialog box when setting a different linetype current. Of the two methods, which do you find easiest?
- ❏ After constructing the drawing objects, set **LTSCALE** to 2, then to .5, and then back to 1. Observe the effects on the linetypes.
- ❏ Save the drawing as EX5-2.

Complex Linetypes

Most of the linetypes contained in the aclt.lin and acltiso.lin definition files are considered *simple* linetypes. These linetypes are composed of dashes, dots, and spaces only. AutoCAD LT also supplies several linetypes that contain embedded shapes or text. Such linetypes are considered *complex* linetypes and are shown in **Figure 5-15.**

Complex linetypes can be used to denote contours, boundaries, utilities, and so forth. They are constructed like simple linetypes and the shapes or text embedded within them are always displayed completely—they are never trimmed.

Figure 5-15.
The complex linetypes included with AutoCAD LT.

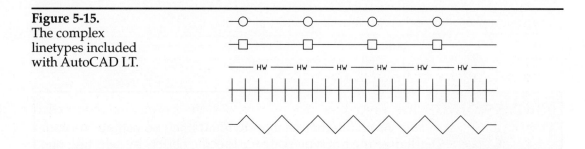

Custom Linetypes

As mentioned previously, AutoCAD LT stores linetype definitions in the external linetype files aclt.lin and acltiso.lin. To create a custom linetype, you must edit one of the existing linetype files or create an entirely new one. There are two ways to accomplish this task. The first method uses the **-LINETYPE** command **Create** option inside AutoCAD LT. The second method permits you to edit the linetype definition file directly with an ASCII *(American Standard Code for Information Interchange)* text editor such as Windows Notepad. A portion of aclt.lin is shown in Notepad in **Figure 5-16.**

Figure 5-16.
A portion of aclt.lin is shown in the Notepad text editor.

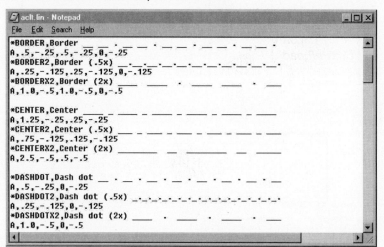

Simple Linetype Definitions

Interpreting a linetype definition is really quite simple. As you can see from the illustration, each linetype name is preceded with an asterisk and followed with a comma and a pictorial representation of the linetype. The **A** on the second line specifies the line pattern alignment used at the ends of individual lines, arcs, and circles. AutoCAD LT refers to this as *A-type alignment*. The pattern alignment ensures that lines and arcs start and end with a dash (or dot).

However, it is the number values that really define a linetype. A positive number specifies the length of the dash segment, while a negative number specifies the length of the space in the line. A 0 (zero) results in a dot being drawn. AutoCAD LT automatically repeats the sequence for any given line length.

Custom Simple Linetype Tutorial

▷ Use the following procedure to create a custom simple linetype called Myborder. It is similar to the Border linetype which draws two dashes and a dot, except that it draws two dots and then a dash.

> Command: **-LINETYPE** *or* **-LT**↵
> ?/Create/Load/Set: **C**↵
> Name of linetype to create: **MYBORDER**↵

▷ When the **Create or Append Linetype File** dialog box appears, enter the name Mylines in the **File name:** text box and then click the **Save** button. See **Figure 5-17.** You are then informed the new linetype file is created, and are prompted to enter some descriptive text. This step is optional.

> Creating new file
> Descriptive text: **TWO DOTS AND A DASH.**↵

▷ After entering the optional descriptive text, enter the linetype pattern definition. Observe that AutoCAD LT automatically places the "A" for A-type alignment at the beginning of the line for you.

> Enter pattern (on next line):
> **A, 0,-.25,0,-.25,.5,-.25** ↵
> New definition written to file.
> ?/Create/Load/Set: **L**↵
> Linetype(s) to load: **MYBORDER.**↵

Figure 5-17.
The **Create or Append Linetype File** dialog box.

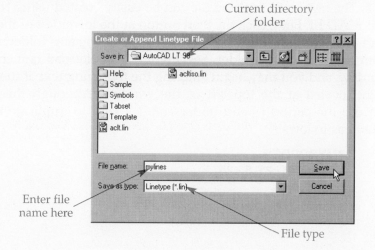

Current directory folder

Enter file name here

File type

⇨ When the **Select Linetype File** dialog box appears, select the file mylines.lin and click the **Open** button.

> Linetype MYBORDER loaded.
> ?/Create/Load/Set: **S**↵
> New object linetype (or ?) ⟨*current*⟩: **MYBORDER.**↵
> ?/Create/Load/Set: ↵

⇨ Remember that you can also use the **Linetype Control** drop-down list or the **CELTYPE** system variable to set the Myborder linetype current. An example of the new linetype is shown in **Figure 5-18**.

Figure 5-18.
A rectangle drawn with the custom MYBORDER linetype.

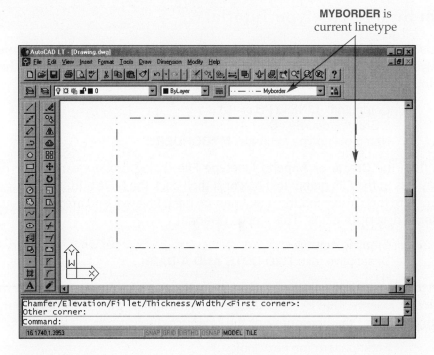

MYBORDER is current linetype

Using the Windows **Notepad** to Create a Custom Linetype

The Notepad program included in Microsoft Windows is a simple ASCII text editor that you can use to edit small text files. This makes Notepad very handy for creating a custom linetype definition file or for editing the existing aclt.lin or acltiso.lin files. The mylines.lin linetype file can be easily created using Notepad without exiting AutoCAD LT. First, click the Start button at the lower left of the Taskbar to display the Start menu. Next, select Accessories from the Programs folder, and then click Notepad from the Accessories folder. See **Figure 5-19**. Notepad launches in its own display window, and you may begin entering the following text at the flashing text insertion point located at the top left of the window. Although this step is optional, you can use the period (.) and underscore (_) keys to duplicate the line representation shown as follows:

        *MYBORDER, . . _ . . _ . . _ . . _
        A, 0,-.25,0,-.25,.5,-.25

Figure 5-19.
Notepad is launched from the Accessories program folder. The Windows 98 desktop is shown.

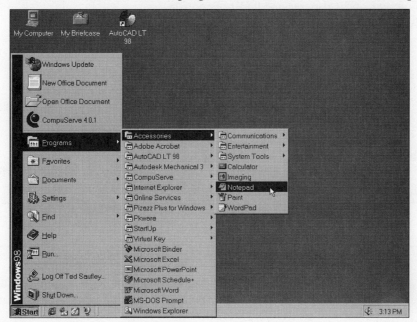

When you have finished entering the text, the Notepad window should appear as shown in **Figure 5-20.** Select Save As... from the File pull-down menu to access the Save As dialog box. Change to the AutoCAD LT 98 folder and save your linetype definition file with the name mylines.lin in the File name: text box. See **Figure 5-21.** Click the Save button to save the file and exit the dialog box. Next, quit Notepad by selecting Exit from the File pull-down menu. You are automatically returned to AutoCAD LT.

Figure 5-20.
The MYBORDER custom linetype pattern definition in Notepad.

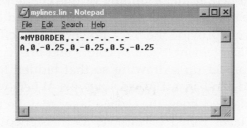

Figure 5-21.
The linetype is saved as mylines.lin in the AutoCAD LT 98 folder.

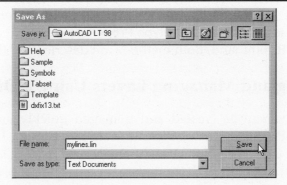

EXERCISE 5-3

❑ Use Notepad to edit the mylines.lin linetype file.
❑ Add these three dotted linetype patterns:

        *MYDOT1,.
        A,0,-.125
        *MYDOT2,.
        A,0,-.1
        *MYDOT3,.
        A,0,-.05

❑ Save the edited mylines.lin linetype file.
❑ Start AutoCAD LT, load your new linetypes and draw several lines with them.
❑ Save the drawing as EX5-3.

PROFESSIONAL TIP

Make backup copies of the original aclt.lin and acltiso.lin linetype files before you experiment with creating or modifying linetype definitions. It might be a good idea to create linetypes in a separate file as described in the two previous examples, and leave the original definition files undisturbed. Check with your instructor or supervisor to verify which procedures should be used.

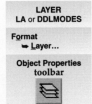

Getting Started Guide 4

Creating and Using Layers

As mentioned at the beginning of this chapter, layers in AutoCAD LT are used much like the transparent overlays used in the traditional paper-based drafting environment. Layers provide the most powerful and efficient means of drawing organization and management. Because colors and linetypes can be assigned to individual layers, you can set up a drawing so that hidden features appear on a layer called Hidden, in red, and in a Dashed linetype. When you wish to view your drawing without the dashed lines, the Hidden layer may be turned off. Dimensions could be placed on a layer called Dimensions and assigned the color green, while drawing annotation could be placed on a yellow layer called Notes. The default layer in AutoCAD LT is layer 0. Layer 0 is assigned color 7 and the Continuous linetype.

There are two ways to create and manage layers in AutoCAD LT. The first method uses the **Layer & Linetype Properties** dialog box and the second method uses the **-LAYER** command. Both methods are described in the following sections.

Creating and Managing Layers Using a Dialog Box

LAYER
LA or DDLMODES

Format
↳ **Layer...**

Object Properties toolbar

Layers

Layers may be created and managed quickly and easily using the **Layer & Linetype Properties** dialog box shown in **Figure 5-22.** To access this dialog box, enter LAYER, or LA or DDLMODES, at the Command: prompt, select **Layer...** from the **Format** pull-down menu, or click the **Layers** button on the **Object Properties** toolbar.

Figure 5-22.
The **Layer & Linetype Properties** dialog box.

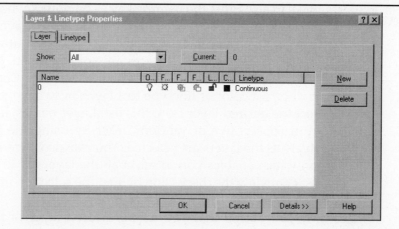

> **NOTE**
>
>
> You may recall the **Layer & Linetype Properties** dialog box from the discussion of the **LINETYPE** command earlier in this chapter. Click the appropriate tab at the top left of this dialog box when you wish to switch between layer and linetype control functions.

Components of the Layer & Linetype Properties dialog box

Observe that there are a number of icons located just to the right of each layer name in the **Layer & Linetype Properties** dialog box. The icons act as switches and are used to toggle the state of selected layers. These icons are illustrated and identified in **Figure 5-23.** Each of the icons and buttons in the dialog box are described as follows:

- **New.** To create a new layer, click the **New** button at the upper right of the dialog box. As shown in **Figure 5-24,** the new layer appears in the layer list with the default name Layer1. Successive clicks of the **New** button create additional layers named Layer2, Layer3, and so on. (After creating the first new

Figure 5-23.
ON—The layer is turned on. **OFF**—The layer is turned off. **THAW**—The layer is thawed. **FREEZE**—The layer is frozen. **VIEWPORT LAYER THAWED**—The layer in the current floating viewport is thawed. **VIEWPORT LAYER FROZEN**—The layer in the current floating viewport is frozen. **LOCK**—The layer is locked. **UNLOCK**—The layer is unlocked. **LAYER COLOR**—The color assigned to the layer. **LINETYPE NAME**—The linetype assigned to the layer.

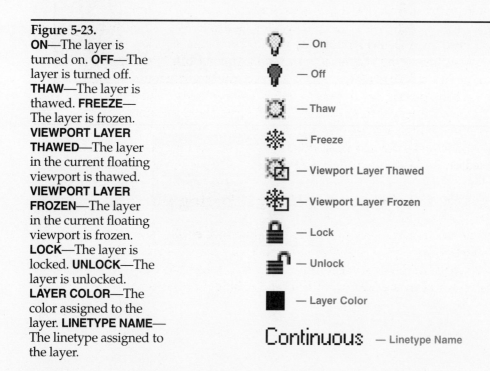

— On
— Off
— Thaw
— Freeze
— Viewport Layer Thawed
— Viewport Layer Frozen
— Lock
— Unlock
— Layer Color

Continuous — Linetype Name

layer, you can also press the comma key (,) on your keyboard to quickly create more new layers.) Simply type over the highlighted layer name with a name you prefer. Layer names, like other named objects in AutoCAD LT, may be up to 31 characters in length, but spaces are not permitted. New layers are automatically assigned color number 7 (white) and the Continuous linetype. To assign a different color or linetype to a layer, or to change its status, you must first select the desired layer from this list. Layer names, like linetypes, may be selected in consecutive or random order by using the [Shift] and [Ctrl] keys respectively as the layers are selected. You can also right-click to access a pop-up menu which enables you to select all the layers or to clear your selection. If necessary, review the discussion of linetype selection in the **Layer & Linetype Properties** dialog box earlier in this chapter.

- **Delete.** If you decide that you do not need a layer in the current drawing, select it from the list using any of the methods previously described and click the **Delete** button. If you select a layer that cannot be deleted, AutoCAD LT displays the alert box shown in **Figure 5-25.**
- **On.** All new layers are on by default. Select one or more layers from the list and click the **On** icon to toggle the layer(s) from on to off. When a layer is turned off, it becomes invisible and does not plot. Keep in mind that a layer that is turned off still redraws and regenerates. AutoCAD LT displays a warning message in a dialog box when you turn off the current layer.
- **Off.** After selecting one or more layers from the list, click the **Off** icon to toggle the layers back on.

Figure 5-24.
The name Layer1 is given to the first new layer created in a drawing.

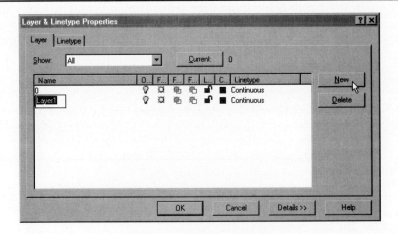

Figure 5-25.
Certain layers cannot be deleted as evidenced by the message in this alert box.

- **Freeze.** Select one or more layers from the list and click the **Thaw** icon to freeze the layer(s). Frozen layers are also not visible. However, unlike objects on layers that are merely turned off, objects on frozen layers do not redraw or regenerate. This can significantly improve system performance. You cannot freeze the current layer, though. Also, keep in mind that frozen layers do not plot. For this reason, it is a good idea to create a special layer in your template(s) for construction purposes. You might name the layer Construct or Temporary. Place objects that you do not want plotted on this layer. Before you plot the drawing, freeze the layer.
- **Thaw.** When you wish to thaw one or more selected layers, click the **Freeze** icon to return the layers to a thawed state.
- **Thawed/Frozen in current viewport:.** These icons set the frozen/thawed status of floating viewport layers in paper space. This capability is covered in *Chapter 17*.
- **Lock/Unlock.** A locked layer is displayed on screen, but not selectable. This is done to prevent accidental editing operations, such as erasing, on the locked layer objects. However, it is possible to draw with a locked layer. To lock or unlock a layer, select one or more layers from the list and click the **Lock** icon.
- **Color.** To assign a color to a layer, first select the desired layer from the layer list and then click the **Color** icon to access the **Select Color** subdialog box. See Figure 5-1. Select one of 255 colors and click **OK**.
- **Linetype.** To assign a linetype to a layer, first select the desired layer from the layer list and then click the linetype name just to the right of the color icon to display the **Select Linetype** subdialog box. See **Figure 5-26.** This subdialog box only displays linetypes that have first been loaded. If the linetype you wish to assign to the new layer is not loaded, click the **Load...** button and load the desired linetype as described earlier in this chapter. Select one of the loaded linetypes and click **OK**.
- **Show.** This drop-down list can be used to restrict the display of layers in the dialog box in several ways. You can show all of the layers (the default), only those that are used in the drawing, or just those that are unused. You may also choose to display any layers that belong to dependent objects. See *Chapter 15* for more information about dependent objects. It is also possible to display only those layers that have been filtered. Layer filtering is described in the next section of this chapter.
- **Current:.** After selecting a layer from the list, click the **Current:** button to set it current. The current layer name is displayed just to the right of the **Current:** button. Any new objects you now create reside on the current layer.

Figure 5-26.
The **Select Linetype** subdialog box lets you load one or more linetypes for layer assignment.

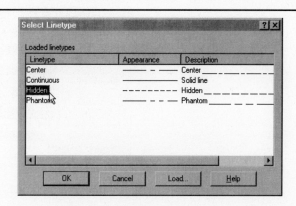

Filtering Layers in the List

For very large drawings that may contain dozens of layers, it is possible to limit the number of layers that appear in the **Layer & Linetype Properties** dialog box listing. The layers may be screened out, or filtered, based on name, color, or linetype. You may also choose to list only those layers that are on or off, thawed or frozen, or locked or unlocked. Consider the layer listing shown in **Figure 5-27.** In this example, the color red has been assigned to the Hidden and Text layers.

To list only the two red layers, do the following:

1. Select **Set Filter dialog** from the **Show:** drop-down list at the upper left of the dialog box to display the **Set Layer Filters** subdialog box shown in **Figure 5-28.**
2. Enter the color name red (or color number 1) in the **Colors:** text box. Click the **OK** button.
3. When the **Layer & Linetype Properties** dialog box reappears, observe that only the red layers are displayed in the layer listing. **See Figure 5-29.**
4. To restore the complete layer list again, select **All** from the **Show:** drop-down list to deactivate the filters.

Keep in mind that layer filters only limit the number of layers that appear in the **Layer & Linetype Properties** dialog box listing. They do not affect the display of layers on screen.

Figure 5-27.
A layer list may be shortened using layer filters.

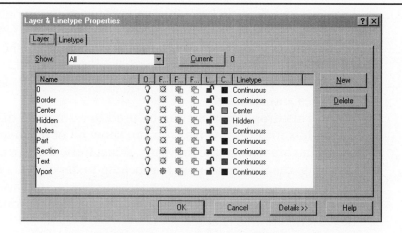

Figure 5-28.
The **Set Layer Filters** subdialog box is used to filter only red layers.

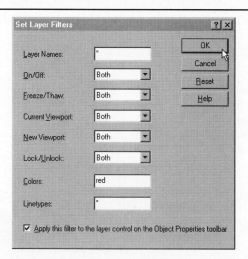

Figure 5-29.
The layer list as it
appears with filters
activated.

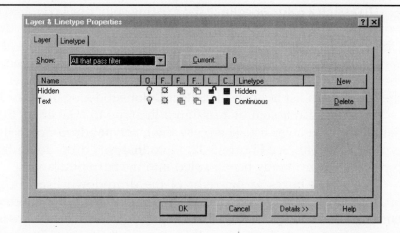

PROFESSIONAL TIP

When filtering layer names and linetypes, you can use
the wild card (*) character. As an example, to display only
those layer names that start with the letter B, place your
cursor in the **Layer Names:** text box and enter B*.

Using the Expanded Dialog Box to Manage Layers

As with linetypes, you can click the **Details»** button at the lower right of the
Layer & Linetype Properties dialog box to obtain an expanded version. Once a layer
has been selected from the list, the text boxes and check boxes are activated and ready
for use. See **Figure 5-30.**

You can rename a layer by first selecting the layer to be renamed from the list of
layer names. The layer name then appears in the **Name:** text box in the **Details** section
at the bottom of the dialog box. Double-click the name in the text box so that it is
highlighted and type over it with a new name. The new name immediately appears
in the layer list at the top.

Figure 5-30.
Layers can also be
managed using the
expanded version of
the **Layer & Linetype
Properties** dialog box.

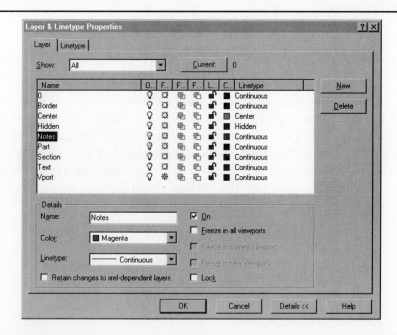

To assign a color, or change the existing color of a layer, first select the layer name from the layer list. Next, select the desired color from the **Color:** drop-down list. Observe from **Figure 5-31** that this drop-down list is identical to the **Color Control** drop-down list located on the **Object Properties** toolbar. If you wish to select one of the nonstandard colors from the full color palette, select **Other...** from the bottom of the drop-down list to open the **Select Color** subdialog box. See Figure 5-1.

You can also assign or reassign a linetype to a layer by first selecting the layer name from the layer list. Then, use the **Linetype:** drop-down list to make your linetype assignment. See **Figure 5-32.** Note that this drop-down list only displays linetypes that have already been loaded into the current drawing.

The check boxes to the right of the drop-down lists allow you to change the on/off, thawed/frozen, and locked/unlocked status of a selected layer. The **Freeze in current viewport** and **Freeze in new viewports** check boxes are inactive until floating viewports are first created in paper space. See *Chapter 17* to learn how to create and manage floating viewports.

Finally, the **Retain changes to xref-dependent layers** check box at the lower left of the dialog box controls the visibility status of layers that belong to external references. This function is also controlled with the **VISRETAIN** system variable and is described fully in *Chapter 15*.

Figure 5-31.
The **Color:** drop-down list can be used to assign a color to a layer.

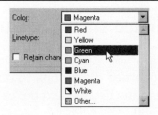

Figure 5-32.
The **Linetype:** drop-down list can be used to assign a linetype to a layer. The linetype must first be loaded.

Setting a Layer Current Quickly

You can quickly change to another layer using the **Layer Control** drop-down list at the left of the **Object Properties** toolbar. This box prominently displays the current layer name. Click the down arrow, or anywhere within the box, and a drop-down list appears that contains all of the layers defined in the current drawing. Click the desired layer name, and that layer is set current. See **Figure 5-33.** When many layers are defined in a drawing, the vertical scroll bar can be used to quickly move up and down through the list.

You can also use the **CLAYER** system variable to make a layer current. The command sequence is as follows:

Command: **CLAYER**↵
New value for CLAYER ⟨*"current layer"*⟩: (*enter the name of an existing layer and press* [Enter])
Command:

AutoCAD LT—Fundamentals and Applications

Figure 5-33.
The **Layer Control** drop-down list on the **Object Properties** toolbar displays the layer names defined in the current drawing as well as their status. You can click on a layer name in the list to change to that layer.

Making an Object's Layer Current

Both AutoCAD LT 98 and AutoCAD LT 97 contain a handy feature that lets you set the current layer to match that of a selected drawing object. To use this powerful function, click the **Make Object's Layer Current** button at the far left of the **Object Properties** toolbar. See **Figure 5-34.** You are then prompted with the following:

Select object whose layer will become current: *(select one drawing object)*

AutoCAD LT then displays a message on the command line that the layer of the object you selected is now the current layer. It is also possible to enter this command at the Command: prompt like this:

Command: **AI_MOLC**⏎

Figure 5-34.
The **Make Object's Layer Current** button lets you set the current layer to match that of a selected drawing object.

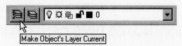

Changing the Status of a Layer Using the **Layer &** **Linetype Properties** List

Apart from displaying each of the layers defined in the current drawing, the **Layer Control** drop-down list also uses small icons to display the current status and assigned color of each layer. These icons are identical to those in the **Layer & Linetype Properties** dialog box and illustrated in **Figure 5-23.**

You can change the locked/unlocked, frozen/thawed, and off/on status of a layer by simply clicking on the appropriate icon. Clicking the layer color icon does nothing, but clicking the layer name sets the selected layer current as previously described.

NOTE	The **Freeze/Thaw** icon is disabled (grayed-out) when working in the default model space environment. This icon is activated automatically when paper space is entered. See *Chapter 17* for more information about paper space.

Creating layers at the **Command:** prompt

Layers may also be created and managed at the Command: prompt using the **-LAYER** command. The command sequence is as follows:

Command: **-LAYER** or **-LA.⌐**
?/Make/Set/New/ ON/OFF/Color/Ltype/Freeze/Thaw/LOck/Unlock:

Each option of the **-LAYER** command is described as follows:

- **?.** Use this option to list any existing layers in the drawing. When you select the list option, you are presented with the following prompt:

  Layer name(s) to list ⟨*⟩: *(press [Enter] to list all layers)*

  The graphics window flips to the text window to display all the layers defined in the drawing. The colors, linetypes, and status of the layers (on/off, frozen/thawed, etc.) also appear in the list. After listing the layers, the -LAYER command option line is redisplayed. Select an option, press [F2] to flip back to the graphics window, or press [Enter] to end the command.

- **Make.** This option makes a new layer and sets it current. Remember that a layer name may be up to 31 characters in length, but no spaces are permitted.

  New current layer ⟨0⟩: *(enter a name for the new layer)*

  The new layer is automatically assigned color 7 and the Continuous linetype.

- **Set.** This option is used to set a different layer current.

  New current layer ⟨current⟩: *(enter the name of an existing layer)*

  If the layer you specify is turned off, it is automatically turned back on.

- **New.** Use this option to create an entirely new layer. When creating multiple layers, separate each layer name with a comma as shown below:

  New layer name(s): **NOTES,DIMS,CENTERLINES.⌐**

  As previously mentioned, color 7 and the Continuous linetype are automatically assigned to new layers. However, unlike the **Make** option, a newly created layer is not automatically set current.

- **ON.** Once turned off, use the **ON** option to turn one or more layers back on. For multiple layers, separate each layer name with a comma. If you enter an asterisk (*), all layers are turned on.

  Layer name(s) to turn On: *(enter layer names separated by commas)*

- **OFF.** Use the **OFF** option to turn one or more layers off. For multiple layers, separate each layer name with a comma. If you enter an asterisk (*), all layers are turned off, including the layer you are presently working with.

  Layer name(s) to turn Off: *(enter layer names separated by commas)*

- **Color.** Use this option to assign a color to a layer. You are first prompted to enter the color. Remember that for the seven standard colors, you can enter a number, the full color name, or just the first letter of the color name. You are then asked to name the layer(s) for the color assignment. In the example that follows, the color green is assigned to a layer called Cables.

  Color: **3** or **GREEN** or **G.⌐**
  Layer name(s) for color 3 (green)⟨current layer⟩: **CABLES.⌐**

AutoCAD LT—Fundamentals and Applications

- **Ltype.** Use this option to assign a linetype to a layer. The linetype must first be loaded into the drawing editor using the **LINETYPE** or **-LINETYPE** commands. You are prompted to enter the linetype and then asked to name the layer(s) for the linetype assignment. Use the **?** option to list the linetypes loaded in the current drawing. In the following example, the Center2 linetype is assigned to the Centerlines layer.

> Linetype (or ?) ⟨*current linetype*⟩: **CENTER2**↵
> Layer name(s) for linetype CENTER2 ⟨*current layer*⟩: **CENTERLINES**↵

- **Freeze.** This option is used to remove one or more layers from the screen display. Remember that you cannot freeze the current layer, however.

> Layer name(s) to Freeze: *(enter layer names separated by commas)*

- **Thaw.** Use this option to thaw one or more frozen layers. The **Thaw** option regenerates the drawing as the frozen layer(s) are restored to the display.

> Layer name(s) to Thaw: *(enter layer names separated by commas)*

- **Lock.** Use this option to lock one or more layers.

> Layer name(s) to Lock: *(enter layer names separated by commas)*

- **Unlock.** Use this option to unlock one or more locked layers.

> Layer name(s) to Unlock: *(enter layer names separated by commas)*

 NOTE   Unlike the **Layer & Linetype Properties** dialog box, using the **-LAYER** command on the command line does not allow you to rename or delete a layer.

Layer Creation Tutorial

To better understand the **-LAYER** command and its options, spend a few moments with the following tutorial.

- ➪ Start AutoCAD LT.
- ➪ Use the **LINETYPE** or **-LINETYPE** commands as described earlier in this chapter to load the Dashed and Center linetypes.
- ➪ Now, use the **-LAYER** command options listed below to create three layers called Object, Hidden, and Centerlines. You will then assign colors and linetypes to your newly created layers.

```
Command: -LAYER or -LA↵
?/Make/Set/New/ ON/OFF/Color/Ltype/Freeze/Thaw/LOck/Unlock: N↵
New layer name(s): OBJECT,HIDDEN,CENTERLINES↵
?/Make/Set/New/ ON/OFF/Color/Ltype/Freeze/Thaw/LOck/Unlock: C↵
Color: 4↵
Layer name(s) for color 4 (cyan)⟨current layer⟩: OBJECT ↵
?/Make/Set/New/ ON/OFF/Color/Ltype/Freeze/Thaw/LOck/Unlock: C↵
Color: 3↵
Layer name(s) for color 3 (green)⟨current layer⟩: HIDDEN↵
?/Make/Set/New/ ON/OFF/Color/Ltype/Freeze/Thaw/LOck/Unlock: L↵
Linetype (or ?) ⟨current linetype⟩: DASHED↵
Layer name(s) for linetype DASHED ⟨current layer⟩: HIDDEN↵
?/Make/Set/New/ ON/OFF/Color/Ltype/Freeze/Thaw/LOck/Unlock: C↵
Color: 2↵
Layer name(s) for color 2 (yellow) ⟨current layer⟩: CENTERLINES↵
?/Make/Set/New/ ON/OFF/Color/Ltype/Freeze/Thaw/LOck/Unlock: L↵
Linetype (or ?) ⟨current linetype⟩: CENTER↵
Layer name(s) for linetype CENTER ⟨current layer⟩: CENTERLINES↵
?/Make/Set/New/ ON/OFF/Color/Ltype/Freeze/Thaw/LOck/Unlock: ?↵
Layer name(s) to list ⟨*⟩: (press [Enter] to list all layers)
?/Make/Set/New/ ON/OFF/Color/Ltype/Freeze/Thaw/LOck/Unlock: S↵
New current layer ⟨current⟩: OBJECT↵
?/Make/Set/New/ ON/OFF/Color/Ltype/Freeze/Thaw/LOck/Unlock: ↵
Command:
```

↪ Draw several lines with the Object layer.
↪ Set the Hidden layer current and draw some more lines.
↪ Set the Centerlines layer current and draw a few more lines.
↪ Turn off the Object layer and then turn it back on.
↪ Try freezing the Centerlines layer. What happens?
↪ Freeze the Object layer and then thaw it.
↪ Lock the Hidden layer and try erasing several lines on that layer. What happens?
↪ It is not necessary to save the drawing when you are finished experimenting.

EXERCISE 5-4

❑ Begin a new drawing using your TEMPLATEA template file from *Chapter 3*.
❑ Load the Hidden, Center, and Phantom linetypes.
❑ Use the **Layer & Linetype Properties** dialog box to create the following layers. Assign the colors and linetypes shown.

Layer Name	Color	Linetype
Objects	White	Continuous
Hidden	Cyan	Hidden
Centerlines	Yellow	Center
Dimensions	Green	Continuous
Hatching	Magenta	Continuous
Notes	Red	Continuous
Cutplane	Blue	Phantom

❑ Set the **Objects** layer current before exiting the **Layer & Linetype Properties** dialog box.
❑ Save the revised drawing as template TEMPLATEA.DWT. It will be used for many of the subsequent drawing exercises and problems in this text.
❑ Begin a new drawing using your TEMPLATEB template from *Chapter 3* and repeat the procedure. Save the revised drawing as template TEMPLATEB.DWT.
❑ Begin a new drawing using your TEMPLATEC template from *Chapter 3* and repeat the procedure. Save the revised drawing as template TEMPLATEC.DWT.
❑ Exit AutoCAD LT.

Renaming Linetypes and Layers

Linetypes and layers may be renamed at any time with the **DDRENAME** command. Remember from *Chapter 4* that this command was used to rename objects, such as saved views, using a dialog box. To activate the **Rename** dialog box, enter DDRENAME, or REN, at the Command: prompt, or select **Rename...** from the **Format** pull-down menu.

DDRENAME
REN

Format
➡ Rename...

The **Named Objects** list appears at the left of the dialog box. This list contains the types of objects that may be named or renamed in AutoCAD LT. Observe in **Figure 5-35A** that Ltype has been selected from the list at the left. A listing of all the linetypes loaded in the current drawing appears at the right of the dialog box. To rename the Center linetype, first select the linetype name from the list. The name of the linetype you select is then displayed in the **Old Name:** text box. With your pointing device, click anywhere inside the **Rename To:** text box and enter the new linetype name. In the example, the Center linetype is renamed to Centerline. When you are done typing, click the **Rename To:** button and the new linetype name appears in the list at the right of the dialog box. When you are finished renaming objects, click the **OK** button to exit the **Rename** dialog box.

A similar procedure is performed with layers in **Figure 5-35B**. In this example, the Part layer is renamed to Object.

Figure 5-35.
A—Renaming a linetype using the **Rename** dialog box. B—Renaming a layer using the **Rename** dialog box.

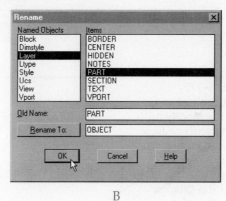

A   B

Renaming Linetypes and Layers at the **Command:** prompt

It is also possible to rename objects at the Command: prompt instead of using a dialog box. In the following example, the **RENAME** command is used to perform the linetype renaming operation described in the previous section.

RENAME
-REN

```
Command: RENAME or -REN.↵
Block/Dimstyle/LAyer/LType/Style/Ucs/VIew/VPort: LT.↵
Old linetype name: CENTER.↵
New linetype name: CENTERLINE.↵
Command:
```

NOTE   Layer 0 and the Continuous linetype *cannot* be renamed and therefore do not appear in the **Rename** dialog box list of named objects.

Changing Object Properties

DDCHPROP
CH

Modify
➥ **P**roperties...

Object Properties
toolbar

Properties

Color, linetype, layer, and linetype scale are considered properties of objects. It is a simple matter to change the properties of existing objects using the **Change Properties** dialog box shown in **Figure 5-36.** To access this dialog box, enter DDCHPROP, or CH, at the Command: prompt, select **P**roperties... from the **Modify** pull-down menu, or click the **Properties** button on the **Object Properties** toolbar. See **Figure 5-37.** The command procedure looks like this:

> Command: **DDCHPROP** *or* **CH**↵
> Select objects: *(select one or more objects)*
> Select objects: ↵

All of the selection set options described in *Chapter 2,* (window, crossing, fence, etc.) are valid at the Select objects: prompt. Select the object(s) whose properties you wish to change, press [Enter], and you are then presented with the **Change Properties** dialog box.

Figure 5-36.
The **Change Properties** dialog box.

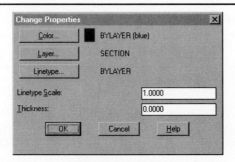

Figure 5-37.
Select **P**roperties... from the **Modify** pull-down menu or click the **Properties** button on the **Object Properties** toolbar to access the **Change Properties** dialog box.

The **Change Properties** Dialog Box

This dialog box displays the current color, layer, and linetype of the object you selected. If you select several objects with different values for the property you wish to change, AutoCAD LT displays the word "varies" as the current value. Each of the components of this dialog box are described as follows:

- **Color....** To change the color of an existing object, click this button to display the **Select Color** subdialog box. Select one of 255 available colors and click **OK**.

- **Layer....** Click this button to display the **Select Layer** subdialog box shown in **Figure 5-38.** To move the selected object to a different layer, select the desired layer from the list or enter the layer name in the **Set Layer Name:** text box. When you are finished, click the **OK** button to exit the subdialog box. Remember that an object placed on a different layer inherits the color and linetype properties of that layer.
- **Linetype....** To change the linetype of an existing object, click this button to display the **Select Linetype** subdialog box. See **Figure 5-39.** Select one of the loaded linetypes from the list or enter the linetype name in the **Linetype:** text box. Click the **OK** button to exit the subdialog box when you are finished.
- **Linetype Scale:.** Use this text box to modify the linetype scale for existing objects. A value greater than one increases the spacing between dashes and dots—a value less than one decreases the spacing.
- **Thickness:.** Thickness is a property of three-dimensional objects. It determines the height of an object above or below the zero elevation plane. See *Chapter 19* of this text for more information on thickness.

When you are finished changing object properties, click the **OK** button to exit the **Change Properties** dialog box. The object(s) you selected are immediately displayed with the new properties.

Figure 5-38.
The **Select Layer** subdialog box is used to move one or more objects to a different layer.

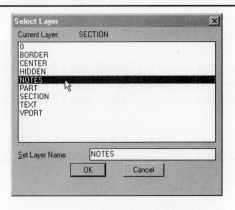

Figure 5-39.
The **Select Linetype** subdialog box is used to change the linetype of one or more objects.

 NOTE   If you select **Properties...** from the **Modify** pull-down menu or click the **Properties** button on the **Object Properties** toolbar and select only *one* object to change, the **DDMODIFY** command is used instead of **DDCHPROP**. **DDMODIFY** displays a dialog box appropriate for the type of drawing object selected. As shown in **Figure 5-40,** the top section of this dialog box may also be used to edit the properties of objects. The **DDMODIFY** command is described fully in *Chapter 10.*

Figure 5-40.
The **DDMODIFY** command displays a dialog box specific to the type of object selected. Properties may also be modified using this dialog box.

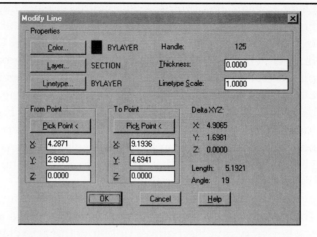

Changing Object Properties at the Command: Prompt

Object properties can also be changed by using the **CHPROP** command at the Command: prompt. In the following example, one or more objects on the Text layer is selected and moved to the Notes layer.

> Command: **CHPROP**↵
> Select objects: *(select one or more objects)*
> Select objects: ↵
> Change what property (Color/LAyer/LType/ltScale/Thickness)? **LA**↵
> New layer ⟨TEXT⟩: **NOTES**↵
> Change what property (Color/LAyer/LType/ltScale/Thickness)? ↵
> Command:

If you select a single object, AutoCAD LT displays the current value of the property in the ⟨⟩ brackets. If you select several objects with different values for the property you wish to change, AutoCAD LT displays ⟨*varies*⟩ as the current value.

Using Property Painter

PAINTER

Standard
Toolbar

Properties

The **Property Painter** is a powerful feature that quickly copies properties of one object to other objects. The properties you can copy include color, layer, linetype, linetype scale factor, and thickness. To use **Property Painter**, enter PAINTER, at the Command: prompt, or click the **Property Painter** button on the **Standard Toolbar**. The command sequence looks like this:

> Command: **PAINTER**↵
> Select Source Object: *(select a single object to be used as the source of properties to be copied)*
> Current active settings = color layer ltype ltscale thickness text dim hatch
> Settings/⟨Select Destination Object(s)⟩: *(select an object to inherit the copied properties)*
> Settings/⟨Select Destination Object(s)⟩: *(select another object or press* [Enter] *to end the command)*
> Command:

You can select the objects to be modified using any of the selection set methods. After making your selection(s), press [Enter] to terminate the command and effect the changes.

Changing the Property Painter Settings

Note from the command syntax shown in the previous section that after selecting a single source object to be copied, AutoCAD LT displays the current active settings, or properties, that will be copied to the destination objects you select. As you can see, color, layer, linetype, linetype scale, and thickness are all copied. In some cases, text, dimension and hatch properties are also copied.

If you wish to change the type of properties to be copied, use the **Settings** option as follows:

Settings/⟨Select Destination Object(s)⟩: **S**↵

The **Property Settings** dialog box is displayed. See **Figure 5-41.** Each of the properties denoted by active check boxes are copied to the destination objects you select. Deactivate the appropriate check box for any property you do not wish to copy and click the **OK** button to exit the dialog box. The command line then displays the new active settings and you are prompted to select the destination object(s) as just described.

Figure 5-41.
The **Property Settings** dialog box is used to set the types of properties to be copied to selected destination objects.

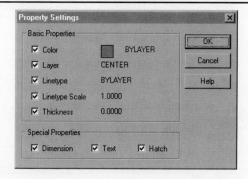

Editing Properties Using the Object Properties Toolbar

As you have learned in this chapter, the **Layer Control**, **Color Control**, and **Linetype Control** drop-down lists on the **Object Properties** toolbar display the current system settings for all newly created objects. However, these drop-down lists can also be used to modify the properties of existing objects.

Consider the example illustrated in **Figure 5-42A**. Observe from the **Object Properties** toolbar that Section is the current layer name. Both color and linetype are set to the default ByLayer mode. Note also that the circle that appears on screen has been drawn with a Hidden linetype.

In **Figure 5-42B**, the circle has been selected with the pointing device and appears highlighted in the drawing window. (The small squares that appear on the circle are called *grips* and are covered in *Chapter 10* of this text.) The **Object Properties** toolbar reports that the selected circle resides on the Hidden layer. To move the circle to a different layer, simply select the desired layer from the **Layer Control** drop-down list. As shown in **Figure 5-42C**, the circle is moved to the Part layer. After changing the objects' layer (or color, or linetype) using this method, press the [Esc] key twice to turn off the displayed grips and remove the highlighting from the select object.

Figure 5-42.
A—The drop-down lists on the **Object Properties** toolbar report the current layer, color, and linetype settings. B—The **Layer Control** drop-down list reports the layer name of the selected circle. C—Selecting a different layer from the **Layer Control** drop-down list moves the circle to the new layer.

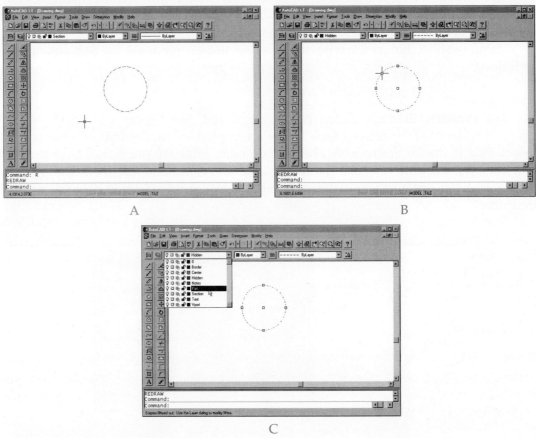

A   B

C

EXERCISE 5-5

❑ Open EX5-2 from earlier in the chapter.
❑ Use the **DDCHPROP** command or the **Properties** button to change the hidden lines from red to yellow.
❑ Repeat the procedure and change the centerline from blue to green.
❑ Try using the **Property Painter** on several of the lines in the drawing.
❑ Finally, try modifying both color and linetype properties using the **Object Properties** toolbar as described in the previous section.
❑ When you are through experimenting, save the drawing as EX5-5.

Restoring Bylayer Mode

You have learned in this chapter that color, linetype, and linetype scale may be explicitly set before drawing any new objects. However, the preferred method is to assign colors and linetypes to layers. This method ensures that drawing objects inherit the color and linetype properties of the layers they are on. AutoCAD LT refers to this convention as *bylayer mode*.

When you explicitly set a different color or linetype current using the **DDCOLOR**, **COLOR**, **DDLTYPE**, or **-LINETYPE** commands, you override bylayer mode. This can be a major source of frustration, because everything drawn will appear in one color, or one linetype, regardless of your layer assignments. Should you experience this problem with colors, use the **COLOR** command as follows:

        Command: **COLOR**↵
        New object color ⟨*current*⟩: **BYLAYER**↵
        Command:

For linetypes, use the **-LINETYPE** command as follows:

        Command: **-LINETYPE**↵
        ?/Create/Load/Set: **S**↵
        New object linetype (or ?) ⟨*current*⟩: **BYLAYER**↵
        ?/Create/Load/Set: ↵
        Command:

It is also possible to restore bylayer mode using the **DDCOLOR** command. Simply click the **BYLAYER** button in the **Logical Colors** section of the **Select Color** dialog box. For linetypes, use **DDLTYPE** and select the linetype labeled ByLayer at the top of the **Layer & Linetype Properties** dialog box. For any existing objects drawn with explicit color or linetype set, use **DDCHPROP** (or **CHPROP**) and change the properties to BYLAYER.

Purging Unused Objects

Unused linetypes and layers can be removed from your drawing at any time during a drawing session with the **PURGE** command. Other named objects that can be purged include blocks, dimension styles, and text styles. These types of objects are explored fully as they are encountered in this text.

Purging in AutoCAD LT 98

In AutoCAD LT 98, purging can be performed using a dialog box. To open the **PURGE** dialog box, enter PURGE, or PU, at the Command: prompt, or select **Purge...** from the **Drawing Utilities** ⟩ cascading submenu found in the **File** pull-down menu. See **Figure 5-43**. The **PURGE** dialog box then appears as shown in **Figure 5-44**.

The two option buttons at the top of the dialog box let you view named objects that can or cannot be purged from your drawing. Remember that you cannot purge any object that is currently used in the drawing. In the example shown in **Figure 5-44**, the Layers tree

Getting Started Guide 5

PURGE
PU

File
➥ Drawing Utilities ⟩
➥ Purge

Figure 5-43.
In AutoCAD LT 98, select **Purge...** in the **Drawing Utilities** cascading menu of the **File** pull-down menu to display the **Purge** dialog box.

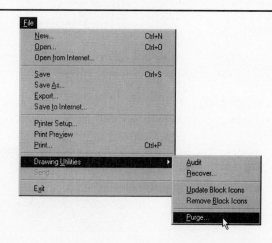

Figure 5-44.
The **Purge** dialog box uses an expandable tree structure to display named objects that can or cannot be purged from the current drawing. In this example, the HIDDEN layer is selected for purging.

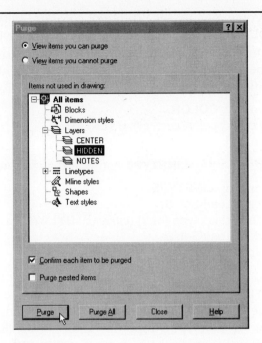

has been expanded to show that the CENTER, HIDDEN, and NOTES layers are unused and may be purged. The HIDDEN layer has been selected and the **Purge** button at the bottom left of the dialog box is clicked. AutoCAD LT 98 then displays the alert box shown in **Figure 5-45.** Click Yes or No as appropriate to confirm the purge operation.

Items that cannot be purged are shown in **Figure 5-46.** In this example, the CENTER linetype has been selected. Observe the message at the bottom of the dialog box notifying the user why this named object cannot be purged.

Figure 5-45.
AutoCAD LT 98 displays the **Confirm Purge** alert box when an object is selected for purging.

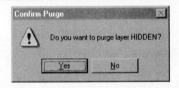

Figure 5-46.
The **Purge** dialog box displays a message at the bottom of the dialog box explaining why a selected object cannot be purged.

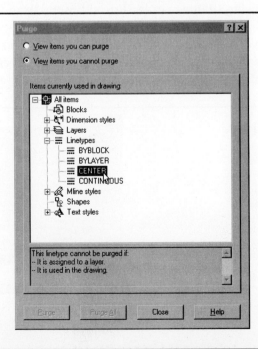

Purging can also be performed on the command line by entering -PURGE, or -PU, at the **Command: prompt.** The procedure for doing so is identical to that described for purging on the command line when using AutoCAD LT 97. That procedure is described in the next section.

NOTE   AutoCAD LT 98 lists **Mline** styles as valid objects for purging. This is an error in the program. **Mline** styles are available in AutoCAD only—not AutoCAD LT.

Purging in AutoCAD LT 97

To purge unused linetypes and/or layers in AutoCAD LT 97, enter PURGE, or PU, at the Command: prompt, or select **Purge** 〉 from the **Drawing Utilities** 〉 cascading submenu found in the **File** pull-down menu. This menu item displays the cascading submenu shown in **Figure 5-47.** The command sequence is as follows:

Command: **PURGE** *or* **PU**↵
Purge unused Blocks/Dimstyles/LAyers/LTypes/Styles/All:

Select an object type to purge, or enter A to purge all named object types from the drawing. Before each item is purged, you are first asked to confirm the operation. Respond with a Y for yes or N for no as required.

Keep in mind that the **PURGE** command removes only one level of reference. It may be necessary to repeat **PURGE** until there are no unreferenced objects remaining in the drawing. Remember that you can use **PURGE** at anytime during a drawing session.

Figure 5-47.
In AutoCAD LT 97, select **Purge** 〉 from the **Drawing Utilities** 〉 cascading submenu found in the **File** pull-down menu to display the purging options.

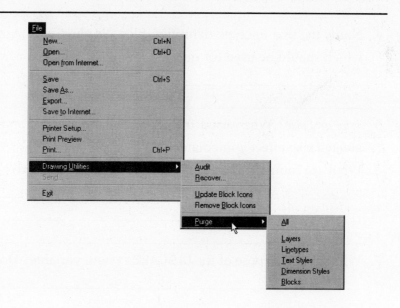

PROFESSIONAL TIP   To avoid losing linetypes or layers that may still be needed, wait until your drawing is finished before using the **PURGE** command.

Chapter 5 Colors, Linetypes, and Layers

EXERCISE 5-6

❏ Begin a new drawing using your TEMPLATEA template. If you have not yet revised this template file as described in Exercise 5-4, do so now.
❏ Draw some lines on both the OBJECT and HIDDEN layers.
❏ Purge the remaining layers and linetypes from the drawing.
❏ Save the drawing as EX5-6.

Chapter Test

Write your answers in the spaces provided.

1. List the seven standard colors and their respective color numbers. What is the maximum number of colors available in AutoCAD LT? _____

   _____

   _____

   _____

   _____

2. You wish to load several linetypes. Identify the keyboard commands used to access the **Layer & Linetype Properties** dialog box for this purpose. _____

   _____

3. *True or False?* A linetype must first be loaded before it can be assigned to a new layer using the **Layer & Linetype Properties** dialog box. _____

   _____

4. Name the two linetype definition files supplied with AutoCAD LT. Of the two, which should be used for metric drawings?

   _____

   _____

5. *True or False?* When used transparently, the **COLOR** and **LINETYPE** commands always take effect immediately. _____

6. What are complex linetypes? Why would they be used? _____

   _____

   _____

   _____

7. What is the purpose of the **LTSCALE** system variable? How is it used?

   _____

   _____

   _____

8. Give the command and entries needed to make the Phantom linetype current.

Command: _____

?/Create/Load/Set: _____

New object linetype (or ?) ⟨*current*⟩: _____

?/Create/Load/Set: _____

Command: _____

9. What is the purpose of A-type alignment? _____

_____

_____

10. You wish to create several new layers. Identify the keyboard commands to access the **Layer & Linetype Properties** dialog box for this purpose. _____

_____

11. *True or False?* It is possible to turn off the current layer. _____

12. Which **LAYER** command option should be used to remove a layer from the display and ensure that it does not redraw or regenerate?

_____

13. How do you obtain an expanded version of the **Layer & Linetype Properties** dialog box? _____

_____

_____

14. *True or False?* Layers that are turned off do not redraw or regenerate. _____

15. What is the purpose of the **LAYER** command **Lock** option? Is a locked layer visible?

_____

_____

_____

16. Identify two ways to rename a layer. _____

_____

_____

17. Identify five ways to make a layer current. _____

_____

_____

_____

_____

_____

18. *True or False?* Layer filters can be used to limit the number of layers displayed on screen._____

19. Identify two commands used to change the properties of existing objects._____

_____

_____

20. Everything you draw is displayed green, regardless of the layer you are drawing on. Yet, each layer is assigned a different color. What is the problem, and how can it be fixed?

_____

_____

21. Your lines are all displayed as phantom lines, but you are drawing on different layers and each layer has a different assigned linetype. What is wrong, and what must be done to fix it?

_____

_____

22. *True or False?* The **PURGE** command can be used at anytime during a drawing session. _____

23. Why is it a good idea to wait until a drawing is complete before issuing the **PURGE** command? _____

_____

_____

24. Identify two ways to remove an unwanted layer from your drawing. _____

_____

_____

Chapter Problems

Mechanical Drafting

1. Use your TEMPLATEB template to draw the object shown. Draw all three views. Place object lines on the Objects layer, hidden lines on the Hidden layer, and centerlines on the Centerlines layer. Do not draw the dimensions. Save the drawing as P5-1.

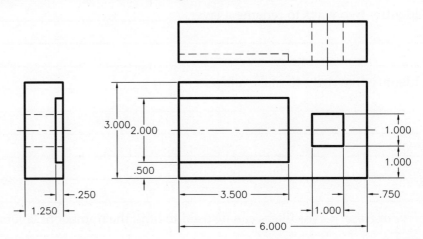

2. Use your **TEMPLATEB** template to draw the object shown. Draw all three views. As with P5-1, place object lines on the Objects layer, hidden lines on the Hidden layer, and centerlines on the Centerlines layer. Do not draw the dimensions. Save the drawing as P5-2.

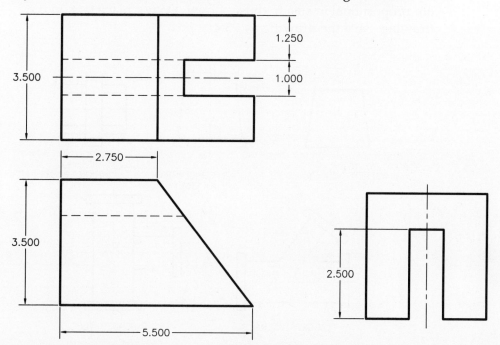

3. Use your **TEMPLATEA** template to draw the object shown. Draw both views. As with the previous two drawing problems, place object lines on the Objects layer, hidden lines on the Hidden layer, and centerlines on the Centerlines layer. Do not draw the dimensions. Save the drawing as P5-3.

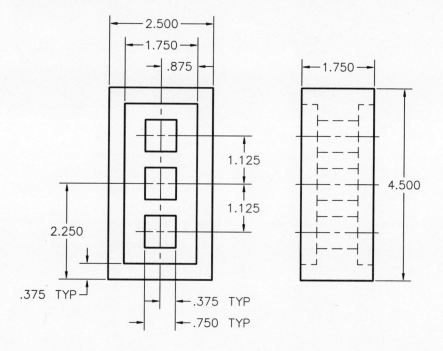

Chapter 5 Colors, Linetypes, and Layers

4. Begin a new drawing without one of your templates. Create two layers named Pipe and Centerlines. Make the Pipe layer cyan and the Centerlines layer green. Assign the Center2 linetype to the Centerlines layer. Using the correct layers, draw the piping symbols so that they are proportional in size to those shown. Do not place text on the drawing. Save the drawing as P5-4.

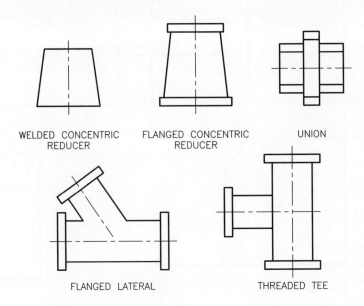

WELDED CONCENTRIC
REDUCER

FLANGED CONCENTRIC
REDUCER

UNION

FLANGED LATERAL

THREADED TEE

Chapter 6

Drawing Commands

AutoCAD LT

Learning Objectives

After you have completed this chapter, you will be able to:
- O Draw curved objects using the **CIRCLE**, **ARC**, **ELLIPSE**, **SPLINE**, and **DONUT** commands.
- O Create double lines and double arcs with **DLINE**.
- O Construct multisided shapes using the **PLINE**, **RECTANG**, and **POLYGON** commands.
- O Explode multisided shapes into individual line segments.
- O Create chamfers and angled corners with the **CHAMFER** command.
- O Draw fillets and rounded corners using the **FILLET** command.
- O Highlight marked-up areas using revision clouds.
- O Construct region objects and perform Boolean operations.

Previous chapters discussed how to set up and save drawings, as well as how to draw and erase lines. You have also learned how to zoom and pan the drawing window using a variety of display control options. In addition, you now have the ability to assign colors and linetypes to layers to help manage drawing elements. It is now time to explore several other AutoCAD LT drawing commands at your disposal to create a wide variety of geometric shapes.

Drawing Circles

The **CIRCLE** command is accessed by entering CIRCLE, or C, at the Command: prompt, or issued by clicking the **Circle** button in the **Draw** toolbar. Selecting **Circle** 〉 from the **Draw** pull-down menu displays a cascading submenu of circle construction options. See **Figure 6-1.**

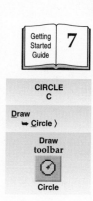

Getting Started Guide 7

CIRCLE
C

Draw
↳ Circle 〉

Draw toolbar

Circle

Figure 6-1.
Select **Circle** 〉 from
the **Draw** pull-down
menu to display a
cascading submenu
of options.

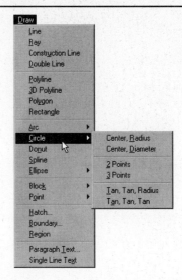

Drawing a Circle Using a Radius

The default method for creating a circle involves locating a point for the circle center, and then providing a radius value as illustrated in **Figure 6-2.** The **CIRCLE** command sequence is as follows:

Command: **CIRCLE** *or* **C**↵
3P/2P/TTR/⟨Center point⟩: *(pick a point for the circle center)*
Diameter/⟨Radius⟩: *(enter a positive radius value and press* [Enter]*)*
Command:

Figure 6-2. First,
locate a point for the
circle center. Next,
enter a radius value
or drag to a point and
pick to set the size.

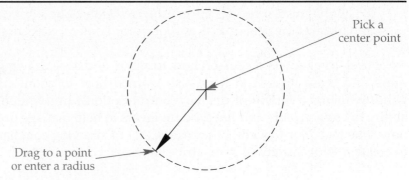

Pick a
center point

Drag to a point
or enter a radius

Drawing a Circle Using a Diameter

If you prefer, you can specify a circle by its diameter. The command sequence is as follows:

Command: **CIRCLE** *or* **C**↵
3P/2P/TTR/⟨Center point⟩: *(pick a point for the circle center)*
Diameter/⟨Radius⟩: *(type* D, *for diameter, and press* [Enter]*)*
Diameter: *(enter a positive diameter value)*
Command:

PROFESSIONAL TIP  Use the **Diameter** option instead of the **Radius** option when you need to draw a circle with a diameter not easily divisible by two.

Drawing a Circle through 3 Points

A circle may also be created by locating three points in the drawing window. The three points define the circumference of the circle as shown in **Figure 6-3.**

Draw
➥ Circle)
➥ 3 Points

> Command: **CIRCLE** *or* **C.**↵
> 3P/2P/TTR/⟨Center point⟩: **3P**
> First point: *(locate point 1 or enter a coordinate value)*
> Second point: *(locate point 2 or enter a coordinate value)*
> Third point: *(locate point 3 or enter a coordinate value)*
> Command:

Figure 6-3. Defining the circumference of a circle through three points.

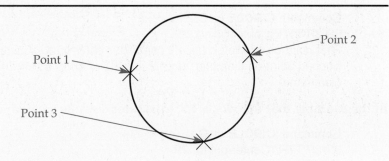

Drawing a Circle Tangent to Two Objects

A circle can also be drawn tangent to two existing objects by selecting the desired points of tangency and providing a radius value for the new circle. See **Figure 6-4.** The circle is drawn with its tangent points closest to the points you select on the existing objects. AutoCAD LT calls this the **TTR** (tangent, tangent, radius) method.

Draw
➥ Circle)
➥ Tan, Tan
    Radius

> Command: **CIRCLE** *or* **C.**↵
> 3P/2P/TTR/⟨Center point⟩: **TTR** *or* **T.**↵
> Enter Tangent spec: *(pick first object)*
> Enter second Tangent spec: *(pick second object)*
> Radius ⟨current⟩: *(enter a positive radius value)*
> Command:

Figure 6-4. The **TTR** option creates a circle tangent to two other objects.

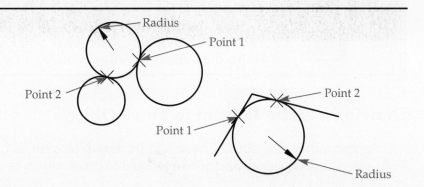

Additional CIRCLE Command Options

Two additional circle construction options have been added to AutoCAD LT 98 that now provide the same **CIRCLE** command functionality as "big brother" AutoCAD. These two additional circle construction options are not available in AutoCAD LT 97. The two new options are described in the following two sections.

Drawing a Circle through 2 Points

A circle may now be created by locating two points in the drawing window. The two points define the diameter endpoints of the circle as shown in **Figure 6-5.**

Draw
➡ Circle ⟩
  ➡ 2 points

Command: **CIRCLE** *or* **C.**↵
3P/2P/TTR/⟨Center point⟩: **2P**↵
First point on diameter: *(locate point 1 or enter a coordinate value)*
Second point on diameter: *(locate point 2 or enter a coordinate value)*
Command:

In the example that follows, a 1.75 diameter circle is created using the **2P** method.

Command: **CIRCLE** *or* **C.**↵
3P/2P/TTR/⟨Center point⟩: **2P**
First point on diameter: *(locate point 1 or enter a coordinate value)*
Second point on diameter: **@1.75⟨0** *or* **@1.75,0.**↵
Command:

Figure 6-5. Defining the diameter of a circle using two points.

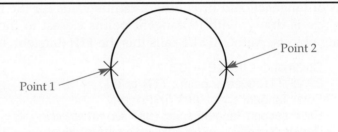

Point 2

Point 1

> **PROFESSIONAL TIP**
>
> Like the **Diameter** option, the **2P** option can also be used instead of the **Radius** option when you need to draw a circle with a diameter not easily divisible by two.

Drawing a Circle Tangent to Three Objects

As previously described, a circle can be drawn tangent to two objects using the **TTR** option. A circle can also be drawn tangent to three objects by selecting the desired points of tangency on the three objects. See **Figure 6-6.** The circle is drawn with its tangent points closest to the points you select on the existing objects. To use this method, you must select **Tan, Tan, Tan** from the **Circle** ⟩ cascading submenu because there is no corresponding tool button. After making your menu selection, the command prompts appear as follows in the command window:

Draw
➡ Circle ⟩
  ➡ Tan, Tan, Tan

Command: _circle 3P/2P/TTR/⟨Center point⟩:_3p First point: _tan to *(pick first object)*
Second point: _tan to *(pick second object)*
Third point: _tan to *(pick third object)*
Command:

Figure 6-6. Selected from the **Circle** ⟩ cascading submenu, the **Tan, Tan, Tan** option creates a circle tangent to three other objects.

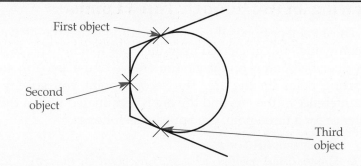

First object

Second object

Third object

From the messages shown on the previous page, you can see that this method invokes the **3P** circle construction option. To ensure the proper tangencies, AutoCAD LT 98 automatically uses a *Deferred tangent object snap*. Object snaps are described fully in *Chapter 7* of this text.

EXERCISE 6-1

❑ Begin a new drawing with your **TEMPLATEA** template, or use your own variables.
❑ Draw a circle with a .75 radius. Draw a second circle with a 1.5625 diameter. Remember to always enter decimal values in full—do not round-off.
❑ Draw several circles through 3 points.
❑ Finally, duplicate the objects illustrated in Figure 6-4. Specify any radius values you like.
❑ If you are using AutoCAD LT 98, draw the objects shown in **Figures 6-5** and **6-6.**
❑ Save the drawing as EX6-1 and quit.

Drawing Arcs

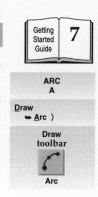

AutoCAD LT offers a variety of ways to draw arcs. An arc can be constructed by locating three points, or specified by its included angle, which is the angle formed between an arc's center, starting point, and ending point. By default, arcs are drawn in a counterclockwise direction. The **ARC** command is accessed by entering ARC, or A, at the Command: prompt, or issued by clicking the **Arc** button in the **Draw** toolbar. Selecting **Arc** from the **Draw** pull-down menu displays a cascading submenu of arc construction options. See **Figure 6-7.**

Figure 6-7. Select **Arc** ⟩ from the **Draw** pull-down menu to display a cascading submenu of options.

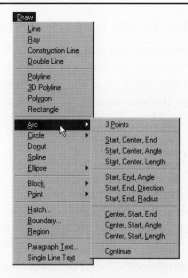

Drawing an Arc through Three Points

Draw
↦ Arc ⟩
↦ 3 Points

The **3 Point** option is the default method when the **ARC** command is issued from the command line or selected from the **Draw** toolbar. This method draws an arc using three specified points on the circumference of the arc. You are first prompted to pick a starting point for the arc. The second point you specify locates a point on the circumference of the arc, and the arc is terminated with a third point. The command sequence for a three-point arc appears as follows:

```
Command: ARC or A↵
Center ⟨Start point⟩: (pick a starting point for the arc)
Center/End/⟨Second point⟩: (pick a second point for the arc)
End point: (pick the arc's endpoint)
Command:
```

Three-point arcs can be drawn clockwise or counterclockwise, depending on the direction of the pick points. A counterclockwise arc is illustrated in **Figure 6-8A.**

Drawing an Arc with Start, Center, and End Points

Draw
↦ Arc ⟩
↦ Start,
Center,
End

There are several other ways to construct arcs with three points. If you know the starting point, center point, and ending point for an arc, select **Start, Center, End** from the **Arc** cascading submenu. An arc drawn using start, center, and ending points is shown in **Figure 6-8B.** The command sequence for this option is as follows:

```
Command: ARC or A↵
Center ⟨Start point⟩: (pick a starting point for the arc)
Center/End/⟨Second point⟩: C↵
Center: (pick a center point for the arc)
Angle/Length of chord/⟨End point⟩: (pick the arc's endpoint)
Command:
```

Drawing an Arc at Its Center Point

Draw
↦ Arc ⟩
↦ Center,
Start,
End

Alternatively, you can start the arc at its center point using the **Center, Start, End** option. The command sequence is as follows:

```
Command: ARC or A↵
Center ⟨Start point⟩: C↵
Center: (pick a center point for the arc)
Start point: (pick a starting point for the arc)
Angle/Length of chord/⟨End point⟩: (pick the arc's endpoint)
Command:
```

Drawing an Arc by Its Included Angle

Draw
↦ Arc ⟩
↦ Start,
Center,
Angle

As stated previously, the angle formed between an arc's center, starting, and ending points is called the *included angle*. When you know the included angle for an arc, you can construct it using a starting point and a center point by selecting **Start, Center, Angle** from the **Arc** cascading submenu. The following command sequence creates an arc with a 45° included angle:

```
Command: ARC or A↵
Center ⟨Start point⟩: (pick a starting point for the arc)
Center/End/⟨Second point⟩: C↵
Center: (pick a center point for the arc)
Angle/Length of chord/⟨End point⟩: A↵
Included angle: 45↵
Command:
```

The **Start, Center, Angle** option can be used to draw the 45° arc shown in **Figure 6-8C.**

Drawing an Arc Using Its Center Point, Start Point, and Included Angle

Draw
➥ Arc 〉
➥ Center, Start, Angle

The **Center, Start, Angle** option allows you to specify the center point first and then the starting point. The command sequence for a 45° arc appears as follows:

> Command: **ARC** *or* **A⏎**
> Center 〈Start point〉: **C**
> Center: *(pick a center point for the arc)*
> Start point: *(pick a starting point for the arc)*
> Angle/Length of chord/〈End point〉: **A⏎**
> Included angle: **45⏎**
> Command:

The **Center, Start, Angle** option can also be used to draw the 45° arc shown in **Figure 6-8C**.

Drawing an Arc Using Its Start Point, End Point, and Included Angle

Draw
➥ Arc 〉
➥ Start, End, Angle

When you know the included angle and you have a starting and ending point for the arc, (but not a center point), select the **Start, End, Angle** option in the **Arc** cascading submenu. The 60° arc shown in **Figure 6-8D** is drawn using the following command sequence:

> Command: **ARC** *or* **A⏎**
> Center 〈Start point〉: *(pick a starting point for the arc)*
> Center/End/〈Second point〉: **E⏎**
> End point: *(pick an endpoint for the arc)*
> Angle/Direction/Radius/〈Center point〉: **A⏎**
> Included angle: **60⏎**
> Command:

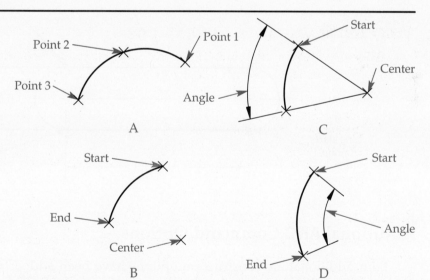

Figure 6-8.
Arcs may be constructed in several ways. A—An arc drawn with the default **3 Point** option. B—An arc drawn by locating center, start, and end points. C—An arc drawn with start and center points and an included angle. D—An arc drawn with start and end points and an included angle.

Using the ARC Continuation Option

In *Chapter 3* you learned that AutoCAD LT provides a means of quickly attaching a new line to a previously drawn line segment using the continuation option. You may continue a new arc from a previous arc in a similar fashion. First, press [Enter] or the [Spacebar] to repeat the **ARC** command and when the Start point: prompt appears, simply press [Enter] or the [Spacebar] again. The new arc is automatically connected to the endpoint of the last arc or line drawn. It is also drawn tangent to the previous arc or line object. Once attached, you can continue to draw more arcs.

Draw
➥ Arc ⟩
　　Continuation

The **Continuation** option can also be used by selecting **C̲ontinue** from the **A̲rc** cascading submenu. For example, the **Continuation** option can be used to produce the fully-radiused slot illustrated in **Figure 6-9.** The command sequence for this object is as follows:

Command: **LINE** *or* **L.**↵
From point: *(pick the starting point P1)*
To point: **@3⟨0.**↵
To point: *(press [Enter] or the [Spacebar] to exit the LINE command)*
Command: **ARC** *or* **A.**↵
Center/Start point: *(press [Enter] or the [Spacebar] to place the starting point of the arc, point P2, at the end of the previous line)*
End point: **@1⟨90.**↵
Command: **LINE** *or* **L.**↵
From point: *(press [Enter] or the [Spacebar] to place the starting point of the line, point P3, at the end of the previous arc)*
Length of line: **3.**↵
To point: *(press [Enter] or the [Spacebar] to exit the LINE command)*
Command: **ARC** *or* **A.**↵
Center/⟨Start point⟩: *(press [Enter] or the [Spacebar] to place the starting point of the arc, point P4, at the end of the previous line)*
End point: **@1⟨270.**↵
Command:

Figure 6-9.
Fully radiused features such as this slot may be drawn quickly and easily using **LINE** and **ARC** command continuation options.

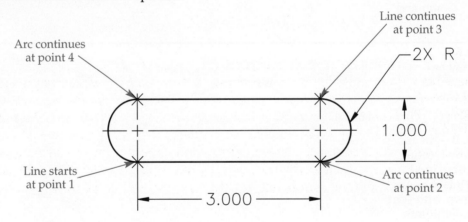

Additional ARC Command Options

Four additional arc construction options have been added to AutoCAD LT 98. These additional arc construction options are not available in AutoCAD LT 97. As with the new **CIRCLE** command options, these new **ARC** command options now provide AutoCAD LT 98 with the same arc construction functionality as "big brother" AutoCAD. There are now two ways to draw an arc when you know the arc's chord length. You can also draw an arc by locating a start point, and end point, and then "dragging" the arc in the desired direction. Finally, an arc can be created by locating its start point, end point, and specifying a radius. The four new options are described in the following sections.

Drawing an arc by the length of its chord

An arc can be defined by locating a starting point, a center point, and providing the chord length. An arc's *chord* is a line segment joining two points on the arc. The arc shown in **Figure 6-10** is drawn using the **Start, Center, Length** option from the **Arc ⟩** cascading submenu. The command sequence is as follows:

Draw
➥ Arc ⟩
    ➥ Start,
       Center,
       Length

> Command: **ARC** *or* **A**↵
> Center ⟨Start point⟩: *(pick a starting point for the arc)*
> Center/End/⟨Second point⟩: **C**
> Center: *(pick a center point for the arc)*
> Angle/Length of chord/⟨End point⟩: **L**↵
> Length of chord: **4**↵
> Command:

As an alternative method, you can first specify the center point and then the start point by selecting the **Center, Start, Length** option from the **Arc ⟩** cascading submenu.

Draw
➥ Arc ⟩
    ➥ Center,
       Start,
       Length

Figure 6-10.
An arc can be constructed by the length of its chord when you know the arc's start point and center point.

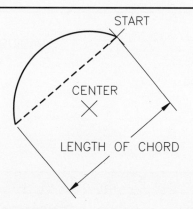

Drawing an arc by indicating its direction

An arc can also be defined by locating a start point, an end point, and then using your pointing device to dynamically "drag" the arc in the desired direction. Several examples of this type of arc are shown in **Figure 6-11.** At A and B in the illustration, the arc length can grow or shrink depending on the amount of cursor movement. At C, the arc length is constrained between the start and end points by turning **Ortho** mode on. To use the direction method, select **Start, End, Direction** from the **Arc ⟩** cascading submenu. On the command line, the sequence looks like this:

Draw
➥ Arc ⟩
    ➥ Start,End
       Direction

> Command: **ARC** *or* **A**↵
> Center ⟨Start point⟩: *(pick a starting point for the arc)*
> Center/End/⟨Second point⟩: **E**↵
> End point: *(pick an end point for the arc)*
> Angle/Direction/Radius/⟨Center point⟩: **D**↵
> Direction from start point: *(locate a point or enter a coordinate)*
> Command:

Figure 6-11.
Three examples of arcs created using the **Start, End, Direction** method.

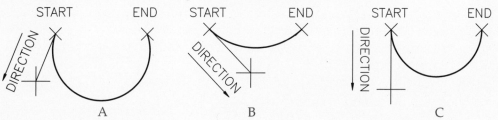

Drawing an arc by specifying its radius

Draw
→ Arc >
→ Start,End
Radius

You can also draw an arc by locating a start point, an end point, and then entering a specific radius value on the command line. An arc constructed using the **Start, End, Radius** method is shown in **Figure 6-12**. The command sequence looks like this:

> Command: **ARC** or **A**↵
> Center ⟨Start point⟩: (*pick a starting point for the arc*)
> Center/End/⟨Second point⟩: **E**↵
> End point: (*pick the arc's endpoint*)
> Angle/Direction/Radius/⟨Center point⟩: **R**↵
> Radius: (*enter a radius value*)
> Command:

Be sure to enter a radius value that is equal to or greater than the distance between the arc's start and end points. Otherwise, AutoCAD LT will display the *Invalid* message in the command window.

Figure 6-12.
After locating the start and end points, the **Start, End, Radius** method requires a radius value to complete the arc.

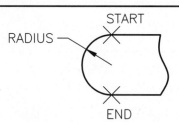

EXERCISE 6-2

❑ Begin a new drawing with your TEMPLATEA template, or use your own variables.
❑ Explore each of the **ARC** command options to construct arcs similar to those shown in **Figure 6-6**.
❑ Use the **Continuation** option to draw the fully-radiused slot shown in **Figure 6-7**. Do not include the dimensions.
❑ If you are using AutoCAD LT 98, draw the objects shown in **Figures 6-10, 6-11,** and **6-12**.
❑ Save the drawing as EX6-2 and quit.

Getting
Started
Guide   7

Drawing Ellipses

ELLIPSE
EL

Draw
→ Ellipse >

Draw
toolbar

Ellipse

When a circle is rotated from the line of sight, an ellipse is created. The longer axis of an ellipse is called the *major axis*, and the shorter axis is called the *minor axis*. In AutoCAD LT, you can draw an ellipse by locating axis endpoints or selecting a center point and a rotation angle. To issue the **ELLIPSE** command, enter ELLIPSE, or EL, at the Command: prompt, click the **Ellipse** button in the **Draw** toolbar, or select **Ellipse** from the **Draw** pull-down menu. See **Figure 6-13**.

Figure 6-13.
Select **Ellipse** ⟩ from the **Draw** pull-down menu to display a cascading submenu of options.

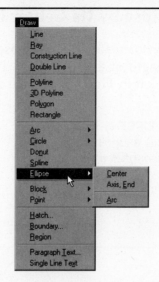

Drawing an Ellipse Using Axis Endpoints

At the keyboard, the default method for creating an ellipse requires that you select two axis endpoints, and then a third point to specify the other axis distance. See **Figure 6-14** and follow the **ELLIPSE** command sequence as follows:

> Command: **ELLIPSE** *or* **EL**↵
> Arc/Center/⟨Axis endpoint 1⟩: *(pick axis endpoint 1)*
> Axis endpoint 2: *(pick axis endpoint 2)*
> Other axis distance/Rotation: *(pick a third point)*
> Command:

Draw
↪ Ellipse ⟩
↪ Axis,End

Using the Rotation option

From **Figure 6-14**, you can see that the two axis endpoints can specify the major axis or minor axis depending on the point selected for the other axis distance. If you select the **Rotation** option after locating the two axis endpoints, AutoCAD LT then assumes that the two points define the major axis for the ellipse. You then provide the angle of the ellipse as it rotated from the line of sight. The **Rotation** option looks like this:

> Command: **ELLIPSE** *or* **EL**↵
> Arc/Center/⟨Axis endpoint 1⟩:*(pick axis endpoint 1)*
> Axis endpoint 2: *(pick axis endpoint 2)*
> Other axis distance/Rotation: **R**↵
> Rotation around major axis: **45**↵
> Command:

A rotation angle from 0° to 89.4° can be entered. However, an angle of 0 produces a circle. The greater the angle, the greater the degree of elongation along the major axis.

Figure 6-14.
An ellipse can be drawn by locating points that define the major and minor axes of the ellipse.

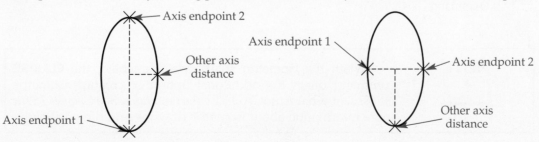

Drawing an Ellipse by Its Center Point

Draw
↪ Ellipse ⟩
   ↪ Center

It is also possible to create an ellipse based on a center point, an endpoint of one axis, and half the length of the other axis. This method is illustrated by the ellipse shown at the upper left in **Figure 6-15.** The command sequence for this ellipse is as follows:

Command: **ELLIPSE** *or* **EL.**↵
Arc/Center/⟨Axis endpoint 1⟩: **C**
Center of ellipse: *(pick a center point)*
Axis endpoint: *(pick a second point)*
⟨Other axis distance/Rotation⟩: *(pick a third point)*
Command:

Figure 6-15.
Ellipses may also be constructed by first locating their centers. At the upper left, three points define the ellipse center, half of its major axis, and half of its minor axis. At the bottom right, two points define the ellipse center and half the major axis. The rotation of the ellipse from the line of sight is specified using the **Rotation** option.

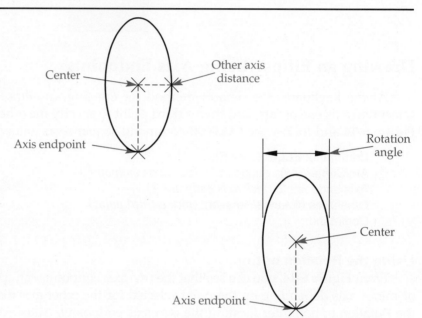

Using the Rotation option

Possibly the best method to use for ellipse construction is shown at the lower right in **Figure 6-15.** With this method, first select a point for the ellipse center, and then select a point that defines half of the length of the major axis. Next, use the **Rotation** option to specify the angle of the ellipse as it is rotated from the line of sight. The following command sequence draws a 60° ellipse with a diameter of 3.50 units.

Command: **ELLIPSE** *or* **EL.**↵
Arc/Center/⟨Axis endpoint 1⟩: **C.**↵
Center of ellipse: *(pick a center point)*
Axis endpoint: **@1.75⟨270** *or* **@0,-1.75.**↵
⟨Other axis distance⟩/Rotation: **R.**↵
Rotation around major axis: **60.**↵
Command:

NOTE

When the **Isometric snap** style is enabled, the **ELLIPSE** command offers the additional option of creating isometric ellipses, or what AutoCAD LT calls *isocircles*. See *Chapter 16* for more information about isometric drawing and dimensioning.

❏ Begin a new drawing with your TEMPLATEA template, or use your own variables.
❏ Use the axis endpoint or **Center** options to draw the ellipses shown at A.
❏ Draw the object illustrated at B using elliptical arcs with the dimensions shown. Use either the **Axis endpoint** or **Center** options to construct the arcs.

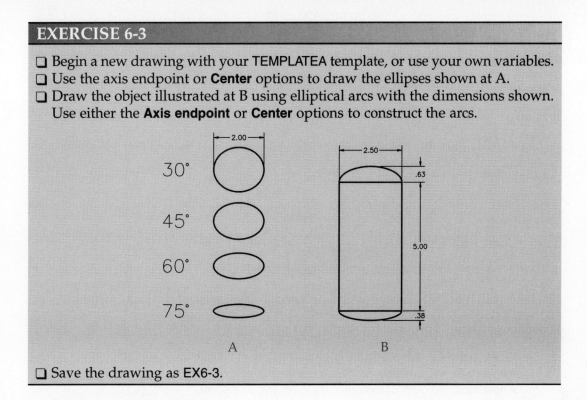

❏ Save the drawing as EX6-3.

Drawing Elliptical Arcs

It is sometimes necessary to construct an ellipse and then trim away a portion to obtain an elliptical arc. AutoCAD LT does this automatically using the **Arc** option of the **ELLIPSE** command. When you use the **Arc** option, you first draw an ellipse using normal construction techniques. That is, you may use axis endpoints or the **Center** option as described in the previous sections. You also define the other axis distance or use the **Rotation** option as you would normally to complete the ellipse as required. After the ellipse is drawn, you are then prompted for the portion of the ellipse to retain.

Drawing an elliptical arc using axis endpoints

As with full ellipses, the default method for creating an elliptical arc requires that you select two axis endpoints, and then a third point to specify the other axis distance. You may want to refer to **Figure 6-14** as you study the command sequence that follows:

Command: **ELLIPSE** *or* **EL**↵
Arc/Center/⟨Axis endpoint 1⟩: **A**↵
⟨Axis endpoint 1⟩/Center: *(pick axis endpoint 1)*
Axis endpoint 2: *(pick axis endpoint 2)*
⟨Other axis distance⟩/Rotation: *(pick a third point)*

You are now prompted to enter start and end angles. These angles determine the start and end location of the elliptical arc relative to the ellipse center. When the default axis endpoint method is used to construct an ellipse, then the angle of the arc is established from the angle of the first axis. The first axis endpoint is assumed to be 0°. This means that a start angle of 45° begins 45° counterclockwise from the first axis endpoint. End angles are also measured in a counterclockwise direction.

Parameter/⟨start angle⟩: *(enter a start angle)*
Parameter/Included/⟨end angle⟩: *(enter an end angle)*
Command:

Several elliptical arcs are shown in **Figure 6-16.** Observe how the start and end-points of the arc are relative to the first axis endpoint.

Figure 6-16.
Several elliptical arcs with varying start and end angles. Observe that the start angle is always located in a counterclockwise direction relative to the first axis endpoint.

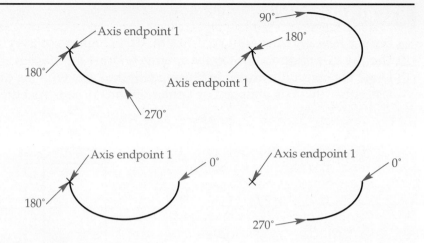

Using the Parameter option

As an alternative to entering start and end angles, you can dynamically pick start and end points with your pointing device using the **Parameter** option. The command sequence looks like this:

> Parameter/⟨start angle⟩: **P**↵
> Angle/⟨start parameter⟩: *(pick the arc start point)*
> Angle/Included/⟨end parameter⟩: *(pick the arc end point)*
> Command:

Drawing an elliptical arc by its included angle

The included angle of an elliptical arc is the angle formed between the start and end points of the arc with the center of the ellipse as the angle vertex. In the command sequence that follows, the start of the arc begins at 0° (axis endpoint 1) and ends at 45° in a counterclockwise direction.

> Command: **ELLIPSE** *or* **EL**↵
> Arc/Center/⟨Axis endpoint 1⟩: **A**↵
> ⟨Axis endpoint 1⟩/Center: *(pick axis endpoint 1)*
> Axis endpoint 2: *(pick axis endpoint 2)*
> ⟨Other axis distance⟩/Rotation: *(pick a third point)*
> Parameter/⟨start angle⟩: **0**↵
> Parameter/Included/⟨end angle⟩: **I**↵
> Included angle ⟨90⟩: **45**↵
> Command:

Remember that the start of the arc is always located in a counterclockwise angular direction from the first axis endpoint.

Defining an elliptical arc by its center

You can use the **Center** option to draw an elliptical arc in the same way that a full ellipse is defined by first locating its center as previously described. Refer to **Figure 6-15** as you study the following command sequence:

> Command: **ELLIPSE** *or* **EL**↵
> Arc/Center/⟨Axis endpoint 1⟩: **A**↵
> ⟨Axis endpoint 1⟩/Center: **C**↵
> Center of ellipse: *(pick a center point)*
> Axis endpoint: *(pick a second point)*
> ⟨Other axis distance⟩/Rotation: *(pick a third point)*
> Parameter/⟨start angle⟩: *(enter a start angle or P for Parameter)*
> Parameter/Included/⟨end angle⟩: *(enter an end angle or select an option)*
> Command:

Rotating an elliptical arc around its major axis

Use the **Rotation** option when you wish to rotate an elliptical arc around its major axis with a known rotation angle. This option is performed identically to that when rotating a full ellipse as previously explained and illustrated in **Figure 6-15.** The command sequence is as follows:

Command: **ELLIPSE** *or* **EL** ↵
Arc/Center/⟨Axis endpoint 1⟩: **A** ↵
⟨Axis endpoint 1⟩/Center: *(pick axis endpoint 1 or use the* **Center** *option)*
Axis endpoint 2: *(pick axis endpoint 2)*
⟨Other axis distance⟩/Rotation: **R** ↵
Rotation around major axis: *(enter a positive rotation angle)*
Parameter/⟨start angle⟩: *(enter a start angle or P for* Parameter*)*
Parameter/Included/⟨end angle⟩: *(enter an end angle or select an option)*
Command:

The PELLIPSE System Variable

The earliest versions of AutoCAD LT did not have NURBS functionality and therefore were unable to create true ellipses. (*NURBS* means Non-Uniform Rational B-Spline.) Instead, ellipses were defined using a polyline representation. (Polylines are described in a later section of this chapter.) You can control the type of ellipse created using the **PELLIPSE** system variable. To create a true ellipse, set **PELLIPSE** to 0. This is the default setting. If you wish to construct a polyline representation of an ellipse, set the variable to 1. The sequence looks like the following:

Command: **PELLIPSE** ↵
New value for PELLIPSE ⟨0⟩: *(enter 0 or 1 as desired)*
Command:

PROFESSIONAL TIP

True ellipses are easier to edit than polyline representations and take up less space in the AutoCAD LT database. Also, you cannot create elliptical arcs if **PELLIPSE** is equal to 1. Therefore, it is recommended that you leave **PELLIPSE** set to 0 unless you have a compelling reason to do otherwise.

EXERCISE 6-4

❑ Begin a new drawing with your TEMPLATEA template, or use your own variables.
❑ Draw the elliptical arcs shown in **Figure 6-16.**
❑ Save the drawing as EX6-4.

Drawing Splines

The **SPLINE** command is used to create wiring, cabling, and other types of curved objects. It may also be used to draw short break lines. As with true ellipses, AutoCAD LT constructs the spline as a *NURBS* curve. Thus, the spline created is considered to be a true spline.

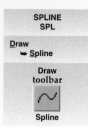

SPLINE
SPL

Draw
→ Spline

Draw
toolbar

Spline

Basically, a spline is drawn by first locating points in the display window. AutoCAD LT then fits the spline curve to the points. You can invoke the **SPLINE** command by selecting **Spline** from the **Draw** pull-down menu, clicking the **Spline** button in the **Draw** toolbar, or entering SPLINE, or SPL, at the Command: prompt. The command sequence for drawing the spline in **Figure 6-17** is as follows:

Command: **SPLINE** *or* **SPL**↵
Object/⟨Enter first point⟩: **3,3**↵
Enter point: **5,5**↵
Close/Fit Tolerance/⟨Enter point⟩: **7,3**↵
Close/Fit Tolerance/⟨Enter point⟩: **9,5**↵
Close/Fit Tolerance/⟨Enter point⟩: **11,3**↵
Close/Fit Tolerance/⟨Enter point⟩: ↵
Enter start tangent: ↵
Enter end tangent: ↵
Command:

Figure 6-17.
A spline is fit between points in the drawing window. The points may be dynamically entered using a pointing device or with coordinates.

NOTE   In the previous example, absolute coordinates are entered to locate the spline points. Points can also be dynamically located using your pointing device. If you locate a point incorrectly, enter U from the keyboard to undo the point. If you are using AutoCAD LT 97, you can also click the **Undo** button on the **Standard Toolbar** to undo the point.

The **SPLINE** command options are described as follows:
- **Object.** It is possible to apply a splined curve to a polyline object. (Applying curves and splines to polylines is described in *Chapter 11* of this text.) The resulting spline is still a polyline but may be converted to a true spline using the **Object** option. If the **DELOBJ** variable is set to 1 (its default setting), the original splined polyline is deleted and replaced with a true spline when the **Object** option is used. The procedure to convert a splined polyline looks like this:

  Command: **SPLINE** *or* **SPL**↵
  Object/⟨Enter first point⟩: **O**↵
  Select objects to convert to splines.
  Select objects: *(pick one or more splined polylines)*
  Select objects: ↵
  Command:

- **Close.** Once two or more spline points are located, you can close the spline back to its starting point using the **Close** option. This feature is handy if you are drawing closed irregular shapes like ponds, lakes, or lagoons for example. An example of a closed spline is shown in **Figure 6-18.**

Figure 6-18.
An example of a
closed spline.

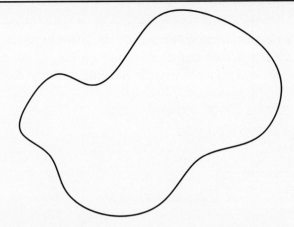

- **Fit Tolerance.** This option changes the tolerance for fitting the spline curve through defined points. By setting a tolerance, the curve can be fit through the same points quite differently. In the example shown in **Figure 6-19**, the original spline passes through the points marked with an "X". After applying a tolerance value of 1, a second spline (shown with a Hidden linetype) is created using the same points. Notice how the spline deviates from the original points but still falls within the specified tolerance. The command sequence for the **Fit Tolerance** option is as follows:

> Command: **SPLINE** *or* **SPL**↵
> Object/〈Enter first point〉: *(pick a point)*
> Enter point: *(pick a second point)*
> Close/Fit Tolerance/〈Enter point〉: **F**↵
> Enter Fit tolerance 〈0.0000〉: **1**↵
> Close/Fit Tolerance/〈Enter point〉: *(continue entering points)*

- **Enter start tangent.** After entering all the required spline points and pressing [Enter], this prompt is displayed. It allows you to specify the tangency of the spline curve at the first point. You may specify a new point or press [Enter].
- **Enter end tangent.** This prompt lets you specify the tangency of the spline curve at the last point. Specify a new point or press [Enter].

Figure 6-19.
Applying a tolerance causes a spline to pass through existing points quite differently. The original spline is shown in bold. The toleranced spline is represented by a Hidden linetype.

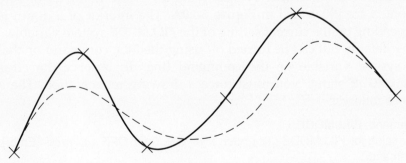

EXERCISE 6-5

❏ Begin a new drawing with your TEMPLATEB template, or use your own variables.
❏ Draw Object A with the dimensions shown. Draw the three vertical lines using any values you choose. Use the **SPLINE** command with the appropriate number of points to duplicate the break line.
❏ Create Object B with a closed spline.

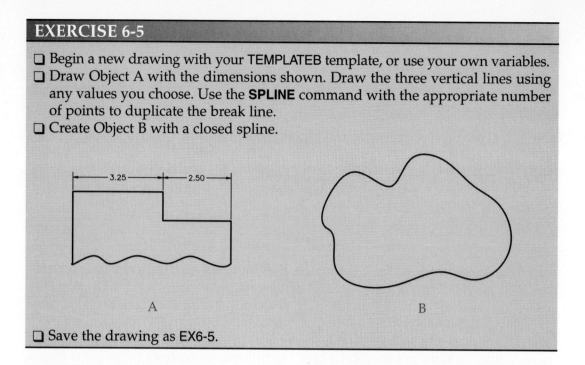

A   B

❏ Save the drawing as EX6-5.

Getting Started Guide 7

Drawing Donuts

A donut in AutoCAD LT is a filled circle or ring constructed with closed polylines comprised of wide polyarc segments. Polylines and polyarcs are covered later in this chapter.

To draw a donut, you must specify a value for the donut's inside diameter, a value for its outside diameter, and then locate the donut's center point. To access the **DONUT** command, enter DONUT, or DO, at the Command: prompt or select **Donut** from the **Draw** pull-down menu. If you are using AutoCAD LT 97, you can also click the **Donut** button in the **Draw** toolbar. The command sequence is as follows:

> Command: **DONUT** or **DO**↵
> Inside diameter ⟨current⟩: (enter a value and press [Enter])
> Outside diameter ⟨current⟩: (enter a value and press [Enter])
> Center of doughnut: (pick a point for the donut center)
> Center of doughnut: (pick another point or press [Enter] to end the command)
> Command:

A filled circle can be drawn by specifying an inside diameter of zero. Several different donuts are illustrated in **Figure 6-20A**. The interior of a donut is filled or unfilled depending on the current setting of the **FILLMODE** system variable. This variable is on by default, but can be turned off using the **FILL** command or changing the **FILLMODE** system variable on the command line. To observe the effects of the changed **FILLMODE** status, you must force a drawing regeneration. The command sequence is as follows:

> Command: **FILLMODE**↵
> New value for FILLMODE ⟨1⟩: (enter 1 for ON, 0 for OFF and press [Enter])
> Command:

Remember that you may also use the **FILL** command as an alternative:

> Command: **FILL**↵
> ON/OFF ⟨ON⟩: (enter ON or OFF as desired)
> Command:

Now, enter **REGEN**, or **RE**, to force a drawing regeneration and see the change.

(Sidebar buttons)
DONUT
DO

Draw
↳ Donut...

The donuts in **Figure 6-20B** are shown with **FILLMODE** turned off. Keep in mind that although **FILL** or **FILLMODE** can be used transparently (**'FILL** or **'FILLMODE**), a regeneration must still be performed to change the drawing display.

Figure 6-20.
A—Various donuts with **FILL** on. B—The same donuts with **FILL** off.

A

B

EXERCISE 6-6

❑ Begin a new drawing with your TEMPLATEA template, or use your own variables.
❑ Draw a variety of donuts with different inside and outside diameters. Be sure to draw a completely filled circle by setting the inside diameter to zero.
❑ As an interesting experiment, load the Gas_line and Fenceline2 linetypes and create additional donuts with these linetypes. Experiment with other linetypes, as well. If necessary, refer to *Chapter 5* to review the procedure to load linetypes.
❑ Turn **FILLMODE** off, regenerate the drawing and observe the effects.
❑ Save the drawing as EX6-6.

Drawing Double Lines with DLINE

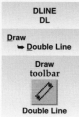

DLINE
DL

Draw
→ Double Line

Draw
toolbar

Double Line

The **DLINE** command can be used to draw continuous double lines and arcs with a specified width. Each line and arc segment is a separate object. For architectural and facilities management applications, **DLINE** is a handy way to draw walls in floor plans. Included among the various **DLINE** options are several that allow you to set the width of the double lines, cap the line ends, undo incorrectly drawn line and arc segments, and break the double lines at intersections. To access the **DLINE** command, enter DLINE, or DL, at the Command: prompt, click the **Double Line** button in the **Draw** toolbar, or select **Double Line** from the **Draw** pull-down menu. The command sequence is as follows:

> Command: **DLINE** *or* **DL**↵
> Break/Caps/Dragline/Offset/Snap/Undo/Width/⟨start point⟩:

Each of the **DLINE** command options is described below.
- **⟨start point⟩**. This is equivalent to the From point: prompt in the **LINE** command. Pick a point on the screen or enter a coordinate for the double line starting point.
- **Break.** This option determines whether a gap is created at the intersection of two double lines. An example of double lines drawn with **Break** on and off is shown in **Figure 6-21**. Break is ON by default, but may be turned off as follows:

> Break/Caps/Dragline/Offset/Snap/Undo/Width/⟨start point⟩: **B**↵
> Break Dline's at start and end points? OFF/⟨ON⟩: **OFF**↵

Figure 6-21.
Using the **DLINE**
Break option.

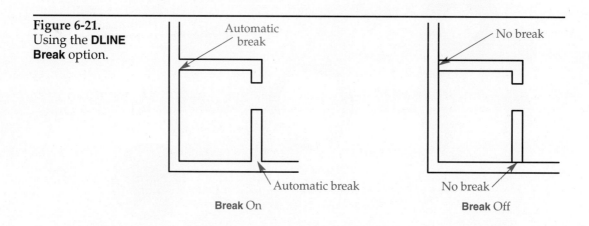

- **Caps.** Use this option to determine the type of endcaps for a double line as shown in **Figure 6-22**. The default **Auto** option automatically closes ends that are not snapped to (intersected with) another object.

> Break/Caps/Dragline/Offset/Snap/Undo/Width/⟨start point⟩: **C**↵
> Draw which endcaps? Both/End/None/Start/⟨Auto⟩:

- **Dragline.** By default, the center of a double line is determined by the starting and ending points you select. You can offset to the left or to the right of the center of the double line using the **Dragline** option. As shown in **Figure 6-23**, the **Left** option sets the pick points to the left side of the double line, while the **Right** option sets the pick points to the right. Left and right are determined by looking from the starting point to the ending point of the double line.

> Break/Caps/Dragline/Offset/Snap/Undo/Width/⟨start point⟩: **D**↵
> Set dragline position to Left/Center/Right/⟨Offset from center=*current*⟩:

Figure 6-22.
The various **DLINE**
Cap options.

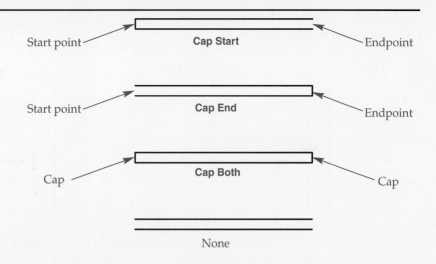

• **Offset.** This option allows you to start a new double line at a specified distance and direction from a base point. You are first prompted to locate the base point, then indicate the direction of the offset, and finally the offset distance. Refer to **Figure 6-24** as you follow the command sequence below:

> Break/Caps/Dragline/Offset/Snap/Undo/Width/⟨start point⟩: **O.**↵
> Offset from: (*pick a base point*)
> Offset toward: (*pick a point to specify the offset direction*)
> Enter the offset distance ⟨*current*⟩: (*enter a value and press* [Enter])

• **Snap.** This option is used to start or end a double line by snapping to an existing object. When both **Snap** and **Break** are on (the defaults) an automatic *clean-up* occurs at the intersection of the two double lines. See **Figure 6-25.**

> Break/Caps/Dragline/Offset/Snap/Undo/Width/⟨start point⟩: **S.**↵
> Set snap size or snap On/Off. Size/OFF/⟨ON⟩: (*select an option*)

Figure 6-24.
Using the **DLINE**
Offset option for a
new double line.

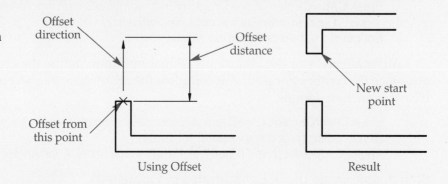

Figure 6-23.
The **Dragline Left**, **Center**, and **Right** options.

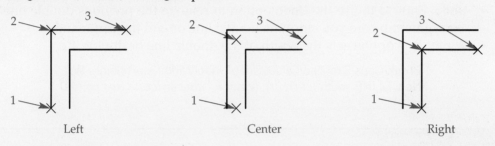

Figure 6-25.
Effects of **DLINE Snap** on and off.

You can use the **Size** option to set the size of the area from the crosshair cursor that is searched for object snapping. This area is called the pixel search area.

Set snap size or snap On/Off. Size/OFF/⟨ON⟩: **S**↵
New snap size (1-10) ⟨3⟩: *(enter a size in pixels and press* [Enter]*)*

- **Undo.** Enter U to use the **Undo** option to remove the previous double line or arc segment before you close the double line or end the command.
- **Width.** This option sets the width of the double line or double arc.

Break/Caps/Dragline/Offset/Snap/Undo/Width/⟨start point⟩: **W**↵
New DLINE width ⟨*current*⟩: *(enter a value or locate two points)*

PROFESSIONAL TIP

If you are doing architectural drafting, first set architectural units and enter a Width value of 6 units to draw exterior walls and 4 units to draw interior walls. Refer to *Chapter 2* to review setting units of measurement in AutoCAD LT.

Drawing Double Arcs

Once you have picked a starting point for the double line, the **Arc** option is added at the beginning of the **DLINE** command options. The default double line arc is constructed like the **ARC** command's **3 Point** option described earlier in this chapter. After picking the double line starting point and entering A for arc, you are then prompted to select a second point and an endpoint for the arc. The command sequence is as follows:

Command: **DLINE** *or* **DL**↵
Break/Caps/Dragline/Offset/Snap/Undo/Width/⟨start point⟩: *(pick a point)*
Arc/Break/CAps/CLose/Dragline/Snap/Undo/Width/⟨next point⟩: **A**↵
Break/CAps/CEnter/CLose/Dragline/Endpoint/Line/Snap/Undo/Width/⟨second point⟩:
    (pick a second point on the arc's circumference)
Endpoint: *(pick an endpoint for the arc)*

Alternatively, you can choose the **CEnter** option to define the center point of the arc. Once the center is located, you complete the arc by selecting an endpoint, or specifying an included angle.

Break/CAps/CEnter/CLose/Dragline/Endpoint/Line/Snap/Undo/Width/⟨second point⟩: **CE**↵
Center point: *(pick a center point for the arc)*
Angle/⟨Endpoint⟩: *(press* [Enter] *for the arc endpoint or* A *for* Angle*)*

Both double arc methods are illustrated in **Figure 6-26.**

Figure 6-26.
Drawing with
DLINE Arcs.

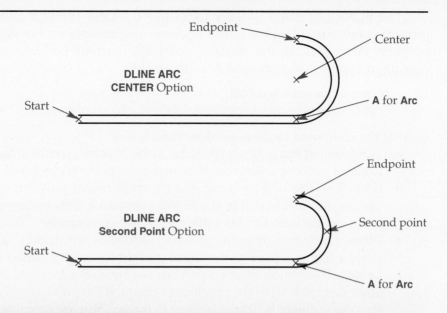

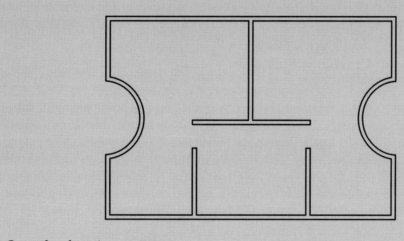

EXERCISE 6-7

❏ Begin a new drawing using the **Quick Setup** wizard.
❏ Set the units to architectural. Next, set the drawing width to 40' and the length to 30'.
❏ Use the **DLINE** command with the width set to 6" to make a drawing similar to that shown below. Do not be concerned with dimensions.
❏ As an additional exercise, try drawing the interior walls with a width of 4".

❏ Save the drawing as EX6-7.

Drawing Polylines

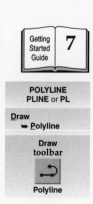

Getting Started Guide 7

POLYLINE
PLINE or PL

Draw
➥ Polyline

Draw
toolbar

Polyline

Polylines are one of the most powerful object types in AutoCAD LT and offer capabilities not found in normal line objects. Multiple polyline segments created in one operation are treated as one object. In addition, a polyline can be drawn with a specified width and contain arc segments (polyarcs). To draw polylines, enter PLINE, or PL, at the Command: prompt, click the **Polyline** button in the **Draw** toolbar, or select **Polyline** from the **Draw** pull-down menu. The command sequence is as follows:

Command: **PLINE** or **PL**↵
From point: (pick a starting point)

The **PLINE** command initially looks like the **LINE** command. At the From point: prompt, locate a point on the screen or enter a coordinate for the starting point of the polyline. After picking the starting point, the current polyline width and **PLINE** command options are displayed as follows:

Current line-width is 0.0000
Arc/CLose/Halfwidth/Length/Undo/Width/⟨Endpoint of line⟩:

Each of the command options are described below:

- ⟨**Endpoint of line**⟩. This is the same as the To point: prompt in the **LINE** command. Locate a point or enter a coordinate to specify the endpoint of the polyline.
- **Undo.** Use this option to remove the most recent polyline segment added to the polyline while still in the **PLINE** command. This option is identical to the **Undo** option found in the **LINE** and **DLINE** commands.
- **Close.** Once two or more polyline segments are drawn, use this option to draw a segment back to the starting point to create a closed shape.
- **Length.** This option draws a polyline segment of a specified length at the same angle (orientation) as the previous segment. If the previous segment is a polyarc, the new segment is drawn tangent to the arc. You are prompted as follows:

Arc/Close/Halfwidth/Length/Undo/Width/⟨Endpoint of line⟩: **L**↵
Length of line: *(enter a positive or negative value)*

- **Width.** Use this option to specify the width of the next polyline segment. The starting width you specify becomes the ending width, by default. The width is maintained for all subsequent polylines until you change the width again. Several examples of wide polylines are illustrated in **Figure 6-27.** The starting and ending points of a wide polyline define the center of the line. In the example below, a uniform width of .25 is assigned for the next polyline segment to be drawn:

Arc/Close/Halfwidth/Length/Undo/Width/⟨Endpoint of line⟩: **W**↵
Starting width ⟨*current*⟩: **.25**
Ending width ⟨0.2500⟩:↵

- **Halfwidth.** This option specifies the width of the next polyline segment from its center to one of its edges. The starting halfwidth you specify becomes the ending halfwidth, by default. The halfwidth is maintained for all subsequent polylines until you change the halfwidth again. Keep in mind that the halfwidth is applied equally to each side of the wide polyline. Thus, it is not possible to assign a halfwidth to just one side of the polyline segment. In the example that follows, a uniform halfwidth of .375 is assigned to the next segment to be drawn:

Arc/Close/Halfwidth/Length/Undo/Width/⟨Endpoint of line⟩: **H**↵
Starting halfwidth ⟨0.1250⟩: **.375**↵
Ending halfwidth ⟨0.3750⟩:↵

Figure 6-27.
A polyline may be drawn with a constant or variable width.

Polyline Tutorial

Because a polyline can be created with variable width, the **PLINE** command can be used to create arrowheads, or any other tapered shape. Try the following tutorial to construct the large cutting-plane line illustrated in **Figure 6-28.**
The tutorial begins as follows:

➪ Load AutoCAD LT and begin a new drawing with the TEMPLATEA template. Set the CUTPLANE layer current. If your template drawing does not yet have a CUTPLANE layer, create one. Assign the Phantom linetype and color blue (5) to the new layer. Set the layer current.

➪ Issue the **PLINE** command and draw the cutting-plane line using the following commands:

```
Command: PLINE or PL↵
From point: (pick a start point near top of screen)
Current line-width is 0.000
Arc/Close/Halfwidth/Length/Undo/Width/〈Endpoint of line〉: W↵
Starting width 〈0.000):↵
Ending width 〈0.000): .75↵
Arc/Close/Halfwidth/Length/Undo/Width/〈Endpoint of line〉: @1.5〈0↵
Arc/Close/Halfwidth/Length/Undo/Width/〈Endpoint of line〉: W↵
Starting width 〈0.750): .05↵
Ending width 〈0.050):↵
Arc/Close/Halfwidth/Length/Undo/Width/〈Endpoint of line〉: L↵
Length of line: 1↵
Arc/Close/Halfwidth/Length/Undo/Width/〈Endpoint of line〉: @6〈270↵
Arc/Close/Halfwidth/Length/Undo/Width/〈Endpoint of line〉: @1〈180↵
Arc/Close/Halfwidth/Length/Undo/Width/〈Endpoint of line〉:W↵
Starting width 〈0.050): .75↵
Ending width 〈0.750): 0↵
Arc/Close/Halfwidth/Length/Undo/Width/〈Endpoint of line〉: L↵
Length of line: 1.5↵
Arc/Close/Halfwidth/Length/Undo/Width/〈Endpoint of line〉:↵
Command:
```

➪ Save the completed drawing with the name CUTPLANE.DWG.

Figure 6-28.
A polyline in a
Phantom linetype is
used to draw a
cutting-plane line.

As with double lines, the **PLINE** command also allows the drawing of arc segments. Each polyline arc (or polyarc) can have an assigned width. The polyarc is drawn tangent to the last polyline or polyarc created. Several polyarcs constructed in this fashion are shown in **Figure 6-29.** You can construct a polyarc by specifying its radius, center point, included angle, or direction. A polyarc may also be constructed through three points that define the radius of the object. Before you can draw a polyarc, you must first specify a starting point as follows:

> Command: **PLINE** *or* **PL**↵
> From point: *(pick a point)*
> Current line-width is ⟨*current*⟩
> Arc/Close/Halfwidth/Length/Undo/Width/⟨Endpoint of line⟩: **A**↵
> Angle/CEnter/CLose/Direction/Halfwidth/Line/Radius/Secondpt/
>   Undo/Width/⟨Endpoint of arc⟩:

Each of the polyarc options are described below:
- **Endpoint of arc.** Locate a point or enter a coordinate to specify the endpoint of the polyarc.
- **Angle.** Use this option to specify the included angle of the arc segment from the starting point of the polyarc. A positive value draws a counterclockwise polyarc; a negative number draws a clockwise polyarc. After providing the included angle, you may then finish the polyarc segment by locating a center point, specifying a radius, or picking an ending point.

> Angle/CEnter/CLose/Direction/Halfwidth/Line/Radius/Second
>   pt/Undo/Width/⟨Endpoint of arc⟩: **A**↵
> Included angle: *(specify an angle and press* [Enter]*)*
> Center/Radius/⟨Endpoint⟩: *(pick an ending point or select an option)*

- **CEnter.** This option specifies the center of the polyarc. After locating the center point, you may then finish the polyarc segment by specifying an included angle, an ending point, or providing the arc chord length. The chord is a line segment joining two points on a circle or an arc.

> Angle/CEnter/CLose/Direction/Halfwidth/Line/Radius/Second
>   pt/Undo/Width/⟨Endpoint of arc⟩: **CE**↵
> Center point: *(pick a center point)*
> Angle/Length/⟨End point⟩: *(pick an ending point or select an option)*

- **CLose.** Use this option to draw a polyarc segment back to the starting point to create a closed shape.

Figure 6-29.
Polyline arcs (polyarcs) may also be drawn with constant or variable widths.

- **Direction.** The direction of polyarc segments is based on the ending direction of the previously drawn segment. This option allows an explicit starting direction to be specified, rather than using the default.

> Angle/CEnter/CLose/Direction/Halfwidth/Line/Radius/Second
> pt/Undo/Width/〈Endpoint of arc〉: **D**↵
> Direction from start point: *(pick a point to indicate direction)*
> End point: *(pick an ending point)*

- **Halfwidth.** Identical to the polyline halfwidth option, this option specifies the width of the next polyarc segment from its center to one of its edges.
- **Line.** Use this option when you are through drawing polyarcs and wish to draw polylines.

> Angle/CEnter/CLose/Direction/Halfwidth/Line/Radius/Second
> pt/Undo/Width/〈Endpoint of arc〉: **L**↵
> Arc/Close/Halfwidth/Length/Undo/Width/〈Endpoint of line〉:

- **Radius.** Use this option to specify an explicit radius for the polyarc. You can then finish drawing the polyarc by locating an ending point, or by specifying an included angle.

> Angle/CEnter/CLose/Direction/Halfwidth/Line/Radius/Second
> pt/Undo/Width/〈Endpoint of arc〉: **R**↵
> Radius: *(enter a value or pick two points)*
> Angle/〈End point〉: *(pick an ending point or type* A, *for angle, and press* [Enter])

- **Second pt.** This option is similar to the **3 Point** option of the **ARC** command. The second point you specify locates a point on the circumference of the polyarc, and the polyarc is terminated with a third point. The polyarc can be drawn clockwise or counterclockwise, depending on the direction of the pick points.

> Angle/CEnter/CLose/Direction/Halfwidth/Line/Radius/Second
> pt/Undo/Width/〈Endpoint of arc〉: **S**↵
> Second point: *(pick a second point for the polyarc)*
> End point: *(pick an ending point for the polyarc)*

- **Undo.** Use this option to remove the most recent polyarc segment added while still in the **PLINE** command.
- **Width.** Identical to the polyline width option, this option specifies the width of the next polyarc segment. By default, the starting width specified also becomes the ending width.

Drawing Fully-Radiused Features with Polylines

Earlier in this chapter, it was stated that the **LINE** and **ARC** command **Continuation** options can be used together to quickly and easily construct fully-radiused features—like slots and cutouts. Similar features can be constructed using polylines and polyarcs in one operation without exiting the **PLINE** command. Consider the fully-radiused slot illustrated in **Figure 6-30**. By constructing this feature with a polyline, editing operations and inquiry commands can be performed much more efficiently than if the feature was constructed from individual lines and arcs. The command sequence is as follows:

Command: **PLINE** *or* **PL**↵
From point: *(pick point 1)*
Current line-width is ⟨*current*⟩
Arc/Close/Halfwidth/Length/Undo/Width/⟨Endpoint of line⟩: **@3⟨0**↵
Arc/Close/Halfwidth/Length/Undo/Width/⟨Endpoint of line⟩: **A**↵
Angle/CEnter/CLose/Direction/Halfwidth/Line/Radius/Second
   pt/Undo/Width/⟨Endpoint of arc⟩: **@190**↵
Angle/CEnter/CLose/Direction/Halfwidth/Line/Radius/Second
   pt/Undo/Width/⟨Endpoint of arc⟩: **L**↵
Arc/Close/Halfwidth/Length/Undo/Width/⟨Endpoint of line⟩: **@3⟨180**↵
Arc/Close/Halfwidth/Length/Undo/Width/⟨Endpoint of line⟩: **A**↵
Angle/CEnter/CLose/Direction/Halfwidth/Line/Radius/Second
   pt/Undo/Width/⟨Endpoint of arc⟩: **CL**↵
Command:

Figure 6-30.
Fully radiused features such as this slot may be drawn quickly and easily in one operation using polylines with polyarcs.

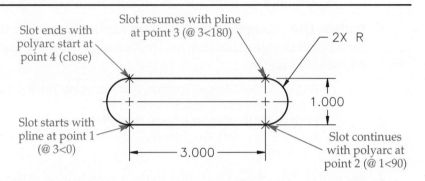

Slot resumes with pline at point 3 (@ 3<180)
Slot ends with polyarc start at point 4 (close)
2X R
Slot starts with pline at point 1 (@ 3<0)
1.000
Slot continues with polyarc at point 2 (@ 1<90)
3.000

NOTE

As an alternative to entering polyline coordinates in the example above, you can use the **PLINE Length** option as you did in the previous tutorial. The **Length** option looks like this:

Arc/Close/Halfwidth/Length/Undo/Width/⟨Endpoint of line⟩: **L**↵
Length of line: **3**

Presetting Polyline Widths

You can preset the constant width of polylines and polyarcs with the **PLINEWID** system variable. Setting the width beforehand can save you valuable drafting time. The **PLINEWID** system variable is entered at the Command: prompt as follows:

Command: **PLINEWID**
New value for PLINEWID ⟨current value⟩: *(enter a width and press* [Enter]*)*

When you are done drawing wide polylines and polyarcs be sure to set the value of **PLINEWID** to 0 (zero).

EXERCISE 6-8

❑ Begin a new drawing with your TEMPLATEA template, or use your own variables.
❑ Draw several polyarc segments using each of the options described in the preceding text.
❑ Using the command options and values shown above, draw the fully-radiused slot illustrated in **Figure 6-30.** Compare this method with that used in EX6-2. Of the two methods, which one do you prefer?
❑ Save the drawing as EX6-8.

Drawing Rectangles

RECTANG
REC

Draw
→ Rectangle

Draw
toolbar

Rectangle

Many of the objects in engineering and architectural drawings are rectangular in shape. Conveniently, AutoCAD LT allows you to quickly draw a rectangular polyline using the **RECTANG** command. To draw rectangles, enter RECTANG, or REC, at the Command: prompt, click the **Rectangle** button in the **Draw** toolbar, or select **Rectangle** from the **Draw** pull-down menu. The rectangle is defined by two diagonal corners as illustrated in **Figure 6-31.** In the following example, a 6 × 4 rectangular polyline is created:

> Command: **RECTANG** *or* **REC**↵
> Chamfer/Elevation/Fillet/Thickness/Width/⟨First corner⟩: *(pick a corner point)*
> Other corner: **@6,4**↵
> Command:

From the syntax above, you can see that AutoCAD LT creates the rectangle by measuring 6 units on the positive X axis and 4 units on the positive Y axis from the first corner to locate the other diagonal corner.

Figure 6-31.
Two diagonal points
define a rectangle.

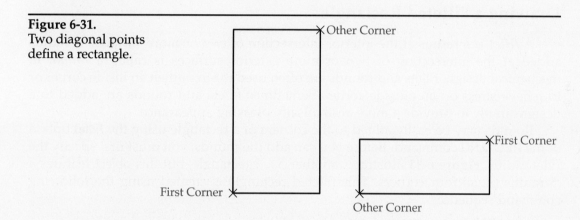

Drawing a Chamfered Rectangle

A *chamfer* is a slight surface angle, or bevel, used to relieve both internal and external sharp edges on mechanical parts. Chamfers are also used to facilitate the assembly of mating parts. An example of this is a bolt or other type of threaded fastener being screwed into a tapped hole. By adding a slight chamfer around the edge of the mating hole, it is easier for an assembler to insert the fastener and engage the threads.

The **RECTANG** command allows you to draw a rectangle that is chamfered on all four corners. The chamfers are created by first setting the first and second chamfer distances. The *chamfer distance* is the amount each corner is trimmed to intersect the chamfer line. A 45° chamfer is created when both chamfer distances are equal. **Figure 6-32** illustrates a 5 × 3 rectangle with .25 × 45° chamfers on all four corners. To create this object, use the following command sequence:

> Command: **RECTANG** *or* **REC**↵
> Chamfer/Elevation/Fillet/Thickness/Width/⟨First corner⟩: **C**↵
> First chamfer distance for rectangles ⟨0.0000⟩: **.25**↵
> Second chamfer distance for rectangles ⟨0.2500⟩: ↵
> Chamfer/Elevation/Fillet/Thickness/Width/⟨First corner⟩: *(pick a corner)*
> Other corner: **@5,3**↵
> Command:

If you need to create a nonstandard chamfer (other than 45°), set the chamfer distances accordingly. The chamfer distances that you set for the rectangle remain in effect during the current drawing session until new distances are entered.

Figure 6-32.
The **Chamfer** option applies chamfers to all four corners of a rectangle in one operation.

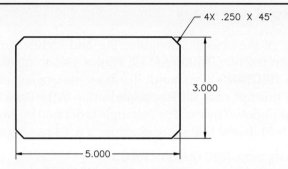

NOTE   The **CHAMFER** command offers additional chamfering options and is covered later in this chapter.

Drawing a Filleted Rectangle

A *fillet* is a radius at the interior intersection of two or more surfaces. A radius added at the intersection of two or more exterior surfaces is called a *round*. In mechanical design, fillets and rounds are often used to strengthen an inside corner or to relieve stress on an outside corner. Sometimes fillets and rounds are added to a design simply to provide a more aesthetically pleasing appearance.

Rounds may be easily added to the corners of a rectangle using the **Fillet** option of the **RECTANG** command. Before you can add the rounds, you must first specify the fillet radius. **Figure 6-33** illustrates another 5 × 3 rectangle, but this object features a .5 radius on all four corners. This filleted rectangle is created using the following command sequence:

> Command: **RECTANG** *or* **REC**↵
> Chamfer/Elevation/Fillet/Thickness/Width/⟨First corner⟩: **F**↵
> Fillet radius for rectangles ⟨0.0000⟩: **.5**↵
> Chamfer/Elevation/Fillet/Thickness/Width/⟨First corner⟩: *(pick a corner)*
> Other corner: **@5,3**↵
> Command:

As with chamfers, the fillet radius that you specify for the rectangle remains in effect during the current drawing session until a different radius is entered.

Figure 6-33.
The **Fillet** option applies rounds to all four corners of a rectangle in one operation.

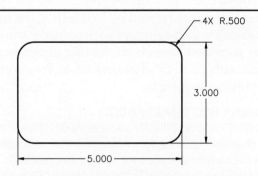

NOTE   The **FILLET** command offers additional filleting options and is covered later in this chapter.

Drawing a 3D Rectangle using the Elevation and Thickness Variables

Elevation and Thickness are system variables that allow you to draw three-dimensional objects. The **Elevation** variable sets the height above or below the zero elevation plane for a drawing object. The **Thickness** variable determines the extrusion distance along the Z axis for an object. Both elevation and thickness may be set to negative values. A positive thickness extrudes a rectangle along the positive Z axis. A negative thickness extrudes a rectangle along the negative Z axis. By default, all objects are drawn with zero elevation and zero thickness and are therefore two-dimensional.

The **Elevation** and **Thickness** variables, as well as an introduction to 3D modeling, are described in greater detail in *Chapter 19* of this text.

PROFESSIONAL TIP

If you would like to jump ahead a bit, use the following command sequence to model the rectangle shown in **Figure 6-34.**

Command: **RECTANG** *or* **REC**↵
Chamfer/Elevation/Fillet/Thickness/Width/⟨First corner⟩: **T**↵
Thickness for rectangles ⟨0.0000⟩: **2**↵
Chamfer/Elevation/Fillet/Thickness/Width/⟨First corner⟩:
 (pick a corner)
Other corner: **@5,3**↵
Command:

Now, obtain a 3D viewing angle with the **VPOINT** command.

Command: **VPOINT** *or* **VP**↵
Rotate/⟨View point⟩ ⟨0.0000,0.0000,1.0000⟩: **1,-1,1**↵
Regenerating drawing.
Command:

To return to a 2D view, use the **PLAN** command as follows:

Command: **PLAN**↵
⟨Current UCS⟩/Ucs/World: **W**↵
Regenerating drawing.
Command:

In the previous example, the **Elevation** variable was not used. See *Chapter 19* for more information about 3D modeling and viewing commands.

Figure 6-34.
Applying thickness to a rectangle adds extrusion height and creates a 3D object.

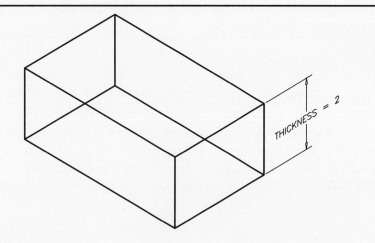

Drawing a Wide Rectangle

Earlier in this chapter you learned that polylines can be drawn with assigned width. Remember that rectangles are also polylines. Therefore, you can assign a constant, or uniform, width to a rectangle using the **Width** option of the **RECTANG** command. The wide rectangle shown in **Figure 6-35** is created using the following command sequence:

> Command: **RECTANG** *or* **REC**↵
> Chamfer/Elevation/Fillet/Thickness/Width/⟨First corner⟩: **W**↵
> Width for rectangles ⟨0.0000⟩: **.21875**↵
> Chamfer/Elevation/Fillet/Thickness/Width/⟨First corner⟩: *(pick a corner)*
> Other corner: **@5,3**↵
> Command:

As with the **POLYLINE** command, the assigned width is applied equally about the center line running around the perimeter of the rectangle.

Figure 6-35.
The **Width** option applies a uniform width to a rectangle.

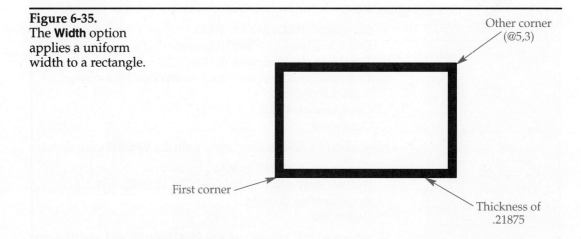

Other corner (@5,3)

First corner

Thickness of .21875

EXERCISE 6-9

❏ Begin a new drawing with your TEMPLATEC template, or use your own variables.
❏ Draw a rectangle that measures 8 units on the X axis and 4 units on the Y axis.
❏ Draw a second rectangle with .125 × 45° chamfers that measure 2.4375 on the X axis and 4.5625 on the Y axis.
❏ Construct a third rectangle with .375 rounds that measures 6.15625 on the X axis and 4.875 on the Y axis.
❏ Finally, create a 3 × 5 rectangle that is .3125 wide.
❏ Save the drawing as EX6-9.

Getting Started Guide 7

Drawing Polygons

A *regular polygon* is a multisided figure with each side of equal length. Several examples of regular polygons include an equilateral triangle, a square, and a hexagon. These shapes, and many others, can be quickly and easily drawn using the **POLYGON** command. Polygons, like rectangles, are constructed with polylines.

To access the **POLYGON** command, enter POLYGON, or POL or PG, at the Command: prompt, click the **Polygon** button in the **Draw** toolbar, or select **Polygon** from the **Draw** pull-down menu. The command sequence is as follows:

POLYGON
POL or PG

Draw
→ Polygon

Draw
toolbar

Polygon

>Command: **POLYGON** *or* **POL** *or* **PG.**↵
>Number of sides ⟨4⟩:

Polygons may be constructed using three different methods. Regardless of the method you select, the **POLYGON** command first prompts you for the desired number of sides. A polygon can have between 3 and 1024 sides—the default number is 4. The three construction methods are described in the following sections.

Drawing a Polygon by Its Center and Radius

The default method for creating a polygon requires you to locate a center point for the polygon. You must then select between an inscribed or circumscribed polygon. An ***inscribed polygon*** is drawn to fit *inside* an imaginary circle. A ***circumscribed polygon*** is drawn *around* an imaginary circle. For both inscribed and circumscribed polygons, you are prompted to enter a radius value for the imaginary circle. Consider the 3-sided inscribed polygon shown at the upper left in **Figure 6-36.** This object can be drawn with the following sequence of steps:

>Command: **POLYGON** *or* **POL** *or* **PG.**↵
>Number of sides ⟨4⟩: **3.**↵
>Edge/⟨Center of polygon⟩: *(pick a center point)*
>Inscribed in circle/Circumscribed about circle (I/C) ⟨I⟩: ↵
>Radius of circle: **1.25**↵
>Command:

The circumscribed option provides a more accurate way to size a polygon. As an example, consider the square shown at the lower-right in **Figure 6-36.** This object is drawn using the following procedure:

>Command: **POLYGON** *or* **POL** *or* **PG.**↵
>Number of sides ⟨4⟩: ↵
>Edge/⟨Center of polygon⟩: *(pick a center point)*
>Inscribed in circle/Circumscribed about circle (I/C) ⟨I⟩: **C**↵
>Radius of circle: **1.25.**↵
>Command:

Whether inscribed or circumscribed, the center and radius method is useful when you know the distance from the center of the polygon to the midpoint of one of its sides.

Figure 6-36.
A—A triangle and square constructed using the default inscribed method. B—The same two objects created using the circumscribed method. Note the difference in the sizes of the objects.

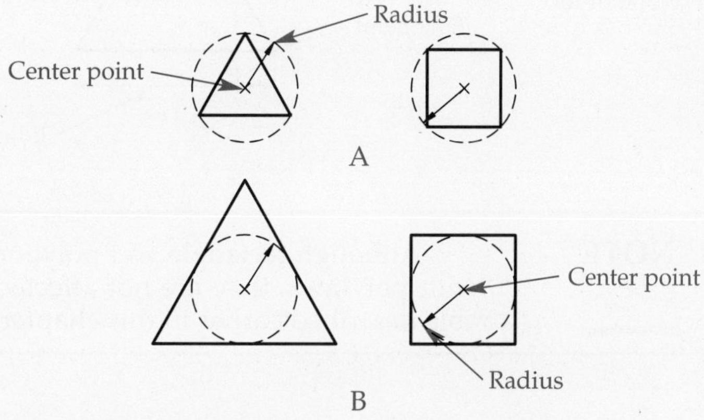

PROFESSIONAL TIP

A six-sided polygon forms a hexagon. This shape is commonly used in mechanical engineering applications to represent hex nuts and bolts. Depending on the object, the hexagon may be dimensioned across its corners or across its flats. See **Figure 6-37.** If a hexagon is dimensioned across its flats, use the circumscribed method. Use the inscribed method when the hexagon is dimensioned across its corners.

Figure 6-37.
Use the inscribed method when creating a hexagon that is dimensioned across its corners. Use the circumscribed method to create a hexagon that is dimensioned across its flats.

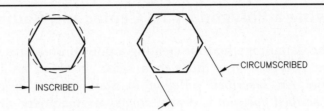

Drawing a Polygon by Specifying the Length of an Edge

The **POLYGON Edge** option provides a handy alternative when you know the length of a polygon segment and where it is to be placed. As an example, look at the 4-sided polygon shown at the right in **Figure 6-38.** This polygon is created using the following command sequence:

```
Command: POLYGON or POL or PG⏎
Number of sides ⟨4⟩: ⏎
Edge/⟨Center of polygon⟩: E⏎
First endpoint of edge: (pick the first endpoint)
Second endpoint of edge: @2.5⟨0⏎
Command:
```

Remember that each side of a polygon is of equal length regardless of the construction method used.

Figure 6-38.
Using the **Edge** option to define a polygon by the length of one of its edges.

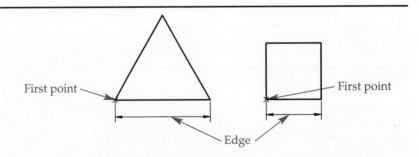

NOTE

Although rectangle and polygon objects are constructed with polylines, they are not affected by the **PLINEWID** variable described earlier in this chapter.

The EXPLODE Command

EXPLODE
X

Modify
→ Explode

Modify
toolbar

Explode

AutoCAD LT defines a compound object as an entity that comprises more than one object. Multiple segmented objects like polylines, rectangles, and polygons are all considered compound objects. You can convert compound objects into their component objects using the **EXPLODE** command. Exploding polylines, rectangles, and polygons converts them into individual line segments. Line and/or arc segments are created when you explode donuts or polyarcs. To access the **EXPLODE** command, enter EXPLODE, or X, at the Command: prompt, click the **Explode** button in the **Modify** toolbar, or select **Explode** from the **Modify** pull-down menu. See **Figure 6-39.** The command sequence is as follows:

> Command: **EXPLODE** *or* **X**↵
> Select objects: *(select one or more compound objects)*
> Select objects:↵
> Command:

All of the selection set options are valid with **EXPLODE** so you can select more than one compound object at a time. However, keep in mind that width is lost when you explode a wide polyline. In those instances, AutoCAD LT displays the following message:

> Exploding this polyline has lost width information.
> The UNDO command will restore it.

Figure 6-39.
Select **Explode** from the **Modify** pull-down menu.

NOTE Other types of compound objects like dimensions and block symbols will be covered as they are encountered in this text.

EXERCISE 6-10

❑ Begin a new drawing with your TEMPLATEB template, or use your own variables.
❑ Using the **POLYGON** command's **Edge** option, draw a square that measures 1.875 along each edge.
❑ Draw a circumscribed octagon with a radius of 3.625 units.
❑ Using a radius of .75 units, duplicate the two hexagons shown in **Figure 6-37.**
❑ Finally, draw a .5 wide polyline that is 6 units long. Explode the polyline and observe the results. Perform an **UNDO** to retrieve the wide polyline.
❑ Save the drawing as EX6-10 and quit.

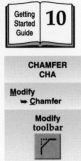

CHAMFER
CHA

Modify
↳ Chamfer

Modify
toolbar

Chamfer

Creating Chamfers

Getting Started Guide **10**

As mentioned earlier in this chapter, a chamfer is a slight surface angle, or bevel, used to relieve both internal and external sharp edges on mechanical parts. A chamfer may be constructed between one line and another line, or between one polyline and another polyline. You can also create a chamfer between a line and a polyline. To construct a chamfer, enter CHAMFER, or CHA, at the Command: prompt, click the **Chamfer** button in the **Modify** toolbar, or select **Chamfer** from the **Modify** pull-down menu.

Creating a Chamfer by Specifying Distances

In the example that follows, the **Distance** option is used to first specify the chamfer distances. Since 45° chamfers are the most common, you will note that the second chamfer distance defaults to the first chamfer distance entered. AutoCAD LT uses a value of .5 units for the default chamfer distances.

> Command: **CHAMFER** *or* **CHA**↵
> (TRIM mode) Current chamfer Dist1 = 0.5000, Dist2 = 0.5000
> Polyline/Distance/Angle/Trim/Method/⟨Select first line⟩: **D**↵
> Enter first chamfer distance ⟨0.5000⟩: **.75**↵
> Enter second chamfer distance ⟨0.7500⟩: ↵
> Command:

Now that the distances are set, press [Enter] to repeat the **CHAMFER** command, and select the lines (or polylines) to be chamfered. See **Figure 6-40.**

> Command: ↵
> CHAMFER
> (TRIM mode) Current chamfer Dist1 = 0.7500, Dist2 = 0.7500
> Polyline/Distance/Angle/Trim/Method/⟨Select first line⟩: *(pick a line or polyline)*
> Select second line: *(pick a second line or polyline)*
> Command:

As soon as you select the second line, the chamfer is created and the lines are automatically trimmed. AutoCAD LT allows you to chamfer nonintersecting lines as well as lines that overlap. Additionally, you can extend two lines to make a corner if you set the chamfer distances to 0 (zero). See **Figure 6-41.**

Figure 6-40.
Creating a chamfer.

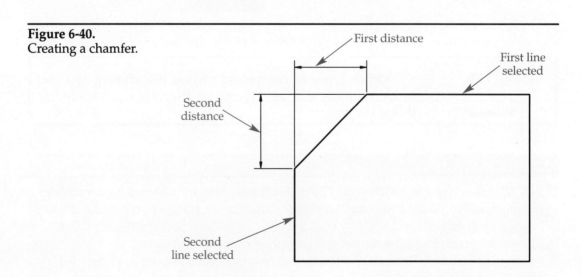

AutoCAD LT—Fundamentals and Applications

Figure 6-41.
Chamfers may be constructed between nonintersecting lines as well as lines that overlap. Setting the chamfer distances to 0 makes a corner.

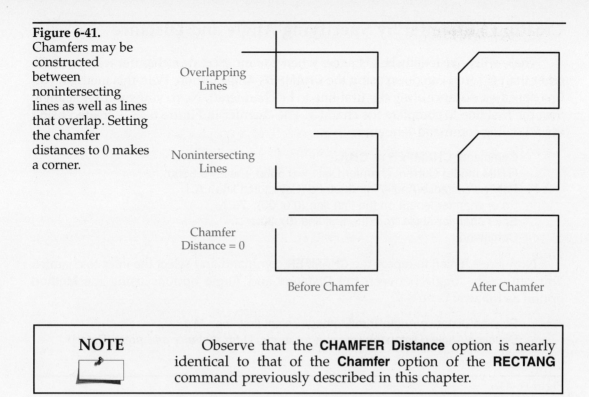

Overlapping Lines

Nonintersecting Lines

Chamfer Distance = 0

Before Chamfer   After Chamfer

NOTE   Observe that the **CHAMFER Distance** option is nearly identical to that of the **Chamfer** option of the **RECTANG** command previously described in this chapter.

Chamfering a 2D Polyline

The **Polyline** option lets you chamfer all the edges of a polyline in one operation. However, only those edges of the polyline long enough to accommodate the new segments are chamfered. Each of the chamfers is joined to the existing polyline as a new polyline segment. The **Polyline** option is used as follows:

Command: **CHAMFER** *or* **CHA**↵
(TRIM mode) Current chamfer Dist1 = 0.5000, Dist2 = 0.5000
Polyline/Distance/Angle/Trim/Method/〈Select first line〉: **P**↵
Select 2D polyline: *(select a polyline, rectangle, or polygon)*
n lines were chamfered
Command:

A polyline with all edges chamfered in one operation is illustrated in **Figure 6-42**. Although the polyline shown is closed, open polylines may also be chamfered using the **Polyline** option.

Figure 6-42.
All contiguous vertices of a polyline are chamfered in one operation. The polyline may be open or closed.

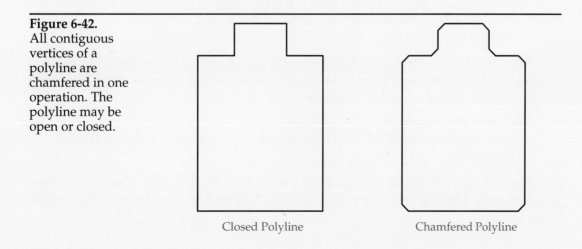

Closed Polyline   Chamfered Polyline

Creating a Chamfer by Specifying Angle and Distance

There will occasionally be instances when you must create a chamfer with an angle other than 45°. You can do so using the **CHAMFER Angle** option. With this method, you first specify a distance *along* the first line to be chamfered, Next, you specify the angle *from* the first line to complete the chamfer. The chamfer in **Figure 6-43** is created using the following command sequence:

> Command: **CHAMFER** *or* **CHA**⏎
> (TRIM mode) Current chamfer Dist1 = 0.5000, Dist2 =0.5000
> Polyline/Distance/Angle/Trim/Method/⟨Select first line⟩: **A**⏎
> Enter chamfer length on the first line ⟨0.0000⟩: **.75**⏎
> Enter chamfer angle from the first line ⟨0⟩: **30**⏎
> Command:

Now Press [Enter] to repeat the **CHAMFER** command and select the lines to chamfer. You can easily toggle between the **Distance** and **Angle** options using the **Method** option as follows:

> Polyline/Distance/Angle/Trim/Method/⟨Select first line⟩: **M**⏎
> Distance/Angle ⟨Distance⟩: *(enter A for angle, D for distance and press* [Enter]*)*

Figure 6-43.
The **CHAMFER Angle** option creates chamfers at angles other than 45°.

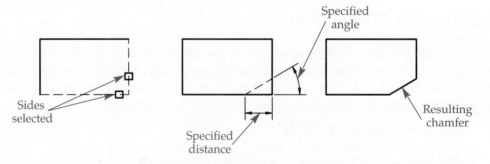

Disabling Chamfer Trimming

By default, corners are automatically trimmed whenever a chamfer is created. If you wish to retain the corners, use the **Trim** option as follows:

> Command: **CHAMFER** *or* **CHA**⏎
> (TRIM mode) Current chamfer Dist1 = 0.5000, Dist2 =0.5000
> Polyline/Distance/Angle/Trim/Method/⟨Select first line⟩: **T**⏎
> Trim/No trim ⟨Trim⟩: **N**⏎

Now construct your nontrimmed chamfer using any of the chamfering options previously described. See **Figure 6-44.** You can also disable chamfer trimming using the **TRIMMODE** system variable as follows:

> Command: **TRIMMODE**⏎
> New value for TRIMMODE ⟨1⟩: *(enter 0 for no trim, 1 for trim and press* [Enter]*)*
> Command:

Keep in mind that changes made to the **TRIMMODE** variable affect the current drawing only. Once a new drawing is begun, **TRIMMODE** is restored to its default value of 1.

Figure 6-44.
Chamfers may be
trimmed or not
trimmed using the
CHAMFER Trim
option.

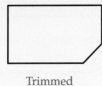 

Trimmed   Not Trimmed

Fillets and Rounds

As stated earlier in this chapter, a fillet is a radius at the interior intersection of two or more surfaces. A radius added at the intersection of two or more exterior surfaces is called a round. Fillets and rounds are created using the **FILLET** command. Before you can draw a fillet, you must first specify the fillet radius. (This value is set to .5 units by default.) You are then prompted to select the objects to fillet. AutoCAD LT allows you to create fillets between lines, polylines, lines and polylines, arcs, and circles. See **Figure 6-45.**

To create a fillet, enter FILLET, or F, at the Command: prompt, click the **Fillet** button in the **Modify** toolbar, or select **Fillet** from the **Modify** pull-down menu. In the following example, the **Radius** option is first used to specify the size of the fillet.

FILLET
F

Modify
→ Fillet

Modify
toolbar

Fillet

> Command: **FILLET** *or* **F**⏎
> (TRIM mode) Current fillet radius = 0.5000
> Polyline/Radius/Trim/⟨Select first object⟩: **R**⏎
> Enter fillet radius ⟨0.5000⟩: **.4375**⏎
> Command:

Now that the radius is set, press [Enter] to repeat the **FILLET** command and select the lines (or polylines), arcs, or circles to be filleted.

> Command: ⏎
> FILLET
> (TRIM mode) Current fillet radius = 0.4375
> Polyline/Radius/Trim/⟨Select first object⟩: *(pick an object)*
> Select second object: *(pick a second object)*
> Command:

As soon as you select the second object, the fillet is created and the objects are automatically trimmed. Like the **CHAMFER** command, AutoCAD LT allows you to fillet nonintersecting lines as well as lines that overlap. You can also extend two lines to make a corner if you set the fillet radius to 0 (zero). See **Figure 6-46.**

Figure 6-45.
Creating a fillet.

First object
selected

Fillet radius

Second
object selected

Fillet radius

First object
selected

Second object
selected

Fillet
radius

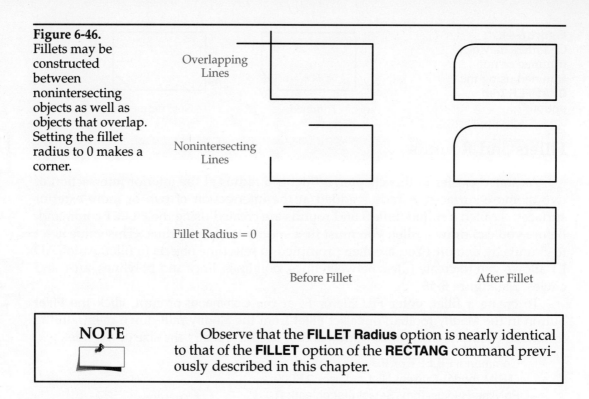

Figure 6-46.
Fillets may be constructed between nonintersecting objects as well as objects that overlap. Setting the fillet radius to 0 makes a corner.

Overlapping Lines

Nonintersecting Lines

Fillet Radius = 0

Before Fillet

After Fillet

NOTE

Observe that the **FILLET Radius** option is nearly identical to that of the **FILLET** option of the **RECTANG** command previously described in this chapter.

Filleting a 2D Polyline

The **FILLET** command also has a **Polyline** option that lets you fillet all the edges of a polyline in one operation. As with the **Polyline** option of the **CHAMFER** command, only those edges of the polyline long enough to accommodate the new segments are filleted. Each of the fillets is joined to the existing polyline as a polyarc segment. The **Polyline** option is used as follows:

    Command: **FILLET** or **F**↵
    (TRIM mode) Current fillet radius = 0.5000
    Polyline/Radius/Trim/⟨Select first object⟩: **P**↵
    Select 2D polyline: *(select a polyline, rectangle, or polygon)*
    n lines were filleted
    Command:

A polyline with all edges filleted in one operation is illustrated in **Figure 6-47.** Although the polyline shown is closed, open polylines may also be filleted using the **Polyline** option.

Figure 6-47.
All contiguous vertices of a polyline are filleted in one operation. The polyline may be open or closed.

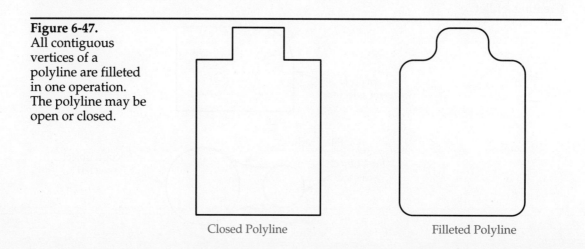

Closed Polyline

Filleted Polyline

Disabling Fillet Trimming

As with chamfers, the corners of lines and polylines are automatically trimmed whenever a fillet is created. If you wish to retain the corners, use the **Trim** option as follows:

Command: **FILLET** *or* **F**↵
(TRIM mode) Current fillet radius = 0.5000
Polyline/Radius/Trim/⟨Select first object⟩: **T**↵
Trim/No trim ⟨Trim⟩: **N**↵

Now construct your nontrimmed fillet using any of the filleting options previously described. See **Figure 6-48.** You can also use the **TRIMMODE** system variable to disable fillet trimming as follows:

Command: **TRIMMODE**↵
New value for TRIMMODE ⟨1⟩: *(enter* 0 *for no trim,* 1 *for trim and press* [Enter]*)*
Command:

Remember that changes made to the **TRIMMODE** variable affect the current drawing only. Once a new drawing is begun, **TRIMMODE** is restored to its default value of 1.

Figure 6-48. Fillets may be trimmed or not trimmed using the **FILLET Trim** option.

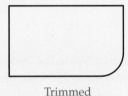   

Trimmed   Not Trimmed

Filleting Parallel Objects

It is possible to create a fillet between two parallel lines at any angle. See **Figure 6-49.** The objects may be lines, rays, and xlines. The procedure is identical to a normal filleting operation, but you need not set a radius value. This is because AutoCAD LT automatically sets the diameter of the fillet arc to be equal to the distance between the two objects you select. As shown in **Figure 6-50,** you can even create a fillet between two objects of unequal length. The procedure looks like this:

Command: **FILLET** *or* **F**↵
(TRIM mode) Current fillet radius = 0.5000
Polyline/Radius/Trim/⟨Select first object⟩: *(pick a line or ray)*
Select second object: *(pick a line, ray, or xline)*
Command:

It is not possible to create a parallel fillet between a line and a polyline or between two polylines. If you attempt to do so, AutoCAD LT displays the following message on the command line:

No intersection can be found between line and polyline line segments.

Figure 6-49. Creating a fillet between parallel lines.

Parallel
Lines

Select
Lines

Resulting
Fillet

Figure 6-50.
Creating a fillet
between parallel
lines of unequal
length.

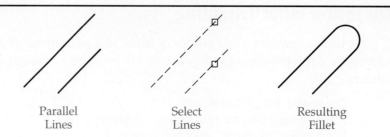

Parallel
Lines

Select
Lines

Resulting
Fillet

NOTE

Remember that it is not necessary to specify a radius value when filleting between parallel objects. However, the first object you select must be a line or ray. The second object may be a line, ray, or xline. See *Chapter 7* for more information about the **RAY** and **XLINE** commands.

EXERCISE 6-11

❑ Begin a new drawing with your TEMPLATEC template, or use your own variables.
❑ Create several shapes similar to those illustrated in **Figure 6-41.** Experiment with different distance values as you chamfer the objects.
❑ Draw two lines or polylines that do not intersect. Set the chamfer distance to 0 and make a corner of the two lines.
❑ Using the **CHAMFER Angle** option, duplicate the rectangle shown in **Figure 6-43.** Use any dimensions you like to construct and chamfer the object.
❑ Create several shapes similar to those illustrated in **Figure 6-46.** Experiment with different radius values as you fillet the objects.
❑ Draw two lines or polylines that do not intersect. Set the radius to 0 and make a corner of the two lines.
❑ Experiment with parallel filleting by duplicating the objects shown in **Figures 6-49** and **6-50.**
❑ Save the drawing as EX6-11 and quit.

Getting
Started
Guide 7

REVCLOUD
RC

Tools
↳ Re**v**ision Cloud

Draw
toolbar

Revcloud

Drawing Revision Clouds with **REVCLOUD**

When drawings are checked for correctness or modified to implement design improvements, it is common to highlight the areas to be revised using a practice called *clouding*. An example of clouding appears in **Figure 6-51.**

You can create your own revision clouds using the new **REVCLOUD** command in AutoCAD LT 98. The **REVCLOUD** command is not available in AutoCAD LT 97. The **REVCLOUD** command draws a cloud-shaped object using sequential polyarcs with a default arc length of .5 units. To create a revision cloud, enter REVCLOUD, or RC, at the Command: prompt, click the **Revcloud** button in the **Draw** toolbar, or select **Re**v**ision Cloud** from the **Tools** pull-down menu. See **Figure 6-52.** This is what the procedure looks like on the command line:

> Command: **REVCLOUD** *or* **RC**↵
> Current arc length = .500
> Arc length/⟨Pick cloud start point⟩: *(locate a point or enter* A *to change the arc length)*
> Guide crosshairs along cloud path...

Figure 6-51.
Clouding is a
technique used to
highlight an area of
a drawing that
requires revision.

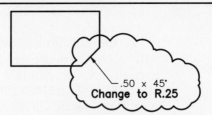

Figure 6-52. Select
Revision Cloud from
the **Tools** pull-down
menu to access the
REVCLOUD
command.

Now, simply move the graphics cursor in a counterclockwise direction around the area you wish to highlight. (Drawing in a clockwise direction results in a convex cloud as shown in **Figure 6-53**.) When the cursor gets near its initial starting point, the following message appears and the command is terminated.

Revision cloud finished.
Command:

Figure 6-53.
A convex cloud is
created by drawing
in a clockwise
direction.

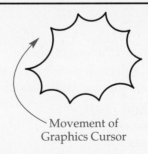

Movement of
Graphics Cursor

NOTE   Because revision clouds are drawn with polyline arc segments, they are affected by the current **PLINEWID** setting. Revision clouds may be edited using grips or with the **PEDIT** command. Grip editing is covered in *Chapter 10* of this text. The **PEDIT** command is covered in *Chapter 11*.

PROFESSIONAL TIP

In the traditional paper-based drafting environment, drafting checkers use a red pen or pencil to mark up drawing changes. You can emulate this convention by creating a layer called REDLINE or MARKUP, and assign the color red to the new layer. Then, set this layer current before using the **REVCLOUD** command.

Creating Regions

A *region* is an object type that encloses an area and can be combined with other regions using Boolean operations. Boolean operations are named after the English logician and mathematician George Boole (1815-1864). Boole's formulation of binary logic operators (AND, OR, NOT, etc.) played a major role in the development of modern digital computers. *Boolean operations* involve adding, subtracting, and intersecting regions with other regions to form entirely new objects called *composite regions*. These types of operations are described in the next section. AutoCAD LT 97 does not have the capability to create regions.

Regions are closed two-dimensional objects created from existing polylines, lines, arcs, circles, ellipses, elliptical arcs, and splines. They may contain holes, slots, or other types of cutouts. The internal features of a region are called *inner loops*, while the closed, outer boundary of a region is called an *outer loop*. Consider the objects shown in **Figure 6-54**. In this example, there is a rectangle, an ellipse, a circle, and two polygons. To convert these five objects into a region with five loops, enter REGION, or REG, at the Command: prompt, or select **Region** from the **Draw** pull-down menu. All of the selection set options may be used to select the objects that comprise the region. The procedure looks like this:

REGION
REG

Draw
➡ Region

> Command: **REGION** *or* **REG.**↵
> Select objects: *(select the objects to make up the region)*
> Select objects: ↵
> 5 loops extracted.
> 5 Regions created.
> Command:

Since regions have no thickness, therefore no height or depth, they can be considered two-dimensional solids. To see this for yourself, issue the **SHADE** command after creating the region. The display will appear similar to that shown in **Figure 6-55.**

> Command: **SHADE** *or* **SH.**↵
> Regenerating drawing.
> Shading complete.
> Command:

Figure 6-54.
Ordinary two-dimensional drawing objects are first drawn before creating a region.

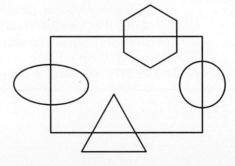

Figure 6-55.
A quick shading operation using the **SHADE** command verifies the region construction.

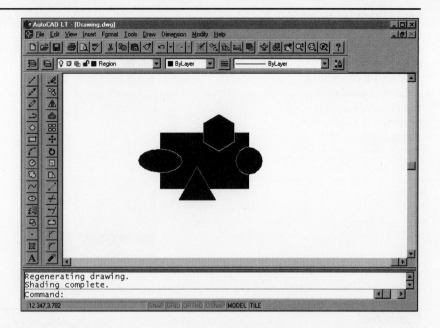

After performing a shading operation, issue the **REGEN** command to restore the normal screen display. See *Chapter 19* to learn more about the **SHADE** command and its options.

Editing Regions Using Boolean Operations

Once a region is created, it may be edited into its final form using Boolean operations. As previously mentioned, these functions perform the union, subtraction, or intersection of regions to form composite regions.

Joining regions together

The **UNION** command combines two or more existing regions to form a new composite region. Although the regions you select to join must lie on the same plane, it is possible to join regions that do not share a common area (overlap). To join one or more region objects together, enter UNION, or UNI, at the Command: prompt, click the **Union** button in the **Modify II** toolbar, or select **Region** from the **Modify** pull-down menu and then select **Union** from the cascading submenu. See **Figure 6-56.** All of the selection set options may be used to join regions together. The procedure appears on the command line as follows:

UNION
UNI

Modify
→ **Region**)
→ **Union**

**Modify II
toolbar**

Union

Command: **UNION** *or* **UNI**↵
Select objects: *(select the objects to join)*
Select objects: ↵
5 loops extracted.
5 Regions created.
Command:

The objects illustrated in **Figure 6-54** are shown unioned together in **Figure 6-57.**

Figure 6-56.
Selecting **Region** ›
from the **Modify**
pull-down menu
displays a cascading
submenu containing
the commands that
perform Boolean
operations.

Figure 6-57.
The results of a
union operation.
Compare this object
with those in
Figure 6-54.

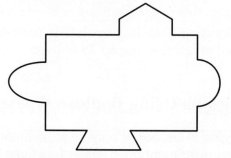

Subtracting regions from one another

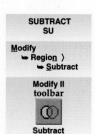

SUBTRACT
SU

Modify
↳ **Region** ›
↳ **Subtract**

Modify II
toolbar

Subtract

The **SUBTRACT** command subtracts one or more regions from another region to form a new composite region. The regions you subtract from other regions must all lie on the same plane. However, it is possible to perform simultaneous subtraction operations by selecting sets of regions that lie on different planes. The results are then separate, subtracted regions on each plane. To subtract a region, enter SUBTRACT, or SU, at the Command: prompt, click the **Subtract** button in the **Modify II** toolbar, or select **Region** from the **Modify** pull-down menu and then select **Subtract** from the cascading submenu. All of the selection set options may be used when subtracting regions from one another. In the example that follows, the ellipse, circle, and two polygons are subtracted from the rectangle shown in **Figure 6-54.** The procedure looks like this on the command line:

    Command: **SUBTRACT** *or* **SU**↵
    Select solids and regions to subtract from...
    Select objects: *(pick the rectangle)*
    Select objects: ↵
    Select solids and regions to subtract...
    Select objects: *(pick the ellipse, circle, and two polygons)*
    Select objects: ↵
    Command:

Essentially, the **SUBTRACT** command works by subtracting objects in the second selection set from objects in the first selection set. The results of the subtraction operation are shown in **Figure 6-58.**

Figure 6-58.
The results of a
subtract operation.
Compare this object
with that shown in
Figure 6-57.

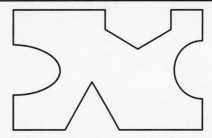

Intersecting regions together

When two or more regions overlap, you can create a new composite region consisting of the overlapping areas using the **INTERSECT** command. The regions you intersect with other regions must all lie on the same plane. However, it is possible to perform simultaneous intersection operations by selecting sets of regions that lie on different planes. The results are then separate, intersected regions on each plane. To intersect a region with another, enter INTERSECT, or IN, at the Command: prompt, click the **Intersect** button in the **Modify II** toolbar, or select **Region** from the **Modify** pull-down menu and then select **Intersect** from the cascading submenu. As with joining and subtracting, all of the selection set options may be used when intersecting regions with each other.

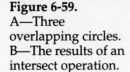

> Command: **INTERSECT** *or* **IN**↵
> Select objects: *(select the objects to intersect)*
> Select objects: ↵
> Command:

Consider the three overlapping circles shown at the left in **Figure 6-59.** The results of an intersection on these objects is shown at the right.

Figure 6-59.
A—Three
overlapping circles.
B—The results of an
intersect operation.

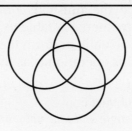

Before Intersection   After Intersection

NOTE

Once a region is created, its mass properties can also be calculated using the **MASSPROP** command. See *Chapter 8* to learn about **MASSPROP** and the other inquiry commands available in AutoCAD LT.

EXERCISE 6-12

❑ Begin a new drawing with your TEMPLATEA template, or use your own variables.

❑ Draw the triangle, square, and circle shown below at the left. Orient the three objects as shown.

❑ Convert the objects to regions.

❑ Join the objects together as shown.

❑ Perform an **UNDO** and subtract the circle from the other objects.

❑ Undo the subtraction and intersect the circle and the square.

❑ Save the drawing as EX6-12.

N-Way Booleans Using the **SUBTRACT** Command

Consider the object shown at the right in **Figure 6-60**. If you were to construct this object as a composite region, and based on what you have learned from the drawing commands described in this chapter, you would probably construct it using a rectangle, two circles, and four polygons as shown at the left of the illustration.

Since you have also learned how to join and subtract regions, you would most likely perform the required Boolean operations by joining the four polygons to the rectangle, and then subtracting the two circles. This would be a reasonable sequence of operations and would produce the finished composite region quite handily. However, there is a more efficient method available to you.

The **SUBTRACT** command can actually perform the union and subtraction in one step. The command sequence for this operation is as follows:

```
Command: SUBTRACT or SU↵
Select solids and regions to subtract from...
Select objects: (select the rectangle and four polygons)
Select objects: ↵
Select solids and regions to subtract...
Select objects: (select both circles)
Select objects: ↵
Command:
```

Figure 6-60.
Using an N-way Boolean, the object at the right can be created using only the **SUBTRACT** command. An automatic union is performed on the rectangle and four polygons at the left when selected as the regions to subtract from.

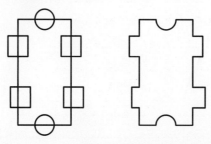

In this example, **SUBTRACT** automatically performs a union of the rectangle and four polygons first. Then it takes the resulting composite region and subtracts the two circles to complete the object. A combination operation such as this is called an *N-way Boolean*, since there are several regions (represented by the letter *N*) involved in the calculation. Because there is a fixed calculation overhead associated with every Boolean operation, it is usually far more efficient to perform several calculations simultaneously using N-way Booleans rather than perform them each separately.

PROFESSIONAL TIP

By using an N-way Boolean in the example above, an entire **UNION** operation was eliminated. This conserves system resources and shortens the drawing process. Utilizing N-way Booleans whenever possible is an excellent way to increase your personal productivity and/or your organization's *profitability*.

Chapter Test

Write your answers in the spaces provided.

1. Describe the **CIRCLE** command's **TTR** option.

   _____

   _____

   _____

2. What is an included angle? _____

   _____

3. Provide the command and entries required to draw a 30° ellipse with a major axis of 4.625 units. The ellipse is to be located by a center point and horizontally oriented.

   Command: _____

   ⟨Axis endpoint 1⟩/Center: _____

   Center of ellipse: _____

   Axis endpoint: _____

   ⟨Other axis distance⟩/Rotation: _____

   Rotation around major axis: _____

4. Define the term *NURBS*. Which two AutoCAD LT drawing objects use NURBS?

   _____

   _____

5. How do you draw a completely filled circle? _____

   _____

   _____

6. What should you do after turning **FILL** mode on or off? _____

   _____

   _____

7. What is the purpose of the **DLINE** command's **Break** option? _____

_____

_____

8. What is the purpose of the **DLINE** command's **Dragline** option? _____

_____

_____

9. *True or False?* Each line and arc segment in a double line is a separate object.

_____

10. How do polylines differ from lines? _____

_____

_____

_____

_____

11. What is the purpose of the **PLINE Length** option? _____

_____

_____

_____

_____

12. Rectangles and polygons are comprised of what type of object? _____

_____

13. What are the minimum and maximum number of sides for a polygon? _____

_____

_____

14. You need to draw a hexagon that is dimensioned across its flats. Which polygon construction option should be used? _____

_____

_____

15. When should the **POLYGON Edge** option be used? _____

_____

_____

_____

16. What is a compound object? Name the command that converts a compound object.

_____

_____

_____

_____

17. What is the purpose of the **PLINEWID** variable?

_____

_____

18. Which two of the following three object types cannot be drawn with assigned width—polylines, polygons, or rectangles?_____
_____
_____

19. Identify the **CHAMFER** option that toggles between the **Distance** and **Angle** options.

_____

20. *Yes or No?* Can a fillet be created between a line and a polyline? _____

21. *True or False?* A polyline must be exploded before it can be chamfered or filleted.

_____

22. How can you bring two lines together to make a corner? _____
_____
_____
_____
_____

23. *True or False?* It is necessary to specify a radius value before filleting between parallel objects. _____

24. Identify the system variable that controls whether corners are trimmed or not on chamfers and fillets._____
_____

25. How do you construct a convex revision cloud? _____
_____

26. What is a *region*?_____
_____
_____

27. Define *Boolean operations*. Identify the commands that perform them. _____
_____
_____
_____
_____

28. What is an *N-way Boolean*? Why would it be used? _____
_____
_____
_____

Chapter Problems

Mechanical
Drafting

1. Using your **TEMPLATEA** template drawing, draw the **GASKET** with the **CIRCLE** and **FILLET** commands. Place object lines on the **OBJECTS** layer and centerlines on the **CENTERLINES** layer. Do not draw the dimensions. Save the drawing as **P6-1**.

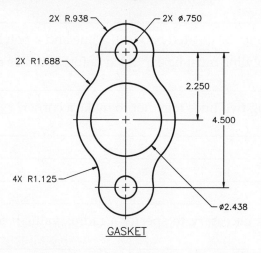

GASKET

Mechanical
Drafting

2. Draw the **ADJUSTING ARM** using fillets, chamfers, and the arc continuation option described in this chapter. Use your **TEMPLATEB** template drawing. As with P6-1, place object lines on the **OBJECTS** layer and centerlines on the **CENTERLINES** layer. Do not draw the dimensions. Save the drawing as **P6-2**.

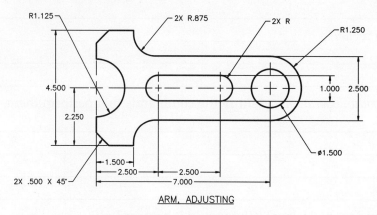

ARM, ADJUSTING

Mechanical
Drafting

3. Use your **TEMPLATEB** template drawing to draw the **CLOSED-END WRENCH**. Rotate the snap and grid as required to draw the hexagon at the proper orientation. As with the previous two drawing problems, place object lines on the **OBJECTS** layer and centerlines on the **CENTERLINES** layer. Do not draw the dimensions. Save the drawing as **P6-3**.

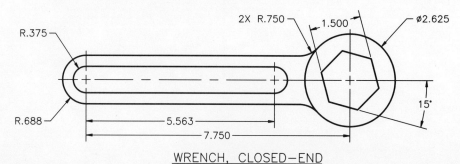

WRENCH, CLOSED-END

4. Use your TEMPLATEB template drawing to draw the object shown. Draw the outer profile with a polyline and chamfer as specified. Draw the inside features with a 4-sided polygon and two rectangles. Save the drawing as P6-4.

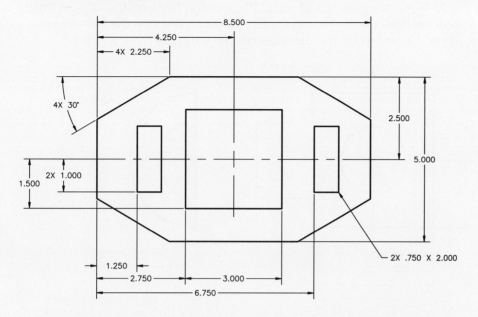

5. On a green layer named FLRPLAN, draw the floorplan shown below using the **DLINE** command. Use architectural units and set the drawing limits to 36',30'. The exterior walls are 6" thick, and the interior walls are 4" thick. Set the **DLINE Width** and **Dragline** options appropriately. Save the drawing as P6-5.

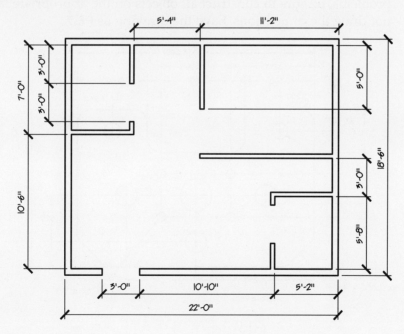

6. Draw the HALF PIN using your TEMPLATEA template drawing. Construct the front view with two rectangles and a circle using the correct dimensions. Use an N-way Boolean as described in this chapter to produce a composite region of the three objects. Draw the side view using lines and arcs. Place object lines on the Objects layer, hidden lines on the Hidden layer, and centerlines on the Centerlines layer. Do not draw the dimensions. Save the drawing as P6-6.

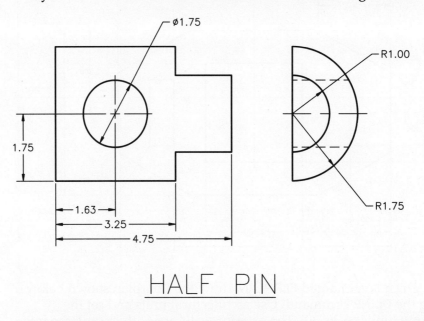

HALF PIN

7. Draw the PULLEY PLATE using fillets and chamfers as specified. Use your TEMPLATEB template drawing. As with the previous drawing problems, be sure to construct all objects on the appropriate layers. Do not draw the dimensions. Save the drawing as P6-7.

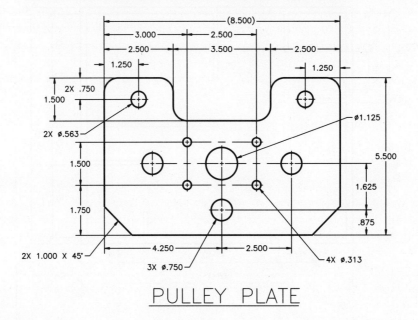

PULLEY PLATE

AutoCAD LT

Chapter 7

Geometry Construction Techniques

Learning Objectives

After you have completed this chapter, you will be able to:
- ○ Select objects at precise pick points using object snap modes.
- ○ Project views and features between views using rays and xlines.
- ○ Use **X** and **Y** coordinate filters to locate and project features and views.
- ○ Describe and use **TRACKING**.
- ○ Select and use **POINT** objects.
- ○ Divide a selected object into a specified number of segments.
- ○ Measure a selected object with specified length segments.
- ○ Offset an object at a specified distance or through a point to create a new object.
- ○ Create auxiliary views.

Perhaps more than anything else, AutoCAD LT is a geometry construction tool. In this chapter, you will learn how to select objects at precise locations to aid in geometry construction and editing. You will also learn how to project features and views using several different methods. This chapter also explains how to divide and measure selected objects with **POINT** objects, create parallel objects, and construct auxiliary views.

Using Object Snap Modes

The AutoCAD LT object snap modes allow you to precisely select objects at designated pick points. This is called *object snap* and means you snap to an object at a precise location. The object snap modes are commonly referred to as *osnaps* and each has a specific application. Some examples of osnaps include selecting a line at its endpoint or midpoint, or picking a circle or arc by its center point. Endpoint, midpoint, and center are three of the twelve object snap modes available.

The greatest advantage of osnaps is the extreme accuracy their use provides. For example, when you use the midpoint object snap on a line, AutoCAD LT always finds the *exact* midpoint of the line. Osnaps are quick and easy to use, too. If you use the endpoint osnap to select the end of a line, you need only pick somewhere near the line's endpoint. The endpoint osnap mode snaps to the exact end of the line you select.

Osnaps are not commands themselves, but modes that are used in conjunction with drawing and editing commands when a point is requested. When entered at the Command: prompt, each osnap mode may be abbreviated by its first three letters. Refer to the circle illustrated at the upper left of **Figure 7-1** as you study the command sequence that follows. In this example, a line is started from the exact center point of the circle.

> Command: **LINE** *or* **L**↵
> From point: **CEN**↵
> of *(locate the cursor over some portion of the circle and pick)*
> To point: *(pick a point for the end of the line)*

Whenever you use an osnap, a marker and **Snap Tip** are displayed as you move your cursor over a snap point. Each of the object snap modes displays a different marker. As shown in **Figure 7-1**, the marker for the **Center** osnap appears as a small circle at the center of circle, arc, ellipse, and donut objects. In this example, the **Snap Tip** clearly identifies the object snap mode in use as the **Center** osnap. This handy feature is called **AutoSnap**. It is described in more detail later in this chapter.

The twelve object snap modes are defined as follows:

- **Center.** Locates the center of a circle, ellipse, donut, or arc. See **Figure 7-1.** When you use the **Center** osnap, do not place the graphics cursor over the center of the object. You must place the cursor directly on the circle, ellipse, donut, or arc. AutoCAD LT will find the object's true center.

- **Endpoint.** As shown in **Figure 7-2**, osnap **Endpoint** finds the endpoint of a line, polyline, spline, or arc.

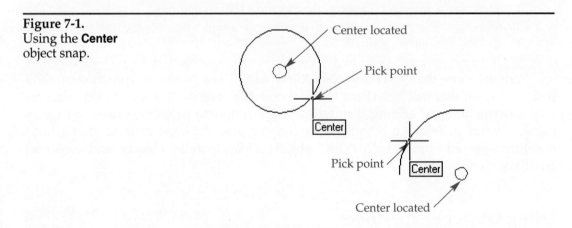

Figure 7-1.
Using the **Center** object snap.

Figure 7-2.
Using the **Endpoint** object snap.

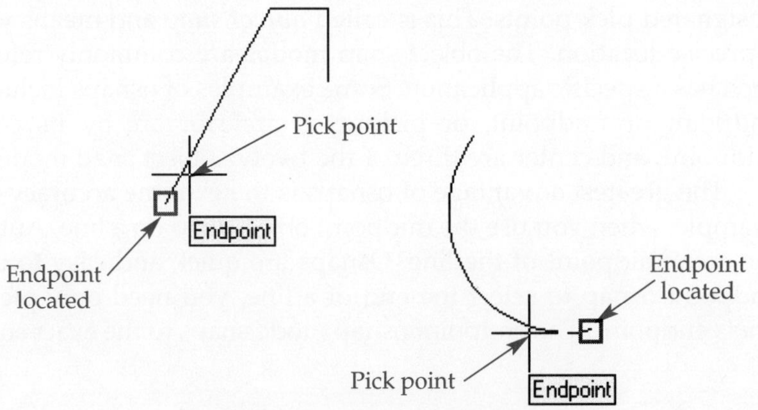

AutoCAD LT—Fundamentals and Applications

- **Insert.** This mode snaps to the insertion point of text or a block. See **Figure 7-3.** Refer to *Chapters 9* and *15* for complete information regarding text and block objects.
- **Intersection.** Picks the closest intersection of two or more objects. When using osnap, place the graphics cursor over the intersecting objects you wish to snap to. See **Figure 7-4.**
- **Midpoint.** As shown in **Figure 7-5**, osnap **Midpoint** locates the midpoint of a line, polyline, spline, or arc.
- **Nearest.** Locates a point on an object nearest to the graphics cursor. Only use this mode when a precise pick location is of secondary importance.
- **Node.** Snaps to a point drawn with the **POINT** command. In the example illustrated in **Figure 7-6**, point objects on the two horizontal lines are connected with lines using osnap **Node.** Points are discussed in a later section of this chapter.

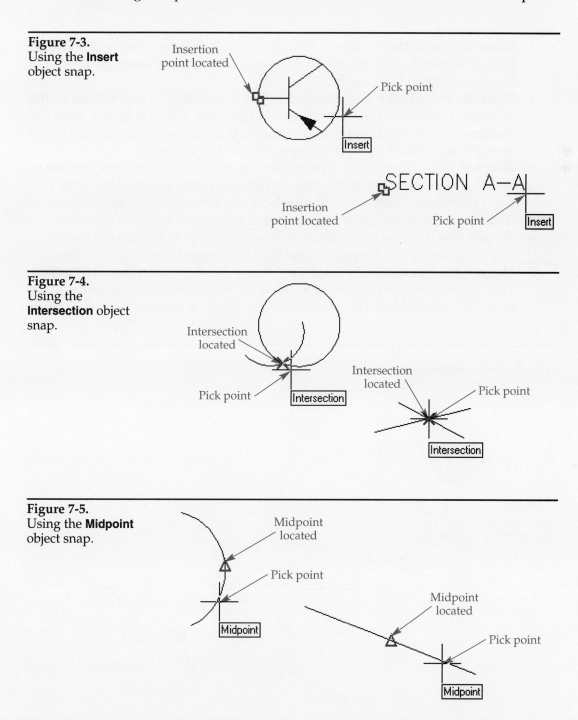

Figure 7-3.
Using the **Insert** object snap.

Figure 7-4.
Using the **Intersection** object snap.

Figure 7-5.
Using the **Midpoint** object snap.

Figure 7-6.
Using the **Node**
object snap.

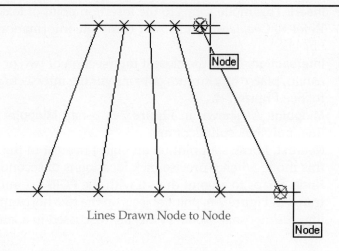

Lines Drawn Node to Node

- **None.** Use osnap **None** to override or turn off one or more running object snap modes. A permanently enabled object snap is called a *running osnap* and is described later in this chapter.
- **Perpendicular.** Creates a perpendicular line or polyline to one feature. In the example illustrated at the upper left of **Figure 7-7**, a line is drawn from the **Quadrant** of a circle perpendicular to a line. At the lower right, a line is drawn from the **Midpoint** of a polygon perpendicular to a rectangle.
- **Quadrant.** Picks one of four quadrants on a circle, ellipse, or donut closest to the target aperture. The quadrants correspond to the 0°, 90°, 180°, and 270° polar coordinate points. See **Figure 7-8A**. As shown in **Figure 7-8B**, osnap **Quadrant** can also be used to snap to the closest quadrant of an arc.
- **Tangent.** Use this object snap mode to draw a line or polyline tangent to a circle, ellipse, spline, or arc. Several examples of the **Tangent** osnap are illustrated in **Figure 7-9**. Observe that the **Snap Tip** displays the description **Deferred Tangent**. This description appears when you select an arc, polyarc, or circle as a starting point for a tangent line. The deferred tangent **Snap Tip** and marker appear when

Figure 7-7.
Using the **Perpendicular** object snap.

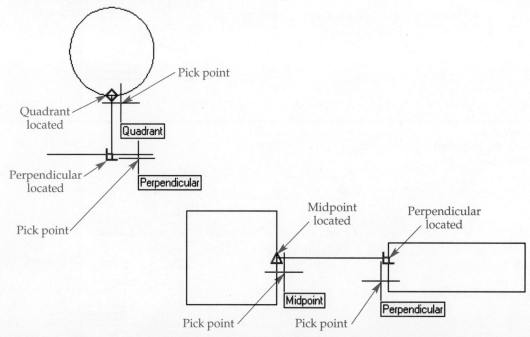

AutoCAD LT—Fundamentals and Applications

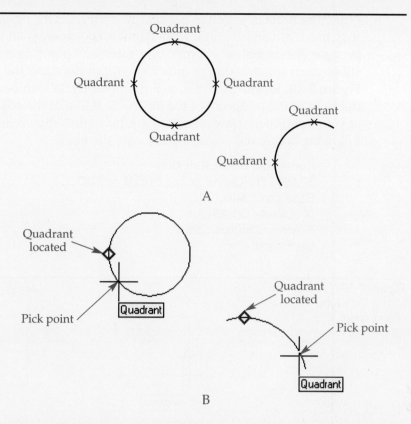

Figure 7-8.
A—**Quadrant** points on circles and arcs.
B—Using the **Quadrant** object snap.

you select the first point, and you are then prompted to enter a second point. As shown at the lower right of **Figure 7-9,** deferred tangent can also be used to create 2- or 3-point circles when the circle to be drawn is tangent to two or three other objects. Be advised that deferred tangent snap points do not work with ellipse or spline objects. If you draw a line that is tangent to an ellipse or spline, you will get a point on the ellipse or spline that is tangent to the last point selected. This usually causes unpredictable results. Also, for both splines and ellipses, the other point you specify must be on the same plane as the snap point.

Figure 7-9.
Using the **Tangent** object snap.

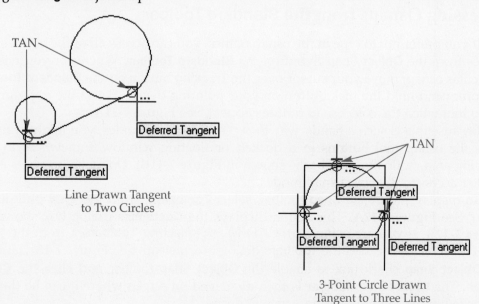

- **From.** The **From** object snap is very different from the other object snap modes. It is used in combination with relative coordinates and other object snaps because it establishes a temporary reference point as a basis for specifying subsequent construction points. To better understand the **From** osnap, refer to **Figure 7-10.** In this example, a .5 diameter circle is to be drawn 1.25 units to the right of the midpoint of the left vertical line of the object. If you are seated at your computer, draw an object similar to that shown in **Figure 7-10**, use the following command sequence to locate the circle:

> Command: **CIRCLE** *or* **C**↵
> 3P/2P/TTR/⟨Center point⟩: **FROM** *or* **FRO**↵
> Base point: **MID**↵
> of ⟨Offset⟩: **@1.25⟨0**↵
> Diameter/⟨Radius⟩: **.25**↵
> Command:

Figure 7-10.
Using the **From** object snap.

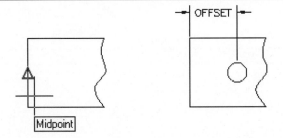

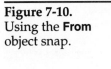

> **NOTE** When the **From** osnap is used in conjunction with the **Tangent** osnap to draw objects other than lines from arcs or circles, the first point drawn is tangent to the arc or circle in relation to the last point selected in the drawing window. Also, you can use an absolute coordinate as a base point, but be sure to specify a relative coordinate for the offset value. This is because specifying an absolute coordinate for the offset cancels the **From** object snap and locates the point at the specified absolute coordinate.

Accessing Osnaps from the Standard Toolbar

If you prefer not to type in the osnap names, you can access all of the object snap modes from the **Object Snap** flyout on the **Standard Toolbar**. Whenever you need a particular osnap, move your cursor over the **Tracking** button on the **Standard Toolbar** and press and hold the pick button on your pointing device. Select the appropriate osnap tool when the object snap buttons appear. See **Figure 7-11A.**

Because this is such a handy way to access the osnap modes, you might want to place the osnap tool buttons in a docked or floating window somewhere in the drawing area, (a floating toolbar is shown in **Figure 7-11B**). Doing so provides even quicker access to the object snap modes.

To display the **Object Snap** toolbar, select **Toolbars...** from the **View** pull-down menu. See **Figure 7-12A.** This action displays the **Customize** dialog box shown in **Figure 7-12B.** If you are using AutoCAD LT 97, selecting **Toolbars...** from the **View** pull-down menu accesses the **Toolbars** dialog box instead. See **Figure 7-13.** Activate the **Object Snap** check box to enable the **Object Snap** toolbar and click the **Close** button. The **Object Snap** toolbar is then displayed on screen where it can be floated or docked in the drawing window as you desire.

View
↪ Toolbars...

AutoCAD LT—Fundamentals and Applications

Figure 7-11.
A—Each of the
object snaps may be
accessed from the
Object Snap flyout
on the **Standard
Toolbar**. B—The
object snaps can
also be found on the
Object Snap toolbar.

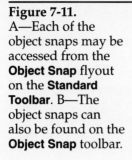

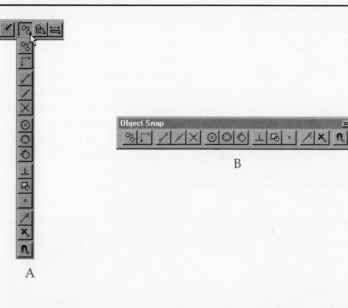

A

B

Figure 7-12.
A—Select **Toolbars...** from the **View** pull-down menu to display the **Customize** dialog box.
B—Activating the **Object Snap** toolbar from the **Customize** dialog box.

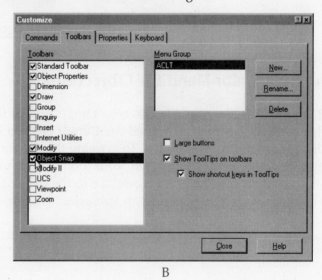

A

B

Figure 7-13. In
AutoCAD LT97,
select **Toolbars...**
from the **View** pull-
down menu to
display the **Toolbars**
dialog box, where
the **Object Snap**
toolbar can be
activated.

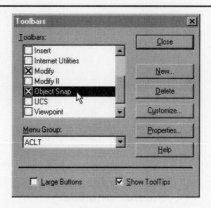

PROFESSIONAL TIP

If you are using AutoCAD LT 97, you can quickly open the **Toolbars** dialog box shown in **Figure 7-13** by placing your pointing device over one of the tool buttons on any toolbar and right-clicking. For AutoCAD LT 98 users, the same action displays the shortcut menu shown in **Figure 7-14.** Use this menu to turn toolbars on and off as desired. The checkmark (√) to the left of the toolbar name indicates that the toolbar is currently open.

Figure 7-14.
The shortcut menu enables AutoCAD LT 98 users to quickly turn toolbars on and off.

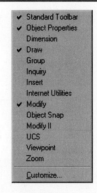

Using the **Cursor Menu** for Object Snaps

It is also possible to access the object snap modes from a floating **Cursor Menu**. See **Figure 7-15.** This menu is called the **Cursor Menu** because it displays at the location of the screen graphics cursor. To activate the **Cursor Menu**, hold down the [Shift] key and click the enter button on your pointing device. When the **Cursor Menu** appears, simply move the pointing device to the desired osnap and click. The **Cursor Menu** disappears and the object snap you select is enabled for one pick only.

Figure 7-15.
The cursor menu provides quick access to object snap modes.

NOTE

If you are using a 3-button mouse, the middle button is often preconfigured by AutoCAD LT to automatically activate the **Cursor Menu.**

PROFESSIONAL TIP

Remember that object snaps are not commands, but modes that are used in conjunction with drawing and editing functions. For example, if you were to type in MID or PER at the Command: prompt, then AutoCAD LT would display an error message.

Setting Running Object Snaps

A *running object snap* is an osnap that is permanently enabled. This is particularly handy if you plan to use the same object snap mode repeatedly. As an example, you might set the **Endpoint** osnap running if you need to connect a series of line endpoints. A running osnap stays on until you turn it off, and you can have more than one osnap mode running at a time.

When you have multiple running osnaps, AutoCAD LT selects the most appropriate osnap to use depending on the object you select or where the object is picked. For example, suppose you set both **Midpoint** and **Endpoint** as running osnaps and then pick a line. Which is selected—the midpoint or endpoint of the line? If you pick closer to the middle of the line, then the midpoint is selected. If you pick closer to the end of the line, then the endpoint of the line is selected. However, be advised that some osnap modes conflict with one another. As an example, if you were to set osnap **Quadrant** and **Center** running simultaneously, **Center** would be ignored and **Quadrant** would take precedence. Can you think of other object snap modes that might conflict?

Setting a Running Object Snap with a Dialog Box

DDOSNAP
OSNAP or OS

Tools
⮡ Object Snap Settings...

Status Bar

OSNAP

To set one or more running osnaps, enter DDOSNAP, or OSNAP or OS, at the Command: prompt, click the **Object Snap Settings** button at the bottom of the **Object Snap** flyout on the **Standard toolbar**, or select **Object Snap Settings...** from the **Tools** pull-down menu. See **Figure 7-16** You may also select **Osnap Settings...** from the cursor menu or double-click **OSNAP** on the status bar at the bottom of the graphics window.

Figure 7-16.
Selecting **Object Snap Settings...** from the **Tools** pull-down menu opens the **Osnap Settings** dialog box.

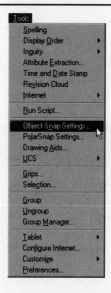

The **Osnap Settings** dialog box is shown in **Figure 7-17.** In this example, both the **Endpoint** and **Center** osnap modes are selected. To turn off a running osnap, click the appropriate check box to deactivate the osnap. If you want to turn off all running osnaps, click the **Clear All** button. Keep in mind that you can override one or more running osnaps at anytime by simply selecting a different osnap for one pick only. Once that pick is completed, any running osnaps are again in effect until overridden once more.

Figure 7-17.
Setting **Endpoint** and **Center** running osnaps from the **Osnap Settings** dialog box.

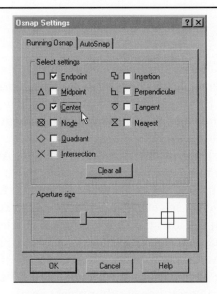

PROFESSIONAL TIP   By double-clicking **OSNAP** on the status bar, you can quickly turn running osnaps on and off. If no osnaps are set, then double-clicking **OSNAP** on the status bar displays the **Osnap Settings** dialog box. An even faster way to toggle running osnaps on and off is by pressing the [F3] function key or using the [Ctrl]+[F] keyboard combination.

Using AutoSnap

As mentioned earlier in this chapter, the **AutoSnap** feature displays a marker and a **Snap Tip** when you move the cursor over a snap point when osnaps are used. **AutoSnap** is automatically turned on when you enter an object snap name on the command line, select an osnap tool from the flyout on the **Standard Toolbar**, or turn on one or more running object snaps using the **Osnap Settings** dialog box.

After entering a drawing or editing command, **AutoSnap** indicates the snap points as you move your pointing device over an object. The cycling feature lets you cycle through all the running osnap points available for a particular object by pressing the [Tab] key. As an example, suppose you have both **Endpoint** and **Midpoint** running osnaps. When you place your cursor over a line, polyline, spline, or arc and press the [Tab] key, **AutoSnap** will cycle between the **Endpoint** and **Midpoint** snap points on the object. Release the [Tab] key when the osnap you want is displayed.

You can change several **AutoSnap** settings by selecting the **AutoSnap** tab in the **Osnap Settings** dialog box. See **Figure 7-18.** The options available are described as follows:

- **Marker.** The marker is a geometric symbol that displays the object snap location when you move your graphics cursor over snap points of an object. Deactivate this check box if you wish to disable markers.
- **Magnet.** On by default, this handy feature forces an automatic movement of the graphics cursor so that the cursor locks onto the snap point.
- **SnapTip.** This is the identifier that describes which part of the object you are snapping to. As with markers and the magnet, snaptips are on by default.
- **Display aperture box.** Versions previous to AutoCAD LT 98 and AutoCAD LT 97 did not have the **AutoSnap** magnet feature. Instead, a small target symbol, called the *aperture box,* was displayed whenever an osnap was used. Although no longer needed, you can toggle the **Display aperture box** on if you wish to use this feature. When enabled, the aperture box is displayed in the center of the graphics cursor when you snap to an object. The size of the aperture box is measured in pixels and defaults to a value of 10 pixels. It can be set to any value between 1 and 50 pixels on the command line using the **APERTURE** system variable as follows:

Command: **APERTURE**⏎
Object snap target height (1-50 pixels) ⟨*current*⟩: (*enter a value 1 to 50*)

You can also change the aperture box size transparently by typing **'APERTURE** in the middle of another command. An example of the aperture box at various sizes appears in **Figure 7-19.**

Figure 7-18.
Click the **AutoSnap** tab in the **Osnap Settings** dialog box to make changes to the **AutoSnap** settings.

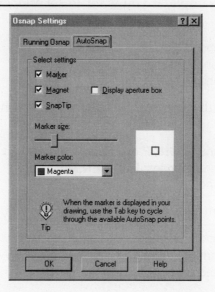

Figure 7-19.
Several examples of various aperture box sizes. When activated, the aperture box can be sized between 1 and 50 pixels with 10 pixels as the default.

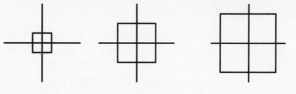

PROFESSIONAL TIP

If you choose to activate the aperture box, be advised that a very large aperture size increases the risk of selecting the wrong object since it is likely that two or more objects may fall into the increased target area. On the other hand, a very small aperture slows you down because it takes more time to position the aperture over the desired object. Most users find that a size of 5–6 pixels works well. Experiment with various sizes to learn which size suits your personal taste and work habits. Once you change the size of the aperture, the new size is used for all subsequent drawing sessions until changed again.

- **Marker si_ze:.** This horizontal slider bar controls the size of the marker. Slide the bar to the right to increase the marker size—slide to the left to decrease the marker size.
- **Marker _color:.** Use this drop-down list if you wish to change the color of markers from the default magenta to one of the other AutoCAD LT standard colors. The standard colors are red, yellow, green, cyan, blue, magenta, and white, respectively. Remember that the color white is white on a dark screen background, but black on a light screen background.

Setting a Running Object Snap on the Command Line

-OSNAP
-OS

To set one or more running object snaps, enter -OSNAP, or -OS, at the Command: prompt. For example, if you want to set **Midpoint** as a running object snap, do the following:

Command: **-OSNAP** *or* **-OS**↵
Object snap modes: **MID**↵
Command:

To set multiple running osnaps, enter the first three letters of each mode separated by commas. For example:

Command: **-OSNAP** *or* **-OS**↵
Object snap modes: **END,CEN,MID**↵
Command:

When you want to turn off any running osnaps, do the following:

Command: **-OSNAP** *or* **-OS**↵
Object snap modes: *(enter* NONE *or* OFF *or press* [Enter]*)*
Command:

PROFESSIONAL TIP

Using osnaps greatly increases your productivity and accuracy. As an additional time-saver, enable those object snap modes you use most often as running object snaps in your template file(s).

EXERCISE 7-1

❏ Begin a new drawing with your **TEMPLATEB** template drawing, or use your own setup variables.

❏ Draw the objects shown below. As a construction hint, start with the two arcs and then draw a rectangle and a circle.

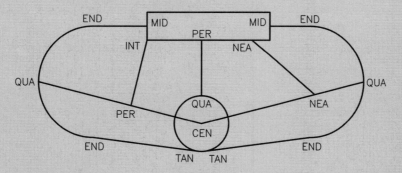

❏ Use the osnap modes indicated to draw the required lines.

❏ Next, try using the **From** object snap mode to draw an object similar to that shown in **Figure 7-10.**

❏ Save the drawing as EX7-1.

Coordinate Filters

Coordinate filters allow you to locate a point by extracting, or *filtering out*, the X, Y, and Z coordinate values of existing objects. You can use one or more filters whenever AutoCAD LT requests a point. The coordinate filters may only be accessed from the command line by entering .X, .Y, or .Z as required.

Using Coordinate Filters

Suppose you wanted to place the center of a circle, ellipse, or polygon at the center of a rectangle or square. See **Figure 7-20.** Coordinate filters accomplish this task by extracting the midpoint X value of one of the horizontal lines, and the midpoint Y value of one of the vertical lines. In the example that follows, the filters are entered on the command line and the X value is filtered before the YZ value. However, the same operation could be performed by filtering the Y value first, and then the XZ value. The command sequence is as follows:

> Command: **CIRCLE** *or* **C**↵
> 3P/2P/TTR/⟨Center point⟩: **.X**↵
> of **MIDPOINT** *or* **MID**↵
> of *(pick the top horizontal line)*
> of (need YZ): **MIDPOINT** *or* **MID** ↵
> of (need YZ): *(pick the right vertical line)*
> Diameter/⟨Radius⟩ ⟨current⟩: *(enter the desired radius at P3)*
> Command:

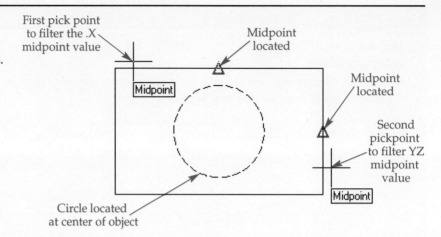

Figure 7-20.
Locating a circle center using X and Y coordinate filters.

First pick point to filter the .X midpoint value

Midpoint located

Midpoint located

Second pickpoint to filter YZ midpoint value

Midpoint

Midpoint

Circle located at center of object

Using X and Y Coordinate Filters to Project Views and View Features

Consider the drawing illustrated in **Figure 7-21A.** If you were drawing this object on a drafting board, you would probably draw the front view first. Then, using conventional drafting instruments, orthogonally project lines and points in the front view to complete the right side view. Coordinate filters can be used to perform similar projection operations. The front view can be drawn very efficiently using the **RECTANG** command, and the circle constructed using X filters and Y filters as previously described. See **Figure 7-21B.** The command sequence to draw the side view is as follows:

> Command: **RECTANG** *or* **REC**↵
> Chamfer/Elevation/Fillet/Thickness/Width/⟨First corner⟩: **.Y**↵
> of **ENDPOINT** *or* **END** ↵
> of *(pick lower-right corner of rectangle, P1)*
> of (need XZ): *(pick point P2 to set distance between the views)*
> Other corner: **@2,3**↵
> Command:

The rectangle that represents the side view is now complete. Because its lower-left corner is located by filtering the Y value of the front view's lower-right corner, it is aligned orthogonally with that view.

Now, using polylines rather than lines, it is also a simple matter to draw the hidden lines which represent the circle seen in the side view. This operation is performed using both **Quadrant** and **Perpendicular** object snap modes. See **Figure 7-22.** The command sequence is as follows:

> Command: **PLINE** *or* **PL**↵
> From point: **.Y**↵
> of **QUADRANT** *or* **QUA**↵
> of *(pick point P1 near circle)*
> of (need XZ): **PERPENDICULAR** *or* **PER**↵
> to *(pick point P2 anywhere on line)*
> Current line-width is 0.0000
> Arc/Close/Halfwidth/Length/Undo/Width/⟨Endpoint of line⟩:**PERPENDICULAR** *or* **PER**↵
> to *(draw to* **Perpendicular** *point P3 on opposite line)*
> Arc/Close/Halfwidth/Length/Undo/Width/⟨Endpoint of line⟩:*(press* [Enter] *or space bar to exit the command)*
> Command:

Now that one of the hidden lines is drawn, repeat the procedure to draw the second hidden line.

AutoCAD LT—Fundamentals and Applications

Figure 7-21.
A—Orthographic views with projected features can be created using X and Y coordinate filters. B—Drawing a side view using plines with X and Y coordinate filters.

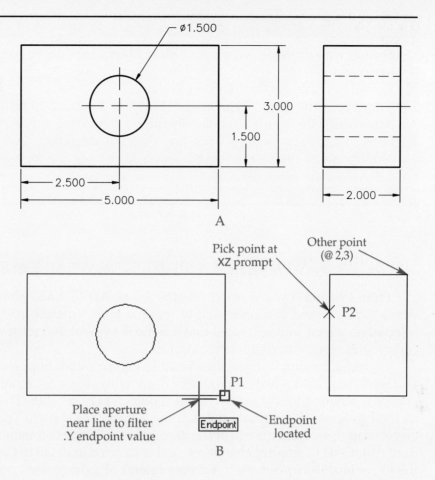

Figure 7-22.
Projecting a pline using X and Y coordinate filters.

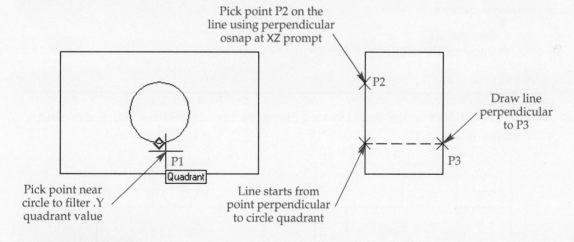

PROFESSIONAL TIP

You can greatly increase your productivity when you use object snap modes in conjunction with X and Y coordinate filters by setting the required object snap modes to be running osnaps. Additionally, it is often helpful to turn blips on when using coordinate filters because they provide points of reference in the drawing window. Set the **BLIPMODE** system variable to 1 to turn on blips.

EXERCISE 7-2

❑ Begin a new drawing with your TEMPLATEA template, or use your own setup variables.
❑ Turn off the grid and snap if they are on.
❑ Draw the front view of the object shown in **Figure 7-20** and locate the circle center using the X and Y coordinate filter technique discussed in this chapter.
❑ Construct the top view (not the side view) of the object using the appropriate running object snap modes and X and Y filters. For the top view, which coordinate values are filtered—X or Y?
❑ Save the drawing as EX7-2.

Using the @ Symbol as a Construction Reference Point

From Chapter 3 you learned that the AutoCAD LT **LASTPOINT** system variable stores the X, Y, and Z coordinates of the last point entered from the keyboard, or selected on screen. You will recall that it is the @ symbol that retrieves the **LASTPOINT** coordinates when entering relative coordinates.

Consider the simple object illustrated in **Figure 7-23A.** Suppose, for example, that you were the drafter who had originally drawn this object. Six months later, a drawing change is required to add the two holes shown in **Figure 7-23B.** There is a very simple method to locate the required holes at the dimensions shown. This method requires object snap modes and the use of the **ID** command. The **ID** command is one of the standard AutoCAD LT inquiry commands and is covered in detail in *Chapter 8.* Essentially, the **ID** command displays the X,Y,Z coordinates of a designated point in the drawing window. The coordinate values returned by the **ID** command are then stored in the **LASTPOINT** system variable, and are therefore accessible using the @ symbol. To locate the 1.250 diameter circle at the dimensions shown in **Figure 7-23A**, use the following command sequence:

> Command: **ID**↵
> Point: *(pick the **Midpoint** of the top line)*

Figure 7-23.
A—Object as originally drawn. B—A Drawing Change Notice requires the addition of two holes.

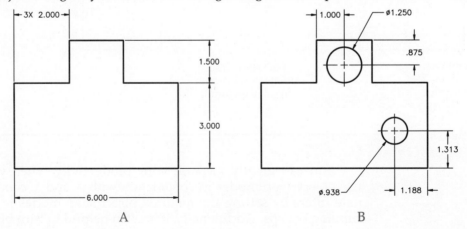

AutoCAD LT—Fundamentals and Applications

The screen coordinates of the line midpoint are displayed on the prompt line and stored in the **LASTPOINT** variable. See **Figure 7-24A**. The required circle is now located relative to that point.

> Command: **CIRCLE** *or* **C**↵
> 3P/2P/TTR/⟨Center point⟩: **@.875⟨270**↵
> Diameter/⟨Radius⟩ ⟨*current*⟩: **.625**↵
> Command:

The .938 diameter circle at the lower right of the object is located in a similar fashion. For this operation, the **Endpoint** object snap mode is used. See **Figure 7-24B**. The command sequence is as follows:

> Command: **ID**↵
> Point: (*pick the right* **Endpoint** *of the bottom line*)

The screen coordinates of the line endpoint are displayed on the prompt line and stored in the **LASTPOINT** variable. The required circle is then located relative to that point.

> Command: **CIRCLE** *or* **C**↵
> 3P/2P/TTR/⟨Center point⟩: **@-1.1875,1.3125**↵
> Diameter/⟨Radius⟩ ⟨*current*⟩: **.46875**↵
> Command:

Figure 7-24.
A—Using **ID** and the **Midpoint** osnap to locate the top hole.
B—Using **ID** and the **Endpoint** osnap to locate the hole at the bottom right.

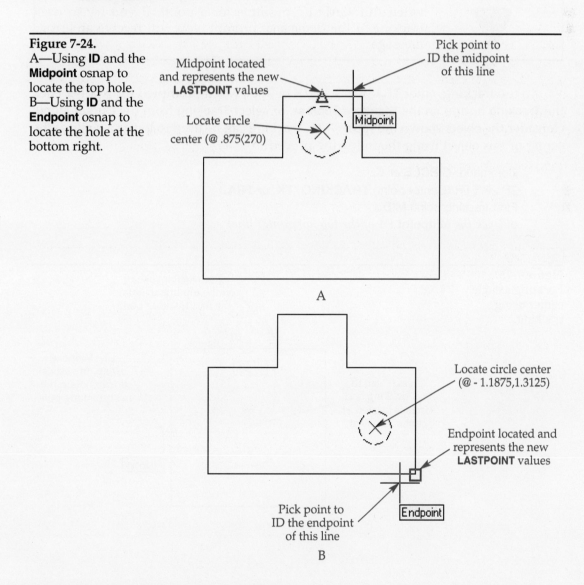

EXERCISE 7-3

❏ Begin a new drawing with your TEMPLATEA template, or use your own setup variables.
❏ Draw the object shown in **Figure 7-23A**.
❏ Add the two circles shown in **Figure 7-23B** using the **ID** command and the method just described.
❏ Save the drawing as EX7-3.

Getting Started Guide 8

Using Tracking

Tracking, like coordinate filters, lets you specify a point relative to existing points. However, unlike coordinate filters, tracking is limited to X and Y values and cannot be used for 3D constructions. This is because tracking is always performed orthogonally, or parallel to the snap axes. If you rotate the snap axes using the **SNAP** command's **Rotate** option, you also rotate the tracking axes.

CAUTION   As with osnaps and point filters, tracking works only when AutoCAD LT prompts for a point. If you try to use tracking at the Command: prompt, you will receive an error message.

TRACKING
TK or TRA

Cursor Menu
➥ Trac**k**ing

Standard
Toolbar

Tracking

To use tracking, enter TRACKING, or TK or TRA, when prompted for a point, click the **Tracking** button on the **Standard Toolbar,** or select **Trac<u>k</u>ing** from the **Cursor Menu.** Consider the object shown in **Figure 7-25.** Tracking can be used to locate a circle at the center of this object using the following procedure:

Command: **CIRCLE** *or* **C**↵
3P/2P/TTR/⟨Center point⟩:**TRACKING, TK,** *or* **TRA**↵
First tracking point: **MID**↵
of *(pick the* **Midpoint** P1 *of the top horizontal line)*

Figure 7-25.
Locating a circle
center using
tracking.

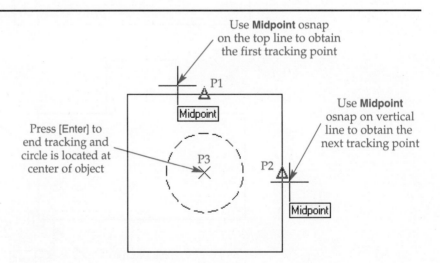

Use **Midpoint** osnap on the top line to obtain the first tracking point

Use **Midpoint** osnap on vertical line to obtain the next tracking point

Press [Enter] to end tracking and circle is located at center of object

Now, move your cursor up and down until you see the rubber-band line. When the rubber-band line appears, you are ready to continue.

> Next point (Press RETURN to end tracking): **MID**↵
> of (pick the **Midpoint** P2 of the right vertical line)
> Next point (Press RETURN to end tracking): ↵
> Diameter/⟨Radius⟩ ⟨*current*⟩: *(enter the desired radius at P3)*
> Command:

When you use tracking, it is very important to move your cursor directly up, down, left, or right until you see the rubber-band line. This is because the direction of your cursor movement affects the tracking direction. If you fail to move your cursor as required, it is likely that tracking will not work properly.

Using Tracking to Project View Features

Tracking can also be used to project views and view features. In **Figure 7-24,** tracking is used to project hidden lines that represent the circle in the top view. Study **Figure 7-26** as you proceed through the following sequence of steps:

> Command: **LINE** *or* **L**↵
> From point: **TRACKING, TK,** *or* **TRA**↵
> First tracking point: **QUA**↵
> of *(pick* **Quadrant** *point P1 on the circle)*

Now, move your cursor up and down until you see the rubber-band line. When the rubber-band line appears, you may continue.

> Next point (Press RETURN to end tracking): **PER**↵
> to *(pick* **Perpendicular** *point P2 anywhere on the top line)*
> Next point (Press RETURN to end tracking): ↵
> To point: **PER**↵
> to *(draw to* **Perpendicular** *point P3 on the bottom line)*
> To point: *(press* [Enter] *or space bar to exit the command)*
> Command:

Do you see how tracking can also be used to project the edges of the top view chamfers to the bottom view?

Figure 7-26.
Projecting lines using tracking.

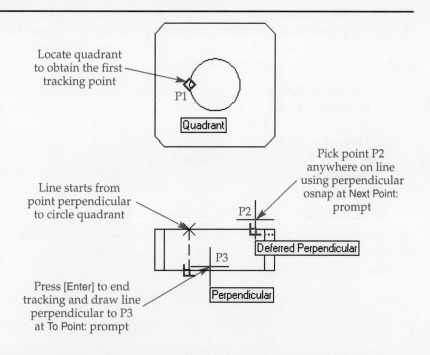

Locate quadrant to obtain the first tracking point

P1

Quadrant

Pick point P2 anywhere on line using perpendicular osnap at Next Point: prompt

Line starts from point perpendicular to circle quadrant

P2

Deferred Perpendicular

P3

Perpendicular

Press [Enter] to end tracking and draw line perpendicular to P3 at To Point: prompt

---

PROFESSIONAL TIP

You can greatly increase your productivity when you use object snap modes in conjunction with tracking by setting the required object snap modes to be running osnaps.

EXERCISE 7-4

❑ Begin a new drawing using your own setup variables.
❑ Using any dimensions you like, draw the object shown in **Figure 7-26**. *Construction hint:* Use the **RECTANG** command to draw both the top and bottom views. As you construct the top view, use the **Chamfer** option of the **RECTANG** command to create the chamfers.
❑ Turn off the grid and snap if they are on.
❑ With **Ortho** mode on, add the circle to the middle of the top view using the tracking method just described and illustrated in **Figure 7-25**.
❑ Project the chamfer edges to the bottom view using the tracking method.
❑ Save the drawing as EX7-4.

Getting Started Guide 8

Projecting Features with Rays and Xlines

The previous sections described coordinate filters and tracking as methods that can be used to project features between views. It is also possible to create construction lines that extend to infinity in one or both directions using the **RAY** and **XLINE** commands. Even though the construction lines are infinite, they do not change the total area of the drawing and therefore have no effect on zooming operations. As an aid to construction, rays and xlines may also be drawn in different layers and assigned linetypes. Once drawn, these infinite length objects may then be trimmed as necessary. An introduction to trimming is provided later in this section.

Projecting in One Direction Using the RAY Command

RAY

Draw
➥ Ray

The **RAY** command may be issued by entering RAY at the Command: prompt, or by selecting **Ray** from the **Draw** pull-down menu. See **Figure 7-27**. To better understand how rays are used to project features between views, refer to **Figure 7-28** as you study the following command sequence:

```
Command: RAY↵
From point: END↵
of (pick P1 using Endpoint osnap)
Through point: PER↵
to (pick P2 using Perpendicular osnap)
Through point: ↵
Command:
```

In this example, the appropriate object snap modes are used to project a ray representing the edge of the chamfer to the side view. Observe how the ray extends infinitely in one direction. **RAY** continues with the Through point: prompt until the command is terminated by pressing [Enter].

Figure 7-27.
Selecting **Ray** from
the **Draw** pull-down
menu.

Figure 7-28.
Using a ray with the
appropriate osnaps
to project the edge
of the chamfer to
the side view.

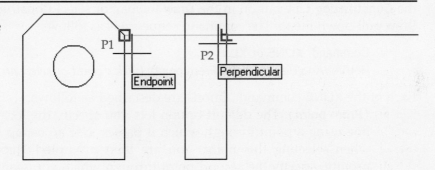

In the next step, a layer with the Hidden linetype assigned is set current and **RAY** is used again to project the edges of the circle quadrants to the side view. Refer to **Figure 7-29** as you study the following command sequence:

```
Command: RAY↵
From point: QUA↵
of (pick P1 using Quadrant osnap)
Through point: PER↵
to (pick P2 using Perpendicular osnap)
Through point: ↵
Command:
```

A second ray is then created to represent the top quadrant of the circle. To complete the side view, the three infinite rays are trimmed as required. The completed object is shown in **Figure 7-30.**

Figure 7-29.
Additional rays
drawn with the
Hidden linetype are
used to project the
circle to the side view.

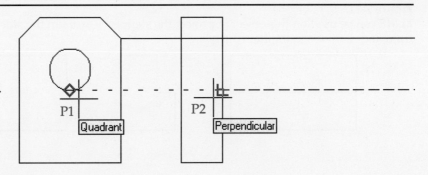

Figure 7-30.
After trimming
away the unneeded
portions of the rays,
the object is
completed.

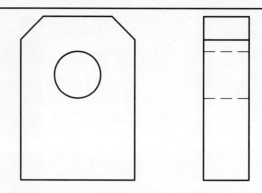

Projecting in Both Directions Using the **XLINE** Command

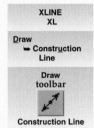

Use the **XLINE** command when you wish to create a construction line that projects in both directions. A typical example appears in **Figure 7-31.** Observe how the stepped feature in the side view can be projected to both the front and rear views simultaneously. To issue the **XLINE** command, enter XLINE, or XL, at the Command: prompt, select the **Construction Line** button in the **Draw** toolbar, or select **Construction Line** from the **Draw** pull-down menu. The command sequence is as follows:

> Command: **XLINE** *or* **XL**↵
> Hor/Ver/Ang/Bisect/Offset/⟨From point⟩: *(pick a point or select an option)*

Each of the **XLINE** command options are described as follows:

- **⟨From point⟩.** The default option lets you specify the location of the infinite line using a point through which it passes. Use an osnap where appropriate when selecting this point. You are then prompted Through point:. At this prompt, specify the second point through which you want the xline to pass. When selecting the second point, be sure to use an appropriate osnap, or turn **Ortho** mode on to force a straight construction line. AutoCAD LT then places the infinite xline through the specified point. Refer to **Figure 7-32** as you follow the command sequence below:

> Command: **XLINE** *or* **XL**↵
> Hor/Ver/Ang/Bisect/Offset/⟨From point⟩: **END**↵
> of *(pick* P1 *using* **Endpoint** *osnap)*
> Through point: **PER**↵
> to *(pick* P2 *using* **Perpendicular** *osnap)*
> Through point: ↵
> Command:

It is now a simple matter to trim away the unneeded portions of the xline, and change the properties of one line segment from the Continuous linetype to the Hidden linetype. Doing so results in the object shown in **Figure 7-31.**

Figure 7-31.
XLINE can be used on this object to project the stepped feature in the side view to both the front and rear views simultaneously.

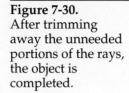

Figure 7-32.
Using **XLINE** with the appropriate object snap modes to project the stepped feature between views.

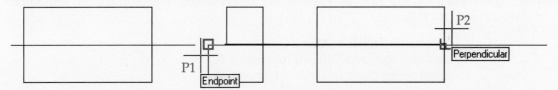

- **Hor.** This option creates a horizontal xline passing through a selected point. You are prompted Through point:. If appropriate, use an osnap to specify the point through which you want the horizontal xline to pass.
- **Ver.** This option creates a vertical xline passing through a selected point. You are prompted Through point:. As with the other xline options, use the appropriate osnap to specify the point through which you want the vertical xline to pass.
- **Ang.** This option creates an xline at a specified angle. A practical example of an object that requires an auxiliary view with xlines at 45° is shown in **Figure 7-33**. (Suggestions for the construction of auxiliary views are presented at the end of this chapter.) The command sequence for angled xlines looks like this:

> Command: **XLINE** *or* **XL**↵
> Hor/Ver/Ang/Bisect/Offset/⟨From point⟩: **A**↵
> Reference/⟨Enter angle (*current*)⟩: **45**↵
> Through point: *(pick a point using an osnap if appropriate)*
> Through point: *(continue picking points or press* [Enter] *to end the command)*
> Command:

You can use the **Reference** suboption to specify an angle from an existing object. The object may be a line, polyline, ray, or another xline. This is handy when you do not know the angle of the construction line, but you do know the required angle between an existing object and the construction line. The **Reference** suboption looks like this:

> Command: **XLINE** *or* **XL**↵
> Hor/Ver/Ang/Bisect/Offset/⟨From point⟩: **A**↵
> Reference/⟨Enter angle (45)⟩: **R**↵
> Select a line object: *(pick an object you want a construction line angled from)*
> Enter angle ⟨current⟩: *(enter an angle)*
> Through point: *(pick a point using the appropriate osnap)*
> Through point: *(continue picking points or press* [Enter] *to end the command)*
> Command:

Figure 7-33.
The **XLINE Ang** option is often used to facilitate the construction of auxiliary views.

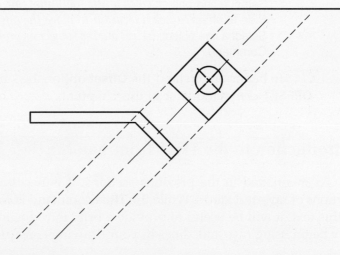

- **Bisect.** This option creates an xline that bisects an existing angle. The xline passes through the selected angle vertex and bisects the angle between the first and second line as shown in **Figure 7-34.** The command sequence appears as follows:

> Command: **XLINE** *or* **XL**↵
> Hor/Ver/Ang/Bisect/Offset/⟨From point⟩: **A**↵
> Angle vertex point: *(pick the angle vertex)*
> Angle start point: *(pick a point on one side of the angle)*
> Angle end point: *(pick a point on the other side of the angle)*
> Angle end point: ↵
> Command:

Figure 7-34.
An xline bisecting an existing angle is created using the **XLINE Bisect** option.

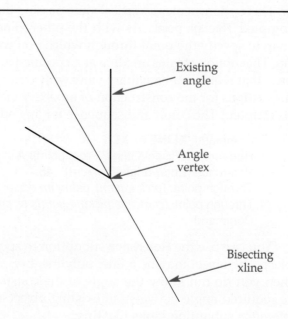

Existing angle

Angle vertex

Bisecting xline

- **Offset.** This option is particularly useful because it quickly creates an xline parallel to an existing object. The object may be a line, polyline, ray, or another xline. You can offset at a specified distance or through an existing point. The procedure looks like this:

> Command: **XLINE** *or* **XL**↵
> Hor/Ver/Ang/Bisect/Offset/⟨From point⟩: **O**↵
> Offset distance or Through ⟨*current*⟩: *(enter a distance value or* T *for the* **Through** *suboption)*
> Select a line object: *(pick a line, polyline, ray, or xline)*
> Side to offset? *(pick a location to place the offset xline)*
> Select a line object: *(select another object or press* [Enter] *to end the command)*
> Command:

To better understand the **Offset** option, be sure to read the section on the **OFFSET** command later in this chapter.

Introduction to the TRIM Command

As mentioned in the previous sections, it is necessary to trim away unneeded portions of rays and xlines. While the **TRIM** command is covered in detail in *Chapter 10* of this text, it will be useful to provide a brief introduction to trimming here so you may begin using rays and xlines in your drawing constructions.

AutoCAD LT—Fundamentals and Applications

Essentially, trimming is performed by first selecting an object to trim against. AutoCAD LT calls this object a *cutting edge*. After selecting one or more cutting edges and pressing [Enter], you are then prompted to select the object(s) to trim. You may continue selecting objects until you terminate the command by pressing [Enter] once again.

To issue the **TRIM** command, enter TRIM, or TR, at the Command: prompt, select the **Trim** button on the **Modify** toolbar, or select **Trim** from the **Modify** pull-down menu. See **Figure 7-35.** The object shown in **Figure 7-36** is very similar to that shown earlier in this chapter in the discussion of the **RAY** command. In this example, a ray has been created to project the edge of the chamfer to the side view. The command sequence to trim the unneeded portions of the ray looks like this:

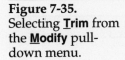

Command: **TRIM** *or* **TR** ↵
Select cutting edges: (Projmode = UCS, Edgemode = No extend)
Select objects: *(select the side view)*
Select objects: ↵

Figure 7-35.
Selecting **Trim** from the **Modify** pull-down menu.

Figure 7-36.
Using the **TRIM** command to trim away unneeded portions of a ray.

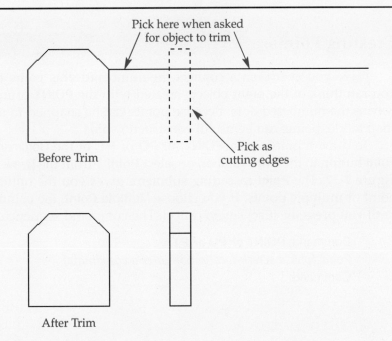

Pick here when asked for object to trim

Pick as cutting edges

Before Trim

After Trim

Because the side view was created using the **RECTANG** command, it is a polyline and is selected with one pick as the cutting edge. If lines had been used to create the side view, each of the vertical lines would have to be selected individually. Next, you are prompted to pick the object to trim:

⟨Select object to trim⟩/Project/Edge/Undo: *(pick one side of the ray)*
⟨Select object to trim⟩/Project/Edge/Undo: *(pick the other side of the ray)*
⟨Select object to trim⟩/Project/Edge/Undo: ↵
Command:

As you select objects to trim, always pick on the side to be trimmed. If you pick incorrectly, enter U for **Undo** and pick again.

> **NOTE** A trimmed xline becomes a ray object while a trimmed ray (if no longer infinite in one direction) is converted to a line object.

EXERCISE 7-5

❏ Begin a new drawing using your TEMPLATEB template.
❏ Using the correct layers, draw an object similar to that shown in **Figure 7-30**. Use any dimensions you like.
❏ Project the chamfer and hole to the side view using the **RAY** command as described in the previous sections. Trim the ray as required to complete the side view.
❏ Next, construct an object similar to that shown in **Figure 7-31**. Once again, use any dimensions you like.
❏ Project the stepped feature between the front and side views using the **XLINE** command as explained in the previous sections. Trim the xline as required, and change the linetype from Continuous to Hidden to complete the views. If necessary, refer to *Chapter 5* of this text to review object property modification.
❏ Save the drawing as EX7-5.

POINT
PO or PT

Draw
↪ P**o**int ⟩

Draw
toolbar

Point

Creating Points

Have you ever seen a connect-the-numbered-dots game that draws a picture? You can think of the point objects created with the **POINT** command much the same way as the numbered dots. Because points can be snapped to using the **NODE** object snap mode, points can be useful construction aids.

To draw a point, enter POINT, or PO or PT, at the Command: prompt, select the **Point** button in the **Draw** toolbar, or select **P**oint ⟩ from the **Draw** pull-down menu. See **Figure 7-37**. The P**o**int cascading submenu gives you the option of creating a single point or multiple points. If you choose **Multiple Point**, the command keeps repeating until you press the [Esc] key to cancel. The command sequence is as follows:

Command: **POINT** *or* **PO** *or* **PT**↵
Point: *(pick a screen location or enter a coordinate)*
Command:

AutoCAD LT—Fundamentals and Applications

Figure 7-37.
You can create
single or multiple
points by selecting
Point from the **Draw**
pull-down menu.

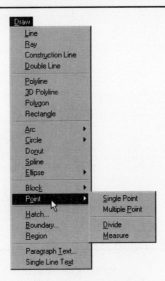

Setting the Point Style and Size in a Dialog Box

Point objects are available in a variety of styles. The default point style is a small dot. This makes the points very difficult to see, especially if the points are located on top of another object. To change the point style using a dialog box, select **Point Style...** from the **Format** pull-down menu. See **Figure 7-38.** The command sequence is as follows:

Command: **DDPTYPE** *or* **'DDPTYPE.**↲

This action displays the **Point Style** dialog box shown in **Figure 7-39.** Each of the available point styles are displayed as image tiles. The default point style, a small dot, is shown at the upper left of the dialog box. To change your point style, simply click the image tile that represents the point style you wish to use and then click the **OK** button. As shown in the illustration, the point style that looks like an "X" has been selected. The other items in this dialog box are described as follows:

- **Point Size: text box.** Use this text box to increase or decrease the size of your points. By default, the size of points is set as a percentage of the screen size.
- **Set Size Relative to Screen.** This is the default point sizing method in AutoCAD LT. The points are sized relative to the screen based on the percentage set in the **Point Size:** text box. Using this method, point sizes do not change as you zoom the display in and out.
- **Set Size in Absolute Units.** Click this option button when you want your points to have an absolute size. Enter the absolute size value in the **Point Size:** text box. With this method, points get larger and smaller as you zoom the display in and out.

Figure 7-38.
Selecting **Point Style...** from the **Format** pull-down menu issues the **DDPTYPE** command.

Figure 7-39.
The **Point Style**
dialog box.

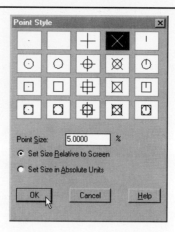

> **NOTE** Changes made to an existing point style or size do not take effect until the next screen regeneration.

The PDMODE and PDSIZE Variables

If you prefer, you can set the point style from the command line using the **PDMODE** (Point Display MODE) system variable:

Command: **PDMODE.⏎**
New value for PDMODE ⟨current⟩: (*enter one of the values from* **Figure 7-39**)
Command:

As shown in **Figure 7-40**, each of the AutoCAD LT points has an identifying value. **PDMODE** values 0, 2, 3, and 4 select a figure to draw for the point. Setting **PDMODE** to 1 selects nothing to be displayed. Adding 32, 64, or 96 to the values on the top line selects a circle, a square, or both to draw around the point figure.

The point size can also be set at the Command: prompt using the **PDSIZE** (Point Display SIZE) system variable.

Command: **PDSIZE.⏎**
New value for PDSIZE ⟨current⟩: (*enter a positive or negative value*)
Command:

When **PDSIZE** is set to zero, a point is created at 5% of the viewport size. This is the default setting for **PDSIZE**. To specify an absolute point size, enter a positive value. A negative value specifies the point size as a percentage of the viewport size.

Figure 7-40.
The available point
styles and their
corresponding
PDMODE values.

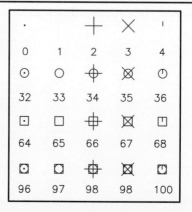

AutoCAD LT—Fundamentals and Applications

PROFESSIONAL TIP

Remember that both **PDMODE** and **PDSIZE** are set to 0 by default in AutoCAD LT. If you want to set a specific point style and/or size, do so in your template(s). It is also a good idea to create a layer named POINTS in your template(s). Create your points on this layer, and when you are ready to plot the finished drawing, turn off or freeze the POINTS layer so your points do not plot.

The DIVIDE Command

Getting Started Guide 8

DIVIDE
DIV

Draw
➥ P**o**int 〉
   Divide

The **DIVIDE** command places point objects along a drawing entity dividing it into a number of user-specified segments. It is important to note that **DIVIDE** does not actually break an object into individual objects. Instead, it uses points as markers to identify the locations of the divisions. Because points are used, be sure to change the point style as previously described so the points are visible. To divide an object, enter DIVIDE, or DIV, at the Command: prompt, or select **Divide** from the **P**o**int** 〉 cascading submenu in the **Draw** pull-down menu. The command sequence is as follows:

> Command: **DIVIDE** *or* **DIV**.↵
> Select object to divide: *(select the object to divide)*
> 〈Number of segments〉/Block: *(enter a number between 2 and 32767)*

In the examples shown in **Figure 7-41**, a line has been divided into 5 equal segments and a circle into 12 equal segments. For a circle, the first dividing point is normally on its circumference just to the right of the circle center (0°). For example, if the snap rotation angle is set to 180°, the first dividing point starts to the left of center. You can see that **PDMODE** has been set appropriately so that the points are visible.

The **DIVIDE** command also provides you with the **Block** option to divide a selected object with a block. You may recall that a block is one or more AutoCAD LT objects grouped together to form a single object. Blocks are an extremely handy way to create special symbols intended for multiple use. See *Chapter 15* of this text for complete information about these powerful objects.

Figure 7-41.
A line and a circle divided into equal segments with the **DIVIDE** command.

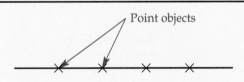

Line Divided into 5 Equal Segments

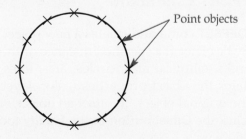

Circle Divided into 12 Equal Segments

Getting Started Guide 8

MEASURE ME

Draw
➥ Point ⟩
    Measure

The **MEASURE** Command

The **MEASURE** command can be used to place point objects at specified length intervals along a selected object. As with the **DIVIDE** command, be sure to change the point style as previously described so that the points are visible. Also like **DIVIDE**, the **MEASURE** command does not actually break an object into individual objects but uses points to identify the ending point of each segment. To measure an object, enter MEASURE, or ME, at the Command: prompt, or select **Measure** from the **Point** ⟩ cascading submenu in the **Draw** pull-down menu. The command sequence is as follows:

Command: **MEASURE** or **ME**↵
Select object to measure: *(select the object to measure)*
⟨Segment length⟩/Block: *(enter a positive value)*

In the examples shown in **Figure 7-42**, points are placed every .625 units along the length of the line object. Note the location of the pick point on the line. Measurement is started at the endpoint closest to the pick point. You can see from the illustration that there may occasionally be an unequal, or short, segment remaining at the end of the line.

For a circle, measurement normally starts on its circumference just to the right of the circle center (0°). If the snap rotation angle is set to 90°, for example, the measurement starts at the top of the circle.

As with the **DIVIDE** command, you may also select the **Block** option to measure an object with a block. See *Chapter 15* for more information about dividing and measuring objects with blocks.

Figure 7-42.
The **MEASURE** command places point markers at specified length segments on a line and a circle.

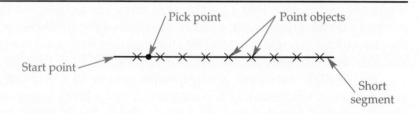

The **OFFSET** Command

The **OFFSET** command creates a new object parallel to a selected object. The new object may be offset at a specified distance or through a point. You can offset 2D polylines, ellipses, elliptical arcs, circles, arcs, lines, xlines, rays, and splines. An offset object retains the object properties (color, layer, linetype, linetype scale, and thickness) of the original object. To offset an object, enter OFFSET, or OF, at the Command: prompt, click the **Offset** button in the **Modify** toolbar, or select **Offset** from the **Modify** pull-down menu.

Offsetting through a Point

You may offset an object to pass through a selected point using the **OFFSET** command's default **Through** option. Refer to the 4-sided polygon shown at the top of **Figure 7-43** as you follow the command sequence below:

> Command: **OFFSET** *or* **OF**↵
> Offset distance or Through ⟨*current*⟩: **T**↵
> Select object to offset: *(pick the polygon)*
> Through point: *(locate a point outside the polygon)*
> Select object to offset: *(pick another object or press* [Enter] *to end)*

In this example, a point is selected outside the perimeter of the object resulting in a larger polygon. Selecting a point inside the polygon would result in a smaller polygon. This same convention applies to arcs, circles, ellipses, elliptical arcs, and splines.

Finally, keep in mind that when prompted **Through point:**, you can enter a coordinate or osnap to an existing object to locate the offset through point.

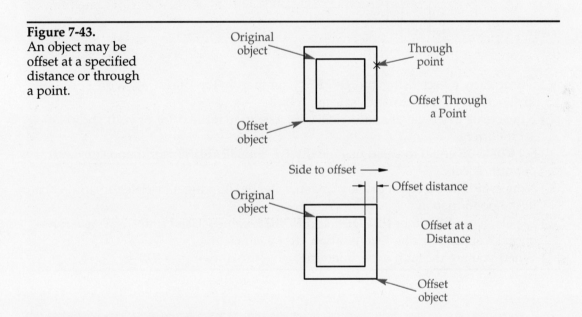

Figure 7-43.
An object may be offset at a specified distance or through a point.

Offsetting at a Distance

It is also possible to create an object at a specified distance from an existing object. Of the two offset methods, this second approach is probably the most commonly used. Refer now to the 4-sided polygon shown at the bottom of **Figure 7-43** as you follow the command sequence below:

> Command: **OFFSET** *or* **OF**↵
> Offset distance or Through ⟨Through⟩: *(enter a positive distance)*
> Select object to offset: *(pick the polygon)*
> Side to offset? *(pick a point to indicate the desired side)*
> Select object to offset: *(pick another object or press* [Enter] *to end)*

As with the **Through** option, picking a point outside the perimeter of an object offsets to the outside. Picking a point on the inside of an object's perimeter offsets to the inside.

❏ Begin a new drawing with your TEMPLATEB template drawing, or use your own setup variables.

❏ Make a drawing similar to that shown here. Be sure to include at least one polyline, ellipse, circle, arc, spline, and line.

POLYLINES   SPLINES

LINES   ARCS   CIRCLES   ELLIPSES

❏ Offset each object using the **OFFSET** command. Try offsetting with specified distances as well as through selected points.

❏ Now create a new layer named POINTS. Assign to it the color of your choice and set it current.

❏ Set **PDMODE** equal to 3 and use the **DIVIDE** and **MEASURE** commands on several of your objects.

❏ Now set **PDMODE** equal to 2 and regenerate the drawing. Observe the difference in the point display.

❏ Experiment with other **PDMODE** and **PDSIZE** values. Use **Figure 7-39** as a reference. Be sure to force a regeneration after each change.

❏ When you are through experimenting, save the drawing as EX7-6.

Auxiliary Views

There may be occasions when the object you are drawing has one or more slanted surfaces. In these instances, an auxiliary view is required to show the true shape and size of the surfaces that are not parallel to the six principal views of orthographic projection. AutoCAD LT provides two different methods to help you construct an auxiliary view. The first method requires you to rotate the snap and grid; the second method involves the creation of a new coordinate system. Both methods are described in the following sections. Before you begin the auxiliary view, however, first draw the principal front, top, and side views as required using coordinate filters, tracking, rays, or xlines to project drawing features between the views.

Using the **SNAP** Rotate Option to Create an Auxiliary View

In *Chapter 2* you learned that the **SNAP** command provides the option to rotate the snap axes around a specified point and at an angle. When you set the snap angle, the grid angle also changes. This method can be useful when constructing an auxiliary view. You can set the snap angle by selecting **Drawing Aids...** from the **Tools** pulldown menu.

This action displays the **Drawing Aids** dialog box illustrated in **Figure 7-44**. In the example shown, the snap rotation angle is set to 60 in the **Snap Angle** text box. Normally, the snap is rotated around the 0,0 drawing origin. If you would like to rotate the snap around a different point, enter the desired X and Y coordinates in the **X Base** and **Y Base** text boxes, respectively. Remember that you can also use this dialog box to set your grid spacing and turn on the grid. Once you have made the necessary changes, click the **OK** button to exit the **Drawing Aids** dialog box.

An example of an auxiliary view with the snap and grid rotated at 60° is shown in **Figure 7-45.** Observe the graphics cursor is realigned to match the new snap angle. As a further aid in the construction of your auxiliary view, be sure to turn **Ortho** mode on. When **SNAP** and **ORTHO** are both on, the cursor movement is constrained to the new rotation alignment.

If you prefer to set the snap angle at the Command: prompt, do the following:

Command: **SNAP** *or* **SN**↵
Snap spacing or ON/OFF/Aspect/Rotate/Style ⟨*current*⟩: **R**↵
Base point ⟨0.0000,0.0000⟩: *(pick a point or accept the default)*
Rotation angle ⟨0⟩: **60**↵
Command:

Remember to set the snap rotation angle back to 0° when you are finished drawing the auxiliary view.

Figure 7-44.
Setting the snap angle in the **Drawing Aids** dialog box.

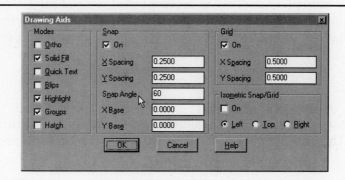

Figure 7-45.
Using a rotated snap and grid to construct an auxiliary view. Note the orientation of both the grid and the graphics cursor.

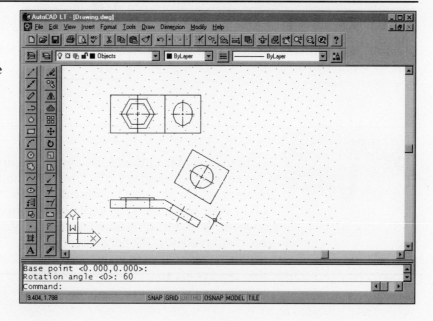

Using a UCS to Define an Auxiliary View

From *Chapter 3*, you learned the Cartesian coordinate system used by AutoCAD LT is fixed in 3D space and may not be moved or altered. AutoCAD LT refers to it as the *World Coordinate System*, or *WCS*. A better way to construct an auxiliary view is by creating your own *User Coordinate System*, or *UCS*. With the UCS, you can redefine the location of 0,0 and the direction of the XYZ axes. Using this method, the whole system is rotated and not just the snap axes. This greatly simplifies detailing and dimensioning operations in the auxiliary view.

Getting
Started 6
Guide

Working with the UCS Icon

The UCS icon is the small graphical marker at the lower left of the drawing window that displays the origin and the viewing plane of the current UCS in model space. See **Figure 7-46.** In its default representation, the X, Y, and Z axes of the UCS icon are positioned 90° relative to one another, with the Z axis perpendicular to the XY plane and along the line of sight. You will notice a box drawn at the vertices of the X and Y axes. The box indicates the viewpoint is from the positive Z direction. Therefore, the viewing angle is from a position above the XY plane looking down. Note also the small W just above the box. The W indicates that the World Coordinate System is active.

UCSICON

View
➥ Display ⟩
➥ UCS Icon ⟩
Origin

When creating your own UCS, it is very helpful to display the UCS icon at the origin of the current UCS. This is accomplished by selecting **Origin** from the **UCS Icon** ⟩ cascading submenu from the **Display** ⟩ cascading menu in the **View** pull-down menu. See **Figure 7-47.** From the command line, the sequence is as follows:

Command: **UCSICON**⏎
ON/OFF/All/Noorigin/ORigin ⟨ON⟩: **OR**⏎
Command:

Note that the **UCSICON** command also allows you to turn the icon on and off if you like. The other options of the **UCSICON** command are covered in *Chapter 19* of this text.

Figure 7-46.
The UCS icon in its default representation.

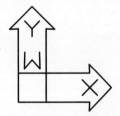

PROFESSIONAL TIP   Some users find the UCS icon distracting. Others dislike it because it occasionally obscures portions of the drawing. To suppress the display in your drawings, turn off the UCS icon in your template(s) as explained in the previous section. However, it is strongly suggested that you leave the UCS icon displayed for 3D constructions. See *Chapter 19* of this text for an introduction to 3D modeling.

Figure 7-47.
Selecting **Display** 〉
from the **View** pull-
down menu and
then **UCS Icon** 〉
displays a cascading
submenu of options.

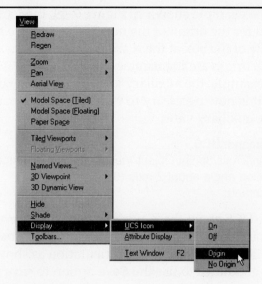

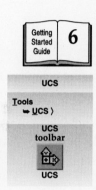

Creating a UCS

Now that the UCS icon is set to the User Coordinate System origin, it is time to create a UCS that represents the orientation of the auxiliary view under construction. Each of the UCS command options may be accessed from a cascading submenu by selecting **UCS** 〉 from the **Tools** pull-down menu. See **Figure 7-48.** You can also access the **UCS** command by entering UCS at the Command: prompt, or clicking the **UCS** button in the **UCS** flyout on the **Standard Toolbar**. On the command line, use the following procedure to locate the UCS origin at a point that coincides with a corner of the auxiliary view:

> Command: **UCS**↵
> Origin/ZAxis/3point/Object/View/X/Y/Z/Prev/Restore/Save/Del/?/〈World〉: **O**↵
> Origin point 〈0,0,0〉: *(pick a point at the desired corner of the auxiliary view)*
> Command:

Figure 7-48.
Selecting **UCS** 〉
from the **Tools** pull-
down menu
displays a cascading
submenu of **UCS**
command options.

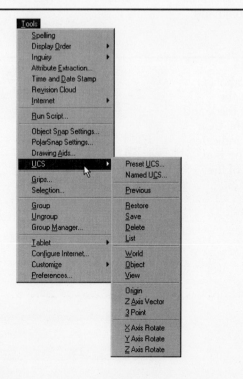

From the example shown in **Figure 7-49**, the UCS icon displays at the point that was selected for the origin of the new UCS. Observe the plus symbol (+) that appears in the middle of the box at the X and Y vertices. This symbol indicates the icon origin and the UCS origin are identical.

In this example, the auxiliary view is projected 60° from the slanted surface in the front view. It is now necessary to rotate the UCS about the Z axis to match the orientation of the auxiliary view.

> Command: **UCS↵**
> Origin/ZAxis/3point/Object/View/X/Y/Z/Prev/Restore/Save/Del/?/⟨World⟩: **Z↵**
> Rotation angle about Z axis ⟨0⟩: **60↵**
> Command:

UCS toolbar

Z Axis Rotate UCS

Rotating the UCS about the Z axis can also be performed by clicking the **Z Axis Rotate UCS** button in the **UCS** flyout on the **Standard Toolbar**.

The UCS is now at the correct orientation as shown in **Figure 7-50**. Before continuing, it is a good idea to use the **Save** option to save the new UCS with a descriptive name. Should you need to return to the auxiliary view for further construction or modification, it is faster to restore a named UCS than to create a new one. A named UCS may contain up to 31 characters, but spaces are not permitted.

> Command: **UCS↵**
> Origin/ZAxis/3point/Object/View/X/Y/Z/Prev/Restore/Save/Del/?/⟨World⟩: **S↵**
> ?/Desired UCS name: **AUXIL↵**
> Command:

If you decide at some point that you wish to change the name of the saved UCS, use the **DDRENAME** command to do so.

Now that the entire system matches the orientation of the auxiliary view, use the projection techniques described in this chapter to project features between the auxiliary view and the slanted surface of the front view.

When you need to return to the World Coordinate System, issue the **UCS** command again and use the default **World** option as follows:

> Command: **UCS↵**
> Origin/ZAxis/3point/Object/View/X/Y/Z/Prev/Restore/Save/Del/?/⟨World⟩: ↵
> Command:

Figure 7-49.
A plus symbol (+) appears at the vertices of the X and Y axes in the UCS icon. This indicates that the icon is at the origin of the current UCS.

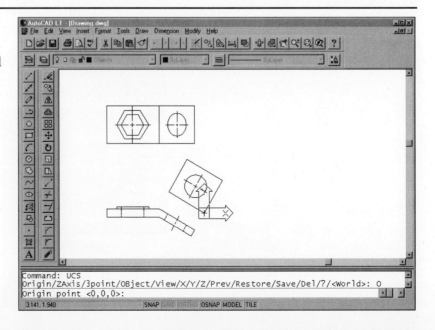

AutoCAD LT—Fundamentals and Applications

Figure 7-50.
The UCS is rotated 60° about the Z axis to match the angle of the auxiliary view.

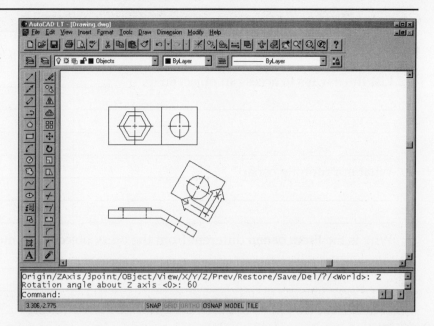

You can also quickly return to the WCS by selecting **World** from the **UCS** 〉 cascading submenu, or clicking the **World UCS** button in the **UCS** flyout on the **Standard Toolbar**.

If you prefer to use a dialog box instead, select **Named UCS...** from the **UCS** 〉 cascading submenu, or click the **Named UCS** button in the **UCS** flyout on the **Standard Toolbar**. This action issues the **DDUCS** command and displays the **UCS Control** dialog box shown in **Figure 7-51**. You can use this dialog box to set a saved UCS current, return to a previous UCS or the WCS, rename an existing UCS, or delete a UCS when no longer needed. As with the **UCSICON** command, each of the other **UCS** command options will be covered in detail in *Chapter 19* of this text.

Figure 7-51.
Selecting a saved UCS from the **UCS Control** dialog box.

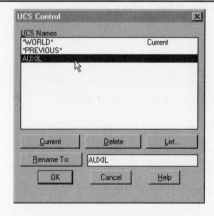

Chapter Test

Write your answers in the spaces provided.

1. List three ways to access an object snap. _____

    _____

    _____

    _____

2. What is a running osnap? _____

    _____

    _____

3. Why is the **From osnap** different from the other object snap modes? _____

    _____

    _____

    _____

4. Give the command and entries required to set **Quadrant** and **Perpendicular** as the running osnaps.

    Command: _____

    Object snap modes: _____

5. List three ways to access the **Object Snap Settings** dialog box. _____

    _____

    _____

    _____

    _____

6. When enabled, name the system variable that changes the size of the cursor target area. Can this system variable be used transparently?_____

    _____

    _____

7. How do you access the cursor menu? _____

    _____

    _____

    _____

8. Give the command and entries required to disable any running osnaps.

    Command: _____

    Object snap modes: _____

9. What is the **AutoSnap** feature? _____

    _____

    _____

    _____

10. What is the **AutoSnap** magnet? _____

    _____

    _____

11. What is the purpose of coordinate filters? _____
_____

_____

12. What must you do with your cursor when using tracking? Why? _____
_____

_____

13. How does an xline differ from a ray? _____
_____

_____

_____

14. What is the purpose of the **PDMODE** variable? _____
_____

15. What is the purpose of the **PDSIZE** variable? Describe its use. _____
_____

_____

_____

16. *True or False?* A drawing can contain several types of points. _____

17. Describe the difference between the **DIVIDE** and **MEASURE** commands. How are they similar? _____
_____

_____

_____

_____

18. What should you do before you divide or measure an object? _____
_____

19. What is the purpose of the **OFFSET** command? _____
_____

_____

20. *True or False?* An offset object inherits the current system color, linetype, linetype scale, and layer._____

21. What is the purpose of the UCS icon? _____
_____

_____

22. Why is it a good idea to save a UCS? _____
_____

_____

Chapter Problems

1. Draw the object shown below using the correct layers in your
   TEMPLATEA template. Make your drawing proportional to that shown.
   Study the object carefully before beginning construction. Determine
   which AutoCAD LT object types best describe the object and draw
   accordingly. Plan to use the **Center**, **Quadrant**, **Endpoint**, **Midpoint**,
   Intersection, and **Tangent** object snap modes as required. Save the
   drawing as P7-1.

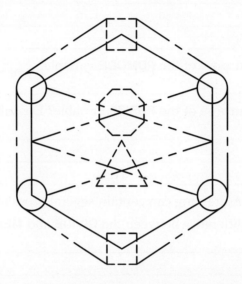

2. Construct the two views of the BEARING CAP using the projection
   techniques described in this chapter. Use your TEMPLATEB template
   and create the objects on the proper layers. Study the drawing carefully to determine if the **OFFSET** command can be used. Do not draw
   the dimensions. Save the drawing as P7-2.

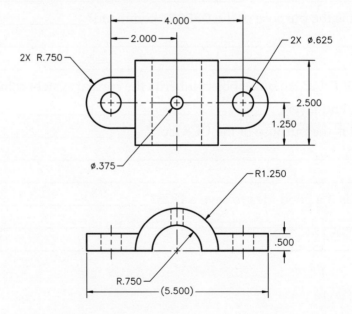

3. Use your TEMPLATEB template to draw the CAM BRACKET. As with P7-2, project views and features using the techniques described in this chapter, and use the **OFFSET** command where appropriate. Do not draw the dimensions. Save the drawing as P7-3.

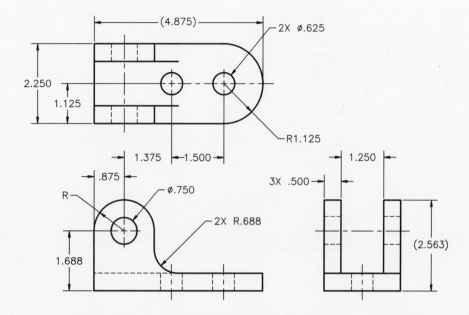

4. Use your TEMPLATEA template to draw the object shown. Create the auxiliary view as described in this chapter. Use any projection technique you like to project the counterbored feature between the auxiliary view and the slanted surface of the front view. Save the drawing as P7-4.

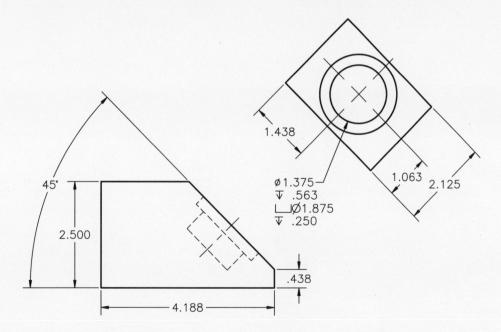

5. Once again, create an auxiliary view drawing of the object shown using your **TEMPLATEB** template. Project the .375 diameter holes between the auxiliary view and the slanted surface of the front view using the projection technique of your choice. Save the drawing as **P7-5**.

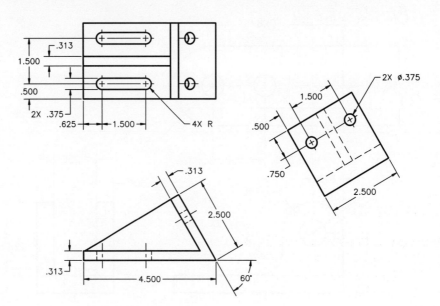

AutoCAD LT

Chapter 8
Inquiry Commands

Learning Objectives

After you have completed this chapter, you will be able to:
- Display the XYZ coordinates of a selected point.
- Find the true 3D distance between two points.
- Obtain the angle between two points.
- Explain the purpose of the **LUPREC** and **AUPREC** system variables.
- Calculate the area and perimeter of an object or shape.
- List the database information for selected objects.
- Display the date and time statistics of a drawing.
- Use the Microsoft Windows **Control Panel** to set your computer's clock and date.
- Calculate the mass properties of region objects.

The AutoCAD LT inquiry commands display useful information about the objects in your drawings. Their proper use will enable you to verify the accuracy and correctness of your designs. The commands are the **ID**, **DIST**, **AREA**, **LIST**, and **TIME** commands. For AutoCAD LT 98 users, the mass properties of regions can be calculated using the **MASSPROP** command. Each of these commands is described fully in this chapter and may be accessed from the **Inquiry** ⟩ cascading submenu found in the **Tools** pull-down menu.

The ID Command

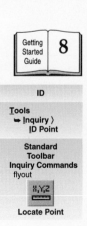

The **ID** command displays the XYZ coordinates of a screen location or a selected point on the command line. You may recall from *Chapter 7* that the coordinate values returned by the **ID** command are stored in the **LASTPOINT** system variable and accessed using the @ symbol. To access the **ID** command, enter ID at the Command: prompt, click the **Locate Point** button in the **Inquiry Commands** flyout on the **Standard Toolbar**, or select **ID Point** from the **Inquiry** ⟩ cascading menu in the **Tools** pull-down menu. See **Figure 8-1.** The command sequence is as follows:

Command: **ID**⏎
Point: *(pick a point)*

Figure 8-1.
Select **Inquiry** from
the **Tools** pull-down
menu and then
select **ID Point** from
the cascading menu
to access the **ID**
command.

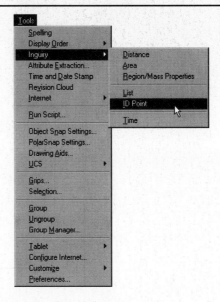

If the point selected is in an empty portion of the drawing window, **ID** displays the XY location and the Z coordinates of the current elevation. Elevation is the Z value above or below the XY plane. The current screen elevation is used whenever a 3D point is requested. By default, elevation is set to 0 (zero). However, if you use an osnap to snap to an object, then **ID** displays the Z coordinate of the selected point on the object and not the current elevation. For 2D constructions, a point on an object and the current elevation will have identical Z values.

EXERCISE 8-1

❏ Begin a new drawing with your **TEMPLATEA** template drawing, or use your own setup variables.
❏ Draw the object shown below with the center of the object located at 5, 4.5. As a construction hint, start with a 4-sided circumscribed polygon and then draw the circles. Be sure to enter all decimal values in full. If necessary, refer to the decimal/fractional equivalency chart in the appendices at the rear of this text.

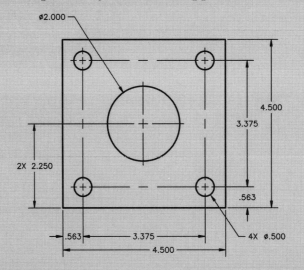

❏ Save the drawing as **EX8-1**, but do not exit AutoCAD LT. This drawing is to be used for several more exercises in this chapter.

AutoCAD LT—Fundamentals and Applications

The DIST Command

Getting Started Guide 8

DIST
DI

Tools
→ Inquiry ⟩
  Distance

Standard
Toolbar
Inquiry Commands
flyout

Distance

The **DIST** (DISTance) command is used to calculate the distance and angle between two points. To access the **DIST** command, enter DIST, or DI, at the Command: prompt, click the **Distance** button in the **Inquiry Commands** flyout on the **Standard Toolbar**, or select **Distance** from the **Inquiry** cascading menu located in the **Tools** pull-down menu. The command sequence is as follows:

> Command: **DIST** *or* **DI**↵
> First point: *(pick a point)* Second point: *(pick a second point)*

To obtain the highest degree of accuracy, be sure to use an osnap when selecting points. **DIST** reports the true 3D distance between the two points. See **Figure 8-2**. The angle in the XY plane is measured relative to the current X axis. The angle from the XY plane is returned for 3D points and is measured relative to the current XY plane. The distance and angle values reported by **DIST** are displayed using the current units format. Delta values are displayed to report the change in XYZ coordinates between the two selected points.

Figure 8-2.
The **DIST** command reports the distance and angle between two points on the command line.

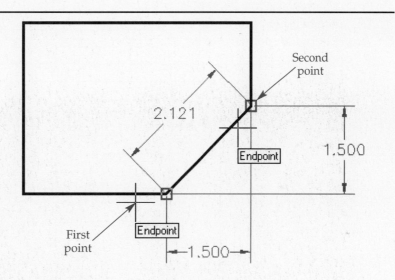

The LUPREC and AUPREC system variables

If you use decimal values in your work, it is helpful to increase the number of displayed decimal places when using the inquiry commands. This provides the greatest degree of accuracy for calculations. **LUPREC** (Linear Units PRECision) is an AutoCAD LT system variable that stores the linear units decimal places. The valid range for **LUPREC** is 0 through 8, with 4 as the default. This value is stored in the drawing and is used for all displayed decimal values including dimensions and tolerances. Use **LUPREC** at the Command: prompt as follows:

> Command: **LUPREC**↵
> New value for LUPREC ⟨4⟩: *(enter a new value and press [Enter])*
> Command:

AUPREC (Angular Units PRECision) is another AutoCAD LT system variable that stores the angular units decimal places. The valid range for **AUPREC** is 0 through 8, with 0 as the default. As with **LUPREC**, this value is also stored in the drawing and is used for all displayed decimal values including dimensions and tolerances. Use **AUPREC** at the Command: prompt as follows:

> Command: **AUPREC**↵
> New value for AUPREC ⟨0⟩: *(enter a new value and press [Enter])*
> Command:

The **LUPREC** and **AUPREC** system variables are a convenient way to set the system decimal places without issuing the **DDUNITS** command.

EXERCISE 8-2

❑ Open EX8-1 if it is not on your screen.
❑ Set the **LUPREC** system variable to 6 and **AUPREC** to 4.
❑ Use the **DIST** and **ID** commands to calculate the following:
Distance between circle centers A & B: _____
Angle between circle centers A & B: _____
Distance between points C & D: _____
Angle between points C & F: _____
ID of point E: _____
ID of point F: _____

❑ When you are done, do not exit AutoCAD LT. This drawing is to be used for several more exercises in this chapter.

The **AREA** Command

The **AREA** command calculates the area and perimeter of objects or of defined areas. **AREA** is also used to combine the areas of two or more objects, as well as to subtract the area of an object from the area of another. To access the **AREA** command, enter AREA, or AA, at the Command: prompt, click the **Area** button in the **Inquiry Commands** flyout on the **Standard Toolbar**, or select **Area** from the **Inquiry** cascading menu located in the **Tools** pull-down menu. The command sequence is as follows:

> Command: **AREA** *or* **AA**↵
> ⟨First point⟩/Object/Add/Subtract: *(select a point or enter an option)*

Each of the **AREA** command options are described below:

- ⟨**First point**⟩. This is the default method for area calculations. With **First point**, first set an **Endpoint** or an **Intersection** running osnap and pick points at each vertex of an object. The area and perimeter of the shape enclosed by the points is reported. This method is illustrated in **Figure 8-3.** If a shape is not closed, the area is calculated as if a line were drawn from the last point selected to the first. That line length is automatically added to the perimeter calculation.

  Therefore, the **First point** method reports the area between three or more points picked on the screen, even if the three points are not connected by lines. The **First point** option appears as follows:

  > Command: **AREA** *or* **AA**↵
  > ⟨First point⟩/Object/Add/Subtract: *(pick a point)*
  > Next point: *(pick a second point)*
  > Next point: *(pick a third point)*
  > Next point: *(pick a fourth point or press* [Enter] *to end)*
  > Area = *nnnn*, Perimeter = *nnnn*
  > Command:

- **Object.** This option is used to find the area and perimeter of a selected object. It is particularly handy because selecting every vertex of an object can be very time-consuming. Additionally, this option allows you to easily calculate the area of shapes that contain fillets and rounds as long as the shape is drawn with a polyline and filleted with the **Polyline** option. If necessary, refer to *Chapter 6* to review the **POLYLINE** and **FILLET** commands. You can use the **Object** option on circles, ellipses, polygons, rectangles, splines, regions, and polylines. For a wide polyline, the area and perimeter (or length) calculations use the centerline of the object. If an open polyline is selected, the area is calculated as if a line were drawn from the last point selected to the first. However, unlike the **First point** option, the line length is not included in the perimeter (or length) calculation of the open polyline. The **Object** option looks like this:

  > Command: **AREA** *or* **AA**↵
  > ⟨First point⟩/Object/Add/Subtract: **O**↵
  > Select objects: *(select a circle, ellipse, polygon, rectangle, spline, region, or polyline)*
  > Area = *nnnn*, Perimeter = *nnnn*
  > Command:

Figure 8-3.
With the **First point** option, each vertex of an object is selected using an appropriate osnap like **Endpoint** or **Intersection.**

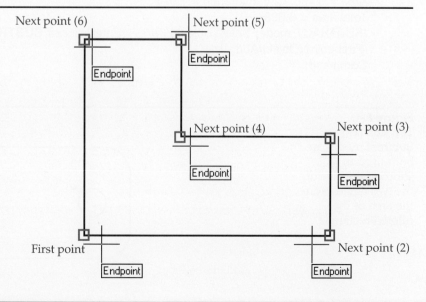

- **Add.** This mode allows you to pick additional points or select another object for area calculation. The additional area and perimeter is automatically added to calculate the total area of all selected objects. The **Add** mode stays in effect until you press [Enter] to end it.

> Command: **AREA** *or* **AA**↵
> ⟨First point⟩/Object/Add/Subtract: **A**↵
> ⟨First point⟩/Object/Subtract:

- **Subtract.** This mode allows you to remove the area and perimeter of selected points or an object from the total area calculated. As with **Add**, the **Subtract** mode stays in effect until you press [Enter] to end it.

> Command: **AREA** *or* **AA**↵
> ⟨First point⟩/Object/Add/Subtract: **S**↵
> ⟨First point⟩/Object/Add:

Adding and subtracting areas

To better understand how the **Add** and **Subtract** modes are used, refer to the object illustrated in **Figure 8-4.** This object is constructed with a rectangle and all four corners filleted with the **Fillet** option of the **RECTANG** command. It is also possible to fillet the rectangle using the **Polyline** option of the **FILLET** command since rectangles (and polygons) are polylines. Study the following command sequence to learn how to subtract the areas of the two circles from the filleted rectangle. Observe how the total area decreases as each circle is subtracted. Notice also that the **AREA** command reports the circumferences of the selected circles.

> Command: **AREA** *or* **AA**↵
> ⟨First point⟩/Object/Add/Subtract: **A**↵
> ⟨First point⟩/Object/Subtract: **O**↵
> (ADD mode) Select objects: *(pick the rectangle)*
> Area = 6.785, Perimeter = 10.142
> Total area = 6.785
> (ADD mode) Select objects: *(press [Enter] to exit **ADD** mode)*
> ⟨First point⟩/Object/Subtract: **S**↵
> ⟨First point⟩/Object/Add: **O**↵
> (SUBTRACT mode) Select objects: *(pick one of the circles)*
> Area = 0.196, Circumference = 1.571
> Total area = 6.589
> (SUBTRACT mode) Select objects: *(pick the other circle)*
> Area = 0.196, Circumference = 1.571
> Total area = 6.393
> (SUBTRACT mode) Select objects: *(press [Enter] to exit **SUBTRACT** mode)*
> ⟨First point⟩/Object/Add: ↵
> Command:

Figure 8-4.
The **Add** and **Subtract** modes are both used to subtract the area of the two circles from the area of the filleted rectangle.

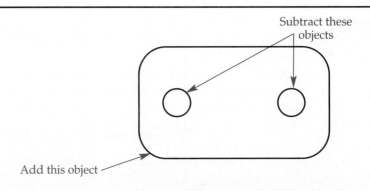

Subtract these objects

Add this object

EXERCISE 8-3

❑ Open EX8-1 if it is not on your screen.
❑ Use the **AREA** command to calculate the following:

Area of Object 1 _____

Perimeter of Object 1 _____

Area of Object 2 _____

Circumference of Object 2 _____

Area of Object 3 _____

Circumference of Object 3 _____

Area of Object 1 minus the area of all circles _____

Total area of Objects 3, 4, 5, and 6 _____

Object 5 ——→
Object 4
Object 2 ——→
Object 1
Object 6 ——
Object 3

❑ When you are done, do not exit AutoCAD LT.

The **LIST** Command

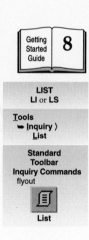

The **LIST** command is particularly useful because it displays the complete database information for a selected object. To access the **LIST** command, enter LIST, or LI or LS, at the Command: prompt, click the **List** button in the **Inquiry Commands** flyout on the **Standard Toolbar**, or select **List** from the **Inquiry** cascading menu in the **Tools** pull-down menu. The command sequence is as follows:

> Command: **LIST** or **LI** or **LS**↵
> Select objects: *(select one or more objects)*

For each object selected, AutoCAD LT lists its type, layer, XYZ position relative to the current UCS, and whether it was created in model space or paper space. If color and linetype are not set to **BYLAYER** mode, then color and linetype information is listed as well. Because so much information is reported by the **LIST** command, AutoCAD LT automatically flips the graphics window to the text window to display it all.

Consider the line and circle objects shown in **Figure 8-5A.** Both objects are selected for listing and the database information for each is displayed in the text window. See **Figure 8-5B.** You can see from the listing that both objects have a handle designation. A *handle* is a unique alphanumeric tag used to identity each object in the drawing database.

For 3D entities, the thickness of an object is displayed if it is not zero. Like color, linetype, linetype scale, and layer, thickness is also a property of AutoCAD LT objects. It represents the distance that a 2D object is extruded above or below its current screen elevation. Remember that the Z coordinate information reported by **LIST** represents the elevation. See *Chapter 19* of this text for more information on thickness and elevation. Once you have obtained the list information that you need, press function key [F2] to flip back to the drawing window.

Figure 8-5.
A—A line and a circle are selected for listing. B—The database information for the selected objects is displayed in the AutoCAD LT text window.

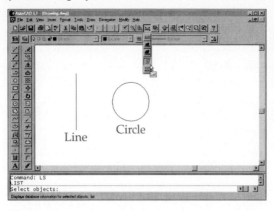

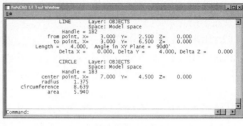

A

B

The TIME Command

TIME
TI

Tools
→ Inquiry ⟩
  Time

The **TIME** command displays the date and time statistics of your drawing in the AutoCAD LT text window. It displays the current time to the nearest millisecond using a 24-hour clock. **TIME** also displays the date and time that the drawing was originally created, when it was last saved, and how much time has elapsed in the current drawing session. To access the **TIME** command, enter TIME, or TI, at the Command: prompt or select **Time** from the **Inquiry** ⟩ cascading menu located in the **Tools** pull-down menu. The command sequence is as follows:

Command: **TIME** *or* **TI**↵

The graphics window automatically flips to the text window as **TIME** displays information similar to the following example:

Current time: 10 Aug 2000 at 01:27:19.520
Times for this drawing:
Created: 27 Feb 2000 at 19:29:08.150
Last updated: 22 July 2000 at 03:22:19.300
Total editing time: 0 days 01:44:10.520
Elapsed timer (on): 0 days 00:07:05.312
Next automatic save in: ⟨disabled⟩
Display/On/OFF/Reset: *(select an option or press* [Enter] *to end the command)*

Each of the **TIME** command options are described as follows:
- **Display.** Use this option to repeat the text window display with update times.
- **On/OFF.** Turns the elapsed timer on and off as desired. The timer is on by default.
- **Reset.** This option resets the elapsed timer to 0 days, 0 hours, 0 minutes, and 0 seconds.

If the **SAVETIME** system variable has been set to automatically save your drawing at specified time intervals, the time remaining until the next automatic save is also displayed. See *Chapter 2* to review how to set the **SAVETIME** variable.

PROFESSIONAL TIP If you are a consultant or contractor, use the **TIME** command to keep accurate time spent in a drawing. This will enable you to bill your clients accurately and fairly.

Setting Your Computer's Date and Time

If the current date and/or time reported by the **TIME** command is incorrect, they can be reset from the Windows Control Panel. The Control Panel provides you with a visual way of modifying your system while working with Microsoft Windows 98, 95, or NT. To launch the Control Panel, click the Start button on the Taskbar and select Control Panel from the Settings folder. See **Figure 8-6.** You need not exit AutoCAD LT to launch the Control Panel.

As shown in **Figure 8-7**, each option that you can change is represented by an icon in the Control Panel window. Using the Date/Time option, you can change your computer's date and time. It is important that your system date and time are always accurate. Date and time changes are recognized by other Windows applications that use the system clock like Explorer. Windows Explorer functions are covered in *Chapter 25* of this text.

To change the system date and time, do the following:

1. Start Microsoft Windows 98, 95, or NT.
2. Click the Start button on the Taskbar and launch Control Panel from the Settings folder.
3. In the Control Panel window, double-click the Date/Time icon to open the Date/Time Properties dialog box.
4. Use the drop-down lists in the Date section to select the correct month and year. Click on the correct day from the calendar to set the day. In the Time section, enter the correct time in the text box and click the up or down arrow to toggle between AM and PM. See **Figure 8-8.**
5. If necessary, click the Time Zone tab at the top of the Date/Time Properties dialog box to set the correct time zone for your location. See **Figure 8-9.** Also, make sure that the Automatically adjust clock for daylight saving changes check box is enabled. With this check box active, your computer's clock will adjust itself automatically when standard time switches to daylight saving time and vice versa.
6. Click the OK button and select Close from the File pull-down menu in the Control Panel window. You are automatically returned to AutoCAD LT if the program was running when Control Panel was launched.

Figure 8-6.
Selecting Control Panel from the Settings folder in the Start menu. The Windows 98 desktop is shown.

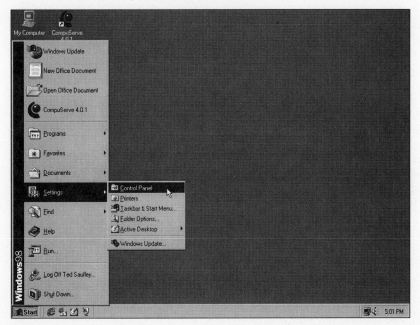

Figure 8-7.
Double-click Date/Time in the Control Panel window to set the date and time on your computer's clock.

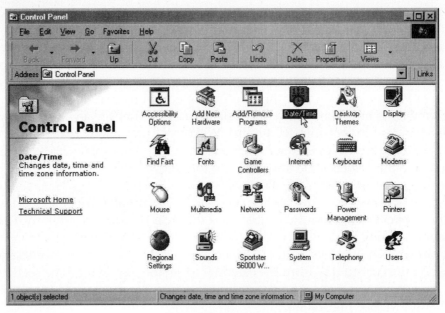

Figure 8-8.
The system date and time may be easily changed in the Date/Time Properties dialog box.

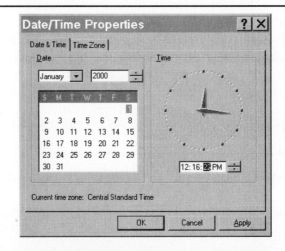

Figure 8-9.
Click the Time Zone tab in the Date/Time Properties dialog box and use the drop-down list at the top to set the correct time for your particular time zone.

PROFESSIONAL TIP

Here is a quick way to access the Date/Time Properties dialog box. Locate your pointing device over the digital clock at the far right of the taskbar and right-click. Select Adjust Date/Time from the shortcut menu.

EXERCISE 8-4

❑ Open any one of your previous drawing exercises or problems.
❑ Use the **TIME** command and study the information that is displayed.
❑ If the current date and time are incorrect, inform your instructor or supervisor. Then use the Windows Control Panel to set the correct date and time.
❑ Use the **Display** option to update the **TIME** display.
❑ If the **SAVETIME** system variable is on, note the remaining time until the next automatic save.
❑ Do not exit AutoCAD LT.

The MASSPROP Command

The **MASSPROP** (MASS PROPerties) command lets you calculate the area, perimeter, bounding box, and centroid (center of area) of regions and composite regions. The **MASSPROP** command is not available in AutoCAD LT 97. Because regions are two-dimensional objects, no mass or volume calculations are performed by **MASSPROP**. However, if the selected region is coplanar with the XY plane of the current UCS, then AutoCAD LT also calculates its moments of inertia, radii of gyration, and principal moments with corresponding principal directions.

AutoCAD LT uses the current units format to report the mass properties calculations of regions performed by **MASSPROP**. A description of these calculations appears below:

- **Area.** The enclosed two-dimensional area of the region.
- **Perimeter.** This value reports the total length of the inside and outside loops of a region. You may recall from the discussion of regions in *Chapter 6* that the internal features of a region, such as holes, slots, and other types of cutouts, are called inner loops. An outer loop represents the closed outer boundary of a region.
- **Bounding Box.** The bounding box is the smallest box that completely encloses the region being analyzed. For regions that are coplanar with the XY plane of the current UCS, the bounding box values represent the diagonally opposite corners of the rectangle that encloses the region. For regions that are not coplanar with the XY plane of the current UCS, the bounding box values represent the diagonally opposite corners of a 3D box that encloses the region.

MASSPROP

Tools
➤ Inquiry ⟩
    Region/Mass
    Properties

Standard
Toolbar
Inquiry Commands
flyout

Region Mass
Properties

PROFESSIONAL TIP

You can also obtain the area, perimeter, and bounding box values for a region using the **LIST** command.

- **Centroid.** This value is a 2D or 3D coordinate that represents the center of area for the region. The coordinate is two-dimensional for a region that is coplanar with the XY plane of the current UCS.

If the region(s) you select are coplanar with the XY plane of the current UCS, the following additional properties are displayed by **MASSPROP**:

- **Moments of Inertia.** This value represents area moments of inertia which are commonly used in structural engineering to compute distributed loads and to calculate the stress on beams or channels.
- **Products of Inertia.** Used to determine the forces causing the motion of an object, the products of inertia are always calculated with respect to two orthogonal planes. The XY value reported here is expressed in mass units times the length squared.
- **Radii of Gyration.** The radius of gyration with respect to a rotation axis represents the distance at which the entire mass of the object should be concentrated, if its moment of inertia with respect to the rotation axis is to remain unchanged. The radii of gyration values are expressed in distance units.
- **Principal Moments and Directions about a Centroid.** These calculations are derived from the products of inertia. The moment of inertia is highest through a certain axis at the centroid of an object. It is lowest through the second axis that is normal to the first axis and also passes through the centroid.

To perform mass properties analysis on one or more region objects, enter MASSPROP at the Command: prompt, click the **Region/Mass Properties** button on the **Standard Toolbar**, or select **Region/Mass Properties** from the **Inquiry** ⟩ cascading menu in the **Tools** pull-down menu. The procedure looks like this:

Command: **MASSPROP**⏎
Select objects: *(select one or more regions)*
Select objects: ⏎

The graphics window automatically flips to the text window to display the analysis results. See **Figure 8-10.** You are then prompted to save the calculated data to an external Mass Properties Results (.mpr) text file.

Write to a file?⟨N⟩ *(answer Y or N as required and press* [Enter]*)*

Figure 8-10.
The results of the mass properties analysis are displayed in the text window.

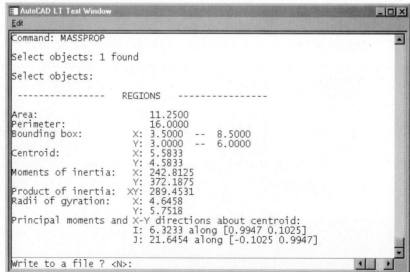

```
AutoCAD LT Text Window
Edit
Command: MASSPROP

Select objects: 1 found

Select objects:

----------------         REGIONS    ----------------

Area:                    11.2500
Perimeter:               16.0000
Bounding box:       X: 3.5000  --  8.5000
                    Y: 3.0000  --  6.0000
Centroid:           X: 5.5833
                    Y: 4.5833
Moments of inertia: X: 242.8125
                    Y: 372.1875
Product of inertia: XY: 289.4531
Radii of gyration:  X: 4.6458
                    Y: 5.7518
Principal moments and X-Y directions about centroid:
                    I: 6.3233 along [0.9947 0.1025]
                    J: 21.6454 along [-0.1025 0.9947]

Write to a file ? <N>:
```

If you answer N, the **MASSPROP** command sequence is terminated. However, if you answer Y, the **Create Mass and Area Properties File** dialog box appears as shown in **Figure 8-11.** By default, the .mpr file assumes the same name as the current drawing and is saved in the current folder. If you wish to change the file name, do so by entering the desired name in the **File name:** text box. AutoCAD LT automatically appends the .mpr extension to the file. Once the file is created, it may be opened by a word processing application or with any ASCII text editor, like the Windows **Notepad.** The file can then be printed and kept for reference.

Figure 8-11.
The **Create Mass and Area Properties File** dialog box is used to store the mass properties calculations in an external text file.

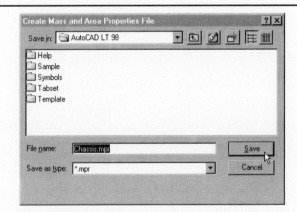

NOTE
All of the selection set options are valid with **MASSPROP**. However, if you select multiple regions, AutoCAD LT accepts only those that are coplanar with the first region you select.

PROFESSIONAL TIP
You can improve the accuracy of the values reported by **MASSPROP** by increasing the value of the **LUPREC** system variable described earlier in this chapter.

EXERCISE 8-5

❑ Open EX8-1.
❑ Convert the polygon and five circles to region objects.
❑ Subtract the five inner loops (the circles) from the outer loop (the polygon). If necessary, review the description of region objects and Boolean operations found in *Chapter 6* of this text.
❑ Use the **MASSPROP** command to calculate the following:
  Area: _____
  Perimeter: _____
  Bounding box: _____
  Centroid: _____
❑ Save the analysis results to a file called PROPERTIES.MPR. Print the file if you are connected to a printer.
❑ Save the drawing as EX8-5.

Chapter Test

Write your answers in the spaces provided.

1. What is the purpose of the **ID** command? Why would you use it? _____

    _____

    _____

    _____

2. Identify the command used to calculate the distance and angle between two points.

    _____

    _____

3. Why should you use osnaps when using the inquiry commands? _____

    _____

    _____

4. Name the system variable that allows you to quickly change the number of displayed decimal places for linear units without using the **DDUNITS** command.

    _____

5. What information is reported by the **AREA** command? _____

    _____

6. You need to calculate the area of an object that is fully radiused at one end. The object has been constructed with a polyline and polyarc. Which **AREA** command option should be used to perform the calculation? _____

    _____

7. What is meant by object thickness?_____

    _____

    _____

    _____

8. Besides the **AREA** command, which other inquiry command reports the area and circumference of a circle? _____

    _____

9. What information is reported by the **TIME** command? _____

    _____

    _____

    _____

10. *True or False?* You must exit AutoCAD LT to reset the date and time. _____

11. What is a *bounding box?* Which inquiry command reports its values? _____

    _____

    _____

12. Why would you save the results of a region calculation?_____

    _____

    _____

Chapter Problems

1. Draw the extrusion shown below with a polyline using your **TEMPLATEA** template. When the object is complete, answer the following:

Mechanical
Drafting

   a. What is the distance between endpoints A and B? _____

   _____

   b. What is the distance between the midpoint of Line C and the midpoint of Line D? _____

   c. What is the distance and angle between point E and the midpoint of Line F? _____

   d. What is the area of the extrusion? _____

   e. What is the perimeter? _____

   Save the drawing as P8-1.

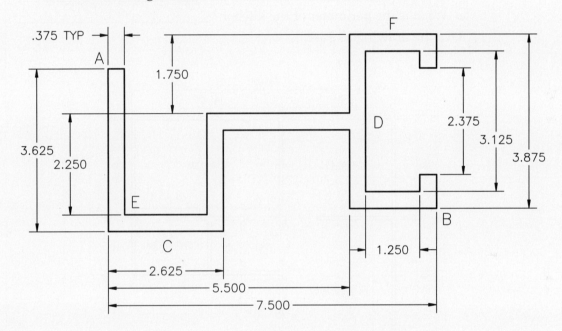

2. Draw the residential floor plan shown below using the **DLINE** command. Each of the walls is 4" thick. Before beginning construction, do the following:

Set architectural units.

Set the limits to 36', 30' and **ZOOM All.**

Set the grid spacing to 4" and the snap spacing to 2".

When the floor plan is complete, answer the following questions:

a. What is the area of the living room? _____

b. What is the combined area of the kitchen and living room?_____

_____

c. What is the total area of the bedroom, bathroom, hall, and closet?

_____

d. What is the area of the entire floor plan minus the area of the hall and closet? _____

e. What is the perimeter of the kitchen? _____

Save the drawing as P8-2.

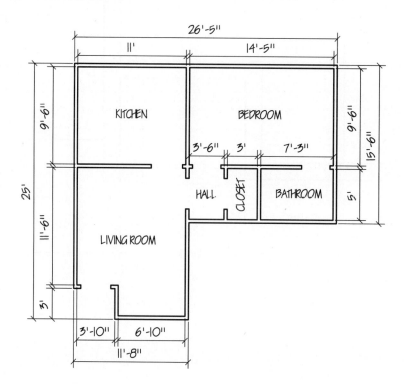

3. Draw the **ADJUSTING ARM** shown below using your **TEMPLATEA** template. This is the identical object from Problem 2 of *Chapter 6*. However, this time draw both the outer profile and the fully radiused inner slot with polylines and polyarcs. When the drawing is complete, answer the following:

a. What is the area of the fully radiused slot? _____

b. What is the slot's perimeter? _____

c. What is the area of the 1.500 diameter hole? _____

d. What is the hole's circumference? _____

e. What is the area of the adjusting arm minus the area of the inner slot and the hole? _____

Save the drawing as **P8-3**.

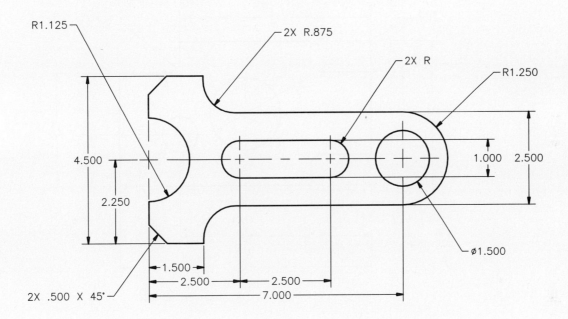

4. Use your TEMPLATEA template to draw the object shown below. Set fractional units current before beginning construction. Convert the objects into regions and subtract the two holes.When the composite region is complete, use the **LIST** command to answer the following:

a. What is the object's area? _____

b. What is its perimeter? _____

c. What are the lower XY values of the bounding box?_____

d. What are the upper XY values of the bounding box? _____

e. Calculate the mass properties of the object using the **MASSPROP** command. Compare these values with those obtained using **LIST**. Save the results of the analysis to a file called P8-4.mpr.

Save the drawing as P8-4.

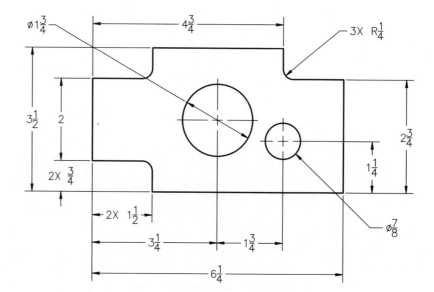

AutoCAD LT

Chapter 9

Creating Drawing Notes

Learning Objectives

After you have completed this chapter, you will be able to:
- ○ Add annotation to your drawings.
- ○ Draw unique characters using special character codes.
- ○ Describe the purpose of the **QTEXT** command.
- ○ Create text with a specified height, orientation, slant, and width factor.
- ○ Understand the difference between font and style.
- ○ Modify and move existing text.
- ○ Correct the spelling of text objects using the spell checker.

No engineering or architectural drawing is complete until it has been annotated. Typical drawing annotation includes local and general notes, tabular data such as door and window schedules, parts lists, and title block information. This chapter describes the use of the **DTEXT**, **TEXT**, and **MTEXT** commands so that you may begin adding notes to your drawings. You will also learn how to create your own text styles using different fonts and orientations. Additionally, several text editing methods are presented as well as how to use the AutoCAD LT spell checker.

Using Dynamic Text

Getting Started Guide **11**

The **DTEXT**, (Dynamic TEXT) command is used to create text. When you use **DTEXT**, the characters you enter from the keyboard are displayed on the screen as well as on the command line. The text can be rotated, justified, and created at any height. The **DTEXT** command also allows you to enter multiple lines of text. When you reach the end of a sentence, press [Enter] and the text insertion cursor drops down one line and aligns itself below the previous line of text. Pressing [Enter] two times in a row terminates the **DTEXT** command.

To use **DTEXT**, enter DTEXT, or DT, at the Command: prompt, or select **Single Line Text** from the **Draw** pull-down menu. See **Figure 9-1.** On the command line, **DTEXT** displays the following prompts and options:

DTEXT
DT

Draw
↳ **Single Line Text**

Command: **DTEXT** *or* **DT**↵
Justify/Style/⟨Start point⟩: *(pick a starting point for the text)*
Height ⟨*current*⟩: *(specify a text height or accept the default)*
Rotation angle ⟨*current*⟩: *(enter the text rotation or accept the default)*
Text: *(enter the desired text and press* [Enter] *to drop down one line)*
Text: *(enter additional text or press* [Enter] *to end the command)*
Command:

Figure 9-1.
Select **Single Line Text** from the **Draw** pull-down menu to issue the **DTEXT** command.

NOTE

If you are using AutoCAD LT 97, in addition to DTEXT and DT you also can enter T at the Command: prompt to access the **DTEXT** command.

If **DTEXT** was the last command entered, pressing [Enter] at the ⟨Start point⟩: prompt skips the additional prompts for height and rotation angle and immediately displays the Text: prompt. The previous text string appears highlighted in the drawing window. Any new text you enter uses the text height and rotation angle previously specified and is placed directly beneath the line of highlighted text.

Each of the **DTEXT** options are described in the following sections.

Text Start Point and Justification

By default, AutoCAD LT text is left justified. That is, the start point is at the lower-left corner of the text string as shown in **Figure 9-2.** You can specify the start point for text by picking a screen location, entering a coordinate, or using one of the object snap modes to snap to an existing object. When selecting a start point, remember that the point specified at the ⟨Start point⟩: prompt can later be accessed using the **Insert** osnap.

Figure 9-2.
Text in AutoCAD LT is left justified by default.

Default text
insertion point

AutoCAD LT—Fundamentals and Applications

Left justification is suitable for most text operations. However, there are occasions when one of the other text justification modes is more appropriate. To change text justification, use the **Justify** option as follows:

Command: **DTEXT** *or* **DT**⏎
Justify/Style/⟨Start point⟩: **J**⏎
Align/Fit/Center/Middle/Right/TL/TC/TR/ML/MC/MR/BL/BC/BR: *(select a justification mode and press* [Enter]*)*

Each of the **Justify** suboptions are described below:

- **Align.** This option justifies text between two selected points. If the two points are not aligned horizontally, the text string is created at a corresponding angle. Regardless of the number of characters entered, AutoCAD LT fits the text between the two points and adjusts the text height as necessary to do so. From **Figure 9-3**, you can see that the longer the character string, the shorter the text height. Fewer characters results in an increased text height. The **Align** option also adjusts the width factor automatically. The *width factor* is the width of a character in proportion to its height. Use the **Align** option as follows:

Align/Fit/Center/Middle/Right/TL/TC/TR/ML/MC/MR/BL/BC/BR: **A**⏎
First text line point: *(select a start point)*
Second text line point: *(select an end point)*
Text: *(enter the text)*

- **Fit.** This option is very similar to the **Align** option with one important difference. With **Fit**, you are prompted to specify a character height after locating the text start and end points. As shown in **Figure 9-4**, the specified height is maintained regardless of the length of the text string. However, the longer the text string, the narrower the characters. A shorter text string results in wider characters. The **Fit** option looks like this:

Align/Fit/Center/Middle/Right/TL/TC/TR/ML/MC/MR/BL/BC/BR: **F**⏎
First text line point: *(select a start point)*
Second text line point: *(select an end point)*
Height ⟨current⟩: *(specify a text height or accept the default)*
Text: *(enter the text)*

Figure 9-3.
An example of three text strings created with the **Align** option.

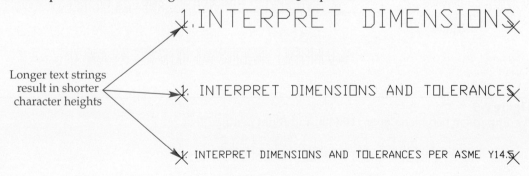

Longer text strings result in shorter character heights

- **Center.** This option centers text horizontally about a selected point. See **Figure 9-5.** This is a handy option when you want to label a detail or section view. Use the **Center** option as follows:

    Align/Fit/Center/Middle/Right/TL/TC/TR/ML/MC/MR/BL/BC/BR: **C.**↵
    Center point: *(pick a point)*
    Height ⟨*current*⟩: *(specify a text height or accept the default)*
    Rotation angle ⟨*current*⟩: *(enter the rotation or accept the default)*
    Text: *(enter the text)*

- **Middle.** As shown in **Figure 9-5,** this option is used to center text both horizontally and vertically about a selected point. The **Middle** option is commonly used to locate text precisely in the middle of an object, like a rectangle or circle. It is also used to accurately place a drawing title or drawing number in the appropriate sections of a title block sheet. Since text is more accurately located using **Middle** justification, this option may be an even better way to label a detail or section view. The **Middle** option looks like this:

    Align/Fit/Center/Middle/Right/TL/TC/TR/ML/MC/MR/BL/BC/BR: **M.**↵
    Middle point: *(pick a point)*
    Height ⟨*current*⟩: *(specify a text height or accept the default)*
    Rotation angle ⟨*current*⟩: *(enter the rotation or accept the default)*
    Text: *(enter the text)*

- **Right.** Use this option when you wish to align the right side of your text at the insertion point. See **Figure 9-5.** The procedure is as follows:

    Align/Fit/Center/Middle/Right/TL/TC/TR/ML/MC/MR/BL/BC/BR: **R.**↵
    End point: *(pick a point)*
    Height ⟨*current*⟩: *(specify a text height or accept the default)*
    Rotation angle ⟨*current*⟩: *(enter the rotation or accept the default)*
    Text: *(enter the text)*

Figure 9-4.
An example of three text strings created using the **Fit** option.

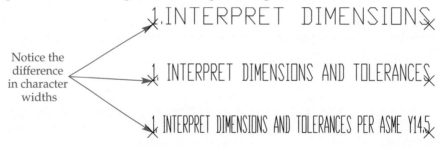

Figure 9-5.
A comparison between **Center**, **Middle**, and **Right** justified text.

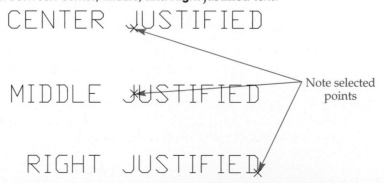

Other Justify suboptions

In addition to the **Justify** suboptions of **Align**, **Fit**, **Center**, **Middle**, and **Right**, you may choose to justify your text using one of the other suboptions illustrated in **Figure 9-6.** Observe that the abbreviations **TL** (top left), **ML** (middle left), **BL** (bottom left), **TC** (top center), **MC** (middle center), **BC** (bottom center), **TR** (top right), **MR** (middle right), and **BR** (bottom right). Although these options are rarely used for uppercase block lettering, they can be quite useful if you have the need to create lowercase characters with specific justification requirements.

As you type in text using one of the fourteen **Justify** suboptions, the text appears on screen as if it were left justified. Do not be alarmed by this. As soon as you are through entering text and terminate the **DTEXT** command, the text will assume the justification mode you specified.

Figure 9-6.
The other text justification suboptions.

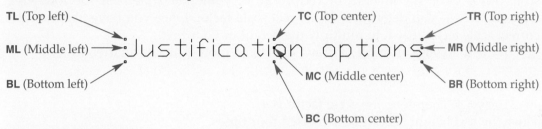

TL (Top left)   **TC** (Top center)   **TR** (Top right)

ML (Middle left)   **MR** (Middle right)

BL (Bottom left)   **MC** (Middle center)   **BR** (Bottom right)

BC (Bottom center)

PROFESSIONAL TIP

You need not enter J for **Justify** when you wish to use one of the justification modes. At the ⟨Start point⟩: prompt, simply enter the first letter of the **Justify** suboption you want. The procedure for middle justification looks like this:

Command: **DTEXT** *or* **DT**↵
Justify/Style/⟨Start point⟩: **M**↵
Middle point: *(pick a point)*
Height ⟨current⟩: *(specify a text height or accept the default)*
Rotation angle ⟨current⟩: *(enter the rotation or accept the default)*
Text: *(enter the text)*

If using the **Top Left**, **Middle Left**, **Bottom Left**, **Top Center**, **Middle Center**, **Bottom Center**, **Top Right**, **Middle Right**, and **Bottom Right** justify suboptions, enter the two letters that uniquely identify each suboption.

Determining the Correct Text Height

If you are using Engineering, Scientific, or Decimal units for your drawings, AutoCAD LT sets the default text height to .200 units. If you are using Architectural or Fractional units, the default text height is set to 3/16 units.

You may recall from *Chapter 2* that AutoCAD LT can draw virtually anything at full scale. Very small objects are scaled up at plot time, while very large objects are scaled down. However, what happens to plotted text height?

If your drawing is to be plotted at 1:1, then you do need not overly concern your-self with text height. On the other hand, if you intend to plot with a specific scale factor, it is very important to set your text height appropriately.

As an example, suppose the object you are drawing is rather small. Therefore, you intend to plot the drawing at a scale of 4:1. Since your text height will be increased by a factor of 4 at plot time, you can compensate by creating your text at 1/4 its normal size. In other words, when **DTEXT** prompts you for the text height, enter .05. The text height will be increased four times at the plotter and thus resume its default height of .200 units.

Consider another example. Suppose that the object you are drawing is very large and you intend to plot with a scale factor of 1:10 (one-tenth). Further, suppose that you want your plotted text height to be .156 (5/32). Since the drawing will be plotted ten times smaller, set your text height to be ten times larger. Therefore, set the text height to 1.56 units for this example.

As you can see, the solution to setting proper text height is to set your drawing scale factor to be the inverse, or reciprocal, of your plot scale. Use the following formula to help you determine the correct scale factor. Once you have obtained the correct scale factor, use it to multiply the height of your text.

In the following example, a drawing is to be plotted at 1:4 (quarter-scale).

$1/4'' = 1''$

$.25'' = 1''$

$1/.25 = 4$. Therefore, the scale factor is 4.

Thus, the text height should be increased four times.

The next example uses a typical architectural scale of $1/2'' = 1'$.

$1/2'' = 1'$

$1/2'' = 12''$

$(2/1)(1/2) = 12/1 \times 2/1$

$1 = 24$. Therefore, the scale factor is 24.

If the architect for this drawing wanted the plotted text height to be 3/16'', then the drawing text height is derived by multiplying the text height by the scale factor as follows:

$3/16 \times 24$

$3/16 \times 24/1$

$72/16 = 4\ 8/16 = 4\ 1/2$

When the drawing is plotted at $1/2'' = 1'$ (1/24), the 4-1/2 units high text characters are reduced 24 times and resume their proper height of 3/16.

This final example calculates the scale factor for a civil engineering drawing that is to be plotted at $1'' = 50'$.

$1'' = 50'$

$1'' = (50 \times 12)$

$1'' = 600''$

$600/1 = 600$. Therefore, the scale factor is 600.

As in the previous examples, multiply what the plotted text height should be by 600 to set the required text height in AutoCAD LT.

Text Rotation Angles

By default, text is generated at 0 degrees. In other words, the text reads from left to right in a horizontal orientation. You can specify a different orientation at the Rotation angle: prompt as follows:

Rotation angle ⟨current⟩: (enter a positive or negative angle)

A positive angle rotates text counterclockwise while a negative angle rotates text clockwise. The ability to rotate the text at any angle is especially useful if you use AutoCAD LT to create charts and graphs. Also, some organizations use title block formats that require drawing titles and numbers to be placed in the right margin of the sheet. If your company or school uses this type of format, set the text rotation angle to 270°. Several examples of rotated text appear in **Figure 9-7.**

Figure 9-7.
Several examples of text at different rotation angles.

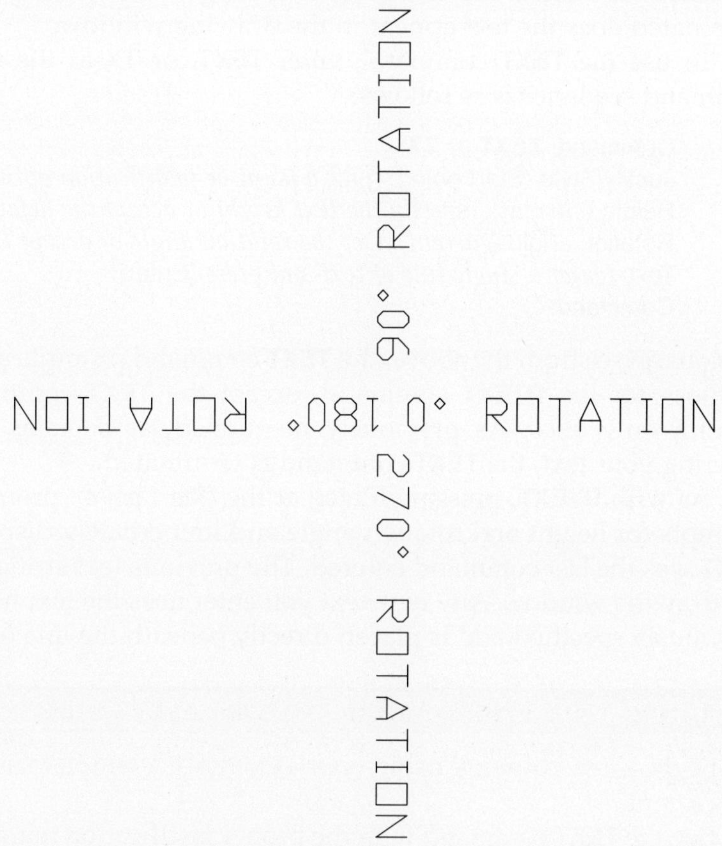

EXERCISE 9-1

❑ Begin a new drawing using your TEMPLATEB template and set the NOTES layer current.
❑ Use **DTEXT** with the proper justification modes to create some text similar to that illustrated in **Figures 9-2** through **9-5**.
❑ Make sure the [Caps Lock] key is off on your keyboard and experiment with several of the other **Justify** suboptions, such as Top Right and Middle Left. Duplicate the character string shown in **Figure 9-6** using several of these options.
❑ Turn the [Caps Lock] key back on and set the **DTEXT** rotation angles appropriately to duplicate the text strings illustrated in **Figure 9-7**.
❑ Save the drawing as EX9-1.

The TEXT Command

The **TEXT** command is similar to the **DTEXT** command with two exceptions. Unlike **DTEXT** that allows you to create multiple lines of text, the **TEXT** command creates only a single line of text. Pressing [Enter] after typing in text ends the **TEXT** command instead of dropping down to a new line. The other difference between **TEXT** and **DTEXT** is that text entered with the **TEXT** command appears on the command line only, and not in the drawing window. Only when the command is terminated does the text appear in the drawing window.

**TEXT
TX**

To use the **TEXT** command, enter TEXT, or TX at the Command: prompt. The command sequence is as follows:

Command: **TEXT** or **TX**.⏎
Justify/Style/⟨Start point⟩: *(pick a point or justification option)*
Height ⟨*current*⟩: *(specify the text height or accept the default)*
Rotation angle ⟨*current*⟩: *(set the rotation angle or accept the default)*
Text: *(enter a single line of text and press* [Enter]*)*
Command:

As you can see from the above, the **TEXT** command prompts and options are the same as those for the **DTEXT** command, except the **TEXT** command displays the **Text:** prompt only once. As previously mentioned, as soon as you press [Enter] after entering your text, the **TEXT** command is terminated.

As with **DTEXT**, pressing [Enter] at the ⟨Start point⟩: prompt skips the additional prompts for height and rotation angle and immediately displays the **Text:** prompt if **TEXT** was the last command entered. The previous text string appears highlighted in the drawing window. Any new text you enter uses the text height and rotation angle previously specified and is placed directly beneath the line of highlighted text.

EXERCISE 9-2

❑ Begin a new drawing using your TEMPLATEA template and set the NOTES layer current.
❑ Use the **TEXT** command with the proper justification modes to create text similar to that shown in **Figures 9-2** through **9-6**.
❑ Using the **TEXT** command, set the text rotation angles as required to duplicate the text strings illustrated in **Figure 9-7**.
❑ Save the drawing as EX9-2. Of the two commands, **DTEXT** and **TEXT**, which do you prefer?

Special Character Codes

Several of the text characters used in engineering and architectural drawings do not appear on a computer keyboard. One example is the Greek letter *phi* (Ø), which is commonly used to represent a diameter symbol. Fortunately, AutoCAD LT provides special character codes that allow you to add these symbols to your drawing notes. Each of the codes is accessed by entering two percent signs (%%) and a designated character. The designated character can be entered in either uppercase or lowercase lettering. Each of the special character codes is listed below:

%%C	Draws a diameter symbol (Ø)
%%D	Draws a degree symbol (°)
%%P	Draws a plus or minus symbol (±)
%%O	Draws overscored characters
%%U	Draws underscored characters

%%%   Forces a single percent sign (%). This code is only used when a single percent sign precedes another control code sequence. As an example, consider the note 42%±1. To create this note you would type in the following: 42%%%%P1. When you need to use a single percent sign, simply press the percent (%) key.

The overscore and underscore character codes act as toggles that can be turned on and off in the middle of a sentence. As an example, suppose you wanted to create the following drawing note:

1. ABSOLUTELY <u>NO PAINT</u> ON THE SURFACES INDICATED.

Use the underscore toggle as follows:

1. ABSOLUTELY %%UNO PAINT%%U ON THE SURFACES INDICATED.

Both overscore and underscore modes can be on simultaneously. When using **DTEXT**, the modes are automatically turned off when you press [Enter] to add another line of text. Also, do not be alarmed to see the character codes displayed in the drawing window as you enter them from the keyboard. As soon as you terminate the **DTEXT** command, the character codes assume the proper symbols. Several examples of text using special character codes appear in **Figure 9-8.**

Figure 9-8.
Text created using special character codes.

DRAFT ANGLE: 3° MAX PER SIDE.

Ø1.875±.005

SECTION B-B

AutoCAD LT

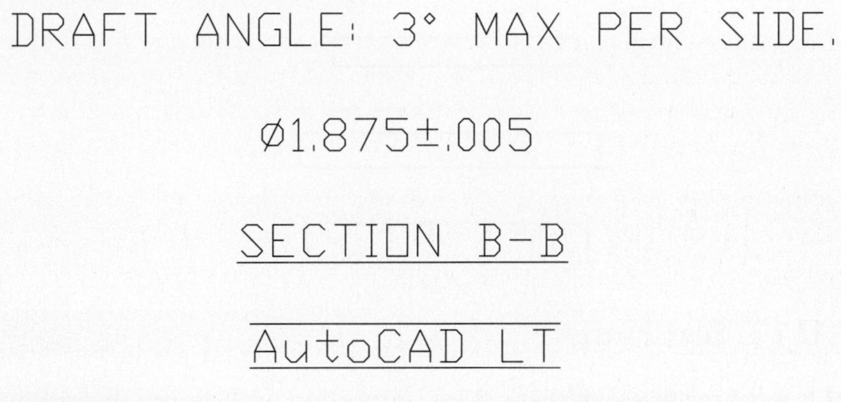

PROFESSIONAL TIP

Many drafters prefer to underline view labels such as <u>DETAIL A</u> or <u>SECTION B-B</u>. Rather than draw a line or polyline under the text, use **Middle** or **Center** justification modes and toggle underscoring on. The view labels are automatically underlined and centered under the views or details they identify.

EXERCISE 9-3

❏ Begin a new drawing using your TEMPLATEA template and set the NOTES layer current.
❏ Use **DTEXT** with the appropriate special character codes to duplicate the text shown in **Figure 9-8.**
❏ Save the drawing as EX9-3.

The QTEXT Command

The **QTEXT** command controls the display and plotting of text and attribute objects. An *attribute* is informational text associated with a block object. Blocks and attributes are covered thoroughly in *Chapter 15.* When **QTEXT** is on, AutoCAD LT displays each text string and attribute with a bounding box around the object. The bounding box represents the approximate height and length of the text string.

In **Figure 9-9**, the identical text from **Figure 9-8** is shown with **QTEXT** turned on. If your drawing contains a lot of text, you can reduce the redraw and regeneration times by turning on **QTEXT** as follows:

QTEXT
QT

> Command: **QTEXT** *or* **QT.↵**
> ON/OFF ⟨*current*⟩: *(enter* ON *or* OFF *and press* [Enter]*)*

A change in **QTEXT** status does not take effect until a regeneration is performed.

> Command: **REGEN** *or* **RE.↵**

Finally, do not forget to turn **QTEXT** off before plotting.

Figure 9-9.
The text from Figure 9-8 is shown with **QTEXT** turned on.

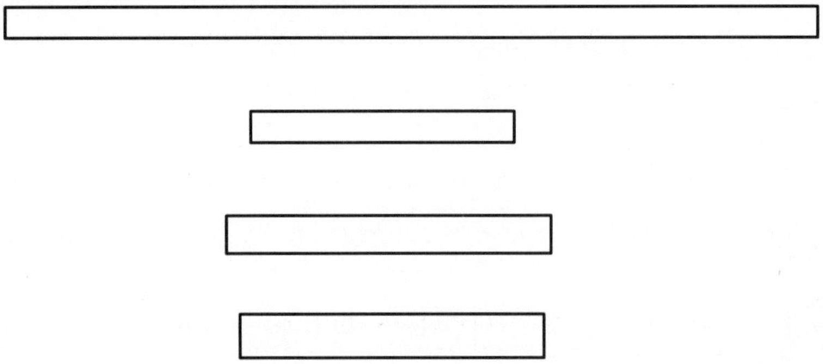

AutoCAD LT Text Fonts

A *font* is a character set of distinctive proportion and design. It contains letters, numerals, punctuation marks, and symbols. The standard AutoCAD LT fonts are shown in **Figure 9-10**. The default text font used by AutoCAD LT is called TXT. This font redraws and regenerates quickly because it contains few vectors. However, it is not particularly attractive. Many users prefer to use the ROMANS (Roman Simplex) font instead. It redraws and regenerates quickly and looks more like the single-stroke Gothic lettering typically used in the traditional paper-based drafting environment.

From **Figure 9-11**, you can see that a variety of special symbol fonts are also included with AutoCAD LT. They include astronomical, mapping, mathematical, meteorological, and musical symbols. Each of these symbols is mapped to a specific key on your keyboard. The character mapping for each symbol font set is shown in **Figure 9-12**.

In addition to AutoCAD LT fonts, you can also use Windows TrueType fonts. You are probably familiar with these types of fonts if you have been using word-processing or other Windows-based software applications. Several examples of TrueType fonts are shown in **Figure 9-13A**. By default, these fonts appear filled (solid) in the drawing window. However, you can display them as outlined text when you print or plot your drawing by setting the **TEXTFILL** variable to 0. An example of TrueType fonts plotted as outlines appears in **Figure 9-13B**. This function is covered in *Chapter 14* of this text.

Figure 9-10.
The standard AutoCAD LT text fonts. (*Autodesk, Inc.*)

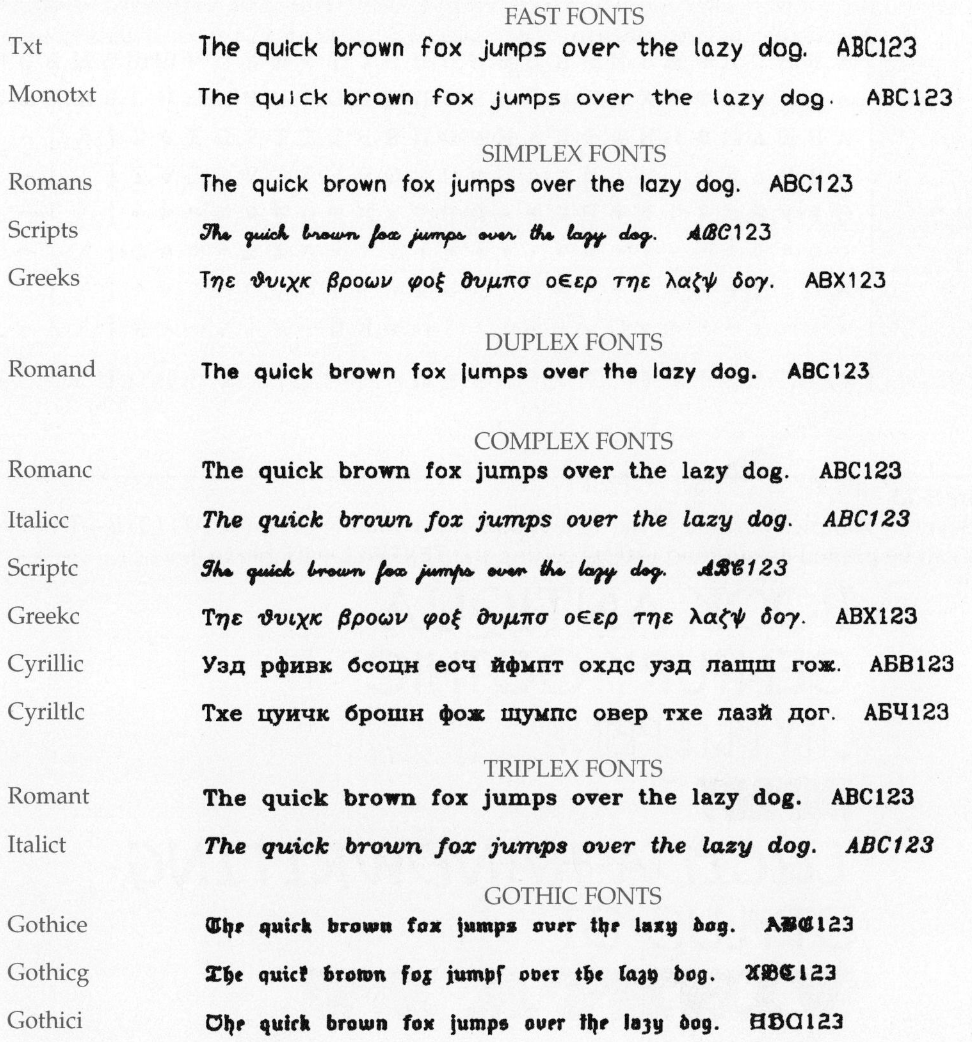

FAST FONTS

Txt   The quick brown fox jumps over the lazy dog. ABC123

Monotxt   The quick brown fox jumps over the lazy dog. ABC123

SIMPLEX FONTS

Romans   The quick brown fox jumps over the lazy dog. ABC123

Scripts   *The quick brown fox jumps over the lazy dog. ABC123*

Greeks   Τηε ϑυιχκ βροων φοξ δυμπσ οϵερ τηε λαζψ δογ. ABX123

DUPLEX FONTS

Romand   The quick brown fox jumps over the lazy dog. ABC123

COMPLEX FONTS

Romanc   **The quick brown fox jumps over the lazy dog. ABC123**

Italicc   *The quick brown fox jumps over the lazy dog. ABC123*

Scriptc   *The quick brown fox jumps over the lazy dog. ABC123*

Greekc   *Τηε ϑυιχκ βροων φοξ δυμπσ οϵερ τηε λαζψ δογ. ABX123*

Cyrillic   Узд рфивк бсоцн еоч йфмпт охдс узд лащш гож. АБВ123

Cyriltlc   Тхе цуичк брошн фож щумпс овер тхе лазй дог. АБЧ123

TRIPLEX FONTS

Romant   **The quick brown fox jumps over the lazy dog. ABC123**

Italict   *The quick brown fox jumps over the lazy dog. ABC123*

GOTHIC FONTS

Gothice   𝕿𝖍𝖊 quick brown fox jumps over the lazy dog. 𝕬𝕭𝕮123

Gothicg   The quick brown fox jumps over the lazy dog. XBC123

Gothici   The quick brown fox jumps over the lazy dog. HBC123

Figure 9-11.
The AutoCAD LT symbol fonts. (*Autodesk, Inc.*)

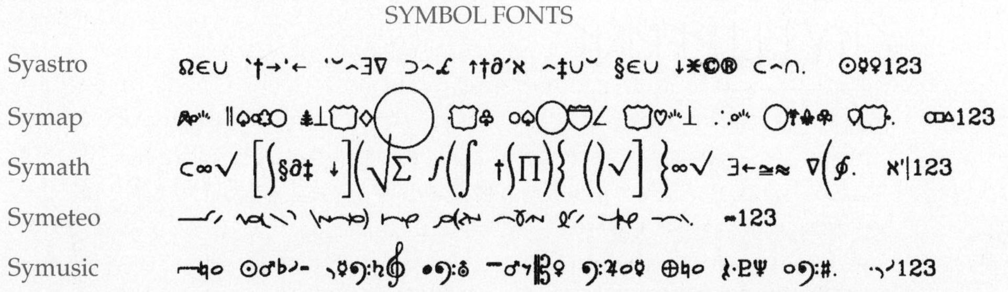

SYMBOL FONTS

Syastro   ΩΕU `†→'← ˙˘∩‡˜ ⊃∧ℒ ℐ⌐ℂ ↑↑∂'χ ⌐‡∪˘ §ΕU ↓✻☉® ⊂⌐∩. ☉♀♀123

Symap   symbols ‖Ω⌂⌂O ‡∏⌂◇◯ ⌂⊕ oϕ◇ ⌐ ⌂'♡∿⊥ .˙.˙˘ ◯†✦✦ ♡◠. ⌂⌂△123

Symath   c∞√ [[§∂‡ ↓](√Σ ʃ∫ †ʃΠ){ ⟨ʃ√] }∞√ ∃←≈÷ ∇(∮. א'|123

Symeteo   ⌐√ ∿⌐\ ⟨∿⌐⟩ ∿⌐ ⌐∿ ⌐∿⌐ ⌐✓ ⌐∿. ⹋123

Symusic   ⌐♩o ☉♂♭✓⌐ ˌ♂♭:♭ ♩♩:♭ ⌐♂ℒ♭♩♀ ♩:♩◇♂ ⊕♩o ʃ:♭♥ o♩:♯. ˌˌʹ123

The standard AutoCAD LT fonts are compiled and have a file extension of .SHX. They are stored in the Program Files\AutoCAD LT 98 folder. The TrueType fonts are located in the Windows\Fonts folder. For AutoCAD LT 97, the fonts are found in the Program Files\AutoCAD LT 97 folder.

Figure 9-12.
Character mapping for nonroman and symbol fonts. (*Autodesk, Inc.*)

Figure 9-13.
A—Several examples of some of the TrueType fonts available in AutoCAD LT. B—TrueType fonts can be plotted as outlined text by setting the **TEXTFILL** variable to 0.

BOOK ANTIQUA
CENTURY GOTHIC
CITY BLUEPRINT
IMPACT
LUCIDA HANDWRITING
STYLUS BT
VINETA BT

A

BOOK ANTIQUA
CENTURY GOTHIC
CITY BLUEPRINT
IMPACT
LUCIDA HANDWRITING
STYLUS BT
VINETA BT

B

PROFESSIONAL TIP   If none of the fonts supplied with the AutoCAD LT program suit your application, there are dozens of third-party fonts commercially available for AutoCAD LT. You can learn about these fonts from your local AutoCAD dealer or from magazines like *CADalyst* and *CADENCE*.

Creating a Text Style

Before you can use any of the available AutoCAD LT fonts, you must first create a text style. A *text style* is a named collection of settings that affect the appearance of text characters for each of the available fonts. For example, text characters can be wide or narrow, slanted or vertical, upside down or backward. Several examples of text styles are illustrated in **Figure 9-14.** Text styles are created with the **STYLE** command and are saved with a name in the current drawing. The name you provide may contain up to 31 characters, but no spaces are allowed. When you begin a new drawing in AutoCAD LT, the default style is used. This style is called STANDARD and has the TXT font assigned to it. You may create a new text style, or modify an existing one, on the command line or by using a dialog box. The two methods are described in the following sections.

Figure 9-14.
A variety of different text styles and fonts.

*THIS IS ROMAN SIMPLEX WITH A 15°
OBLIQUING ANGLE.*

WIDE   ROMAN   DUPLEX

NARROW ITALIC COMPLEX

BACKWARDS TECHNICBOLD

UPSIDE DOWN ROMAN TRIPLEX

VERTICAL TXT

Creating a Text Style Using a Dialog Box

To create or modify a text style, enter DDSTYLE, or STYLE or ST, at the Command: prompt, or select **Text Style...** from the **Format** pull-down menu. See **Figure 9-15.** The **Text Style** dialog box is then displayed. See **Figure 9-16.** Each of the sections of this dialog box are described below.

The **Style Name** section at the top of the dialog box features the following:

- **Style Name drop-down list.** This drop-down list includes the names of all existing text styles in the current drawing. The default STANDARD style is shown in the list in **Figure 9-16.**

**DDSTYLE
STYLE or ST**

**Format
➥ Text Style...**

- **New....** When you wish to create a new text style, click this button to display the **New Text Style** subdialog box. See **Figure 9-17.** Enter the desired style name in the **Style Name:** text box and click the **OK** button. Make the style name descriptive of the style you wish to create, such as SLANTED or ARCHSTYLE. Remember that the style name may contain up to 31 characters, but no spaces are permitted. If you do not wish to enter a name, AutoCAD LT automatically provides the name STYLE1 to the new text style. Any subsequently created text styles take the default names STYLE2, STYLE3, and so on.
- **Rename....** Click this button to rename an existing text style using the **Rename Text Style** subdialog box. First, select the style name you wish to rename from the **Style Name** drop-down list so that it becomes the highlighted selection. After clicking the **Rename...** button, enter the new name in the **Style Name:** text box. Finally, click the **OK** button to finish renaming the text style.

Figure 9-15.
Select **Text Style...** from the **Format** pull-down menu to open the **Text Style** dialog box.

Figure 9-16.
The **Text Style** dialog box is used to create a new text style or modify an existing one.

Default style

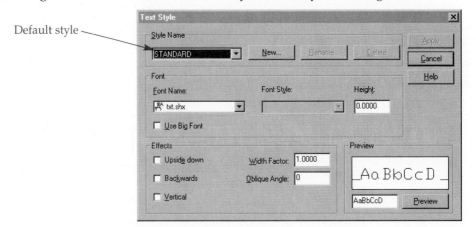

Figure 9-17.
The **New Text Style** subdialog box is used to enter a name for a new text style. If a name is not provided, AutoCAD LT supplies the name style1.

Enter new style name here

AutoCAD LT—Fundamentals and Applications

NOTE You cannot rename the STANDARD text style using the **Rename...** button in the **Text Style** dialog box. If you wish to rename the STANDARD text style, use the **DDRENAME** or **RENAME** commands, instead.

- **Delete....** To delete a text style, first select the style name you wish to delete from the **Style Name** drop-down list so that it becomes the highlighted selection. After clicking the **Delete...** button, AutoCAD LT prompts you to confirm the deletion using an alert box. Click the **Yes** or **No** buttons as desired.

NOTE A text style may not be deleted if any text exists in the current drawing using that style. To delete the text style, you must first edit the text so that it is in a different style. This is accomplished using the **DDMODIFY** or **CHANGE** commands described later in this chapter.

The **Font** section in the middle of the dialog box features the following:
- **Font Name drop-down list.** After providing a name for your new text style, select the desired font for the style using this drop-down list. See **Figure 9-18.** The font names followed with a .SHX file extension are AutoCAD LT compiled fonts. Observe that many of the fonts appearing in the list are TrueType fonts. These fonts are compatible with other Windows 98, 95, or NT applications, as well.
- **Font Style:. drop-down list.** Several of the supplied TrueType fonts may also be created in Italic and Bold styles. If the font you select supports these styles, the Italic and Bold styles can be selected from the **Font Style:** drop-down list. See **Figure 9-19.**
- **Height:.** You can use this text box to assign a text height to the new style. However, it is strongly recommended that you leave the height set to 0. Doing so allows you to specify the text height each time you enter text using this style. If you specify an explicit height here, then the text height you enter is always used for this style and you are not prompted for height.

Figure 9-18.
Selecting a font
from the **Font Name:**
drop-down list.

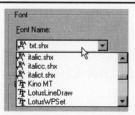

Figure 9-19.
An Italic, Bold,
or Bold Italic style
can be selected
for some fonts using
the **Font Style:**
drop-down list.

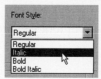

The **Effects** section at the bottom of the dialog box features the following:

- **Upside down.** Activate this check box if you want text generated upsidedown.
- **Backwards.** Activate this check box if you want text generated backward.
- **Vertical.** Activate this check box if you want text generated in a vertical format. An example of vertical text is shown at the far right in **Figure 9-14.** This aspect of style might be useful for charts and graphs. However, keep in mind that TrueType fonts cannot be set to a vertical orientation.
- **Width Factor:.** The width factor is the width of a character in proportion to its height. Entering a value less than 1 in this text box condenses characters, making them narrow. A value greater than 1 expands the characters, making them wider.
- **Oblique Angle:.** The oblique angle is used to create a slanted text style. You may use this text box to enter a value greater than 0 and less than 85. A positive value slants text forward, while a negative value slants text backward. Slanted text created with an obliquing angle of 15° is shown at the top of **Figure 9-14.**
- **Preview section.** This section at the lowerright of the dialog box displays sample text (AaBbCcD) that changes dynamically as you change fonts and modify the effects. See **Figure 9-20.** This area also displays the results when a width factor or oblique angle is applied to the text style. However, the **Preview** box cannot display changes when height or a vertical orientation has been applied to text. To change the sample text in the **Preview** box, enter characters in the box below the character preview image and click the **Preview** button to the right. The sample text you enter is then displayed in the **Preview** box.
- **Apply.** Click this button to apply style changes made in the dialog box to text of the current style in the drawing.
- **Cancel.** This button changes to **Close** whenever a change is made to any of the options available in the **Text Style** dialog box. However, keep in mind that changing, renaming, or deleting the current style and creating a new style are operations that take place immediately and cannot be canceled.

Figure 9-20.
Using the **Preview** section at the lower right of the dialog box to preview a sample of a new text style.

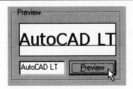

Creating a Text Style on the Command Line

-STYLE

To create a text style on the command line, enter -STYLE at the Command: prompt. The **-STYLE** command displays the following prompts and options:

```
Command: -STYLE↵
Text style name (or ?) ⟨STANDARD⟩: ↵
Specify full font name or font filename ⟨txt⟩: ↵
Height ⟨0.0000⟩: ↵
Width factor ⟨1.0000⟩: ↵
Obliquing angle ⟨0⟩: ↵
Backwards? ⟨N⟩ ↵
Upside-down? ⟨N⟩ ↵
Vertical? ⟨N⟩ ↵
Command:
```

Each of the **-STYLE** command options are described as follows:

- **Text style name (or ?).** Enter a descriptive name for the new text style at this prompt or press [Enter] to accept the default text style. You can use the **?** option to list any existing text styles defined in the current drawing.
- **Height.** As previously mentioned, it is strongly recommended that you leave the height set to 0. Doing so allows you to specify the text height each time you enter text using this style.
- **Width factor.** As mentioned previously, the width factor is the width of a character in proportion to its height. A value less than 1 condenses characters, making them narrow. A value greater than 1 expands the characters, making them wider.
- **Obliquing angle.** The obliquing angle is used to create a slanted text style. You may enter a value greater than 0 and less than 85. Remember that a negative value slants text backwards. The default is 0.
- **Backwards.** Answer Y or N if you want text generated backwards. The default is N.
- **Upside-down.** Answer Y or N if you want text generated upside-down. The default is N.
- **Vertical.** Answer Y or N if you want text generated in a vertical format. The default is N. Remember that the vertical orientation cannot be applied to TrueType fonts.

Once each of the prompts has been answered, **-STYLE** displays a message stating the style name you specified is now the current text style.

EXERCISE 9-4

❏ In this exercise, you will create a new text style named SLANTED on the command line. The style will use the Roman Simplex font with an obliquing angle of 15°.

❏ Begin a new drawing using your TEMPLATEA template.

❏ Enter the **-STYLE** command and answer the prompts as shown below:

```
Command: -STYLE↵
Text style name (or ?) 〈STANDARD〉: SLANTED↵
Specify full font name or font filename 〈txt〉: ROMANS↵
New style. Height 〈0.000〉: ↵
Width factor 〈1.000〉: ↵
Obliquing angle 〈0〉: 15↵
Backwards? 〈N〉 ↵
Upside-down? 〈N〉 ↵
Vertical? 〈N〉 ↵
SLANTED is now the current text style.
Command:
```

❏ Set the NOTES layer current and create some text with your new text style.

❏ Next, perform an **UNDO Back** operation to undo everything in the drawing.

❏ Now, use the **Text Style** dialog box to recreate the SLANTED text style with the font and obliquing angle previously specified. Of the two methods, which do you prefer?

❏ When you are done experimenting, save the drawing as EX9-4.

Setting a Text Style Current

Once you have two or more text styles defined in your drawing, it is a simple matter to make one of them current. There are several ways to accomplish this. One method is to use the **Style** option offered by both the **DTEXT** and **TEXT** commands. This option looks like this:

Command: **DTEXT** *or* **DT**↵
Justify/Style/⟨Start point⟩: **S**↵
Style name (or ?) ⟨*current*⟩: *(enter an existing text style name)*

After providing a valid name, the **DTEXT** (or **TEXT**) command resumes as usual. If you enter a text style name that does not exist, AutoCAD LT displays an error message. If this happens, use the **?** option to list the styles defined in the current drawing or to double-check the correct spelling of the style names.

TEXTSTYLE

You can also preset the text style name before you create any text. This is done using the **TEXTSTYLE** system variable. In the following example, the SLANTED style is set current.

Command: **TEXTSTYLE**↵
New value for TEXTSTYLE ⟨"STANDARD"⟩: **SLANTED**↵
Command:

Setting a Text Style Current Using the **Text Style** Dialog Box

It is also possible to set a text style current using the **Text Style** dialog box. Simply select the desired text style from the **Style Name:** drop-down list as shown in **Figure 9-21.** When you are through, click the **Close** button at the upper right of the dialog box. The style name you selected from the list is now the current text style.

Figure 9-21.
Setting a different text style current using the **Style Name:** drop-down list in the **Text Style** dialog box.

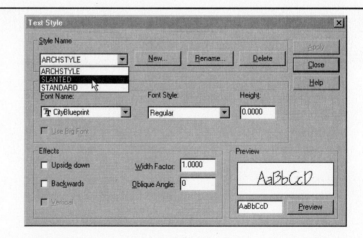

PROFESSIONAL TIP

As with layers, create various text styles in your templates so that they are always available when needed.

Renaming a Text Style

Text styles, like views, linetypes, and layers, can be renamed at any time with the **DDRENAME** command. You may recall from previous chapters that this command permits you to rename objects using the **Rename** dialog box. To do so, enter DDRENAME, or REN, at the Command: prompt, or select **Rename...** from the **Format** pull-down menu.

DDRENAME
REN

Format
➡ Rename...

The **Named Objects** list appears at the left of the dialog box and contains the types of objects that can be named or renamed in AutoCAD LT. From the example shown in **Figure 9-22**, observe that Style has been selected from the list at the left. A listing of all the text styles defined in the current drawing appears at the right of the dialog box. To rename the SLANTED text style, first select the style name from the list. The name of the text style you select is then displayed in the **Old Name:** text box. With your pointing device, click anywhere inside the **Rename To:** text box and enter the new style name. In the example, the SLANTED text style is renamed to OBLIQUE. When you are done typing, click the **Rename To:** button and the new style name appears in the list at the right of the dialog box. When you are finished renaming objects, click the **OK** button to exit the **Rename** dialog box.

It is also possible to rename text styles from the command line instead of using the dialog box. In the following example, the **RENAME**, or **-REN**, command is used to perform the identical renaming operation described above.

> Command: **RENAME** *or* **-REN**↵
> Block/Dimstyle/LAyer/LType/Style/Ucs/VIew/VPort: **S**↵
> Old text style name: **SLANTED**↵
> New text style name: **OBLIQUE**↵
> Command:

Figure 9-22.
Using the **Rename** dialog box to rename a text style.

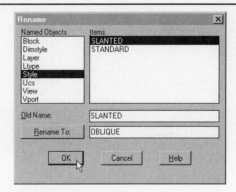

Creating Multiline Text with the MTEXT Command

Earlier in this chapter, you learned how the **DTEXT** command can be used to create multiple lines of text. However, each line of text created with **DTEXT** is a single object. The **MTEXT** command also allows you to enter multiple lines of text by creating paragraphs that fit within a nonprinting text boundary. The text boundary you specify determines the width of the paragraph and the type of text justification within the paragraph. Although not printed or plotted, the text boundary remains part of the object's framework. Also, unlike **DTEXT**, each multiline text object is a single object, regardless of the number of lines it contains.

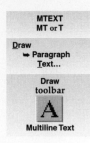

MTEXT
MT or T

Draw
➥ Paragraph
  Text...

Draw
toolbar

A

Multiline Text

To issue the **MTEXT** command, enter MTEXT, or MT or T, at the Command: prompt, click the **Multiline Text** button in the **Draw** toolbar or select **Paragraph Text...** from the **Draw** pull-down menu. The command sequence is as follows:

Command: **MTEXT** or **MT** or **T**↵
Current text style: STANDARD. Text height: 0.2000
Specify first corner: *(pick the first corner of the text boundary)*
Specify opposite corner or [Height/Justify/Rotation/Style/Width]: *(specify a second point or enter an option)*

As you drag your pointing device to specify the opposite corner of the text boundary, a rectangle is displayed to show the location and size of the multiline text paragraph. See **Figure 9-23.** The arrow within the rectangle indicates the direction of the paragraph's text flow. After you specify the second corner of the text boundary, AutoCAD LT displays the **Multiline Text Editor** dialog box. This dialog box is described in detail in a later section of this chapter.

Figure 9-23.
Two diagonal corners define the height and width of the paragraph-oriented text created with **MTEXT**.

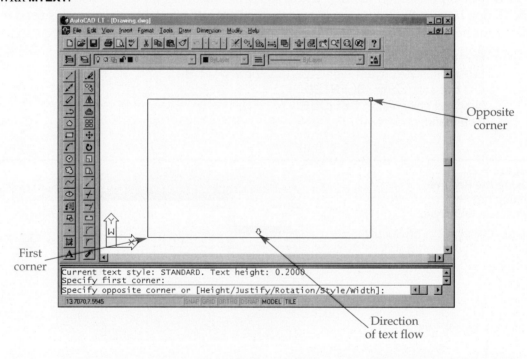

First corner

Opposite corner

Direction of text flow

NOTE   If you are using AutoCAD LT 98 or AutoCAD 97, the following message is displayed the first time the **MTEXT** command is invoked:

Please wait while one-time initialization completes...
...done.

Remember also that in AutoCAD LT 97, entering T from the keyboard invokes the **DTEXT** command, not **MTEXT**.

From the command sequence shown on previous page, note that you can select an option before locating a second corner of the text boundary. The **MTEXT** options are described as follows:

- **Height.** This option specifies the text height to use for multiline text. The default height is the height of the current text style; otherwise it is the height stored in the **TEXTSIZE** system variable. You are prompted with:

  Specify height ⟨current⟩: *(enter a height value)*

  After specifying a new height, AutoCAD LT once again prompts you to specify the opposite corner of the text box.

- **Justify.** This option determines both text justification and text flow relative to the text boundary. The current justification (top left by default) is applied to new text. The text is justified within the specified rectangle based on one of nine justification points on the rectangle. Text is center-, left-, or right-justified with respect to the width of the rectangle. Text flow controls whether text is aligned from the middle, the top, or the bottom of a paragraph. You are prompted with:

  Enter justification [TL/TC/TR/ML/MC/MR/BL/BC/BR] ⟨TL⟩: *(enter an option and press [Enter])*

  The **Justify** options are defined as **TL** (top left), **TC** (top center), **TR** (top right), **ML** (middle left), **MC** (middle center), **MR** (middle right), **BL** (bottom left), **BC** (bottom center), **BR** (bottom right). Refer to **Figure 9-24** to obtain a better understanding of the different options. After specifying a **Justify** option, AutoCAD LT once again prompts you to specify the opposite corner of the text box.

- **Rotation.** This option specifies the rotation angle of the text boundary. You are prompted with:

  Specify rotation angle ⟨0⟩: *(enter a positive value)*

  After specifying a different rotation angle, AutoCAD LT once again prompts you to specify the opposite corner of the text box.

Figure 9-24.
The different justification options available with **MTEXT**.

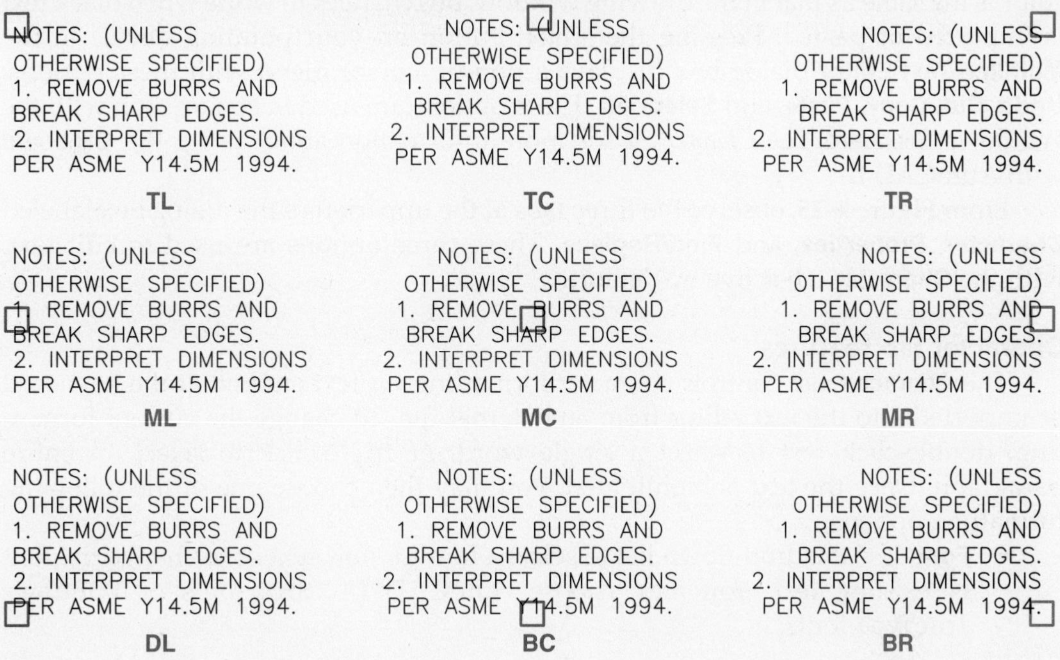

NOTES: (UNLESS OTHERWISE SPECIFIED)
1. REMOVE BURRS AND BREAK SHARP EDGES.
2. INTERPRET DIMENSIONS PER ASME Y14.5M 1994.

TL

NOTES: (UNLESS OTHERWISE SPECIFIED)
1. REMOVE BURRS AND BREAK SHARP EDGES.
2. INTERPRET DIMENSIONS PER ASME Y14.5M 1994.

TC

NOTES: (UNLESS OTHERWISE SPECIFIED)
1. REMOVE BURRS AND BREAK SHARP EDGES.
2. INTERPRET DIMENSIONS PER ASME Y14.5M 1994.

TR

NOTES: (UNLESS OTHERWISE SPECIFIED)
1. REMOVE BURRS AND BREAK SHARP EDGES.
2. INTERPRET DIMENSIONS PER ASME Y14.5M 1994.

ML

NOTES: (UNLESS OTHERWISE SPECIFIED)
1. REMOVE BURRS AND BREAK SHARP EDGES.
2. INTERPRET DIMENSIONS PER ASME Y14.5M 1994.

MC

NOTES: (UNLESS OTHERWISE SPECIFIED)
1. REMOVE BURRS AND BREAK SHARP EDGES.
2. INTERPRET DIMENSIONS PER ASME Y14.5M 1994.

MR

NOTES: (UNLESS OTHERWISE SPECIFIED)
1. REMOVE BURRS AND BREAK SHARP EDGES.
2. INTERPRET DIMENSIONS PER ASME Y14.5M 1994.

DL

NOTES: (UNLESS OTHERWISE SPECIFIED)
1. REMOVE BURRS AND BREAK SHARP EDGES.
2. INTERPRET DIMENSIONS PER ASME Y14.5M 1994.

BC

NOTES: (UNLESS OTHERWISE SPECIFIED)
1. REMOVE BURRS AND BREAK SHARP EDGES.
2. INTERPRET DIMENSIONS PER ASME Y14.5M 1994.

BR

- **Style.** Use this option to specify an existing text style to use for multiline text. The prompt looks like this:

    Enter style name (or "?") ⟨*current*⟩: (*enter an existing style name, enter ?, or press* [Enter] *to accept the current style*)

    After specifying a different style name, AutoCAD LT once again prompts you to specify the opposite corner of the text box.

- **Width.** This option is used to specify the width of the paragraph text object. If you use your pointing device to specify a point in the drawing window, the width is calculated as the distance between the starting point (first corner) and the specified point. Word wrap is turned off and the multiline text object appears on a single line, if you specify a width of zero. You are prompted as follows:

    Specify width: (*specify a point or enter a positive value*)

    After specifying a width, AutoCAD LT once again prompts you to specify the opposite corner of the text box. Once both corners of the text boundary are specified, the **Multiline Text Editor** dialog box is displayed. See **Figure 9-25.**

Figure 9-25.
The **Multiline Text Editor** dialog box.

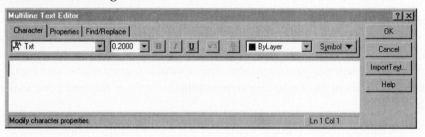

Using the Multiline Text Editor Dialog Box

The **Multiline Text Editor** dialog box lets you insert special characters, underscore text, and apply bold and italic formatting. It displays characters that have been entered from the keyboard or imported from other files. By default, the background color is the same as that in the drawing window, but changes to white when black text is imported or pasted. Pressing the [Enter] button on your pointing device in the **Multiline Text Editor** dialog box displays a pop-up cursor menu with these options: **Undo, Cut, Copy, Paste,** and **Select All**. These options are used in conjunction with the Windows Clipboard. See *Chapter 24* for more information about using the Clipboard with AutoCAD LT.

From **Figure 9-25,** observe the three tabs at the upperleft of the dialog box labeled **Character, Properties,** and **Find/Replace.** These three options are used to edit text, with the **Character** tab active by default.

Character tab features

The **Character** tab controls character formatting for text entered at the keyboard or imported into the text editor from an external file. To change the current formatting, double-click text to select a single word, or triple-click to select an entire paragraph. Once the text is highlighted, you may then choose one of the following formatting options:

- **Font.** Use the drop-down list to select a font for new text or to change the font of existing text. You may choose AutoCAD LT .SHX fonts or Windows TrueType fonts.

- **Height.** This text box is used to enter the height for new text or to change the height of existing text. If there is varying height in the multiline text object, the different heights will appear in a drop-down list.
- **B (Bold).** This button is used to turn bold formatting on and off for new or selected text. Bold formatting cannot be applied to nonTrueType fonts, however.
- **I (Italic).** Use this button to turn italic formatting on and off for new or selected text. As with bold formatting, italics cannot be applied to nonTrueType fonts.
- **U (Underline).** This button turns underlining on and off for new or selected text.
- **Undo.** This button is used to reverse the last edit action. Remember that you may also press [Ctrl]+[Z] to perform an **Undo** operation.
- **Stack.** Use this button to stack text or fractions in a vertical alignment. AutoCAD LT uses the forward slash (/) and caret (^) characters to indicate where selected text should be stacked. Several examples of stacked text are shown in **Figure 9-26.** Enter 3/8 to stack the fraction shown in the top example. Enter .250^.252 to stack the decimal values shown in the bottom example. To use the **Stack** button, first select the text you wish to stack by pressing and holding the pick button on your pointing device as you "drag" it over the text. Once the text is highlighted, click the **Stack** button. The stacked text then appears in the **Multiline Text Editor** dialog box. Next, click the **OK** button to display the stacked text in the drawing window.
- **Color.** Select a different color for new or selected text from the drop-down list labeled ByLayer at the right of the **Multiline Text Editor** dialog box. Selecting **Other...** from the bottom of the drop-down list displays the **Select Color** dialog box previously described in *Chapter 5* of this text.
- **Symbol.** Use this drop-down list when you wish to insert a degree symbol, plus/minus symbol, or diameter symbol in new or selected text. See **Figure 9-27.** As an alternative, you can still use the %%D, %%P, or %%C special character codes described earlier in this chapter. Selecting **Other...** from the bottom of the drop-down list launches the Windows Character Map application. See **Figure 9-28.** Use the Character Map dialog box to cut and paste special characters into your AutoCAD LT text. Be advised that Character Map cannot be used with the compiled (.SHX) AutoCAD LT fonts, however.

Figure 9-26.
Use the **Stack** button to stack fractions and text in a vertical alignment.

$$3/8 \qquad \frac{3}{8}$$

$$.250^{\char`\^}.252 \qquad \frac{.250}{.252}$$

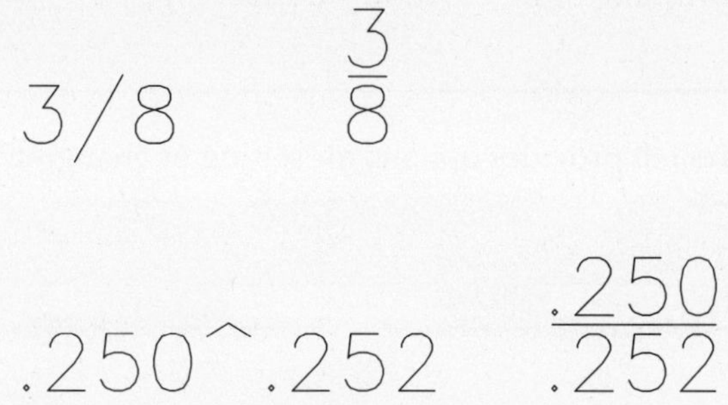

Figure 9-27.
Selecting a special character from the **Symbol** drop-down list.

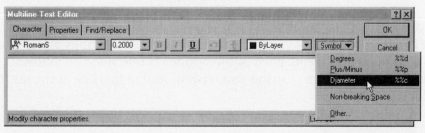

Figure 9-28.
Special characters may be selected for TrueType fonts using **Character Map**.

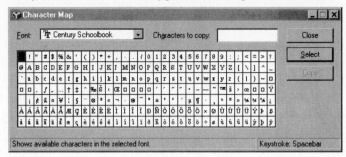

Properties tab features

Clicking the **Properties** tab provides access to the options that control the properties applicable to multiline objects. See **Figure 9-29**. These properties are described as follows:

- **Style.** Use this drop-down list to apply an existing text style to new or selected text. The character formatting for font, height, and bold or italic attributes is overridden if you apply a new style to existing multiline text. However, stacking, underlining, and color are retained in characters to which a new style is applied. Any styles that have backwards or upside-down effects are not applied. If you have a style with a vertical effect and apply it to an .SHX font, the text is displayed horizontally in the **Multiline Text Editor** dialog box.
- **Justification.** This drop-down list sets justification and alignment for new or selected text. The **MTEXT Justify** options are described in a previous section of this chapter.
- **Width.** This drop-down list applies a specified paragraph width to new or selected text. If you select the (**no wrap**) option at the bottom of the drop-down list, word wrap is turned off and the resulting multiline text object appears on a single line. This **Width** option does not affect the width of individual characters.
- **Rotation.** This drop-down list sets the rotation angle in 15° increments for new or selected text. Gradians or radians, rather than degrees, are used if those are the angular units currently in use.

Figure 9-29.
The **Properties** tab provides options for setting or changing the properties of multiline text.

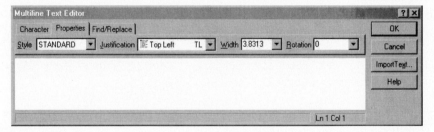

Find/Replace features

The **Find/Replace** tab lets you search for specified text strings and replace them with new text. See **Figure 9-30**. Each of the options is described as follows:

- **Find box.** Enter the text string you wish to find in this box at the far left of the dialog box.

Figure 9-30.
You can search for specified text strings and replace them with new text using the
Find/Replace tab.

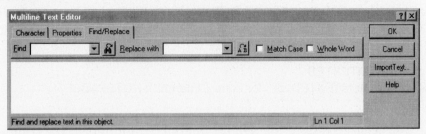

- **Find button.** This button is represented by a pair of binoculars. Click it to start the search for the text string entered in the **Find** box. To continue the search for the next occurrence of the text string, click the **Find** button again.
- **Replace with box.** This box is used to enter the text string intended to replace the text in the **Find** box.
- **Replace button.** Clicking this button replaces the highlighted text with the text in the **Replace with** box.
- **Match Case.** When this check box is active, AutoCAD LT finds text only if the case of all characters in the multiline text object is identical to the case of the text in the **Find** box. When deactivated, a match is found for specified text strings regardless of the case of the characters.
- **Whole Word.** When this check box is active, AutoCAD LT matches the text in the **Find** box only if it is a single word. If the text is part of another text string, it is ignored. When deactivated, a match is found on text strings whether they are single words or part of other words.

Importing text into AutoCAD LT

When you wish to import text files created with other computer applications, click the **Import Text...** button at the far right of the dialog box. This action displays the **Open** dialog box. You can import text files created in RTF *(Rich Text Format)* or ASCII *(American Standard Code for Information Interchange)* formats. The text you insert inherits the properties of the current layer, but retains its original character formatting and style properties. In other words, bold characters are still bold, italic characters are still italicized, etc. After selecting a text file to import, you can choose to replace either selected text or all the text in the multiline text object. You can also append inserted text to the current selection within the text editor. The **Character** tab can be used to control character formatting for text imported into the text editor from an external file.

Keep in mind that imported text is limited to 16KB in size. Also, the background color of the **Multiline Text Editor** dialog box automatically changes from its current color to white when black characters are inserted.

NOTE   It is also possible to insert a text file into the AutoCAD LT drawing window using the Windows *drag and drop* function. See *Chapter 25* for more information about this handy feature.

Using Another Text Editor with **MTEXT**

MTEXTED

If you prefer, you can use other text editors with **MTEXT** instead of the **Multiline Text Editor** supplied with AutoCAD LT. This editor is called the *internal editor*. Use the **MTEXTED** system variable to specify a different text editor. In the following example, the Windows Notepad is specified.

Command: **MTEXTED**↵
New value for MTEXTED, or . for none ⟨"Internal"⟩: **NOTEPAD**↵
Command:

When you wish to restore the default internal editor, repeat the command and enter a period (.) when prompted for a value.

Using **-MTEXT** on the Command Line

If you enter -MTEXT, or -MT, at the Command: prompt, **MTEXT** displays prompts on the command line and no dialog boxes are displayed. The procedure looks like this:

Command: **-MTEXT** *or* **-MT**↵
Current text style: STANDARD. Text height: 0.2000
Specify first corner: *(pick the first corner of the text boundary)*
Specify opposite corner or [Height/Justify/Rotation/Style/Width]: *(specify a second point or enter an option)*
MText: *(enter a string of text)*
MText: *(continue entering text or press [Enter] to end the command)*
Command:

However, be advised that since the **-MTEXT** command does not use the **Multiline Text** editor dialog box, you give up the ability to insert special characters, underscore text, and apply bold and italic formatting. You also cannot use the **Find/Replace** functions described earlier in this chapter.

EXERCISE 9-5

❑ Begin a new drawing using your TEMPLATEA template. Set the NOTES layer current.
❑ Using **MTEXT** with a .156 (5/32) character height, duplicate the drawing notes shown in **Figure 9-24.** For your convenience, they are repeated below:

NOTES: (UNLESS OTHERWISE SPECIFIED)
1. REMOVE BURRS AND BREAK SHARP EDGES.
2. INTERPRET DIMENSIONS PER ASME Y14.5M 1994.

❑ After entering the text, select it all and change the height to .1875 (3/16).
❑ Change the color of the first sentence to magenta. Apply bold formatting to the word BURRS in the second sentence. Change the entire third sentence to italics.
❑ Using the **Find/Replace** tab, replace the word SHARP with ALL.
❑ Experiment with several of the other **MTEXT** editor options described in the previous sections.
❑ When you are finished, save the drawing as EX9-5.

Editing Existing Text

It will occasionally be necessary to modify the notes on your drawings. You can edit text in a dialog box by using the **DDEDIT** command. To do so, enter DDEDIT, or ED, at the Command: prompt , or select **Text...** from the **Object** cascading menu in the **Modify** pull-down menu. See **Figure 9-31**. The command sequence is as follows:

Command: **DDEDIT** *or* **ED.**⏎
⟨Select an annotation object⟩/Undo: *(select one line of text)*

An annotation object is a text or attribute object. (As mentioned earlier in this chapter, an attribute is informational text associated with a block object. Attributes are covered in *Chapter 15* of this text.) Only one object may be selected at a time with **DDEDIT**. In the example shown in **Figure 9-32A**, the following note has been selected and appears in the **Edit Text** dialog box:

NOTS: (UNLESS OTHERWISE SPECIFIED)

To correct the typing error, move the text insertion cursor (the flashing vertical bar) between the T and the S in the word NOTS. Now, type in the letter E and click the **OK** button (or press [Enter]) to exit the dialog box. See **Figure 9-32B**. You are prompted to select another object for editing, or to use the **Undo** option to undo the editing operation that you just performed. When you are finished, press [Enter] to end the **DDEDIT** command.

Figure 9-31.
The **DDEDIT** command is issued by first selecting **Object** from the **Modify** pull-down menu and then selecting **Text...** from the cascading submenu.

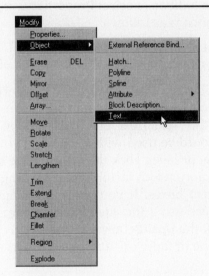

Figure 9-32.
A—The cursor is located at the desired text insertion point. B—After editing the text, click the **OK** button or press [Enter] to exit the **Edit Text** dialog box.

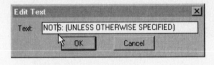

A   B

DDEDIT Editing Methods

The text string that you select for editing with **DDEDIT** appears highlighted in the **Edit Text** dialog box. If you begin entering any new text, the highlighted text is automatically removed. You can also remove the highlighted text by pressing the space bar, by using the [Ctrl]+[X] key combination, or by pressing the [Delete] or [Backspace] keys on your keyboard. If you make a typing error, use the [Backspace] key or click the **Cancel** button and reselect the text you wish to edit.

You can freely pick with your pointing device to locate the text insertion cursor at the desired point in the character string. You can also use several of the editing keys on your keyboard. The left and right arrow keys move the cursor one character to the left or to the right, respectively. The [End] key places the text cursor at the very end of the character string. The [Home] key places the text cursor at the very start of the character string. The [Delete] key deletes the character just to the right of the text cursor.

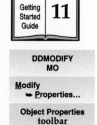

Getting Started Guide 11

DDMODIFY
MO

Modify
→ Properties...

Object Properties
toolbar

Properties

Changing Other Aspects of DTEXT, TEXT and MTEXT

The **DDEDIT** command described above is very handy when you need to correct a spelling error or amend some existing text. However, when you need to change style aspects such as height and rotation, or the color or layer of text, use the **DDMODIFY** command instead. To issue the **DDMODIFY** command, enter DDMODIFY, or MO, at the Command: prompt, click the **Properties** button at the far right of the **Object Properties** toolbar, or select **Properties...** from the **Modify** pull-down menu. The command sequence is as follows:

Command: **DDMODIFY** *or* **MO**↵
Select one object to modify: *(select one text object)*

Select one object created with the **DTEXT**, **TEXT**, or **MTEXT** commands and the **Modify Text** dialog box is displayed. As shown in **Figure 9-33,** the selected text is highlighted in the **Text:** text box and can be edited using the same keyboard techniques as would be used with **DDEDIT**. If you wish to change the text properties of color, linetype, or layer, click the appropriate buttons at the top of the dialog box. Text height, rotation, width factor, and obliquing angle can all be changed using the corresponding text boxes. If you wish to change the existing justification or style, make your choices using the **Justify:** and **Style:** drop-down lists at the right of the dialog box. Click the **Upside Down** or **Backward** check boxes if you want the selected text to assume one of these orientations. (Observe that the **Vertical** style format is not

Figure 9-33.
The **Modify Text** dialog box can be used to change nearly every aspect of existing text created with the **DTEXT** or **TEXT** commands.

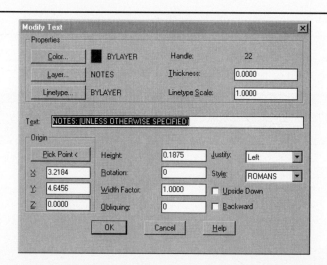

available in this dialog box.) If you need to change the location of the text, you can enter new X and Y coordinates in the **X:** and **Y:** text boxes. It is faster and easier, however, to click the **Pick Point** ⟨ button. Doing so removes the dialog box and you are prompted on the command line with:

Insertion point:

Move your cursor to select a new insertion point for the text in the drawing window and pick. The **Modify Text** dialog box is redisplayed and the coordinates of the new insertion point are shown in the **X:** and **Y:** text boxes. Click **OK** to exit the dialog box, and the selected text appears at the new location.

The **Modify MText** dialog box is displayed if you select a multiline text object. You will observe from **Figure 9-34** that this text box is nearly identical to the **Modify Text** dialog box. Note that the **Full editor...** button at the right-center of the dialog box provides quick access to the **Multiline Text Editor**.

Figure 9-34.
The **Modify MText** dialog box is displayed when a multiline text object is selected. Note the **Full editor...** button providing quick access to the **Multiline Text Editor**.

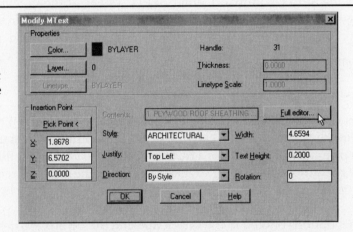

NOTE
If you select **Properties...** from the **Modify** pull-down menu, or click the **Properties** button on the **Object Properties** toolbar and select more than one object, the **DDCHPROP** command is issued instead of **DDMODIFY**. If necessary, refer to *Chapter 5* of this text to review **DDCHPROP**.

The CHANGE Command

As an alternative to changing text using a dialog box, you can issue the **CHANGE** command to modify or move selected text created with the **DTEXT** or **TEXT** commands on the command line. However, **CHANGE** cannot be used with multiline text created with the **MTEXT** command. The procedure looks like the following:

CHANGE
-CH

Command: **CHANGE** *or* **-CH**↵
Select objects: *(select one or more text strings to be changed)*
Select objects: ↵
Properties/⟨Change point⟩: ↵
Enter text insertion point: *(pick a new text location or press* [Enter]*)*
Text style: STANDARD
New style or press ENTER for no change: *(enter an existing style name or* [Enter]*)*
New height ⟨current⟩: *(specify a new text height or press* [Enter]*)*
New rotation angle ⟨current⟩: *(specify a new text rotation or press* [Enter]*)*
New text ⟨selected text string⟩: *(enter a new text string or press* [Enter]*)*
Command:

The **CHANGE** command allows you to select more than one text object. If several text strings are selected, you receive the prompts shown on the previous page for each text object as it is encountered in the selection set. After all the selected text has been changed, the Command: prompt returns.

Both the **DDMODIFY** and **CHANGE** commands may be used to edit other object types, as well. This capability is described in *Chapter 10* of this text.

Using the Spell Checker

The **SPELL** command uses the **Check Spelling** dialog box to correct the spelling of text objects created with **TEXT**, **DTEXT**, **LEADER**, and **MTEXT** commands. (**LEADER** is a dimensioning command and is covered in *Chapter 12* of this text.) However, this dialog box is displayed only if AutoCAD LT finds a questionable word in the specified text.

To issue the **SPELL** command, enter SPELL, or SP, at the Command: prompt, click the **Spelling** button on the **Standard Toolbar,** or select **Spelling** from the **Tools** pull-down menu. See **Figure 9-35.** Enter the following at the Command: prompt:

Command: **SPELL** *or* **SP**⏎
Select objects: *(select one or more text objects)*
Select objects: ⏎

Select one or more **DTEXT**, **TEXT**, or **MTEXT** objects and press [Enter] to display the **Check Spelling** dialog box. In the example shown in **Figure 9-36**, the spell checker has caught the spelling error in the word NOTS. The drop-down list at the left of the dialog box provides a number of spelling suggestions. To fix the error, select the word NOTES: from the drop-down list and click the **Change** button. Once spell checking is complete a message box is displayed. See **Figure 9-37.** Click the **OK** button to continue.

The other options offered in the **Check Spelling** dialog box are described as follows:
- **Current dictionary.** The spell checker provides two main dictionaries with several variations for a total of six choices. They are American English (the default), British English (ise), British English (ize), French (unaccented capitals), French (accented capitals), and a sample custom dictionary. Custom dictionaries are described later in this chapter. The name of the current dictionary is displayed at the top of the **Check Spelling** dialog box.

Figure 9-35.
Select **Spelling** from the **Tools** pull-down menu to issue the **SPELL** command.

Figure 9-36.
The **Check Spelling**
dialog box.

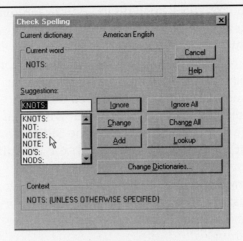

Figure 9-37.
AutoCAD LT
displays a message
when the spell
check is complete.

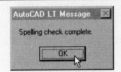

- **Current word.** This section identifies a suspected misspelling.
- **Suggestions:.** This box displays the word being checked and provides alternatives in a drop-down list.
- **Ignore.** Many schools and commercial firms use acronyms that are specific to the institution or company. Naturally, the spell checker would have difficulty identifying these proprietary acronyms. It would also have trouble with most proper names. When such a name or acronym is encountered, click this button to skip the current word.
- **Ignore All.** Similar to the **Ignore** button, this button skips all remaining words that match the current word.
- **Change.** Click the **Change** button to replace the current word with a selected word in the **Suggestions:** box.
- **Change All.** Similar to the **Change** button, the **Change All** button replaces the current word in all selected text objects.
- **Add.** Click this button to add the current word to the current custom dictionary. The maximum word length is 63 characters. By default, the custom dictionary supplied with AutoCAD LT 98 and AutoCAD LT 97 is called sample.cus.
- **Lookup.** This button is used to check the spelling of the word in the **Suggestions:** box.
- **Change Dictionaries….** Click this button to display the **Change Dictionaries** subdialog box. This subdialog box is covered in the next section.
- **Context.** This area at the bottom of the dialog box displays the phrase in which AutoCAD LT located the current word.

The Change Dictionaries Subdialog Box

When a spelling check is performed, AutoCAD LT matches the words in the drawing to the words in the current main dictionary and current custom dictionary. Any spelling exceptions that you identify with the **Add** button are stored in the custom dictionary that is current at the time of the spelling check. As previously mentioned, this dictionary is named sample.cus, and is stored in the Program Files\AutoCAD LT 98\ folder. If you are using AutoCAD LT 97, sample.cus is stored in the Program Files\AutoCAD LT 97\ folder.

If you want to check spelling in another language, you can change to one of five supplied different main dictionaries. You can also create any number of custom dictionaries and switch to them as needed using the **Change Dictionaries** subdialog box. See **Figure 9-38.** To display this subdialog box, click the **Change Dictionaries...** button in the **Check Spelling** dialog box. The options offered in the **Change Dictionaries** subdialog box are described below:

- **Main dictionary.** Use the drop-down list at the top of the subdialog box to change the dictionary used by the **SPELL** command. The dictionary you select is then used in conjunction with the default custom dictionary, or any other custom dictionary you may have loaded.
- **Custom Dictionary.** Use the text box to enter the drive, folder, and file name of the custom dictionary you want to use for the spell check. To create a new custom dictionary, enter a name with the file extension .cus and click the **OK** button.
- **Browse....** Click this button to display the **Select Custom Dictionary** subdialog box. See **Figure 9-39.** Use this subdialog box to select or find a custom dictionary, as well as to define the location of a new custom dictionary. The default sample.cus custom dictionary appears in the subdialog box listing.

Figure 9-38.
The **Change Dictionaries** subdialog box is used to select a different main dictionary, as well as to select or create a custom dictionary.

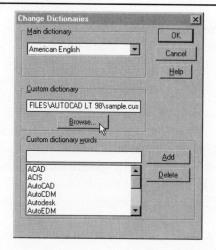

Figure 9-39.
Selecting a custom dictionary using the **Select Custom Dictionary** subdialog box.

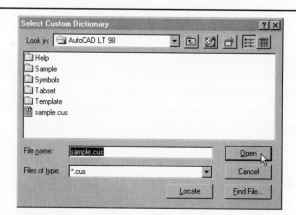

AutoCAD LT—Fundamentals and Applications

- **Custom dictionary words.** This area at the bottom of the subdialog box displays a list of words that have been added to the custom dictionary. Enter a new word or acronym in the text box and click the **Add** button to add to the dictionary. To delete a word from the custom dictionary, select a word you wish to remove from the list and click the **Delete** button. The default sample.cus custom dictionary contains the following *Autodesk, Inc.*-specific words: ACAD, ACIS, AutoCAD, AutoCDM, Autodesk, AutoEDM, AutoFlix, AutoLathe, AutoLISP, AutoShade, AutoSketch, AutoSolid, AutoSurf, and AutoVision.

Once you are finished, click the **OK** button to return to the **Check Spelling** dialog box.

PROFESSIONAL TIP
Make a list of words or names specific to your school or company and add them to the custom dictionary supplied with AutoCAD LT. Doing so will save you from clicking the **Ignore** button in the **Check Spelling** dialog box every time the spell checker encounters an unrecognized word.

Spell checker system variables

As an alternative to the dialog box methods just described, you can use the **DCTCUST** system variable on the command line to display and change the current custom spelling dictionary path and file name. The procedure looks like this:

Command: **DCTCUST**⏎
New value for DCTCUST, or . for none ⟨"C:\PROGRAM FILES\AUTOCAD LT 98\sample.cus"⟩: *(enter a different custom dictionary name and press* [Enter]*)*
Command:

Use the **DCTMAIN** system variable like this to display the current main spelling dictionary file name:

Command: **DCTMAIN**⏎
New value for DCTMAIN, or . for none ⟨"enu"⟩: *(enter a different main dictionary name and press* [Enter]*)*
Command:

Main dictionary files have the .dct file extension. The English dictionary is named enu.dct and the French dictionary is fr.dct.

EXERCISE 9-6

❑ Begin a new drawing using your TEMPLATEA template. Set the NOTES layer current.
❑ Using **MTEXT** or **DTEXT** with the default character height, type the notes shown below. Duplicate the spelling errors *exactly* as shown:

   NOTS: (UNLISS OTHERWYSE SPECIFED)
   1. REMOV BURS AND BREEK SHIRP EDGES.
   2. INTERPRAT DIMENSIONS PER ASME Y14.5M 1994.

❑ Use **SPELL** as described in this chapter to correct the spelling errors. Which words were unrecognized by the spell checker? Why?
❑ Add the unrecognized words to the custom dictionary and repeat the **SPELL** command.
❑ It is not necessary to save the exercise when you are finished.

Chapter Test

Write your answers in the spaces provided.

1. Identify two ways to access the **MTEXT** command. _____
   _____
   _____

2. List the differences between the **MTEXT** , **DTEXT** , and **TEXT** commands. _____
   _____
   _____
   _____
   _____

3. Why would the **Middle** justification mode be used?_____
   _____
   _____
   _____

4. You are drawing an architectural floor plan that is to be plotted at 1/4″ = 1′. The plotted text height is to be 3/16″. What is the drawing scale factor, and what size should you make the text in AutoCAD LT? _____
   _____
   _____

5. Provide the special character codes for the following text strings:
   a. Ø7.625_____
   b. 2° MAX DRAFT _____
   c. 375±.010 _____
   d. DETAIL A _____

6. *True or False?* Special character codes must always be entered in uppercase lettering._____

7. What is a font? _____
   _____
   _____

8. What is a style?_____
   _____
   _____

9. What is **QTEXT**? Why would it be used? _____
   _____
   _____
   _____

10. Which check box in the **Text Style** dialog box should be active to create slanted text?
    _____
    _____
    _____

11. What is meant by width factor?_____

_____

_____

12. How many characters may be used in a text style name?_____

_____

_____

13. Why should you leave the style height set to 0 (zero)? _____

_____

_____

14. Identify three ways to set a text style current. _____

_____

_____

15. Describe how to insert an external text file into AutoCAD LT. What happens to the properties of the inserted text? _____

_____

_____

_____

16. What are the disadvantages of using the **-MTEXT** command? _____

_____

_____

_____

17. Name three commands that may be used to modify text created with the **DTEXT** or **TEXT** commands. Of the three, which command cannot be used with multiline text?

_____

_____

_____

18. Why would you use a custom dictionary with the AutoCAD LT spelling checker?

_____

_____

_____

_____

Chapter Problems

Electronic Drafting

1. Use the layers in your TEMPLATEB template to draw the block diagram of the modulator receiver shown below. Use the **POLYLINE**, **POLYGON**, and **RECTANG** commands to your advantage. Make the symbols proportional in size to those illustrated. Create a style with the Roman Simplex font and use **MTEXT** to letter the diagram. Save the drawing as P9-1.

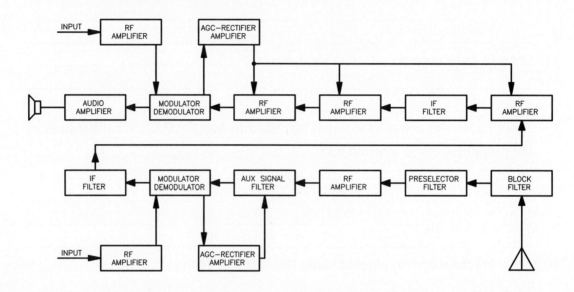

Architectural Drafting

2. Draw the map title shown below using your TEMPLATEA template. Create a text style using the Roman Triplex font and place all lettering on the NOTES layer. Using **DTEXT**, set the text height appropriately to approximate the lettering height shown. Use **DDMODIFY** to increase the width factor as required to duplicate the "IN THE" and "SCALE~MILES" text strings. Draw the solid lines in the legend with wide polylines. Save the drawing as P9-2.

MAP SHOWING

IRON ORE DEPOSITS

IN THE

WESTERN STATES

SCALE~MILES   0 50 100   200   300   400

3. Draw the architectural title shown below using your TEMPLATEA template. Create a text style using the City Blueprint font and place all lettering on the NOTES layer. Save the drawing as P9-3.

Architectural
Drafting

4. Use the layers in your TEMPLATEB template to draw the flow diagram of the digital numerical control (DNC) system shown below. Make the diagram proportional in size to that illustrated and use the **POLYLINE** and **RECTANG** commands to your advantage. Create a style with the Roman Simplex font and use **DTEXT** to letter the diagram. Save the drawing as P9-4.

Electronic
Drafting

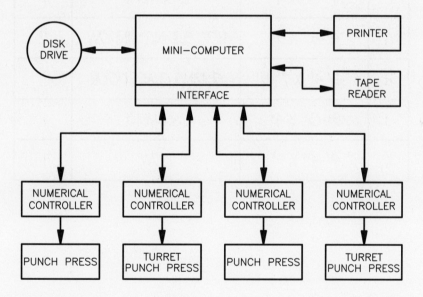

5. Create the window schedule shown below using your TEMPLATEA
template. Create a text style using the City Blueprint font and place all
lettering on the NOTES layer. Save the drawing as P9-5.

WINDOW SCHEDULE			
SYM.	SIZE	MODEL	QUAN.
A	5'-0" X 4'	CASEMENT	1
B	6' X 4'	CASEMENT	1
C	3' X 3'	HOR. SLIDING WINDOW	1
D	6' X 7'-5"	SLIDING GLASS DOOR	1
E	3'-6" X 6'-8"	FIXED\GRID	2
F	4'-0" X 4'	CASEMENT	1
G	4'-6" X 5'	HOR. SLIDING WINDOW	2
H	5'-1/4" X 7'-5"	SLIDING GLASS DOOR	1
J	5'-0" X 4'	CASEMENT	1
K	9'-4" X 5'	BOW	1

Chapter *10*

Modifying the Drawing

Learning Objectives

After you have completed this chapter, you will be able to:
- ○ Trim one or more objects against an edge.
- ○ Extend one or more objects to a boundary.
- ○ Break an object at selected points.
- ○ Move and rotate drawing objects.
- ○ Resize objects using the **SCALE**, **LENGTHEN**, and **STRETCH** commands.
- ○ Use the **CHANGE** command to modify line endpoints and the size of circles.
- ○ Create a mirror image of an object.
- ○ Make one or more copies of selected objects using the **COPY** and **ARRAY** commands.
- ○ Edit a selected object using a dialog box.
- ○ Use grips to modify objects.

Regardless of the technical discipline, most detail drawings are eventually revised to implement design improvements, reduce costs, and to correct drafting errors. Fortunately, AutoCAD LT provides a vast array of editing commands that allow you to quickly and easily modify your drawings. These editing commands are also used to aid in the construction of new drawings and are described in this chapter.

Trimming Objects

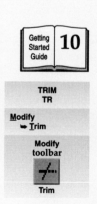

The **TRIM** command is used to trim one or more objects against existing objects. You can trim arcs, circles, ellipses, elliptical arcs, donuts, lines, rays, xlines, splines, rectangles, polygons, and open 2D and 3D polylines. The objects that you trim against are called *cutting edges*. To use the **TRIM** command, enter TRIM, or TR, at the Command: prompt, click the **Trim** button in the **Modify** toolbar, or select **Trim** from the **Modify** pull-down menu. See **Figure 10-1.** The command sequence is as follows:

```
Command: TRIM or TR↵
Select cutting edges: (Projmode = UCS, Edgemode = No extend)
Select objects: (select one or more objects to trim against)
Select objects: ↵
```

Figure 10-1.
Select **Trim** from the
Modify pull-down
menu to issue the
TRIM command.

After selecting the cutting edge(s), it is very important to terminate the selection by pressing [Enter]. The prompt now changes to:

⟨Select object to trim⟩/Project/Edge/Undo: *(select an object to trim)*
⟨Select object to trim⟩/Project/Edge/Undo: *(select another object or press* [Enter] *to end)*
Command:

As shown in **Figure 10-2A**, select the objects on the side that you wish to trim. If you select the wrong object, or the wrong side, use the **Undo** option to undo the selection and try again. Occasionally, there may be instances when more than one cutting edge exists. Such an example is illustrated by the "D" hole shown in **Figure 10-2B.**

Figure 10-2.
A—An example of
several lines
trimmed against
one cutting edge.
B—Trimming with
two cutting edges.

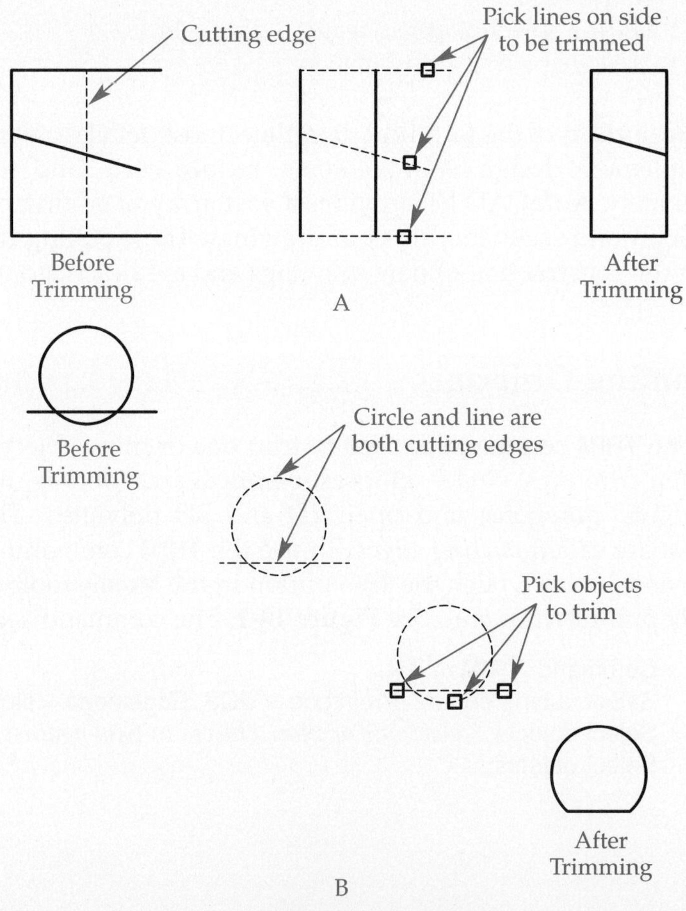

Cutting edge

Pick lines on side
to be trimmed

Before
Trimming

After
Trimming

A

Before
Trimming

Circle and line are
both cutting edges

Pick objects
to trim

After
Trimming

B

> **NOTE** A trimmed circle becomes an arc; trimmed ellipses become elliptical arcs. A trimmed xline is converted to a ray, while a trimmed ray becomes a line object.

Using the **Project** Option

Trimming is normally performed when objects intersect in the same two-dimensional plane. However, objects with different Z values cannot be trimmed against one another when modeling in 3D. In these cases, it becomes necessary to project such objects into the same plane so that trimming can be performed. This can be accomplished in several ways using the **Project** option of the **TRIM** command. After selecting the cutting edge(s) to cut against, the **Project** option is selected as follows:

⟨Select object to trim⟩/Project/Edge/Undo: **P**↵
None/Ucs/View⟨current⟩: *(select an option or accept the default)*

The three **Project** suboptions are described as follows:

- **None.** This suboption specifies no projection and is how the **TRIM** command works by default. As shown in **Figure 10-3,** only objects that intersect the cutting edge(s) in 3D space are trimmed.
- **UCS.** This allows you to trim objects that do not intersect in 3D space by specifying projection onto the XY plane of the current UCS. Refer to **Figure 10-4** to help you visualize this suboption.

Figure 10-3.
Only objects that intersect the cutting edges in 3D space are trimmed.

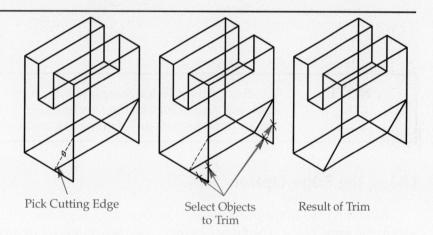

Pick Cutting Edge   Select Objects to Trim   Result of Trim

Figure 10-4.
The **UCS** suboption allows you to trim objects that do not intersect in 3D space.

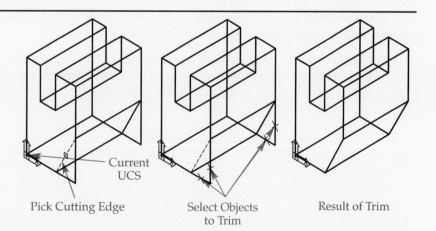

Pick Cutting Edge   Select Objects to Trim   Result of Trim

- **View.** This suboption specifies projection along the current view direction. As shown in **Figure 10-5,** objects that intersect the cutting edge(s) in the current view are trimmed. This method can be conveniently used to convert a 3D wireframe model into an isometric drawing.

You can also set the current projection mode for trim operations on the command line using the **PROJMODE** system variable as follows:

Command: **PROJMODE.**⏎
New value for PROJMODE ⟨*current*⟩: *(enter 0, 1, or 2 and press* [Enter]*)*
Command:

Enter a 0 (the default) for no projection. Enter a 1 to project to the XY plane of the current UCS. Enter a 2 to project to the current viewing plane.

Figure 10-5.
With the **View** suboption, objects that intersect the cutting edge in the current view are trimmed.

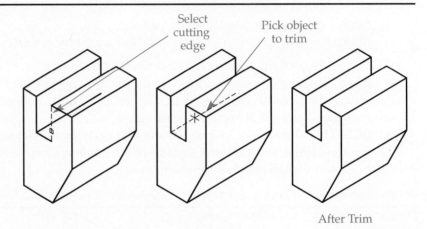

Select cutting edge

Pick object to trim

After Trim

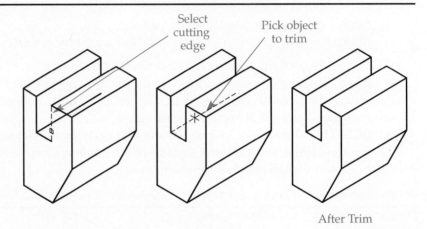

> **NOTE** See *Chapter 16* for complete information about isometric drawing and dimensioning techniques. Refer to *Chapter 19* for an introduction to 3D modeling and viewing commands.

Using the Edge Option

As mentioned in the previous section, trimming is performed when objects intersect in the same plane. The **Edge** option is used when objects do not have a true intersection, but have an implied intersection. An ***implied intersection*** is the point where two objects would meet if they were extended. After selecting the cutting edge(s) to cut against, the **Edge** option is selected as follows:

⟨Select object to trim⟩/Project/Edge/Undo: **E.**⏎
Extend/No extend ⟨*current*⟩: *(select an option or accept the default)*

AutoCAD LT—Fundamentals and Applications

With the default **No extend** suboption, trimming can only occur when there is a true intersection. Conversely, the **Extend** suboption extends a cutting edge along its natural path to trim an object at an implied intersection in 3D space. As shown in **Figure 10-6,** this suboption is used to trim the horizontal line against the vertical line at its implied intersection. The procedure looks like this:

Command: **TRIM** *or* **TR.⏎**
Select cutting edges: (Projmode = UCS, Edgemode = No extend)
Select objects: *(select the vertical line)*
Select objects: ⏎
⟨Select object to trim⟩/Project/Edge/Undo: **E.⏎**
Extend/No extend⟨No extend⟩: **E.⏎**
⟨Select object to trim⟩/Project/Edge/Undo: *(select the horizontal line at the right end)*
⟨Select object to trim⟩/Project/Edge/Undo: ⏎
Command:

You can also enable or disable the **Edge** option using the **EDGEMODE** system variable on the command line as follows:

Command: **EDGEMODE.⏎**
New value for EDGEMODE ⟨1⟩: *(enter 0 or 1 and press [Enter])*
Command:

Enter 1 to enable **Extend** mode. Enter 0 (zero) to restore the default **No extend** mode.

Figure 10-6.
The **Extend** suboption extends a cutting edge along its natural path to trim an object at an implied intersection in 3D space.

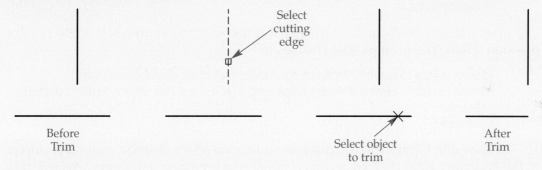

Before Trim   Select cutting edge   Select object to trim   After Trim

PROFESSIONAL TIP

Here is a handy method to speed up a trim operation. Simply press [Enter] at the Select objects: prompt when asked to select cutting edges. Now, select the object you wish to trim at the ⟨Select object to trim⟩ prompt. AutoCAD LT automatically searches the drawing database and trims the object you select against the closest object it encounters. More than one object may be selected for trimming using this method.

EXERCISE 10-1

❏ Draw an object similar to that illustrated in **Figure 10-2A** and use **TRIM** as shown.
❏ Undo the trim operation and try picking the lines on the other side of the cutting edge.
❏ Now, draw a line and circle like that shown in **Figure 10-2B**. Use **TRIM** to produce the "D" hole illustrated.
❏ Draw two lines similar to those shown in **Figure 10-6**. Use the **Edge** option to trim the horizontal line against the vertical line as shown.
❏ Save the drawing as EX10-1.

EXTEND
EX

Modify
↳ Extend

Modify
toolbar

Extend

Extending Objects

The **EXTEND** command extends an object to meet, or intersect, another object. The intersecting object is called the *boundary edge*. Both 2D and 3D polylines, arcs, circles, ellipses, elliptical arcs, lines, rays, xlines, splines, and text are all valid boundary edges. Objects that you may extend include arcs, elliptical arcs, lines, rays, and open 2D and 3D polylines. Since polygons and rectangles are considered closed polylines, these object types may not be extended. To use **EXTEND**, enter EXTEND, or EX, at the Command: prompt, click the **Extend** button in the **Modify** toolbar, or select **Extend** from the **Modify** pull-down menu. The command sequence is as follows:

Command: **EXTEND** *or* **EX**↵
Select boundary edges: (Projmode = None, Edgemode = No extend)
Select objects: *(select one or more objects to extend to)*
Select objects: ↵

After selecting the boundary edge(s), it is necessary to terminate the selection by pressing [Enter]. The prompt now changes to:

⟨Select object to extend⟩/Project/Edge/Undo: *(select an object to extend)*
⟨Select object to extend⟩/Project/Edge/Undo: *(select another object or press* [Enter] *to end)*
Command:

As shown in **Figure 10-7A**, an arc and a line are selected at the endpoints closest to the boundary edge they are to meet. When two boundary edges are selected, it is then possible to extend an object in two directions. This method is illustrated in **Figure 10-7B.** As with the **TRIM** command, if you select the wrong object, or the wrong endpoint, use the **Undo** option to undo the selection and try again. If you attempt to extend an object where no intersection exists, AutoCAD LT displays the following error message:

Object does not intersect an edge.

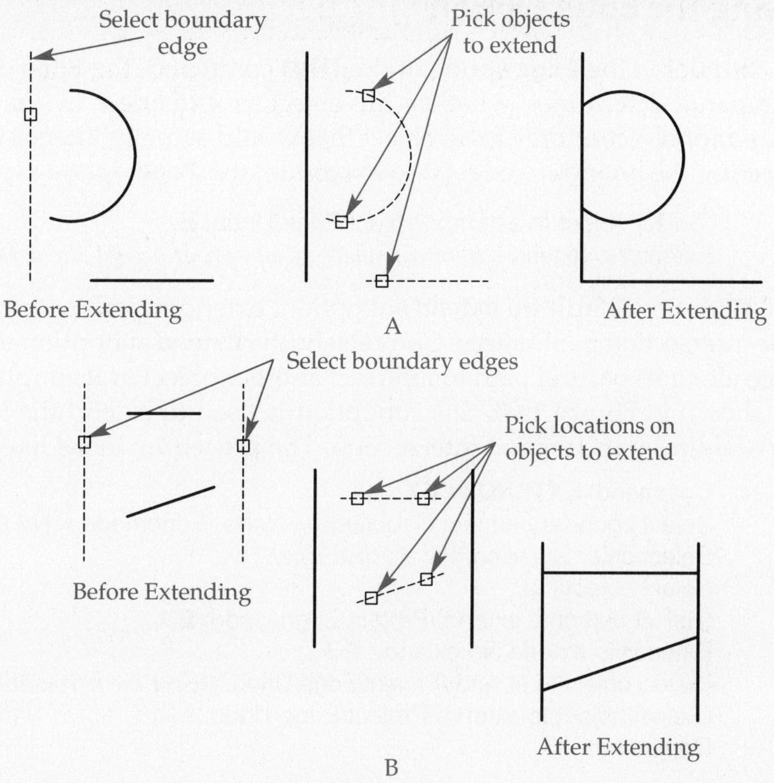

Figure 10-7.
A—An example of an arc and a line extended to one boundary. B—Extending several lines to two boundary edges.

Select boundary edge

Pick objects to extend

Before Extending

After Extending

A

Select boundary edges

Pick locations on objects to extend

Before Extending

After Extending

B

NOTE You cannot trim against, or extend to, a block. See *Chapter 15* for complete information about block objects.

Using the **Project** Option

As with trimming, objects are normally extended to boundaries they intersect with in the same 3D plane. The **Project** option of the **EXTEND** command determines the projection method used when extending objects in different 3D planes. After selecting the boundary edge(s) to extend to, the **Project** option is selected as follows:

⟨Select object to extend⟩/Project/Edge/Undo: **P**↵
None/Ucs/View⟨current⟩: *(select an option or accept the default)*

The three **Project** suboptions are described as follows:
- **None.** This suboption specifies no projection and is how the **EXTEND** command works by default. Only objects that would intersect the boundary edge in 3D space are extended.
- **UCS.** This suboption specifies projection onto the XY plane of the current UCS. Objects that do not intersect with the boundary objects in 3D space are extended with this suboption.
- **View.** This suboption specifies projection along the current view direction.

As with trimming, you can set the current projection mode for extend operations on the command line using the **PROJMODE** system variable as follows:

Command: **PROJMODE**↵
New value for PROJMODE ⟨current⟩: *(enter 0, 1, or 2 and press* [Enter]*)*
Command:

Enter a 0 (the default) for no projection. Enter a 1 to project to the XY plane of the current UCS. Enter a 2 to project to the current viewing plane.

Using the Edge Option

Similar to the **Edge** option of the **TRIM** command, the **Edge** option of the **EXTEND** command determines whether an object is extended to the implied edge of a boundary object or only to an object that would actually intersect it in 3D space. After selecting the boundary edge(s) to extend to, the **Edge** option is selected as follows:

⟨Select object to extend⟩/Project/Edge/Undo: **E**↵
Extend/No extend ⟨*current*⟩:*(select an option or accept the default)*

With the default **No extend** suboption, extending can only occur when there is a true intersection in 3D space. Conversely, the **Extend** suboption extends the boundary edge along its natural path to intersect another object or its implied edge in 3D space. As shown in **Figure 10-8,** this suboption is used to extend the horizontal line to the vertical line at its implied intersection. The procedure looks like this:

Command: **EXTEND** *or* **EX**↵
Select boundary edges: (Projmode = None, Edgemode = No extend)
Select objects: *(select the vertical line)*
Select objects: ↵
⟨Select object to extend⟩/Project/Edge/Undo: **E**↵
Extend/No extend⟨No extend⟩: **E**↵
⟨Select object to extend⟩/Project/Edge/Undo: *(select the horizontal line at the right end)*
⟨Select object to extend⟩/Project/Edge/Undo:↵
Command:

Remember you can also enable or disable the **Edge** option using the **EDGEMODE** system variable on the command line as follows:

Command: **EDGEMODE**↵
New value for EDGEMODE ⟨1⟩: *(enter 0 or 1 and press [Enter])*
Command:

Enter 1 to enable **Extend** mode. Enter 0 (zero) to restore the default **No extend** mode.

Figure 10-8.
The **Extend** suboption extends the boundary edge along its natural path to intersect another object or its implied edge in 3D space.

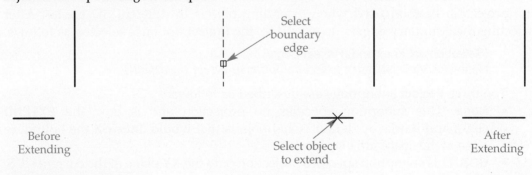

Before Extending   Select object to extend   After Extending

PROFESSIONAL TIP

You can easily speed up an extend operation by simply pressing [Enter] at the Select objects: prompt when asked to select boundary edges. Now, select the object you wish to extend at the ⟨Select object to extend⟩ prompt. AutoCAD LT automatically searches the drawing database and extends the object you select to the closest object it encounters. More than one object may be selected for extending using this method.

EXERCISE 10-2

❏ Draw two lines and an arc similar to those illustrated in **Figure 10-7A** and use **EXTEND** as shown.

❏ Next, draw the line pattern shown in **Figure 10-7B**. Extend both lines to the two boundary edges as shown.

❏ Draw two lines similar to those shown in **Figure 10-8** Use the **Edge** option to extend the horizontal line to the vertical line as shown.

❏ Draw a rectangle with the **RECTANG** command, and a square with the **POLYGON** command. Try to extend these objects to a line. What happens? Why?

❏ Save the drawing as EX10-2.

Breaking Objects

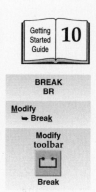

The **BREAK** command allows you to put a space in an object by breaking out a section. You can also break an object at a selected point, resulting in two separate objects. To use the **BREAK** command, enter BREAK, or BR, at the Command: prompt, click the **Break** button in the **Modify** toolbar, or select **Break** from the **Modify** pull-down menu. Using the **BREAK** command is described in the following two sections.

Breaking Between Two Points

The **BREAK** command is most commonly used to remove a section from an object by breaking between two selected points. While the **TRIM** command is a faster and more reliable way to remove a section from an object, there are certain instances where **BREAK** must be used. One example occurs when there are no cutting edges to trim against. Another example exists when the edge you need to trim against belongs to a block object. As mentioned previously, blocks cannot be used as cutting edges.

There are several ways to use **BREAK** to remove a section. The first method requires that you select the object to break and then pick the two points to break between. This method is illustrated using a circle in **Figure 10-9**. The procedure looks like the following:

> Command: **BREAK** or **BR**↵
> Select object: *(select the circle)*
> Enter second point (or F for first point): **F**↵
> Enter first point: *(pick the first point on the circle)*
> Enter second point: *(pick the second point on the circle)*
> Command:

For circles, ellipses, and arcs, the order in which points are selected determines whether the break is performed in a clockwise or counterclockwise direction. See **Figure 10-9**.

Figure 10-9.
Sections removed
from circles using
the **Break** command.

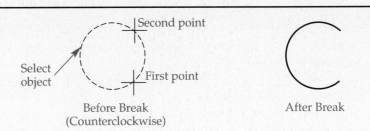

Before Break
(Counterclockwise)

After Break

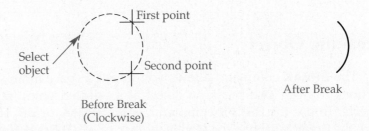

Before Break
(Clockwise)

After Break

When you use **BREAK** to remove a section from an object, be sure to use the appropriate object snap mode if necessary. As an example, consider the portion of an electronic schematic diagram shown in **Figure 10-10.** Here, a line passes completely through a transistor symbol and must be removed where it intersects with the transistor. Since the transistor is a block object, the **TRIM** command cannot be used. To break the line accurately, osnap **Intersection** is used twice at the intersections of the transistor and the line. The procedure looks like this:

Command: **BREAK** *or* **BR**↵
Select object: *(select the line)*
Enter second point (or F for first point): **F**↵
Enter first point: **INT**↵
of *(pick the first intersection of the line and the block)*
Enter second point: **INT**↵
of *(pick the second intersection of the line and the block)*
Command:

Figure 10-10.
Using **Break** on a
line object.

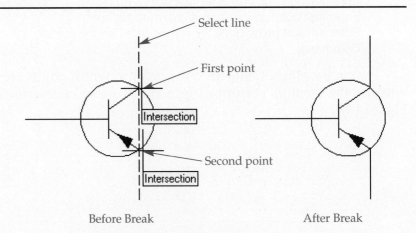

Before Break

After Break

You can also break a section out of an object without explicitly selecting the first point with the **F** option. With this method, the point you select on the object when prompted **Select object:** automatically becomes the first break point. To ensure precision, use an osnap if necessary when picking the first point.

> Command: **BREAK** *or* **BR**⏎
> Select object: *(pick the first point on the object)*
> Enter second point (or F for first point): *(pick a second point on the object)*
> Command:

Breaking at a Single Point

As mentioned previously, the **BREAK** command may also be used to break an object at a selected point, resulting in two separate objects. This procedure uses the **@** symbol and is shown below:

> Command: **BREAK** *or* **BR**⏎
> Select object: *(select an object)*
> Enter second point (or F for first point): **@**⏎
> Command:

Using this method, an object is broken at precisely the point at which it is selected. Therefore, be sure to use the appropriate osnap when selecting the object to break. For example, if you want to break a line at its midpoint into two separate lines, do the following:

> Command: **BREAK** *or* **BR**⏎
> Select object: *(select the line using osnap **Midpoint**)*
> Enter second point (or F for first point): **@**⏎
> Command:

EXERCISE 10-3

❏ Draw several lines, polylines, arcs, ellipses, and circles. Experiment with the **BREAK** command as described in the preceding sections. For the arcs, ellipses, and circles, try selecting points in both counterclockwise and clockwise directions.

❏ When you are done experimenting with the **BREAK** command, begin a new drawing without saving the current drawing. It is not necessary to use one of your templates for the new drawing.

❏ Construct the object shown below. *Construction hint:* Draw all radiused features with circles and use the **TRIM** command to produce the arcs. Connect the arcs with the **Tangent** object snap mode.

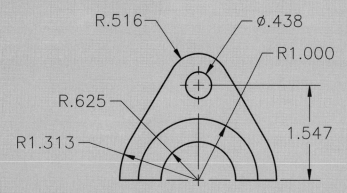

❏ Save the drawing as EX10-3 when you are finished, but do not exit AutoCAD LT.

Moving Objects

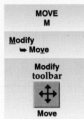

The **MOVE** command is used to move one or more selected objects to a new location in your drawing. Because all of the AutoCAD LT selection set options are valid with **MOVE**, you can select objects with a **Window**, **Crossing**, **Fence**, etc. (If necessary, refer to *Chapter 3* to review the various selection set options and their use.)

After selecting the objects, you are prompted to select a basepoint or enter a displacement. The basepoint is a reference point from which to move. After selecting the basepoint, you are prompted for the second displacement point. The two points you specify define the distance and direction the objects are to be moved. To issue the **MOVE** command, enter MOVE, or M, at the Command: prompt, click the **Move** button in the **Modify** toolbar, or select **Mo̲ve** from the **M̲odify** pull-down menu.

Moving from a Reference Point

Moving an object relative to a known basepoint, or reference point is quite commonly used and is described as follows:

> Command: **MOVE** *or* **M**↵
> Select objects: *(select the object(s) to move)*
> Select objects: ↵
> Base point or displacement: *(pick a point close to the selected objects)*
> Second point of displacement: *(pick the point to move to)*
> Command:

Be sure to use the appropriate object snap modes when the basepoint and/or displacement point must be precisely selected. As an example, consider the object shown in **Figure 10-11.** This is the same object that you constructed in *Exercise 10-3.* In this example, the lower-left corner of the object is selected as the basepoint using osnap **Endpoint**. The object is then dynamically "dragged" with the pointing device to a new screen location. Once the object is located to your satisfaction, click to set the object and end the command.

Moving a circle to its correct location on an object using the **Center** osnap is shown in **Figure 10-12.** In this example, the basepoint of the circle is its center and the second point of displacement is the center of the arc.

Figure 10-11.
Using the **MOVE** command.

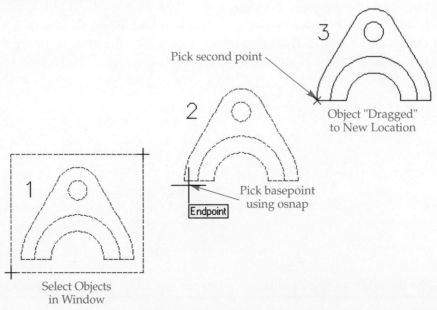

Figure 10-12.
Using object snap
modes with the
MOVE command.

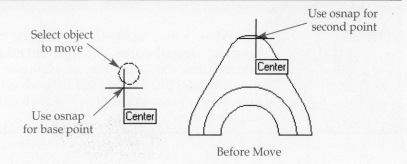

Select object
to move

Use osnap for
second point

Center

Center

Use osnap
for base point

Before Move

After Move

Moving with a known displacement

If you know the exact distance that an object must be moved, you can enter that
distance on the command line. For example, suppose that an object needs to be relocated 4 units to the right. There are two ways to accomplish this. The first method
looks like this:

>Command: **MOVE** *or* **M.**⏎
>Select objects: *(select the object)*
>Select objects: ⏎
>Base point or displacement: *(pick a point or use an osnap)*
>Second point of displacement: **@4,0**⏎
>Command:

Since polar coordinates may also be used, you can use the method just described
to move selected objects at any distance and at any angle from a known basepoint.
For example, @4⟨0.

An even faster method exists to move an object at a known displacement. With
this second method, only the displacement is entered—no basepoint is selected at all.

>Command: **MOVE** *or* **M.**⏎
>Select objects: *(select the object)*
>Select objects: ⏎
>Base point or displacement: **4,0** ⏎
>Second point of displacement: ⏎
>Command:

As shown above, AutoCAD LT still prompts for a second point of displacement
even though the displacement has been entered. If you press [Enter] at this prompt,
the values you originally entered are then interpreted as the relative X, Y, and Z
displacement from the 0,0,0 drawing origin and the object is moved accordingly.

<table>
<tr>
<td>

PROFESSIONAL TIP

</td>
<td>

When using **MOVE** to increase or decrease the space between views, be sure to toggle **ORTHO** mode on. Doing so ensures that the views stay in alignment during the move operation. **ORTHO** can be used for both orthogonal and auxiliary views. Refer to *Chapter 7* to review the construction of auxiliary views.

</td>
</tr>
</table>

EXERCISE 10-4

❑ Open EX10-3 if it is not on your screen.
❑ Move the entire object 3 units straight down.
❑ Next, move the circle off the object at an unspecified distance and angle.
❑ Using the example shown in **Figure 10-12,** move the circle back to its original position.
❑ When you are through, save the drawing as EX10-4 but do not exit AutoCAD LT.

ROTATE
RO

Modify
➥ Rotate

Modify
toolbar

Rotate

Rotating Objects

The **ROTATE** command rotates objects around a selected basepoint at a specified angle. As with the **MOVE** command, all of the AutoCAD LT selection set options are valid. To use the **ROTATE** command, enter ROTATE, or RO, at the Command: prompt, click the **Rotate** button in the **Modify** toolbar, or select **Rotate** from the **Modify** pull-down menu. The command options are described in the following sections.

Rotating Around a Reference Point

The default method for rotating objects involves selecting a basepoint and then specifying a rotation angle. A positive rotation angle rotates in a counterclockwise direction and a negative angle rotates in a clockwise direction. As with other editing commands, the proper use of object snap modes helps to facilitate the operation. In the example shown in **Figure 10-13,** the object is first selected in a window and then rotated 45° about the center of the arc. The command sequence is as follows:

```
Command: ROTATE or RO↵
Select objects: W↵
First corner: (pick a point) Other corner: (pick a diagonal point)
Select objects: ↵
Base point: (use osnap Center and pick the innermost arc)
⟨Rotation angle⟩/Reference: 45↵
Command:
```

Remember that implied windowing can be used as an efficient alternative to entering W at the Select objects: prompt.

Figure 10-13.
Using an osnap with the **ROTATE** command.

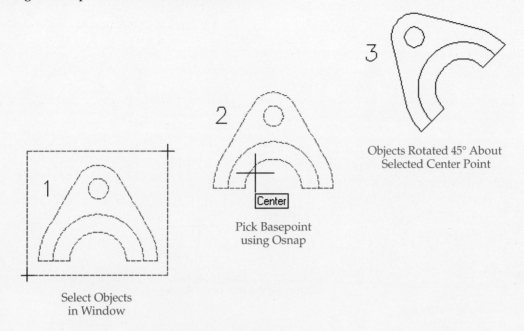

Objects Rotated 45° About
Selected Center Point

Pick Basepoint
using Osnap

Select Objects
in Window

Rotating Using the **Reference** Option

The **Reference** option of the **ROTATE** command allows you to rotate objects relative to an existing angle or object. With this method, you are prompted to specify the reference (existing) angle and then the new angle. When you know the reference angle, it may be entered at the keyboard. If you do not know the reference angle, you can use osnaps to select two specific points on an object. The angle between the two points you select defines the reference angle. This method is illustrated in **Figure 10-14.** In this example, the object previously rotated 45° is rotated another 15° relative to the angle specified by the two selected endpoints. The procedure looks like the following:

> Command: **ROTATE** *or* **RO**⏎
> Select objects: **W**⏎
> First corner: *(pick a point)* Other corner: *(pick a diagonal point)*
> Select objects: ⏎
> Basepoint: *(select a basepoint)*
> ⟨Rotation angle⟩/Reference: **R**⏎
> Reference angle ⟨0⟩: *(pick two points using osnap* **Endpoint***)*
> New angle: **15**⏎
> Command:

Figure 10-14.
The **Reference** option rotates objects relative to an existing object or angle.

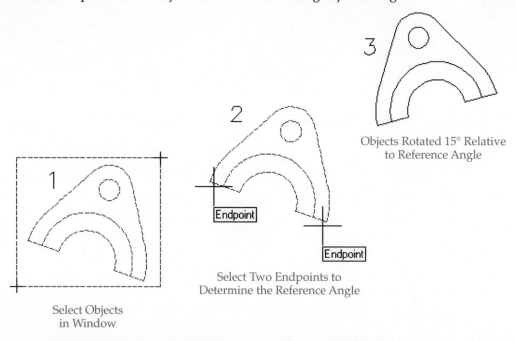

Objects Rotated 15° Relative
to Reference Angle

Select Two Endpoints to
Determine the Reference Angle

Select Objects
in Window

EXERCISE 10-5

❏ Open EX10-4 if it is not on your screen.
❏ Rotate the object 45° as shown in **Figure 10-13.**
❏ Next, use the **Reference** option to rotate the object 15° as shown in **Figure 10-14.**
❏ Finally, rotate the object back to its original orientation.
❏ Do not save the drawing and do not exit AutoCAD LT.

Getting
Started
Guide **10**

SCALE
SC

Modify
↪ Scale

Modify
toolbar

Scale

Scaling Objects

The **SCALE** command is used to reduce or enlarge selected objects. When you use the scale command, objects are scaled equally in the X, Y, and Z directions. To issue the **SCALE** command, enter SCALE, or SC, at the Command: prompt, click the **Scale** button in the toolbox, or select **Scale** from the **Modify** pull-down menu. As with the **MOVE** and **ROTATE** commands, all of the AutoCAD LT selection set options are valid with **SCALE**. The **SCALE** command options are described in the following two sections.

Scaling with a Known Scale Factor

The default scaling method scales objects with a known scale factor relative to a selected basepoint. A scale factor greater than 1 enlarges the objects, while a scale factor between 0 and 1 shrinks the objects. A negative value is disallowed. Once again, consider the familiar object shown in **Figure 10-15.** In the two examples illustrated, the object is scaled from a basepoint at the lower left and with a specified scale factor. The procedure looks like this:

> Command: **SCALE** *or* **SC**↵
> Select objects: *(select the object using any selection set option)*
> Select objects: ↵
> Base point: *(pick a basepoint)*
> ⟨Scale factor⟩/Reference: **2**↵
> Command:

Figure 10-15.
Scaling objects with the **SCALE** command.

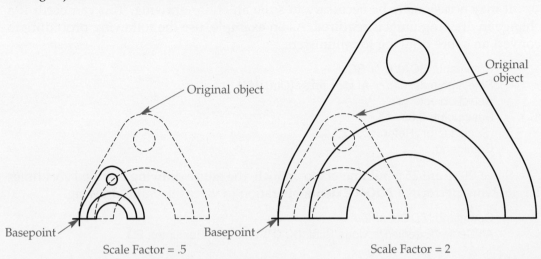

In the example above, the object is doubled in size. It is also possible to scale an object dynamically by "dragging" the object to the desired size at the ⟨Scale factor⟩ prompt. Using this method, a rubberband line connected to the selected basepoint follows the motion of your graphics cursor. Move your pointing device up or down, or left and right to scale the object. Once the object is scaled to your satisfaction, click the pick button on your pointing device to set the new size and end the command.

Scaling Using the **Reference** Option

The **Reference** option allows you to scale an object using an existing dimension as the basis for a new size. You are first prompted to specify the current length and then to enter a new length. In the example shown in **Figure 10-16,** a line is changed from 5 units to 7 units in length using the **Reference** option. The procedure is as follows:

       Command: **SCALE** *or* **SC**↵
       Select objects: *(select the line)*
       Select objects: ↵
       Base point: *(pick the basepoint using osnap* **Endpoint***)*
       ⟨Scale factor⟩/Reference: **R**↵
       Reference length ⟨1⟩: **5**↵
       New length: **7**↵

Figure 10-16.
Using the **SCALE** command's
Reference option.

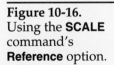
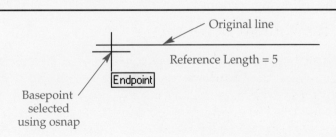

New Length = 7

Scaling the entire drawing

It may occasionally be necessary to scale an entire drawing. This can occur if a change in drawing units is required. As an example, use the following procedure to convert an entire drawing to millimeters:

Command: **SCALE** *or* **SC**↵
Select objects: *(enter* ALL *or press* [Ctrl]+[A]*)*
Select objects: ↵
Base point: **0,0**↵
〈Scale factor〉/Reference: **25.4.**↵
Command:

Since there are 25.4 millimeters to an inch, the entire drawing is scaled 25.4 times larger. Now, perform a **ZOOM Extents** operation to view the entire drawing.

Command: **ZOOM** *or* **Z**↵
All/Center/Extents/Previous/Scale(X/XP)/Window/〈Realtime〉: **E**↵

Also, do not forget to set the appropriate drawing limits for a metric drawing.

PROFESSIONAL TIP You can also use the procedure described above to convert a metric drawing to Imperial units. Enter .03937 when prompted for the scale factor.

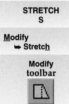

STRETCH
S

Modify
↳ Stret**ch**

Modify
toolbar

Stretch

Stretching Objects

The **STRETCH** command stretches (or shrinks) selected objects. To use **STRETCH** properly, you must use a crossing box or crossing polygon to select the objects. This is because AutoCAD LT can only stretch objects that cross the selection window. The endpoints that lie inside the crossing box are moved, while those that are outside the crossing box are unchanged. To issue the **STRETCH** command, enter STRETCH, or S, at the Command: prompt, click the **Stretch** button in the **Modify** toolbar, or select **Stret**ch from the **Modify** pull-down menu.

The **STRETCH** command options are identical to the **MOVE** command options discussed earlier in this chapter. In other words, you may stretch from a selected base-point, with a known displacement, or both. These **STRETCH** command options are described in the following sections.

Stretching from a Reference Point

Consider the simple object shown at the top of **Figure 10-17.** This object is to be stretched to the right. Observe that the crossing box only encloses those objects that are to be moved. The remainder of the object is outside the crossing box and stays *anchored* at its current location. This is very important because if you select the entire object in the selection set, the objects are moved and not stretched. Additionally, it is a good idea to toggle **ORTHO** mode on before stretching an object. This ensures that objects do not get skewed, or misaligned, during the operation. The procedure for stretching the object shown at the top of **Figure 10-17** is given below:

> Command: **STRETCH** *or* **S**↵
> Select objects to stretch by crossing-window or crossing-polygon...
> Select objects: **C**↵
> First corner: *(pick the point indicated)* Other corner: *(pick the diagonal point)*
> Select objects: ↵
> Base point or displacement: *(select the circle using osnap* **Center***)*
> Second point of displacement: *(pick a location to the right of the object)*
> Command:

Remember that implied windowing can be used as an efficient alternative to entering C at the Select objects: prompt.

Figure 10-17.
Using the **STRETCH** command.

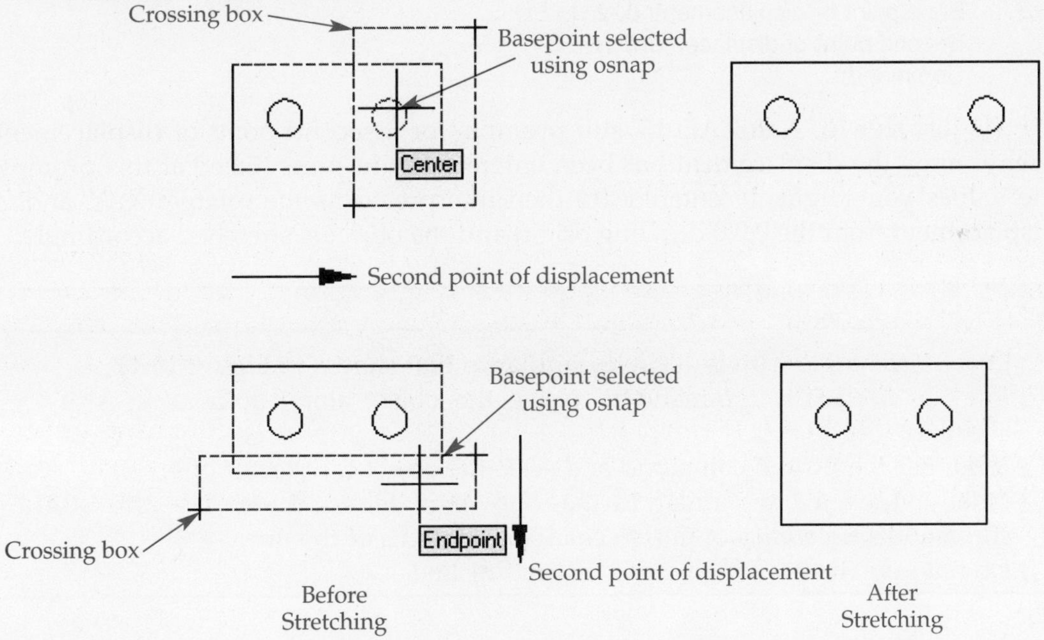

Crossing box — Basepoint selected using osnap — Center — Second point of displacement

Crossing box — Basepoint selected using osnap — Endpoint — Second point of displacement

Before Stretching — After Stretching

Stretching with a Known Displacement

If you know the exact distance that an object must be stretched, you can enter that distance on the command line. For example, suppose that the object shown at the bottom of **Figure 10-17** needs to be stretched 2 units straight down. There are two ways to accomplish this stretching. The first method looks like this:

Command: **STRETCH** *or* **S**↵
Select objects to stretch by crossing-window or crossing-polygon...
Select objects: **C**↵
First corner: *(pick the point indicated)* Other corner: *(pick the diagonal point)*
Select objects: ↵
Base point or displacement: *(pick the lower-right corner using osnap* **Endpoint***)*
Second point of displacement: **@2⟨270**↵
Command:

Since both cartesian and polar coordinates may be used as shown above, you can use the method just described to stretch selected objects at any distance and at any angle from a known basepoint.

An even faster method exists to stretch an object at a known displacement. With this second method, only the displacement is entered—no basepoint is selected at all.

Command: **STRETCH** *or* **S**↵
Select objects to stretch by crossing-window or crossing-polygon...
Select objects: **C**↵
First corner: *(pick the point indicated)* Other corner: *(pick the diagonal point)*
Select objects: ↵
Base point or displacement: **0,-2** ↵
Second point of displacement: ↵
Command:

As just shown, AutoCAD LT still prompts for a second point of displacement even though the displacement has been entered. If you press [Enter] at this prompt, the values you originally entered are then interpreted as the relative X, Y, and Z displacement from the 0,0,0 drawing origin and the object is stretched accordingly.

EXERCISE 10-6

❏ Draw a rectangle with two circles similar to that shown in **Figure 10-17**.
❏ Use the **STRETCH** command to resize the object along both axes. Also try shrinking the object.
❏ Next, use the **SCALE** command and scale the object by a factor of 4.
❏ Finally, draw a line similar to that shown in **Figure 10-16**. Use the **SCALE** command's **Reference** option to change the length of the line.
❏ Do not save the drawing when you are finished.

Editing Lines and Circles with the CHANGE Command

The **CHANGE** command was introduced in *Chapter 9* as a means of modifying existing text. You may recall that **CHANGE** allows you to change the text insertion point, height, rotation angle, style, and character string. However, **CHANGE** may also be used to modify the endpoint of a line or the radius of a circle. When changing the endpoint of a line, you are prompted ⟨Change point⟩. The *change point* is the point you select for the new endpoint of the line. You can pick a point on the screen, enter a coordinate, or osnap to an existing object. To gain a clearer understanding of how **CHANGE** modifies the endpoints of lines, see **Figure 10-18**. At the top of the illustration, a line endpoint is modified to intersect with the endpoint of a horizontal line. The procedure is as follows:

> Command: **CHANGE** *or* **-CH**↵
> Select objects: *(pick the diagonal line nearest the endpoint to change)*
> Select objects: ↵
> Properties/⟨Change point⟩: **END**↵
> of *(select the endpoint of the horizontal line)*
> Command:

Because all of the AutoCAD LT selection set options are valid with **CHANGE**, you can select more than one line at a time. When you specify a new endpoint for several lines, the endpoints of the selected lines closest to the change point move to the new point. This is illustrated by the three lines shown near the bottom of **Figure 10-18**. In this example, the change point for the three lines selected is the **Midpoint** of the horizontal line. However, if **Ortho** mode is on, the lines are forced parallel to either the X or the Y axis, rather than moving their endpoints to the specified change point. In the example shown in **Figure 10-18,** the three lines would be forced vertical with **Ortho** on since their original orientation was more vertical than horizontal.

Figure 10-18.
Using the **CHANGE** command to change line endpoints.

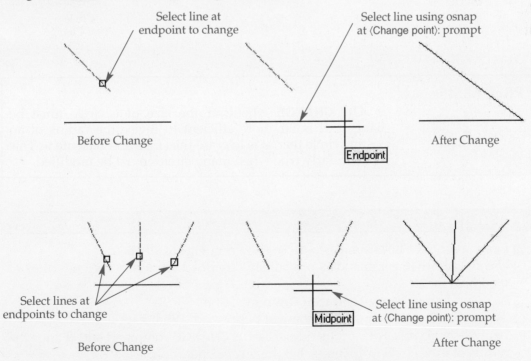

You can use **CHANGE** to specify a new circle radius for an existing circle in two different ways. The first method is to simply pick a screen location that the circle is to pass through. See **Figure 10-19.** The procedure looks like this:

Command: **CHANGE** *or* **-CH**↵
Select objects: *(pick the circle to change)*
Select objects: ↵
Properties/⟨Change point⟩: *(pick a point through which the circle is to be drawn)*
Command:

When you need to be more precise for the new circle radius, do the following:

Command: **CHANGE** *or* **-CH**↵
Select objects: *(pick the circle to change)*
Select objects: ↵
Properties/⟨Change point⟩: ↵
Enter circle radius: *(enter a positive value)*
Command:

If more than one circle is selected, AutoCAD LT repeats the prompt for each object encountered in the selection set.

Figure 10-19. Changing the radius of a circle with the **CHANGE** command.

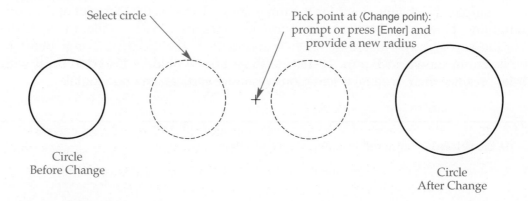

Select circle

Pick point at ⟨Change point⟩: prompt or press [Enter] and provide a new radius

Circle
Before Change

Circle
After Change

PROFESSIONAL TIP

Use **CHANGE** whenever the size of a circle must be changed. It is far more efficient to revise the radius of an existing circle than it is to erase the circle and recreate it. This is particularly true when many circles must be modified.

EXERCISE 10-7

❑ Draw a series of lines similar to those shown in **Figure 10-18.**
❑ Use the **CHANGE** command as previously described to modify the endpoints of the lines.
❑ Now, undo the changes and turn **Ortho** mode on.
❑ Repeat the **CHANGE** operation you just performed. What happens?
❑ Draw several circles of various sizes. Use the **CHANGE** command and change the radius of each circle to 1.5 units. Do this in *one* operation.
❑ Save the drawing as EX10-7.

AutoCAD LT—Fundamentals and Applications

Lengthening Objects

Previous discussions in this chapter described how to change the length of lines using the **EXTEND**, **SCALE**, **STRETCH**, and **CHANGE** commands. It is also possible to change the length of lines using the **LENGTHEN** command. Other object types that may be lengthened include open polylines, open splines, arcs, and elliptical arcs. Closed objects, like rectangles and polygons, cannot be lengthened, however.

To issue the **LENGTHEN** command, enter LENGTHEN, or LEN, at the Command: prompt, click the **Lengthen** button in the **Modify** toolbar, or select **Lengthen** from the **Modify** pull-down menu. The command sequence is as follows:

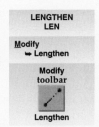

> Command: **LENGTHEN** or **LEN**↵
> DElta/Percent/Total/DYnamic/⟨Select object⟩: *(select one object)*

If the object you select is a line, open polyline, ellipse, elliptical arc, or spline, AutoCAD LT reports the object's current length in the command window. If an arc is selected, both the current length and the included angle of the arc are displayed.

Once you have selected an object, you may choose from one of four options to lengthen it. The four options are described as follows:

- **DElta.** This option changes the length of an object by a specified increment, measured from the endpoint of the selected object closest to the pick point. See **Figure 10-20.** This option can also be used to change the angle of an arc or elliptical arc by a specified increment measured from the endpoint of the object. A positive value extends an object, while a negative value trims it. After selecting **DElta**, you are prompted with:

> Angle/⟨Enter delta length⟩(⟨*current*⟩): *(specify a distance, enter A, or press [Enter])*

- **⟨Enter delta length⟩**—This is the default suboption. It changes the length of an object by the distance you specify. You are prompted with:

> ⟨Select object to change⟩/Undo: *(select one object or enter U)*

  The prompt is repeated until you press [Enter] to end the command.

- **Angle**—This suboption changes the included angle of a selected arc or elliptical arc by a specified angle value. See **Figure 10-21.** The prompts look like this:

> Enter delta angle⟨*current*⟩: *(specify an angle or press [Enter])*
> ⟨Select object to change⟩/Undo: *(select one object or enter U)*

  The prompt is repeated until you press [Enter] to end the command.

Figure 10-20.
Using the **DElta** option to lengthen or shorten an object.

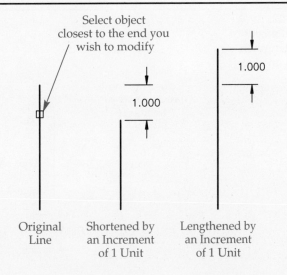

Select object closest to the end you wish to modify

1.000

1.000

Original Line

Shortened by an Increment of 1 Unit

Lengthened by an Increment of 1 Unit

Figure 10-21.
Using the **Angle**
suboption to increase
or decrease the
included angle of an
arc or elliptical arc.

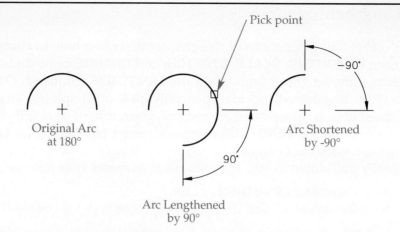

Pick point

Original Arc
at 180°

Arc Shortened
by -90°

Arc Lengthened
by 90°

- **Percent.** This option sets the length of an object by a specified percentage of its total length. As an example, to double the length of an object, enter a value of 200. To reduce the length of an object by one-half, enter a value of 50. See **Figure 10-22.** The **Percent** option can also be used to change the angle of an arc or elliptical arc by a specified percentage of the total included angle of the object. After selecting **Percent** , you are prompted with:

    Enter percent length⟨*current*⟩: (*enter a positive nonzero value or press* [Enter]*)*
    ⟨Select object to change⟩/Undo: (*select one object or enter* U*)*

    The prompt is repeated until you press [Enter] to end the command.

- **Total.** This option sets the length of a selected object by specifying the total absolute length from the fixed endpoint. For arcs and elliptical arcs, this option sets the included angle of the selected object by a specified total angle. After selecting **Total**, you are prompted with:

    Angle/⟨Enter total length⟩(⟨*current*⟩): (*specify a distance, enter* A*, or press* [Enter]*)*

    - **⟨Enter total length⟩**—This is the default suboption. It lengthens (or shortens) an object to the specified value from the endpoint nearest the selection point. See **Figure 10-23.** The prompt is as follows:

        ⟨Select object to change⟩/Undo: (*select one object or enter* U*)*

        The prompt is repeated until you press [Enter] to end the command.

Figure 10-22.
Using the **Percent**
option to lengthen
or shorten an object.

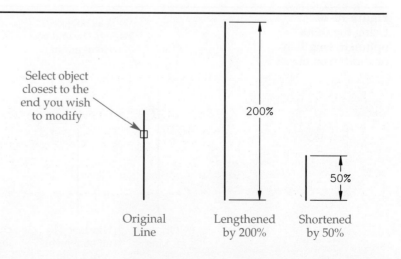

Select object
closest to the
end you wish
to modify

200%

50%

Original
Line

Lengthened
by 200%

Shortened
by 50%

Figure 10-23.
Using the **Total**
option to lengthen
or shorten an object.

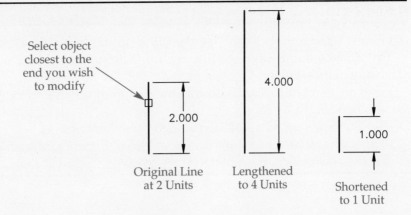

Select object closest to the end you wish to modify

2.000

4.000

1.000

Original Line
at 2 Units

Lengthened
to 4 Units

Shortened
to 1 Unit

- **Angle**—As previously mentioned, the **Angle** suboption sets the included angle of a selected arc or elliptical arc to a specified value. Refer again to **Figure 10-21.** The prompts look like this:

   Enter total angle⟨*current*⟩: *(specify an angle or press* [Enter]*)*
   ⟨Select object to change⟩/Undo: *(select one object or enter* U*)*

   This prompt is repeated until you press [Enter] to end the command.
- **DYnamic.** This option enables the *Dynamic Dragging* mode. With it, you change the length of a selected object by dragging one of its endpoints—the other end remains fixed. In the example shown in **Figure 10-24,** the length of an arc is dynamically lengthened and shortened using this method. After selecting **DYnamic,** you are prompted with:

   ⟨Select object to change⟩/Undo: *(select one object or enter* U*)*

   The prompt is repeated until you press [Enter] to end the command.

Figure 10-24.
Using the **DYnamic**
option to lengthen
or shorten an object.

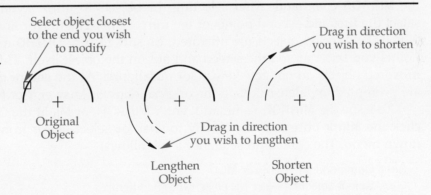

Select object closest
to the end you wish
to modify

Drag in direction
you wish to shorten

Original
Object

Drag in direction
you wish to lengthen

Lengthen
Object

Shorten
Object

PROFESSIONAL TIP

The **LENGTHEN DYnamic** option is a handy alternative to the **EXTEND** command. Also, keep in mind that the **LENGHTEN Total** option is a much faster method for lengthening lines and polylines than the **Reference** option of the **SCALE** command.

EXERCISE 10-8

❑ Draw a line 5 units long. Use the **DElta** option to increase the length of the line by .75 increments until the line is 8 units long. Now shorten the line to 4.5 units using .5 increments.

❑ Use the **Percent** option to double the length of the line to 9 units. Now, decrease the line length by 25%.

❑ Set the line length to 7.625 units using the **Total** option.

❑ Draw several arcs and some additional lines. Experiment with the **DYnamic** option on the new objects. It is not necessary to save the drawing when you are finished.

Commands that Duplicate Existing Objects

Perhaps the greatest value in using CAD is never having to draw the same object twice. AutoCAD LT provides several commands that allow you to duplicate existing objects. One of these commands, **OFFSET**, was introduced in *Chapter 7*. You may recall that **OFFSET** allows you to duplicate an object at a distance or through a selected point. The following sections describe the **MIRROR**, **COPY**, and **ARRAY** commands. These commands allow you to duplicate many objects at once using a variety of methods.

Creating Mirror Images

The **MIRROR** command creates a mirror image of selected objects. This makes **MIRROR** particularly useful in the construction of complex symmetrical objects. For these types of shapes, simply draw one half of the object and mirror it across its symmetrical centerline. All of the AutoCAD LT selection set options are valid with the **MIRROR** command. After selecting the objects to mirror, you are prompted to select the first and second points of the mirror line. The mirror line is the axis about which the selected objects are mirrored. Be sure to turn **ORTHO** mode on if the two points you select are on the screen and not on the object itself. This ensures that the mirrored objects do not get skewed, or misaligned. At the end of the command, you are prompted to delete or retain the original objects. Answer Y or N accordingly.

To issue the **MIRROR** command, enter MIRROR, or MI, at the Command: prompt, click the **Mirror** button in the **Modify** toolbar, or select **Mirror** from the **Modify** pull-down menu. The command sequence is as follows:

MIRROR
MI

Modify
↳ Mirror

Modify
toolbar

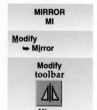

Mirror

Command: **MIRROR** *or* **MI**↵
Select objects: *(select the object(s) to be mirrored)*
Select objects: ↵
First point of mirror line: *(pick a point)* Second point: *(pick a second point)*
Delete old objects? ⟨N⟩ **Y** *or* **N**↵
Command:

Refer to **Figure 10-25** to obtain a better understanding of the **MIRROR** procedure. At the left, the objects to be mirrored are first selected using a crossing box. Observe that the two horizontal lines of the object are purposely excluded from the selection set. This is to ensure that these lines are not duplicated upon themselves during the **MIRROR** operation. Next, osnap **Endpoint** is used to select two points that define the axis about which the objects are to be mirrored. At the far right, the object is mirrored, the original objects are retained, and the two original horizontal lines are erased. The two lines could also have been erased prior to the **MIRROR** procedure.

Figure 10-25.
Using the **MIRROR** command.

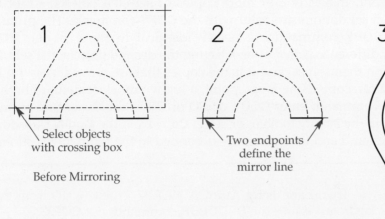
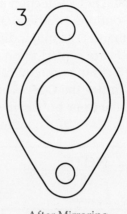

Select objects with crossing box

Before Mirroring

Two endpoints define the mirror line

After Mirroring

The **MIRRTEXT** System Variable

It is important to realize that the **MIRROR** command also mirrors text and dimensions. This is controlled by the **MIRRTEXT** system variable. By default, **MIRRTEXT** is turned on, which causes text and dimensions to mirror. To eliminate mirrored text and dimensions, turn **MIRRTEXT** off as follows:

Command: **MIRRTEXT**⏎
New value for MIRRTEXT ⟨1⟩: **0**⏎

Block attributes, (textual information attached to blocks), are mirrored regardless of the **MIRRTEXT** setting. See *Chapter 15* for complete information about blocks and block attributes.

PROFESSIONAL TIP

To ensure that text and dimensions are not mirrored in any of your drawings, set **MIRRTEXT** to 0 in your template file(s). When you do want to mirror some text or dimensions, turn **MIRRTEXT** back on in the current drawing, only.

EXERCISE 10-9

❏ Open drawing EX10-4.
❏ Using the **MIRROR** command, create a mirror image of the object as shown in **Figure 10-25.**
❏ Save the drawing as EX10-9.

Copying Objects

The **COPY** command makes one or more copies of selected objects. All of the AutoCAD LT selection set options are valid with the **COPY** command. The prompts and options of the **COPY** command are nearly identical to those of the **MOVE** command. The major difference is that after selecting the desired objects, the selected objects are copied upon themselves, and it is the copies that are moved. As with the **MOVE** command, you can copy using a basepoint, a known displacement, or both.

To use the **COPY** command, enter COPY, or CO or CP, at the Command: prompt, click the **Copy** button in the **Modify** toolbar, or select **Copy** from the **Modify** pull-down menu. The **COPY** command and its options are described in the following sections.

```
COPY
CO or CP

Modify
  ⤷ Copy

Modify
toolbar

Copy
```

> **NOTE**
>
> If you are using AutoCAD LT 97, entering CO from the keyboard issues the **DDCOLOR** command, not **COPY**.

Copying from a reference point

Consider the partial schematic diagram shown in **Figure 10-26.** In this example, a resistor symbol is copied to another location in the diagram using the appropriate object snap modes. Study the illustration as you follow the command sequence given below:

```
Command: COPY or CO or CP↵
Select objects: W↵
First corner: (pick the first corner) Other corner: (pick a diagonal corner)
Select objects: ↵
⟨Base point or displacement⟩/Multiple: CEN↵
of (select the center of the donut at the top of the resistor)
Second point of displacement: NEA↵
to (select a point on the top line to the right of the resistor)
Command:
```

Figure 10-26.
Using the **COPY** command.

Copying with a known displacement

If you know the exact distance that a copied object is to be moved, you can enter that distance on the command line. For example, suppose that an object needs to be copied 3 units to the left. There are two ways to accomplish this. The first method looks like this:

> Command: **COPY** *or* **CO** *or* **CP**↵
> Select objects: *(select the object(s) to copy)*
> Select objects: ↵
> ⟨Base point or displacement⟩/Multiple: *(pick a point or use an osnap)*
> Second point of displacement: **@-3,0**↵
> Command:

Since polar coordinates may also be used, you can use the method just described to copy selected objects at any distance and at any angle from a known basepoint.

An even faster method exists to copy an object at a known displacement. With this second method, only the displacement is entered—no basepoint is selected at all.

> Command: **COPY** *or* **CP**↵
> Select objects: *(select the object(s) to copy)*
> Select objects: ↵
> ⟨Base point or displacement⟩/Multiple: **-3,0**↵
> Second point of displacement: ↵
> Command:

As shown above, AutoCAD LT still prompts for a second point of displacement even though the displacement has been entered. If you press [Enter] at this prompt, the values you originally entered are then interpreted as the relative X, Y, and Z displacement from the 0,0,0 drawing origin and the object is copied to the new location accordingly.

Making Multiple Copies

It is often necessary to make more than one copy of an object. The **COPY** command's **Multiple** option allows you to do so. After selecting the objects to copy, enter M for multiple. Then, select a basepoint as usual and a second point of displacement to place the copy. The Second point of displacement: prompt is repeated to allow multiple copies. When you are through copying, press [Enter] to end the command. The command sequence is as follows:

> Command: **COPY** *or* **CO** *or* **CP**↵
> Select objects: *(select the object(s) to copy)*
> Select objects: ↵
> ⟨Base point or displacement⟩/Multiple: **M**↵
> Base point: *(pick a point or use an osnap)*
> Second point of displacement: *(pick a point or use an osnap)*
> Second point of displacement: *(pick another point or use an osnap)*
> Second point of displacement: *(locate another copy or press* [Enter] *to end)*
> Command:

The ARRAY Command

The **ARRAY** command creates multiple copies of objects in a rectangular or polar (circular) pattern. This command and its options are described in the following sections.

Creating a Rectangular Array Using a Dialog Box

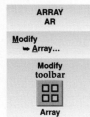

ARRAY
AR

Modify
➥ Array...

Modify
toolbar

Array

A rectangular array copies objects in a pattern defined by a number of rows and columns. The rows correspond to the Y axis, and the columns correspond to the X axis. Consider the rectangular array of electronic resistors shown in **Figure 10-27.** The first resistor in this array is located at the lower left. This is the original object that is copied and is called the *cornerstone element*. Each of the other objects in a rectangular array are called *cells*. Each cell remains a separate, discrete drawing object that may be erased, or otherwise modified, independently from the rest of the array. In this example, there are 4 rows and 3 columns in the array. The distance between the rows and columns, or *offsets*, must also be specified. To create the rectangular array shown in **Figure 10-27** using a dialog box, enter ARRAY, or AR, at the Command: prompt, click the **Array** button in the **Modify** toolbar, or select **Array...** from the **Modify** pull-down menu. The command sequence is as follows:

Command: **ARRAY** *or* **AR**↵

Figure 10-27.
In a rectangular array, the columns correspond to the X direction and the rows correspond to the Y direction.

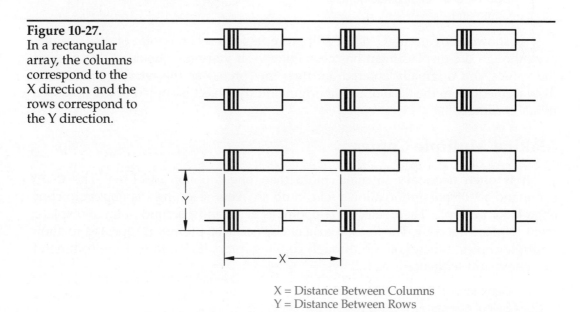

X = Distance Between Columns
Y = Distance Between Rows

NOTE If you are using AutoCAD LT 97, using the **Array** dialog box is not an option. If any of the previously mentioned entry methods are used, the **ARRAY** command is initiated at the command line. The command line method is describe later in this chapter.

The **Array** dialog box appears as shown in **Figure 10-28**. Each of the options available in this dialog box are described as follows:

- **Rectangular/Polar Array option buttons.** Located at the very top of the dialog box, these buttons are used to specify the type of array to create. The **Rectangular Array** button is active by default.

- **Rows: text box.** Enter the required number of rows in this text box. The default value is 4. Remember that the rows correspond to the Y direction.

- **Columns: text box.** Enter the required number of columns in this text box. As with rows, the default value is 4. Remember that the columns correspond to the X direction.

- **Row offset:.** Specify the required distance between rows using this text box. The default value is 1 unit.

- **Pick Row Offset button.** This is the top square button at the far right of the **Row offset:** text box. It allows you to specify the distance between rows by picking two points in the drawing window with your pointing device. Clicking this button temporarily removes the dialog box and you are prompted with:

    Specify the distance between rows: *(pick the first point)*
    Second point: *(pick the second point)*

Figure 10-28.
Creating a rectangular array using the **Array** dialog box.

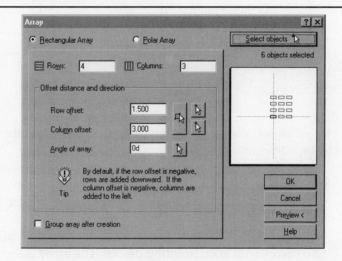

Once the two points have been selected, the **Array** dialog box is redisplayed.

- **Column offset:.** Use this text box to enter the required spacing between columns. As with the row offset, this value defaults to 1 unit.

- **Pick Column Offset button.** This is the bottom square button at the far right of the **Column offset:** text box. It allows you to specify the distance between columns by picking two points in the drawing window with your pointing device. Clicking this button temporarily removes the dialog box and you are prompted with:

    Specify the distance between columns: *(pick the first point)*
    Second point: *(pick the second point)*

Once the two points have been selected, the **Array** dialog box is redisplayed.

- **Pick both offsets button.** This is the large rectangular button located just to the right of the **Row offset:** and **Column offset:** text boxes. It allows you to specify the distance between cells by picking two diagonal corners in the drawing window with your pointing device. This method is illustrated in **Figure 10-29.** As previously mentioned, cells are each of the objects in a rectangular array. Clicking this button temporarily removes the dialog box and you are prompted with:

> Specify unit cell: *(pick the first corner)*
> Other corner: *(pick the second corner)*

Figure 10-29.
Two diagonal corners define the unit cell distance.

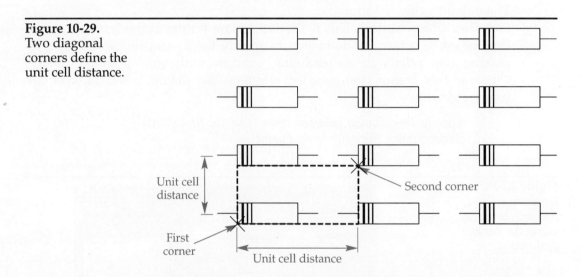

Once you have selected two diagonal corners representing both unit cell offsets, the **Array** dialog box is redisplayed.

- **Angle of array: text box.** You can create a rotated array by entering the desired rotational value in degrees using this text box. An example of a rotated array with one row and three columns is shown in **Figure 10-30.**
- **Pick Angle of Array button.** This is the square button at the far right of the **Angle of array:** text box. It allows you to specify the angle of a rotated array by picking two points with your pointing device. The array is then rotated with the identical angle defined between the two selected points. Clicking this button temporarily removes the dialog box and you are prompted with:

> Specify angle of array: *(pick the first point)*
> Second point: *(pick the second point)*

Figure 10-30.
A rotated rectangular array.

Once the two points have been selected, the **Array** dialog box is redisplayed.

- **Group array after creation check box.** Inactive by default, this check box creates a new group object from the rectangular array when activated. A *group* is a saved selection set. The **GROUP** command is described in *Chapter 15* of this text.

- **Select objects button.** After specifying the requirements for your array in the **Offset distance and direction** section of the **Array** dialog box, click the **Select objects** button at the top right of the dialog box. The dialog box is temporarily removed and the familiar Select objects: prompt is displayed in the command window. Use any of the AutoCAD LT selection set options to select the objects you wish to array. Once the objects are selected, the dialog box returns and the number of objects selected for the array is reported just below the **Select objects** button. **See Figure 10-28.** Notice also that the image tile at the right of the dialog box graphically illustrates the rectangular array with the precise parameters you have specified.

- **Preview⟨.** Once you have entered all the required values and selected the objects for your array, click this button to see the new array as it will appear in the drawing window. An alert box like that shown in **Figure 10-31** prompts you to accept or modify the array as required.

  - **Cancel**—Click this button if you decide not to create the array.
  - **Modify**—If you click this button, the **Array** dialog box is redisplayed so you can edit any of the array values and then preview the array again.
  - **Accept**—Clicking this button creates the rectangular array in the drawing window as specified and terminates the **ARRAY** command.

Figure 10-31.
The **Array** alert box is displayed when you preview an array.

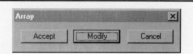

Creating a Rectangular Array with AutoCAD LT 97

The **Array** dialog box is a feature unique to AutoCAD LT 98. As previously mentioned, for users of AutoCAD LT 97 the rectangular arrays must be created using command line input. Refer once again to **Figure 10-27** as you follow the procedure below:

  Command: **ARRAY** *or* **AR**↵
  Select objects: *(select the resistor)*
  Select objects: ↵
  Rectangular or Polar array (⟨R⟩/P) ⟨*current*⟩: **R**↵
  Number of rows (–) ⟨1⟩: **4**↵
  Number of columns (| | |) ⟨1⟩: **3**↵
  Unit cell or distance between rows (–): **1.5**↵
  Distance between columns (| | |): **3**↵
  Command:

Remember that the cornerstone element is usually assumed to be at the lower left so that an array is created up and to the right. However, an array can be created down and/or to the left by entering negative values for the distances between the rows and columns. It is also possible to specify the distance between unit cells by picking two diagonal corners with your pointing device. This method is illustrated in **Figure 10-29** and is performed as follows:

Command: **ARRAY** *or* **AR**↵
Select objects: *(select the resistor)*
Select objects: ↵
Rectangular or Polar array (⟨R⟩/P) ⟨*current*⟩: **R**↵
Number of rows (−) ⟨1⟩: **4**↵
Number of columns (| | |) ⟨1⟩: **3**↵
Unit cell or distance between rows (−): *(pick the first corner)*
Other corner: *(pick a diagonal corner)*
Command:

PROFESSIONAL TIP

Although the **ARRAY** command in AutoCAD LT 97 does not offer the option to generate a rectangular array at an angle other than 0°, you can still do so by setting the **SNAP Rotation** angle appropriately before issuing the **ARRAY** command. If necessary, refer to *Chapter 2* to review the **SNAP** command.

NOTE

AutoCAD LT 98 users can also create rectangular arrays on the command line as shown in the example above, by entering **-AR** instead of **ARRAY** or **AR**.

EXERCISE 10-10

❏ Use a circle and a six-sided polygon to draw one of the hexagonal features shown in this exercise. Do not draw the centerlines or dimensions.
❏ Finish the construction using a rectangular array.

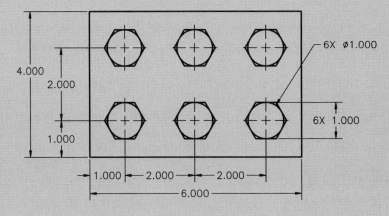

❏ Save the drawing as EX10-10.

Creating a Polar Array Using a Dialog Box

A polar array copies selected objects in a circular pattern around a specified center point. As shown in **Figure 10-32**, a small circle with a centerline is copied 8 times around the center point of the large circle. The objects may be rotated as they are copied as shown in the illustration. Observe the difference in the centerlines when the array is not rotated. You can array an object through a full 360°or only through a portion of the 360°. AutoCAD LT calls this the *angle to fill*. A positive value copies in a counterclockwise direction, while a negative value copies in a clockwise direction.

To create the polar array shown in **Figure 10-32** using a dialog box, enter ARRAY, or AR, at the Command: prompt, click the **Array** button in the **Modify** toolbar, or select **Array...** from the **Modify** pull-down menu.

Figure 10-32 .
An example of a rotated and nonrotated polar array.

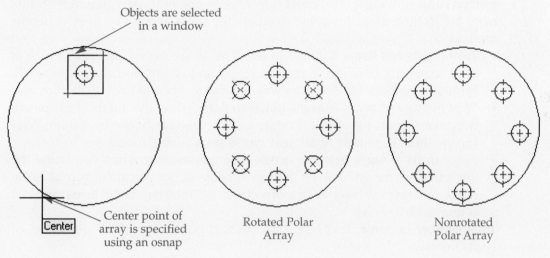

NOTE	As previously mentioned, using the **Array** dialog box is not an option for AutoCAD LT 97 users. If any of the previously mentioned entry methods are used, the **ARRAY** command is initiated at the command line. The command line method is describe later in this chapter.

When the **Array** dialog box appears, activate the **Polar Array** option button at the top of the dialog box as shown in **Figure 10-33**. Each of the options available for polar arrays using this dialog box are described as follows:

- **Center point: text boxes.** You can use these text boxes to enter the X and Y cartesian values for the center point about which to array. However, it is far more efficient to locate a point in the drawing window by clicking the **Pick Center Point** button just to the right of the text boxes. Clicking this button temporarily removes the dialog box and you are prompted with:

    Specify center point of array: *(pick a center point)*

    Use an appropriate osnap to locate the center point as shown at the far left in **Figure 10-32.** Once the center point is selected, the **Array** dialog box is redisplayed.

Figure 10-33.
Creating a polar
array using the
Array dialog box.

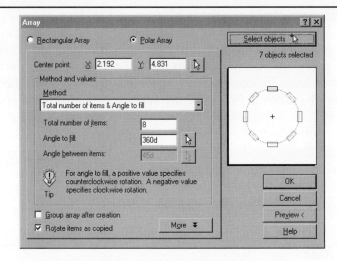

- **Method drop-down list.** You must now choose one of three different methods from the **Method** drop-down list to create the polar array. The three different methods are:
  - **Total number of items & Angle to fill**—This is the default method which is used to specify how many items to copy and rotate, and the angle to fill. With this method, the **Angle between items:** text box is unavailable for use.
  - **Total number of items & Angle between items**—Use this method to specify how many items to copy and rotate and the angle between each item. With this method, the **Angle to fill:** text box is unavailable for use.
  - **Angle to fill & Angle between items**—Use this method when you know the angle that must exist between the arrayed objects, but you are unsure as to the number of items to copy. With this method, the **Total number of items:** text box is unavailable for use.
- **Total number of items: text box.** Use this text box to specifiy the number of items to copy.
- **Angle to fill: text box.** This text box is used to specify whether you wish to array through a full circle (the default), or some portion thereof.
- **Angle between items: text box.** Use this text box to enter an explicit angle between items.
- **Group array after creation check box.** Inactive by default, this check box creates a new group object from the polar array when activated. As previously mentioned, a *group* is a saved selection set and is described in *Chapter 15* of this text.
- **Rotate items as copied check box.** This check box is active by default. Refer once again to **Figure 10-32** to compare rotated and nonrotated polar arrays.
- **Select objects button.** After specifying the requirements for your array in the **Method and values** section of the **Array** dialog box, click the **Select objects** button at the top right of the dialog box. The dialog box is temporarily removed and the familiar Select objects: prompt is displayed in the command window. Use any of the AutoCAD LT selection set options to select the objects you wish to array. Once the objects are selected, the dialog box returns and the number of objects selected for the array is reported just below the **Select objects** button. See **Figure 10-33**. Notice also that the image tile at the right of the dialog box graphically illustrates the polar array with the precise parameters you have specified.

- **Preview** ⟨. Once you have entered all the required values and selected the objects for your array, click this button to see the new array as it will appear in the drawing window. An alert box like that shown in **Figure 10-31** prompts you to accept or modify the array as required.
  - **Cancel**—Click this button if you decide not to create the array.
  - **Modify**—If you click this button, the **Array** dialog box is redisplayed so you can edit any of the array values and then preview the array again.
  - **Accept**—Clicking this button creates the rectangular array in the drawing window as specified and terminates the **ARRAY** command.

Creating a Polar Array with AutoCAD LT 97

As previously mentioned, the **Array** dialog box is a feature unique to AutoCAD LT 98. For users of AutoCAD LT 97, polar arrays must be created using command line input. To create the polar array shown in **Figure 10-32** on the command line, do the following:

> Command: **ARRAY** or **AR**↵
> Select objects: *(select the object(s) to array)*
> Select objects: ↵
> Rectangular or Polar array (⟨R⟩/P) ⟨current⟩: **P**↵
> Base/⟨Specify center point of array⟩: *(pick the large circle using osnap* **Center***)*
> Number of items: **8**↵

When specifying the number of items to array, be sure to include the original selection set.

> Angle to fill (+=ccw,-=cw) ⟨360⟩:↵

You can array an object through a full 360°or only through a portion of the 360°. A positive value copies in a counterclockwise direction, while a negative value copies in a clockwise direction.

> Rotate objects as they are copied? ⟨Y⟩:↵
> Command:

The default is to rotate objects as they are arrayed. If you prefer not to rotate the objects, answer N accordingly.

There may be instances when you know the angle that must exist between the arrayed objects, but you are unsure as to the number of items. In the following example, an angle of 60° is specified between the arrayed objects:

> Command: **ARRAY** or **AR**↵
> Select objects: *(select the object(s) to array)*
> Select objects: ↵
> Rectangular or Polar array (⟨R⟩/P) ⟨current⟩: **P**↵
> Base/⟨Specify center point of array⟩: *(pick the center point)*
> Number of items: ↵
> Angle to fill (+=ccw,-=cw) ⟨360⟩: ↵
> Angle between items: **60**↵
> Rotate objects as they are copied? ⟨Y⟩: ↵
> Command:

NOTE	AutoCAD LT 98 users can also create polar arrays on the command line as shown in the example above, by entering **-AR** instead of **ARRAY** or **AR**.

Using the **Base** Option with Polar Arrays

When objects are not rotated in a polar array, they often appear to not rotate correctly around the specified center point of the array. This is apparent with the nonrotated circles and centerlines shown at the far right in **Figure 10-32** . This occurs because AutoCAD LT determines the distance from the center point of the array to a reference point on the *last object* encountered in the selection set. The reference point varies depending on the type of object selected. AutoCAD LT uses one endpoint of a line, the start point of text, and the center point of an arc, circle, or ellipse as the reference point. If you pick objects singly with your pointing device, the last object selected determines the reference point. On the other hand, if you use a crossing or window box, the last object encountered in the selection set is arbitrary. This is the reason why a nonrotated polar array appears nonsymmetric around the center.

You can avoid this problem by using the **Base** option which lets you specify a new basepoint to be used as the reference point. The procedure looks like this:

    Base/⟨Specify center point of array⟩: **B.**↵
    Specify basepoint of objects: *(locate a point in the drawing window)*

You can locate a new reference point by entering coordinates or by using an osnap. Once the point is located, the polar array command continues as previously described.

Accessing the **Base** option in the Array Dialog Box

A new basepoint can be specified by first expanding the **Array** dialog box. To do so, click the button labeled **M<u>o</u>re** at the bottom of the dialog box. **See Figure 10-33**. The expanded portion displays the **Object base point** section of the dialog box shown in **Figure 10-34**. To specify a new basepoint, do the following:

1. First, deactivate the **Set to object's default** check box.
2. Next, use the **<u>X</u>** and **<u>Y</u>** text boxes to explicitly enter the cartesian coordinates of the new basepoint. However, it is far more efficient to dynamically locate the basepoint in the drawing window.
3. To do so, click the **Pick Base Point** button just to the right of the **Base point:** text boxes. The dialog box temporarily disappears and you are prompted with:

    Specify the base point of objects:*(pick the basepoint)*

4 After locating the new basepoint, the **Array** dialog box reappears and the remainder of the operation is completed as previously described. To return the dialog box to its unexpanded condition, click the button labeled **Less** at the bottom of the dialog box.

Figure 10-34.
A new reference point can be selected by expanding the **Array** dialog box.

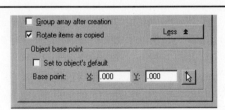

❑ Use a polar array to draw the object shown in this exercise. Do not draw the center-lines or dimensions. *Construction hint:* Study the geometry carefully to identify how the **OFFSET** and **TRIM** commands can speed the construction of this object.

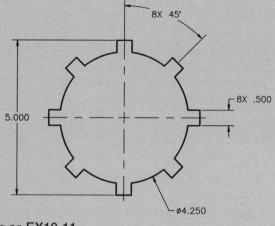

❑ Save the drawing as EX10-11.

Modifying Objects Using a Dialog Box

The **DDMODIFY** command was introduced in *Chapter 9* as a means of editing a string of text characters. However, **DDMODIFY** can be used on any object type in AutoCAD LT . Remember, **DDMODIFY** also permits you to change the properties (color, layer, linetype, linetype scale, thickness) of a selected object. To issue the **DDMODIFY** command, enter DDMODIFY, or MO, at the Command: prompt, or click the **Properties** button at the far right of the **Object Properties** toolbar. The command sequence is as follows:

> DDMODIFY
> MO
>
> Object Properties toolbar
>
> Properties

    Command: **DDMODIFY** *or* **MO**⏎
    Select object to modify: *(select one object)*

DDMODIFY allows only one object to be selected for modification. After picking the object, a dialog box appropriate for the object type you selected is displayed. As shown in **Figure 10-35A**, the **Modify Circle** dialog box displays when a circle is selected. Observe that the circle's radius, diameter, circumference, and area are displayed at the right of the dialog box. Use the **Radius:** text box to change the size of the circle. At the left of the dialog box, the XYZ coordinates of the circle's center are displayed in the corresponding text boxes. You can edit the values in these text boxes to move the circle to a new location, or click the **Pick Point** ⟨ button instead. When you use this button, the dialog box temporarily disappears and you receive the **Center point:** prompt.

Pick a point on the screen, enter a coordinate, or osnap to an existing object to locate the circle at a new origin. The dialog box then reappears showing the new XYZ coordinates of the circle's center. Click **OK** to exit the dialog box.

When a line is selected, **DDMODIFY** displays the **Modify Line** dialog box shown in Figure 10-35B. You can change the starting and ending points of a line by changing the values in the appropriate text boxes, or click the **Pick Point** ⟨ buttons to interactively change the line points. The **Delta XYZ:** values, length, and angle for the selected line are displayed at the right of the dialog box. When you are through modifying the line, click **OK** to exit the dialog box.

Figure 10-35.
A—The **Modify Circle** dialog box. B—The **Modify Line** dialog box.

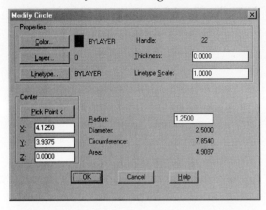

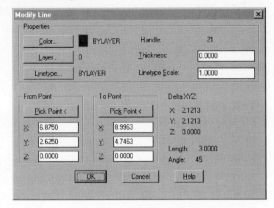

A

B

EXERCISE 10-12

❑ Open EX10-11 from the previous polar array exercise.
❑ Use **DDMODIFY** to change the length of one of the lines and the radius of one of the arcs. Select any values you like.
❑ Next, draw a circle with a diameter of 2.3125 units. Use **DDMODIFY** to change the diameter to 4.375 units.
❑ Try moving an object using **DDMODIFY**. Of the two methods, **MOVE** and **DDMODIFY**, which do you prefer to use when moving objects? Why?
❑ Do not save the drawing when you are through experimenting.

Introduction to Grips and Grip Editing

Grips are the small squares that appear on an object when an object is selected at the Command: prompt. They provide a quick way to edit AutoCAD LT objects without using the standard editing commands. As shown in **Figure 10-36,** grips are strategically placed on objects in locations that correspond to object snap points, such as the midpoint or endpoints of a line.

Figure 10-36.
Grips appear at specific points on each object type. The points correspond with object snap mode locations.

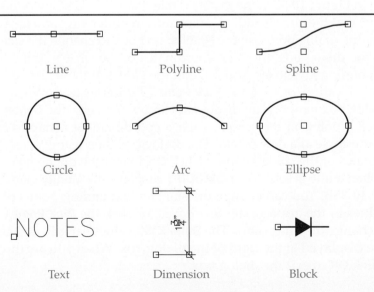

Grips can be either warm, hot, or cold. The grips that appear when an object is selected at the **Command:** prompt are called warm grips. By default, they display as unfilled blue squares. Selecting a warm grip with your pointing device makes the grip hot. It then displays as a filled red square. Once a grip is hot, it can be used to stretch, move, copy, rotate, scale, or mirror an object.

Grips are made cold by pressing the [Esc] key to perform a **Cancel** operation. Object highlighting is also removed when grips are made cold. See **Figure 10-37**.

Figure 10-37.
A visual comparison between warm, hot, and cold grips.

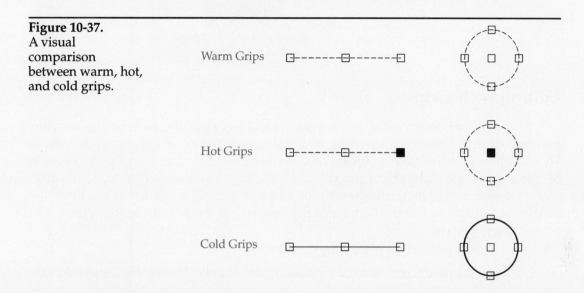

The Grips Dialog Box

There are several system variables that control the use of grips. These variables can be changed using a dialog box by selecting **Grips...** from the **Tools** pull-down menu, or by entering DDGRIPS, or GR, at the Command: prompt.

DDGRIPS
GR

Tools
↪ Grips...

The **DDGRIPS** command activates the **Grips** dialog box shown in **Figure 10-38**. Each of the components of this dialog box are described below.

- **Select Settings.** If you wish to disable grips, click to remove the checkmark (√) from the **Enable Grips** check box. This action sets the **GRIPS** system variable to 0 (off). If you wish to turn on the display of grips within block objects, activate the **Enable Grips Within Blocks** check box. The new setting is stored in the **GRIPBLOCK** system variable.
- **Grip Colors.** As previously mentioned, unselected (warm) grips are blue and selected (hot) grips are red. Use the appropriate buttons in this section if you wish to assign different colors to your grips. The color selected for warm grips is stored in the **GRIPCOLOR** system variable, and the color selected for hot grips is stored in the **GRIPHOT** system variable.
- **Grip Size.** Use the horizontal slider bar in this section to dynamically increase or decrease the size of grips. By default, grips are 3 pixels in size (the same as the object pickbox). The new grip size is stored in the **GRIPSIZE** system variable.

Once you have made your changes, click **OK** to exit the **Grips** dialog box.

Figure 10-38.
The **Grips** dialog box.

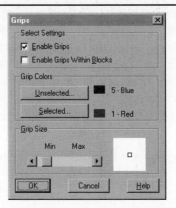

Editing with Grips

To modify an object using grips, select the object with the pick button on your pointing device. The object is highlighted and unselected grips appear on the object. To select a grip, move your pointing device over the desired grip and pick. There is no need to use one of the object snap modes—the cursor will snap directly to the grip. Once the grip is selected, it becomes hot and appears solid. At the same time, the following is displayed in the Command: prompt area at the bottom of the screen:

> **STRETCH**
> 〈Stretch to point〉/Base point/Copy/Undo/eXit:

If you pick a new screen location at the 〈Stretch to point〉/Base point/Copy/Undo/eXit: prompt, the object will stretch from the hot grip origin to the new selected point. See **Figure 10-39.** Each of the other **STRETCH** options are described as follows:

- **Base point.** Enter B and press [Enter] to select a different basepoint as the point of reference from which to stretch.
- **Copy.** If you wish to make one or more copies of the selected object, enter C and press [Enter]. This activates **Multiple** mode, allowing you to make multiple copies until you exit the operation.
- **Undo.** Use the **Undo** option to undo the **Basepoint** or **Copy** selection.
- **eXit.** Enter X and press [Enter] to exit the grip editing procedure. The hot grip is removed from the object, but the unselected (warm) grips remain. As previously mentioned, the warm grips are made cold by pressing the [Esc] key on your keyboard. Press [Esc] twice, or click the **Undo** button on the **Standard Toolbar** to remove the cold grips, turn off object highlighting, and return to the Command: prompt.

Stretching is the default grip editing mode. This mode is very powerful because it allows you to move and copy as well. To move a line using stretch, simply select the middle grip of the line and move it to a new location. If you wish to move a circle or ellipse, pick the grip at the very center of the object. Only one grip appears on text objects when text is left-justified. This grip corresponds to the text insertion point at the lower left of the text string. Pick this grip to move the text. For the other text justification options, a grip appears at the lower left of the text string, as well as at the text insertion point for the specified justification mode. Either grip can be used to move the text.

Figure 10-39.
Stretching with grips.

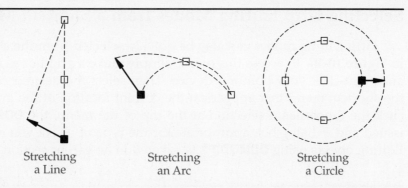

Stretching
a Line

Stretching
an Arc

Stretching
a Circle

PROFESSIONAL TIP

More than one grip can be hot at a time. This is particularly useful when you stretch using grips. To make more than one grip hot, press and hold the [Shift] key while picking other warm grips. Once all of the required grips are selected, release the [Shift] key and pick the grip that represents the desired basepoint.

Other Grip Editing Modes

You can also use the **MOVE, ROTATE, SCALE,** and **MIRROR** functions on grips. If you successively press [Enter] when you see **STRETCH** appear on the command line, you can cycle through each of the other available grip editing modes. These modes appear as follows:

MOVE
⟨Move to point⟩/Base point/Copy/Undo/eXit:

ROTATE
⟨Rotation angle⟩/Base point/Copy/Undo/Reference/eXit:

SCALE
⟨Scale factor⟩/Base point/Copy/Undo/Reference/eXit:

MIRROR
⟨Second point⟩/Base point/Copy/Undo/eXit:

As an alternative to pressing [Enter] to cycle through each of the grip editing modes, you may enter the first two characters of the desired command from the keyboard as follows: MO for **MOVE**, RO for **ROTATE**, SC for **SCALE**, MI for **MIRROR**, and ST for **STRETCH**.

The **Base point, Copy,** and **Undo** options work identically for all the grip editing modes. The **Reference** options appear only for the **ROTATE** and **SCALE** modes, and are identical to the **ROTATE** and **SCALE** command **Reference** options described earlier in this chapter.

When mirroring with grips, the hot grip automatically becomes the first point of the mirror line. Use the **Copy** option if you want to retain the original object.

Selecting Grip Editing Modes from a Shortcut Menu

Grip editing modes can also be quickly selected from the shortcut menu shown in **Figure 10-40**. To access this menu, simply make a grip hot as previously described and right-click your pointing device. Then select the desired editing function from the shortcut menu that appears at the current location of the graphics cursor. If you click the **Properties...** selection at the top of the menu, the **DDMODIFY** command is issued and a dialog box appropriate for the type of object you selected is displayed. Editing objects using **DDMODIFY** is covered in an earlier section of this chapter.

Figure 10-40.
Grip editing modes can also be selected from a shortcut menu.

EXERCISE 10-13

❑ Make a drawing similar to that shown in **Figure 10-39.**
❑ Use grips to stretch the line and arc endpoints to new locations.
❑ Use a grip to move the circle to a different origin.
❑ Draw one or more simple objects of your choice. Experiment with the other grip editing modes, as well.
❑ Do not save the drawing when you are finished.

Chapter Test

Write your answers in the spaces provided.

1. What are cutting edges? What are boundary edges? _____
   _____
   _____
   _____

2. What is the purpose of the **BREAK** command? _____
   _____
   _____
   _____

3. When using the **MOVE** or **COPY** commands, what is meant by *basepoint*? _____
   _____
   _____

4. Give the command and entries required to move an object 5 units to the right and 2 units straight up *without using a basepoint.*

Command: _____

Select objects: _____

Select objects: _____

Base point or displacement: _____

Second point of displacement: _____

5. What is the purpose of the **ROTATE** command's **Reference** option? How is it used?

_____

_____

_____

6. Give the command and entries required to reduce the size of an object by 1/4th.

Command: _____

Select objects: _____

Select objects: _____

Base point: _____

⟨Scale factor⟩/Reference: _____

7. Which two selection set options are valid with the **STRETCH** command? _____

_____

_____

8. Why is it a good idea to turn **Ortho** on before stretching?_____

_____

_____

_____

9. A stretch operation has just been performed on an object. Instead of stretching, however, the object has moved to a new location. Why did this occur?

_____

_____

_____

10. What happens when more than one line is selected using the **CHANGE** command? _____

_____

_____

11. *True or False?* It is more efficient to erase and redraw a circle rather than change its size. _____

12. How many options are offered by the **LENGTHEN** command? Briefly describe them.

_____

_____

_____

_____

_____

13. *True or False?* The **LENGTHEN** command may be used with closed objects, like rectangles and polygons. _____

14. What is the mirror line?_____

_____

_____

15. Name the system variable that controls the mirroring of text and dimensions.

_____

16. Give the command and entries required to make two copies of a selected object.

Command: _____

Select objects: _____

Select objects: _____

⟨Base point or displacement⟩/Multiple: _____

Base point: _____

Second point of displacement: _____

Second point of displacement: _____

Second point of displacement: _____

17. In a rectangular array, what do the rows and columns represent?_____

_____

_____

18. What must you do to create an array that goes down and to the right?_____

_____

_____

19. How does a polar array differ from a rectangular array? _____

_____

_____

_____

20. How do you specify the angle between items when creating a polar array?

21. Describe the differences between a warm grip and a hot grip. _____

_____

_____

_____

_____

22. Identify the six editing operations that may be performed using grips. _____

_____

_____

_____

23. List two ways to access the **Grips** dialog box._____

_____

_____

_____

24. *True or False?* It is not necessary to select grips with an osnap. _____

Chapter Problems

Beginning with this chapter, many of the drawing problems throughout the remainder of this text require the title block format templates created in Chapter 2. If you have not yet created these templates, you should do so now before proceeding.

1. Use your TITLEA template to draw the COVER PLATE shown below. Use the **ARC** and **TRIM** commands to construct the object. Do not draw the centerlines or dimensions. Save the drawing as P10-1.

Mechanical
Drafting

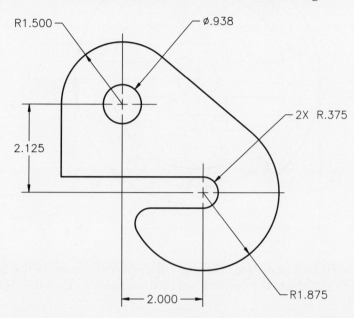

2. Use a polar array to draw the KNOB below using your TITLEA template with the proper layers. Draw the centerlines, but do not draw the dimensions. Save the drawing as P10-2.

Mechanical
Drafting

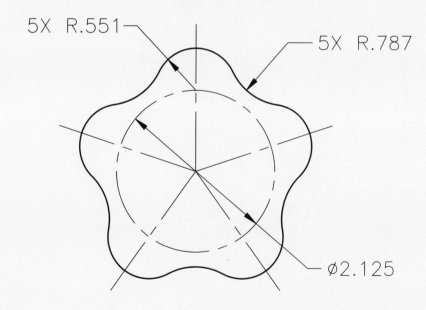

---

3. Draw the object shown using your TITLEB template with the correct layers. Use the **ARRAY** and **MIRROR** commands to aid in the construction. Do not draw the centerlines or dimensions. Save the drawing as P10-3.

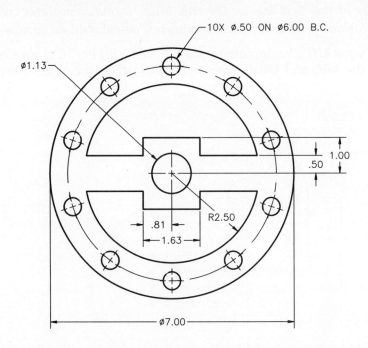

4. Use your TITLEA template with the proper layers to draw the SAW below. Do not draw the centerlines or dimensions. Save the drawing as P10-4.

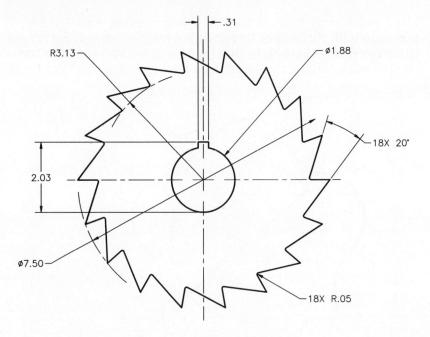

5. Draw the CUP WASHER shown below using your TITLEA template. Be sure to use the proper layers. Use a polar array to speed the construction of the top view. Project points and lines to the bottom view using rays or tracking as described in *Chapter 7*. Do not draw the centerlines or dimensions. Save the drawing as **P10-5**.

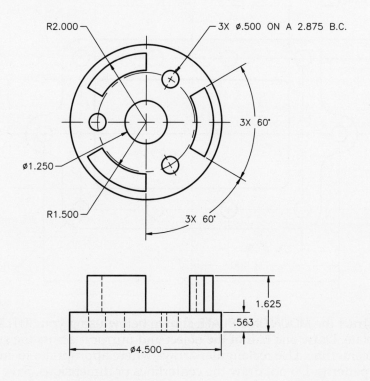

6. Draw the SLOTTED CAM shown below using your TITLEA template. Use the **TRIM** and **ARRAY** commands to your advantage. Do not draw the centerlines or dimensions. Save the drawing as **P10-6**.

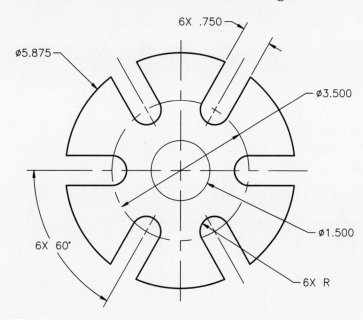

7. Use your TITLEB template drawing to draw the GASKET shown below. Use the **RECTANG** and **ARRAY** commands to help you construct the object. Do not draw the centerlines or dimensions. Save the drawing as P10-7.

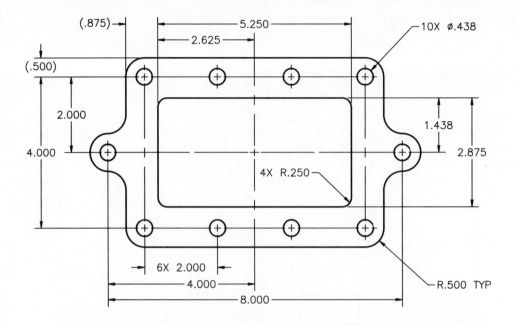

8. Construct the MOUNTING PLATE shown below using your TITLEC template. Draw one half of the object and mirror it across the symmetrical centerline. Use rectangular arrays where appropriate to create the hole patterns. Do not draw the centerlines or dimensions. Save the drawing as P10-8.

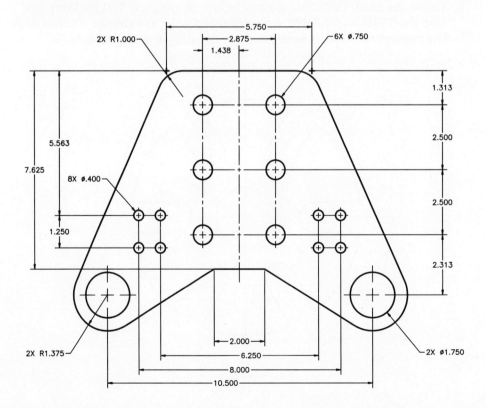

9. Although one of your template files is not required for this problem, use the following guidelines to draw the **CLASSROOM** shown below:

A. Use architectural units.

B. Set the limits to 0',0' and 60',40'.

C. Do not draw the Desk, Chair, and Cabinet details. They are provided for reference purposes so that you may construct the main drawing accurately.

D. Do not draw the dimensions.

Save the drawing as P10-9.

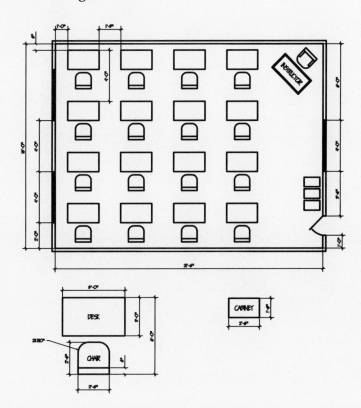

AutoCAD LT—Fundamentals and Applications

Chapter *11*

AutoCAD LT

Editing Polylines and Splines

Learning Objectives

After you have completed this chapter, you will be able to:
- ○ Open the **Modify II** toolbar.
- ○ Perform various polyline editing operations on polylines and splines.

This chapter describes the **PEDIT** and **SPLINEDIT** commands that are used to perform advanced editing operations on polylines and splines. Before continuing, you may wish to open the **Modify II** toolbar that provides quick access to the **Edit Polyline** and **Edit Spline** tool buttons.

Opening the Modify II Toolbar

To open the **Modify II** toolbar, select **Toolbars...** from the **View** pull-down menu. See **Figure 11-1.** When the **Customize** dialog box appears, activate the **Modify II** check box. See **Figure 11-2.** The **Modify II** toolbar is then displayed. Click the **Close** button to exit the **Customize** dialog box.

View
⤷ Toolbars...

> **NOTE**
>
> If you are using AutoCAD LT 97, the **Customize** dialog box is called the **Toolbars** dialog box. See **Figure 11-3A.** Additionally, the AutoCAD LT 97 **Modify II** toolbar shown in **Figure 11-3B** does not feature tool buttons for the **UNION, SUBTRACT,** and **INTERSECT** commands as shown in **Figure 11-2A.**

Polyline Editing

The **PLINE** command was introduced in *Chapter 6.* You may recall that polylines offer capabilities not found in normal line objects. As an example, multiple polyline and polyarc segments created in one operation may be drawn with variable widths and are treated as one object. Polylines may be edited in a variety of ways using the **PEDIT** command.

Figure 11-1.
Select **Toolbars**…
from the **View**
pull-down menu to
display the
Customize
dialog box.

Figure 11-2.
A—Activating the **Modify II** check box. B—The **Modify II** toolbar.

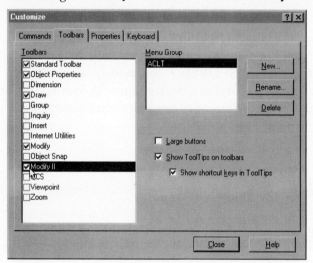

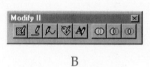

B

A

Figure 11-3.
A—Activating the **Modify II** check box in AutoCAD LT 97. B—The **Modify II** toolbar in
AutoCAD LT 97.

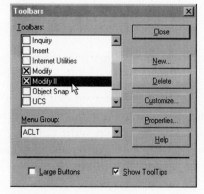

B

A

To issue the **PEDIT** command, enter PEDIT, or PE, at the Command: prompt, click the **Edit Polyline** button in the **Modify II** toolbar, or select **Polyline** from the **Object** ⟩ cascading submenu in the **Modify** pull-down menu. See **Figure 11-4.** The command sequence is as follows:

PEDIT
PE

Modify
→ Object
→ Polyline

Modify II
toolbar

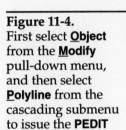

Edit Polyline

> Command: **PEDIT** *or* **PE**↵
> Select polyline: *(select the object)*

If you select a line or an arc, AutoCAD LT informs you that you did not select a polyline. You are then given the option to automatically convert the object to a polyline by simply pressing [Enter].

> Object selected is not a polyline
> Do you want to turn it into one? ⟨Y⟩ ↵
> Close/Join/Width/Edit Vertex/Fit/Spline/Decurve/Ltype gen/Undo/eXit ⟨X⟩:

Each of the **PEDIT** command options are described in the following sections.

Figure 11-4.
First select **Object** from the **Modify** pull-down menu, and then select **Polyline** from the cascading submenu to issue the **PEDIT** command.

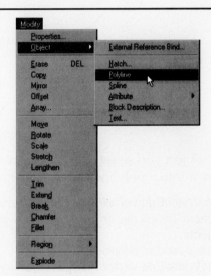

Closing and Opening a Polyline

If the polyline you select is open, then the first **PEDIT** command option is **Close**. This option draws the closing segment of the polyline by connecting the last segment with the first. On the other hand, if the polyline you select is already closed, then the first command option is **Open**. An example of a closed and open polyline is shown in **Figure 11-5.**

Figure 11-5.
The **PEDIT** command can close an open polyline and open a closed one.

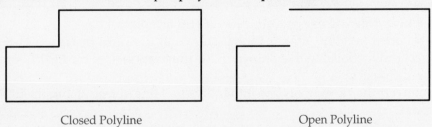

Closed Polyline   Open Polyline

Joining Objects Together into One Polyline

The **PEDIT Join** option allows you to join line, arc, and polyline objects together into one polyline as long as their endpoints touch. See **Figure 11-6.** If a line or polyline crosses the end of a polyline in a T-shape, the objects cannot be joined. Additionally, you cannot join objects to a closed polyline. The **Join** option appears as follows:

Command: **PEDIT** *or* **PE**↵
Select polyline: *(select the object)*

Figure 11-6.
Separate objects can be joined into one polyline using the **PEDIT Join** option.

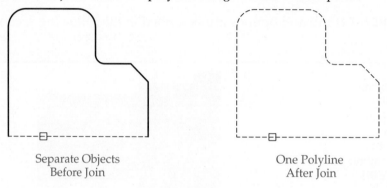

Separate Objects
Before Join

One Polyline
After Join

Remember if the object you select is a line or an arc, you are then prompted to automatically convert it into a polyline.

Close/Join/Width/Edit Vertex/Fit/Spline/Decurve/Ltype gen/Undo/eXit ⟨X⟩: **J**↵
Select objects: *(select one or more objects to join together)*
Select objects: ↵
n segments added to polyline
Close/Join/Width/Edit Vertex/Fit/Spline/Decurve/Ltype gen/Undo/eXit ⟨X⟩: ↵
Command:

PROFESSIONAL TIP
The **PEDIT Join** option is particularly handy when you have a shape drawn with lines and would like to fillet or chamfer each vertex of the object in one operation. Once the objects are joined together into a polyline, use the **Polyline** option of the **FILLET** or **CHAMFER** commands to modify all contiguous vertices in one step.

EXERCISE 11-1

❑ Begin a new drawing using your TEMPLATEB template.
❑ Draw an open polyline similar to that shown at the right in **Figure 11-5.** Make the object proportional to that shown in the illustration. Use the **PEDIT** command to close the object.
❑ Next, convert the closed polyline into individual line objects using the **EXPLODE** command.
❑ Now, use the **PEDIT Join** option to join the objects back into a closed polyline.
❑ Save the drawing as EX11-1.

Changing the Width of a Polyline

Use the **PEDIT Width** option to add a width or specify a new width for an existing polyline. As shown in **Figure 11-7,** the width you specify is uniform over the entire length of the polyline. The **Width** option looks like this:

Command: **PEDIT** *or* **PE**↵
Select polyline: *(select the polyline)*
Close/Join/Width/Edit Vertex/Fit/Spline/Decurve/Ltype gen/Undo/eXit ⟨X⟩: **W**↵
Enter new width for all segments: *(enter a positive value)*
Close/Join/Width/Edit Vertex/Fit/Spline/Decurve/Ltype gen/Undo/eXit ⟨X⟩: ↵
Command:

Figure 11-7.
The **PEDIT Width** option is used to add or modify polyline width.

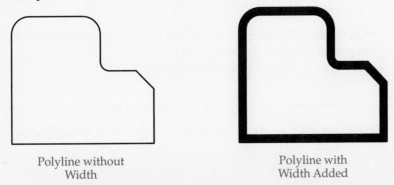

Polyline without
Width

Polyline with
Width Added

EXERCISE 11-2

❏ Open EX11-1 if it is not on your screen.
❏ Use the **PEDIT Width** option to change the width of the object to .25 units, then .125 units, and finally .0625 units.
❏ Save the drawing as EX11-2.

Editing the Vertices of a Polyline

Each vertex of a polyline may be individually modified using the **PEDIT Edit Vertex** option. When this option is selected, AutoCAD LT places a marker shaped like an X at the first vertex of the selected polyline. You then move the marker to the vertex you wish to edit using the **Next** (for next vertex) and **Previous** (for previous vertex) suboptions. The **PEDIT Edit Vertex** option appears as follows:

Command: **PEDIT** *or* **PE**↵
Select polyline: *(select the polyline)*
Close/Join/Width/Edit Vertex/Fit/Spline/Decurve/Ltype gen/Undo/eXit ⟨X⟩: **E**↵
Next/Previous/Break/Insert/Move/Regen/Straighten/Tangent/Width/eXit ⟨N⟩:

Each of the **Edit Vertex** suboptions are described below:
- **Next/Previous.** As mentioned above, use these suboptions to move the X shaped marker forward or backward to the vertex you wish to edit. The **Next** suboption is the default.

- **Break.** Use this suboption to remove one or more segments from a polyline. See **Figure 11-8.** The break is performed between the first selected vertex and the last selected vertex as marked by the **Next** and **Previous** suboptions. Once you have identified the last vertex, use the **Go** suboption to effect the break. The **Break** suboption looks like this:

  Next/Previous/Break/Insert/Move/Regen/Straighten/Tangent/Width/eXit ⟨N⟩: **B.**↵
  Next/Previous/Go/eXit ⟨N⟩:

- **Insert.** This suboption allows you to insert a new vertex at a selected location after the vertex that is currently marked with the X. See **Figure 11-9.** The **Insert** suboption appears as follows:

  Next/Previous/Break/Insert/Move/Regen/Straighten/Tangent/Width/eXit ⟨N⟩: **I.**↵
  Enter location of new vertex: *(locate a point)*

- **Move.** Use this suboption to move an X marked vertex to a new screen location. See **Figure 11-10.**

  Next/Previous/Break/Insert/Move/Regen/Straighten/Tangent/Width/eXit ⟨N⟩: **M.**↵
  Enter new location: *(locate a point)*

Figure 11-8.
The **Edit Vertex Break** suboption removes one or more segments from a polyline.

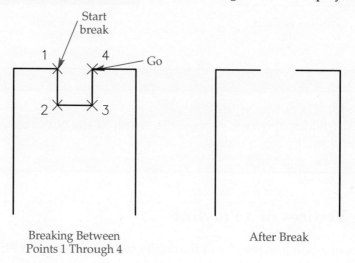

Breaking Between   After Break
Points 1 Through 4

Figure 11-9.
Using the **Edit Vertex Insert** suboption to add a new vertex.

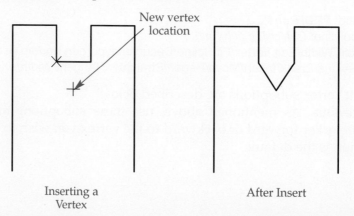

Inserting a   After Insert
Vertex

- **Regen.** After using the **Edit Vertex Width** suboption, **Regen** is used to display the changes. The **Width** suboption is described in a later section.
- **Straighten.** This suboption is used to straighten both polyline and polyarc segments between selected vertices. See **Figure 11-11.** The straightening is performed between the first selected vertex and the last selected vertex as marked by the **Next** and **Previous** suboptions. Once you have identified the last vertex, use the **Go** suboption to straighten the polyline. The **Straighten** suboption looks like this:

> Next/Previous/Break/Insert/Move/Regen/Straighten/Tangent/Width/eXit ⟨N⟩: **S**↵
> Next/Previous/Go/eXit ⟨N⟩:

- **Tangent.** The **Tangent** suboption is used to change the tangent direction of a polyline vertex when curve fitting has been used. Curve fitting is described in a later section.

Figure 11-10.
The **Edit Vertex Move** suboption is used to move an existing vertex.

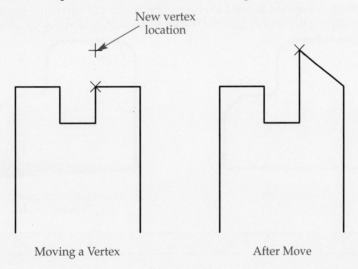

Moving a Vertex   After Move

Figure 11-11.
The **Edit Vertex Straighten** suboption may be used to straighten both polyline and polyarc segments.

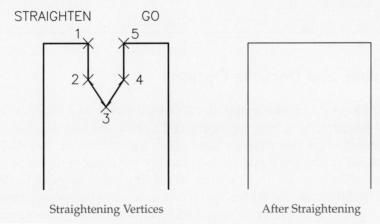

Straightening Vertices   After Straightening

- **Width.** This suboption allows you to change the width of individual segments within a polyline. The polyline segment that immediately follows the X marked vertex is the segment whose width is changed. As shown in **Figure 11-12,** the segment width may be uniform or tapered. After changing the width, use the **Regen** suboption as previously described to display the change. In the following example, a starting width of 0 and an ending width of .25 is specified to produce a tapered polyline segment. The **Regen** suboption is then used to display the new width.

> Next/Previous/Break/Insert/Move/Regen/Straighten/Tangent/Width/eXit ⟨N⟩: **W.**↵
> Enter starting width ⟨*current*⟩: **0.**↵
> Enter ending width ⟨0.0000⟩: **.25.**↵
> Next/Previous/Break/Insert/Move/Regen/Straighten/Tangent/Width/eXit ⟨N⟩: **R.**↵

- **eXit.** Once you are finished editing the polyline vertices, press X for exit to end the operation. You are then returned to the **PEDIT** command options.

Figure 11-12.
The **Edit Vertex Width** suboption is used to change the width of individual segments within a polyline. After changing the width, use the **Regen** suboption to display the change.

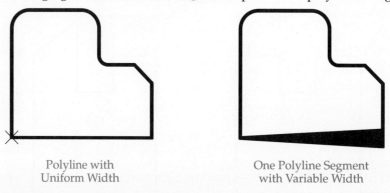

Polyline with
Uniform Width

One Polyline Segment
with Variable Width

EXERCISE 11-3

❑ Begin a new drawing using your TEMPLATEA template.
❑ Draw a polyline object similar to that shown in **Figure 11-8.** Do not be concerned with dimensions.
❑ Try each of the **Edit Vertex** suboptions on the object as described and illustrated in the preceding sections.
❑ Do not save the drawing when you are finished.

The Fit, Spline, and Decurve Options

The **PEDIT Fit** option creates a smooth curve by converting a polyline from straight line segments into arcs. As shown in **Figure 11-13,** there are two arcs for every pair of vertices. Observe that the curve passes through all the vertices of the polyline. Use the **Edit Vertex Tangent** suboption if you wish to modify the tangent direction of the arcs.

It is also possible to create a spline from an existing polyline using the **PEDIT Spline** option. Unlike the **Fit** option, the **Spline** option creates a curve that passes through the first and last control points only. The curve is pulled toward the other control points but does not always pass through them. The more control points on the polyline, the more pull they exert on the curve. This type of curve is called a *B-spline* (for *Bezier spline*) and it produces a much smoother curve than that produced by the **Fit** option. Use the **PEDIT Decurve** option when you want to remove the curve or spline applied to a polyline.

Figure 11-13.
The **PEDIT Fit** option is applied to a polyline.

Polyline Before Fit

Polyline After Fit

PROFESSIONAL TIP

Use the **Fit** and **Spline** options to create wiring, cabling, and other types of curved objects. **Fit** and **Spline** can also be used to draw short break lines.

System Variables that Control B-Splines

You can control the type of spline created by AutoCAD LT using the **SPLINETYPE** system variable. When **SPLINETYPE** is set to 5, a quadratic B-spline is generated. Setting **SPLINETYPE** to 6 (the default value) creates a cubic B-spline.

```
Command: SPLINETYPE.⏎
New value for SPLINETYPE ⟨6⟩: (enter a 5 or 6 and press [Enter])
Command:
```

The two spline types are illustrated in **Figure 11-14.**

Figure 11-14.
AutoCAD LT creates a quadratic or cubic spline based on the setting of the **SPLINETYPE** system variable.

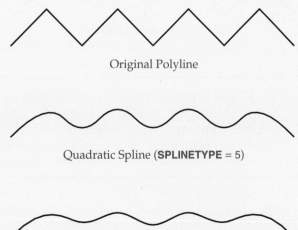

Original Polyline

Quadratic Spline (**SPLINETYPE** = 5)

Cubic Spline (**SPLINETYPE** = 6)

The **SPLFRAME** and **SPLINESEGS** System Variables

When a spline is applied to a polyline, AutoCAD LT remembers the original polyline *frame* so that it can be restored when you use the **Decurve** option. Normally, the spline frames are not displayed on screen. If you want to see them, use the **SPLFRAME** variable as follows at the Command: prompt:

Command: **SPLFRAME**↵
New value for SPLFRAME ⟨0⟩: **1**↵
Command:

After the next screen regeneration, the spline frames are displayed. See **Figure 11-15.** Finally, you can change the fineness or coarseness of displayed splines by using the **SPLINESEGS** variable as follows on the command line:

Command: **SPLINESEGS**↵
New value for SPLINESEGS ⟨8⟩: *(enter a higher or lower value as desired)*
Command:

After changing the **SPLINESEGS** value, use the **PEDIT Spline** option to respline an existing curve to the new setting. Although a higher value draws more line segments and produces a more precise spline approximation, keep in mind the new spline takes up more space in the drawing file and takes longer to redraw and regenerate.

Figure 11-15.
Spline frames are shown when **SPLFRAME** is enabled.

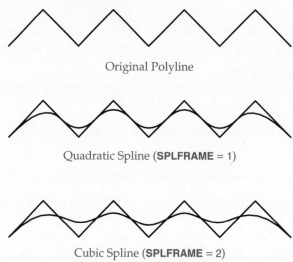

Original Polyline

Quadratic Spline (**SPLFRAME** = 1)

Cubic Spline (**SPLFRAME** = 2)

NOTE If you wish to convert a spline fitted polyline to a true spline object, you can do so using the **Object** option of the **SPLINE** command. This option is not valid if the **PEDIT Fit** option has been applied to a polyline, however. See *Chapter 6* for more information on the **SPLINE** command.

The PEDIT Ltype gen Option

When **Ltype gen** is turned off (the default), linetype generation is performed so that dashes start and stop at each vertex of an object. This is in accordance with good drafting practice. When **Ltype gen** is turned on, linetypes are drawn in a continous pattern through polylines, disregarding the vertices. An example of **Ltype gen** turned on and off is shown in **Figure 11-16.** In the unlikely event that you need to enable **Ltype gen**, there are several ways to do so. They are listed below:

- Use the **PEDIT Ltype gen** option as follows:

> Command: **PEDIT** *or* **PE**↵
> Select polyline: *(select the polyline)*
> Close/Join/Width/Edit Vertex/Fit/Spline/Decurve/Ltype gen/Undo/eXit ⟨X⟩: **L**↵
> Full PLINE linetype ON/OFF ⟨Off⟩: **ON**↵

Or,

- Use the **PLINEGEN** system variable at the Command: prompt as follows:

> Command: **PLINEGEN**↵
> New value for PLINEGEN ⟨0⟩: **1**↵
> Command:

Remember that linetype generation affects polyline objects only. These include polygons and rectangles. Tapered polylines are not affected.

Figure 11-16.
An example of several polylines with **Ltype gen** on and off. Observe the dashes at the vertices of each polyline. The default in AutoCAD LT is to have **Ltype gen** turned off.

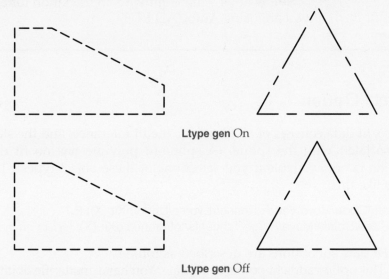

Ltype gen On

Ltype gen Off

EXERCISE 11-4

❏ Draw a polyline similar to that shown at the top in **Figure 11-13.** Use **DDMODIFY** to change it to a curve, then a cubic B-spline, and finally a quadratic B-spline.
❏ Make a copy of the spline fitted polyline.
❏ Next, use the **Object** option of the **SPLINE** command to convert the copy of the polyline to a true spline.
❏ Use the **LIST** command on both objects and compare the output returned by AutoCAD LT.
❏ It is not necessary to save the drawing when you are through.

Editing Splines

You can edit splines created with **SPLINE** as well as spline-fit polylines created with **PEDIT** using the **SPLINEDIT** command. With it, you can fit data to a selected spline, close an open spline, open a closed spline, move spline vertices, refine, or reverse a spline.

To issue the **SPLINEDIT** command, enter SPLINEDIT, or SPE, at the Command: prompt, click the **Edit Spline** button in the **Modify II** toolbar, or select **Object** from the **Modify** pull-down menu, and then select **Spline** from the cascading submenu.

SPLINEDIT
SPE

Modify
➥ Object
➥ Spline

Modify II
toolbar

Edit Spine

> **NOTE**   Refer to the beginning of this chapter to review how to enable the **Modify II** toolbar.

The **SPLINEDIT** command sequence is as follows:

> Command: **SPLINEDIT** or **SPE.**↵
> Select spline: *(select a spline)*
> Fit Data/Close/Move Vertex/Refine/rEverse/Undo/eXit ⟨X⟩:

Grips automatically appear at the control points when you select a spline or spline-fit polyline. Each of the **SPLINEDIT** command options are described in the following sections.

> **NOTE** SPE is not a valid command abbreviation for **SPLINEDIT** if you are using AutoCAD LT 97.

The Fit Data Option

A spline's fit data consists of all fit points, the fit tolerance, and the start and end tangents associated with the spline. (A spline-fit polyline has no fit data, so the **Fit Data** option is not available if you select one of these object types.) The **Fit Data** option looks like this:

> Fit Data/Close/Move Vertex/Refine/rEverse/Undo/eXit ⟨X⟩: **F**↵
> Add/Close/Delete/Move/Purge/Tangents/toLerance/eXit ⟨X⟩: *(select an option)*

Each of the **Fit Data** suboptions are described as follows:

- **Add.** This option adds fit points to a spline. You have greater flexibility in editing a spline's definition when more control points exist. You are prompted with:

  > Select point: *(select a fit point)*
  > Enter new point: *(specify a point)*
  > Enter new point: *(specify another point or press [Enter])*

  When you select a point, it and the next point along the spline are highlighted. AutoCAD LT adds the new point between the highlighted points. Use the **Undo** option to remove the last point added. Selecting the last point on an open spline highlights only that point, and the new point is added after the last point.

If the spline you select is open, you have the option of placing a new point before or after the first point on the open spline. The prompt appears as follows:

> After/⟨Before⟩ ⟨Enter new point⟩: *(specify a point, enter an option, or press* [Enter]*)*

Whether the spline you select is open or closed, AutoCAD LT adds the point and refits the spline through the new set of points.

- **Close.** This suboption closes an open spline by connecting the last segment of the spline with the first. On the other hand, if the spline you select is already closed, then this option appears as **Open**. See **Figure 11-17.**
- **Open.** This suboption opens a closed spline.
- **Delete.** This suboption removes fit points from a spline and refits the spline through the remaining points. See **Figure 11-18.**
- **Move.** Use this suboption to move a fit point to a new location. You are prompted with:

> Next/Previous/Select Point/eXit/⟨Enter new location⟩:⟨N⟩: *(specify a point, enter an option, or press* [Enter]*)*

The default **Next** suboption changes the selected point to be the next point. **Previous** changes the point to the previous point. The **Select Point** suboption lets you select from any of the fit points on the spline. **(Enter new location)** moves the selected point when you specify a point. When you are finished, enter X for exit to return to the main prompt of the **SPLINEDIT** command. An example of a moved fit point appears in **Figure 11-19.**

- **Purge.** Choose this suboption with caution since it removes a spline's fit data from the drawing database. After purging the spline's fit data, the **SPLINEDIT** main prompt is displayed without the **Fit Data** option.

Figure 11-17.
A—An open spline.
B—A closed spline.

A

B

Figure 11-18.
A—The original spline and fit points.
B—A fit point is selected for deletion. C—The revised spline.

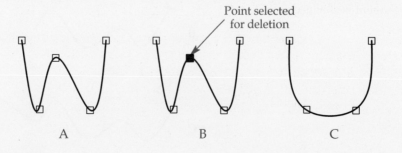

Point selected for deletion

A   B   C

- **Tangents.** Use this suboption to edit the start and end tangents of a spline. You are prompted with:

  System Default/⟨Enter start tangent⟩: *(specify a point, enter an option, or press [Enter])*
  System Default/⟨Enter end tangent⟩: *(specify a point, enter an option, or press [Enter])*

  The **(Enter start tangent)** option changes to **(Enter tangent)** if the spline you select is closed. The **System Default** option calculates the default tangents at the ends of the spline. See **Figure 11-20.** You can specify new points or use **Tangent** or **Perpendicular** osnaps to make the spline tangential or perpendicular existing objects.

- **toLerance.** This suboption refits the spline to the existing fit points with new tolerance values. You are prompted with:

  Enter fit tolerance ⟨*current*⟩: *(enter a value)*

- **eXit.** Returns to the main prompt of the **SPLINEDIT** command.

Figure 11-19.
A—The original spline and fit points. B—A fit point is selected. C—The revised spline. Note the new location of the fit point.

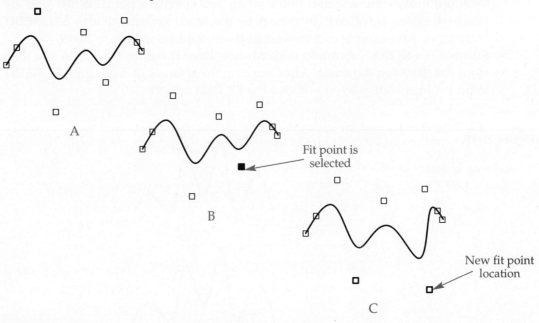

Figure 11-20.
A—The original spline. B—The spline's start tangent is changed. C—The spline's end tangent is changed.

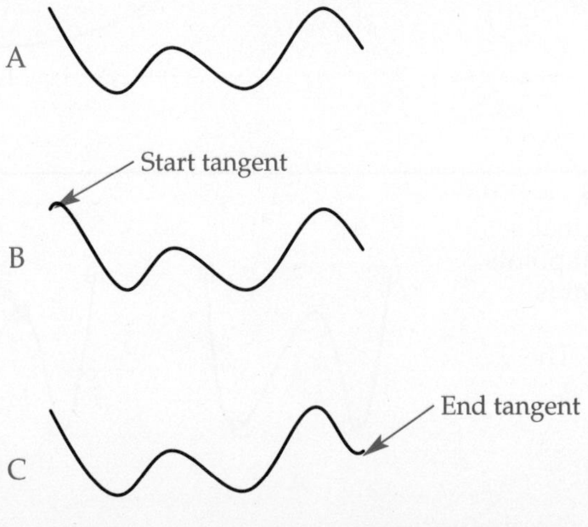

AutoCAD LT—Fundamentals and Applications

CAUTION	Be advised that a spline can lose its fit data if you do any of the following:

- Trim, break, stretch, or lengthen the spline.
- Use the **Purge** suboption while editing fit data.
- Refine the spline by elevating the order, adding a control point, or changing the weight of a control point.
- Change the fit tolerance.
- Move a control point.

Other SPLINEDIT Options

The other options offered by **SPLINEDIT** are described below:
- **Close.** The **Close** option closes an open spline by connecting the last segment of the spline with the first. On the other hand, if the spline you select is already closed, then this option appears as **Open**. See **Figure 11-17.**
- **Open.** Opens a closed spline.
- **Move Vertex.** This option relocates the control vertices of a spline. Its options are identical to those displayed by the **Fit Data Move** suboption previously described. See **Figure 11-18.** You are prompted with:

> Next/Previous/Select Point/eXit/⟨Enter new location⟩:⟨N⟩: *(specify a point, enter an option, or press* [Enter]*)*

- **Refine.** The **SPLINEDIT Refine** option is used to *tweak* a spline definition. It allows you to add more control points, elevate the order of the spline, or add weight to the existing spline points. The **Refine** option looks like this:

> Fit Data/Close/Move Vertex/Refine/rEverse/Undo/eXit ⟨X⟩: **R↵**
> Add control point/Elevate Order/Weight/eXit ⟨X⟩: *(select an option)*

Each of the **Refine** suboptions are described as follows:
- **Add Control Point**—Increases the number of points that control a portion of a spline. The new control point is added close to the location you select between two existing control points. You are prompted:

> Select a point on the spline: *(select a point)*

- **Elevate Order**—Increases the order of the spline by uniformly increasing the number of control points across the spline. See **Figure 11-21.** You are prompted with:

> Enter new order ⟨*current*⟩: *(enter an integer value between 4 and 26)*

Figure 11-21.
A—Original spline with an order of 4.
B—The spline order elevated to a value of 6.

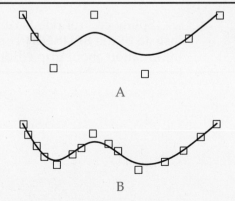

- **Weight**—This option changes the weight of a selected spline control point. A larger value pulls the spline closer to the control point. You are prompted with the following:

  Next/Previous/Select Point/eXit/⟨Enter new weight⟩ ⟨*current*⟩ ⟨N⟩: *(enter an integer, select an option, or press* [Enter]*)*

  The default **Next** suboption changes the selected point to be the next point. **Previous** changes the point to the previous point. The **Select Point** suboption lets you select from any of the points on the spline. **Enter new weight** recalculates the spline based on the new weight value at the selected control point. The larger the value, the more the spline is pulled toward the control point. When you are finished, enter X for exit to return to the main prompt of the **Refine** option. The example shown in **Figure 11-22** displays the results when a weight of 6 is applied to a selected spline point.
- **rEverse.** This option reverses the direction of a spline and is intended primarily for third-party applications that are added to AutoCAD LT.
- **Undo.** Cancels the last **SPLINEDIT** operation.
- **eXit.** Enter X to end the command and return to the Command: prompt.

Figure 11-22.
A—The original spline and fit points. B—A fit point is selected. C—A weight of 6 is applied to the spline point. Observe how the spline is pulled toward the weighted point.

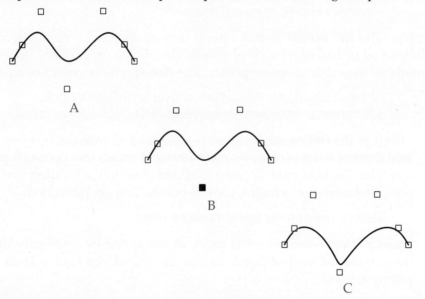

PROFESSIONAL TIP
Spline control points can be quickly moved using grips instead of the **SPLINEDIT** command. See *Chapter 10* for more information about grip editing.

Chapter Test

Write your answers in the spaces provided.

1. What is the purpose of the **PEDIT Join** option?_____
    _____
    _____

2. Which **Edit Vertex** suboption allows you to remove one or more segments from a polyline? _____
    _____

3. Which **Edit Vertex** suboption allows you to add a segment to a polyline?_____

4. What must you do after changing the starting and ending width of a polyline segment? _____
    _____
    _____

5. Describe the difference between the **PEDIT Fit** and **Spline** options._____
    _____
    _____
    _____
    _____
    _____

6. What must you do to create a quadratic B-spline?_____
    _____
    _____

7. *True or False?* The **SPLINEDIT Fit Data** option can be used with spline-fit polylines.
    _____

8. Why would you add more control points to a spline? _____
    _____
    _____

9. What happens when you change the weight of a control point?_____
    _____
    _____

10. Why should you use caution with the **Purge** suboption? _____
    _____
    _____

Chapter Problems

Mechanical Drafting

1. Begin a new drawing using the TEMPLATEA template. Draw the object shown using a polyline with a polyarc in one operation. Do not be concerned with dimensions. Save the drawing as P11-1.

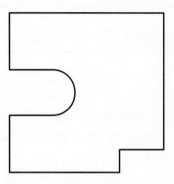

Mechanical Drafting

2. Open P11-1. Use the **Edit vertex** option of the **PEDIT** command to produce the new shape shown. Apply a uniform width of 1/32 to the polyline. Save the drawing as P11-2.

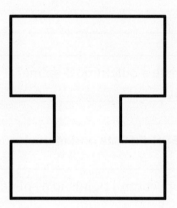

AutoCAD LT—Fundamentals and Applications

3. Begin a new drawing using the TEMPLATEA template. Draw the three arrowheads at the left with polyarcs using the following values:

General

Arrow body start: 3/16

Arrow body end: 1/16

Arrowhead start: 1/2

Arrowhead end: 0

Make a copy of the three arrowheads and place the copy to the right of the original objects. Use the **Edit vertex** option of the **PEDIT** command to change the polyarc values as follows:

Arrow body start: 3/8

Arrow body end: 1/8

Arrowhead start: 3/4

Arrowhead end: 0

Save the drawing as P11-3.

4. Begin a new drawing using the TEMPLATEC template. Construct the four preliminary swimming pool designs using splines. Start at the upper left with a single closed spline. Copy the object as required, and use **SPLINEDIT** to complete the other three designs. Add new fit points and apply weights if necessary. Draw the objects to appear proportional to those shown in the text. Save the drawing as P11-4.

General

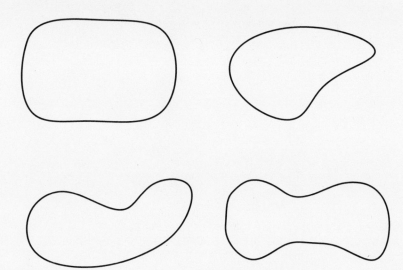

5. Begin a new drawing using the TEMPLATEB template. Draw the objects on the correct layers with the dimensions shown. Do not draw the dimensions. Use a polyline to create the break lines on the top object. Use splines for the break lines on the remaining two objects. Use **SPLINEDIT** where necessary on the bottom object. Save the drawing as P11-5.

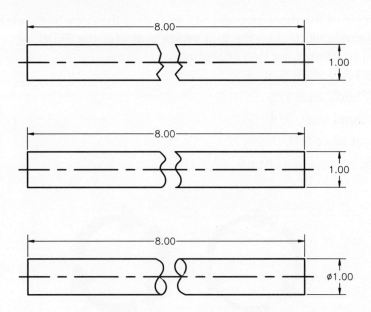

AutoCAD LT

Dimensioning the Drawing

Learning Objectives

After you have completed this chapter, you will be able to:
- O Add linear, angular, radial, and ordinate dimensions to your drawings.
- O Use dimension variables to control the appearance and format of dimensions.
- O Create center lines through arcs and circles.
- O Use leaders to place feature callouts.
- O Modify existing dimensions.
- O Construct feature control frames and datum symbols.
- O Create and use dimension styles.

Drawing dimensions convey feature size and location and may well be the most important aspect of any engineering or architectural drawing. AutoCAD LT provides a variety of dimensioning commands and options that enable you to quickly and accurately place dimensions on your drawings. This chapter describes each of these functions as well as the dimension variables that control the appearance and format of dimensions. Additionally, you will learn how to edit existing dimensions and create your own dimension styles.

Dimensioning Commands

Unlike the first two versions of AutoCAD LT, Release 1 and Release 2, it is no longer necessary to enter dimensioning mode to issue most dimensioning commands. The commands that perform many dimensioning and dimension editing functions can now be issued at the Command: prompt. Each of these commands starts with the letters *DIM*.

However, it is still possible, and sometimes necessary, to enter dimensioning mode. The procedure looks like this:

> Command: **DIM**⏎
> Dim:

The Dim: prompt indicates that dimensioning mode is active and most of the available dimensioning commands and all of the dimension variables may now be issued. Once you enter dimensioning mode, the mode remains active until you return to normal command mode. To exit dimensioning mode and return to the Command: prompt, enter E for exit or press the [Esc] key to cancel dimensioning mode.

NOTE

Commands that work strictly in dimensioning mode are listed at the end of this chapter. Entering D invokes the DDIM command, which is described later in this chapter. If you are using AutoCAD LT 97, the single letter D can also be typed to enter dimensioning mode.

As an alternative to keyboard entry, the dimensioning commands can also be accessed through the **Dimension** pull-down menu, or the **Dimensioning** toolbar. See **Figure 12-1.** To use the toolbar, first select **Toolbars...** from the **View** pull-down menu. When the **Customize** dialog box appears, activate the **Dimension** check box and click the **Close** button. If you are using AutoCAD LT 97, this dialog box is labeled **Toolbars**. The **Dimension** toolbar is then displayed on the screen. You may move the toolbar to either a floating or docked position as described in *Chapter 1* of this text. As with other toolbars, the **Dimension** toolbar position is automatically saved for future drawing sessions.

Figure 12-1.
A—The dimensioning commands may be accessed from the **Dimension** pull-down menu.
B—Once activated, the **Dimension** toolbar can also be used to issue dimensioning commands.

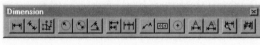

B

A

Introduction to Dimension Variables

The appearance and format of AutoCAD LT dimensions is controlled through the use of dimension variables, or *dimvars*. Each of the dimvars begins with the three letters *DIM*. The remaining letters are a code that describes the purpose of the variable. You can change the variables at the Command: prompt, the Dim: prompt, or in the **Dimension Styles** dialog box using the **DDIM** command. At the Dim: prompt, you can save yourself some typing and enter the dimension variable name by its last three or four letters. This convention is shown in the examples throughout this chapter where appropriate.

NOTE

Remember that the shortened versions of the dimension variable names can only be used at the Dim: prompt—not the Command: prompt. Additionally, you may notice some slight differences in the dimvar prompts when entering the variable names at the Command: prompt. Regardless of the method you choose to access a dimension variable, the variable functions in a consistent manner.

To check the current status of the dimensioning variables at any time while in dimensioning mode, enter the following dimensioning command at the Dim: prompt.

Dim: **STATUS** *or* **STA**⏎

The graphics window automatically flips to the text window and all the dimvars and their respective values are displayed in a format similar to that shown below and on the next page. From the list, you can see that some dimvars contain numeric values while others are listed as on or off. You can turn a dimvar on by entering **ON** or the numeral **1**. Turn a dimvar off by entering **OFF** or a **0** (zero). Observe also that several of the dimvars show no values at all. These dimvars are set with user-specified characters.

DIMALT	Off	Alternate units selected
DIMALTD	2	Alternate unit decimal places
DIMALTF	25.4000	Alternate unit scale factor
DIMALTTD	2	Alternate tolerance decimal places
DIMALTTZ	0	Alternate tolerance zero suppression
DIMALTU	2	Alternate units
DIMALTZ	0	Alternate unit zero suppression
DIMAPOST		Prefix and suffix for alternate text
DIMASO	On	Create associative dimensions
DIMASZ	0.1800	Arrow size
DIMAUNIT	0	Angular unit format
DIMBLK		Arrow block name
DIMBLK1		First arrow block name
DIMBLK2		Second arrow block name
DIMCEN	0.0900	Center mark size
DIMCLRD	BYBLOCK	Dimension line and leader color
DIMCLRE	BYBLOCK	Extension line color
DIMCLRT	BYBLOCK	Dimension text color
DIMDEC	4	Decimal places
DIMDLE	0.0000	Dimension line extension
DIMDLI	0.3800	Dimension line spacing
DIMEXE	0.1800	Extension above dimension line
DIMEXO	0.0625	Extension line origin offset
DIMFIT	3	Fit text
DIMGAP	0.0900	Gap from dimension line to text
DIMJUST	0	Justification of text on dimension line
DIMLFAC	1.0000	Linear unit scale factor
DIMLIM	Off	Generate dimension limits
DIMPOST		Prefix and suffix for dimension text
DIMRND	0.0000	Rounding value
DIMSAH	Off	Separate arrow blocks
DIMSCALE	1.0000	Overall scale factor
DIMSD1	Off	Suppress the first dimension line
DIMSD2	Off	Suppress the second dimension line
DIMSE1	Off	Suppress the first extension line
DIMSE2	Off	Suppress the second extension line
DIMSHO	On	Update dimensions while dragging
DIMSOXD	Off	Suppress outside dimension lines
DIMSTYLE	STANDARD	Current dimension style (read-only)
DIMTAD	0	Place text above the dimension line
DIMTDEC	4	Tolerance decimal places
DIMTFAC	1.0000	Tolerance text height scaling factor
DIMTIH	On	Text inside extensions is horizontal
DIMTIX	Off	Place text inside extensions
DIMTM	0.0000	Minus tolerance
DIMTOFL	Off	Force line inside extension lines
DIMTOH	On	Text outside horizontal

DIMTOL	Off	Tolerance dimensioning
DIMTOLJ	1	Tolerance vertical justification
DIMTP	0.0000	Plus tolerance
DIMTSZ	0.0000	Tick size
DIMTVP	0.0000	Text vertical position
DIMTXSTY	STANDARD	Text style
DIMTXT	0.1800	Text height
DIMTZIN	0	Tolerance zero suppression
DIMUNIT	2	Unit format
DIMUPT	Off	User positioned text
DIMZIN	0	Zero suppression

When you are done checking the current dimvar status, press [F2] to return to the graphics window. This chapter describes each of the dimensioning variables in the context for which they are most appropriate. Changing the value of a dimvar from the Dim: prompt or using the **Dimension Styles** dialog box is also presented.

PROFESSIONAL TIP   The dimension variables can be set to comply with mechanical, architectural, or civil engineering drafting standards. Set the variables appropriately for your application in your template(s) so that they are always ready for use.

Getting Started Guide 12

DIMUNIT UNIT

Dimension
➥ Style...
or
Format
➥ Dimension
Style...

Dimension
toolbar

Dimension Style

Dimension Units

The **DIMUNIT** variable determines the system of units used by AutoCAD LT for linear and radial dimensioning. This variable can be set using the **Dimension Styles** dialog box. To do so, click the **Dimension Style** button in the **Dimension** toolbar, or select **Style...** from the **Dimension** pull-down menu. You can also select **Dimension Style...** from the **Format** pull-down menu to open this dialog box. See **Figure 12-2.**

Once the **Dimension Styles** dialog box is displayed, click the **Annotation...** button as shown in **Figure 12-3.** When the **Annotation** subdialog box appears, click the **Units...** button. This activates the **Primary Units** subdialog box as shown in **Figure 12-4.** You may now select the desired system of units from the **Units** drop-down list. When you are through, click the **OK** button to exit. Click **OK** again to exit the **Annotation** dialog box, and then click **OK** a third time to exit the **Dimension Styles** dialog box. From the command line, the **DIMUNIT** variable may be set as follows:

Dim: **DIMUNIT** *or* **UNIT.**⏎
Current value ⟨*current*⟩ New value: *(enter a value between* 1 *and* 8*)*
Dim:

The **DIMUNIT** values represent the following systems of units:
   1 Scientific
   2 Decimal (default)
   3 Engineering
   4 Architectural (stacked)
   5 Fractional (stacked)
   6 Architectural
   7 Fractional

Figure 12-2.
A—Selecting **Style...** from the **Dimension** pull-down menu issues the **DDIM** command and displays the **Dimension Styles** dialog box. B—Selecting **Dimension Style...** from the **Format** pull-down menu also opens the **Dimension Styles** dialog box.

A

B

Figure 12-3.
A—Clicking the **Annotation...** button in the **Dimension Styles** dialog box accesses the **Annotation** subdialog box. B—Clicking the **Units...** button accesses the **Primary Units** subdialog box.

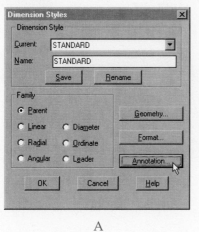

A

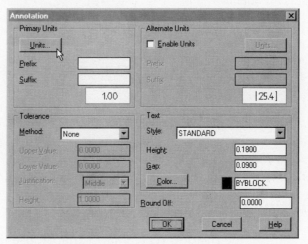

B

Figure 12-4.
The desired system of dimensioning units is set from the **Units** drop-down list in the **Primary Units** subdialog box.

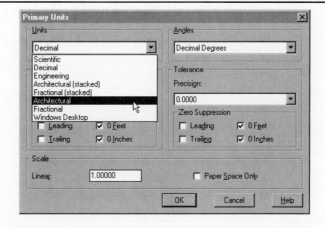

Setting Units for Angular Dimensions

DIMAUNIT
AUNIT

The **DIMAUNIT** (Angular UNIT) variable is used to specify the system of units for angular dimensions. This variable is set using the **Angles** drop-down list in the **Primary Units** dialog box. See **Figure 12-5**. From the command line, the **DIMAUNIT** variable may be set as follows:

> Dim: **DIMAUNIT** *or* **AUNIT**↵
> Current value ⟨*current*⟩ New value: *(enter a value between* 0 *and* 4*)*
> Dim:

The **DIMAUNIT** values represent the following systems of units:

   0 Decimal degrees (default)
   1 Degrees/Minutes/Seconds
   2 Gradians
   3 Radians
   4 Surveyor's units

Figure 12-5.
The desired system of dimensioning units for angular dimensions is set from the **Angles** drop-down list in the **Primary Units** subdialog box.

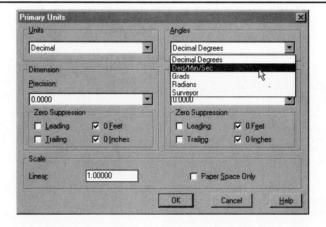

Setting Dimension Precision

DIMDEC
DEC

To set the **DIMDEC** (DECimal) variable, use the **Precision:** drop-down list in the **Primary Units** dialog box. This variable sets the precision of your dimension values. The precision is for display purposes only and is independent of the true accuracy stored in the drawing database. In the example shown in **Figure 12-6**, three decimal places to the right of the decimal point are selected from the drop-down list. From the command line, use the variable as follows:

> Dim: **DIMDEC** *or* **DEC**↵
> Current value ⟨*current*⟩ New value: *(enter a value between* 0 *and* 8*)*
> Dim:

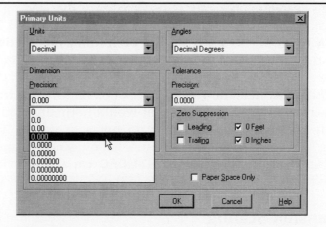

Figure 12-6.
Dimension precision is selected from the **Precision:** drop-down list in the **Primary Units** subdialog box.

Setting the Zero Inch Variable

The **DIMZIN** (Zero Inch) variable controls the display of leading and trailing zeros that occur in certain types of dimensions. For architectural dimensions, **DIMZIN** may contain the value 0 (the default), 1, 2, or 3. The following list provides an example of each setting:

DIMZIN = 0	Suppresses zero feet and zero inches	5/8″	4″	3′	3′-0 ½″
DIMZIN = 1	Includes zero feet and zero inches	0′-0 5/8″	0′-4″	3′-0″	3′-0 ½″
DIMZIN = 2	Includes zero feet suppresses zero inches	0′-0 5/8″	0′-4″	3′	3′-0 ½″
DIMZIN = 3	Suppresses zero feet includes zero inches	5/8″	4″	3′-0″	3′-0 ½″

For mechanical dimensions with inch units, set **DIMZIN** = 4 or 7 to omit leading zeros. As an example:

$$\textbf{DIMZIN} = 0 \qquad \textbf{DIMZIN} = 4 \text{ or } 7$$
$$0.75 \qquad\qquad .75$$

Changing DIMZIN using a dialog box

To change **DIMZIN** using the **Dimension Styles** dialog box, open the **Primary Units** subdialog box as previously described. As shown in **Figure 12-7**, the **Zero Suppression** section is at the lower left of the subdialog box with the **0 Feet** and **0 Inches** check boxes active by default. The **0 Feet** check box omits the 0′ value for a feet and inches dimension that is less than one foot. Therefore, a six inch dimension reads as 6″ when this box is checked, and as 0′-6″when it is not checked. The **0 Inches** check box removes the 0″ portion of a dimension, such as 24′. When this box is not checked, the same dimension would read as 24′-0″.

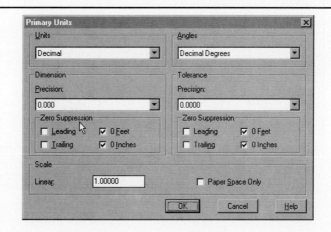

Figure 12-7.
The **Zero Suppression** section of the **Primary Units** subdialog box controls the leading and trailing zeros for various types of dimensions.

The **Leading** check box is used to drop the leading zero from a decimal inch dimension. This is equivalent to setting **DIMZIN** = 4 or 7 as previously described. Leave this box unchecked if you are performing metric dimensioning, however, since metric dimensioning standards state that dimensions less than one millimeter in size require a 0 before the decimal point.

When activated, the **Trailing** check box removes all trailing zeros from a decimal dimension. Thus, a dimension that would normally read as 7.500 becomes 7.5. It is strongly recommended that you do not activate the **Trailing** check box because trailing zeros usually have tolerance significance in mechanical engineering and manufacturing. Instead, use the **DIMDEC** variable previously described to set the required number of decimal places to the right of the decimal point.

Dimension Scaling

You may recall from the scaling discussions in previous chapters that AutoCAD LT can draw virtually anything at full scale. Very small objects are scaled up at plot time, while very large objects are scaled down. What happens, then, to dimension text height?

If your drawing is to be plotted at 1:1, then you need not concern yourself with dimension text height. If, on the other hand, you intend to plot with a specified scale factor, it is critically important to set your dimension height appropriately. This also applies to other components of a dimension as well, such as the arrowhead lengths and the distance that an extension line is offset from an object line.

Fortunately, the size of all dimensioning objects can be controlled with the **DIMSCALE** dimension variable. As an example, suppose the object you are dimensioning is somewhat small. You intend, therefore, to plot the drawing at a scale of 2:1. Since the size of your dimensions will be increased by a factor of two at plot time, you can compensate by setting **DIMSCALE** equal to .5 (1/2). As shown at the left in **Figure 12-8**, all the components of the dimension are then reduced by a factor of 1/2. When plotted at 2:1, the drawing geometry increases by a factor of 2 and the dimensions are restored to their normal sizes.

Consider another example. Suppose that the object you are drawing is rather large and you intend to plot with a scale factor of 1:2. Since the drawing geometry will be plotted two times smaller, you must ensure that the dimensions do not reduce in scale also. As shown at the right of **Figure 12-8**, setting **DIMSCALE** equal to 2 creates dimension objects two times larger, thus compensating for the reduced drawing size at the plotter.

Figure 12-8.
An example of identical objects dimensioned with different **DIMSCALE** values.

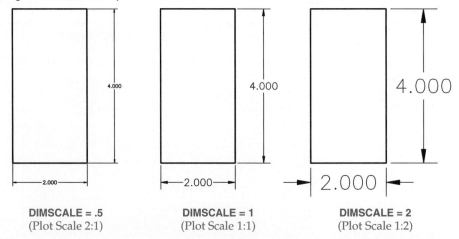

DIMSCALE = .5
(Plot Scale 2:1)

DIMSCALE = 1
(Plot Scale 1:1)

DIMSCALE = 2
(Plot Scale 1:2)

Changing DIMSCALE using a dialog box

To change **DIMSCALE** using the **Dimension Styles** dialog box, access the **Dimension Styles** dialog box and click the **Geometry...** button to open the **Geometry** subdialog box. Enter the desired **DIMSCALE** value in the **Overall Scale:** text box at the lower left of the subdialog box. **DIMSCALE** is set to 4 in the example illustrated in **Figure 12-9.** On the command line, **DIMSCALE** may be changed as follows:

DIMSCALE
SCALE

> Dim: **DIMSCALE** *or* **SCALE.**↵
> Current value ⟨*current*⟩ New value: *(enter a new scale factor)*
> Dim:

Figure 12-9.
The desired **DIMSCALE** value is entered in the **Overall Scale:** text box at the lower left of the **Geometry** subdialog box.

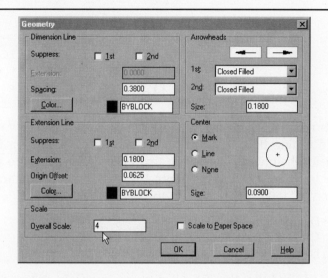

Dimension Text Style and Height

Dimensions can be created in any text style. After creating the text style with the **STYLE** command, you must tell AutoCAD LT to use that style for dimensions using the **DIMTXSTY** (TeXt STYle) variable. To do so using the **Dimension Styles** dialog box, return to the **Annotation** subdialog box as previously described. Use the **Style:** drop-down list to select one of the text styles defined in the current drawing. As shown in **Figure 12-10**, two text styles, ARCHITECTURAL and MECHANICAL appear along with the default STANDARD style. At the Dim: prompt, **DIMTXSTY** may be set as follows:

> Dim: **DIMTXSTY** *or* **TXSTY.**↵
> Current value ⟨STANDARD⟩ New value: *(enter an existing text style name)*
> Dim:

PROFESSIONAL TIP

Create the text styles you use most often in your template(s) so that they may quickly be used for dimensioning purposes as well.

Figure 12-10.
Setting **DIMTXSTY**
using the **Style:**
drop-down list in
the **Annotation**
subdialog box.

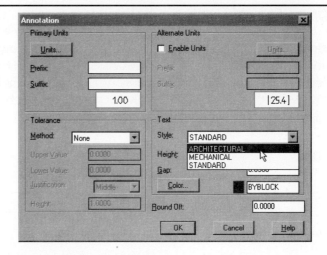

Setting Dimension Text Height

Dimension text height is set using the **DIMTXT** (TeXT) variable. To change **DIMTXT**
using a dialog box, return to the **Annotation** subdialog box and enter the desired
dimension height in the **Height:** text box. In the example shown in **Figure 12-11**, the
height is set to .125 (1/8) units. In the following example, dimension height is
changed to .156 (5/32) units on the command line:

DIMTXT
TXT

> Dim: **DIMTXT** *or* **TXT**↵
> Current value ⟨0.1800⟩ New value: **.156**↵
> Dim:

Be advised that the default dimension height differs from the default text height
in AutoCAD LT if you are using decimal units as your system of measurement. The
program sets the dimension text height at 3/16 units which is in accordance with
industry standards. AutoCAD LT text height, on the other hand, is .200 units by
default. Be sure to set text height and dimension height equally in your template(s)
to ensure uniformity. Also be sure to use the same text style for both general annotation and dimensions to comply with industry drafting standards.

Figure 12-11.
Setting **DIMTXT**
using the **Height:**
text box in the
Annotation
subdialog box.

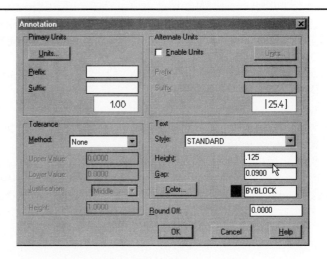

The DIMLFAC Variable

The **DIMLFAC** (Length FACtor) variable sets a global scale factor for linear and radial dimensioning measurements. The size and distance values measured by the dimensioning commands are multiplied by the **DIMLFAC** setting before being converted to dimension text. Angular dimensions are not affected, however.

DIMLFAC is extremely convenient when dimensioning detail or section views that are scaled differently from the main views of the drawing. As an example, suppose you wanted to dimension a detail view that is at a scale of 4:1. Simply set **DIMLFAC** to a value of .25 as follows:

DIMLFAC
LFAC

> Dim: **DIMLFAC** *or* **LFAC**⏎
> Current value ⟨1.0000⟩ New value: **.25**⏎
> Dim:

When you dimension the view, AutoCAD LT automatically divides the true dimension values by a factor of 1/4 and displays the dimensions as if the view were drawn at 1:1. Be sure to set **DIMLFAC** back to 1 when you wish to resume full scale dimensioning.

To set **DIMLFAC** in a dialog box, return to the **Primary Units** subdialog box as previously described and enter the desired **DIMLFAC** value in the **Linear:** text box at the lower left of the subdialog box. See **Figure 12-12**.

Figure 12-12.
The desired **DIMLFAC** value is entered in the **Linear:** text box at the lower left of the **Primary Units** subdialog box.

NOTE   The **Paper Space Only** check box shown in **Figure 12-12** is used to calculate the scale factor based on the scaling between the current model space viewport and paper space. Activating this check box disables **DIMSCALE**. Floating viewports in paper space are covered in *Chapter 17* of this text.

Setting Dimension Colors

Like other objects in AutoCAD LT , dimensions are created on the current layer. This is why it is a good idea to create a separate dimensioning layer for your dimensions. The dimensions may then be turned on and off, or frozen and thawed as desired. You may recall from the discussion of colors and layers in *Chapter 5* that objects (including dimensions) normally inherit the color of the layer on which they are created. AutoCAD LT calls this *bylayer mode*. Remember that it is possible to override bylayer mode by explicitly setting colors using the **COL** or **COLOR** commands.

It is also possible to set explicit colors for dimension lines, extension lines, and dimension text using dimension variables. The three dimvars that are used for these settings are called **DIMCLRD**, **DIMCLRE**, and **DIMCLRT**. **DIMCLRD** sets the color of dimension lines, arrowheads, and leaders. **DIMCLRE** sets the color of extension lines, and **DIMCLRT** is used to assign color to the dimension text.

Remember that when specifying a color, you can enter the name of the color or its AutoCAD Color Index, or ACI, number. In the following example, the color of dimension text is changed to red:

Dim: **DIMCLRT** *or* **CLRT**↵
Current value ⟨BYBLOCK⟩ New value: **RED, R,** *or* **1**↵
Dim:

NOTE   The **BYBLOCK** mode differs from **BYLAYER** mode such that objects assume the current color until grouped into a block. When the block is inserted into a drawing, it inherits the current color setting of that drawing. See *Chapter 15* for more information about block objects.

Setting dimension colors using a dialog box

You can also change dimension colors quickly and easily using the **Dimension Styles** dialog box. To change the color of dimension lines and extension lines, click the **Geometry...** button to open the **Geometry** subdialog box. Click the **Color...** button in the **Dimension Line** section of the subdialog box as shown in **Figure 12-13A.** The **Select Color** subdialog box is then displayed. In the example shown in **Figure 12-13B,** cyan (ACI number 4) has been selected from the standard colors at the top of the subdialog box. After making your color selection, click **OK** to exit the **Select Color** subdialog box.

To change the color of extension lines, click the **Color...** button in the **Extension Line** section of the **Geometry** subdialog box. Select the color you wish to use from the **Select Color** subdialog box as previously described.

If you wish to change the color of dimension text, open the **Annotation** subdialog box and click the **Color...** button in the **Text** section at the lower right. See **Figure 12-14.** Once again, select the color you wish to use from the **Select Color** subdialog box.

Figure 12-13.
A—Setting the color of dimension lines (**DIMCLRD**) in the **Geometry** subdialog box. Notice that extension line color (**DIMCLRE**) is also changed using this subdialog box. B—The desired color is selected from the color palette in the **Select Color** subdialog box.

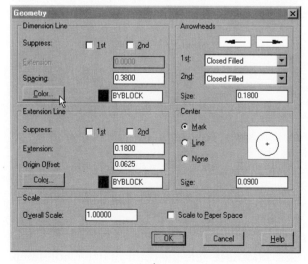

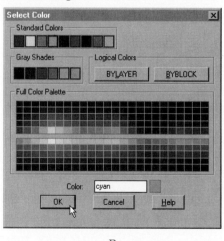

A

B

Figure 12-14.
The color of dimension text (**DIMCLRT**) is changed using the **Annotation** subdialog box.

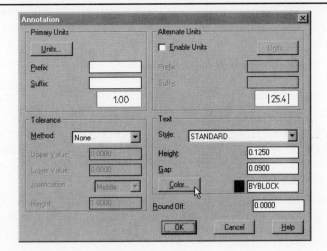

PROFESSIONAL TIP

When plotting, color numbers can be assigned to individual pens of varying widths. Use the **DIMCLRT** variable if you want dimension text plotted bold so that it stands out from dimensions lines, extension lines, and arrowheads. This is common practice in many architectural offices. See *Chapter 14* for complete information regarding color and pen assignments when plotting.

Linear Dimensions

Linear dimensioning measures lines that are horizontal, vertical, or neither. A linear dimension includes dimension text, dimension lines, extension lines, and arrowheads. See **Figure 12-15.** Each of the dimension components is grouped together into a single dimension object. AutoCAD LT allows you to create four types of linear dimensions; horizontal, vertical, aligned, and rotated. An example of each type is shown in **Figure 12-16.**

Figure 12-15.
Components of a linear dimension.

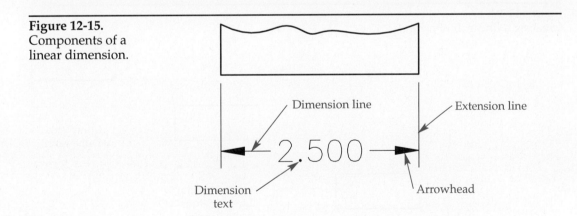

The **DIMLINEAR** command creates horizontal, vertical, and rotated linear dimensions. (Aligned, or parallel, dimensions are created with the **DIMALIGNED** command which is described in a later section.) When creating a linear dimension, you are prompted to select the first and second extension line origins. These are the ends of the feature to be dimensioned. You are then asked to pick a location for the dimension line. As you move your cursor, the dimension is dynamically "dragged" to the location you specify. The only difference among the linear dimension types is the angle at which the dimension line is drawn. If you move your pointing device to the left or right when dragging the dimension, a horizontal dimension is created. A vertical dimension is drawn if you move your cursor up or down.

The **DIMLINEAR** command may be accessed by entering DIMLINEAR, or DLI, at the Command: prompt, clicking the **Linear Dimension** button in the **Dimension** toolbar, or by selecting **Linear** from the **Dimension** pull-down menu. On the command line, **DIMLINEAR** appears as follows. Refer to **Figure 12-17** as you follow the command sequence below:

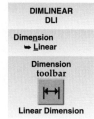

DIMLINEAR
DLI

Dimension
➥ **L**inear

Dimension
toolbar

Linear Dimension

Command: **DIMLINEAR** *or* **DLI**↵
First extension line origin or press ENTER to select: (*pick one end of the feature to dimension*)
Second extension line origin: (*pick the other end of the feature to dimension*)
Dimension line location (Mtext/Text/Angle/Horizontal/Vertical/Rotated): (*pick a location*)
Dimension text = 2.500
Command:

Figure 12-16.
Examples of the four types of linear dimensions available in AutoCAD LT.

Figure 12-17.
Creating a linear dimension.

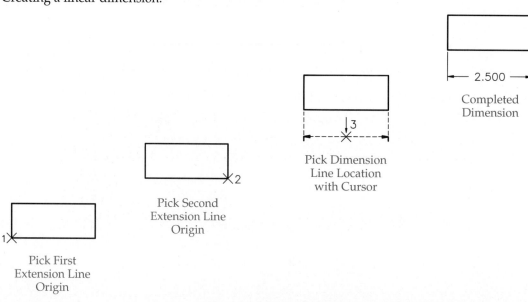

Be sure to use an appropriate object snap mode, such as **Endpoint**, to precisely select the extension line origins. If your drawing geometry is accurate, and you have used osnaps correctly, the dimension created will be accurate. However, if the dimension is not correct, start over again making sure that the extension line origins are selected correctly. If the dimension is still incorrect, correct your drawing geometry before continuing.

Notice from the command syntax on the previous page that you can specify whether a horizontal or vertical dimension is required. However, it is faster and easier to simply drag the dimension to the desired orientation with your pointing device as previously mentioned.

Using the Mtext or Text Options

When creating dimensions, AutoCAD LT allows you to preface or append the dimension with additional text. This can be accomplished using the **Mtext** or **Text** options. For example, suppose that you wish to append a dimension with the letters **TYP**, for **TYPICAL**. After selecting the extension line origins, follow the procedure given below to use the **Mtext** option:

Dimension line location (Mtext/Text/Angle/Horizontal/Vertical/Rotated): **M**↵

Entering M for **Mtext** displays the **Multiline Text Editor** dialog box. As shown in **Figure 12-18**, the brackets (⟨⟩) indicate the current dimension value found by AutoCAD LT . Use your pointing device, or the text editing keys on your keyboard, to move the cursor to the end of the brackets. Once at the end, press the [Spacebar] and type the characters TYP. (The [Spacebar] is pressed so that a space appears between the dimension and the letters TYP.) Click the **OK** button when you are through. The dialog box disappears and the command line is redisplayed. Continue with the procedure as follows:

Dimension line location (Mtext/Text/Angle/Horizontal/Vertical/Rotated): *(pick a location)*
Dimension text = *nnn*
Command:

You can perform the same operation on the command line using the the **Text** option as follows:

Dimension line location (Mtext/Text/Angle/Horizontal/Vertical/Rotated): **T**↵
Dimension text ⟨2.500⟩: ⟨⟩ **TYP**↵
Dimension line location (Mtext/Text/Angle/Horizontal/Vertical/Rotated): *(pick a location)*
Dimension text = 2.500
Command:

Figure 12-18.
The **Mtext** option edits dimension text using the **Multiline Text Editor** dialog box.

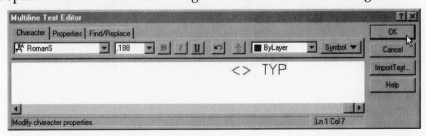

In this example, you instruct AutoCAD LT to "take the value in the brackets and place a space and the letters TYP after it." Although you may do so, there is no need to reenter the 2.500 value. The resulting dimension is displayed as 2.500 TYP.

You can also use the **Text** option to add a prefix to a dimension. In the following example, the characters "2X" are added to indicate that a dimension occurs two places:

Dimension line location (Mtext/Text/Angle/Horizontal/Vertical/Rotated): **T.**↲
Dimension text ⟨2.500⟩: **2X ⟨⟩** ↲
Dimension line location (Mtext/Text/Angle/Horizontal/Vertical/Rotated): *(pick a location)*
Dimension text = 2.500
Command:

The resulting dimension is displayed as 2X 2.500. Adding a prefix to a dimension can also be performed using the **Mtext** option. Whether you add a prefix or a suffix, the dimension is still one object.

Using the Angle Option

The **Angle** option allows you to change the angle of the dimension text. By default, all dimensions are created in a unidirectional fashion. In other words, dimensions read horizontally from left to right. If you wish to place dimension text at a different angle as shown in **Figure 12-19**, do the following:

Dimension line location (Mtext/Text/Angle/Horizontal/Vertical/Rotated): **A.**↲
Enter text angle: **270.**↲
Dimension line location (Mtext/Text/Angle/Horizontal/Vertical/Rotated): *(pick a location)*
Dimension text = 2.625
Command:

In architectural drafting, it is common practice to rotate dimensions so that they are aligned with the features being dimensioned. While the **Angle** option may be used for this purpose, it is far more efficient to use the **DIMTIH** and **DIMTOH** dimension variables. These two dimvars are covered later in this chapter.

Figure 12-19.
An example of a dimension rotated at 270° using the **Angle** option.

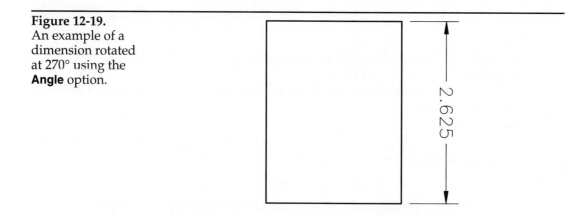

PROFESSIONAL TIP

Here is another example of how you might preface or append a dimension with additional text. AutoCAD LT does not place a diameter symbol in front of a dimension when using the **DIMLINEAR** or **DIMALIGNED** commands. However, it is common practice to place a diameter symbol in front of a linear dimension when detailing a cylindrical feature. In the example shown below, a diameter symbol is added using the **Text** option and entering the %%C special character control code.

Dimension line location
    (Mtext/Text/Angle/Horizontal/Vertical/Rotated): **T**⏎
Dimension text ⟨2.500⟩: **%%C ⟨⟩ TYP**⏎

This instructs AutoCAD LT to "take the value in the brackets and place a diameter symbol in front of it and then a space and the word TYP after it." The resulting dimension is displayed as Ø2.500 TYP and is still a single object.

You can also use the **Mtext** option to place a special character in front of dimension text. When the **Multiline Text Editor** dialog box appears, locate your cursor in front of the brackets (⟨⟩) and select **Diameter** from the **Symbol** drop-down list at the upper right of the dialog box. Click the **OK** button when you are finished. If necessary, refer to *Chapter 9* to review the other special character control codes.

Using the DIMLINEAR Rotated Option

A rotated dimension is very similar to a horizontal or vertical dimension with one important distinction. With a rotated dimension, you must specify the dimension line angle after selecting the extension line origins. An example of a rotated dimension is shown in **Figure 12-16.** Use **DIMLINEAR** as follows to create a rotated dimension:

Command: **DIMLINEAR** *or* **DLI**⏎
First extension line origin or press ENTER to select: *(pick one end of the feature to dimension)*
Second extension line origin: *(pick the other end of the feature to dimension)*
Dimension line location (Mtext/Text/Angle/Horizontal/Vertical/Rotated): **R**⏎
Dimension line angle ⟨0⟩: *(specify an angle)*
Dimension line location (Mtext/Text/Angle/Horizontal/Vertical/Rotated): *(pick a location)*
Dimension text = *nnn*
Command:

There may be instances when you do not know the required dimension line angle. You can use the **LIST** command to query the system for the angle or, better yet, pick two points on the line to be dimensioned when prompted for the dimension line angle. Be sure to use an osnap to pick the points precisely. If necessary, refer to *Chapter 8* to review the **LIST** command.

Creating an Aligned Dimension

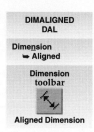

DIMALIGNED
DAL

Dime_n_sion
➥ Aligned

Dimension
toolbar

Aligned Dimension

The **DIMALIGNED** command aligns a dimension so that the dimension line is parallel with a horizontal, vertical, or angled feature. An example of an aligned dimension is shown in **Figure 12-16**. The procedure and options of **DIMALIGNED** are nearly identical to that of the **DIMLINEAR** command. To issue the **DIMALIGNED** command, enter DIMALIGNED, or DAL, at the Command: prompt, select **Aligned** from the **Dime_n_sion** pull-down menu, or click the **Aligned Dimension** button in the **Dimension** toolbar. The command sequence is as follows:

> Command: **DIMALIGNED** *or* **DAL**↵
> First extension line origin or press ENTER to select: *(pick one end of the feature to dimension)*
> Second extension line origin: *(pick the other end of the feature to dimension)*
> Dimension line location (Mtext/Text/Angle): *(pick a location)*
> Dimension text = *nnn*
> Command:

> **PROFESSIONAL TIP**
>
> Since the **DIMALIGNED** command can dimension horizontal and vertical features, as well as angled surfaces, it can be used in place of the **DIMLINEAR** command. The **DIMALIGNED** command is also a convenient way to dimension auxiliary views. Refer to *Chapter 7* to review auxiliary view construction.

The **or press ENTER to select** Option

In each of the previous linear dimensioning examples, you may have noticed the or press ENTER to select: prompt. As shown in **Figure 12-20**, this powerful option allows you to place a horizontal, vertical, aligned, or rotated dimension on a line, arc, or circle without specifying the extension line origins. When the or press ENTER to select: prompt appears, simply press [Enter] and pick the object you wish to dimension. Refer to the dimensioned circle at the far right of **Figure 12-20** as you follow the command procedure below:

> Command: **DIMLINEAR** *or* **DLI**↵
> First extension line origin or press ENTER to select: ↵
> Select object to dimension: *(pick anywhere on circle)*
> Dimension line location (Mtext/Text/Angle/Horizontal/Vertical/Rotated): **T**↵
> Dimension text 〈1.500〉: **%%C〈〉** ↵
> Dimension line location (Mtext/Text/Angle/Horizontal/Vertical/Rotated): *(pick a location below the circle)*
> Dimension text = 1.500
> Command:

The **or press ENTER to select** option may also be used on polylines, donuts, rectangles, and polygons.

Figure 12-20.
Using the **press ENTER to select** option.

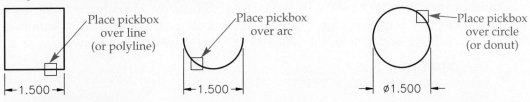

Place pickbox over line (or polyline)

Place pickbox over arc

Place pickbox over circle (or donut)

|← 1.500 →|

|← 1.500 →|

|→ ⌀1.500 ←|

PROFESSIONAL TIP

Dimensioning in AutoCAD LT , like dimensioning on a conventional drafting board, should be performed as accurately and as neatly as possible. You can achieve consistently professional results by adhering to the following guidelines:

- Always construct drawing geometry as precisely as possible. Never truncate, or round-off, decimal values when entering coordinates. In other words, enter .4375 for 7/16—not .43 or .44.

- For decimal dimensioning, set the dimension variable DIMDEC to the desired number of decimal places before creating any dimensions. Leave the system variable **LUPREC** (Linear Units PRECision) set to 4 so that the text boxes in the **Dimension Styles** subdialog boxes display more accurate values.

- *Do not* use the **DIMRND** (RouND) variable. This dimension variable rounds linear and radial dimension distances to a specified value. For example, if **DIMRND** is set to .5, all distances round to the nearest .5 unit. All dimensions round to the nearest integer when **DIMRND** is set to 1. A value of 0 (the default) turns off **DIMRND**.

- Use running object snap modes like **Endpoint** and **Intersection** to your advantage to snap to exact extension line origins.

- *Never* type in a different dimension value than that created by AutoCAD LT . If a dimension needs to change, revise the drawing geometry accordingly. The ability to change a dimension using the **DIMLINEAR** and **DIMALIGNED Mtext** or **Text** options is provided so that a different text format may be specified for the dimension. As you will learn in later sections of this chapter, this ability is provided for angular and radial dimensions as well. Additionally, prefixes and/or suffixes may be added to the dimension in the brackets as previously described. A typical example of a prefix might be to specify the number of times a dimension occurs, such as: 4X 1.750. The same callout can be expressed with a suffix as follows: 1.750 4 PLCS.

Adding Text to Dimensions Using the DIMPOST Variable

Another way to add a prefix or suffix to a dimension is with the dimension variable **DIMPOST**. Suppose, for example, that you wish to create a series of dimensions each appended with the word "TYP". Set **DIMPOST** as follows:

DIMPOST
POST

Dim: **DIMPOST** *or* **POST**↵
Current value ⟨⟩ New value: **TYP**↵
Dim:

Every dimension you now create will automatically include the letters "TYP". However, be sure to type a space before entering the suffix. Doing so ensures that a space exists between the dimension and the suffix. To clear the **DIMPOST** variable, type a period (.) as follows:

Dim: **DIMPOST** *or* **POST**↵
Current value ⟨⟩ New value: **.**↵
Dim:

You can also use **DIMPOST** to add a prefix to a dimension. In the following example, the prefix "APPROX." is added to a series of dimensions. Note the use of the angle brackets. Entering the brackets after the **DIMPOST** value instructs AutoCAD LT to use the value as a prefix rather than a suffix.

Dim: **DIMPOST** *or* **POST**↵
Current value ⟨⟩ New value: **APPROX. ⟨⟩** ↵
Dim:

Changing DIMPOST with a dialog box

To change **DIMPOST** using the **Dimension Styles** dialog box, issue the **DDIM** command and click the **Annotation...** button in the **Dimension Styles** dialog box. This displays the **Annotation** subdialog box. See **Figure 12-21**. In the example shown, APPROX. appears in the **Prefix:** text box and FT. is entered in the **Suffix:** text box. Every newly created dimension will now look like the following: APPROX. *nnn* FT. Be sure to include spaces in the text boxes where appropriate as previously described.

Figure 12-21.
Adding a prefix and a suffix to dimensions using the **Annotation** subdialog box.

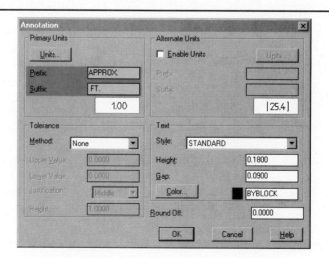

NOTE

In an effort to maintain compatibility with previous versions of AutoCAD LT, the following linear dimensioning commands may still be entered at the Dim: prompt. The **HORIZONTAL**, or **HOR**, command is used to dimension a horizontal feature. The **VERTICAL**, or **VE**, command places dimensions for vertical features. The **ALIGNED**, or **AL**, command aligns a dimension so that the dimension line is parallel with a feature. The feature may be horizontal, vertical, or angled. The **ROTATED**, or **RO**, command is used to create a linear dimension with dimension lines drawn at a user-specified angle. A list of dimensioning commands that can be issued at the Dim: prompt only (like those just mentioned) appears at the end of this chapter.

EXERCISE 12-1

❏ Begin a new drawing using your TEMPLATEB template.
❏ Set **Fractional** units and construct the object shown below on the OBJECTS layer.

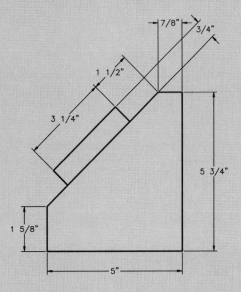

❏ Set the DIMS layer current and dimension the drawing exactly as shown, (refer to **Figure 12-16** as a guide). Use the **or press ENTER to select:** option where appropriate.
❏ Save the drawing as EX12-1.

More Dimensioning Variables

As previously stated, dimension variables control the appearance and format of all AutoCAD LT dimensions. The *dimvars* described in the following sections control the placement of dimension text and the appearance of dimension lines and extension lines. Four of these variables are shown in **Figure 12-22** and are described in the following sections.

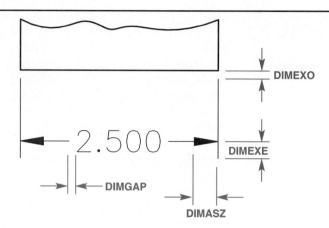

Figure 12-22.
The **DIMGAP**, **DIMASZ**, **DIMEXE**, and **DIMEXO** dimension variables.

The DIMEXO and DIMEXE Variables

The **DIMEXO** (EXtension line Offset) variable controls the size of the space between the end of an object line and the start of an extension line. By default, that value is set to .0625 (1/16) units in accordance with current drafting standards. To change the extension line offset, do the following:

DIMEXO
EXO

> Dim: **DIMEXO** *or* **EXO**↵
> Current value ⟨0.0625⟩ New value: *(enter a positive value)*
> Dim:

The distance that an extension line extends past the end of a dimension line is controlled with the **DIMEXE** (EXtension line Extension) variable. This value is .18 (approx. 3/16) units by default and is also in accordance with drafting standards. To change this value, do the following:

DIMEXE
EXE

> Dim: **DIMEXE** *or* **EXE**↵
> Current value ⟨0.1800⟩ New value: *(enter a positive value)*
> Dim:

Changing DIMEXO and DIMEXE using a dialog box

You can also use the **Dimension Styles** dialog box to change the values of both **DIMEXO** and **DIMEXE**. First, issue the **DDIM** command and then click the **Geometry...** button to display the **Geometry** subdialog box shown in **Figure 12-23.** Change the **DIMEXE** variable by entering the desired new value in the **Extension:** text box. Use the **Origin Offset:** text box to change the value of **DIMEXO.**

Figure 12-23.
The **Extension:** and **Origin Offset:** text boxes in the **Extension Line** section of the **Geometry** subdialog box are used to change **DIMEXE** and **DIMEXO,** respectively.

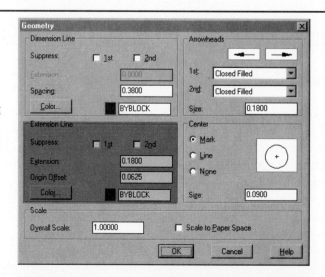

Controlling the Gap Between the Dimension Line and Dimension Text

The **DIMGAP** variable is used to control the spacing between the end of a dimension line and the start of the dimension text. By default, that spacing is .09 (approx. 3/32) units. It is rarely necessary to change this value. However, setting **DIMGAP** to a negative value creates a dimension like that shown in **Figure 12-24.** This type of dimension is called a *basic dimension* and represents a theoretically exact dimension used in *geometric dimensioning and tolerancing (GD&T).* To create a basic dimension using **DIMGAP**, do the following:

DIMGAP
GAP

> Dim: **DIMGAP** *or* **GAP**↵
> Current value ⟨0.0900⟩ New value: **-.09**↵
> Dim:

A larger negative value creates a larger box around the dimension, while a smaller negative value draws a smaller box.

Figure 12-24.
Setting **DIMGAP** to a negative value creates a basic dimension.

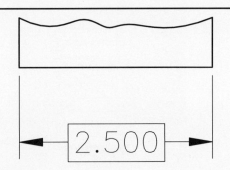

2.500

Changing DIMGAP using a dialog box

To increase or decrease the positive value of **DIMGAP** using the **Dimension Styles** dialog box, issue the **DDIM** command and click the **Annotation...** button to display the **Annotation** subdialog box. Enter the desired value in the **Gap:** text box in the **Text** section. See **Figure 12-25A.** To create a basic dimension, select **Basic** from the **Method:** drop-down list in the **Tolerance** section of the **Annotation** subdialog box. See **Figure 12-25B.** The other options available in the **Method:** drop-down list are described later in this chapter.

Setting the Size of Arrowheads

The length of the arrowheads at the end of dimension lines and leader lines is controlled with the **DIMASZ** (Arrowhead SiZe) variable. This value is set to .18 units (approx. 3/16) by default. If you wish to change the length of your arrowheads, enter DIMASZ, or ASZ, at the Command: prompt. The command sequence is as folllows:

DIMASZ
ASZ

> Dim: **DIMASZ** *or* **ASZ**↵
> Current value ⟨0.1800⟩ New value: *(enter a larger or smaller value)*
> Dim:

Changing DIMASZ using a dialog box

You can also use the **Dimension Styles** dialog box to change the value of **DIMASZ.** First, issue the **DDIM** command and then click the **Geometry...** button to display the **Geometry** subdialog box shown in **Figure 12-26.** Enter an appropriate value in the **Size:** text box to lengthen or shorten arrowheads.

Figure 12-25.
A—Changing the positive value of **DIMGAP** using the **Annotation** subdialog box. B—Specifying a basic dimension in the **Tolerance** section of the **Annotation** subdialog box.

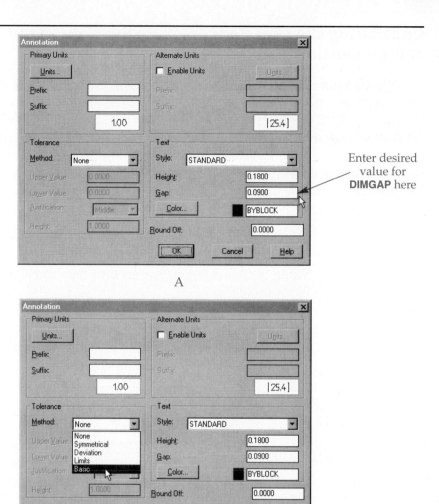

Enter desired value for **DIMGAP** here

A

B

Figure 12-26.
Using the **Geometry** subdialog box to change the value of **DIMASZ**.

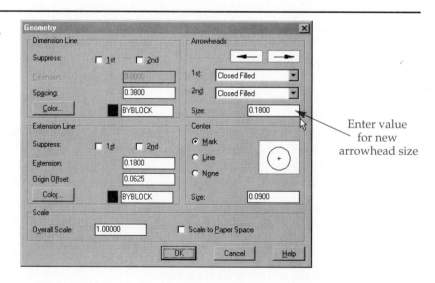

Enter value for new arrowhead size

Updating the Appearance and Format of Existing Dimensions

It is often necessary to change the dimension variable status for one or more existing dimensions. As an example, suppose you need to change the arrowhead lengths for a drawing that is already completely dimensioned. It is not necessary to erase the existing dimensions and recreate them. Instead, set **DIMASZ** as required and issue the **UPDATE** command by entering UPDATE, or UP or UPD, at the Dim: prompt, clicking the **Dimension Update** button in the **Dimension** toolbar, or selecting **Update** from the **Dimension** pull-down menu. At the Dim: prompt, enter the following:

> Dim: **UPDATE, UP,** *or* **UPD**↵
> Select objects: *(select the dimension(s) to change)*
> Select objects: ↵
> Dim:

Since all of the AutoCAD LT selection set options are valid with **UPDATE**, you can select many dimensions at one time using a **Window** or **Crossing** box. Be advised, however, that selected dimensions are updated to the current status of *all* dimension variables. More information about the **UPDATE** command is provided later in this chapter.

Controlling the Placement of Text and Arrowheads

AutoCAD LT always places text and arrowheads between the extension lines of a dimension when space is available. The **DIMFIT** variable determines the placement of text and arrowheads when space between the extension lines is inadequate. As shown in **Figure 12-27**, **DIMFIT** may be set to the following values:

- **0.** Places both dimension text and arrowheads outside the extension lines.
- **1.** Places the dimension text between the extension lines and places arrowheads outside them. When not enough space is available for text, both text and arrowheads are placed outside extension lines.
- **2.** Places arrowheads between the extension lines and places the dimension text outside. When not enough space is available for arrowheads, both the text and arrowheads are placed outside the extension lines.
- **3.** Places the dimension text between the extension lines and places the arrowheads outside the extension lines. When enough space is available for arrowheads only, they are placed between the extension lines and the text outside the extension lines. When not enough space is available for either the text or the arrowheads, both are placed outside the extension lines. This is the default **DIMFIT** setting.
- **4.** Creates a leader line when there is not enough space for dimension text between the extension lines. Horizontal justification controls whether the text is drawn to the right or the left of the leader.
- **5.** When enough space is available for arrowheads only, they are placed between the extension lines and the text is placed above the dimension line. When not enough space is available for both text and arrowheads, the text can be placed anywhere, independent of the dimension line.

> **NOTE**
> When you move dimension text, the dimension line moves with it if **DIMFIT** is set to a value of 0, 1, 2, or 3. If **DIMFIT** is set to a value of 4 or 5, the dimension line does not move when you move dimension text.

Figure 12-27.
The effects of the **DIMFIT** variable on linear dimensions.

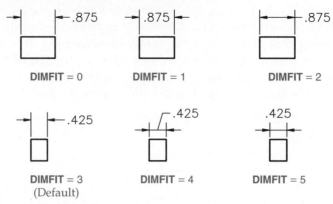

Setting DIMFIT with a dialog box

You can also set **DIMFIT** using the **Dimension Styles** dialog box by first issuing the **DDIM** command and then clicking the **Format…** button to display the **Format** subdialog box. The values may be changed by selecting the desired choice from the **Fit:** drop-down list at the left of the subdialog box. See **Figure 12-28.** Each of the drop-down list options are described as follows:

- **Text and Arrows.** This selection places the dimension text and arrows outside the extension lines if they will not fit between the extension lines. When you move the dimension text, the dimension line moves with it. This is the equivalent of **DIMFIT** set to 0.
- **Text Only.** Places the arrows inside and the dimension text outside the extension lines if both will not fit between the extension lines. If there is still not enough space for the text, it is placed outside the extension lines with the arrowheads. When you move the dimension text, the dimension line moves with it. This is the equivalent of **DIMFIT** set to 1.
- **Arrows Only.** Places the dimension text inside and the arrowheads outside the extension lines if both do not fit between the extension lines. If there is still not enough space for the text, it is placed outside the extension lines with the arrowheads. When you move the dimension text, the dimension line moves with it. This is the equivalent of **DIMFIT** set to 2.
- **Best Fit.** If space is available, this option places the text, arrowheads, or text and arrowheads inside the extension lines. When you move the dimension text, the dimension line moves with it. This is the equivalent of **DIMFIT** set to the default setting of 3.
- **Leader.** This option creates a leader line to the text if it does not fit between the extension lines. When you move the dimension text, it is independent of the dimension line. This is the equivalent of **DIMFIT** set to 4.
- **No Leader.** Places text above the dimension line without a leader line if it does not fit between the extension lines. When you move the dimension text, it is independent of the dimension line. This is the equivalent of **DIMFIT** set to 6.

Figure 12-28.
DIMFIT values may
also be set using
the **Format**
subdialog box.

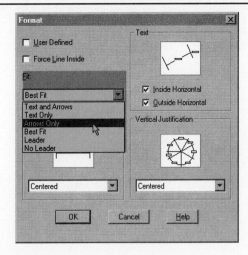

The DIMTIX, DIMSOXD, and DIMTOFL Variables

Releases prior to AutoCAD LT for Windows 95 (Release 3) did not feature the **DIMFIT** variable. If you are a user of one of those earlier releases, you probably use the **DIMTIX** (Text Inside eXtensions) dimension variable to control the placement of dimension text inside or outside extension lines. As shown in **Figure 12-29**, when **DIMTIX** = 1 (on), dimension lines and arrowheads are placed outside, and dimension text is placed between, the extension lines. When off (equal to 0), the dimension is placed on the side of the last extension line origin selected. **DIMTIX** is off by default. As shown below, it may be turned on by entering the numeral 1 or the word ON as follows:

> Dim: **DIMTIX** *or* **TIX**⏎
> Current value ⟨Off⟩ New value: *(type* 1 *or* ON *and press* [Enter]*)*
> Dim:

Turn off **DIMTIX** by entering a 0 or OFF.

When **DIMTIX** is on, arrowheads and dimension lines are always placed outside when they cannot be fit between the extension lines. To force text and arrowheads inside the extension lines, the **DIMSOXD** (Suppress Outside Dimension lines) variable is used. As shown at the lower right of **Figure 12-29**, **DIMSOXD** automatically suppresses arrowheads and dimension lines if they do not fit inside. **DIMSOXD** has no effect when **DIMTIX** is off. **DIMSOXD** looks like this:

> Dim: **DIMSOXD** *or* **SOXD**⏎
> Current value ⟨Off⟩ New value: *(type* 1 *or* ON *and press* [Enter]*)*
> Dim:

Turn off **DIMSOXD** by entering a 0 or OFF.

The **DIMTOFL** (Text Outside, Force Line inside) variable draws a dimension line between the extension lines when the text is placed outside the extensions. This can be seen at the lower left of **Figure 12-29**. **DIMTOFL** is off by default, but may be turned on as follows:

> Dim: **DIMTOFL** *or* **TOFL**⏎
> Current value ⟨Off⟩ New value: *(type* 1 *or* ON *and press* [Enter]*)*
> Dim:

Turn off **DIMTOFL** by entering a 0 or OFF.

Figure 12-29.
The effects of the
DIMTIX, DIMTOFL,
and **DIMSOXD**
variables.

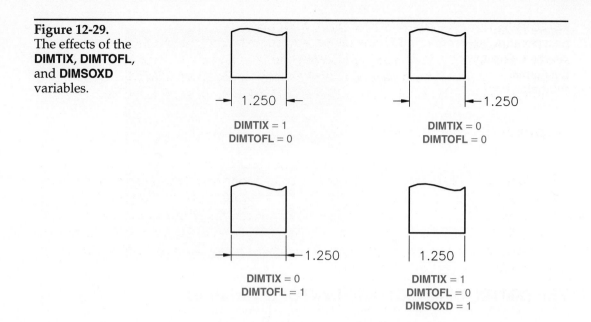

NOTE   Although **DIMTIX** and **DIMTOFL** are still available in AutoCAD LT 98 and AutoCAD LT 97 , their use has been essentially replaced by the **DIMFIT** variable.

Suppressing Extension Lines

Linear and angular dimensions in AutoCAD LT are automatically drawn with extension lines. You may choose to suppress one of both extension lines using the **DIMSE1** (Suppress Extension line 1) and **DIMSE2** (Suppress Extension line 2) dimension variables. Several examples of extension line suppression are shown in **Figure 12-30.** To activate extension line suppression, enter the following at the Dim: prompt:

DIMSE1
SE1

DIMSE2
SE2

Dim: **DIMSE1, SE1, DIMSE2,** *or* **SE2**↵
Current value ⟨Off⟩ New value: *(type* 1 *or* ON *and press* [Enter])
Dim:

Figure 12-30.
The **DIMSE1** and **DIMSE2** variables control extension line suppression.

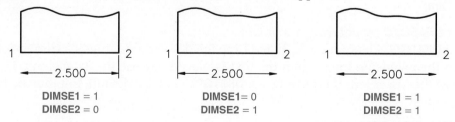

Changing DIMSE1 and DIMSE2 with a dialog box

You can also use the **Dimension Styles** dialog box to change the values of both **DIMSE1** and **DIMSE2**. First, issue the **DDIM** command and click the <u>Geometry...</u> button to open the **Geometry** subdialog box. As shown in **Figure 12-31**, **DIMSE1** is activated by clicking the check box labeled **1st** in the **Extension Line** section of the subdialog box.

Suppressing Dimension Lines

All linear and angular dimensions in AutoCAD LT are also automatically drawn with dimension lines. You may choose to suppress one or both dimension lines using the **DIMSD1** (Suppress Dimension line 1) and **DIMSD2** (Suppress Dimension line 2) dimension variables. Several examples of dimension line suppression are shown in **Figure 12-32.** Compare the dimension illustrated at the lower right with the dimension shown at the lower right in **Figure 12-29.** To activate dimension line suppression, enter the following at the Dim: prompt:

> Dim: **DIMSD1**, **SD1**, **DIMSD2**, *or* **SD2**.↵
> Current value ⟨Off⟩ New value: *(type* 1 *or* ON *and press* [Enter]*)*
> Dim:

DIMSD1	SD1
DIMSD2	SD2

Figure 12-31.
Using the **Suppress:** check boxes in the **Extension Line** section of the **Geometry** subdialog box to control extension line suppression.

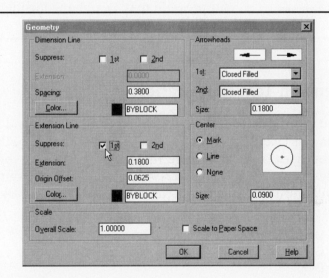

Figure 12-32.
The **DIMSD1** and **DIMSD2** variables control dimension line suppression.

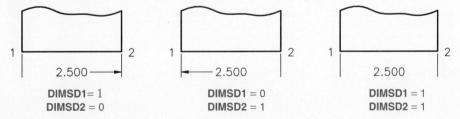

| DIMSD1= 1 | DIMSD1 = 0 | DIMSD1 = 1 |
| DIMSD2 = 0 | DIMSD2 = 1 | DIMSD2 = 1 |

Changing DIMSD1 and DIMSD2 with a dialog box

You can also use the **Dimension Styles** dialog box to change the values of both **DIMSD1** and **DIMSD2**. First, issue the **DDIM** command and click the <u>Geometry...</u> button to open the **Geometry** subdialog box. As shown in **Figure 12-33**, **DIMSD2** is activated by clicking the check box labeled **2nd** in the **Dimension Line** section of the subdialog box.

Figure 12-33.
Using the **Suppress:** check boxes in the **Dimension Line** section of the **Geometry** subdialog box to control dimension line suppression.

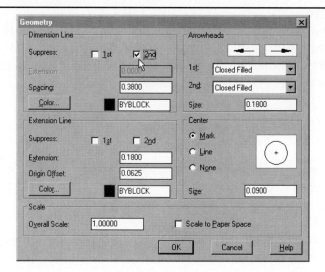

> **NOTE**
>
> Although **DIMSOXD** is still available in AutoCAD LT 98 and AutoCAD LT 97, greater control over dimension line suppression may be obtained using the **DIMSD1** and **DIMSD2** variables.

Dimension Text Justification

You probably noticed in performing *Exercise 12-1*, and from the examples shown so far in this chapter, that AutoCAD LT automatically centers dimension text within extension lines. You can change this convention using the **DIMJUST** (JUSTification) variable. As shown in **Figure 12-34**, various **DIMJUST** settings produce a variety of horizontal justification options. To change **DIMJUST**, enter the following at the Dim: prompt:

DIMJUST
JUST

> Dim: **DIMJUST** *or* **JUST.**↵
> Current value ⟨*current*⟩ New value: *(type 0, 1, 2, 3, or 4 and press* [Enter]*)*
> Dim:

Figure 12-34.
The **DIMJUST** variable provides a variety of dimension text justification options.

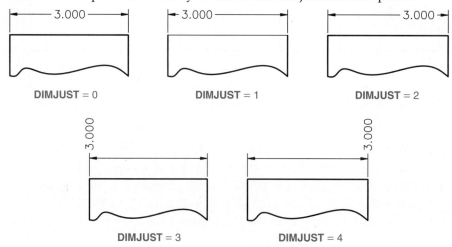

Changing DIMJUST with a dialog box

If you wish to change the **DIMJUST** values using the **Dimension Styles** dialog box, enter the **DDIM** command and click the **F̲ormat...** button. As shown in **Figure 12-35**, the drop-down list in the **Horizontal Justification** section of the **Format** subdialog box provides easy access to the five **DIMJUST** options.

Figure 12-35.
DIMJUST values
may be set using
the **Format**
subdialog box.

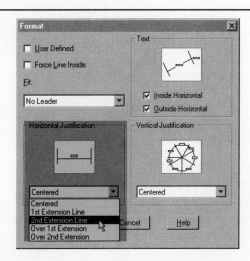

Using Your Cursor to Determine Dimension Text Placement

The **DIMUPT** (User Positioned Text) variable provides a great deal of flexibility in placing dimension text. When enabled, **DIMJUST** settings are virtually ignored and you can place your dimension text anywhere inside or outside extension lines as you desire. Although off by default, **DIMUPT** may be turned on as follows:

> Dim: **DIMUPT** *or* **UPT**↵
> Current value ⟨Off⟩ New value: *(type* 1 *or* ON *and press* [Enter]*)*
> Dim:

DIMUPT
UPT

Turn off **DIMUPT** by entering a 0 or OFF.

Changing DIMUPT with a dialog box

To enable **DIMUPT** using the **Dimension Styles** dialog box, enter DDIM and click the **F̲ormat...** button to open the **Format** subdialog box. As shown in **Figure 12-36**, activate the **U̲ser Defined** check box at the upper left to turn on **DIMUPT**.

PROFESSIONAL TIP

The **DIMUPT** variable may also be used with radius and diameter dimensions. These functions are covered later in this chapter. To obtain the greatest flexibility in dimension text placement for all dimension types, turn **DIMUPT** on and set **DIMFIT** = 1 in your template file(s).

Also, observe from **Figure 12-36** the **Force L̲ine Inside** check box located just below the **U̲ser Defined** check box. Activating the **Force L̲ine Inside** check box is the equivalent of turning on the **DIMTOFL** variable. This dimension variable was described in a previous section of this chapter.

Figure 12-36.
Setting **DIMUPT**
using the **Format**
subdialog box.

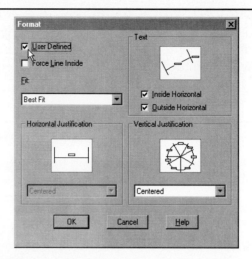

EXERCISE 12-2

❑ Open drawing EX12-1 if it is not still on your screen.
❑ Try changing the values of each of the dimension variables described in the preceding sections.
❑ After changing one or more dimvars, use the **UPDATE** command on your dimensions to see the effect.
❑ Next, turn **DIMUPT** on and create some additional linear dimensions. Compare the differences in placing dimensions with **DIMUPT** on and **DIMUPT** off.
❑ Do not save the drawing when you are finished experimenting.

Architectural Dimensioning Variables

AutoCAD LT offers several dimension variables that are more appropriate for architectural drafting practices. These dimvars are illustrated in **Figure 12-37** and are described in this section.

Figure 12-37.
The dimension variables shown here are appropriate for architectural applications.

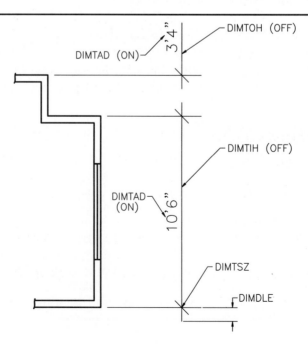

Using Oblique Strokes in Place of Arrowheads

Architects often use oblique strokes (tick marks) at the end of dimension lines instead of arrowheads. This capability is provided with the **DIMTSZ** (Tick SiZe) variable and is illustrated in **Figure 12-37.** When set to 0 (the default), arrowheads are drawn. Enter a positive value to draw tick marks in place of arrowheads.

> Dim: **DIMTSZ** *or* **TSZ**⏎
> Current value ⟨0.0000⟩ New value: *(enter a positive value)*
> Dim:

Once **DIMTSZ** is set, **DIMASZ** is ignored.

Changing DIMTSZ with a dialog box

Another way to use oblique ticks in place of arrowheads is provided with the **Dimension Styles** dialog box. Issue the **DDIM** command and click the **Geometry...** button to open the **Geometry** subdialog box. Next, use the **Arrowheads** drop-down list at the upper right of the subdialog box to display a variety of arrowhead choices. See **Figure 12-38.** Select Oblique as shown in the illustration. Note that you can choose to have bold oblique strokes by selecting Architectural Tick located just below Oblique in the list. Set the desired arrowhead length using the **Size:** text box at the bottom of the **Arrowheads** section of the subdialog box. See **Figure 12-58** later in this chapter for a complete graphical listing of available arrowheads in AutoCAD LT.

Figure 12-38
Selecting an arrowhead type using the **Geometry** subdialog box.

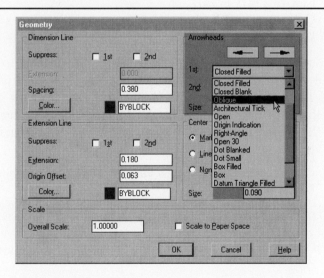

Extending a Dimension Line Past Extension Lines

It is also common in architectural drafting to extend the dimension line such that it crosses over the extension lines. This practice is shown in **Figure 12-37** and may be accomplished with the **DIMDLE** (DIMension Line Extension) variable as follows:

> Dim: **DIMDLE** *or* **DLE**⏎
> Current value ⟨0.0000⟩ New value: *(enter a positive value)*
> Dim:

Keep in mind that **DIMTSZ** must be set before **DIMDLE** can be used.

Changing DIMDLE with a dialog box

You can set **DIMDLE** using the **Dimension Styles** dialog box by first issuing the **DDIM** command and clicking the **Geometry** button to display the **Geometry** subdialog box. Next, select the desired arrowhead style as previously described. Observe that once you have selected an arrowhead type, the **Extension:** text box located in the **Dimension Line** section at the upper left of the dialog box becomes active. Normally, this text box is grayed-out. See **Figure 12-38.** Enter an appropriate value in the **Extension:** text box to set the dimension line extension.

PROFESSIONAL TIP

Setting the **DIMTSZ** and **DIMDLE** values equal provides a more pleasing appearance to architectural dimensions.

Placing Dimension Text Above or Below the Dimension Line

Dimensions are often placed above the dimension line in architectural and structural drafting. See **Figure 12-37.** This capability is provided with the **DIMTAD** (Text Above Dimension) variable. Off by default, **DIMTAD** may be turned as follows:

Dim: **DIMTAD** *or* **TAD**↵
Current value ⟨Off⟩ New value: *(type* 1 *or* ON *and press* [Enter]*)*
Dim:

Another dimension variable somewhat similar to **DIMTAD** is **DIMTVP** (Text Vertical Position). The similarities between **DIMTAD** and **DIMTVP** are illustrated in **Figure 12-39.** As shown in the illustration, **DIMTVP** can be used to place dimension text below the dimension line as well as above it. Entering 1 places the dimension text above the dimension line. Text is placed below the dimension line when –1 is entered.

Dim: **DIMTVP** *or* **TVP**↵
Current value ⟨0.0000⟩ New value: *(enter* 1 *or* –1 *as appropriate and press* [Enter]*)*
Dim:

To obtain a dimension text location that is not centered within the dimension line, but not completely above or below it, set **DIMTVP** to any value between 1 and –1. The **DIMTVP** variable may not be changed using the **Dimension Styles** dialog box.

Figure 12-39.
Comparisons between **DIMTAD** and **DIMTVP**.

5'–6"   5'–6"

DIMTAD = 0   DIMTAD = 1

5'–6"   5'–6"   5'–6"

DIMTVP = 0   DIMTVP = 1   DIMTVP = –1

Changing DIMTAD with a dialog box

In addition to the **DIMTAD** settings previously described, there are other **DIMTAD** options available using the **Dimension Styles** dialog box. First issue the **DDIM** command and click the **Format...** button to display the **Format** subdialog box. As shown in **Figure 12-40**, the drop-down list in the **Vertical Justification** section at the lower right of the subdialog box offers the following four **DIMTAD** choices:

- **Centered.** This option centers the dimension text between the extension lines and sets **DIMTAD** to 0.
- **Above.** Places the dimension text above the dimension line and sets **DIMTAD** to 1 as previously described.
- **Outside.** Places the dimension text on the side of the dimension line farthest from the first defining point. This option sets **DIMTAD** to 2.
- **JIS.** Places the dimension text in conformance to a *Japanese Industrial Standards* (JIS) representation and sets **DIMTAD** to 3.

Figure 12-40.
DIMTAD values may be set using the **Vertical Justification** drop-down list in the **Format** subdialog box.

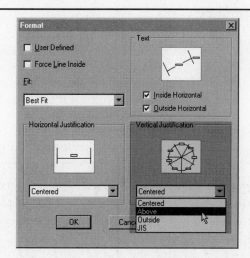

Alignment of Dimension Text Inside and Outside Extension Lines

By default, dimensions in AutoCAD LT are created unidirectionally. That is, the dimensions read from left to right in a horizontal fashion. It is common practice in architectural drafting to align dimension text with dimension lines, however. This capability is provided with two dimension variables called **DIMTIH** (Text Inside Horizontal) and **DIMTOH** (Text Outside Horizontal). As shown in **Figure 12-37**, **DIMTIH** controls the alignment of dimension text when the text is placed inside the extension lines. **DIMTOH** performs the same function when dimension text is located outside the extension lines. By default, **DIMTIH** and **DIMTOH** are both on. To create aligned dimensions, turn one or both of them off as follows:

Dim: **DIMTIH** *or* **TIH** *or* **DIMTOH** *or* **TOH.**⏎
Current value ⟨On⟩ New value: *(enter* 0 *or* OFF *and press* [Enter]*)*
Dim:

Changing DIMTIH and DIMTOH with a dialog box

To change the status of **DIMTIH** or **DIMTOH** using the **Dimension Styles** dialog box, issue the **DDIM** command and click the **Format...** button to display the **Format** subdialog box. As shown in **Figure 12-41**, deactivating the **Inside Horizontal** and **Outside Horizontal** check boxes in the **Text** section at the top right of the subdialog box turns off **DIMTIH** and **DIMTOH**.

Figure 12-41.
DIMTIH and **DIMTOH**
may be turned on
and off using the
appropriate check
boxes in the **Format**
subdialog box.

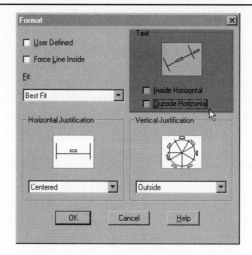

PROFESSIONAL TIP

For architectural applications, create a text style using the City Blueprint or Country Blueprint fonts. These fonts closely resemble the lettering style commonly used in architectural drafting. As a matter of efficiency, create the text style in your template(s) so that it is always available for your use. Be sure to set the **DIMTXSTY** variable so that AutoCAD LT uses your text style for dimensioning. See *Chapter 9* for more information about text styles and fonts.

EXERCISE 12-3

❏ Begin a new drawing using your TEMPLATEC template.
❏ Make architectural units current and set the drawing limits to 60', 40'. Perform a **ZOOM All** after changing the limits.
❏ Next, create a text style named ARCH using the City Blueprint font.
❏ Use the **DLINE** command to draw the partial floor plan shown below. All wall thicknesses are 6".

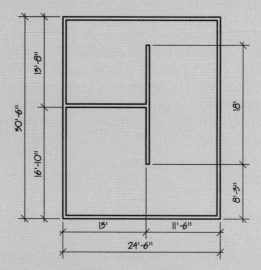

❏ The plot scale of the drawing is 1" = 1'. Set **DIMSCALE** appropriately and all other dimension variables as required to dimension the drawing exactly as shown. Be sure to create all dimensions on the DIMS layer.
❏ Save the drawing as EX12-3.

Baseline Dimensioning

The **DIMBASELINE** command continues a linear dimension from the baseline, or datum, of the previous linear dimension. This is why baseline dimensioning is also called *datum dimensioning*. An example of baseline dimensioning appears in **Figure 12-42**. As shown in the illustration, **DIMBASELINE** draws a series of related dimensions measured from the same baseline. In the example, the baseline is at the left of the object. Before you can use the **DIMBASELINE** command, you must first create a linear dimension using **DIMLINEAR** or **DIMALIGNED** to serve as the *base dimension*. In the example shown, a horizontal or aligned dimension can be used to create the 2.500 base dimension.

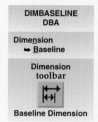

To issue the **DIMBASELINE** command, enter DIMBASELINE, or DBA, at the Command: prompt, select **Baseline** from the **Dimension** pull-down menu, or click the **Baseline Dimension** button in the **Dimension** toolbar. After first creating the 2.500 linear dimension, the two baseline dimensions shown in **Figure 12-42** are created as follows:

> Command: **DIMBASELINE** *or* **DBA**↵
> Specify a second extension line origin or (Undo/⟨Select⟩): *(pick point 1)*
> Dimension text = 5.750
> Specify a second extension line origin or (Undo/⟨Select⟩): *(pick point 2)*
> Dimension text = 8.375
> Specify a second extension line origin or (Undo/⟨Select⟩): ↵
> Select base dimension: ↵
> Command:

AutoCAD LT uses the first extension line origin of the previous dimension for the first extension line origin of the baseline dimension. After you select a second extension line origin, the baseline dimension is drawn and AutoCAD LT redisplays the Specify a second extension line origin prompt so that you may continue dimensioning. Press [Enter] twice when you are through dimensioning to terminate the command.

Figure 12-42.
An example of baseline (datum) dimensioning.

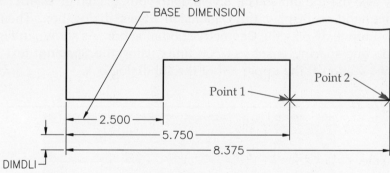

Selecting a Different Baseline Origin

AutoCAD LT automatically uses the last dimension created as the baseline reference for the next dimension. However, there may be occasions when you wish to use a different dimension as the base for subsequent dimensions. To select a different baseline origin, do the following:

Command: **DIMBASELINE** *or* **DBA**↵
Specify a second extension line origin or (Undo/⟨Select⟩): ↵
Select base dimension: *(pick the dimension you wish to use as the new baseline reference)*
Specify a second extension line origin or (Undo/⟨Select⟩): *(pick a point)*

After you select the new base dimension, the Specify a second extension line origin prompt is redisplayed. Pick a point for the second extension and the baseline dimension is drawn.

Setting the Dimension Line Increment

DIMDLI
DLI

As shown in **Figure 12-42**, AutoCAD LT uses a baseline increment value to offset each new dimension line to avoid writing over the previous dimension line. This value is stored in the **DIMDLI** (DIMension Line Increment) variable. By default, **DIMDLI** is set to .38 units (3/8) in accordance with drafting standards. While acceptable for most horizontal dimensions, the default value may be too close for vertical dimensions. This is particularly true if the vertical dimensions include tolerances. To change the value of **DIMDLI**, do the following:

Dim: **DIMDLI** *or* **DLI**↵
Current value ⟨0.3800⟩ New value: *(enter a positive value and press* [Enter]*)*
Dim:

Changing DIMDLI with a dialog box

You may also use the **Dimension Styles** dialog box to change **DIMDLI**. First, issue the **DDIM** command to display the **Dimension Styles** dialog box. Then, click the **Geometry...** button to display the **Geometry** subdialog box. As shown in **Figure 12-43,** the dimension line spacing is set to .7500 units using the **Sp_acing:** text box in the **Dimension Line** section at the upper left of the subdialog box.

Figure 12-43.
The value of **DIMDLI** may be changed using the **Sp_acing:** text box in the **Geometry** subdialog box.

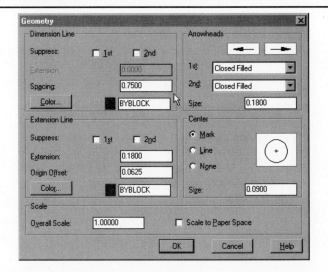

AutoCAD LT—Fundamentals and Applications

Continue Dimensioning

The **DIMCONTINUE** command continues a linear dimension from the second extension line of the previously created linear dimension. Continued dimensioning is also known as *chain dimensioning*. As shown in **Figure 12-44**, AutoCAD LT uses the origin of the previous dimension's second extension line for the origin of the next dimension's first extension line. As with baseline dimensioning, you must first create a base dimension using **DIMLINEAR** or **DIMALIGNED** before using the **DIMCONTINUE** command.

To issue the **DIMCONTINUE** command, enter DIMCONTINUE, or DCO, at the Command: prompt, select **Continue** from the **Dimension** pull-down menu, or click the **Continue Dimension** button in the **Dimension** toolbar. After first creating the 2.500 linear dimension, the two continue dimensions shown in **Figure 12-44** are created using the following procedure:

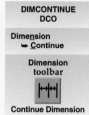

DIMCONTINUE
DCO

Dimension
↳ Continue

Dimension
toolbar

Continue Dimension

> Command: **DIMCONTINUE** *or* **DCO**↵
> Specify a second extension line origin or (Undo/⟨Select⟩): *(pick point 1)*
> Dimension text = 3.250
> Specify a second extension line origin or (Undo/⟨Select⟩): *(pick point 2)*
> Dimension text = 2.625
> Specify a second extension line origin or (Undo/⟨Select⟩): ↵
> Select continued dimension: ↵
> Command:

As with the **DIMBASELINE** command, AutoCAD LT automatically uses the last dimension created as the reference for the next continued dimension. If you wish to use a different dimension as the base for subsequent dimensions, do the following:

> Command: **DIMCONTINUE** *or* **DCO**↵
> Specify a second extension line origin or (Undo/⟨Select⟩): ↵
> Select continued dimension: *(pick the dimension you wish to use as the new continue reference)*
> Specify a second extension line origin or (Undo/⟨Select⟩): *(pick a point)*

After you select the new base dimension, the Specify a second extension line origin prompt is redisplayed. Pick a point for the second extension and the continued dimension is drawn. Finally, if it is necessary to increment a continued dimension to avoid writing over an existing dimension, the current value of **DIMDLI** is used to set the dimension line spacing.

Figure 12-44.
An example of continue (chain) dimensioning.

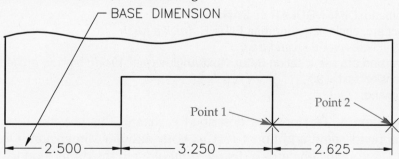

EXERCISE 12-4

❏ Begin a new drawing using your TEMPLATEA template.
❏ Draw the object shown below on the OBJECTS layer.

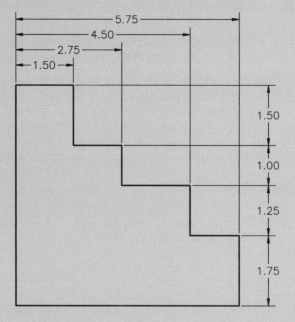

❏ Set the DIMS layer current and use baseline dimensioning to create the horizontal dimensions. Use continued dimensioning to create the vertical dimensions.
❏ Save the drawing as EX12-4.

Angular Dimensions

Angular dimensions are most commonly used to measure the angle between two selected lines. An angular dimension can also be used to measure the angle between two points on a circle, or the angle between the two endpoints of an arc. After selecting the extension line origins, you are then prompted to pick the dimension line arc location.

To issue the **DIMANGULAR** command, enter DIMANGULAR, or DAN, at the Command: prompt, select **Angular** from the **Dimension** pull-down menu, or click the **Angular Dimension** button in the **Dimension** toolbar. Refer to the angular dimension used with lines shown at the top of **Figure 12-45** as you follow the command procedure below:

DIMANGULAR
DAN

Dimension
⇨ Angular

Dimension
toolbar

Angular Dimension

> Command: **DIMANGULAR** *or* **DAN**↵
> Select arc, circle, line, or press ENTER: *(pick a line)*
> Second line: *(pick a second line)*
> Dimension arc line location (Mtext/Text/Angle): *(pick the dimension arc location)*
> Dimension text = 90
> Command:

Use the **Mtext** or **Text** options described earlier in this chapter if you wish to preface or append some additional text to your angular dimension. Observe that AutoCAD LT automatically adds a degree symbol (°) to the dimension text.

Figure 12-45.
Creating angular dimensions with lines, a circle, and an arc.

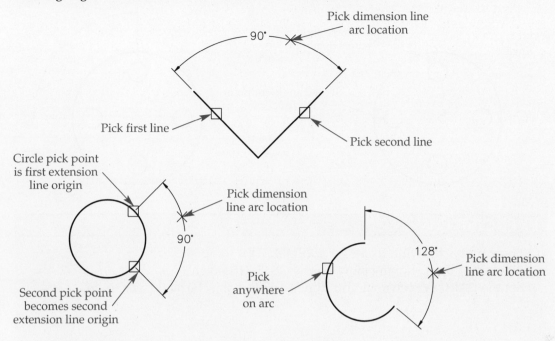

As previously mentioned, angular dimensions may also be used with circles and arcs. At the lower left of **Figure 12-45**, an angular dimension is used to measure the angle between two selected points on a circle. The first pick point on the circle becomes the first extension line origin. The second pick point is the second extension line origin (the second point need not be on the circle).

As shown at the lower right of **Figure 12-45**, the center of an arc becomes the angle vertex when placing an angular dimension. The two endpoints of the arc become the extension line origins.

Creating an Angular Dimension Through Three Points

It is also possible to create an angular dimension through three points. With this method, you first specify the angle vertex and then select the extension line origins. A practical application for this type of angular dimension is shown in **Figure 12-46.** Refer to the illustration as you follow the procedure below:

Command: **DIMANGULAR** *or* **DAN.**↵
Select arc, circle, line, or press ENTER: ↵
Angle vertex: *(pick the* **Center** *of the large circle)*
First angle endpoint: *(pick the* **Quadrant** *of the top circle)*
Second angle endpoint: *(pick the* **Quadrant** *of the circle at the right)*
Dimension arc line location (Mtext/Text/Angle): *(pick the dimension arc location)*
Dimension text = 90
Command:

NOTE

Remember that the appearance of your angular dimensions is dependent on the current **DIMAUNIT** and **DIMDEC** values. These dimension variables are discussed at the beginning of this chapter. Also, keep in mind that except for **DIMLFAC** and **DIMRND**, each of the dimvars described so far in this chapter are also applicable to angular dimensions.

Figure 12-46.
Creating an angular dimension through three points.

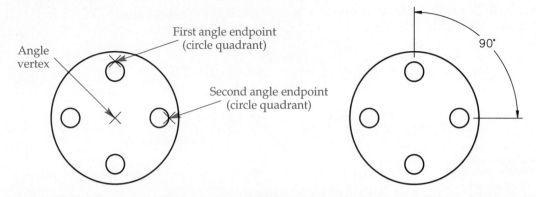

EXERCISE 12-5

❑ Begin a new drawing using your TEMPLATEA template.
❑ Draw the object shown below on the OBJECTS layer.
❑ Set the DIMS layer current and dimension the object exactly as shown.

❑ Create the centerline through the object on the CENTERLINES layer.
❑ Save the drawing as EX12-5.

Getting Started Guide 12

Radial Dimensions

Radial dimensions include both diameter and radius dimensions. This section describes radial dimensioning operations, as well as how to place center marks and centerlines through arcs and circles.

Drawing Center Marks and Centerlines

Good drafting practice dictates that center marks be drawn through small arcs and circles when detailing a drawing. For larger arcs and circles, drawing centerlines is the preferred method. To draw center marks or centerlines, enter DIMCENTER, or DCE, at the Command: prompt, select **Center Mark** from the **Dimension** pull-down menu, or click the **Center Mark** button in the **Dimension** toolbar. The command sequence is as follows:

DIMCENTER
DCE

Dimension
➥ Center Mark

Dimension
toolbar

Center Mark

Command: **DIMCENTER** *or* **DCE**↵
Select arc or circle: *(pick an arc or circle)*
Command:

AutoCAD LT places a center mark in the selected arc or circle. (Center marks may also be placed in donut objects, but not ellipses.) You can control the size of the center mark, and whether centerlines are drawn instead of center marks, using the **DIMCEN** (CENter) variable as follows:

Dim: **DIMCEN**↵
Current value ⟨0.0900⟩ New value: *(enter a positive or negative value)*
Dim:

As shown in **Figure 12-47**, a positive value (the default) draws a center mark. The larger the value, the larger the center mark. A negative value draws a centerline that extends past an arc or circle at the distance specified. The larger the negative value, the greater the extension of the centerline.

Changing **DIMCEN** with a dialog box

You can also use the **Dimension Styles** dialog box to change the value of **DIMCEN**. First, issue the **DDIM** command to display the **Dimension Styles** dialog box. Then, click the **Geometry...** button to display the **Geometry** subdialog box. Locate the **Center** section at the middle right of the subdialog box. Enter the desired value in the **Size:** text box to lengthen or shorten the center mark through small arcs and circles. To draw centerlines instead of center marks, activate the **Line** option button as shown in **Figure 12-48**. Once the **Line** option is activated, it is not necessary to enter a negative value in the **Size:** text box.

Figure 12-47.
The **DIMCEN** variable controls whether center marks or centerlines are drawn.

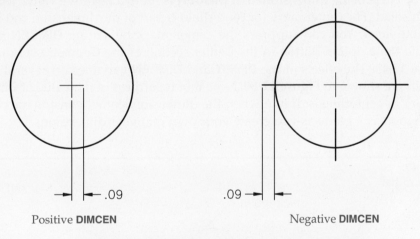

Positive **DIMCEN**   Negative **DIMCEN**

Figure 12-48.
Using the **Geometry** subdialog box to set the **DIMCEN** variable.

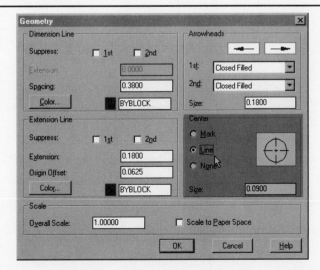

Diameter Dimensions

The **DIMDIAMETER** command is used to place a diameter dimension on a circle. Although possible, it should not be used with arc objects because the command automatically places a diameter symbol (Ø) in front of the dimension text. For arcs, use the **DIMRADIUS** command instead. The dimension arrowhead is placed at the point at which the circle or arc is selected. This applies to both diameter and radius dimensions as shown in **Figure 12-49.**

To create a diameter dimension, enter DIMDIAMETER, or DDI, at the Command: prompt, select **Diameter** from the **Dimension** pull-down menu, or click the **Diameter Dimension** button in the **Dimension** toolbar. The command sequence is as follows:

DIMDIAMETER
DDI

Dimension
➥ Diameter

Dimension
toolbar

Diameter Dimension

Command: **DIMDIAMETER** *or* **DDI**↵
Select arc or circle: *(pick an arc or circle)*
Dimension text = *nnn*
Dimension line location (Mtext/Text/Angle): *(drag to a point, select an option, or press* [Enter]*)*
Command:

If you press [Enter] at the Dimension line location prompt, AutoCAD LT draws a small leader equal to the length of two arrowheads. For a longer leader, use your cursor to dynamically "drag" the leader to the desired position. You can change the angle of the leader and also the corresponding arrowhead location by moving your cursor in a radial fashion.

Keep in mind that the **DIMDIAMETER** command automatically places a center mark through the circle being dimensioned. If **DIMCEN** is set to a negative value, a centerline is placed instead. The center mark (or centerline) is part of the dimension and is created on the same layer. You can suppress the center mark by setting **DIMCEN** = 0 or by clicking the **None** option button in the **Center** section of the **Geometry** subdialog box. See **Figure 12-48.** The effects of the **DIMFIT** and **DIMCEN** variables on several diameter dimensions are shown in **Figure 12-50.** Note that regardless of the value of **DIMCEN**, no center mark or centerline is drawn when the dimension leader is inside the circle. Use this illustration as a guide as you create your own diameter dimensions.

Figure 12-49.
Creating a radial dimension.

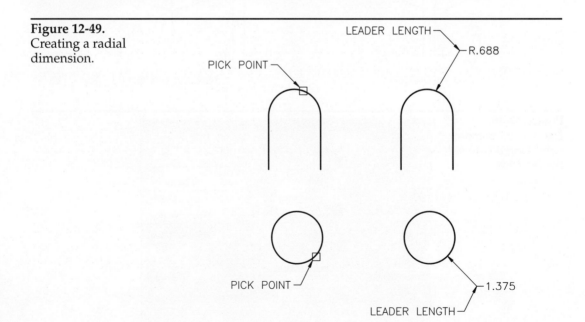

Figure 12-50.
The effects of **DIMFIT** and **DIMCEN** on diameter dimensions.

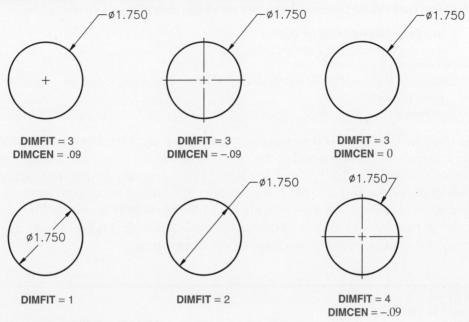

DIMFIT = 3
DIMCEN = .09

DIMFIT = 3
DIMCEN = −.09

DIMFIT = 3
DIMCEN = 0

DIMFIT = 1

DIMFIT = 2

DIMFIT = 4
DIMCEN = −.09

PROFESSIONAL TIP

Center marks and centerlines are drawn on the same layer as dimensions if **DIMCEN** has a positive or negative value when diameter dimensions are created. If you prefer to keep center marks and centerlines on a separate centerline layer, set **DIMCEN** to 0 when creating diameter dimensions. When center marks and centerlines are desired, set **DIMCEN** to the required value and use the **DIMCENTER** command on a separate centerline layer.

EXERCISE 12-6

- ❏ Begin a new drawing using your TEMPLATEA template.
- ❏ Draw the Ø1.750 circles shown in **Figure 12-50** on the OBJECTS layer.
- ❏ Set the DIMS layer current. Using the appropriate dimension variables, dimension each circle exactly as shown.
- ❏ Save the drawing as EX12-6.

Radius Dimensions

The **DIMRADIUS** command is used to place a radius dimension on an arc and automatically places an "R" (for radius) in front of the dimension text. As with diameter dimensions, the dimension arrowhead is placed at the point at which the arc is selected.

DIMRADIUS
DRA

Dime**n**sion
➡ **R**adius

Dimension
toolbar

Radius Dimension

To create a radius dimension, enter DIMRADIUS, or DRA, at the Command: prompt, select **R**adius from the **Dime**nsion pull-down menu, or click the **Radius Dimension** button in the **Dimension** toolbar. The command sequence is as follows:

Command: **DIMRADIUS** *or* **DRA**↵
Select arc or circle: *(pick an arc or circle)*
Dimension text = *nnn*
Dimension line location (Mtext/Text/Angle): *(drag to a point, select an option, or press* [Enter]*)*
Command:

As with the **DIMDIAMETER** command, pressing [Enter] at the Dimension line location prompt draws a small leader equal to the length of two arrowheads. For a longer leader, use your cursor to dynamically "drag" the leader to the desired position. You can change the angle of the leader and also the corresponding arrowhead location by moving your cursor in a radial fashion. As shown in **Figure 12-51**, the **DIMFIT** and **DIMCEN** variables affect the appearance of radius dimensions also. As with **Figure 12-50**, use this illustration for reference when you create radius dimensions.

Figure 12-51.
The effects of **DIMFIT** and **DIMCEN** on radius dimensions.

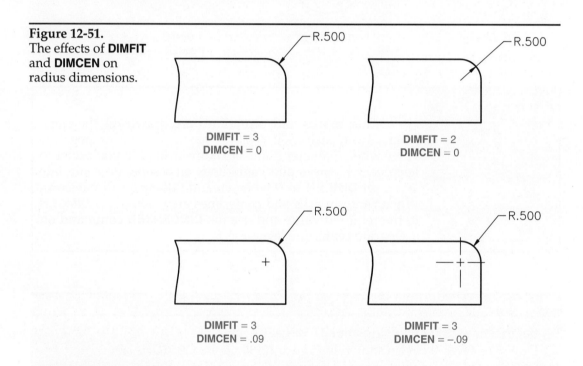

R.500   R.500

DIMFIT = 3   DIMFIT = 2
DIMCEN = 0   DIMCEN = 0

R.500   R.500

DIMFIT = 3   DIMFIT = 3
DIMCEN = .09   DIMCEN = −.09

PROFESSIONAL TIP

As with diameter dimensions, center marks and center-lines are drawn on the same layer as dimensions if **DIMCEN** has a positive or negative value when radius dimensions are created. If you prefer to keep center marks and centerlines on a separate centerline layer, set **DIMCEN** to 0 when creating radius dimensions. When center marks and centerlines are desired, set **DIMCEN** to the required value and use the **DIMCENTER** command on a separate centerline layer.

EXERCISE 12-7

❏ Begin a new drawing using your TEMPLATEA template.
❏ With the OBJECTS layer set current, draw an object similar to that shown in
Figure 12-51. Use the SPLINE command to draw the break line.
❏ Use the COPY Multiple command or a rectangular array with two rows and two
columns to create three additional copies of the object.
❏ Set the DIMS layer current. Using the appropriate dimension variables, dimen-
sion each fillet exactly as shown.
❏ Save the drawing as EX12-7.

The LEADER Command

The **LEADER** command creates a leader similar to that drawn by the **DIMDIAMETER**
and **DIMRADIUS** commands. Its purpose is to draw a leader with appended text for
specification callouts. Unlike a diameter or radius dimension which is one complete
object, a leader is drawn with separate **Mtext** and **Line** objects. Because the text is created
with **Mtext**, you may have multiple lines of text on a single leader. The arrowhead at the
end of the leader is a filled solid, (the **SOLID** command is described in *Chapter 13*).

To draw a simple leader, enter LEADER, or LE, at the Command: prompt, select
Le̲ader from the **Dime̲nsion** pull-down menu, or click the **Leader** button in the
Dimension toolbar. Refer to **Figure 12-52** as you follow the procedure shown below.

> Command: **LEADER** *or* **LE**⏎
> From point: *(pick a point on the feature to be dimensioned—object snap mode*
>   **Nearest** *is often a good choice here)*

As shown above, you are first prompted From point:. This is the point at which the
leader arrowhead will touch. Be sure to use an appropriate object snap mode when
picking the From point. The command then begins to resemble the **LINE** command as
you are presented with the To point: prompt.

> To point: *(pick the second leader point—the start of the horizontal hook line)*
> To point (Format/Annotation/Undo)⟨Annotation⟩: ⏎

Use your cursor to dynamically "drag" the leader to the desired length and angle
and pick to set the second point. AutoCAD LT repeats the To point: prompt allowing
you to draw multiple leader segments until you press [Enter] as shown above. (As
with the **LINE** command, enter U and press [Enter] to undo an incorrectly drawn
segment.) You are then prompted to enter the leader annotation:

> Annotation (or press ENTER for options): **1/2 X 45%%D**⏎
> Mtext: ⏎
> Command:

Figure 12-52.
Creating a simple
leader.

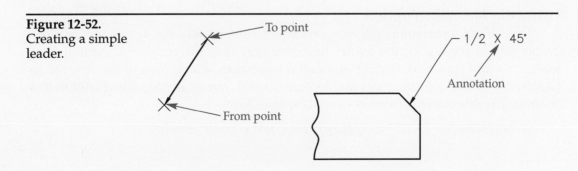

After entering the desired annotation and terminating the command as shown above, AutoCAD LT draws the horizontal hook line segment for you automatically and displays the annotation you entered.

The previous example illustrated a leader drawn in its simplest form using straight line segments. However, a leader can also be composed of an arrowhead attached to a spline. You may also choose to omit the arrowhead at the start of the leader if you like. As with other dimensioning objects, various dimvars are used to control the appearance of leader lines, such as placing the text above the hook line with **DIMTAD**.

LEADER Command Options

As shown by the command syntax repeated below, the **LEADER** command offers a variety of options.

To point (Format/Annotation/Undo)⟨Annotation⟩:

These options are described in the following sections.

Using the Format option

The **Format** option controls the way the leader is drawn and whether it has an arrowhead. You are prompted with the following:

Spline/STraight/Arrow/None/⟨Exit⟩: *(enter an option or press [Enter])*

After each suboption, you are returned to the (Format/Annotation/Undo)⟨Annotation⟩: prompt. Each **Format** suboption is described below:

- **Spline.** This suboption draws the leader line as a spline rather than a straight segment. See **Figure 12-53.** The vertices of the leader are the control points, each of equal weight.
- **Straight.** This suboption draws the leader line as a set of straight line segments. This is the default.
- **Arrow.** This suboption draws an arrowhead at the start point of the leader line. As with straight leader segments, this is the default.
- **None.** This suboption draws a leader line with no arrowhead at the start point. See **Figure 12-53.**
- **⟨Exit⟩.** This suboption exits the **Format** option.

Figure 12-53.
Examples of leaders created using the **Format** option.

A SPLINED LEADER WITH AN ARROWHEAD

A STRAIGHT LEADER WITH NO ARROWHEAD

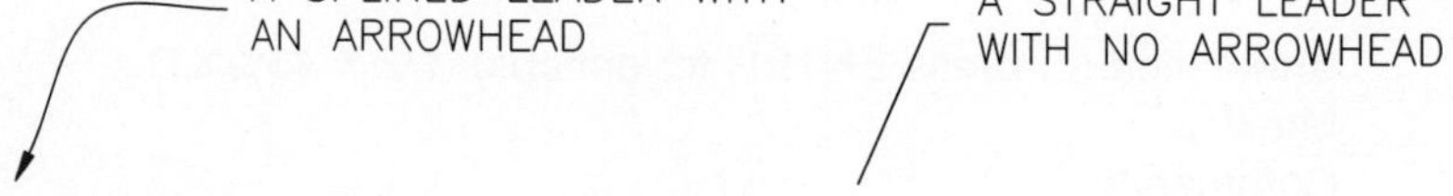

Using the Annotation option

The default **Annotation** option inserts annotation, such as single line text or paragraph text, at the end of the leader line. You may also insert a block symbol, or a feature control frame containing geometric tolerances. Block objects are covered in *Chapter 15.* Geometric tolerances and feature control frames are described later in this chapter. The **Annotation** option is described as follows:

Annotation (or ENTER for options): *enter text or press [Enter])*

After entering the desired text and pressing [Enter], AutoCAD LT places the text you entered at the end of the leader line and terminates the command. If you press [Enter] without entering text, the following prompt is displayed:

Tolerance/Copy/Block/None/⟨Mtext⟩: *(enter an option or press* [Enter]*)*

Each of these **Annotation** suboptions are described as follows:

- **Tolerance.** This option creates a feature control frame containing geometric tolerance symbols. See **Figure 12-54.** It can also create datum indicators and basic dimension notation. For more information, see the description of the **TOLERANCE** command later in this chapter. After you specify the geometric tolerance, the **LEADER** command ends.
- **Copy.** Copies existing text, paragraph text, a feature control frame with geometric tolerances, or a block symbol and connects the copy to the end of the leader line. With this option you are prompted to:

  Select an object: *(use any object selection method)*

  AutoCAD LT places the object at the end of the leader and terminates the **LEADER** command. The text is inserted at a location determined by the current **DIMGAP** value.
- **Block.** This suboption inserts a block at the end of the leader line. See **Figure 12-54.** AutoCAD LT uses the same prompts as the **INSERT** command (covered in *Chapter 15*). The block reference is inserted at an offset from the end of the leader line and is associated to the leader line. Keep in mind that no hook line is created for you when this option is used. Therefore, be sure to draw the hook after drawing the leader segment.
- **None.** Terminates the command without adding any annotation to the leader line.
- **⟨Mtext⟩.** The default option creates multiline text using the **Multiline Text Editor** dialog box. The current text style determines the appearance of the text. As shown in **Figure 12-55,** the City Blueprint font is used to create paragraph oriented architectural annotation. The paragraph of text is vertically centered, and is horizontally aligned according to the X axis direction of the last two vertices of the leader line. The text is offset from the hook line by the current **DIMGAP** value. If this value is negative, the paragraph text is enclosed in a box as a basic dimension. See *Chapter 9* for a complete description of the **Multiline Text Editor** dialog box.

Figure 12-54.
The **Annotation** option can place geometric tolerance symbols or a block at the end of a leader. Note that the **Block** suboption does not automatically draw a hook line at the end of the leader.

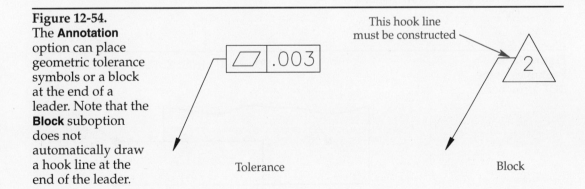

Tolerance

This hook line must be constructed

Block

Figure 12-55.
The **Multiline Text Editor** dialog box is used to create paragraph-oriented leader annotation.

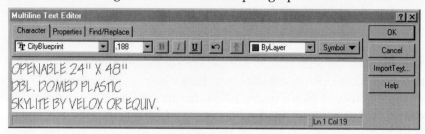

> **NOTE**
>
> The length of a hook line is equal to the length of one arrowhead. Its length can therefore be increased or decreased using the **DIMASZ** variable. The hook line is automatically included if the angle of the leader line is greater than 15° from horizontal. To position text above the hook line, as it is in JIS (Japanese Industrial Standards), set **DIMTOH** to 0 and **DIMTAD** to 1.

More On Arrowheads

As previously mentioned, AutoCAD LT provides you with a variety of arrowheads for your dimensioning applications. One of these arrowheads is in the form of a dot. Like tick marks, dot arrowheads are often used in architectural drafting. Several examples of the **DOT** arrowhead are shown in **Figure 12-56.** The size of the dot is controlled with the **DIMASZ** (Arrowhead SiZe) variable described earlier in this chapter. To use the **DOT** arrowhead, set the **DIMBLK** (BLocK) variable as follows:

```
Dim: DIMBLK or BLK↵
Current value ⟨⟩ New value: DOT↵
Dim:
```

When you wish to restore normal arrowheads for your dimension lines and leaders, clear the **DIMBLK** variable by typing a period (.) as follows:

```
Dim: DIMBLK or BLK↵
Current value ⟨⟩ New value: .↵
Dim:
```

Figure 12-56.
Examples of the
DOT arrowhead.

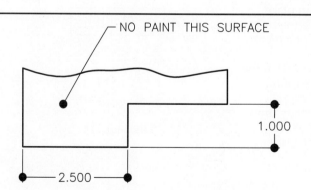

Setting the DOT Arrowhead with a Dialog Box

You can also use the **Dimension Styles** dialog box to set the **DOT** arrowhead. First, issue the **DDIM** command to display the **Dimension Styles** dialog box. Then, click the **Geometry...** button to display the **Geometry** subdialog box. Next, select **Dot Small** from the **Arrowheads** drop-down list at the upper right of the subdialog box. See **Figure 12-57**. The **Dot Blanked** option can also be used when you wish to use open circles as terminators at the end of your dimension lines. For both dot arrowhead types, enter an appropriate value in the **Size:** text box to increase or decrease the diameter of the dots.

Figure 12-57.
Using the **Arrowheads** drop-down list in the **Geometry** subdialog box to draw dot arrowheads.

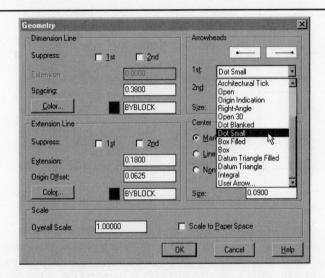

Specifying Separate Arrowheads

The **Arrowheads** drop-down list in the **Geometry** subdialog box allows you to specify a separate arrowhead at each end of a dimension line. This is accomplished by selecting one type of arrowhead from the **1st:** drop-down list, and a different type from the **2nd:** drop-down list. Doing so sets the **DIMBLK1** and **DIMBLK2** dimension variables, respectively. Specifying separate arrowheads also turns on the **DIMSAH** (Separate ArrowHeads) variable. Each of the arrowhead types available in AutoCAD LT are shown in **Figure 12-58**.

NOTE

When using separate arrowheads, the **LEADER** command uses the arrowhead specified by **DIMBLK1**. Diameter and radius dimensions use the arrowhead specified by **DIMBLK2**.

Creating Your Own Arrowheads

If the arrowhead type you need is not included with AutoCAD LT , you have the option of creating your own. A custom arrowhead must first be drawn 1 unit in size and saved as a block with a name that cannot exceed 31 characters in length, (block objects are covered in *Chapter 15*). In the example that follows, a user has created a custom arrowhead and saved it as a block object with the name MYARROW. This name is then entered for the **DIMBLK** value.

Dim: **DIMBLK** *or* **BLK**↵
Current value 〈〉 New value: **MYARROW**↵

Figure 12-58.
The arrowhead types available in AutoCAD LT 98 and AutoCAD LT 97. The CLOSED FILLED type is the default.

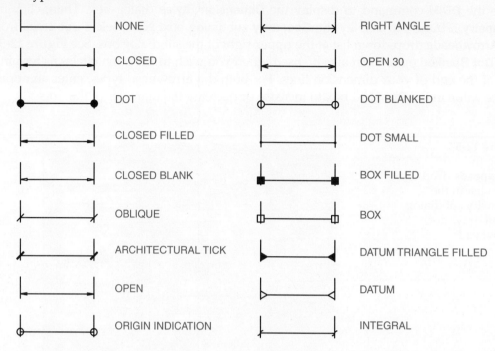

Whenever a linear, angular, or radial dimension is now created, AutoCAD LT inserts your block where the arrowheads are normally placed. The custom arrowhead is then sized using the formula **DIMASZ** × **DIMSCALE**. Also, be sure to draw an extra "tail" with your arrowheads so that they connect properly with the dimension lines. The tail is trimmed at each end of the dimension line using the formula **DIMGAP** × **DIMSCALE**.

Setting custom arrowheads current with a dialog box

You can also use the **Dimension Styles** dialog box to set your custom arrowheads current. Issue the **DDIM** command to display the **Dimension Styles** dialog box. Then, click the **Geometry...** button to display the **Geometry** subdialog box. Next, select **User Arrow...** from the very bottom of the **Arrowheads** drop-down list at the upper right of the subdialog box. When the **User Arrow** subdialog box appears, enter the name of your custom arrowhead block in the **Arrow Name:** text box. Be sure to repeat the procedure for the second arrowhead as well.

Ordinate Dimensioning

Ordinate dimensions, also known as *arrowless dimensions*, display the X or Y coordinate of a feature on a single leader line. As shown in **Figure 12-59**, no arrowheads are used with ordinate dimensions. Before dimensioning with ordinate dimensions, you must first create a UCS (User Coordinate System). This is because AutoCAD LT uses the origin of the current UCS to determine the measured X or Y coordinates. The leader lines are then drawn parallel to the coordinate axes of the current UCS. For most applications, the UCS is created at the lower left of the object. That point then becomes the 0,0 datum for all subsequent ordinate dimensions. Certain applications may require the datum to be located on a specific feature, like the center of a hole. Such a datum is shown in **Figure 12-60**. Although the two objects are physically identical, compare the dimensions in this illustration with those in **Figure 12-59**.

Figure 12-59.
Ordinate dimensions display the X or Y coordinate of a feature on a single leader.

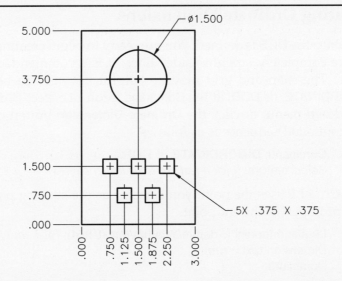

Figure 12-60.
A UCS is defined at the datum origin of the object. Note the docked **Dimension** toolbar at the left of the drawing window.

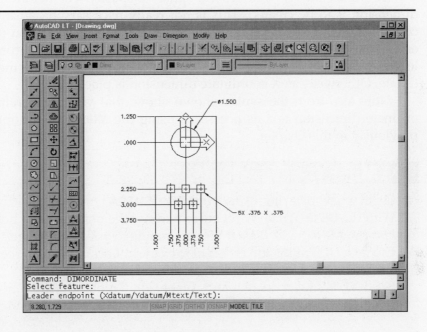

The UCS and UCSICON Commands Revisited

You may recall that the **UCS** command was introduced in *Chapter 7* as a means of facilitating the creation of auxiliary views. The **UCS** command may be issued at the Command: prompt, or by selecting **UCS** from the **Tools** pull-down menu. Each of the **UCS** command options are then displayed in a cascading submenu. Refer to **Figure 12-60** as you follow the procedure given below to create a UCS that represents the 0,0 datum:

> Command: **UCS↵**
> Origin/ZAxis/3point/OBject/View/X/Y/Z/Prev/Restore/Save/Del/?/⟨World⟩: **O↵**
> Origin point ⟨0,0,0⟩: *(select the circle using osnap* **Center***)*
> Command:

Now that the required UCS is created, it is helpful to display the UCS icon at the origin of the current UCS. You can move the origin of the UCS icon using the **UCSICON** command at the Command: prompt like this:

> Command: **UCSICON↵**
> ON/OFF/All/Noorigin/ORigin ⟨ON⟩: **OR↵**
> Command:

UCS

Tools
➥ UCS ⟩
➥ Origin

UCSICON

Creating Ordinate Dimensions

DIMORDINATE
DOR

Dimension
➥ Ordinate

Dimension
toolbar

Ordinate Dimension

Once the UCS is defined, you are ready to begin creating ordinate dimensions. To ensure completely straight leader lines, it is recommended that you turn on Ortho mode. The snap and grid may be helpful, as well. To begin dimensioning, enter DIMORDINATE, or DOR, at the Command: prompt, select **Ordinate** from the **Dimension** pull-down menu, or click the **Ordinate Dimension** button on the **Dimension** toolbar. The command sequence is as follows:

> Command: **DIMORDINATE** *or* **DOR**↵
> Select feature: (*pick a feature to be dimensioned*)

AutoCAD LT uses the point you selected as the starting point of the leader line and then prompts for the endpoint.

> Leader endpoint (Xdatum/Ydatum/Mtext/Text): (*pick an endpoint for the leader*)
> Dimension text = *nnn*
> Command:

As shown above, you have the option to specify whether an Xdatum or Ydatum dimension is to be created. This is not really necessary because the **DIMORDINATE** command makes the determination based on the direction you pick for the leader endpoint. If the difference in the X coordinate between the feature location and the leader endpoint is greater than the Y coordinate, the dimension measures the Y coordinate. Otherwise, an X coordinate dimension is placed.

Note also from the syntax shown above that you may preface or append the ordinate dimension text as necessary using the **Mtext** or **Text** options as described previously in this chapter.

EXERCISE 12-8

❑ Begin a new drawing using your **TEMPLATEA** template.
❑ With the OBJECTS layer set current, draw the object shown below.
❑ Use the **ARRAY** and **CHAMFER** commands to your advantage.
❑ Create a UCS at the lower left of the object. Locate the UCS icon at the origin of the UCS.
❑ Set the DIMS layer current and dimension the object using ordinate dimensions exactly as shown. Turn on **Ortho** mode to ensure straight leader lines.

4X Ø.625

1.000

.750 X 45°

3.500
2.750
2.250
2.000
1.000

.750
.000

.000   1.500   3.750   4.750   5.250

❑ Save the drawing as EX12-8.

Associative Dimensions

AutoCAD LT defines an *associative dimension* as a dimension that adapts as the associated geometry is modified. In other words, if you stretch a dimensioned object, the dimension updates automatically. This powerful capability permits you to quickly revise drawings without having to redimension them. Consider the simple object illustrated in **Figure 12-61.** In this example, an object is stretched 1.375 units to the right. Because the dimension is included in the **Crossing** selection set, its value is automatically updated both during and after the stretch operation.

Dimension associativity is controlled with the **DIMASO** (ASsOciativity) variable. When **DIMASO** is off (0), there is no association between the various elements of a dimension. The lines, arcs, arrowheads, and text of a dimension are drawn as separate objects and must be edited individually. When **DIMASO** is on (the default), there is association between each element of a dimension forming it into a single object. If the *definition point* of the dimension moves, the dimension value is updated. Definition points are used by AutoCAD LT to maintain associativity between geometry and dimensions. These points define extension line and dimension line origins, as well as the selected points and centers of circles and arcs for diameter and radius dimensions. Although it is recommended that **DIMASO** be left on, it may be turned off as follows:

Dim: **DIMASO** *or* **ASO**⏎
Current value ⟨On⟩ New value: *(type* 0 *or* OFF *and press* [Enter]*)*
Dim:

Figure 12-61.
Dimension associativity ensures that dimensions are updated during a **STRETCH** operation.

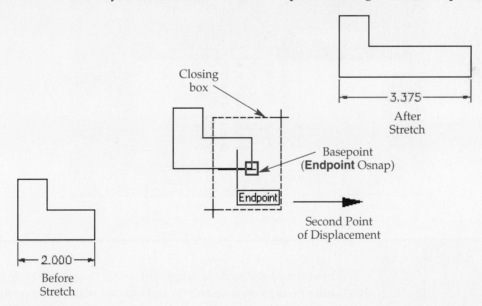

NOTE

Associative dimensions recompute dynamically as they are dragged. This can be a slow process on older computers, or machines that have insufficient physical memory (RAM). If you find that dimension dragging is adversely affecting system performance, it may be turned off with the **DIMSHO** variable. When turned on (the default), **DIMSHO** controls the redefinition of linear, angular, and radial dimensions while dragging. Observe that neither **DIMSHO** or **DIMASO** may be controlled using the **Dimension Styles** dialog box.

The **DEFPOINTS** Layer

As mentioned previously, definition points are used to maintain associativity between geometry and dimensions. When **DIMASO** is on and the first associative dimension is created in a drawing, AutoCAD LT automatically creates a new layer called **Defpoints**. See **Figure 12-62.** This layer contains the definition points needed for dimension associativity. The definition points are displayed, but not plotted, whether the Defpoints layer is turned on or off. When stretching dimensioned geometry, be sure to include the definition points in the selection set or the dimensions will not update.

Figure 12-62.
The Defpoints layer is shown in the **Layer and Linetype Properties** dialog box.

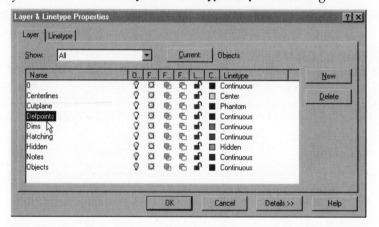

PROFESSIONAL
TIP

There may be instances when you wish to include proprietary information on a drawing, but do not want to have the information appear on the finished plot. The information could be created on a separate layer and then turned off or frozen before plotting. Another alternative would be to create the information on the **Defpoints** layer. Since this layer does not plot, you need not be concerned about the layer visibility.

Exploding a Dimension

An associative dimension is all one object. The **EXPLODE** command returns an associative dimension to its constituent elements and associativity is lost. This is the equivalent of creating a dimension with **DIMASO** turned off. Also, the objects that once comprised the dimension (lines and text) are automatically placed on layer 0. Should you inadvertently explode one or more dimensions, an **UNDO** operation will restore them.

Editing Dimensions

Eventually, one or more of the associative dimensions on your drawings may require modification. AutoCAD LT provides several dimension editing commands for that purpose. However, keep in mind that the dimension editing commands cannot be used with exploded, or non-associative, dimensions.

The **DIMTEDIT** Command

The **DIMTEDIT** (DIMension Text EDIT) command is used to shift a linear or angular dimension left, right, up, or down within the dimension line. See **Figure 12-63.** It is often used to obtain staggered dimensions. For vertical dimensions, shifting to the left moves the dimension text down; shifting to the right moves the dimension text up. Rather than explicitly specifying the **Left** or **Right** options, you can also use your cursor to dynamically "drag" the dimension after issuing the **DIMTEDIT** command. Doing so gives you greater control over the dimension placement.

DIMTEDIT can also be used with radial dimensions. It is particularly handy with radial dimensions because it allows you to change the direction of the hook and text at the end of the dimension leader line.

Use the **Home** option to return dimension text in linear dimensions to its original (centered) position. As shown in **Figure 12-63**, the **Angle** option rotates dimension text at any angle (positive or negative) within the dimension line. This option is useful for orienting dimensions correctly in auxiliary views. To return angled dimension text to its default text angle, enter a 0 (zero).

Figure 12-63.
Using the **DIMTEDIT** command with associative dimensions.

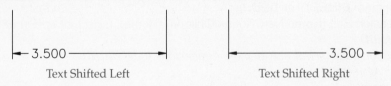

| Text Shifted Left | Text Shifted Right |

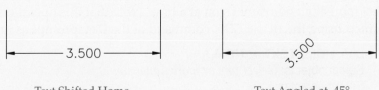

| Text Shifted Home | Text Angled at 45° |

DIMTEDIT

Dime**n**sion
→ Align Te**x**t ⟩

Dimension
toolbar

Dimension Text Edit

The **DIMTEDIT** command looks like this:

Command: **DIMTEDIT**⏎
Select dimension: *(select a dimension)*
Enter text location (Left/Right/Home/Angle): *(select an option or use your pointing device to dynamically move the dimension text)*
Command:

At the Dim: prompt, enter the following to issue the **DIMTEDIT** command:

Dim: **TEDIT** *or* **TE**⏎

DIMTEDIT may also be issued by clicking the **Dimension Text Edit** button in the **Dimension** toolbar. Each of the **DIMTEDIT** command options are also accessible from the **Dime_n_sion** pull-down menu. As shown in **Figure 12-64**, clicking the **Align Te_x_t ⟩** selection displays a cascading submenu containing these options: **_H_ome**, **_A_ngle**, **_L_eft**, **_C_enter**, and **_R_ight**.

Figure 12-64.
Clicking **Align Te_x_t ⟩** in the **Dime_n_sion** pull-down menu displays a cascading submenu containing the **DIMTEDIT** command options.

The DIMEDIT Command

DIMEDIT
DED

Dimension
toolbar

Dimension Edit

DIMEDIT is another dimension editing command that contains several options. It may be quickly accessed by entering DIMEDIT, or DED, at the Command: prompt, or by clicking the **Dimension Edit** button in the **Dimension** toolbar. The command sequence is as follows:

Command: **DIMEDIT** *or* **DED**⏎
Dimension Edit (Home/New/Rotate/Oblique) ⟨Home⟩: *(select an option or accept the default)*
Select objects: *(select one or more dimensions to be edited)*
Select objects: ⏎
Command:

Each of the **DIMEDIT** command options are described as follows:

*   **Home.** This option returns linear dimension text to its original (centered) position. In other words, it performs the same function as the **Home** option of the **DIMTEDIT** command. The difference is that the **DIMEDIT Home** option allows you to select more than one dimension at a time. Note that this operation can also be performed using the **HOMETEXT** command at the Dim: prompt as follows:

    Dim: **HOMETEXT** *or* **HOM**⏎
    Select objects: *(select one or more dimensions)*
    Select objects: ⏎
    Dim:

- **New.** This option can be used to edit the text format of, or add a prefix or suffix to, one or more existing dimensions. In the example shown in **Figure 12-65**, a diameter symbol (Ø) has been inadvertently omitted from the 1.125 vertical dimension. To correct the error, issue the **DIMEDIT** command and select the **New** option as follows:

  Command: **DIMEDIT** *or* **DED**↵
  Dimension Edit (Home/New/Rotate/Oblique) ⟨Home⟩: **N**↵

  When the **Multiline Text Editor** dialog box appears, enter %%C in front of the angle brackets (⟨⟩) or select **Diameter** from the **Symbol** drop-down list and then click the **OK** button. You are then prompted with:

  Select objects: *(select the 1.125 dimension)*
  Select objects: ↵
  Command:

  As with the **Home** option, the **New** option may also be performed at the Dim: prompt like this:

  Dim: **NEWTEXT** *or* **N**↵
  Enter new dimension text: %%C⟨⟩↵
  Select objects: *(select the 1.125 dimension)*
  Select objects: ↵
  Dim:

CAUTION

Never use the **DIMEDIT New** option (or the **NEWTEXT** command) to type in a different dimensional value than appears in the brackets. Doing so destroys the associativity between the dimension and the associated feature. Should the dimensioned object then be stretched, the dimension *will not* update. If a dimension needs to change, revise the drawing geometry accordingly. Only use **DIMEDIT New** (or **NEWTEXT**) to change the existing dimension text format or add a prefix/suffix to a dimension.

- **Rotate.** Similar to the **Angle** option of the **DIMTEDIT** command, the **DIMEDIT Rotate** option rotates dimension text at any angle (positive or negative) within the dimension line. The difference is that this option allows you to rotate more than one dimension at a time. The procedure looks like this:

  Command: **DIMEDIT** *or* **DED**↵
  Dimension Edit (Home/New/Rotate/Oblique) ⟨Home⟩: **R**↵
  Enter text angle: *(enter a positive or negative value)*
  Select objects: *(select one or more dimensions)*
  Select objects: ↵
  Command:

Figure 12-65.
The **DIMEDIT New** option is used to add prefixes and/or suffixes to associative dimensions.

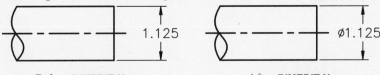

Before **DIMEDIT New**   After **DIMEDIT New**

This function may also be performed at the Dim: prompt using the **TROTATE** command as follows:

> Dim: **TROTATE** *or* **TR**↵
> Enter text angle: *(enter a positive or negative value)*
> Select objects: *(select one or more dimensions)*
> Select objects: ↵
> Dim:

- **Oblique.** The **Oblique** option is used to change the angle of extension lines for existing associative dimensions. This option is occasionally used on curved surfaces when dimensions are crowded or diffficult to read. As shown at the right in **Figure 12-66,** an obliquing angle of 30° has been applied to two vertical dimensions. The procedure looks like this:

> Command: **DIMEDIT** *or* **DED**↵
> Dimension Edit (Home/New/Rotate/Oblique) ⟨Home⟩: **O**↵
> Select objects: *(select one or more linear dimensions)*
> Select objects: ↵
> Enter obliquing angle (press ENTER for none): *(enter a positive or negative value)*
> Command:

The identical function can be performed at the Dim: prompt using the **OBLIQUE** command as follows:

> Dim: **OBLIQUE** *or* **OB**↵
> Select objects: *(select one or more linear dimensions)*
> Select objects: ↵
> Enter obliquing angle (press ENTER for none): *(enter a positive or negative value)*
> Dim:

Oblique dimensions are also used to dimension isometric drawings. This capability is explored in *Chapter 16.*

Figure 12-66.
A—Linear dimensions on a curved object. B—Two dimensions with oblique extension lines.

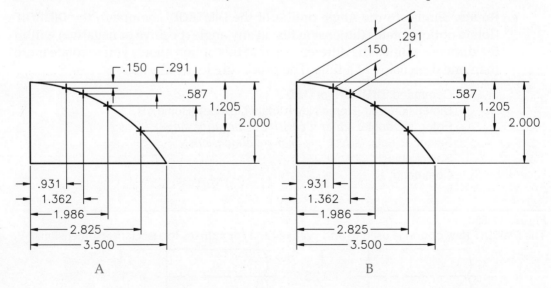

PROFESSIONAL TIP
You can quickly invoke the **DIMEDIT** Oblique by selecting **Oblique** from the **Dimension** pull-down menu.

Editing Dimensions Using DDEDIT and DDMODIFY

The **DDEDIT** command was introduced in *Chapter 9* as a means of editing AutoCAD LT text objects. It may also be used to edit a dimension. To do so, enter **DDEDIT**, or **ED**, at the Command: prompt, or select **Text...** from the **Object** ⟩ cascading submenu in the **Modify** pull-down menu. See **Figure 12-67.** The command sequence is as follows:

    Command: **DDEDIT** *or* **ED**↵
    ⟨Select an annotation object⟩/Undo: *(select one dimension)*

After selecting a dimension to edit, the **Multiline Text Editor** dialog box appears. Use the dialog box to add a prefix or suffix to the selected dimension. If you wish to add a special character code (like a diameter symbol), select it from the **Symbol** drop-down list at the upper right of the dialog box. However, do not change the dimension value represented by the angle brackets. Remember that doing so destroys the associativity between the dimension and the geometry to which it is related. Click the **OK** button when you are through editing the dimension. The dialog box closes and you are again prompted with:

    ⟨Select an annotation object⟩/Undo: *(select another dimension or press* [Enter] *to end the command)*

If necessary, refer to *Chapter 9* to review the editing features offered by the **Multiline Text Editor** dialog box.

Dimension text, as well as dimension properties, may also be edited using the **DDMODIFY** command. You may recall that this command was described in *Chapter 10* as a means of editing single drawing objects. As shown in **Figure 12-68**, you can use **DDMODIFY** to change the color, layer, linetype, thickness, linetype scale, contents, and text style of a selected dimension. You can also use the **Multiline Text Editor** dialog box with **DDMODIFY** by clicking the **Full editor...** button at the right of the **Modify Dimension** dialog box.

Figure 12-67.
Selecting **Object** ⟩ from the **Modify** pull-down menu and then selecting **Text...** from the cascading submenu issues the **DDEDIT** command.

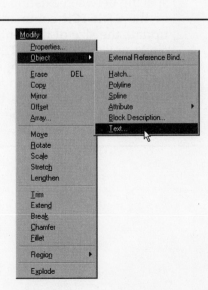

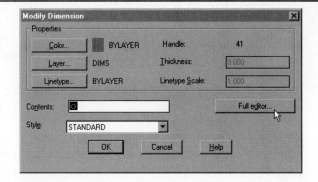

Figure 12-68.
The **Modify Dimension** dialog box is displayed when **DDMODIFY** is used to edit a dimension.

To issue the **DDMODIFY** command, enter DDMODIFY, or MO, at the Command: prompt, or click the **Properties** button on the far right of the **Object Properties** toolbar. The command sequence is as follows:

    Command: **DDMODIFY** or **MO**↵
    Select one object to modify: *(select one dimension)*

The UPDATE Command Revisited

As mentioned earlier in this chapter, the **UPDATE** command is used to update one or more dimensions to the current dimension variables. Since all of the AutoCAD LT selection set options are valid with **UPDATE**, you can select many dimensions at one time using a **Window** or **Crossing** box. Exploded, or nonassociative, dimensions cannot be updated, however. Issue the **UPDATE** command by clicking the **Dimension Update** button in the **Dimension** toolbar or by selecting **Update** from the **Dimension** pull-down menu. At the Dim: prompt, enter the following:

    Dim: **UPDATE** or **UP** or **UPD**↵
    Select objects: *(select one or more dimensions)*
    Select objects: ↵
    Dim:

NOTE

The **UPDATE** command cannot be used to increase the dimension line increment (**DIMDLI**) between **BASELINE** and **CONTINUE** dimensions. Should you need to increase the spacing between existing linear dimensions, use grip editing or the **STRETCH** command instead. Also, **UPDATE** will not update the size of the centerlines drawn through an arc or a circle with the **DIMCENTER** command. You must erase the existing centerlines, change the value of **DIMCEN**, and reissue the **DIMCENTER** command. However, the centerlines created through arcs and circles by the **DIMRADIUS** and **DIMDIAMETER** commands may be updated to a new **DIMCEN** value using **UPDATE**.

Using the DIMOVERRIDE Command

A major drawback of the **UPDATE** command is that dimensions are created anew—not edited—when updated. This is why the selected dimensions assume the characteristics of *all* the current dimension variables, and not just the one or two variables you wish to update to. For this reason, you may want to use the **DIMOVER-RIDE** command instead. This command allows you to specify one or more dimvar values to change without recreating the entire dimension. If you are using a dimension style (covered later in this chapter), **DIMOVERRIDE** overrides the variable settings that are associated with a dimension but does not affect the current dimension style.

As an example, suppose that you would like to create a basic dimension by setting the **DIMGAP** variable to a negative value. You could set the variable and then create a new dimension, or update an existing dimension using the **UPDATE** command. After doing so, however, you then have to return the **DIMGAP** variable back to its previous value before creating any new, or updating any existing, dimensions. Otherwise, those dimensions also assume the revised **DIMGAP** setting and become basic dimensions. To avoid this problem, use the **DIMOVERRIDE** command as follows:

DIMOVERRIDE
DOV

> Command: **DIMOVERRIDE** *or* **DOV**↵
> Dimension variable to override (or Clear to remove overrides): **DIMGAP** ↵
> Current value ⟨0.0900⟩ New value: **–.09.**↵
> Dimension variable to override: ↵
> Select objects: *(select one or more dimensions)*
> Select objects: ↵
> Command:

The identical function can be performed at the Dim: prompt using the **OVERRIDE** command as follows:

> Dim: **OVERRIDE** *or* **OV.**↵
> Dimension variable to override (or Clear to remove overrides): **DIMGAP.**↵
> Current value ⟨0.0900⟩ New value: **-.09.**↵
> Dimension variable to override: ↵
> Select objects: *(select one or more dimensions)*
> Select objects: ↵
> Command:

Observe from the command syntax examples shown above that **DIMOVERRIDE** continues to prompt for the dimension variable to override until you press [Enter]. Thus, you can override multiple dimension variables. Note also the **Clear to remove overrides** option. This option clears any overrides on selected dimensions. The procedure looks like this:

> Command: **DIMOVERRIDE** *or* **DOV.**↵
> Dimension variable to override (or Clear to remove overrides): **C.**↵
> Select objects: *(select one or more dimensions)*
> Select objects: ↵
> Command:

AutoCAD LT clears the override(s) on the dimension you select, and it returns to its previous settings (defined by its dimension style).

A *tolerance* is the total amount of variation in size from a specified dimension. Tolerances may be expressed as plus and minus (+/−) values or as dimensional limits. A horizontal dimension expressed with tolerance limits is shown at the upper right in **Figure 12-69.** The three dimension variables that control this type of dimension are **DIMLIM** (LIMits), **DIMTP** (Tolerance Plus), and **DIMTM** (Tolerance Minus). In the example shown, **DIMTP** and **DIMTM** are both set to .005.

To express the same dimension with plus and minus values, the **DIMTOL** (TOLerance) variable is used in place of **DIMLIM**. (Turning **DIMTOL** on automatically disables **DIMLIM**, and vice-versa.) When **DIMTP** and **DIMTM** are set equal, the dimension is created with an equal bilateral tolerance. This type of dimension is shown at the lower left of **Figure 12-69.** An unequal bilateral tolerance is shown at the lower right. To create this tolerance, do the following:

> Dim: **DIMTOL** *or* **TOL**⏎
> Current value ⟨Off⟩ New value: *(enter* 1 *or* ON *and press* [Enter]*)*
> Dim: **DIMTP** *or* **TP**⏎
> Current value ⟨.000⟩ New value: **.006**⏎
> Dim: **DIMTM** *or* **TM** ⏎
> Current value ⟨.000⟩ New value: **.002**⏎
> Dim:

Any new dimension you now create automatically includes the +.006/−.002 tolerance. Use the **UPDATE** or **DIMOVERRIDE** commands to add the tolerance to one or more existing dimensions.

Figure 12-69.
The **DIMLIM**, **DIMTOL**, **DIMTP**, and **DIMTM** variables control dimension tolerances.

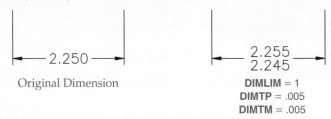

2.250
Original Dimension

2.255
2.245
DIMLIM = 1
DIMTP = .005
DIMTM = .005

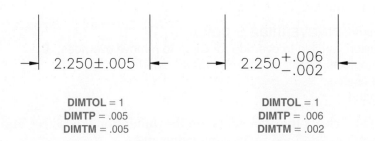

2.250±.005
DIMTOL = 1
DIMTP = .005
DIMTM = .005

$2.250^{+.006}_{-.002}$
DIMTOL = 1
DIMTP = .006
DIMTM = .002

Setting Tolerance Height

As shown in **Figure 12-69**, AutoCAD LT sets the tolerance height equal to the height of the dimension text. This is in accordance with industry drafting standards. If you wish to set the tolerance height to be slightly smaller (or larger) than the dimension height, use the **DIMTFAC** (Tolerance FACtor) variable. In the following example, tolerance height is set to 3/4th the dimension height:

    Dim: **DIMTFAC** *or* **TFAC**⏎
    Current value ⟨1.000⟩ New value: **.75**⏎
    Dim:

Setting Tolerance Justification

AutoCAD LT lets you set the vertical justification for tolerance values relative to the nominal dimension text. This feature is controlled using the **DIMTOLJ** (TOLerance Justification) variable. As shown in **Figure 12-70**, **DIMTOLJ** may be set to one of three values. The values are:

    0 = Bottom justification
    1 = Middle justification (the default setting)
    2 = Top justification

In the unlikely event that you need to change **DIMTOLJ**, do the following:

    Dim: **DIMTOLJ** *or* **TOLJ**⏎
    Current value ⟨*current*⟩ New value: *(enter 0, 1, or 2 and press* [Enter]*)*
    Dim:

Figure 12-70.
Tolerance justification is controlled with the **DIMTOLJ** variable.

     DIMTOLJ = 1   DIMTOLJ = 0   DIMTOLJ = 2

Other Tolerance Settings

You may recall from earlier in this chapter that the number of decimal places in decimal dimensions is controlled with the **DIMDEC** variable. Good drafting practice dictates that the number of decimal places in a tolerance should be equal to the number of decimal places specified in the nominal dimension. You can set the number of tolerance decimal places using the **DIMTDEC** (Tolerance DECimals) variable like this:

    Dim: **DIMTDEC** *or* **TDEC**⏎
    Current value ⟨*current*⟩ New value: *(enter 0 – 8 and press* [Enter]*)*
    Dim:

Also discussed earlier in this chapter, the **DIMZIN** variable is used to drop leading or trailing zeroes from dimension values. You can also drop leading and trailing zeroes from tolerances using the **DIMTZIN** (Tolerance Zero INch) variable. Refer to the table of **DIMZIN** values shown on page 421 as a guide in helping you select the appropriate **DIMTZIN** value for your tolerances.

See **Figure 12-71** to get a better idea how **DIMTDEC** and **DIMZIN** affect the appearance of decimal tolerances.

Figure 12-71.
The effects of the **DIMDEC**, **DIMTDEC**, and **DIMTZIN** variables on toleranced dimensions.

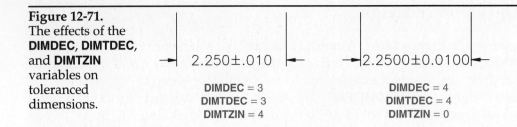

2.250±.010

DIMDEC = 3
DIMTDEC = 3
DIMTZIN = 4

2.2500±0.0100

DIMDEC = 4
DIMTDEC = 4
DIMTZIN = 0

PROFESSIONAL TIP

Set **DIMTZIN** to 4 (or 7) to drop leading zeroes from decimal tolerances. Leave **DIMTZIN** set to 0 (the default setting) if you are dimensioning with metric units. This is because metric dimensioning standards specify leading zeroes in metric tolerances.

Controlling Tolerances Using a Dialog Box

Tolerances may also be set using the **Dimension Styles** dialog box. To access this dialog box, enter DDIM at the Command: prompt, pick **Style...** from the **Dimension** pull-down menu, or click the **Dimension Style** button on the **Dimension** toolbar. Once the **Dimension Styles** dialog box is displayed, click the **Annotation...** button to display the **Annotation** subdialog box. Next, locate the **Tolerance** section at the lower left of the subdialog box. Each of the options available in this section are described as follows:

- **Method.** Use this drop-down list to specify the type of tolerance you wish to use. As shown in **Figure 12-72**, this drop-down list contains five options. They are:
  - **None**—When this default option is selected, dimensions are created without tolerances.
  - **Symmetrical**—Select this option when you wish to create an equal bilateral tolerance. An example would be ±.002. After selecting **Symmetrical** from the drop-down list, enter the desired tolerance value in the **Upper Value:** text box.
  - **Deviation**—Use this option when you wish to create an unequal tolerance. Enter the appropriate tolerance values in the **Upper Value:** and **Lower Value:** text boxes.
  - **Limits**—Select this option when you wish to express a tolerance as dimensional limits. As with the **Deviation** option, enter the appropriate tolerance values in the **Upper Value:** and **Lower Value:** text boxes.
  - **Basic**—Select this option when you wish to create a basic dimension. A basic dimension is described as a theoretically exact dimension when using geometric dimensioning and tolerancing symbols. Selecting the **Basic** option from the drop-down list is equivalent to setting the **DIMGAP** variable to a negative value as discussed earlier in this chapter.
- **Upper Value:**. Enter the appropriate tolerance upper value in this text box when using the **Symmetrical** or **Deviation** tolerance options.
- **Lower Value:**. Enter the appropriate tolerance lower value in this text box when using the **Deviation** tolerance option.
- **Justification.** This drop-down list offers three choices—**Top, Middle** (the default), and **Bottom.** These choices equate to setting the **DIMTOLJ** variable equal to 0, 1, and 2, respectively.
- **Height.** If you wish to set the tolerance height to be slightly smaller (or larger) than the dimension height, enter the desired height value in this text box. This is the equivalent of setting the **DIMTFAC** variable.

Figure 12-72.
The **Tolerance** section in the **Annotation** subdialog box is used to control the types and values of tolerances created by AutoCAD LT.

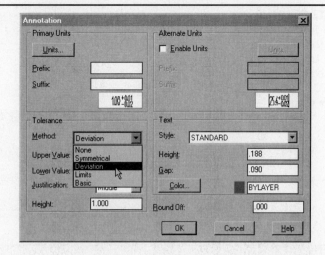

PROFESSIONAL TIP

Keep in mind that AutoCAD LT omits the + (or –) in a unilateral or unequal bilateral tolerance when one of the tolerance values is zero. This is acceptable for metric tolerances, but inch tolerances should display the + (or –) in accordance with ANSI and ASME standards. You can "trick" AutoCAD LT into placing a + (or –) in front of a zero tolerance by setting the **DIMTP** or **DIMTM** variables to a greater number of decimal places than are actually required. For example, suppose you are dimensioning and tolerancing a drawing using three-place decimals (**DIMDEC** = 3 and **DIMTDEC** = 3). Several dimensions on your drawing require a tolerance of +.000, –.005. Set **DIMTM** to .005, but set **DIMTP** to .0001. Because dimension and tolerance decimal places are displayed as stored in the **DIMDEC** and **DIMTDEC** system variables, AutoCAD LT does not show the numeral 1 in the fourth decimal place. Thus, the tolerance displays on screen as +.000.

Also, be advised that the number of decimal places displayed in dialog boxes is determined by the **LUPREC** (Linear Units PRECision) variable. If this variable is set to 3, then you cannot use the **Annotation** dialog box to set a tolerance value to 4 places as described in the tip above. The tolerance values must then be set on the command line. If you wish to use the dialog box, be sure to set **LUPREC** to 4, its default value.

Using the Primary Units Dialog Box with Tolerances

As previously mentioned, you will need to set the number of decimal places for your decimal tolerances using the **DIMTDEC** variable. Use **DIMTZIN** if you need to drop any leading zeroes. You can perform these tasks in the **Dimension Styles** dialog box by issuing the **DDIM** command. Then, click the **Annotation...** button to display the **Annotation** subdialog box. Now, click the **Units...** button at the upper left to open the **Primary Units** subdialog box. See **Figure 12-73.**

Set **DIMTDEC** by selecting the required number of tolerance decimal places from the **Precision** drop-down list in the **Tolerance** section at the right of the subdialog box. Activating the **Leading** check box sets the **DIMTZIN** variable. Remember, do not activate this check box for metric tolerancing applications.

Figure 12-73.
Use the **Tolerance** section in the **Primary Units** subdialog box to set **DIMTDEC** and **DIMTZIN** values.

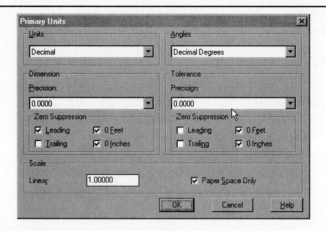

EXERCISE 12-9

❏ Open EX12-5.
❏ Set the appropriate dimension variables to create the toleranced dimensions shown below. Use the **UPDATE** command to revise the existing dimensions.

$$\varnothing 1.250^{+.005}_{-.000}$$

.120
.122

3.875±.010

❏ Save the drawing as EX12-9.

Dual Dimensioning

The practice of including metric equivalents with inch dimensions on a drawing is called *dual dimensioning*. AutoCAD LT refers to it as alternate units dimensioning. Two examples of dual dimensions are shown in **Figure 12-74.** The dimension variables that create dual dimensions are described below:

- **DIMALT.** When **DIMALT** is on (**DIMALT** = 1), alternate units are displayed in brackets to the right of the primary units. The default alternate units are millimeters.
- **DIMALTD.** This variable sets the number of alternate unit decimal places. The default value is 2. **DIMALTD** is independent of **DIMDEC** (DIMension DECimal places).
- **DIMALTF.** This is the alternate unit scale factor. The default value is 25.4 because there are 25.4 millimeters to an inch. However, **DIMALTF** may be set to any scale factor you choose. As an example, if you wish to use millimeters as the primary units and inches as the alternate units, set **DIMALTF** to .039370078 (1÷25.4). Enter this value in full to prevent round-off error.
- **DIMALTU.** This variable sets the system of alternate units.
- **DIMALTZ.** Similar to **DIMZIN**, **DIMALTZ** sets the alternate unit zero suppression.
- **DIMAPOST.** Similar to **DIMPOST**, **DIMAPOST** adds a suffix to an alternate unit dimension. Both **DIMPOST** and **DIMAPOST** are used to produce the 5.000 IN. [127.00 MM] dimension shown at the right in **Figure 12-74.** As with **DIMPOST**, enter a period (.) to clear the **DIMAPOST** value.

If your alternate dimensions require tolerances, then you will also need to consider the following two dimvars:

- **DIMALTTD.** Sets the number of alternate tolerance decimal places.
- **DIMALTTZ.** Similar to **DIMTZIN**, **DIMALTTZ** sets the alternate tolerance zero suppression.

Setting Alternate Units Using a Dialog Box

To set alternate units using a dialog box, issue the **DDIM** command to display the **Dimension Styles** dialog box. Then, click the **Annotation...** button to display the **Annotation** subdialog box. The **Alternate Units** section is at the upper right. As shown in **Figure 12-75**, **DIMALT** is turned on by activating the **Enable Units** check box. Note that **DIMPOST** and **DIMAPOST** may be set using the **Prefix** and **Suffix** text boxes in the **Primary Units** and **Alternate Units** sections of the subdialog box.

- Click the **Units...** button at the upper right to display the **Alternate Units** subdialog box shown in **Figure 12-76.** Set **DIMALTU** by selecting the desired system of units from the **Units** drop-down list at the upper left of the subdialog box. **DIMALTD** is set by selecting the required number of decimal places from the **Precision:** drop-down list. Activate the **Leading** check box in the **Zero Suppression** section to set the **DIMALTZ** variable. Once you have alternate units enabled, the **Linear:** text box at the lower left automatically displays the current **DIMALTF** value of 25.4. Use this text box if you wish to enter a different scale factor. For example, if you wish to use millimeters as the primary units and inches as the alternate units, enter .039370078 in the **Linear:** text box.

Figure 12-74.
Using dual dimensions.

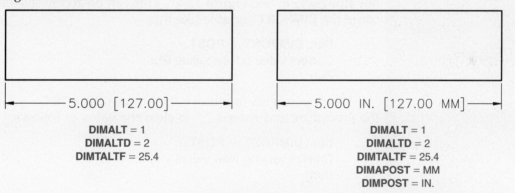

5.000 [127.00]

DIMALT = 1
DIMALTD = 2
DIMTALTF = 25.4

5.000 IN. [127.00 MM]

DIMALT = 1
DIMALTD = 2
DIMTALTF = 25.4
DIMAPOST = MM
DIMPOST = IN.

Figure 12-75.
Several of the dual dimensioning variables are controlled in the **Alternate Units** section at the upper right of the **Annotation** subdialog box.

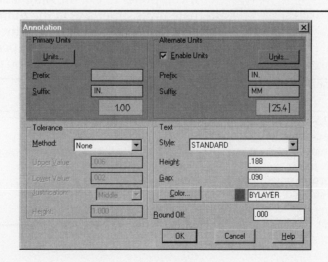

Figure 12-76.
Additional variables that control the format of alternate units are enabled in the
Alternate Units subdialog box.

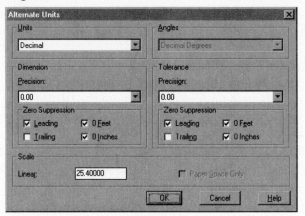

If you require tolerances on your alternate units, use the **Precision** drop-down list
in the **Tolerance** section at the right of the subdialog box to set the number of alternate tolerance decimal places (**DIMALTTD**). To set **DIMALTTZ**, activate the **Leading**
check box in the **Zero Suppression** area at the right.

PROFESSIONAL TIP

From the examples shown in **Figure 12-74**, you will
observe that AutoCAD LT places the alternate units to the
right of the primary dimension. However, it is the preferred
practice to place alternate units *below* the primary dimension,
not alongside it. See **Figure 12-77**. This can be accomplished
using the **DIMPOST** variable like this:

> Dim: **DIMPOST** *or* **POST**↵
> Current value ⟨⟩ New value: **\P**↵
> Dim:

When you wish to remove the **\P** from **DIMPOST**, repeat
the procedure and enter a "." to clear the value as follows:

> Dim: **DIMPOST** *or* **POST**↵
> Current value ⟨⟩ New value: **.**
> Dim:

If you prefer to use the **Annotation** subdialog box to stack
alternate units, enter a \P in the **Suffix:** text box in the **Primary
Units** section at the upper left of the subdialog box.
　　Be advised that whether you perform this function on the
command line or in a dialog box, you *must* use an uppercase "P".

Figure 12-77.
A—The default
representation of
alternate units.
B—Alternate units
may be stacked
by setting
DIMPOST
to \P.

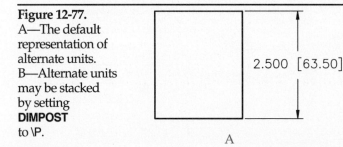

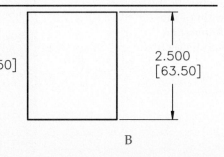

A　　　　　　　　　　　　　　　　　B

Using AutoCAD LT for Metric Dimensioning Only

It may occasionally be necessary to create and dimension a drawing in millimeters only. This can easily be accomplished by adhering to the following guidelines:

- Set the drawing limits in millimeters and **ZOOM All**. Remember that one inch equals 25.4 millimeters.
- Set the value of the **DIMDEC** dimension variable to 1 or 2 decimal places as required.
- Set the **DIMSCALE** variable to 25.4. Remember that **DIMSCALE** controls the size of *all* dimensioning objects, so you need not set each variable individually.
- When using the **MTEXT**, **DTEXT**, or **TEXT** commands to create the drawing annotation, be sure to set the text height in millimeters to match that of the dimension text height.
- Adjust the **LTSCALE** variable as necessary to ensure that hidden lines, phantom lines, centerlines, etc., are scaled correctly.
- For sectioned views, set the hatch pattern scale to 25.4. Hatching parameters are discussed in *Chapter 13*.
- Plot the finished drawing at 1 (plotted inch) = 25.4 (drawing units). Plotting and plot scale factors are covered in *Chapter 14*.

EXERCISE 12-10

❑ Open EX12-4.
❑ Enable the appropriate alternate units dimension variables and update the dimensions as shown below. Be sure to set **DIMPOST** as described to obtain stacked dimensions.
❑ If necessary, use the **STRETCH** command or grips to adjust the placement of the dimensions.

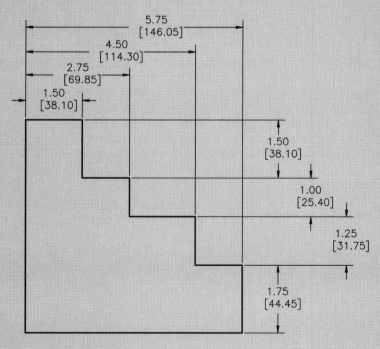

❑ Save the drawing as EX12-10.

The **TOLERANCE** Command

The **TOLERANCE** command is used for geometric dimensioning and tolerancing operations. Geometric tolerances define the maximum allowable variations of form or profile, orientation, location, and runout from the drawing geometry. Thus, their use specifies the required accuracy for proper function and fit of the objects drawn in AutoCAD LT.

Using the **TOLERANCE** command, mechanical drafters and engineers can easily create datum identifier and form tolerance symbols, as well as feature control frames. These are frames divided into compartments that contain the geometric characteristic symbols followed by one or more tolerance values. Where applicable, the tolerance is preceded by the diameter symbol (for a cylindrical tolerance zone) and followed by datums and symbols for their material conditions. A typical feature control frame is shown in **Figure 12-78**.

To issue the **TOLERANCE** command, enter TOLERANCE, or TOL, at the Command: prompt, select **Tolerance...** from the **Dimension** pull-down menu, or click the **Tolerance** button in the **Dimension** toolbar. On the command line, enter the following:

Command: **TOLERANCE** *or* **TOL.**⏎

TOLERANCE
TOL

Dimension
➥Tolerance...

Dimension
toolbar

Tolerance

The **Symbol** dialog box is now displayed. See **Figure 12-79A.** This dialog box contains the geometric characteristic symbols for location, orientation, form, profile, and runout. These symbols and their meanings are listed in **Figure 12-79B**.

Figure 12-78.
The components of a typical feature control frame. Feature control frames like this one are easily created using the **TOLERANCE** command.

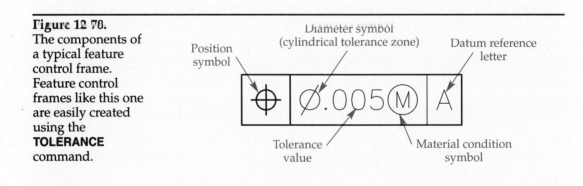

Position symbol — Diameter symbol (cylindrical tolerance zone) — Datum reference letter — Tolerance value — Material condition symbol

---

Figure 12-79.
A—The **Symbol** dialog box contains geometric characteristic symbols for location, orientation, form, profile, and runout. B—The geometric characteristic symbols and descriptions.

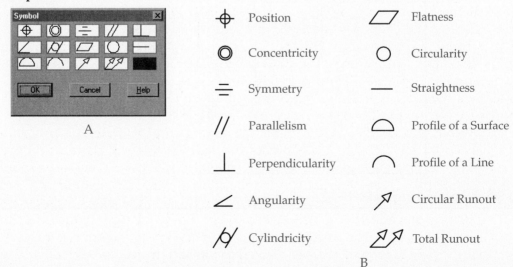

A

⊕ Position	▱ Flatness
◎ Concentricity	○ Circularity
꞊ Symmetry	— Straightness
// Parallelism	⌓ Profile of a Surface
⊥ Perpendicularity	⌒ Profile of a Line
∠ Angularity	⤴ Circular Runout
⌭ Cylindricity	⤴⤴ Total Runout

B

Select the symbol you wish to use from the **Symbol** dialog box. The dialog box is closed and the symbol is then inserted into the **Sym** box in the **Geometric Tolerance** dialog box. As shown in **Figure 12-80**, the symbol for Position has been selected and appears in the **Sym** box at the upper left of the **Geometric Tolerance** dialog box. Each of the options available in the **Geometric Tolerance** dialog box are described in the next section.

Figure 12-80.
The **Geometric Tolerance** box is used to specify the symbols and values required for a feature control frame.

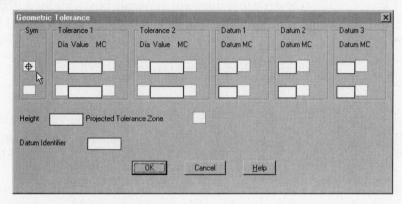

The **Geometric Tolerance** Dialog Box

The **Geometric Tolerance** dialog box is used to specify the symbols and values for a feature control frame. It is also used to define form tolerance and datum identifier symbols. Each of the components of the **Geometric Tolerance** dialog box are described as follows:

- **Sym.** This box contains the geometric characteristic symbol that was selected in the **Symbol** dialog box. If you wish to select a different symbol, simply click the **Sym** box and the **Symbol** dialog box reappears. You can then make a new selection.
- **Tolerance 1.** Use this box to create the first tolerance value in the feature control frame. The tolerance value indicates the amount by which the geometric characteristic can deviate from a perfect form.
- **Dia.** Clicking this box inserts a diameter symbol in front of the tolerance value to indicate a cylindrical tolerance zone.
- **MC.** Click this box to display the **Material Condition** subdialog box. See **Figure 12-81A.** The material condition symbols act as modifiers to the geometric characteristic and the tolerance value of features that can vary in size. The three symbols and what they represent are listed in **Figure 12-81B.**

Select the material condition symbol you wish to use and click the **OK** button to exit the **Material Condition** subdialog box. When you wish to remove a material condition symbol, click the empty box at the far right of the **Material Condition** subdialog box.

- **Tolerance 2.** Use this box to create the second tolerance value in the feature control frame. The second tolerance value is specified the same way as the first. As with the first tolerance value, diameter (Dia) and material condition (MC) symbols can be included with the tolerance value, if necessary.
- **Datum 1.** This box is used to enter the primary datum reference letter in the feature control frame. A datum is a theoretically exact geometric reference used to establish the tolerance zone for a feature. The datum reference can consist of a letter and a material condition modifying symbol (MC).

- **Datum 2.** If applicable, use this text box to enter the secondary datum reference letter in the feature control frame. Specify the secondary datum reference and material condition modifier (MC) in the same way as the primary datum reference.
- **Datum 3.** If applicable, use this text box to enter the tertiary (third) datum reference in the feature control frame. Specify the tertiary datum reference and material condition modifier (MC) in the same way as the primary and secondary datum references.

NOTE

Observe that there are duplicate boxes for **Sym, Tolerance 1**, and **Tolerance 2**, as well as for **Datum 1, Datum 2**, and **Datum 3**. These duplicate boxes are used when a composite feature control frame is required. See *Exercise 12-11* for an example of a composite feature control frame.

- **Height.** Use this box to enter a projected tolerance zone value in the feature control frame. A projected tolerance zone controls the height of the extended portion of a fixed perpendicular part and refines the tolerance to that specified by positional tolerances.
- **Projected Tolerance Zone.** Clicking this box inserts a projected tolerance zone symbol to the right of the height value. See **Figure 12-82**.
- **Datum Identifier.** A datum is a theoretically exact geometric reference from which the location and tolerance zones of other features can be established. A point, line, plane, or cylinder can be used as a datum. To create a datum identifier only, click the empty box at the lower right of the **Symbol** dialog box and then click the **OK** button. When the **Geometric Tolerance** subdialog box appears, use the **Datum Identifier** text box at the lower left to create a datum-identifying symbol. This symbol consists of a reference letter preceded and followed by a dash. For example: –A–. You must enter the necessary dashes – they are not automatically created for you.

Figure 12-81.
A—The **Material Condition** subdialog box. B—The material condition symbols and descriptions.

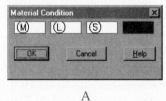

A

Ⓜ Maximum Material Condition

Ⓛ Least Material Condition

Ⓢ Regardless of Feature Size

B

Figure 12-82.
An example of a feature control frame with a height value and a projected tolerance zone symbol.

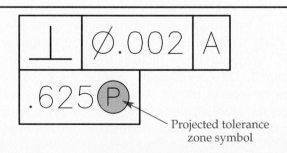

Projected tolerance zone symbol

AutoCAD LT—Fundamentals and Applications

After selecting the required geometric characteristic symbols and clicking the **OK** button, the **Geometric Tolerance** dialog box closes and the following prompt is displayed on the command line:

Enter tolerance location: *(specify a location)*

The feature control frame appears in the drawing window with the graphics cursor attached to the far left midpoint of the object. Place the feature control frame at the desired location using an object snap mode if appropriate. After placing the feature control frame, the **TOLERANCE** command is terminated and the Command: prompt is redisplayed.

PROFESSIONAL TIP

For complete information regarding geometric tolerancing methods, refer to *Geometric Dimensioning and Tolerancing* by David Madsen and published by Goodheart-Willcox Company.

NOTE

Unfortunately, the datum identifier symbol created by AutoCAD LT does not represent the latest drafting standard. The current standard is *ASME Y14.5M-1994*. The new symbol with the proper dimensions appears in **Figure 12-83**. See *Chapter 15* to learn how to save this symbol as a block object for multiple use.

Figure 12-83.
The datum identifier symbol as specified by *ASME Y14.5M-1994*. The "h" indicates dimension lettering height.

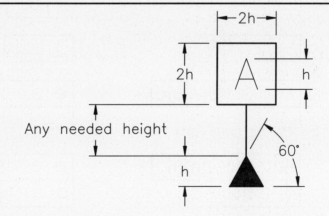

Editing Feature Control Frames

Existing feature control frames may be edited using the **DDEDIT** and **DDMODIFY** commands. Use **DDEDIT** when you wish to only modify the symbols within a feature control frame. Use **DDMODIFY** when you wish to also edit feature control frame properties like color, layer, and linetype, etc. To modify the symbols within a feature control frame using **DDMODIFY**, enter DDMODIFY, or MO, at the Command: prompt. Then, open the **Geometric Tolerance** dialog box by clicking the **Edit...** button in the center of the **Modify Tolerance** dialog box. See **Figure 12-84.**

Figure 12-84.
Both the properties and the symbols of a geometric tolerance may be edited using the **DDMODIFY** command.

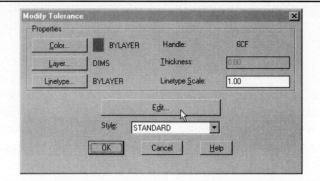

PROFESSIONAL TIP

Feature control frame properties may also be edited using the **DDCHPROP** command.

EXERCISE 12-11

❏ Begin a new drawing using your TEMPLATEA template.
❏ Set the DIMS layer current and create the geometric tolerances shown at A below.
❏ Revise the tolerances using **DDEDIT** to produce the objects shown at B.

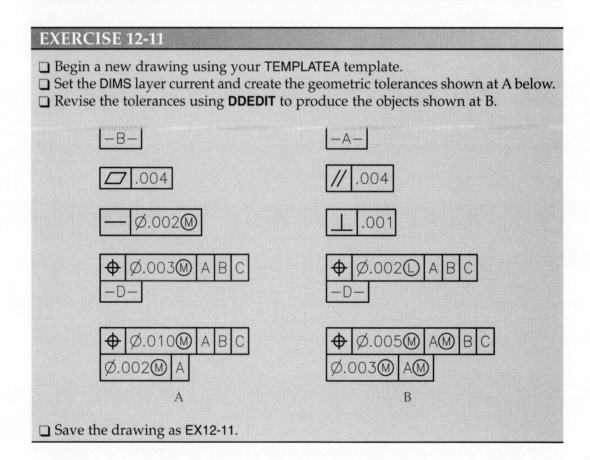

❏ Save the drawing as EX12-11.

Using Geometric Dimensioning and Tolerancing Symbols in Text and Dimensions

As discussed in the previous section, the **TOLERANCE** command provides you with the ability to create feature control frames, form tolerances, and datum identifier symbols. The symbols can be located anywhere in the drawing window, or placed at the end of extension lines or leaders. Unfortunately, the **TOLERANCE** command does not provide symbols for counterbore, countersink, depth, etc. As a result, many users in the mechanical and manufacturing disciplines are still making blocks for these symbols and inserting them as needed.

However, there is a way to place geometric dimensioning and tolerancing symbols in drawings by entering them directly from the keyboard using lower-case characters.

To do so requires the creation of a new text style using the gdt.shx font. This font is a Simplex type that redraws and regenerates quickly and is located in the **Program Files\AutoCAD LT 98** folder. Users of AutoCAD LT 97 will find gdt.shx located in the Program Files\AutoCAD LT 97 folder.

Creating the Required Text Style

The easiest way to create the new text style is to use the **Text Style** dialog box accessed by the **STYLE** command. To do so, enter STYLE, or ST, at the Command: prompt, or select **Text Style...** from the **Format** pull-down menu to open the dialog box.

STYLE
ST

Format
➥ Text Style...

You can also create the new text style from the command line. To do so, use the **–STYLE** command as follows:

```
Command: –STYLE↵
Text style name (or ?) ⟨current⟩: MECHANICAL ↵
New style.
Specify full font name or font filename ⟨current⟩: GDT↵
Height ⟨0.000⟩: ↵
Width factor ⟨1.000⟩: ↵
Obliquing angle ⟨0d⟩: ↵
Backwards? ⟨N⟩ ↵
Upside-down? ⟨N⟩ ↵
Vertical? ⟨N⟩ ↵
MECHANICAL is now the current text style.
Command:
```

Using the New Text Font Symbols in Dimensions

Now that the MECHANICAL text style is current, set the **DIMTXSTY** variable to MECHANICAL so that the new style is used for dimensions as well as text. You can use the new style in notes and dimensions by entering lower case characters. As an example, typing in a lowercase "x" places a depth symbol in front of a dimension. A lowercase "v" places a counterbore symbol. You can indicate squareness by entering a lowercase "o". Best of all, instead of entering %%c to force a diameter symbol, you can now simply enter a lowercase "n." However, you can still enter %%c if you wish.

To use the new style when dimensioning, simply create a dimension as you would normally. When prompted for the dimension line location, do the following:

```
Dimension line location (Mtext/Text/Angle/Horizontal/Vertical/Rotated): M↵
```

The **Multiline Text Editor** is then displayed. Enter the special lowercase character you require directly in front of the angle brackets (⟨⟩). Remember that these brackets represent the current dimension value. To comply with ANSI/ASME dimensioning standards, do *not* put a space between the special character and the dimension. After entering the lowercase character, click the **OK** button. The previous prompt is once again displayed.

> Dimension line location (Mtext/Text/Angle/Horizontal/Vertical/Rotated): *(place the dimension)*

If you prefer, you can ignore the **Multiline Text Editor** and enter the special character on the command line instead using the **Text** option. In the following example, the symbol for squareness is placed before a .875 dimension.

> Dimension line location (Mtext/Text/Angle/Horizontal/Vertical/Rotated): **T**↵
> Dimension text ⟨.875⟩: **o**⟨⟩ ↵

Each of the characters in gdt.shx are mapped and shown in **Figure 12-85**.

NOTE   Remember that you must enter lowercase characters to generate the special symbols listed in **Figure 12-85**.

Figure 12-85.
Mapping the lower-case characters of the gdt.shx font to their respective geometric dimensioning and tolerancing symbols.

Character	Symbol	Description	Character	Symbol	Description
a	∠	Angularity	n	Ø	Diameter Symbol
b	⊥	Perpendicularity	o	□	Square Symbol
c	▱	Flatness	p	Ⓟ	Projected Tolerance Zone
d	⌓	Profile of a Surface	q	₵	Centerline Symbol
e	○	Circularity	r	◎	Concentricity
f	//	Parallelism	s	Ⓢ	Regardless of Feature Size
g	⌭	Cylindricity	t	⫫	Total Runout
h	⌲	Circular Runout	u	—	Straightness
i	⩵	Symmetry	v	⊔	Counterbore Symbol
j	⌖	Position	w	∨	Countersink Symbol
k	⌒	Profile of a Line	x	↧	Depth Symbol
l	Ⓛ	Least Material Condition	y	⊳	Conical Taper Symbol
m	Ⓜ	Maximum Material Condition	z	⊐	Slope Symbol

A *dimension style* is a stored group of dimensioning variables with unique values. The style is saved with a name and can be recalled for use at any time. This capability allows you to create several styles to be used for different drafting applications or industry standards. The current dimension style name is stored in the **DIMSTYLE** variable. The default dimension style name is called STANDARD. You can verify the current style at the Dim: prompt using the **DIMSTYLE** variable as follows:

> Dim: **DIMSTYLE**↵
> Current value 〈STANDARD〉↵
> Dim:

DIMSTYLE cannot be used to change the current style because it is a *read only* type of dimensioning variable. This means that it only stores a value.

Using a Dialog Box to Manage Dimension Styles

Thus far in this chapter you have seen how the **Geometry...**, **Format...**, and **Annotation...** buttons in the **Dimension Styles** dialog box provide quick access to dimensioning variables. The **Dimension Styles** dialog box can also be used to create, list, and restore a dimension style. To create a dimension style, enter the **DDIM** command or click the **Dimension Style** button in the **Dimension** toolbar. Alternatively, you may select **Style...** from the **Dimension** pull-down menu or **Dimension Style...** from the **Format** pull-down menu to open the **Dimension Styles** dialog box.

The name of the current dimension style is shown in the **Current:** drop-down list at the top of the **Dimension Styles** dialog box. Enter the desired name for your new style in the **Name:** text box and click the **Save** button. A dimension style name may contain up to 31 characters, but no spaces are allowed. As shown in **Figure 12-86**, the name ASME (for the American Society of Mechanical Engineers) is entered. Also, note the message at the bottom of the dialog box. This message appears because AutoCAD LT makes a complete copy of the current dimension style. The style name you enter then appears in the **Current:** drop-down list at the top of the dialog box.

If you wish to rename a dimension style, first make the style current. Next, enter the new name in the **Name:** text box and click the **Rename** button.

Figure 12-86.
Creating a dimension style using the **Dimension Styles** dialog box.

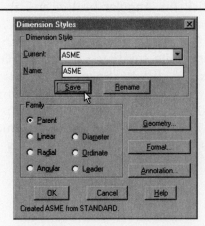

Using the Family Option Buttons

The option buttons that appear in the **Family** section at the lower left of the **Dimension Styles** dialog box allow you to create a dimension style that can have a variety of settings. For example, within a dimension style you may create a variation such that no center mark (or centerline) is created for radius and diameter dimensions. As an example, the following procedure can be performed if you are at your computer:

1. Begin a new drawing using your TEMPLATEA template.
2. Issue the **DDIM** command and create a dimension style named **MYDIMSTYLE**. Be sure to click the **Save** button after entering the style name in the **Name:** text box.
3. Click the **Radial** button and then click the **Geometry...** button to display the **Geometry** subdialog box. See **Figure 12-87**.
4. Locate the **Center** section at the right of the dialog box and click the **None** option button. Click the **OK** button when you are finished.
5. When the **Dimension Styles** dialog box reappears, click the **Save** button to save the modified style. AutoCAD LT displays the **Alert** box shown in **Figure 12-88** if you forget to save your changes.
6. Now, click the **Diameter** option button and reopen the **Annotation** subdialog box. Once again, click the **None** button and select **OK**.
7. Save the modified style again and click the **OK** button to exit the **Dimension Styles** dialog box.
8. Draw several arcs and circles and dimension them using the **DIMRADIUS** and **DIMDIAMETER** commands as described earlier in this chapter. Be sure to use the proper layers. Observe that no centermarks are created through the arcs and circles.
9. Finally, set the **CENTER** layer current and use the **DIMCENTER** command to manually force a centerline through several arcs and circles.

From the exercise above, do you see how AutoCAD LT uses the appropriate dimension style family member for the type of dimension you create? If there are no differences in settings for a dimension type, the **Parent** dimension style settings are used. To explain further, suppose you want to dimension a drawing using two decimal places. If you leave the **Parent** option button checked and set the **DIMDEC** variable to 2, then *all* of your dimensions will appear with two decimal places. This may be fine for linear and radial dimensions, but what about your angular dimensions? Depending on your application, the angular dimensions may be better expressed with no decimal places.

To do so, click the **Angular** button and then click the **Annotation...** button to display the **Annotation** subdialog box. Next, click the **Units...** button to open the **Primary Units** subdialog box. Set **DIMDEC** = 0 using the **Precision** drop-down list at the left of the **Primary Units** subdialog box. Click **OK** twice to return to the **Dimension Styles** dialog box and click the **Save** button to save your changes.

Now when you create linear and radial dimensions, they will appear with two decimal places of accuracy. Any angular dimensions you create will display no decimal places. Remember that the key to successfully using the **Family** option buttons is to first select the appropriate **Family** button and then set the dimension variable(s).

Figure 12-87.
Disabling center
marks and
centerlines in
the **Geometry**
subdialog box.

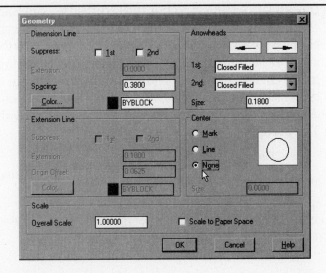

Figure 12-88.
AutoCAD LT displays an **Alert** box if you fail to save your changes to a dimension style.

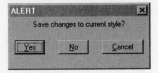

Other Dimension Style Options

Although it is much easier to use the **Dimension Styles** dialog box, dimension styles may also be created and managed at the Dim: prompt with the following commands:

- **SAVE.** After setting the dimension variables as required, use the **SAVE** command to save them with a name. This command also features the **?** option allowing you to list all existing dimension styles in the current drawing.

  > Dim: **SAVE** *or* **SA**↵
  > ?/Name for new dimension style: *(enter the style name)*

- **RESTORE.** The **RESTORE** command is used to restore a previously saved dimension style. It may also be used to list existing dimension styles.

  > Dim: **RESTORE** *or* **RES**↵
  > dimension style: STANDARD
  > ?/Enter dimension style name or press ENTER to select dimension:

  Enter the name of the style you wish to set current. If you press [Enter], you are then prompted to select a dimension. The style used to create the dimension you select then becomes the current dimension style.

- **VARIABLES.** This command lists all of the current dimension variable settings for a specified dimension style. The graphics window flips to the text window to display the complete dimension variable listing.

  > Dim: **VARIABLES** *or* **VA**↵
  > dimension style: STANDARD
  > ?/Enter dimension style name or press ENTER to select dimension:

  As with the **RESTORE** command, you can enter the name of the style whose variable settings you wish to list, or select a dimension on the screen.

- **OVERRIDE.** Identical to the **DIMOVERRIDE** command described earlier in this chapter, the **OVERRIDE** command allows you to change one or more dimension variables and update selected dimensions to the new variable settings. As an example, suppose you have an architectural dimension style named ARCH in the current drawing. You would like to change the arrowheads on a single dimension to the DOT arrowhead style, but wish to retain the tick marks defined in the ARCH dimension style for any new dimensions you may create. The procedure looks like this:

> Dim: **OVERRIDE** *or* **OV**⏎
> Dimension variable to override (or Clear to remove overrides): **DIMBLK**⏎
> Current value ⟨⟩ New value: **DOT**⏎
> Dimension variable to override: ⏎
> Select objects: *(pick the dimension to change)*
> Select objects: ⏎
> Dim:

PROFESSIONAL TIP

Keep in mind that there is no limit to the number of dimension styles that you can create. This means that you may have dimension styles that represent a wide variety of drafting standards and applications. Create your dimension styles in your template files so that they are always available. Whenever you wish to use one of your saved dimension styles, issue the **DDIM** command and select its name from the **Current** drop-down list. The style name you select then appears in the **Name:** text box and becomes the current dimension style.

EXERCISE 12-12

❑ Open your TITLEA template file created in *Chapter 2*.
❑ Create a text style named ARCH. Assign to it the City Blueprint font.
❑ Next, create a text style named MECH. Assign to it the gdt.shx font as described in this chapter.
❑ Use the **Dimension Styles** dialog box to create a dimension style named ARCHITECTURAL. Set the following dimvars to these values:

DIMTSZ = 1/8	**DIMTIH** = OFF	**DIMUNIT** = 4
DIMDLE = 1/8	**DIMTOH** = OFF	**DIMSCALE** = 48
DIMTAD = ON	**DIMTXSTY** = ARCH	**DIMZIN** = 2

❑ Be sure to click the **Save** button to save the new dimension style.
❑ Use the **Dimension Styles** dialog box to restore the STANDARD dimension style.
❑ Create another new dimension style named MECHANICAL. Set the following dimvars to these values:

DIMCEN = −.09	**DIMFIT** = 1	**DIMUPT** = ON
DIMDEC = 3	**DIMUNIT** = 2	
DIMZIN = 4	**DIMTXSTY** = MECH	

❑ Once more, be sure to click the **Save** button to save the new dimension style. There should now be three dimension styles in the TITLEA template file—STANDARD, ARCHITECTURAL, and MECHANICAL.
❑ Save the revised TITLEA.DWT.
❑ Repeat the procedure for the TITLEB and TITLEC templates.

Dimensioning Mode Commands

As stated at the beginning of this chapter, most dimensioning and dimension editing functions in AutoCAD LT are performed in *dimensioning mode.* Once you enter dimensioning mode, each of the dimensioning commands can be abbreviated to the capital letters indicated in **Figure 12-89.**

If you plan to use only one dimensioning command, type the following at the Command: prompt to enter **DIM1** mode:

> Command: **DIM1** *or* **D1.**⏎
> Dim:

After performing the one dimensioning task, AutoCAD LT automatically exits dimensioning mode and returns to the Command: prompt.

Figure 12-89.
The dimensioning mode commands, abbreviations, and descriptions.

Abbreviation	Description
ALigned	A linear dimension that is aligned with the extension line origins.
ANgular	Angular dimension.
Baseline	Continues from the first extension line of the previous dimension.
CEnter	Draws a center mark or centerlines through circles and arcs.
COntinue	Continues from the second extension line of the previous dimension.
Diameter	Diameter dimension.
Exit	Returns to normal command mode (Command: prompt).
HORizontal	A linear dimension with a horizontal dimension line.
Leader	Draws a leader to the dimension text.
ORdinate	Ordinate point (arrowless) dimensioning.
RAdius	Radius dimension.
Redraw	Redraws the display.
REStore	Changes to a previously stored dimension style.
ROtated	A linear dimension at a specified angle.
SAve	Stores the current variable settings as a dimension style.
STAtus	Lists dimensioning variables and their current values.
STYle	Switches to a new text style.
Undo	Reverses the last dimensioning command.
VErtical	A linear dimension with a vertical dimension line.

The following *dimension* editing commands operate on a selection set of existing dimensions:

Abbreviation	Description
HOMetext	Moves dimension text back to its home (default) position.
Newtext	Modifies the text of selected dimensions.
OBlique	Sets the oblique angle of dimension extension lines.
OVerride	Overrides a subset of the dimension variable settings.
TEdit	Changes the position of the dimension text.
TRotate	Rotates the dimension text.
UPdate	Redraws the dimensions in the current settings of all dimensioning variables.
VAriables	Lists variable settings.

Chapter Test

Write your answers in the spaces provided.

1. What is an associative dimension? _____
   _____
   _____

2. What happens to an exploded dimension? _____
   _____
   _____

3. What is an aligned dimension? _____
   _____
   _____

4. How does a rotated dimension differ from an aligned dimension? _____
   _____
   _____

5. What is the purpose of the **press ENTER to select:** option? _____
   _____
   _____

6. Why should you never type in a different dimension value than appears in the brackets? _____
   _____
   _____
   _____

7. What is the purpose of the **UPDATE** command? _____
   _____
   _____

8. Identify the commands that perform datum and chain dimensioning.
   _____
   _____
   _____

9. *True or False?* Angular dimensions can only be used with lines. _____

10. How can you prevent the **DIMDIAMETER** and **DIMRADIUS** commands from automatically creating a centerline? _____

_____

11. What must you do to create a centerline that extends past an arc or a circle? ___

_____

12. *True or False?* The **DIMLEADER** command cannot create multiple lines of text.___

_____

13. What must you do before using ordinate dimensions? Why? _____

_____

_____

_____

14. What is the purpose of the **DEFPOINTS** layer? _____

_____

_____

15. Identify the command used to create a staggered dimension._____

_____

16. Identify two commands that can be used to change the angle of extension lines.

_____

_____

17. How does the **DIMOVERRIDE** command differ from the **UPDATE** command?____

_____

_____

_____

18. Which two commands can be used to change the contents of a feature control frame?_____

_____

19. What is a dimension style?_____

_____

_____

20. Describe the **Dim1** mode._____

_____

_____

_____

_____

For Questions 21 through 45, identify the dimension variable that:

21. Controls the placement of dimension text and arrowheads inside extension lines.

22. Sets dimension text height.

23. Controls the overall scaling of all dimensions.

24. Suppresses the first dimension line.

25. Controls the size of arrowheads.

26. Controls trailing and leading zeros on dimensions.

27. Sets the distance that an extension line is offset from an object line.

28. Places dimension text above, but not below, a dimension line.

29. Turns on and sets the size of tick marks.

30. Sets the plus tolerance value.

31. Sets the minus tolerance value.

32. Turns on limits dimensioning.

33. Enables dual dimensioning.

34. Assigns a color to dimension text.

35. Controls the dimension text alignment outside extension lines.

36. Sets dimension line spacing for baseline and continue dimensions.

37. Creates dimension lines that extend past extension lines.

38. Suppresses the second extension line.

39. Disables associative dimensioning. _____

_____

40. Controls the dimension text alignment inside extension lines. _____

_____

41. Adds a prefix and/or suffix to a dimension. _____

_____

42. Specifies the text style to be used for dimensioning. _____

_____

43. Sets the number of significant places for decimal dimensions. _____

_____

44. Specifies the system of units for angular dimensions. _____

_____

45. Determines the justification mode for dimension text. _____

_____

Chapter Problems

Use the appropriate dimension style (as specified in Exercise 12-12 of this chapter) for the following problems. Also, draw all objects on the proper layers and dimension each in accordance with industry standards.

1. Use the layers in your TITLEA template to draw and dimension the CONTROL PLATE shown below. Use the **RECTANG** and **CHAMFER** commands to your advantage. Save the drawing as P12-1.

Mechanical Drafting

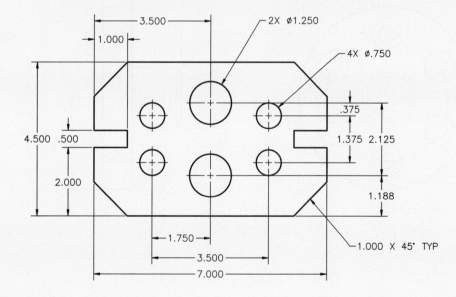

2. Draw and dimension the SHAFT shown below using your TITLEB template. Do not draw the WOODRUFF KEY detail. It is provided for your reference. Save the drawing as P12-2.

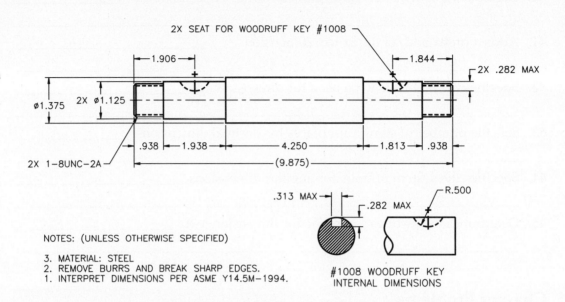

NOTES: (UNLESS OTHERWISE SPECIFIED)

3. MATERIAL: STEEL
2. REMOVE BURRS AND BREAK SHARP EDGES.
1. INTERPRET DIMENSIONS PER ASME Y14.5M−1994.

#1008 WOODRUFF KEY
INTERNAL DIMENSIONS

3. Draw and dimension the HUB shown below using your TITLEA template. Use a polar array to aid in the construction of the front view. Save the drawing as P12-3.

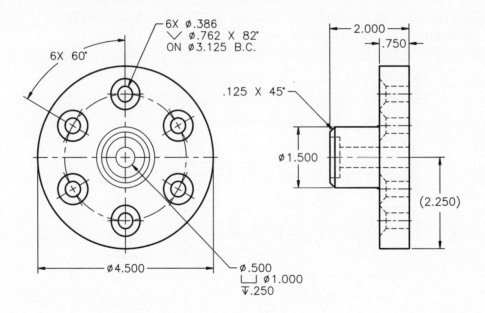

4. Draw the **TRANSISTOR** shown below using your **TITLEA** template. An object this small would probably be plotted at 4:1. Set the **DIMSCALE** variable accordingly before dimensioning. Save the drawing as **P12-4**.

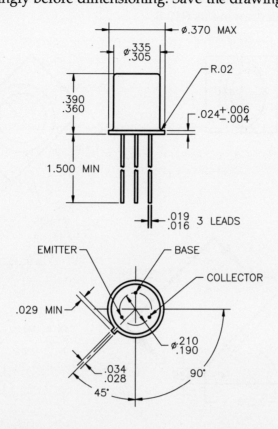

5. Draw the **TRANSISTOR** shown below using your **TITLEA** template. This object would probably be plotted at 2:1. As with **P12-4**, set the **DIMSCALE** variable accordingly before dimensioning. Save the drawing as **P12-5**.

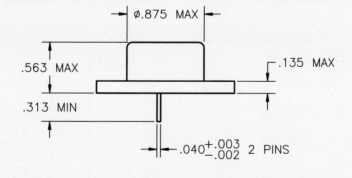

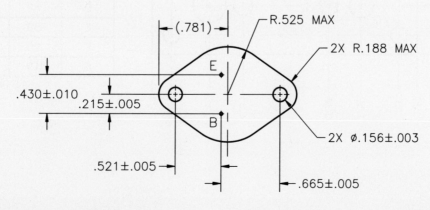

Chapter 12 Dimensioning the Drawing

6. Draw and dimension the **SLANTED BLOCK** shown below using your **TITLEC** template. Draw the viewing plane line on the **CUTPLANE** layer. If necessary, refer to *Chapter 7* to review auxiliary view construction. Save the drawing as **P12-6**.

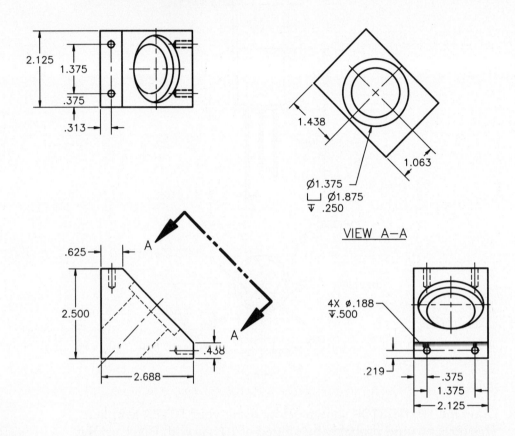

VIEW A–A

7. Use your **TITLEB** template to draw the **COMPONENT CHASSIS** shown below. Create all dimensions using the **DIMORDINATE** command. Include the hole schedule on the face of the drawing.

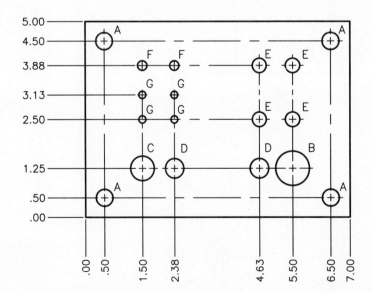

HOLE SCHEDULE		
SYMBOL	SIZE	QTY
A	.44	4
B	.88	1
C	.63	1
D	.50	2
E	.38	4
F	.25	2
G	.19	4

8. Draw the house plan shown using your TITLEE template. Set architectural units and limits appropriately. A drawing this large might be plotted with a scale of ¼″ = 1′. Set the **DIMSCALE** variable accordingly. Save the drawing as P12-8.

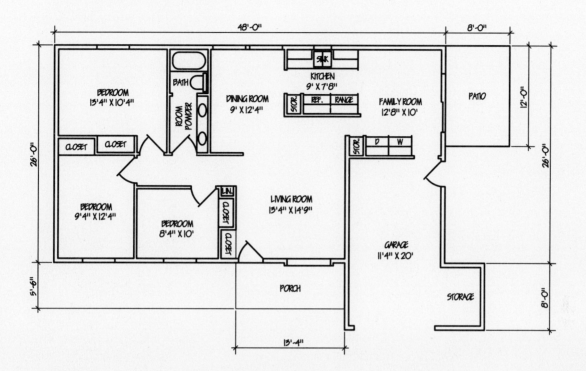

9. Use your TITLEB template to draw and dimension the MOUNTING PLATE shown below. Use the **TOLERANCE** command to create the dimensioning and tolerancing symbols. Save the drawing as P12-9.

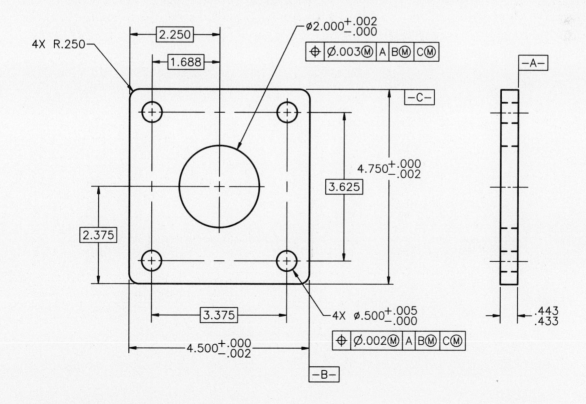

AutoCAD LT

Chapter 13

Hatching Patterns and Techniques

Learning Objectives

After you have completed this chapter, you will be able to:

- O Draw a cutting-plane line.
- O Hatch a closed area with a specified hatch pattern, angle, and spacing.
- O Edit existing hatched areas.
- O Interpret a hatch pattern definition and create custom hatch patterns using the Windows Notepad.
- O Create solid-filled polygons with the **SOLID** command.
- O Construct polylines from the boundaries of objects.

Many objects designed by engineers contain complex internal structures. Attempting to convey these features using hidden lines is often confusing, and sometimes impossible. When this is the case, a sectional view, which shows a portion of the object cut away, is used. A sectional view must show which portions of the object are empty spaces and which contain solid material. This is accomplished using section lines, called *hatching*, in the areas that contain material.

In this chapter, you will learn how hatching is performed in AutoCAD LT and how to create your own custom hatch patterns. The **BOUNDARY** and **SOLID** commands are also introduced.

Cutting-Plane Lines

Cutting-plane lines are used to identify the plane through an object from which a sectional view is taken. As shown in **Figure 13-1,** sometimes the section is obvious and the cutting-plane line is unnecessary. In other objects, the cutting-plane line helps to describe the precise area viewed in section. See **Figure 13-2.**

Cutting-plane lines are constructed with phantom or hidden linetypes. Each end of the line terminates with a large arrowhead. The arrowheads are drawn perpendicular to the line and are used to indicate the direction of sight for viewing the section.

When more than one sectional view exists in a drawing, letters are placed near the arrowheads to help identify the associated view. Additionally, cutting-plane lines are drawn thick to stand out clearly.

In *Chapter 6*, you learned that a polyline can be created with variable width and can be used to create arrowheads. This makes polylines ideal objects for cutting-plane lines. A tutorial appeared in *Chapter 6* to construct a large cutting-plane line. Another tutorial is presented to draw the cutting-plane line illustrated in **Figure 13-3.**

Figure 13-1.
The cutting-plane line identifies the direction of sight for the sectional view.

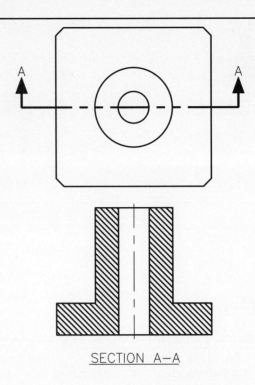

SECTION A–A

Figure 13-2.
This cutting-plane line describes the precise area being sectioned.

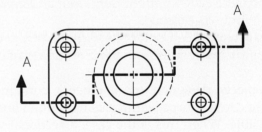

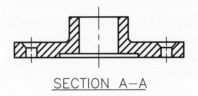

SECTION A–A

Figure 13-3.
The **PLINE** command with a phantom linetype is used to draw a cutting-plane line.

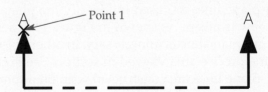

Cutting-Plane Line Tutorial

➪ Begin a new drawing using your TEMPLATEA template.

➪ If your template drawing does not have a Cutplane layer, create one. Assign the Phantom linetype and color blue (5) to the new layer. Set the layer current.

➪ Use the **PLINE** command to draw the cutting-plane line:

```
Command: PLINE or PL↵
From point: (pick point 1)
Current line-width is 0.000
Arc/Close/Halfwidth/Length/Undo/Width/⟨Endpoint of line⟩: W↵
Starting width ⟨0.000⟩: ↵
Ending width ⟨0.000⟩: .375↵
Arc/Close/Halfwidth/Length/Undo/Width/⟨Endpoint of line⟩: @.5⟨270↵
Arc/Close/Halfwidth/Length/Undo/Width/⟨Endpoint of line⟩: W↵
Starting width ⟨0.375⟩: .04 ↵
Ending width ⟨0.040⟩: ↵
Arc/Close/Halfwidth/Length/Undo/Width/⟨Endpoint of line⟩: L↵
Length of line: .75↵
Arc/Close/Halfwidth/Length/Undo/Width/⟨Endpoint of line⟩: @5⟨0↵
Arc/Close/Halfwidth/Length/Undo/Width/⟨Endpoint of line⟩: @.75⟨90↵
Arc/Close/Halfwidth/Length/Undo/Width/⟨Endpoint of line⟩: W↵
Starting width ⟨0.040⟩: .375↵
Ending width ⟨0.375⟩: 0↵
Arc/Close/Halfwidth/Length/Undo/Width/⟨Endpoint of line⟩: L↵
Length of line: .5↵
Arc/Close/Halfwidth/Length/Undo/Width/⟨Endpoint of line⟩: ↵
Command:
```

➪ After drawing the cutting-plane line, use the **DTEXT** command to create the identification letters. Use a height of .25. It is not necessary to save the drawing when you are finished.

AutoCAD LT Hatch Patterns

Getting Started Guide 7

There are 68 predefined hatch patterns supplied with AutoCAD LT. Each pattern has a descriptive name and is stored in an external file called aclt.pat. This file is located in the **Program Files\AutoCAD LT 98 folder.** If you are using AutoCAD LT 97, the file may be found in the Program Files\AutoCAD LT 97 folder.

The default hatch pattern is ANSI31. This pattern represents cast iron, but is used for general purpose hatching. Each of the patterns are shown in **Figure 13-4.**

Many other hatch patterns are available from software vendors. Creating a custom hatch pattern is described later in this chapter.

Figure 13-4.
Standard AutoCAD LT hatch patterns. (*Autodesk, Inc.*)

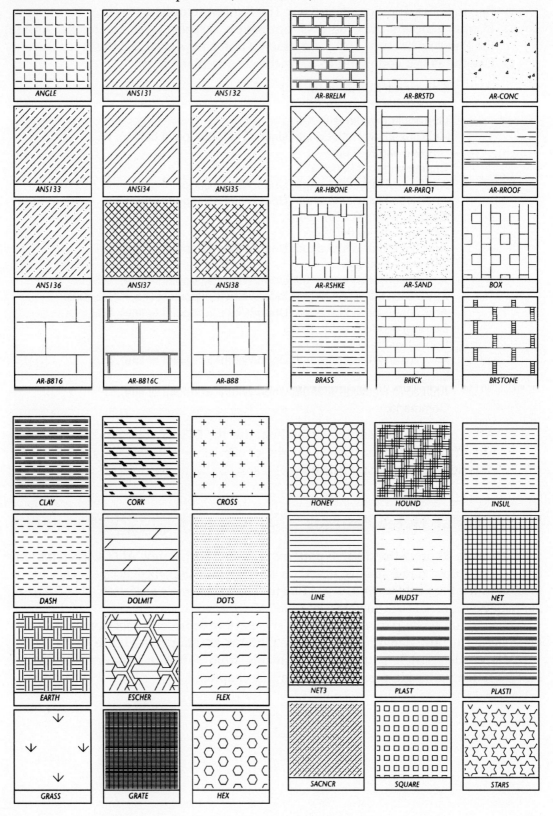

AutoCAD LT—Fundamentals and Applications

Figure 13-4.
(continued)

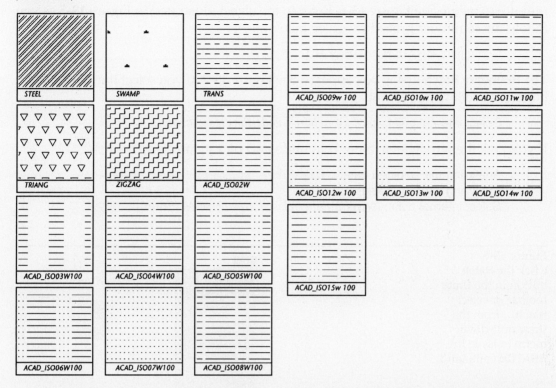

Boundary Hatching

The **BHATCH** (Boundary HATCH) command is used to apply hatching. After you select a point, the command recognizes the surrounding boundary and hatches the enclosed area.

The **BHATCH** command has several steps. After picking an internal point, a polyline boundary is created using the objects defining the enclosed area. The boundary is highlighted. The hatch can be previewed before it is applied. Once the hatch is applied, the temporary polyline boundary is erased.

The object shown in **Figure 13-5** has four areas that require hatching. The four internal points can all be selected in one operation. The areas that are not hatched are called *islands*. The **BHATCH** command detects these areas automatically.

Figure 13-5.
The **BHATCH** command creates a temporary polyline boundary around the enclosed area to be hatched.

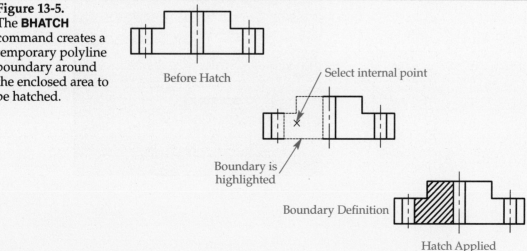

Before Hatch

Select internal point

Boundary is highlighted

Boundary Definition

Hatch Applied

BHATCH
BH or H

Draw
↳ Hatch...

Draw
toolbar

Hatch

To perform boundary hatching, enter BHATCH, or BH, or H at the Command: prompt, click the **Hatch** button in the **Draw** toolbar or select **Hatch...** from the **Draw** pull-down menu. See **Figure 13-6.** Refer to the object illustrated in **Figure 13-5** as you follow the command procedure given below:

Command: **BHATCH** *or* **BH** *or* **H.**↵

The **Boundary Hatch** dialog box appears. See **Figure 13-7.** If you select the **Pick Points** ⟨ button, the following prompt appears:

Select internal point: *(pick anywhere inside the closed area)*

If you pick the wrong area, enter U to undo and pick again.

Analyzing the selected data...
Analyzing internal islands...
Select internal point: *(select another closed area or press* [Enter]*)*

Figure 13-6.
Click the **Hatch** button in the **Draw** toolbar or select **Hatch...** from the **Draw** pull-down menu to issue the **BHATCH** command.

Figure 13-7.
The **Boundary Hatch** dialog box.

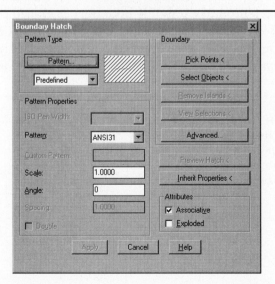

Once you press [Enter], the **Boundary Hatch** dialog box is redisplayed. To preview the hatch within the area specified before applying it, click the **Preview Hatch** ⟨ button. A preview of the hatching appears. A small subdialog box then appears, prompting you to continue. See **Figure 13-8.** Click the **Continue** button and the **Boundary Hatch** dialog box reappears. If the hatch preview was correct, the **Apply** button creates the hatching and terminates the command.

The area to be hatched must be enclosed. If the area is open, AutoCAD LT displays the alert box shown in **Figure 13-9.** Click the **OK** button, and then cancel the command. Close the open geometry using the appropriate editing commands and try again.

Figure 13-8.
Click the **Continue** button to return to the **Boundry Hatch** dialog box.

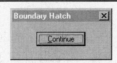

Figure 13-9.
The **Boundary Definition Error** alert box is displayed if you attempt to hatch an area that is not closed.

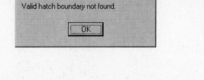

NOTE

The **BHATCH** command alias BH is not available in AutoCAD LT 97.

The Boundary Hatch Dialog Box

The **Boundary Hatch** dialog box, shown in **Figure 13-7**, contains various options for basic and advanced hatching operations. Each of the buttons and options of this dialog box are described in the following sections:

- **Pattern Type.** As mentioned previously, there are 68 predefined hatch patterns. There are three ways to select a different pattern using the **Boundary Hatch** dialog box. Observe that a graphical representation of the current hatch pattern is displayed in the image tile in the **Pattern Type** section at the upper-left of the dialog box. If you place your pointing device over the image tile and successively click the pick button, a different pattern appears in the image tile with each click. Stop clicking when the pattern you wish to use is displayed. You can also select a pattern from the **Pattern:** drop-down list in the **Pattern Properties** area. As shown in **Figure 13-10,** the pattern for steel (ANSI32) is selected from the list and appears in the image tile at the top. A third, (and perhaps the easiest) way to select a hatch pattern is by clicking the **Pattern...** button at the top-left of the dialog box. Doing so opens the **Hatch pattern palette** subdialog box shown in **Figure 13-11.** With this method, each hatch pattern is graphically displayed for your convenience. You may select a pattern from the scroll list at the left of the subdialog box, or by clicking the hatch pattern image tile with your pointing device. Click the **Next** button to display the next page of available hatch patterns. The **Previous** button is used to return to the previous page. After selecting a pattern, click **OK** to close the **Hatch pattern palette** subdialog box.

Figure 13-10.
Selecting a different hatch pattern from the **Pattern:** drop-down list. Note that the pattern appears in the image tile at the top.

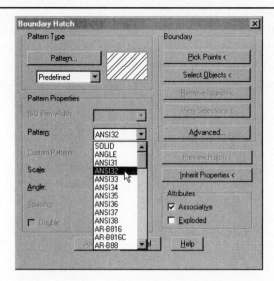

Figure 13-11.
The **Hatch pattern palette** subdialog box graphically displays each hatch pattern on multiple pages.

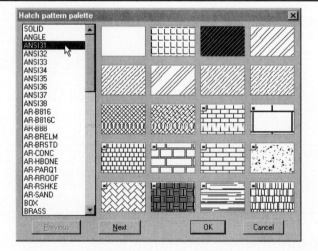

- **Scale: text box.** Use this text box to increase or decrease the spacing between hatch lines. In most cases, the default hatch scale works well. If you intend to plot at a different scale, be sure to set the hatch scale accordingly. Hatch scale should be the inverse of the plot scale. For example, if your drawing is to be plotted at 2:1, set the hatch scale to .5. For metric drawings, set the hatch scale to 25.4 units.
- **Angle: text box.** Use this text box to specify the desired hatch angle. Predefined hatch patterns are set to 0°. Several examples of hatch scales and angles appear in **Figure 13-12.**
- **Pick Points ⟨ button.** As previously mentioned, this button is used to select internal points. From the example in **Figure 13-13,** you can see that the text string 'TEXT' is automatically recognized as an island. No hatching is applied in an island.
- **Select Objects ⟨ button.** This button can be used to select objects to be hatched. When you use this option, the **Boundary Hatch** dialog box disappears and you receive the familiar Select objects: prompt. Pick one or more objects to hatch and press [Enter]. In **Figure 13-14,** both the rectangle and text are selected. Because there is no island or boundary detection with the **Select Objects** option, the text must be selected or hatching will pass through it. The results of the hatch operation are shown at the right. Note that the overlapping area is also hatched.

Figure 13-12.
Examples of hatching with different scales and angles.

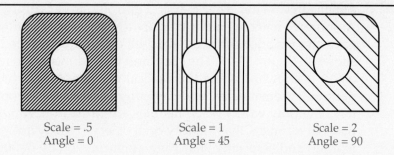

Scale = .5
Angle = 0

Scale = 1
Angle = 45

Scale = 2
Angle = 90

Figure 13-13.
A—Islands are detected automatically when picking points. B—The hatch results.

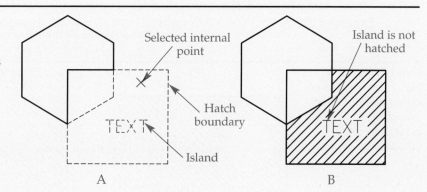

Selected internal point

Hatch boundary

Island

TEXT

A

Island is not hatched

TEXT

B

Figure 13-14.
A—Islands are not detected with the **Select Objects** option. B—The hatch results.

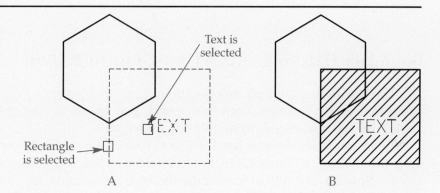

Text is selected

TEXT

Rectangle is selected

A

TEXT

B

- **Remove Islands ⟨ button.** This button allows you to remove islands detected when using the **Pick Points ⟨** button. You cannot remove the outer boundary, however. When you use this option, the **Boundary Hatch** dialog box disappears and the prompt Select island to remove: is displayed on the command line. Select one or more islands to remove and press [Enter] to redisplay the **Boundary Hatch** dialog box.

- **View Selections ⟨ button.** This button displays all currently defined boundary sets. A small subdialog box also appears on screen prompting you to continue. Click the **Continue** button and the **Boundary Hatch** dialog box reappears.

- **Preview Hatch ⟨ button.** As mentioned previously, click this button to preview the hatching before applying it. If the hatching is correct, click the **Apply** button to add it to the drawing.

- **Inherit Properties ⟨ button.** This button allows you to select an existing hatch in your drawing to be used as the current hatch pattern. This is particularly convenient when there are several hatch patterns being used in one drawing and you wish to quickly set one of them current. When you click the **Inherit Properties ⟨** button, the **Boundary Hatch** dialog box disappears and you receive the prompt Select hatch object: on the command line. Pick the existing hatch pattern that you wish to use.

- **Associative.** This check box controls associativity in hatched areas. Associative hatching automatically updates a hatch pattern when the boundaries and islands within the hatched object are modified. Consider the object shown in **Figure 13-15.** The circle and text are moved to new locations, and the object is stretched along the vertical axis. Because of associativity, the hatch pattern automatically updates after each editing operation. Associative hatching only works when handles are turned on. *Handles* are unique hexadecimal numbers that identity each object in the AutoCAD LT database. Both handles and associative hatching are turned on by default.
- **Exploded check box.** AutoCAD LT creates a hatch pattern as a single object. Thus, a large hatched area may be selected with a single pick. If you activate the **Exploded** check box, the hatch pattern is drawn with separate line segments.

Figure 13-15.
Hatching is updated automatically after islands and boundaries are edited.

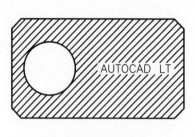 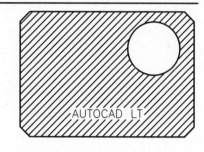

Original Drawing   Modified Drawing

Boundary Hatching with a User-Defined Pattern

The **BHATCH** command also permits you to create a user-defined hatch pattern using the current linetype. With this option, you specify an explicit hatch scale and angle. You can also choose to double hatch an area.

To create a user-defined hatch pattern, select **User-defined** from the **Pattern Type** drop-down list. See **Figure 13-16.** Enter the desired hatch angle in the **Angle:** text box. Use the **Spacing:** text box to specify the distance between the hatch lines. Activate the check box labeled **Double** if you wish to use double hatching. Several examples of user-defined hatching are shown in **Figure 13-17.**

Figure 13-16.
Selecting **User-defined** from the **Pattern Type** drop-down list.

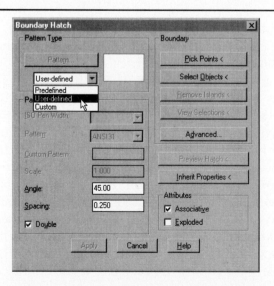

Figure 13-17.
Examples of user-defined hatch patterns.

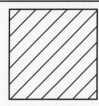
45° Angle
.25 Spacing
Single Hatch

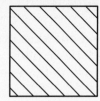
135° Angle
.25 Spacing
Single Hatch

45° Angle
.125 Spacing
Double Hatch

EXERCISE 13-1

❏ Begin a new drawing using your TEMPLATEA template.
❏ Set the Objects layer current and draw three shapes similar to those shown in **Figure 13-12.** Do not be concerned with dimensions.
❏ Set the Hatching layer current. Use the **BHATCH** command and the ANSI31 pattern to hatch the three objects. Set the hatch scale and angle as shown.
❏ Next, draw the three squares illustrated in **Figure 13-17.** Use the **User-defined** option to hatch the squares with the parameters specified.
❏ Save the drawing as EX13-1.

Advanced Boundary Hatch Options

Getting Started Guide 7

The **BHATCH** command offers additional options that are accessed by clicking the **Advanced...** button in the **Boundary Hatch** dialog box. This displays the **Advanced Options** subdialog box shown in **Figure 13-18.** The properties of the **Advanced Options** subdialog box are described in the following sections.

Figure 13-18.
The **Advanced Options** subdialog box.

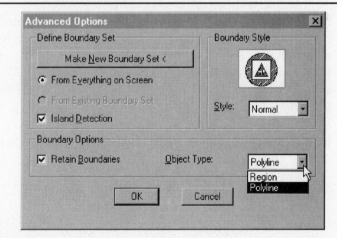

Defining a Boundary Set

The **BHATCH** command analyzes every object displayed on screen when determining islands and boundaries. This is a time-consuming process for very large or complex drawings. You can limit the area to be evaluated by defining a boundary set. There are three options:

- **From Everything on Screen.** When this is set, the entire screen is examined to determine islands and boundaries. This option button is active by default.
- **From Existing Boundary Set.** This option is not available until a new boundary set is created.
- **Make New Boundary Set ⟨.** Use this button to limit what is evaluated during the hatching operation. When the Select Objects: prompt appears, use a window box to define the area of the screen to be evaluated for hatching. This area remains the only area examined during future hatching operations. Creating another boundary set replaces the existing set.

PROFESSIONAL TIP You can also speed the hatching process using the **ZOOM** command to magnify the area to be hatched. Since only the area displayed on screen is evaluated, zooming provides a convenient alternative to making a new boundary set.

Selecting a Hatch Style

There are three hatch styles: Normal, Outer, and Ignore, as shown in **Figure 13-19.** The **Style:** drop-down list is used to choose one of the three styles. A graphical representation of the current hatch style appears in the image tile just above the drop-down list. The hatch styles are described as follows:

- **Normal.** This is the default style. Normal hatches inward from the outermost boundary. When an internal boundary is encountered, hatching is turned off and remains off until another boundary is encountered. The Normal style hatches every other boundary.
- **Outer.** This style also hatches inward and turns off hatching when an internal boundary is encountered. However, the hatching is not turned back on. Only the outermost areas are hatched.
- **Ignore.** This option ignores all internal areas and hatches through the entire object.

Figure 13-19.
The three hatching styles. **Normal** is the default.

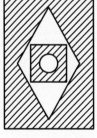 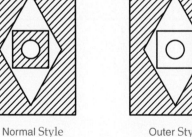 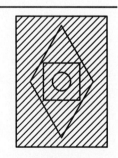

Normal Style   Outer Style   Ignore Style

Island Detection

The **Island Detection** check box is used to determine whether objects within the outermost boundary are used as boundary objects. These internal objects are known as islands. It is recommended this check box remain activated.

Retaining Hatch Boundaries

The **BHATCH** command creates a temporary polyline boundary using the objects that define an enclosed area. Once the hatching is applied, the temporary polyline is erased. You can choose to keep the boundary as a permanent polyline object by activating the **Retain Boundaries** check box. By default, this check box is not active. AutoCAD LT 98 users can choose between a polyline boundary (the default) or a region boundary by selecting the desired object type from the **Object Type:** drop-down list at the lower-right of the **Advanced Options** subdialog box. Region objects are described in *Chapter 6* of this text. Selecting a region boundary is not an option for users of AutoCAD LT 97.

The **HATCH** Command

The **HATCH** command can be used if you do not wish to use boundary hatching. Because there is no island or boundary detection, the **HATCH** command functions like the **Select Objects** ⟨ button option of the **BHATCH** command. The **HATCH** command displays the following prompts and options:

> Command: **HATCH** *or* **-H**↵
> Enter pattern name or [?/Solid/User defined] ⟨ANSI31⟩: *(enter a pattern name or accept the default)*
> Scale for pattern ⟨1.0000⟩: *(enter the hatch scale)*
> Angle for pattern ⟨0⟩: *(enter the hatch angle)*
> Select hatch boundaries or press ENTER for direct hatch option,
> Select objects: *(select one or more objects)*
> Select objects: ↵
> Command:

HATCH
-H

Listing Available Hatch Patterns

If you forget the name of a hatch pattern, a list of the available hatch patterns can be displayed:

> Command: **HATCH** *or* **-H**↵
> Enter pattern name or [?/Solid/User defined] ⟨ANSI31⟩: **?**↵
> Pattern(s) to list ⟨*⟩: ↵

An alphabetical list of hatch pattern names and descriptions is then displayed in the text window. See **Figure 13-20.** When the listing is finished, press [F2] to flip back to the graphics window.

Figure 13-20.
The list of available hatch patterns is displayed in the text window.

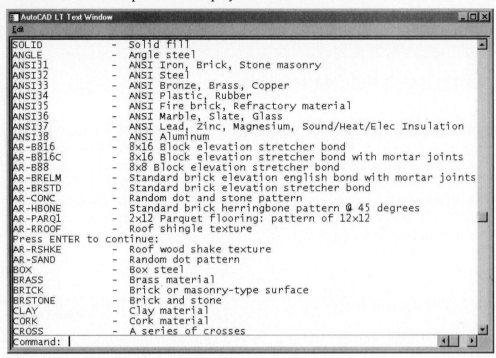

```
AutoCAD LT Text Window                                        _□×
Edit
SOLID            -  Solid fill                                    ▲
ANGLE            -  Angle steel
ANSI31           -  ANSI Iron, Brick, Stone masonry
ANSI32           -  ANSI Steel
ANSI33           -  ANSI Bronze, Brass, Copper
ANSI34           -  ANSI Plastic, Rubber
ANSI35           -  ANSI Fire brick, Refractory material
ANSI36           -  ANSI Marble, Slate, Glass
ANSI37           -  ANSI Lead, Zinc, Magnesium, Sound/Heat/Elec Insulation
ANSI38           -  ANSI Aluminum
AR-B816          -  8x16 Block elevation stretcher bond
AR-B816C         -  8x16 Block elevation stretcher bond with mortar joints
AR-B88           -  8x8 Block elevation stretcher bond
AR-BRELM         -  Standard brick elevation english bond with mortar joints
AR-BRSTD         -  Standard brick elevation stretcher bond
AR-CONC          -  Random dot and stone pattern
AR-HBONE         -  Standard brick herringbone pattern @ 45 degrees
AR-PARQ1         -  2x12 Parquet flooring: pattern of 12x12
AR-RROOF         -  Roof shingle texture
Press ENTER to continue:
AR-RSHKE         -  Roof wood shake texture
AR-SAND          -  Random dot pattern
BOX              -  Box steel
BRASS            -  Brass material
BRICK            -  Brick or masonry-type surface
BRSTONE          -  Brick and stone
CLAY             -  Clay material
CORK             -  Cork material
CROSS            -  A series of crosses                           ▼
Command: |                                              ◄│   │►
```

Hatching with the Solid Option

The **Solid** option lets you specify a solid fill pattern. This is useful when showing thin features like gaskets and seals in section. It can also be used to hatch a solid-filled wall for architectural applications. To use the **Solid** option, do the following:

> Command: **HATCH** *or* **-H**↵
> Enter pattern name or [?/Solid/User defined] ⟨ANSI31⟩: **S**↵
> Select hatch boundaries or press ENTER for direct hatch option,
> Select objects: *(select one or more objects)*
> Select objects: ↵
> Command:

Keep in mind that selecting part of a block for solid fill selects the entire block. See *Chapter 15* for complete information about block objects.

The User defined Option

The **User defined** option of the **HATCH** command allows you to specify a user-defined pattern. This means that you set the hatch angle and spacing. You may also specify double hatching, if required. The **User defined** option looks like this:

> Command: **HATCH** *or* **-H**↵
> Enter pattern name or [?/Solid/User defined] ⟨ANSI31⟩: **U**↵
> Angle for crosshatch lines ⟨0⟩: **45**↵
> Spacing between lines ⟨1.0000⟩: **.125**↵
> Double hatch area? ⟨N⟩ *(enter Y or N)*
> Select hatch boundaries or press ENTER for direct hatch option,
> Select objects: *(select one or more objects)*
> Select objects: ↵
> Command:

Specifying a Hatch Style

The **HATCH** command permits you to specify one of the three hatch style options (**Normal, Outer,** and **Ignore**), described previously in this chapter. Remember that the Normal style is the default. When you use this method, it is more efficient to select the objects to be hatched with a window or crossing box. In the following example, the **Outer** option is being used with the ANSI32 pattern. Separate the hatch style option from the pattern name with a comma, as shown.

> Command: **HATCH** *or* **-H.**↵
> Enter pattern name or [?/Solid/User defined] ⟨ANSI31⟩: **ANSI32,O.**↵
> Scale for pattern ⟨1.0000⟩: ↵
> Angle for pattern ⟨0⟩: ↵
> Select objects: *(pick a corner)* Other corner: *(pick a diagonal point)*
> Select objects: ↵
> Command:

Using the **Direct Hatch Option**

You will note from the syntax shown in several of the previous examples that the or press ENTER for direct hatch option, is given. The direct hatch option lets you specify points, rather than objects, to define the boundary of the hatching area. Therefore, it can be used to hatch an area that may overlap another by isolating the area to be hatched with a temporary polyline. The polyline passes through the points you select. You may choose to retain the polyline if you wish. The direct option looks like this:

> Command: **HATCH** *or* **-H.**↵
> Enter pattern name or [?/Solid/User defined] ⟨ANSI31⟩: *(enter a pattern name or accept the default)*
> Scale for pattern ⟨1.0000⟩: *(enter the hatch scale)*
> Angle for pattern ⟨0⟩: *(enter the hatch angle)*
> Select hatch boundaries or press ENTER for direct hatch option,
> Select objects: ↵
> Retain polyline? ⟨N⟩: *(enter Y to retain the hatching boundary after the area is hatched or N to discard it)*
> From point: *(locate a start point for the polyline boundary)*
> Arc/Close/Length/Undo/⟨Next point⟩: *(pick a point, enter an option, or press [Enter])*

Observe that the options shown above are also found in the **PLINE** command. (If necessary, see *Chapter 6* of this text to review polyline construction.) When the polyline boundary is complete, you are prompted to create additional polyline boundaries as follows:

> From point or press ENTER to apply hatch: *(pick a point or press [Enter])*
> Command:

Be sure to use the appropriate object snap modes when using the direct hatch option to isolate existing geometry. Doing so ensures the highest degree of accuracy as the polyline is traced over the objects.

Drag and Drop Hatching Using Content Explorer

One of the most useful features of AutoCAD LT 98 and 97 is the **Content Explorer**. It provides a powerful method for inserting blocks and attaching external references. These object types, and **Content Explorer**, are fully described in *Chapter 15* of this text. If you are using AutoCAD LT 98, **Content Explorer** can also be used to drag and drop a hatch pattern into any enclosed area on your drawing. If you are using AutoCAD LT 97, the **Content Explorer** cannot be used to drag and drop a hatch pattern. Like the **BHATCH** command, the hatching you create with **Content Explorer** is fully associative.

To access **Content Explorer**, enter CONTENT, or CE, at the Command: prompt, click the **Content Explorer** button in the **Draw** toolbar or select **Content Explorer...** from the **Insert** pull-down menu. See **Figure 13-21**.

Command: **CONTENT** *or* **CE**↵

The **Content Explorer** window appears at the right side of the drawing window. Click the tab labeled **Hatch** to graphically display each of the available hatch patterns in the **Content Explorer** window. Next, click the desired hatch pattern from the window using your pointing device as shown in **Figure 13-22**. Use the horizontal slider bar at the bottom of the window to display more of the available hatch patterns.

CONTENT
CE

Insert
➥ Content
Explorer...

Draw
toolbar

Content Explorer

Figure 13-21.
Click the **Content Explorer** button in the **Draw** toolbar or select **Content Explorer...** from the **Insert** pull-down menu to issue the **CONTENT** command.

Figure 13-22.
Click the **Hatch** tab in the **Content Explorer** window to display all of the available hatch patterns.

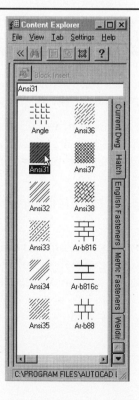

Once you have selected the hatch pattern that you wish to use, the command **_.drginsert** is echoed in the command window and you are prompted to select an insertion point. Press and hold the pick button on your pointing device as you "drag" the pattern into the area you wish to hatch. Observe that your cursor displays the selected hatch pattern as shown in **Figure 13-23**. Once your cursor is located over the area to be hatched, release the pick button on your pointing device and the hatch is created. The following messages are displayed in the command window during the drag and drop operation.

```
Selecting everything...
Selecting everything visible...
Analyzing the selected data...
Analyzing internal islands...
Command:
```

Figure 13-23.
Dragging a hatch pattern into the area to be hatched. Observe that the graphics cursor displays the selected hatch pattern.

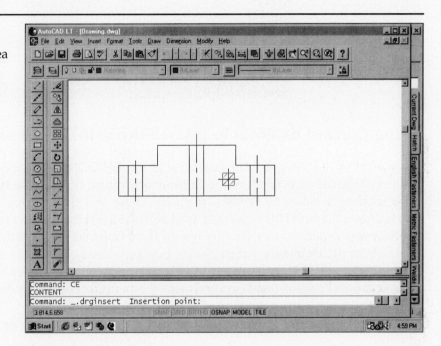

Selecting multiple pick points

By default, **Content Explorer** allows only one pick point for drag and drop hatching. If you wish to select more than one point, you can do so by selecting **Multiple Pick Points** from the shortcut menu shown in **Figure 13-24**. This menu is accessed by right-clicking anywhere within the **Content Explorer** window.

Now, when you drag a selected hatch pattern into the drawing window, the Insertion point: prompt is automatically repeated allowing you to pick as many enclosed areas as desired for hatching. When you are through selecting pick points, press the [Esc] key to cancel drag and drop hatching. An example of multiple pick point selection is illustrated in **Figure 13-25**.

Figure 13-24.
Right-clicking your pointing device in the **Content Explorer** window displays a shortcut menu featuring several hatching options

Figure 13-25.
Selecting multiple
pick points for
hatching using
Content Explorer.

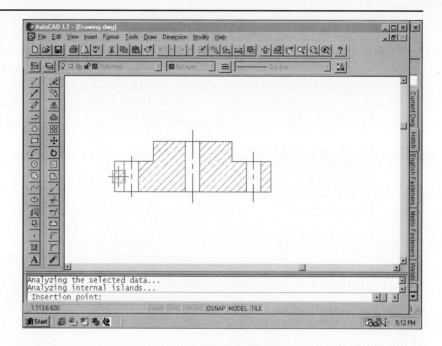

Using **Content Explorer** to invoke the **BHATCH** command

Earlier in this chapter you learned that the **BHATCH** command can be issued by entering BHATCH, or BH or H, at the Command: prompt, clicking the **Hatch** button in the **Draw** toolbar or selecting **Hatch...** from the **Draw** pull-down menu. Another way to quickly issue the **BHATCH** command is to activate the **Hatch** tab in the **Content Explorer** window and double-click over any one of the displayed hatch pattern images. Doing so displays the **Boundary Hatch** dialog box previously described and illustrated in **Figure 13-7**. Once this dialog box is displayed, make any necessary changes to pattern type, scale, and rotation and proceed with the boundary hatch operation.

Specifying hatch properties using **Content Explorer**

As previously mentioned, you can right-click anywhere within the **Content Explorer** window to display a shortcut menu with various options. See **Figure 13-24**. If you select **Hatch Properties...** located at the bottom of the shortcut menu, the **Hatch Properties** dialog box is displayed as shown in **Figure 13-26**. The options provided by this dialog box have been discussed in previous sections of this chapter. However, notice the **Regenerate Hatch Icons** check box located at the bottom of the dialog box. When this check box is activated (the default), any changes you make to hatch scale and angle in the **Hatch Properties** dialog box forces a regeneration of each of the hatch patterns that appear in **Content Explorer.** Every hatch pattern is then displayed showing the new scale and/or angle modifications. Since the regeneration of each hatch pattern is somewhat time-consuming, it is recommended that you deactivate this check box to improve system performance.

NOTE	The **Hatch Properties** dialog box can also be displayed by selecting **Hatch Properties...** from the **Settings** pull-down menu in the **Content Explorer** window. It can also be opened by first selecting the **Hatch** tab and then clicking the **Hatch Properties** button on the **Content Explorer** toolbar.

Figure 13-26.
The **Hatch Properties**
dialog box.

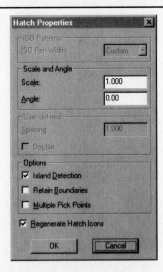

EXERCISE 13-2

❑ Proceed with this exercise if you are using AutoCAD LT 98 only.
❑ Begin a new drawing using your TEMPLATEA template.
❑ Once again, set the Objects layer current and draw three shapes similar to those shown in **Figure 13-12.** Do not be concerned with dimensions.
❑ Set the Hatching layer current.
❑ Use **Content Explorer** and the ANSI31 pattern to hatch the three objects. Set the hatch scale and angle as shown.
❑ Save the drawing as EX13-2.

Modifying Hatched Areas

The **HATCHEDIT** command allows you to modify associative hatching. To edit an existing hatched area, enter HATCHEDIT, or HE, at the Command: prompt or select **Hatch** from the **Object** cascading submenu in the **Modify** pull-down menu. See **Figure 13-27.** To use the **Hatch Edit** button shown in the margin, you must first open the **Modify II** toolbar. This is accomplished by first selecting **Toolbars...** from the **View** pull-down menu. The **Customize** dialog box is then displayed. Users of AutoCAD LT 97 are presented with the **Toolbars** dialog box. For either version, scroll down until you locate the **Modify II** selection in the list. Select **Modify II** and then close the dialog box by clicking the **Close** button. The **Modify II** toolbar then appears on screen. You may dock the toolbar or leave it in a floating state as you desire. The **HATCHEDIT** command looks like this:

Command: **HATCHEDIT** or **HE**⏎
Select hatch object: *(select the hatching to change)*

Only one hatched area may be edited at a time. After selecting the hatch to change, the **Hatch Edit** dialog box appears. See **Figure 13-28.** This dialog box is identical to the **Boundary Hatch** dialog box. However, many of the buttons are "grayed-out" and are unavailable for use.

The **Hatch Edit** dialog box displays all of the characteristics of the selected hatch. Change one or more of the hatch properties and click the **Apply** button. The dialog box disappears and the hatching is modified to the new specifications.

Figure 13-27.
Select **Object** from
the **Modify** pull-
down menu, and
the select **Hatch**
from the cascading
submenu to issue
the **HATCHEDIT**
command.

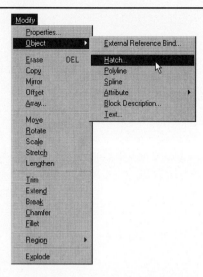

Figure 13-28.
The **Hatch Edit**
dialog box displays
the characteristics of
the selected hatch.

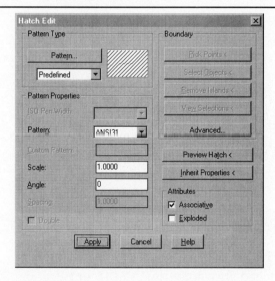

NOTE

Although hatching created with the **HATCH** command is
not fully associative, it may still be modified with
HATCHEDIT.

EXERCISE 13-3

❑ Open EX13-1.
❑ Using **HATCHEDIT**, change the three ANSI31 patterns to Brick, Escher, and Earth
as shown below.

  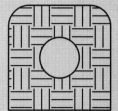

❑ Use any pattern, angle, or spacing you choose to modify the remaining three
hatched squares.
❑ Save the drawing as EX13-3.

AutoCAD LT—Fundamentals and Applications

Creating a Custom Hatch Pattern

Like linetypes, hatch patterns are stored in an external library file (aclt.pat). This file can be modified to create your own custom hatch patterns. Unlike linetypes, custom hatch patterns cannot be modified or created using AutoCAD LT. The aclt.pat file must be edited with an ASCII *(American Standard Code for Information Exchange)* text editor, such as Windows Notepad.

The aclt.pat library file contains the definitions for the standard hatch patterns. Three of the patterns, Line, Net, and Net3, are shown in **Figure 13-29.** These patterns are defined in the aclt.pat file as follows:

```
*LINE,Parallel horizontal lines
0, 0,0, 0,.125
*NET,Horizontal / vertical grid
0, 0,0, 0,.125
90, 0,0, 0,.125
*NET3,Network pattern 0-60-120
0, 0,0, 0,.125
60, 0,0, 0,.125
120, 0,0, 0,.125
```

Deciphering a hatch pattern definition is not difficult. The word after the asterisk (*) is the hatch pattern name. The text string after the comma is a description of the pattern. This description is displayed in the text window when you list hatch patterns.

Each line of numbers under the pattern description represents a group of repeated parallel lines. The numbers represent the angle, X-origin, Y-origin, delta-X, and delta-Y, respectively. Dashes, dots, and gaps can also be included.

In the first hatch pattern example, Line, the first 0 represents the angle at which the lines are drawn. The 0,0 is the X and Y origin, and the last pair of numbers specifies where to start subsequent parallel lines. After drawing the first horizontal line of the pattern, the second line starts 0 units to the left and .125 units up from the starting point of the first line.

The net pattern has two parallel line groups, with the first pattern being identical to the Line pattern group. It then draws a second group of 90° lines spaced .125 apart. The Net3 pattern is very similar, but it has three groups of lines, at 0°, 60°, and 120°.

There are many types of hatch patterns designed for specific drawing applications. Many of these patterns are included with AutoCAD LT , others can be purchased.

Figure 13-29.
The Line, Net, and
Net3 hatch patterns.

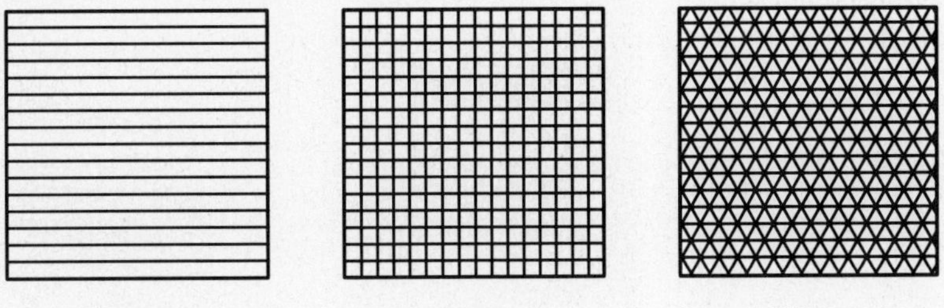

Line   Net   Net3

Using the Windows Notepad to Create a Custom Hatch Pattern

The Microsoft Windows Notepad is an ASCII text editor that can edit small text files (less than 50K in size). It can be used to create a custom hatch pattern by editing the aclt.pat file.

Consider the custom roof shingle hatch pattern shown in **Figure 13-30.** This pattern can be easily created using Notepad without exiting AutoCAD LT. First, use the Start button on the Windows 98/95/NT task bar. Next, open the Programs folder and select Notepad from the Accessories menu as shown in **Figure 13-31.**

Notepad launches in its own display window, and you can begin entering the following lines of text:

```
*ROOF,Custom shingles
0, 0,0, 0,6
90, 0,0, 6,18, 6,-6
90, 12,0, 6,18, 3,-9
90, 24,0, 6,18, 3,-9
```

Figure 13-30.
The Roof custom shingle hatch pattern.

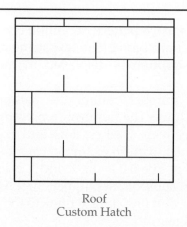

Roof
Custom Hatch

Figure 13-31.
Notepad is launched from the Accessories menu located in the Programs folder. The Windows 98 desktop is shown.

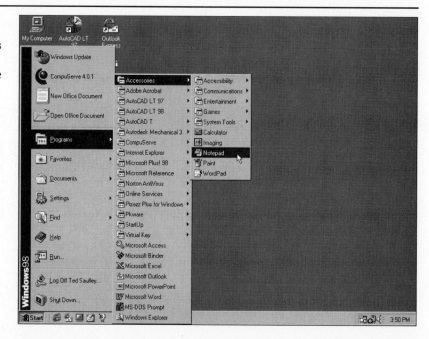

When you have finished entering the text, the Notepad window should appear as shown in **Figure 13-32.** Select Save <u>A</u>s... from the <u>F</u>ile pull-down menu. Change to the Program Files\AutoCAD LT 98 folder and save your hatch pattern file with the name roof.pat. If you are using AutoCAD LT 97, you will save your hatch pattern file in the Program Files\AutoCAD LT 97 folder. See **Figure 13-33.** Quit Notepad by selecting E<u>x</u>it from the <u>F</u>ile pull-down menu and you are returned to AutoCAD LT.

A custom hatch pattern does not need to be included in the aclt.pat library file. The pattern can be stored in a separate file, as long as the file name matches the hatch pattern name. In this example, the Roof pattern resides in a file called roof.pat.

To use your custom hatch patterns, select **Custom** from the **Pattern Type** drop-down list in the **Boundary Hatch** dialog box. Enter the hatch pattern name in the **<u>C</u>ustom Pattern:** text box, as shown in **Figure 13-34.**

Figure 13-32.
The Roof custom hatch pattern definition as entered in Notepad.

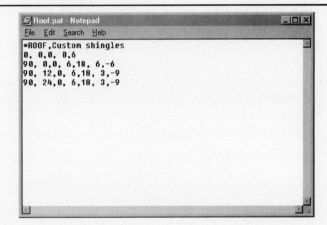

Figure 13-33.
The hatch pattern is saved with the name roof.pat in the Program Files\AutoCAD LT 98 folder.

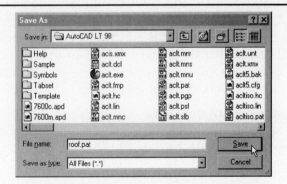

Figure 13-34.
Selecting Custom from the **Pattern Type** drop-down list. The Roof custom hatch pattern is entered in the **<u>C</u>ustom Pattern:** text box.

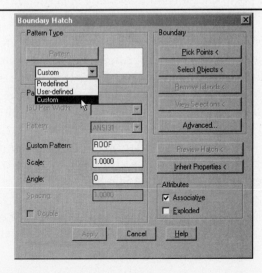

Chapter 13 Hatching Patterns and Techniques

PROFESSIONAL TIP

Be sure to make a backup copy of the original aclt.pat file before you experiment with creating or modifying hatch patterns. It is a good idea to create hatch patterns in separate files as described in the previous section and leave the aclt.pat file undisturbed. Check with your instructor or supervisor to verify which procedures should be used.

EXERCISE 13-4

❏ Use Notepad to create the Roof hatch pattern described in the preceding text.
❏ Be sure to save the Notepad file with the name roof.pat in the Program Files\AutoCAD LT 98 or Program Files\AutoCAD LT 97 folder as appropriate.
❏ Start AutoCAD LT using the TEMPLATEC template file. Set **DDUNITS** to architectural, **LIMITS** to 80′, 60′, and **ZOOM All**.
❏ Use the **RECTANG** command on the Objects layer to draw a 60′ × 30′ rectangle.
❏ Set the Hatching layer current and use **BHATCH** to hatch the rectangle with the Roof pattern.
❏ Use **HATCHEDIT** to experiment with different hatch pattern scales.
❏ Save the drawing as EX13-4.

The SOLID Command

Polylines, polyarcs, and donuts may be filled in solid when **FILL** mode is on. When **FILL** is off, these objects are drawn as outlines. As an alternative to the solid fill pattern offered by the **BHATCH** and **HATCH** commands, the **SOLID** command can be used to fill shapes that are already drawn, or to fill an area defined by points that you pick. To draw a solid-filled object, issue the **SOLID** command by entering the following at the Command: prompt:

> Command: **SOLID** *or* **SO**↵
> First point: *(pick a point)*
> Second point: *(pick a second point)*

The first two points that you select define one edge of the solid.

> Third point: *(pick a point diagonally opposite the second point)*
> Fourth point: *(pick point 4 or press* [Enter] *to end the command)*

If you press [Enter] at the Fourth point: prompt, AutoCAD LT creates a filled triangle. However, picking a fourth point can also create a quadrilateral area, depending on the four point locations. Several examples of solids are shown in **Figure 13-35**. Observe how the picking sequence determines the final shape of the solid.

When drawing a solid, the last two points selected form the first edge of the next filled area. This helps to create multiple connected triangles and four-sided polygons in a single solid-filled object. AutoCAD LT repeats the Third point: and Fourth point: prompts so that you can create additional figures in a single operation. When you are through, press [Enter] to end the **SOLID** command.

Although the solid fill hatch pattern is a better choice, the **SOLID** command can also be used when sectioning very thin features, like seals and gaskets. Such an application is shown in **Figure 13-36**. A wide polyline can also be conveniently used for this type of application.

Figure 13-35.
Several examples of solids defined with different picking sequences.

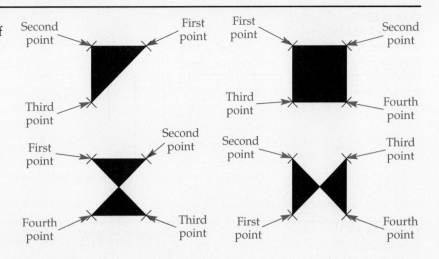

Figure 13-36.
This gasket between mating parts is a practical application for the solid command.

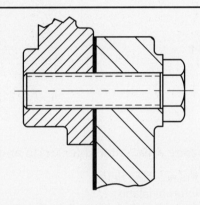

Creating Polylines Using the BOUNDARY Command

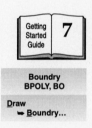

Getting Started Guide 7

Boundry
BPOLY, BO

Draw
➥ Boundry...

The **BOUNDARY** command creates a polyline object from overlapping objects. This function is the same as the component of the **BHATCH** command that creates a boundary object.

To create a polyline boundary, enter BOUNDARY, or BPOLY or BO, at the Command: prompt or select **Boundary...** from the **Draw** pull-down menu.

> **NOTE**
>
> The **BOUNDARY** command alias BO is not available in AutoCAD LT 97.

Refer to **Figure 13-37** as you follow the command procedure described below.

Command: **BOUNDARY** *or* **BPOLY** *or* **BO.**↵

The **Boundary Creation** dialog box appears. See **Figure 13-38.** Note that the options are identical to those offered by the **Advanced Options** subdialog box in the **BHATCH** command. You can choose between creating a boundary comprised of a polyline (the default) or a region object. If you are using AutoCAD LT 97, you can only create a boundary comprised of a polyline. Use the **Object Type:** drop-down list at the top of the **Boundary Creation** dialog box to make your choice. After making your choice, click the **Pick Points** 〈 button. The dialog box disappears and you receive the following prompt:

Select internal point: *(pick anywhere inside the closed area)*

Figure 13-37.
The **BOUNDARY** command creates a permanent polyline boundary around the enclosed area.

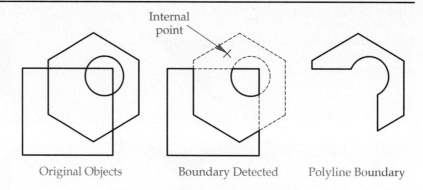

Internal point

Original Objects   Boundary Detected   Polyline Boundary

Figure 13-38.
The **Boundary Creation** dialog box offers the same options as the **Advanced Options** subdialog box of the **BHATCH** command.

If you pick the wrong area, enter U for undo and pick again.

    Analyzing the selected data...
    Analyzing internal islands...
    Select internal point: *(select another closed area or press* [Enter]*)*

Pressing [Enter] ends the **BOUNDARY** command and you are informed as to the number of polylines (or regions) created. The boundary is created in the current layer, color, and linetype. If a polyline object type was selected, it can be edited using the **PEDIT** command. **REGION** objects are described in *Chapter 6* of this text. See *Chapter 11* to review polyline editing.

PROFESSIONAL TIP
    If you need to calculate the area enclosed by overlapping objects, create a polyline or region object using **BOUNDARY**. The boundary can then be selected with a single pick using the **Object** option of the **AREA** command. Use the **ERASE** command or perform several undo operations if you do not wish to retain the polyline or region boundary.

Chapter Test

Write your answer in the space provided.

1. What is the aclt.pat file? _____
   _____
   _____
   _____

2. Identify two ways to access the **BHATCH** command. _____
   _____
   _____
   _____

3. How does the **BHATCH** command differ from the **HATCH** command? _____
   _____
   _____
   _____

4. Which button in the **Boundary Hatch** dialog box lets you use an existing hatch pattern in your drawing as the pattern for the next hatch operation? _____
   _____
   _____

5. What is associative hatching? _____
   _____
   _____
   _____

6. List the three hatch style options. Of the three, which style hatches completely through an object? _____
   _____
   _____

7. Identify two ways to specify multiple pick points when hatching using **Content Explorer.** _____
   _____

8. A hatch boundary is comprised of what type of object? What are the choices for users of AutoCAD LT 97? _____
   _____

9. Name the command that allows you to change existing hatched areas. In which toolbar is it located? _____
   _____

10. *True or False?* Hatching created with the **HATCH** command may be edited. _____

11. What is the purpose of the **SOLID** command? _____
    _____
    _____
    _____

12. Name two alternatives to using the **SOLID** command. _____

_____

_____

13. *True or False?* As with **BHATCH**, the polyline created with the **BOUNDARY** command is automatically erased when the command is terminated._____

Chapter Problems

Electronics Drafting

1. Use the layers in your TEMPLATEA template file to draw and hatch the cross-section of the multilayer circuit board shown below. Use the solid fill pattern of the **BHATCH** command to draw the conductor patterns. Save the drawing as P13-1.

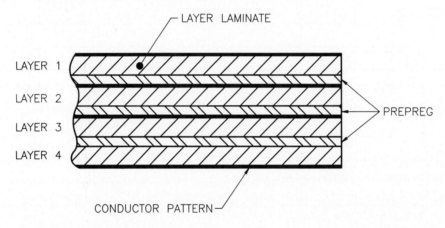

General Drafting

2. Draw, label, and hatch the pie chart using your TEMPLATEA template file. Create the text and hatch patterns exactly as shown using separate layers. Save the drawing as P13-2.

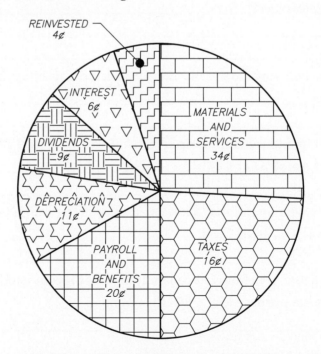

MAPLETON POWER & LIGHT CO.
REVENUE DISPOSITION

3. Draw, dimension, and hatch the HUB LEVER using your TITLEB template file. Save the drawing as P13-3.

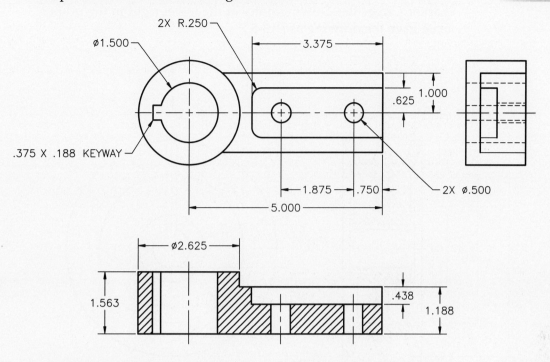

4. Draw, dimension, and hatch the BELL CRANK using your TITLEC template file. Construct the cutting plane line as described in this chapter. Create the drawing notes at the lower left in the proper layer. Save the drawing as P13-4.

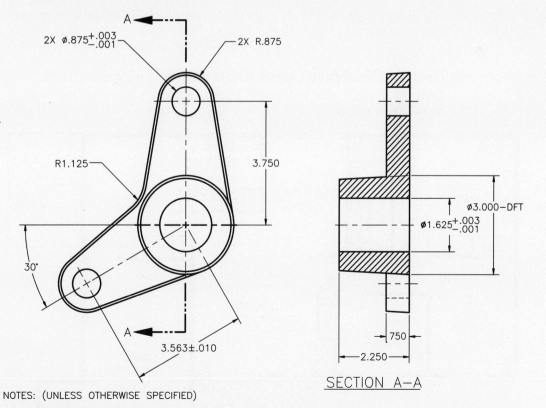

SECTION A–A

NOTES: (UNLESS OTHERWISE SPECIFIED)

1. DRAFT ANGLE: 3° MAX PER SIDE.
2. MATERIAL: CAST IRON
3. INTERPRET DIMENSIONS PER ASME Y14.5M–1994.

Chapter 13 Hatching Patterns and Techniques

5. Draw, dimension, and hatch the V-BELT PULLEY using your TITLEC template file. Construct the cutting plane line as described in this chapter. Create the drawing notes at the lower right in the proper layer. Save the drawing as **P13-5**.

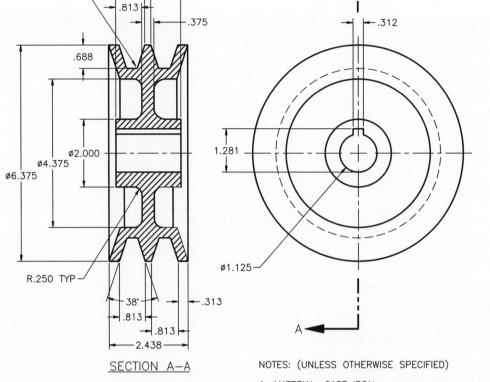

SECTION A—A

NOTES: (UNLESS OTHERWISE SPECIFIED)

1. MATERIAL: CAST IRON
2. INTERPRET DIMENSIONS PER ASME Y14.5M−1994.

6. Open Problem 8 from *Chapter 12* and add the appropriate hatch patterns to the walls, patio, and porch as shown. Save the revised drawing as **P13-6**.

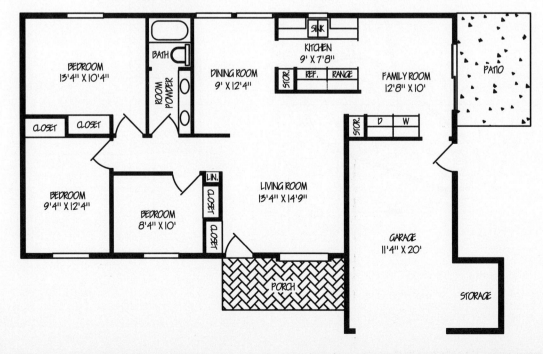

7. Draw, dimension, and hatch the **CONNECTOR BRACKET** using your TITLEC template file. Construct the cutting plane line as described in this chapter. Create the drawing notes at the lower right in the proper layer. Save the drawing as P13-7.

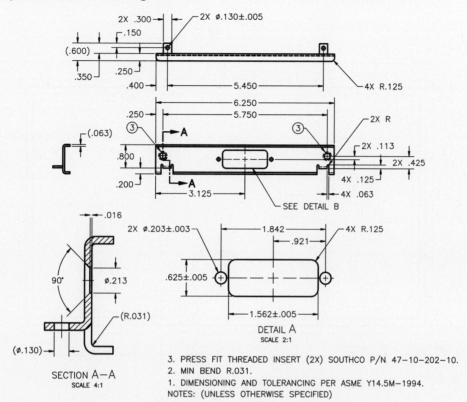

3. PRESS FIT THREADED INSERT (2X) SOUTHCO P/N 47−10−202−10.
2. MIN BEND R.031.
1. DIMENSIONING AND TOLERANCING PER ASME Y14.5M−1994.
NOTES: (UNLESS OTHERWISE SPECIFIED)

8. Draw, dimension, and hatch the **BALL CAP** using your TITLEB template file. Save the drawing as P13-5.

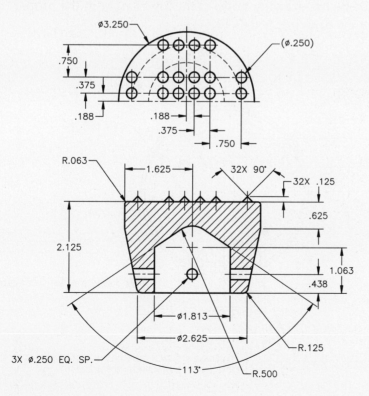

9. Create the FOUNDATION PLAN using your TEMPLATEC template file. Dimension and hatch the object as shown using the AR-CONC hatch pattern. Be sure to set units, limits, and **DIMSCALE** appropriately for an architectural drawing. Save the file as P13-9.

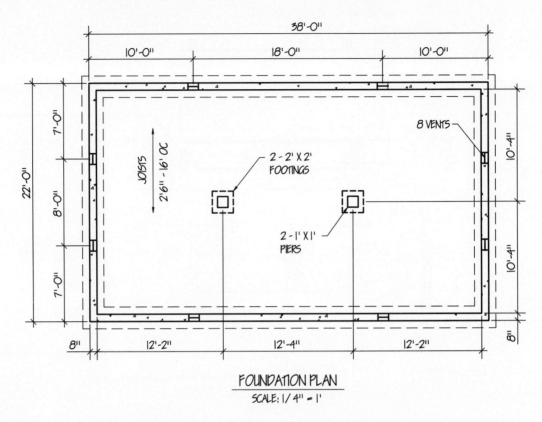

FOUNDATION PLAN
SCALE: 1/4" = 1'

10. Draw, dimension, and hatch the PRESSURE PLATE using your TITLEC template file. Construct the cutting plane line as described in this chapter. Create the drawing notes at the lower right in the proper layer. Save the drawing as P13-10.

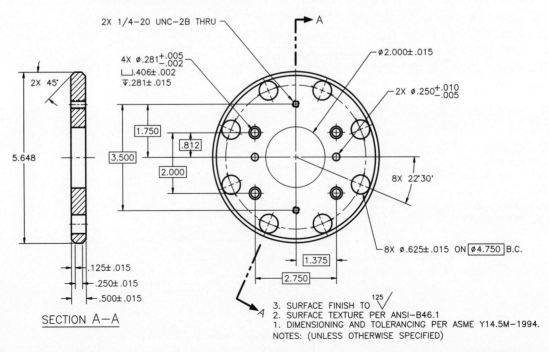

SECTION A—A

3. SURFACE FINISH TO $\sqrt{}$ 125
2. SURFACE TEXTURE PER ANSI–B46.1
1. DIMENSIONING AND TOLERANCING PER ASME Y14.5M–1994.
NOTES: (UNLESS OTHERWISE SPECIFIED)

AutoCAD LT

Chapter *14*

Plotting the Drawing

Learning Objectives

After you have completed this chapter, you will be able to:
- ○ Print or plot a drawing.
- ○ Save printing and plotting parameters for various configurations and output devices.
- ○ Output a drawing in a variety of raster graphics formats.
- ○ Export a drawing in PostScript format.

The **PLOT** Command

The **PLOT** command enables you to reproduce your drawing on a printer or plotter. This chapter describes the **PLOT** command and each of its options. AutoCAD LT supports a variety of output devices for producing hard copy. Before printing or plotting, make sure that your device is configured properly, as described in *Chapter 15* and *Appendix A* of the *AutoCAD LT 98 Getting Started Guide*. (When you install AutoCAD LT, the current system printer is automatically configured as your output device.)

PLOT
PP or [Ctrl]+[P]

File
➥ **Print...**

Standard toolbar

Print

Once your output device is properly configured, the **PLOT** command can be entered in several ways. You can enter PLOT, or PP, at the Command: prompt, click the **Print** button on the **Standard Toolbar**, press [Ctrl]+[P], or select **Print...** from the **File** pull-down menu. See **Figure 14-1**. At the Command: prompt, the sequence is as follows:

    Command: **PLOT** *or* **PP**↵

Figure 14-1.
Selecting **Print...**
from the **File** pull-
down menu issues
the **PLOT** command.

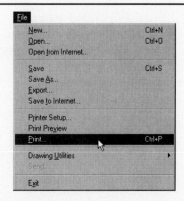

Any one of these methods presents you with the **Print/Plot Configuration** dialog box, **Figure 14-2.** This dialog box allows you to define and then preview each one of the parameters you specify for the final printing or plotting of your drawing.

Unlike the other dialog boxes in AutoCAD LT that are controlled with the **FILEDIA** system variable, the **Print/Plot Configuration** dialog box is controlled with the system variable **CMDDIA.** By default, **CMDDIA** is set to 1 (on) and will display the **Print/Plot Configuration** dialog box. When **CMDDIA** is set to 0 (off), all printing and plotting parameters are specified in response to prompts on the command line. Each of the areas and options of the **Print/Plot Configuration** dialog box are described in the following sections.

Figure 14-2.
The **Print/Plot Configuration** dialog box.

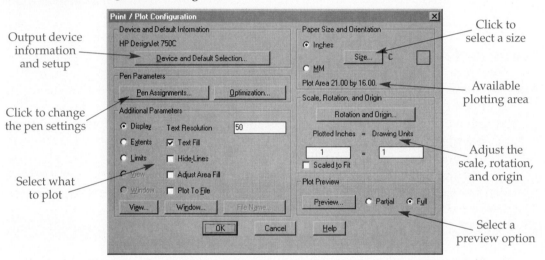

Selecting the Output Device

The **Device and Default Information** section at the top left of the **Print/Plot Configuration** dialog box is used to select the type of output device you will be using. Click the **Device and Default Selection...** button to display the **Device and Default Selection** subdialog box, **Figure 14-3.** A list of available output devices appears at the top of this subdialog box. As shown in the illustration, the Default System Printer is selected from the list. This is the device that is used for printing all Microsoft Windows 98/95/NT applications.

NOTE

It is also possible to change your output device by selecting **Printer Setup...** from the **File** pull-down menu. This method opens the **Preferences** dialog box and is covered in *Chapter 20.*

Figure 14-3.
Opening the **Device and Default Selection** subdialog box allows you to select the desired output device.

Select an output device

Save or retrieve plot configuration files

Click to review or change device settings

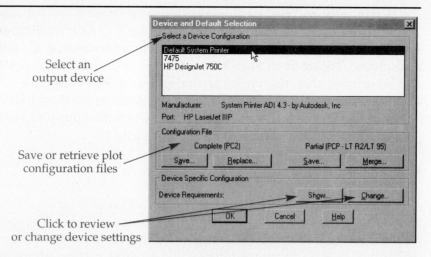

Use the buttons in the **Device Specific Configuration** area to review or change your printer or plotter settings. The **Show...** button displays the **Show Device Requirements** subdialog box, **Figure 14-4A.** This subdialog box displays the manufacturer of the currently configured device and the port to which it is connected. In the example given, the device requirements for the currently configured system printer are shown. Check the device settings and click **OK** when you are satisfied.

Click the **Change...** button in the **Device Specific Configuration** area of the **Device and Default Selection** subdialog box to make any changes. If your currently configured device is the system printer, AutoCAD LT uses the default printer specified in the Windows 98/95/NT settings and the Windows **Print Setup** dialog box is displayed. See **Figure 14-4B.** The name of the currently configured device appears in the **Name:** drop-down list. If you wish to use a different printer, select the desired printer from the drop-down list.

Figure 14-4.
A—The **Show Device Requirements** subdialog box for the currently configured system printer. B—Clicking the **Change...** button in the **Device and Default Selection** subdialog box opens the **Print Setup** subdialog box. C—Clicking the **Properties...** button in the **Print Setup** subdialog box offers additional printer setup options.

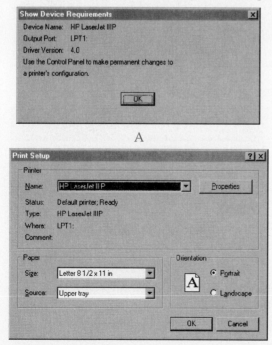

A

B

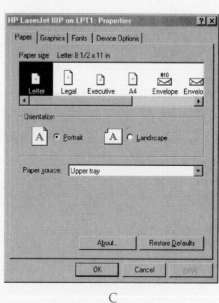

C

If you wish to view or change additional options for the currently configured device, such as paper size or the font to be printed, click the **Properties** button in the **Print Setup** dialog box. A subdialog box listing properties specific to the system printer is displayed, **Figure 14-4C.** Make any changes as required and click **OK** to continue.

Remember that the types of dialog boxes presented are a function of your currently configured printer or plotter. Regardless of the output device you are using, be sure to refer to the manufacturer's instructions supplied with your printer or plotter to help you configure the device properly.

Saving and Reusing Plot Parameters

There are two ways to save plot specifications to external files for reuse. The first method saves the complete plot configuration as a .PC2 file. The second method saves a partial configuration that is device-independent as a plot configuration parameters (PCP) file. A .PCP file stores information such as pen assignments, plot area, scale, paper size, and rotation for an unspecified device. A .PC2 file stores all the information found in a .PCP file, plus *device-specific* information that would otherwise be defined in the aclt5.cfg file. If you are using AutoCAD LT 97, this information is stored in the aclt4.cfg file.

The .PC2 file format is unique to AutoCAD LT 98 and 97 and AutoCAD Release 14. A typical .PC2 file can contain information about the output device, pens, plot scale, and rotation, for example. You can have multiple configuration files for various size drawings, printers, and plotters.

Before creating a .PC2 file, first specify all the required plot parameters. Then, click the **Save...** button located under the **Complete (PC2)** area in the **Configuration File** section of the **Device and Default Selection** subdialog box. The **Save PC2 File** subdialog box is displayed, **Figure 14-5A.** Enter a name in the **File name:** text box that is descriptive of the settings you are saving and click the **Save** button. By default, the .PC2 file is stored in the Program Files\AutoCAD LT 98 folder. For AutoCAD LT 97 users, the .PC2 file is stored in the Program Files\AutoCAD LT 97 folder.

When you wish to retrieve a saved .PC2 file, click the **Replace...** button located under the **Complete (PC2)** area in the **Device and Default Selection** subdialog box. Any saved files appear in the **Replace from PC2 File** subdialog box, **Figure 14-5B.** Select the file that you wish to use from the file list, or enter the desired file name in the **File name:** text box. Click the **Open** button when you are finished.

Figure 14-5.
A—Saving a .PC2 file. B—Replacing plot parameters with a saved .PC2 file.

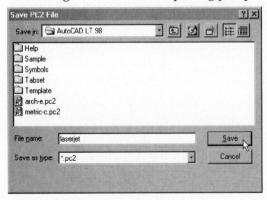

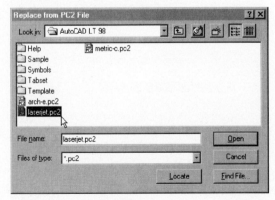

A   B

AutoCAD LT—Fundamentals and Applications

Using partial configuration files

A .PCP file is designated as a partial configuration file because it does not contain information about the output device. Therefore, a .PCP file is useful if you only have a single plotter (or printer). Since the .PCP file format is compatible with earlier versions of AutoCAD LT and AutoCAD, it may be used to share device-independent plot configuration information with files from those programs.

NOTE

A .PCP file is known as a *partial file*, while a .PC2 file is known as a *complete file*. The methods for creating and retrieving both types of files are very similar. The different methods are distinguished by the two sets of buttons in the **Configuration File** section of the **Device and Default Selection** subdialog box.

To save a .PCP file, first specify the plot parameters. Then, click the **Save...** button located under the **Partial (PCP-LT R2/LT 95)** area in the **Device and Default Selection** subdialog box. This will open the **Save PCP file** subdialog box. This subdialog box is virtually identical to the **Save PC2 File** subdialog box. Enter the desired file name in the **File name:** text box and click the **Save** button. Use a file name that is descriptive of the settings that you are saving.

When you wish to retrieve a saved .PCP file, click the **Merge...** button located under the **Partial (PCP-LT R2/LT 95)** area in the **Device and Default Selection** subdialog box. The **Merge from PCP file** subdialog box is displayed (the options are the same as those in the **Replace from PC2 File** subdialog box). Select the file that you wish to use from the file list, or enter the desired file name in the **File name:** text box. Click the **Open** button when you are finished.

Even if you do not have a plotter, you can use the .PCP file format to specify the required plotting parameters for your drawing. The file may then be given to a plotting service that can plot the drawing for you.

PROFESSIONAL TIP

Keep backup copies of your saved .PC2 and .PCP files on a floppy disk. Should you need to reinstall AutoCAD LT, or upgrade to a new version, simply copy your saved configuration files onto your hard disk to avoid recreating the plotting parameters again. Also, you can use the Windows 98/95/NT Notepad program, or any other ASCII text editor, to edit .PC2 and .PCP files.

Pen Assignments

The **Pen Parameters** area of the **Print/Plot Configuration** dialog box allows you to set pen parameters based on your drawing standards or the type of output device you are using. To change the pen parameters, click the **Pen Assignments...** button to display the **Pen Assignments** subdialog box, **Figure 14-6.** Selecting a pen from the list displays the current pen values in the **Modify Values** text boxes at the right of the subdialog box. The values that may be changed include the pen number, linetype, and width. If you are using a pen or inkjet plotter, the speed may also be changed.

Figure 14-6.
The **Pen Assignments** subdialog box allows you to change the pen parameters for the output device you are using.

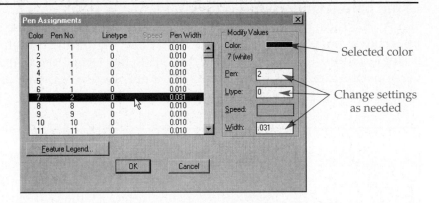

To ensure the proper line weight for plotted drawing objects, you must assign the color numbers used for your screen objects to the correct pen number(s) in the output device. As an example, suppose you have created a drawing using the first seven colors available in AutoCAD LT. These colors — red, yellow, green, cyan, blue, magenta, and white (or black) — are mapped to color numbers 1 through 7, respectively. These numbers are automatically assigned to matching pen numbers by AutoCAD LT.

In other words, all red objects displayed on screen are plotted with pen number 1, all yellow objects with pen number 2, all green objects with pen number 3, and so on. If you did nothing to change this convention, and you were using a pen plotter, you would need a separate pen for every color used in your drawing!

It is far more efficient and cost-effective to map the various colors used in your drawing to only a few pens. To further illustrate, refer to the **Pen Assignments** subdialog box shown in **Figure 14-6.** In this example, colors 1 through 6 have been assigned to pen number 1. The objects drawn with these colors are to be plotted with a thin pen. These objects would include dimensions, text, hatch objects, and centerlines. The object lines in the drawing have been drawn with color number 7. Since object lines should be drawn thick, color number 7 has been assigned to pen number 2. This pen has a tip size that produces a line weight, or thickness, of .031" to conform to the ASME/ANSI standards for object lines. Therefore, only two pens are required to accurately plot all the drawing objects.

Fortunately, most pen plotters are capable of using various pen sizes. These types of pens are similar to the ink pens used for inking on mylar and are therefore available in a range of tip sizes. If your pen plotter is compatible with these types of pens, you need not set the pen width in the **Pen Assignments** subdialog box. Simply insert the correct pen size in the assigned pen position on your plotter.

Other types of output devices, such as laser printers, inkjet printers, and electrostatic plotters, do not use pens. However, you can still produce plots with the proper line weights by assigning the desired pen widths to the color numbers used in your drawing.

Also note that a specific linetype may be assigned to a pen using the **Ltype:** text box in the **Pen Assignments** subdialog box. For most plotters, the drawing linetypes are controlled by the installed plotter driver. Therefore, objects drawn in linetypes other than continuous will plot correctly as a function of the software itself. It is very unlikely that you will need to change the linetype assignments, unless everything in your drawing has been drawn using the continuous linetype.

To make a linetype assignment, click the **Feature Legend...** button in the lower-left portion of the **Pen Assignments** subdialog box to display the **Feature Legend** subdialog box. See **Figure 14-7.** The linetypes and the respective values shown in this subdialog box reflect the linetypes that are generated by your plotter firmware. They are different than the linetypes created in your drawing by AutoCAD LT. Thus, assigning linetype value 6 to a pen in the **Pen Assignments** subdialog box will plot a

Figure 14-7.
The **Feature Legend** subdialog box displays the linetypes generated by the currently configured output device—not AutoCAD LT.

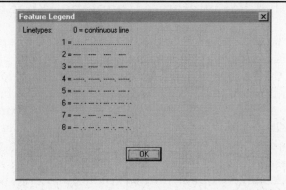

phantom line rather than a continuous line. Keep in mind the linetype values displayed in the **Feature Legend** subdialog box vary from one device to another. Remember that it is also highly unlikely that you will ever need to change the line-type assignment settings in the **Feature Legend** subdialog box.

Optimizing Pen Motion

By increasing the efficiency of your pens, you can minimize wasted pen motion and reduce plot time. For example, pens can be prevented from retracing duplicate lines and other drawing objects. Also, if your drawing uses many colors or line widths, you can reduce the time needed to change pens by sorting the pens. This enables AutoCAD LT to plot every object that uses one particular pen before switching to another.

To optimize your pens, click the **Optimization...** button in the **Pen Parameters** section of the **Print/Plot Configuration** dialog box. This displays the **Optimizing Pen Motion** subdialog box, **Figure 14-8.** With the exception of the **No Optimization** option, the optimization level is increased with each successive check box selected. In other words, selecting **Adds elimination of overlapping diagonal vectors** selects all preceding check boxes except **No Optimization.** The default settings shown depend on the configured output device. Note that the optimization options have no effect on raster (inkjet) printers and most are not available for the Windows system printer.

Figure 14-8.
The **Optimizing Pen Motion** subdialog box.

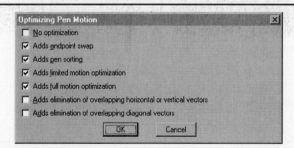

PROFESSIONAL TIP

In many cases, depending on the speed of your computer, your pen plotter, and the pen change mechanism, optimizing can actually be counterproductive. When in doubt, leave the optimization values at their default settings.

Additional Parameters—Choosing What to Plot

After selecting the desired output device and the necessary pen parameters, you must decide what part of the drawing you want to plot. The **Additional Parameters** section of the **Print/Plot Configuration** dialog box provides options for determining the portion of the drawing to be plotted and how it is to be plotted. Refer to **Figure 14-2.**

There are five option buttons labeled **Display, Extents, Limits, View,** and **Window** in the **Additional Parameters** section. Their functions are described below:

- **Display.** Using this option prints or plots only what is currently displayed on screen.
- **Extents.** This option prints or plots every object in the drawing without regard to the current screen display or limits. To verify exactly what will be plotted, be sure to perform a **ZOOM Extents** before using this option.
- **Limits.** This option prints or plots everything inside the defined drawing limits. If necessary, refer to *Chapter 2* to review setting the drawing limits.
- **View.** Views saved with the **VIEW** command (see *Chapter 4*) are plotted using this option. Until a view name has been provided, this option button is grayed-out (unavailable). To specify a view name, pick the **View...** button at the bottom of the **Additional Parameters** section of the **Print/Plot Configuration** dialog box. This displays the **View Name** subdialog box. Select the name of the view you want printed or plotted and then click **OK.** The view name you select does not have to be currently displayed on screen, but the **TILEMODE** system variable must be on (1) to output any saved view from either model space or paper space. See *Chapter 17* of this text to learn more about the **TILEMODE** system variable.
- **Window.** This option allows you to plot a defined area in your drawing by using a window to select the area. It is automatically activated by clicking the **Window...** button in the **Additional Parameters** section of the **Print/Plot Configuration** dialog box. This displays the **Window Selection** subdialog box, **Figure 14-9.** The **Window** option requires you to define two diagonally opposite corners of a window around the portion of the drawing to be plotted. The corners can be chosen with your pointing device or entered as absolute coordinates.

    If you are using absolute coordinates, enter the **First Corner** and **Other Corner** coordinates of the desired window in the appropriate **X:** and **Y:** text boxes. If you want to define the window with your pointing device, click the **Pick <** button in the upper-left portion of the subdialog box. This clears the dialog boxes and redisplays the drawing window. You are then prompted on the command line to pick the window corners that surround the part of the drawing you want printed or plotted. After you have picked the corners, the **Window Selection** subdialog box reappears and displays the X and Y coordinate locations of the window to be printed or plotted. Click **OK** to return to the **Print/Plot Configuration** dialog box.

Figure 14-9.
The **Window Selection** subdialog box is used to specify a plot window for a portion of your drawing.

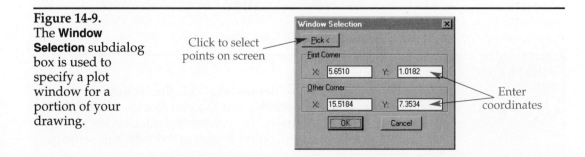

Click to select points on screen

Enter coordinates

AutoCAD LT—Fundamentals and Applications

Other Additional Parameters

A number of other plot configuration settings can be made using options in the **Additional Parameters** section of the **Print/Plot Configuration** dialog box. The functions of these options are discussed next.

The **Text Resolution** text box is used to set the resolution, in dots per inch, of TrueType fonts while plotting or exporting PostScript files with the **PSOUT** command. (The **PSOUT** command is covered later in this chapter.) Lower values decrease the text resolution and increase the plotting speed, while higher values increase the text resolution and decrease the plotting speed. The default value of 50 is adequate for most applications.

The **Text Fill** check box controls the filling of TrueType fonts while plotting or exporting with **PSOUT.** This check box is active by default. When it is inactive, text is output as outlines. The value for this entry (on or off) is stored in the **TEXTFILL** system variable.

Enabling the **Hide-Lines** check box allows you to plot a 3D model with hidden lines removed. This option serves the same function as the **HIDE** command, which is described in *Chapter 19.* Plotting takes somewhat longer when removing hidden lines, since AutoCAD LT must calculate each of the objects to be removed. Do not check this box when plotting a 2D drawing.

The **Adjust Area Fill** check box should be activated when you want objects such as wide polylines, solid hatch patterns, donuts, and 2D solids filled with a higher degree of precision. AutoCAD LT accomplishes this by adjusting the pen inside the boundary of the solid object by one-half the pen width. This option is only necessary for very precise applications, such as printed circuit board artwork. The pen plots at the center of the boundary when this check box is not active.

Creating a Plot File

Some computer operating systems allow you to continue working on a drawing while other instructions are being handled by the computer. This capability is called *multitasking* and is a standard feature of the Windows 98, Windows 95, and Windows NT operating systems.

Although it is not necessary for multitasking operating systems, it is possible to redirect plot output to an external file that has a .PLT extension. Redirecting plot output to a .PLT file is especially handy if there is only one department or classroom lab computer connected to a printer or plotter. The plot file may be written to a floppy disk and reloaded onto the hard disk of the computer connected to the output device and plotted accordingly.

If you want to redirect plot output to a file, click the **Plot To File** check box in the **Additional Parameters** section of the **Print/Plot Configuration** dialog box. The plot file name automatically defaults to the current drawing name. If you have not yet provided a name for the current drawing, the plot file is saved with the name DRAWING.PLT. If you wish to enter a different file name, click the **File Name...** button to display the **Create Plot File** subdialog box. See **Figure 14-10.** Saved plot files are automatically given the extension .PLT. To provide a different name for the plot file, enter the desired name in the **File name:** text box and click the **Save** button. You are then returned to the **Print/Plot Configuration** dialog box. Click **OK** once more to close the dialog box and create the plot file. When the file is complete, a message from AutoCAD LT appears on the command line.

Figure 14-10.
A plot file from
your drawing can
be saved by using
the **Create Plot File**
subdialog box.

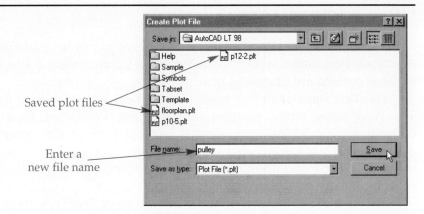

Saved plot files

Enter a
new file name

NOTE   A plot file is a series of instructions for pen motions
(such as pen up, pen down, draw, etc.) and is written in
HP-GL (Hewlett-Packard Graphics Language). Even if your
plotter is from a different manufacturer, it is likely to
conform to the HP-GL standard.

Paper Size and Orientation

The area in the upper-right corner of the **Print/Plot Configuration** dialog box illustrated in **Figure 14-2** controls the paper size and orientation for your drawing. Click either the **Inches** or **MM** option button to specify the appropriate units for your drawing. Clicking the **Size...** button displays the **Paper Size** subdialog box, **Figure 14-11.** Select the desired size from the list given, or enter your own width and height specifications in one of the **USER:** text boxes. If you enter your own size specifications, make sure the values do not exceed the maximum size indicated in the list (the maximum size is the largest size plot media your plotter can accommodate). Therefore, the sizes listed in the **Paper Size** subdialog box will vary according to the size of your printer or plotter.

Keep in mind that all pen plotters require margins around the edges of the plot media. The margin space is used to secure the media to the plotter drum with clamps, grit wheels, or other holding devices. As a result, the available plotting area is smaller than the standard sheet sizes specified by industry standards. Whether you select a standard size from the **Paper Size** subdialog box or enter your own specifications, the available plotting area is indicated in the **Paper Size and Orientation** area of the **Print/Plot Configuration** dialog box.

Figure 14-11.
Available sheet sizes
for the current
output device are
listed in the **Paper
Size** subdialog box.

Enter a
custom size

Select a
paper size

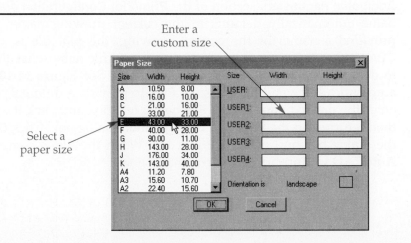

Plot Rotation

Options to control the plot scale, rotation, and origin are located in the **Scale, Rotation, and Origin** area of the **Print/Plot Configuration** dialog box. Refer to **Figure 14-2.** Clicking the **Rotation and Origin...** button displays the **Plot Rotation and Origin** subdialog box, **Figure 14-12.** AutoCAD LT rotates plots clockwise in 90° increments. A degree rotation setting can be chosen from the **0, 90, 180,** and **270** option buttons in the **Plot Rotation and Origin** subdialog box. The results of different plot rotation values are shown in **Figure 14-13.**

When using the system printer, the **Portrait** and **Landscape** options in the **Orientation** section of the **Print Setup** subdialog box can be used to make a plot rotation setting. Refer to **Figure 14-4B.** As shown in **Figure 14-13A,** a *portrait orientation* corresponds to a 0° rotation. The *landscape orientation* shown in **Figure 14-13B** corresponds to a 90° rotation.

Figure 14-12.
The **Plot Rotation and Origin** subdialog box can be used to rotate plots and set the plot origin.

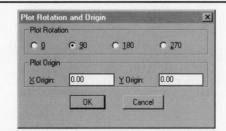

Figure 14-13.
Plot rotations are performed in 90° clockwise increments. When using the Windows system printer, rotation settings can be made in either portrait or landscape format.

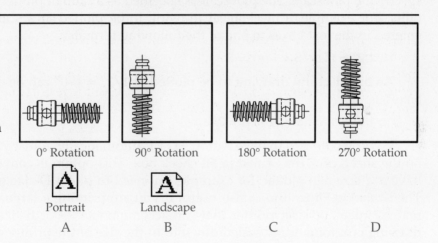

0° Rotation   90° Rotation   180° Rotation   270° Rotation

Portrait   Landscape

A   B   C   D

Plot Origin

The plot origin for a pen plotter is the lower-left corner of the plot media. The origin can be changed by entering coordinate values in the **Plot Origin** area of the **Plot Rotation and Origin** subdialog box. If you wish to use the default plot origin, leave the **X Origin:** and **Y Origin:** text box values at 0.00. If you wish to shift the drawing away from the default origin, set the required values in the text boxes accordingly. For example, to shift the drawing one unit to the right and one-half unit above the plotter origin, enter 1 in the **X Origin:** text box and .5 in the **Y Origin:** text box.

For printers, the plot origin is the upper-left corner of the paper. The coordinates presented above would shift the print origin one unit to the right and one-half unit down from the origin. Remember that the units you enter should be consistent with the units specified (inches or millimeters) in the **Paper Size and Orientation** area of the **Print/Plot Configuration** dialog box. Refer to **Figure 14-2.**

Setting the Plot Scale

Scaling the text height and dimensions in your drawing has been covered in previous chapters. You may recall from those discussions that unless a drawing is to be plotted at 1:1, the plot scale factor is always the reciprocal of the drawing scale. For example, if you wish to plot an architectural drawing at a scale of 1/8″ = 1′-0″, you would calculate the scale factor as follows:

> 1/8″ = 1′-0″
> .125″ = 12″
> 12 ÷ .125 = 96 *(The scale factor is 96)*

A mechanical drawing to be plotted at a scale of 1:4 is calculated as follows:

> 1″ = 4″
> 1″ / 4″
> 1/4 = .25 *(The scale factor is .25)*

Finally, the plot scale factor of a civil engineering drawing with a drawing scale of 1″ = 50′ is calculated as:

> 1″ = 50′
> 1″ = (50 x 12) = 600 *(The scale factor is 600)*

As explained in previous chapters, AutoCAD LT drawing geometry should *always* be created at full scale. The drawing is then scaled up or down accordingly at the plotter to fit the sheet size. The **Plotted Inches = Drawing Units** text boxes in the **Scale, Rotation, and Origin** area of the **Print/Plot Configuration** dialog box are used to specify the plot scale. The plot scale is specified as a ratio of plotted units to drawing units. For example, a mechanical drawing to be plotted at a scale of 1/2″ = 1″ is entered in the text boxes in one of the following formats:

> 1/2″ = 1″ *or* .5 = 1 *or* 1= 2

An architectural drawing to be plotted at 1/2″ = 1′-0″ can be entered in the text boxes as:

> 1/2″ = 1′ *or* .5 = 12 *or* 1 = 24

If you would like to have AutoCAD LT automatically adjust your drawing to fit on the sheet, click the **Scaled to Fit** check box. This option is convenient if you only have a C-size pen plotter, for example, but need to plot a D-size or E-size drawing. The **Scaled to Fit** feature is also useful if you are printing a large drawing on a dot matrix, inkjet, or laser printer that can accommodate A- or B-size sheets only. The drawing is automatically scaled down to fit the size of the printer paper.

Previewing the Plot

Because of the size and complexity of some drawings, it often takes a long time to finish a plot. By previewing a plot before it is sent to the output device, you can save ink, paper, and time. Preview options are offered in the **Plot Preview** area of the **Print/Plot Configuration** dialog box. Refer to **Figure 14-2.** You can choose between a partial or full preview before clicking the **Preview...** button. The two preview options are described below:

- **Partial.** Clicking this option button displays the **Preview Effective Plotting Area** subdialog box, **Figure 14-14.** It is used to verify the position of the plotted drawing on the sheet. Two outlines are displayed. The red outline represents the paper size. The blue outline represents the area occupied by the plotted image and is called the *effective area.* The dimensions of both the paper size and the effective area are reported just below the outlines. The **Warnings:** text box alerts you if the plotted image is too large for the paper size.

Figure 14-14.
The **Preview Effective Plotting Area** subdialog box outlines the appearance of the plotted drawing on the sheet.

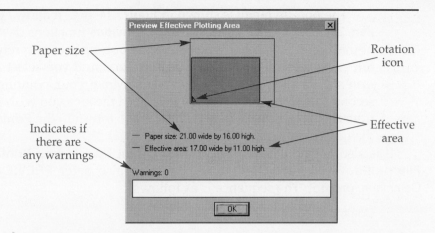

Paper size

Rotation icon

Indicates if there are any warnings

Effective area

When the effective area and the paper size are the same, AutoCAD LT displays a red and blue dashed line. In the example shown in **Figure 14-14,** the reported values indicate that a B-size drawing is being plotted on a C-size sheet. Also, notice the small triangular symbol in the lower-left corner of the effective area. This symbol is called the *rotation icon.* The 0° default rotation angle is indicated when the icon is in the lower-left corner. The icon displays in the upper-left corner when the plot rotation is 90°. It appears in the upper-right corner for a 180° rotation and in the lower-right corner for a 270° rotation.

- **Full.** This option displays the plot in the drawing window as it will appear on the plotted hard copy. When you use this function, the realtime zoom icon appears and allows you to inspect details on the drawing before plotting. See **Figure 14-15.** Press and hold the pick button of your pointing device and drag up or down (not left or right) to change the magnification of the plot preview. When the image is zoomed to your satisfaction, press [Esc] or [Enter] on the keyboard to terminate the function. As shown in **Figure 14-15,** the following message is also displayed on the command line when you preview a plot:

Press Esc or Enter to exit, or right-click to activate pop-up menu.

Figure 14-15.
The **Full** preview option displays the drawing as it will appear on the plotted hard copy.

Realtime zoom icon

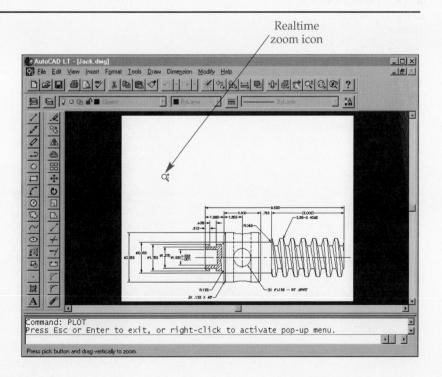

The pop-up menu is shown in **Figure 14-16A.** It allows you to perform the **Pan**, **Zoom**, **Zoom Window**, and **Zoom Previous** functions described in *Chapter 4* of this text. Click **Zoom Previous** in the pop-up menu to return to the original full preview display after performing a zoom. If you select **Zoom Window**, the icon shown in **Figure 14-16B** appears. Move your pointing device to pick a second corner forming a rectangle around the area you wish to zoom. Click **Exit** from the pop-up menu when you wish to return to the **Print/Plot Configuration** dialog box.

It is also possible to quickly preview a plot by selecting **Print Preview** from the **File** pull-down menu, **Figure 14-17.** You can also enter PREVIEW, or PRE, at the Command: prompt. The sequence is as follows:

Command: **PREVIEW** *or* **PRE**↵

When you use this method to preview a plot, the full preview option is used. A partial preview cannot be performed.

Once you are satisfied with all printer or plotter parameters and are ready to plot, click the **OK** button to exit the **Print/Plot Configuration** dialog box. However, before doing so, be sure that your printer or plotter is turned on and that all cabling is secure. For inkjet and pen plotters, make sure that the correct size and number of pens are in place, and that the plot media is properly loaded in the plotter. After plotting, the following messages are displayed on the command line:

Effective plotting area: (*xx*) wide by (*yy*) high
Plot complete.
Command:

Figure 14-16.
A—Pan and zoom options are offered in the full plot preview pop-up menu.
B—The **Zoom Window** option allows you to inspect details of your drawing before plotting.

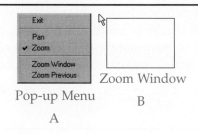

Pop-up Menu
A

Zoom Window
B

Figure 14-17.
Selecting **Print Preview** from the **File** pull-down menu allows you to quickly preview a plot.

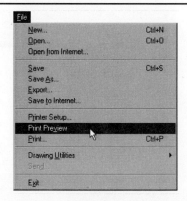

Exporting a Raster File

The **PLOT** command also allows you to export a drawing in one of four industry-standard raster file formats. A *raster file* is one in which graphical objects are defined by the location and color of screen pixels. Raster file formats are used in a variety of Windows 98, Windows 95, and Windows NT-based presentation graphics and desktop publishing applications. The four available raster formats are:

- Windows bitmap (.BMP)
- Targa (.TGA)
- Z-Soft (.PCX)
- Tagged Image File Format (.TIF)

Each of the four formats offers a range of screen resolutions from 320×200 pixels to 1600×1280 pixels. In the following example, a .PCX file at 800×600 pixels is selected as the export file type. If you are seated at your computer, try the following:

1. Issue the **PREFERENCES** command by selecting **Preferences...** from the **Tools** pull-down menu, or by entering PR on the command line. (You can also enter CONFIG to display the **Preferences** dialog box.)
2. When the **Preferences** dialog box appears, click the **Printer** tab. Next, click the **New...** button. See **Figure 14-18.**
3. The **Add a Printer** subdialog box is displayed, **Figure 14-19.** Select Raster file export ADI 4.3 - by Autodesk, Inc. from the list of available drivers. Next, use the **Add a description:** text box to enter an appropriate description for the type of export file you wish to create. In the example shown in **Figure 14-19**, the description entered is 800×600 .PCX format. After entering a description, click the **OK** button.

Figure 14-18.
Click the **New...** button in the **Preferences** dialog box to configure a raster export driver.

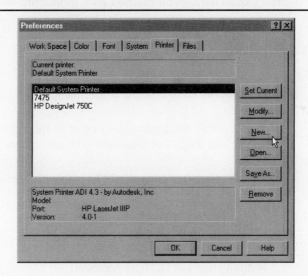

Figure 14-19.
The **Add a Printer** subdialog box contains a list of available raster file export drivers. After making a selection, enter an appropriate description for the raster format in the **Add a description:** text box.

Select a raster file export driver

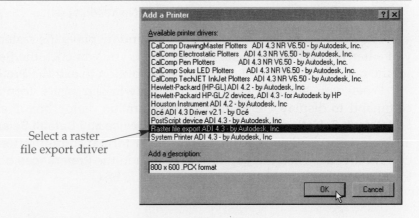

---

4. The graphics window then flips to the text window and you are presented with the following:

    1. 320 × 200 (CGA/MCGA Color)
    2. 640 × 200 (CGA Monochrome)
    3. 640 × 350 (EGA)
    4. 640 × 400
    5. 640 × 480 (VGA)
    6. 720 × 540
    7. 800 × 600
    8. 1024 × 768
    9. 1152 × 900 (Sun standard)
  10. 1600 × 1280 (Sun hi-res)
  11. User-defined

Enter selection, 1 to 11 ⟨1⟩: **7** ↵

You can export the drawing in any of the following raster file formats. Please select the format you prefer.

    1. Microsoft Windows Device-independent Bitmap (.BMP)
    2. TrueVision TGA Format
    3. Z-Soft PCX Format
    4. TIFF (Tag Image File Format)

Enter selection, 1 to 4 ⟨1⟩: **3**↵

The export file can be created as a monochrome or color image.

    1. Monochrome
    2. Color -16 colors
    3. Color -256 colors

Enter selection, 1 to 3 ⟨3⟩: **3** ↵

You can specify the background color to be any of AutoCAD LT's 256 standard colors. The default of 0 selects a black screen background.

Enter selection, 0 to 255 ⟨0⟩: **255** ↵ *(sets the background color to white)*

Sizes are in Inches and the style is landscape
Plot origin is at (0.00,0.00)
Plotting area is 800.00 wide by 600.00 high (MAX size)
Plot is NOT rotated
Hidden lines will NOT be removed
Plot will be scaled to fit available area

Do you want to change anything? (No/Yes/File) ⟨N⟩: ↵

The **Preferences** dialog box reappears and displays the raster export description you entered. See **Figure 14-20**. At this point, you can click the **Set Current** button to set the raster driver current or click the **OK** button to exit the **Preferences** dialog box.

When you are ready to export a drawing in raster format, issue the **PLOT** command to display the **Print/Plot Configuration** dialog box. Next, click the **Device and Default Selection** button to display the **Device and Default Selection** subdialog box and select the configured format. (The raster format configuration will already be set current if you clicked the **Set Current** button in the **Preferences** dialog box.) Click **OK** to return to the **Print/Plot Configuration** dialog box.

Figure 14-20.
The newly configured raster export format appears in the **Preferences** dialog box.

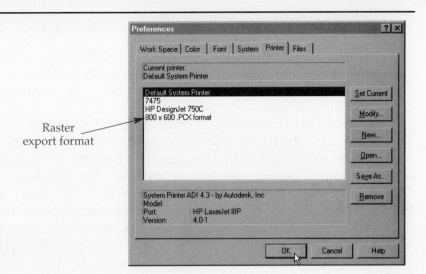

Raster export format

Next, specify any required plot parameters, such as scale and rotation, as described in this chapter. When all parameters are set to your satisfaction, click the **OK** button to exit the **Print/Plot Configuration** dialog box. The output file is then saved to disk in the raster format you specified. Keep in mind that the raster file name defaults to the current drawing name and is saved in the Program Files\AutoCAD LT 98 folder. For users of AutoCAD LT 97, the raster file is saved in the Program Files\AutoCAD LT 97 folder. If you wish to change this convention, click the **File Name...** button in the **Print/Plot Configuration** dialog box and save the file with a different name and/or folder designation. An example of an AutoCAD LT drawing in .PCX monochrome format appears in the Windows 98/95/NT Paint program. See **Figure 14-21.**

Figure 14-21.
An AutoCAD LT drawing in .PCX format displayed in the Windows 98/95/NT Paint program.

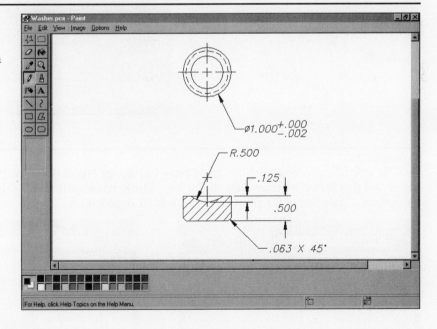

PROFESSIONAL TIP

The .PCX and .TGA formats are smaller in size than the .BMP and .TIF formats, and therefore take up far less disk space. Also, monochrome files are smaller than color files. See *Chapter 25* for more information about file export options.

Exporting in PostScript Format

PostScript is a page description language commonly used in desktop publishing applications. You can export an AutoCAD LT drawing in PostScript format by using the **PSOUT** or **EXPORT** commands. The output file is saved with a .EPS (Encapsulated PostScript) file extension.

The **PSOUT** command may be issued by entering **PSOUT** on the command line. This displays the **Create PostScript File** dialog box. You can also issue the **EXPORT** command to export a drawing by entering **EXPORT** at the command line or by selecting **Export...** from the **File** pull-down menu. See **Figure 14-22.**

As previously mentioned, entering the **PSOUT** command displays the **Create PostScript File** dialog box shown in **Figure 14-23A.** Observe that the encapsulated PostScript file name defaults to the current drawing name. If you wish to change this convention, enter the desired file name in the **File name:** text box and click the **Save** button.

Alternatively, you can enter the **EXPORT** command which displays the **Export Data** dialog box. See **Figure 14-23B.** Select Encapsulated PS (*.eps) from the **Save as type:** drop-down list at the bottom of the dialog box. Once again, note that the encapsulated PostScript file name defaults to the current drawing name. To change this convention, enter the desired file name in the **File name:** text box and click the **Save** button.

As with the **PLOT** command, AutoCAD LT reports the actual dimensions of the effective plotting area. The file now resides on disk and may be used with a PostScript application like Adobe Illustrator or output to a printer with PostScript capability.

Figure 14-22.
To export a file, select **Export...** from the **File** pull-down menu.

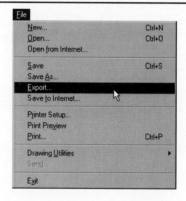

Figure 14-23.
A—The **PSOUT** command displays the **Create PostScript File** dialog box. B—The **EXPORT** command displays the **Export Data** dialog box. Either command may be used to create an encapsulated PostScript file from an AutoCAD LT drawing.

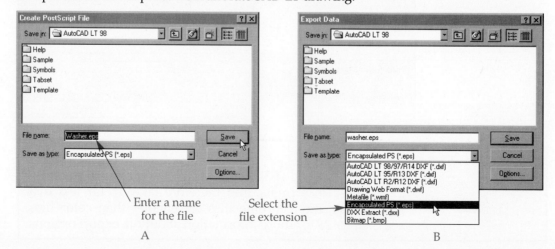

A   B

Chapter Test

Do not write in this text. Answer the following questions on a separate sheet of paper.

1. What is the system printer? _____
   _____
   _____
   _____

2. Define HP-GL. _____
   _____
   _____
   _____

3. What is a .PC2 file? Why would it be used? _____
   _____
   _____
   _____
   _____

4. How does a .PCP file differ from a .PC2 file? Give an example of how a .PCP file
   would be used. _____
   _____
   _____
   _____
   _____
   _____

5. What is the purpose of the **Pen Assignments** subdialog box? _____
   _____
   _____
   _____

6. List several reasons why you would choose to optimize pen motion. _____
   _____
   _____
   _____

7. Why would you create a plot file? _____
   _____
   _____
   _____
   _____

8. *True or False?* Plots are rotated in 90° counterclockwise increments._____

9. Describe the purpose and appearance of the **Preview Effective Plotting Area** subdialog box._____

_____

_____

_____

_____

_____

_____

10. Aside from the **Print/Plot Configuration** dialog box, how else may a plot be previewed? _____

_____

_____

11. Identify the system variable that controls the display of the **Print/Plot Configuration** dialog box. _____

_____

12. What is a raster file? List the file extensions of the four types of raster files that can be output by AutoCAD LT.

_____

_____

_____

13. What is PostScript and where is it used? Identify the keyboard command that allows you to export a drawing in PostScript format.

_____

_____

_____

Chapter Problems

1. Open Problem 3 from *Chapter 9* (P9-3). Obtain a print on your printer.

   General

2. Open Problem 8 from *Chapter 10* (P10-8). Set the line weights accordingly using the **Pen Assignments** dialog box. Use the **Scaled to Fit** option in the **Print/Plot Configuration** dialog box to obtain a print on your printer.

   General

3. Open the BELL CRANK from *Chapter 13* (P13-4).

   General

   a. Zoom in on SECTION A-A and produce a pen plot using the **Display** option. Be sure to make all required pen assignments before plotting.

   b. Next, make a pen plot of the entire drawing.

4. If you have a color output device, open Problem 2 from *Chapter 13* (P13-2). Create a color plot of the pie chart using a different color for each hatch pattern in the drawing.

   General

5. Open Problem 1 from *Chapter 13* (P13-1). Export the drawing in Windows bitmap format and then in Z-Soft format. Compare the two file sizes. Open one of the files in the Windows 98/95/NT Paint program and use the **Print** command to obtain a printed copy.

   General

6. If you have access to Adobe Illustrator, or some other PostScript-compatible program, try exporting an AutoCAD LT drawing of your choice using the **PSOUT** command. Then, import the file into the PostScript program and compare the two files.

   General

AutoCAD LT

Blocks, Attributes, and External References

Learning Objectives

After you have completed this chapter, you will be able to:
- ○ Create, insert, and redefine a block.
- ○ Save a block to disk.
- ○ Divide and measure selected objects with blocks.
- ○ Assign and edit block attributes.
- ○ Use attributes to automate drafting documentation tasks.
- ○ Extract attribute information in a bill of materials.
- ○ Link existing drawings to new drawings.
- ○ Use **Content Explorer** to insert blocks and attach external references.
- ○ Define and manage selection sets using **Group Manager**.

Many types of drawing symbols exist in the engineering and architectural fields. Symbols can be used for items such as fasteners, gears, doors, windows, pipes, resistors, and diodes. In traditional drafting, plastic templates are used to quickly draw common symbols. In computer-aided drafting, a symbol is drawn once and then saved for insertion into other drawings.

Symbols in AutoCAD LT are created as *blocks.* Text objects containing information about block symbols, called *attributes,* can be included with blocks if desired. This chapter describes how blocks and block attributes can be used to automate repetitive drafting tasks. You will also learn how one drawing can be linked, or attached, to another drawing using the **XREF** command. Finally, this chapter will explain how to save and manage selection sets using the **GROUP** command.

Creating a Block

Getting Started Guide 13

There are two types of blocks in AutoCAD LT. The first type remains in the drawing where it was created. This type of block is created with either the **BMAKE** or **BLOCK** command. The second type of block is called a *wblock.* This type of block is saved to disk so that it can be used with any number of different drawings. Wblocks are created with the **WBLOCK** command. Both types of blocks take up much less space in a drawing file than other types of objects. Therefore, it is practical to use blocks whenever there are multiple occurrences of a symbol or feature in a drawing.

Regardless of the type of block you define, the procedure for creating a block is very simple. The following steps are used:

1. Construct the object to be made into a block. Draw it as completely and accurately as possible. Any layers, colors, and linetypes used to create the object are retained when the object is made into a block and inserted. However, if the object is constructed on layer 0, the block will assume the properties of the drawing layer it is inserted on.
2. Name the block. A block name cannot exceed 31 characters. No spaces are permitted.
3. Select an *insertion base point*. This is a point of reference on the block that is used when the block is inserted into a drawing. Use an appropriate object snap mode or enter a known set of coordinates to ensure accuracy. The location should be logical for the symbol. For example, the center of a hex nut or the corner of a door are good insertion base points, **Figure 15-1.**
4. Select the objects that will comprise the block using any of the selection set methods.

Figure 15-1.
Creating a block. Choose a logical place for the insertion base point, such as the center of the nut shown here.

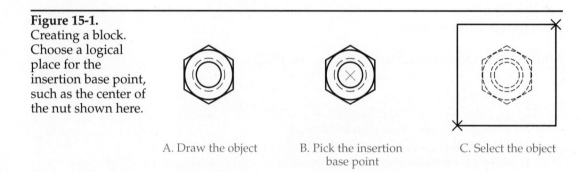

A. Draw the object

B. Pick the insertion base point

C. Select the object

Creating a Block Using a Dialog Box

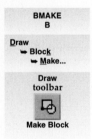

BMAKE
B

Draw
↪ Block
  ↪ Make...

Draw
toolbar

Make Block

The **BMAKE** command lets you define a block using the **Create Block** dialog box, **Figure 15-2.** To access this dialog box, click the **Make Block** button in the **Draw** toolbar, or select **Block** from the **Draw** pull-down menu, and then select **Make...** from the cascading submenu. See **Figure 15-3.** You can also enter the command as follows:

Command: **BMAKE** or **B**↵

Figure 15-2.
The **Create Block** dialog box.

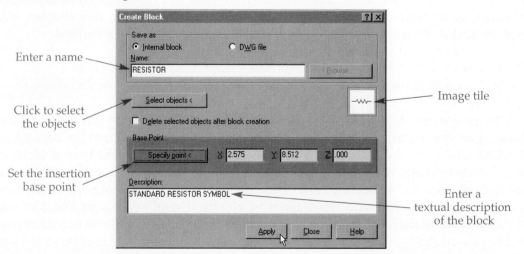

AutoCAD LT—Fundamentals and Applications

Figure 15-3.
Select **Block** from
the **Draw** pull-down
menu, and then
select **Make...** from
the cascading
submenu to issue
the **BMAKE**
command.

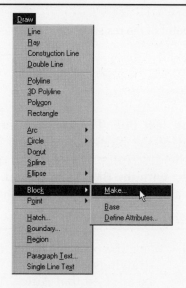

NOTE

For users of AutoCAD LT 97, entering **-B** on the command line is another option for invoking the **BMAKE** command and opening the **Create Block** dialog box. In AutoCAD LT 98, the **-B** command alias issues the **BLOCK** command, which is discussed in the next section.

The **Create Block** dialog box can be used to create internal blocks or wblocks. The different components of this dialog box are described below and on the next page:

- **Internal block.** Activate this option button when you want to create a block that will reside in the current drawing only.
- **DWG file.** This option button should be activated when you want to write a block to disk as a .dwg file to create a wblock. This button serves the same function as the **WBLOCK** command, which is described later in this chapter.
- **Name: text box.** Enter a name for the block in this text box. Remember that a block name cannot exceed 31 characters and no spaces are permitted.
- **Select objects ⟨ button.** After providing the block name, click this button to select the objects that will make up the block. When this button is clicked, the dialog box disappears and the Select objects: prompt is displayed on the command line. Use any selection set method to select the objects. The dialog box is redisplayed and an image of the objects you selected appears in the image tile at the right of the dialog box. Refer to **Figure 15-2.**
- **Delete selected objects after block creation.** Activate this check box if you want AutoCAD LT to automatically delete the selected objects after they have been defined in the block. Since block symbols take up less space than the objects they were created from, you may want to activate this check box to reduce the size of your drawing file.
- **Base Point section.** Use this area to specify the insertion base point for the block. You can enter a known coordinate using the **X:**, **Y:**, and **Z:** text boxes, but it is easier to click the **Specify point ⟨** button. When you do, the dialog box disappears and you are prompted for the insertion base point on the command line. Pick the point using an object snap mode to ensure accuracy. The endpoint of the resistor shown in **Figure 15-4** was selected using the **Endpoint** object snap mode. After selecting the insertion base point, the **Create Block** dialog box reappears.

Figure 15-4.
The insertion base point of the resistor symbol is selected using the **Endpoint** object snap mode.

Insertion basepoint

- **Description: text box.** This area of the dialog box lets you enter a textual description of the block using up to 256 characters. Although this step is optional, the description you enter is displayed in **Content Explorer** and can be modified with the **BMOD** command. Both **Content Explorer** and the **BMOD** command are described later in this chapter.

> **CAUTION**
>
> If your school or organization is using AutoCAD LT drawings with AutoCAD Release 14 and/or AutoCAD 2000, be advised that AutoCAD is unable to display AutoCAD LT textual descriptions for blocks.

- **Apply.** Clicking this button creates the specified block (or drawing file if the **DWG file** option button is activated). After clicking the **Apply** button, you can continue creating additional blocks or drawings.
- **Close.** Click this button to exit the **Create Block** dialog box and terminate the **BMAKE** command. Be sure to first click the **Apply** button or your work will be discarded.

The block is now created and may be inserted into the current drawing as many times as necessary using the **INSERT** or **DDINSERT** commands. These commands are described in a later section of this chapter.

> **PROFESSIONAL TIP**
>
> If you wish to change the name of an existing block, use the **DDRENAME** or **RENAME** command as described in previous chapters.

Creating a Block on the Command Line

If you prefer, you can define a block on the command line using the **BLOCK** command. The command sequence is as follows:

```
Command: BLOCK or -B↵
Block name (or ?): RESISTOR↵
Insertion base point: (pick the insertion point)
Select objects: (select the objects that make up the symbol)
Select objects: ↵
Command:
```

> **NOTE**
>
> For users of AutoCAD LT 97, entering -B on the command line issues the **BMAKE** command and opens the **Create Block** dialog box.

Unlike the **BMAKE** command, the **BLOCK** command automatically erases the original objects after the block is defined. If you wish to restore the original objects, enter OOPS or OO at the Command: prompt. The erased objects then reappear in their original locations.

To verify that the block was saved properly, repeat the **BLOCK** command. Enter the **?** option at the Block name (or ?): prompt, as shown below:

    Command: **BLOCK**↵
    Block name (or ?): **?**↵
    Block(s) to list ⟨*⟩: ↵

After pressing [Enter], the names of all blocks defined in the current drawing are reported in the **AutoCAD LT Text Window.** See **Figure 15-5.** The column labeled **User Blocks** lists the number of blocks created using the **BMAKE** or **BLOCK** command. The number of drawings that are referenced, or attached, with the **XREF** command is listed in the column labeled **External References.** (The **XREF** command is discussed later in this chapter.) Any blocks that are part of a referenced drawing are indicated under **Dependent Blocks.** The **Unnamed Blocks** column reports the number of anonymous blocks. Anonymous blocks are associative dimensions that have been erased in the current drawing.

Figure 15-5.
The **?** option of the **BLOCK** command lists all blocks defined in the current drawing in the **AutoCAD LT Text Window.**

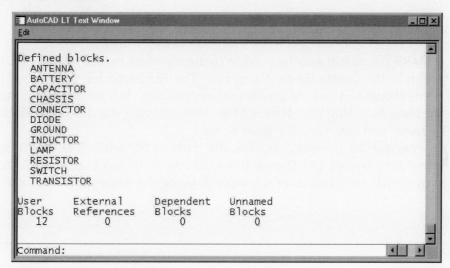

PROFESSIONAL TIP

Depending on the application, some block symbols will vary in size from one drawing to another. In these instances, it is helpful to draw the symbol so that it fits inside a one-unit square. When the block is inserted, it can then be scaled to the required size. As an example, create a circle measuring one unit in diameter. Next, place a centerline (or center mark) through the circle as described in *Chapter 12.* Create a block of the circle and the centerline. Now, whenever a hole of a given diameter is required, insert the circle block at the required scale. You then have a circle drawn with the correct diameter and a centerline, scaled accordingly in one operation.

EXERCISE 15-1

❏ Begin a new drawing using the **Start from Scratch** option button.
❏ Draw the resistor symbol shown in **Figure 15-4** on Layer 0. Leave the color set to white and the linetype set as continuous.
❏ Use the **BMAKE** command to create a block named RESISTOR. Activate the **Delete selected objects after block creation** check box.
❏ Select the insertion base point as described in this chapter. Enter the description STANDARD RESISTOR SYMBOL in the **Description:** text box.
❏ Save the drawing as EX15-1.

Saving a Block to Disk—the WBLOCK Command

An object saved as a *block* exists in the current drawing only and cannot be used in another drawing. A *wblock* is a block saved to disk so that it can be used in other drawings. A wblock can be created from an existing block in a drawing, or it can be created from an object and saved as a separate file in one operation.

To create a wblock, use the **WBLOCK** (Write Block) command. When using **WBLOCK**, you are first prompted to provide a file name for the block. The file name can be entirely different from the block name, but it must conform to Windows 98/95/NT file naming conventions.

Creating a Wblock Using a Dialog Box

The **BMAKE** command may be used to create a wblock by activating the **DWG file** option button in the **Create Block** dialog box. The file name for the wblock is then entered in the **Name:** text box. As an alternative, you can click the **Browse...** button to display the **Save As** dialog box, **Figure 15-6.** After entering the desired wblock name in the **File name:** text box, click the **Save** button.

When you use the **Browse...** option, the path to the wblock is then displayed in the **Name:** text box of the **Create Block** dialog box. See **Figure 15-7.** You can now continue with the creation of the wblock using the same methods for creating a block.

Figure 15-6.
After clicking the **Browse...** button in the **Create Block** dialog box, enter the desired wblock file name in the **Save As** dialog box.

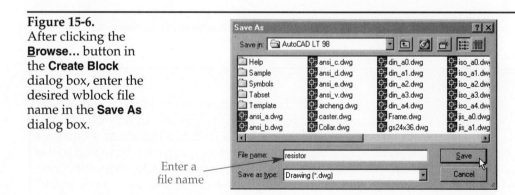

Enter a file name

Figure 15-7.
After exiting the
Save As dialog box,
the path to the
wblock is displayed
in the **Name:** text
box in the **Create
Block** dialog box.

Specified
path and
file name

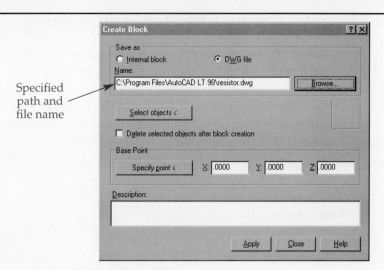

Creating a Wblock on the Command Line

A wblock can also be created on the command line. Enter the following at the
Command: prompt:

Command: **WBLOCK** *or* **W**↵

The **Create Drawing File** dialog box appears, **Figure 15-8.** Enter the desired file
name in the **File name:** text box. Note that blocks written to disk assume the .dwg file
extension (just like an AutoCAD LT drawing). After entering a file name, click the
Save button to exit the **Create Drawing File** dialog box. The following prompt is then
displayed on the command line:

Block name:

If you want to specify a block name that is different from the file name, enter the
desired name. If you have previously saved the object as a block and wish to make
the file name identical to the block name, you can enter an equal symbol (=) at the
Block name: prompt after entering the same block name in the **File name:** text box of
the **Create Drawing File** dialog box.

Block name: =↵
Command:

Once the block has been saved to disk, it may be used in the current drawing or
in any other drawing at any time. It is a good idea to make a backup copy of the
wblock on a floppy disk so that it may be shared with coworkers and clients.

Figure 15-8.
The **Create Drawing
File** dialog box is
displayed after
issuing the
WBLOCK command.

Create Drawing File

Save in: AutoCAD LT 98

Help	ansi_c.dwg	din_a0.dwg	iso_a0.dw
Sample	ansi_d.dwg	din_a1.dwg	iso_a1.dw
Symbols	ansi_e.dwg	din_a2.dwg	iso_a2.dw
Tabset	ansi_v.dwg	din_a3.dwg	iso_a3.dw
Template	archeng.dwg	din_a4.dwg	iso_a4.dw
ansi_a.dwg	caster.dwg	Frame.dwg	jis_a0.dwg
ansi_b.dwg	Collar.dwg	gs24x36.dwg	jis_a1.dwg

File name: resistor   Save

Save as type: Drawing (*.dwg)   Cancel

Enter a
file name

Creating and Saving a Block Simultaneously

It is also possible to define a block and write it to disk at the same time with the **WBLOCK** command. This option is convenient because you do not need to use the **BLOCK** command at all. First, draw the object. Then, issue the **WBLOCK** command. Enter a file name for the object when the **Create Drawing File** dialog box appears and click the **Save** button. Since a block has not yet been defined, press [Enter] when prompted for a block name and continue as follows:

> Block name: ↵
> Insertion base point: *(pick the insertion point)*
> Select objects: *(select the objects that make up the block)*
> Select objects: ↵
> Command:

Compressing a Drawing with WBLOCK

Suppose you have a drawing in which several linetypes have been loaded, but not used, and there are some layers that contain no drawing objects. The **WBLOCK** command can be used to remove unneeded linetypes, layers, blocks, and other named objects from a drawing. AutoCAD LT refers to unused named objects as *unreferenced objects.* Removing unreferenced objects compresses a drawing and saves disk space. To compress a drawing, use the following procedure:

> Command: **WBLOCK** *or* **W**↵

Enter the current drawing file name when the **Create Drawing File** dialog box appears and click **Save.** An alert box appears indicating that the current drawing file exists and asks if you want to replace it. Click the **Yes** button. When prompted for a block name on the command line, enter an asterisk (*) as follows:

> Block name: *↵
> Command:

Because an asterisk is used, this procedure is often called *star-blocking.* As the drawing is saved to disk, unreferenced objects are discarded and every object is stored in a new sequential order. The reordering process closes "gaps" in the data structure and helps greatly to reduce the overall file size.

CAUTION

Do not save the drawing after star-blocking or you will write over the new compressed version on disk with the earlier uncompressed version.

PROFESSIONAL TIP

It is best to perform star-blocking when a drawing is complete and you are certain that the unreferenced objects are no longer needed.

Compressing a drawing with the PURGE command

You may recall from *Chapter 5* that unreferenced objects can be removed from the drawing database at any time during a drawing session with the **PURGE** command. However, since no reordering of the drawing database occurs, the file reduction is not as great as that performed by the star-blocking method just described. To issue the **PURGE** command, first select **Drawing Utilities** from the **File** pull-down menu. Next, select **Purge...** to display the **Purge** dialog box. See **Figure 15-9**. A full description of this dialog box and its options is given in *Chapter 5*. The same purging options can be listed on the command line by entering -PU at the Command: prompt as follows:

    Command: **-PU**↵
    Purge unused Blocks/Dimstyles/LAyers/LTypes/SHapes/STyles/Mlinestyles/All:

The **-PU** command and the **Purge** dialog box are new features in AutoCAD LT 98. However, users of AutoCAD LT 97 can still remove unreferenced objects by entering PURGE or PU on the command line, or by selecting **Drawing Utilities** from the **File** pull-down menu and then selecting the type of object to purge from a cascading submenu.

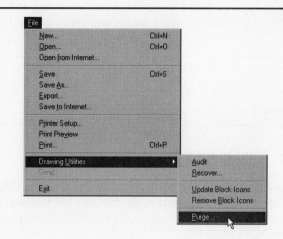

Figure 15-9. Selecting **Drawing Utilities** from the **File** pull-down menu and then selecting **Purge...** displays the **Purge** dialog box. The functions of this dialog box are described in *Chapter 5* of this text.

PROFESSIONAL TIP

Unused layers and linetypes can also be removed by using the **Delete** button in the **Layer & Linetype Properties** dialog box. Remember that only layers and linetypes that are not referenced in any way can be deleted. Referenced layers include the 0 and Defpoints layers, layers containing objects, the current layer, and xref-dependent layers (external references are described later in this chapter). The linetypes that cannot be deleted include the ByLayer, ByBlock, and Continuous linetypes.

Inserting a Block

The **INSERT** command allows you to insert a defined block or an entire drawing into the current drawing at a specified point, applying scale factors and rotation. If the block is not defined in the current drawing, but another drawing with that name exists on disk, a block definition is first created from the other drawing. The **INSERT** command displays the following prompts and options:

    Command: **INSERT** *or* **-I**↵
    Block name (or ?): **RESISTOR**↵

Enter ? to list each of the blocks currently defined in the drawing. If you wish to insert a drawing rather than a block, enter a tilde (~) to display the **Select Drawing File** dialog box. You can then select the drawing name from the dialog box file list (instead of entering it on the command line). After the block or drawing is selected, the command sequence continues as follows:

Insertion point: *(locate the insertion point)*
X scale factor ⟨1⟩/Corner/XYZ: *(enter the X scale factor or select an option)*
Y scale factor (default=X): *(enter a different Y scale factor or accept the default)*
Rotation angle ⟨0⟩: *(enter a rotation angle or press* [Enter]*)*
Command:

If you wish to separate the block or drawing into its individual drawing objects while inserting it, preface the block name with an asterisk (*) as shown below. Keep in mind, however, that you can only specify an X scale factor (not a separate Y scale factor) when exploding a block during insertion.

Command: **INSERT** *or* **-I**↵
Block name (or ?): ***RESISTOR**↵

Once a block has been inserted, or referenced, into a drawing, it can be selected with a single pick. Use the **Insert** object snap mode to select a block at its insertion point.

> **NOTE**
> Users of AutoCAD LT 97 can also enter the command alias IN on the command line to issue the **INSERT** command.

Insertion Scaling Options

By default, blocks are inserted at full scale (1:1). The X and Y scale factor prompts allow you to provide different scale factors for both axes of a block. When you wish for both the X and Y dimensions of a block to be identical, specify the X scale factor and press [Enter] when prompted for the Y scale factor (the Y scale factor defaults to the X scale factor). To give the block different X and Y scale factors, enter the desired values at the prompts. For example, suppose you have created a block that is one unit square. However, when inserted, you want the block to be 4.5 units long and 2.25 units high. When prompted for the scale factors, enter the following:

X scale factor ⟨1⟩/Corner/XYZ: **4.5**↵
Y scale factor (default=X): **2.25**↵

You can obtain mirror images of inserted blocks by entering negative values for the X and Y scale factors. The effects of this technique on a block are illustrated in **Figure 15-10.**

The **Corner** option allows you to specify the X and Y scale factors simultaneously by using the insertion point as the lower-left corner of a box, and a new diagonal point as the upper-right corner. The procedure is as follows:

X scale factor ⟨1⟩/Corner/XYZ: **C**↵
Other corner: *(pick a diagonal point)*

The block is then scaled to fit between the two diagonal corners. For three-dimensional blocks, enter XYZ when prompted for the X scale factor to specify different scale factors as follows:

X scale factor ⟨1⟩/Corner/XYZ: **XYZ**↵
X scale factor ⟨1⟩/Corner: *(enter an X scale factor or C for* **Corner***)*
Y scale factor (default=X): *(enter a Y scale factor)*
Z scale factor (default=X): *(enter a Z scale factor)*

See *Chapter 19* of this text for more information on three-dimensional objects.

Figure 15-10.
Negative scale
factors produce
mirrored images of
an inserted block.

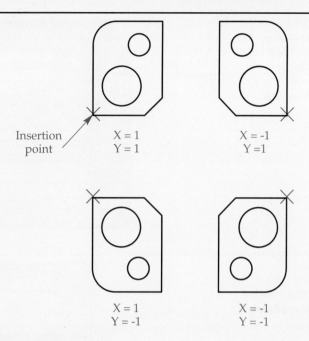

Insertion point

X = 1
Y = 1

X = -1
Y = 1

X = 1
Y = -1

X = -1
Y = -1

Inserting a Block Using a Dialog Box

DDINSERT
I

Insert
➥ Block...

Insert
toolbar

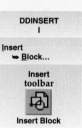

Insert Block

You can use the **Insert** dialog box to insert a block or drawing. To access this dialog box, click the **Insert Block** button located on the **Insert** toolbar. (To open this toolbar, select **Toolbars...** from the **View** pull-down menu and select it from the list in the **Customize** dialog box. This dialog box is labeled **Toolbars** in AutoCAD LT 97).

The **Insert** dialog box can also be opened by selecting **Block...** from the **Insert** pull-down menu. See **Figure 15-11.** Or, you can type DDINSERT or I at the Command: prompt:

       Command: **DDINSERT** *or* **I**↵

The **Insert** dialog box is shown in **Figure 15-12.** If you know the name of the block or file, you can enter it in the appropriate text box. If not, click the **Block...** button to display the **Defined Blocks** subdialog box, **Figure 15-13.** Select the block that you wish to insert from the list or enter the desired block name in the **Selection:** text box. When you are finished, click the **OK** button. The **Insert** dialog box then reappears.

If you wish to insert a drawing file rather than a block, click the **File...** button. When the **Select Drawing File** dialog box appears, select the drawing you wish to insert and click **Open**. The **Insert** dialog box is then redisplayed.

Notice in **Figure 15-12** that the **Insertion Point**, **Scale**, and **Rotation** text boxes are grayed out. This is because the **Specify Parameters on Screen** check box is active by default. When this check box is active, the insertion point, scale, and rotation for the block are entered on the command line. If you wish to enter these parameters in the corresponding text boxes, deactivate the check box. If you wish to separate the block into individual objects during insertion, activate the **Explode** check box near the bottom of the **Insert** dialog box.

Figure 15-11.
Select **Block...** from
the **Insert** pull-down
menu to display the
Insert dialog box.

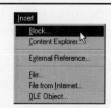

Figure 15-12.
The **Insert** dialog box can be used to insert a block or drawing file into the current drawing.

Click to select a name from a list

Enter a name

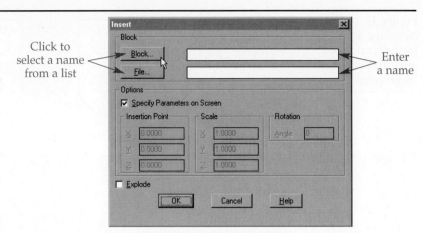

Figure 15-13.
Select a block for insertion from the list in the **Defined Blocks** subdialog box.

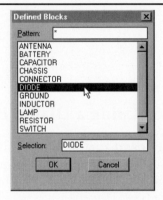

PROFESSIONAL TIP

It is common practice in industry to refer to other drawing prints to check features or dimensions while working on a drawing. Unfortunately, the hard copy prints are occasionally out of date, resulting in erroneous information. In other instances, the prints are not available and must be plotted. This is usually handled by a Document Control department after a formal Print Request is issued. You can avoid such problems and delays by using the **INSERT** or **DDINSERT** commands. When you need to reference another drawing, insert it into your current drawing. When you are done checking the features or dimensions you need, simply undo the insert operation or erase the inserted drawing. Drawings can also be inserted into other drawings using the "drag and drop" capability of Windows Explorer. See *Chapter 25* for a complete discussion of this powerful feature.

Inserting Blocks with Long File Names

The Windows 98, Windows 95, and Windows NT operating systems support long file names (a file name may contain up to 256 characters). Characters that cannot be included in a file name include the backslash (\), forward slash (/), colon (:), asterisk (*), question mark (?), quotation mark ("), less-than sign (⟨), greater-than sign (⟩), and piping symbol (|). While spaces may be used in a file name, AutoCAD LT block names cannot contain spaces. Therefore, when you insert a drawing that has a long file name, specify the name using quotation marks:

    Command: **INSERT** or **-I**↵
    Block name (or ?): **BLOCKNAME="PIVOT PLATE ASSEMBLY"**↵

NOTE Long file names cannot be selected from a file list in a dialog box because the necessary quotation marks are not included. Therefore, you must use the **INSERT** command—not **DDINSERT**—to insert drawings with long file names.

EXERCISE 15-2

❏ Open EX15-1 if it is not on your screen.
❏ Create three layers named Red, Green, and Blue. Assign the corresponding color to each of the layers.
❏ Set the Red layer current and use **INSERT** or **DDINSERT** to insert the RESISTOR block at 1:1 (full scale).
❏ Set the Green layer current and insert the RESISTOR block at 2:1.
❏ Set the Blue layer current and insert the RESISTOR block at 4:1 with a 270° rotation angle.
❏ What color are the three inserted blocks? Why?
❏ Save the drawing as EX15-2.

The BASE Command

When an entire drawing is inserted, it automatically becomes a block object. If you want to modify it, you must explode the block into individual objects. Also, when the drawing is inserted, AutoCAD LT uses the 0,0 drawing origin of the inserted file as the base point. You can change the insertion base point for a drawing using the **BASE** command.

To access the **BASE** command, select **Block** from the **Draw** pull-down menu, and then select **Base** from the cascading submenu. See **Figure 15-14**. You can also enter the following on the command line:

> Command: **BASE** or **BA.**↵
> Base point 〈0.0000,0.0000,0.0000〉: *(pick a point or enter new coordinates)*
> Command:

BASE
BA

Draw
➥ Block
   ➥ Base

Figure 15-14.
Issue the **BASE** command by first selecting **Block** from the **Draw** pull-down menu, and then **Base** from the cascading submenu.

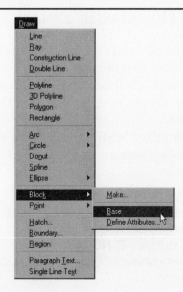

NOTE   Use the **BASE** command only if the current drawing is to be inserted into another drawing and requires a base point other than the drawing origin (0,0).

Dividing an Object with a Block

In *Chapter 7*, you learned that the **DIVIDE** command can be used to divide an object into a number of user-specified segments with point objects. The **DIVIDE** command also allows you to divide a selected object with a block. When using a block, you can choose whether or not to align the block with the divided object. In **Figure 15-15,** a spline is divided into five equal segments with a block named D-hole. The block is shown both aligned and unaligned with the spline.

DIVIDE
DIV

Draw
➥ P**o**int
➥ **Divide**

To divide an object with a block, first select **Point** from the **Draw** pull-down menu and then click **Divide** in the cascading submenu. You can also enter the following at the Command: prompt:

```
Command: DIVIDE or DIV↵
Select object to divide: (select the object to divide)
⟨Number of segments⟩/Block: B↵
Block name to insert: D-HOLE↵
Align block with object? ⟨Y⟩ (enter Y or N as required)
Number of segments: 5↵
Command:
```

Figure 15-15.
Dividing an object with a block. You can choose whether to align the block with the divided object.

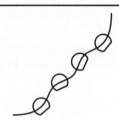 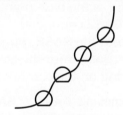

Blocks aligned
with divided object

Blocks not aligned
with divided object

Measuring an Object with a Block

You may also recall from *Chapter 7* that the **MEASURE** command is used to place points at user-specified lengths along an object. The **MEASURE** command can also be used to place a block at specified lengths along an object. As with the **DIVIDE** command, you can decide whether to align the block with the object you are measuring, **Figure 15-16.**

MEASURE
ME

Draw
➥ P**o**int
➥ **Measure**

To measure an object with a block, first select **Point** from the **Draw** pull-down menu and then click **Measure** in the cascading submenu. You can also enter the command as follows:

```
Command: MEASURE or ME↵
Select object to measure: (select the object to measure)
⟨Segment length⟩/Block: B↵
Block name to insert: D-HOLE↵
Align block with object? ⟨Y⟩ (enter Y or N as required)
Segment length: .75↵
Command:
```

Figure 15-16.
Measuring an object with a block. The block can be aligned with the measured object or left unaligned.

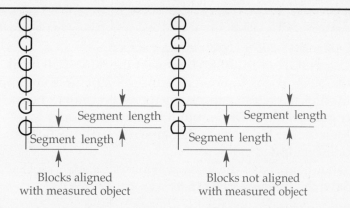

Blocks aligned with measured object

Blocks not aligned with measured object

Redefining a Block

Getting Started Guide **13**

It is sometimes necessary to modify or edit an existing block. AutoCAD LT refers to the modification of a block as *block redefinition.* To modify a block, the block must first be exploded. If you change an unexploded block and attempt to make a new block from it using the same name, the following error message is displayed:

    Block (name) references itself
    Regenerating drawing.
    Invalid

This message indicates that the block already exists. To redefine a block, use the following procedure:

1. Insert the block to be redefined anywhere in the drawing.
2. Explode the inserted block. Remember that you can explode the block as it is inserted by prefacing the block name with an asterisk (*), or by activating the **Explode** check box in the **Insert** dialog box.
3. Make any required changes.
4. Issue the **BLOCK** command and provide the same name as previously used for the block. Enter Y when AutoCAD LT prompts you with the following:

    Block (name) already exists.
    Redefine it? ⟨N⟩ **Y**↵

5. Be sure to specify the same insertion base point as the one previously used.
6. Finally, select all of the objects that will comprise the block.

Once the block has been redefined, any existing occurrences of the block in the drawing are automatically updated to reflect the modifications. Therefore, changing one block changes them all.

Using **BMAKE** to Redefine a Block

If you use the **BMAKE** command to redefine a block, AutoCAD LT displays the alert box shown in **Figure 15-17.** Click the **Yes** button to proceed with the block redefinition.

Figure 15-17.
Using the **BMAKE** command to redefine a block displays this alert box.

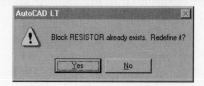

EXERCISE 15-3

❑ Open EX15-2 if it is not on your screen.
❑ Use **INSERT** or **DDINSERT** to insert the RESISTOR block in the drawing. Explode the block as it is inserted. The insertion point is not important.
❑ Modify the resistor to match the object shown below. (*Hint:* Use the **LEADER** command at the Dim: prompt to draw the leader line.)
❑ Make a new block using the same name (RESISTOR) and the same insertion base point indicated.
❑ What happens to the three previously inserted blocks?
❑ Save the drawing as EX15-3.

Managing Blocks

You will probably create a large number of blocks as your experience with AutoCAD LT grows. A collection of block symbols is called a *symbol library.* Remember to use the **WBLOCK** command to store your blocks on disk so that they may be used in other drawings and shared with coworkers and clients. Many users prefer to keep their symbol libraries in one or more separate folders or on floppy disks. As an example, you might create a folder called Symbols under the Program Files\AutoCAD LT 98 folder. The path to the folder would look like this:

C:\Program Files\AutoCAD LT 98\Symbols

If you work with many block symbols representing various professional applications, you might create several folders with specific names, such as the following:

C:\Program Files\AutoCAD LT 98\Architectural
C:\Program Files\AutoCAD LT 98\Civil
C:\Program Files\AutoCAD LT 98\Electronic
C:\Program Files\AutoCAD LT 98\Mechanical

Refer to *Chapter 25* of this text to learn how to create folders. To create a path to your new folders so that AutoCAD LT can find your blocks, see *Chapter 20* of this text.

In a networked environment, all of the block symbols should be stored on the network server so that they are easily accessible to everyone in the office or classroom. The CAD Manager or Network Administrator should have the responsibility to manage the symbol library. It is also this person's duty to inform everyone concerned when a block has been added to (or deleted from) the library.

Storing a Symbol Library in a Separate Drawing

As an alternative to storing your blocks on disk or on a network, you can also use a separate drawing file as a symbol library. With this method, all of your blocks are created and stored in a drawing that is named to reflect the kind of blocks it contains. For example, you can create a drawing named Mechanical that contains only mechanical symbols. Another drawing named Architectural might contain only architectural symbols, and so forth. An example of a drawing that contains only electronic schematic symbols, called Elec.dwg, is shown in **Figure 15-18.**

When you create a symbol library drawing, be sure to include the name of the block and a marker, such as a point or an X, to identify the insertion point of the block. Make 8-1/2″ × 11″ printed copies of the drawing to be shared with everyone who will use the blocks in your office or school. A larger plotted copy might also be displayed on a wall where it can be easily seen.

Figure 15-18.
A block symbol library for electronic schematic symbols. The name of each symbol is included in the drawing, along with the insertion base point (shown in color).

Electronic Schematic Symbols

RESISTOR	CAP	XSISTOR	DIODE
SWITCH	BATTERY	LAMP	INDUCTOR
CONNECT	GROUND	ANTENNA	CHASSIS

Inserting a Symbol Library

Once you have a symbol library drawing, it may be inserted into another drawing whenever the block symbols are needed. In the following example, the drawing Elec.dwg shown in **Figure 15-18** is inserted:

    Command: **INSERT** *or* -I↵
    Block name (or ?): **ELEC**↵
    Insertion point: *(press* [Esc] *to cancel the insertion)*

After the drawing name is entered, AutoCAD LT first searches the current drawing for a block with that name. When the block is not found, the current working folder is then searched for a drawing with that name. Once the drawing is located, the objects defined in the drawing appear briefly on screen. At this point, if you cancel the command, the objects disappear. However, all of the blocks defined in the symbol library now reside in the current drawing and are accessible to you. To remove any unneeded blocks from the drawing and reduce the file size, use the **WBLOCK** or **PURGE** commands as described earlier in this chapter.

Remember that block names cannot contain spaces. Therefore, if the drawing you are inserting has a long file name, such as Electronic symbols.dwg, use the following procedure:

    Command: **INSERT** *or* -I↵
    Block name (or ?): **BLOCKNAME="ELECTRONIC SYMBOLS"**↵
    Insertion point: *(press* [Esc] *to cancel the insertion)*

PROFESSIONAL TIP

Inserting one drawing into another also inserts layers, linetypes, text styles, and dimension styles along with blocks. This is a very convenient way to transfer named objects from one drawing to another. As an example, suppose you start a new drawing but forget to use a template file that contains your layers. Simply insert an existing drawing with the desired layers into the new drawing and press [Esc] at the Insertion point: prompt as described above. The layers, as well as any other named objects defined in the inserted drawing, are now in the new drawing.

Block Attributes

Attributes are objects that contain textual information and can be assigned to any object that is part of a block. Several examples of blocks with attributes appear in **Figure 15-19.** Other examples of attributes include part numbers, vendor names, prices, and sizes. Attributes can be made visible or invisible in your drawing. This capability is useful when you wish to suppress the display of proprietary information, such as the price or supplier.

Attributes can be edited both before and after becoming part of a block. Attribute data can also be extracted from a drawing to help produce a drawing parts list, or bill of materials.

Figure 15-19.
Block attributes are text objects that contain information about block symbols.

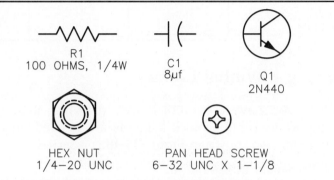

R1
100 OHMS, 1/4W

C1
8μf

Q1
2N440

HEX NUT
1/4–20 UNC

PAN HEAD SCREW
6–32 UNC X 1–1/8

Creating Attributes with the ATTDEF Command

Attributes can be created on the command line using the **ATTDEF** (ATTribute DEFinition) command. An attribute has four separate optional modes that may be assigned. The four modes are described below:

- **Invisible.** When invisible, attributes are not displayed or plotted. By default, attributes are visible.
- **Constant.** This mode assigns a fixed value to an attribute that cannot be changed without redefining the block. It is best to assign the **Constant** mode only to attributes that will not change.
- **Verify.** This mode prompts for verification that the attribute value is correct when you insert the block.
- **Preset.** This mode is similar to the **Constant** mode, except that the attribute value can be changed without redefining the block.

After issuing the **ATTDEF** command, enter I, C, V, or P to specify one or more of the modes. You are then prompted to provide a tag for the attribute. The *tag* is simply an identifier for the attribute and can contain any characters except spaces and exclamation marks. You *must* provide an attribute tag.

Next, you are asked to provide an attribute prompt. This step is omitted if you have specified **Constant** mode. The prompt is used to help define the attribute when the block is inserted. Typical prompts include Enter the manufacturer's name: or What is the price? If you do not specify a prompt, the attribute tag is automatically used in its place.

AutoCAD LT then asks for a default attribute value. This is the value that appears with the block on screen. You do not need to assign a default value. Even if a value is assigned, you can change it as you insert the block. If **Constant** mode is active, however, you *must* assign a default value.

After specifying one of the four optional modes, assigning a tag, and providing a prompt and default value, the **ATTDEF** command issues prompts that are similar to those used by the **TEXT** and **DTEXT** commands. You are prompted for the starting point of the attribute, the text height, and the text rotation. Looking at the resistor symbol in **Figure 15-20,** four attributes are first defined using middle text justification directly underneath the resistor. The attribute tags are displayed on screen until they are included in a block definition. The resistor and attribute definitions are then made into a single block and inserted into the drawing. When inserted, the tags are replaced with the attribute values entered while inserting. Refer to the illustration as you follow the **ATTDEF** command sequence given below:

> Command: **ATTDEF**↵
> Attribute modes—Invisible:N Constant:N Verify:N Preset:N
> Enter (ICVP) to change, or press ENTER when done: ↵
> Attribute tag: **RESISTOR**↵
> Attribute prompt: **REFERENCE DESIGNATOR?**↵
> Default attribute value: **R1**↵
> Justify/Style/⟨Start point⟩: **J**↵
> Align/Fit/Center/Middle/Right/TL/TC/TR/ML/MC/MR/BL/BC/BR: **M**↵
> Middle point: *(locate a middle point under the resistor)*
> Height ⟨0.2000⟩: *(enter a value or accept the default)*
> Rotation angle ⟨0⟩: ↵
> Command:

Figure 15-20.
At left, attribute tags are displayed underneath the resistor symbol before being included in a block. At right, the inserted attribute values appear under the resistor after the block is defined and inserted into the drawing.

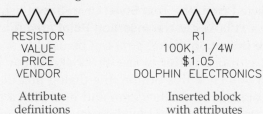

RESISTOR	R1
VALUE	100K, 1/4W
PRICE	$1.05
VENDOR	DOLPHIN ELECTRONICS

Attribute definitions   Inserted block with attributes

To create additional attributes, press [Enter] to repeat the command. When you reach the Justify/Style/⟨Start point⟩: prompt, note that the previously created attribute appears highlighted on screen. Simply press [Enter] to place the new attribute tag directly below the previous tag. Using this method, the new tag also inherits the text justification of the previous tag.

Once you have created the necessary attribute definitions, use the **BLOCK** or **WBLOCK** command to define the block as described earlier in this chapter. Be sure to include the attributes in the selection set when you create the block.

Creating Attributes with a Dialog Box

Block attributes can also be created using the **Attribute Definition** dialog box, **Figure 15-21.** To access this dialog box, first select **Block** from the **Draw** pull-down menu and then select **Define Attributes...** from the cascading submenu. You can also enter the following on the command line:

DDATTDEF
AT or DAD

Draw
➥ Block
➥ Define
Attributes...

> Command: **DDATTDEF** *or* **AT** *or* **DAD**↵

Figure 15-21.
The **Attribute Definition** dialog box.

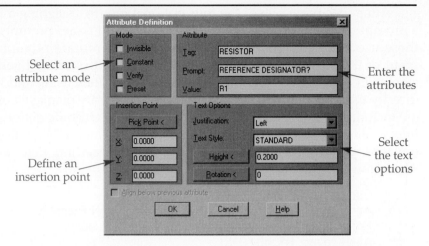

Select an attribute mode

Define an insertion point

Enter the attributes

Select the text options

If you wish to enable any of the four optional attribute modes, activate the appropriate check box in the **Mode** area (located in the upper-left portion of the dialog box). Use the text boxes in the **Attribute** area to enter the attribute tag, prompt, and default value. Each of the text boxes can contain up to 256 characters. Remember that entering a default value is strictly optional unless you have activated the **Constant** check box. Also, the **Prompt:** text box is not available if **Constant** mode is active.

The **Text Options** section allows you to set the attribute justification, height, rotation, and text style. Use the **Justification:** drop-down list to specify the desired text justification for your attribute. Enter the attribute text height and rotation in the appropriate text boxes. However, if you click either the **Height** ⟨ or **Rotation** ⟨ buttons, the **Attribute Definition** dialog box disappears and you are prompted for height and rotation values on the command line. If more than one text style is defined in the drawing, it can be selected from the **Text Style:** drop-down list.

The **X:**, **Y:**, and **Z:** text boxes in the **Insertion Point** area (located in the lower-left portion of the **Attribute Definition** dialog box) can be used to specify the origin of the attribute. However, it is much easier to use the **Pick Point** ⟨ button to specify the attribute origin. When you click this button, the dialog box disappears and you are prompted for the text start point on the command line. Pick a point on the screen as desired. The **Attribute Definition** dialog box then reappears, and the XYZ coordinates of the origin you selected are displayed in the appropriate text boxes.

When you are finished entering all necessary information in the **Attribute Definition** dialog box, click the **OK** button. The dialog box disappears and the attribute tag appears at the origin you specified.

If you wish to define another attribute, press [Enter] to repeat the command. Then, enter all necessary information as required in the appropriate sections. If you want to place the new attribute directly underneath the previous attribute using the same text justification, activate the **Align below previous attribute** check box near the bottom of the **Attribute Definition** dialog box. As with the **ATTDEF** command, once you have created the necessary attribute definitions, create a block making sure that the attributes are included in the selection set.

PROFESSIONAL TIP

When attribute definitions are selected using a Window or Crossing selection set, the prompts are issued in a random order as the block is inserted. If you prefer to be prompted in a specific order, select the attribute definitions using the same order in which you wish to be prompted when you create the block.

Editing Attribute Definitions

You may need to change certain aspects of attribute text before it is included in a block or wblock. The **CHANGE** command can be used to redefine the attribute text insertion point, text style, height, and rotation angle of selected attribute definitions. This is similar to editing normal text. The **CHANGE** command also allows you to revise the attribute tag, prompt, and default value (if initially provided). The following sequence is an example of using the **CHANGE** command to edit an attribute definition:

> Command: **CHANGE** *or* **-CH**↵
> Select objects: *(select the attribute definition to change)*
> Select objects: *(press* [Enter] *to close the selection set)*
> Properties/⟨Change point⟩: *(press* [Enter]*)*
> Enter text insertion point: *(pick a new insertion point or press* [Enter]*)*
> Text style: STANDARD
> New style or press ENTER for no change: *(enter an existing style name or press* [Enter]*)*
> New height ⟨0.2000⟩: *(enter a new height or press* [Enter]*)*
> New rotation angle ⟨0⟩: *(enter a new angle or press* [Enter]*)*
> New tag ⟨RESISTOR⟩: *(provide a new tag or press* [Enter]*)*
> New prompt ⟨REFERENCE DESIGNATOR?⟩: *(enter a new prompt or press* [Enter]*)*
> New default value ⟨R1⟩: *(provide a new default value or press* [Enter]*)*

If you only want to change the tag, prompt, or default value assigned to an attribute, you can do so quickly using the **Edit Attribute Definition** dialog box. See **Figure 15-22.** Unlike the **CHANGE** command, however, this dialog box only allows you to change one attribute definition at a time. To access this dialog box, click the **Edit Text** button in the **Modify II** toolbar, or select **Object** from the **Modify** pull-down menu and then **Text...** from the cascading submenu. See **Figure 15-23.** You are then prompted with the following:

> ⟨Select an annotation object⟩/Undo:

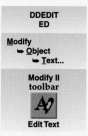

DDEDIT
ED

Modify
→ **Object**
→ **Text...**

Modify II toolbar

Edit Text

Figure 15-22.
An attribute's tag, prompt, and default values may be edited in the **Edit Attribute Definition** dialog box.

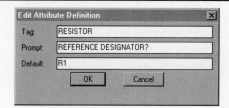

Figure 15-23.
Selecting **Object** from the **Modify** pull-down menu and then **Text...** from the cascading submenu allows you to access the **Edit Attribute Definition** dialog box.

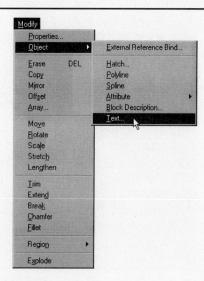

After selecting an attribute definition, the **Edit Attribute Definition** dialog box appears. You can also enter the following on the command line to edit an attribute definition:

Command: **DDEDIT** *or* **ED.**↵
⟨Select an annotation object⟩/Undo: *(select an attribute definition to change)*

Revise the tag, prompt, or default value in the corresponding text box. If necessary, refer to *Chapter 9* to review the editing techniques available in this type of dialog box. When you are done making changes, click the **OK** button and the dialog box is closed. The **DDEDIT** prompt remains on the command line if you want to select another object or undo the changes you made. If you are finished, press [Enter] to end the command.

Editing Attribute Definitions in a Dialog Box

DDMODIFY
MO

Modify
↳ Properties...

Object Properties
toolbar

Properties

The **Modify Attribute Definition** dialog box provides expanded editing capabilities for attribute text. See **Figure 15-24.** To access this dialog box, click the **Properties** button on the **Object Properties** toolbar or select **Properties...** from the **Modify** pull-down menu. Then, select a single attribute definition to edit. You can also use the **DDMODIFY** command to edit a single attribute definition using the **Modify Attribute Definition** dialog box:

Command: **DDMODIFY** *or* **MO.**↵
Select one object to modify: *(select a single attribute definition)*

You can change the color, linetype, layer, thickness, or linetype scale properties of the selected attribute in the **Properties** section at the top of the **Modify Attribute Definition** dialog box. Just below the **Properties** section are the **Tag:**, **Prompt:**, and **Default:** text boxes. These text boxes provide the same functions as the **Edit Attribute Definition** dialog box.

You can change the origin of the text attribute by selecting the **Pick Point ⟨** button and picking a new point on the screen, or by entering new X, Y, or Z coordinates in the appropriate text boxes. There are also options to change the text height, rotation angle, width factor, and obliquing angle. The **Justify:** drop-down list can be used to select a new text justification. To change the attribute's text style, use the **Style:** drop-down list. If another text style is defined in the current drawing, it appears in the list. Click the **Upside Down** or **Backward** check box if you want one of these conditions applied to your text attribute.

Figure 15-24.
Every aspect of an attribute definition may be changed in the **Modify Attribute Definition** dialog box.

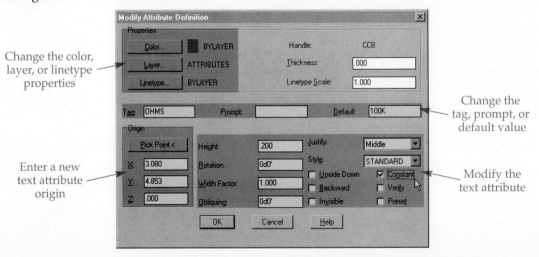

Perhaps the most powerful feature of the **Modify Attribute Definition** dialog box is the ability to change the attribute modes originally defined for a text attribute. You may recall from the discussion of the **ATTDEF** and **DDATTDEF** commands in this chapter that an attribute can be defined with **Invisible**, **Constant**, **Verify**, or **Preset** modes. Remember that the **Constant** mode assumes that the values of an attribute will remain unchanged. Therefore, no prompt is defined for the attribute and no prompt is presented when the attribute is inserted. The example shown in **Figure 15-24** illustrates this restriction. Since the **Constant** check box is activated, no prompt appears in the **Prompt:** text box. To revise the attribute definition for normal prompting, deactivate the **Constant** check box and enter a prompt in the **Prompt:** text box. If you want to toggle the **Verify** or **Preset** modes, or change an attribute from visible to invisible, click the appropriate check box.

Inserting Blocks with Attributes

Normally, attribute prompts are answered on the command line as a block is inserted. To accept the default attribute value, you simply press [Enter] or provide a new value as required. However, you can answer attribute prompts using a dialog box if the **ATTDIA** (ATTribute DIAlog) system variable is turned on as follows:

Command: **ATTDIA**↵
New value for ATTDIA ⟨0⟩: **1**↵

After entering the **INSERT** or **DDINSERT** command and specifying the block name, insertion point, scale, and rotation angle, the **Enter Attributes** dialog box appears. As shown in **Figure 15-25,** this dialog box can list up to eight attributes at one time. If a block has more than eight attributes, click the **Next** button to display additional attributes.

Responding to attribute prompts in a dialog box has distinct advantages over answering the prompts on the command line. With the dialog box, you can see at a glance whether all the attribute values are correct. It is therefore not necessary to use the **Verify** mode. If you decide to change a value, simply move to the incorrect value and enter a new one. You can quickly navigate forward through the attribute values and buttons in this dialog box by using the [Tab] key. Using the [Shift]+[Tab] key combination cycles through the attribute values and buttons in reverse order. When you are finished, click **OK** to close the dialog box. The inserted block with attributes then appears on screen.

Figure 15-25.
Attribute values
may be changed
during a block
insertion by using
the **Enter Attributes**
dialog box.

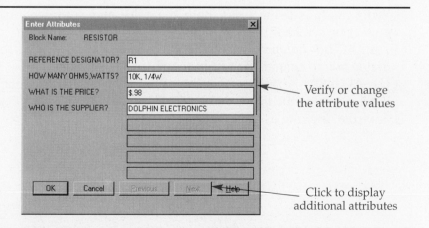

Verify or change
the attribute values

Click to display
additional attributes

<table>
<tr><td>**PROFESSIONAL TIP**</td><td></td><td>Set the value of **ATTDIA** to 1 in your template file(s) to automatically activate the **Enter Attributes** dialog box whenever you insert a block with attributes.</td></tr>
</table>

Controlling the Display of Attributes

All attributes are displayed on screen unless they are defined as invisible. You can control attribute visibility using the **ATTDISP** system variable as follows:

Command: **ATTDISP** *or* **AD**⏎
Normal/ON/OFF ⟨Normal⟩: *(select an option)*

Turning **ATTDISP** on displays all attributes, even those that are defined as invisible. Turning **ATTDISP** off removes the display of all attributes. The **Normal** option returns the display of attributes as originally defined. Keep in mind that **ATTDISP** is a global variable and controls the display of all attributes defined in the drawing.

EXERCISE 15-4

❑ Open EX15-1.
❑ Insert the RESISTOR block in the drawing using the **INSERT** or **DDINSERT** command. Explode the block as it is inserted. The insertion point is not important.
❑ Use **ATTDEF** or **DDATTDEF** to create four attributes with the values given below. You can use **Center** or **Middle** text justification for the attributes.

Mode	Tag	Prompt	Value
(none)	RESISTOR	Reference designator?	R1
(none)	VALUES	How many Ohms, Watts?	10K, 1/4W
Invisible & Verify	PRICE	What is the price?	$.98
Invisible	SUPPLIER	Who is the supplier?	DOLPHIN ELECTRONICS

❑ Make a new block using the same name (RESISTOR) and the same insertion base point. Be sure to include the attribute definitions in the selection set.
❑ Next, insert the block several times into the drawing. Enter different values for the attributes if you wish. You will be prompted twice for the price because the **Verify** mode is being used. Both the price and supplier attributes should not appear on screen if the **Invisible** mode was set properly.
❑ Turn **ATTDIA** on and insert the resistor one more time. Use the **Enter Attributes** dialog box to change the attribute values.
❑ Use **ATTDISP** to display all attributes. Next, turn off the display of the attributes. Finally, restore the display of attributes to the original definitions.
❑ Save the drawing as EX15-4.

RESISTOR
VALUES
PRICE
SUPPLIER

R1
10K, 1/4W
$.98
DOLPHIN ELECTRONICS

Editing Block Attributes

As discussed earlier, you can freely edit attribute definitions with the **CHANGE**, **DDEDIT**, or **DDMODIFY** commands before the attributes are included in the definition of a block. Once the block is created, however, the attributes are part of it and must be changed using the **DDATTE** or **ATTEDIT** commands. The **DDATTE** (dynamic dialog attribute editing) command is used to edit attribute text values only. The **ATTEDIT** (attribute editing) command can be used to change both attribute text and attribute properties. These properties include attribute position, height, angle, style, layer, and color.

The DDATTE Command

The **DDATTE** command allows you to edit attribute text values using the **Edit Attributes** dialog box, **Figure 15-26**. To issue the **DDATTE** command, click the **Edit Attribute** button in the **Modify II** toolbar or select **Object** from the **Modify** pull-down menu. Next, select **Attribute** and then **Single...** from the cascading submenus. See **Figure 15-27**. To issue the command from the command line, enter the following:

> Command: **DDATTE** *or* **ATE**↵
> Select block: *(pick a block with attributes)*

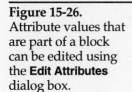

DDATTE
ATE

Modify
➥ Object
➥ Attribute
➥ Single...

Modify II
toolbar

Edit Attribute

Each of the attribute text values of the selected block then appears in the **Edit Attributes** dialog box. To make a change, simply move to the value you wish to edit and enter a new one. Remember that you can quickly move through the attribute values by using the [Tab] key. When you are finished editing the attributes, click **OK** to close the dialog box. The edited block attributes are then displayed on screen.

Figure 15-26.
Attribute values that are part of a block can be edited using the **Edit Attributes** dialog box.

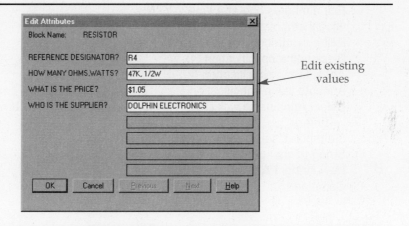

Edit existing values

Figure 15-27.
To issue the **DDATTE** command, first select **Object** from the **Modify** pull-down menu. Next, select **Attribute** and then select **Single...** from the cascading submenus.

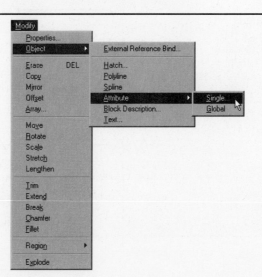

The ATTEDIT Command

The **ATTEDIT** command allows you to edit attribute text values as well as properties. Attributes can be edited one at a time or globally. Attributes must be visible to be edited one at a time, so use the **ATTDISP** system variable if necessary (this restriction does not apply to global editing). The **ATTEDIT** command displays the prompts below:

> Command: **ATTEDIT** *or* **AE** *or* **-ATE**↵
> Edit attributes one at a time? ⟨Y⟩ *(enter* Y *or* N*)*
> Block name specification ⟨*⟩: ↵
> Attribute tag specification ⟨*⟩: ↵
> Attribute value specification ⟨*⟩: ↵

If you enter N when prompted to edit attributes one at a time, a global edit of text values is performed. Global editing, however, limits you to replacing one text string with another. Entering Y at the prompt allows you to edit the attribute properties one at a time. You can choose to restrict the attribute selection to block name, tag, or value specifications. It is usually faster to simply press [Enter] after each of the prompts, as shown above.

Global attribute editing

To gain a clearer understanding of global editing, refer to the resistors illustrated in **Figure 15-28.** In this example, the supplier is changed from DOLPHIN ELECTRONICS to PARKER SUPPLY on all three resistors. The procedure to change all three attributes in one operation is as follows:

> Command: **ATTEDIT** *or* **AE** *or* **-ATE**↵
> Edit attributes one at a time? ⟨Y⟩ **N**↵
> Global edit of attribute values.
> Edit only attributes visible on screen? ⟨Y⟩ ↵
> Block name specification ⟨*⟩: ↵
> Attribute tag specification ⟨*⟩: ↵
> Attribute value specification ⟨*⟩: ↵
> Select Attributes: *(pick* DOLPHIN ELECTRONICS *on all three resistors and press* [Enter]*)*
> 3 attributes selected.
> String to change: **DOLPHIN ELECTRONICS**↵
> New string: **PARKER SUPPLY**↵
> Command:

Figure 15-28.
Global editing is used to change the same attribute value on multiple block insertions.

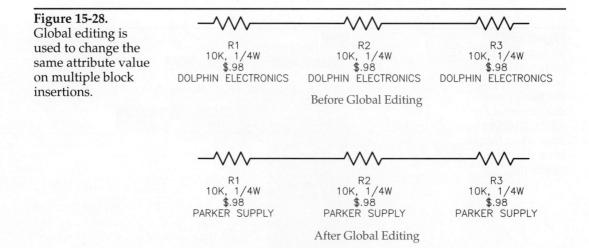

Before Global Editing

After Global Editing

Attributes do not need to be displayed when performing global editing. As an example, if you enter N at the Edit only attributes visible on screen? prompt in the previous sequence, the graphics window automatically flips to the **AutoCAD LT Text Window** and you are not prompted to select attributes. You are, however, asked for the text string to change, as well as the new text string. Be careful using this method since every occurrence of the old text string (visible or invisible) changes to the new text string you enter.

PROFESSIONAL TIP

Attribute text strings are case-sensitive. This means that they recognize both uppercase and lowercase letters. Therefore, it is a good idea to turn on **ATTDISP** so that you can verify and enter attribute values exactly as they appear on screen.

Editing attributes one at a time

Individual attribute editing allows you to change a variety of properties for a selected attribute. The properties you can change include value, position, height, angle, style, layer, and color. When you perform individual editing, the first attribute encountered in the selection set is marked with a small X. After changing the first attribute, if you press [Enter] to accept the default **Next** option, the X moves to the next attribute it encounters in the selection set.

For example, looking at the resistor shown on the left in **Figure 15-29,** the symbol was inserted with a 270° rotation angle. The text attributes must now be rotated to 0° so that they can be read horizontally. The attributes also require a new text position. Use the **Angle** and **Position** options of the **ATTEDIT** command to make the necessary changes as follows:

>   Command: **ATTEDIT** or **AE** or **-ATE**↵
>   Edit attributes one at a time? ⟨Y⟩ ↵
>   Block name specification ⟨*⟩: ↵
>   Attribute tag specification ⟨*⟩: ↵
>   Attribute value specification ⟨*⟩: ↵
>   Select Attributes: *(pick both resistor attributes and press* [Enter]*)*
>   2 attributes selected.

An X appears on the first attribute selected.

>   Value/Position/Height/Angle/Style/Layer/Color/Next ⟨N⟩: **A**↵
>   New rotation angle ⟨270⟩: **0**↵
>   Value/Position/Height/Angle/Style/Layer/Color/Next ⟨N⟩: **P**↵
>   Enter text insertion point: *(move the text string as required)*
>   Value/Position/Height/Angle/Style/Layer/Color/Next ⟨N⟩: ↵

The X moves to the next attribute in the selection set. The same operations are now performed for the remaining attribute.

>   Value/Position/Height/Angle/Style/Layer/Color/Next ⟨N⟩: **A**↵
>   New rotation angle ⟨270⟩: **0**↵
>   Value/Position/Height/Angle/Style/Layer/Color/Next ⟨N⟩: **P**↵
>   Enter text insertion point: *(move the text string as required)*
>   Value/Position/Height/Angle/Style/Layer/Color/Next ⟨N⟩: ↵
>   Command:

Because there are no other attributes in the selection set, pressing [Enter] to accept the **Next** option automatically terminates the command. The edited attributes are shown on the right in **Figure 15-29.**

Figure 15-29.
Individual attribute editing is used to change selected attribute properties, such as text angle and position.

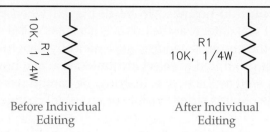

Before Individual Editing

After Individual Editing

NOTE

The **ATTEDIT** command displays the following messages if you attempt to edit an inserted block attribute with a **Constant** mode setting:

Select Attributes: 0 found
0 attributes selected. *Invalid*

The inserted block must then be exploded and redefined as described earlier in this chapter.

EXERCISE 15-5

❑ Open EX15-4 and erase all block objects on screen.
❑ Draw the partial schematic diagram shown by inserting the RESISTOR block three times into the drawing. Resistors R1 and R2 are to be rotated 270° as they are inserted. Accept the default attribute values.
❑ Edit the attribute text values to match those shown using the **DDATTE** command.
❑ Change the angle and position attribute properties for resistors R1 and R2 using the **ATTEDIT** command.
❑ Save the drawing as EX15-5.

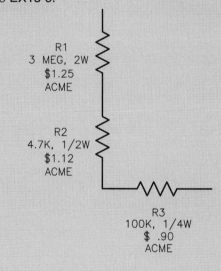

R1
3 MEG, 2W
$1.25
ACME

R2
4.7K, 1/2W
$1.12
ACME

R3
100K, 1/4W
$ .90
ACME

Using Attributes to Automate Drafting Documentation

So far you have seen that attributes are extremely powerful tools for assigning textual information to drawing symbols. However, attributes can also be used to automate any type of detailing or documentation task that requires a great deal of text. Such tasks include the creation of title block information, revision block data, and parts lists or bills of materials.

AutoCAD LT—Fundamentals and Applications

Attributes and Title Blocks

After a drawing is completely drawn and dimensioned, the next task is to fill out the information in the drawing title block. This is usually one of the more time-consuming operations associated with drafting documentation. Using the following suggested guidelines, this task can be efficiently automated using block attributes.

* The title block format is first drawn using the correct layer(s) and industry or company standards. You can use one of the title block formats provided by AutoCAD LT as discussed in *Chapter 2*, or you can create your own. Be sure to include your company or school logo in the title block. If you work in an industry that produces items for the federal government, also include the applicable CAGE code in the title block (see Note below). A typical A-size title block following the ASME Y14.1 *Drawing Sheet Size and Format* standard is illustrated in **Figure 15-30**.

Figure 15-30.
A title block format sheet must be drawn in compliance with industry or company standards.

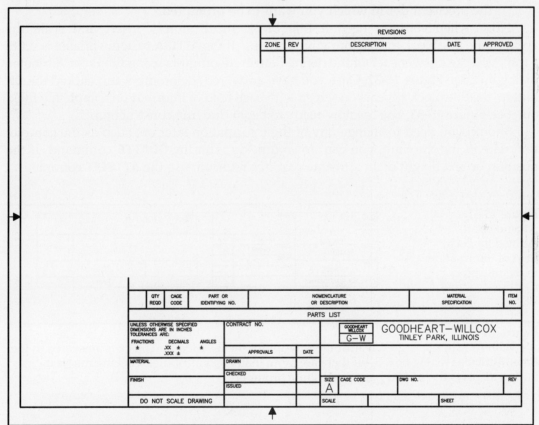

NOTE   The CAGE *(Commercial and Government Entity)* code is a five-digit numerical code identifier applicable to all activities that have produced, or are providing, items used by the federal government. For the commercial sector, where there is no requirement for this code, the CAGE code attribute may be eliminated from the title block.

- After drawing the title block, create a separate layer for the title block attributes. By doing this, you can easily suppress the title block information by freezing the layer that contains the attributes. This can greatly reduce redraw and regeneration times. When you are ready to plot the finished drawing, simply thaw the frozen layer.
- Define attributes for each area of the title block. As you create the attributes, determine the appropriate text height and justification for each definition. Define attributes for the drawing title, drawing number, drafter, checker, dates, scale, sheet size, material, finish, revision letter, and tolerance information, as shown in **Figure 15-31.** Include any other information that may be specific to your organization or application.
- Assign default values to attributes wherever possible. As an example, if your organization consistently specifies the same overall tolerances on drawing dimensions, the tolerance attributes can be assigned default values.
- Once you have defined each attribute, use the **WBLOCK** command to save the entire drawing to disk with a descriptive file name. For example, an A-size title block might be saved as titlea or formata. Be sure to use 0,0 as the insertion point. Also, as you create the wblock, remember to select the attributes using the precise order in which you want to be prompted.

Now, whenever you need a title block sheet, simply insert and scale the appropriate title block format into your drawing. If the **ATTDIA** system variable is set to 1 (on), you can answer each of the defined attribute prompts using the **Enter Attributes** dialog box. See **Figure 15-32.** Once you have answered the prompts and clicked the **OK** button, the title block appears on screen with each field of information completely filled out. See **Figure 15-33.** You are now ready to begin drawing construction.

Should you need to change any of the information later on, such as the completion date of the drawing, you can do so quickly with the **DDATTE** command. If the position or text height of an attribute requires revision, use the **ATTEDIT** command.

Figure 15-31.
Attributes are defined for each field of information in the title block.

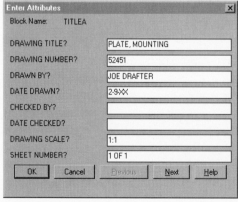

Figure 15-32.
A—With **ATTDIA** set to 1, each attribute prompt for the inserted title block is answered in the **Enter Attributes** dialog box. B—If there are more than eight attributes, clicking the **Next** button displays the second page of attribute prompts.

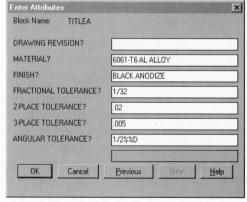

A   B

Figure 15-33.
The title block after insertion. When the drawing is complete, dates and checker information can be conveniently added with the **DDATTE** command.

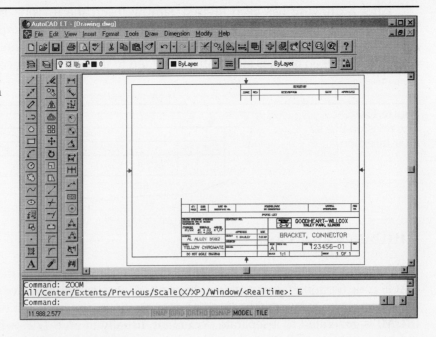

Attributes and Revision Blocks

It is almost certain that a detail drawing will require revision at some time in the life of a product. Typical changes that occur include design improvements and the correction of drafting errors. The first time that a drawing is revised, it is usually assigned the revision letter A. If necessary, revision letters continue with B through Z. (The letters I, O, and Q are not used because they might be confused with numbers.)

Title block sheets include an area for revision information called the *revision block*. See **Figure 15-34.** This area is designated to record all drawing changes. It is normally located at the upper-right corner of the title block sheet. The revision block provides space for the revision letter, a description of the change, the revision date, and approvals. Zones appear in the margins of a title block sheet and are indicated by alphabetical and numerical entries. They are used for reference purposes in much the same way that reference letters and numbers are used to identify a street or feature on a road map. Although A-size and B-size title block sheets may include zones, they are rarely needed for these smaller formats.

Block attributes provide an easy way to complete the necessary information in a revision block. Refer to **Figure 15-34** as you follow the guidelines below.

- First, create a revision block on the appropriate drawing layer(s).
- On a separate layer, define attributes that describe the zone (optional), revision letter, description of change, and change approval.
- Use left-justified text for the change description attribute, and middle-justified text for the remaining attributes.
- Use the **WBLOCK** command to save the revision block on disk with a descriptive name, such as revblk. Use the upper-left endpoint of the revision block as the insertion point.

Figure 15-34.
Revision blocks are used to record changes to your drawing. Defined attributes appear in each area as shown.

After a drawing has been revised, simply insert the revision block at the correct location. If **ATTDIA** is set to 1, you can answer the attribute prompts using the **Enter Attributes** dialog box. After providing the new information, click the **OK** button and the completed revision block is automatically added to the title block sheet. See **Figure 15-35.**

Figure 15-35.
The revision block after insertion.

ZONE	REV	DESCRIPTION	DATE	APPROVED
		REVISIONS		
D4	A	ADDED R.375 FILLET	11–18–XX	

Attributes and Parts Lists

Assembly drawings require a parts list, or list of materials, that includes the quantity, CAGE code (optional), part number, description, and item number for each component of the assembly or subassembly. In some organizations, the parts list or *Bill of Materials (BOM)* is generated as a separate document, usually in an 8-1/2" × 11" format. In other companies, the parts list is included on the assembly drawing. Whether they are separate documents, or part of the assembly drawing itself, parts lists and bills of materials provide another example of how attributes can be used to automate the documentation process.

Refer once again to the title block sheet in **Figure 15-30.** A section specifically designated for a parts list is located just above the title block area. To create a similar list, refer to the example in **Figure 15-36** and use the following guidelines:
- First, create a parts list block using the appropriate drawing layer(s).
- Define the attributes on a separate layer. Define attributes that describe the quantity, CAGE code (optional), part number, item description, material specification, and item number for the components of an assembly drawing.
- Use left-justified text for the item description attribute, and middle-justified text for the remaining attributes.
- Use the **WBLOCK** command to save the parts list block on disk with a descriptive name, such as PL for parts list or BOM for bill of materials. Use the lower-left endpoint of the block as the insertion point.

After an assembly drawing has been completed, simply insert the parts list block at the correct location on the drawing. If the system variable **ATTDIA** is set to 1, you can answer the attribute prompts in the **Enter Attributes** dialog box. After providing the information, click the **OK** button and the completed parts list block is automatically added to the title block sheet. See **Figure 15-37.** Repeat the procedure as many times as required for each component of the assembly drawing.

Figure 15-36.
A parts list can be created as a block with defined attributes.

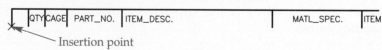

QTY CAGE PART_NO. ITEM_DESC. MATL_SPEC. ITEM
Insertion point

Figure 15-37.
The parts list block after insertion.

1		52451	PLATE, MOUNTING	6061–T6 ALUM	1
QTY REQD	CAGE CODE	PART OR IDENTIFYING NO.	NOMENCLATURE OR DESCRIPTION	MATERIAL SPECIFICATION	ITEM NO.

PARTS LIST

Attribute information can be taken from a drawing to create a separate text file, or *extract file,* that can serve as a parts list or bill of materials. Extract files can be created in several different formats to be used with spreadsheet or database programs, or other CAD programs.

Before you can extract attribute data from a drawing, you must first create a template file using an ASCII text editor (such as Windows Notepad). Once the template file is created with a text editor, the extract file is created in AutoCAD LT.

Creating a Template File

The template file is used to tell AutoCAD LT what type of attribute data is to be extracted from the drawing. The file contains information about the attribute tag name, block name, insertion point coordinates, data type (character or numeric), field length, and number of decimal places associated with the information you wish to extract.

To gain a clearer understanding of the structure required for the template file, see **Figure 15-38.** The template file starts at the left with a field name of any length. The list of data in the second column begins with a C or an N to indicate whether the type of data is character or numeric. The next three characters represent the total field width, including spaces for a decimal point and decimal values. The last three characters represent the number of decimal places for numeric data. Notice in **Figure 15-38** that the price data does not begin with an N for numeric data, as you might think. This is because the price information for this particular attribute begins with a dollar symbol character ($), rather than a numeral.

Figure 15-38.
A template file contains information about the attribute data to be extracted from a drawing.

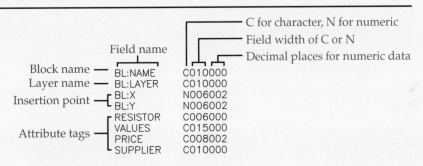

	Field name	C for character, N for numeric
		Field width of C or N
		Decimal places for numeric data
Block name —	BL:NAME	C010000
Layer name —	BL:LAYER	C010000
Insertion point —	BL:X	N006002
	BL:Y	N006002
	RESISTOR	C006000
Attribute tags —	VALUES	C015000
	PRICE	C008002
	SUPPLIER	C010000

NOTE

See *Chapter 13* of the *AutoCAD LT 98 Getting Started Guide* for a complete listing of acceptable field names and their respective formats in a template file. Also, you may use a tab between fields if you are using the Windows 98/95 or NT Notepad text editor to create a template file. Other types of text editors may require that you use a space between fields.

❏ In this exercise, you will construct a template file for the drawing EX15-5. Use Windows Notepad to create the file.

❏ Open EX15-5 if it is not already on your screen.

❏ Click the Start button on the Windows taskbar and open the Programs folder. Next, select Accessories and then Notepad to launch the Notepad text editor.

❏ Enter the following text at the text insertion point (identified by the flashing vertical cursor) in the Notepad window. With Notepad, you may place either a tab or several spaces between the columns:

BL:NAME	C010000
BL:LAYER	C010000
RESISTOR	C006000
VALUES	C015000
PRICE	C008002
SUPPLIER	C010000

❏ Select Save As... from the File pull-down menu, and save the file with the name EX15-6. Notepad automatically appends a .txt extension to the file name.

❏ Select Exit from the File pull-down menu to exit Notepad and return to AutoCAD LT.

Attribute Extraction Using a Dialog Box

DDATTEXT

Tools
↦ Attribute
  ↦ Extraction...

Once a template file is created, you can extract the attribute data from a drawing file. Attribute extraction can be performed using a dialog box with the **DDATTEXT** (Dynamic Dialog ATTribute EXTraction) command. The **DDATTEXT** command may be entered on the command line or issued by selecting **Attribute Extraction...** from the **Tools** pull-down menu. See **Figure 15-39.**

    Command: **DDATTEXT**↵

Figure 15-39.
Selecting **Attribute Extraction...** from the **Tools** pull-down menu issues the **DDATTEXT** command.

The **Attribute Extraction** dialog box then appears, **Figure 15-40.** The options available in this dialog box are described below:

- **Comma Delimited File (CDF).** As shown in **Figure 15-41,** the CDF format uses a comma to separate the fields for each block record in the extract file. Each character field is enclosed with single quotation marks. Select this option button when you wish to transfer attribute data to an external database program.
- **Space Delimited File (SDF).** The SDF format uses spaces to separate block attribute fields, **Figure 15-42.** It does not use commas or quotation marks. This format is easier to read (many spreadsheet programs use this type of file format).
- **Drawing Interchange File (DXF).** The DXF format is used to transfer drawing data between AutoCAD LT and other CAD software programs. Using this option does not require a template file. The extract file is given the .dxx file extension, not .dxf. See *Chapter 25* for more information about the DXF file format.
- **Attribute Template File...** Once you have specified the desired format for the extract file, click this button to display the **Attribute Template File** dialog box, **Figure 15-43.** Select the template file from the list of files, or enter the file name in the **File name:** text box. Click the **Open** button when you are finished and the **Attribute Extraction** dialog box is redisplayed.
- **Output File...** Click this button to display the **Output File** dialog box, **Figure 15-44.** You must provide a file name in the **File name:** text box. Be sure to enter a different file name than the name used for the template file, or the extract file will overwrite the template file. As shown in **Figure 15-44,** the name ex15-7 is entered in the **File name:** text box. The file extension .txt is automatically appended to the file name you provide. Click **Save** when you are finished and the **Attribute Extraction** dialog box is redisplayed.
- **Select Objects ⟨.** You are now ready to select the blocks with attribute data for extraction. When you click this button, the **Attribute Extraction** dialog box disappears and the prompt Select objects: appears on the command line. If you want the attribute data to be listed in a specific order in the extract file, be sure to select the blocks using the corresponding sequence. When you are done selecting the blocks with attributes, press [Enter]. The **Attribute Extraction** dialog box reappears and reports the number of blocks found. Click **OK** to exit the dialog box and create the extract file.

Figure 15-40.
The **Attribute Extraction** dialog box.

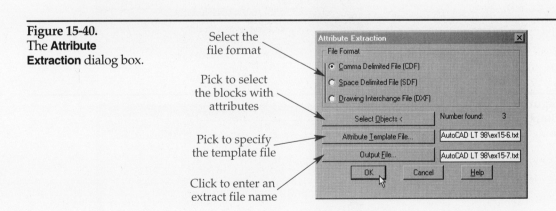

Select the file format

Pick to select the blocks with attributes

Pick to specify the template file

Click to enter an extract file name

Figure 15-41.
An extract file
displayed in CDF
format in the
Windows Notepad
text editor.

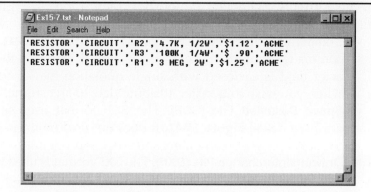

Figure 15-42.
An extract file
displayed in SDF
format in Windows
Notepad.

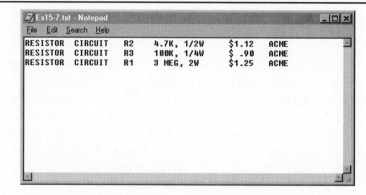

Figure 15-43.
The **Attribute
Template File** dialog
box.

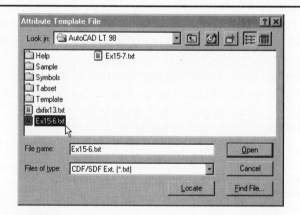

Figure 15-44. The
Output File dialog
box.

Enter a new
file name

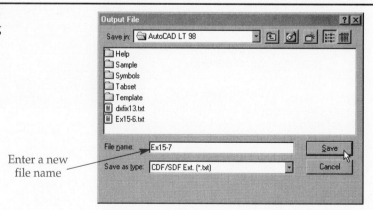

Performing Attribute Extraction on the Command Line

If you do not wish to use the **Attribute Extraction** dialog box, you can perform attribute extraction on the command line. The sequence is as follows:

Command: **ATTEXT** *or* **AX.**⏎
CDF, SDF or DXF Attribute extract (or Objects)? ⟨C⟩: *(select a format option)*

After entering the desired file format, the **Select Template File** dialog box appears. Specify a template file and click the **Open** button to display the **Create extract file** dialog box. The **Select Template File** dialog box and the **Create extract file** dialog box are used just as the **Attribute Template File** and **Output File** dialog boxes previously described. After you create the extract file, AutoCAD LT reports the number of records in the extract file on the command line.

EXERCISE 15-7

❑ Open EX15-5 if it is not still on your screen.
❑ Issue the **DDATTEXT** command and specify the attribute template file that you created in the previous exercise.
❑ Create an extract file called EX15-7 in CDF format. When the extraction is complete, open the file in Notepad. Print the file if you have a printer.
❑ Now create another extract file with the same name, but in SDF format. Open the file in Notepad and print it if you have a printer.

External References

A drawing that is linked, or attached, to another drawing is called an *external reference.* The drawing that it is attached to is called the *master drawing.* A referenced drawing is visible within the master drawing and may be plotted, but it *cannot* be modified in any way. This is because the referenced drawing's database is completely separate from the database of the master drawing.

This concept is very different from inserting a block, which becomes part of the database of the drawing it is inserted into. If the original drawing that is inserted is modified, the current drawing must also be modified to reflect the same changes. Additionally, an inserted block or drawing increases the size of the current drawing, which consumes more disk space.

An external reference, on the other hand, is only *attached* to the current drawing and is not permanent. It appears in the master drawing as a single object, like a block, but it cannot be exploded. Also, the file size of the master drawing is increased by only a few bytes. These bytes store the name of the external reference and its drive and path. Best of all, if the original external reference is modified, the changes are automatically reflected when the master drawing is opened in the AutoCAD LT drawing editor.

To more fully appreciate the value of external references, consider the sheet metal panel drawing in **Figure 15-45.** Since the panel is part of a test instrument, a subassembly drawing is required. The assembly drawing is shown in **Figure 15-46.** Rather than inserting the panel into the assembly drawing, the panel drawing is referenced to the new assembly drawing. Thus, the panel appears in the assembly drawing as required, but it is not part of the drawing's database.

To remove the display of dimensions and centerlines, the appropriate layers are frozen. Next, the rotary switch, fasteners, and BNC connectors are drawn and callouts are added to complete the assembly. The finished assembly drawing takes up far less disk space than if the panel had been inserted into the assembly.

Now consider the following scenario. Later in the life of the product, it is decided to add rounded corners to the panel to protect the user's fingers from injury. Fillets are applied to the object in the detail drawing, as shown in **Figure 15-47.** The very next time the assembly drawing is opened, AutoCAD LT automatically reloads the external reference and the assembly drawing is updated to show the filleted edges. See **Figure 15-48.** Such automatic updating cannot occur when a drawing is inserted rather than referenced.

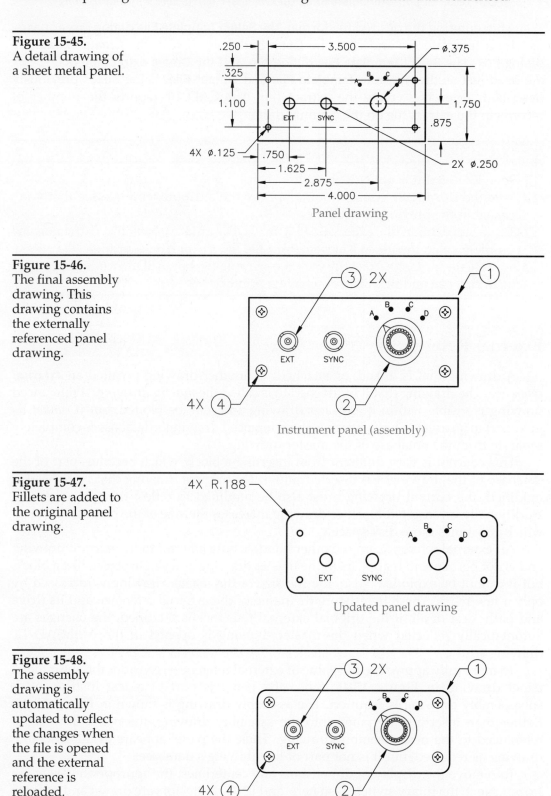

Figure 15-45.
A detail drawing of a sheet metal panel.

Panel drawing

Figure 15-46.
The final assembly drawing. This drawing contains the externally referenced panel drawing.

Instrument panel (assembly)

Figure 15-47.
Fillets are added to the original panel drawing.

Updated panel drawing

Figure 15-48.
The assembly drawing is automatically updated to reflect the changes when the file is opened and the external reference is reloaded.

New assembly drawing

AutoCAD LT—Fundamentals and Applications

The XREF Command

XREF
XR

Insert
↳ External
Reference...

Standard
toolbar

External Reference

External references are called *xrefs* for short. They are linked and managed using the **External Reference** dialog box, **Figure 15-49.** To access this dialog box, select **External Reference...** from the **Insert** pull-down menu, or click the **External Reference** button on the **Insert** toolbar. You can also enter the following at the Command: prompt:

Command: **XREF** *or* **XR**↵

Figure 15-49.
The **External Reference** dialog box.

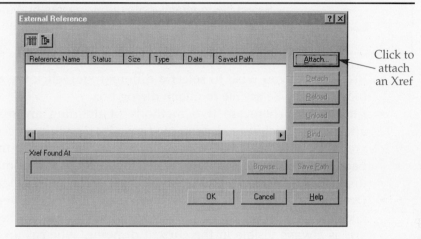

Click to attach an Xref

Attaching an External Reference

When you wish to attach an external reference to your drawing, click the **Attach...** button in the **External Reference** dialog box to display the **Select file to attach** dialog box. See **Figure 15-50.** Use this dialog box to attach an AutoCAD LT drawing file from any of the folders on your hard disk or network drives. Select the file you wish to attach or enter a file name in the **File name:** text box and click the **Open** button.

Figure 15-50.
The **Select file to attach** dialog box is used to attach a drawing file to the current drawing.

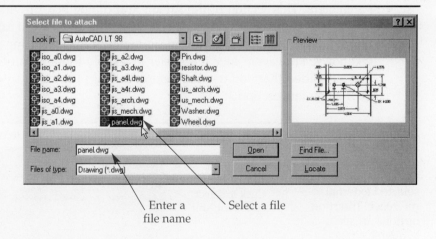

Enter a file name

Select a file

Although many external references may be linked to a master drawing, only one may be attached at a time. In the example shown, the panel drawing (panel.dwg, located in the AutoCAD LT 98 folder) is being attached. After selecting the drawing to be attached, the **Attach Xref** dialog box is displayed. The selected xref name appears at the top of the dialog box and various insertion options are provided. See **Figure 15-51.** The options offered in the **Attach Xref** dialog box are described below.

NOTE The **XATTACH** command can also be used to display the **Select file to attach** dialog box. Normally, AutoCAD LT displays this dialog box when the first xref is attached to a drawing. The **Attach Xref** dialog box is displayed for all subsequent xrefs.

- **Browse....** If you wish to select a different xref, click the **Browse...** button to redisplay the **Select file to attach** dialog box.
- **Attachment.** There are two methods of defining an xref—overlaying and attaching. Attaching a drawing is typically a one-time occurrence for a given xref and is intended for permanent use and plotting in the master drawing. Each time you open the master drawing, the xref is automatically loaded and displayed. The **Attachment** option button is active by default.
- **Overlay.** Overlays are typically used when you need to temporarily view the geometry in another drawing, but do not intend to plot that data. An attached xref is always visible in the current drawing, whereas an overlay is not. The other difference between overlays and attachments is the way nested references are handled. *Nesting* occurs when an xref drawing that is attached contains an xref to another drawing. An overlay displays xrefs that have been *attached* to the xref, but not xrefs that have been *overlaid*.
- **Include Path.** Active by default, this check box determines whether the full path to the xref is saved in the drawing database. If it is not selected, the name of the xref drawing is saved in the database without a path. AutoCAD LT then searches for the xref in the AutoCAD LT Support File Search Path specified in the **Preferences** dialog box. See *Chapter 20* of this text to learn more about AutoCAD LT search paths and the **Preferences** dialog box.
- **Parameters.** This section of the **Attach Xref** dialog box provides options that are identical to those available with the **INSERT** command. You can specify the insertion point, scale factors, and rotation angle of an xref using the corresponding text boxes. However, since it is easier to specify these parameters on screen, it is recommended that you use the default settings provided by the check boxes in the **Parameters** section.

Figure 15-51.
The **Attach Xref** dialog box displays the name of the selected external reference. Insertion options are also available.

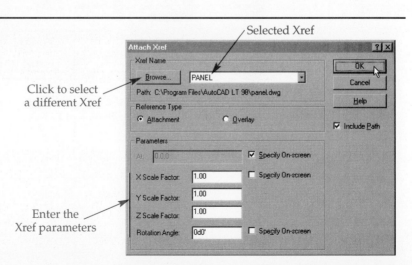

AutoCAD LT—Fundamentals and Applications

Click the **OK** button in the **Attach Xref** dialog box when you are ready to attach (or overlay) the external reference. The following messages appear on the command line, and you are prompted to specify an insertion point for the xref:

Attach Xref PANEL: C:\Program Files\AutoCAD LT 98\panel.dwg
PANEL loaded.
Insertion point: *(locate the insertion point)*
Command:

CAUTION

The alert box shown in **Figure 15-52** is displayed if you attempt to attach a drawing with an illegal name, or a name that exceeds eight characters. AutoCAD LT then assigns the name XREF1 to the attached drawing unless you enter a different name in the **New Block Name** text box.

Figure 15-52.
An alert box appears if you attempt to attach a drawing with an unacceptable name or a name that exceeds eight characters.

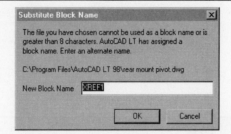

Other Features of the **External Reference** Dialog Box

Once a drawing is attached and has been highlighted in the **External Reference** dialog box, the option buttons that were previously grayed out become activated. The functions these buttons perform are described below.

- **List View.** The **List View** button is located in the top-left portion of the dialog box. See **Figure 15-53.** By default, it displays a flat listing of the attached xrefs and their associated data. You can sort the list of xrefs by name, status, size, type, file date, or by the saved path and file name. Selecting the xref name highlights the xref, as shown in **Figure 15-53.**

Figure 15-53.
The **External Reference** dialog box shown in the default list view.

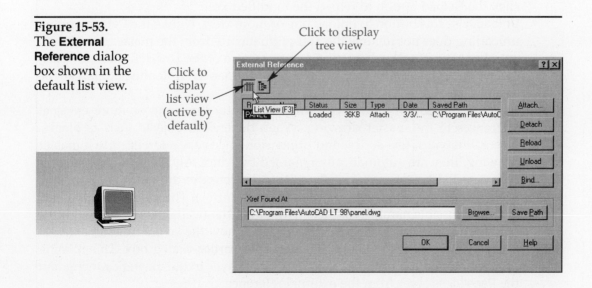

- **Tree View.** The **Tree View** button is located to the right of the **List View** button in the **External Reference** dialog box. Clicking this button displays a hierarchical representation of the xrefs and illustrates the relationships between xref definitions. This display, called a *tree view*, is shown in **Figure 15-54.** The tree view shows the nesting levels that exist within the attached xrefs and indicates whether the xrefs are attached or overlaid. The tree view also shows whether the xrefs are loaded, unloaded, marked for reload or unload, not found, unresolved, or unreferenced.

Figure 15-54.
Clicking the **Tree View** button displays a tree view listing of xrefs in the **External Reference** dialog box.

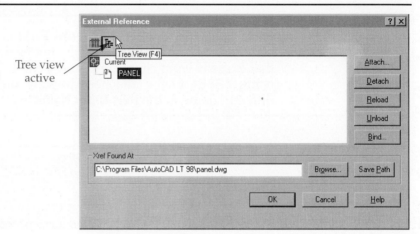

PROFESSIONAL TIP

You can also use the [F3] and [F4] function keys to toggle between **List View** and **Tree View**, respectively.

- **Detach.** The **Detach** button allows you to remove one or more external references from the master drawing.
- **Reload.** Xrefs are automatically reloaded each time the master drawing is opened in the AutoCAD LT drawing editor. However, you can force a reload at any time by selecting an xref from the list and clicking the **Reload** button. This option is particularly useful if another individual is currently editing a drawing that appears as an external reference in your drawing. As soon as the changes are completed and saved to the network drive by the other person, click the **Reload** button to reload the modified xref.
- **Unload.** Use this button to unload one or more xrefs. Unlike the **Detach** option, unloading does not remove the xref permanently from the master drawing. It merely suppresses the display and regeneration of the xref definition to speed current session editing and improve performance. Unloaded xrefs can be easily reloaded using the **Reload** button.
- **Bind....** This option allows you to permanently bind one or more external references to the master drawing. When dependent objects such as blocks, layers, linetypes, text styles, and dimension styles are referenced to a master drawing, they are automatically renamed by AutoCAD LT. The object names are preceded by the name of the external reference; the xref name and the object name are separated by the pipe character (|). This convention is used to avoid possible naming conflicts with other identically named objects in the master drawing. In **Figure 15-55,** you can see how the layers from an external reference appear in the **Layer & Linetype Properties** dialog box. This naming convention avoids conflict between the Dims layer in the master drawing and the Panel|dims layer from the external reference.

Figure 15-55.
Layers from an external reference are preceded by the xref name, as shown in the **Layer & Linetype Properties** dialog box.

Xref-dependent layers

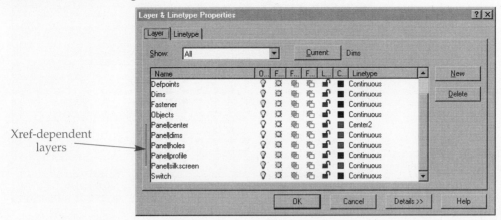

It is important to remember that you cannot edit the dependent objects contained within an external reference unless you first *bind* the xref to the master drawing. When you bind an external reference, *all* dependent objects (including blocks, layers, linetypes, text styles, and dimension styles) in the former xref become part of the master drawing and are then accessible to you. However, a bound xref becomes a block object and must be exploded if it is to be modified.

To permanently bind one or more external references to the master drawing, click the **Bind...** button in the **External Reference** dialog box. The **Bind Xrefs** subdialog box appears and offers two options. See **Figure 15-56.** Clicking the default **Bind** option button binds one or more xrefs to the master drawing. Once an xref is bound, the dependent objects within it are once again automatically renamed by AutoCAD LT. As shown in **Figure 15-57,** layer names such as Panellcenter and Panelldims become Panel0center and Panel0dims, respectively. Once the dependent objects within an xref are bound, they become part of the master drawing and you may do with them as you please.

The other option available in the **Bind Xrefs** subdialog box is provided by the **Insert** option button. Using this option binds the xref to the current drawing in a way that is similar to detaching the xref and then inserting it with the **INSERT** command. When you bind an xref using the **Insert** option, all objects in the xref are converted to blocks in the drawing, but the xref name is not included with the object names and no renaming of layers occurs. All named objects retain their names as specified in the xref.

Figure 15-56.
The **Bind Xrefs** subdialog box is used to bind an xref to the master drawing. The two options allow you to specify how xref-dependent objects are to be incorporated.

Figure 15-57.
Named objects, such as layers, are renamed when an xref is bound to the master drawing.

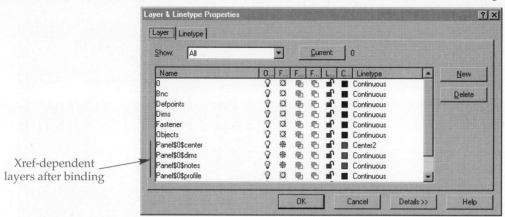

Xref-dependent
layers after binding

- **Xref Found At.** This section displays the path name associated with a specified external reference and allows you to change the path or xref name. It should be used if you move an xref to a different drive or folder, or if you rename the xref. For example, if you open a drawing containing an xref that has been moved to a different folder other than the one that was saved with the xref, and it cannot be found in the AutoCAD LT Support File Search Path, the **External Reference** dialog box displays its status as **Not found** in the xref list, and the **Xref Found At** text box appears blank. You can then click the **Browse...** button and select a new path and file name in the **Select New Path** subdialog box. The new path and file name are subsequently displayed in the **Saved Path** column in the list view and also in the **Xref Found At** text box. You can remove the path from the file name or specify a new path by directly editing the path in the **Xref Found At** text box and then clicking the **Save Path** button. Keep in mind that only one xref path can be changed at a time.

Binding Dependent Objects Individually Using a Dialog Box

As previously discussed, using the **Bind...** button in the **External Reference** dialog box allows you to permanently bind an external reference to the master drawing. *All* dependent objects in the former xref then become part of the master drawing. Until such named objects from the xref are bound, they are not available for your use.

XBIND
XB

Modify
➥ Object
➥ External
Reference
Bind...

There may be occasions when you wish to bind only *some* of the named objects from an xref to the master drawing. This is accomplished using the **XBIND** command. You can issue this command by first selecting **Object** from the **Modify** pull-down menu and then **External Reference Bind...** from the cascading submenu. You can also type the following on the command line:

Command: **XBIND** *or* **XB**↵

This displays the **Xbind** dialog box, **Figure 15-58.** Click the plus sign (+) icon next to the xref name in the **Xrefs** list to expand the list of named objects that can be bound. These items include blocks, dimension styles, layers, linetypes, and text styles. If you wish to bind a layer, for example, click the plus sign icon next to **Layer** in the list. An expanded tree of xref layer names then appears, as shown in **Figure 15-59A.** Click the layer name you wish to bind so that it is highlighted and then click the **Add->** button. The layer name you select is then bound to the master drawing, and it appears in the **Definitions to Bind** list at the right of the dialog box. See **Figure 15-59B.** If you change your mind, click the **<-Remove** button to remove the named object from the **Definitions to Bind** list. This action is essentially the same as performing an undo operation.

Figure 15-58.
The **Xbind** dialog box displays an expanded tree listing of xref-dependent objects that may be bound to the master drawing.

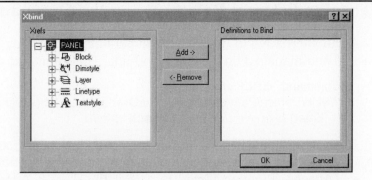

Figure 15-59.
A—Selecting an xref-dependent layer name to be bound. B—After selecting the object to bind, click the **Add->** button. The object is added to the **Definitions to Bind** list.

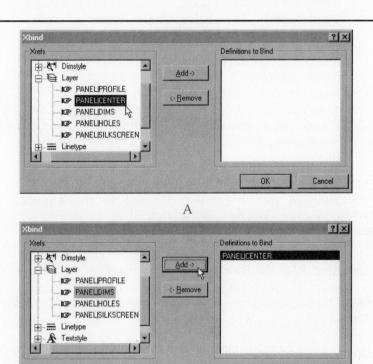

A

B

Binding Dependent Objects on the Command Line

It is also possible to bind xref-dependent objects on the command line using the **-XBIND** command. In the example that follows, two layers from a referenced drawing are bound to the master drawing:

Command: **-XBIND** *or* **-XB**↵
Block/Dimstyle/LAyer/LType/Style: **LA.**↵
Dependent Layer name(s): **PANEL|CENTER,PANEL|DIMS.**↵
2 Layer(s) bound.
Command:

As previously mentioned, once a dependent object is bound to the master drawing, it is automatically renamed by AutoCAD LT. All bound objects are renamed using the 0 naming convention.

Managing External References on the Command Line

As an alternative to using the **External Reference** dialog box, xrefs may also be attached and managed on the command line. The command sequence is as follows:

Command: **-XREF** *or* **-XR**↵
?/Bind/Detach/Path/Unload/Reload/Overlay/⟨Attach⟩: *(select an option or press* [Enter] *to accept the default* **Attach** *option)*

The options available are similar to those found in the **External Reference** dialog box and the **Attach Xref** dialog box. The **-XREF** command options are described below.

- ⟨**Attach**⟩. Pressing [Enter] to accept the default **Attach** option displays the **Select file to attach** dialog box. Select the file you wish to attach and click the **Open** button. The dialog box is removed and you are prompted on the command line with the following:

  Attach Xref PANEL: panel.dwg
  PANEL loaded.
  Insertion point: *(locate the insertion point)*
  X scale factor ⟨1⟩/Corner/XYZ: *(enter the X scale factor or select an option)*
  Y scale factor (default=X): *(enter a different Y scale factor or accept the default)*
  Rotation angle ⟨0⟩: *(enter a rotation angle or press* [Enter]*)*
  Command:

- **?.** This option allows you to list the xref name, path, and total number of xrefs attached to the current drawing in the **AutoCAD LT Text Window**. The following prompt is displayed:

  Xref(s) to list ⟨*⟩: *(enter a name or press* [Enter]*)*

- **Bind.** Use the **Bind** option to permanently bind one or more external references to the master drawing. As discussed earlier, a bound xref becomes a block object and must be exploded if it is to be modified. The following prompt is displayed:

  Xref(s) to bind: *(enter a name or several names separated by commas and press* [Enter]*)*

- **Detach.** Use the **Detach** option to remove one or more external references from the master drawing. The following prompt is displayed:

  Xref(s) to detach: *(enter a name or several names separated by commas and press* [Enter]*)*

- **Path.** This option displays the path name associated with a specified external reference and allows you to change the path. This function is identical to that served by the **Xref Found At** section in the **External Reference** dialog box. In the following example, a new path to a different folder and drive is entered for the panel xref:

  Edit path for which xref(s): **PANEL**↵
  Xref name: **PANEL**↵
  Old path: panel.dwg
  New path: **D:\PARTS\PANEL**↵

- **Unload.** This option is used to unload one or more xrefs. Remember that unloading does not remove the xref permanently from the master drawing. It merely suppresses the display and regeneration of the xref definition to speed current session editing and improve performance. An unloaded xref can be reloaded using the **Reload** option.

- **Reload.** As previously mentioned, xrefs are automatically reloaded each time the master drawing is opened in the AutoCAD LT drawing editor. However, you can force a reload at any time by using the **Reload** option. The following prompt is displayed:

> Xref(s) to reload: *(enter a name or several names separated by commas and press* [Enter]*)*

- **Overlay.** This option attaches a drawing as an external reference overlay. If you reference a drawing that itself contains an overlaid xref, the overlaid xref does not appear in the current drawing. Unlike blocks and attached xrefs, overlaid xrefs cannot be nested. AutoCAD LT overlays the most recently saved version if another person is currently editing the xref.

Controlling the Visibility of Xref Layers—the **VISRETAIN** Variable

It is sometimes desirable to change the visibility or other properties of xref-dependent layers in the master drawing. As shown in **Figure 15-60**, the layers Panellcenter, Panelldims, and Panellnotes are frozen. This suppresses the display of objects on those layers. When you wish to change the color, linetype, on/off, or freeze/thaw status of layers from an external reference, make sure that the **Re̱tain changes to xref-dependent layers** check box (located near the bottom of the **Layer & Linetype Properties** dialog box) is activated as shown.

You can also use the **VISRETAIN** (VISibility RETAIN) system variable on the command line to control the visibility of xref layers. Enter the following at the Command: prompt:

Command: **VISRETAIN**↵
New value for VISRETAIN ⟨*current setting*⟩: **1**↵

Figure 15-60.
Activating the **Re̱tain changes to xref-dependent layers** check box in the **Layer & Linetype Properties** dialog box ensures that changes to the visibility status of xref-dependent layers are retained through subsequent drawing sessions.

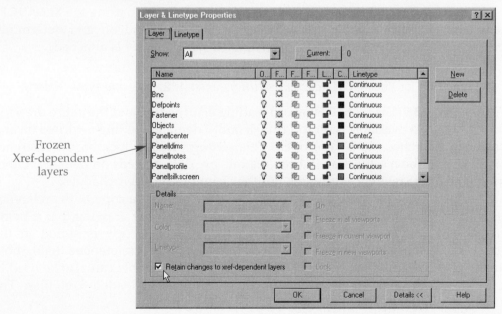

Frozen
Xref-dependent
layers

When **VISRETAIN** is set to the default of 1 (on), the color, linetype, on/off, and freeze/thaw settings for xref-dependent layers in the master drawing take precedence over the layer status settings in the xref drawing. This ensures that any changes made to the status of xref-dependent layers in the master drawing are retained when the xref is reloaded. To increase your drawing efficiency, **VISRETAIN** should be turned on in your template file(s).

When **VISRETAIN** is set to 0 (off), the layer status settings in the xref drawing take precedence over the following settings for xref-dependent layers in the master drawing: color, linetype, on/off, and freeze/thaw.

Creating an Xref Log File—The XREFCTL Variable

AutoCAD LT can keep a record of **Attach**, **Detach**, and **Reload** operations for each drawing that contains external references. The record is in ASCII text format and is called a *log file.* A log file has the same name as the current drawing with an *.xlg* file extension.

By default, the **XREFCTL** system variable is off and log files are not created. To have AutoCAD LT create log files, set the **XREFCTL** variable as follows:

Command: **XREFCTL**⏎
New value for XREFCTL ⟨0⟩: **1**⏎

The current status of the **XREFCTL** system variable is stored in the aclt5.cfg file. Therefore, it is saved for each drawing session until changed. If you are using AutoCAD LT 97, this file is called aclt4.cfg.

Using Demand Loading to Maximize Xref Performance

When an xref is attached to a drawing, *demand loading* ensures that only the external reference data necessary to regenerate the current drawing is loaded into memory. This feature increases performance because the entire xref file is not loaded into the master drawing. As an example, when demand loading is enabled, only thawed layers are read into the master drawing (frozen layers are ignored). Demand loading is on by default, but it may be turned off in the **Preferences** dialog box. See *Chapter 20* for more information about using the **Preferences** dialog box.

You can also control demand loading on the command line using the **XLOADCTL** system variable. This variable turns demand loading on and off and determines whether the original drawing or a copy is opened when an xref is attached.

Command: **XLOADCTL**⏎
New value for XLOADCTL ⟨*current setting*⟩: (*enter* 1, 2, *or* 3, *and press* [Enter]*)*

When **XLOADCTL** is set to 0, demand loading is turned off and the entire drawing is loaded. When the variable is set to 1 (the default), demand loading is turned on and the external reference file is kept open. This setting places a lock on the reference drawing so that the master drawing can read in any data it needs on demand. Other users can open the reference drawing, but they cannot save their changes.

A setting of 2 turns on demand loading and ensures that a copy of the reference file is opened. This setting allows others to modify a reference drawing that is being demand loaded into another drawing. The reference file copy is stored in the AutoCAD LT Temporary Drawing File Location (defined in the **Preferences** dialog box) or in a user-specified directory. The **XLOADPATH** system variable can also be used to specify the path for storing temporary copies of demand-loaded xref files. The sequence is as follows:

Command: **XLOADPATH**⏎
New value for XLOADPATH, or . for none ⟨"C:\TEMP\"⟩: (*specify a different path or press* [Enter] *to accept the default*)

PROFESSIONAL TIP  Unless there is a compelling reason to do otherwise, it is recommended that you leave **XLOADCTL** at its default setting of 1 for the best xref performance.

Using Content Explorer

One of the most exciting features of AutoCAD LT 98 and AutoCAD LT 97 is **Content Explorer**. It provides an easy, powerful method for inserting blocks, inserting hatch patterns (AutoCAD LT 98 only), and attaching xrefs. You can also use it to locate drawing files and blocks, view block icon images and textual descriptions, and create tabs associated with drawings and folders on your computer or network drive.

To access **Content Explorer**, click the **Content Explorer** button in either the **Draw** or **Insert** toolbar or select **Content Explorer...** from the **Insert** pull-down menu. You can also enter CONTENT or CE on the command line. However, be advised that **CE** is not a valid command alias if you are using AutoCAD LT 97.

> Command: **CONTENT** *or* **CE**↵

The **Content Explorer** window appears on the right side of the graphics window. It consists of three primary components:

- **Content View.** This area displays the names and icons of blocks, hatch patterns, and drawing files, **Figure 15-61.** You can insert one of the displayed blocks or hatch patterns by clicking the desired icon and pressing and holding the pick button on your pointing device as you drag the icon into the current drawing. This function is called "drag and drop." Other examples of the drag and drop feature are provided in *Chapter 13* and *Chapter 25* of this text.

CONTENT
CE

Insert
➥ Content
  Explorer...

Draw *or* Insert
toolbar

Content Explorer

Figure 15-61.
The **Content View** area of the **Content Explorer** window displays blocks, hatch patterns, and drawing files that are available for insertion into your drawing.

Click to display the block description

Click to display tree view

Click to locate a file or block

Click to display an image preview

Select a block or drawing file

The symbols shown in **Figure 15-61** are from the mechanical block library supplied with AutoCAD LT. This library is called a *tab set*. The other supplied tab sets, located at the right of the **Content Explorer** window, feature architectural and electrical symbols. You select the default tab set of your choice during the installation of AutoCAD LT. However, you can easily open one of the other tab sets at any time. Tab sets are covered later in this chapter.

> **PROFESSIONAL TIP**
>
> Unfortunately, using the drag and drop feature to insert a block symbol does not permit you to specify scale and rotation options. The inserted block comes in at 1:1. If you wish to specify a different scale factor or rotation angle, double-click the block icon in the **Content Explorer** window instead of using drag and drop.

- **Tree View.** This is an expanded area of the **Content Explorer** window. It is accessed by clicking the **Tree View** (《) button on the **Content Explorer** toolbar. When displayed, the tree view provides space to navigate through the drives and folders on the left side of the **Content Explorer** window. You can create tabs and assign them to drawings and folders for easier navigation. Clicking the **Tree View** button again collapses the tree view area.
- **Find button.** The **Find** button is identified by an icon representing a pair of binoculars on the **Content Explorer** toolbar. Clicking this button displays the **AutoCAD LT Find:** dialog box, which is used for finding files and blocks. This dialog box is described later in this chapter.

Browsing for Content Using **Tree View**

As previously mentioned, you can expand the tree view in **Content Explorer** to browse for drawing files and blocks. To do so, enable tree view and then click a drive or folder icon to display a list of drawing files on the left side of the **Content Explorer** window. See **Figure 15-62.** You can then click a drawing file to display a list of any blocks it may contain in the **Content View** area on the right side of the **Content Explorer** window.

Finding Content

The **Current Dwg** tab, located at the far right of the **Content Explorer** window, lists all of the block definitions in the current drawing. To locate external blocks and drawing files, you can browse through drives and folders using the tree view as previously discussed, or you can specify criteria by clicking the **Find** button and using the **AutoCAD LT Find:** dialog box.

Locating Content Using the **AutoCAD LT Find: Dialog Box**

The **AutoCAD LT Find:** dialog box, shown in **Figure 15-63**, accepts various types of criteria for locating drawing files and blocks. The criteria you can specify includes:
- A drawing name, drive, and folder.
- The date the file was created or modified.
- A block name, block attribute tag name, and related criteria.

AutoCAD LT searches the specified drives and folders for drawing files and blocks that match the criteria you enter. The search results are then displayed in a list at the bottom of the **AutoCAD LT Find:** dialog box. Double-clicking on a name in the list displays the drawing name or icon in the **Content View** area, along with other drawings in the folder.

Figure 15-62.
The **Content Explorer** tree view provides a means to browse for drawing files, hatch patterns, and blocks by navigating through the drives and folders shown. The contents of a selected folder are displayed on the right side of the **Content Explorer** window.

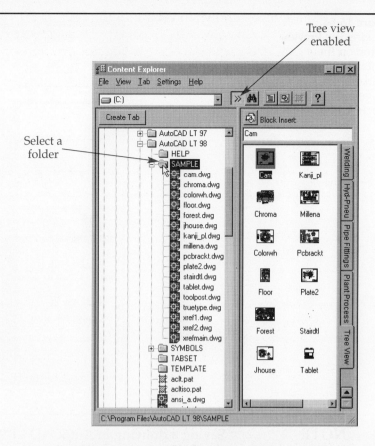

Tree view enabled

Select a folder

Figure 15-63.
The **AutoCAD LT Find:** dialog box can be used to locate drawing files and blocks by specifying various criteria.

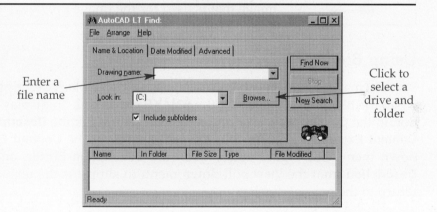

Enter a file name

Click to select a drive and folder

Examining Content in Content View

When blocks and drawings are shown in the **Content View** area of the **Content Explorer** window, you can display an enlarged image preview of the block or drawing. To do this, click the **Preview** button on the **Content Explorer** toolbar or select **Preview** from the **Content Explorer View** pull-down menu.

A preview of the hex bolt block is shown in **Figure 15-64.** Click the **Preview** button once again or select **Preview** from the **View** pull-down menu to collapse the preview window and return to the normal display.

To exit **Content Explorer** after you are finished, click the close window icon in the upper-right corner of the window. You can also select **Close** from the **File** pull-down menu.

Figure 15-64.
Clicking the **Preview**
button on the
Content Explorer
toolbar displays an
image preview of a
selected block.

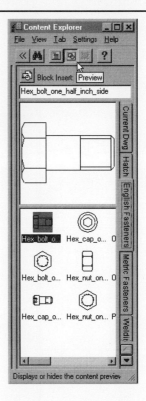

NOTE Saving a drawing in AutoCAD LT 98 or AutoCAD LT 97 automatically creates an icon image of a drawing. It is this image that is used for the image preview.

Using Block Descriptions

You may recall from earlier in this chapter that a block description can be entered when the block is created using the **BMAKE** command. To display the block description in the **Content View** area of **Content Explorer**, click the **Description** button on the **Content Explorer** toolbar or select **Description** from the **Content Explorer View** pull-down menu. See **Figure 15-65.** Click the **Description** button once again or select **Description** from the **View** pull-down menu to suppress the textual description and return to the normal display.

Changing the block description

BMOD

Modify
↳ **Object**
  ↳ **Block**
    Description...

When you wish to change the existing description of a block or the current drawing, enter the **BMOD** command at the Command: prompt or select **Object** and then **Block Description...** from the **Modify** pull-down menu. The **Modify Block Description** dialog box appears, **Figure 15-66.** The components of this dialog box are described below:

- **Internal Blocks:.** This list displays the names of all blocks defined in the current drawing. Click one of the block names to display an image preview and its textual description.
- **Filter:.** This text box lets you use standard wildcard characters to limit the listing of internal blocks. For example, entering c* lists only the block names beginning with the letter "c".
- **Export.** The **Export** button is used to create a new drawing file from a selected block. Clicking this button opens the **Save As** dialog box. You can then provide a file name for the exported block. This procedure is the equivalent of using the **WBLOCK** command as described earlier in this chapter.

Figure 15-65.
The textual description of a block can be displayed by highlighting a block icon and clicking the **Description** button.

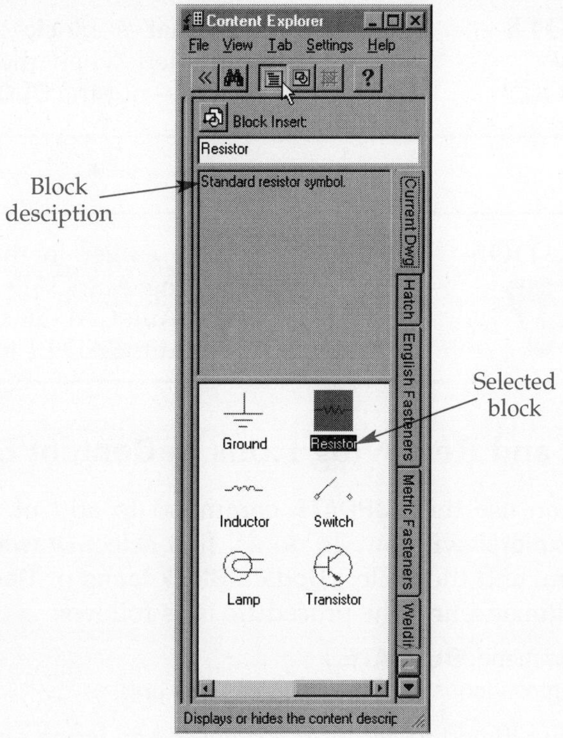

Block desciption

Selected block

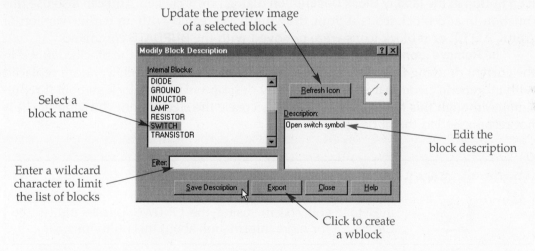

Figure 15-66.
The **Modify Block Description** dialog box allows you to change the description for a block or the current drawing.

Update the preview image of a selected block

Select a block name

Edit the block description

Enter a wildcard character to limit the list of blocks

Click to create a wblock

- **Refresh Icon.** Selecting this button allows you to update the preview image of the currently selected block after a block redefinition occurs.
- **Description:.** This text box is used to display and edit the textual description of a selected block. The description can be up to 256 characters long.
- **Save Description.** Click this button to apply changes to the description of the currently selected block. If you select a different block name to edit, any changes you make to the previous block description are stored automatically.
- **Close.** This button is used to close the **Modify Block Description** dialog box.

NOTE
Remember that a block description is initially (and optionally) provided when the block is created using the **BMAKE** command—not the **BLOCK** command.

CAUTION
As mentioned earlier in this chapter, if your school or organization is using AutoCAD LT drawings with AutoCAD Release 14 and/or AutoCAD 2000, be advised that AutoCAD is unable to display AutoCAD LT textual descriptions for blocks.

Adding and Removing Icons in **Content Explorer**

You can use the **BUPDATE** command to add or remove block icons from the **Content Explorer** window. To do so, first select **Drawing Utilities** from the **File** pull-down menu and then select **Update Block Icons** or **Remove Block Icons** as required. On the command line, the procedure is as follows:

Command: **BUPDATE**↵
Remove icons/⟨Add icons⟩: *(select an option)*

Pressing [Enter] to accept the default **Add icons** option lets you add icons to the existing block definitions or refresh block icons in the current drawing. This function is typically performed after the redefinition of one or more blocks as described earlier in this chapter. Once a block is redefined, its new graphical icon is not updated in the **Content Explorer** window until the **BUPDATE** command is issued, or until the **Refresh Icon** button in the **Modify Block Description** dialog box is clicked. You can also use this function to add block icons if your drawing was created with an earlier version of AutoCAD LT, or if block icons were removed with the **BUPDATE** command.

The **Remove icons** option allows you to remove the icons of the blocks defined in the current drawing from the **Content Explorer** window. The block icons are replaced with a "generic" icon that is not graphically descriptive of the block symbol it represents. Although this function can slightly decrease the size of your drawing file, it is not recommended that it be used.

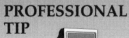

PROFESSIONAL TIP
You can also add or remove block icons from a list of drawings that you specify using the LT DWG Update utility. See *Chapter 25* for more information about this utility program.

Managing Tabs and Tab Sets

The displayed tabs on the right side of the **Content Explorer** window are designed to help you quickly select blocks, hatch patterns, and folders. Three tabs are loaded by default:
- **Current Dwg.** This tab lists all of the blocks defined in the current drawing.
- **Hatch.** This tab displays each of the hatch patterns available in AutoCAD LT 98. (As mentioned earlier, for users of AutoCAD LT 97, hatch patterns are not provided in **Content Explorer** and this tab is not displayed.) See *Chapter 13* for a complete description of drag and drop hatching using **Content Explorer**.
- **Tree View.** This tab is only displayed when the tree view area is expanded. Clicking this tab lists the blocks in the currently selected drawing or the drawings in the currently selected folder.

You can create additional tabs as shortcuts to file folders. Once you create additional tabs, they can be saved for future use in a tab set. You can also rename or delete an existing tab, delete all currently loaded tabs except **Current Dwg**, **Hatch**, and **Tree View**, retrieve a saved set of tabs, change the order in which tabs are displayed by dragging them, or merge saved tab sets together. In addition, you can suppress loading of the default tab set when you create a new drawing or open an existing drawing that lacks a tab set. Tabs can also be used to move drawing files between folders by dragging and dropping any drawing file from the current tab to another tab.

Controlling the default tab set and opening a tab set

A default tab set is displayed in the **Content Explorer** window when you create a new drawing, or when you open an existing drawing that was saved without an associated tab set.

The default tab set that you selected when installing AutoCAD LT is stored as aclt.set for drawings with English (imperial) settings and acltiso.set for drawings with metric settings. You can change your default tab set by opening the desired tab set and saving it as aclt.set or acltiso.set.

To open a tab set, select **Open Tab Set...** from the **Content Explorer Tab** pull-down menu. This displays a list of tab sets to choose from in the **Open** dialog box, **Figure 15-67.** These tab sets, as well as any additional tab sets you might create, are stored in the Program Files\AutoCAD LT 98\Tabset folder. Select the tab set you wish to use and click the **Open** button. The tab set you select then replaces the previously current tab set.

Figure 15-67.
After selecting **Open Tab Set...** from the **Content Explorer Tab** pull-down menu, a list of existing tab sets appears in the **Open** dialog box.

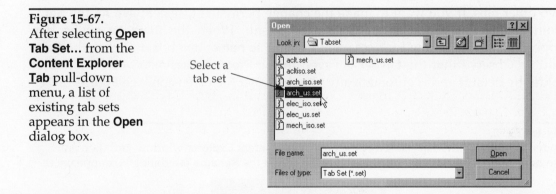

Creating a new tab set

To create a new tab set, first expand the **Content Explorer** window to display tree view. Next, use tree view to select a folder in which you want to create a tab. Now click the **Create Tab** button located above the tree view area, or select **Create...** from the **Content Explorer Tab** pull-down menu. When the **Create Tab** dialog box appears, enter the desired name for the new tab in the **Tab name:** text box and click the **OK** button. See **Figure 15-68.** The dialog box disappears and the new tab is displayed along the right edge of the **Content Explorer** window.

Deleting a tab set

To delete a tab set, first select the tab to delete from the right edge of the **Content Explorer** window. Next, select **Delete** from the **Content Explorer Tab** pull-down menu. The **Delete Tab** dialog box appears, displaying the name of the tab set you selected. See **Figure 15-69.** Click the **OK** button to proceed with the deletion.

If you wish to delete all tab sets, select **Delete All** from the **Content Explorer Tab** pull-down menu. An alert dialog box appears and asks you to confirm your action. Click the **Yes** or **No** button as appropriate. Keep in mind that the **Delete All** selection deletes all tabs except **Current Dwg**, **Hatch**, and **Tree View**.

Figure 15-68.
A new tab set can be
created using the
Create Tab dialog
box.

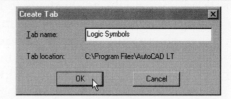

Figure 15-69.
The **Delete Tab**
dialog box is used
to delete an existing
tab set.

Renaming a tab set

If you wish to rename an existing tab set, first select the tab set to rename from the right edge of the **Content Explorer** window. Then, select **Rename...** from the **Content Explorer Tab** pull-down menu. When the **Rename Tab** dialog box appears, enter the new tab set name in the **Tab name:** text box and click the **OK** button. See **Figure 15-70.**

Moving a tab set to a different position

You may find it convenient to move a tab to a different position in the row of tabs in **Content Explorer**. To do so, drag and drop the tab you want to reposition between two other tabs. If you want to make the change permanent, select **Save As Tab Set...** from the **Content Explorer Tab** pull-down menu. When the **Save As** dialog box appears, enter the desired tab set name in the **File name:** text box and click the **Save** button. Observe that the tab set is saved to the Program Files\AutoCAD LT 98\Tabset folder by default and is automatically given the .set file extension. See **Figure 15-71.**

Figure 15-70.
To rename an existing tab set, select the tab in the **Content Explorer** window and then enter the new tab set name in the **Tab name:** text box when the **Rename Tab** dialog box appears.

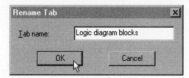

Figure 15-71.
To save a new tab set, enter the desired tab set name in the **File name:** text box when the **Save As** dialog box appears. Tab sets are saved to the Program Files\AutoCAD LT 98\Tabset folder by default.

Enter a new
tab set name

Merging tab sets

It is often desirable to work with more than one tab set at a time. This can be accomplished by merging one tab set with another. The merged tab set is appended to the end of the existing tab set. To merge a tab set, select **Merge Tab Set...** from the **Content Explorer Tab** pull-down menu. When the **Merge** dialog box appears, select the tab set to merge and click the **Open** button, **Figure 15-72**. The tabs for the merged tab set then appear below the tabs of the existing tab set in the **Content Explorer** window. The two tab sets remain merged for the current drawing session only.

Figure 15-72.
A second tab set can be merged with an existing tab set after selecting the new tab set in the **Merge** dialog box.

New tab set to be merged

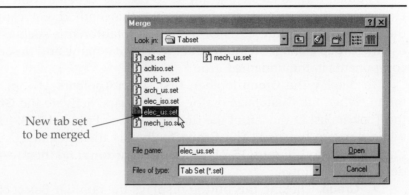

EXERCISE 15-8

❑ Begin a new drawing from scratch.
❑ Open **Content Explorer** and open the elec_us tab set. Activate the **Electrical Power** tab and drag and drop the Alarm block into the current drawing.
❑ Double-click the Fan block and insert it into the drawing at a scale of 2:1 and a rotation angle of 90°.
❑ Experiment with several other blocks and tabs.
❑ Finally, merge the arch_us tab set with the elec_us tab set.
❑ Do not save the drawing when you are finished.

Saving Selection Sets with the GROUP Command

A *group* is a collection of objects that are associated into a selection set to make editing operations more convenient. A group can be given a name and a description. As with other named objects in AutoCAD LT, a group name cannot exceed 31 characters and spaces are not permitted. Groups are created and managed using the **GROUP** command.

> **NOTE**
> The **GROUP** command and its various functions are offered in AutoCAD LT 98 only. This command is not available to users of AutoCAD LT 97.

Like blocks, groups can be used to streamline mundane drafting tasks and help organize your drawing. For example, you could create three groups that represent the top, front, and side views of a drawing object. Once a group is created, each of the components within the group can be edited individually, but the group itself can still be moved and/or copied as a single unit.

Drawing objects can be members of more than one group, and groups themselves can be nested within other groups. You can ungroup a nested group to restore the original group configuration.

The objects in your drawing can be quickly grouped and ungrouped using the **Group** toolbar. More advanced group functions are available using the **Group Manager** window. Both features are described in the following sections.

Creating a Simple Group Using the Group Toolbar

A quick way to create a group is to use the **Group** button on the **Group** toolbar. However, keep in mind that when you use this method, you cannot assign a name to the group because AutoCAD LT assigns a default name such as *A1 or *A2. You can use the **Group Manager** window later to assign a name and description or change the components in the unnamed group.

To display the **Group** toolbar, first select **Toolbars...** from the **View** pull-down menu. When the **Customize** dialog box appears, activate the **Group** check box from the Toolbars list at the left of the dialog box. See **Figure 15-73.** Click the Close button when you are finished. The **Group** toolbar is then displayed in the AutoCAD LT graphics window, **Figure 15-74.** The toolbar buttons and their respective functions are described as follows:

- **Group.** Clicking this button displays the familiar Select objects: prompt in the command window. Use any of the selection set methods to select the objects that you wish to include in the group. Once the group is created, it may then be selected with one pick. You can also quickly create a group by selecting **Group** from the **Tools** pull-down menu.
- **Ungroup.** Click this button when you wish to remove the grouping and restore each object in the group to a single object. Selecting **Ungroup** from the **Tools** pull-down menu is also a quick way to perform this function.
- **Group Manager.** Clicking this button displays the **Group Manager** window, **Figure 15-75.** You can also access the **Group Manager** window by selecting **Group Manager...** from the **Tools** pull-down menu. Each of the functions offered by **Group Manager** is described in the next section.
- **Group Selection On/Off (Ctrl+H).** Click this button when you wish to edit individual objects within a group. When you are through, click this button again to restore the full grouping. Observe that the same operation can be performed on the command line by using the [Ctrl]+[H] key combination. This is equivalent to toggling the **PICKSTYLE** system variable between on (1) and off (0).

Figure 15-73.
To display the **Group** toolbar, activate the **Group** check box from the **Toolbars** list in the **Customize** dialog box.

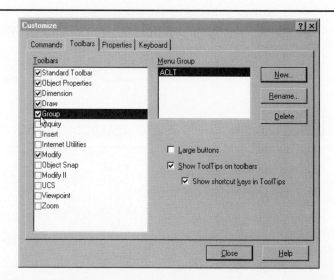

Figure 15-74.
The four tool buttons in the **Group** toolbar.

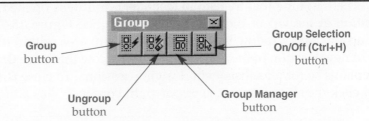

Group button
Ungroup button
Group Manager button
Group Selection On/Off (Ctrl+H) button

Figure 15-75.
The **Group Manager** window in its undocked state.

> **NOTE**
>
> Because the **PICKSTYLE** system variable is global, every group in a drawing is affected by its current value.

EXERCISE 15-9

❑ Begin a new drawing using the TEMPLATEA template file.
❑ With the Objects layer set current, draw the circle, rectangle, and six-sided polygon with the same proportions as shown.
❑ Open the **Group** toolbar as previously described.
❑ Create a group of the three objects. Copy the group to the right of the original objects. Observe how all three objects can be selected with one pick.
❑ Click the **Group Selection On/Off (Ctrl+H)** button so that individual editing can be performed on the copied group. Move the circle on the right to the Centerlines layer, the rectangle to the Cutplane layer, and the polygon to the Hidden layer.
❑ Click the **Group Selection On/Off (Ctrl+H)** button again to restore the groupings.
❑ Save the drawing as EX15-9 when you are finished.

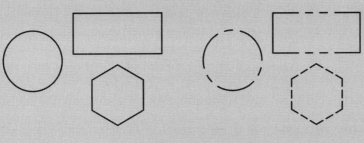

Advanced Group Functions Using **Group Manager**

The **Group Manager** window can be used to add or remove members in a group. Erasing an object that is defined as a group member deletes that object from the group definition. You can also use **Group Manager** to revise the name or description of a group.

As described in the previous section, you can open the **Group Manager** window by clicking the **Group Manager** button in the **Group** toolbar, or by selecting **Group Manager...** from the **Tools** pull-down menu. You can also enter the following on the command line:

    Command: **GROUP** or **G↵**

GROUP
G

Tools
➥ Group
   Manager...

Group
toolbar

Group Manager

The first time that the **Group Manager** window is opened, it appears in a docked position at the top of the graphics window. See **Figure 15-76.** You can undock the **Group Manager** window by clicking in a vacant area within its borders and dragging it to a new location in the graphics window. Note that once **Group Manager** is opened, it remains so for all subsequent drawing sessions. To close **Group Manager**, undock it and click the close icon in the upper-right corner.

Figure 15-76.
When the **Group Manager** window is first displayed, it is docked at the top of the graphics window. It must be undocked before it can be closed.

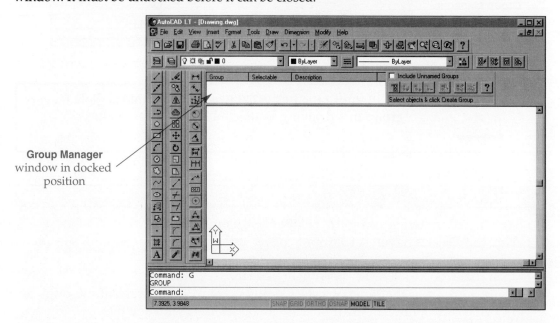

Group Manager window in docked position

Each of the toolbar buttons in the **Group Manager** window is illustrated in **Figure 15-77.** The buttons and other features are described as follows:

- **Create Group.** To create a group, first select the desired objects using any valid selection set method so that grips appear on all the objects. Next, click the **Create Group** button. A flashing text cursor appears in the column labeled **Group** at the top of the **Group Manager** window. Enter the desired name for the group and press [Enter]. Remember that the name you enter cannot exceed 31 characters, and no spaces are permitted. The group name is automatically converted to uppercase characters. If you wish to add a description for the new group, click in the **Description** column and enter the textual description using any combination of uppercase and lowercase characters. Press [Enter] when you are through entering descriptive text. See **Figure 15-78.** To adjust the width of the columns, drag the lines between the columns. You may create as many groups as necessary using this method. Be sure to provide a different name for each group. Regardless of the order in which the groups are created, their names appear alphabetically in the Group column.

- **Ungroup.** To remove a group definition, first select the group name in the **Group Manager** window so that the name is highlighted. Next, click the **Ungroup** button to remove the group. Although the group is removed, no drawing objects are erased. If you wish to remove several groups simultaneously, press and hold the [Ctrl] key as you select the group names in the **Group Manager** window. AutoCAD LT then displays the alert box shown in **Figure 15-79.** Click the **OK** or **Cancel** button as required to complete the operation.

AutoCAD LT—Fundamentals and Applications

Figure 15-77.
The **Group Manager** toolbar buttons provide a number of options for managing groups in your drawing.

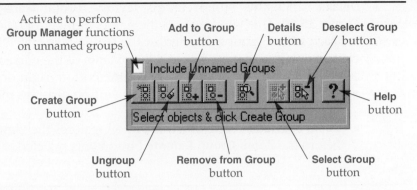

Figure 15-78.
The new group name, FRONT, appears in the **Group** column and descriptive text is entered in the **Description** column in the **Group Manager** window.

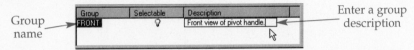

Figure 15-79.
AutoCAD LT displays the **Group Manager** alert box when you attempt to ungroup multiple groups.

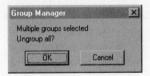

PROFESSIONAL TIP

If you want to quickly select all of the groups in the **Group Manager** window, place your pointing device over one of the group names and right-click. When the shortcut menu appears, pick **Select All** from the menu. Select **Clear All** from the menu if you want to clear the selection.

- **Add to Group.** When you wish to add one or more objects to an existing group, first highlight the group name in the **Group Manager** window. Next, select the object(s) you wish to add and click the **Add to Group** button. The objects are added to the group and the increased number of group objects is reported just below the **Group Manager** toolbar.

- **Remove from Group.** To remove one or more objects from an existing group, first highlight the group name in the **Group Manager** window. Next, click the light bulb icon in the column labeled **Selectable**. Once the light bulb icon is disabled (grayed out), individual drawing objects can be selected from the group. Select one or more objects to remove, and then click the **Remove from Group** button. The selected objects are removed from the group, but not erased from your drawing. The decreased number of objects in the group is reported just below the **Group Manager** toolbar.

- **Details.** Click this button to display the **Group Manager-Details** window, **Figure 15-80.** This window lists the name, number of objects, and description for each of the groups selected in the **Group Manager** window. If any group contains objects that are beyond the extents of the current viewport, you can select one of the following buttons at the bottom right of the window:
  - **Zoom Group Extents—** Clicking this button displays the drawing extents of the current group.
  - **Zoom Previous—** Clicking this button restores the view that was displayed before the **Zoom Group Extents** button was selected.

Figure 15-80.
The **Group Manager-Details**

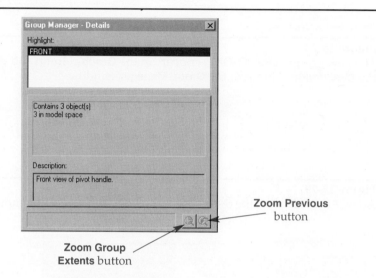

Zoom Previous
button

Zoom Group
Extents button

- **Select Group.** This button is used to identify a group in the graphics window. This can be handy when you cannot remember the group associated with a group name, or you are working with a drawing file from another user. To identify a group, first select the group name in the **Group Manager** window, and then click the **Select Group** button. AutoCAD LT then highlights the identified group and displays its grips.
- **Deselect Group.** Once a group has been selected using the **Select Group** button, use this button to remove the highlighting and grips from the group.
- **Help.** Clicking this button invokes online help specific to the **GROUP** command.
- **Include Unnamed Groups.** Activating this check box allows you to perform **Group Manager** operations on any unnamed groups created by using the **Group** button in the **Group** toolbar, or by selecting **Group** from the **Tools** pull-down menu.

Performing Group Operations on the Command Line

If you enter -GROUP or -G at the Command: prompt, AutoCAD LT displays prompts listing the **GROUP** command options on the command line. The sequence is as follows:

Command: **-GROUP** *or* **-G**↵
?/Add/Remove/Ungroup/REName/Selectable/⟨Create⟩: *(select an option or press* [Enter] *to accept the default)*

Specifying a Group Name at the **Select Objects:** Prompt

Whenever the Select objects: prompt is displayed in the command window, you can specify a group name instead of selecting objects. In the following example, the **MOVE** command is issued and a group name is entered:

Command: **MOVE** *or* **M**↲
Select objects: **GROUP** *or* **G**↲
Enter group name: **FRONT**↲
n found
Select objects: ↲
Base point or displacement: *(continue with the editing operation as required)*

Chapter Test

Write your answers in the spaces provided.

1. What is the maximum number of characters permitted for a block name? _____

2. Identify the command that uses a dialog box to create a block. _____
_____

3. A block is created on layer 0. What happens to the block when it is inserted on another layer? _____
_____

4. What is an anonymous block? Provide an example. _____
_____
_____

5. Why is it helpful to create a block to fit inside a one-unit square? _____
_____
_____

6. You are saving a block to disk. What should you enter at the Block name: prompt when the file name and block name are identical?_____

7. When using the **WBLOCK** command to compress a drawing file, what should you enter when prompted for the block name? _____

8. *True or False?* The **PURGE** command may be used at any time during a drawing session._____

9. Name the command that allows you to insert a block or drawing file using a dialog box. Which pull-down menu and menu option is used to access the same dialog box? _____

10. What must you do to create a mirrored image of a block as it is inserted? _____
_____
_____

11. What must be done before a block can be redefined? _____
_____
_____

12. Identify two ways to explode a block as it is inserted. _____

_____

_____

13. What is the function of the **BASE** command? Why would it be used? _____

_____

_____

14. Name the two commands that allow you to align a block with an object. _____

_____

15. What are block attributes? _____

_____

16. What is the difference between the **Constant** and **Preset** modes for attributes?

_____

_____

17. Identify the three commands that may be used to edit attributes *before* they are included within a block. _____

18. Which command allows you to change an attribute mode definition from **Visible** to **Invisible**? _____

19. Name the system variable that permits you to answer attribute prompts using a dialog box. _____

20. How do the **DDATTE** and **ATTEDIT** commands differ? _____

_____

21. Why would you use global attribute editing? _____

_____

22. What must you do before extracting attribute information? _____

_____

23. What is CDF format? Why would it be used? _____

_____

_____

24. Why must you provide a different name for the attribute extract file than that used by the template file? _____

_____

25. *True or False?* Drawings that use external references take up less disk space than drawings that use inserted blocks. _____

26. You have changed the display status of one or more xref layers. Which system variable should be used to store the changes? _____

27. What is the purpose of the **-XREF Bind** option? _____

_____

28. Several xrefs have been moved to a new directory on the hard drive. Which **-XREF** command option must be used so that AutoCAD LT can locate the files?

_____

29. You are working in a networked CAD environment. Another user has just modified and saved a drawing file that appears as an xref in your current drawing. Identify two ways to load the modified xref into your drawing. _____

_____

_____

30. Name the system variable that controls the creation of xref log files.

_____

31. *True or False?* An unloaded xref is permanently removed from the drawing.

_____

32. How does demand loading maximize xref performance? Identify the system variable that controls demand loading. _____

_____

_____

33. Name the command used to change the textual description of a block.

_____

34. What is the purpose of **Content Explorer**? _____

_____

35. Why would you merge tab sets? _____

_____

36. *True or False?* You can provide a name for a group by clicking the **Group** button in the **Group** toolbar. _____

37. Identify the internal naming convention used by AutoCAD LT when a user creates an unnamed group. Can this name be changed? _____

38. What must be done before closing the **Group Manager** window? _____

_____

_____

39. Identify the command used to perform **Group Manager** functions on the command line. _____

40. How do you specify a group name at the Select objects: prompt?_____

_____

_____

Chapter Problems

General

1. Open the TITLEA.DWT template file from Problem 4 of *Chapter 2*. Define attributes for the title block information, revision block, and parts list as described in this chapter. Save the revised template file. Repeat the procedure for the TITLEB.DWT and TITLEC.DWT template files.

Mechanical Drafting

2. Open Problem 9 from *Chapter 12*. Erase the existing A, B, and C datum identifier symbols. Create a new datum identifier symbol in accordance with ASME Y14.5M-1995 using a *single* block with an attribute. The correct dimensions for the symbol are provided in *Chapter 12*. Insert the blocks in the locations shown and rotate as necessary as you insert them. Use the **ATTEDIT** command to orient the datum letters properly. Save the revised drawing as P15-2.

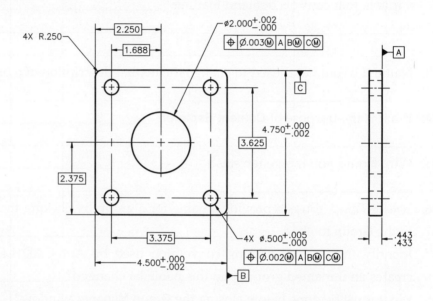

Electronic Drafting

3. Draw the electrical diagram of the motor control circuit shown below using your TITLEC template file. Use blocks with attributes where appropriate. Save the drawing as P15-3.

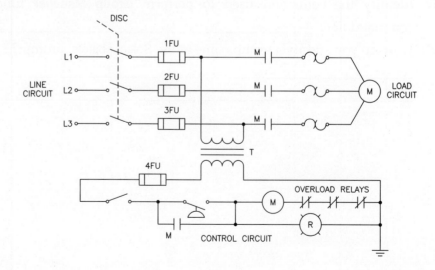

4. Using blocks with attributes, draw the schematic diagram of the plug-in card shown below using your TITLEB template file. Save the drawing as P15-4.

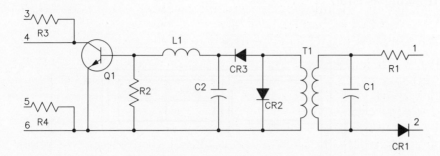

5. Draw the schematic diagram of the fine tuning indicator shown below using your TITLEB template file. Be sure to use the blocks from P15-4 where required. Save the drawing as P15-5.

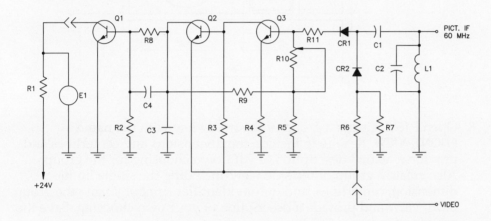

6. Draw the partial logic diagram shown below using your TITLEB template file. As with P15-5, use previously created blocks wherever appropriate. Save the drawing as P15-6.

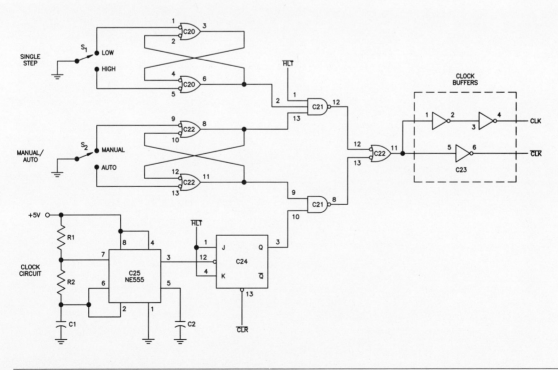

Chapter 15 Blocks, Attributes, and External References

7. Draw the bathroom/laundry room plan shown below using blocks for the doors, window, tub, toilet, vanity, washer, and dryer. Dimension as shown using the appropriate layers and dimension variables. Save the drawing as P15-7.

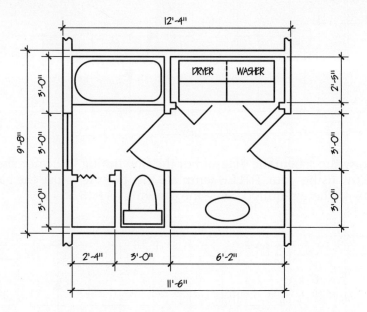

8. Open P15-2. Create a group of the front view with the name FRONT_VIEW. Be sure to include the dimensions and centerlines and provide a textual description of your own choosing for the group. Also create a group of the side view, including the single limits dimension, centerlines, and datum identifier symbol. Name the group SIDE_VIEW and provide a description of your own choosing. Save the revised drawing as P15-8.

AutoCAD LT

Chapter *16*

Isometric Drawing and Dimensioning

Learning Objectives

After you have completed this chapter, you will be able to:
- Assign an isometric snap style and draw isometric objects.
- Define and use isometric text styles.
- Set up an isometric template drawing.
- Create isometric dimensions.

Drafting is the science of fully describing three-dimensional objects using two-dimensional views. Such two-dimensional drawings are called *orthogonal* drawings. *Pictorial* drawings use three-dimensional views to describe height, width, and depth.

An *isometric* drawing is a pictorial drawing. An object drawn isometrically has the X, Y, and Z axes spaced 120° apart, with the Z axis projected vertically. Although an isometric view is two-dimensional in shape, it gives the illusion of three dimensions because several faces appear in one view. For this reason, isometric drawings are often used in technical documentation to assist in visualizing an object. An example of a typical isometric assembly drawing appears in **Figure 16-1.**

This chapter describes how to draw and dimension isometric objects. In addition, guidelines are provided for creating an isometric template drawing.

Figure 16-1.
An isometric drawing of an exploded assembly. Such drawings help in visualizing objects.

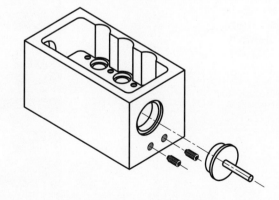

Setting the Isometric Snap Style

When you create orthogonal drawings in AutoCAD LT , the snap style is in the default **Standard** mode. This mode sets the graphics cursor in a vertical and horizontal orientation. The **Standard** mode also ensures that the grid and snap are aligned with the graphics cursor.

When creating an isometric drawing, the width and depth of objects must be drawn with lines angled 30° from the horizontal plane. Any vertical measurement, or height, is drawn using 90° lines. This convention is illustrated in **Figure 16-2.**

Figure 16-2.
In an isometric drawing, width and depth dimensions are measured on isometric axes drawn 30° from the horizontal plane. Vertical dimensions are drawn using 90° lines.

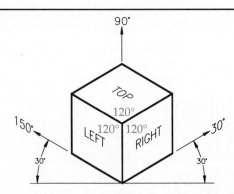

The **SNAP** command is used to toggle the snap style from **Standard** to **Isometric** and to align the grid and snap with the isometric axes. The procedure is as follows:

Command: **SNAP** *or* **SN**↵
Snap spacing or ON/OFF/Aspect/Rotate/Style ⟨*current*⟩: **S**↵
Standard/Isometric ⟨S⟩: **I**↵
Vertical spacing ⟨*current*⟩: **.25**↵
Command:

**DDRMODES
RM**

Tools
↳ Drawing Aids...

The **Isometric** snap style can also be set using a dialog box by entering DDRMODES, or RM, at the Command: prompt, or by selecting **Drawing Aids...** from the **Tools** pull-down menu. See **Figure 16-3.** The **Drawing Aids** dialog box is shown in **Figure 16-4.**

Figure 16-3.
To set the **Isometric** snap style using a dialog box, select **Drawing Aids...** from the **Tools** pull-down menu.

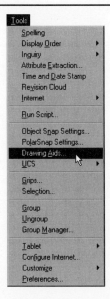

Figure 16-4.
The **Isometric** snap style is enabled using the **Drawing Aids** dialog box.

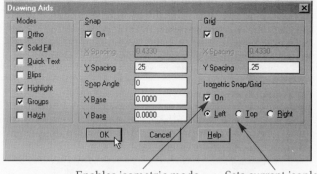

Enables isometric mode   Sets current isoplane

Click the check box labeled **On** in the **Isometric Snap/Grid** section of the dialog box to enable the **Isometric** snap style. Set the snap and grid vertical spacing using the **Y Spacing** text boxes. Since horizontal grid and snap spacing is not used in isometric mode, the **X Spacing** text boxes are grayed out and unavailable.

PROFESSIONAL TIP

    ORTHO mode is extremely helpful when constructing isometric drawings. If you are using the **Drawing Aids** dialog box to set up isometric mode, be sure to also enable the **Ortho** check box at the top left of the dialog box. It is also quite helpful to have the coordinate display on the status bar set at polar coordinates (distance⟨angle⟩) rather than Cartesian coordinates (X,Y). Keep in mind, however, that the polar display is available only when you draw lines or other object types that prompt for more than one point. You may recall from *Chapter 3* that the coordinate display can be toggled on and off, and from Cartesian to polar coordinates, by using function key [F6] or the [Ctrl]+[D] key combination. You can also toggle the coordinate display by simply double-clicking the coordinate display on the status bar with your pointing device. Any one of these methods may be used to cycle through the different coordinate display states, or you can use the **COORDS** system variable to set polar coordinates as follows:

        Command: **COORDS**↵
        New value for COORDS ⟨*current*⟩: **2**↵

The coordinate display on the status bar will then switch to polar coordinates when you perform a drawing command.

Toggling the Cursor Orientation

It is easier to draw an isometric shape if the angles of the graphics cursor align with the isometric axes. The isometric cursor positions are called *isoplanes*. The graphics cursor positions for the three isoplane modes are shown in **Figure 16-5.**

When the **Isometric** snap style is first enabled, AutoCAD LT defaults to the left isoplane. You can toggle between the three isoplanes by pressing [F5] or [Ctrl]+[E]. As the isoplane modes are toggled, their states are displayed on the command line for reference as follows:

    Command: ⟨Isoplane Left⟩
    Command: ⟨Isoplane Top⟩
    Command: ⟨Isoplane Right⟩

Figure 16-5.
A—The graphics cursor aligned with the left isoplane. B—The graphics cursor aligned with
the top isoplane. C—The graphics cursor aligned with the right isoplane.

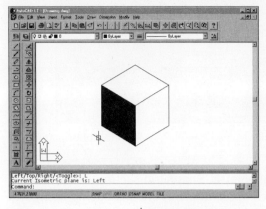

A

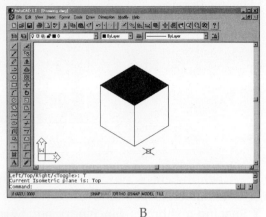

B

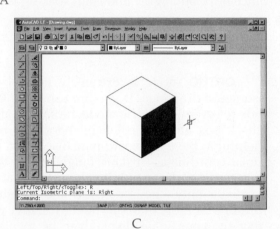

C

The desired isoplane can also be selected by picking the **Left**, **Top**, or **Right** option
buttons in the **Drawing Aids** dialog box. Another method to toggle the cursor orientation is to use the **ISOPLANE** command. The sequence is as follows:

> Command: **ISOPLANE** *or* **IS.**↵
> Left/Top/Right/⟨Toggle⟩: ↵

Press [Enter] to toggle the isoplane to the next position. Rather than repeatedly
pressing the [Enter] key, you can specify the desired isoplane by entering the first
letter of the isoplane:

> Left/Top/Right/⟨Toggle⟩: **T**↵
> Current Isometric plane is: Top

PROFESSIONAL TIP    Although using function key [F5] or the [Ctrl]+[E] key
combination is a more efficient means to toggle the isoplane
orientation while inside another command, the **ISOPLANE**
command can be used transparently to accomplish the same
purpose.

When the isometric snap style is in effect, the graphics cursor is normally in one
of the three isoplanes. When a multiple selection set method (such as **Window** or
Crossing) is used, the graphics cursor orientation reverts to the horizontal and vertical

positions. At the completion of the command, the graphics cursor automatically resumes the isoplane orientation.

EXERCISE 16-1

❑ Begin a new drawing.
❑ Set the grid spacing to .5.
❑ Set the snap style to **Isometric** and set the vertical spacing to .25.
❑ Draw the object shown using the dimensions given.
❑ Activate **ORTHO** mode and change the coordinate display to aid in construction of the object. Toggle the isoplane orientation as required.
❑ Save the drawing as EX16-1.

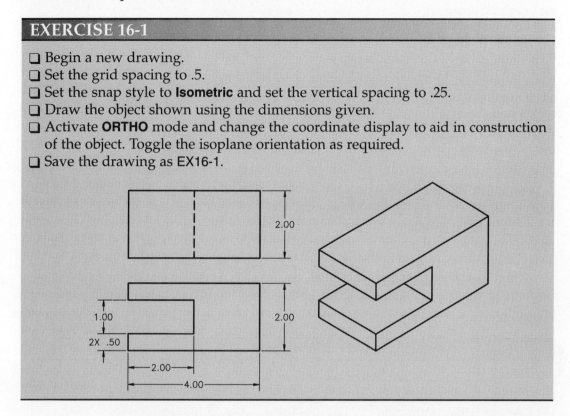

Drawing Isocircles

Circles appear as ellipses in isometric mode, as shown in **Figure 16-6.** A true isometric ellipse is rotated 35°16′ about its major axis. Whenever the **Isometric** snap style is enabled, AutoCAD LT adds an additional option called **Isocircle** to the **ELLIPSE** command.

An *isocircle* is a true isometric ellipse and can be specified by either its radius or diameter. To create an isocircle, enter ELLIPSE, or EL, at the Command: prompt, click the **Ellipse** button in the **Draw** toolbar, or select **Ellipse** from the **Draw** pull-down menu, **Figure 16-7.** The sequence at the Command: prompt is as follows:

ELLIPSE
EL

Draw
↳ Ellipse...

Draw
toolbar

Ellipse

> Command: **ELLIPSE** *or* **EL**↵
> Arc/Center/Isocircle/⟨Axis endpoint 1⟩: **I**↵
> Center of circle: *(pick a point)*
> ⟨Circle radius⟩/Diameter: *(enter a radius value or type* D *for diameter)*
> Command:

Figure 16-6.
Isometric ellipses are drawn using the **Isocircle** option of the **ELLIPSE** command. Note the orientation of the graphics cursor for each isoplane.

Figure 16-7.
Select **Ellipse** from
the **Draw** pull-down
menu and then pick
Axis, End from the
cascading submenu
to issue the **ELLIPSE**
command. Next,
use the **Isocircle**
option from the
command line.

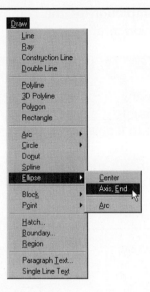

After locating a center point, the isocircle appears on screen in the current
isoplane. Press [F5] or [Ctrl]+[E] to toggle the correct isoplane. Remember, the **Isocircle**
option is only available when the **Isometric** snap style is enabled.

EXERCISE 16-2

❏ Open EX16-1 if it is not still on your screen.
❏ Make the modifications shown using the **Isocircle** option of the **ELLIPSE** command.
❏ Use the **TRIM** command to obtain the fully radiused feature.
❏ Save the drawing as EX16-2.

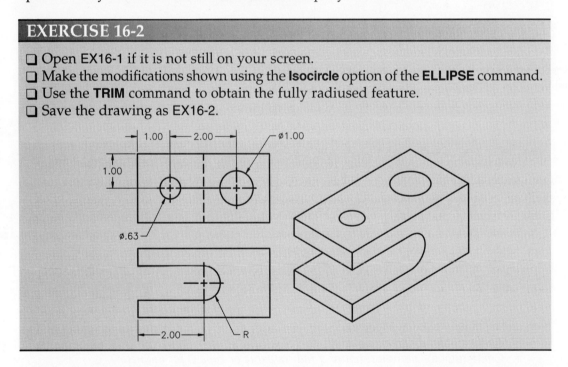

Creating Isometric Text

The appearance of isometric drawings is improved through the use of isometric
text. Before creating isometric text, you must first create two isometric text styles using
the **STYLE** command. In the example shown in **Figure 16-8,** two styles are used to label
each isoplane. These styles are named ISOM-F (forward) and ISOM-B (backward).

The ISOM-F style has an obliquing angle of positive 30° so that the text leans
forward. The ISOM-B style has a negative 30° obliquing angle so that the text leans backward. The obliquing angles of the two styles are shown in comparison to the orientation of the STANDARD text style. Each style is assigned the roman simplex font
(ROMANS.SHX), but any font can be used for isometric text styles.

Figure 16-8.
Examples of
isometric text.

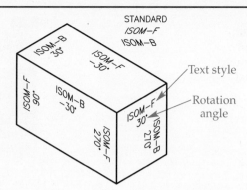

The isometric text should be aligned with the corresponding isoplane. This is accomplished by using the proper text style and setting the text rotation angle as required. In the examples shown in **Figure 16-8,** the rotation angle is indicated below the text style name for each isoplane and orientation.

Like other text styles, an isometric text style can be created using the **STYLE** command and the **Text Style** dialog box. This was discussed in *Chapter 9.* An isometric text style can also be created on the command line without using a dialog box by entering -STYLE at the Command: prompt. The sequence is as follows:

> Command: **-STYLE**↵
> Text style name (or ?) ⟨STANDARD⟩: **ISOM-F**↵
> New style.
> Specify full font name or font filename ⟨txt⟩: **ROMANS**↵
> Height ⟨0.0000⟩:↵
> Width factor ⟨1.0000⟩:↵
> Obliquing angle ⟨0⟩: **30**↵
> Backwards? ⟨N⟩↵
> Upside-down? ⟨⟩↵
> Vertical? ⟨N⟩↵
> ISOM-F is now the current text style.
> Command:

Now press [Enter] to repeat the **-STYLE** command, and create the ISOM-B text style with a -30° obliquing angle.

Before inserting isometric text in your drawing, you must set the appropriate style current. You can set a text style current at the command line by using the **TEXTSTYLE** system variable. The following sequence is used to make the ISOM-F text style current:

> Command: **TEXTSTYLE**↵
> New value for TEXTSTYLE ⟨"STANDARD"⟩: **ISOM-F**↵
> Command:

If you wish to set a current style using a dialog box, select **Text Style...** from the **Format** pull-down menu. See **Figure 16-9.**

When the **Text Style** dialog box appears, select the desired style from the **Style Name** drop-down list, as shown in **Figure 16-10.** In this example, ISOM-B is the current style as evidenced by the **Preview** box at the lower right of the dialog box, and the ISOM-F style is selected to replace it. After selecting a different style, AutoCAD LT displays an alert box. Click the **No** button in this alert box and then click the **Close** button at the upper right to exit the **Text Style** dialog box and return to the Command: prompt. (Remember that you can also use this dialog box to create the required isometric text styles.) Refer to *Chapter 9* if you wish to review style and text options.

Figure 16-9.
Select **Text Style...**
from the **Format**
pull-down menu to
set a current text
style.

Figure 16-10.
Setting the ISOM-F
style current using
the **Text Style** dialog
box. An alert box is
displayed whenever
a new style is set
current using the
Text Style dialog box.

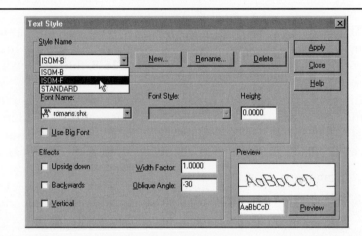

EXERCISE 16-3

❏ Draw an object similar to the one shown in **Figure 16-8.** Use any dimensions you like.
❏ Create two isometric text styles with the roman simplex font.
❏ Using **Figure 16-8** as a guide, add text to all three isoplanes with the correct styles and rotation angles.
❏ Save the drawing as EX16-3.

Isometric Template (Isoproto.dwt) Tutorial

Because isocircles are constructed with ellipses, it is not possible to draw a center-line through them with the **DIMCENTER** command. The Isoproto.dwt tutorial enables you to create an isometric template file for isocircles with centerlines generated in each isoplane. Each isocircle is defined with a diameter of 1 unit. The isocircles are saved as individual blocks and remain in the isometric template file.

After completion of this tutorial, whenever an isocircle with a centerline is required, the appropriate block can be inserted and scaled to the proper diameter. This tutorial also serves the following functions:

- It provides you with more practice in defining text styles and creating and inserting block objects.
- It demonstrates how blocks can be utilized to streamline otherwise mundane drafting tasks.
- It illustrates the global changes made to linetypes by the **LTSCALE** system variable.

The Isoproto.dwt tutorial begins as follows:

↪ Start a new drawing using your TEMPLATEA template. See **Figure 16-11.**

↪ Make sure that the Objects layer is set current. (If you have not yet created a template file with the necessary layers and linetypes, first complete Exercise 5-4 from *Chapter 5* before continuing with this procedure.)

↪ Set the grid spacing to .25.

↪ Set the snap style to **Isometric** and the vertical snap spacing to .25.

↪ With **ORTHO** mode on, toggle between the proper isoplanes and draw a 1.50 isometric cube using the **LINE** command.

↪ Turn **ORTHO** off and use the **COPY** command to copy the cube. Place the copy to the right of the original cube. Perform a **ZOOM Extents** and then a **ZOOM Scale(X)** at .8X. Your drawing should appear similar to the one shown in **Figure 16-12.**

↪ Using the **Isocircle** option of the **ELLIPSE** command, place an isocircle with a .5 radius (or a diameter of one unit) in the center of each isoplane on the original (left) cube. See **Figure 16-13.**

↪ Set the Centerlines layer current.

↪ Use the **DDOSNAP** command to access the **Osnap Settings** dialog box and set the running object snap mode to **Midpoint.**

↪ Toggle the grid [F7] and snap [F9] off.

Figure 16-11.
Click the **Use a Template** button in the **Create New Drawing** dialog box and select Templatea.dwt as your template file.

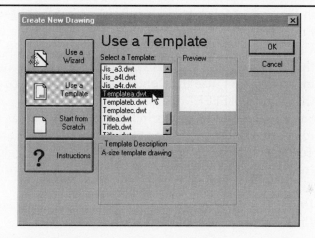

Figure 16-12.
After drawing the isometric cube, make a copy to the right of the original object and perform a **ZOOM Scale(X)** at .8x.

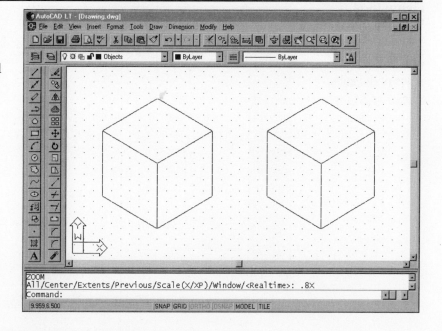

Figure 16-13.
Three isocircles with a diameter of one unit are added to the cube surfaces.

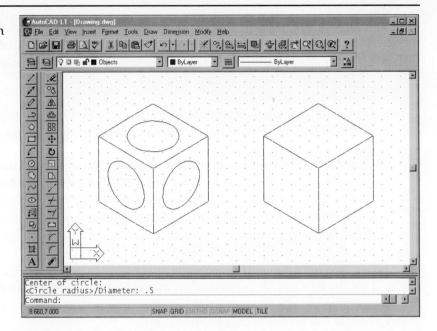

- ◇ Using the **LINE** command, draw lines bisecting the surfaces of the cube, as shown in **Figure 16-14.** When you are finished, set the Objects layer current again.
- ◇ Erase the left cube, leaving the isocircles and the centerlines.
- ◇ Using the **BLOCK** (or **BMAKE**) command, save the isocircle and centerlines on the left side as a block. A crossing box will be helpful for this step. For the insertion point, use the **Center** osnap on the isocircle. See **Figure 16-15.** Name the block HOLELEFT.
- ◇ Save the top and right isocircles and centerlines as blocks. It is not necessary to toggle the isoplanes. Name the blocks HOLETOP and HOLERGHT, respectively.
- ◇ Turn off any running object snap modes and toggle the grid and snap back on.
- ◇ Insert the block Holeleft at the center of the left isoplane on the remaining cube. Enter .75 for the insertion scale.
- ◇ Insert the block Holetop at the center of the top isoplane on the cube. Enter .5 for the insertion scale.

Figure 16-14.
Centerlines are constructed by drawing lines from the midpoints of the sides of the cube.

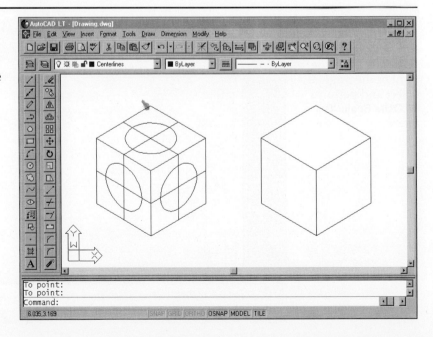

Figure 16-15.
Select the center of
the isocircle as the
insertion base point
for the block.

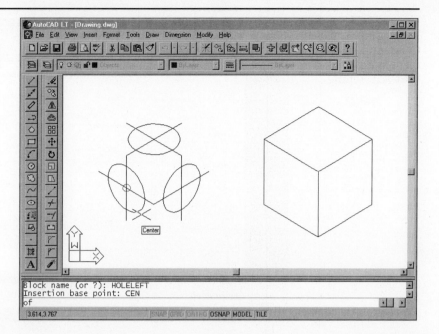

- Insert the block Holerght at the center of the right isoplane on the cube. Enter 1.125 for the insertion scale.
- Look carefully at the centerlines of the inserted blocks. See **Figure 16-16.** Set **LTSCALE** to .625 and observe the results. Now, set **LTSCALE** to .375 and once again note the changes. See **Figure 16-17.**
- Experiment with the inserted blocks by using varying scales and different **LTSCALE** values.
- Remember that the linetype scale may also be changed on individual lines by using the **DDMODIFY** and **DDCHPROP** commands.
- When you are through experimenting, erase all displayed geometry.
- Create two isometric text styles as described earlier in this chapter. Assign the font of your choice to the styles.
- Make any dimension variable and system variable changes appropriate to your application. Also, add drawing layers or rename them as desired.

Figure 16-16.
The inserted blocks
with an **LTSCALE**
setting of 1.

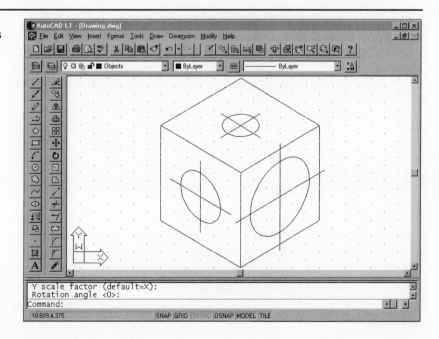

Figure 16-17.
The appearance of the inserted blocks after changing the **LTSCALE** setting to .375.

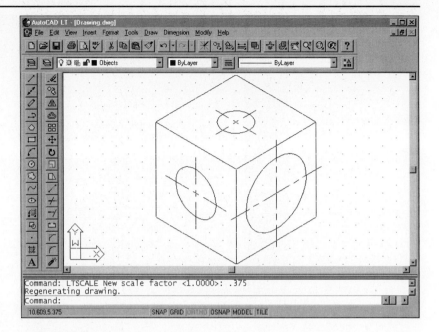

⟳ Finally, use the **SAVEAS** command to save the template file with the name Isoproto.dwt. Repeat the **SAVEAS** command and save the file as Isoproto.dwg.

⟳ Use Isoproto.dwt whenever a new isometric drawing is required. Remember that Isoproto.dwg may be inserted into another drawing when needed. Simply press [Esc] to cancel when prompted for the insertion point. The isocircle blocks, isometric text styles, and layers defined in Isoproto.dwg then become part of the current drawing. This insertion method is described more fully in *Chapter 15*.

NOTE

It is not necessary to create three separate isocircle blocks for Isoproto.dwt. As a quicker alternative, a single isocircle block can be saved and rotated into the other isoplanes when it is inserted.

EXERCISE 16-4

❑ Open your TITLEA template file from the *Chapter 15* drawing problems.
❑ Insert Isoproto.dwg into your title block. Press [Esc] when prompted for an insertion point. Save the revised TITLEA template file.
❑ Repeat the procedure for your TITLEB and TITLEC templates.

Creating Isometric Dimensions

AutoCAD LT does not automatically create isometric dimensions. However, it is possible to perform isometric dimensioning by editing linear dimensions.

The first step in creating an isometric dimension is to select the correct isometric text style. As an example, consider the object shown in **Figure 16-18A.** Two aligned dimensions and one vertical dimension have been applied to this object. The table on the following page lists the linear dimensions and dimension text styles used for the drawing.

AutoCAD LT—Fundamentals and Applications

Dimension	Dimension Type	Text Style	Obliquing Angle	Rotation Angle
2.50	Aligned	ISOM-F	90°	30°
1.50	Vertical	ISOM-F	30°	30°
1.75	Aligned	ISOM-B	30°	30°

After the dimensions are drawn, an obliquing angle is applied to the extension lines. You may recall from *Chapter 12* that the **OBLIQUE** command can be issued at the Dim: prompt to change the extension line angles for existing associative dimensions. Enter the command by clicking the **Dimension Edit** button in the **Dimension** toolbar or by selecting **Oblique** from the **Dimension** pull-down menu, **Figure 16-19.** You can also enter the following at the Command: prompt:

Command: **DIMEDIT**↵
Dimension Edit (Home/New/Rotate/Oblique) ⟨Home⟩: **O**↵
Select objects: *(select the 2.50 dimension)*
Select objects:↵
Enter obliquing angle (press ENTER for none): **90**↵
Command:

Figure 16-18.
A—Linear dimensions are applied to the object using the proper isometric text styles.
B—The **OBLIQUE** command is used to modify the angle of the extension lines. C—The dimension text is rotated into the correct orientation using either the **DIMTEDIT** command or the **TROTATE** command at the Dim: prompt.

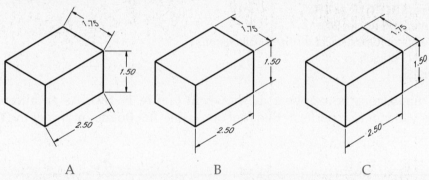

A   B   C

Figure 16-19.
The **Oblique** option of the **DIMEDIT** command may be quickly issued by selecting **Oblique** from the **Dimension** pull-down menu.

The procedure may also be performed at the Dim: prompt as follows:

Command: **DIM** *or* **D**↵
Dim: **OBLIQUE** *or* **OB**↵
Select objects: *(select the 2.50 dimension)*
Select objects:↵
Enter obliquing angle (press ENTER for none): **90**↵
Dim:

At this point, the **OBLIQUE** command is repeated and a 30° obliquing angle is applied to the two remaining dimensions. The results are shown in **Figure 16-18B.**

The final step is to apply the correct text rotation to the dimensions. The **Angle** option of the **DIMTEDIT** command rotates dimension text within the dimension lines. Issue the command by clicking the **Dimension Text Edit** button in the **Dimension** toolbar or by selecting **Align Text** from the **Dimension** pull-down menu, and then selecting **Angle** from the cascading submenu. See **Figure 16-20.** You can also enter the following at the Command: prompt:

Command: **DIMTEDIT**↵
Select dimension: *(select one dimension)*
Enter text location (Left/Right/Home/Angle): **A**↵
Enter text angle: **30**↵
Command:

When you wish to select and rotate several dimensions in one operation, use the **TROTATE** command at the Dim: prompt. The sequence is as follows:

Command: **DIM** *or* **D**↵
Dim: **TROTATE** *or* **TR**↵
Enter text angle: **30**↵
Select objects: *(select all three dimensions)*
Select objects:↵
Dim:

The dimensions now appear as shown in **Figure 16-18C.** As an alternative to **TROTATE,** you can also perform this function using the **Rotate** option of the **DIMEDIT** command.

Figure 16-20.
The **Angle** option of
the **DIMTEDIT**
command is entered
by first selecting
Align Text from the
Dimension pull-
down menu, and
then selecting **Angle**
from the cascading
submenu.

AutoCAD LT—Fundamentals and Applications

PROFESSIONAL TIP

Whether you use **TROTATE** or **DIMEDIT**, applying rotation angles to isometric text can be confusing. Use **Figure 16-8** as a reference when you create isometric text and dimensions.

EXERCISE 16-5

❑ Begin a new drawing using your ISOPROTO.DWT template file.
❑ Draw the object shown in **Figure 16-18** on the Objects layer.
❑ Set the Dims layer current and apply dimensions as described in this chapter.
❑ Save the drawing as EX16-5.

Chapter Test

Write your answers in the spaces provided.

1. Identify the command and option to enable isometric mode. _____
_____
_____

2. Name the system variable that controls the state of displayed coordinates on the status bar._____
_____
_____

3. What is an *isoplane*? _____
_____
_____
_____

4. Identify two methods to toggle the current isoplane. _____
_____
_____

5. *True or False?* The current isoplane can be changed transparently. _____

6. Identify the command that draws an isocircle. Is the isocircle function available at any time?_____
_____
_____

7. What is the true rotation of an isometric ellipse (in degrees and minutes)? _____
_____

8. How many text styles are required to adequately create isometric text and dimensions? Which characteristic distinguishes the isometric styles from one another?

_____

_____

_____

_____

9. *True or False?* Horizontal dimensions can be used when dimensioning isometric objects. _____

10. Identify two dimension editing commands that are required to create isometric dimensions. _____

_____

_____

Chapter Problems

Mechanical Drafting

1. Draw and dimension the **CLAMP BLOCK** shown below using your **TITLEB** template file. Save the drawing as **P16-1**.

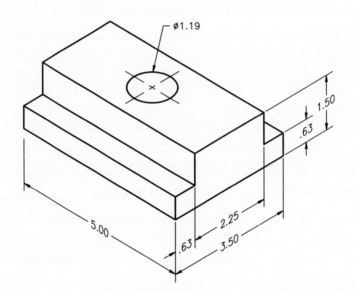

2. Draw the **STARTING CATCH** shown below using your **TITLEB** template file. Do not dimension the drawing. Save the drawing as P16-2.

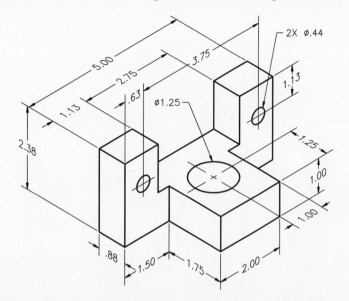

3. Draw and dimension the **BEARING CAP** shown below using your **TITLEB** template file. Save the drawing as P16-3.

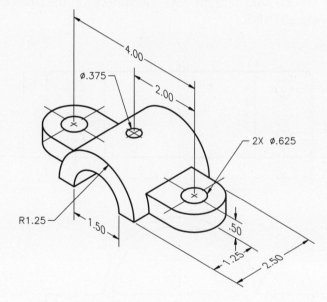

4. Draw the GUIDE shown below as an isometric drawing using your TITLEB template file. Do not dimension the drawing. Save the drawing as P16-4.

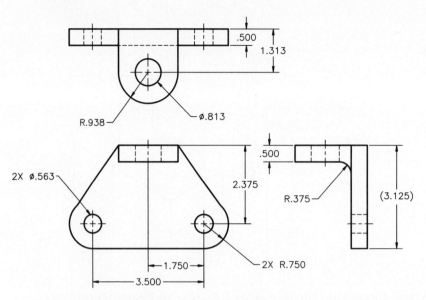

5. Draw the PIPE CLAMP shown below as an isometric drawing using your TITLEB template file. Do not dimension the drawing. Save the drawing as P16-5.

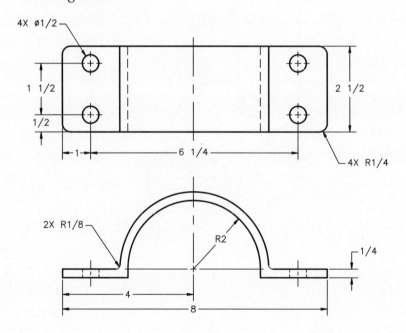

6. Draw the FLANGED ROLLER shown below as an isometric drawing using your TITLEA template file. Do not dimension the drawing. Save the drawing as P16-6.

Mechanical Drafting

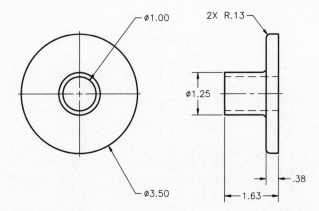

7. Draw the MOUNTING PLATE shown below as an isometric drawing using your TITLEB template file. Do not dimension the drawing. Save the drawing as P16-7.

Mechanical Drafting

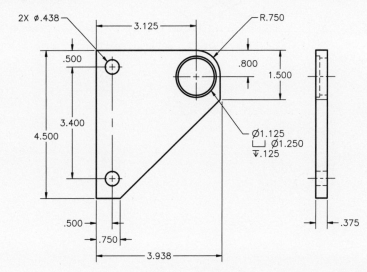

8. Draw the **TABLE** shown below as an isometric drawing using your **TEMPLATEC** template file. Do not dimension the drawing. Save the drawing as P16-8.

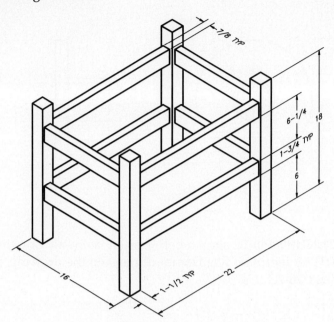

AutoCAD LT

Chapter 17

Model Space and Paper Space

Learning Objectives

After you have completed this chapter, you will be able to:
- O Describe the differences between model space and paper space.
- O Define and use floating viewports.
- O Create and manage viewport-specific layers.
- O Use external references in floating viewports to reduce drawing size.

There are two primary environments in which AutoCAD LT drawing objects reside. The first environment is called *model space*. Model space represents "real-world," three-dimensional coordinate space and is the default working environment. This is where you construct and detail your drawings. In this text, all of the drafting and design work you have done with AutoCAD LT has been in model space.

The second drawing environment is called *paper space*. The paper space environment was developed to aid in multiview plotting, particularly when the views are scaled differently. It is used to arrange the final layout of your drawing prior to plotting.

Paper space represents the paper on which your drawing is to be plotted. By creating windows, or *viewports,* in the paper, you can "see" your drawing that exists behind the viewports in model space. Independent viewports are used for each view of an object. Local and general notes are added to complete the drawing.

AutoCAD LT refers to paper space viewports as *floating* viewports. These are created using the **MVIEW** command. You can draw, edit, dimension, and annotate in one viewport without affecting other viewports. This is accomplished by freezing layers, or turning off layers on a viewport-specific basis, using the **VPLAYER** command.

This chapter describes the differences between model space and paper space viewports, as well as each of the **MVIEW** and **VPLAYER** command options. A drawing tutorial is included in this chapter to help reinforce paper space concepts.

Model Space vs. Paper Space Viewports

You may recall from *Chapter 4* that using the **VPORTS** command is a means to create multiple viewports in model space. Viewports in model space are called *tiled* viewports. They are adjacent to one another and cannot be spaced apart or overlapped.

Viewports in paper space, on the other hand, are actual drawing objects that can be moved, scaled, stretched, copied, or erased. Floating viewports can be created in any layer or color, but they can only be displayed with a continuous linetype. The distance between floating viewports can be specified so that they are close together or far apart. Additionally, floating viewports can overlap one another. It is even possible to create a floating viewport within another viewport.

Unlike viewports created in model space, viewports in paper space can be turned on or off. All displayed viewports—active or inactive—can be plotted.

The TILEMODE System Variable

The **TILEMODE** system variable must be set to 0 (off) to enter paper space and create floating viewports. When **TILEMODE** is set to 1, its default setting, you are limited to model space. You can quickly turn **TILEMODE** off and enter paper space by selecting **Paper Space** from the **View** pull-down menu. See **Figure 17-1A.** Selecting **Model Space (Tiled)** from the **View** pull-down menu turns **TILEMODE** back on and returns you to the model space environment. See **Figure 17-1B. TILEMODE** may also be turned on and off at the command line as follows:

> Command: **TILEMODE**↵
> New value for TILEMODE ⟨1⟩: **0**↵
> Entering Paper space. Use MVIEW to insert Model space viewports.
> Regenerating paperspace.
> Command:

Once paper space is entered, any model space objects on screen disappear until you create a floating viewport. Floating viewports are created using the **MVIEW** command, which is discussed in this chapter.

Figure 17-1.
A—To enter paper space, turn off **TILEMODE** by selecting **Paper Space** from the **View** pull-down menu. B—Selecting **Model Space (Tiled)** from the **View** pull-down menu turns **TILEMODE** on and restores model space.

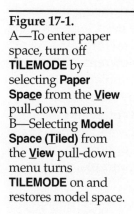

A   B

Guideposts in Paper Space

When paper space is active, the model space UCS *(User Coordinate System)* icon, shown in **Figure 17-2A,** is replaced with an icon that resembles a 30°-60° drafting triangle. See **Figure 17-2B.** Also, once paper space is entered, the **PAPER** button on the status bar at the bottom of the graphics window is activated. See **Figure 17-3.** This button, and the UCS icon, serve as reminders that you are working in paper space.

After paper space is enabled and you have created a floating viewport, you can double-click the **PAPER** button to toggle between paper space and model space. (In model space, the button is labeled **MODEL**.) The equivalent commands are **PSPACE** (or **PS**) and **MSPACE** (or **MS**). If you attempt to return to model space without having at least one floating viewport on and active, AutoCAD LT displays the following error message:

> There are no active Model space viewports.

If you receive this message, simply create a viewport in paper space and then repeat the **MSPACE** command. You can return to model space without creating any floating viewports by setting **TILEMODE** back to 1 (on).

Figure 17-2.
The appearance of the UCS icon in model space and paper space.
A—Model space is activated. B—Paper space is activated.

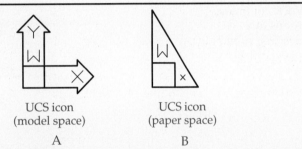

UCS icon
(model space)

UCS icon
(paper space)

A

B

Figure 17-3.
Once paper space is enabled, the **PAPER** button on the status bar can be used to toggle between paper space and model space. Observe the appearance of the UCS icon when paper space is active.

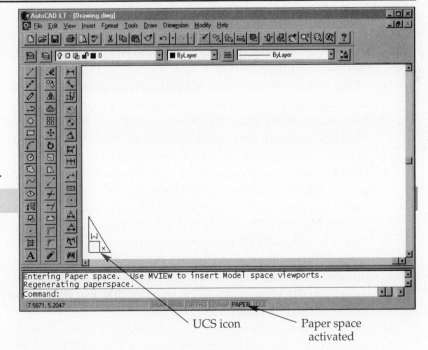

UCS icon

Paper space activated

NOTE

The ability to switch between model space and paper space using the status bar **MODEL** or **PAPER** button or the **MSPACE** and **PSPACE** commands is only possible when **TILEMODE** is off.

Creating Floating Viewports with MVIEW

The **MVIEW** (Make VIEWport) command creates floating viewports in paper space. **MVIEW** is also used to turn the contents of the viewports on and off, and to remove hidden lines in selected viewports when plotting. The **MVIEW** command can be issued by selecting **Model Space (Floating)** from the **View** pull-down menu.

To display all of the **MVIEW** command options in a cascading submenu, select **Floating Viewports** from the **View** pull-down menu. See **Figure 17-4.** When the **MVIEW** command is issued at the Command: prompt, the sequence is as follows:

> Command: **MVIEW** *or* **MV**↵
> ON/OFF/Hideplot/Fit/2/3/4/Restore/⟨First Point⟩: *(select an option)*

MVIEW
MV

View
⮕ Floating
  Viewports

Figure 17-4.
Selecting **Floating Viewports** from the **View** pull-down menu displays the **MVIEW** command options in a cascading submenu.

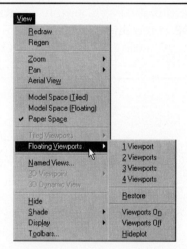

Floating viewports can be created and manipulated in a number of ways, depending on the requirements for your drawing. Each one of the **MVIEW** command options is described below:

- ⟨**First Point**⟩. The default **MVIEW** option prompts for two points that define the diagonal corners of a new floating viewport. Once the first point is specified, AutoCAD LT displays a box cursor to help you size the viewport. The viewport corners can also be specified with coordinates. The new viewport becomes the current, or active, viewport.
- **ON/OFF.** By default, newly created viewports are visible (on). When a viewport is edited (and moved or resized), its contents are regenerated. You can avoid waiting for viewports to regenerate by turning them off. You can also use the **MVIEW OFF** option to control which viewports appear on the finished plot. The **MAXACTVP** (maximum active viewports) system variable is used to control the number of viewports that can be visible at one time. The minimum number is 2 and the maximum number is 48. If you turn on an additional viewport, the viewport will be marked **ON**, but its contents will not be visible until you turn another viewport off.
- **Hideplot.** This option removes hidden lines from 3D models when plotting in paper space. You are prompted to enter **ON** or **OFF** and then select one or more viewports. The hidden lines are removed from the plotted output only—not the drawing window. For more information on 3D models and hidden line displays, see *Chapter 19* of this text.
- **Fit.** The **Fit** option creates a floating viewport that completely fills the current paper space screen display.

- **2/3/4.** These options permit you to choose between two, three, or four floating viewports.
  - **2**—This option creates a horizontal or vertical (default) division between two viewports for the paper space area you specify on your screen.
  - **3**—Selecting this option divides the specified paper space area into three viewports with the following options:

    Horizontal/Vertical/Above/Below/Left/⟨Right⟩:

    The dominant viewport may be placed to the right (by default), to the left, or above or below the other two viewports.
  - **4**—This option divides the specified paper space area into four equally sized viewports. You are prompted with the following:

    Fit/⟨First Point⟩:

    If **Fit** is selected, the viewports are scaled to completely fill the current paper space area in the drawing window. As an alternative, you may use the **⟨First Point⟩** option to locate two points that define the diagonal corners of the screen area to fill with the new viewports. Once the first point is specified, AutoCAD LT displays a window cursor to help you visualize and size the area for the four viewports. The corners may also be specified with X,Y coordinates.
- **Restore.** Model space viewport configurations can be saved using the **VPORTS** command. The **Restore** option is used to translate the viewports from model space to paper space. You are prompted as follows:

  ?/Name of window configuration to insert ⟨*ACTIVE⟩:

  Enter the name of a previously saved viewport configuration or use the **?** option to list all saved configurations. (If you press [Enter], the currently displayed view will be placed into a floating viewport.) If a configuration has already been restored, its name will appear as the default configuration. As with the other viewport options, you are presented with the Fit/⟨First point⟩: prompt after entering the viewport name.

PROFESSIONAL TIP

A floating viewport is automatically created when you begin a new drawing if you use the advanced paper space layout capabilities in the **Step 7: Layout** tab of the **Advanced Setup** subdialog box. Use the **Step 6: Title Block** tab of the **Advanced Setup** subdialog box to insert a title block or border, as well as a date and time stamp on your drawing. Refer to *Chapter 2* to review the drawing setup wizards.

Working in Floating Viewports

Once you have created a floating viewport, you must switch from paper space to model space to work within it. Only one floating viewport can be active at a time. The active viewport contains the graphics cursor and is surrounded by a wide border. The cursor appears as an arrow in the other viewports.

The viewports are interactive; a drawing or editing command can be started in one viewport and completed in another. An inactive viewport can be made current by picking anywhere within its border with the pick button on your pointing device. You can also toggle between active and inactive viewports with the [Ctrl]+[R] key combination.

NOTE	Because floating viewports can only be created in paper space, the following message appears if model space is active when the **MVIEW** command is used.

** Command not allowed unless TILEMODE is set to 0 **

EXERCISE 17-1

❏ Begin a new drawing using the **Advanced Setup** wizard.

❏ Click the **Step 6: Title Block** tab in the **Advanced Setup** subdialog box.

❏ Select ANSI A (in) from the **Title Block Description:** drop-down list and click the **Next** 》 button in the lower-right portion of the subdialog box.

❏ Activate the **Yes** option button to use advanced paper space layout capabilities. Also activate the **Work on my drawing while viewing the layout.** option button. Click the **Done** button when you are through. These option buttons should be active by default.

❏ Move your cursor around the drawing window. Observe that the graphics cursor is confined within the floating viewport, as shown below.

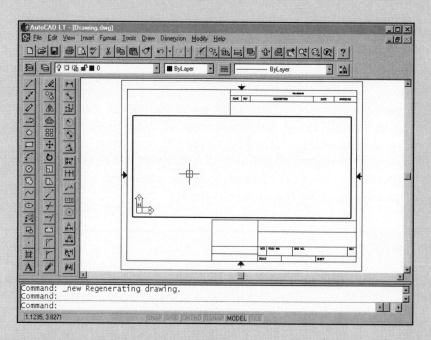

❏ Issue the **PSPACE** or **PS** command or double-click the **MODEL** button on the status bar to enable paper space.

❏ Toggle back and forth between paper space and model space by double-clicking the **PAPER** or **MODEL** button on the status bar or by using the **MSPACE** and **PSPACE** commands.

❏ With model space active, try drawing a line outside of the floating viewport. What happens? Why?

❏ Save the drawing as EX17-1.

AutoCAD LT—Fundamentals and Applications

Zooming and Scaling in Floating Viewports

Whether you are drawing microelectronic components or a shopping mall, the drawings that you create are *always* constructed at full scale. As you detail and dimension an object in a floating viewport, you can freely zoom and pan within the viewport using familiar display control commands.

When the contents of a viewport are to be dimensioned and plotted at 1:1, leave the dimension variable **DIMSCALE** at its default setting (1). Then, issue the **ZOOM** command and enter 1XP to scale the view relative to paper space. The **XP** option of the **ZOOM** command scales the model space within a viewport relative to paper space (**XP** means "times paper space"). To zoom the model space display relative to paper space, simply append XP to the scale factor, as shown in the following example (using a scale factor of .5):

Command: **ZOOM** *or* **Z**↵
All/Center/Extents/Previous/Scale(X/XP)/Window/⟨Realtime⟩: **.5XP**↵

There will be instances when your drawings will be plotted at 10:1, quarter-scale, or at some other scale factor. If the drawing is to be plotted at 10:1, zoom the viewport to 10XP and set **DIMSCALE** at .1. At quarter-scale, the viewport would be zoomed to .25XP and **DIMSCALE** would be set to 4. For an architectural drawing that is to be plotted at 1/4"=1', set **DIMSCALE** to 48 and zoom the viewport to 1/48XP.

Remember that drawings are always created at full scale. The viewport zoom magnification is scaled relative to paper space. Typical mechanical and architectural floating viewport scales are provided in the table below.

4 = 1	**ZOOM 4XP**
2 = 1	**ZOOM 2XP**
1 = 2	**ZOOM .5XP**
1″ = 2.54 mm	**ZOOM .3937XP**
2.54 mm = 1″	**ZOOM 2.54XP**
3″ = 1′	**ZOOM 1/4XP**
3/4″ = 1′	**ZOOM 1/16XP**
1/2″ = 1′	**ZOOM 1/24XP**
3/8″ = 1′	**ZOOM 1/32XP**
1/4″ = 1′	**ZOOM 1/48XP**
1/8″ = 1′	**ZOOM 1/96XP**

You can even plot a drawing so that identical views in different viewports are scaled differently. This is useful when a detail view is to appear on the face of the drawing at a different scale.

You can verify the zoom scale factor for a floating viewport with the **LIST** command. While in paper space, enter LIST, or LS, at the Command: prompt and select the viewport border to display the text window. The XP scale factor for the selected viewport is listed on the line labeled Scale relative to Paper space:.

NOTE

Regardless of the scale factor set for floating viewports, title blocks used for paper space plotting are *always* inserted at full scale (1:1) and the completed drawing is plotted at full scale. Also, be sure to set your paper space limits to match the size of the media on which you will plot.

EXERCISE 17-2

❑ Open EX17-1 if it is still not on your screen.
❑ Activate model space and insert any one of your previous drawing problems or exercises in the floating viewport.
❑ Enter 0,0 as the insertion point and accept the defaults for scale and rotation.
❑ Perform a **ZOOM Extents** on the inserted drawing. Now, zoom the display 1XP. Next, zoom the display .5XP. Experiment with different XP scale factors.
❑ Return to paper space. Try to erase one or more objects from within the floating viewport. What happens? Why?
❑ Save the drawing as EX17-2.

Viewport-Specific Layers and the VPLAYER Command

You have learned from previous chapters that the **LAYER** command is used to turn layers on and off, as well as freeze or thaw them. These operations are global in nature and thus affect all displayed viewports in your drawing. In paper space, it is possible to isolate layers and control their visibility in selected viewports with the **VPLAYER** (viewport layer) command.

With **VPLAYER**, you can determine which layers are visible in a given viewport, freeze or thaw layers in one or more viewports, reset a layer to its default visibility, create a new layer that will be frozen in all viewports, and set the default visibility for layers in viewports yet to be created. As with the **MVIEW** command, the **VPLAYER** functions can only be used when **TILEMODE** is turned off. If you attempt to use **VPLAYER** when **TILEMODE** is set at 1, the following error message is displayed:

** Command not allowed unless TILEMODE is set to 0 **

VPLAYER
VL

The **VPLAYER** command can be issued by entering VPLAYER, or VL, at the Command: prompt. The following options appear when the command is entered:

Command: **VPLAYER** *or* **VL**⏎
?/Freeze/Thaw/Reset/Newfrz/Vpvisdflt: *(select an option)*

Using the **VPLAYER** command is an effective way to manage the layers in your drawing. Each one of the command options is described below:

- **?.** This option allows you to list the frozen layers in a viewport. If model space is active when the **?** option is invoked, you are temporarily switched to paper space for viewport selection.
- **Freeze.** You can use this option to freeze layers in different viewports. After providing the layer name(s), you are prompted to select the viewports in which the layers are to be frozen.
- **Thaw.** This option thaws one or more frozen viewport layers. It will only thaw layers that have been frozen using the **Freeze** option of **VPLAYER** or **DDLMODES**. It will *not* thaw a layer that has been globally frozen with the **LAYER** command. You are prompted to enter the layer(s) you wish to thaw and select the viewports in which to thaw each layer.
- **Reset.** The **Reset** option restores the default visibility setting for viewport layers.
- **Newfrz.** This option permits you to create new layers that are frozen in *all* floating viewports. Whenever a viewport-specific layer is needed, it can be thawed in the appropriate viewport. The layer remains frozen in all other viewports. If a new viewport is added, the layer is frozen in it.

- **Vpvisdflt.** Using the **Freeze** and **Thaw** options of **VPLAYER** only affects *existing* floating viewports. The **Vpvisdflt** option sets the frozen or thawed default status of layers for viewports that are yet to be created. You are prompted to enter both the layer names and whether the layers should be frozen or thawed in any newly created viewports.

For **VPLAYER** options that request layer names, you can respond with a single name or a list of names, separated by commas. You can also use any of the AutoCAD LT selection set options, such as Window or Crossing, when prompted to select viewports.

Paper Space Tutorial

In the following tutorial, you will layout a drawing of mechanical details for a caster assembly using model space and paper space. You will create five floating viewports using the **MVIEW** command, externally reference a different drawing in each viewport, scale each view with the **XP** option of the **ZOOM** command, and freeze layers with the **VPLAYER** command. The completed drawing appears in **Figure 17-5.**

Figure 17-5.
The mechanical details for a caster assembly.

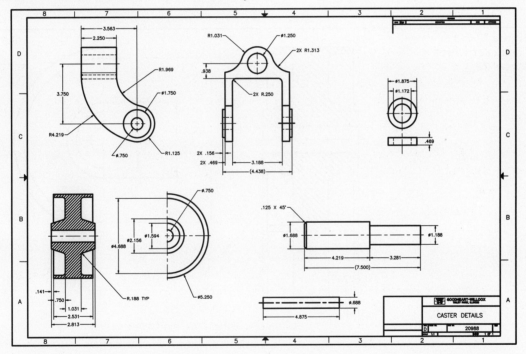

Before beginning this tutorial, draw and dimension the Frame, Wheel, Shaft, Collar, and Pin mechanical objects shown in **Figures 17-6** through **17-10.** Each object is to be created as a separate drawing using the proper layers and an appropriately sized template file. Do not use title blocks for the drawings. Once you have completed the five detail drawings, begin the paper space tutorial as described below.

Figure 17-6.
The caster frame (Frame.dwg).

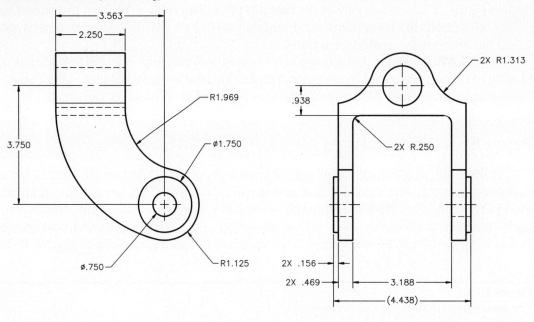

Figure 17-7.
The caster wheel
(Wheel.dwg).

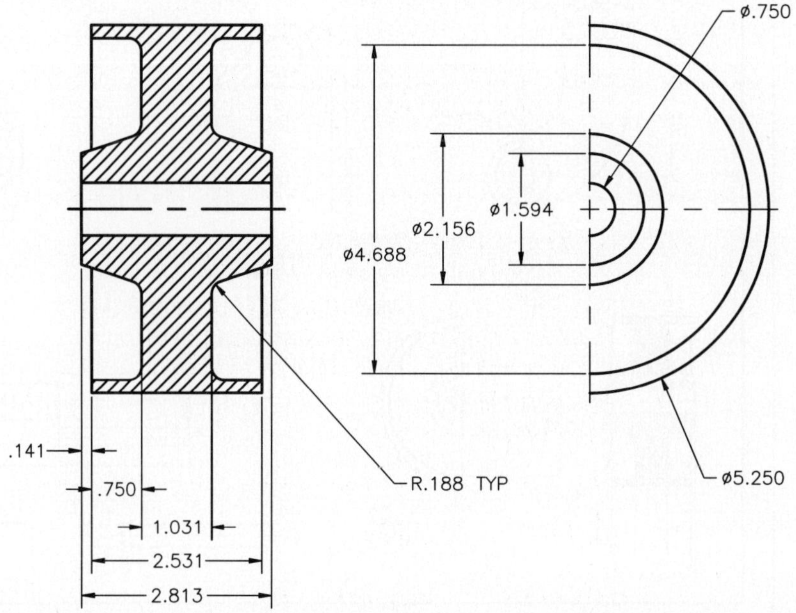

Figure 17-8.
The frame shaft
(Shaft.dwg).

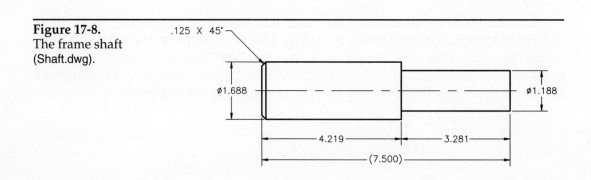

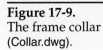

Figure 17-9.
The frame collar
(Collar.dwg).

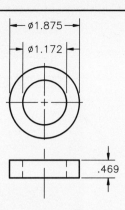

Figure 17-10.
The wheel pin
(Pin.dwg).

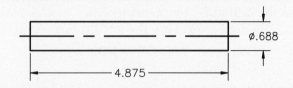

⇨ Start a new drawing from scratch using English settings. Do not use one of your templates. Set the **TILEMODE** system variable to 0 (zero) to enter paper space:

> Command: **TILEMODE**↵
> New value for TILEMODE ⟨1⟩: **0**↵
> Entering Paper space. Use MVIEW to insert Model space viewports.
> Regenerating paperspace.
> Command:

⇨ Set the paper space limits to 0,0 and 34,22 (D-size) and then perform a **ZOOM All.**

> Command: **LIMITS** *or* **LM**↵
> Reset Paper space limits:
> ON/OFF/⟨Lower left corner⟩ ⟨0.0000,0.0000⟩: ↵
> Upper right corner ⟨12.0000,9.0000⟩: **34,22**↵
> Command: **ZOOM** *or* **Z**↵
> All/Center/Extents/Previous/Scale(X/XP)/Window/⟨Realtime⟩: **A**↵
> Command:

⇨ Next, make the following layer and color assignments.

Layer	Color
Notes	Blue
Viewports	Magenta
Xref	White

After creating each of the layers, set the Viewports layer current. The **Layer & Linetype Properties** dialog box should appear as shown in **Figure 17-11.** Next, create the first floating viewport using the **MVIEW** command.

> Command: **MVIEW** *or* **MV**↵
> ON/OFF/Hideplot/Fit/2/3/4/Restore/⟨First Point⟩: **1.5,.75**↵
> Other corner: **14,10**↵
> Regenerating drawing:
> Command:

Figure 17-11.
The required layers
are shown in the
**Layer & Linetype
Properties** dialog
box.

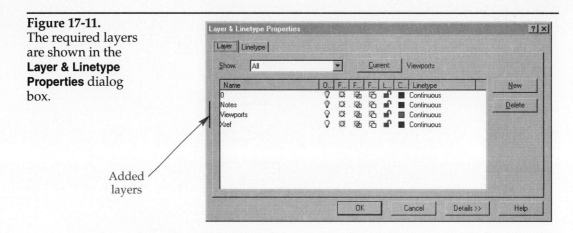

Added
layers

⇨ Use the **MSPACE** command to enter model space. You can also enter model
space by double-clicking the **PAPER** button on the status bar.

> Command: **MSPACE** or **MS**⏎
> Command:

Observe that the graphics cursor is confined to the new viewport when model space
is enabled. This is the active viewport. Your drawing should look like **Figure 17-12.**

⇨ Now, set the Xref layer current and use the **-XREF** command to externally
attach the drawing named Wheel. Insert it at 0,0 into the viewport. Accept the
defaults for scale and rotation.

> Command: **-XREF** or **-XR**⏎
> ?/Bind/Detach/Path/Unload/Reload/Overlay/⟨Attach⟩:⏎

⇨ When the **Select file to attach** dialog box appears, select Wheel.dwg from the file
list or enter the drawing name in the **File name:** text box. Click the **Open** button
when you are finished, **Figure 17-13.** The following prompt is then issued:

> Attach Xref WHEEL: wheel.dwg
> WHEEL loaded.
> Insertion point: **0,0**⏎
> X scale factor ⟨1⟩/Corner/XYZ: ⏎
> Y scale factor (default=X): ⏎
> Rotation angle ⟨0⟩: ⏎
> Command:

Figure 17-12.
After the first
floating viewport is
created, model
space is enabled.

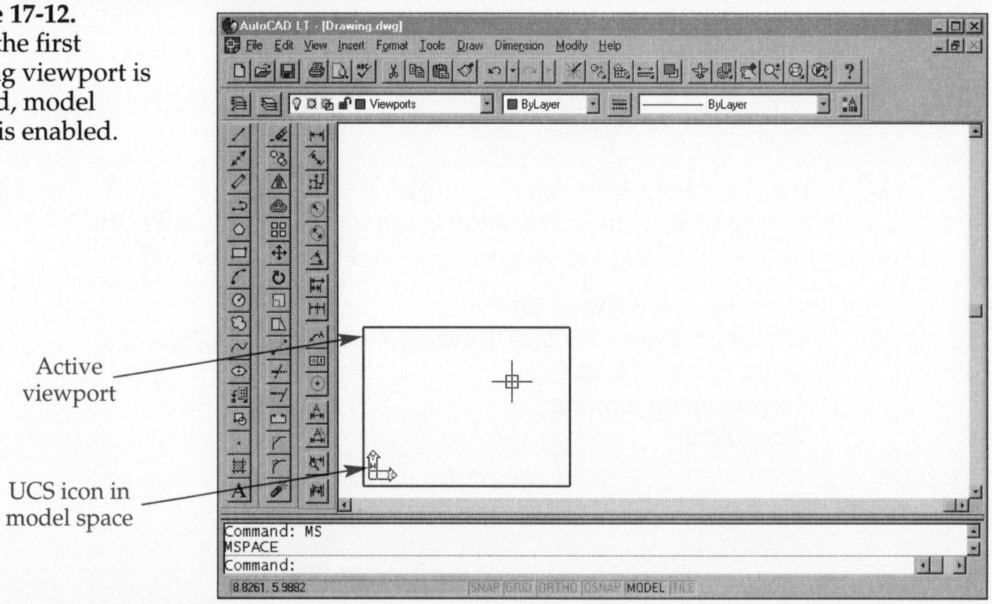

Active
viewport

UCS icon in
model space

Figure 17-13.
After displaying the
Select file to attach
dialog box, select
Wheel.dwg for
insertion into the
first viewport.

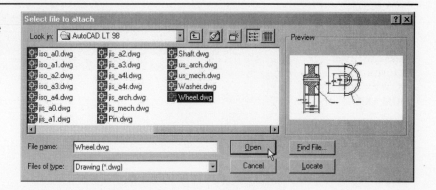

NOTE   The **-XREF** command was used for the first external reference in this tutorial to show the command sequence and prompts. If you prefer, you can attach the remainder of the drawings in this tutorial using the **XREF** command and the **External Reference** dialog box. If necessary, refer to *Chapter 15* to review the differences between the **-XREF** and **XREF** commands.

 ⇨ Perform a **ZOOM Extents** to view the entire Wheel drawing, and then reissue the **ZOOM** command and enter 1XP. Remember that the **XP** option scales model space units relative to paper space units.

      Command: **ZOOM** *or* **Z**⏎
      All/Center/Extents/Previous/Scale(X/XP)/Window/⟨Realtime⟩: **E**⏎
      Command: ⏎
      ZOOM
      All/Center/Extents/Previous/Scale(X/XP)/Window/⟨Realtime⟩: **1XP**⏎
      Command:

After this operation, your drawing should appear as shown in **Figure 17-14.** Now you will use the **VPLAYER** command to control the visibility of the layers in the Wheel drawing for each subsequently created viewport. Use the **Vpvisdflt** option and a wildcard character (*) to specify all layer names that begin with Wheel.

      Command: **VPLAYER** *or* **VL**⏎
      ?/Freeze/Thaw/Reset/Newfrz/Vpvisdflt: **V**⏎
      Layer name(s) to change default viewport visibility ⟨⟩: **WHEEL***⏎
      Change default viewport visibility to Frozen/⟨Thawed⟩: **F**⏎
      ?/Freeze/Thaw/Reset/Newfrz/Vpvisdflt: ⏎
      Command:

 ⇨ Next, enter the **LAYER** command to display the **Layer & Linetype Properties** dialog box. Look at the layer names beginning with Wheel. You may recall from *Chapter 15* that when a drawing is referenced, the layers that are inserted into the file have the original drawing file name prefixed to their names. The drawing names are separated from the layer names with the pipe character (|). Observe that the snowflake icon appears in the **Freeze/Thaw in new viewports** settings for each of the referenced layers. See **Figure 17-15.** This indicates that each layer is frozen in any new viewports.

Figure 17-14.
The appearance of the attached file Wheel.dwg after performing a **ZOOM Extents** and a **ZOOM 1XP.**

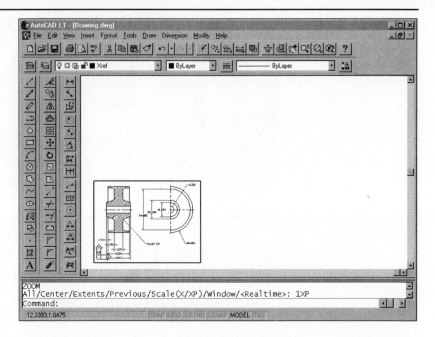

Figure 17-15.
Snowflake icons appear in the **Freeze/Thaw in new viewports** settings for the Wheel drawing layers in the **Layer & Linetype Properties** dialog box. The icons indicate that all of the layers in the Wheel drawing are frozen in any newly created floating viewports.

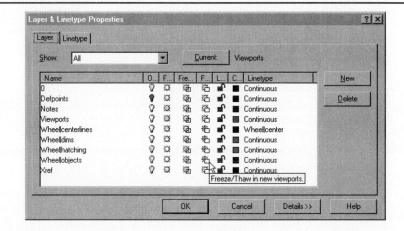

⇨ Next, set the Viewports layer current and return to paper space. Create another viewport with the **MVIEW** command.

> Command: **MVIEW** or **MV**↵
> ON/OFF/Hideplot/Fit/2/3/4/Restore/⟨First Point⟩: **1.5,10.25**↵
> Other corner: **20.5,20.125**↵
> Regenerating drawing.
> Command:

Your drawing should appear as the one shown in **Figure 17-16.** Notice that none of the objects in the Wheel drawing appear in the new viewport.

⇨ Set the Xref layer current and enter MSPACE, or MS, at the Command: prompt so that you can externally reference the next drawing into model space.

⇨ The upper-left viewport should be the active viewport. If it is not, click the viewport with your pointing device or use [Ctrl]+[R] to make it the active viewport. Now, attach the Frame drawing to the viewport.

> Command: **-XREF** or **-XR**↵
> ?/Bind/Detach/Path/Unload/Reload/Overlay/⟨Attach⟩: ↵

AutoCAD LT—Fundamentals and Applications

Figure 17-16.
Since they are
frozen, the layers
from Wheel.dwg are
not displayed in the
new viewport.

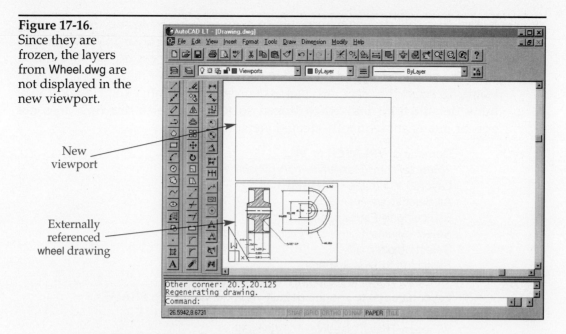

New
viewport

Externally
referenced
wheel drawing

⇨ Select Frame.dwg from the **Select file to attach** dialog box. Use a 0,0 insertion
point and accept the defaults for scale and rotation.

> Attach Xref FRAME: frame.dwg
> FRAME loaded.
> Insertion point: **0,0**↵
> X scale factor ⟨1⟩/Corner/XYZ: ↵
> Y scale factor (default=X): ↵
> Rotation angle ⟨0⟩: ↵
> Command:

⇨ Use the **PAN** command to center the drawing in the viewport and then scale
the model space units relative to paper space.

> Command: **ZOOM** or **Z**↵
> All/Center/Extents/Previous/Scale(X/XP)/Window/⟨Realtime⟩: **1XP**↵
> Command:

If necessary, reissue the **PAN** command to position the Frame drawing in the
viewport as shown in **Figure 17-17.**

Figure 17-17.
The Frame drawing
is externally
referenced into the
second floating
viewport. Note that
it also appears in
the lower viewport.

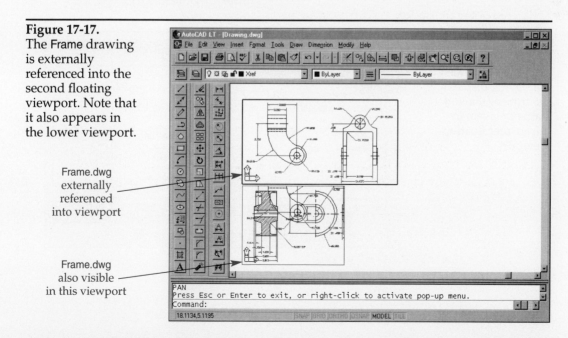

Frame.dwg
externally
referenced
into viewport

Frame.dwg
also visible
in this viewport

⮑ Notice that this drawing is visible in both viewports. Using the following sequence with the **VPLAYER** command will allow you to freeze the layer names beginning with Frame in the lower-left viewport. Remember that a wildcard character (*) can be used to freeze all the layer names prefixed with Frame. To select the viewport, pick its border. Also, change the viewport visibility default from thawed to frozen so that the Frame drawing does not appear in any subsequently created viewports.

> Command: **VPLAYER** *or* **VL**↵
> ?/Freeze/Thaw/Reset/Newfrz/Vpvisdflt: **F**↵
> Layer(s) to Freeze ⟨⟩: **FRAME***↵
> All/Select/⟨*current*⟩: **S**↵
> Switching to Paper space.
> Select objects: *(select the lower left viewport)*
> Select objects: ↵
> Switching to Model space.
> ?/Freeze/Thaw/Reset/Newfrz/Vpvisdflt: **V**↵
> Layer name(s) to change default viewport visibility ⟨⟩: **FRAME***↵
> Change default viewport visibility to Frozen/⟨Thawed⟩: **F**↵
> ?/Freeze/Thaw/Reset/Newfrz/Vpvisdflt: ↵
> Command:

⮑ The **Vpvisdflt** option freezes the Frame layers for all subsequent viewports. Enter the **LAYER** command to display the **Layer & Linetype Properties** dialog box again and scroll through all the layers, **Figure 17-18**. Observe that the snowflake icon appears in the **Freeze/Thaw in current viewport** settings for the layer names beginning with Wheel. This is because these layers are frozen in the current (top) viewport.

⮑ Notice also that the snowflake icon appears in the **Freeze/Thaw in new viewports** settings for the layer names beginning with Wheel and Frame. This indicates that these layers will be frozen for any newly created viewports. Next, set the Viewports layer current, return to paper space, and create another viewport.

> Command: **MVIEW** *or* **MV**↵
> ON/OFF/Hideplot/Fit/2/3/4/Restore/⟨First Point⟩: **15.5,1**↵
> Other corner: **23.5,3.5**↵
> Regenerating drawing.
> Command:

Figure 17-18.
The **Layer & Linetype Properties** dialog box displays the frozen/thawed status of layers in the current floating viewport.

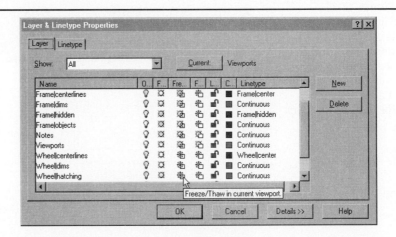

Your drawing should now appear as shown in **Figure 17-19.** Notice that the Wheel and Frame drawings do not appear in the new viewport. To save regeneration time, turn off the contents of the first two viewports using the following command sequence.

Command: **MVIEW** *or* **MV**↵
ON/OFF/Hideplot/Fit/2/3/4/Restore/⟨First Point⟩: **OFF**↵
Select objects: *(select the two left viewports)*
Select objects: ↵
Command:

Figure 17-19.
A third floating
viewport is created.

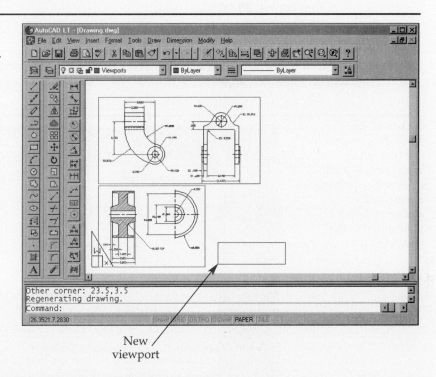

New
viewport

▷ Set the Xref layer current and enter model space so that you can externally reference another drawing into the new viewport. The lower-right viewport should be the active viewport. If it is not, make it so. Now, attach the Pin drawing.

Command: **-XREF** *or* **-XR**↵
?/Bind/Detach/Path/Unload/Reload/Overlay/⟨Attach⟩: ↵

▷ Select Pin.dwg from the **Select file to attach** dialog box. Enter 0,0 for the insertion point and accept the defaults for scale and rotation.

Attach Xref PIN: pin.dwg
PIN loaded.
Insertion point: **0,0**↵
X scale factor ⟨1⟩/Corner/XYZ: ↵
Y scale factor (default=X): ↵
Rotation angle ⟨0⟩: ↵
Command:

▷ Use the **PAN** command to center the drawing in the viewport. Next, scale the model space units relative to paper space.

Command: **ZOOM** *or* **Z**↵
All/Center/Extents/Previous/Scale(X/XP)/Window/⟨Realtime⟩: **1XP**↵
Command:

If necessary, use the **PAN** command again to position the drawing as shown in **Figure 17-20.** Now return to paper space, set the Viewports layer current, and create the last two required viewports.

Command: **MVIEW** *or* **MV**↵
ON/OFF/Hideplot/Fit/2/3/4/Restore/⟨First Point⟩: **15.5,4**↵
Other corner: **28.5,9.5**↵
Regenerating drawing.
Command: ↵
MVIEW
ON/OFF/Hideplot/Fit/2/3/4/Restore/⟨First Point⟩: **22.5,10.25**↵
Other corner: **28,16.75**↵
Regenerating drawing.
Command:

Observe that the Pin drawing appears in the two new viewports. See **Figure 17-21.** This will be remedied shortly.

Figure 17-20.
With the contents of the two left viewports turned off, the Pin drawing is externally referenced and positioned in the new viewport.

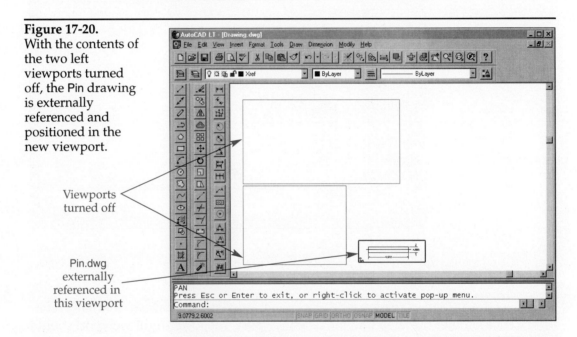

Viewports turned off

Pin.dwg externally referenced in this viewport

Figure 17-21.
After creating two new floating viewports, the Pin drawing is displayed inside both viewports.

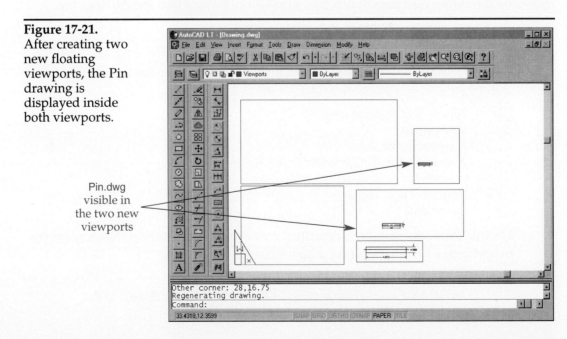

Pin.dwg visible in the two new viewports

AutoCAD LT—Fundamentals and Applications

⟳ Return to model space and set the Xref layer current. The upper-right view-port should be the active viewport. If it is not, make it active. Now, reference the Collar drawing and attach it to the viewport.

> Command: **-XREF** *or* **-XR**↵
> ?/Bind/Detach/Path/Unload/Reload/Overlay/⟨Attach⟩: ↵

⟳ Select Collar.dwg from the **Select file to attach** dialog box. Use a 0,0 insertion point and accept the defaults for scale and rotation.

> Attach Xref COLLAR: collar.dwg
> COLLAR loaded.
> Insertion point: **0,0**↵
> X scale factor ⟨1⟩/Corner/XYZ: ↵
> Y scale factor (default=X): ↵
> Rotation angle ⟨0⟩: ↵
> Command:

⟳ Now use the **ZOOM** command to scale the model space units relative to paper space. Enter 1XP as the zoom scale factor. Next, center the drawing in the viewport with the **PAN** command. After completing this step, activate the middle-right viewport and reference the Shaft drawing.

> Command: **-XREF** *or* **-XR**↵
> ?/Bind/Detach/Path/Unload/Reload/Overlay/⟨Attach⟩: ↵

⟳ Select Shaft.dwg from the **Select file to attach** dialog box. Use a 0,0 insertion point and accept the defaults for scale and rotation.

> Attach Xref SHAFT: shaft.dwg
> SHAFT loaded.
> Insertion point: **0,0**↵
> X scale factor ⟨1⟩/Corner/XYZ: ↵
> Y scale factor (default=X): ↵
> Rotation angle ⟨0⟩: ↵
> Command:

⟳ Once again, use the **ZOOM** command to scale model space relative to paper space. Enter 1XP as the zoom scale factor. Finally, center the Shaft drawing in the viewport with the **PAN** command. Your drawing should appear as shown in **Figure 17-22.**

Figure 17-22.
The Collar and Shaft drawings are externally referenced and positioned in the two remaining viewports.

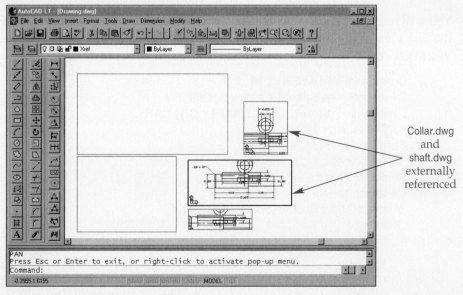

Collar.dwg
and
shaft.dwg
externally
referenced

↪ The middle-right viewport should still be active. If it is not, make it active. You will now freeze all layer names beginning with Pin and Collar in the current viewport, then freeze all layer names beginning with Pin and Shaft in the upper-right viewport. Finally, you will freeze all layer names beginning with Collar and Shaft in the lower-right viewport. Follow the command sequence below:

> Command: **VPLAYER** *or* **VL**↵
> ?/Freeze/Thaw/Reset/Newfrz/Vpvisdflt: **F**↵
> Layer(s) to Freeze ⟨⟩: **PIN*,COLLAR***↵
> All/Select/⟨*current*⟩: *(press* [Enter] *to select the current viewport)*
> ?/Freeze/Thaw/Reset/Newfrz/Vpvisdflt: **F**↵
> Layer(s) to Freeze ⟨⟩: **PIN*,SHAFT***↵
> All/Select/⟨*current*⟩: **S**↵
> Switching to Paper space.
> Select objects: *(select the upper-right viewport)*
> Select objects: ↵
> Switching to Model space.
> ?/Freeze/Thaw/Reset/Newfrz/Vpvisdflt: **F**↵
> Layer(s) to Freeze ⟨⟩: **COLLAR*,SHAFT***↵
> All/Select/⟨*current*⟩: **S**↵
> Switching to Paper space.
> Select objects: *(select the lower-right viewport)*
> Select objects: ↵
> Switching to Model space.
> ?/Freeze/Thaw/Reset/Newfrz/Vpvisdflt: ↵
> Command:

↪ The viewports on the right now display the required layers. However, you need to freeze the layers whose names begin with Pin, Shaft, and Collar in the two viewports on the left. You can turn on the two left viewports with the **MVIEW** command.

> Command: **MVIEW** *or* **MV**↵
> Switching to Paper Space.
> ON/OFF/Hideplot/Fit/2/3/4/Restore/⟨First Point⟩: **ON**↵
> Select objects: *(select the two left viewports)*
> Select objects: ↵
> Regenerating drawing.
> Switching to Model space.
> Command:

↪ You will notice that the last three externally referenced drawings are visible in the two viewports, **Figure 17-23.** Freeze the layers of these drawings using the **VPLAYER** command.

> Command: **VPLAYER** *or* **VL**↵
> ?/Freeze/Thaw/Reset/Newfrz/Vpvisdflt: **F**↵
> Layer(s) to Freeze ⟨⟩: **PIN*,SHAFT*,COLLAR***↵
> All/Select/⟨*current*⟩: **S**↵
> Switching to Paper space.
> Select objects: *(select the two left viewports)*
> Select objects: ↵
> Switching to Model space.
> ?/Freeze/Thaw/Reset/Newfrz/Vpvisdflt: ↵
> Command:

Figure 17-23.
Turning on the two left viewports displays the last three externally referenced drawings.

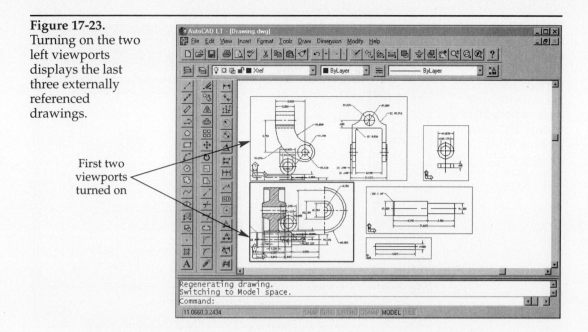

First two viewports turned on

↪ Next, return to paper space and insert the drawing Ansi_d.dwg at 0,0. This drawing is supplied with AutoCAD LT and is located in the Program Files\AutoCAD LT 98 folder. If you are using AutoCAD LT 97, the drawing Ansi_d.dwg is located in the Program Files\AutoCAD LT 97 folder. Accept the defaults for scale and rotation.

    Command: **INSERT** or **–I**↵
    Block name (or ?): **ANSI_D**↵
    Insertion point: **0,0**↵
    X scale factor ⟨1⟩/Corner/XYZ: ↵
    Y scale factor (default=X): ↵
    Rotation angle ⟨0⟩: ↵
    Command:

↪ Perform a **ZOOM Extents** to center the drawing in the drawing window.

    Command: **ZOOM** or **Z**↵
    All/Center/Extents/Previous/Scale(X/XP)/Window/⟨Realtime⟩: **E**↵
    Regenerating drawing.
    Command:

↪ Now, freeze the Viewports layer to suppress the display of the floating viewport borders. Your drawing should appear as shown in **Figure 17-24.**

↪ If you wish, set the Notes layer current and complete the title block information. Add any other drawing annotation as desired. The mechanical detail sheet is now complete and ready for plotting at full scale (1:1). Save the finished drawing with the name **CASTER.**

Figure 17-24.
A D-size title block
is inserted, a **ZOOM**
Extents is
performed to center
the drawing, and
the Viewports layer is
frozen. The drawing
is ready to be
plotted at full scale.

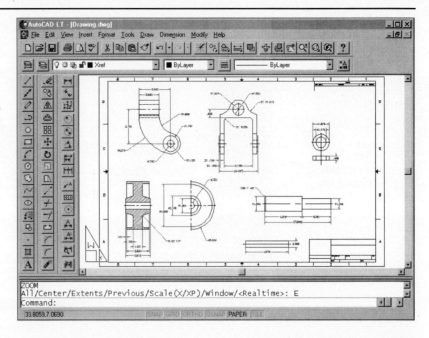

Summary

In the preceding paper space tutorial, each one of the detail drawings was externally referenced into the master drawing. This method reduces file size and conserves disk space. The **INSERT** or **DDINSERT** commands can be used if external references are not desired. Remember, however, that using **INSERT** or **DDINSERT** will increase the drawing file size.

A separate layer, Viewports, was created for the floating viewports. Creating a separate layer allows you to turn off or freeze your viewport borders before plotting.

Also, all of the floating viewports were scaled at 1:1 (1XP). As an experiment, try repeating the tutorial and scale the Collar and Pin viewports at 2XP.

The **XP** option of the **ZOOM** command allows you to scale the contents of a floating viewport at any scale. This makes paper space the ideal environment for mixing details with varying scales while still plotting at full scale.

As a final guideline, always use model space to construct, dimension, and detail your drawings. Use paper space only to add annotation and to arrange multiple views to fit the sheet size you designate for plotting.

Chapter Test

Write your answers in the spaces provided.

1. Identify the system variable that determines whether model space or paper space is active. _____

_____

2. What are tiled viewports? What command is used to create them? _____

_____

_____

_____

3. What must be done before the **PAPER** button on the status bar can be used? ___

_____

_____

4. What is the purpose of the **MAXACTVP** system variable? What is its maximum value?

_____

_____

_____

5. Identify the command that creates one or more floating viewports. What must be done before this command can be used? _____

_____

_____

6. Which keyboard combination is used to toggle between multiple floating viewports?

_____

_____

7. What is the purpose of the **ZOOM XP** option and what does "XP" mean? _____

_____

_____

_____

8. How does the **VPLAYER** command differ from the **LAYER** command? _____

_____

_____

_____

9. What is the purpose of the **VPLAYER Vpvisdflt** option? _____

_____

_____

_____

10. Why is it a good idea to turn off the contents of some floating viewports? Which command is used to do so? _____

_____

_____

_____

Chapter Problems

1. Begin a new drawing using the **Advanced Setup** wizard and select a C-size title block. Externally reference Problem 4 from *Chapter 12* and pick a point in the middle of the floating viewport as the insertion point. Accept the defaults for scale and rotation. Use the correct **ZOOM XP** value to scale the viewport. Stretch the viewport border to reduce its size and position the transistor as shown below. Complete the title block information and add annotation as desired. Freeze the Viewport layer before plotting. Save the drawing as P17-1.

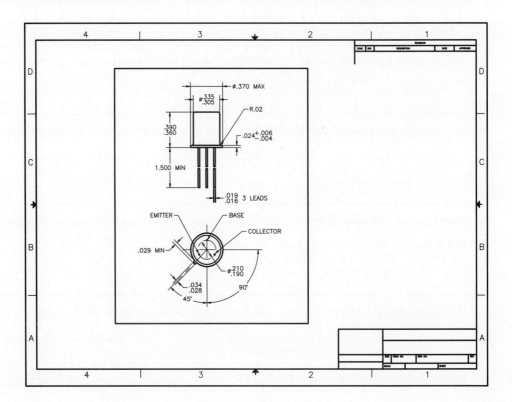

2. Once again, begin a new drawing using the **Advanced Setup** wizard and select a C-size title block. Externally reference Problem 5 of *Chapter 6* at full scale into the floating viewport. Use 0,0 as the insertion point. Perform a **ZOOM Extents** and then use the correct **ZOOM XP** value to scale the viewport. Stretch the viewport border to reduce its size and position the floor plan as shown below. Complete the title block information and add annotation as desired. Freeze the Viewport layer before plotting. Save the drawing as P17-2.

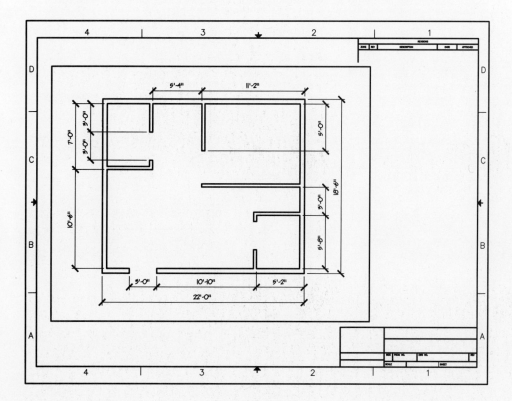

AutoCAD LT—Fundamentals and Applications

Chapter 18

AutoCAD LT   Command Aliases, Script Files, and Slide Shows

Learning Objectives

After you have completed this chapter, you will be able to:
- ○ Edit the aclt.pgp file to create command aliases.
- ○ Write a script file using the Windows Notepad or WordPad text editors.
- ○ Make and view slides of AutoCAD LT drawings and create a running slide show.
- ○ Create a slide library using the **SLIDELIB** command.

As you become more experienced with AutoCAD LT , you will want to modify the program to suit your personal tastes and needs. *Command aliasing* allows you to define your own abbreviated command names using an ordinary text editor.

A text editor is also used in the creation of script files. A *script file* is a set of AutoCAD LT commands automatically executed in sequence. In this chapter, you will learn how to create your own command aliases and script files. You will also learn how to create slide files, slide shows, and slide libraries.

Text Editors

Text editor programs write ASCII *(American Standard Code for Information Interchange)* text files. In the Microsoft Windows 95, 98, and NT operating systems, the Notepad program provides a convenient method of creating script files. While Notepad is quite capable of performing most of the text editing tasks appropriate for AutoCAD LT, it cannot accommodate files exceeding 50K (50,000 bytes) in size.

There are also a variety of commercial text editors available. The more powerful text editors are called *programmer's editors.* Programmer's editors usually feature sophisticated search and find, cut and copy, and word wrap functions. TextPad, from Helios Software Solutions, is one example of an excellent programmer's editor.

Word Processors

You can also use a word processing program to create text files. The WordPad program is a text editor for short documents that is included with Microsoft Windows 98, 95, and NT. You can format documents in WordPad with various font and paragraph styles. Like Notepad, WordPad may be accessed by clicking the Start button on the Windows taskbar, then selecting Programs from the Start menu and opening the Accessories folder. See **Figure 18-1.** Other Windows-compatible programs include Ami Pro, WordPerfect, and Microsoft Word for Windows.

Figure 18-1.
Both the Notepad
ASCII text editor
and the WordPad
word processor can
be accessed from
the Accessories
folder after selecting
Programs from the
Start menu. The
Windows 98
desktop is shown.

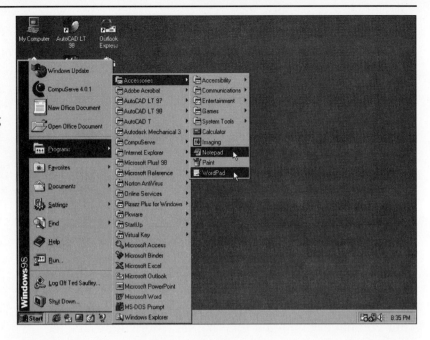

While most commercial word processing programs are excellent tools for producing written documentation, their capabilities exceed what is required to create text files for AutoCAD LT. However, if you use a word processor, be sure to save the file in ASCII format so that it is readable by AutoCAD LT.

PROFESSIONAL TIP

When working in Windows, use Notepad to create or edit text files smaller than 50,000 bytes. If the file you are working with exceeds this size, edit the file with WordPad and use the Save As function to save the file as a text document (in ASCII format).

Using MS-DOS Prompt

One of the advantages of using multitasking operating systems like Windows 98, 95, or NT is the ability to have an application open in one window while working in another window. This allows you to edit a text file without exiting AutoCAD LT. Many of the text files you create will be designed and then applied while running AutoCAD LT.

There are times when it is convenient to run a non-Windows application without exiting AutoCAD LT. This capability is provided with a Windows application called MS-DOS Prompt. You can access MS-DOS Prompt by opening the Programs folder in the Start menu, **Figure 18-2.**

After MS-DOS Prompt is selected, you are presented with a prompt similar to that shown in **Figure 18-3.** By pressing [Alt]+[Enter], you can toggle between the window shown and a full screen display.

You can now use DOS commands or run a non-Windows application when you are ready to exit MS-DOS Prompt, simply type EXIT and press [Enter].

Figure 18-2.
MS-DOS Prompt is located in the Programs folder.

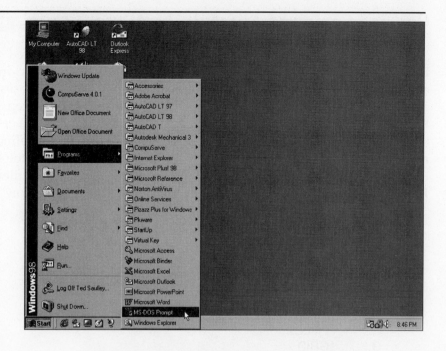

Figure 18-3.
The MS-DOS Prompt window. Press [Alt]+[Enter] to toggle between the window and a full screen display.

PROFESSIONAL TIP

Be sure to save your drawing before using MS-DOS Prompt. This will ensure that no work is lost in case your computer should "crash" while you are temporarily exited from AutoCAD LT. Keep in mind that certain DOS commands cannot be used when running MS-DOS Prompt. These commands include UNDELETE and CHKDSK with the /F switch. Also, never use disk compression and optimization programs when running MS-DOS Prompt.

Creating Command Aliases—The **ACLT.PGP** File

As discussed earlier in this chapter, you can create abbreviated command names in AutoCAD LT. Many predefined command aliases have been introduced where appropriate throughout this text. These predefined command aliases are contained in a file called aclt.pgp (program parameters), which is located in the **Program Files\AutoCAD LT 98** folder. For users of AutoCAD LT 97, the aclt.pgp file is located in the Program Files\AutoCAD LT 97 folder. The command aliases defined in aclt.pgp are automatically loaded into the current drawing session when AutoCAD LT is started.

You can display the contents of aclt.pgp by opening the file in Notepad. See **Figure 18-4.** A small sample of the command aliases is given below.

E,	*ERASE
ED,	*DDEDIT
EL,	*ELLIPSE
EM,	*DDEMODES
EX,	*EXTEND
EXIT,	*QUIT
EXP,	*EXPORT
F,	*FILLET
G,	*GRID
GR,	*DDGRIPS

You can create your own command aliases by editing the aclt.pgp file using Notepad or some other ASCII text editor. You may recall that Notepad was used in *Chapter 13* as a means to add a customized hatch pattern to the aclt.pat file. It was used again in *Chapter 15* to create a template file for attribute extraction. If necessary, refer to those chapters to refresh your memory on the use of Notepad.

Figure 18-4.
Command aliases for AutoCAD LT are listed in the aclt.pgp file, which can be opened in the Windows Notepad program.

PROFESSIONAL TIP

Always make backup copies of text files (such as aclt.lin, aclt.pat, and aclt.pgp) before editing them. If you corrupt one of these files through incorrect editing techniques, simply delete the file and restore the original.

AutoCAD LT—Fundamentals and Applications

From the previous examples, observe that an asterisk precedes the command name. This tells AutoCAD LT that the character string is an alias. Since each command alias uses a small amount of memory, you should keep the number of aliases to a minimum if your computer has little memory.

AutoCAD LT already provides the command alias **DCE** for the **DIMCENTER** command. If you wanted to create a shorter alias for **DIMCENTER**, use the following procedure. First, position your cursor between the **DIMBASELINE** and existing **DIMCENTER** command aliases in the aclt.pgp file. Then, enter the following:

    DC,   *DIMCENTER

Keep in mind that the revised.pgp file will not work until you exit AutoCAD LT and reenter the program, which reloads the aclt.pgp file. You can also reload the aclt.pgp file by entering REINIT at the Command: prompt. This displays the **Re-initialization** dialog box. See **Figure 18-5**. Activating the **PGP File** check box and then clicking the **OK** button re-initializes the aclt.pgp file so that your new command alias(es) will work.

Figure 18-5.
The **Re-initialization** dialog box allows you to reload the aclt.pgp file without exiting AutoCAD LT.

NOTE

The **Re-initialization** dialog box can also be used if you have one of your serial ports, such as COM1, configured for a plotter and a digitizer. If you physically change the cable from plotter to digitizer, click the **Digitizer** check boxes in both areas of the dialog box and then select **OK**. The digitizer will be re-initialized. If you are using a mouse instead of a digitizer, the two **Digitizer** check boxes will be grayed out. See *Chapter 23* to learn more about digitizers and how to calibrate the digitizer tablet.

EXERCISE 18-1

Obtain the permission of your instructor or supervisor before performing this exercise.
❑ Make a backup copy of aclt.pgp.
❑ Use Notepad to add the shortened **DIMCENTER** command alias as previously described.
❑ Define an alias for the **RAY** command. Make sure that your new alias does not conflict with an existing one.
❑ Save the file and exit Notepad. Start AutoCAD LT and test your two new command aliases.

As discussed earlier in this chapter, a script file is a set of AutoCAD LT commands that are automatically executed in sequence. The script file can be created with Notepad or any other ASCII text editor, but it must be given a .scr file extension. The example that appears below, csetup.scr, can be used to begin a new C-size drawing.

LIMITS 0,0 22,17	*Sets the limits to C-size*
SNAP .5	*Sets the snap spacing to .5 units*
GRID SNAP	*Sets the grid spacing equal to the snap spacing*
ZOOM ALL	*Zooms to the new limits*
	Blank line

Although a script file can contain several commands per line, it is good practice to put one command on each line. This makes the file easier to *debug* if the script does not run correctly. For this same reason, try to avoid using command aliases and single-letter command options.

When creating a script file, you can use lowercase or uppercase letters. However, be sure to put a space between the command and its option, as shown in the example. Just as you must press [Enter] after entering a command, you must also press [Enter] after typing each line of the script file. The blank line at the end of the script file is interpreted as an [Enter] and ensures that the **ZOOM** command is executed.

If you wish to add comments to your script file, you can do so by placing a semi-colon (;) at the start of the line. These lines are ignored when the script file is run.

CAUTION

Commands that use dialog boxes will not work in a script file. If the script file is to open or close files, be sure to set the **FILEDIA** system variable to 0 to disable the file dialog boxes. If you are automating plotting procedures, turn the **CMDDIA** system variable off. This variable controls the display of the **Print/Plot Configuration** dialog box. See *Chapter 14* for more information about plotting.

Running the Script File

SCRIPT
SCR

Tools
➡ Run Script...

Once the script file is complete, it is run within AutoCAD LT using the **SCRIPT** command. Select **Run Script...** from the **Tools** pull-down menu, **Figure 18-6,** or enter the following at the Command: prompt:

Command: **SCRIPT** *or* **SCR**↵

The **Select Script File** dialog box is displayed, **Figure 18-7.** In the example shown, the Csetup.scr file is selected from the file list. Click the **Open** button to exit the dialog box and execute the script file one line at a time. Each one of the commands in the script file appears in the command line window as the file is run.

Figure 18-6.
The **SCRIPT** command can be issued by selecting **Run Script...** from the **Tools** pull-down menu.

Figure 18-7.
The **Select Script File** dialog box.

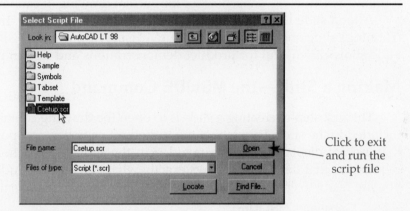

Click to exit and run the script file

Script Commands

The commands listed below are used in association with script files. With the exception of the **RSCRIPT** command, each can be invoked transparently by preceding the command with an apostrophe (**'TEXTSCR,** for example). The following is an explanation of each script command:

- **DELAY.** This command delays the execution of the next script command for a specified amount of time (in milliseconds). For example, DELAY 2000 delays execution of the next script command by about two seconds. The longest value allowed is 32767, which creates a delay of slightly less than 33 seconds.
- **RESUME.** This command resumes an interrupted script file.
- **RSCRIPT.** This command repeats a script from its beginning.
- **TEXTSCR.** The text window is displayed when this command is entered.
- **GRAPHSCR.** The text window flips back to the graphics window when this command is entered.

You can pause execution of a script file by pressing the [Backspace] key. Enter RESUME at the Command: prompt to start the script file where it left off. To restart the script file from its beginning, use the **RSCRIPT** command instead. Press the [ESC] key to cancel a running script file.

EXERCISE 18-2

❏ Use Notepad to write a script file named myscript.scr. The script file should do the following:
  ❏ Set the current color to green.
  ❏ Construct a circumscribed hexagon (a six-sided polygon) at coordinates 6,4 with a radius of 2 units.
  ❏ Change the current color to cyan.
  ❏ Draw a circle with a radius of 1.5 units centered on the hexagon.
❏ Start AutoCAD LT and use the **SCRIPT** command to run myscript.scr.
❏ If the script file does not run correctly or stops before completion, use Notepad to correct it. Run the script file again until it works.
❏ Save the drawing as EX18-2.

Slide Files and Slide Shows

A *slide file* is a raster image of the drawing window display. It is not a drawing itself; it is only a picture, or "snapshot," of the current drawing. It cannot be edited or plotted.

After a slide file has been made, it can be viewed in any drawing. A continuous (running) slide show can be viewed by displaying multiple slide files in sequence. Slide shows are useful for product demonstrations and design proposals.

Making a Slide—the MSLIDE Command

The first step in creating a slide is to open the drawing containing the objects to be included in the slide. Layers that are turned off or frozen and portions of the drawing that are not displayed are not included in the slide. Adjust the drawing window as required so that the display shows exactly what you want included in the slide. When you are ready to create the slide, enter the following at the Command: prompt:

MSLIDE

Command: **MSLIDE**↵

The **Create Slide File** dialog box is then displayed. See **Figure 18-8.** Slides are automatically given the file extension .sld. Also, the slide file name defaults to the current drawing name. If you wish to enter a different name, do so by entering the new name in the **File name:** text box.

When you are finished, pick the **Save** button. The slide file is created and the Command: prompt reappears.

The **MSLIDE** command makes a slide file from the current viewport only if you are working in model space. In paper space, **MSLIDE** makes a slide file of the entire paper space display, including all floating viewports and their contents.

Figure 18-8.
The **Create Slide File** dialog box. Unless otherwise specified, the slide file name defaults to the current drawing name.

Name of slide file to be saved

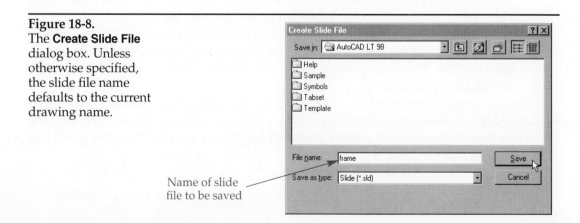

Viewing a Slide—the VSLIDE Command

Once you have created a slide, it can be displayed for viewing. Enter the following at the Command: prompt:

Command: **VSLIDE** *or* **VS**↵

VSLIDE
VS

When the **Select Slide File** dialog box appears, select a slide file from the file list and click **Open**. See **Figure 18-9.** The slide file you select remains displayed until you enter REDRAW or REGEN at the Command: prompt, or until you use one of the **ZOOM** or **PAN** command options.

Figure 18-9.
A slide file is
selected for viewing
using the **Select
Slide File** dialog box.

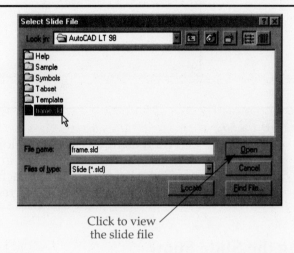

Click to view
the slide file

Making a Slide Show

A slide show can be viewed by creating a script file that displays multiple slide files in sequence. The speed at which slide files are displayed is a function of the number of disk accesses required to read the file. To expedite the process, you can preload a slide file into memory with a script file command that follows the command for display of the previously viewed slide. This is accomplished by placing an asterisk (*) before the slide file name.

An example of a typical slide show script file, Details.scr, is shown in **Figure 18-10.** A line-by-line explanation is given below. In this example, five slides have been created from the detail drawings used in the *Chapter 17* paper space tutorial. Note how the **VSLIDE** and **DELAY** commands are used in the script file.

VSLIDE Frame	*Begin the slide show by loading the* Frame *slide*
VSLIDE *Wheel	*Preload the* Wheel *slide*
DELAY 3000	*Let the audience view the* Frame *slide*
VSLIDE	*Display the* Wheel *slide*
VSLIDE *Shaft	*Preload the* Shaft *slide*
DELAY 3000	*Let the audience view the* Wheel *slide*
VSLIDE	*Display the* Shaft *slide*
VSLIDE *Collar	*Preload the* Collar *slide*
DELAY 3000	*Let the audience view the* Shaft *slide*
VSLIDE	*Display the* Collar *slide*
VSLIDE *Pin	*Preload the* Pin *slide*
DELAY 3000	*Let the audience view the* Collar *slide*
VSLIDE	*Display the* Pin *slide*
DELAY 3000	*Let the audience view the* Pin *slide*
RSCRIPT	*Repeat the slide show until canceled with* [ESC]

Figure 18-10.
The sequence of script commands making up the Details.scr slide show script file.

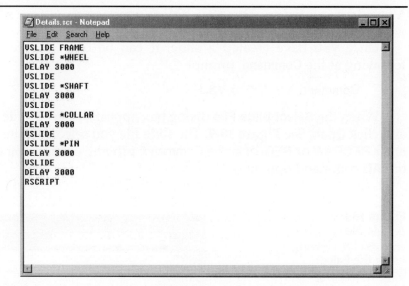

```
Details.scr - Notepad
File  Edit  Search  Help
VSLIDE FRAME
VSLIDE *WHEEL
DELAY 3000
VSLIDE
VSLIDE *SHAFT
DELAY 3000
VSLIDE
VSLIDE *COLLAR
DELAY 3000
VSLIDE
VSLIDE *PIN
DELAY 3000
VSLIDE
DELAY 3000
RSCRIPT
```

PROFESSIONAL TIP

When using slide files on floppy disks, be sure to include the disk drive letter and path in front of the slide file name (for example, A:Frame.sld). Each **VSLIDE** command in the script file must include the correct path.

Viewing the Slide Show

After completing the script file, the slide show can be viewed. Issue the **SCRIPT** command to open the **Select Script File** dialog box. Then, select the script file and click **Open** to begin the show.

EXERCISE 18-3

❑ Use the **MSLIDE** command to create slide files of the five detail drawings from the *Chapter 17* paper space tutorial. If you did not complete the tutorial, select five other drawings of your choice.

❑ Using Notepad, create the script file Details.scr as described above. Be sure to press [Enter] after the **RSCRIPT** command to ensure that the script file is repeated. Place the script file and the slide files in the Program Files\AutoCAD LT 98 folder. If you are using AutoCAD LT 97 place them in the Program Files\AutoCAD LT 97 folder.

❑ Use the **SCRIPT** command to run the slide show.

❑ Edit the script file and experiment with different delay times.

Creating a Slide Library—the **SLIDELIB** Utility Program

You can create a library of slide files using the slidelib.exe utility program, which is supplied with AutoCAD LT. The library is saved with a name of your choice and is automatically given a .slb file extension.

Before you create the slide library, you must first create a list of the slides to appear in the library. Since the slide list must be saved with a .txt file extension, use an ASCII text editor, such as Notepad.

A list of the caster details used in the previous script file example can be entered in a file called Details.txt. The list would appear in the text editor as follows:

```
Frame.sld
Wheel.sld
Shaft.sld
Collar.sld
Pin.sld
```

After completing the slide list file, use the **SLIDELIB** command to make the slide library. The slidelib.exe program is located in the Program Files\AutoCAD LT 98 folder. If you are using AutoCAD LT 97 it is located in the Program Files\AutoCAD LT 97 folder. Be sure to place the Details.txt file in the same folder so the slidelib utility can find it to create the slide library. Since the slide list represents the detail drawings required for a caster assembly, an appropriate slide library name would be Caster.slb.

The slidelib utility must be executed at the DOS prompt, so it cannot be used within AutoCAD LT. However, it can be used from the MS-DOS Prompt window. Keep in mind that MS-DOS cannot accommodate names longer than eight characters for files or folders. Therefore, some folder and file names will appear truncated in the MS-DOS Prompt window. As an example, the Program Files folder might appear as PROGRA~1, while the AutoCAD LT 98 folder might appear as AUTOCA~1.

Once you are in the MS-DOS Prompt window, enter the DIR command to verify the correct folder names on your particular workstation. Then, using the appropriate folder names, enter the following to switch to the AutoCAD LT 98 folder and create the slide library:

```
C:\WINDOWS⟩ CD \PROGRA~1\AUTOCA~1.⌐
C:\Program Files\AutoCAD LT 98⟩SLIDELIB CASTER ⟨ DETAILS.TXT.⌐
SLIDELIB 1.2 (3/8/89)
(C) Copyright 1987-1989,1994,1995 Autodesk, Inc.
    All Rights Reserved
C:\Program Files\AutoCAD LT 98⟩ EXIT.⌐
```

In the example above, the less-than sign (⟨) instructs the slidelib utility to take its input from the Details.txt slide list to create a file called Caster.slb. To display a slide from the slide library, you must first disable the **Select Slide File** dialog box using the **FILEDIA** system variable:

```
Command: FILEDIA.⌐
New value for FILEDIA ⟨1⟩: 0.⌐
Command:
```

Now, issue the **VSLIDE** command and enter the library file name and the slide file name. The following format is used when prompted for the file names after entering VSLIDE at the Command: prompt:

```
LIBRARY NAME(SLIDE NAME)
```

Enter any one of the five detail drawings saved as a slide file. As an example, enter the following to display the Wheel slide from the Caster slide library:

```
Command: VSLIDE.⌐
Slide file ⟨Drawing⟩: CASTER(WHEEL).⌐
Command:
```

When you are through viewing slides, be sure to set the **FILEDIA** system variable back to 1 (on). This will re-enable the display of all dialog boxes.

Updating the Slide Library

It is possible that slides will be added or deleted from a slide list over a period of time. However, the slide library is not automatically updated. You must revise the slide list file and then recreate the slide library.

Using the Slide Library to Make a Slide Show

It is more efficient to create a slide show from a slide library (rather than from a basic script file) because there is no need to preload slides. Compare the following script file, which uses a slide library, to the Details.scr script file created earlier in this chapter:

```
VSLIDE Caster(Frame)
DELAY 2000
VSLIDE Caster(Wheel)
DELAY 2000
VSLIDE Caster(Shaft)
DELAY 2000
VSLIDE Caster(Collar)
DELAY 2000
VSLIDE Caster(Pin)
DELAY 2000
RSCRIPT
```

Since slides do not have to be preloaded, delay times can be shortened. The **RSCRIPT** command repeats the slide show until canceled. Use the **REDRAW** command at the end of the script file if you want to run the show once and then clear the screen and replace the previous display.

Chapter Test

Write your answers in the spaces provided.

1. What is the purpose of a script file? _____
   _____
   _____
   _____

2. Name the file that contains the AutoCAD LT command aliases._____
   _____
   _____

3. If you use a word processing program to create a script file, in what format must the file be saved? _____
   _____
   _____

4. What is the maximum file size (in bytes) that can be handled by the Windows Notepad program?_____
   _____
   _____

5. *True or False?* New command aliases can be used immediately after the aclt.pgp file is edited. _____

6. Identify the command that allows you to use a revised aclt.pgp file without restarting AutoCAD LT. _____
_____
_____

7. *True or False?* All DOS commands and program utilities may be executed from MS-DOS Prompt. _____

8. What must you do to place a comment in a script file? _____
_____
_____
_____

9. *True or False?* Dialog boxes may be used with a script file. _____

10. What is the purpose of the **RSCRIPT** command in a script file? _____
_____
_____

11. Which key should you press to interrupt a running script? _____
_____

12. Identify the two commands used to create and view slide files. _____
_____

13. *True or False?* A slide file cannot be edited. _____

14. Identify the utility program that creates a slide library. Where is this program located? _____
_____
_____

15. List all of the required steps to view a slide named DESK contained in a slide library named OFFICE. _____
_____
_____
_____

Chapter Problems

1. Write a script file named P18-1.scr that does the following:
   A. Sets the limits to A-size and zooms to the new limits.
   B. Sets the grid spacing to 1 unit and the snap spacing to .5 units.
   C. Changes the current color to blue.
   D. Draws a 6 × 4 rectangle with the first corner of the rectangle at 3,2.
   E. Sets the current color to red.
   F. Uses the **TEXT** command to create the character string THE END in the middle of the rectangle with a text height of .75 units.

General

2. Create a group of slides that are related to your professional discipline or field of interest. The slides could feature electronic components, such as resistors, capacitors, and diodes. An architectural collection could include doors, windows, and bath fixtures. As you create the drawings for the slides, label each drawing with descriptive text. After the slide files are saved, create a slide list file. Use the slidelib utility to produce a slide library and create a script file to run the slide show. Name the script file P18-2.SCR.

AutoCAD LT

Chapter **19**

Introduction to 3D Modeling

Learning Objectives

After you have completed this chapter, you will be able to:

- ○ Use the **UCSICON** command to control the display of the UCS icon.
- ○ Identify the various model space UCS icon representations and match them with the viewing angles they depict.
- ○ Use the **VPOINT** command to establish 3D views.
- ○ Describe elevation and thickness and apply both properties to objects.
- ○ Remove hidden lines and shade 3D objects.
- ○ Create and save multiple viewports in model space.
- ○ Construct 3D polyline objects using the **3DPOLY** command.
- ○ Develop and apply user-defined coordinate systems.
- ○ Control and alter 3D viewing aspects with **DVIEW**.

Although AutoCAD LT is primarily a two-dimensional (2D) design drafting tool, it can also be used to construct simple three-dimensional (3D) objects. This chapter describes the commands used to establish 3D viewing angles and construct 3D geometry. Display control functions applicable to 3D models are also introduced.

Thinking in Three Dimensions

Creating 3D geometry is not very different from creating 2D geometry. The 3D point entry methods in AutoCAD LT use the *Cartesian* coordinate system that you are already familiar with. With this system, all X, Y, and Z values are related to the drawing origin. The origin is usually at the very lower left of the drawing screen, and it is where X = 0, Y = 0, and Z = 0. Point distances are measured along the horizontal X axis and the vertical Y axis. Positive X values are to the right (east), and positive Y values are to the top (north). The Z axis is perpendicular to the screen. Positive Z values come out of the screen toward you, while negative Z values go into the screen away from you. The three axes form perpendicular planes.

The World Coordinate System vs. the User Coordinate System

The coordinate system described in the last section is fixed in 3D space and cannot be moved or altered. Because this coordinate system is universal, AutoCAD LT refers to it as the *World Coordinate System (WCS)*. Whenever a new drawing file is created in AutoCAD LT , the drawing window defaults to a single viewport that corresponds to the WCS. In this view, the user is looking down the positive Z axis onto the XY plane. This viewing angle is referred to as the *plan view*, or *plan to the WCS*. All coordinates are measured along the X and Y axes relative to the 0,0,0 drawing origin at the lower left of the screen.

An alternative to the WCS is the *User Coordinate System (UCS)*. With the UCS, a user can redefine the location of the drawing origin and the direction of the XYZ axes. While the vast majority of the 2D drawings you have created using this text have been in the WCS, several UCS options were introduced in previous chapters as a way to help construct 2D auxiliary views and perform ordinate dimensioning operations. The UCS is absolutely essential for the construction of 3D geometry. It will be discussed more fully later in this chapter.

Figure 19-1.
The model space
UCS icon. The W
above the box
indicates that the
World Coordinate
System is active.

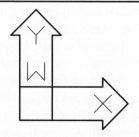

Getting Started Guide **6**

The Model Space UCS Icon

The *UCS icon* is a small graphical marker located at the lower left of the drawing window. It displays the drawing origin and the viewing plane of the current UCS in model space. The icon is shown in **Figure 19-1.** In the default representation, the X, Y, and Z axes of the UCS icon are positioned 90° relative to one another, with the Z axis perpendicular to the XY plane and along the line of sight. Notice that the icon has a box drawn at the vertices of the X and Y axes. The box indicates that the viewpoint is from the positive Z direction. Therefore, the viewing angle is from a position above the XY plane looking down. Also notice the small W just above the box. The W indicates that the World Coordinate System is active.

The **UCSICON** Command

UCSICON

View
➥ Display
  UCS icon

You can control the visibility and placement of the UCS icon using the **UCSICON** command. The **UCSICON** command options may be accessed by first selecting **Display** from the **View** pull-down menu, and then selecting **UCS Icon** from the cascading submenu. See **Figure 19-2.** You can also enter the following at the Command: prompt:

    Command: **UCSICON**↵
    ON/OFF/All/Noorigin/ORigin ⟨ON⟩: *(select an option)*
    Command:

Figure 19-2.
Clicking the **View** pull-down menu and selecting **UCS Icon** from the **Display** cascading submenu displays the **UCSICON** command options.

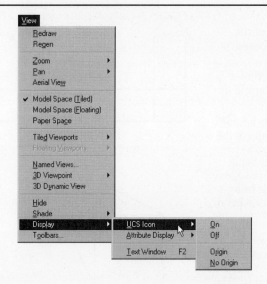

The command options allow you to decide how the UCS icon is to be displayed. The options are described as follows:

- **ON.** This option displays the UCS icon. It is the default setting.
- **OFF.** This option turns off the icon display.
- **All.** When this option is selected, changes to the icon display are shown in all viewports.
- **Noorigin.** This option displays the icon at the lower-left corner of the viewport, regardless of the current UCS definition.
- **Origin.** This option displays the icon at the origin (0,0,0) of the current UCS. If the origin of the current UCS is outside the viewing area on screen, the icon is displayed at the lower-left corner of the drawing window.

The **All** option is actually a modifier to the other **UCSICON** command options. It tells AutoCAD LT to display any changes made to the UCS icon in *all* model space viewports. When **All** is selected, the **UCSICON** command option line is redisplayed and you can then select the desired display option for all viewports. For example, suppose you want to display the UCS icon at the origin of the current UCS in four different viewports. The command sequence is as follows:

```
Command: UCSICON↵
ON/OFF/All/Noorigin/ORigin ⟨ON⟩: A↵
ON/OFF/All/Noorigin/ORigin ⟨ON⟩: OR↵
Command:
```

Other UCS Icon Representations

As you begin working in 3D, you will learn that the UCS icon can assume several different forms. See **Figure 19-3.** Each of these representations has a specific meaning for the 3D user. When the icon is displayed with a plus symbol (+), it is located at the origin of the current UCS. When a box appears in the icon, the viewing angle is from the positive Z direction, or *above* the current UCS. When no box is displayed on the icon, the viewing angle is from the negative Z direction, or *below* the current UCS. The icon assumes the appearance of a cube in perspective whenever the **Distance** option of the **DVIEW** command is enabled. The **DVIEW** command is discussed at the end of this chapter. Finally, the UCS icon appears as a "broken pencil" enclosed in a box if the viewing angle is perpendicular to the XY plane of the current UCS. While these different icon representations may be hard to understand initially, they will soon become quite familiar.

Figure 19-3.
The display of the UCS icon is based on a specific representation of the viewing angle in your drawing.

A—The icon is located at the origin of the current UCS.

B—The UCS is being viewed from above.

C—The UCS is being viewed from below.

D—Perspective viewing is on.

E—The "broken pencil" display indicates that the XY plane of the current UCS is perpendicular to the viewing plane.

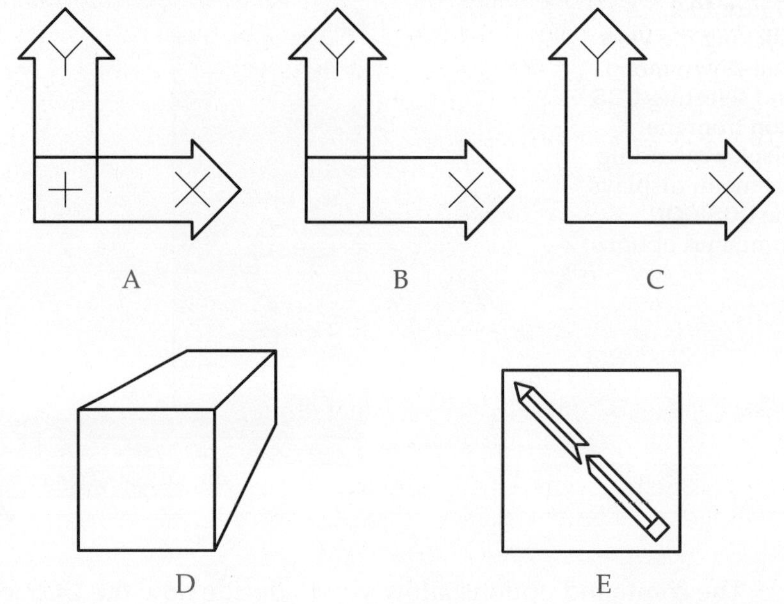

The Right-Hand Rule

The *right-hand rule* of 3D modeling is a graphic representation of the positive coordinate directions used by most 3D CAD systems. The UCS in AutoCAD LT is based on this simple concept of visualization that requires nothing more than the thumb, index finger, and middle finger on your right hand. Try positioning your hand as illustrated in **Figure 19-4.** With your right hand open in front of you, extend your thumb straight out to the right, and your index finger straight up. Keep your last two fingers curled into your palm and extend your middle finger straight toward you.

Now imagine that your thumb is the positive X axis, your index finger is the positive Y axis, and your middle finger is the positive Z axis. Think of your palm as being the 0,0,0 drawing origin. Like the axes represented by the UCS icon, the three axes formed by your thumb and first two fingers lie perpendicular to each other.

Figure 19-4.
Position your hand as shown to understand the relationship shared by the X, Y, and Z axes.

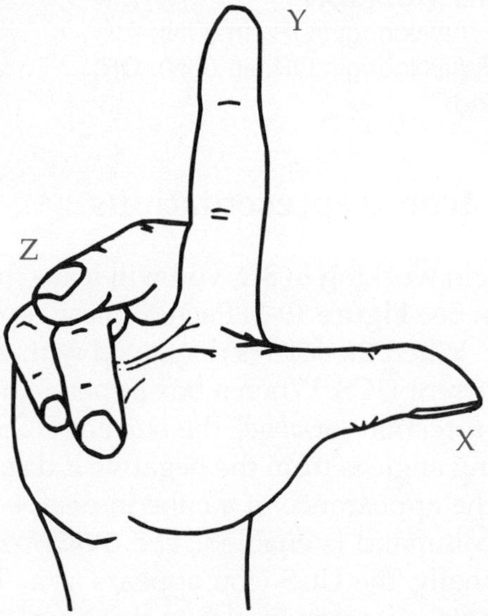

The greatest advantage of the UCS is the ability to rotate the coordinate axes to any orientation desired. You can use the right-hand rule to visualize how the UCS can be rotated about any one of the three axis lines. To rotate the X axis, for example, keep your thumb stationary and turn your hand toward or away from you. To visualize Y axis rotation, keep your index finger pointed straight up and turn your hand to the left or right. Rotation about the Z axis can be envisioned by keeping your middle finger pointed toward you and rotating your entire arm to the left or right.

Establishing a 3D Viewpoint with VPOINT

New drawing files opened in AutoCAD LT default to a single viewport where the UCS and WCS are the same, and the viewing angle is the plan view (plan to the WCS). This viewing orientation suits 2D drawing methods quite nicely, but 3D objects are more easily visualized and constructed when viewed from an angle.

Several techniques exist for establishing 3D views in AutoCAD LT , but perhaps the most common method involves the **VPOINT** (ViewPOINT) command. With **VPOINT**, a user can specify the direction that an object will be viewed from. The object itself remains fixed in 3D space. Only the line of sight changes. In other words, the *view* rotates, not the object.

The **VPOINT** command options may be selected from a cascading submenu by selecting **3D Viewpoint** from the **View** pull-down menu. See **Figure 19-5.** On the command line, enter the following:

> Command: **VPOINT** *or* **VP**↵
> Rotate/⟨View point⟩ ⟨0.0000,0.0000,1.0000⟩: *(select an option)*

| VPOINT |
| VP |
| View |
| ↦ 3D Viewpoint |

Figure 19-5.
Selecting **3D Viewpoint** from the **View** pull-down menu displays a cascading submenu of **VPOINT** command options.

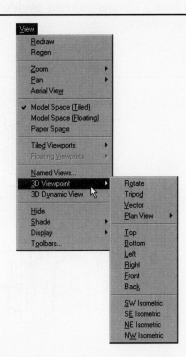

Observe that **VPOINT** offers two options on the command line for view rotation. Using the default option, which is equivalent to selecting **Vector** in the **3D Viewpoint** cascading submenu, allows you to rotate the view with XYZ coordinates. However, these coordinates are not *distance* coordinates, but rather *direction* (vector) coordinates. The default values shown above in the angle brackets describe coordinates for a plan view. They are interpreted as follows:

- **The X value is zero.** Therefore, the viewing angle is *not* along the X axis.
- **The Y value is also zero.** Therefore, the viewing angle is *not* along the Y axis.
- **The Z value is positive.** A positive Z value extends out of the screen toward the viewer. Therefore, the viewing angle is along the positive Z axis above the XY plane.

You may be confused by the Z coordinate having a numeric value equal to 1. A Z value equal to 1 does *not* mean that the viewing angle is located one unit above the object being viewed. In reality, the XYZ values used by **VPOINT** are not units of measurement at all; they are *directional* units. Thus, direction values such as 0,0,2 or 0,0,10 produce exactly the same plan view as 0,0,1.

The **VPOINT** Rotate Option

Using the **VPOINT Rotate** option allows you to define a 3D view by specifying two angles. The first angular value specified rotates the view (not the object) in the XY plane, **Figure 19-6.** The second angular value rotates the view away from the XY plane, **Figure 19-7.** The procedure for using the **Rotate** option is shown below:

Command: **VPOINT** *or* **VP**↵
Rotate/⟨View point⟩ ⟨0.0000,0.0000,1.0000⟩: **R**↵
Enter angle in XY plane from X axis ⟨*current angle*⟩: *(enter an angle)*
Enter angle from XY plane ⟨*current angle*⟩: *(enter an angle)*
Regenerating drawing.
Command:

Figure 19-6.
VPOINT rotation in the XY plane is performed about the Z axis.

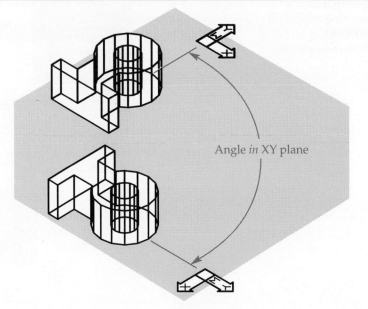

Angle *in* XY plane

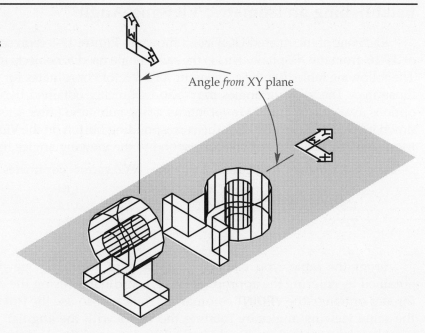

Figure 19-7.
VPOINT rotation from the XY plane is performed about the X axis.

Angle *from* XY plane

To visualize the direction of rotation in the XY plane, refer to **Figure 19-8**. Starting at the upper-left viewport and moving in a clockwise direction, the XY plane is rotated 45°, 135°, 225°, and finally 315°. From the right-hand rule, you will see that all rotation in the XY plane is done about the Z axis.

On the other hand, angles measured *from* the XY plane are rotated about the X axis. Using the right-hand rule, rotate your hand *away* from you so that your thumb, index finger, and palm are in a horizontal position (parallel to the floor), and your middle finger (the Z axis) is pointed straight up. In this orientation, the XY plane is considered to be at 0°. Slowly return your hand once more into a vertical position so that your middle finger is once again pointed toward you. You can now see that rotation from the XY plane is performed about the X axis (your thumb). Since the direction of rotation is positive, the angle from the XY plane is now 90°. Continue rotating your hand so that your index finger, the Y axis, is pointed straight at you. In this orientation, the angle from the XY plane is 180°.

Figure 19-8.
Establishing a view orientation using angular rotation in the XY plane. Clockwise from the upper-left viewport: XY rotation = 45°, XY rotation = 135°, XY rotation = 225°, XY rotation = 315°.

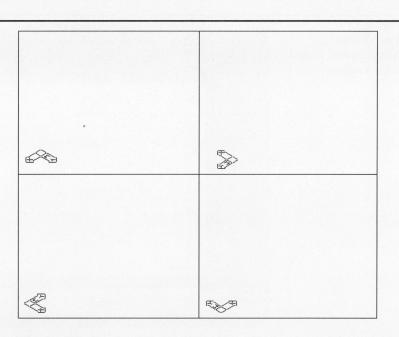

Establishing an Isometric Viewing Angle

Each one of the rotated UCS icons shown in **Figure 19-8** represents a rotation angle of 35°16′ from the XY plane. This is the same angle used for objects in an isometric view. The following table lists the equivalent XYZ vector coordinates for the viewing angles illustrated. The viewing angles may also be quickly obtained by using the **Isometric** options available in the **3D Viewpoint** cascading submenu (after selecting the **View** pull-down menu). You can also click the corresponding button on the **Viewpoint** toolbar. The four isometric viewing options correspond to the viewing angles listed below:

Angle in XY plane	Angle from XY plane	XYZ vector coordinates	Viewing option
45°	35°16′	1,1,1	**NE Isometric**
135°	35°16′	–1,1,1	**NW Isometric**
225°	35°16′	–1,–1,1	**SW Isometric**
315°	35°16′	1,–1,1	**SE Isometric**

From the table, you can see that the four isometric viewing angles can be obtained by entering the appropriate XYZ coordinates (using the default vector coordinates option of the **VPOINT** command). You can also use the **Rotate** option to obtain the same viewing angles by rotating the views with the angular values shown (use proper values for both the angle *in* the XY plane and the angle *from* the XY plane). If you use the second method, you can specify 35°16′ on the command line by entering 35d16′. However, the simplest way to establish an isometric viewing angle is to select the **View** pull-down menu and use one of the four **Isometric** viewing options that appear in the **3D Viewpoint** cascading submenu.

The VPOINT Compass and Tripod Axes

Another quick and easy way to define a 3D viewing angle is to use the **VPOINT** "axes and compass" display. To use this method, click the **View** pull-down menu and then select **Tripod** from the **3D Viewpoint** cascading submenu, or simply press [Enter] after issuing the **VPOINT** command. Whichever method is used, the axes and compass display appears in the drawing window. See **Figure 19-9.** The compass display represents the north and south poles and the equator. For this reason, the compass is sometimes referred to as the "globe icon."

Figure 19-9.
The **VPOINT** compass and tripod axes display.

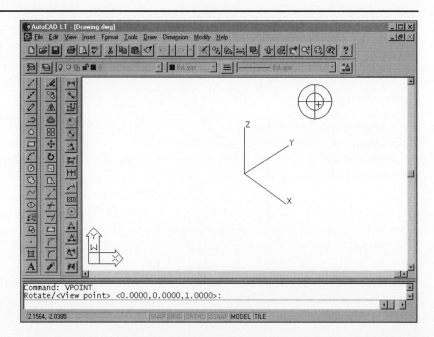

The very center of the compass represents the north pole, the small circle represents the equator, and the large circle represents the south pole. The normal graphics cursor changes to a very small crosshair cursor, as shown within the compass. The cursor controls the movement of the tripod axes. By positioning the cursor within one of the compass quadrants and clicking with the pick button on your pointing device, a 3D view is created. Clicking inside any one of the four inner (north pole) quadrants places the viewing angle *above* the XY plane. In this view, you are looking down on the object. Clicking inside any one of the four outer (south pole) quadrants places the viewing angle *below* the XY plane. In this view, you are looking up at the object.

Notice that the compass is bisected along both the horizontal and vertical axes. Positioning the cursor *below* the horizontal axis places the viewer in front of the object. Positioning the cursor *above* the horizontal axis places the viewer behind the object. In similar fashion, the vertical axis controls the viewing angle from left or right. By positioning the cursor to the *left* of the vertical axis, the object is viewed from the left side. When the cursor is positioned to the *right* of the vertical axis, the object is viewed from the right side. A top view, or plan view, can be established by turning the **Snap** mode on and placing the cursor at the precise intersection of the horizontal and vertical axes.

Just to the left and below the compass are the tripod axes. The motion of the tripod axes follows the principles of the right-hand rule. See **Figure 19-10.** As you move your pointing device about the compass, the tripod axes revolve to reflect the view orientation.

Figure 19-10.
The **VPOINT** tripod axes illustrate the principles of the right-hand rule.

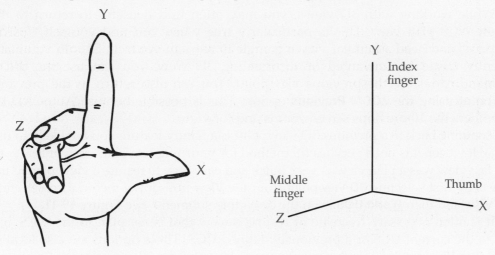

Saving the 3D View

It is always a good idea to save the view you select so that you can easily return to it at any time without reissuing the **VPOINT** command. Views, whether in 2D or 3D, are saved with names using either the **DDVIEW** or **VIEW** commands introduced in *Chapter 4.* As with other named objects in AutoCAD LT , a view name may contain up to 31 characters, but no spaces or punctuation marks are permitted.

Remember you can save as many views as needed. The views can be restored or deleted as necessary. Since you may occasionally forget the names of saved views, they can be listed for quick reference. This option is particularly handy when you find yourself working with a drawing file that was created some time ago, or with a file created by another user.

DDVIEW
V

View
➥ Named Views...

Standard
Toolbar

Named Views

Views can be saved, restored, listed, and deleted using the **View Control** dialog box. This dialog box is accessed by clicking the **Named Views** button on the **Standard Toolbar**, selecting **Named Views...** from the **View** pull-down menu, or entering DDVIEW, or V, at the Command: prompt. If you do not wish to use a dialog box, you can issue the **VIEW** command:

Command: **VIEW** *or* **-V**↵
?/Delete/Restore/Save/Window: *(select an option)*

The **VIEW** command options allow you to define and manipulate views on the command line. The options are discussed below:

- **?.** This option allows you to list all saved views in the **AutoCAD LT Text Window.** An M (for model space) or a P (for paper space) appears next to each view name in the list to indicate how the view was defined.
- **Delete.** This option is used to remove one or more defined views. Multiple view names must be separated by commas.
- **Restore.** This option displays a saved view in the current viewport.
- **Save.** This option allows you to name and save the current viewport display. Unlike the **DDVIEW** command, however, no warning is issued if a view is saved with the same name of an existing view.
- **Window.** Selecting this option enables you to define a view with two diagonal points. The view is named and saved, but it is not displayed until the **Restore** option is used.

Restoring the Plan View with the PLAN Command

While working with 3D views, you may often find it useful to return to the default WCS plan view. This is particularly true when you find yourself "lost in 3D space" and need a familiar viewing angle to reorient yourself. Should you inadvertently create an unwanted or disorienting 3D view, you can use the **UNDO** command to restore the previous viewpoint. You can also return to the previous viewpoint using the **ZOOM Previous** option. This is possible because AutoCAD LT remembers the 10 previous screen zooms and/or views.

Zooming back to a previous 3D viewpoint is a handy feature you are likely to use often. However, it is not a very useful method for returning to a plan view unless your very last view was a plan view. A very quick and easy way to restore a view plan to the WCS is by first selecting **3D Viewpoint** from the **View** pull-down menu, then selecting **Plan View** and then **World UCS** from the cascading submenu. See **Figure 19-11.**

PLAN

View
➥ 3D Viewpoint
  ➥ Plan View

It is often necessary to create or restore a view that is *not* plan to the WCS, but plan to the current UCS or a previously defined UCS. These options are also located in the **Plan View** cascading submenu. You can also enter the following at the Command: prompt:

Command: **PLAN**↵
⟨Current UCS⟩/Ucs/World: *(select an option or accept the default)*

The **PLAN** command allows you to define or restore a view at the command line. The command options are described below:

- ⟨**Current UCS**⟩. The default option creates or restores a view that is plan to the current UCS (where X = 0, Y = 0, and Z = 1). If no UCS has been defined, this option restores the plan view of the WCS because the UCS is the same as the WCS in this case.
- **Ucs.** This option allows you to define a plan view or restore the plan view of a previously defined UCS.
- **World.** This option restores the plan view of the WCS.

Figure 19-11.
Selecting **3D Viewpoint** from the **View** pull-down menu and then selecting **Plan View** displays the **PLAN** command options in a cascading submenu.

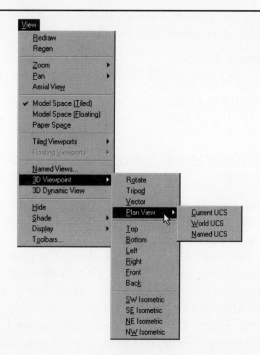

Elevation and Thickness

Every object created in AutoCAD LT , whether it is 2D or 3D, has a Z value. The *elevation* of an object is the Z value of the XY plane that it was constructed on. By default, the base XY plane has a Z value of zero. Thus, all objects created in AutoCAD LT have zero elevation. A positive elevation creates objects *above* the base XY plane, while a negative elevation creates objects *below* the XY plane. Therefore, an object's elevation is simply the height of the object above or below the plane of construction.

Object elevation is illustrated by the three circles shown in **Figure 19-12.** The three circles all have the same diameter, and each one has the same center point on the XY plane. However, the circle in the middle has a default base elevation of zero. The circle on top has an elevation of 4, which places it 4 units *above* the middle circle. The circle at the bottom has an elevation of –4, which places it 4 units *below* the middle circle.

Figure 19-12.
Elevation is the height, or depth, of an object above or below the base XY plane.

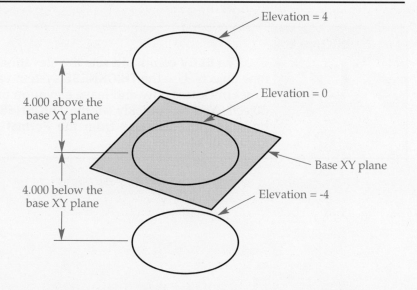

Changing the system base elevation, or Z value, is performed with the **ELEV** command. The sequence is as follows:

Command: **ELEV⏎**
New current elevation ⟨0.0000⟩: *(enter a positive or negative value)*

After specifying a value for the elevation, you are then prompted to enter a thickness value. Like the elevation value, the object thickness can be a positive or negative value:

New current thickness ⟨0.0000⟩: *(enter a positive or negative value)*
Command:

Thickness is a property of an object, just as color, layer, linetype scale, and linetype are object properties. Objects with thickness are often called *extrusions*. A thickness value sets the distance that a 2D object is "extruded" above or below its elevation. A positive value extrudes along the positive Z axis and a negative value extrudes along the negative Z axis. This is illustrated by the three circles shown in **Figure 19-13.** As you can see, an object with zero thickness is strictly two-dimensional. Also from the illustration, notice the lines connecting the two circles with thickness. These lines are called *tessalation lines*. AutoCAD LT creates them automatically along the curved surfaces of an extrusion to help you visualize its location and curvature.

Figure 19-13.
Thickness values set the distance that 2D objects are extruded above or below their elevation.

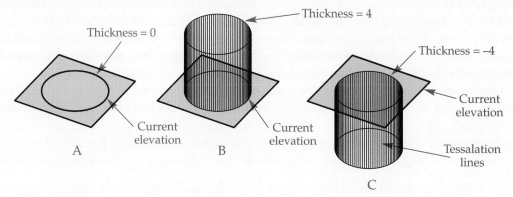

PROFESSIONAL TIP

The **ELEV** command sets the elevation and thickness for new objects. Use the **THICKNESS** system variable if you wish to set thickness only and leave elevation unchanged for new objects. You can quickly set the **THICKNESS** system variable by selecting **Thickness** from the **Format** pull-down menu, **Figure 19-14.**

Figure 19-14.
The **THICKNESS**
system variable can
be quickly changed
by selecting
Thickness from the
Format pull-down
menu.

Changing the Thickness of Existing Objects

Just as other object properties can be modified in AutoCAD LT, thicknesses can be edited, or added to existing objects, using the **CHPROP** and **DDCHPROP** commands. Use the **CHPROP** command as follows:

Command: **CHPROP**↵
Select objects: *(select one or more objects to change)*
Change what property (Color/LAyer/LType/ltScale/Thickness)? **T**↵
New thickness ⟨*current value*⟩: *(enter a positive or negative value and press* [Enter])
Change what property (Color/LAyer/LType/ltScale/Thickness)? ↵
Command:

If you wish to use a dialog box to change the thickness of an object, click the **Properties** button on the **Object Properties** toolbar, or select **Properties...** from the **Modify** pull-down menu. If you select several objects to change, **DDCHPROP** is invoked and the **Change Properties** dialog box is displayed. See **Figure 19-15A.** You can change the thickness of the selected objects by entering a value in the **Thickness:** text box. When only one object is selected for modification, the **DDMODIFY** command is issued instead of **DDCHPROP**.

The **DDMODIFY** command displays a dialog box appropriate for the one object selected. In **Figure 19-15B,** the thickness of a circle is revised using the **Modify Circle** dialog box.

Figure 19-15.
A—The **DDCHPROP** command displays the **Change Properties** dialog box when the thickness of several existing objects is modified. B—When only one object is selected for thickness modification, such as a circle, the **DDMODIFY** command is used and the appropriate dialog box is displayed.

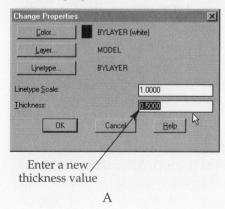

Enter a new
thickness value

A

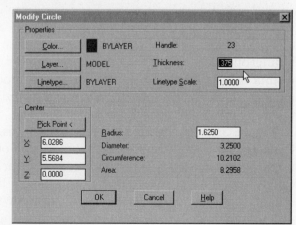

B

EXERCISE 19-1

❑ Use the following procedure to create a 3D model of the object shown below.
❑ Start a new drawing from scratch. Leave the elevation set at 0 but set the thickness to .375.
❑ Draw a 4 × 2 rectangle and fillet all four corners in one operation using the **Fillet** option of the **RECTANG** command.
❑ Set the elevation to .375 and change the thickness to .25.
❑ Create the circle and the six-sided circumscribed polygon using the dimensions given.
❑ Using **DDCHPROP**, change the thickness of the circle to .625.
❑ Use the **VPOINT** command to establish a 3D viewing angle of the model. Once you have a view to your liking, save it with the name 3DVIEW using the **DDVIEW** command.
❑ Return to the plan view using the **PLAN** command.
❑ Save the model as EX19-1.

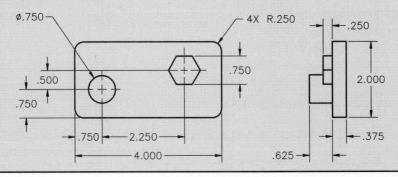

The HIDE Command

The type of 3D geometric construction that can be performed in AutoCAD LT is called *wireframe modeling*. In a wireframe model, all edges of an object are shown as lines. Arc, circle, and spline objects are used to define curved features. The resulting model assumes the appearance of a frame constructed out of wire, or a "wireframe." Unfortunately, all of the lines that would normally be hidden are clearly visible. Consequently, interpreting the image is often difficult.

There is a way to remove, or suppress, hidden lines from view in AutoCAD LT . This is done with the **HIDE** command. While this command is quite useful, it has several significant limitations. For wireframe displays, **HIDE** only evaluates circles, wide polylines, and solids. Line, polyline, and circle objects extruded with an assigned thickness are also evaluated. These objects behave as opaque surfaces, hiding other objects behind them. The model shown in **Figure 19-16** illustrates the results of using **HIDE** with the wireframe model constructed in Exercise 19-1. The normal display of the model is shown in the left viewport, while the hidden-line display appears in the right viewport.

Since circles are treated as opaque surfaces, only the portion of the model behind the hole is hidden. Also notice that extruded objects, or objects with thickness (such as the extruded rectangle and polygon), appear open at the top. After using **HIDE**, you can redraw the screen display without losing the hidden-line display. However, any operation that requires a screen regeneration will restore the original display. You can also manually restore the original display using the **REGEN** command.

Figure 19-16.
The results of a **HIDE** operation on the wireframe model from Exercise 19-1. The normal display of the model is shown in the left viewport, while the hidden-line display appears in the right viewport.

Wireframe model

Model after using the **HIDE** command

A Few Warnings About HIDE

Be aware that the **HIDE** command will only work in the current viewport. Using this command can also be a very compute-intensive operation. Therefore, **HIDE** can be quite time-consuming on very large models or on slower computers. Also, layers that are turned off may still obscure other features. Even though the layers are invisible, they are *still evaluated* during a **HIDE** operation. Frozen layers, however, are *not* evaluated by **HIDE**. To improve system performance, freeze any unnecessary layers in your drawing since frozen layers are not evaluated during a **HIDE** operation.

Finally, hidden-line displays can only be plotted by picking the **Hide-Lines** check box in the **Additional Parameters** section of the **Print/Plot Configuration** dialog box. See *Chapter 14* for more information about printing and plotting.

PROFESSIONAL TIP

Once hidden lines have been suppressed with the **HIDE** command, they remain suppressed until the screen is regenerated. To save a hidden-line display, use the **MSLIDE** command to make a slide of the current screen. Whenever the hidden-line display is required, simply restore it with the **VSLIDE** command. If necessary, refer to *Chapter 18* to review the **MSLIDE** and **VSLIDE** commands.

Shading an Image with the SHADE Command

Once an object is extruded, it may be shaded with the **SHADE** command. *Shading* is another way of removing lines that are not normally hidden from view in a wireframe display. The **SHADE** command can be entered at the keyboard or issued by selecting **Shade** from the **View** pull-down menu. When using the pull-down menu, several shading options appear in a cascading submenu. See **Figure 19-17.** These options are covered in the next section.

Figure 19-17.
Selecting **Shade**
from the **View** pull-
down menu
displays the
shading options in a
cascading submenu.
Observe that the
HIDE command may
also be issued from
the **View** pull-down
menu.

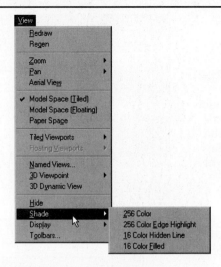

The speed of a shading operation is largely dependent on the available RAM in the system and also on the area of the screen taken up by the model. Therefore, shading in a smaller viewport is faster. A shading operation in progress may be canceled by pressing the [Esc] key.

Once an object is shaded, the operation cannot be reversed with the **UNDO** command. To return to the original display, the **REGEN** command must be issued. Also, you cannot select or plot objects in a shaded image.

The **SHADEDGE** System Variable

Several kinds of shaded renderings can be performed with the **SHADE** command, depending on the number of colors available and the current values of the **SHADEDGE** and **SHADEDIF** system variables. The **SHADEDGE** variable determines what kind of shaded rendering will be produced by specifying how faces and edges are displayed. The **SHADEDIF** variable is covered in the next section.

You can quickly set the **SHADEDGE** variable and perform a shade in one operation by clicking the **View** pull-down menu and selecting one of the options in the **Shade** cascading submenu. The menu options are described as follows:

- **256 Color.** This option requires a 256-color display. All faces are shaded with diffuse light, but edges are not highlighted. Selecting this option sets the **SHADEDGE** variable to 0.
- **256 Color Edge Highlight.** Use of this option also requires a 256-color display. All faces are shaded with diffuse light, and edges are highlighted with the screen background color. Selecting this option sets the **SHADEDGE** variable to 1.
- **16 Color Hidden Line.** This option performs a simulated hidden-line rendering and works with any display regardless of the number of available colors. Selecting this option sets the **SHADEDGE** variable to 2.
- **16 Color Filled.** When this option is selected, faces are not shaded with diffuse light, but they are filled in their original color (flat shading). Selecting this option sets the **SHADEDGE** variable to 3. This is the default **SHADEDGE** setting if the **SHADE** command is entered from the keyboard. It works with any number of colors.

The model from Exercise 19-1 is shown in **Figure 19-18** shaded with each of the four **SHADEDGE** settings. Compare the hidden-line display in the lower-right viewport with the display shown in **Figure 19-16.**

Figure 19-18.
The model from
Exercise 19-1 is
shaded with each of
the four **SHADEDGE**
system variable
settings. Clockwise
from the upper-left
viewport:
SHADEDGE=0,
SHADEDGE =1,
SHADEDGE=2,
SHADEDGE=3.

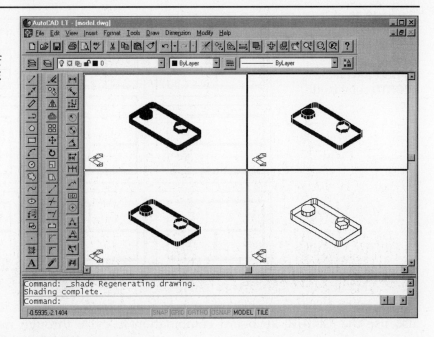

The SHADEDIF System Variable

AutoCAD LT calculates the shading of objects using only one light source. When **SHADEDGE** is set to 0 or 1, the image is shaded based on the angle the faces form with the viewing direction. The diffuse reflection and ambient light in the shaded image are controlled with the **SHADEDIF** system variable. The **SHADEDIF** variable can be set to any value between 0 and 100. By default, it is set to 70. This means that 70% of the light is diffuse reflection from the light source, and 30% is ambient light. Increasing the value of **SHADEDIF** increases diffuse lighting, thereby adding more reflectivity and contrast to an image. Observe that **SHADEDIF** has no effect when **SHADEDGE** is set to 2 (hidden) or 3 (filled).

EXERCISE 19-2

❏ Open drawing EX19-1 if it is not still on your screen.
❏ Try each of the four shading options on the model.
❏ Experiment with different **SHADEDIF** variable settings as you shade the model.
❏ Do not save the file when you are finished.

Setting up Multiple Views with the VPORTS Command

You may recall from *Chapter 17* that the **VPORTS** command allows you to divide the model space display into a maximum of 48 multiple viewing windows (viewports). Some typical viewport configurations are shown in **Figure 19-19.** The viewports are adjacent to one another with no gaps in between. Thus, the viewports are *tiled*. Each viewport can display a different view of your 3D model, and you can pan or zoom independently in each viewport. The **REDRAW** and **REGEN** commands affect *all* displayed viewports.

Only one viewport can be active at one time. The active viewport is surrounded by a wider border, and the graphics cursor is only displayed within that viewport. For the other displayed viewports, the cursor appears as the Windows arrow cursor. All viewports are *interactive*. This means that a drawing or editing command can be started in one viewport and completed in another.

Figure 19-19.
Typical model space
viewport
configurations
produced with the
VPORTS command.

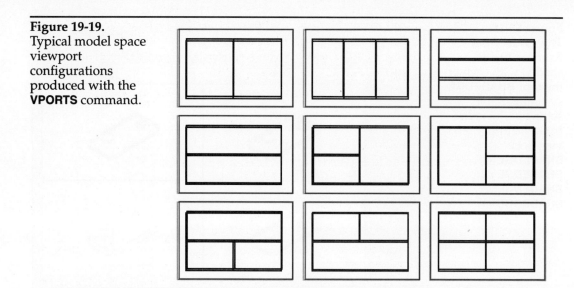

To make a viewport current, simply pick anywhere within its border. You can also use the [Ctrl]+[R] keyboard combination to cycle through multiple viewports, making each one current in succession. When plotting multiple viewports, however, only the current viewport is plotted.

You may also recall from *Chapter 4* that a multiple viewport configuration can be named and saved. It can then be restored, listed, or deleted. Single viewports can be returned to at any time, and more than one configuration can be saved. Like view names, viewport configuration names can have up to 31 characters. The same naming restrictions apply. Also, an inactive viewport can be joined to an active viewport providing the resulting viewport forms a rectangle. The newly joined viewport inherits all aspects of the dominant viewport that it is joined to, such as **LIMITS**, **GRID**, and **SNAP** settings.

By default, the **VPORTS** command divides the screen into three viewports with the *dominant viewport* (the active viewport) located to the right and the two inactive viewports arranged vertically to the left. Selecting **Tiled Viewports** from the **View** pull-down menu displays the **VPORTS** command options in a cascading submenu. See **Figure 19-20.** At the Command: prompt, the **VPORTS** command is issued as follows:

VPORTS
VW

View
↳ Tiled Viewports

Command: **VPORTS** *or* **VW**↵
Save/Restore/Delete/Join/SIngle/?/2/⟨3⟩/4: *(select an option)*

Figure 19-20.
The **VPORTS**
command options
can be displayed in
a cascading
submenu by
selecting **Tiled
Viewports** from the
View pull-down
menu.

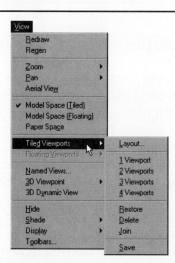

AutoCAD LT—Fundamentals and Applications

The **VPORTS** command allows you to manage the display of viewports in your drawing at the command line. The command options are described as follows:

- **Save.** This option is used to save a defined viewport configuration with a name. The name cannot exceed 31 characters.
- **Restore.** Entering this option allows you to redisplay a saved viewport configuration.
- **Delete.** This option is used to delete a saved viewport configuration.
- **Join.** You can use this option to combine two adjacent viewports into one viewport, providing the new viewport forms a rectangle.
- **SIngle.** This option disables multiple viewports and displays the current viewport as a single view.
- **?.** Selecting this option allows you to display a list of any or all saved viewport configurations in the **AutoCAD LT Text Window.**
- **2.** This option divides the current viewport into two viewports. You can choose between a horizontal or vertical division.
- **⟨3⟩.** This option divides the current viewport into three viewports. The dominant viewport can be placed to the right (by default), to the left, or above the other two viewports.
- **4.** This option divides the current viewport into four equally sized viewports.

Creating Viewports Using a Dialog Box

Predefined multiple viewport configurations can be selected from a dialog box using the following procedure. Click the **View** pull-down menu and then select **Layout...** from the **Tiled Viewports** cascading submenu to display the **Tiled Viewport Layout** dialog box, **Figure 19-21.** Observe that this dialog box features several viewport configurations that are unavailable when the **VPORTS** command is issued on the command line. Select a viewport configuration from the list inside the dialog box, or click the image tile that corresponds to the desired configuration. Click the **OK** button when you are finished.

Figure 19-21.
A predefined viewport configuration can be quickly selected from the **Tiled Viewport Layout** dialog box.

Select a viewport configuration

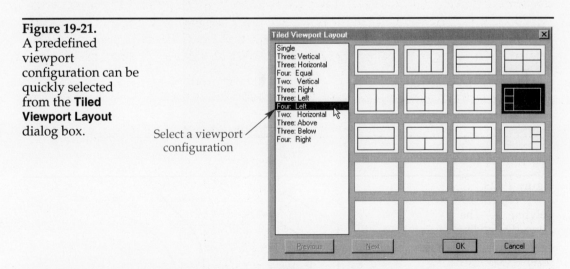

EXERCISE 19-3

❑ Open drawing EX19-1 if it is not still on your screen.
❑ Divide the screen into four viewports using the **VPORTS** command.
❑ Save the viewport configuration with the name 4VIEWS.
❑ Use the **VPOINT** command to establish a different 3D viewing angle in each viewport.
❑ Save the drawing as EX19-3.

Drawing 3D Polylines

The **3DPOLY** command enables you to draw 3D polylines. With the exception of the third dimension (the Z value), these objects are identical to regular 2D polylines. To draw a 3D polyline, select **3D Polyline** from the **Draw** pull-down menu, **Figure 19-22**, or enter the command at the Command: prompt:

> Command: **3DPOLY**↵
> From point: **5,4,7**↵
> Close/Undo/⟨Endpoint of line⟩: **@3,0,2**↵

As with regular polylines, two or more segments can be closed using the **Close** option, and the **Undo** option can be used to remove the last polyline segment without exiting the command.

A 3D polyline can be edited using the **PEDIT** command. However, not all of the **PEDIT** options are available with 3D polylines, as shown below:

> Command: **PEDIT**↵
> Select polyline: *(select a 3D polyline)*
> Open/Edit vertex/Spline curve/Decurve/Undo/eXit ⟨X⟩: *(select an option)*

A typical 3D polyline is illustrated in **Figure 19-23A**. The same 3D polyline with a spline curve applied appears in **Figure 19-23B**.

Figure 19-22.
Selecting **3D Polyline** from the **Draw** pull-down menu issues the **3DPOLY** command.

Figure 19-23.
A—A typical 3D polyline. B—The same 3D polyline after applying a spline curve with the **PEDIT** command.

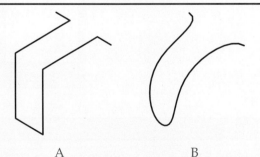

A   B

The User Coordinate System (UCS)

As mentioned at the beginning of this chapter, the World Coordinate System (WCS) in AutoCAD LT is fixed in 3D space and cannot be modified. However, by using the **UCS** command, you can create your own User Coordinate System. A UCS can be defined by:

- Specifying a new 0,0,0 drawing origin.
- Selecting a new XY plane or Z axis direction.
- Copying the 3D orientation of an existing object.
- Rotating the current UCS around its X, Y, or Z axes.
- Aligning a new UCS with the current viewing direction.

Like views and viewport configurations, a UCS can be saved with a name and then restored, listed, deleted, or renamed. Any number of coordinate systems can be defined in a drawing, but only one can be current at any given time.

Elevation and the UCS

Earlier in this chapter, you learned that changing the elevation can be quite handy for 3D construction. Unfortunately, you may often forget the current system elevation and objects will be inadvertently generated above or below the plane that you intended. However, creating a UCS permits you to define a construction plane at any *height*, any *angle*, and any *orientation*. Since the origin of a UCS can be placed at any height, you really do not need to be concerned with Z values at all. Geometry is generated in the UCS-defined XYZ plane using familiar absolute, relative, or polar coordinates. The UCS icon serves as a marker for the current construction plane when displayed at the origin of the current UCS, so you are far less likely to construct geometry with incorrect Z values.

The two circles shown in **Figure 19-24A** both have the same 2.500 diameter, and both have the same center point on the XY plane. However, the lower circle has a default base elevation of zero. The upper circle has an elevation of 4, placing it 4 units *above* the lower circle. In **Figure 19-24B**, two circles with the same diameter and XY plane center point are shown. Both of the lower circles were created in the same way. However, for the upper circle in **Figure 19-24B**, a UCS was defined with its origin 4 units up from the Z axis. The circle was generated by putting the UCS into effect, rather than setting the system elevation. Note the appearance of the UCS icon. The plus symbol at the juncture of the X and Y axes indicates that the icon is at the origin of the current UCS. Also, observe that the "W" has disappeared from the icon. Once a UCS is created, the World Coordinate System is no longer in effect.

Figure 19-24.
A—An object created with elevation. B—An object created with a defined UCS.

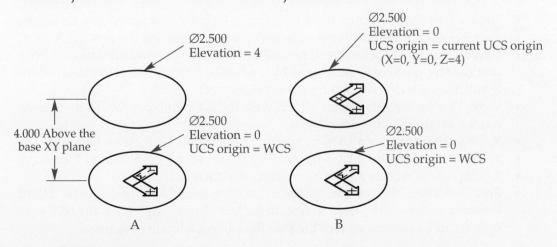

Figure 19-25.
Selecting **UCS** from
the **Tools** pull-down
menu displays each
of the **UCS**
command options
in a cascading
submenu.

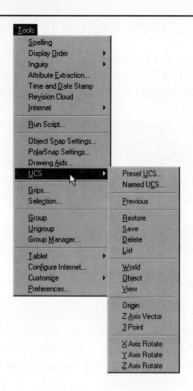

The UCS Command Options

Each of the **UCS** command options may be selected from a cascading submenu by selecting **UCS** from the **Tools** pull-down menu, **Figure 19-25.** You can also access the **UCS** command options by clicking the **UCS** button on the **Standard Toolbar.** Or, enter UCS at the command line:

Command: **UCS**↲
Origin/ZAxis/3point/OBject/View/X/Y/Z/Prev/Restore/Save/Del/?/⟨World⟩:

The **UCS** command is a powerful tool for manipulating the drawing origin and displaying different viewing orientations for construction. The command options are described below:

- **Origin.** Entering this option allows you to define a UCS by shifting the origin of the current UCS to a new location. The direction of the X, Y, and Z axes remains unchanged.
- **ZAxis.** This option establishes a UCS with two points. The first point specifies the UCS origin. The second point determines the direction for the positive Z axis.
- **3point.** This option can be used to define a UCS by first specifying its origin, then a point on the positive X axis, and finally a point on the positive Y axis.
- **OBject.** This option allows you to create a UCS with the same extrusion direction (on the positive Z axis) used by a selected object. The orientation of the X and Y axes is determined by the type of object selected.
- **View.** This option establishes a UCS with the XY plane parallel to the screen, but the origin remains unchanged.
- **X.** This option creates a UCS by rotating the current UCS about its X axis.
- **Y.** This option creates a UCS by rotating the current UCS about its Y axis.
- **Z.** This option creates a UCS by rotating the current UCS about its Z axis.
- **Prev.** Selecting this option restores the previous UCS. Just as the **ZOOM Previous** option can be used to restore the last 10 drawing views, the **UCS Prev** option can be used to restore the previous 10 coordinate systems.

- **Restore.** This option restores a saved UCS so that it becomes the current UCS. Entering a question mark (?) allows you to list any or all defined coordinate systems.
- **Save.** This option is used to name and save the current coordinate system. UCS names can contain up to 31 characters, but they must conform to the standard AutoCAD LT naming convention. Responding with a question mark (?) allows you to list any or all defined coordinate systems.
- **Del.** This option can be used to delete a saved UCS. More than one UCS can be deleted by separating the UCS names with commas.
- **?.** This option allows you to list the name, origin, and XYZ axes for each UCS you specify. Entering the asterisk wildcard character (*) lists all coordinate systems. If the current UCS is unnamed, it is listed as *NO NAME* or *WORLD*, depending on whether it is the same as the WCS.
- **⟨World⟩.** The default option to the **UCS** command, **World** restores the WCS.

PROFESSIONAL TIP

It is a good idea to save a UCS once it is created. Saving a UCS is easier and faster than defining a new one, and it can always be renamed or deleted later.

Using the UCS Control Dialog Box

A UCS can be set current, listed, renamed, or deleted using the **UCS Control** dialog box. To display this dialog box, type DDUCS or UC at the Command: prompt or click the **Tools** pull-down menu and select **Named UCS...** from the **UCS** cascading submenu. You can also click the **Named UCS** button on the **UCS** toolbar. The **UCS Control** dialog box lists every UCS in your drawing—named or unnamed, **Figure 19-26.** The **UCS Names** field always displays *WORLD* for the World Coordinate System. If a previous UCS has been defined but remains nameless (unsaved), the entry *PREVIOUS* is displayed. If the current UCS has not yet been named, then *NO NAME* appears in the **UCS Names** field.

DDUCS
UC

Tools
→ UCS
→ Named UCS...

UCS toolbar

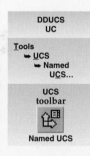

Named UCS

Figure 19-26.
You can list every UCS in your drawing by displaying the **UCS Control** dialog box.

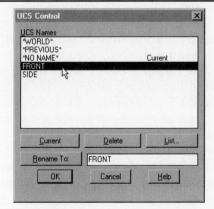

Using the UCS Orientation Dialog Box

When you wish to define a UCS, you can use the **UCS Orientation** dialog box to select from nine preset UCS configurations. To do so, enter DDUCSP, or UCP, at the Command: prompt, or click the **Tools** pull-down menu and select **Preset UCS...** from the **UCS** cascading submenu. You can also click the **Preset UCS** button on the **UCS** toolbar. The **UCS Orientation** dialog box, shown in **Figure 19-27**, lets you select a new

DDUCSP
UCP

Tools
→ UCS
→ Preset UCS...

UCS toolbar

Preset UCS

Figure 19-27.
Nine preset UCS
configurations are
available in the
UCS Orientation
dialog box.

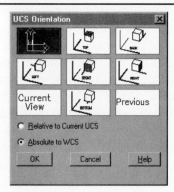

UCS that is created at right angles to either the current UCS or the WCS. To specify your choice, select the appropriate UCS configuration and then click the **OK** button. Also, you can restore the WCS or previous UCS, or set the UCS to the current view. This procedure is equivalent to using the **View** option of the **UCS** command.

3D Modeling Methodology

Despite the diverse geometry used in engineering and architecture, nearly all objects have one very important similarity—a common profile. Any single object usually has at least one feature that reflects a profile that is duplicated at its top, bottom, sides, or anywhere in between. For example, a circle might represent a hole, or a polygonal feature might represent a hex head. The key to successful 3D modeling is to first identify the common profile for the object you wish to model. Once you have identified the profile, create a new UCS if necessary and construct the profile using ordinary AutoCAD LT drawing and editing commands. When the profile is complete, copy it along the Z axis at the required dimension and connect the two profiles using lines or polylines.

For example, the common profile of the object in **Figure 19-28A** is shown in **Figure 19-28B**. Refer to **Figure 19-29** as you follow the procedure below:

1. Establish a 3D viewing angle with the **VIEWPOINT** command.
2. Rotate the UCS 90° about the X axis to help with the construction of the common profile. Save the UCS with a name such as FRONT.
3. Create the closed profile with line or polyline objects as shown in **Figure 19-29A**.
4. Next, copy the profile along the Z axis as required, **Figure 19-29B**. You can copy along the positive or negative Z axis (the negative axis is used in this example).
5. Referring to **Figure 19-29C**, connect the two profiles using line or polyline objects. Set the running object snap mode to **Endpoint** and use the **MULTIPLE** command modifier to help simplify this task.
6. Return to the WCS or rotate the UCS –90° about the X axis. Move the UCS origin to the top corner of the object as shown in **Figure 19-29D**. Save the UCS with a name such as TOP.
7. Draw the two circles at the top of the object. Copy them along the negative Z axis as required to show the hole bottoms. Connect the coaxial circles by their quadrants. Making connections at all four quadrants is unnecessary—connecting two quadrants is sufficient.
8. Use the **UCS 3point** option to create the UCS shown in **Figure 19-29E**. Save it with a name such as AUXILIARY or SLANTED and create the counterbore feature using two circles with different Z values.

The 3D wireframe model is now complete. See **Figure 19-29F.**

Figure 19-28.
A—Nearly every object has a common profile. Can you identify the common profile of this object? B—The profile is shown here highlighted.

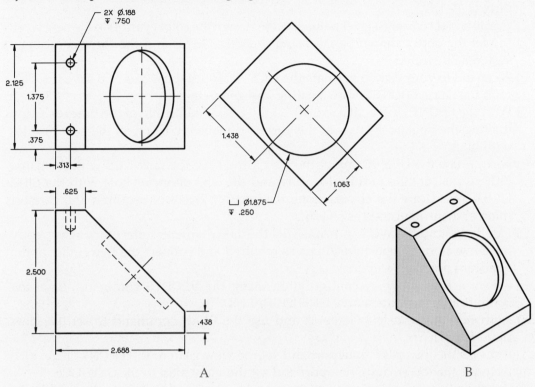

A

B

Figure 19-29.
A through E—The suggested sequence of steps required to construct the 3D wireframe model. F—The completed wireframe model.

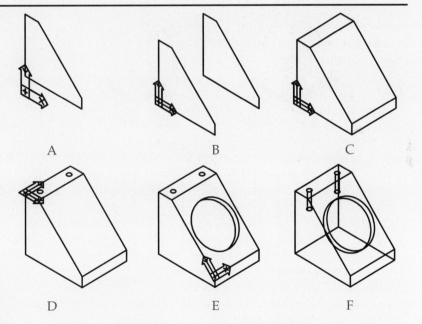

A

B

C

D

E

F

PROFESSIONAL TIP

Create and save a UCS for each plane of your 3D model that represents an orthographic view (top, front, and side). When organizing multiple viewport configurations in an orthographic fashion, simply activate the desired viewport and set the view plan to the named UCS that represents that view.

EXERCISE 19-4

❏ Begin a new drawing from scratch. Establish a 3D view with the viewpoint coordinates 1,–1,1.
❏ Create and set current a layer named Model. Assign the color cyan (4) to the new layer.
❏ Model the object shown below using the Model layer and the three coordinate systems illustrated.
❏ As an aid to your drawing, rotate the UCS 90° about the X axis and save the UCS with the name FRONT before creating any geometry.
❏ With the FRONT UCS active, construct the L-shaped profile of the bracket. Copy it along the negative Z axis at the correct dimension. Connect the two profiles with lines.
❏ Next, rotate the UCS 90° about the Y axis and save the new UCS with the name SIDE. Construct the radiused feature and the .750 diameter hole with the SIDE UCS active. Copy the objects along the positive Z axis as required and connect them at their quadrants as shown.
❏ Finally, restore the WCS and construct the .500 diameter hole. Once again, copy the circle along the positive Z axis as required and connect the two circles at the quadrant points as shown.
❏ Create a four-viewport configuration using the **VPORTS** command. Save the configuration with the name ORTHOGRAPHIC.
❏ Activate the upper-left viewport and use the **PLAN** command to set the view plan to the WCS.
❏ Activate the lower-left viewport and set the view plan to the FRONT UCS.
❏ Activate the lower-right viewport and set the view plan to the SIDE UCS.
❏ Zoom and pan in each viewport as required to arrange the views orthographically.
❏ Save the 3D model as EX19-4.

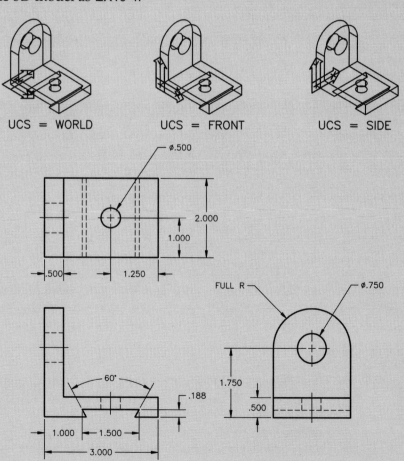

UCS = WORLD   UCS = FRONT   UCS = SIDE

AutoCAD LT—Fundamentals and Applications

The UCSFOLLOW System Variable

As you begin modeling in 3D, you will probably find it convenient to do most of your work in an oblique (3D) view. This is easily accomplished by creating UCS configurations that correspond to each construction plane of your model. Creating the entire model in this fashion does have some drawbacks, however.

As you may have noticed, the wireframe representation of a 3D model can sometimes play tricks on your eyes. The model seems to reverse its orientation at times or "flip" on you. Because a 3D model is a true three-dimensional object and a computer display screen is two-dimensional, things are not always what they seem to be. Therefore, it is a good idea to build your model in two vertical (or horizontal) viewports. One viewport can contain a 3D view and the other can contain an orthographic view. As you construct geometry with a UCS in the oblique view, the orthographic view can be set parallel, or plan to the current UCS, to serve as a guide. This will verify the correct location of features on the XYZ axes. Having a plan view also enables you to better visualize the shape and orientation of the object under construction.

Earlier in this chapter, you learned how the **PLAN** command can be used to set a view plan to the current UCS, a different UCS, or to the WCS. For multiple viewport configurations, the **UCSFOLLOW** system variable allows you to do this automatically. In the two-viewport configuration suggested above, **UCSFOLLOW** can be turned on in one of the viewports. Then, whenever a UCS is created or restored in the 3D viewport, the other viewport automatically displays a view plan to the changed UCS. The **UCSFOLLOW** system variable can be turned on or off as follows:

> Command: **UCSFOLLOW**↵
> New value for UCSFOLLOW ⟨0⟩: *(type* 0 *to turn it off or* 1 *to turn it on and press* [Enter]*)*

The **UCSFOLLOW** system variable is off by default. Enter a 1 to turn it on. Just as different viewports can have individual settings for **GRID**, **SNAP**, and **LIMITS**, each viewport can have a different setting for **UCSFOLLOW**.

Dynamic Viewing with DVIEW

So far you have learned that a 3D view can be established with the **VPOINT** command and its various options. Remember that **VPOINT** only changes the viewing angle to the object, and not the orientation of the object or its distance from the viewer. Using the **DVIEW** (dynamic view) command is a far more powerful and flexible way of manipulating a 3D model. Several of the **DVIEW** command options provide you with a horizontal slider bar where values can be set. As you change the view with the slider bar, 3D objects move dynamically, providing greater control of every aspect of the display.

An analogy can be made with the **DVIEW** command and photography. With **DVIEW**, the location of the viewer's eyes is the *camera* and the 3D model is the *target*. Because these two points form the line of sight and each can be adjusted to any angle, the user can control both the orientation and the distance that an object is viewed from—just as a camera can be equipped with a wide-angle or telephoto lens to alter distance. The distance from the camera to the target can also be adjusted to produce a "vanishing point" perspective display, which **DVIEW** calls *distance*. In addition, the camera can be rotated around the line of sight to produce a different tilt, or *twist* angle. You can also eliminate, or *clip*, the front or back planes of an object to reveal (or hide) certain features. Should you create an unsatisfactory display, **DVIEW** includes an **Undo** option to restore the previous view. Finally, a hidden-line display can also be established from within **DVIEW** if thickness has been applied to the model.

DVIEW Selection Set and Command Options

DVIEW
DV

View
↳ 3D Dynamic
View

The **DVIEW** command can be issued by selecting **3D Dynamic View** from the **View** pull-down menu. You can also enter the following at the Command: prompt:

    Command: **DVIEW** *or* **DV**↵
    Select objects:

When the **DVIEW** command is entered, the Select objects: prompt appears. All selection set options are valid. However, since the position of the selected objects is constantly updated on screen, large selection sets can quickly use up system resources. Therefore, select only a few objects. Once these objects are displayed to your satisfaction, simply exit the **DVIEW** command and the rest of the objects will match the new view orientation.

    *** Switching to the WCS ***
    CAmera/TArget/Distance/POints/PAn/Zoom/TWist/CLip/Hide/Off/Undo/⟨eXit⟩:

After selecting an option and manipulating a model, you can end the command using the default **eXit** option. Each of the **DVIEW** command options is described below.

- **CAmera.** This option is similar to the **VPOINT Rotate** option. Select the angle from the camera to the target, both *from* the XY plane and *in* the XY plane (around the Z axis).
- **TArget.** This option is similar to the **CAmera** option, except the viewing angle is determined from the target to the camera. In other words, the target moves and not the camera.
- **Distance.** This option sets the distance from the camera to the target and turns perspective viewing on. When perspective viewing is on, the UCS icon is displayed as a cube seen in perspective, and only a subset of AutoCAD LT commands are active.
- **POints.** With this option, you select both the target and the camera to change the view.
- **PAn.** This option permits dynamic panning of the view.
- **Zoom.** This option permits dynamic zooming of the view. If perspective viewing is on, the focal length of the camera can be adjusted. The default focal length is 50 mm. Increasing the focal length is similar to using a telephoto lens. Decreasing the focal length produces a wide-angle lens effect. When perspective viewing is off, entering the **Zoom** option is similar to using the **Center** option of the **ZOOM** command.
- **TWist.** This option allows you to rotate the camera's viewing angle around the target. The target remains fixed in 3D space.
- **CLip.** This option sets the front or back clipping planes. To return the front clipping plane to the default camera position after removing portions of the view, select the **Eye** option.
- **Hide.** This option produces a hidden-line display of the **DVIEW** selection set you provide.
- **Off.** Selecting this option turns perspective viewing off.
- **Undo.** This option reverses the last **DVIEW** option used.
- **⟨eXIT⟩.** This option exits the **DVIEW** command, regenerates the display to reflect the new view, and restores the UCS, if one was in effect.

Using Dviewblock

A sample drawing named Dviewblock offers an easy way to set a desired view orientation after entering the **DVIEW** command. Dviewblock is a predefined block object provided by AutoCAD LT . This block appears as a house in a wireframe representation with an open door, a window, and a chimney. See **Figure 19-30.** Although it is a very simple object, it can be quite useful for manipulating a view to your liking. To use Dviewblock, simply press [Enter] when prompted to select objects after issuing the **DVIEW** command.

If no 3D view has yet been created, the house will display the plan to the WCS. Select any of the **DVIEW** options to position the house in the orientation you want your 3D model to be. When you exit **DVIEW,** your model will display the same view characteristics that were assigned to the house.

Figure 19-30.
The Dviewblock sample drawing used in conjunction with the **DVIEW** command.

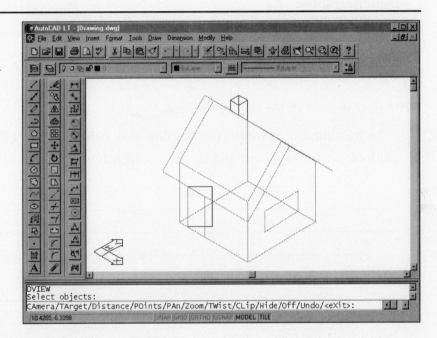

The WORLDVIEW System Variable

By default, dynamic viewing angles are based on the WCS. Therefore, if a UCS is current when the **DVIEW** command is issued, the display is temporarily switched to the WCS (a message informs you of this action). Once the **DVIEW** command is ended, the display is switched back to the previous UCS automatically. When the **WORLDVIEW** system variable is set to 1 (the default setting), the display switches to the WCS after the **DVIEW** command is issued. In most cases, this convention eliminates much of the disorientation that might otherwise occur by viewing the model through an unfamiliar viewing angle. To perform dynamic viewing with the angles set by the current UCS, set the **WORLDVIEW** system variable to 0 (off).

❏ Begin a new drawing from scratch.
❏ Issue the **DVIEW** command and press [Enter] at the Select objects: prompt.
❏ Using the **CAmera** option, rotate the house 45° from the XY plane and –45° in the XY plane.
❏ Use the **DVIEW Zoom** and **PAn** options to change the display.
❏ Rotate the camera about the Z axis with a **TWist** angle of 120°.
❏ Experiment with the **POints** option. Pick a corner of the house window as the target and the top of the door as the camera. Be sure to use the appropriate object snap modes.
❏ Create a perspective view with the **Distance** option and then enter the **Hide** option.
❏ Turn perspective viewing off and enter the **CLipping** option. Try clipping the front plane, then the back plane. Use the **Undo** option if you are not satisfied with the display.
❏ Exit the **DVIEW** command and do not save the drawing.

Chapter Test

Write your answer in the space provided.

1. Which command controls the display and origin of the UCS icon? List the options to this command and the function each one performs._____

_____

_____

_____

_____

_____

_____

_____

2. When the UCS icon is displayed on screen as a "broken pencil," what does this representation mean?_____

_____

_____

3. Describe the *right-hand rule.* What is its purpose? _____

_____

_____

_____

4. What is a *plan view?* _____

_____

_____

_____

5. List three methods used for obtaining a 3D view with the **VPOINT** command.

_____

_____

6. What do the coordinates 1,–1,1 represent when entered with the **VPOINT** command? Are these distance or direction coordinates? _____

_____

_____

7. What does the **VPOINT** compass display icon represent? _____

_____

_____

8. What is the purpose of the **VIEW** command? Why is it useful for 3D work?

_____

_____

_____

9. What are *tessalation lines?* _____

_____

10. What is meant by *elevation?* _____

11. What is *thickness* and how is it used? _____

_____

_____

_____

12. How do the system variables **SHADEDIF** and **SHADEDGE** affect a shaded display?

_____

_____

_____

13. How many viewports can be displayed with the **VPORTS** command? How many can be plotted? _____

_____

14. What is the UCS? How does it differ from the World Coordinate System?

_____

_____

_____

15. What does the plus sign at the juncture of the UCS icon X and Y axes represent?

_____

16. Assume the UCS icon is displayed with no box at the juncture of the X and Y axes. From which direction is the XY plane being viewed? _____

_____

17. *Yes or No?* Does the direction of the X and Y axes change when using the **UCS Origin** command option? _____

18. Why should you save a defined UCS? _____

_____

_____

19. How do you arrange multiple viewports in an orthographic representation?

_____

_____

20. How can a view be automatically made plan to the current UCS in a multiple viewport configuration? _____

_____

_____

_____

21. Describe the difference between the **CAmera** and **TArget** options of the **DVIEW** command. How are they similar? _____

_____

_____

_____

22. Which **DVIEW** command option allows you to create a perspective view? _____

_____

23. List the advantages of the **DVIEW** command over the **VPOINT** command. _____

_____

_____

_____

24. What purpose does the Dviewblock drawing serve? _____

_____

_____

25. Is dynamic viewing performed in the WCS or the UCS? Why? _____

_____

_____

Chapter Problems

Mechanical Drafting

1. Model the object shown in **Figure 19-28A.** Set up three viewports with the dominant viewport to the right. Display the top view of the object in the upper-left viewport and the front view in the lower-left viewport. Display a 3D view in the dominant viewport on the right. Save the model as P19-1.

Mechanical Drafting

2. Model the CLAMP BLOCK from Problem 1 of *Chapter 16*. Set up three viewports with the dominant viewport above the others. Save the configuration with the name 3VIEWS. Display the top view of the object in the lower-left viewport and the side view in the lower-right viewport. Display a 3D view in the top viewport. Save the model as P19-2.

Mechanical Drafting

3. Model the STARTING CATCH from Problem 2 of *Chapter 16*. Set up four viewports and save the configuration with the name 4VIEWS. Display the top view of the object in the upper-left viewport, the front view in the lower-left viewport, and the side view in the lower-right viewport. Display a 3D view in the upper-right viewport. Save the model as P19-3.

Chapter **20**

Customizing the AutoCAD LT Environment

Learning Objectives

After you have completed this chapter, you will be able to:
- Control the size of the graphics cursor displayed on screen.
- Assign colors and fonts to the graphics window and the **AutoCAD LT Text Window**.
- Enable or disable the creation of backup files.
- Perform automatic drawing saves at specified time intervals.
- Select between a mouse and digitizer as your pointing device.
- Specify the search paths for support folders and the placement of temporary files.
- Resize and reposition the AutoCAD LT windows.
- Use command line switches to create a custom configuration.
- Create your own desktop shortcuts and shortcut icons.

AutoCAD LT provides a variety of options to customize the user interface and working environment. These customization options allow you to configure the software to suit personal preferences or satisfy organizational requirements. This chapter explores these options, which include the following: defining colors for the individual window elements; assigning preferred fonts to both the graphics window and the **AutoCAD LT Text Window**; sizing and positioning the window displays; and creating different shortcut configurations.

Setting Preferences

The options for customizing the AutoCAD LT user interface and working environment are found in the **Preferences** dialog box. This dialog box is accessed by selecting **Preferences...** from the **Tools** pull-down menu, **Figure 20-1.** You can also open the **Preferences** dialog box by locating your pointing device anywhere over the command line window and right-clicking. When the shortcut menu appears, select **Preferences...** at the bottom, **Figure 20-2.** The **Preferences** dialog box may also be displayed by entering the following on the command line:

Command: **PREFERENCES** *or* **PR**↵

The **Preferences** dialog box contains six different tabs that can be selected to make customization settings. The tabs and various options in this dialog box are described in the following sections.

Figure 20-1.
Selecting
Preferences... from
the **Tools** pull-down
menu displays the
Preferences dialog
box.

Figure 20-2.
The **Preferences** dialog
box may also be accessed
from a shortcut menu
after right-clicking
anywhere within the
command line window.

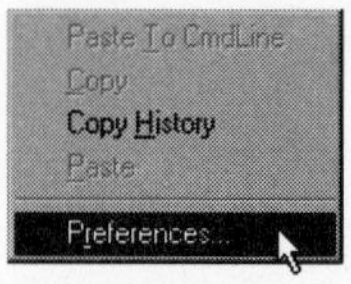

The Work Space Tab Window

The **Work Space** tab window is the default open tab when the **Preferences** dialog box initially opens. See **Figure 20-3.** The options available in this tab window are primarily used to control the AutoCAD LT 98 user interface. Each of the options is described as follows:

- **Show Start Up dialog.** You may recall from *Chapter 2* that the **Start Up** dialog box is used to specify settings for a new drawing session. The **Show Start Up dialog** check box controls whether the **Start Up** dialog box is displayed when you start AutoCAD LT. Deactivating the check box disables the dialog box. You can also disable the **Start Up** dialog box by deactivating the **Show this dialog at start up** check box at the lower-left corner of the **Start Up** dialog box. See **Figure 20-4.**

- **Beep on error.** Activate this check box if you wish to hear a beep signal when you enter an unknown command or attempt to perform a function that is not permitted. The beep is off by default.

- **Display Scrollbars.** This check box controls whether the scrollbars are displayed on the bottom and right sides of the AutoCAD LT graphics window. The scroll-bars provide a handy means to pan the drawing display. See *Chapter 4* of this text for more information about pan and zoom functions.

- **Right-click mouse button.** This area, located at the upper right of the **Work Space** tab window, provides the following two options:
  - **AutoCAD classic (Enter)**—When this option button is selected, the right-click button on your pointing device behaves the same way as the [Enter] key on the keyboard by repeating the last command. This convention was used in releases of AutoCAD LT prior to AutoCAD LT 98 and 97.
  - **Shortcut menu**—This is the default setting. When the right button on your pointing device is clicked, a pop-up menu containing selections relevant to the previous action is displayed.

Figure 20-3.
The **Work Space** tab is used to set user interface options in AutoCAD LT 98. It is displayed when the **Preferences** dialog box is initially opened.

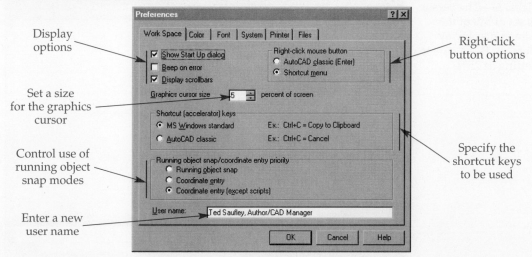

Display options

Set a size for the graphics cursor

Control use of running object snap modes

Enter a new user name

Right-click button options

Specify the shortcut keys to be used

Figure 20-4.
Deactivating the **Show this dialog at start up** check box offers another way to disable the **Start Up** dialog box.

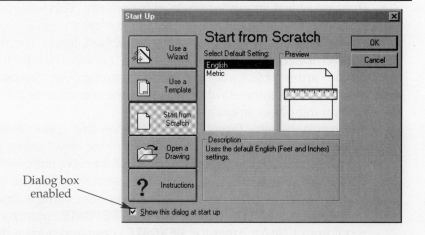

Dialog box enabled

- **Graphics cursor size.** Use the up and down arrows or the text box to set the size of the screen graphics cursor. The allowable range is from 1 to 100 percent of the total screen area. At 100%, the ends of the cursor are never visible. When the size is decreased to 99% or below, the cursor crosshairs have a finite size, and the ends are visible when moved to the edge of the graphics window. The default size is 5%. See **Figure 20-5.**
- **Shortcut (accelerator) keys.** This area in the middle of the **Preferences** dialog box is used to specify how shortcut keys are interpreted by AutoCAD LT. The following two options are provided:
  - **MS Windows standard**—The default setting follows Microsoft Windows 98/95/NT standards in interpreting shortcut keys. For example, the [Ctrl]+[C] key combination issues the **COPYCLIP** command. See *Chapter 24* for more information about the **COPYCLIP** command and clipboard functions.
  - **AutoCAD classic**—Activating this option button causes AutoCAD LT to interpret shortcut keys using standards from AutoCAD LT Releases 1 and 2, rather than Microsoft Windows 98, 95, and NT. For example, the [Ctrl]+[C] key combination can be used to issue a cancel operation (providing an alternative to the [Esc] key).

Figure 20-5.
A comparison of graphics cursor sizes. A—The cursor is set at 5% of the screen display by default. B—A cursor setting at 25%.

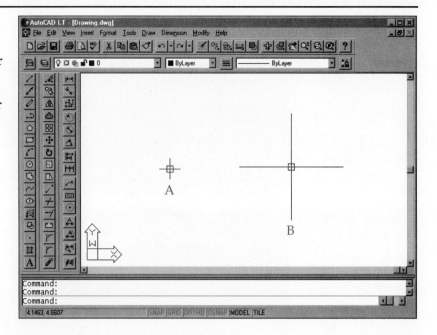

- **Running object snap/coordinate entry priority.** This section of the **Work Space** tab window offers the following three options:
  - **Running object snap**—Setting this option forces running object snaps to override coordinate entry at all times. If necessary, refer to *Chapter 7* to review the various object snap modes and running object snaps.
  - **Coordinate entry**—With this option, the coordinates that you enter override running object snaps at all times.
  - **Coordinate entry (except scripts)**—When this option button is activated, the coordinates that you enter override running object snaps, except in script files. This is the default setting. See *Chapter 18* for more information about script files.
- **User Name:** This text box displays the user name that was specified during the initial AutoCAD LT 98/97 installation. The user name is stored in the Windows system registry and is accessed when the **REVDATE** command is issued. You may recall from *Chapter 2* that the **REVDATE** command adds a date and time stamp and inserts the user name into a drawing. Use the **User Name:** text box to change the name if more than one person works on the drawing.

The Color Tab Window

By customizing the colors displayed in the AutoCAD LT graphics window and the **AutoCAD LT Text Window**, you can add your own personal touch and make the displays stand out from other active Windows applications. The color options can be listed by clicking the **Color** tab in the **Preferences** dialog box, **Figure 20-6.**

The **Window Element:** drop-down list, located at the upper right of the **Color** tab window, allows you to change individual color elements in both AutoCAD LT windows. These color elements include the colors of the graphics and command line windows, the **AutoCAD LT Text Window** background, the text in the command line window and the **AutoCAD LT Text Window**, the graphics cursor, and the UCS icon. To customize the colors displayed in AutoCAD LT, do the following:

1. First, display the **Color** tab window. If you have a monochrome display monitor, the **Monochrome Vectors** check box is activated. If you have a grayscale display monitor and you are experiencing problems displaying elements of AutoCAD LT, try clicking this check box.
2. Click an area in the Graphics Window or text window samples at the left, or select the element to change from the **Window Element:** drop-down list.

Figure 20-6.
The **Color** tab window is used to set the colors displayed by the graphics window and the **AutoCAD LT Text Window**.

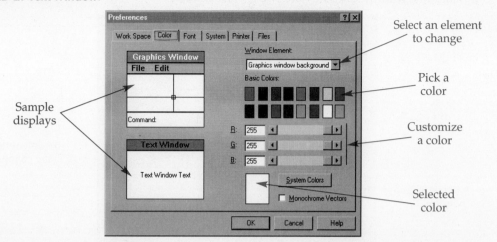

3. Select the color you want from the available colors displayed in the **Basic Colors:** section. The sample window is updated to reflect your selection. The color also appears in the color swatch near the bottom of the dialog box. You can modify the selected color by using the horizontal slider controls labeled **R:**, **G:**, and **B:** to change the red, green, and blue components of the color. You can also type a number between 0 and 255 in the respective text box.

4. If you are not satisfied with your color selections, click the **System Colors** button just below the RGB horizontal slider controls to restore the default AutoCAD LT colors. Once you have made your color selections, click the **OK** button at the bottom of the **Color** tab window to implement the changes and terminate the **PREFERENCES** command. If you modified the colors for the **AutoCAD LT Text Window** as well, press the [F2] function key, or select **Display** from the **View** pull-down menu and then select **Text Window** from the cascading submenu to observe the color changes.

The Font Tab Window

Apart from choosing your own display colors, you can also change the text font used in the command line area and the **AutoCAD LT Text Window**. The options for changing the text fonts are provided in the **Font** tab window of the **Preferences** dialog box. The type of font you select has no effect on the text in your drawings and is not used in the AutoCAD LT dialog boxes. To change the command window or **AutoCAD LT Text Window** text fonts, do the following:

1. Click the **Font** tab in the **Preferences** dialog box. This displays the **Font** tab window, where you can select a font, font style, and font size. See **Figure 20-7.**

2. Note the two option buttons at the lower left of the **Font to Change** section. Click the **Command Window** button to modify the text font on the command line. To modify the **AutoCAD LT Text Window** text font, click the **Text Window** button.

3. To select a different font, select the new font from the **Font:** drop-down list. In the example shown in **Figure 20-8**, the Lucida Console TrueType font is selected from the drop-down list. The style is changed to Bold Italic and the font size is changed to 12 points. The **Sample Text Window Font** section at the bottom of the tab window displays a sample of the selected font as it will appear in the **AutoCAD LT Text Window**. If you are selecting a font for use on the command line, this box is labeled **Sample Command Window Font.**

4. Once you have selected the desired font, font style, and font size for the command window and/or **AutoCAD LT Text Window**, click the **OK** button to implement the changes and close the **Preferences** dialog box. Click **Cancel** to keep the previous font.

Figure 20-7.
The **Font** tab window provides options to set font types, styles, and sizes used by the command line window and the **AutoCAD LT Text Window**.

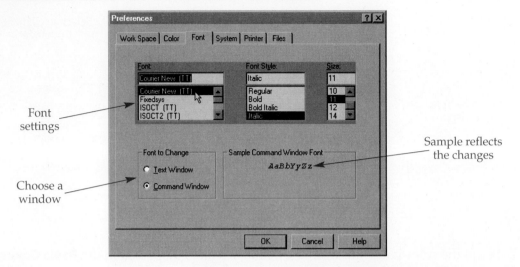

Font settings

Choose a window

Sample reflects the changes

Figure 20-8.
In this example, the Lucida Console TrueType font is set current using the **Font:** drop-down list. The font style and size are also changed.

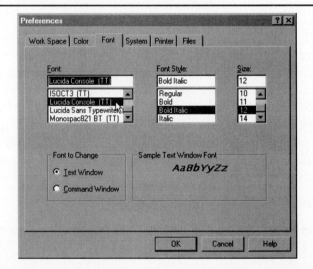

EXERCISE 20-1

❏ Begin a new drawing from scratch.
❏ Use the **Color** and **Font** tabs in the **Preferences** dialog box to change the color elements and fonts of the graphics window and the **AutoCAD LT Text Window** to your personal liking.

The System Tab Window

The **System** tab window is used to specify several general AutoCAD LT operating preferences. As shown in **Figure 20-9**, the **System** tab window offers the following options:

- **Always create backups (BAK).** Active by default, this check box setting specifies whether a backup copy is created when you save a drawing. It is recommended that you do not change this setting. Remember that you must rename the .bak file extension to .dwg before using a backup file. See *Chapter 25* of this text to learn how to rename files and file extensions using Windows Explorer.

Figure 20-9.
The **System** tab window provides settings for a number of general AutoCAD LT operating options.

Click to disable backup files

Click to write **AutoCAD LT Text Window** data to a file

Click to disable drawing preview images

Click to disable automatic saves

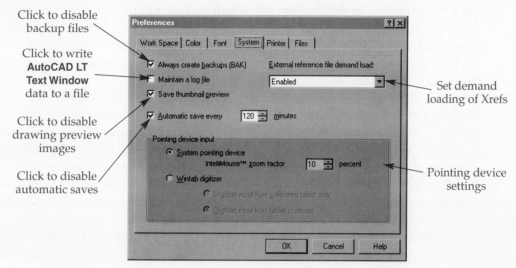

Set demand loading of Xrefs

Pointing device settings

- **Maintain a log file.** When activated, this option writes the prompts and messages that appear in the **AutoCAD LT Text Window** to a log file. The name of the log file defaults to aclt.log. Each individual log session is separated by a line of 40 dashes. The aclt.log file is in ASCII format and may be viewed using Windows Notepad or any other text editor. To specify the location and name of the log file, use the **Files** tab in the **Preferences** dialog box. The **Files** tab window is described later in this chapter. You can also enable the log file using the **LOGFILEMODE** system variable. To specify a different log file name, use the **LOGFILENAME** system variable.

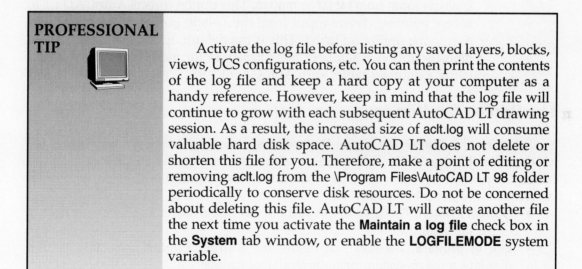

PROFESSIONAL TIP

Activate the log file before listing any saved layers, blocks, views, UCS configurations, etc. You can then print the contents of the log file and keep a hard copy at your computer as a handy reference. However, keep in mind that the log file will continue to grow with each subsequent AutoCAD LT drawing session. As a result, the increased size of aclt.log will consume valuable hard disk space. AutoCAD LT does not delete or shorten this file for you. Therefore, make a point of editing or removing aclt.log from the \Program Files\AutoCAD LT 98 folder periodically to conserve disk resources. Do not be concerned about deleting this file. AutoCAD LT will create another file the next time you activate the **Maintain a log file** check box in the **System** tab window, or enable the **LOGFILEMODE** system variable.

- **Save thumbnail preview.** Active by default, this check box setting determines whether an image of a drawing is saved with the drawing and then displayed in the **Preview** area of the **Select File** dialog box when the drawing is opened. The preview image function is also controlled by the **RASTERPREVIEW** system variable.

- **Automatic save every.** You may recall from *Chapter 2* that the **SAVETIME** system variable can be set to save your work automatically at regular time intervals. You can set this variable on the command line or use the **Automatic save every** option in the **System** tab window. Use the text box or the up and down arrows to set the desired time interval (in minutes). When this feature is enabled, AutoCAD LT saves your drawing with the name auto.sv$. As with backup files, before the saved file can be used, it must be renamed using the filename.dwg format.
- **External reference file demand load:.** This drop-down list controls the demand loading of external references (xrefs). You may recall from *Chapter 15* that demand loading improves system performance by loading only the parts of an externally referenced drawing that are needed to regenerate the current drawing. If necessary, refer to *Chapter 15* to review the demand loading options.
- **Pointing device input.** This section of the **System** tab window offers several options for setting the AutoCAD LT pointing device. These options are described as follows:
  - **System pointing device**—This is the default option. It is used to specify the system pointing device, usually a two- or three-button mouse, as the AutoCAD LT pointing device.
  - **IntelliMouse™ zoom factor**—This option controls the response rate of zooming with the IntelliMouse wheel. See *Chapter 4* of this text for more information regarding the use of the Microsoft IntelliMouse.
  - **Wintab digitizer**—Activate this option button when you wish to use a WINTAB-compatible digitizing tablet as the AutoCAD LT pointing device. This setting offers two additional options:
    - **Digitizer input from calibrated tablet only.** This option directs AutoCAD LT to accept pointing device input from the digitizing tablet *only*, and only when the tablet is calibrated and the tablet mode is on. If you have no tablet calibrated, this option is unavailable.
    - **Digitizer input from tablet or mouse.** This option directs AutoCAD LT to accept pointing device input from the system pointing device in addition to the digitizing tablet. This is the default option when the **Wintab digitizer** option is selected. See *Chapter 23* for more information about using a digitizer tablet with AutoCAD LT 98.

The Printer Tab Window

Selecting the **Printer** tab in the **Preferences** dialog box displays the **Printer** tab window. See **Figure 20-10.** This window allows you to set the current printer and customize printer or plotter settings. The various sections and buttons in the **Printer** tab window are described below:
- **Current Printer:.** This area displays the name of the current printer near the top of the tab window.
- **List of printers.** Located just below the **Current Printer:** area, this section displays a list of system printers available for use.
- **Printer description.** This area near the bottom of the tab window displays information about the currently selected printer.
- **Set Current button.** After selecting an output device from the list of printers, click this button to make your selection current.
- **Modify... button.** This button is used to reconfigure a selected output device from the list of printers and plotters. You have the option to provide a new description for the device using the **Description:** text box in the **Reconfigure a Printer** subdialog box. See **Figure 20-11A.** After entering the description, click the **Reconfigure** button. If you reconfigure the default system printer, a subdialog box

AutoCAD LT—Fundamentals and Applications

Figure 20-10.
The **Printer** tab window provides options for setting a printer current and customizing printer or plotter settings.

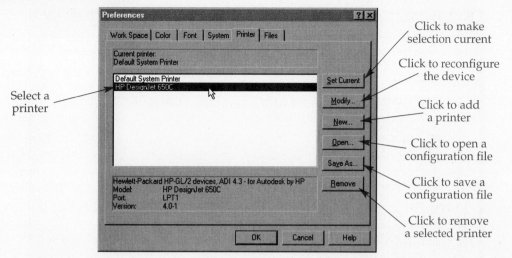

labeled **AutoCAD LT System Printer Configuration** displays over the **AutoCAD LT Text Window.** If you do not have a color printer, deactivate the **Allow dithered output** check box to obtain the highest degree of line quality from your AutoCAD LT printed drawings. See **Figure 20-11B.** As shown in **Figure 20-12,** AutoCAD LT then displays the **AutoCAD LT Text Window** with prompts for printer settings. If you just want to update the printer description, click the **OK** button instead of the **Reconfigure** button in the **Reconfigure a Printer** subdialog box.

● **New... button.** Clicking this button displays the **Add a Printer** subdialog box, **Figure 20-13.** To add a printer, select a device from the list of available output devices, provide a description in the **Add a description:** text box, and then click the **OK** button. AutoCAD LT then displays the **AutoCAD LT Text Window** with prompts for printer settings.

Figure 20-11.
A—The **Reconfigure a Printer** subdialog box can be used to change the description of a selected output device. B—The **AutoCAD LT System Printer Configuration** subdialog box is displayed when you reconfigure the default system printer.

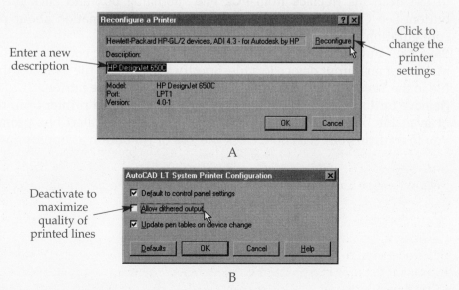

Figure 20-12.
Clicking the **Reconfigure** button in the **Reconfigure a Printer** subdialog box displays prompts for printer settings in the **AutoCAD LT Text Window**.

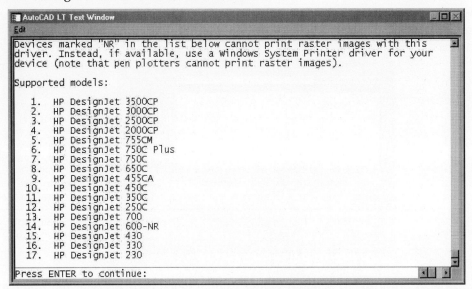

Figure 20-13.
The **Add a Printer** subdialog box is used to add an output device.

Select a new output device

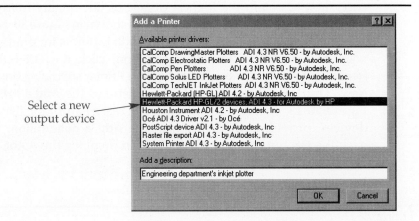

- **Open... button.** Clicking this button allows you to open a saved printer configuration file. Select the configuration file for the output device you wish to use from the **Replace from PC2 File** subdialog box and click the **Open** button. See *Chapter 14* of this text for complete information about printer configuration files.
- **Save As... button.** Click this button to save the complete configuration information for an output device to a file. Specify a folder and file name for the .pc2 file in the **Save PC2 File** subdialog box and click the **Save** button.
- **Remove button.** This button is used to remove a selected printer from the list of available output devices. AutoCAD LT displays an alert box prompting you to confirm your selection. Click the **Yes** or **No** button as appropriate.

The Files Tab Window

The **Files** tab window is used to specify the folders where AutoCAD LT looks for menus, text fonts, drawings to insert, linetypes, and hatch patterns that are not in the current folder. See **Figure 20-14**. It is also used to specify settings for other AutoCAD LT user-defined options, such as where to search for template files and which dictionary to use for spell checking. The search paths, file names, file locations, and other elements displayed in the **Files** tab window are described as follows:

- **Browse... button.** The **Files** tab window displays a list of the folders and files used by AutoCAD LT 98. To specify a location for a folder or file, select the desired folder or file from the list. If you wish to use a different file or folder after making a selection, click the **Browse...** button and use the **Browse for Folder** subdialog box to locate the desired file or folder, **Figure 20-15**.

Figure 20-14.
The **Files** tab window is used to specify folders, search paths, and other user-defined settings.

Existing search path

Click to specify a new file or folder location

Click to add a folder to the search path

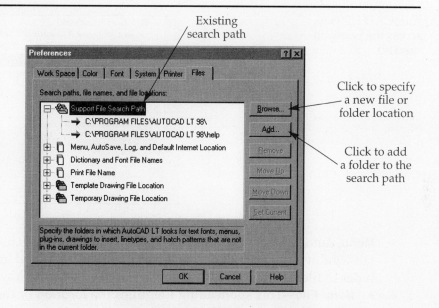

Figure 20-15.
The **Browse for Folder** subdialog box is displayed after clicking **Browse...** in the **Files** tab window.

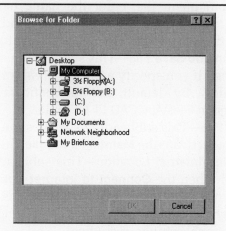

- **Support File Search Path.** Click the icon labeled with a plus symbol (+) to the left of the Support File Search Path heading to display all of the folders AutoCAD LT searches for support files. You can add a path to any new folder you create that may contain support files. As an example, suppose you store all of the blocks you typically use in a separate folder named Program Files\AutoCAD LT 98\blocks on the C: drive. Unless this folder name is placed in the Support File Search Path, AutoCAD LT will not be able to find your blocks when you attempt to insert them. To add this folder to the existing search path, click the **Add...** button in the tab window and enter the path name for the desired folder, as shown in **Figure 20-16**.

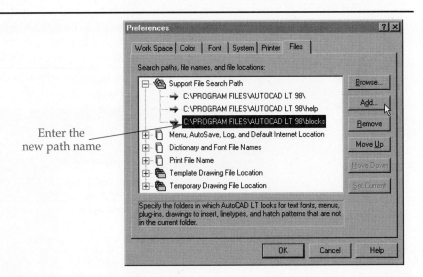

Figure 20-16.
Adding a folder to the Support File Search Path allows AutoCAD LT 98 to access the path you specify.

Enter the new path name

- **Menu, AutoSave, Log, and Default Internet Location.** This heading in the **Files** tab window contains subheadings that list the names and locations of various types of files. The four subheadings are described as follows:
  - **Menu File**—This subheading identifies the location of the AutoCAD LT 98 menu file. The default menu file is named aclt.mnu. If you wish to use a custom menu file, enter the name here. The current menu file is also controlled by the **MENULOAD** command. Only one menu file may be active at a time. See *Chapter 22* to learn how to create custom menus.
  - **Automatic Save File**—This subheading specifies the path for the file that is created if you specify a time interval for automatic saves in the **System** tab window. By default, the automatic saves file (auto.sv$) is stored in the \Program Files\AutoCAD LT 98 folder.
  - **Log File**—This subheading specifies the path for the log file that is created if you activate the **Maintain a log file** check box in the **System** tab window.
  - **Default Internet Location**—This subheading specifies the Internet location used when the **Connect to Internet** option is selected from the **Help** pull-down menu. By default, this location is http://www.autodesk.com/acltuser.
- **Dictionary and Font File Names.** This heading contains a number of subheadings with optional settings, including:
  - **Main Dictionary**—This subheading specifies the dictionary to use by the spell checker. You can specify an American, British, or French dictionary. The dictionary can also be specified by using the **DCTMAIN** system variable. See *Chapter 9* for more information about the AutoCAD LT 98 spell checker.
  - **Custom Dictionary File**—This subheading specifies the name and location of a custom dictionary if one has been created. You can also use the **DCTCUST** system variable for this purpose.

- **Alternate Font File**—This subheading specifies the font file to use if AutoCAD LT 98 cannot locate the original font and an alternate font is not specified in the font mapping file. This value defaults to simplex.shx and can be changed using the **FONTALT** system variable.
- **Font Mapping File**—This subheading specifies the name and location of the AutoCAD LT 98 font mapping file. The default file (aclt.fmp) defines how AutoCAD LT 98 should convert fonts that it cannot locate. The file name and location can also be specified using the **FONTMAP** system variable.
- **Print File Name.** This heading specifies the name to use for a saved plot file. The default name is the name of the current drawing plus the file extension .plt.
- **Template Drawing File Location.** This heading is used to specify the folder for the template files used by the start-up wizards. By default, this folder is \Program Files\AutoCAD LT 98\template.
- **Temporary Drawing File Location.** AutoCAD LT 98 creates several temporary files as it is running. These files are placed in the C:\Windows\Temp folder by default. When you exit AutoCAD LT, the temporary files are automatically deleted. Use the Temporary Drawing File Location heading if you wish to specify a different folder for the placement of these files.

NOTE Your temporary drawing file folder name and location may be different, depending on whether you are running Windows 98, Windows 95, or Windows NT.

EXERCISE 20-2

❑ Create the following folder for your block symbols:

C:\Program Files\AutoCAD LT 98\symbols

❑ Add the folder to the AutoCAD LT 98 search path as described in this chapter.

Positioning the Graphics Window and the AutoCAD LT Text Window

Perhaps the greatest advantage offered by the Microsoft Windows operating system is the ability to have several applications running in separate windows simultaneously. As a result, it is simple to click anywhere within an open window and use the application within it.

The first time AutoCAD LT 98 is loaded after the initial software installation, the graphics window normally fills the majority of the display screen. The **Content Explorer** window appears at the far right and slightly overlaps the graphics window. The **AutoCAD LT Text Window** is hidden behind the graphics window. It is only displayed when you press the [F2] function key, or when you select **Display** and then **Text Window** from the **View** pull-down menu. You can scale and position both windows so that each one is readily displayed. However, this is best accomplished on a 17" or larger monitor with a screen resolution of at least 800 × 600 (pixels).

Look at the screen display arrangement in **Figure 20-17**. The graphics window has been positioned below and to the left of the **AutoCAD LT Text Window**. With this window orientation, you can activate the **AutoCAD LT Text Window** by clicking anywhere within its border with the pick button on your pointing device. The window is then brought to the front, but a portion of the graphics window is still visible. When you want to return to the graphics window, simply click anywhere within its border. Also notice the position of the floating **Draw** and **Modify** toolbars. They have been relocated out of the graphics window so that they obscure very little of the active drawing area.

Figure 20-17.
The graphics window and the **AutoCAD LT Text Window** may be sized and positioned as desired. Note the location of the floating **Draw** and **Modify** toolbars.

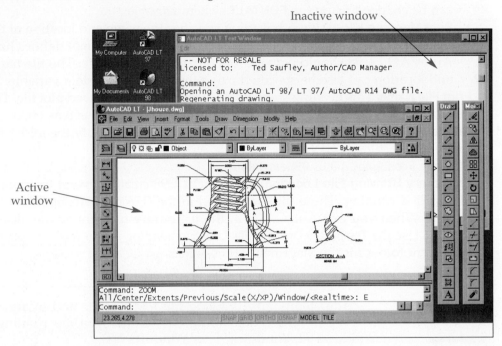

You can reposition an AutoCAD LT window by first clicking within the active title bar at the top of the window. Press and hold the pick button on your pointing device, drag the window to the desired location, and release the pick button. Once you have placed the graphics window and the **AutoCAD LT Text Window** where you want them, the windows will remain at the defined locations for all subsequent AutoCAD LT sessions until you relocate them.

Sizing the AutoCAD LT Windows

Resizing a window is as easy as moving its location. To stretch or shrink a window along its vertical axis, simply click and hold at the top or bottom border of the window. The pointer assumes the shape of a double arrow, **Figure 20-18A**. Drag the border to the desired size and release the pick button. To stretch or shrink a window along its horizontal axis, click and hold at the left or right border of the window. The pointer again assumes the shape of a double arrow. Drag the border to the desired size and release the pick button. To stretch or shrink a window along both axes simultaneously, click and hold at one of the four corners of the window. The pointer changes to the double arrow, **Figure 20-18B**. Drag the corner to the desired position and release the pick button. This method also helps to maintain the correct aspect ratio of the window.

By increasing the width of a window border, you may find it easier to select within the border. To do so, first select Settings from the Start menu on the Windows taskbar, and then select Control Panel. When the Control Panel window appears, double-click the Display icon. Click the Appearance tab when the Display Properties dialog box appears. Next, select Active Window Border from the Item: drop-down list. See **Figure 20-19**. Use the up and down arrows or the text box to increase or decrease the window border width. The window border width is measured in pixels.

Figure 20-18.
A—Clicking the top or bottom border of a window allows you to adjust its size vertically. The right or left border can be clicked to adjust the horizontal size of the window. B—A window can be resized along both axes simultaneously by clicking one of the window corners and dragging the pointing device.

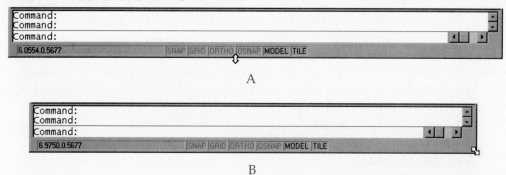

A

B

Figure 20-19.
Select Active Window Border from the Item: drop-down list in the Display Properties dialog box to increase or decrease the window border width.

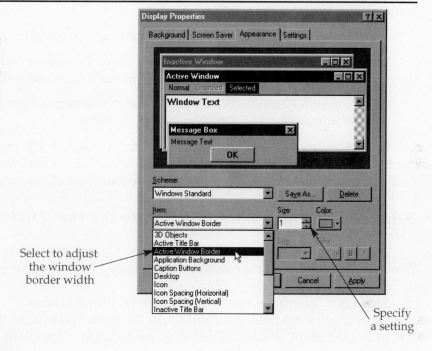

Select to adjust the window border width

Specify a setting

PROFESSIONAL TIP

The following is a quick way to open the Display Properties dialog box. Place your cursor over an open area on the Microsoft Windows desktop and click the right button of your pointing device. When the pop-up menu appears, select Properties from the bottom of the menu to display the dialog box.

EXERCISE 20-3

❑ Using the methods previously described, change the position and size of both AutoCAD LT windows and the **Draw** and **Modify** toolbars to resemble those illustrated in **Figure 20-17**.

❑ Try several different window and toolbar configurations until you are satisfied with the screen display.

Starting AutoCAD LT Using Command Line Switches

Command line switches can be used to specify several start-up options when AutoCAD LT starts. For example, you can instruct AutoCAD LT to start with a specified template drawing, run a script file, and display a saved view when a drawing is opened. Using command line switches, you can also set up several AutoCAD LT icons, each with different start-up options.

Command line switches are parameters that are added to the aclt.exe command line file. The command lines in this file are associated with a Windows shortcut icon or the Windows Run dialog box. Several switches can be included within a single command line. The valid switches are as follows:

/b Script name *("b" stands for batch process)*
/t Template file name
/c Configuration folder
/v View name

The proper syntax must be used when typing command line switches. The syntax is as follows:

"drive:pathname\aclt.exe" ["drawing_name"] [/switch "name"]

When using a switch option, you must follow the switch with a space and then the name of the file, path, or view in quotation marks. Consider the following:

"C:\Program Files\AutoCAD LT 98\aclt.exe" /t "C:\Program Files\AutoCAD LT 98\template\mech" /v "revision_history" /b "setup"

In this example, the first switch starts AutoCAD LT from the C:\Program Files\AutoCAD LT 98 folder with a template drawing named mech. The next two switches restore a view named revision_history and execute the setup.scr script file.

Adding Command Line Switches to the Run Dialog Box

As previously mentioned, the aclt.exe command line file is associated with a Windows shortcut icon or the Windows Run dialog box. To set switches using the Run dialog box, do the following:

1. Select Run... from the Start menu on the Windows taskbar.
2. Enter the desired path and switches in the Open: text box. In the example shown in **Figure 20-20**, AutoCAD LT 98 is started and a template file named arch is loaded by entering the following:

   "C:\Program Files\AutoCAD LT 98\aclt.exe" /t "C:\Program Files\AutoCAD LT 98\template\arch"

3. Click the **OK** button when you are finished.

Figure 20-20.
Setting a command line switch using the Windows Run dialog box.

Enter the command line switch

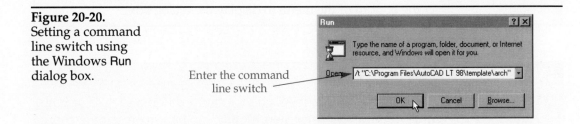

AutoCAD LT—Fundamentals and Applications

Adding Command Line Switches to the AutoCAD LT 98 Desktop Shortcut

When AutoCAD LT 98 is first installed on your computer, the setup.exe program automatically creates the AutoCAD LT 98 shortcut icon on the Microsoft Windows desktop, **Figure 20-21A**. If desired, you can modify the properties associated with the shortcut. These properties include command line switches, a defined folder that contains an original item or some related files that AutoCAD LT 98 needs, the use of a shortcut key to start AutoCAD LT 98, and the icon that AutoCAD LT 98 uses to represent the application.

To modify the properties, place your pointing device over the AutoCAD LT 98 shortcut icon and right-click. When the pop-up shortcut menu appears, select Properties to display the AutoCAD LT 98 Properties dialog box. Click the Shortcut tab to open the Shortcut tab window, **Figure 20-21B**. The various elements of this tab window are described as follows:

- **Target:** This text box displays the name of the item that the shortcut points to. A shortcut can point to a file, folder, printer, or computer on a network.
- **Start in:** This text box specifies the folder that contains the original item or some related files. Occasionally, programs need to use files from other locations. Use this text box to specify the folder where these files reside so the program can find them.

Figure 20-21.
A—The AutoCAD LT 98 shortcut icon. B—The default settings in the Shortcut tab window of the AutoCAD LT 98 Properties dialog box.

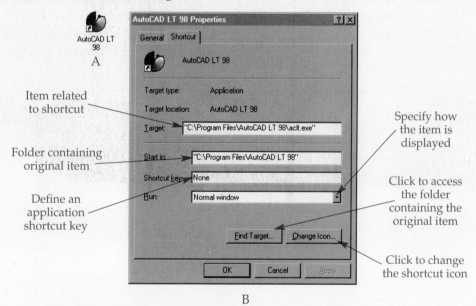

B

- **Shortcut key:** The Microsoft Windows operating systems provide a special feature called an *application shortcut key.* This feature permits you to launch AutoCAD LT 98, or any other application, with a key combination that you define. No matter where you are in Windows 98, 95, or NT, and regardless of which application is currently running, you can quickly start AutoCAD LT 98 by using the shortcut key. A shortcut key must include a [Ctrl] key and/or [Alt] key and another key. You cannot use the [Esc], [Enter], [Tab], [Print Screen], [Backspace], or space bar keys, however. Since AutoCAD LT 98 does not use the [F11] or [F12] function keys, one of these would make a good choice. To create a shortcut key, click anywhere within the Shortcut key: text box. The flashing vertical cursor immediately appears at the end of the word None. Now, press the [Ctrl] key and/or [Alt] key and the key you want to assign, such as [F12]. The character combination you press then appears in the text box. Click the Apply button and then click the Close button to exit the AutoCAD LT 98 Properties dialog box. Since any changes you make take effect immediately, there is no need to restart Windows.
- **Run:** This drop-down list is used to specify how you want the window to display the item when you open the shortcut. You can choose from a normal window (the default), a full screen (the maximized option), or a button on the taskbar (the minimized option).
- **Find Target...** Clicking this button opens the folder containing the original item that the shortcut points to.
- **Change Icon...** Click this button when you wish to change the shortcut icon used by AutoCAD LT 98 on the Microsoft Windows desktop. When the Change Icon subdialog box appears, click the Browse... button and then select the \Program Files\AutoCAD LT 98 folder. Next, select aclt.exe from the list of files and click the Open button. Select the icon you wish to use and click the OK button to exit the Change Icon subdialog box. See **Figure 20-22**. Your icon selection is now displayed in the upper-left corner of the AutoCAD LT 98 Properties dialog box.

Figure 20-22.
Selecting an icon from the Windows 98 Change Icon subdialog box.

Select a new icon

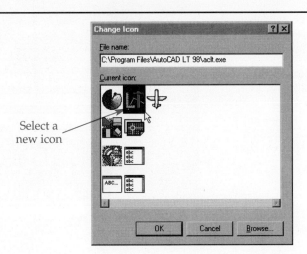

Defining a New Desktop Shortcut

It is possible to create different configurations of AutoCAD LT 98 by defining your own desktop shortcuts. Each configuration can utilize different command line switches. To create a desktop shortcut, use the following procedure:

1. Place your pointing device over an empty area on the Microsoft Windows desktop and right-click.
2. When the pop-up menu appears, **Figure 20-23**, click New and then select Shortcut from the cascading submenu.
3. The Create Shortcut dialog box appears, **Figure 20-24**. Click the Browse... button and select aclt.exe from the \Program Files\AutoCAD LT 98 folder in the Browse subdialog box. Add the desired command line switch(es) as described earlier in this chapter. Click the Next > button when you are finished.
4. Provide a name for the shortcut in the Select a Title for the Program subdialog box and click the Finish button. See **Figure 20-25**.
5. If desired, select a different icon for the new desktop shortcut as described in this chapter. An example is shown in **Figure 20-26**.

Figure 20-23.
To create a desktop shortcut, select New from the desktop pop-up menu and then select Shortcut from the cascading submenu.

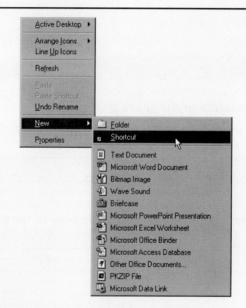

Figure 20-24.
The Create Shortcut dialog box.

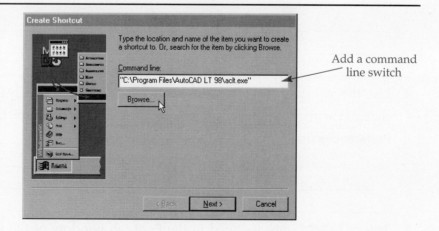

Add a command line switch

Figure 20-25.
When the Select a
Title for the Program
subdialog box
appears, enter a
name for the
shortcut.

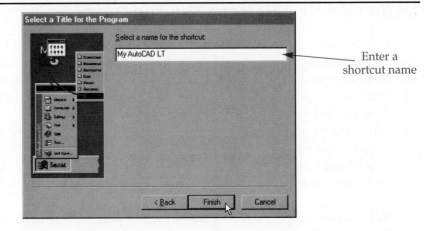

Enter a
shortcut name

Figure 20-26. The
new desktop
shortcut displays the
name you provide
and (by option) a
different icon.

My AutoCAD
LT

Chapter Test

Write your answers in the space provided

1. List two methods to access the **Preferences** dialog box. _____

   _____

   _____

   _____

2. Explain two ways to control the display of the **Start Up** dialog box when you start
   AutoCAD LT. _____

   _____

   _____

3. Describe the steps required to change the size of the graphics cursor displayed on
   screen._____

   _____

   _____

   _____

4. List the windows and other display elements of AutoCAD LT that can be
   changed with the color customization options in the **Color** tab window of the
   Preferences dialog box._____

   _____

   _____

   _____

5. *True or False?* Fonts assigned in the **Font** tab window of the **Preferences** dialog
   box may be used in an AutoCAD LT drawing. _____

6. Which tab window and check box in the **Preferences** dialog box is used to activate or deactivate the automatic creation of backup drawing files? _____

   _____

7. Which system variable allows you to enable the creation of a log file to record the prompts and messages that appear in the **AutoCAD LT Text Window**?_____

   _____

8. Explain the steps used to save your drawing files at specified time intervals using the **Preferences** dialog box. _____

   _____

   _____

   _____

9. Describe how to direct AutoCAD LT to accept pointing device input from the system pointing device as well as a digitizing tablet. _____

   _____

   _____

10. How can you access the **Add a Printer** dialog box to specify a different output device? _____

   _____

   _____

11. AutoCAD LT resides in the C:\Program Files folder on your workstation. You have created two folders under \Program Files named projects and symbols. You want to store your drawings in the projects folder and your blocks in the symbols folder. What should you enter under the Support File Search Path in the **Files** tab window of the **Preferences** dialog box so that these folders are added to the existing search path?_____

   _____

12. By default, which folder contains temporary files that are created during a drawing session in AutoCAD LT?_____

   _____

13. Describe how to reposition an AutoCAD LT window. _____

   _____

   _____

14. How do you increase the width of an AutoCAD LT window border?

   _____

   _____

   _____

15. Describe how to set command line switches using the Windows Run dialog box.

   _____

   _____

16. Which AutoCAD LT file is used to create a desktop shortcut by defining a configuration with command line switches? _____

Chapter Problems

General

1. Create an alternate configuration that starts AutoCAD LT with the TITLEA.DWT template file. Use the following instructions to complete this problem.

   A. Assign a different program item icon to the A-size configuration.
   B. Name the program item label AutoCAD LT A-size.
   C. Define a shortcut key for the configuration.

General

2. Create an alternate configuration that starts AutoCAD LT with the TITLEB.DWT template file. Use the following instructions to complete this problem.

   A. Assign a different program item icon to the B-size configuration.
   B. Name the program item label AutoCAD LT B-size.
   C. Define a shortcut key for the configuration.

General

3. Create an alternate configuration that starts AutoCAD LT with the TITLEC.DWT template file. Use the following instructions to complete this problem.

   A. Assign a different program item icon to the C-size configuration.
   B. Name the program item label AutoCAD LT C-size.
   C. Define a shortcut key for the configuration.

Chapter 21

AutoCAD LT

Toolbar Customization and Creating Keyboard Command Shortcuts

Learning Objectives

After you have completed this chapter, you will be able to:
- ○ Display any or all of the AutoCAD LT toolbars.
- ○ Change the description of an existing tool button.
- ○ Create a toolbar command micro.
- ○ Add buttons to existing toolbars.
- ○ Create your own custom toolbar.
- ○ Design a custom tool button.
- ○ Create a custom flyout.
- ○ Assign keyboard shortcuts to commands.

The graphical tool buttons that appear on the AutoCAD LT toolbars provide a quick and easy way to issue commands. When you move your pointing device over a tool button, the tooltips balloon displays the name of the tool. Tool buttons with a small black triangle in the lower-right corner have flyouts that contain related commands. With your cursor over the tool icon, press and hold the pick button on your pointing device until the flyout appears. In this chapter, you will learn to create your own tool buttons and toolbars, as well as how to modify existing tool buttons and toolbars. Additionally, you will learn how to create a custom flyout containing your favorite, or most frequently used commands. For users of AutoCAD LT 98, assigning keyboard shortcuts to commands is also described.

Working with Toolbars

Getting Started Guide 2

When first installed, AutoCAD LT displays four toolbars. They are the **Standard Toolbar**, the **Object Properties** toolbar, the **Draw** toolbar, and the **Modify** toolbar. All four toolbars are in docked positions by default. The **Standard Toolbar** and **Object Properties** toolbar are docked at the top of the drawing window, while the **Draw** and **Modify** toolbars are docked at the left side of the drawing window. See **Figure 21-1A**.

A toolbar can be floating or docked. A floating toolbar can be located anywhere in the AutoCAD LT drawing window. The **Draw** and **Modify** toolbars are shown floating at the right side of the drawing window in **Figure 21-1B**. You can drag a floating toolbar to a new location, resize it, or dock it so that it is attached to any edge of the drawing area. You can move a docked toolbar by undocking it and dragging it to a new docking location.

To remove a toolbar from the display, first place the toolbar in a floating state. Then click the **Close** button (represented by an "X") at the upper-right corner of the toolbar.

Figure 21-1.
A—The toolbars in their default docked positions. B—The **Draw** and **Modify** toolbars in a floating state.

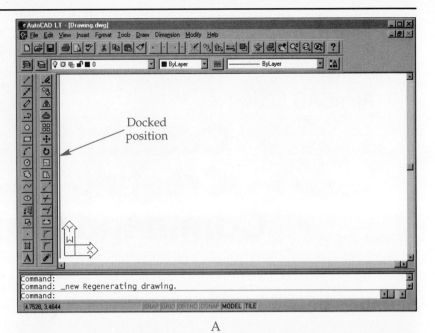

A

B

Resizing Floating Toolbars

Although you cannot change the shape of a docked toolbar, a floating toolbar can be resized along its horizontal or vertical axes. To resize a toolbar horizontally, select the toolbar at its left or right vertical edge. The pointer on your pointing device changes to a double-arrow. Press and hold the pick button on your pointing device as you drag the toolbar in a horizontal direction. See **Figure 21-2A**. When the toolbar assumes the shape you want, release the pick button on your pointing device.

To resize a toolbar vertically, select the toolbar at its top or bottom edge. Once again, press and hold the pick button on your pointing device as you drag the toolbar in a vertical direction. See **Figure 21-2B**. Release the pick button when the toolbar is in the desired orientation. The toolbar will retain its new size for subsequent drawing sessions.

Figure 21-2.
A—Resizing a
floating toolbar
horizontally. B—
Resizing a floating
toolbar vertically.

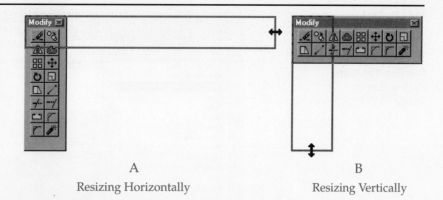

A
Resizing Horizontally

B
Resizing Vertically

Turning on Additional Toolbars

There are a total of 14 toolbars available to you in AutoCAD LT 98. There are 13 toolbars available for AutoCAD LT 97 users. Each of these toolbars is shown for your reference on the inside rear cover of this textbook. To open a toolbar, enter TOOLBAR, or TO, at the Command: prompt or select **Toolbars...** from the **View** pull-down menu. See **Figure 21-3.** The command sequence is as follows:

Command: **TOOLBAR** *or* **TO**↵

The Customize dialog box appears. See **Figure 21-4A.** For users of AutoCAD LT 97, the **Toolbars** dialog box is presented, instead. See **Figure 21-4B.** Use the vertical scroll bar to locate the toolbar you wish to display. Then, click the check box to the left of the toolbar name to activate and display the toolbar. The **Dimension** toolbar is activated in the examples shown in **Figure 21-4.** Click the **Close** button when you are finished. The other options available in these dialog boxes are described more fully later in this chapter.

TOOLBAR
TO

View
➥ Toolbar...

Figure 21-3.
Selecting **Toolbars...**
from the **View** pull-down menu issues
the **TOOLBAR**
command.

Figure 21-4.
A—The **Customize** dialog box in AutoCAD LT 98.
B—The **Toolbars** dialog box in AutoCAD LT 97.

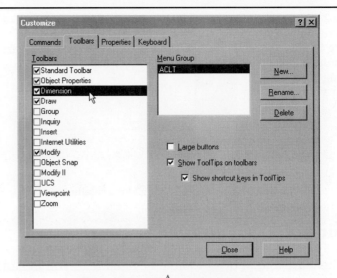

A

B

Using the Toolbar Short-Cut Menu

Users of AutoCAD LT 98 can quickly open or close a single toolbar by placing your pointing device over any tool button and right-clicking. The short-cut menu then appears. See **Figure 21-5**. Select the toolbar you wish to open (or close). As soon as you make your selection, the short-cut menu disappears and the operation is completed. Observe that selecting **Customize...** from the bottom of the short-cut menu enables the **Customize** dialog box.

Figure 21-5.
With the short-cut menu, toolbars can be opened or closed, and the **Customize** dialog box enabled.

Opening and Closing a Toolbar Quickly in AutoCAD LT 97

Although there is no toolbar short-cut menu for users of AutoCAD LT 97, multiple toolbars can still be opened or closed quickly by placing your pointing device over a tool button and right-clicking. The **Toolbars** dialog box then appears, and one or more toolbars can be selected for opening (or closing). When you are finished making your selection(s), click the **Close** button to terminate the operation.

Managing Toolbars on the Command Line

Toolbars can also be opened, hidden, and placed by entering the **-TOOLBAR** command at the keyboard. In the following example, the **Object Snap** toolbar is opened. Note the use of the underscore character when a toolbar name contains more than one word.

        Command: **-TOOLBAR**⏎
        Toolbar name (or ALL): **OBJECT_SNAP**⏎
        Show/Hide/Left/Right/Top/Bottom/Float: ⟨Show⟩: *(select an option or press* [Enter]*)*
        Command:

When prompted for the toolbar name, you can use the **ALL** option to display or close *all* toolbars. You are then prompted with:

        Show/Hide: *(enter* S *or* H *and press* [Enter]*)*

The **Show** option displays all toolbars—the **Hide** option closes all toolbars. Each of the other **-TOOLBAR** command options are described as follows:

- ⟨**Show**⟩. This default option displays the specified toolbar in a floating state. You can then move or dock it as desired.
- **Hide.** This option closes the specified toolbar.
- **Left.** Docks the specified toolbar at the left side of the graphics window. You are then prompted to specify a position which sets the position of the toolbar in columns and rows relative to a toolbar dock. The first value is horizontal. The second value is vertical.

        Position ⟨0,0⟩: *(specify a position or press* [Enter]*)*

- **Right.** Docks the specified toolbar at the right side of the graphics window. As with the **Left** option, you are prompted to specify a position.
- **Top.** Docks the specified toolbar at the top of the graphics window. As with the **Left** and **Right** options, you are prompted to specify a position.
- **Bottom.** Docks the specified toolbar at the bottom of the graphics window. As with the **Left**, **Right**, and **Top** options, you are prompted to specify a position.
- **Float.** Use this option to change the toolbar from docked to floating. You are prompted as follows:

        Position ⟨0,0⟩: *(specify a position or press* [Enter]*)*
        Rows ⟨1⟩: *(specify a value)*

The Position prompt specifies the location of the floating toolbar in screen coordinate values. The Rows prompt specifies the number of rows in the floating toolbar.

PROFESSIONAL TIP   Use the default **Show** option when entering the **-TOOLBAR** command. You can then move and/or resize the toolbar much faster and easier than by entering position and row values.

Displaying Large Tool Buttons

You can increase the size of the tool buttons by opening the **Customize** dialog box and activating the **Large Buttons** check box. This option changes the size of the buttons from 16 by 15 pixels to 24 by 22 pixels. An example of large buttons at 800 x 600 screen resolution is shown in **Figure 21-6.** Observe that when large buttons are enabled at lower screen resolutions, fewer tool buttons can be displayed on your screen.

Figure 21-6.
The graphics window as it appears with large tool buttons.

Large toolbar buttons

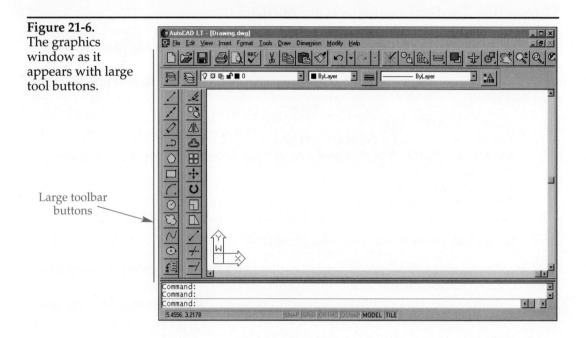

Disabling Tooltips

A *tooltip* is a pop-up label describing each tool button as your cursor passes over it. Although not recommended, you can turn off the tooltips by opening the **Customize** dialog box and deactivating the **Show ToolTips on toolbars** check box. For users of AutoCAD LT 97, this capability is provided within the **Toolbars** dialog box. For both versions of AutoCAD LT, you can also control the display of tooltips using the **TOOLTIPS** system variable like this:

    Command: **TOOLTIPS**↵
    New value for TOOLTIPS ⟨current⟩: (enter 0 or 1 and press [Enter])

A value of 0 (zero) turns off the display of tooltips—the default value of 1 turns the display on.

EXERCISE 21-1

❑ Begin a new drawing from scratch.
❑ Change the **Draw** and **Modify** toolbars to a floating state. Resize and locate them as shown in **Figure 21-1B.**
❑ Open the **Dimensioning** toolbar and dock it at the left edge of the drawing window.
❑ Next, change the size of the tool buttons from small to large. If you are dissatisfied with their appearance, change them back to small. Also, try toggling the tooltips display off and back on.
❑ Finally, experiment with each of the options of the **-TOOLBAR** command.

Redefining the Properties of an Existing Tool Button

You can easily change the function of an existing tool button without any knowledge of programming techniques. In the following example, the **Multiline Text** tool button on the **Draw** toolbar is changed to invoke the **DTEXT** command instead of **MTEXT**. The procedure is as follows:

1. Open the **Customize** dialog box using any of the methods previously described.
2. When the **Customize** dialog box appears, click the **Properties** tab to display the **Properties** window. See **Figure 21-7**.
3. Next, click the **Multiline Text** tool button in the **Draw** toolbar and the **Button Properties** window appears. This window displays the properties of the selected **Multiline Text** tool button. See **Figure 21-8A**.
4. Change the tool button name from Multiline Text to Dynamic Text in the **Name:** text box. See **Figure 21-8B**. The name(s) you enter is used for the tool button's tooltip.
5. Edit the description of the button in the **Description**: text box. This description is displayed on the status bar at the bottom of the graphics window when you pass your cursor over the tool button.
6. Next, edit the **Macro associated with this button:** text box to read, ^C^C_dtext. The macro definition controls the command or set of commands associated with a tool button. Separate a series of commands using a semicolon (;). In case you are wondering about the underscore character (_) in the macro, here is the reason. If you develop menus that can be used with a foreign-language version of AutoCAD LT, the standard AutoCAD LT commands and key words are translated automatically if you precede each command or key word with the underscore character.
7. The carat (^) and letter C perform a cancel function. Two cancels are provided in the event that the button is clicked while in dimensioning mode. The first cancel operation cancels the dimensioning command in progress and the second cancel operation cancels dimensioning mode before issuing the **DTEXT** command.
8. When you are through, click the **Apply** button at the lower right of the **Button Properties** window and then click the **Close** button. The tool button properties are now redefined.

Figure 21-7.
The **Properties** tab window in the **Customize** dialog box.

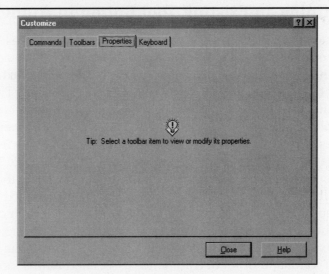

Figure 21-8.
A—The **Button Properties** window displays the properties of the selected tool button. B—Changing the **Multiline Text** tool button properties to **Dynamic Text**.

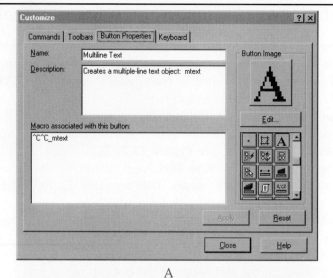

A

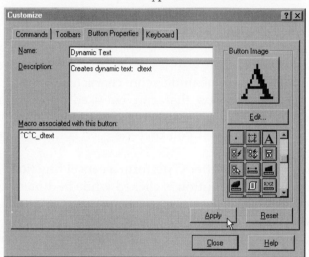

B

Redefining an Existing Tool Button in AutoCAD LT 97

AutoCAD LT 97 users can also edit the properties of existing tool buttons. However, the procedure is slightly different from that used in AutoCAD LT 98. The following example once again modifies the **Multiline Text** tool button on the **Draw** toolbar to invoke the **DTEXT** command instead of **MTEXT**. The procedure is as follows:

1. Double right-click with your pointing device over the button you wish to redefine. The **Toolbars** dialog box is displayed and then the **Button Properties** subdialog box appears. This subdialog box displays the properties of the **Multiline Text** button. See **Figure 21-9A.**

2. Change the button name from Multiline Text to Dynamic Text in the **Name:** text box. See **Figure 21-9B.** The name(s) you enter is used for the button's tooltip.

3. Edit the description of the button in the **Help:** text box. This description is displayed on the status bar at the bottom of the graphics window when you pass your cursor over the tool button.

4. Next, edit the **Macro:** text box to read, ^C^C_dtext. The macro definition controls the command or set of commands associated with a tool button. Separate a series of commands using a semicolon (;). Observe the use of the underscore character that precedes the command. As with AutoCAD LT 98, if you develop menus that can be used with a foreign-language version of AutoCAD LT 97, the standard AutoCAD LT commands and key words are translated automatically if you precede each command or key word with the underscore character.

Figure 21-9.
A—In AutoCAD LT 97, the **Button Properties** subdialog box displays the properties of the selected tool button. B—Changing the **Multiline Text** tool button properties to **Dynamic Text**.

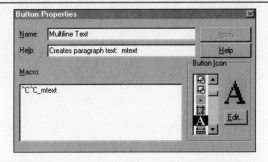

A

B

5. The carat (^) and letter C perform a cancel function. Two cancels are provided in the event that the button is clicked while in dimensioning mode. The first cancel operation cancels the dimensioning command in progress and the second cancel operation cancels dimensioning mode before issuing the **DTEXT** command.

6. When you are through, click the **Apply** button at the upper right of the **Button Properties** subdialog box and then click the **Close** button in the **Toolbars** dialog box. The tool button is now redefined.

NOTE

The AutoCAD LT menu files are stored in the C:\Program Files\AutoCAD LT 98 or the C:\Program Files\AutoCAD LT 97 folder by default. They are described more fully in *Chapter 22* of this text. The menu file names are aclt.mnc, aclt.mnr, aclt.mns, and aclt.mnu, respectively. Changing toolbars and tool button descriptions, as well as modifying the pull-down menus or digitizer tablet menu overlay, automatically changes several of the AutoCAD LT menu files. Therefore, it is always a good idea to make backup copies of these menu files before customizing tool buttons and/or toolbars. You can then easily restore the original menu files if something goes wrong or if you are dissatisfied with your modifications. It is also possible to restore the original menus using the **MENULOAD** command, which is described later in this chapter.

Adding Command Macros to Tool Buttons

A command macro is a character string containing up to 255 uppercase or lower-case characters that can perform one or more AutoCAD LT commands with the click of a single tool button. As an example, consider the following command macro string:

    ^C^C_limits 0,0 22,17;_zoom all;_snap .5;_grid s

As previously mentioned, each command is separated by a semicolon. Therefore, this button macro performs the following functions:
- Sets the drawing limits to 22,17 for a C-size drawing.
- Performs a **ZOOM All** to zoom to the new screen limits.
- Sets the snap spacing to .5 units.
- Sets the grid spacing to match the snap spacing.

Tool button command macros can be used in a variety of ways. As an example, the template files that you created in *Chapter 5* of this textbook contain four layers named Objects, Centerlines, Hatching, and Notes. You can modify any of the tool buttons to automatically set the appropriate layer current using the **CLAYER** system variable before creating any drawing objects. Consider the following tool button macro examples:

    ^C^C_clayer objects;_line
    ^C^C_clayer centerlines;_dimcenter
    ^C^C_clayer hatching;_bhatch
    ^C^C_clayer notes;_dtext

You can see that from the examples above that when you click the **Line** tool button, the layer is automatically changed to the Objects layer for any new lines you draw. Clicking the **Bhatch** tool button automatically sets the Hatching layer current, and so on.

PROFESSIONAL TIP

Do not forget to add the character string ^C at the start of the tool button macro if you want to cancel a command in progress. The string ^C^C is even better because if you are in dimensioning mode when you click the modified button, dimensioning mode is canceled before executing the macro.

EXERCISE 21-2

❏ Check with your instructor or supervisor before beginning this exercise.
❏ Make backup copies of the aclt.mnr and aclt.mns files.
❏ Change the function of the **Multiline Text** button to **Dynamic Text** as described in the previous section.
❏ Try changing the functions of several other tool buttons as well.
❏ Using the examples shown in the previous section, add command macros that change the current layer before executing a drawing or dimensioning command. Select any four tool buttons of your choice.

Adding Tool Buttons to Existing Toolbars

It is a simple matter to add additional tool buttons to existing toolbars. To do so, open the **Customize** dialog box previously described. When the dialog box appears, click the **Commands** tab to display the categories and commands that can be modified. See **Figure 21-10.** The **Commands** tab window offers the following categories from which to choose:

File
Edit
View
Insert
Format
Tools
Draw
Dimension
Modify
Help
All Commands
User defined
Flyouts

Figure 21-10.
The **Commands** tab window in the **Customize** dialog box.

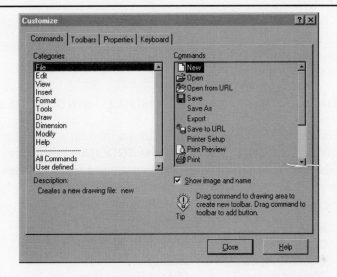

In the example shown in **Figure 21-11, Modify** is selected from the **Categories** list at the left of the window, and the **Edit Text** tool button (**DDEDIT**) is selected from the **Commands** list at the right. Once you locate the tool button you wish to add from the **Commands** list, select it and press and hold the pick button on your pointing device as you drag the tool button to the desired toolbar. An outline of the tool button appears on screen as it is dragged. See **Figure 21-11.** Drag the tool button to the toolbar of your choice and position it where you want it to be located. Positioning the tool button between two existing tool buttons places the new tool button between them. Once the tool button is located to your satisfaction, release the pick button on your pointing device to place it. As shown in **Figure 21-12,** the **Edit Text** tool button has been added between the **Erase** and **Copy Object** tool buttons on the **Modify** toolbar.

If you are dissatisfied with your modifications, simply drag the new button off the toolbar where it was added. Do this while the **Commands** tab window is still open, however. AutoCAD LT then displays an alert box asking you to confirm the deletion of the tool button from the toolbar. Click the **OK** or **Cancel** buttons in the alert box as appropriate.

When you are finished adding tool buttons, click the **Close** button to exit the **Commands** tab window and return to the Command: prompt.

Figure 21-11.
An outline of the
tool button appears
as it is dragged to
an existing toolbar.

Tool button
outline

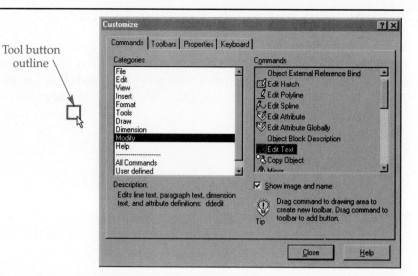

Figure 21-12.
The **Edit Text** tool button is added between the **Erase** and **Copy Object** tool buttons on the **Modify** toolbar.

Adding Tool Buttons to Existing Toolbars in AutoCAD LT 97

It is also a simple matter to add additional tool buttons to existing toolbars in AutoCAD LT 97. To do so, issue the **TOOLBAR** command as previously described. When the **Toolbars** dialog box appears, click the **Customize...** button. The **Customize Toolbars** subdialog box is then displayed. This subdialog box contains a drop-down list offering the following toolbar categories from which to choose:

Attribute	**External Reference**
Custom	**Internet**
Custom Flyout	**Modify**
Dimensioning	**Object Properties**
Draw	**Standard**

In the example shown in **Figure 21-13,** the **Edit Text** button (**DDEDIT**) is selected from the **Modify** category in the drop-down list. Keep in mind that tooltips are not used when passing your cursor over the tool buttons in the **Customize Toolbars** subdialog box. When you wish to see the description of a tool button, click the button of interest. Its description then appears at the bottom of the subdialog box.

Once you locate the tool button you wish to add, select it and press and hold the pick button on your pointing device as you drag the tool button to the desired toolbar. An outline of the tool button appears on screen as it is dragged. See **Figure 21-14.** Drag the tool button to the toolbar of your choice and position it where you want it to be located. Positioning the tool button between two existing tool buttons places the new button between them. Once the tool button is located to your satisfaction, release the pick button on your pointing device to place it. As shown in **Figure 21-15,** the **Edit Text** tool button has been added between the **Fillet** and **Explode** tool buttons on the **Modify** toolbar.

If you are dissatisfied with your modifications, simply drag the new tool button off the toolbar where it was added. Do this while the **Customize Toolbars** subdialog box is still open, however. When you are finished adding tool buttons, click each **Close** button to exit the dialog boxes and return to the Command: prompt.

AutoCAD LT—Fundamentals and Applications

Figure 21-13.
Selecting a tool button from the **Customize Toolbars** subdialog box in AutoCAD LT 97.

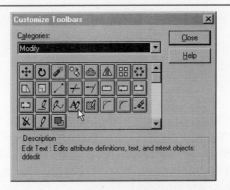

Figure 21-14.
An outline of the tool button appears as it is dragged to an existing toolbar.

Tool button outline

Figure 21-15.
The **Edit Text** tool button is added between the **Fillet** and **Explode** tool buttons on the **Modify** toolbar.

EXERCISE 21-3

❑ Check with your instructor or supervisor before beginning this exercise.
❑ Make backup copies of the aclt.mnr and aclt.mns files if you have not already done so.
❑ Add the **Ray** tool button to the **Draw** toolbar. Locate it between the **Line** and **Construction Line** tool buttons.
❑ Add the **Oops!** tool button to the **Modify** toolbar. Locate it between the **Erase** and **Copy Object** tool buttons.
❑ Try adding some additional tool buttons of your choice to the **Standard Toolbar** and **Object Properties** toolbar.

It is a simple matter to create a completely new toolbar that contains your most frequently used tools. Perform the following tutorial to create a toolbar that contains tool buttons appropriate for attribute definitions, attribute editing, and block creation and insertion.

⇨ Open the **Customize** dialog box and click the **Toolbars** tab to display the **Toolbars** window (if not already displayed). Then, click the **New...** button.

⇨ The **New Toolbar** subdialog box appears. Enter the name Attribute Management in the **Toolbar name:** text box as shown in **Figure 21-16.** Click the **OK** button when you are finished.

⇨ The new toolbar name now appears in the **Toolbars** list in the **Customize** dialog box. See **Figure 21-17.** Observe that the new toolbar is automatically placed near the top of the graphics window. You can freely move the toolbar to a more convenient location if desired.

⇨ Click the **Commands** tab to display the list of available categories and commands in the **Commands** window. Select **All Commands** from the **Categories** list at the left of the window. Then scroll down the **Commands** list at the right and select the **Make Block (BMAKE)** tool. (To help you locate the tool button command you desire, the tool button descriptions are listed in alphabetical order.) Once you have found and selected a command from the **Commands** list, a description of the command is displayed at the lower left of the dialog box. See **Figure 21-18.**

⇨ Now, press and hold the pick button on your pointing device and drag the **Make Block** command button to the **Attribute Management** toolbar.

⇨ Next, locate the **Define Attribute**, **Edit Attribute**, and **Edit Attribute Globally** command buttons. Drag each of these buttons (one at a time) to the **Attribute Management** toolbar also. The three buttons perform the **DDATTDEF, DDATTE,** and **ATTEDIT** commands, respectively.

⇨ Also add the **Insert Block (DDINSERT)** and **Edit Text (DDEDIT)** buttons to your toolbar. Your new toolbar should appear as shown in **Figure 21-19.** Click the **Close** button to return to the Command: prompt.

⇨ You can now dock the new **Attribute Management** toolbar, or leave it in a floating state as you desire. Remember that you can also resize the toolbar along its horizontal or vertical axes if you wish.

Figure 21-16.
Providing a name
for the new toolbar.

Enter new
toolbar name
here

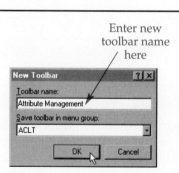

Figure 21-17.
The new toolbar name appears in the **Toolbars** list at the left of the **Customize** dialog box.

New toolbar name

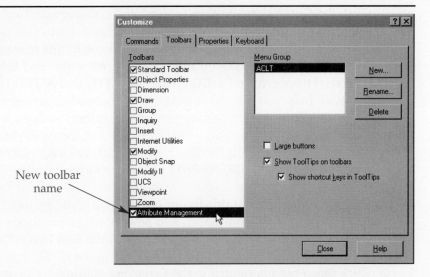

Figure 21-18.
The **Make Block** tool button is selected from the **Commands** list at the right of the **Customize** dialog box.

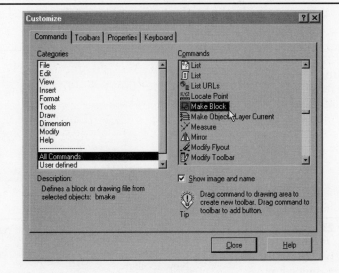

Figure 21-19.
The completed **Attribute Management** toolbar.

Create a New Toolbar Tutorial—AutoCAD LT 97

Although the procedure is slightly different, it is also a simple matter to create a completely new toolbar in AutoCAD LT 97. Like the preceding AutoCAD LT 98 tutorial, this AutoCAD LT 97 tutorial also creates a toolbar named **Attribute Management** that contains tool buttons appropriate for attribute definitions, attribute editing, and block creation and insertion.

⇨ Open the **Toolbars** dialog box and click the **New...** button.

⇨ The **New Toolbar** subdialog box appears. Enter the name **Attribute Management** in the **Toolbar Name:** text box as shown in **Figure 21-20.** Click the **OK** button when you are finished.

⇨ The new toolbar name now appears in the **Toolbars** dialog box. See **Figure 21-21.** Observe that the new toolbar is automatically placed near the top of the graphics window. You can freely move the toolbar to a more convenient location if desired.

➪ Click the **Customize...** button to display the **Customize Toolbars** subdialog box. The **Attributes** category is displayed by default. From this category, select three buttons (one at a time) and drag them to the **Attribute Management** toolbar. The three buttons are the **Define Attribute**, **Edit Attribute**, and **Edit Attribute Globally** buttons. They perform the **DDATTDEF**, **DDATTE**, and **ATTEDIT** commands, respectively. To help you identify a button, a command description is provided at the bottom of the dialog box when you select a button with your pointing device.

➪ Go to the **Draw** category in the drop-down list, locate the **Make Block (BMAKE)** button and also drag it to your new toolbar. See **Figure 21-22**.

➪ Also add the **Insert (DDINSERT)** flyout button to your toolbar. This button is located at the very end of the bottom row of displayed buttons in the **Draw** category. Observe that this flyout button also contains tool buttons for **Content Explorer**, the **XREF** command, and several other functions.

➪ Finally, go to the **Modify** category and add the **Edit Text (DDEDIT)** button. Your new toolbar should appear as shown in **Figure 21-23**.

➪ Click **Close** twice to return to the Command: prompt. You can now dock the new **Attribute Management** toolbar, or leave it in a floating state as you desire. Remember that you can also resize the toolbar along its horizontal or vertical axes if you wish.

Figure 21-20.
Providing a name for the new toolbar in AutoCAD LT 97.

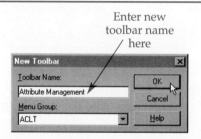

Figure 21-21.
The new toolbar name appears in the **Toolbars** dialog box.

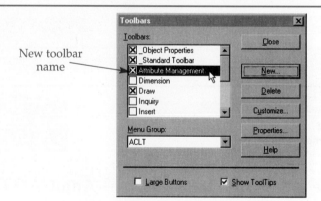

Figure 21-22.
The **Make Block** button is selected from the **Draw** category in the **Customize Toolbars** subdialog box.

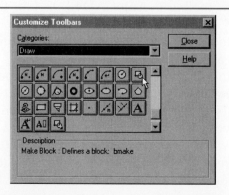

Figure 21-23.
The completed **Attribute Management** toolbar in AutoCAD LT 97.

Renaming a Toolbar

You can easily change the name of any toolbar in AutoCAD LT 98 by doing the following:
1. Open the **Customize** dialog box.
2. Click the **Toolbars** tab to open the **Toolbars** window if it is not already open.
3. Select the toolbar you wish to rename from the **Toolbars** list at the left of the **Toolbars** window and click the **Rename...** button. See **Figure 21-24.**
4. When the **Rename Toolbar** subdialog box appears, enter the new toolbar name in the **Toolbar name:** text box as shown in **Figure 21-25.** In the example shown, the **Attribute Management** toolbar is renamed **Block & Attribute Control**.

Figure 21-24.
After selecting a toolbar to rename from the **Toolbars** list at the left of the **Customize** dialog box, click the **Rename...** button.

Select toolbar to be renamed

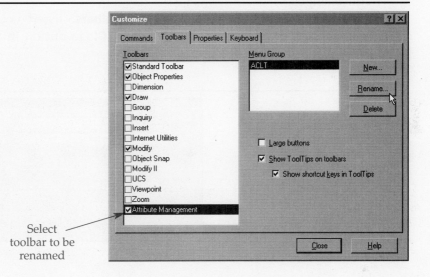

Figure 21-25.
The **Attribute Management** toolbar is renamed the **Block & Attribute Control** toolbar.

Enter new toolbar name

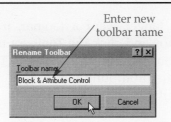

Editing Toolbar Properties—AutoCAD LT 97

In AutoCAD LT 97, you can change a toolbar name or revise the help text using the **Toolbar Properties** subdialog box. To open this subdialog box, first open the **Toolbars** dialog box and select the toolbar name you wish to edit from the **Toolbars:** list. Next, click the **Properties…** button to display the **Toolbar Properties** subdialog box. In the example shown in **Figure 21-26,** the **Attribute Management** toolbar that was created in the previous AutoCAD LT 97 tutorial has been selected. The options available in this subdialog box are described as follows:

- **Name:.** This text box is used to specify or change the toolbar name.
- **Help:.** The help text that you enter here is displayed at the left end of the status bar when your pointing device moves over the toolbar.
- **Alias:.** This area at the bottom of the subdialog box displays the toolbar name that AutoCAD LT 97 uses internally. The name includes a prefix that represents the toolbar's menu group, followed by the toolbar name as it appears in the aclt.mnu file. The toolbar alias is used in the **TOOLBAR** command and cannot be edited. See *Chapter 22* to learn more about menu groups.
- **Apply.** When you are finished entering text, click the **Apply** button to activate the changes.

Select another toolbar name from the **Toolbars:** list if you wish to continue editing toolbar properties. Otherwise, click the **Close** button in the **Toolbars** dialog box to close both displayed dialog boxes.

Figure 21-26.
The toolbar description and help text is added using the **Toolbar Properties** subdialog box in AutoCAD LT 97.

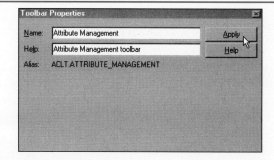

Deleting a Toolbar

When you no longer want a toolbar, it may be deleted. To do so, open the **Customize** dialog box and click the **Toolbars** tab to open the **Toolbars** window. Now, select the toolbar you wish to delete from the **Toolbars** list, and click the **Delete** button. An **Alert** box appears prompting you to confirm your choice. See **Figure 21-27.** Click the **OK** or **Cancel** buttons as appropriate.

Figure 21-27.
An **Alert** box is displayed when you delete a toolbar.

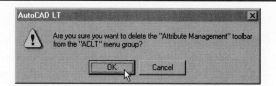

Deleting a Toolbar—AutoCAD LT 97

To delete an unwanted toolbar from AutoCAD LT 97, open the **Toolbars** dialog box, select the toolbar you wish to delete from the **Toolbars:** list, and click the **Delete** button. An alert box appears prompting you to confirm your choice. See **Figure 21-28.** Click the **Yes** or **No** buttons as appropriate.

Figure 21-28.
The **Alert** box displayed by AutoCAD LT 97 when you delete a toolbar.

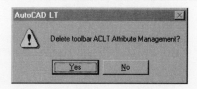

 CAUTION

Neither the **UNDO** or **OOPS** commands can recover a toolbar. Therefore, slow down and think carefully before deleting any toolbars. Also be aware that if you delete one of the toolbars supplied with AutoCAD LT, it can only be retrieved using the **MENULOAD** command. Unfortunately, this command removes any toolbar modifications you have made. The **MENULOAD** command is described later in this chapter.

Defining a Custom Tool Button

You can design your own custom tool button to perform a specific function, or modify an existing button using the **Properties** tab in the **Customize** dialog box. For example, do the following to create a completely new toolbar button that issues the **REGEN** command:

1. Open the **Customize** dialog box and click the **Commands** tab to display the **Commands** window.
2. Select **User defined** near the bottom of the **Categories** list at the left of the dialog box. Now, drag the blank **User Defined** button from the **Commands** list at the right of the dialog box to an empty area in the drawing window. AutoCAD LT creates a new toolbar named **TOOLBAR 1** containing the single blank button. Your display should appear similar to that shown in **Figure 21-29.**
3. Now, left-click the blank button in the new toolbar to display the **Button Properties** window.
4. Use the **Name:** text box to enter the name Regen for the new button.
5. Type Regenerates the drawing display in the **Description:** text box. The help text that you enter here is displayed at the left end of the status bar when your pointing device moves over the tool button.
6. Enter the word _regen directly after the character string ^C^C.
7. When you are finished, click the **Apply** button. The **Button Properties** window should appear as shown in **Figure 21-30.**

Now that the tool button properties have been defined, it is time to design an icon for the new button using the **Button Editor**. This procedure is described in the next section.

Figure 21-29.
Dragging the **User Defined Button** to an empty area in the drawing window.

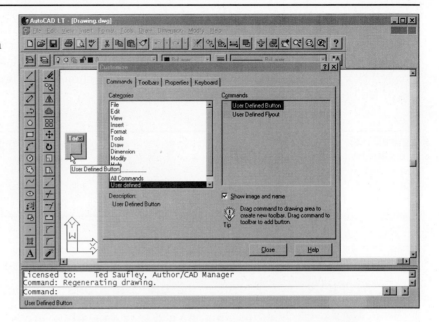

Figure 21-30.
Entering the new tool button properties in the **Button Properties** window.

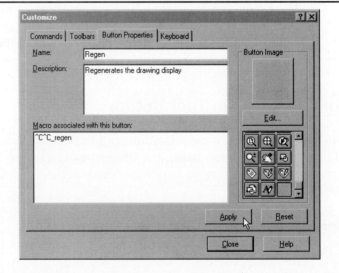

Using the Button Editor

The **Edit...** button in the **Button Properties** window opens the **Button Editor**. See **Figure 21-31.** This subdialog box offers several tools and options for creating a graphical icon for a new tool button, or for modifying an existing button icon. The tools and options available in the **Button Editor** are described below:

- **Button Image.** This area at the upper left of the **Button Editor** displays the button at its actual size.
- **Editing Tools.** The four editing tools at the top of the **Button Editor** provide the following functions:
  - **Pencil**—Located at the far left, the pencil tool edits one pixel at a time in the selected color. Drag the pointing device to edit several pixels at once.
  - **Line**—This tool creates lines in the selected color. Press and hold the pick button on your pointing device to set the first endpoint of the line. Drag to draw the line. Release the pick button to complete the line. In the example shown in **Figure 21-31**, a simple letter **R** (for **Regen**) is created using the Line tool. You may wish to be more creative as you create your own button icons.

AutoCAD LT—Fundamentals and Applications

Figure 21-31.
The **Button Editor** is used to create a graphic image for a new tool button or to modify an existing button.

- **Circle**—This tool draws circles in the selected color. Press and hold the pick button on your pointing device to set the center of the circle. Drag to set the radius. Release the pick button to complete the circle.
- **Erase**—This tool sets individual pixels to white. To set all pixels to white, double-click the **Erase** tool with your pointing device.
- **Editing Area.** The large square in the middle of the **Button Editor** provides a close-up view of the button icon for pixel editing.
- **Color Palette.** Located at the far right of the **Button Editor**, the color palette lets you select 1 of 16 colors to set the current color.
- **Grid.** This check box turns on the grid, which is very helpful for pixel editing. Each grid dot represents one pixel.
- **Clear.** Clicking this button clears the editing area.
- **Open....** This button opens a dialog box where you can retrieve an existing button icon for editing. Button icons are stored as .BMP (bitmap) files in the Program Files\AutoCAD LT 98 or Program Files\AutoCAD LT 97 folder.
- **Undo.** Undoes the last action.
- **Save As....** Click this button to save the button icon with a specific name. A .BMP extension is automatically appended to the file name you provide.
- **Save.** AutoCAD LT saves the customized button icon as a .BMP file with an arbitrary name, like ICON.BMP. The next time an image is saved, the file name may be something like ICON2537.BMP. Use the **Save As** button instead if you wish to provide a more specific name for your tool button icon.
- **Close.** Click this button to close the **Button Editor** and return to the **Button Properties** window.

Once you return to the **Button Properties** window, click the **Apply** button to apply the icon to the new tool button. Then, click the **Close** button in the **Customize** dialog box to terminate the procedure. You can then dock the new tool button or leave it floating as you desire.

Defining a Custom Tool Button Tutorial—AutoCAD LT 97

The procedure for creating or modifying a custom tool button is slightly different in AutoCAD LT 97. Like the previous AutoCAD LT 98 tutorial, the following tutorial creates a completely new button that issues the **REGEN** command:

⇨ Open the **Toolbars** dialog box and click the **Customize...** button to display the **Customize Toolbars** subdialog box.

⇨ Select **Custom** from the **Categories:** drop-down list.

⇨ Drag and drop the blank button at the left into the drawing window. AutoCAD LT 97 creates a new toolbar named **TOOLBAR 1** containing the single blank button.

⇨ Place your cursor over the blank button in the new toolbar and click the right button on your pointing device. The **Button Properties** subdialog is displayed at the lower right of the graphics window. See **Figure 21-32.**

⇨ Use the **Name:** text box to enter the name **Regen** for the new button.

⇨ Type Regenerates the drawing display in the **Help:** text box. The help text that you enter here is displayed at the left end of the status bar when your pointing device moves over the tool button.

⇨ Enter the word _regen directly after the character string ^C^C.

⇨ When you are finished, click the **Apply** button. The **Button Properties** subdialog box should appear as shown in **Figure 21-33.**

⇨ Now that the button properties have been defined, you can design a graphical icon for the new tool button using the **Button Editor** as described in the previous section.

Figure 21-32.
Creating a custom tool button in AutoCAD LT 97.

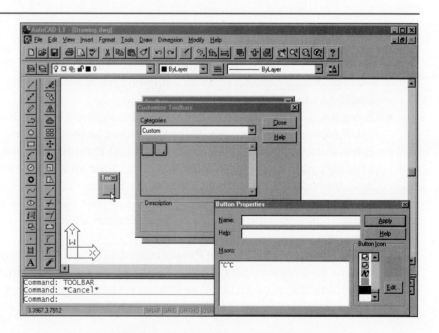

Figure 21-33.
The AutoCAD LT 97 **Button Properties** subdialog box.

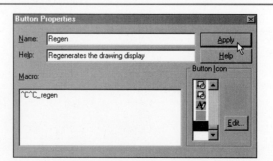

AutoCAD LT—Fundamentals and Applications

❏ Check with your instructor or supervisor before beginning this exercise.
❏ Make backup copies of the aclt.mnr and aclt.mns files.
❏ Create a custom button that performs a drawing regeneration as described in the previous sections.
❏ Draw the letter "R" in red using the **Line** tool. Then, clear the icon and try drawing something a bit more creative to represent the **REGEN** command.
❏ Save the bitmap file with the name REGEN.BMP.

Creating a Custom Flyout

You may find it convenient to create your own custom flyout button that contains your favorite, or most frequently used commands. The flyout can contain buttons from any of the toolbar categories available in AutoCAD LT 98. However, you must create a new toolbar before you can create a custom flyout. This is because the custom flyout buttons have to be associated with an existing toolbar. In the tutorial that follows, command buttons are first added to a new toolbar called My Buttons. A custom flyout is then created that is associated with the My Buttons toolbar. The procedure begins as follows:

1. Open the **Customize** dialog box and click the **Toolbars** tab to display the **Toolbars** window (if not already displayed). Then, click the **New...** button.
2. The **New Toolbar** subdialog box appears. Enter the name My Buttons in the **Toolbar name:** text box as shown in **Figure 21-34**. Click the **OK** button when you are finished.
3. The new toolbar name now appears in the **Toolbars** window and the new toolbar is automatically placed near the top of the graphics window. You can freely move the toolbar to a more convenient location if desired.
4. Click the **Commands** tab to display the list of available categories and commands in the **Commands** window. Select **All Commands** from the **Categories** list at the left of the window. Then scroll down the **Commands** list at the right and select the **Edit Polyline** (**PEDIT**) tool. (To help you locate the tool button command you desire, the tool button descriptions are listed in alphabetical order.) Once you have found and selected a command from the **Commands** list, a description of the command is displayed at the lower-left of the dialog box.
5. Now, press and hold the pick button on your pointing device and drag the **Edit Polyline** command button to the **My Buttons** toolbar.

Figure 21-34.
Providing a name for the new **My Buttons** toolbar.

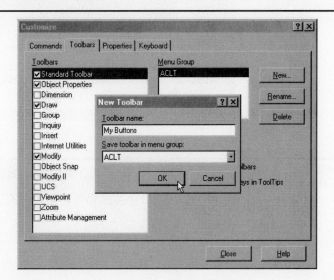

6. Next, locate the **Edit Spline**, **Edit Text**, **Edit Hatch, Oops!**, and **Purge** command buttons. Drag each of these buttons (one at a time) to the **My Buttons** toolbar also. These five additional tool buttons perform the **SPLINEDIT**, **DDEDIT**, **HATCHEDIT**, **OOPS**, and **PURGE** commands, respectively. When you are through, the **My Buttons** toolbar should appear as shown in **Figure 21-35**.

7. Select **User defined** near the bottom of the **Categories** list at the left of the **Command** window. Now, drag the blank **User Defined Flyout** button from the **Commands** list at the right of the dialog box to an empty area in the drawing window. (This button has a small black arrow at the lower right.) AutoCAD LT then creates a new toolbar named **TOOLBAR 1** containing the single blank flyout button. Your display should appear similar to that shown in **Figure 21-36**.

8. Now, left-click the blank flyout button in the new toolbar. An **Alert** box is displayed informing you that a toolbar must be associated with the new flyout. See **Figure 21-37**. Click the **OK** button to acknowledge the message and close the **Alert** box.

9. Once the **Alert** box is closed, AutoCAD LT displays the **Flyout Properties** window. Select the **My Buttons** toolbar from the list and click the **Apply** button as shown in **Figure 21-38**. Next, click the **Close** button to close the **Customize** dialog box and terminate the procedure.

10. Finally, move the new flyout button to a docked or floating location of your choice. As shown in **Figure 21-39**, the new flyout is docked just to the right of the **Object Properties** toolbar at the top of the drawing window.

Figure 21-35.
The completed **My Buttons** toolbar.

Figure 21-36.
Dragging the **User Defined Flyout** button to an empty area in the drawing window.

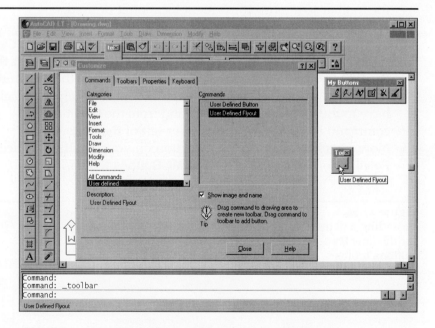

Figure 21-37.
An **Alert** box is displayed informing you to associate a toolbar with the new flyout button.

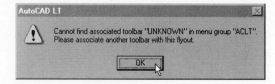

AutoCAD LT—Fundamentals and Applications

Figure 21-38.
Assigning a toolbar to the new flyout button using the **Flyout Properties** window.

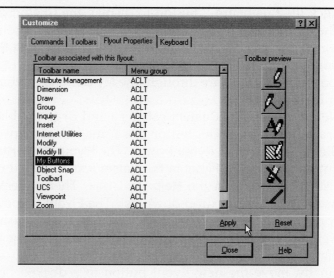

Figure 21-39.
The custom flyout is docked just to the right of the **Object Properties** toolbar above the drawing window.

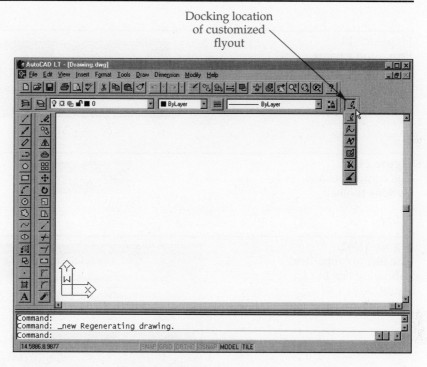

Docking location of customized flyout

Creating a Custom Flyout—AutoCAD LT 97

Although the procedure is somewhat different, a custom flyout can also be created in AutoCAD LT 97. However, as with AutoCAD LT 98, you must first create a new toolbar before you can create a custom flyout. In the tutorial that follows, buttons from the **Modify** category are added to a new toolbar called **My Buttons**. A custom flyout is then created that is associated with the **My Buttons** toolbar. The procedure begins as follows:

1. Open the **Toolbars** dialog box and click the **New...** button.
2. The **New Toolbar** subdialog box appears. Enter the name **My Buttons** in the **Toolbar Name:** text box as shown in **Figure 21-40.** Click the **OK** button when you are finished. The new toolbar name now appears in the **Toolbars** dialog box. Observe that the **My Buttons** toolbar is automatically placed near the top of the graphics window. You can freely move the toolbar to a more convenient location if desired.

3. Click the **Customize...** button to display the **Customize Toolbars** subdialog box. The **Attributes** category is displayed by default. Scroll down to the **Modify** category. From this category, select the **Edit Polyline**, **Edit Spline**, **Edit Text**, **Edit Hatch**, **Oops!**, and **Change** buttons (one at a time) and drag them to the **My Buttons** toolbar. When you are through, the **My Buttons** toolbar should appear as shown in **Figure 21-41**.

4. Next, move to the **Custom** category and drag the blank flyout button into the drawing window. (This button has a small black arrow at the lower right.) Right-click over the blank flyout button. The **Flyout Properties** subdialog box appears.

5. Enter the name My Flyout in the **Name:** text box. Add the character string Various editing commands in the **Help:** text box. Then, select ACLT.MyButtons from the **Associated Toolbar:** drop-down list. The **Flyout Properties** subdialog box should appear as shown in **Figure 21-42**. When you are finished, click the **Apply** button. Next, click the **Close** button in the **Toolbars** dialog box to close all displayed dialog boxes and terminate the procedure.

6. Finally, move the new flyout button to a docked or floating location of your choice. Refer once again to **Figure 21-39**.

Figure 21-40.
Providing a name for the new **My Buttons** toolbar in AutoCAD LT 97.

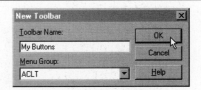

Figure 21-41.
The completed **My Buttons** toolbar.

Figure 21-42.
The **Flyout Properties** subdialog box in AutoCAD LT 97.

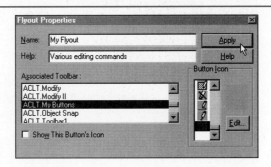

NOTE   Take note of the **Show This Button's Icon** check box at the lower-left of the **Flyout Properties** subdialog box. If this check box is activated, AutoCAD LT 97 always uses the blank flyout icon for the flyout. Otherwise, the displayed flyout icon is the icon of the last flyout tool button selected. Therefore, it is recommended that you leave this check box inactive.

❏ Check with your instructor or supervisor before beginning this exercise.
❏ Make backup copies of the aclt.mnr and aclt.mns files.
❏ Depending on the version of AutoCAD LT that you are using, create a custom flyout button identical to one of those described in the previous sections.
❏ Locate the new flyout where desired.

Restoring the Original Toolbars

If you are dissatisfied with your toolbar modifications and would like to start over again, or if you would like to restore the toolbars to their original definitions, you can do so using the **MENULOAD** command. This command can be entered at the Command: prompt or issued by selecting **Customize** from the **Tools** pull-down menu, and then selecting **Menus...** from the cascading submenu. See **Figure 21-43.** AutoCAD LT 97 users, simply select **Customize Menus...** from the **Tools** pull-down menu.

The **Menu Customization** dialog box is displayed which is used to load a template menu file. The default template menu file is called ACLT.MNU. Menu files are described more fully in *Chapter 22* of this text.

To restore the default template menu file, enter aclt.mnu in the **File Name:** text box. Next, activate the **Replace All** check box and click the **Load** button at the lower right of the dialog box. See **Figure 21-44.** You are then presented with an **Alert** box warning you that any toolbar changes you have made will be lost. See **Figure 21-45.** Click the **Yes** button if you wish to proceed. Expect a slight delay as the original menu file is loaded. When complete, click the **Close** button to exit the **Menu Customization** dialog box and terminate the function. The toolbars are now restored to their default states.

Figure 21-43.
Selecting **Customize** from the **Tools** pull-down menu and then selecting **Menus...** from the cascading submenu issues the **MENULOAD** command.

Figure 21-44.
The **Menu Customization** dialog box is used to load a template menu file.

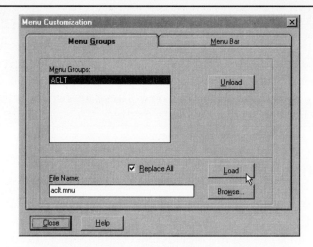

Figure 21-45.
An **Alert** box is displayed when you attempt to load the ACLT.MNU template menu file.

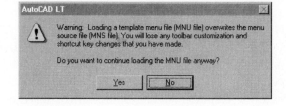

PROFESSIONAL TIP You can also replace your original menu files by restoring the backup copies of the aclt.mnr and aclt.mns files as previously mentioned in this chapter.

Assigning Keyboard Shortcuts to Commands

AutoCAD LT provides numerous keyboard shortcuts to frequently used commands. Pressing one of the function keys on the keyboard accesses some of these shortcuts, while others use a control-key combination, such as [Ctrl]+[O]. Each of these keyboard shortcuts are listed and described in *Chapter 1* of this text.

Users of AutoCAD LT 98 can create their own keyboard shortcuts to favorite, or frequently used, commands. You can choose from one of three categories:

- Commands found in the standard pull-down menus.
- Commands found in any of the AutoCAD LT toolbars.
- Any AutoCAD LT command.

To create a keyboard shortcut, first open the **Customize** dialog box and click the **Keyboard** tab to display the **Keyboard** window. The **Keyboard** window can also be quickly opened by selecting **Customize** from the **Tools** pull-down menu, and then selecting **Keyboard...** from the cascading submenu. Once the **Keyboard** window is open, **Figure 21-46**, it is a good idea to click the **Show All...** button to display a list of existing keyboard shortcuts in the **Shortcut Keys** window. See **Figure 21-47**. When you wish to define a shortcut key, first check this list to make sure that you will not be duplicating an existing shortcut. Click the **OK** button when you wish to return to the **Keyboard** window.

Figure 21-46.
The **Keyboard** tab window in the **Customize** dialog box.

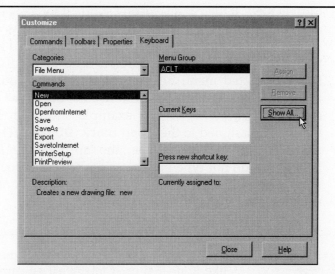

Figure 21-47.
Each of the keyboard shortcuts in AutoCAD LT are listed in the **Shortcut Keys** window. User-defined shortcuts also appear in this window.

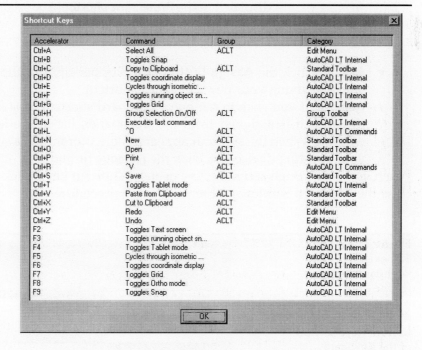

Each of the areas of the **Keyboard** window are described as follows:

- **Categories.** This drop-down list at the top left of the **Keyboard** window lets you select one of the three available categories previously mentioned.

- **Commands.** Once you have selected one of the menus, toolbars, or AutoCAD LT commands from the **Categories** drop-down list, the associated items are displayed in the **Commands** list at the left of the **Keyboard** window. When you select an item from the **Commands** list, its description appears in the **Description:** section at the lower-left of the **Keyboard** window.

- **Menu Group.** This area at the top-right of the **Keyboard** window displays the current menu group. By default, the menu group is called **ACLT** for aclt.mns. The keyboard shortcuts you assign are stored in the **Accelerators** section of the aclt.mns file. If you are using a third-party application that runs with AutoCAD LT, the menu group name may be different. See *Chapter 22* for more information about menu files.

- **Current Keys.** If there is an existing shortcut for a selected command, the shortcut appears in this section of the **Keyboard** window. As shown in **Figure 21-48**, the existing keyboard shortcut for the **PRINT** command is displayed.
- **Press new shortcut key.** This area is used to specify a new keyboard shortcut for the selected menu item, toolbar item, or AutoCAD LT command. Two formats are permissible. You can use the keyboard combinations [Ctrl]+[*letter*], or [Ctrl]+[Shift]+[*letter*]. In the example shown in **Figure 21-49**, the [Ctrl]+[I] shortcut is assigned to the **Insert Block (DDINSERT)** toolbar button. When you make the assignment, press the appropriate key combination on the keyboard—do not type in the letters. If the shortcut you specify is already in use, the message Currently assigned to: *(command name)* appears at the lower right of the **Keyboard** window.

NOTE Shortcut keys internally assigned to Microsoft Windows like [Ctrl]+[F4] or [Ctrl]+[Alt]+[Del] cannot be reassigned. If you press an invalid key combination, AutoCAD LT will not display it in the **Press new shortcut key** section of the **Keyboard** window. In these instances, use another key combination.

- **Assign.** Click the **Assign** button at the upper-right of the **Keyboard** window after specifying your new keyboard shortcut.
- **Remove.** If you wish to remove a keyboard shortcut, first select the command to which it is assigned from the **Commands** list at the left of the **Keyboard** window. When the shortcut appears in the **Current Keys** section, select it with your pointing device and click the **Remove** button.

When you are through assigning one or more shortcut keys, click the **Close** button to close the **Keyboard** window and terminate the procedure.

Figure 21-48.
The existing keyboard shortcut for the **Print** command is displayed in the **Current Keys** section of the **Keyboard** window.

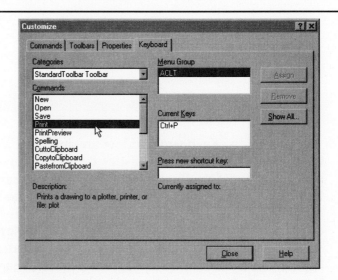

Figure 21-49.
Assigning the
[Ctrl]+[I] keyboard
shortcut to the
Insert Block
(**DDINSERT**) toolbar
button.

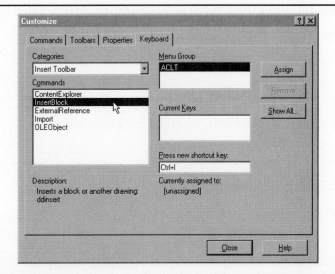

EXERCISE 21-6

❏ Open the **Shortcut Keys** window as described in the previous section.
❏ Identify the keyboard letters that are available for shortcut assignments. Make a note of the available letters for future reference.
❏ Assign [Ctrl]+[I] to the **INTERSECT** command, [Ctrl]+[M] to the **Make Object's Layer Current** function, and [Ctrl]+[U] to the **UNION** command.
❏ Close the **Keyboard** tab window and test your new keyboard shortcuts.

Chapter Test

Answer the following questions. Write your answer in the space provided.

1. How can you use your pointing device to quickly display the **Customize** dialog box? For users of AutoCAD LT 97, how can you quickly display the **Toolbars** dialog box using your pointing device?_____

_____

_____

_____

_____

2. Identify the command that allows you to control the display of toolbars on the command line. _____

_____

3. Why is it not a good idea to display large tool buttons at low screen resolutions?

_____

_____

_____

_____

4. What are tooltips? What is the command and value needed to disable them on the command line? _____

_____

_____

_____

5. Why is it a good idea to make backup copies of menu files before customizing tool buttons and/or toolbars? _____

_____

_____

6. Why is an underscore character (_) used in a tool button macro? _____

_____

_____

_____

_____

_____

7. What is the purpose of the ^C^C character string in a tool button macro? _____

_____

_____

_____

_____

_____

8. You have just deleted one of your customized toolbars. Which command will restore it—**UNDO** or **OOPS**? _____

_____

9. Where is tool button **Help** text displayed? _____

_____

10. How many colors can be used to create a custom tool button? _____

_____

11. Which **Button Editor** function should be used to save a custom button icon with a specific name? _____

_____

_____

12. *True or False?* A custom flyout need not be associated with an existing toolbar.

_____

13. You are dissatisfied with the changes you have made to the AutoCAD LT toolbars. Unfortunately, you neglected to make backup copies of the menu files before beginning your modifications. What command can be used to restore the original toolbars? _____

_____

14. You would like to define a new keyboard command shortcut. What should you do to check if the shortcut you wish to use is not already assigned? List all required steps._____

_____

_____

_____

15. *True or False?* It is possible to override the keyboard shortcuts defined by Microsoft Windows._____

Chapter Problems

1. Create a toolbar named Circle that contains each of the tool buttons that perform **CIRCLE** command options. Create a custom flyout of this toolbar. The toolbar and flyout for AutoCAD LT 98 users should appear as shown at the left below. The toolbar and flyout for users of AutoCAD LT 97 should appear as shown at the right.

General

LT 98   LT 98

2. Create another toolbar named Arc that contains each of the tool buttons that perform **ARC** command options. Create a custom flyout of this toolbar. The toolbar and flyout for AutoCAD LT 98 users should appear as shown at the left below. The toolbar and flyout for users of AutoCAD LT 97 should appear as shown at the right.

General

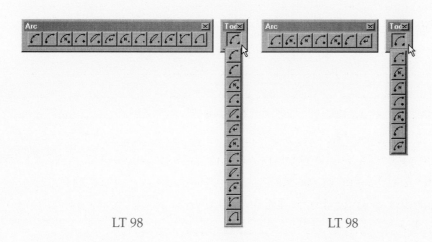

LT 98   LT 98

AutoCAD LT

Chapter **22**

Introduction to Pull-Down and Button Menu Customization

Learning Objectives

After you have completed this chapter, you will be able to:
- Describe the four AutoCAD LT menu types.
- Add or remove pull-down menus to the menu bar.
- Assign a menu macro to one or more pointing device buttons.
- Modify and create pull-down menus and cascading submenus.
- Add help strings to pull-down menu items.
- Define menu accelerator and mnemonic shortcut keys.
- Create image tile menus using slides and the **SLIDELIB** program.

In *Chapter 21* you learned how to modify existing tool buttons and toolbars as well as how to create your own. It is also possible to customize the AutoCAD LT menus. You can modify the standard menus, rearrange their order on the menu bar, or create an entirely new menu system to suit your personal tastes. You may also assign command string macros to pointing device buttons and create menus that use image tiles to facilitate block insertion. By mastering the fundamentals of menu customization, you can increase your productivity, knowledge, and enjoyment of AutoCAD LT. This chapter provides a brief introduction to customizing pull-down and button menus. The procedures it describes are applicable to both AutoCAD LT 98 and AutoCAD LT 97.

Menu Files

The base menu in AutoCAD LT is called aclt.mnu and is the menu that is initially loaded. The aclt.mnu menu file is a complete menu description and usually contains button, image, and other sections as well as the pull-down menu definitions found in the sections labeled **POP***n*. POP menus are another term for pull-down menus. The POP sections are covered later in this chapter. A menu file is actually a group of files that work together to define and control the appearance and functionality of AutoCAD LT menus. By default, the various AutoCAD LT menu files are stored in the C:\Program Files\AutoCAD LT 98 folder or C:\Program Files\AutoCAD LT 97 folder depending on the software used. Menu files define the following:
- Pointing device button menus
- Pull-down and cursor menus
- Toolbars

- Image tile menus
- Digitizing tablet menus
- Help strings and tooltips
- Menu access keys
- Shortcut keys

AutoCAD LT has four kinds of menu files that are described in **Figure 22-1**.

Figure 22-1.
The four kinds of AutoCAD LT menu files and their description.

File Name	Description
aclt.mnu	The template menu file. This file is in ASCII format and can be edited.
aclt.mnc	The compiled (machine-readable) menu file. This is a binary file that contains the command strings and menu syntax that define the functionality and appearance of the menu.
aclt.mnr	This is the menu resource file. It contains the bitmaps used for the tool buttons in the toolbars.
aclt.mns	This is the source file which is generated by AutoCAD LT. This file is also in ASCII text format and can be edited.

AutoCAD LT finds and loads the specified file according to the sequence shown below. This same sequence is used when AutoCAD LT loads a new menu.

1. AutoCAD LT looks for a menu source (.mns) file of the given name in the search path. After locating the .mns file, AutoCAD LT looks for a compiled menu (.mnc) file of the same name in the same folder. If it finds a matching .mnc file with the same or later date and time as the .mns file, AutoCAD LT loads the .mnc file. Otherwise, AutoCAD LT compiles the .mns file, generating a new .mnc file in the same folder, and loads that file.
2. If AutoCAD LT does not find a .mns file in step 1, it looks for a compiled menu (.mnc) file of the given name in the search path. If AutoCAD LT finds the .mnc file, it loads that file.
3. If AutoCAD LT does not find either a .mns or a .mnc file, it searches the path for a menu template (.mnu) file of the given name. If this file is found, it compiles a .mnc and a .mns file, then loads the .mnc file.
4. If AutoCAD LT does not find any menu files of the given names, it displays an error message and prompts you for another menu file name.
5. Each time AutoCAD LT compiles a .mnc file it generates a menu resource (.mnr) file, which contains the bitmaps used by the menu. The .mns file is an ASCII file that is initially the same as the .mnu file, but lacks comments or special formatting. The .mns file is modified by AutoCAD LT each time you make changes to the contents of the menu file through the user interface, such as modifying the contents of a toolbar as described in *Chapter 21* of this text.
6. The initial positioning of the AutoCAD LT toolbars is defined in the .mnu or .mns file. However, any changes you make to the show/hide and docked/floating status of toolbars, or to their positions in the graphics window, are recorded in the Windows system registry. After a .mns file has been created, it is used as the source for generating future .mnc and .mnr files. If you modify the .mnu file after a .mns file has been generated, you must use the **MENULOAD** command to explicitly load the .mnu file so that AutoCAD LT will generate new menu files and your changes will be recognized.

Adding a Pull-Down Menu with the MENULOAD Command

The **MENULOAD** command uses the **Menu Customization** dialog box that lets you add a partial menu file to an existing base menu file like aclt.mnu. Both base and partial menu files have an associated menu group name. From each menu group, you can access each pull-down menu (POP menu) that resides in the associated menu file. Once you have loaded a base or partial menu file, you can then customize the AutoCAD LT menu bar at the top of the graphics window by adding or removing pull-down menus.

You can enter MENULOAD at the Command: prompt, or select **Customize** from the **Tools** pull-down menu and then select **Menus...** from the cascading submenu. See **Figure 22-2**. If you are using AutoCAD LT 97, simply select **Customize Menus...** from the **Tools** pull-down menu to issue the **MENULOAD** command.

Figure 22-2.
Selecting **Customize** from the **Tools** pull-down menu and then selecting **Menus...** from the cascading submenu issues the **MENULOAD** command.

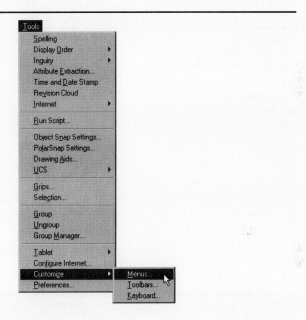

The **Menu Customization** dialog box appears as shown in **Figure 22-3**. Click the **Menu Bar** tab at the upper right of the **Menu Customization** dialog box to display the **Menu Bar** window shown in **Figure 22-4**. This window is used to add or remove pull-down menus from the menu bar. A list of available menus appears in the **Menus:** list at the left. The order of pull-down menus as they currently appear on the menu bar appears in the **Menu Bar:** list on the right. To add an additional pull-down menu, do the following:

1. Use the vertical scrollbar to scroll down to the bottom of the **Menus:** list.
2. Select **Clipboard Tools** from the bottom of the list as shown in **Figure 22-5**.
3. To insert the **Clipboard Tools** pull-down menu between the **Modify** and **Help** pull-down menus, select **Help** from the **Menu Bar:** list at the right.
4. Click the **Insert》** button in the middle of the **Menu Bar** window.
5. Finally, click the **Close** button at the lower left to end the procedure.

Your menu bar should now appear like that shown in **Figure 22-6**.

Figure 22-3.
The **Menu Customization** dialog box.

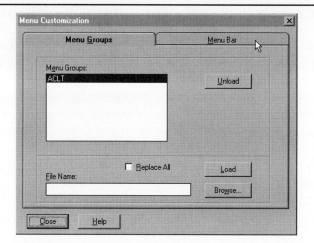

Figure 22-4.
The **Menu Bar** window lets you add or remove pull-down menus from the AutoCAD LT menu bar.

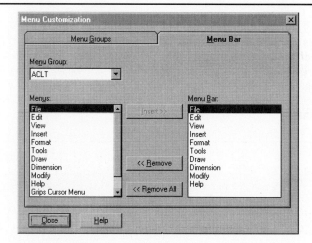

Figure 22-5.
Adding the **Clipboard Tools** pull-down menu between the **Modify** and **Help** pull-down menus.

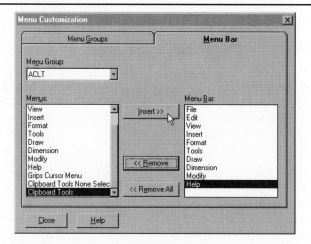

Figure 22-6.
The new **Clipboard Tools** pull-down menu on the menu bar.

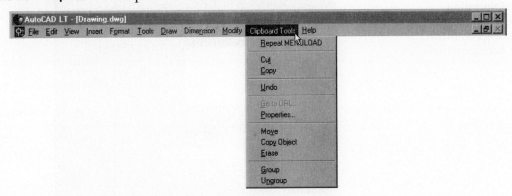

Removing a Pull-Down Menu

To remove a pull-down menu from the menu bar, do the following:
1. Open the **Menu Bar** window as previously described or issue the **MENULOAD** or **MENUUNLOAD** command.
2. Select the menu you wish to remove from the **Menu Bar:** list at the right of the window.
3. Click the ⟨⟨**Remove** button in the middle of the **Menu Bar** window. See **Figure 22-7**.
4. Finally, click the **Close** button at the lower left to end the procedure.

Figure 22-7.
Removing the
Clipboard Tools
pull-down menu
from the menu bar.

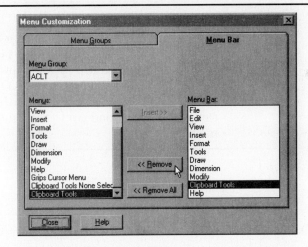

Restoring the Original Menu Bar Configuration

If you are dissatisfied with your modifications to the menu bar and would like to start over again, or if you would like to restore the menu bar to its original configuration, do the following:
1. Issue the **MENULOAD** command.
2. Enter aclt.mnu in the **File Name:** text box at the bottom of the **Menu Groups** window.
3. Next, activate the **Replace All** check box and click the **Load** button at the lower right of the dialog box. See **Figure 22-8**.
4. You are then presented with an alert box warning you that loading a template menu file (.mnu) file overwrites a menu source file (.mns). See **Figure 22-9**.
5. Click the **Yes** button if you wish to proceed. Expect a slight delay as the original aclt.mnu menu file is loaded. When complete, click the **Close** button to exit the **Menu Customization** dialog box and terminate the function. The menu bar is now restored to its original state.

Figure 22-8.
Using the **Menu Customization** dialog box to restore the original menu bar configuration.

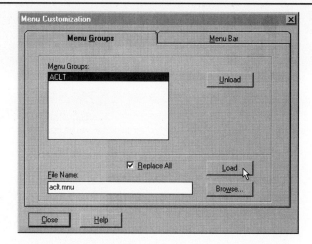

Figure 22-9.
An alert box warns you that the template menu file will overwrite the menu source file.

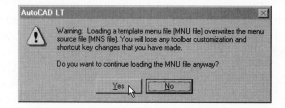

PROFESSIONAL TIP

When you use **MENULOAD** or **MENUUNLOAD** to alter the loaded menus or customize the menu bar with **POP** menus, the changes are saved to the Windows system registry. The next time you start up AutoCAD LT, the menus that were loaded last and the menu bar configuration are restored. You can load and unload up to 8 partial menus and up to 16 POP menus.

EXERCISE 22-1

❑ Check with your supervisor or instructor before beginning this exercise.
❑ Begin a new drawing. It is not necessary to use one of your template files.
❑ Add the **Grips Cursor Menu** between the **Draw** and **Dimension** pull-down menus.
❑ Experiment with moving the remaining pull-down menus to different locations on the menu bar.
❑ When you are through experimenting, restore the menu bar to its original configuration as described in the preceding section.

Specifying a Menu File Using the Preferences Dialog Box

As an alternative to the **MENULOAD** command, you can also specify a different menu file using the **Files** tab in the **Preferences** dialog box. See **Figure 22-10**. See *Chapter 20* for complete information about the **Files** tab window.

Figure 22-10.
The **Files** window in
the **Preferences**
dialog box specifies
the current menu
file.

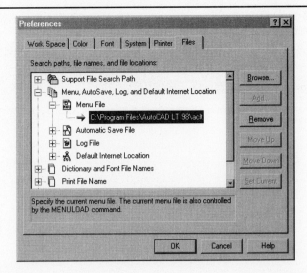

NOTE

Observe the name ACLT in the **Menu Groups:** section at the left of the **Menu Customization** dialog box. See **Figure 22-3.** If you are using a third-party application that runs with AutoCAD LT, that application may have its own menu file. The name of that file would then appear in place of ACLT.

When you wish to use a third-party menu file, or a menu file that you have customized yourself, enter the menu file name and extension in the **File Name:** text box. You can also click the **Browse...** button at the lower right of the dialog box to display the **Select Menu File** subdialog box. This subdialog box lets you select a .mnc or .mns menu file from a different folder or disk drive. Use the **Files of type:** drop-down list if you wish to select a .mnu template file, instead. Once the desired menu file is found, click the **Load** button to load it. When you wish to completely replace the current menu file with an alternate, or customized version, activate the **Replace All** check box before clicking the **Load** button.

Menu Structure and Sections

Before continuing, it would be a good idea to spend a few moments studying the aclt.mnu menu template file. Remember that the file is in ASCII format and may easily be printed. Having a printout makes interpretation and modification of the file much simpler. You can load aclt.mnu into the Windows WordPad or any other text editor you care to use. See **Figure 22-11.**

Figure 22-11.
The aclt.mnu file as it appears in Windows WordPad.

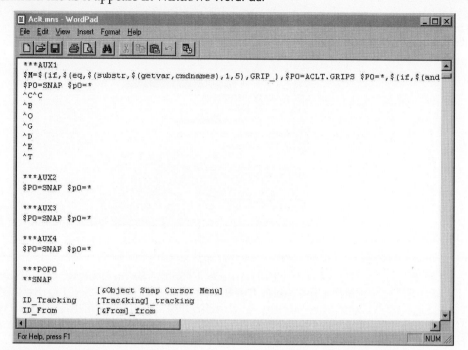

PROFESSIONAL TIP

You may choose to customize the aclt.mnu file, or create an entirely new one. However, be sure to make a backup copy before customizing aclt.mnu. You can then restore the original menu file if the customized version becomes corrupted.

A better alternative would be to make a copy of the existing menu file and give the copy a different name like *mymenu.mnu.* This method preserves the integrity of the original aclt.mnu and allows you to freely edit the new menu file to suit your needs.

You can also choose to customize the aclt.mns source file instead of the aclt.mnu file. Make a copy of aclt.mns and provide a name like *mymenu.mns.* Whether you choose to customize the menu template file (aclt.mnu) or the menu source file (aclt.mns), it is always a good idea to preserve the original files.

As you study the menu file, observe that it is divided into sections that relate to specific menu areas or types. Menu labels identify the menu sections. The sections and the types of menus they represent are as follows:

- *****MENUGROUP.** This section reads =ACLT to define the base menu system.
- *****AUX*n*.** These sections are for customized pointing device button functions (where *n* is a number from 1 to 4). The button menu and key/button sequences are defined below. However, keep in mind that the Windows driver used with your pointing device takes precedence over the key/button sequences shown.

AUX1	Simple button press
AUX2	[Shift] + *[button press]*
AUX3	[Ctrl] + *[button press]*
AUX4	[Ctrl] + [Shift] + *[button press]*

- *****POP*n*.** These sections define the pull-down and cursor menus (where *n* is a number from 0 to 16). The section labeled ***POP0 defines the cursor menu. The remaining sections, ***POP1 through ***POP10, define the **File** through **Help** pull-down menus, respectively. **POP17 defines the **Grips Cursor Menu**, ***POP18 defined the **Clipboard Tools None Selected** menu, and ***POP19 defines the **Clipboard Tools** menu. These three menus are accessible using the **Menu Customization** dialog box described earlier in this chapter. The cursor menu, plus its cascading submenus, can have a total of 499 menu items. The pull-down menus, plus their cascading submenus, may have a total of 999 menu items. However, the maximum number of menu items that can be displayed is determined by the current screen resolution.
- *****TOOLBARS.** This section contains the toolbar definitions.
- *****IMAGE.** This section describes an image tile menu. Only one image tile menu is predefined in AutoCAD LT. It can be seen in the **Tile Viewport Layout** dialog box. Selecting **Tiled Viewports** from the **View** pull-down menu, and then selecting **Layout...** from the cascading submenu open this dialog box.
- *****ACCELERATORS.** This section contains shortcut (or accelerator) key definitions.
- *****HELPSTRINGS.** This section defines the text that is displayed in the status bar when a pull-down or cursor menu item is highlighted, or when your pointing device is over a tool button.
- *****TABLET*n*.** These four sections define the menu commands that are accessible if you are using a digitizer tablet as your pointing device. See *Chapter 23* to learn more about using a digitizer with AutoCAD LT.

Interpreting the Pointing Device (AUX*n*) Menus

The buttons (**BUTTONS*n*) and auxiliary (***AUX*n*) menus are identical in format. However, their use depends on the type of pointing device you are using. The auxiliary menus define the buttons on the system mouse. Any other pointing device, like a digitizing puck, uses the button menus. Regardless of the type of pointing device you are using, you may not reassign the pick button of the device. Take a look at the ***AUX1 section of the menu file shown below.

```
***AUX1
$M=$(if,$(eq,$(substr,$(getvar,cmdnames),1,5),GRIP_),$P0=ACLT.GRIPS
    $P0=*,$(if,$(and,$(and,$(and,$(=,$(getvar,rtclickmenu),1),$(=,$(getvar,cmdac-
    tive),0),$(eq,$(getvar,curcmdln),"")))),$(=,$(getvar,pickfirst),1)),$P0=*));
$P0=SNAP $p0=*
^C^C
^B
^O
^G
^D
^E
^T
```

The first several lines in the ***AUX1 section define whether the right-click grips menu or the shortcut menu that repeats a command should be activated when you press button 2 on your mouse. Do not concern yourself with these lines.

Choosing button 3 ($P0=*) displays the menu assigned to the P0 menu area which is the cursor menu. Typically, the ***POP0 section of the menu file is assigned to the P0 menu area. Each remaining line in the section assigns a command sequence to each subsequent button on the pointing device: for example, ^C^C ([Esc] twice) to button 4, ^B (**Snap** mode toggle) to button 5, and so on. Can you interpret the functions of the remaining lines?

PROFESSIONAL TIP

Keep in mind that your pointing device (mouse or puck) can recognize as many lines as it has assignable buttons. Each of the control functions mentioned in the ***AUX1 section are listed in Chapter 1 of this text.

The menu section labeled ***AUX2 is used when you press the [Shift] key and click the right mouse button simultaneously. This action displays the popup cursor menu.

```
***AUX2
// Shift + button
$P0=SNAP $p0=*
```

The line $p0=* is interpreted as follows:

- **$.** Loads a menu area.
- **P0.** Identifies the POP*n* menu area. Remember that POP0 defines the cursor menu.
- **=*.** Displays what is currently loaded to the specified menu area.

If you were to edit the ***AUX2 section to read $p3=* , which menu would be displayed in place of the cursor menu?

The menu section labeled ***AUX3 is used when you press the [Ctrl] key and click the right mouse button simultaneously. By default, this button assignment also enables the cursor menu. However, keep in mind that you can also assign menu macros to the mouse buttons. A *menu macro* is a character string that can perform one or more AutoCAD LT commands. It is similar to the tool button macros described in *Chapter 21*. Consider the following menu macro:

```
***AUX3
// Control + button
grid .5 snap .25 limits 0,0 17,11 zoom all
```

From this example, the grid, snap, and limits are set and a **ZOOM All** operation is performed whenever the [Ctrl] key is pressed and the right mouse button is clicked simultaneously. If a menu macro does not fit on one line, it may be continued to the next line by entering a plus sign (+) as the last character of the line to be continued.

Finally, remember that you may add a fourth section, ***AUX4, so that a specialized function is performed when you press both the [Shift] and [Ctrl] keys simultaneously as you click the right mouse button.

EXERCISE 22-2

❑ Before beginning this exercise make a backup copy of the aclt.mnu file.
❑ Edit the ***AUX3 menu section to add a button macro that performs the following operations:
❑ Sets the limits to a C-size drawing (22 × 17).
❑ Sets the grid spacing to 1 unit and the snap spacing to .5 units.
❑ Performs a **ZOOM All**.
❑ Turns on **Ortho** mode.
❑ Turns off the grid, snap, and coordinate display.
❑ Turns off the **UCS** icon.
❑ Remember to use the plus sign (+) if your macro does not fit on one line.
❑ Save the revised menu file with the name EX22-2.MNU.
❑ Begin a new drawing. Load the revised menu as described in the preceding text. If there is an error in the menu file, you will receive an alert message from AutoCAD LT as the file is loading. Should this occur, check the menu file for errors.
❑ After correcting any errors, reload the corrected menu file.
❑ Test your new button assignment. Do not save the drawing when you are finished.

Interpreting the Cursor and Pull-Down Menus

As you study the aclt.mnu file, locate the ***POP0 heading just below the ***AUX*n* sections. The ***POP0 section defines the cursor menu which is used for quick access to tracking, object snap modes, and the **Osnap Settings** dialog box. Both the cursor menu and its definition in aclt.mnu appear in **Figure 22-12**. Notice that the words enclosed in brackets ([ ]) appear in the on-screen cursor menu. The brackets are used to enclose labels for all of the ***POP*n* menu sections. Each label can be up to 14 characters long.

Observe that several lines are used to separate items within a POP menu. These separator lines are specified by enclosing two hyphens in brackets [– –].

Note also that one of the characters in each menu label within the brackets is preceded by an ampersand symbol [&]. The character preceded by an ampersand in a cursor or pull-down menu label defines the keyboard accelerator shortcut key combination used to enable that menu. To illustrate further, locate the ***POP1 section just below ***POP0 in the menu file. The ***POP1 section defines the **File** pull-down menu on the menu bar. Observe that the title of the **File** pull-down menu is defined as [&File] in aclt.mnu; thus pressing [Alt]+[F] accesses the **File** menu.

Remember also that once a pull-down menu is displayed, a menu item within it may be selected using a single mnemonic character key. The mnemonic keys defined for the **New...** and **Open...** commands in the **File** pull-down menu appear in aclt.mnu as [&New...] and [&Open...]. Therefore, these menu items are enabled with the single keys N and O, respectively.

Figure 22-12.
The cursor menu as it appears on the screen (left) and how it is defined in the menu file (right).

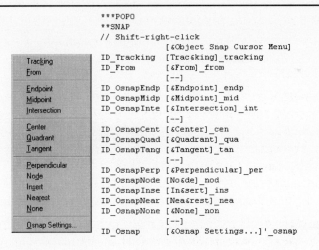

```
***POP0
**SNAP
// Shift-right-click
                    [&Object Snap Cursor Menu]
ID_Tracking    [Trac&king]_tracking
ID_From        [&From]_from
               [--]
ID_OsnapEndp   [&Endpoint]_endp
ID_OsnapMidp   [&Midpoint]_mid
ID_OsnapInte   [&Intersection]_int
               [--]
ID_OsnapCent   [&Center]_cen
ID_OsnapQuad   [&Quadrant]_qua
ID_OsnapTang   [&Tangent]_tan
               [--]
ID_OsnapPerp   [&Perpendicular]_per
ID_OsnapNode   [No&de]_nod
ID_OsnapInse   [In&sert]_ins
ID_OsnapNear   [Nea&rest]_nea
ID_OsnapNone   [&None]_non
               [--]
ID_Osnap       [&Osnap Settings...]'_osnap
```

Special Label Characters

For pull-down menus, the first label defines the menu bar title; succeeding labels define menu and submenu items. The following example is the top portion of the POP3 pull-down menu section:

```
***POP3
ID_MnView      [&View]
ID_Redraw      [&Redraw]'_redraw
ID_Regen       [Re&gen]^C^C_regen
               [– –]
               [-)&Zoom]
ID_ZoomRealt   [&Realtime]'_zoom;
               [– –]
```

Compare the example on the previous page with the actual **View** pull-down menu in AutoCAD LT. Observe that on the first line after the ***POP3 section label, the label [&View] specifies the word View to be displayed as the menu bar title. Because the letter V is preceded with an ampersand, it appears underscored in the pull-down **View** menu to denote that it is the menu accelerator key. The name tag ID_Redraw points to the appropriate line in the ***HELPSTRINGS section that defines the help text that is displayed in the status bar at the bottom of the graphics window when a pull-down or cursor menu item is highlighted. The help text is also displayed when you pause your pointing device over a tool button. The syntax for the help strings section is a name tag followed by a label. When a menu item is selected, the name tag for that item is queried for a corresponding entry in the ***HELPSTRINGS section. If such a match occurs, then the string contained within the label is displayed on the status bar. The entry for ID_Redraw appears in the ***HELPSTRINGS section like this:

ID_Redraw   [Refreshes the display of the current viewport: redraw]

Figure 22-13 shows the characters that perform a special function when included in a cursor or pull-down menu label.

Figure 22-13.
Shown are the characters that perform a special function when included in a cursor or pull-down menu label.

Character	Description
[label]	Identifies the menu item as it appears in the menu.
[--]	As previously mentioned, two hyphens enclosed in brackets draw a separator line between menu items.
-)	Identifies the beginning of a cascading submenu.
(-	Identifies the end of a cascading submenu.
***	Identifies the beginning of a menu section.
^C^C	A single ^C cancels most commands. However, ^C^C is required to return to the Command: prompt from a dimensioning command.
&	Placed directly before a character, it specifies that character as the accelerator or mnemonic key in a pull-down or cursor menu label.
~	As a prefix, the tilde character makes a menu item unavailable. Any characters following the tilde appear grayed out.
!	As a prefix, an exclamation point and a period mark a menu item with a checkmark. An example can be seen with the **Model Space (Tiled)** item in the **View** pull-down menu.
\t	Specifies that all label text to the right of these characters is pushed to the right side of the menu. This is the convention used when a keyboard equivalent appears in a pull-down menu. Here is an example: **Open... Ctrl+O.**

Creating a New Pull-Down Menu Tutorial

As with tool button and toolbar customization, the best way to learn how to customize a pull-down menu is to try it! In the following tutorial, you will create a new base menu system called mymenu.mnu that features an additional pull-down menu labeled **Custom**. The new menu is to be placed directly after the **Help** pull-down menu. See **Figure 22-14**.

Figure 22-14.
The new **Custom** pull-down menu is located at the far right of the menu bar.

The menu contains three items labeled **Lines**, **Shapes**, and **Curves**. Each of these items features a cascading submenu with additional drawing commands as shown in **Figure 22-15**. Observe from **Figure 22-16** that the **Arc**, **Circle**, and **Ellipse** menu items also feature their own cascading submenus.

↳ Begin the tutorial as follows:

↳ Make a copy of the aclt.mnu file. Name the copy mymenu.mnu.

↳ Use Windows WordPad or your own word processing program to edit mymenu.mnu. However, be sure to save the menu file in text-only format when you are done editing it.

↳ Use the **Find** function or scroll down through mymenu.mnu until you locate the section labeled ***POP10.

↳ Move your cursor down to the blank line just before the ***POP17 section and begin inserting text there. Be sure to leave a blank line between pull-down menus.

↳ Now, enter the following lines listed on the next page. Although indentations are shown for greater readability and consistency with the remainder of the menu file, they are not necessary and may be omitted. **HINT:** Use **Cut** and **Paste** functions to eliminate typing and reduce the risk of errors. In other words, cut the required lines from aclt.mnu and paste them into mymneu.mnu wherever possible.

Figure 22-15.
Each of the menu items displays a cascading submenu.

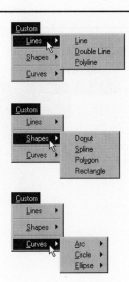

```
***POP11
ID_Custom    [&Custom]
[-)&Lines]
  ID_Line        [&Line]^C^C_line
  ID_Dline       [&Double Line]^C^C_dline
  ID_Pline       [⟨-&Polyline]^C^C_pline
[- -]
[->&Shapes]
  ID_Donut       [Do&nut]^C^C_donut
  ID_Spline      [&Spline]^C^C_spline
  ID_Polygon     [Pol&ygon]^C^C_polygon
  ID_Rectang     [⟨-Rectan&gle]^C^C_rectang
[- -]
[-)&Curves]
[-)&Arc]
  ID_Arc3point   [3 &Points]^C^C_arc
  ID_ArcStCeEn   [&Start, Center, End]^C^C_arc \_c
  ID_ArcStCeAn   [S&tart, Center, Angle]^C^C_arc \_c \_a
  ID_ArcStCeLe   [St&art, Center, Length]^C^C_arc \_c \_l
  ID_ArcStEnAg   [Start, E&nd, Angle]^C^C_arc \_e \_a
  ID_ArcStEnDi   [Start, End, &Direction]^C^C_arc \_e \_d
  ID_ArcStEnRa   [Start, End, &Radius]^C^C_arc \_e \_r
  ID_ArcCeStEn   [&Center, Start, End]^C^C_arc _c
  ID_ArcCeStAn   [C&enter, Start, Angle]^C^C_arc _c \\_a
  ID_ArcCeStLe   [Center, Start, &Length]^C^C_arc _c \\_l
  ID_ArcContin   [⟨-C&ontinue]^C^C_arc ;
[-)&Circle]
  ID_CircleRad   [Center, &Radius]^C^C_circle
  ID_CircleDia   [Center, &Diameter]^C^C_circle \_d
  ID_Circle2pt   [&2 Points]^C^C_circle _2p
  ID_Circle3pt   [&3 Points]^C^C_circle _3p
  ID_CircleTTR   [&Tan, Tan, Radius]^C^C_circle _ttr
  ID_CircleTTT   [⟨-T&an, Tan, Tan]^C^C_circle _3p _tan \_tan \_tan \
[-)&Ellipse]
  ID_EllipseCe   [&Center]^C^C_ellipse _c
  ID_EllipseAx   [Axis, &End]^C^C_ellipse
  ID_EllipseAr   [⟨Arc]^C^C_ellipse _a
```

Figure 22-16.
The **Arc**, **Circle**, and **Ellipse** menu items each feature their own cascading submenus.

- Be sure to leave a blank line between the last line you entered and the line labeled ***POP17.
- Now, scroll down to the ***HELPSTRINGS section and add the following line right after the ID_CtrlUndo line:

  ID_Custom   [Creates lines, shapes, and curves]

- Save mymenu.mnu in text-only format.
- Start AutoCAD LT. Issue the **MENULOAD** command and enter mymenu.mnu in the **File Name:** text box as shown in **Figure 22-17**. Activate the **Replace All** check box and click the **Load** button to load your new menu.
- When the **Alert** box appears asking if you want to continue loading the menu file, click the **Yes** button.
- Click the **Close** button when you are finished.
- If there is an error in the new menu file, you will receive a message as the file is loading. Should this occur, reopen the menu file and check for any open brackets or illegal characters.
- After correcting any errors, reload the menu using the **MENULOAD** command previously described in this tutorial.
- Try using the new **Custom** menu. Make sure that each of the help string messages is displayed on the **Status** bar at the bottom of the graphics window.

Figure 22-17.
Loading the new menu file in the **Menu Customization** dialog box.

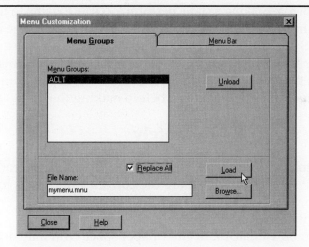

Image Tile Menus

As mentioned earlier in this chapter, the section of the menu file labeled ***IMAGE describes an image tile menu. An example of an image tile menu can be seen in the **Tiled Viewport Layout** dialog box. See **Figure 22-18**. Observe from the illustration that image tile menus use a dialog box to display slides in groups of 20. If there are more than 20 slides in the menu, the **Next** and **Previous** buttons are used to leaf through additional menu pages.

Image tile menus are particularly useful for displaying and selecting block symbols for insertion. The following sections describe how to prepare slides and add an image tile menu representing electronic schematic symbols to AutoCAD LT.

Figure 22-18.
The **Tiled Viewport Layout** dialog box is an example of an image tile menu.

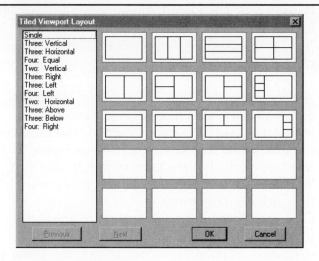

Preparing Slides for Image Tile Menus

In *Chapter 18*, you learned how to create slides using the **MSLIDE** command. You can greatly improve the appearance of your image tile menus by adhering to the following guidelines as you make your slides:
- Keep the slides simple. Complex slides slow the display of the image tile menu.
- Before making a slide, perform a **ZOOM Extents** to fill the screen with the graphic image. Use the **PAN** command to center the image in the drawing window.
- Solid filled areas are not displayed in image tiles. If you are using solids, wide polylines, arrowheads, solid hatch, or donuts in your slides, turn off **FILLMODE** to see how the slide will appear in the image tile. Make any required modifications before making the slide.

Sizing the Slide Accurately

AutoCAD LT displays image tiles with an aspect ratio of 1.5 to 1 (1.5 units wide by 1 unit high). You can assure the correct proportions for your image tiles by doing the following:
1. Begin a new drawing.
2. Turn off **TILEMODE** to enter paper space. You may do so by selecting **Paper Space** from the **View** pull-down menu.
3. Issue the ⟨**First Point**⟩ option of the **MVIEW** command by first selecting **Floating Viewports** from the **View** pull-down menu and then selecting **1 Viewport** from the cascading submenu.
4. Enter the coordinates 0,0 for the first corner of the viewport and 3,2 for the other corner.
5. Enter MSPACE (or MS) to enter model space.
6. Construct the desired graphics symbol in the viewport. If the symbol already exists on disk, insert it into the viewport using the **INSERT** or **DDINSERT** commands. When complete, perform a **ZOOM Extents** to fill the viewport. Pan as necessary to center the image.
7. Use the **MSLIDE** command to make the slide.

NOTE	If necessary, refer to *Chapter 17* to review the **TILEMODE** system variable and paper space commands.

Organizing the Slides

Once the necessary slides are created, you can create a slide library using the slidelib.exe utility program introduced in *Chapter 18*. Before you create the slide library, use Windows Notepad or another ASCII text editor to create a list of the slides to appear in the library.

In the following example, a list of slide files representing electronic components for schematic diagrams is prepared and saved with the name elecsym.txt. The list might appear in the text editor as follows:

```
cap
diode
resistor
xsistor
inductor
lamp
switch
battery
```

After completing and saving the slide list file, use the **SLIDELIB** command to make the slide library. Since the **SLIDELIB** program is located in the C:\Program Files\AutoCAD LT 98 folder, place the elecsym.txt file in the same folder so that slidelib can find it to create the slide library. If you are using AutoCAD LT 97 it is located in the Program Files\AutoCAD LT 97 folder. Place the elecsym.txt file in this folder.

Remember that the slidelib utility must be executed at the DOS prompt and cannot be used within AutoCAD LT. If you are already in Windows, use the MS-DOS Prompt application covered in *Chapter 18* to switch to the DOS prompt. Also, keep in mind that MS-DOS cannot accommodate names longer than eight characters for files or folders. Therefore, some folder and file names will appear truncated in the MS-DOS Prompt window. As an example, the Program Files folder might appear as PROGRA~1, while the AutoCAD LT 98 folder might appear as AUTOCA~1.

Once you are in the MS-DOS Prompt window, enter the DIR command to verify the correct folder names on your particular workstation. Then, using the appropriate folder names, enter the following to switch to the AutoCAD LT 98 or AutoCAD LT 97 folder as appropriate and create the slide library:

```
C:\WINDOWS⟩ CD \PROGRA~1\AUTOCA~1↵
C:\Program Files\AutoCAD LT 98⟩ SLIDELIB ELECSYM ⟨ ELECSYM.TXT↵
SLIDELIB 1.2 (3/8/89)
(C) Copyright 1987-1989,1994,1995 Autodesk, Inc.
     All Rights Reserved
C:\Program Files\AutoCAD LT 98⟩ EXIT↵
```

In the example above, the slide library is given the same name as the list of slide files. When complete, the slide library resides in the AutoCAD LT folder with the name elecsym.slb. Remember that you may use any names you choose when creating slide libraries and slide lists providing the file names conform to DOS naming conventions.

Creating an Image Tile Menu

Now that the slide library is created, the menu file may be edited. First, page down to the section labeled ***IMAGE and make your entries similar to the examples shown below:

```
***IMAGE
**ELECSYM
[Insert Electronic Component]
[elecsym(cap,Capacitor)]^C^Cinsert cap
[elecsym(Diode)]^C^Cinsert diode
[elecsym(Resistor)]^C^Cinsert resistor
[elecsym(xsistor,Transistor)]^C^Cinsert xsistor
[elecsym(Inductor)]^C^Cinsert inductor
[elecsym(Battery)]^C^Cinsert battery
[elecsym(Lamp)]^C^Cinsert lamp
[elecsym(Switch)]^C^Cinsert switch
```

The label **Insert Electronic Components...** will appear in the title bar of the new image tile menu dialog box. Now study the syntax of the next line just below the label. The string [elecsym(cap,Capacitor)] instructs AutoCAD LT to locate the cap slide file in the elecsym slide library.

Note the addition of the word Capacitor after the cap, character string. By adding an additional field after the slide name, you can specify any name you choose in the image tile menus. This is particularly useful when a component name like capacitor or transistor exceeds 8 characters and cannot be used for the slide file name.

The next character string in the field, ^C^Cinsert cap, performs two cancel operations and inserts the block named cap into the drawing. Remember that two cancels are required to return to the Command: prompt from a dimensioning command.

Adding the Image Tile Menu to a Pull-Down Menu

Before you can view the new image tile menu, you must add a menu selection that displays it on the screen. A logical place to put the menu selection would be in the **Insert** pull-down menu. It is also a good idea to add an ID reference to a help string. The following line is added to the **Insert** pull-down menu (***POP4) between the **Block...** and the **Content Explorer...** menu items:

```
ID_Ddinsert    [&Block...]^C^C_ddinsert
ID_Inselec     [&Electronic Components...]$I=elecsym $I=*
ID_Content     [&Content Explorer...]^C^C_content
```

The label **Electronic Components...** appears as a new menu item in the **Insert** pull-down menu. See **Figure 22-19**. Note that the ampersand character placed immediately before the capital E in Electronic denotes the mnemonic key and the inclusion of an ellipsis (...) to denote that this item opens a dialog box.

The next part of the entry, $I=elecsym, calls the new electronic component image tile menu. The last part of the entry, $I=*, displays the image tile menu and makes the items within it selectable.

Figure 22-19.
The new image tile menu item is added to the **Insert** pull-down menu.

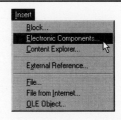

AutoCAD LT—Fundamentals and Applications

Adding a Help String to the Menu Item

As you did in the previous pull-down menu tutorial, add a help string for the new menu item in the ***HELPSTRINGS section at the end of the menu file. Insert the following line between the ID_Import and ID_Insertobj help strings:

ID_Inselec [Inserts electronic component symbols]

Save the menu file and load it as described earlier in this chapter. The completed image tile menu is shown in **Figure 22-20**. Because image tiles cannot display solid filled areas, note the appearance of the diode and transistor symbols.

Figure 22-20.
The new **Insert Electronic Component** dialog box displays the image tiles.

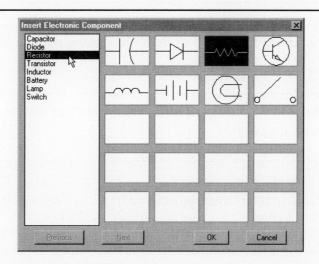

Chapter Test

Write your answers in the spaces provided.

1. What is a .mns file?_____

_____

_____

2. Name the file that contains the default AutoCAD LT menu template._____

_____

3. Why is it a good idea to make a backup copy of the original menu file?_____

_____

_____

_____

4. Identify the required steps to load a menu file using the **Menu Customization** dialog box._____

_____

_____

_____

_____

_____

_____

5. Which section of the menu file is used to customize mouse buttons? _____

_____

6. *True or False?* The pick button on your pointing device may be reassigned. _____

7. Which section of the menu file is used to modify or add pull-down menus?

_____

_____

8. What is the maximum number of pull-down menus that may appear on the menu bar? _____

_____

_____

9. What character is used to continue a menu macro on another line?_____

_____

_____

10. What character is used in a menu label to define a keyboard accelerator or mnemonic key?_____

_____

_____

11. What characters must be entered to place a separator line between menu items?

_____

_____

12. What is the purpose of the ***HELPSTRINGS section in the menu file? _____

_____

_____

_____

_____

13. Which section of the menu file is used to add image tile menus?_____

_____

14. How many slides may be displayed on one page of an image tile menu? _____

_____

_____

15. *True or False?* Solid areas cannot be displayed in an image tile._____

16. What aspect ratio is used to display an image tile? _____

_____

_____

_____

Chapter Problems

1. Create a new pull-down menu named **Special**. The new menu should include the following drawing and editing commands:

General

Line	**Move**
Arc	**Copy**
Circle	**Stretch**
Polyline	**Trim**
Dline	**Extend**
Spline	**Lengthen**
Polygon	**Chamfer**
Rectangle	**Fillet**
Mtext	**Erase**

Use cascading submenus as desired. Include a separator line between the drawing and editing commands, and specify appropriate accelerator keys.

2. Create a group of slides of block symbols that are pertinent to your professional discipline or field of interest. As an example, the slides might feature mechanical fasteners such as nuts, washers, bolts, etc. An architectural collection of slides would include blocks of doors, windows, receptacles, and so forth. Create a minimum of four slides and be sure to size the blocks as described in this chapter. When the slide files are created, write a slide list and use the slidelib utility to produce a slide library. Edit the menu file and add your slides to the ***IMAGE section. Add a new menu item called **My Symbols...** to the **Insert** pull-down menu.

General

Chapter 23

Configuring a Digitizing Tablet

Learning Objectives

After you have completed this chapter, you will be able to:
- O Configure and use the AutoCAD LT tablet menu overlay with a digitizing tablet.
- O Calibrate a tablet to be used for tracing over drawings or photographs.

A digitizing tablet is an input device that works like a miniature drawing board with AutoCAD LT. A polyester film tablet menu overlay featuring graphical icons that represent AutoCAD LT commands is attached to the top surface of the digitizer. Items can then be selected directly from the tablet menu with a pointing device.

There are two types of pointing devices used with digitizing tablets. The most commonly used device is called a *puck*. This device attaches to the digitizer with a wire and features from 1 to 16 buttons. The bottom surface of the puck slides atop the digitizer surface. A set of crosshairs mounted in the puck serve as the target point for this device. The position of the graphics cursor on the screen reflects the position of the puck's crosshairs on the tablet surface. One button on the puck serves as the pick button and is used to enter points and select tablet menu commands. The tablet manufacturer typically pre-programs the other pick buttons to perform specific commands or functions. However, a user may customize these buttons if desired.

The other type of pointing device used with a digitizing tablet is called a *stylus*. Like a puck, the stylus is attached to the digitizer with a wire, but is pen-shaped. The point of the stylus is pressed down on the surface of the digitizer to enter a point or select a command. An example of a digitizer tablet with a puck is shown in **Figure 23-1**.

Bear in mind that there are several disadvantages when using a digitizing tablet. One disadvantage is that you must take your eyes from the screen as you search for the desired command on the tablet menu overlay. Another disadvantage is the size of the tablet itself. Although some digitizers are very small, (6″ square), most tablets have a 12″ × 12″ working area. These tablets measure approximately 16″ × 16″ overall and require a lot of desktop space. Some digitizers are even larger; ranging in size up 44″ × 60″ and are used to digitize points on existing paper drawings or photographs.

Figure 23-1.
A 12″ × 12″ digitizer tablet with a puck.

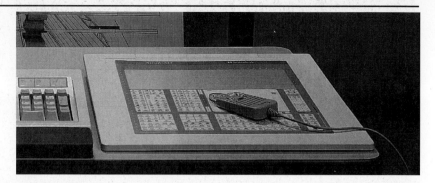

Wintab Compatibility

A digitizing tablet can only be used with AutoCAD LT if it is Wintab-compatible. *Wintab* is a Windows specification that permits you to use your tablet both as a system pointer like a mouse, or as an absolute pointing device. An absolute pointing device lets you digitize points and trace drawings into AutoCAD LT. Using your tablet as a digitizer in this manner is called *tablet mode.*

When you are using a Wintab driver, the tablet puck (or stylus) is used in place of a conventional mouse for *all* your Windows programs, not just AutoCAD LT. Keep in mind that Wintab drivers are not supplied with AutoCAD LT. You must obtain the driver from the manufacturer of your tablet. If the driver you require did not come with your tablet, you can usually download it from the manufacturer's Web site free of charge.

PROFESSIONAL TIP If you are looking for a Wintab driver, or any other type of device driver, point your Internet browser to *http://www.driverguide.com.* This site has links to drivers for a wide variety of computer peripheral devices.

Configuring the Tablet as the System Pointing Device

The default tablet menu overlay supplied with AutoCAD LT 98 is shown in **Figure 23-2.** The drawing for this tablet menu is stored in the C:\Program Files \AutoCAD LT 98\Sample folder. To configure your tablet to serve as your system pointer, do the following:

1. First obtain and install the Wintab driver for your particular tablet as previously mentioned. You will probably have to restart your computer after installing the driver.
2. Start AutoCAD LT.
3. Open the **Preferences** dialog box by selecting **Preferences...** from the **Tools** pull-down menu, or enter PREFERENCES, or PR, at the Command: prompt. Remember that you can also quickly issue this command by placing your pointing device anywhere in the command window and right-clicking to display a pop-up shortcut menu. Select **Preferences...** from the bottom of the shortcut menu.
4. When the **Preferences** dialog box appears, click the **System** tab to display the **System** window.
5. Activate the **Wintab digitizer** option button in the **Pointing device input** area of the window. Do not be alarmed if the dialog box flashes momentarily—this is normal behavior.
6. Now activate the **Digitizer** input from tablet or mouse option button. The dialog box should appear as shown in **Figure 23-3.**
7. Click **OK** to exit the **Preferences** dialog box.

Figure 23-2.
The AutoCAD LT 98 tablet menu.

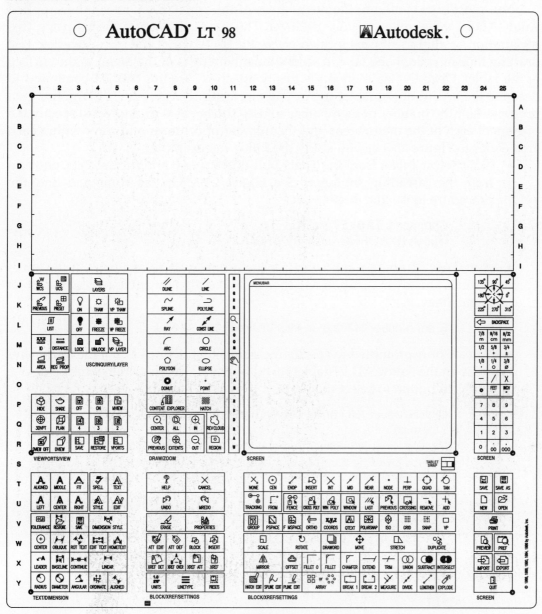

Figure 23-3.
Specifying the digitizer as the system pointing device in the **System** window of the **Preferences** dialog box.

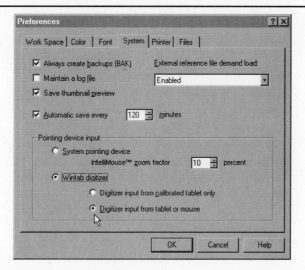

Configuring the Tablet Menu Areas

You must now configure the menu areas of the tablet. First, attach the supplied AutoCAD LT tablet menu to your digitizer. This is usually accomplished using two registration or alignment pins located along the top edge of the menu overlay. Use drafting tape or cellophane tape to secure the other edges of the menu to the surface of the tablet. Once the tablet menu is firmly attached, use the **TABLET** command to describe the layout of the tablet menu you are using to AutoCAD LT. You are then prompted for the number of menu areas to use. You are also prompted to specify the corners of each of the menu areas and the number of columns and rows within each area. Refer to **Figure 23-4** as you study the following example.

- Now, select **Tablet** from the **Tools** pull-down menu and then select **Configure** from the cascading submenu. See **Figure 23-5**. On the command line, the procedure looks like this:

  Command: **TABLET** *or* **TA**↵
  Option (ON/OFF/CAL/CFG): **CFG**↵

- AutoCAD LT now prompts you for the number of tablet menus. If the tablet menu is already in use, you will then be asked if you want to realign the tablet menu areas.

  Enter number of tablet menus desired (0-4) ⟨0⟩: **4**↵

- You are now prompted to specify the points that define each of the four menu areas on the AutoCAD LT tablet menu overlay. Use the tablet pointing device and pick button to select the points.

  Digitize upper left corner of menu area 1: *(pick the donut at the upper-left corner)*
  Digitize lower left corner of menu area 1: *(pick the point)*
  Digitize lower right corner of menu area 1: *(pick the point)*
  Enter the number of columns for menu area 1, (*n-nnn*) ⟨25⟩: ↵
  Enter the number of rows for menu area 1, (*n-nnn*) ⟨9⟩: ↵

Figure 23-4.
Small donuts identify the corners of the menu areas on the AutoCAD LT tablet menu overlay.

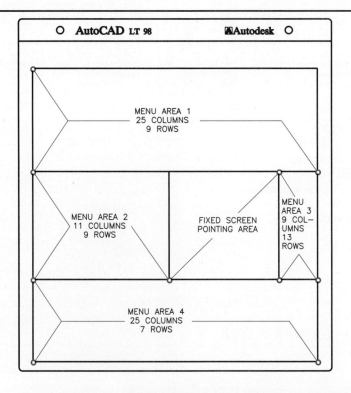

Figure 23-5.
Start the tablet configuration procedure by selecting **Configure** from the **Tablet** cascading submenu in the **Tools** pull-down menu.

- Now that the location of menu area 1 and the required number of columns and rows have been specified, you are then prompted to specify the required information for menu areas 2, 3, and 4.

> Digitize upper left corner of menu area 2: *(pick the point)*
> Digitize lower left corner of menu area 2: *(pick the point)*
> Digitize lower right corner of menu area 2: *(pick the point)*
> Enter the number of columns for menu area 2, (*n-nnn*) ⟨11⟩: ↵
> Enter the number of rows for menu area 2, (*n-nnn*) ⟨9⟩: ↵
> Digitize upper left corner of menu area 3: *(pick the point)*
> Digitize lower left corner of menu area 3: *(pick the point)*
> Digitize lower right corner of menu area 3: *(pick the point)*
> Enter the number of columns for menu area 3, (*n-nnn*) ⟨9⟩: ↵
> Enter the number of rows for menu area 3, (*n-nnn*) ⟨13⟩: ↵
> Digitize upper left corner of menu area 4: *(pick the point)*
> Digitize lower left corner of menu area 4: *(pick the point)*
> Digitize lower right corner of menu area 4: *(pick the point)*
> Enter the number of columns for menu area 4, (*n-nnn*) ⟨25⟩: ↵
> Enter the number of rows for menu area 4, (*n-nnn*) ⟨7⟩: ↵

- You are now prompted to locate opposite corners of the screen pointing area. This is a rectangular area of the tablet that translates the motion of the tablet pointing device to the movement of the graphics cursor in the AutoCAD LT graphics window. You can specify two screen pointing areas for a tablet—one fixed and one floating.
- With a *fixed screen area*, the tablet pointer behaves like a mouse. The next prompt in the tablet configuration procedure lets you set the size of the fixed screen area. It is recommended that you specify a small screen area on your tablet. This area is then used to map the entire screen of your display monitor. Once again, refer to **Figure 23-4** as you continue with the procedure.

> Do you want to respecify the Fixed Screen Pointing Area? ⟨N⟩ **Y**↵
> Digitize lower left corner of Fixed Screen pointing area: *(pick a point)*
> Digitize upper right corner of Fixed Screen pointing area: *(pick a point)*

- Keep in mind that you cannot use the fixed screen pointing area if you wish to use **Tablet** mode and digitize points, drawings, or photographs. This is because there is a one-to-one correspondence between the digitizer and the drawing when **Tablet** mode is enabled. However, the configuration procedure allows you to specify a *floating screen area* that can expand the pointing area of your tablet and be used with Tablet mode. If you choose this alternative, you can then press the [F12] function key whenever you wish to toggle between the fixed screen and floating screen areas. You can also designate one of the buttons on the digitizer puck to serve as the toggle. You cannot select the pick button, though.

> Do you want to specify the Floating Screen pointing area? ⟨N⟩ **Y**↵
> Do you want the Floating Screen Pointing Area to be
> the same size as the Fixed Screen Pointing Area? ⟨Y⟩ ↵
> The F12 key will toggle the Floating Screen
> Area ON and OFF. Would you also like to specify a button to
> toggle the Floating Screen Area? ⟨N⟩ **Y**↵
> Press any non-pick button that will become the
> toggle for the Floating Screen Area, now: *(pick a button on your puck)*
> Command:

- The new tablet configuration is saved in the aclt5.cfg file which is in the C:\Program Files\AutoCAD LT 98 folder. If you are using AutoCAD LT 97, the tablet configuration is saved in the aclt4.cfg file, which is in the C:\Program Files\AutoCAD LT 97 folder.

Using Tablet Mode

If you want to use a digitizing tablet for digitizing points or tracing drawings and/or photographs, the tablet must first be calibrated. As previously mentioned, using a digitizing tablet in this manner is called **Tablet** mode. The purpose of calibration is to align the paper drawing or photograph with the tablet and to establish a proportional relationship between point locations on the drawing and locations on the surface of the tablet. The first step in tablet calibration is to open the **Preferences** dialog box as described earlier in this chapter. Click the **System** tab to open the **System** window and activate the **Digitizer input from calibrated tablet only** option button. Click the **OK** button when you are finished to close the **Preferences** dialog box.

After the tablet is calibrated, you can enter any of the AutoCAD LT drawing commands to trace an existing drawing. If the drawing is too big to fit on your tablet, you can trace the drawing in portions. However, be sure to calibrate the tablet with each portion in turn. Also, any command that requires you to select objects with the tablet pointer still works in **Tablet** mode. For example, to erase an object, issue the **ERASE** command and move your tablet pointer until the pickbox is over the object. Use the pick button on the pointing device to select the object.

You can quickly turn **Tablet** mode on and off by selecting **Tablet** from the **Tools** pull-down menu and then selecting **On** or **Off** from the cascading submenu, pressing the [F4] function key, or using the [Ctrl]+[T] keyboard combination. On the command line, do the following:

> Command: **TABLET** *or* **TA**↵
> Option (ON/OFF/CAL/CFG): **ON** *or* **OFF**↵
> Command:

Calibrating the Tablet

From the previous discussion of fixed and floating screen areas, remember that you can keep the tablet menus configured and still digitize points and trace drawings. However, make sure that the configured area does not overlap the area you intend to trace. Depending on the size of your digitizer and the size of the drawing, you may have to turn off the tablet menu area until you have finished digitizing your drawing. This is accomplished by using the **CFG** option of the **TABLET** command as previously described. However, this time when prompted for the number of tablet menus desired, enter 0 (zero).

You are now ready to calibrate the tablet. Calibration creates a mapping of the points on the tablet to the points on the drawing or photograph you want to trace. The **Calibrate** option of the **TABLET** command requires that you specify points on the tablet with the tablet pointer and then give those points X,Y coordinate values. A minimum of two points defining a rectangular area can be specified, but specifying five points is recommended. Choose points for which you can enter precise X,Y coordinate values and that are not too close to one another. Use the following procedure to calibrate your tablet:

1. Use drafting tape or cellophane tap to firmly attach the drawing you wish to trace to the top surface of the digitizing tablet.
2. Enter TABLET, or TA, at the Command: prompt and then enter CAL at the next prompt to select the **Calibrate** option. Alternatively, you can select **Calibrate** from the **Tablet** cascading submenu in the **Tools** pull-down menu. See **Figure 23-5**.
3. Using the pick button on your puck or stylus, pick a point on the tablet for which you know the *X,Y* coordinate values. It is recommended that you hold the puck in both hands and, looking down from the top, align the puck crosshairs as accurately as possible with the specified location in the drawing. An error or inaccuracy when picking the calibration points represents a residual error throughout your work.
4. Use your keyboard to enter the X,Y coordinate values for the point you specified.
5. Repeat steps 2 and 3 until five points have been calibrated.
6. Press [Enter] to end the calibration.

Once the computations are complete, a table is displayed in the AutoCAD LT text window with the number of calibration points and a column for each transformation type. (The three transformation types are described below.) The following information is provided under each column: Outcome of fit, RMS error, Standard deviation, Largest residual/At point, and Second largest residual/At point. Descriptions of the three transformation types are as follows:

- **Orthogonal.** This option specifies translation, uniform scaling, and rotation with two calibration points. Use this option for dimensionally accurate drawings. Also use this option for drawings where the portion to be digitized is long and narrow, with most points confined to single lines. If you only specify two points to be calibrated, AutoCAD LT automatically uses this transformation type.
- **Affine.** This option specifies arbitrary linear transformation in two dimensions consisting of translation, independent X and Y scaling, rotation, and skewing with three calibration points. Use this option when horizontal dimensions in a drawing are stretched with respect to vertical dimensions and lines that are supposed to be parallel actually are parallel.
- **Projective.** This option specifies a transformation that is equivalent to a perspective projection of one plane in space onto another plane with four calibration points. A projective transformation provides a limited form of what is called *rubber sheeting* by cartographers. This is where different portions of the tablet surface are stretched by varying amounts. Straight lines map into straight lines, but parallel lines do not necessarily remain parallel. Projective transformation corrects parallel lines that appear to converge.

If three or more points are specified during calibration, AutoCAD LT computes the transformation in each of the three types to determine which type best fits the calibration points. However, computing the best fitting projective transformation can take a long time if more than four points are entered. If necessary, press the [Esc] key to cancel the process.

If there have been no failures of projection transformation, you are prompted with the following:

Select transformation type...
Orthogonal/Affine/Projective?⟨Repeat table⟩: *(select an option or press [Enter])*

Only transformation types for which the outcome was Success, Exact, or Canceled are included in this prompt. A projective transformation can be specified even if you canceled the computation process. In this case, AutoCAD LT uses the result computed at the time you canceled.

After you have calibrated the tablet, the coordinates showing on your screen should be coincident with the coordinates in the paper drawing. You can now enter an AutoCAD LT drawing command and use the digitizer pointer to specify points on the drawing or photograph you are tracing. The specified points become digitized to create a drawing.

Chapter Test

Write your answers in the spaces provided.

1. Describe the function of a digitizer tablet. _____
   _____
   _____
   _____
   _____

2. How many menu areas are defined in the default AutoCAD LT tablet menu overlay? _____
   _____

3. Identify the command and option used to specify the size of the menu areas.
   _____
   _____

4. List three methods to quickly turn the tablet on and off. _____
   _____
   _____
   _____

5. *True or False?* You can use the pick button on the tablet pointing device to toggle between a fixed screen area and a floating screen area. _____

6. What is the name of the driver that must first be installed before you can configure a digitizer tablet as the system pointing device? _____

7. Why is it important to hold the digitizer puck with both hands and look straight down when calibrating points? _____

_____

_____

_____

8. List several disadvantages in using a digitizer tablet. _____

_____

_____

_____

_____

9. What is the minimum number of points required to calibrate a tablet? What is the recommended number of points? _____

_____

_____

10. How do you tell AutoCAD LT to use a tablet as the system pointing device or as a digitizer only? _____

_____

_____

_____

_____

Chapter Problems

1. If you have access to a digitizer tablet, install and configure it as the system pointing device as described in this chapter. Make at least one complete drawing using the tablet menus. In your opinion, which input device is more convenient or easier to use—a mouse or a digitizer tablet?

    General

2. Calibrate your tablet as a digitizing device only. Obtain a simple line drawing of your choice from a drafting textbook and trace over it using the digitizer. Save the drawing as P23-2.

    General

AutoCAD LT

Chapter 24

Advanced AutoCAD LT Features and OLE

Learning Objectives

After you have completed this chapter, you will be able to:
- ○ Identify and use advanced clipboard text and graphics.
- ○ Import and export Windows Metafiles.
- ○ Link AutoCAD LT drawings into other applications.
- ○ Embed AutoCAD LT drawings into other applications.
- ○ Launch applications and load files from linked or embedded images.
- ○ Create Universal Resource Locators.
- ○ Modify Universal Resource Locators.
- ○ Create Drawing Web Format files for use on the Internet.

The Microsoft NT and Windows 98/95 operating systems provide options for sharing information between AutoCAD LT sessions as well as other compatible applications. With these operating systems, AutoCAD LT text and drawing objects can be copied in bitmap (raster) or metafile (vector) formats to the Windows Clipboard before pasting into other Windows compatible programs. AutoCAD LT drawing objects and even entire drawings can be linked into other applications such as word processors and graphics presentation programs. This chapter introduces you to these unique features, including Clipboard support, Object Linking and Embedding (OLE), importing and exporting metafiles and the use of .DWF files.

Advanced Clipboard Support

The Windows Clipboard is one of the applications included in Windows 98/95/NT. Since most users of AutoCAD LT operate in the Windows 98/95 environment, this chapter describes the Clipboard found in those systems. Although both the Windows NT and Windows 98/95 Clipboards operate in an identical manner, Windows NT users have a greater range of options, including both *Clipboard* and *Clipbook*.

The Clipboard is a storage device for text and graphics used by the Microsoft Windows operating systems. The contents of the Clipboard can be viewed using the Clipboard Viewer. See **Figure 24-1**. The Clipboard Viewer in Windows 98/95 is found in the System Tools ⟩ cascading folder. This folder can be accessed from the Accessories folder group. See **Figure 24-2**.

Entities from all Windows-compatible programs, including AutoCAD LT, can be copied to the Clipboard. Once an image is copied to the Clipboard, it can then be pasted into another Windows-compatible application.

Keep in mind that the Clipboard can only hold one image at a time. The image remains in the Clipboard until it is replaced by some other image, or until you turn off or reboot your computer. You may save the contents of the Clipboard, if you wish. Saved Clipboard images have a .CLP file extension.

Figure 24-1.
The Windows 98
Clipboard Viewer

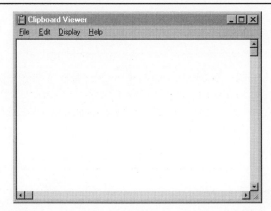

Figure 24-2.
Opening the
Clipboard Viewer.

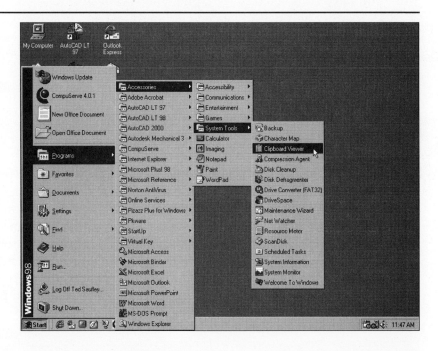

Copying Images to the Clipboard

The objects in the AutoCAD LT drawing window can be copied to the Clipboard in Windows bitmap format and then pasted into another Windows application. The bitmap image is in raster format but displays very quickly. It requires a fixed amount of memory regardless of its size or complexity. Keep in mind, though, that a clipped image is an exact replica of what currently appears on the screen. Therefore, if you are operating at a low screen resolution, such as 640 × 480, the clipped image will also be at the same resolution. This is generally referred to as *WYSIWYG* or *What You See Is What You Get.* Also, be aware that bitmap images are not scaleable and become blocky when scaled up or down. Therefore, a scaled bitmap image results in a poor image when printed. This can be a major drawback if you need to scale a bitmap after pasting it into a word processing document, graphics presentation program, or some other Windows-compatible application.

Images of AutoCAD LT drawing objects can be clipped and copied to the Clipboard by clicking the **Copy to Clipboard** button on the **Standard Toolbar** or selecting **Copy** from the **Edit** pull-down menu. See **Figure 24-3**. Alternatively, you may enter the command from the keyboard using the [Ctrl]+[C] shortcut combination or by entering COPYCLIP on the command line as follows:

Command: **COPYCLIP**⏎
Select objects: *(select one or more objects)*
Select objects: ⏎
Command:

At the Select objects: prompt, select the AutoCAD LT objects you wish to copy using any selection set method. An image of the selected objects is then transferred to the Clipboard. Note that the **COPYCLIP** command captures only the objects within the AutoCAD LT drawing window.

Figure 24-3.
Selecting **Copy** from the **Edit** pull-down menu issues the **COPYCLIP** command.

Viewing and Saving the **Clipboard** Contents

In the example of the Plate2.dwg sample drawing from the AutoCAD LT\Sample folder shown in **Figure 24-4A**, only a portion of the drawing is copied to the Clipboard using the Window selection set option. The portion that has been copied appears in the Clipboard Viewer as shown in **Figure 24-4B**. Observe that the image appears elongated. This is the result of Clipboard adjusting the aspect ratio of the captured image to fit inside the Clipboard Viewer window. When the Clipboard contents are pasted back into AutoCAD LT, or some other Windows application, the correct aspect ratio is automatically restored.

Figure 24-4.
A—The Window selection set option is used to copy just a portion of the drawing to the Clipboard. B—The selected objects as they appear in Clipboard Viewer. The objects appear distorted because they are adjusted to fit within the Clipboard Viewer window.

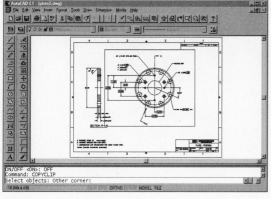
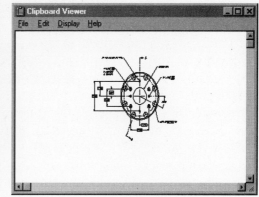

A   B

Chapter 24 Advanced AutoCAD LT Features and OLE

To save the image in the Clipboard Viewer, select **Save As...** from the **File** pull-down menu. The bitmap image is then saved with a .CLP extension. Be aware that bitmap images are very large. Therefore, once you have saved the image, open the **Edit** pull-down menu and select **Delete** to delete the image. Clearing the contents of the Clipboard conserves your computer's memory and improves system performance.

Improving the Quality of the Copied Image

You can improve the quality of a clipped AutoCAD LT image in several ways. First, turn off the UCS icon unless it is required in the copied image. To change the visibility of the UCS icon, enter UCSICON at the Command: prompt. If necessary, refer to *Chapter 7* to review the **UCSICON** command options.

A second important consideration is the background color of the AutoCAD LT image. In general, users of AutoCAD LT prefer a black background with white or light colored drawing objects. A black background has lower glare and reduces eye fatigue.

However, if you intend to copy an image of your AutoCAD LT screen to another document, you must consider its background color as well. Word processing documents, for instance, are printed on white paper. In such circumstances, the image of your AutoCAD LT screen will be a rectangular, black blob. To avoid this problem, change the background color of your AutoCAD LT drawing window prior to clipping an image.

To do so, select **Preferences** from the **Tools** pull-down menu, or enter PREFERENCES, or PR or PF, at the Command: prompt. Select the **Color** tab, as shown in **Figure 24-5**. Pick the image of the AutoCAD LT graphics window, or select Graphics window background from within the **Window Element:** drop-down list. Then, select a new background color from the palette provided. When you are finished, click the **OK** button to exit.

A third way to improve the quality of an image is to modify the colors of the AutoCAD LT layers after you have changed the background color. For instance, yellow contrasts well with the standard AutoCAD LT background, but is hard to see against the white background.

Figure 24-5.
Changing the AutoCAD LT background color using the **Color** tab window in the **Preferences** dialog box.

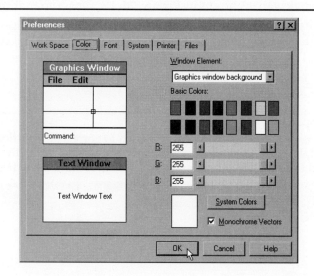

Pasting the Clipboard Contents

You can paste the contents of the Clipboard, or a saved .CLP file, into other Windows-compatible programs. To paste the contents of the Clipboard, launch the appropriate Windows-based application and open the target document. Specify the position within the target document where the image is to appear. To paste a Clipboard image into AutoCAD LT, click the **Paste from Clipboard** button on the **Standard Toolbar**, press [Ctrl]+[V], select **Paste** from the **Edit** pull-down menu, or enter PASTECLIP at the Command: prompt as follows:

> Command: **PASTECLIP**↵
> Command:

Once the image is pasted, it can be moved or resized as necessary.

The **COPYCLIP** command creates a temporary file of the AutoCAD LT clipped vectors in the default temporary folder, typically C:\Windows\Temp. If the clipped image is pasted into AutoCAD LT, the temporary file is automatically deleted. However, if the image is pasted into a non-AutoCAD LT Windows application, the temporary file might not be deleted. Make a point of periodically checking the Temp folder on your workstation to delete any unnecessary files. Ideally, it should be empty if your computer has just started. If you detect large numbers of temporary files building up in your system, you should delete them

---

PROFESSIONAL TIP  You can use the **COPYCLIP** and **PASTECLIP** commands as a handy alternative to the **WBLOCK** command to quickly copy and paste views, details, sections, and notes from one drawing to another.

Clipping the Entire AutoCAD LT Drawing Window

You can quickly clip the entire contents of the AutoCAD LT drawing window by selecting **Copy Link** from the **Edit** pull-down menu, or by entering COPYLINK, or CL, at the Command: prompt as follows:

> Command: **COPYLINK** or **CL**↵
> Command:

You may also "print" an image of an active window, including AutoCAD LT, to the Clipboard. The [Print Scrn] key transfers a copy of *all* the windows displayed on your desktop to the Clipboard. The keyboard combination [Alt]+[Print Scrn] copies an image of the *active window only* to the clipboard. These images are handled like all other clipped images.

Creating and Using Bitmap Images

AutoCAD LT can create standard bitmap image files with a .BMP extension. These .BMP images cannot be used directly by AutoCAD LT. However, other programs, such as "big-brother" AutoCAD, Paint, and most word processors for example, can use these images.

To create a bitmap image file, select **Export...** from the **File** pull-down menu to display the **Export Data** dialog box. Be sure to select Bitmap [*.bmp] from the **Save as type:** drop-down list at the bottom of the dialog box. Observe that the bitmap file is saved with the same name as the current drawing. Use the **File name:** text box if you wish to save the file with a different name. Click the **Save** button when you are through. See **Figure 24-6**. On the command line, the procedure looks like this:

Command: **EXPORT** *or* **EXP**↵
Select objects: *(select one or more objects to be included in the bitmap file)*
Select objects: ↵
Command:

Once a bitmap is created, it can be inserted into other Windows-based applications. A bitmap image of the Plate2 sample drawing is shown inserted into a Microsoft Word document in **Figure 24-7**.

Figure 24-6.
Saving a bitmap (.bmp) file using the **Export Data** dialog box.

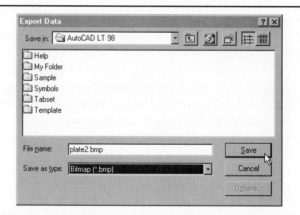

Figure 24-7.
The Plate2 bitmap file shown inserted into a Microsoft Word document.

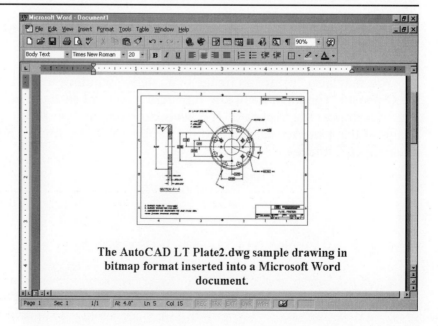

The AutoCAD LT Plate2.dwg sample drawing in bitmap format inserted into a Microsoft Word document.

NOTE

You can also use the **BMPOUT** command as a quick means to export AutoCAD LT drawing objects in bitmap format.

Creating and Using Windows Metafiles

Saved bitmap files, whether saved as .CLP or as .BMP files, are large and cumbersome. Both file types can also be difficult to scale and to print. By using the Windows *metafile* format, many of these problems can be avoided.

AutoCAD LT drawings can be saved in a metafile format that has a .WMF file extension. To create a metafile, select **Export...** from the **File** pull-down menu to display the **Export Data** dialog box. Be sure to select Metafile [*.wmf] from the **Save as type:** drop-down list at the bottom of the dialog box. As with bitmap files, the metafile is saved with the same name as the current drawing. Use the **File name:** text box if you wish to save the metafile with a different name. Click the **Save** button when you are through. Then, at the Select objects: prompt, select the objects to be saved in the metafile.

Once a metafile is created, it can be inserted into other Windows-based applications. To insert a Windows metafile into AutoCAD LT, select **File** from the **Insert** pull-down menu. See **Figure 24-8.** You can also enter IMPORT, or IMP, at the Command: prompt to open the **Import File** dialog box. When the dialog box appears, select Metafile [*.wmf] from the **Save as type:** drop-down list at the bottom. Then, select the file you wish to insert and click the **Open** button.

Notice that .WMF files are inserted into AutoCAD LT in the form of a block. These .WMF images can be moved, copied or scaled, just like other blocks. However, be aware that exploding the block is not recommended. This is because instead of reverting to usable AutoCAD LT drawing objects, the .WMF file dissolves into a myriad of short line segments.

Figure 24-8.
Selecting **File...** from the **Insert** pull-down menu opens the **Import File** dialog box.

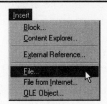

PROFESSIONAL TIP

You can also use the **WMFOUT** and **WMFIN** commands to quickly export and import Windows metafiles. Both commands display dialog boxes that are designed to work with metafiles only.

Object Linking and Embedding (OLE)

Object Linking and Embedding (OLE) allows you to share data or images between programs. With OLE, you can create compound documents with data from several applications. For instance, a word processing document might contain an AutoCAD LT drawing or vice versa.

Linking vs. Embedding

The difference between linking and embedding is similar to the difference between an xref and an inserted block. A *linked object* is like an xref because it maintains a connection with the original document. When the original changes, the linked object also changes. An *embedded object* is like an inserted block because it has no connection to the original document. When the original document changes, the embedded object remains unchanged. If necessary, refer to *Chapter 15* to review the differences between inserted objects and external references.

The OLE-related commands for all Windows-compatible applications are found in the **Edit** pull-down menu. See **Figure 24-3**. A summary of the command functions are provided as follows:

- **Cut.** Clears the selected object(s) from the application and places the object(s) in the Windows Clipboard.
- **Copy.** Makes a copy of the selected object(s) and places the object(s) in the Windows Clipboard
- **Copy Link.** Makes a copy of the current AutoCAD LT drawing window and places it in the Windows Clipboard.
- **Paste.** Makes a copy of the object(s) in the Windows Clipboard and places the object(s) in the AutoCAD LT drawing window.
- **Paste Special....** Makes a copy of the object(s) in the Windows Clipboard and places the object(s) in the AutoCAD LT drawing window, allowing the user to determine whether the object(s) will be linked or embedded.
- **Clear.** Issues the **ERASE** command and is used to remove pasted objects from the AutoCAD LT drawing window.
- **OLE Links....** Opens a dialog box allowing you to view and manage linked objects in an AutoCAD LT drawing.

Embedding an Image Tutorial

- ▷ Launch AutoCAD LT and open the drawing Plate2 from the C:\Program Files\AutoCAD LT 98\Sample folder. Save the drawing as Plate2-Test.
- ▷ Select **Copy Link** from the **Edit** pull-down menu. This will create a copy of the Plate2-Test drawing in the Windows Clipboard.
- ▷ Open Microsoft Word (or your own word processor) and begin a new document. Press the [Enter] key several times to move the cursor lower on the page.
- ▷ Open the Edit pull-down menu and select Paste. A copy of the Plate2-Test drawing will appear at the cursor's position. Click to paste the image and save the document as Test1.
- ▷ Return to AutoCAD LT by clicking anywhere inside its open window. Exit AutoCAD LT.

The image of the AutoCAD LT drawing you have just embedded in the Microsoft Word document is completely adjustable. Whenever you click the image with your pointing device, small boxes appear at each corner of the image as well as at the midpoint of each edge. These boxes, or handles, are used in the same manner as you would to manipulate the size or shape of a window. When the cursor is placed inside of an active image, it takes the form of the AutoCAD LT **Move** tool button icon. By pressing and holding the pick button on your pointing device, you can move the image within the document. To deactivate the image, simply click the document outside of the image's boundary.

Embedding an image destroys most of the connections to the original document. One important connection is maintained, however. The image is always connected to its parent document and the software application that created it. Like the film character ET, it can always "call home". By double-clicking the image of the AutoCAD LT drawing inside the Microsoft Word document, you can launch AutoCAD LT and open the original drawing.

Launching a Program From an Embedded Image Tutorial

↪ Double-click the AutoCAD LT drawing inside the Microsoft Word document. AutoCAD LT starts up and the Plate2-Test drawing is loaded. Notice the title of the drawing in the title bar reads: Drawing in test1.doc.

↪ Make a change in the Plate2-Test drawing and save it.

↪ Switch to Microsoft Word. Notice that the image of the drawing inside the Microsoft Word document reflects your drawing changes.

↪ Click the image of the AutoCAD LT drawing. Now, select Clear from the Edit pull-down menu.

↪ Return to AutoCAD LT. Follow the steps in the *Embedding an Image Tutorial* to embed the new image of the Plate2-Test drawing into the Microsoft Word document.

Linking an Image

Linking an image and embedding an image are similar. Both begin with either cutting or copying the original document. The difference between linking and embedding occurs in the Paste Special step of the procedure.

Linking an Image Tutorial

↪ Select New... from the Microsoft Word File pull-down menu to create a new document.

↪ Switch to AutoCAD LT and select **Copy Link** from the **Edit** pull-down menu. Exit AutoCAD LT.

↪ Switch to Microsoft Word and select Paste Special... from the Edit pull-down menu to open the Paste Special dialog box. Activate the Paste Link option button and select AutoCAD LT Drawing Object from the As: selection box. See **Figure 24-9**.

↪ AutoCAD LT starts up and the Plate2-Test drawing is loaded.

↪ Switch to Microsoft Word to see the inserted image of the drawing.

↪ Save this document as Test2 and close the document.

The image of the AutoCAD LT drawing you have just linked to the Microsoft Word document is completely adjustable. Whenever you click the image with your pointing device, small boxes appear at each corner of the image as well as at the midpoint of each edge. As previously mentioned, these boxes are used in the same manner as you would to manipulate the size or shape of a window. When the cursor is placed inside an active image, it takes the form of the AutoCAD LT **Move** tool button icon. By pressing and holding the pick button on your pointing device, you can move the image within the document. To deactivate the image, simply click the document outside the image's boundary.

Linking an image creates a dynamic connection to the original document. As with the embedded document, you can launch AutoCAD LT and open the original drawing by double-clicking the image inside the Microsoft Word document. Additionally, the Microsoft Word document is automatically updated to reflect the changes you make in the AutoCAD LT drawing.

Figure 24-9.
The **Paste Special**
dialog box.

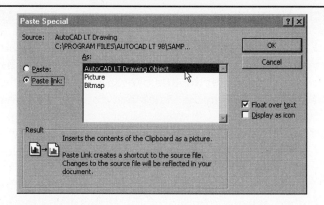

Modifying Linked Images Tutorial

⇨ In AutoCAD LT, modify the Plate2-Test drawing and save it.
⇨ Open the Test2 document in Microsoft Word. Notice that the Word document has already been updated with the changes you made to the Plate2-Test drawing in AutoCAD LT.
⇨ Switch to AutoCAD LT. Modify the Plate2-Test drawing again and save it.
⇨ Switch to Microsoft Word. Notice that the changes implemented in AutoCAD LT have also occurred in the Microsoft Word document.

Opening a document, including an AutoCAD LT drawing, will always update any linked files it contains. However, when both the original and destination programs are actively in use, the updating process may be delayed. When this occurs, you can force the update by using the Links dialog box shown in **Figure 24-10**. Selecting Links... from the Edit pull-down menu opens this dialog box.

The Update Now button in the Links dialog box forces the application to reread the source file and update the linked data based upon the current saved version. The Links dialog box also contains buttons to launch the source and open the linked document. It also allows you to change sources. Finally, the Links dialog box permits you to break the link between the source and destination object. Doing so would change a linked file into an embedded file. This would be like binding an external reference to the master drawing resulting in an inserted drawing. Be aware that the Update Now button can also be used to launch a second AutoCAD LT session. This second session will load the most recent version of the linked drawing before transferring the updated data to the object file. This activity can be rather disconcerting, but it is a normal part of a complex process. Once the object file has been updated, you may terminate the newly launched AutoCAD LT session. Closing the session will not destroy your drawing.

Figure 24-10.
The **Links** dialog
box.

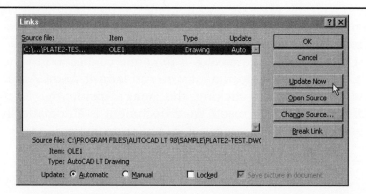

Internet Utilities

AutoCAD LT has a variety of tools allowing you to annotate, publish, download, and view drawings on the Internet. These tools can be divided into two types:
- Tools used to prepare your drawing to be published on the Internet.
- Tools used to publish, download, and view drawings on the Internet.

Universal Resource Locators (URL)

Universal Resource Locators are used to embed text within a document. The embedded text may be attached to an area in the drawing window or to a single AutoCAD LT object. The URL may redirect you to another drawing, access the Internet through your browser, or access files though a network (Intranet). In AutoCAD LT, the URL commands can be accessed from the **Internet** cascading submenu in the **Tools** pull-down menu. See **Figure 24-11**.

Figure 24-11.
Selecting **Internet** from the **Tools** cascading submenu displays several URL (Universal Resource Locators) command options.

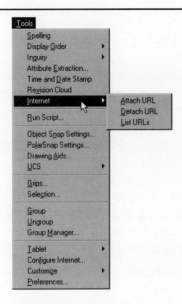

NOTE   Keep in mind that the URL commands can also be accessed from the **Internet Utilities** toolbar shown in **Figure 24-12**. See *Chapter 21* to learn how to open one of the nonstandard AutoCAD LT toolbars.

Figure 24-12.
The **Internet Utilities** toolbar.

To attach a URL redirecting the user to the Internet address www.autodesk.com, select **Attach URL** from the **Internet** cascading submenu. On the command line the procedure is as follows:

Command: **ATTACHURL**↵
URL by (Area/⟨Objects⟩): **O**↵
Select objects: *(select one or more objects)*
Select objects: ↵
Enter URL: **http://www.autodesk.com**↵
Command:

To list the URLs attached to an object(s) or area, select **List URLs** from the **Internet** cascading submenu. The URLs are listed on the command line as follows:

Command: **LISTURL**↵
Select objects: *(select the object(s))*
Select objects: ↵
URL for selected object is: http://www.autodesk.com
Command:

The Drawing Web Format (.DWF) File

AutoCAD LT drawings cannot be viewed by Web browsers. If you are going to publish your drawing on the Internet, you must create a new file type that can be seen with a Web browser. These new file types are called *Drawing Web Format* files.

AutoCAD LT drawing files have a .DWG extension. Internet compatible versions of these drawings have .DWF extensions. These .DWF files cannot be viewed using AutoCAD LT. Instead, you view them through a Web browser like Netscape Navigator or Internet Explorer.

Any AutoCAD LT drawing can be converted into a Drawing Web Format file. Since it will be used on the Internet, be sure to have your URLs attached before creating the .DWF file. To easily create a .DWF file using a dialog box, you can issue the **DWFOUT** command as follows:

Command: **DWFOUT**↵

When the **Create DWF File** dialog box appears, enter the desired name for the file in the **File name:** text box, or accept the default file name. See **Figure 24-13**. When you are through, click the **Save** button. The dialog box is closed and a subdialog box appears briefly on your screen informing you that the .DWF file is being created.

Figure 24-13.
The Create DWF File dialog box is used to save an AutoCAD LT drawing in Web format.

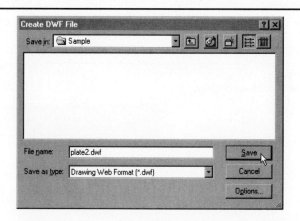

AutoCAD LT—Fundamentals and Applications

Once the .DWF file is posted on your Internet site, other people will be able to log into your server and view your drawing. However, they will not be able to download the actual drawing unless you load a copy of the drawing into the same folder as the .DWF file.

To see your .DWF file, launch the application from inside of Windows Explorer. See **Figure 24-14**. Launching applications using Windows Explorer is explained in *Chapter 25* of this text.

Figure 24-14.
The .DWF file is shown in the Microsoft Internet Explorer Web browser.

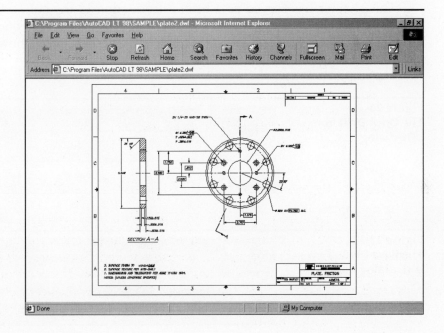

Other Internet Functions

AutoCAD LT also permits you to save drawings to other servers through the Internet or open drawings posted on the Internet. These two functions are available from the **Internet Utilities** toolbar shown in **Figure 24-12**, or from the **File** pull-down menu. See **Figure 24-15**.

Figure 24-15.
AutoCAD LT drawings can be opened from, and saved to, the Internet using the functions in the **File** pull-down menu.

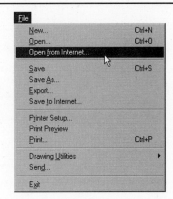

To open a drawing posted on the Internet, select **Open from Internet...** from the **File** pull-down menu. The **Open DWG from URL** dialog box appears. See **Figure 24-16**. Enter the required Web address and click the **Open** button at the upper right of the dialog box to access the Internet server.

When you wish to save a drawing to an Internet server, select **Save to Internet...** from the **File** pull-down menu. The **Save DWG to URL** dialog box appears. See **Figure 24-17**. As before, enter the required Web address and click the **Open** button at the upper right of the dialog box to access the server.

This chapter has served as a brief introduction to the cut and paste, OLE, and Internet functions available to you with AutoCAD LT. You are encouraged to learn more about these functions using online **Help** to increase your knowledge and enjoyment of the program.

Figure 24-16.
The **Open DWG from URL** dialog box.

Figure 24-17.
The **Save DWG to URL** dialog box.

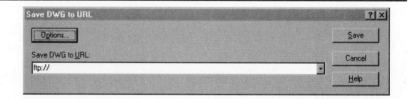

Chapter Test

Write your answers in the spaces provided.

1. What is the difference between the **COPYCLIP** and **COPYLINK** commands? _____
   _____
   _____

2. You pasted a clipped image of an AutoCAD LT drawing into Microsoft Word. The image is a black rectangle and it is impossible to see anything within it. What should you do? _____
   _____
   _____
   _____

3. You have been cutting and embedding images from AutoCAD LT into Microsoft Word for a report. Your computer seems to be slowing down. What is wrong?
   _____
   _____
   _____

4. *Yes or No?* You exported a bitmap of a drawing. Can it be pasted into an AutoCAD LT drawing? _____

5. *Yes or No?* You have just inserted a .WMF file into your AutoCAD LT drawing as a block. If you explode the block, will you be able to use the parts you want and erase the rest? _____

6. What is the difference between a linked object and an embedded object? _____
   _____

   _____

   _____

7. When pasting an object into the AutoCAD LT drawing window, how do you determine whether you are linking the object rather then embedding it? _____
   _____

   _____

8. What is a *URL?* _____
   _____

   _____

   _____

9. *True or False?* Both .DWG and .DWF files can be directly accessed with AutoCAD LT.
   _____

10. *True or False?* AutoCAD LT drawing files can be directly viewed over the Internet.
    _____

11. *True or False?* When users view your .DWF file with their Internet browser, they automatically have access to the drawing file. _____

Chapter Problems

1. If you have not already done so, complete the tutorials in this chapter.

   General

2. Create a rectangle in the Plate2 sample drawing. This drawing is located in the C:\Program Files\AutoCAD LT 98\Sample folder. If this drawing cannot be found, notify your instructor or supervisor. Create a URL inside the rectangle, directing the user to www. autodesk.com. Save the drawing as P24-2.

   General

3. Create a Drawing Web Format file from P24-2. If you have a Web browser, view the .DWF file you just created.

   General

AutoCAD LT

Chapter 25

Drawing Management, File Formats, and Using Windows Explorer

Learning Objectives

After you have completed this chapter, you will be able to:
- O Evaluate the integrity of drawing data using the **AUDIT** command.
- O Repair a damaged drawing file using the **RECOVER** command.
- O Import and export Drawing Interchange Format (DXF) files.
- O Convert drawings from previous AutoCAD LT versions to AutoCAD LT 98/97 format.
- O Identify the various elements of the Windows Explorer.
- O Start applications and print drawing files from Explorer.
- O Drag and drop AutoCAD LT-related files into the AutoCAD LT drawing window.
- O Move, copy, delete, undelete, and rename files on floppy and hard disks.
- O Create and manage folders and subfolders.

Prudent file and disk management is of paramount importance to every computer user. This is particularly true in the case of AutoCAD LT. The loss of a large or complex drawing file through carelessness or negligence is a painful experience. Losing an entire folder of drawing files can be devastating. A variety of suggestions and procedures for managing AutoCAD LT-related files have been offered throughout the preceding chapters of this text.

This chapter describes the AutoCAD LT commands that enable you to examine and correct drawing errors and repair damaged drawings. Additionally, how to import and export drawings from other CAD programs into, and out of, AutoCAD LT is also covered. You will also learn how to quickly convert drawing files created with earlier versions of AutoCAD LT into AutoCAD LT 98/97 format.

Finally, you are introduced to an excellent method of file and folder maintenance using the Microsoft Windows Explorer program. With Windows Explorer, you can perform a wide variety of file manipulation tasks with remarkable ease and assurance. This powerful tool also enables you to create, delete, rename, copy, and move files and entire folders. What is more, Windows Explorer can be used to open a drawing file and simultaneously start AutoCAD LT in one simple operation. Additionally, the "drag and drop" capability of Windows Explorer is explored as a means of inserting drawing and text files into the AutoCAD LT drawing window, as well as printing a drawing with the Windows Print Manager.

<table>
<tr><td>NOTE</td><td>If you are a Windows NT user, Windows Explorer is called Windows NT Explorer. Apart from the name difference, Explorer is identical between Windows 95 and Windows NT. However, the *Active Desktop*, (a feature common to Windows 98 and Internet Explorer 4.0 and 5.0), changes the appearance of Windows Explorer a bit. The screen captures shown in this chapter are from Windows 98 and thus reflect these "cosmetic" changes. Therefore, do not be alarmed if your screen display appears somewhat different. Be assured that the functions of Windows Explorer described in this chapter are applicable to all users of Windows 95, Windows 98, or Windows NT.</td></tr>
</table>

Using the AUDIT Command

AUDIT

File
➥ Drawing Utilities 〉
Audit

The **AUDIT** command is a diagnostic tool that allows you to examine the current drawing and correct errors. You should use **AUDIT** if you suspect that your drawing has been corrupted. To issue the command, enter AUDIT at the Command: prompt, or select **Audit** from the **Drawing Utilities** 〉 cascading submenu in the **File** pull-down menu. See **Figure 25-1**. The command sequence is as follows:

Command: **AUDIT**↵
Fix any errors detected? 〈N〉 *(answer Y to correct any errors)*

AutoCAD LT then makes several passes through the drawing database looking for errors and displays a report on the command line similar to the following:

0 Blocks audited
Pass 1 224 objects audited
Pass 2 224 objects audited
Total errors found 0 fixed 0
Command:

Note that errors are listed, but not fixed, if you answer N to the Fix any errors detected? prompt.

If the system variable **AUDITCTL** is set to 1 (ON), AutoCAD LT creates an audit report that lists the corrections made. This report is given the same name as the current drawing, but has an .ADT file extension. The file is in *ASCII (American Standard Code for Information Interchange)* text format and is placed in the same folder as the current drawing. You may open the file for viewing using Windows Notepad or any other standard text editor.

Figure 25-1.
Selecting **Audit** from the **Drawing Utilities** cascading submenu issues the **AUDIT** command.

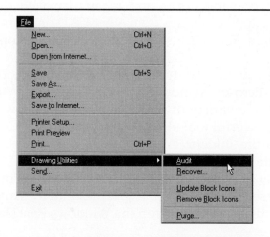

Recovering a Damaged Drawing

There may be occasions when the **AUDIT** command is unable to correct the drawing errors it encounters. In those instances, use the **RECOVER** command instead. Typically, **RECOVER** is run automatically if AutoCAD LT detects damage in a drawing's header information when you attempt to open a corrupted drawing file. To issue the command manually, enter RECOVER at the Command: prompt or select **Recover...** from the **Drawing Utilities** 〉 cascading submenu in the **File** pull-down menu.

Select the drawing file you wish to recover from the **Select File** dialog box and click **OK**. The results of the drawing recovery operation are then displayed in the **AutoCAD LT Text Window**. If the operation is successful, AutoCAD LT displays a message box informing you that no errors were detected in the recovered database.

Keep in mind that AutoCAD LT will discard any corrupted data that cannot be repaired. For this reason, be sure to obtain a print or plot of the recovered drawing to verify any missing drawing objects.

```
RECOVER
File
 ↳ Drawing Utilities 〉
  ↳ Recover...
```

PROFESSIONAL TIP   One of the most common reasons for corrupted drawing files occurs when a user attempts to save a drawing file to a floppy disk, but removes the floppy from the disk drive before the save operation is complete. To avoid this problem, always wait for the green LED light on your floppy disk drive to go out before removing the floppy disk. Other tips for using your floppy disks are provided later in this chapter.

Drawing Interchange File (DXF) Format

The *Drawing Interchange File* (DXF) format was developed by Autodesk, Inc. to allow the translation of drawing files between AutoCAD LT and other CAD programs. A file in DXF format is written in standard ASCII format so that any computer may read it. To translate a drawing from a different CAD system into AutoCAD LT, the **DXFIN** command is used. Use the **DXFOUT** command when you wish to transfer an AutoCAD LT drawing to a different CAD program.

The DXFIN Command

The **DXFIN** command is used to load a .DXF file into AutoCAD LT. To use **DXFIN**, first begin a new drawing and click the **Start from Scratch** button in the Create New Drawing dialog box. Next, enter DXFIN, or DN, at the Command: prompt, or select **File...** from the **Insert** pull-down menu. See **Figure 25-2**.

Select the file to convert when the **Select DXF File** dialog box appears and click the **Open** button. See **Figure 25-3**. The drawing conversion is aborted if AutoCAD LT detects any errors during input. Once the drawing is converted, save it as a .DWG file.

```
DXFIN
DN
Insert
 ↳ File...
```

Figure 25-2.
Selecting **File...**
from the **Insert** pull-
down menu imports
DXF and other file
types.

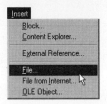

Figure 25-3.
Selecting a DXF file
to convert using the
Select DXF File
dialog box.

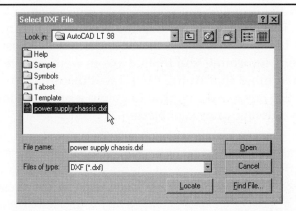

The **DXFOUT** Command

The DXFOUT command creates a drawing interchange file from an AutoCAD LT drawing so that it may be used by another CAD program. To create a DXF file, enter DXFOUT, or DX, at the Command: prompt to display the **Create DXF File** dialog box. See **Figure 25-4.** Alternatively, you can select **Export...** from the **File** pull-down menu to open the **Export File** dialog box. Either dialog box can be used to export a drawing in DXF format.

Regardless of the dialog box you use, observe that the DXF file assumes the same name as the current drawing file. If you wish to change this convention, specify the desired file name in the **File name:** text box and click the **Save** button. The file is then written to disk with a .DXF extension and is ready to be translated into another CAD program.

Figure 25-4.
Specifying a DXF file
name in the **Create
DXF File** dialog box.

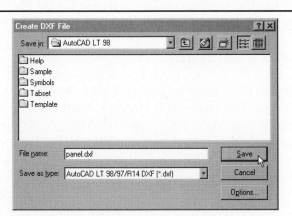

NOTE　　　　AutoCAD LT and AutoCAD share the same drawing file format. Therefore, it is not necessary to use the DXF translator when you wish to transfer drawings between AutoCAD LT and AutoCAD. However, remember that AutoCAD LT Releases 1 & 2 for Windows 3.1 use the AutoCAD Release 12 format, AutoCAD LT for Windows 95 shares the AutoCAD Release 13 format, and AutoCAD LT 98 and AutoCAD LT 97 are compatible with AutoCAD Release 14.

Using the LT DWG Update Utility

The **LT DWG Update** utility converts drawing files created by earlier versions of AutoCAD LT to the AutoCAD LT 98 format. Although an earlier drawing is converted automatically once it has been opened and saved under AutoCAD LT 98, only one drawing can be converted at a time. The **LT DWG Update** utility lets you convert multiple drawings in one operation. It does so by first opening a dialog box that lets you specify one or more drawings to convert. It then starts AutoCAD LT, loads the first drawing you specified, saves it under AutoCAD LT 98, and then repeats the process for the next drawing in the list. When the procedure is complete, AutoCAD LT is automatically exited. No user interaction is required at all.

There are two ways to access the **LT DWG Update** utility. One way is from the Start menu on the Windows taskbar. First, select Programs and then select AutoCAD LT 98 ⟩ LT DWG Update. See **Figure 25-5.**

The other way to launch the utility program is to open Windows Explorer, go to the Program Files\AutoCAD LT 98 folder and double-click LTUpdate.exe as shown in **Figure 25-6.** Starting programs from Explorer is covered in detail later in this chapter.

Figure 25-5.
Launching the LT DWG Update utility from the Windows Start menu.

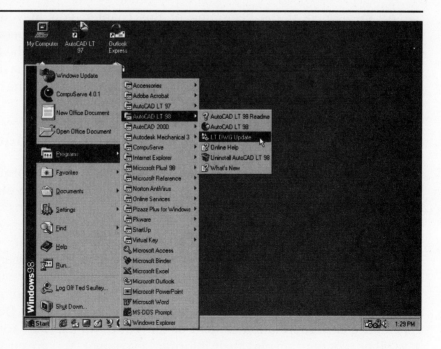

Figure 25-6.
Launching the **LT DWG Update** utility, LTUpdate.exe, from the Program Files\AutoCAD LT 98 folder in Windows Explorer.

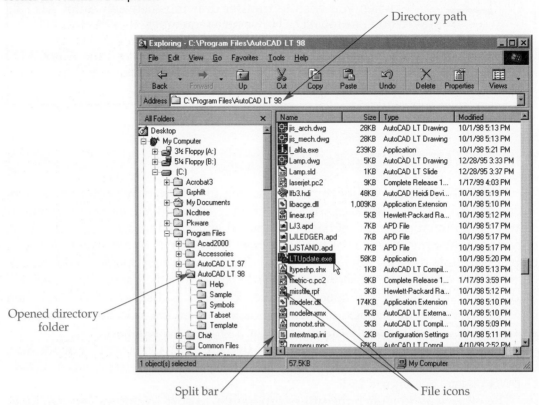

Directory path

Opened directory folder

Split bar

File icons

Introduction to Windows Explorer

As mentioned at the beginning of this chapter, you may use the Windows Explorer to perform numerous file and folder maintenance operations. To launch Windows Explorer, click the Start button on the taskbar to open the Start menu. Next, open the Programs folder and select Windows Explorer. An even faster way to launch Explorer is to place your pointing device over the Start button on the taskbar and right-click. Now, select Explore from the pop-up short-cut menu.

Elements of the Windows Explorer Directory Window

When you use Windows Explorer, all of your work is performed in a directory window. A *directory window* is a graphic representation of the directory, or folder, structure of your disk, and each of the files and folders it contains. See **Figure 25-7.**

The View menu

The View menu has several options. See **Figure 25-8.** The Toolbars and Explorer Bar menu items each display cascading submenus offering a variety of viewing choices. The Status Bar item is used to turn the status bar at the bottom of the directory window on and off. Selecting Large Icons, Small Icons, List, or Details changes the appearance and information content of the Windows Explorer. You may also affect how other programs display their information content. You are encouraged to experiment with each of the viewing options to discover which option best fits your personal style and work preferences.

As shown in **Figure 25-8** the **Details** method is the current viewing method. With this format, you can see the names of the drives, files, and folders in one column on

Figure 25-7.
The Windows Explorer directory window.

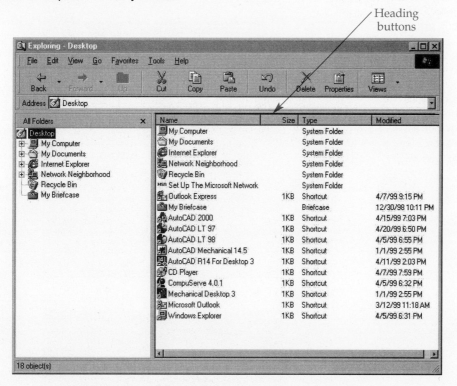

the left side of the directory window. The individual files are shown on the right side of the directory window. The size of the files and the dates that each was last modified is also displayed. Each heading button on the right side of the directory window can be individually sized to view long names as required. Further, these heading buttons can be used to sort the columns of information. Clicking a heading button causes the information to be sorted in ascending or descending order.

If you chose to view the contents as either large or small icons, you may arrange these icons by Name, File Type, Size, or Date. Optionally, you may simply line up your icons.

If you select Folder Options... from the bottom of the View menu, the Folder Options dialog box is displayed. See **Figure 25-9A.** This dialog box provides options that let you change the appearance of the Windows desktop. Clicking the View tab in the Folder Options dialog box displays the View tab window shown in **Figure 25-9B.** In the View tab, you may select which types of files are displayed. For instance, hidden or system files are seldom of interest to most users. You may also check boxes to Display the Full MS-DOS path in title bars, to hide MS-DOS file extensions or to show file attributes when using Detail view. Since information regarding file extensions can be important to all users, it is suggested that you do not hide files extensions for known file types.

Figure 25-8. The Windows Explorer View Menu.

Figure 25-9.
A—The General tab in the Folder Options dialog box provides several options for viewing the Windows desktop. B—The View tab in the Folder Options dialog box lets you choose which aspects of files and folders you care to view.

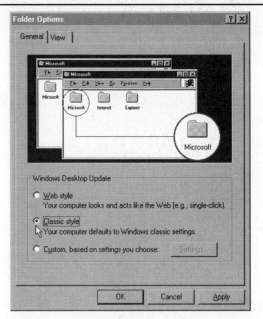

A

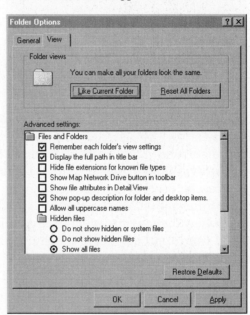

B

NOTE

The Folder Options dialog box tab windows shown in **Figures 25-9A** and **25-9B** are exclusive to Windows 98. If you are using Internet Explorer 4.0, this dialog box is also available to users of Windows 95 or 5.0 Windows NT.

AutoCAD LT—Fundamentals and Applications

The Tools menu

The Tools menu is shown in **Figure 25-10.** This menu is used for several purposes. First, use the Find option to search for files, directory folders, network nodes, and Internet addresses. Second, use the Map Network Drive... and Disconnect Network Drive... options to map network drives or to disconnect existing maps, respectively.

The Panes

The lower portion of Windows Explorer is divided into two panes. These two panes work together to help you find files and folders. The one on the left is the Folder and Program pane. The one on the right is the File and Subfolder pane. The left and right panes are separated by a split bar that you can move.

The Folder and Program pane shows the contents of your *desktop*. With the Desktop icon active, the left pane contains three or more collapsed icons, including My Computer, My Documents, Recycle Bin, and possibly Network Neighborhood, Internet Explorer, and Briefcase. The right pane shows the Desktop, including icons for all short-cuts to your programs.

Picking an icon or a name in the left pane will display the item's contents in the right pane. By picking My Computer, the entire list of available drives is shown. See **Figure 25-11.**

A box containing a plus sign precedes each icon in the Folder and Program pane. By clicking the box, you can expand the icon to view its contents. Clicking the plus box in front of the My Computer icon changes the "plus" sign to a "minus" sign and displays the storage drives on the left side as well as on the right. See **Figure 25-12.**

Figure 25-10.
The Windows
Explorer Tools menu.

Figure 25-11.
Windows Explorer with My Computer selected.

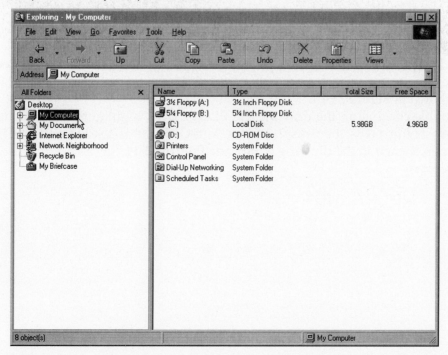

Figure 25-12.
Windows Explorer with My Computer expanded.

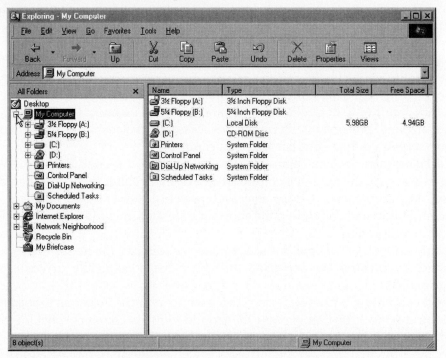

Viewing a Drive's Contents

You can view a drive's contents in one of two ways. You can pick a drive's icon or name in the left pane and see its contents in the right pane. Alternatively, you can pick a drive's box to open its contents in the left pane. In this way, the two panes can be operated independently to see the contents of two different drives, folders, or subfolders.

Launching Applications with Windows Explorer

Many of the files that appear in Windows Explorer's panes are associated with application programs. By double-clicking on the file icon, or on the filename itself, you can load the file and simultaneously start the application with which it is associated. As an example, consider the contents of the C:\Program Files\AutoCAD LT 98\Sample folder shown in **Figure 25-13.**

Double-clicking on the drawing file PLATE2.DWG highlights the filename. The Windows hourglass is then displayed as AutoCAD LT is loaded and the PLATE2 drawing is opened in the drawing editor. See **Figure 25-14.**

AutoCAD LT—Fundamentals and Applications

Figure 25-13.
Selecting a drawing file from Windows Explorer.

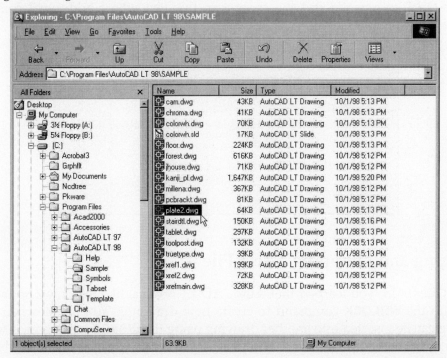

Figure 25-14.
AutoCAD LT is launched and the plate.dwg file is opened automatically.

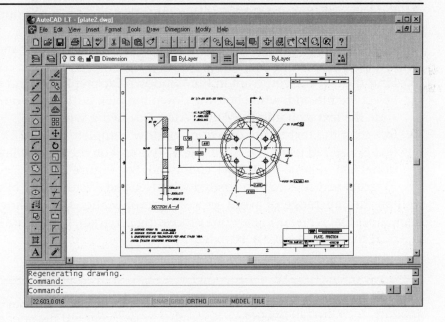

Drag and Drop Operations with Windows **Explorer**

Windows Explorer can also be used to dynamically "drag and drop" file icons into the AutoCAD LT drawing window. This powerful capability allows you to insert drawing files as blocks, insert text files as dynamic text, and to import DXF and PostScript files. Drag and drop can also be used to load template, linetype, script, and slide files. A file selected for drag and drop operations with AutoCAD LT must have a .dwg, .dwt, .dxf, .eps, .lin, .sld, .scr, or .txt extension.

The following table lists the different kinds of drag and drop operations that can be used in AutoCAD LT. Also listed are the required filename extensions, the related AutoCAD LT commands and the chapter in this text where additional command information can be found.

Operation	File Extension	Commands	Chapter
Load linetype	.lin	–LINETYPE	5
Load template	.dwt	NEW, OPEN	2
Load Text	.txt	DTEXT	9
Insert Drawing	.dwg	INSERT	15
Load Slide	.sld	VSLIDE	18
Import	.dxf	DXFIN	25

Dragging and Dropping a Text File

In *Chapter 15*, you learned that AutoCAD LT objects, like text, may be saved to disk with the **WBLOCK** command to create new drawings. You also learned that a drawing can be inserted into another drawing using the **INSERT** command. A text file created with a text editor outside of AutoCAD LT may also be inserted into a drawing using Windows Explorer. For example, consider the Note1.txt text file shown in **Figure 25-15.** To drag this text file into AutoCAD LT, do the following:

1. Launch both AutoCAD LT and Windows Explorer. Arrange your windows so that both are visible.
2. Issue the **DTEXT** command. Select a start point, a text height and a rotation angle as usual. Stop when the Text: prompt appears.
3. Find the text file you want in the Windows Explorer Folder and Icons pane.
4. Select the file and, while holding down the pick button on your pointing device, slide the text icon into the AutoCAD LT drawing window.
5. Inserting the text in the drawing window completes the **DTEXT** command. The text is inserted using the current text style and on the current layer. To enter additional text, reissue the **DTEXT** command. See **Figure 25-16.**

External text files can be created with Notepad, WordPad, or other text editors as well as the full range of word processing applications, including Microsoft Word. Remember that when using a word processing program, the document must be saved in ASCII format and have a .txt extension.

Figure 25-15.
External text files with .txt extensions (like this one shown in Notepad) can be dragged and dropped into the drawing window. Remember to save your text file prior to dragging it.

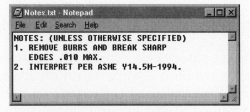

Figure 25-16.
After issuing the
DTEXT command
and answering the
prompts, the text
file is dragged and
dropped into the
AutoCAD LT
drawing window.

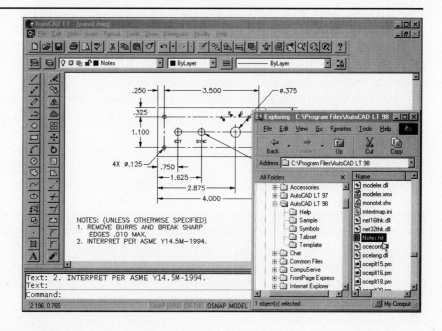

Dragging and Dropping to Print a Drawing

Drag and drop may also be used to print an AutoCAD LT drawing file by dragging the drawing file icon directly to the Windows system printer icon on the desktop. AutoCAD LT must be loaded beforehand or the file must have been linked to the printer before initiating the drag and drop procedure.

When you drag a print file to the printer icon, an alert box appears in the AutoCAD LT drawing window if the current drawing has not yet been saved. You can then save or discard any changes made to the current drawing before the new drawing to be printed is opened. The procedure to drag and drop a drawing on the desktop printer icon is provided as follows:

1. From the Start button on the Windows task bar, select Settings and then Printers.
2. Click the System Printer icon in the Printers dialog box.
3. Right-click the pick button on your pointing device and select Create Shortcut button from the pop-up menu. An alert box appears informing you that a shortcut cannot be created here. You are then asked if you would like to place the shortcut on the desktop instead. Click the Yes button.
4. Next, close the Printers dialog box by selecting Close from the File pull-down menu or by clicking the X at the upper-right corner of the dialog box.
5. Drag the drawing file you wish to print from Windows Explorer onto the printer icon on the Windows desktop.
6. If you have not yet saved the current drawing, an alert box appears prompting you to do so. Click Yes or No as required.
7. AutoCAD LT automatically loads the drawing you selected from Explorer and the Print/Plot Configuration dialog box appears.
8. Make any necessary changes to the printing configuration and click OK to print your drawing.

Dragging and Dropping to Insert a Drawing File

Drag and drop can also be used to insert any drawing into the current drawing session. This method is very similar to the **INSERT** command. Like **INSERT**, the drawing that you drag and drop becomes a block.

1. Launch both AutoCAD LT and Windows Explorer, arranging the two windows so that both are visible. Be sure you can see the AutoCAD LT Command: prompt
2. Drag the drawing file icon you want to insert into the AutoCAD drawing window and release the pick button on your pointing device.
3. The **INSERT** command is echoed on the command line. Answer the prompts in the usual manner, exploding the block after insertion if necessary.

EXERCISE 25-1

○ Launch Windows Explorer.
○ Open the AutoCAD LT 98 folder and the Sample folder inside.
○ Double-click the Plate2 drawing to open AutoCAD LT and load the drawing.
○ Arrange the windows as previously shown in **Figure 25-16.**
○ Use Notepad to create a simple text file. Save it using a .txt extension.
○ Activate the AutoCAD LT window, and issue the **DTEXT** command.
○ Pick a start point and accept the default height and rotation.
○ When the command line prompts Text:, drag your text file into the AutoCAD LT drawing window.
○ Save the drawing under a new name.
○ If you are connected to a printer, try to drag and drop the new drawing onto the system printer icon.

Working with Files and Directory Folders

Managing files and directory folders with Windows Explorer can be a simple task, made even easier because more than one instance of Explorer can be launched. You may create, delete, or rename files or folders with the commands found in the File pull-down menu. As with the AutoCAD LT pull-down menus, several of the menu items are followed by a triangular arrowhead. These arrows indicate that additional items will be found within a cascading submenu. See **Figure 25-17.**

To create a folder, select the drive and folder within which you wish to create a new folder. For instance, if you wish to create your personal folder within the AutoCAD LT folder, begin by selecting the C:\Program Files\AutoCAD LT 98 (or C:\Program Files\AutoCAD LT 97) folder in the left pane. In the File pull-down menu select New) Folder. The new folder appears in the right pane. The default name of this folder is New Folder, which appears highlighted in

---

Figure 25-17.
The Windows Explorer File pull-down menu.

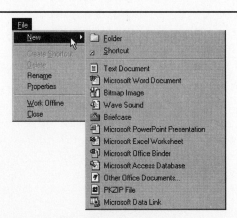

AutoCAD LT—Fundamentals and Applications

blue inside of a black rectangle. Simply type the desired folder name to replace the default and press [Enter]. If you wish to rename the folder at a later date, select the folder and from the File pull-down menu select Rename. The folder's name is again highlighted in blue and appears inside a rectangle. Simply type the new folder name and press [Enter].

Files and folders can be deleted by first selecting the file or folder you wish to remove and then using the Delete option in the File pull-down menu. When you select Delete, you will be prompted to confirm your decision. If you choose to delete the file or folder, it will be sent to the Recycle Bin on your desktop.

The Properties selection in the File pull-down menu provides context-sensitive information about the item selected. The user should use the Properties selection with a degree of caution since file or folder attributes may get changed inadvertently.

The Edit pull-down menu contains the commands to cut, copy, and paste selected items, as well as to undelete deleted items. The commands that perform these functions are located in the File or Edit pull-down menus. A keyboard shortcut is associated with the Select All option and appears to the right of the menu item. See **Figure 25-18.**

Figure 25-18.
The Windows
Explorer's Edit
pull-down menu.

Selecting Files and Folders

Before you can work with a file or folder, it must first be selected. As mentioned earlier, you select a file or folder by placing your cursor arrow over the desired item and clicking it with the pick button on your pointing device. Occasionally, you will want to select more than one item. Selecting several items simultaneously is called *extending a selection.* Extending a selection can be done in two different ways.

If you want to select more than one item in a consecutive sequence, pick the first item. Then, while pressing and holding one of the [Shift] keys on your keyboard, pick the last item in the series. If you want to select items out of sequence, pick the first item, as before. Then, while pressing and holding the [Ctrl] key, pick any other items you wish. Also, if you inadvertently select an item, hold down the [Ctrl] key and reselect the file or folder.

Moving Files and Folders

You can move or copy files and folders using Drag-and-Drop, however the procedure can be slightly different depending upon the source and the destination. In the case shown in **Figure 25-19**, the process of moving or copying a drawing from the Sample folder of AutoCAD LT to My Folder is accomplished as follows:
1. Select the Sample folder, displaying its contents in the right pane.
2. Select the drawing file(s) to be moved or copied.
3. Using the right-click button on your pointing device, drag the file over the My Folder icon and release the button.
4. A pop-up menu appears , asking whether to move or to copy the item(s).

You can also drag and drop files and folders from one disk drive to another. In the example shown in **Figure 20-20**, a file is dragged from the Sample folder in the right pane to the B: floppy disk drive in the left pane. As long as both the source and the destination can be seen within the two sides of the Windows Explorer, both move and copy are readily accomplished.

Figure 25-19.
Dragging and dropping a file in Windows Explorer between folders on the same hard drive.

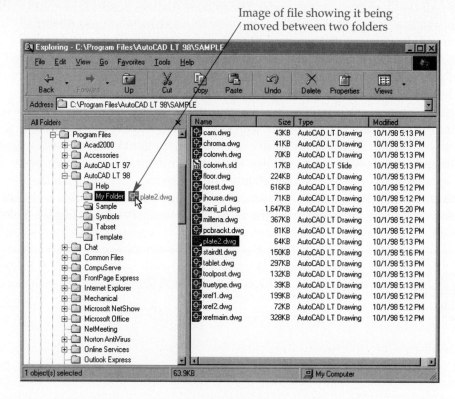

Image of file showing it being moved between two folders

Figure 25-20.
Dragging and dropping a file from the hard drive to a floppy disk drive using Windows Explorer.

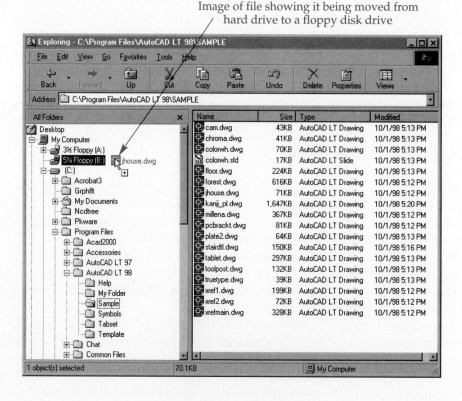

Image of file showing it being moved from hard drive to a floppy disk drive

AutoCAD LT—Fundamentals and Applications

PROFESSIONAL TIP

Here is another easy way to copy one or more files or folders from your hard drive to a floppy disk. After making your selection(s) from the right pane, make sure your cursor arrow is still over a highlighted selection and then right-click with your pointing device. From the pop-up shortcut menu that appears at your cursor location, select Send To. Next, select 3-1/2 Floppy (A) or 5-1/4 Floppy (B) as desired from the cascading submenu. (Do not be concerned if your computer does not have a second floppy disk drive.) Get in the habit of using this method to make quick backups of your drawings and other important files.

Windows Explorer also lets you use Windows Cut, Copy, and Paste commands. For instance, after highlighting one or more files or folders, choose either Cut or Copy from the Edit pull-down menu. Select the drive and folder you wish to paste the files or folders into. Then, select Paste from the Edit pull-down menu to complete the process. Remember that you can also use keyboard shortcuts to accomplish Cut, Copy, and Paste functions. The shortcuts are [Ctrl]+[X], [Ctrl]+[C], and [Ctrl]+[V], respectively.

Deleting and Undeleting Files and Folders

To delete files or folders, first select the items with your pointing device. Next, select Delete from the File pull-down menu, or press the [Delete] key on your keyboard, and confirm the deletion when queried. This procedure does not permanently remove the files or folders from your hard drive. Instead, the deleted items are placed in the Recycle Bin where they can later be recovered. However, be advised that deleted items cannot be recovered if the Recycle Bin has been emptied.

To retrieve items from the Recycle Bin, go to the Desktop and double-click on the Recycle Bin icon. A pop-up menu appears as shown in **Figure 25-21.** Select Open from the pop-up menu to display the contents of the Recycle Bin. If the item you wish to undelete is still in the Recycle Bin, select it with your pointing device and then select Restore from the File pull-down menu in the Recycle Bin. See **Figure 25-22.** The file or folder you select for undeletion is then restored to its original folder and/or drive.

Figure 25-21.
Opening the
Recycle Bin.

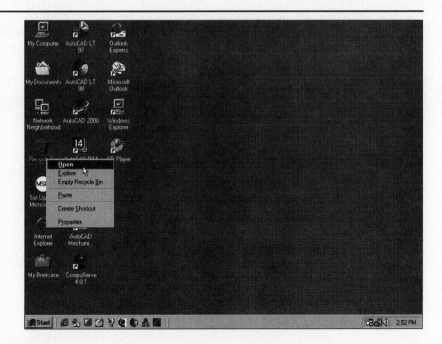

Figure 25-22.
Using the Restore option of Recycle Bin.

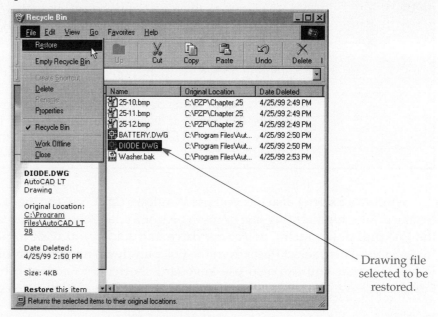

Drawing file
selected to be
restored.

Disk Operations

There may be occasions when you need to format or copy a floppy disk. The following sections detail how to perform these tasks.

Formatting a Floppy Disk

Whenever you use unformatted floppy disks, you must format them before they will accept data. The processes of formatting and labeling of disks are not handled by Windows Explorer. Instead, these functions are handled by the My Computer icon on the Windows Desktop. Use the following procedure to format a disk:

1. Select the My Computer icon with the pick button on your pointing device, right-click the icon, and then select the Open option in the pop-up menu. This accesses the My Computer dialog box . You can also access this dialog box by double-clicking the My Computer icon. Icons representing the storage devices available on your computer appear, as well as the Printers folder, the Control Panel folder and other selections.

2. Place a new floppy disk in the floppy drive. Double-click the floppy drive icon in the My Computer window to see its contents. If it is an unformatted disk an **Alert** box will appear saying that the disk media is not recognized and the disk may not be formatted.

3. Click the floppy drive icon with the right-click button on your pointing device to bring up the pop-up menu shown in **Figure 25-23.** Select Format... from the pop-up menu. Notice that the selection is followed by an ellipsis (…). As in AutoCAD LT, the ellipsis indicates that a dialog box is used with this command. See **Figure 25-24.**

4. Begin by selecting the type of drive to be formatted. Some 3.5″ floppy disks are formatted to a 720 KB capacity, some to the more standard 1.44 MB and others to 2.88 MB and higher. Be sure to select the value that is correct for your drive and floppy disk.

AutoCAD LT—Fundamentals and Applications

Figure 25-23.
The My Computer pop-up menu.

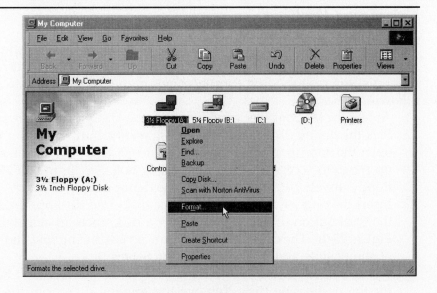

Figure 25-24.
The Format command dialog box.

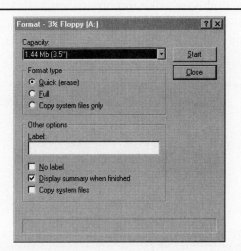

5. Next, choose the type of formatting you want. The Quick format erases any files or folders on the floppy disk, but does not reformat the floppy. To reformat an existing floppy disk, or to format one for the first time, chose the Full option. The Copy system files only option transfers special files to make a formatted floppy disk bootable. This type of disk is also called a *system disk*. You may enter a disk label in the Label text box. Also, you may select to see a summary, have no disk label, or copy system files.

6. Once you have made all your selections, click the Start button at the upper right of the dialog box. When the formatting is complete, a subdialog box appears informing you that the formatting is complete. Click the OK button.

7. If you wish to format another disk, insert the next disk, make your formatting selections, and click the Start button. When you are done formatting disks, click the Close button to return to the My Computer window. Select Close from the File pull-down menu to exit My Computer.

Copying a Disk

Throughout this text you have been advised to make backup copies of your AutoCAD LT drawings or related files. It is also a good idea to have a second copy of these disks in case the first copy becomes damaged. To make these copies, use the following procedure:

1. Access the My Computer window using the My Computer icon on your desktop.
2. Pick the floppy drive icon with the right-click button on your pointing device to open the pop-up menu shown in **Figure 25-23.** Select Copy Disk... from the pop-up menu to access the Copy Disk dialog box. See **Figure 25-25.** If you have two floppy drives, both will appear in the dialog box.
3. Insert the original floppy disk (source disk) into the appropriate drive and click the Start button. If you do not insert a disk, then an alert box will appear. See **Figure 25-26.** The dialog box will show an advancing line, indicating the percent of completion, and the words Reading Source Disk.
4. When this half of the procedure is completed, another alert box appears asking for the destination disk. Remove the original disk from the floppy drive and insert the disk you wish to copy to, and click the OK button.
5. If you wish to make another copy, insert the original source disk, and repeat the procedure. When you are done copying disks, click the Close button.

Figure 25-25.
The Copy Disk dialog box.

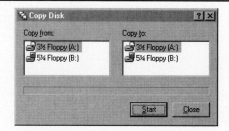

Figure 25-26.
An alert box prompts you to insert a source disk.

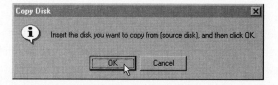

 CAUTION

The Copy Disk command automatically formats the destination disk before copying files to it. Be certain that your destination disk does not contain any files that you might need, since the formatting process will destroy them.

 NOTE

This chapter has introduced you to only a subset of the features within Windows Explorer. Make a point of becoming familiar with all of the functions offered by this useful tool. By making Windows Explorer an integral part of your daily work, you can greatly increase your productivity and your knowledge of Microsoft Windows.

Chapter Test

Write your answer in the space provided.

1. What is the purpose of the **AUDIT** command? Why would you use it? _____
    _____
    _____

2. Name the command used to repair a damaged drawing file. _____
    _____

3. What is a DXF file? Explain how it is used. _____
    _____
    _____
    _____

4. Explain the purpose of the **LT DWG Update** utility._____
    _____
    _____
    _____

5. What is a directory window?_____
    _____

6. How do you select more than one file or folder in consecutive order from the
    directory window?_____
    _____
    _____

7. How do you select more than one file or folder out of sequence from the directory
    window? _____
    _____
    _____

8. Once a file or folder is selected, how do you cancel your selection?_____
    _____
    _____

9. What is the purpose of the directory window split bar?_____
    _____
    _____

10. Which AutoCAD LT command must be used when dragging and dropping an
    external text file—**TEXT, DTEXT,** or **MTEXT**? _____
    _____
    _____

11. What action should be performed after dragging and dropping a drawing file
    into the AutoCAD LT drawing window?_____
    _____

12. *True or False?* When you delete a file or folder using Windows Explorer, the file or
    folder is permanently removed from your hard drive. _____

---

13. What are the keyboard equivalents of the Cut, Copy, and Paste commands?_____

_____

_____

_____

14. What is the purpose of the Recycle Bin? _____

_____

_____

_____

15. *True or False?* You must first format a floppy disk before using the Copy Disk function._____

Chapter Problems

General

1. This problem involves making new folders and copying drawing files to them using Windows Explorer.
   A. Make a folder under C:\Program Files\AutoCAD LT 98 named Student.
   B. Copy all of your drawing problem files starting with the letter P from one floppy disk to the new Student folder.
   C. Delete all files with a .BAK extension from the Student folder.
   D. Make another folder under C:\Program Files\AutoCAD LT 98 named Exercises.
   E. Copy all of your drawing exercise files starting with EX* from one floppy disk to the new Exercises folder.

General

2. Label four floppy disks with the following names: PROBLEMS, PROBSBACKUP, XERCISES, and XERSBACKUP. Use the floppy disks to store the drawing problems and exercises presented in this text. If necessary, format the disks before labeling them.

Appendix A

System Requirements for AutoCAD LT

AutoCAD LT 98

AutoCAD LT 98 has the following system requirements:

Software

- Windows 95, Windows 98, or Windows NT 4.0
- .DWF (*Drawing Web Format*) files are designed to be viewed on the Internet or company Intranets using a Web browser. To view .DWF files, you must download and install the *WHIP!* Browser Accessory. *WHIP!* is available as a Netscape Navigator plug-in and as a Microsoft Internet Explorer ActiveX control. For information on downloading and using *WHIP!*, point your browser to *www.autodesk.com*.

Hardware (required)
- Intel 486 with math coprocessor or compatible processor (Pentium recommended)
- VGA video display (800 × 600 or higher resolution required)
- CD-ROM drive for initial installation and running *Learning Assistance*
- Windows-supported display adapter
- Mouse or other pointing device (Microsoft Intellimouse recommended)

Hardware (optional)

- Printer or plotter
- Digitizing tablet

RAM and Hard Disk Space

- 16 MB of RAM (16 MB minimum, 32 MB recommended)
- 34- 56 MB minimum of hard disk space depending on your configuration
- An additional 45 MB for Microsoft Explorer (MSIE) 4.0 on your system drive
- 64 MB of disk swap space (64 MB minimum, 100 MB recommended)
- 8 MB of additional RAM for each concurrent AutoCAD LT 98 session
- 5 MB of free disk space during installation only (this space is used for temporary files that are removed when installation is complete)

NOTE　　　For MSIE 4.0, an additional 10 MB to 14 MB of disk space may be required for files installed in the system folder. This does not need to be on the same drive as the program folder where you launch AutoCAD LT 98.

AutoCAD LT 97

AutoCAD LT 97 has the following system requirements:

Software

- Windows 95 or Windows NT 4.0

NOTE　　　While AutoCAD LT 97 runs under Windows 98, be advised that this operating system is not officially supported for AutoCAD LT 97 by Autodesk, Inc.

- .DWF (*Drawing Web Format*) files are designed to be viewed on the Internet or company Intranets using a Web browser. To view .DWF files, you must download and install the *WHIP!* Browser Accessory. *WHIP!* is available as a Netscape Navigator plug-in and as a Microsoft Internet Explorer ActiveX control. For information on downloading and using *WHIP!*, point your browser to *www.autodesk.com*.

Hardware (required)

- Intel 486 with math coprocessor or compatible processor (Pentium recommended)
- VGA video display (800 × 600 or higher resolution required)
- CD-ROM drive for initial installation and running *Learning Assistance*
- Windows-supported display adapter
- Mouse or other pointing device (Microsoft Intellimouse recommended)

Hardware (optional)

- Printer or plotter
- Digitizing tablet

RAM and Hard Disk Space

- 16 MB of RAM (16 MB minimum, 32 MB recommended)
- 34- 56 MB minimum of hard disk space depending on your configuration
- 64 MB of disk swap space (64 MB minimum, 100 MB recommended)
- 8 MB of additional RAM for each concurrent AutoCAD LT 97 session
- 5 MB of free disk space during installation only (this space is used for temporary files that are removed when installation is complete)

Appendix B
AutoCAD LT Command Reference

AutoCAD LT 98

The following listing contains a brief description for each of the AutoCAD LT 98 commands. Command aliases are shown if applicable. An apostrophe (') at the beginning of a command name indicates a command that can be used transparently. (Transparent commands may be used while another command is running.)

Command Name	Shortcut(s)	Description
3DPOLY	-	Creates a 3D polyline using straight line segments
'ABOUT	-	Displays information about the current version of AutoCAD LT 98
'APERTURE	-	Sets the size of the object snap target box (in pixels)
ARC	A	Draws an arc
AREA	AA	Computes the area and perimeter of objects or of defined areas
ARRAY	AR	Creates multiple copies of objects in a rectangular or circular (polar) pattern using a dialog box
-ARRAY	-AR	Creates multiple copies of objects in a rectangular or circular (polar) pattern on the command line
ATTACHURL	-	Attaches a URL to objects or areas
ATTDEF	-AT	Creates an attribute definition
'ATTDISP	AD	Globally controls the visibility of attributes
ATTEDIT	AE,-ATE	Edits attribute information independent of its block definition
ATTEXT	AX	Extracts attribute data in CDF, SDF, or DXF formats
AUDIT	-	Evaluates the integrity of a drawing file
'BASE	BA	Sets the insertion basepoint for the current drawing
BHATCH	BH	Hatches an enclosed area with an associative hatch pattern
'BLIPMODE	BM	Controls the display of marker blips
BLOCK	-B	Creates a block definition of selected objects
BMAKE	B	Creates blocks using a dialog box

Command Name	Shortcut(s)	Description
BMOD	-	Modifies the description of a block definition
BMPOUT	-	Saves selected objects to a file in device-independent format
BOUNDARY	**BO**	Creates a polyline or region around a closed boundary using a dialog box
-BOUNDARY	**-BO**	Creates a polyline or region around a closed boundary on the command line
BREAK	**BR**	Splits an object in two or erases parts of a selected object
BROWSER	-	Launches the default web browser defined in your system's registry
BUPDATE	-	Adds or removes block icons displayed in **Content Explorer**
CHAMFER	**CHA**	Creates bevels, or chamfers, on the edges of lines and polylines
CHANGE	**-CH**	Changes the properties and/or parameters of selected objects
CHPROP	**CR**	Changes the color, layer, linetype, linetype scale, and thickness of selected objects
CIRCLE	**C**	Draws a circle
'COLOR	-	Sets the system color for new objects
CONTENT	**CE**	Launches the **Content Explorer** window
CONVERT	-	Updates hatching and 2D polylines created in previous versions of AutoCAD LT
COPY	**CO,CP**	Copies objects
COPYCLIP	-	Copies text and graphics to the Windows Clipboard
COPYHIST	-	Copies the text in the command line history window to the Windows Clipboard
COPYLINK	**CL**	Copies the current view to the Clipboard for linking into other OLE programs
CUSTOMIZE	-	Lets you customize toolbars, tool buttons, and create keyboard shortcuts using a dialog box
CUTCLIP	-	Copies objects to the Windows Clipboard and erases them from the drawing
DDATTDEF	**AT,DAD**	Creates an attribute definition using a dialog box
DDATTE	**ATE**	Edits the textual attributes of a block
DDATTEXT	-	Extracts attribute data using a dialog box
DDCHPROP	**CH**	Changes the color, layer, linetype, linetype scale, and thickness of objects using a dialog box
DDCOLOR	**COL**	Sets the color for new objects using a dialog box

Command Name	Shortcut(s)	Description
DDEDIT	ED	Edit text and attribute definitions using a dialog box
'DDGRIPS	GR	Turns on and sets the color of grips using a dialog box
DDIM	D,DM	Creates and modifies dimension styles using a dialog box
DDINSERT	I	Inserts a block or drawing using a dialog box
'DDLMODES	-	Creates and manages layers using a dialog box
'DDLTYPE	LT	Creates and manages linetypes using a dialog box
DDMODIFY	MO	Edits all aspects of an object using a dialog box
'DDOSNAP	OS	Sets one or more running object snap modes using a dialog box
'DDPTYPE	-	Sets the display mode and size of point objects using a dialog box
DDRENAME	REN	Uses a dialog box to rename named objects
'DDRMODES	RM	Enables the **Drawing Aids** dialog box
'DDSELECT	SE	Controls object selection modes in a dialog box
DDUCS	UC	Manages and lists defined user coordinate systems
DDUCSP	UCP	Uses a dialog box to select a preset user coordinate system
'DDUNITS	UN	Sets linear and angular formats as well as the displayed precision in a dialog box
DDVIEW	V	Saves and restores named views using a dialog box
'DELAY	-	Used in script files to provide a timed pause
DETACHURL	-	Detaches URLs from blocks or other objects
DIM	-	Enters dimensioning mode
DIM1	D1	Enters dimensioning mode for one dimensioning operation only
DIMALIGNED	DAL	Creates an aligned linear dimension
DIMANGULAR	DAN	Creates an angular dimension
DIMBASELINE	DBA	Creates a linear, angular, or ordinate dimension from the baseline of the previous or selected dimension
DIMCENTER	DCE	Creates center marks or centerlines for arcs and circles
DIMCONTINUE	DCO	Creates a linear, angular, or ordinate dimension from the second extension line of the previous or selected dimension
DIMDIAMETER	DDI	Creates diameter dimensions for arcs and circles
DIMEDIT	DED	Edits dimensions
DIMLINEAR	DLI	Creates linear dimensions
DIMORDINATE	DOR	Creates ordinate (arrowless) dimensions

Command Name	Shortcut(s)	Description
DIMOVERRIDE	**DOV**	Overrides dimension variables (dimvars)
DIMRADIUS	**DRA**	Creates radial dimensions for arcs and circles
DIMSTYLE	**DST**	Creates and modifies dimension styles on the command line
DIMTEDIT	**-**	Moves and rotates dimension text
'DIST	**DI**	Calculates the distance and angle between two selected points
DIVIDE	**DIV**	Places evenly spaced point markers or blocks along an object
DLINE	**DL**	Draws a double line using separate line and arc segments
DONUT	**DO**	Draws filled rings and filled circles
DRAWORDER	**DR**	Changes the display order of images and other objects
DSVIEWER	**DS**	Activates the **Aerial View** window
DTEXT	**DT**	Displays multiline text on screen as it is entered
DVIEW	**DV**	Creates parallel projection or perspective views for 3D objects
DWFOUT	**-**	Exports a Drawing Web Format (DWF) file
DXFIN	**DN**	Imports a Drawing Interchange Format (DXF) file
DXFOUT	**DX**	Creates a Drawing Interchange Format (DXF) file of the current drawing
'ELEV	**-**	Sets the elevation and extrusion thickness for new objects
ELLIPSE	**EL**	Draws an ellipse or elliptical arc
ERASE	**E**	Removes selected drawing objects
EXPLODE	**X**	Returns a compound object to its component objects
EXPORT	**EXP**	Saves objects to other file formats
EXTEND	**EX**	Extends an object to intersect another object
FILEOPEN	**-**	Opens a drawing file
'FILL	**-**	Controls the filling of wide polylines, donuts, and 2D solids
FILLET	**F**	Draws fillets and rounds on selected objects
'GETENV	**-**	Displays specified variables
'GRAPHSCR	**-**	Switches from the text window to the graphics window
'GRID	**-**	Activates and sets the grid X and Y spacing
GROUP	**G**	Creates and manages saved selection sets using a dialog box
-GROUP	**-G**	Creates and manages saved selection sets on the command line

Command Name	Shortcut(s)	Description
HATCH	-H	Hatches an enclosed area with a non-associative hatch pattern
HATCHEDIT	HE	Modifies an existing associative hatch pattern
'HELP	?	Activates online help
HIDE	HI	Suppresses the hidden lines in a 3D model
'ID	-	Displays the XYZ coordinates of a selected point or screen location
IMAGE	-	Lists and modifies the paths of images inserted into a drawing file
IMAGEFRAME	-	Controls whether image frames are displayed or hidden
IMPORT	IMP	Imports various file formats into AutoCAD LT 98
INETCFG	-	Configures the default browser information for Internet access
INSERT	-I	Places a block or drawing into the current drawing
INSERTOBJ	IO	Inserts a linked or embedded object
INSERTURL	-	Inserts a drawing file from an Internet address
INTERSECT	IN	Combines selected regions by intersection
'ISOPLANE	IS	Sets the current isometric plane
'LAYER	LA	Creates and manages layers using a dialog box
-'LAYER	-LA	Creates and manages layers on the command line
LEADER	LE	Creates a line that connects annotation to a feature
LENGTHEN	LEN	Changes the length of lines and polylines and the included angles of arcs
'LIMITS	LM	Sets the drawing boundaries
LINE	L	Draws straight line segments
'LINETYPE	LT	Lists, creates, loads, and sets linetypes using a dialog box
-'LINETYPE	-LT	Lists, creates, loads, and sets linetypes on the command line
LIST	LI,LS	Displays database information for selected objects
LISTURL	-	Lists all the URLs in a drawing file
LOGFILEOFF	-	Terminates the recording and closes the log file (ACLT.LOG)
LOGFILEON	-	Creates ACLT.LOG (ASCII) and begins recording the contents of the text window
'LTSCALE	LTS	Globally sets the linetype scale factor
MASSPROP	-	Calculates the mass properties of regions
MEASURE	ME	Places point markers or blocks at measured intervals along an object

Command Name	Shortcut(s)	Description
MENULOAD	-	Loads partial menu files
MENUUNLOAD	-	Unloads partial menu files
MIRROR	**MI**	Creates a reflected image copy of selected objects
MOVE	**M**	Moves selected objects at a specified distance and direction
MREDO	**MR**	Reverses the effects of several previous **U** or **UNDO** commands
MSLIDE	-	Creates a slide file of the current viewport
MSPACE	**MS**	Returns to model space from paper space
MTEXT	**MT,T**	Creates paragraph-oriented text using a dialog box
-MTEXT	**-MT**	Creates paragraph-oriented text on the command line
MULTIPLE	-	Repeats the previous command until canceled
MVIEW	**MV**	Creates and activates floating viewports in paper space
NEW	**N**	Begins a new drawing
OFFSET	**O,OF**	Duplicates a single object at a distance or through a point
OLELINKS	-	Updates, cancels, and changes existing links
OOPS	**OO**	Reverses the last **ERASE** operation
OPEN	**OP**	Opens an existing drawing file
OPENURL	-	Opens a drawing file from an Internet address
'ORTHO	**OR**	Constrains cursor motion to the horizontal or vertical axes
-'OSNAP	**-OS**	Sets running object snaps on the command line
PAINTER	-	Copies the properties of one object to other objects
'PAN	**P**	Shifts the drawing display in the current viewport in realtime
-'PAN	**-P**	Shifts the drawing display in the current viewport
PASTECLIP	-	Inserts text and graphics data from the Windows Clipboard
PASTESPEC	**PA**	Inserts text and graphics data from the Windows Clipboard and controls the format of the data
PEDIT	**PE**	Edit 2D polylines and polyarcs
PLAN	-	Displays the plan view of a user coordinate system
PLINE	**PL**	Draws 2D polylines and polyarcs
PLOT	**PP,PRINT**	Plots a drawing to a printer, plotter, or file
POINT	**PO,PT**	Draws a point object

Command Name	Shortcut(s)	Description
'POLAR	-	Constrains cursor motion to specified angles and radial distances
POLYGON	PG,POL	Draws an equilateral, multisided object
PREFERENCES	PF,PR	Customizes the drawing environment using a dialog box
PREVIEW	PRE	Shows how the drawing will look when it is printed or plotted
PSOUT	-	Outputs an Encapsulated PostScript (.EPS) file
PSPACE	PS	Returns to paper space from model space
PSUPDATE	-	Adjusts the size of all PostScript text in a drawing
PURGE	PU	Removes unused named objects, such as linetypes and blocks, from the drawing using a dialog box
-PURGE	-PU	Removes unused named objects, such as linetypes and blocks, from the drawing on the command line
QSAVE	-	Saves the current drawing
'QTEXT	QT	Displays each text and attribute object as a bounding box around the text object
QUIT	EXIT	Exits an AutoCAD LT 98 drawing session
RAY	-	Creates an infinite line in one direction
RECOVER	-	Repairs a corrupted drawing
RECTANG	REC	Creates a rectangular polyline
REDO	RE	Reverses the effects of the previous **U** or **UNDO** command
'REDRAW	R	Refreshes the display of all viewports
REGEN	RE	Regenerates (recalculates) the display in all viewports
REGION	REG	Converts a closed object into a region object
REINIT	RI	Reinitializes the input/output ports, digitizer, display, and Program Parameters (PGP) file
RENAME	-REN	Changes the name of named objects on the command line
'RESUME	-	Continues an interrupted script file
REVCLOUD	RC	Creates a polyline of sequential arcs to form a cloud shape
REVDATE	RD,REV	Inserts a revision time, date, file name, and user name into a drawing
ROTATE	RO	Rotates objects about a basepoint
RSCRIPT	-	Repeats a script file continuously
SAVE	SA	Saves an existing drawing with the current file name
SAVEAS	-	Saves an unnamed drawing with a name or renames the current drawing

Command Name	Shortcut(s)	Description
SAVEURL	-	Saves a drawing file to an Internet address
SCALE	SC	Reduces or enlarges objects equally in the X, Y, and Z directions
'SCRIPT	SCR	Executes a sequence of commands from a script file
SELECT	-	Used to place objects in the **Previous** selection set
SELECTURL	-	Selects all the URLs attached to a drawing file
'SETENV	-	Changes the value of a registry variable
'SETVAR	SET	Lists or changes values of system variables
SHADE	SH,SHA	Creates a flat-shaded image of a 3D model in the current viewport
'SNAP	SN	Restricts cursor movement to user-specified increments
SOLID	SO	Draws solid-filled polygons
SPELL	SP	Launches the spell checker
SPLINE	SPL	Creates a quadratic or cubic spline (NURBS) curve
SPLINEDIT	SPE	Edits a spline object or spline-fit polyline
STRETCH	S	Stretches or shrinks objects
'STYLE	ST	Creates and modifies named text styles
SUBTRACT	SU	Subtracts one or more regions from another region
TABLET	TA	Calibrates and configures a digitizing tablet and turns Tablet mode on and off
TEXT	TX	Creates a single line of text
'TEXTSCR	-	Switches from the graphics window to the text window
'TIME	TI	Displays time and date information of a drawing in the text window
TOLERANCE	TOL	Creates geometric tolerances
TOOLBAR	TO	Displays, hides, and positions toolbars
-TOOLBAR	-	Displays, hides, and positions toolbars using the command line
TRIM	TR	Trims objects against the edges of other objects
U	-	Reverses the most recent operation
UCS	-	Creates and manages user coordinate systems on the command line
UCSICON	-	Controls the visibility and origin of the UCS icon
UNDO	-	Provides various options to reverse the effects of previous commands

Command Name	Shortcut(s)	Description
UNION	UNI	Joins one or more regions with another region
'UNITS	-UN	Sets linear and angular formats as well as the displayed precision on the command line
'VIEW	-V	Saves and manages named views on the command line
VPLAYER	VL	Controls layer visibility in floating viewports
VPOINT	VP,-VP	Sets the viewing direction for 3D objects
VPORTS	VW	Divides the drawing window into multiple tiled viewports
VSLIDE	VS	Displays a slide file in the current viewport
WBLOCK	W	Writes objects to disk in a new drawing file
WMFIN	WI	Imports a Windows metafile
WMFOPTS	-	Sets options for importing metafiles
WMFOUT	WO	Saves objects in Windows metafile format
XATTACH	XA	Attaches an external reference to the current drawing
XBIND	XB	Binds dependent symbols of an xref to the current drawing using a dialog box
-XBIND	-XB	Binds dependent symbols of an xref to the current drawing on the command line
XLINE	XL	Creates an infinite line in two directions
XREF	XR	Controls external references (xrefs) using a dialog box
-XREF	-XR	Controls external references (xrefs) on the command line
'ZOOM	Z	Increases or decreases the apparent size of objects in the current viewport

AutoCAD LT 97

The following listing contains a brief description for each of the AutoCAD LT 97 commands. Command aliases are shown if applicable. An apostrophe (') at the beginning of a command name indicates a command that can be used transparently. (Transparent commands may be used while another command is running.)

Command Name	Shortcut(s)	Description
3DPOLY	-	Creates a 3D polyline using straight line segments
'ABOUT	-	Displays information about the current version of AutoCAD LT 97
'APERTURE	-	Sets the size of the object snap target box (in pixels)
ARC	A	Draws an arc
AREA	AA	Computes the area and perimeter of objects or of defined areas
ARRAY	AR	Creates multiple copies of objects in a rectangular or circular (polar) pattern
ATTACHURL	-	Attaches a URL to objects or areas
ATTDEF	-AT	Creates an attribute definition
'ATTDISP	AD	Globally controls the visibility of attributes
ATTEDIT	AE,-ATE	Edits attribute information independent of its block definition
ATTEXT	AX	Extracts attribute data in CDF, SDF, or DXF formats
AUDIT	-	Evaluates the integrity of a drawing file
'BASE	BA	Sets the insertion basepoint for the current drawing
BHATCH	H	Hatches an enclosed area with an associative hatch pattern
'BLIPMODE	BM	Controls the display of marker blips
BLOCK	-	Creates a block definition of selected objects
BMAKE	B,-B	Creates blocks using a dialog box
BMOD	-	Modifies the description of a block definition
BMPOUT	-	Saves selected objects to a file in device-independent format
BOUNDARY	-	Creates a polyline around a closed boundary
BREAK	BR	Splits an object in two or erases parts of a selected object
BROWSER	-	Launches the default Web browser defined in your system's registry
BUPDATE	-	Adds or removes block icons displayed in **Content Explorer**

Command Name	Shortcut(s)	Description
CHAMFER	**CHA**	Creates bevels, or chamfers, on the edges of lines and polylines
CHANGE	**-CH**	Changes the properties and/or parameters of selected objects
CHPROP	**CR**	Changes the color, layer, linetype, linetype scale, and thickness of selected objects
CIRCLE	**C**	Draws a circle
'COLOR	**-**	Sets the system color for new objects
CONTENT	**CE**	Launches the **Content Explorer** window
CONVERT	**-**	Updates hatching and 2D polylines created in previous versions of AutoCAD LT
COPY	**CP**	Copies objects
COPYCLIP	**-**	Copies text and graphics to the Windows Clipboard
COPYHIST	**-**	Copies the text in the command line history window to the Windows Clipboard
COPYLINK	**CL**	Copies the current view to the Clipboard for linking into other OLE programs
CUTCLIP	**-**	Copies objects to the Windows Clipboard and erases them from the drawing
DDATTDEF	**AT,DAD**	Creates an attribute definition using a dialog box
DDATTE	**ATE**	Edits the textual attributes of a block
DDATTEXT	**-**	Extracts attribute data using a dialog box
DDCHPROP	**CH**	Changes the color, layer, linetype, linetype scale, and thickness of objects using a dialog box
DDCOLOR	**CO,COL**	Sets the color for new objects using a dialog box
DDEDIT	**ED**	Edit text and attribute definitions using a dialog box
'DDGRIPS	**GR**	Turns on and sets the color of grips using a dialog box
DDIM	**DM**	Creates and modifies dimension styles using a dialog box
DDINSERT	**I**	Inserts a block or drawing using a dialog box
'DDLMODES	**-**	Creates and manages layers using a dialog box
'DDLTYPE	**LT**	Creates and manages linetypes using a dialog box
DDMODIFY	**MO**	Edits all aspects of an object using a dialog box
'DDOSNAP	**OS**	Sets one or more running object snap modes using a dialog box
'DDPTYPE	**-**	Sets the display mode and size of point objects using a dialog box

Command Name	Shortcut(s)	Description
DDRENAME	REN	Uses a dialog box to rename named objects
'DDRMODES	RM	Enables the **Drawing Aids** dialog box
'DDSELECT	SE	Controls object selection modes in a dialog box
DDUCS	UC	Manages and lists defined user coordinate systems
DDUCSP	UCP	Uses a dialog box to select a preset user coordinate system
'DDUNITS	UN	Sets linear and angular formats as well as the displayed precision in a dialog box
DDVIEW	V	Saves and restores named views using a dialog box
'DELAY	-	Used in script files to provide a timed pause
DETACHURL	-	Detaches URLs from blocks or other objects
DIM	D	Enters dimensioning mode
DIM1	D1	Enters dimensioning mode for one dimensioning operation only
DIMALIGNED	DAL	Creates an aligned linear dimension
DIMANGULAR	DAN	Creates an angular dimension
DIMBASELINE	DBA	Creates a linear, angular, or ordinate dimension from the baseline of the previous or selected dimension
DIMCENTER	DCE	Creates center marks or centerlines for arcs and circles
DIMCONTINUE	DCO	Creates a linear, angular, or ordinate dimension from the second extension line of the previous or selected dimension
DIMDIAMETER	DDI	Creates diameter dimensions for arcs and circles
DIMEDIT	DED	Edits dimensions
DIMLINEAR	DLI	Creates linear dimensions
DIMORDINATE	DOR	Creates ordinate (arrowless) dimensions
DIMOVERRIDE	DOV	Overrides dimension variables (dimvars)
DIMRADIUS	DRA	Creates radial dimensions for arcs and circles
DIMSTYLE	DST	Creates and modifies dimension styles on the command line
DIMTEDIT	-	Moves and rotates dimension text
'DIST	DI	Calculates the distance and angle between two selected points
DIVIDE	DIV	Places evenly spaced point markers or blocks along an object
DLINE	DL	Draws a double line using separate line and arc segments
DONUT	DO	Draws filled rings and filled circles

Command Name	Shortcut(s)	Description
DRAWORDER	DR	Changes the display order of images and other objects
DSVIEWER	DS	Activates the **Aerial View** window
DTEXT	DT,T	Displays multiline text on screen as it is entered
DVIEW	DV	Creates parallel projection or perspective views for 3D objects
DWFOUT	-	Exports a Drawing Web Format (DWF) file
DXFIN	DN	Imports a Drawing Interchange Format (DXF) file
DXFOUT	DX	Creates a Drawing Interchange Format (DXF) file of the current drawing
'ELEV	-	Sets the elevation and extrusion thickness for new objects
ELLIPSE	EL	Draws an ellipse or elliptical arc
ERASE	E	Removes selected drawing objects
EXPLODE	X	Returns a compound object to its component objects
EXPORT	EXP	Saves objects to other file formats
EXTEND	EX	Extends an object to intersect another object
FILEOPEN	-	Opens a drawing file
'FILL	-	Controls the filling of wide polylines, donuts, and 2D solids
FILLET	F	Draws fillets and rounds on selected objects
'GETENV	-	Displays specified variables
'GRAPHSCR	-	Switches from the text window to the graphics window
'GRID	G	Activates and sets the grid X and Y spacing
HATCH	-H	Hatches an enclosed area with a non-associative hatch pattern
HATCHEDIT	HE	Modifies an existing associative hatch pattern
'HELP	?	Activates online help
HIDE	HI	Suppresses the hidden lines in a 3D model
'ID	-	Displays the XYZ coordinates of a selected point or screen location
IMAGE	-	Lists and modifies the paths of images inserted into a drawing file
IMAGEFRAME	-	Controls whether image frames are displayed or hidden
IMPORT	IMP	Imports various file formats into AutoCAD LT 97
INETCFG	-	Configures the default browser information for Internet access
INSERT	IN	Places a block or drawing into the current drawing

Command Name	Shortcut(s)	Description
INSERTOBJ	**IO**	Inserts a linked or embedded object
INSERTURL	**-**	Inserts a drawing file from an Internet address
'ISOPLANE	**IS**	Sets the current isometric plane
'LAYER	**LA**	Creates and manages layers using a dialog box
-'LAYER	**-LA**	Creates and manages layers on the command line
LEADER	**LE**	Creates a line that connects annotation to a feature
LENGTHEN	**LEN**	Changes the length of lines and polylines and the included angles of arcs
'LIMITS	**LM**	Sets the drawing boundaries
LINE	**L**	Draws straight line segments
'LINETYPE	**LT**	Lists, creates, loads, and sets linetypes using a dialog box
-'LINETYPE	**-LT**	Lists, creates, loads, and sets linetypes on the command line
LIST	**LI,LS**	Displays database information for selected objects
LISTURL	**-**	Lists all the URLs in a drawing file
LOGFILEOFF	**-**	Terminates the recording and closes the log file (ACLT.LOG)
LOGFILEON	**-**	Creates ACLT.LOG (ASCII) and begins recording the contents of the text window
'LTSCALE	**LTS**	Globally sets the linetype scale factor
MEASURE	**ME**	Places point markers or blocks at measured intervals along an object
MENULOAD	**-**	Loads partial menu files
MENUUNLOAD	**-**	Unloads partial menu files
MIRROR	**MI**	Creates a reflected image copy of selected objects
MOVE	**M**	Moves selected objects at a specified distance and direction
MSLIDE	**-**	Creates a slide file of the current viewport
MSPACE	**MS**	Returns to model space from paper space
MTEXT	**MT**	Creates paragraph-oriented text using a dialog box
-MTEXT	**-MT**	Creates paragraph-oriented text on the command line
MULTIPLE	**-**	Repeats the previous command until canceled
MVIEW	**MV**	Creates and activates floating viewports in paper space
NEW	**N**	Begins a new drawing
OFFSET	**OF**	Duplicates a single object at a distance or through a point

Command Name	Shortcut(s)	Description
OLELINKS	-	Updates, cancels, and changes existing links
OOPS	**OO**	Reverses the last **ERASE** operation
OPEN	**OP**	Opens an existing drawing file
OPENURL	-	Opens a drawing file from an Internet address
'ORTHO	**OR**	Constrains cursor motion to the horizontal or vertical axes
-'OSNAP	**-OS**	Sets running object snaps on the command line
PAINTER	-	Copies the properties of one object to other objects
'PAN	**P**	Shifts the drawing display in the current viewport in realtime
-'PAN	**-P**	Shifts the drawing display in the current viewport
PASTECLIP	-	Inserts text and graphics data from the Windows Clipboard
PASTESPEC	**PA**	Inserts text and graphics data from the Windows Clipboard and controls the format of the data
PEDIT	**PE**	Edit 2D polylines and polyarcs
PLAN	-	Displays the plan view of a user coordinate system
PLINE	**PL**	Draws 2D polylines and polyarcs
PLOT	**PP,PRINT**	Plots a drawing to a printer, plotter, or file
POINT	**PO,PT**	Draws a point object
'POLAR	-	Constrains cursor motion to specified angles and radial distances
POLYGON	**PG**	Draws an equilateral, multisided object
PREFERENCES	**PF,PR**	Customizes the drawing environment using a dialog box
PREVIEW	**PRE**	Shows how the drawing will look when it is printed or plotted
PSOUT	-	Outputs an Encapsulated PostScript (.EPS) file
PSPACE	**PS**	Returns to paper space from model space
PSUPDATE	-	Adjusts the size of all PostScript text in a drawing
PURGE	**PU**	Removes unused named objects, such as linetypes and blocks, from the drawing
QSAVE	-	Saves the current drawing
'QTEXT	**QT**	Displays each text and attribute object as a bounding box around the text object
QUIT	**EXIT**	Exits an AutoCAD LT 97 drawing session
RAY	-	Creates an infinite line in one direction
RECOVER	-	Repairs a corrupted drawing
RECTANG	**REC**	Creates a rectangular polyline

Command Name	Shortcut(s)	Description
REDO	RE	Reverses the effects of the previous **U** or **UNDO** command
'REDRAW	R	Refreshes the display of all viewports
REGEN	RE	Regenerates (recalculates) the display in all viewports
REINIT	RI	Reinitializes the input/output ports, digitizer, display, and Program Parameters (PGP) file
RENAME	-REN	Changes the name of named objects on the command line
'RESUME	-	Continues an interrupted script file
REVDATE	RD,REV	Inserts a revision time, date, file name, and user name into a drawing
ROTATE	RO	Rotates objects about a base point
RSCRIPT	-	Repeats a script file continuously
SAVE	SA	Saves an existing drawing with the current file name
SAVEAS	-	Saves an unnamed drawing with a name or renames the current drawing
SAVEURL	-	Saves a drawing file to an Internet address
SCALE	SC	Reduces or enlarges objects equally in the X, Y, and Z directions
'SCRIPT	SCR	Executes a sequence of commands from a script file
SELECT	-	Used to place objects in the **Previous** selection set
SELECTURL	-	Selects all the URLs attached to a drawing file
'SETENV	-	Changes the value of a registry variable
'SETVAR	SET	Lists or changes values of system variables
SHADE	SH	Creates a flat-shaded image of a 3D model in the current viewport
'SNAP	SN	Restricts cursor movement to user-specified increments
SOLID	SO	Draws solid-filled polygons
SPELL	SP	Launches the spell checker
SPLINE	SPL	Creates a quadratic or cubic spline (NURBS) curve
SPLINEDIT	-	Edits a spline object or spline-fit polyline
STRETCH	S	Stretches or shrinks objects
'STYLE	ST	Creates and modifies named text styles
TABLET	TA	Calibrates and configures a digitizing tablet and turns Tablet mode on and off
TEXT	TX	Creates a single line of text
'TEXTSCR	-	Switches from the graphics window to the text window

Command Name	Shortcut(s)	Description
'TIME	TI	Displays time and date information of a drawing in the text window
TOLERANCE	TOL	Creates geometric tolerances
TOOLBAR	TO	Displays, hides, and positions toolbars
-TOOLBAR	-	Displays, hides, and positions toolbars using the command line
TRIM	TR	Trims objects against the edges of other objects
U	-	Reverses the most recent operation
UCS	-	Creates and manages user coordinate systems on the command line
UCSICON	-	Controls the visibility and origin of the UCS icon
UNDO	-	Provides various options to reverse the effects of previous commands
'UNITS	-	Sets linear and angular formats as well as the displayed precision on the command line
'VIEW	-V	Saves and manages named views on the command line
VPLAYER	VL	Controls layer visibility in floating viewports
VPOINT	VP	Sets the viewing direction for 3D objects
VPORTS	VW	Divides the drawing window into multiple tiled viewports
VSLIDE	VS	Displays a slide file in the current viewport
WBLOCK	W	Writes objects to disk in a new drawing file
WMFIN	WI	Imports a Windows metafile
WMFOPTS	-	Sets options for importing metafiles
WMFOUT	WO	Saves objects in Windows metafile format
XATTACH	XA	Attaches an external reference to the current drawing
XBIND	XB	Binds dependent symbols of an xref to the current drawing using a dialog box
-XBIND	-XB	Binds dependent symbols of an xref to the current drawing on the command line
XLINE	XL	Creates an infinite line in two directions
XREF	XR	Controls external references (xrefs) using a dialog box
-XREF	-XR	Controls external references (xrefs) on the command line
'ZOOM	Z	Increases or decreases the apparent size of objects in the current viewport

Appendix C
AutoCAD LT Menu Trees

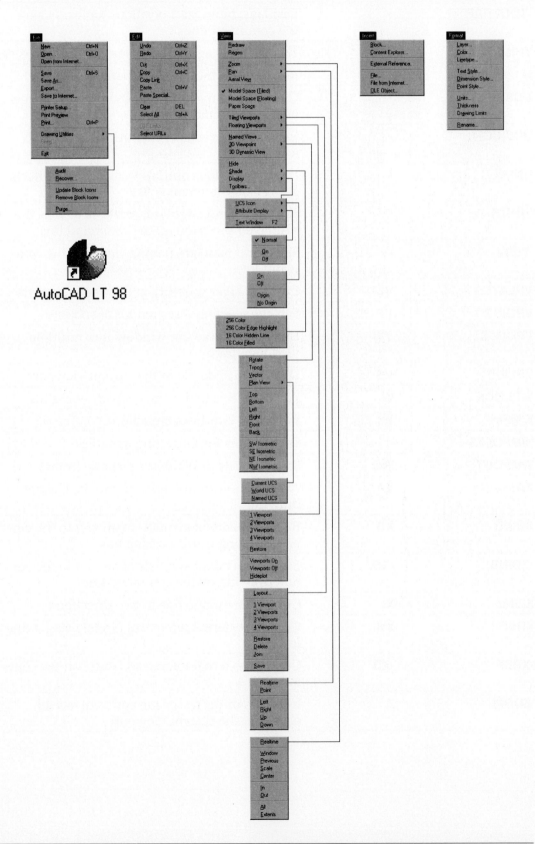

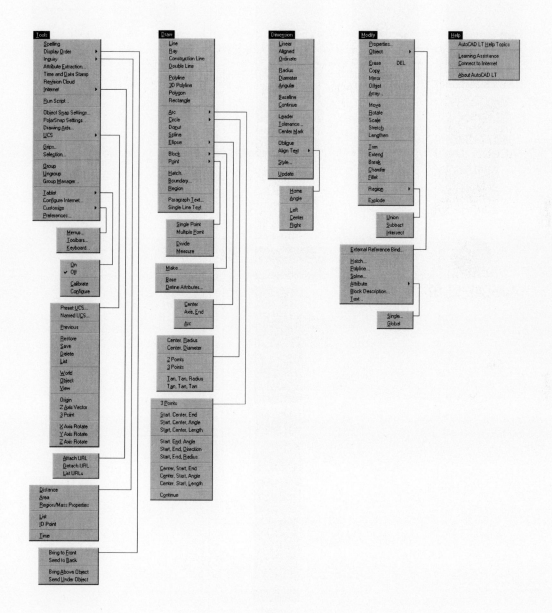

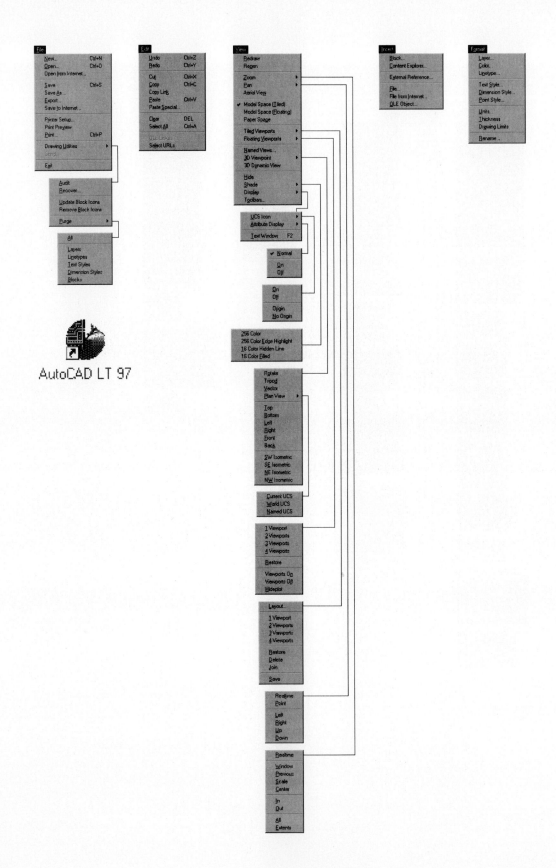

AutoCAD LT 97

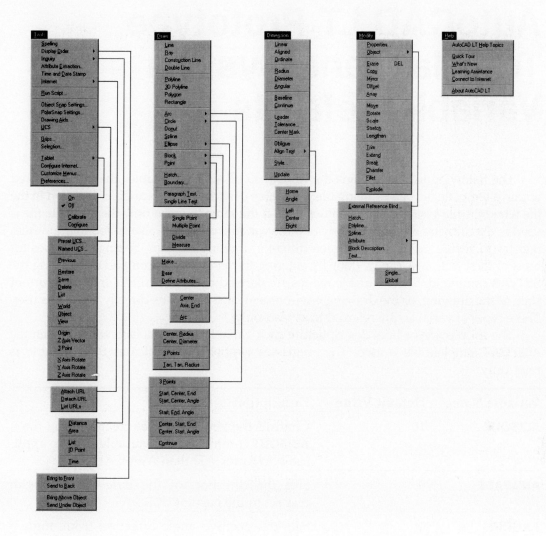

Appendix D

AutoCAD LT Prototype Template and System Variable Defaults

The following listing contains the AutoCAD LT system variables that can be stored within a template file or a drawing file. The value of each of these variables is stored in the file when the file is saved, so the values remain the same the next time the template file is used or the drawing is opened. Many of these variable values are also stored in the system registry to ensure uniformity between different drawing sessions. Setting the values for most of these variables can be done by entering the associated command or by using the **SETVAR** command. Some variable names are derived by AutoCAD LT from the current state of the drawing, or the drawing environment, and cannot be directly set by the user. These types of variables are referred to as read-only.

The list provides a brief description of each variable and its default setting when the ACLT.DWT template file is used. The eyeglasses symbol ($\mathcal{O}$) indicates that variable is read-only.

Variable Name	Default Value	Description
ACISOUT	16	Controls the version of files created using the **ACISOUT** command (this variable is more applicable to AutoCAD than AutoCAD LT)
ANGBASE	0	Sets the direction of the base angle 0 with respect to the current UCS
ANGDIR	0	Sets the positive angle direction from angle 0 with respect to the current UCS
ATTDIA	0	Controls whether a dialog box is used for attribute value entry
ATTMODE	1	Controls the **Attribute Display** mode
ATTREQ	1	Determines whether default attribute settings are used during insertion of blocks
AUNITS	0	Format used for angular units
AUPREC	0	Sets the decimal precision display of angular units
BACKZ	$\mathcal{O}$	Stores the back clipping plane offset from the target plane
BLIPMODE	0	Controls the visibility of marker blips
CECOLOR	"BYLAYER"	Sets the color of newly-created objects
CELTSCALE	1	Individual linetype scaling for new objects
CHAMFERA	0.5000	Sets the first chamfer distance
CHAMFERB	0.5000	Sets the second chamfer distance
CHAMFERC	1.0000	Chamfer length

Variable Name	Default Value	Description
CHAMFERD	0	Chamfer angle
CLAYER	"0"	Sets the current layer
COORDS	1	Controls dynamic coordinate updating
CVPORT	2	Sets the identification number of the current viewport
DIMADEC	-1	Sets the decimal places for angular dimensions
DIMALT	Off	Alternate units selected
DIMALTD	2	Alternate unit decimal places
DIMALTF	25.4000	Alternate unit scale factor
DIMALTTD	2	Sets the decimal places for alternate units tolerance values
DIMALTU	2	Units format for alternate units dimensions
DIMALTZ	0	Zero suppression for alternate units dimension values
DIMAPOST	""	Suffix for alternate text
DIMASO	On	Create associative dimensions
DIMASZ	0.1800	Arrow size
DIMAUNIT	0	Unit format for angular dimensions
DIMBLK	""	Arrow block name
DIMBLK1	""	First arrow block name for separate arrowheads
DIMBLK2	""	Second arrow block name for separate arrowheads
DIMCEN	0.0900	Center mark size
DIMCLRD	BYBLOCK	Dimension line color
DIMCLRE	BYBLOCK	Extension line and leader color
DIMCLRT	BYBLOCK	Dimension text color
DIMDLE	0.0000	Dimension line extension
DIMDLI	0.3800	Dimension line increment for continuation
DIMEXE	0.1800	Extension above dimension line
DIMEXO	0.0625	Extension line origin offset
DIMGAP	0.0900	Gap from dimension line to text
DIMJUST	0	Horizontal justification of dimension text
DIMLFAC	1.0000	Linear unit scale factor
DIMLIM	Off	Generate dimension limits
DIMPOST	""	Default suffix for dimension text
DIMRND	0.0000	Rounding value
DIMSAH	Off	Separate arrow blocks
DIMSCALE	1.0000	Overall scale factor
DIMSD1	Off	Suppress the first dimension line

Variable Name	Default Value	Description
DIMSD2	Off	Suppress the second dimension line
DIMSE1	Off	Suppress the first extension line
DIMSE2	Off	Suppress the second extension line
DIMSHO	On	Update dimensions while dragging
DIMSOXD	Off	Suppress outside extension dimension
DIMSTYLE	ᔢ	Current dimension style (read-only)
DIMTAD	0	Place text above the dimension line
DIMTDEC	4	Decimal units for primary tolerance values
DIMTFAC	1.0000	Tolerance text height scaling factor
DIMTIH	On	Text inside extensions is horizontal
DIMTIX	Off	Place text inside extensions
DIMTM	0.0000	Minus tolerance
DIMTOFL	Off	Force line inside extension lines
DIMTOH	On	Text outside extensions is horizontal
DIMTOL	Off	Generate dimension tolerances
DIMTOLJ	1	Vertical justification for dimension tolerance text
DIMTP	0.0000	Plus tolerance
DIMTSZ	0.0000	Tick size
DIMTVP	0.0000	Text vertical position
DIMTXSTY	"Standard"	Current style used for dimension text
DIMTXT	0.1800	Text height
DIMTZIN	0	Zero suppression for primary units tolerance values
DIMUNIT	2	Units format for primary dimensions
DIMUPT	Off	Controls user placement of dimension line and text
DIMZIN	0	Zero suppression
DWGCHECK	0	Checks the drawing file format to see if the drawing was last saved by AutoCAD or AutoCAD LT
DWGCODEPAGE	ᔢ	Set equal to **SYSCODEPAGE** when a new drawing is created
ELEVATION	0.0000	Stores the current 3D elevation relative to the current UCS
EXTMAX	ᔢ	Upper-right extents of drawing
EXTMIN	ᔢ	Lower-left extents of drawing
FILLETRAD	0.5000	Stores the current fillet radius
FILLMODE	1	Specifies whether objects are filled in
FRONTZ	ᔢ	Stores the front clipping plane offset from the target plane

Variable Name	Default Value	Description
GRIDMODE	0	Toggles **GRID** on and off
GRIDUNIT	0.0000,0.0000	Specifies the X and Y grid spacing for the current viewport
HANDLES	∽	Object handles are enabled and can be accessed by applications
INDEXCTL	0	Controls creation and saving of layer and spatial indexes
INSBASE	0.0000,0.0000	Insertion base point set by **BASE** command, expressed in UCS coordinates
LASTPOINT	0.0000,0.0000	Stores the last point entered, expressed in UCS coordinates
LENSLENGTH	∽	Stores the length of the lens (in millimeters) used in perspective viewing
LIMCHECK	0	Controls object creation outside the current drawing limits
LIMMAX	12.0000,9.0000	Stores upper-right drawing limits, expressed in world coordinates
LIMMIN	0.0000,0.0000	Stores lower-left drawing limits, expressed in world coordinates
LTSCALE	1.0000	Sets the global linetype scale factor
LUNITS	2	Sets the current linear units decimal places
LUPREC	4	Sets the decimal precision display of linear units
MBUTTONPAN	1	Controls the behavior of the third button or wheel on pointing devices
MEASUREINIT	0	Sets initial drawing units for new drawings as English (0) or metric (1)
MEASUREMENT	0	Sets initial drawing units for existing drawings as English (0) or metric (1). This variable overrides **MEASUREINIT**
MIRRTEXT	1	Controls how **MIRROR** reflects text and dimensions
ORTHOMODE	0	Toggles **ORTHO** mode on and off
OSMODE	0	Stores the bit code of the current object snap
PDMODE	0	Sets the point object display mode
PDSIZE	0.0000	Sets the point object display size
PELLIPSE	0	Controls the object type created with **ELLIPSE**
PICKSTYLE	1	Controls group and associative hatch selection
PLINEGEN	0	Determines the linetype pattern generation around the vertices of a 2D polyline
PLINEWID	0.0000	Sets the current polyline width
PLOTROTMOD	1	Controls the orientation of plots

Variable Name	Default Value	Description
POLARANG	15.0000	Sets the **PolarSnap** angle relative to the current UCS
POLARDIST	1.0000	Sets the distance from the last point for **PolarSnap** intervals
POLARMODE	0	Controls whether **PolarSnap** is constrained for distance, angle, or both
PSLTSCALE	1	Paper space linetype scale factor
QTEXTMODE	0	Toggles the quick text display mode
RASTERPREVIEW	1	Toggles drawing preview saving and sets format
REGENMODE	1	Toggles automatic drawing regeneration
RTCLICKMENU	1	Controls the right-click action of the pointing device
SHADEDGE	3	Controls the shading of edges during rendering
SHADEDIF	70	Sets ratio of diffuse reflective light to ambient light during rendering
SNAPANG	0	Sets the snap/grid rotation angle for the current viewport
SNAPBASE	0.0000,0.0000	Stores the origin point of the snap/grid in the current viewport
SNAPISOPAIR	0	Controls the isometric plane (isoplane) for the current viewport
SNAPMODE	0	Toggles **SNAP** mode on and off
SNAPSTYL	0	Sets the snap style between Standard and Isometric
SNAPUNIT	0.5000,0.5000	Sets the snap spacing for the current viewport
SPLFRAME	0	Controls the display of spline-fit polylines
SPLINESEGS	8	Sets the number of line segments to be generated for each spline-fit polyline
SPLINETYPE	6	Determines the type of spline curve to be generated by **PEDIT Spline**
SYSCODEPAGE	∿	Stores the system code page specified in AUTO.XMF
TARGET	∿	Stores location of the target point for the current viewport (in UCS coordinates)
TDCREATE	∿	Stores the time and date when the current drawing was created
TDINDWG	∿	Stores the total editing time for the current drawing
TDUPDATE	∿	Stores the time and date of last drawing update/save
TDUSRTIMER	∿	Stores user timer time elapsed

Variable Name	Default Value	Description
TEXTFILL	1	Controls the filling of Bitstream, TrueType, and Adobe Type 1 fonts
TEXTQLTY	50	Sets the resolution for TrueType fonts when plotting or exporting with the **PSOUT** command
TEXTSIZE	0.2000	Sets the text height for the current style
TEXTSTYLE	"Standard"	Sets the current text style name
THICKNESS	0.0000	Sets the current 3D thickness
TILEMODE	1	Toggles between model space and paper space
UCSICON	1	Controls the display of the UCS icon
UCSNAME	∿	Stores the name of the current UCS for the current space
UCSORG	∿	Stores the origin point of the current UCS for the current space
UCSXDIR	∿	Stores the X direction of the current UCS for the current space
UCSYDIR	∿	Stores the Y direction of the current UCS for the current space
UNITMODE	0	Controls the units display format
USERNAME	∿	Stores the name of the current user
VIEWCTR	∿	Stores the center of view in the current viewport, expressed in UCS coordinates
VIEWDIR	∿	Stores the viewing direction in the current viewport, expressed in UCS coordinates
VIEWMODE	∿	Controls the **DVIEW** viewing mode for the current viewport using bit-code
VIEWSIZE	∿	Stores the height of view in the current viewport, expressed in drawing units
VIEWTWIST	∿	Stores the view twist angle for the current viewport
VISRETAIN	1	Controls the visibility of layers in xref files
VSMAX	∿	Upper-right corner of the current viewport's virtual screen
VSMIN	∿	Lower-left corner of the current viewport's virtual screen
WORLDVIEW	1	Controls whether the UCS changes to the WCS during **DVIEW** or **VPOINT** operations
XCLIPFRAME	0	Controls visibility of xref clipping boundaries
XLOADCTL	1	Controls xref demand loading
XLOADPATH	"C:\Windows\Temp"	The path for storage of temporary copies of demand loaded xref files

The following listing contains the AutoCAD LT system variables that are saved with the AutoCAD LT configuration file, and not within the drawing file. The configuration file is named ACLT5.CFG if you are using AutoCAD LT 98. If you are using AutoCAD LT 97, the file is called ACLT4.CFG. The values stored in the configuration file are identical between all drawing sessions. The default values shown here represent the values existing prior to the initial configuration of AutoCAD LT. The eyeglasses symbol (👓) indicates that variable is read-only.

Variable Name	Default Value	Description
APBOX	0	Turns the **AutoSnap** aperture box on or off
APERTURE	10	Sets the object snap target height (in pixels)
AUDITCTL	1	Toggles the creation of an audit file (.ADT)
AUTOSNAP	7	Controls the display of the AutoSnap marker and SnapTip and turns the AutoSnap magnet on or off
CMDDIA	1	Controls the display of the **PLOT** and **BHATCH** command dialog boxes
CURSORSIZE	5	Controls the size of the graphics cursor crosshairs as a percentage of screen size
DCTCUST	"C:\Program Files\ AutoCAD LT 98\ sample.cus"	Current custom dictionary filename and path
DCTMAIN	(varies by country)	Main dictionary filename
FILEDIA	1	Controls the display of all dialog boxes except **PLOT** and **BHATCH**
FONTALT	"simplex.shx"	Font file to be used when a specified font file cannot be found
FONTMAP	"C:\Program Files\ AutoCAD LT 98\ aclt.fmp"	Font mapping file to be used when a specified file cannot be found
GRIPBLOCK	0	Controls the assignment of grips within blocks
GRIPCOLOR	5	Sets the color of nonselected (warm) grips
GRIPHOT	1	Sets the color of selected (hot) grips
GRIPS	1	Toggles grips on and off
GRIPSIZE	3	Sets the size of the grip box (in pixels)
HPBOUND	1	Controls the object type created by **BHATCH** and **BOUNDARY**
INETLOCATION	"www.autodesk. com/acltuser"	Internet location used by the **BROWSER** command
LOGFILEMODE	0	Specifies whether the text window contents are written to a log file
LOGFILENAME	"C:\Program Files\ AutoCAD LT 98\ aclt.log"	Specifies the name and path for the log file

Variable Name	Default Value	Description
MAXSORT	200	Maximum number of symbols or filenames sorted by listing commands
MTEXTED	"Internal"	Name of text editor for editing **MTEXT** objects
OSNAPCOORD	2	Controls whether typed coordinates override object snap settings
PICKADD	1	Controls the additive selection of objects
PICKAUTO	1	Controls automatic windowing at Select objects: prompt
PICKBOX	3	Sets the object selection target height (in pixels)
PICKDRAG	0	Controls how a selection window is drawn
PICKFIRST	1	Allows objects to be selected before a command is issued
PLINETYPE	2	Specifies whether AutoCAD LT uses light-weight polylines
PLOTID	"Default System Printer"	Stores the current printer/plotter description
PLOTTER	0	Integer describing current printer/plotter configuration
PROJMODE	1	Controls the projection mode for the **TRIM** and **EXTEND** commands
RTDISPLAY	1	Controls the display of raster objects during realtime zooming and panning operations
SAVEFILE	*varies*	Stores the current auto-save file name
SAVETIME	120	Sets the automatic save time interval (in minutes)
SORTENTS	96	Controls object sort order operations
TOOLTIPS	1	Toggles tooltips on and off
TRIMMODE	1	Controls whether the **FILLET** and **CHAMFER** commands trim corners
XREFCTL	0	Determines whether AutoCAD LT writes .XLG files (external reference log files)
ZOOMFACTOR	10	Controls the response rate of zooming with an Intellimouse wheel

This final listing shows the AutoCAD LT variables that are not saved at all. These variables revert to default values when opening an existing or beginning a newdrawing. Many of these variables are read-only, and reference drawing or operating system-specific information. Other variables in this section are used to change standard features of AutoCAD LT and are restored to their default values in future drawing sessions to avoid unexpected results during common drawing operations. The eyeglasses symbol (👓) indicates that variable is read-only.

Variable Name	Default Value	Description
ACLTPREFIX	👓	Stores the directory path specified in the **PREFERENCES** dialog box
ACLTVER	👓	Stores the version number of AutoCAD LT
AFLAGS	0	Current attribute flag settings
AREA	👓	Stores the last area value computed by the **AREA** or **LIST** commands
CDATE	👓	Shows date and time in calendar and clock format: YYYYMMDD.HHMMSSmsec
CHAMMODE	0	Current chamfer method
CIRCLERAD	0.0000	Radius of last circle drawn
CMDACTIVE	👓	Indicates what type of command is active
CMDNAMES	👓	Displays the name of the currently active command and transparent command
CURCMDLN	👓	Controls whether a pop-up menu is displayed when you right-click
DATE	👓	Stores the current date and time as a Julian date and fraction in a real number
DISTANCE	👓	Stores the distance calculated by the **DIST** command
DONUTID	0.5000	Sets the inside diameter of a donut object
DONUTOD	1.0000	Sets the outside diameter of a donut object
DWGNAME	👓	Stores the current drawing name
DWGPREFIX	👓	Stores the drive/directory path of the current drawing
DWGTITLED	👓	Specifies whether the current drawing has been saved
EXEDIR	👓	Displays the directory path of the AutoCAD LT executable file
EXPERT	0	Suppresses the level of warning prompts and messages
HIGHLIGHT	1	Toggles object highlighting on and off
HPANG	0	Sets the hatch pattern angle

Variable Name	Default Value	Description
HPDOUBLE	0	Specifies hatch pattern doubling for user-defined (U) patterns
HPNAME	"ANSI31"	Sets the default hatch pattern name. Enter a period (.) to set no default
HPSCALE	1.0000	Sets the current hatch pattern scale
HPSPACE	1.0000	Sets the hatch pattern spacing for user-defined (U) patterns
INSNAME	""	Sets the default block name for the **DDINSERT** and **INSERT** commands
LASTANGLE	ᨆ	Stores end angle of last arc entered, relative to the XY plane of the current UCS
LASTCMD	ᨆ	Stores the last string echoed to the command line
LOCALE	ᨆ	ISO language code of the current running AutoCAD LT version
MAXACTVP	16	Sets the maximum number of viewports to regenerate at one time
MENUECHO	0	Suppresses the level of menu echo prompts
MODEMACRO	""	Displays a text string on the toolbar written in the DIESEL macro language
OFFSETDIST	−1.0000	Sets the default offset distance
PERIMETER	ᨆ	Stores the last perimeter value computed by the **AREA** or **LIST** commands
PLATFORM	ᨆ	Displays the current operating system
POLYSIDES	4	Sets the default number of polygon sides
SAVENAME	ᨆ	Stores the filename and path of a saved drawing
TABMODE	0	Turns **Tablet** mode on and off
UNDOCTL	ᨆ	Current status of **UNDO** command
UNDOMARKS	ᨆ	The number of **UNDO** marks that have been placed
WORLDUCS	ᨆ	Comparison of current UCS and World UCS

Appendix E

AutoCAD LT Hatch Pattern Descriptions

Hatch Pattern Name	Description
SOLID	Solid fill
ANGLE	Angle Steel
ANSI31	ANSI Iron, Brick, Stone masonry
ANSI32	ANSI Steel
ANSI33	ANSI Bronze, Brass, Copper
ANSI34	ANSI Plastic, Rubber
ANSI35	ANSI Fire brick, Refractory material
ANSI36	ANSI Marble, Slate, Glass
ANSI37	ANSI Lead, Zinc, Magnesium, Sound/Heat/Elec Insulation
ANSI38	ANSI Aluminum
AR-B816	8×16 Block elevation stretcher bond
AR-B816C	8×16 Block elevation stretcher bond with mortar joints
AR-B88	8×8 Block elevation stretcher bond
AR-BRELM	Standard brick elevation English bond with mortar joints
AR-BRSTD	Standard brick elevation stretcher bond
AR-CONC	Random dot and stone pattern
AR-HBONE	Standard brick herringbone pattern @ 45°
AR-PARQ1	2×12 Parquet flooring: pattern of 12×12
AR-RROOF	Roof shingle texture
AR-RSHKE	Roof wood shake texture
AR-SAND	Random dot pattern
BOX	Box Steel
BRASS	Brass material
BRICK	Brick or masonry-type surface
BRSTONE	Brick and stone
CLAY	Clay material
CORK	Cork material
CROSS	A series of crosses
DASH	Dashed lines
DOLMIT	Geological rock layering
DOTS	A series of dots
EARTH	Earth or ground (subterranean)
ESCHER	Escher pattern
FLEX	Flexible material
GRASS	Grass area
GRATE	Grated area
HEX	Hexagons
HONEY	Honeycomb pattern
HOUND	Houndstooth check
INSUL	Insulation material

Hatch Pattern Name	Description
LINE	Parallel horizontal lines
MUDST	Mud and sand
NET	Horizontal/vertical grid
NET3	Network pattern 0-60-120
PLAST	Plastic material
PLASTI	Plastic material
SACNCR	Concrete
SQUARE	Small aligned squares
STARS	Star of David
STEEL	Steel material
SWAMP	Swampy area
TRANS	Heat transfer material
TRIANG	Equilateral triangles
ZIGZAG	Staircase effect
ACAD_ISO02W100	Dashed line
ACAD_ISO03W100	Dashed space line
ACAD_ISO04W100	Long dashed dotted line
ACAD_ISO05W100	Long dashed double-dotted line
ACAD_ISO06W100	Long dashed triplicate dotted line
ACAD_ISO07W100	Dotted line
ACAD_ISO08W100	Long dashed short dashed line
ACAD_ISO09W100	Long dashed double-short-dashed line
ACAD_ISO10W100	Dashed dotted line
ACAD_ISO11W100	Double-dashed dotted line
ACAD_ISO12W100	Dashed double-dotted line
ACAD_ISO13W100	Double-dashed double-dotted line
ACAD_ISO14W100	Dashed triplicate-dotted line
ACAD_ISO15W100	Double-dashed triplicate-dotted line

Appendix F

Drafting Standards and Related Documents

The following is a list of ANSI/ASME drafting standards or related documents. They are ANSI/ASME adopted, unless another standard developing organization, such as ANSI/NFPA, is indicated.

Abbreviations

Y1.1-1989, *Abbreviations for Use on Drawings and in Text*

Charts and Graphs (Y15)

Y15.1M-1979 (R1993), *Illustrations for Publication and Projection*
Y15.2M-1979 (R1986), *Time-Series Charts*
Y15.3M-1979 (R1986), *Process Charts*

Dimensions

B4.1-1967 (R1987), *Preferred Limits and Fits for Cylindrical Parts*
B4.2-1978 (R1994), *Preferred Metric Limits and Fits*
B4.3-1978 (R1994), *General Tolerances for Metric Dimensioned Products*
B4.4M-1981 (R1987), *Inspection of Workpieces*
B32.1-1952 (R1994), *Preferred Thickness for Uncoated, Thin, Flat Metals (Under 0.250/in.)*
B32.2-1969 (R1994), *Preferred Diameters for Round Wire-0.500 Inches and Under*
B32.3M-1984 (R1994), *Preferred Metric Sizes for Flat Metal Products*
B32.4M-1980 (R1994), *Preferred Metric Sizes for Round, Square, Rectangle, and Hexagon Metal Products*
B32.5-1977 (R1994), *Preferred Metric Sizes for Tubular Metal Products Other Than Pipe*
B32.6M-1984 (R1994), *Preferred Metric Equivalents of Inch Sizes for Tubular Metal Products Other Than Pipe*
B36.10M-1985, *Welded and Seamless Wrought Steel Pipe*
B36.19M-1985, *Stainless Steel Pipe*

Drafting Standards

Y14.1-1980 (R1987), *Drawing Sheet Size and Format*
Y14.1M-1992, *Metric Drawing Sheet Size and Format*
Y14.2M-1992, *Line Conventions and Lettering*
Y14.3M-1992, *Multi- and Sectional-View Drawings*
Y14.4M-1989 (R1994), *Pictorial Drawings*
Y14.5M-1994, *Dimensioning and Tolerancing*
Y14.5.1-1994, *Mathematical Definition of Y14.5*
Y14.5.2, *Certification of GD&T Professionals*

Y14.6M-1978 (R1993), *Screw Thread Representation*

14.6aM-1981 (R1993), *Engineering Drawing and Related Documentation Practices (Screw Thread Representation) (Metric Supplement)*

Y14.7.1-1971 (R1993), *Gear Drawing Standards-Part 1-Spur, Helical, Double Helical, and Rack*

Y14.7.2-1978 (R1994), *Gear and Spline Drawing Standards-Part 2-Bevel and Hypoid Gears*

Y14.8M-1989 (R1993), *Castings and Forgings*

Y14.13M-1981 (R1992), *Engineering Drawing and Related Documentation Practices-Mechanical Spring Representation*

Y14.18M-1986 (R1993), *Engineering Drawings and Related Documentation Practices-Optical Parts*

Y14.24M-1989, *Types and Applications of Engineering Drawings*

14.34M-1989 (R1993), *Parts Lists, Data Lists, and Index Lists*

Y14.35M-1992, *Revision of Engineering Drawings and Associated Documents*

Y14.36-1978 (R1993), *Surface Texture Symbols*

Y14 Report 1, *Digital Representation of Physical Object Shapes*

Y14 Report 2, *Guidelines for Documenting of Computer Systems Used in Computer-Aided Preparation of Product Definition Data-User Instructions*

Y14 Report 3, *Guidelines for Documenting of Computer Systems Used in Computer-Aided Preparation of Product Definition Data-Design Requirements*

Y14 Report 4-1989, *A Structural Language Format for Basic Shape Description*

ANSI/US PRO/IPO-100-1993, *Digital Representation for Communication of Product Definition Data (Replaced ANSI Y14.26M-1981)*

Graphic Symbols

Y32.2-1975, *Electrical and Electronic Diagrams*

Y32.2.3-1949 (R1988), *Pipe Fittings, Valves, and Piping*

Y32.2.4-1949 (R1993), *Heating, Ventilating, and Air Conditioning*

Y32.2.6-1950 (R1993), *Heat/Power Apparatus*

Y32.4-1977 (R1987), *Plumbing Fixture Diagrams Used in Architectural and Building Construction*

Y32.7-1972 (R1987), *Railroad Maps and Profiles*

Y32.9-1972 (R1989), *Electrical Wiring and Layout Diagrams Used in Architecture and Building*

Y32.10-1967 (R1987), *Fluid Power Diagrams*

Y32.11-1961 (R1993), *Process Flow Diagrams in the Petroleum and Chemical Industries*

Y32.18-1972 (R1993), *Mechanical and Acoustical Elements as Used in Schematic Diagrams*

ANSI/AWS A2.4-91, *Symbols for Welding, Brazing, and Nondestructive Examination*

ANSI/IEEE 200-1975 (R1989), *Reference Designations for Electrical and Electronics Parts and Equipment*

ANSI/IEEE 315-1975 (R1989), *Electrical and Electronics Diagrams (Including Reference Designation Class Designation Letters)*

ANSI/IEEE 623-1976 (R1989), *Grid and Mapping Used in Cable Television Systems*

ANSI/ISA S5.1-1984 (R1992), *Instrumentation Symbols and Identification*

ANSI/NFPA 170-1991, *Public Fire Safety Symbols*

Letter Symbols

Y10.1-1972 (R1988), *Glossary of Terms Concerning Letter Symbols*
Y10.3M-1984, *Mechanics and Time-Related Phenomena*
Y10.4-1982 (R1988), *Heat and Thermodynamics*
Y10.11-1984, *Acoustics*
Y10.12-1955 (R1988), *Chemical Engineering*
Y10.17-1961 (R1988), *Greek Letters Used as Letter Symbols for Engineering Math*
Y10.18-1967 (R1977), *Illuminating Engineering*
ANSI/IEEE 260-1978 (R1992), *SI Units and Certain Other Units of Measurement*

Metric System

SI-1, *Orientation and Guide for Use of SI (Metric) Units*
SI-2, *SI Units in Strength of Materials*
SI-3, *SI Units in Dynamics*
SI-4, *SI Units in Thermodynamics*
SI-5, *SI Units in Fluid Mechanics*
SI-6, *SI Units in Kinematics*
SI-7, *SI Units in Heat Transfer*
SI-8, *SI Units in Vibration*
SI-9, *Metrification of Codes and Standards SI (Metric) Units*
SI-10, *Steam Charts, SI (Metric) and U.S. Customary Units*

Drafting Symbols

Standard Dimensioning Symbols

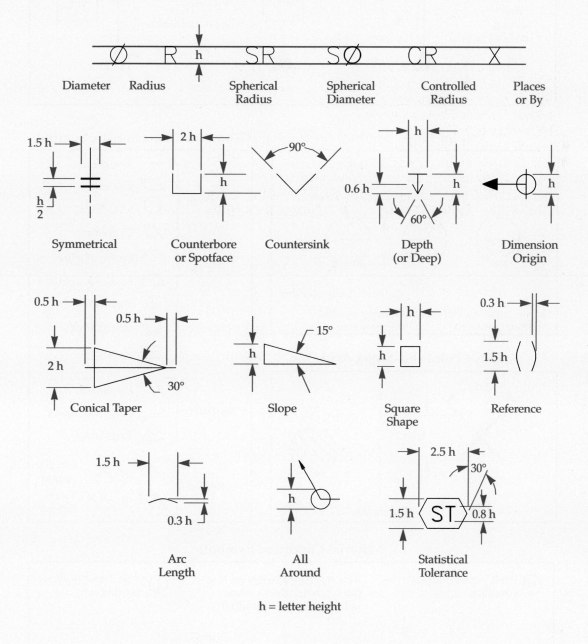

h = letter height

Geometric Dimensioning and Tolerancing Symbols

Datum Feature Symbol

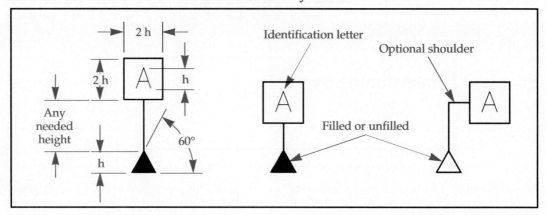

Datum Target Symbol

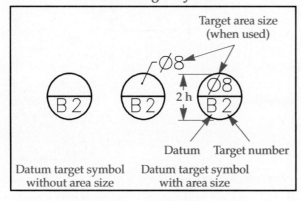

Datum target symbol without area size

Datum target symbol with area size

Target Point and Target Area

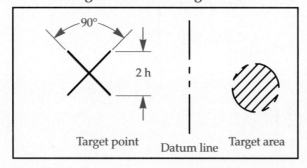

Target point

Datum line

Target area

Geometric Characteristic Symbols

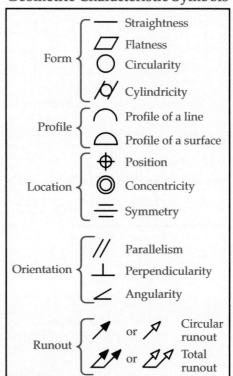

Form
- — Straightness
- ▱ Flatness
- ○ Circularity
- ⌀ Cylindricity

Profile
- ⌒ Profile of a line
- ⌓ Profile of a surface

Location
- ⊕ Position
- ◎ Concentricity
- ≡ Symmetry

Orientation
- // Parallelism
- ⊥ Perpendicularity
- ∠ Angularity

Runout
- ↗ or ↗ Circular runout
- ↗↗ or ↗↗ Total runout

Material Condition Symbols

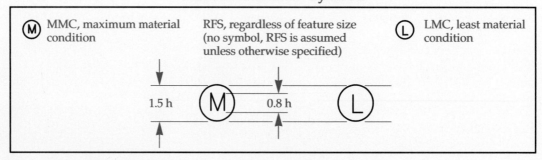

Ⓜ MMC, maximum material condition

RFS, regardless of feature size (no symbol, RFS is assumed unless otherwise specified)

Ⓛ LMC, least material condition

Geometric Dimensioning and Tolerancing Symbols (cont.)

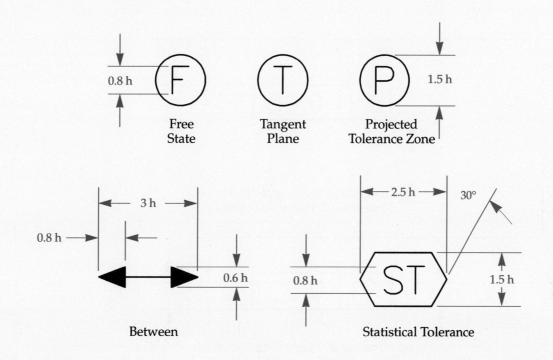

Free State

Tangent Plane

Projected Tolerance Zone

Between

Statistical Tolerance

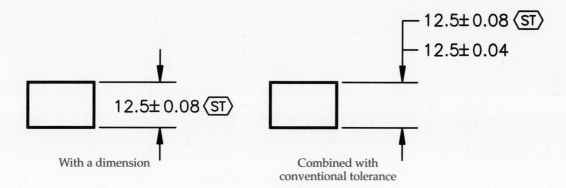

With a dimension

Combined with conventional tolerance

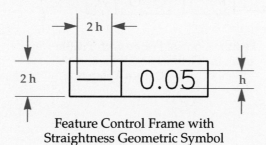

In the feature control frame

Statistical Tolerancing Methods

Feature Control Frame with
Straightness Geometric Symbol

h = lettering height

Geometric Dimensioning and Tolerancing Symbols (cont.)

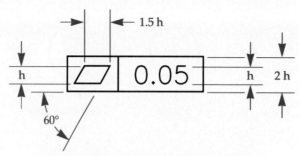

Feature Control Frame with the Flatness
Geometric Characteristic Symbol

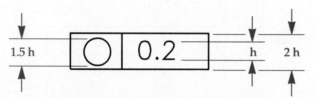

Feature Control Frame with Circularity
Geometric Characteristic Symbol

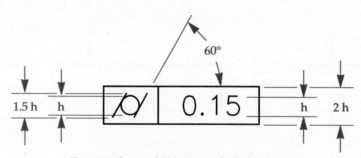

Feature Control Frame with Cylindricity
Geometric Characteristic Symbol

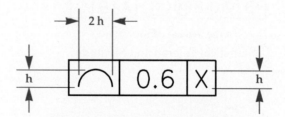

Feature Control Frame with Profile
of a Line Geometric Characteristic
Symbol and a Datum Reference   h = lettering height

Geometric Dimensioning and Tolerancing Symbols (cont.)

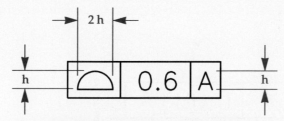

Feature Control Frame with Profile
of a Surface Geometric Characteristic
Symbol and a Datum Reference

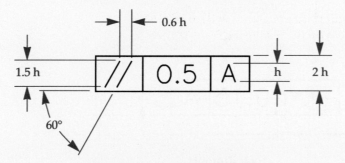

Feature Control Frame with
Parallelism Geometric Characteristic
Symbol and a Datum Reference

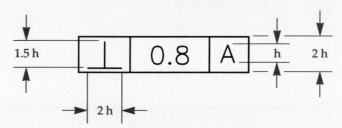

Feature Control Frame with
Perpendicularity Geometric Characteristic
Symbol and a Datum Reference

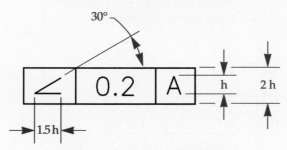

Feature Control Frame with
Angularity Geometric Characteristic
Symbol and a Datum Reference

h = lettering height

Geometric Dimensioning and Tolerancing Symbols (cont.)

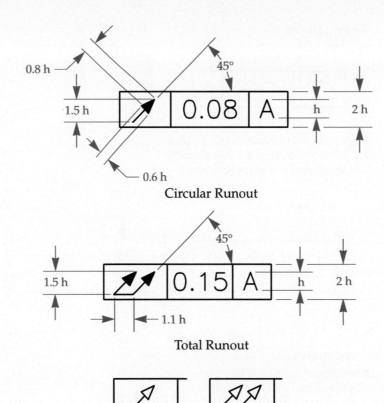

Circular Runout

Total Runout

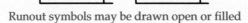

Runout symbols may be drawn open or filled

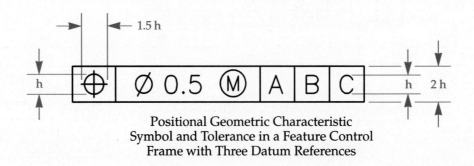

Positional Geometric Characteristic
Symbol and Tolerance in a Feature Control
Frame with Three Datum References

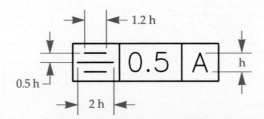

Feature Control Frame with Symmetry
Geometric Characteristic
Symbol and a Datum Reference

h = lettering height

Geometric Dimensioning and Tolerancing Symbols (cont.)

SYMBOL FOR:	ANSI Y14.5M	ASME Y14.5M	ISO
STRAIGHTNESS	—	—	—
FLATNESS	▱	▱	▱
CIRCULARITY	○	○	○
DYLINDRICITY	⌭	⌭	⌭
PROFILE OF A LINE	⌒	⌒	⌒
PROFILE OF A SURFACE	⌓	⌓	⌓
ALL AROUND	⟜⊕	⟜⊕	⟜⊕ (proposed)
ANGULARITY	∠	∠	∠
PERPENDICULARITY	⊥	⊥	⊥
PARALLELISM	//	//	//
POSITION	⊕	⊕	⊕
CONCENTRICITY	◎	◎	◎
SYMMETRY	NONE	≡	≡
CIRCULAR RUNOUT	*↗	*↗	↗
TOTAL RUNOUT	*↗↗	*↗↗	↗↗
AT MAXIMUM MATERIAL CONDITION	Ⓜ	Ⓜ	Ⓜ
AT LEAST MATERIAL CONDITION	Ⓛ	Ⓛ	Ⓛ
REGARDLESS OF FEATURE SIZE	Ⓢ	NONE	NONE
PROJECTED TOLERANCE ZONE	Ⓟ	Ⓟ	Ⓟ
TANGENT PLANE	Ⓣ	Ⓣ	NONE
FREE STATE	Ⓕ	Ⓕ	Ⓕ
DIAMETER	⌀	⌀	⌀
BASIC DIMENSION	50	50	50
REFERENCE DIMENSION	(50)	(50)	(50)
DATUM FEATURE	–A–	*⟍▥Ⓐ	*⟍▥Ⓐ or *⟍▥Ⓐ
DIMENSION ORIGIN	⊕→	⊕→	⊕→
FEATURE CONTROL FRAME	⊕ ⌀0.5Ⓜ A B C	⊕ ⌀0.5Ⓜ A B C	⊕ ⌀0.5Ⓜ A B C
CONICAL TAPER	▷	▷	▷
SLOPE	◿	◿	◿
COUNTERBORE\SPOTFACE	⌴	⌴	NONE
COUNTERSINK	⌵	⌵	NONE
DEPTH\DEEP	↧	↧	NONE
SQUARE	□	□	□
DIMENSION NOT TO SCALE	<u>15</u>	<u>15</u>	<u>15</u>
NUMBER OF TIMES\PLACES	8X	8X	8X
ARC LENGTH	⌒105	⌒105	⌒105
RADIUS	R	R	R
SPHERICAL RADIUS	SR	SR	SR
SPHERICAL DIAMETER	S⌀	S⌀	S⌀
CONTROLLED RADIUS	NONE	CR	NONE
BETWEEN	NONE	*←→	NONE
STATISTICAL TOLERANCE	NONE	⟨ST⟩	NONE
DATUM TARGET	⌀6/A1	⌀6/A1 or A1/⌀6	⌀6/A1 or A1/⌀6
TARGET POINT	✕	✕	✕

* MAY BE FILLED OR NOT FILLED

Single Line Piping Symbols

Name	Screwed			Buttwelded		
	Left Side	Front	Right Side	Left Side	Front	Right Side
90° Elbow						
45° Elbow						
Tee						
45° Lateral						
Cross						
Cap						
Concentric Reducer						
Eccentric Reducer						
Union						
Coupling						

Common Symbols for Electrical Diagrams

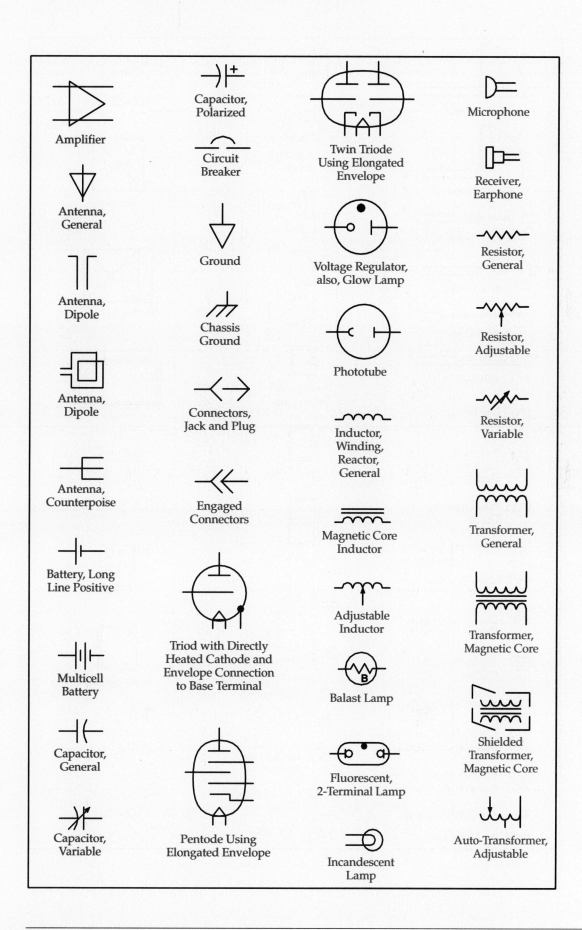

Amplifier

Antenna, General

Antenna, Dipole

Antenna, Dipole

Antenna, Counterpoise

Battery, Long Line Positive

Multicell Battery

Capacitor, General

Capacitor, Variable

Capacitor, Polarized

Circuit Breaker

Ground

Chassis Ground

Connectors, Jack and Plug

Engaged Connectors

Triod with Directly Heated Cathode and Envelope Connection to Base Terminal

Pentode Using Elongated Envelope

Twin Triode Using Elongated Envelope

Voltage Regulator, also, Glow Lamp

Phototube

Inductor, Winding, Reactor, General

Magnetic Core Inductor

Adjustable Inductor

Balast Lamp

Fluorescent, 2-Terminal Lamp

Incandescent Lamp

Microphone

Receiver, Earphone

Resistor, General

Resistor, Adjustable

Resistor, Variable

Transformer, General

Transformer, Magnetic Core

Shielded Transformer, Magnetic Core

Auto-Transformer, Adjustable

Common Architectural Symbols

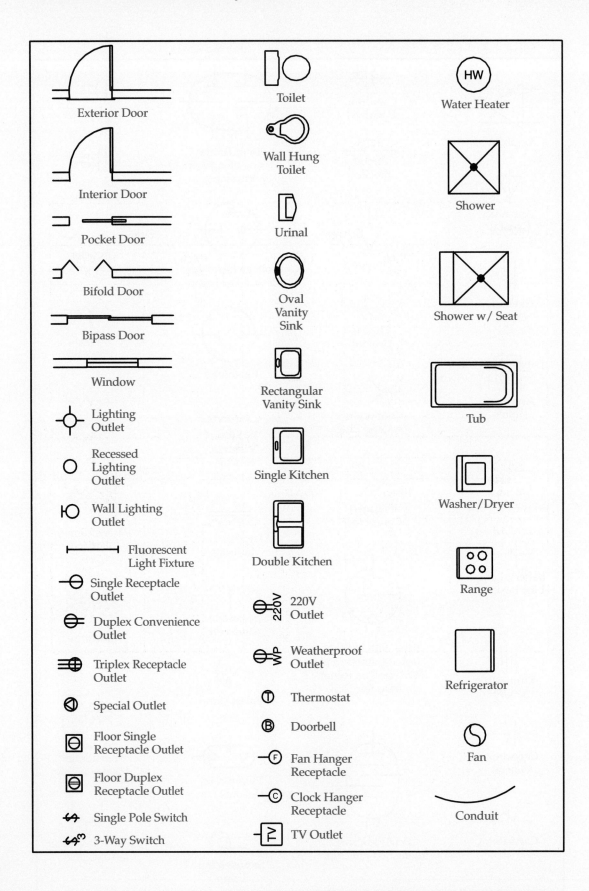

Exterior Door

Interior Door

Pocket Door

Bifold Door

Bipass Door

Window

Lighting Outlet

Recessed Lighting Outlet

Wall Lighting Outlet

Fluorescent Light Fixture

Single Receptacle Outlet

Duplex Convenience Outlet

Triplex Receptacle Outlet

Special Outlet

Floor Single Receptacle Outlet

Floor Duplex Receptacle Outlet

Single Pole Switch

3-Way Switch

Toilet

Wall Hung Toilet

Urinal

Oval Vanity Sink

Rectangular Vanity Sink

Single Kitchen

Double Kitchen

220V Outlet

Weatherproof Outlet

Thermostat

Doorbell

Fan Hanger Receptacle

Clock Hanger Receptacle

TV Outlet

Water Heater

Shower

Shower w/ Seat

Tub

Washer/Dryer

Range

Refrigerator

Fan

Conduit

Appendix H

Standard Tables and Symbols

Tap Drill Sizes for ISO Metric Threads

Nominal Size mm	Series			
	Coarse		Fine	
	Pitch mm	Tap Drill mm	Pitch mm	Tap Drill mm
1.4	0.3	1.1	—	—
1.6	0.35	1.25	—	—
2	0.4	1.6	—	—
2.5	0.45	2.05	—	—
3	0.5	2.5	—	—
4	0.7	3.3	—	—
5	0.8	4.2	—	—
6	1.0	5.0	—	—
8	1.25	6.75	1	7.0

Nominal Size mm	Series			
	Coarse		Fine	
	Pitch mm	Tap Drill mm	Pitch mm	Tap Drill mm
10	1.5	8.5	1.25	8.75
12	1.75	10.25	1.25	10.50
14	2	12.00	1.5	12.50
16	2	14.00	1.5	14.50
18	2.5	15.50	1.5	16.50
20	2.5	17.50	1.5	18.50
22	2.5	19.50	1.5	20.50
24	3	21.00	2	22.00
27	3	24.00	2	25.00

Tap Drill Sizes Unified Standard Screw Heads

Screw Thread		Tap Drill	Screw Thread		Tap Drill
Major Diameter	Threads Per Inch	Size Or Number	Major Diameter	Threads Per Inch	Size Or Number
0	80	3/64	3/8	16	5/16
				24	Q
1	64	53			
	72	53	7/16	14	U
				20	25/64
2	56	50			
	64	50	1/2	13	27/64
				20	29/64
3	48	47			
	56	45	9/16	12	31/64
				18	33/64
4	40	43			
	48	42	5/8	11	17/32
				18	37/64
5	40	38			
	44	37	3/4	10	21/32
				16	11/16
6	32	36			
	40	33	7/8	9	49/64
				14	13/16
8	32	29			
	36	29	1	8	7/8
				12	59/64
10	24	25			
	32	21	1 1/8	7	63/64
				12	1 3/64
12	24	16			
	28	14	1 1/4	7	1 7/64
				12	1 11/64
1/4	20	7			
	28	3	1 3/8	6	1 7/32
				12	1 19/64
5/16	18	F			
	24	I	1 1/2	6	1 11/32
				12	1 27/64

Number and Letter Drills

Drill No.	Frac	Deci	Drill No.	Frac	Deci	Drill No.	Frac	Deci
80	—	.0135		9/64	.140	S	—	.348
79	—	.0145	28	—	.141	T	—	.358
	1/64	.0156	27	—	.144		23/64	.359
78	—	.0160	26	—	.147	U	—	.368
77	—	.0180	25	—	.150		3/8	.375
76	—	.0200	24	—	.152	V	—	.377
75	—	.0210	23	—	.154	W	—	.386
74	—	.0225		5/32	.156		25/64	.391
73	—	.0240	22	—	.157	X	—	.397
72	—	.0250	21	—	.159	Y	—	.404
71	—	.0260	20	—	.161		13/32	.406
70	—	.0280	19	—	.166	Z	—	.413
69	—	.0292	18	—	.170		27/64	.422
68	—	.0310		11/64	.172		7/16	.438
	1/32	.0313	17	—	.173		29/64	.453
67	—	.0320	16	—	.177		15/32	.469
66	—	.0330	15	—	.180		31/64	.484
65	—	.0350	14	—	.182		1/2	.500
64	—	.0360	13	—	.185		33/64	.516
63	—	.0370		3/16	.188		17/32	.531
62	—	.0380	12	—	.189		35/64	.547
61	—	.0390	11	—	.191		9/16	.562
60	—	.0400	10	—	.194		37/64	.578
59	—	.0410	9	—	.196		19/32	.594
58	—	.0420	8	—	.199		39/64	.609
57	—	.0430	7	—	.201		5/8	.625
56	—	.0465		13/64	.203		41/64	.641
	3/64	.0469	6	—	.204		21/32	.656
55	—	.0520	5	—	.206		43/64	.672
54	—	.0550	4	—	.209		11/16	.688
53	—	.0595	3	—	.213		45/64	.703
	1/16	.0625		7/32	.219		23/32	.719
52	—	.0635	2	—	.221		47/64	.734
51	—	.0670	1	—	.228		3/4	.750
50	—	.0700	A	—	.234		49/64	.766
49	—	.0730		15/64	.234		25/32	.781
48	—	.0760	B	—	.238		51/64	.797
	5/64	.0781	C	—	.242		13/16	.813
47	—	.0785	D	—	.246		53/64	.828
46	—	.0810		1/4	.250		27/32	.844
45	—	.0820	E	—	.250		55/64	.859
44	—	.0860	F	—	.257		7/8	.875
43	—	.0890	G	—	.261		57/64	.891
42	—	.0935		17/64	.266		29/32	.906
	3/32	.0938	H	—	.266		59/64	.922
41	—	.0960	I	—	.272		15/16	.938
40	—	.0980	J	—	.277		61/64	.953
39	—	.0995		9/32	.281		31/32	.969
38	—	.1015	K	—	.281		63/64	.984
37	—	.1040	L	—	.290		1	1.000
36	—	.1065	M	—	.295			
	7/64	.1094		19/64	.297			
35	—	.1100	N	—	.302			
34	—	.1110		5/16	.313			
33	—	.1130	O	—	.316			
32	—	.116	P	—	.323			
31	—	.120		21/64	.328			
	1/8	.125	Q	—	.332			
30	—	.129	R	—	.339			
29	—	.136		11/32	.344			

Metric Drills

MM	DEC.	MM	DEC.	MM	DEC.	MM	DEC.
1.	.0394	3.2	.1260	6.3	.2480	9.5	.3740
1.05	.0413	3.25	.1280	6.4	.2520	9.6	.3780
1.1	.0433	3.3	.1299	6.5	.2559	9.7	.3819
1.15	.0453	3.4	.1339	6.6	.2598	9.75	.3839
1.2	.0472	3.5	.1378	6.7	.2638	9.8	.3858
1.25	.0492	3.6	.1417	6.75	.2657	9.9	.3898
1.3	.0512	3.7	.1457	6.8	.2677	10.	.3937
1.35	.0531	3.75	.1476	6.9	.2717	10.5	.4134
1.4	.0551	3.8	.1496	7.	.2756	11.	.4331
1.45	.0571	3.9	.1535	7.1	.2795	11.5	.4528
1.5	.0591	4.	.1575	7.2	.2835	12.	.4724
1.55	.0610	4.1	.1614	7.25	.2854	12.5	.4921
1.6	.0630	4.2	.1654	7.3	.2874	13.	.5118
1.65	.0650	4.25	.1673	7.4	.2913	13.5	.5315
1.7	.0669	4.3	.1693	7.5	.2953	14.	.5512
1.75	.0689	4.4	.1732	7.6	.2992	14.5	.5709
1.8	.0709	4.5	.1772	7.7	.3031	15.	.5906
1.85	.0728	4.6	.1811	7.75	.3051	15.5	.6102
1.9	.0748	4.7	.1850	7.8	.3071	16.	.6299
1.95	.0768	4.75	.1870	7.9	.3110	16.5	.6496
2.	.0787	4.8	.1890	8.	.3150	17.	.6693
2.05	.0807	4.9	.1929	8.1	.3189	17.5	.6890
2.1	.0827	5.	.1968	8.2	.3228	18.	.7087
2.15	.0846	5.1	.2008	8.25	.3248	18.5	.7283
2.2	.0866	5.2	.2047	8.3	.3268	19.	.7480
2.25	.0886	5.25	.2067	8.4	.3307	19.5	.7677
2.3	.0906	5.3	.2087	8.5	.3346	20.	.7874
2.35	.0925	5.4	.2126	8.6	.3386	20.5	.8071
2.4	.0945	5.5	.2165	8.7	.3425	21.	.8268
2.45	.0965	5.6	.2205	8.75	.3445	21.5	.8465
2.5	.0984	5.7	.2244	8.8	.3465	22.	.8661
2.6	.1024	5.75	.2264	8.9	.3504	22.5	.8858
2.7	.1063	5.8	.2283	9.	.3543	23.	.9055
2.75	.1083	5.9	.2323	9.1	.3583	23.5	.9252
2.8	.1102	6.	.2362	9.2	.3622	24.	.9449
2.9	.1142	6.1	.2402	9.25	.3642	24.5	.9646
3	.1181	6.2	.2441	9.3	.3661	25.	.9843
3.1	.1220	6.25	.2461	9.4	.3701		

Decimal and Metric Equivalents

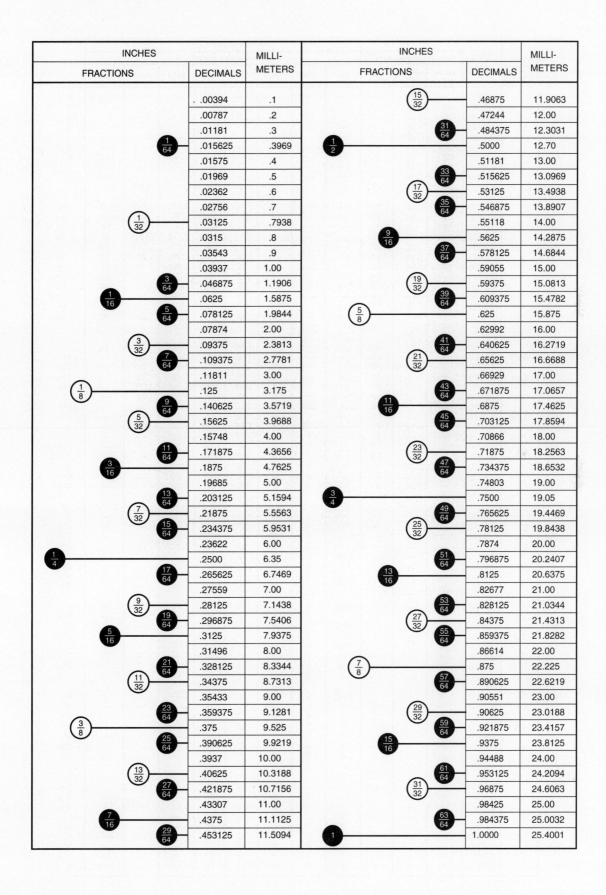

INCHES			MILLI-	INCHES			MILLI-
FRACTIONS		DECIMALS	METERS	FRACTIONS		DECIMALS	METERS
		.00394	.1	15/32		.46875	11.9063
		.00787	.2			.47244	12.00
		.01181	.3		31/64	.484375	12.3031
	1/64	.015625	.3969	1/2		.5000	12.70
		.01575	.4			.51181	13.00
		.01969	.5		33/64	.515625	13.0969
		.02362	.6	17/32		.53125	13.4938
		.02756	.7		35/64	.546875	13.8907
1/32		.03125	.7938			.55118	14.00
		.0315	.8	9/16		.5625	14.2875
		.03543	.9		37/64	.578125	14.6844
		.03937	1.00			.59055	15.00
	3/64	.046875	1.1906	19/32		.59375	15.0813
1/16		.0625	1.5875		39/64	.609375	15.4782
	5/64	.078125	1.9844	5/8		.625	15.875
		.07874	2.00			.62992	16.00
3/32		.09375	2.3813		41/64	.640625	16.2719
	7/64	.109375	2.7781	21/32		.65625	16.6688
		.11811	3.00			.66929	17.00
1/8		.125	3.175		43/64	.671875	17.0657
	9/64	.140625	3.5719	11/16		.6875	17.4625
5/32		.15625	3.9688		45/64	.703125	17.8594
		.15748	4.00			.70866	18.00
	11/64	.171875	4.3656	23/32		.71875	18.2563
3/16		.1875	4.7625		47/64	.734375	18.6532
		.19685	5.00			.74803	19.00
	13/64	.203125	5.1594	3/4		.7500	19.05
7/32		.21875	5.5563		49/64	.765625	19.4469
	15/64	.234375	5.9531	25/32		.78125	19.8438
		.23622	6.00			.7874	20.00
1/4		.2500	6.35		51/64	.796875	20.2407
	17/64	.265625	6.7469	13/16		.8125	20.6375
		.27559	7.00			.82677	21.00
9/32		.28125	7.1438		53/64	.828125	21.0344
	19/64	.296875	7.5406	27/32		.84375	21.4313
5/16		.3125	7.9375		55/64	.859375	21.8282
		.31496	8.00			.86614	22.00
	21/64	.328125	8.3344	7/8		.875	22.225
11/32		.34375	8.7313		57/64	.890625	22.6219
		.35433	9.00			.90551	23.00
	23/64	.359375	9.1281	29/32		.90625	23.0188
3/8		.375	9.525		59/64	.921875	23.4157
	25/64	.390625	9.9219	15/16		.9375	23.8125
		.3937	10.00			.94488	24.00
13/32		.40625	10.3188		61/64	.953125	24.2094
	27/64	.421875	10.7156	31/32		.96875	24.6063
		.43307	11.00			.98425	25.00
7/16		.4375	11.1125		63/64	.984375	25.0032
	29/64	.453125	11.5094	1		1.0000	25.4001

Unified Standard Screw Thread Series

SIZES Primary	SIZES Secondary	BASIC MAJOR DIAMETER	Coarse UNC	Fine UNF	Extra fine UNEF	4UN	6UN	8UN	12UN	16UN	20UN	28UN	32UN	SIZES
0		0.0600	—	80	—	—	—	—	—	—	—	—	—	0
	1	0.0730	64	72	—	—	—	—	—	—	—	—	—	1
2		0.0860	56	64	—	—	—	—	—	—	—	—	—	2
	3	0.0990	48	56	—	—	—	—	—	—	—	—	—	3
4		0.1120	40	48	—	—	—	—	—	—	—	—	—	4
5		0.1250	40	44	—	—	—	—	—	—	—	—	—	5
6		0.1380	32	40	—	—	—	—	—	—	—	—	UNC	6
8		0.1640	32	36	—	—	—	—	—	—	—	—	UNC	8
10		0.1900	24	32	—	—	—	—	—	—	—	—	UNF	10
	12	0.2160	24	28	32	—	—	—	—	—	—	UNF	UNEF	12
1/4		0.2500	20	28	32	—	—	—	—	—	UNC	UNF	UNEF	1/4
5/16		0.3125	18	24	32	—	—	—	—	—	20	28	UNEF	5/16
3/8		0.3750	16	24	32	—	—	—	—	UNC	20	28	UNEF	3/8
7/16		0.4375	14	20	28	—	—	—	—	16	UNF	UNEF	32	7/16
1/2		0.5000	13	20	28	—	—	—	—	16	UNF	UNEF	32	1/2
9/16		0.5625	12	18	24	—	—	—	UNC	16	20	28	32	9/16
5/8		0.6250	11	18	24	—	—	—	12	16	20	28	32	5/8
	11/16	0.6875	—	—	24	—	—	—	12	16	20	28	32	11/16
3/4		0.7500	10	16	20	—	—	—	12	UNF	UNEF	28	32	3/4
	13/16	0.8125	—	—	20	—	—	—	12	16	UNEF	28	32	13/16
7/8		0.8750	9	14	20	—	—	—	12	16	UNEF	28	32	7/8
	15/16	0.9375	—	—	20	—	—	—	12	16	UNEF	28	32	15/16
1		1.0000	8	12	20	—	—	UNC	UNF	16	UNEF	28	32	1
	1 1/16	1.0625	—	—	18	—	—	8	12	16	20	28	—	1 1/16
1 1/8		1.1250	7	12	18	—	—	8	UNF	16	20	28	—	1 1/8
	1 3/16	1.1875	—	—	18	—	—	8	12	16	20	28	—	1 3/16
1 1/4		1.2500	7	12	18	—	—	8	UNF	16	20	28	—	1 1/4
	1 5/16	1.3125	—	—	18	—	—	8	12	16	20	28	—	1 5/16
1 3/8		1.3750	6	12	18	—	UNC	8	UNF	16	20	28	—	1 3/8
	1 7/16	1.4375	—	—	18	—	6	8	12	16	20	28	—	1 7/16
1 1/2		1.5000	6	12	18	—	UNC	8	UNF	16	20	28	—	1 1/2
	1 9/16	1.5625	—	—	18	—	6	8	12	16	20	—	—	1 9/16
1 5/8		1.6250	—	—	18	—	6	8	12	16	20	—	—	1 5/8
	1 11/16	1.6875	—	—	18	—	6	8	12	16	20	—	—	1 11/16
1 3/4		1.7500	5	—	—	—	6	8	12	16	20	—	—	1 3/4
	1 13/16	1.8125	—	—	—	—	6	8	12	16	20	—	—	1 13/16
1 7/8		1.8750	—	—	—	—	6	8	12	16	20	—	—	1 7/8
	1 15/16	1.9375	—	—	—	—	6	8	12	16	20	—	—	1 15/16
2		2.0000	4 1/2	—	—	—	6	8	12	16	20	—	—	2
	2 1/8	2.1250	—	—	—	—	6	8	12	16	20	—	—	2 1/8
2 1/4		2.2500	4 1/2	—	—	—	6	8	12	16	20	—	—	2 1/4
	2 3/8	2.3750	—	—	—	—	6	8	12	16	20	—	—	2 3/8
2 1/2		2.5000	4	—	—	UNC	6	8	12	16	20	—	—	2 1/2
	2 5/8	2.6250	—	—	—	4	6	8	12	16	20	—	—	2 5/8
2 3/4		2.7500	4	—	—	UNC	6	8	12	16	20	—	—	2 3/4
	2 7/8	2.8750	—	—	—	4	6	8	12	16	20	—	—	2 7/8
3		3.0000	4	—	—	UNC	6	8	12	16	20	—	—	3
	3 1/8	3.1250	—	—	—	4	6	8	12	16	—	—	—	3 1/8
3 1/4		3.2500	4	—	—	UNC	6	8	12	16	—	—	—	3 1/4
	3 3/8	3.3750	—	—	—	4	6	8	12	16	—	—	—	3 3/8
3 1/2		3.5000	4	—	—	UNC	6	8	12	16	—	—	—	3 1/2
	3 5/8	3.6250	—	—	—	4	6	8	12	16	—	—	—	3 5/8
3 3/4		3.7500	4	—	—	UNC	6	8	12	16	—	—	—	3 3/4
	3 7/8	3.8750	—	—	—	4	6	8	12	16	—	—	—	3 7/8
4		4.0000	4	—	—	UNC	6	8	12	16	—	—	—	4
	4 1/8	4.1250	—	—	—	4	6	8	12	16	—	—	—	4 1/8
4 1/4		4.2500	—	—	—	4	6	8	12	16	—	—	—	4 1/4
	4 3/8	4.3750	—	—	—	4	6	8	12	16	—	—	—	4 3/8
4 1/2		4.5000	—	—	—	4	6	8	12	16	—	—	—	4 1/2
	4 5/8	4.6250	—	—	—	4	6	8	12	16	—	—	—	4 5/8
4 3/4		4.7500	—	—	—	4	6	8	12	16	—	—	—	4 3/4
	4 7/8	4.8750	—	—	—	4	6	8	12	16	—	—	—	4 7/8
5		5.0000	—	—	—	4	6	8	12	16	—	—	—	5
	5 1/8	5.1250	—	—	—	4	6	8	12	16	—	—	—	5 1/8
5 1/4		5.2500	—	—	—	4	6	8	12	16	—	—	—	5 1/4
	5 3/8	5.3750	—	—	—	4	6	8	12	16	—	—	—	5 3/8
5 1/2		5.5000	—	—	—	4	6	8	12	16	—	—	—	5 1/2
	5 5/8	5.6250	—	—	—	4	6	8	12	16	—	—	—	5 5/8
5 3/4		5.7500	—	—	—	4	6	8	12	16	—	—	—	5 3/4
	5 7/8	5.8750	—	—	—	4	6	8	12	16	—	—	—	5 7/8
6		6.0000	—	—	—	4	6	8	12	16	—	—	—	6

ISO Metric Screw Thread Standard Series

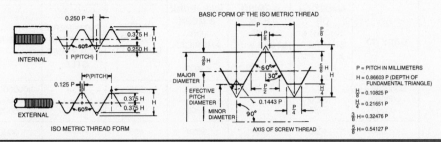

P = PITCH IN MILLIMETERS
H = 0.86603 P (DEPTH OF FUNDAMENTAL TRIANGLE)
$\frac{H}{8}$ = 0.10825 P
$\frac{H}{4}$ = 0.21651 P
$\frac{3}{8}$ H = 0.32476 P
$\frac{5}{8}$ H = 0.54127 P

Nominal Size Diam. (mm)			Pitches (mm)														Nominal Size Diam. (mm)
Column[a]			Series With Graded Pitches		Series With Constant Pitches												
1	2	3	Coarse	Fine	6	4	3	2	1.5	1.25	1	0.75	0.5	0.35	0.25	0.2	
0.25			0.075	—	—	—	—	—	—	—	—	—	—	—	—	—	0.25
0.3			0.08	—	—	—	—	—	—	—	—	—	—	—	—	—	0.3
	0.35		0.09	—	—	—	—	—	—	—	—	—	—	—	—	—	0.35
0.4			0.1	—	—	—	—	—	—	—	—	—	—	—	—	—	0.4
	0.45		0.1	—	—	—	—	—	—	—	—	—	—	—	—	—	0.45
0.5			0.125	—	—	—	—	—	—	—	—	—	—	—	—	—	0.5
	.055		0.125	—	—	—	—	—	—	—	—	—	—	—	—	—	0.55
0.6			0.15	—	—	—	—	—	—	—	—	—	—	—	—	—	0.6
	0.7		0.175	—	—	—	—	—	—	—	—	—	—	—	—	—	0.7
0.8			0.2	—	—	—	—	—	—	—	—	—	—	—	—	—	0.8
	0.9		0.225	—	—	—	—	—	—	—	—	—	—	—	—	—	0.9
1			0.25	—	—	—	—	—	—	—	—	—	—	—	—	0.2	1
	1.1		0.25	—	—	—	—	—	—	—	—	—	—	—	—	0.2	1.1
1.2			0.25	—	—	—	—	—	—	—	—	—	—	—	—	0.2	1.2
	1.4		0.3	—	—	—	—	—	—	—	—	—	—	—	—	0.2	1.4
1.6			0.35	—	—	—	—	—	—	—	—	—	—	—	—	0.2	1.6
	1.8		0.35	—	—	—	—	—	—	—	—	—	—	—	—	0.2	1.8
2			0.4	—	—	—	—	—	—	—	—	—	—	—	0.25	—	2
	2.2		0.45	—	—	—	—	—	—	—	—	—	—	—	0.25	—	2.2
2.5			0.45	—	—	—	—	—	—	—	—	—	—	0.35	—	—	2.5
3			0.5	—	—	—	—	—	—	—	—	—	—	0.35	—	—	3
	3.5		0.6	—	—	—	—	—	—	—	—	—	—	0.35	—	—	3.5
4			0.7	—	—	—	—	—	—	—	—	—	0.5	—	—	—	4
	4.5		0.75	—	—	—	—	—	—	—	—	—	0.5	—	—	—	4.5
5			0.8	—	—	—	—	—	—	—	—	—	0.5	—	—	—	5
		5.5	—	—	—	—	—	—	—	—	—	0.5	—	—	—	—	5.5
6			1	—	—	—	—	—	—	—	—	0.75	—	—	—	—	6
		7	1	—	—	—	—	—	—	—	—	0.75	—	—	—	—	7
8			1.25	1	—	—	—	—	—	—	1	0.75	—	—	—	—	8
		9	1.25	—	—	—	—	—	—	—	1	0.75	—	—	—	—	9
10			1.5	1.25	—	—	—	—	—	1.25	1	0.75	—	—	—	—	10
	11		1.5	—	—	—	—	—	—	—	1	0.75	—	—	—	—	11
12			1.75	1.25	—	—	—	—	1.5	1.25	1	—	—	—	—	—	12
	14		2	1.5	—	—	—	—	1.5	1.25[b]	1	—	—	—	—	—	14
		15	—	—	—	—	—	—	1.5	—	1	—	—	—	—	—	15
16			2	1.5	—	—	—	—	1.5	—	1	—	—	—	—	—	16
		17	—	—	—	—	—	—	1.5	—	1	—	—	—	—	—	17
	18		2.5	1.5	—	—	—	2	1.5	—	1	—	—	—	—	—	18
20			2.5	1.5	—	—	—	2	1.5	—	1	—	—	—	—	—	20
	22		2.5	1.5	—	—	—	2	1.5	—	1	—	—	—	—	—	22
24			3	2	—	—	—	2	1.5	—	1	—	—	—	—	—	24
		25	—	—	—	—	—	2	1.5	—	1	—	—	—	—	—	25
		26	—	—	—	—	—	—	1.5	—	1	—	—	—	—	—	26
	27		3	2	—	—	—	2	1.5	—	1	—	—	—	—	—	27
		28	—	—	—	—	—	2	1.5	—	1	—	—	—	—	—	28
30			3.5	2	—	—	(3)	2	1.5	—	1	—	—	—	—	—	30
		32	—	—	—	—	—	2	1.5	—	—	—	—	—	—	—	32
	33		3.5	2	—	—	(3)	2	1.5	—	—	—	—	—	—	—	33
		35[c]	—	—	—	—	—	—	1.5	—	—	—	—	—	—	—	35[c]
36			4	3	—	—	—	2	1.5	—	—	—	—	—	—	—	36
		38	—	—	—	—	—	—	1.5	—	—	—	—	—	—	—	38
	39		4	3	—	—	—	2	1.5	—	—	—	—	—	—	—	39
		40	—	—	—	—	3	2	1.5	—	—	—	—	—	—	—	40
42			4.5	3	—	4	3	2	1.5	—	—	—	—	—	—	—	42
	45		4.5	3	—	4	3	2	1.5	—	—	—	—	—	—	—	45

a Thread diameter should be selected from columns 1, 2, or 3; with preference being given in that order.
b Pitch 1.25 mm in combination with diameter 14 mm has been included for spark plug applications.
c Diameter 35 mm has been included for bearing locknut applications.
The use of pitches shown in parentheses should be avoided wherever possible.
The pitches enclosed in the bold frame, together with the corresponding nominal diameters in Columns 1 and 2, are those combinations which have been established by ISO Recommendations as a selected "coarse" and "fine" series for commercial fasteners. Sizes 0.25 mm through 1.4 mm are covered in ISO Recommendation R 68 and, except for the 0.25 mm size, in **AN Standard ANSI B1.10.**   **(ANSI)**

Sheet Metal and Wire Gage Designation

GAGE NO.	AMERICAN OR BROWN & SHARPE'S A.W.G. OR B. & S.	BIRMING-HAM OR STUBS WIRE B.W.G.	WASHBURN & MOEN OR AMERICAN S.W.G.	UNITED STATES STANDARD	MANU-FACTURERS' STANDARD FOR SHEET STEEL	GAGE NO.
0000000	- - - -	- - - -	.4900	.500	- - - -	0000000
000000	.5800	- - - -	.4615	.469	- - - -	000000
00000	.5165	- - - -	.4305	.438	- - - -	00000
0000	.4600	.454	.3938	.406	- - - -	0000
000	.4096	.425	.3625	.375	- - - -	000
00	.3648	.380	.3310	.344	- - - -	00
0	.3249	.340	.3065	.312	- - - -	0
1	.2893	.300	.2830	.281	- - - -	1
2	.2576	.284	.2625	.266	- - - -	2
3	.2294	.259	.2437	.250	.2391	3
4	.2043	.238	.2253	.234	.2242	4
5	.1819	.220	.2070	.219	.2092	5
6	.1620	.203	.1920	.203	.1943	6
7	.1443	.180	.1770	.188	.1793	7
8	.1285	.165	.1620	.172	.1644	8
9	.1144	.148	.1483	.156	.1495	9
10	.1019	.134	.1350	.141	.1345	10
11	.0907	.120	.1205	.125	.1196	11
12	.0808	.109	.1055	.109	.1046	12
13	.0720	.095	.0915	.0938	.0897	13
14	.0642	.083	.0800	.0781	.0747	14
15	.0571	.072	.0720	.0703	.0673	15
16	.0508	.065	.0625	.0625	.0598	16
17	.0453	.058	.0540	.0562	.0538	17
18	.0403	.049	.0475	.0500	.0478	18
19	.0359	.042	.0410	.0438	.0418	19
20	.0320	.035	.0348	.0375	.0359	20
21	.0285	.032	.0317	.0344	.0329	21
22	.0253	.028	.0286	.0312	.0299	22
23	.0226	.025	.0258	.0281	.0269	23
24	.0201	.022	.0230	.0250	.0239	24
25	.0179	.020	.0204	.0219	.0209	25
26	.0159	.018	.0181	.0188	.0179	26
27	.0142	.016	.0173	.0172	.0164	27
28	.0126	.014	.0162	.0156	.0149	28
29	.0113	.013	.0150	.0141	.0135	29
30	.0100	.012	.0140	.0125	.0120	30
31	.0089	.010	.0132	.0109	.0105	31
32	.0080	.009	.0128	.0102	.0097	32
33	.0071	.008	.0118	.00938	.0090	33
34	.0063	.007	.0104	.00859	.0082	34
35	.0056	.005	.0095	.00781	.0075	35
36	.0050	.004	.0090	.00703	.0067	36
37	.0045	- - - -	.0085	.00624	.0064	37
38	.0040	- - - -	.0080	.00625	.0060	38
39	.0035	- - - -	.0075	- - - -	- - - -	39
40	.0031	- - - -	.0070	- - - -	- - - -	40
41	.0028	- - - -	.0066	- - - -	- - - -	41
42	.0025	- - - -	.0062	- - - -	- - - -	42
43	.0022	- - - -	.0060	- - - -	- - - -	43
44	.0020	- - - -	.0058	- - - -	- - - -	44
45	.0018	- - - -	.0055	- - - -	- - - -	45
46	.0016	- - - -	.0052	- - - -	- - - -	46
47	.0014	- - - -	.0050	- - - -	- - - -	47
48	.0012	- - - -	.0048	- - - -	- - - -	48

Index

D

Date stamp, 55–56
Date resetting, 295–297
Date/Time Properties dialog box, 295–297
Datum dimensioning, 451
DCTCUST system variable, 337
DCTMAIN system variable, 337
DDATTE command, 585
DDATTEXT command, 594
DDCHPROP command, 178, 701
DDCOLOR command, 150
DDEDIT command, 331–332
   editing dimensions, 475
   editing feature control frames, 489
DDGRIPS command, 383
DDIM command, 416
DDINSERT command, 571, 572
DDMODIFY command, 332–334, 701
   changing object properties, 179
   editing dimensions, 475–476
   editing feature control frames, 489
   modifying objects, 381
DDOSNAP command, 253
DDRENAME command, 138, 177, 280, 323
DDRMODES command, 69
DDUCS command, 281
DDUNITS command, 63
DDVIEW command, 134–135
Decimal places, setting, 289–290
Defpoints layer, 470
DELAY command, 681
Demand loading, 608
Desktop shortcut,
   adding command line switches, 737–738
   defining, 739
Device and Default Selection... button, 540
Dialog box, 26–29
Diameter dimension, 458–459
Digitizing tablet, 29, 799–807
   calibrating the tablet, 805–806
   configuring the tablet as the system pointing device, 800–801
   configuring the tablet menu areas, 802–804
   using tablet mode, 804
   Wintab compatibility, 800
DIM1 mode, 497
DIMALIGNED command, 432
DIMALT variable, 482, 483

DIMALTD variable, 482, 483
DIMALTF variable, 482
DIMALTTD variable, 483, 484
DIMALTTZ variable, 483, 484
DIMALTU variable, 482, 483
DIMALTZ variable, 482, 483
DIMANGULAR command, 454–455
DIMAPOST variable, 482, 483
DIMASO variable, 469–470
DIMASZ variable, 437
DIMAUNIT variable, 420
DIMBASELINE command, 451–452
DIMBLK variable, 464, 465
DIMCEN variable, 457, 458
DIMCENTER command, 456–457
DIMCLRD variable, 425
DIMCLRE variable, 425
DIMCLRT variable, 426, 427
DIMCONTINUE command, 453
DIMDEC variable, 420
DIMDIAMETER command, 458
DIMDLE variable, 447–448
DIMDLI variable, 452
DIMEDIT command, 472–474, 642–643
Dimension Edit button, 472, 641
Dimensioning,
   commands, 415–416
   guidelines, 433
   isometric, 640–642
   mode, 415
Dimensioning mode commands, 497
Dimension line,
   extending past extension lines, 447–448
   increment setting, 452
   suppressing, 443
Dimensions,
   adding tolerances, 478–481
   angular, 454–455
   arrowless, 466
   associative, 469–471
   dual, 482–485
   editing, 471–477
   linear, 427–435
   radial, 456–460
Dimension style, 493–496
   creating and managing at Dim: prompt, 495–496
   managing with dialog box, 493
   using **Family** option buttons, 494
Dimension Style button, 418, 480, 493
Dimension Styles dialog box, 418, 423, 426, 434, 436, 437, 440, 443, 445, 447–449, 452, 457, 465, 480, 481, 483, 493–494

M

Make Object's Layer Current button, 173
MASSPROP command, 297–299
Master drawing, 597
MAXACTVP system variable, 652
MEASURE command, 274
  measuring an object with a block, 574
Measurement style,
  changing, 63
  setting with Quick Setup, 47
Menu bar, 19
  restoring original configuration, 781
Menu Customization dialog box,
  769, 779
Menu files, 777–783
  adding a help string to the menu
    item, 795
  adding and removing pull-down
    menus, 779–781
  AUXn menus, 785–786
  creating a new pull-down menu,
    789–791
  cursor and pull-down menus,
    787–788
  image tile menus, 791–795
  restoring original menu bar configu-
    ration, 781
  specifying a menu file using
    Preferences dialog box, 782–783
  structure and sections, 783–785
MENULOAD command, 769, 779, 781, 791
Menu macro, 786
MENUUNLOAD command, 781
Metafile, 815
Metric dimensioning, 485
Microsoft IntelliMouse, 131
Mirror button, 368
MIRROR command, 368–369
Mirror images, 368–369
Mirror line, 368
MIRRTEXT system variable, 369
Mnemonic key, 25, 787–788
.MNS file, 778
MODEL button, 651
Model space, 49, 649
Modify II toolbar, opening, 395
Modify Attribute Definition dialog box,
  582–583
Modify Block Description dialog box,
  612–613
Modify Dimension dialog box, 475
Modifying objects, using a dialog box, 381
Modify MText dialog box, 333

Modify Text dialog box, 332–333
Modify toolbar, converting to floating
  state, 20
Moments of inertia, 298
Move button, 354
MOVE command, 354
Moving objects, 354–355
MREDO command, 114–115
MS-DOS Prompt, 676–677
MSLIDE command, 682
MSPACE command, 651
MTEXT command, 323–326, 330
MTEXTED system variable, 330
Multiline text button, 324
Multiline text, creating, 323–326
Multiline Text Editor dialog box, 429, 475
  Character tab, 326–327
  Find/Replace tab, 328–329
  Properties tab, 328
MULTIPLE command, 87
Multiple copies, 371
Multiple Pick Points, 523
Multiple Viewports, 140–143
MVIEW command, 652–655

N

N-Way Boolean, 238–239
Named UCS button, 281
Named Views button, 134, 698
NEW command, 62–63
Noun/Verb selection, 105, 110
NURBS, 205

O

Object cycling, 109
Object Linking and Embedding (OLE),
  815–816
Object properties, changing, 178–180
Object Properties toolbar, 23, 181
Object Selection Settings dialog box,
  109–111
Object snap modes (osnaps), 245–252
  accessing from Standard Toolbar,
    250–252
  using the Cursor Menu, 252
Object Snap Settings button, 253
Object Sort Method... button, 111
OBLIQUE command, and isometric
  dimensions, 641–642
Oblique strokes, 447

modifying linked images, 818
polyline, 215

Dedication

Ted Saufley wishes to dedicate this text to...

  Liz Saufley and Matt Shivell